The Thomas Guide®

S0-AHH-724

Portland
street guide

TELL US
comment card on last page
WHAT YOU THINK

Contents

Introduction

Using Your Street Guide   A

PageFinder™ Map   B

Legend   D

We've Got You Covered   E

Maps

Downtown Map   F

Street Guide Detail Maps   384-837

Vicinity Map   Inside back cover

Lists and Indexes

Cities & Communities Index   1

List of Abbreviations   3

Street Index and   4
Points of Interest Index

Comment Card   Last page

RAND MCNALLY

Rand McNally Consumer Affairs
P.O. Box 7600
Chicago, IL 60680-9915
randmcnally.com

For comments or suggestions, please call
(800) 777-MAPS (-6277)
or email us at:
consumeraffairs@randmcnally.com

NAVTEQ
ON BOARD™

Legend

123 Interstate highway

BUS 123 Interstate (Business) highway

123 U.S. highway

123 State/provincial highway

123 Secondary state/provincial highway/county highway

1 Trans-Canada Highway

123 Canadian autoroute

123 Mexican highway

123 Other highway designation

456 Exit number

Free limited-access highway (with tunnel)

Toll highway, toll plaza

Interchange

Ramp

Highway

Primary road

Secondary road

Minor road, unpaved road

Restricted road

Walkway or trail

One-way road

Ferry, waterway

Levee

Trolley

Railroad, station, mass transit line

Bus station

Park and ride

Rest area, service area

Airport

1200 Block number

International boundary, state boundary

County boundary

Township/range boundary, section corner

12345 ZIP code boundary, ZIP code

45°33'30" 90°33'30" Latitude, longitude

H Hospital

School

University or college

Information/visitor center/ welcome center

Police/sheriff, etc.

FS Fire Station

City/town/village hall and other government buildings

Courthouse

Post office

Lib Library

Museum

Border crossing/ Port of entry

Theater/ performing arts center

Golf course

Other point of interest

we've got you COVERED

Rand McNally's broad selection of products is perfect for your every need. Whether you're looking for the convenience of write-on wipe-off laminated maps, extra maps for every car, or a Road Atlas to plan your next vacation or to use as a reference, Rand McNally has you covered.

Street Guides

Portland

Folded Maps

EasyFinder® Laminated Maps

Oregon State

Portland

Willamette Valley to Astoria

Paper Maps

Beaverton & Hillsboro

Oregon City/ Lake Oswego/ Clackamas County

Oregon State

Portland

Salem

Vancouver/ Camas/ Washougal, WA

Road Atlases

Pacific Northwest Road Atlas

Road Atlas

Road Atlas & Travel Guide

Large Scale Road Atlas

Midsize Road Atlas

Deluxe Midsize Road Atlas

Pocket Road Atlas

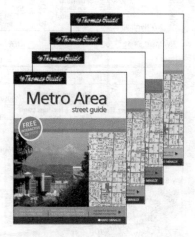

Downtown Portland

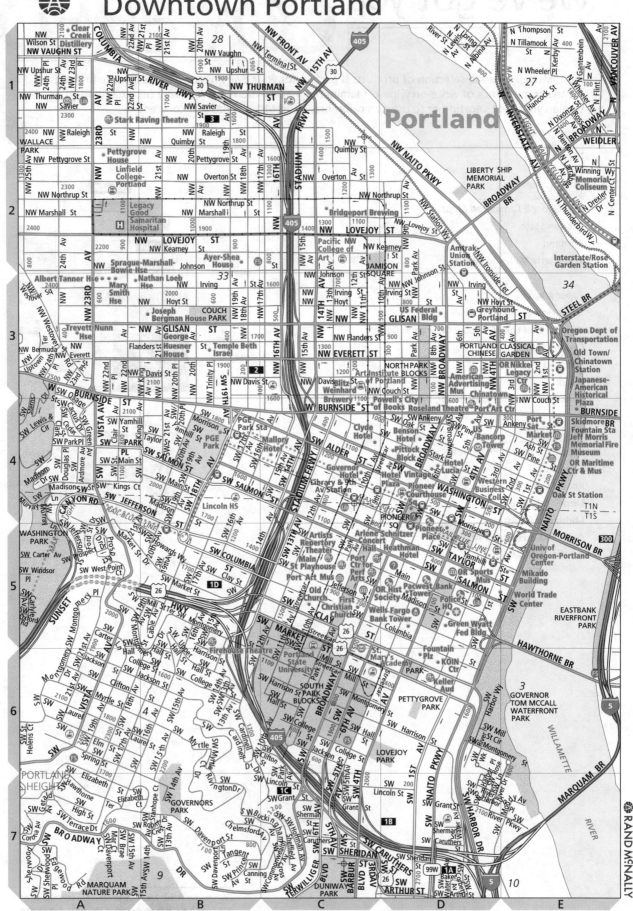

Note: This grid references this map only

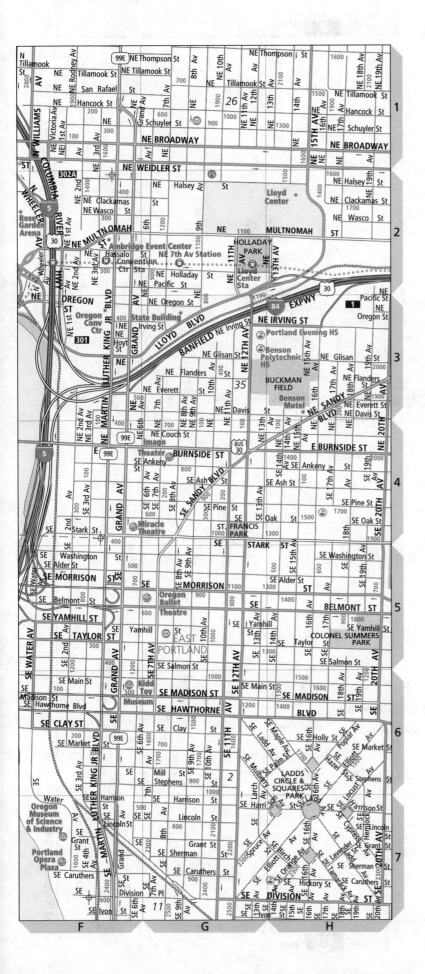

Points of Interest

American Advertising Museum	D3
Amtrak-Union Station	D2
Arlene Schnitzer Concert Hall	C5
Art Institute of Portland	C3
Benson Hotel	D4
Central Library	C4
Chinatown	D3
Clyde Hotel	C4
Federal Courthouse	D5
Fountain Plaza	D6
Governor Hotel	C4
Greyhound-Portland	D3
Heald College School of Business & Technology-Portland	D4
Heathman Hotel	D5
Hotel Lucia	D4
Hotel Vintage Plaza	D4
Japanese-American Historical Plaza	E4
Jeff Morris Memorial Fire Museum	E4
Keller Auditorium	D6
KOIN Center	D6
Legacy Good Samaritan Hospital	A2
Linfield College-Portland	A2
Lloyd Center	H2
Mallory Hotel	C4
Marquam Nature Park	A7
Memorial Coliseum	E2
Multnomah County District Court	D5
Northwest Library	A1
Old Church	C5
Oregon Convention Center	F3
Oregon Department of Transportation	E3
Oregon Historical Society	C5
Oregon Maritime Center & Museum	E4
Oregon Museum of Science & Industry	F7
Oregon Sports Hall of Fame & Museum	D5
Pacific Northwest College of Art	C2
PGE Park	B4
Pioneer Courthouse	D4
Pioneer Place	D5
Pittock Block	D4
Port of Portland Library	E3
Portland Art Center	D4
Portland Art Museum	C5
Portland Center for Performing Arts	C5
Portland City Hall	D5
Portland Classical Chinese Garden	D3
Portland Opera Plaza	F7
Portland State University	C6
Powell's City of Books	C4
Rose Garden Arena	F2
State Building	F3
University of Oregon-Portland Center	D5
US Bancorp Tower	D4
US Federal Building	D3
Wells Fargo Bank Tower	C5
Western Business College	D4
World Trade Center	E5

1 in. = 1400 ft.

0   0.25   0.5

miles

MAP
384

1:24,000
1 in. = 2000 ft.
0   0.25   0.5
miles

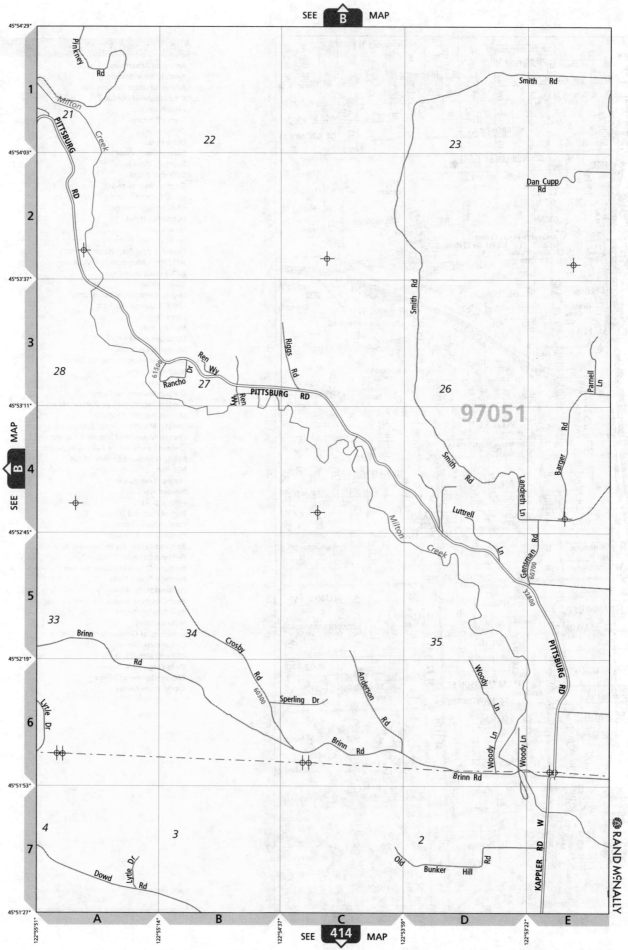

SEE B MAP

Pinkney Rd

Milton Creek

Smith Rd

21

PITTSBURG RD

22

23

Dan Cupp Rd

28

Smith Rd

3

Riggs Rd

Ren Wy
Ren Wy
61500
Rancho Dr

27

PITTSBURG RD

26

97051

Parnell Ln

Barger Rd

Smith Rd

Landreth Ln

Luttrell Ln

Milton Creek

Gentsman Rd
60700

31400

33

Brinn Rd

34

Crosby Rd
60300

35

PITTSBURG RD

Sperling Dr

Anderson Rd

Woody Ln

Woody Ln

Lytle Dr

Brinn Rd

Woody Ln

Brinn Rd

4

3

2

Old Bunker Hill Rd

KAPPLER RD W

Dowd Rd
Lytle Dr

SEE 414 MAP

A   B   C   D   E

45°54'29"
45°54'03"
45°53'37"
45°53'11"
45°52'45"
45°52'19"
45°51'53"
45°51'27"

122°55'51"
122°55'14"
122°54'37"
122°53'59"
122°53'22"

SEE B MAP

1:24,000
1 in. = 2000 ft.
0   0.25   0.5
miles

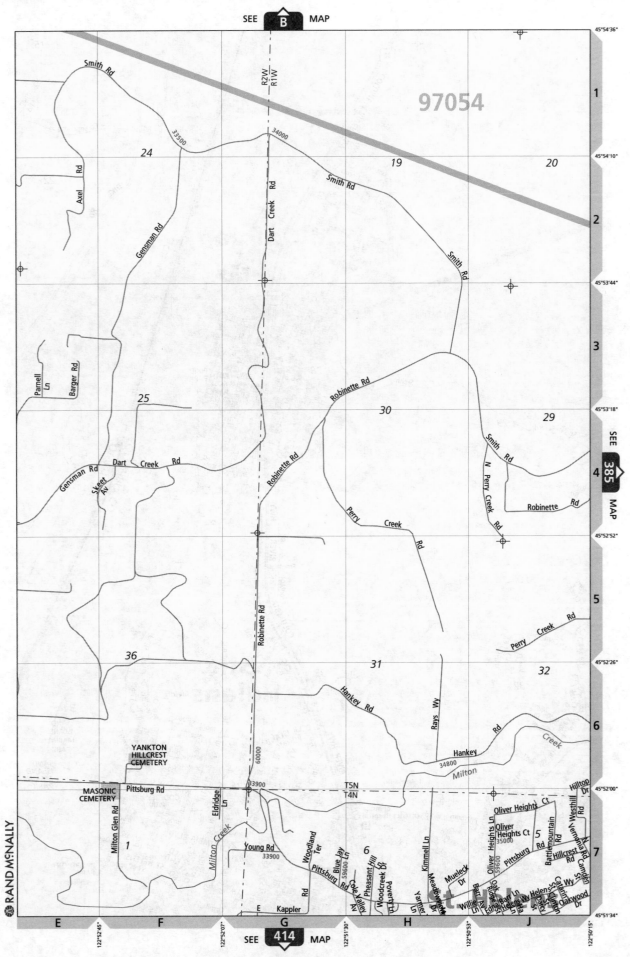

MAP
384

SEE **B** MAP

97054

Smith Rd

R2W
R1W

33500   34000

24   19   20

Smith Rd

Axel Rd

Gensman Rd

Dart Creek Rd

Smith Rd

Parnell Ln

Barger Rd

Robinette Rd

25   30   29

Gensman Rd

Dart Creek Rd

Skeet Av

Robinette Rd

N Perry Creek Rd

Smith Rd

Robinette Rd

Perry Creek Rd

36   31   32

Robinette Rd

Perry Creek Rd

Hankey Rd

Rays Wy

Rd   Creek

YANKTON
HILLCREST
CEMETERY

60000

Hankey

34800

Milton

MASONIC
CEMETERY

Pittsburg Rd

33900

Eldridge Ln

T5N
T4N

Hilltop Dr

Oliver Heights Ct

Milton Glen Rd

1

Milton Creek

Young Rd

33900

Woodland Ter

Blue Jay   59600 Ln

Pheasant Hill

6

Kimmell Ln

Muelck Dr

Oliver Heights Ln

Oliver Heights Ct

35000

Nemonia Rd

Westhill Rd

N Camden

Battlemountain Rd

Hillcrest Rd

5

Pittsburg Rd

59600

Pittsburg Rd

Cole Valley Av

Woodcreek Dr

poverty Ln

Meadowick Dr

Barr Ln

Willie Ln

Edna Rae

S Helens St

S Helens Wy

Catamin Wy

Clifman St

Oakwood Dr

E   Kappler

Yanmer Dr

RAND McNALLY

E   F   G   H   J

45°54'36"
45°54'10"
45°53'44"
45°53'18"
45°52'52"
45°52'26"
45°52'00"
45°51'34"
45°51'15"

1
2
3
4
5
6
7

122°52'45"   122°52'07"   122°51'30"   122°50'53"   122°50'15"

MAP
385

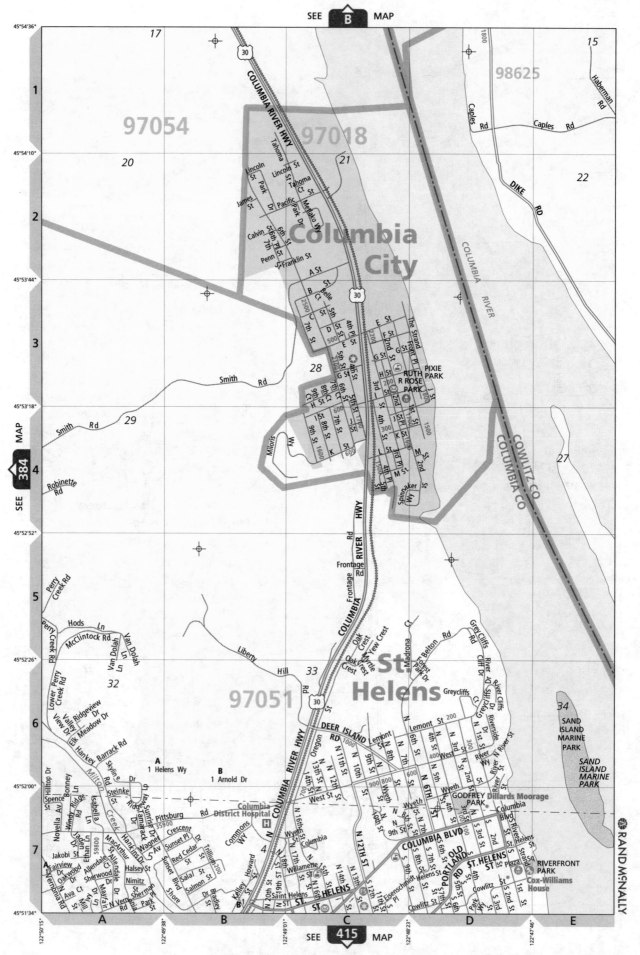

 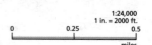

1:24,000
1 in. = 2000 ft.

0   0.25   0.5
miles

97054

97018

98625

17   15

20   21   22

Columbia City

Lincoln St
Lincoln St
Tahoma
Tahoma
Ct
James St
Pacific
Calvin St
6th St
7th
Penn
Franklin St

Caples Rd
Caples Rd

Haberman Rd

DIKE RD

COLUMBIA RIVER HWY

COLUMBIA RIVER

A St
Belle
B St
2500
C St 5th
7th St
D
5000
E
St
4th Pl St
4th St

E St
The Strand
Front St
2nd St
G St
H St
RUTH R ROSE PARK
PIXIE PARK
J St
I St

28

Smith Rd

30

5th 6th St 7th St
8th Ct
9th St
H St
8th Ct
600
7th St
J St
K
300

Milioris Wy
9th St 8th St
K
600
L
3rd St
M St
4th Pl St
M St
5th
Spinnaker Wy

COWLITZ CO
COLUMBIA CO

27

29
Smith Rd

Robinette Rd

SEE 384 MAP

Perry Creek Rd
Hods Ln
McClintock Rd
Van Dolah Ln
Van Dolah Ln
Perry Creek Rd
Lower Perry Creek Rd
32

Liberty
Hill
Rd

33

COLUMBIA RIVER HWY

Oak Crest
View Crest
Myrtle
Oak Crest

Madrona Ct
Belton Rd
Grey Cliffs
River Cliffs
Cliff Dr
Riverside

34
SAND ISLAND MARINE PARK
SAND ISLAND MARINE PARK

97051

St. Helens

Greycliffs

30

Valley View Dr
Ridgeview Dr
Elk Meadow Dr
Hankey Rd
Barrack Rd
Skyline Dr
Sunrise Dr

DEER ISLAND RD
Lemont St
Lemont St
N 6th St
N 4th St
N 3rd St
N 1st St
West
River
River Wy

DEER ISLAND RD 1000
Oregon
N 11th St
N 10th St
N 9th St
N 8th St
N 7th St
400
600
N 5th St
N 2nd St

Hilltop Dr
Spence St
Bonney Ln
Windy Ridge Rd
Isabella Ln
Steinke Ln
Ridge Dr
Pittsburg Rd
35900
Amarack Dr
Ethan
Oakwood Dr
S'Allendale Dr
Sherwood
Nimitz St
N Vernonia Rd
MacArthur Dr
Hankins Dr
Wagner
Crescent
Red Cedar
Trillium 200
Salal
Salmon St
Bradley
Shore Dr
Sunset Blvd
Sunset Pl

A 1 Helens Wy
B 1 Arnold Dr

Columbia District Hospital
H

Commons WY

West St
Wyeth
900 800
Wyeth
N 6th St
N 5th St
GODFREY PARK
Dillards Moorage
700
3rd St
2nd
River
Helens
Columbia Plaza
RIVERFRONT PARK

Columbia
Wyeth
N 9th St
COLUMBIA BLVD
OLD PORTLAND RD
ST. HELENS
Cox-Williams House

Jakobi St
Fairview Dr
Daylen
Ava St
Mayfair St
N Vernonia Rd Park
Halsey St
Kelley Howard
Willamette
Saint Helens
S 20th St
Willamette
N 13th St
N 14th St
S 12th St
Eisenschmidt
Helens
Cowlitz
S 4th
S 3rd
Strand Sq

ST. HELENS ST

Columbia Creek

122°50'15"
122°49'38"
122°49'01"
122°48'23"
122°47'46"

45°54'36"
45°54'10"
45°53'44"
45°53'18"
45°52'52"
45°52'26"
45°52'00"
45°51'34"

A   B   C   D   E

MAP
385

1:24,000
1 in. = 2000 ft.
0   0.25   0.5
miles

N

SEE B MAP

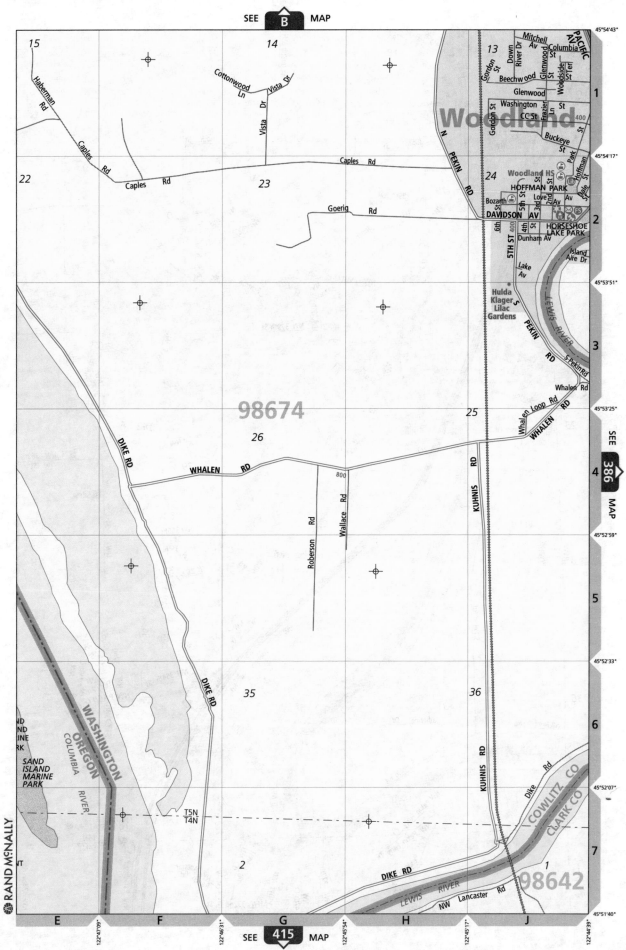

15

14

45°54'43"

Mitchell Av
PACIFIC AV
13
Columbia St
Down
Gordon St
River Dr
Beechwood
Glenwood St
Woodside St
Washington St Ter
1
Glenwood
Washington
St
Frazier
CC St
400
Woodland

Haberman Rd

Cottonwood Ln
Vista Dr
Vista Dr

Buckeye St

45°54'17"

22

Caples Rd

Caples Rd

Caples Rd

23

Caples Rd

N PEKIN RD

24

Woodland HS
HOFFMAN PARK
Hoffman
Dale St
Park
St

Goerig Rd

Bozarth St
5th St
Love Av
2nd
3rd St
Av
DAVIDSON AV

45°53'51"

5TH ST
400
4th St
Dunham Av
6th St
HORSESHOE LAKE PARK
Island Aire Dr

Lake Av

Hulda Klager Lilac Gardens
S PEKIN RD

LEWIS RIVER

3

S Pekin Rd

98674

Whalen Rd

Whalen Loop Rd
WHALEN RD

45°53'25"

25

SEE 386 MAP

26

DIKE RD

WHALEN RD

800

4

Roberson Rd
Wallace Rd

KUHNIS RD

45°52'59"

5

45°52'33"

DIKE RD

35

36

KUHNIS RD

6

WASHINGTON
OREGON
COLUMBIA

SAND ISLAND MARINE PARK

RIVER

Dike Rd
COWLITZ CO
CLARK CO

45°52'07"

T5N
T4N

7

DIKE RD

98642

LEWIS RIVER
NW Lancaster Rd

45°51'40"

E   F   G   H   J

122°47'09"   122°46'31"   122°45'54"   122°45'17"   122°44'39"

MAP
386

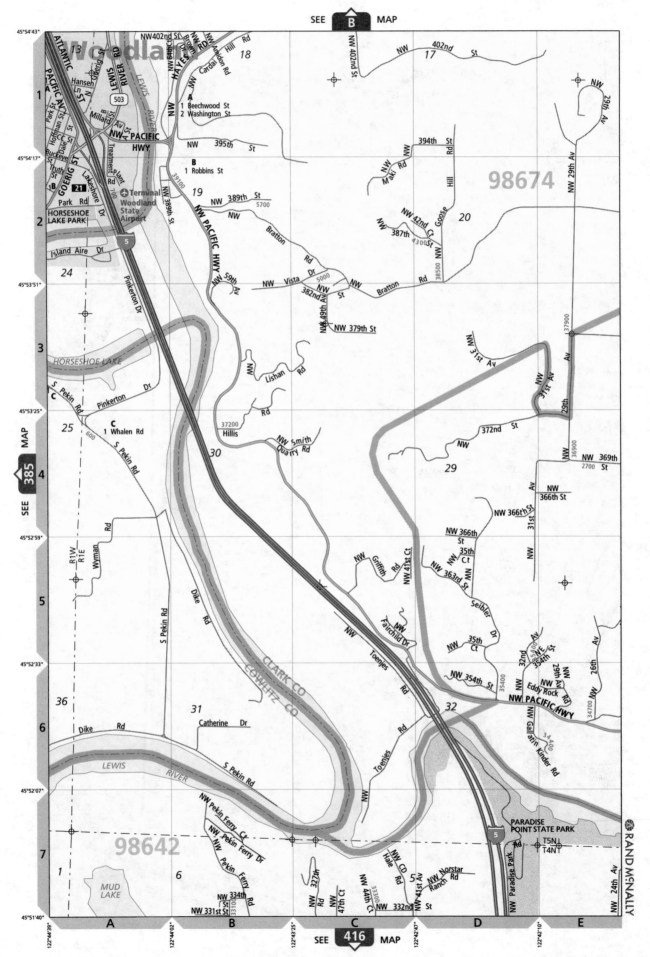

1:24,000
1 in. = 2000 ft.
0   0.25   0.5
miles

SEE B MAP

45°54'43"

Woodland

13

NW 402nd St

NW 64th Ct

NW Brown Rd

18

Arndon Rd

NW Cardal Rd

Hill Rd

NW 402nd St

NW   402nd   St

17

ATLANTIC PACIFIC AV

LEWIS ST

GOERIG ST

HAYES Rd

LEWIS RIVER

LEWIS RIVER

503

Hanseh Ln

Millard Av

1

A
1 Beechwood St
2 Washington St

NW PACIFIC HWY

NW 395th St

B
1 Robbins St

19

NW 389th St

NW 389th St

5700

NW 394th St

NW Maki Rd

NW 42nd Ct

NW 387th St

4300

Goose Hill Rd

NW 29th Av

98674

20

NW 29th Av

45°54'17"

Park St
Dale St
Buckeye St
Truth St

1B

21

Park Rd

Treatment Plant Rd

Lakeshore Dr

700

NW PACIFIC HWY

Bratton Rd

NW Vista Dr

5000

NW 59th Av

NW 382nd St

NW 49th Av

NW Bratton Rd

38500

2

HORSESHOE LAKE PARK

5

Island Aire Dr

24

Pinkerton Dr

45°53'51"

NW 379th St

31st Av

NW 31st Av

NW 29th Av

37900

3

HORSESHOE LAKE

Pinkerton Dr

NW Lishan Rd

Rd

37200 Hillis

NW Smith Quarry Rd

372nd St

NW 369th St

36900

2700

45°53'25"

C
1 Whalen Rd

S Pekin Rd

Pinkerton

C

25

600

S Pekin Rd

30

NW 366th St

NW 366th St

NW 366th St

31st Av

45°53'25"

SEE 385 MAP

Wyman Rd

R1W R1E

29

NW Griffith Rd

NW 41st Ct

NW 363rd St

35th Ct

31st Av

45°52'59"

4

45°52'33"

S Pekin Rd

Dike Rd

CLARK CO
COWLITZ CO

NW Fairchild Dr

NW

NW Toenjes Rd

Seibler Dr

35th Ct

32nd Av

NW 5400

29th St

NW 354th St

26th Av

5

45°52'33"

36

Dike Rd

31

Catherine Dr

S Pekin Rd

Toenjes Rd

32

35400

NW 354th St

Eddy Rock

29th NW

NW PACIFIC HWY

34700

NW Gallatin Kinder Rd

34400

6

LEWIS RIVER

NW Pekin Ferry Ct

NW Pekin Ferry Dr

NW Pekin Ferry Rd

NW Toenjes Rd

5

PARADISE POINT STATE PARK

NW Paradise Park

Rd

T5N T4N

45°52'07"

7

98642

1

MUD LAKE

6

NW 334th St

33100

NW 331st St

NW 327th Rd

NW 47th Ct

NW 44th Ct

33300

NW 332nd St

NW 41st Av

NW Hale Rd

NW CD Rd

5

NW Norstar Ranch Rd

NW 24th Av

45°51'40"

A   B   C   D   E

122°44'39"   122°44'02"   122°43'25"   122°42'47"   122°42'10"

SEE 416 MAP

RAND MCNALLY

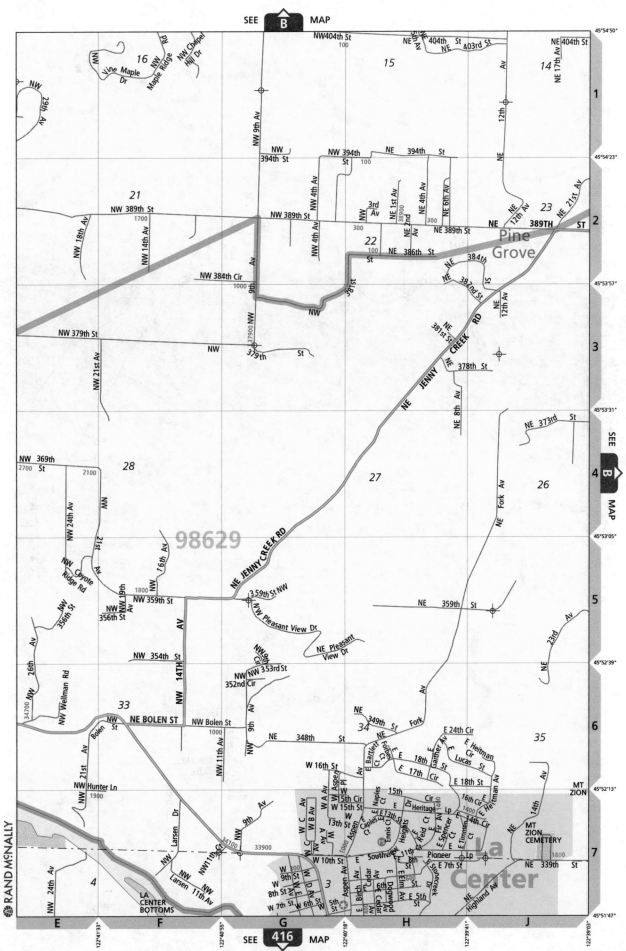

MAP
386

1:24,000
1 in. = 2000 ft.

0   0.25   0.5
miles

SEE B MAP

45°54'50"

NW 404th St
100
NE 404th St
NE 403rd St
NE 404th St

16
NW Maple Ridge Rd
NW Chapel Hill Dr
Vine Maple Dr
MN
15
14
NE 17th Av

1

NW 29th Av
NW
NW 9th Av
12th Av

45°54'23"

NW 394th St
NW 394th St
100
NE 394th St
NE

NE 21st Av

21
NW 389th St
1700
NW 389th St
3rd Av
NW
NE 1st Av
NE 2nd
38900
NE 4th Av
NE 6th Av
300
300
NE
12th Av
23
NE 389TH ST

2

NW 18th Av
NW 14th Av
NW 4th Av
22
100
St
NE 386th St
NE 389th St
Pine Grove

NW 384th Cir
1000
9th
Av
NW
381st
NE 386th St
384th
NE 382nd St

45°53'57"

NW 379th St
NW
37900
NW
379th St
NW
NE JENNY CREEK RD
NE 381st St
NE
12th Av

3

NW 21st Av
NE 378th St

NE 8th Av

45°53'31"

NE 373rd St

NW 369th St
2700
2100
28
NE Fork Av
26
SEE B MAP

4

98629
27
NE

45°53'05"

NW 24th Av
21st Av
NW 16th
NW Coyote Ridge Rd
1800
NW
NE JENNY CREEK RD
359th St NW
NW Pleasant View Dr
NE 359th St
NE 23rd Av

5

NW 18th
NW 356th St
NW 356th St
NW
NE Pleasant View Dr
NE

45°52'39"

NW 26th Av
NW Wellman Rd
NW 354th St
NW 14TH AV
NW 9th
NW 353rd St
NW 352nd Cir
Av

33
34700
NW Bolen
NE BOLEN ST
NW Bolen St
1000
NE 348th St
NE Fork
NE 349th St
34
E 24th Cir
E Heitman Cir
Lucas
35

6

NW 21st Av
NW Hunter Ln
1900
NW 11th Av
NW 9th
NE 348th St
W 16th St
E Bartlett Ct
E Forbes Ct
E 18th
E Gaither
E
E 17th Cir
E 18th St
Av
MT ZION

45°52'13"

W Aspen Pl
W 15th Cir
W 15th St
15th
E Naples Ct
E Heritage Dr
16th Cir
1400
E Heitman Av
14th
MT ZION CEMETERY
1800

RAND M°NALLY
Larsen Dr
34100
33900
W C
W B Av
W A A
W 13th St
1000
E Caples Ct
E 12th St
E Ennis Ct
Heights
E Reid Ct
E Fir Av
E Spencer
1400
E Timmen
E 14th Cir
1400
NE 14th

7

NW 24th Av
4
NW Larsen 11th Av
NW 11th Av
W 10th St
W 9th St
8th St
W 8th St
3
W 7th St
W 6th St
5th St
W Aspen Av
E Birch Av
E Cedar
6th Cedar
E Dogwood
E Elm
E 5th St
E Stonecreek
E 7th St
Pioneer
1800
E 7th St
La Center
NE 339th St

45°51'47"

LA CENTER BOTTOMS

E   F   G   H   J

122°41'33"   122°40'55"   122°40'18"   122°39'41"   122°39'03"

MAP
414

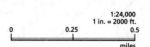

1:24,000
1 in. = 2000 ft.
0   0.25   0.5
miles

SEE 384 MAP

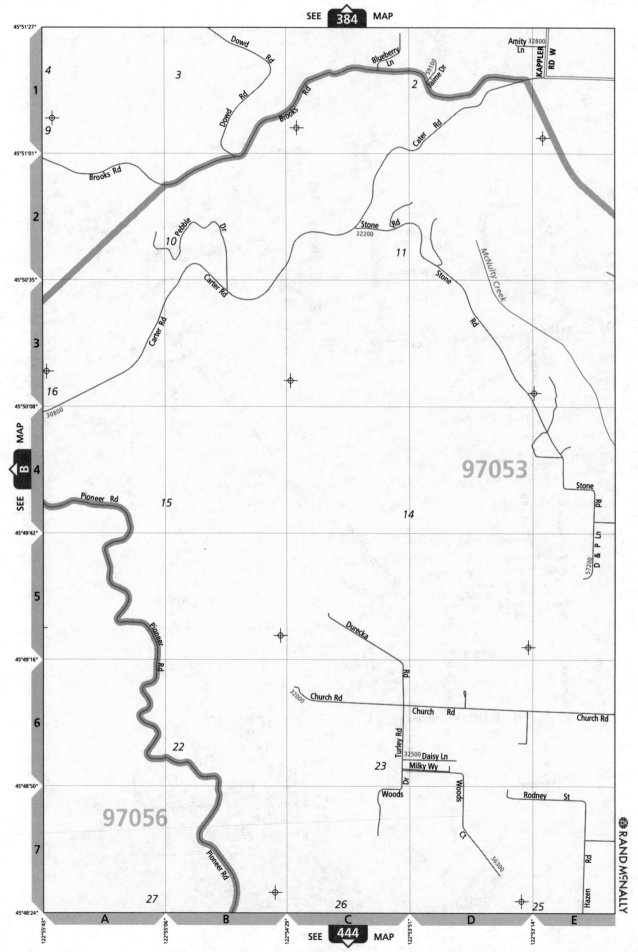

97053

97056

SEE MAP B 4

SEE 444 MAP

RAND McNALLY

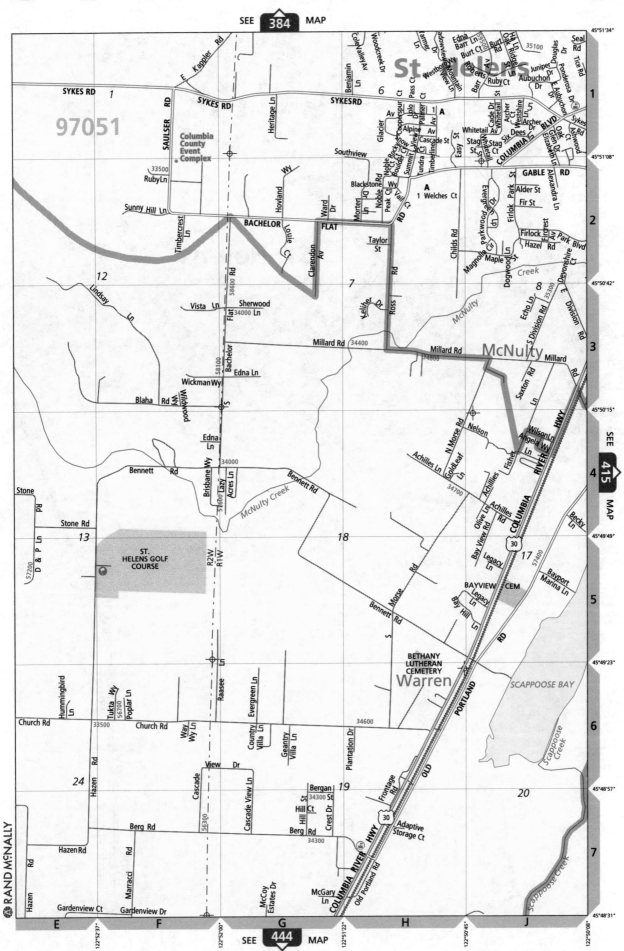

MAP
414

1:24,000
1 in. = 2000 ft.

0   0.25   0.5
miles

SEE 384 MAP

45°51'34"

97051

St. Helens

SYKES RD   1
SYKES RD
SYKESRD

Columbia County Event Complex

45°51'08"

GABLE   RD

45°50'42"

Bachelor   FLAT

McNulty

Millard Rd   34400
Millard Rd
Millard

St. Helens Golf Course

SEE 415 MAP

45°50'15"

45°49'49"

BAYVIEW CEM

Bayport Marina Ln

BETHANY LUTHERAN CEMETERY

Warren

SCAPPOOSE BAY

45°49'23"

Church Rd   33500   Church Rd

45°48'57"

45°48'31"

E   F   G   H   J

SEE 444 MAP

122°52'37"   122°52'00"   122°51'22"   122°50'45"   122°50'08"

MAP
415

1:24,000
1 in. = 2000 ft.

0   0.25   0.5

miles

N

SEE 385 MAP

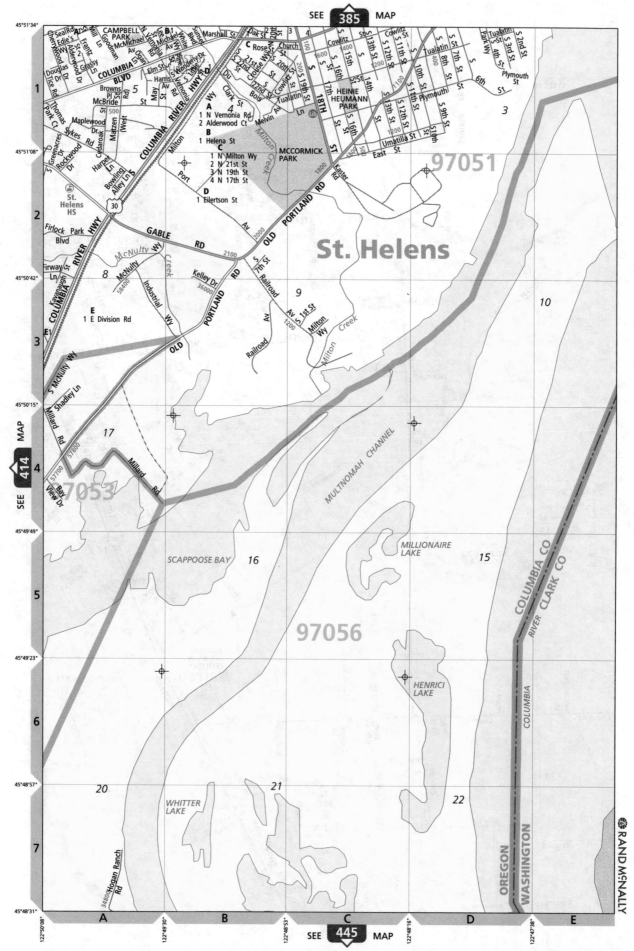

SEE 414 MAP

SEE 445 MAP

RAND McNALLY

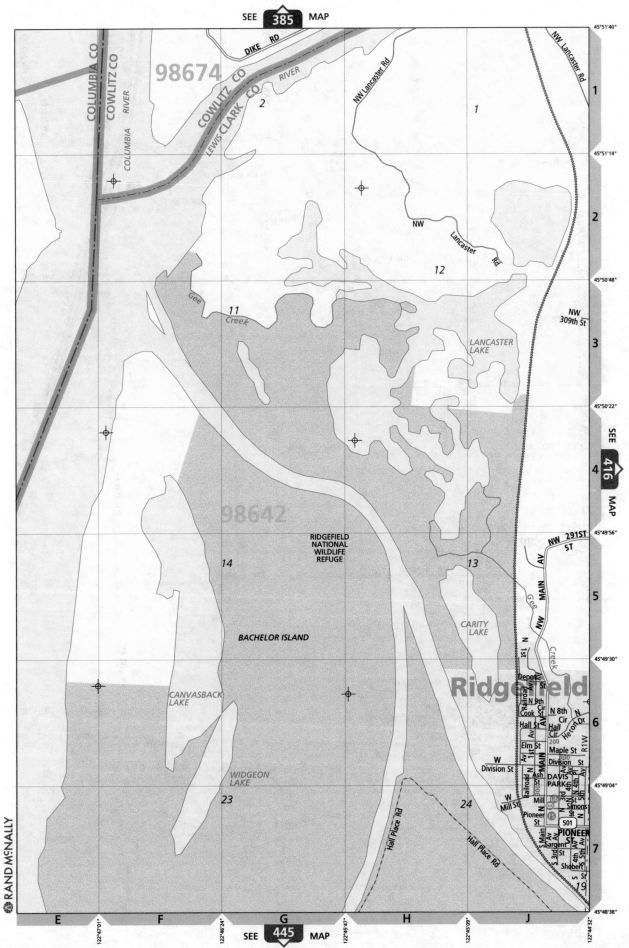

1:24,000
1 in. = 2000 ft.

0   0.25   0.5
miles

MAP
415

SEE 385 MAP

98674

COLUMBIA CO
COWLITZ CO

COWLITZ CO
LEWIS CLARK CO

COLUMBIA RIVER

COWLITZ RIVER

DIKE RD

NW Lancaster Rd

NW Lancaster Rd

2

1

1

45°51'40"

45°51'14"

NW Lancaster Rd

NW

2

12

45°50'48"

Gee Creek

11

LANCASTER LAKE

NW 309th St

3

45°50'22"

SEE 416 MAP

4

98642

RIDGEFIELD NATIONAL WILDLIFE REFUGE

14

13

NW 291ST ST

MAIN AV

Gee Creek

45°49'56"

5

BACHELOR ISLAND

CARITY LAKE

45°49'30"

CANVASBACK LAKE

Ridgefield

Depot St

N 9th Cir
Cook Av
N 8th Cir
Hall St
Hall Cir
Heron Dr

6

Elm St
1st Av
Maple St
200
Division St
500

W Division St

MAIN
R1W
R1E

WIDGEON LAKE

Railroad Av
Ash St
DAVIS PARK
800
N 3rd Av
N 4th Av
N 5th Av

45°49'04"

23

24

W Mill St
Mill St
Pioneer St
Simons
501

Hall Place Rd

Hall Place Rd

PIONEER ST

S Main Av
Sargent
3rd St
4th St
5th St
Shobert St

7

19

45°48'38"

E   F   G   H   J

SEE 445 MAP

122°47'01"   122°46'24"   122°45'47"   122°45'09"   122°44'32"

RAND MCNALLY

MAP
416

1:24,000
1 in. = 2000 ft.

0   0.25   0.5
miles

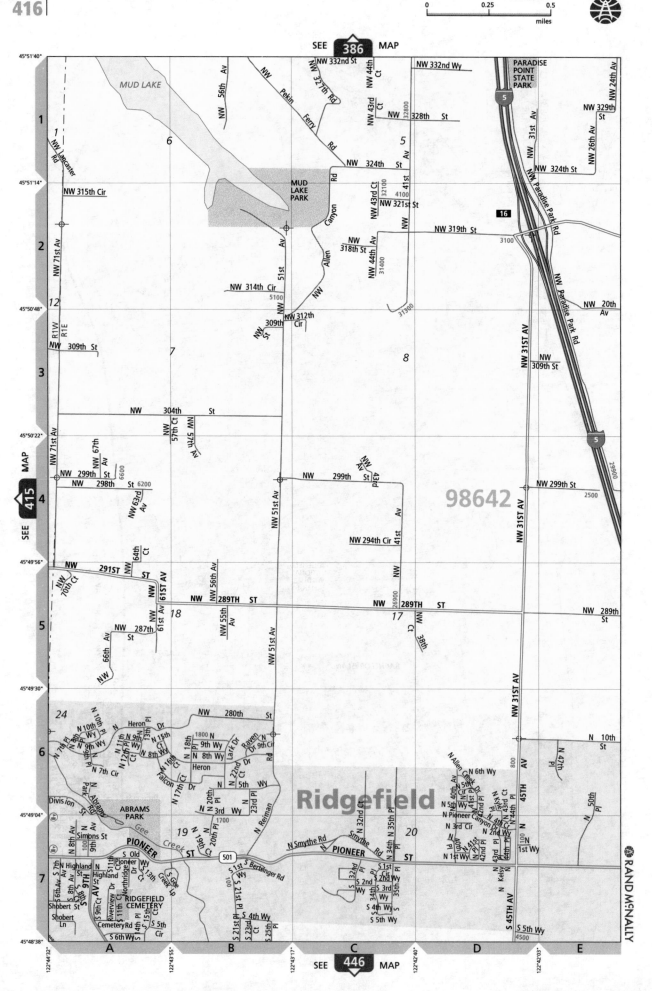

SEE 386 MAP

PARADISE POINT STATE PARK

MUD LAKE

MUD LAKE PARK

98642

Ridgefield

ABRAMS PARK

RIDGEFIELD CEMETERY

PIONEER ST

PIONEER ST

501

MAP 415 SEE

SEE 446 MAP

A   B   C   D   E

RAND McNALLY

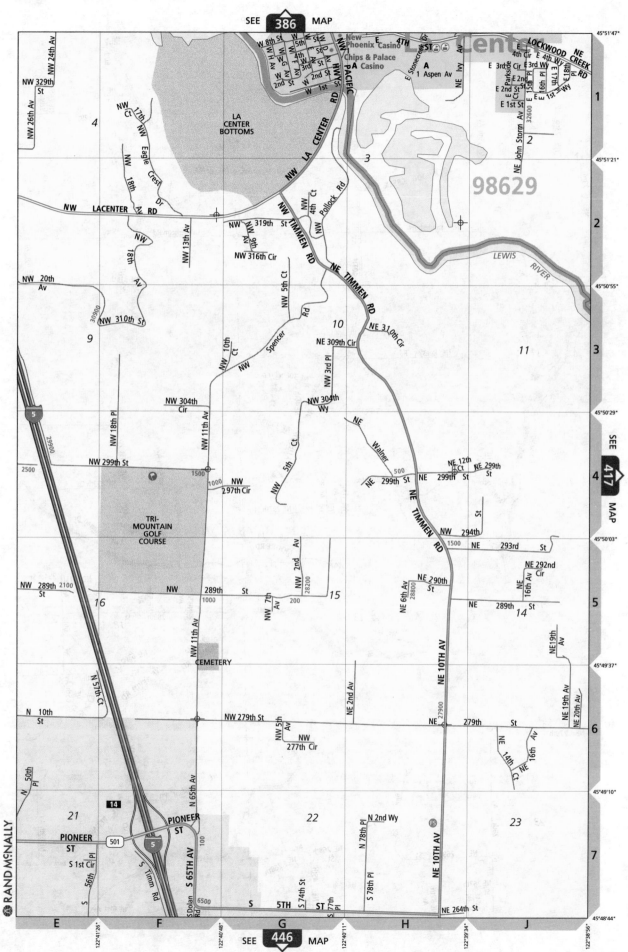

MAP
416

1:24,000
1 in. = 2000 ft.

0   0.25   0.5
miles

SEE 386 MAP

New Phoenix Casino
Chips & Palace Casino

La Center

NW 24th Av
NW 329th St
NW 26th Av

NW 17th Ct
NW Eagle Crest Dr
NW 18th

LA CENTER BOTTOMS

W 8th St
W 5th
W 4th St
W 3rd St
W 2nd St
W 1st St
NW PACIFIC HWY

NE 4TH ST
E Stonecreek Dr
A 1 Aspen Av
NE Ivy Av
NE John Storm Av

LOCKWOOD CREEK RD
NE
4th Cir E 4th Wy
E 3rd E 3rd Wy
E Parkside Cir
E 2nd E 1st
E 2nd St
E 16th Pl
E 1st St
E 18th Pl
32600

98629

45°51'47"
45°51'21"
45°50'55"

1

2

NW LACENTER RD
NW 13th Av
NW 18th Av
NW 20th Av
30900
NW 310th St

NW LA CENTER RD
NW TIMMEN RD
NW 319th Av
NW 9th Av
NW 316th Cir
NW 4th Ct
NW Pollock Rd

NE TIMMEN RD

LEWIS RIVER

45°51'21"

2

9

NW 5th Ct
NW 10th Ct
NW Spencer Rd
NW 3rd Pl

10
NE 309th Cir
NE 310th Cir

11

3

45°50'55"

NW 304th Cir
NW 18th Pl
NW 11th Av
NW 304th Wy

NE Walher
NE 12th Ct

5
29900

2500
NW 299th St
1500
1000
NW 297th Cir

NE 299th Av
NE 299th St
500
NE 299th St
NE 299th St

45°50'29"

SEE 417 MAP

4

TRI-MOUNTAIN GOLF COURSE

NW 2nd Av
28200

NE Timmen RD
NW 294th St
1500
NE 293rd St

NE 292nd Cir
NE 16th Av

45°50'03"

NW 289th St
2100
NW 289th St
1000
NW 7th Av
200
15

NE 6th Av
28800
NE 290th St
NE 289th St
NE 289th St

14

16

NW 11th Av
CEMETERY

45°49'37"

NE19th Av
NE 19th Av
NE 20th Av

N 57th Ct
N 10th St

NW 279th St
NW 5th Av
NW 277th Cir

NE 2nd Av

NE 279th St
27900

NE 14th Ct
NE 16th Av

6

45°49'10"

N 50th Pl
14
21

PIONEER ST
PIONEER ST
501
5
S 1st Cir
56th Pl
S Timm Rd
S 65th AV
S 5th AV

100
22
N 78th Pl
N 2nd Wy
S 78th Pl

NE 10TH AV
F5
23

NE 10TH AV

7

S Dolan Rd
6500
S 5TH ST
S 74th St
S 77th Pl
NE 264th St

45°48'44"

E   F   G   H   J

122°41'26"   122°40'48"   122°40'11"   122°39'34"   122°38'56"

SEE 446 MAP

MAP
417

1:24,000
1 in. = 2000 ft.

0   0.25   0.5
miles

SEE **B** MAP

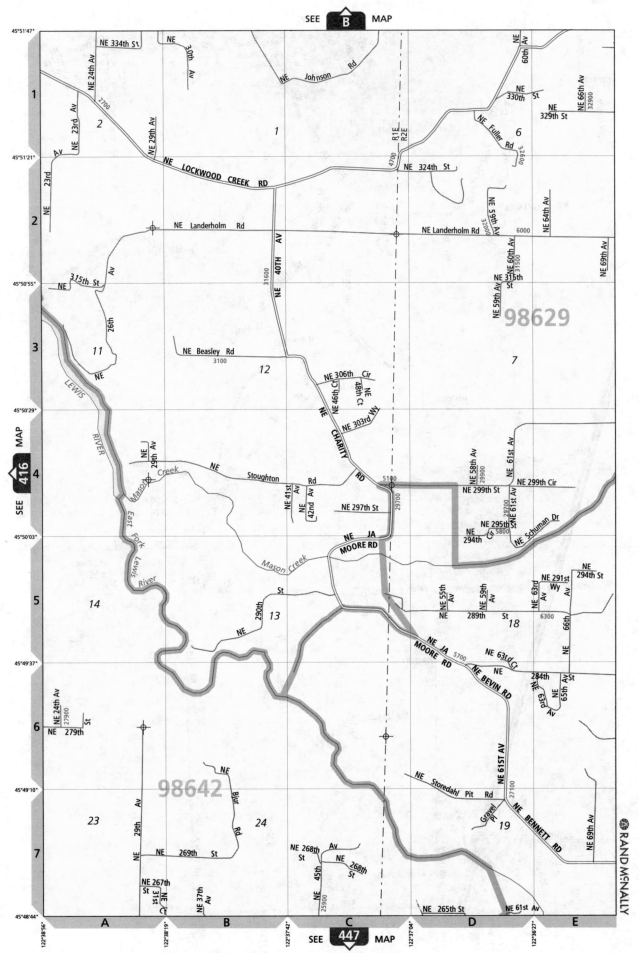

NE 334th St

NE 24th Av

NE 30th Av

NE Johnson Rd

NE 60th Av

NE 330th St

NE 66th Av

32900

NE 329th St

2700

1

R1E R2E

6

NE Fuller Rd

33600

NE 23rd Av

2

NE 29th Av

45°51'21"

NE LOCKWOOD CREEK RD

4700

NE 324th St

NE 23rd Av

NE Landerholm Rd

NE Landerholm Rd

NE 40TH AV

NE 59th Av

NE 60th Av

31500

6000

NE 64th Av

31000

315th St

NE Av

45°50'55"

NE 315th St

NE 69th Av

31600

26th

98629

NE Beasley Rd

3100

11

12

7

NE 306th Cir

NE 48th Ct

NE 46th Ct

NE CHARITY RD

45°50'29"

NE 303rd Wy

NE 29th Av

LEWIS

RIVER

Mason Creek

NE Stoughton Rd

NE 58th Av

NE 61st Av

29900

NE 299th Cir

MAP
416
SEE

4

5100

NE 299th St

NE 41st Av

NE 42nd Av

NE 297th St

29700

NE 295th Cir

NE 61st Av

29700

NE Schuman Dr

45°50'03"

NE JA

MOORE RD

NE 294th

5800

NE 294th St

Mason Creek

East Fork Lewis River

NE 290th St

13

NE 55th Av

NE 59th Av

NE 63rd Av

NE 291st Wy

14

NE 289th St

18

6300

NE 66th Av

45°49'37"

NE JA MOORE RD

5700

NE 63rd Ct

NE BEVIN RD

NE 284th Av

NE 65th Av

NE 63rd Av

NE 24th Av

27900

NE 279th St

45°49'37"

6

NE 279th St

NE 61ST AV

NE Storedahl Pit Rd

27100

45°49'10"

98642

29th Av

Blur Rd

Gravel Pit

NE BENNETT RD

23

24

19

NE 69th Av

NE 29th Av

NE 269th St

NE 268th St

NE 268th St

NE 267th St

NE 31st Ct

NE 37th Av

NE 45th Av

25900

NE 265th St

NE 61st Av

45°51'47"

45°48'44"

122°38'56"   122°38'19"   122°37'42"   122°37'04"   122°36'27"

MAP
417

1:24,000
1 in. = 2000 ft.

0   0.25   0.5
miles

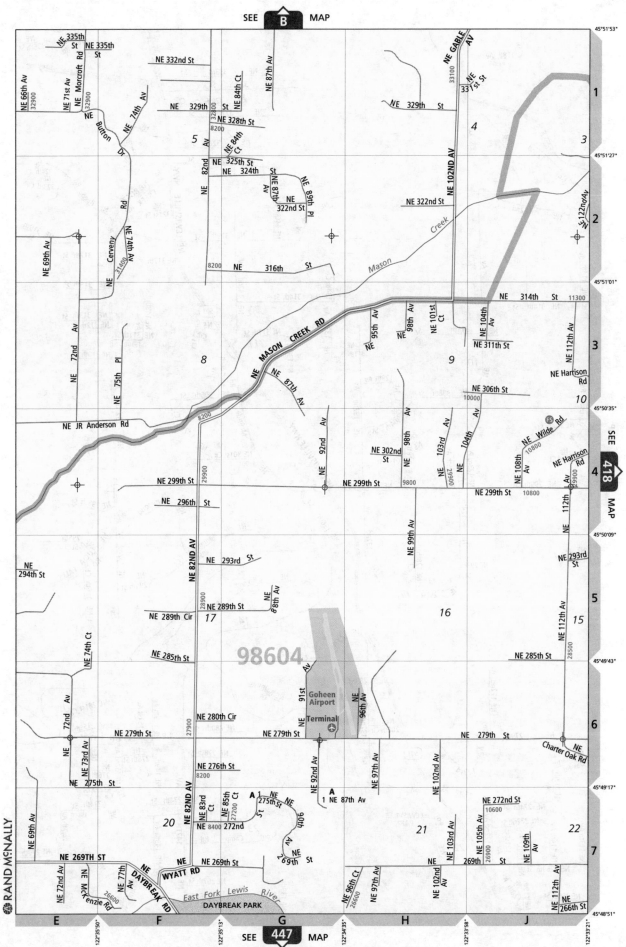

SEE **B** MAP

NE 335th St
NE 335th St
NE 332nd St
NE 87th Av
NE GABLE AV
33100
NE 331st St

NE 66th Av
32900
NE 71st Av
NE Morcroft Rd
32900
NE 74th Av
NE 329th St
3200
NE 84th Ct
NE 329th St
NE 4
NE 328th St
8200
NE 84th Ct
5
NE 82nd Av
NE 325th St
NE 324th St
NE 322nd St
NE 102ND AV
NE 122nd Av

Burton Dr
NE 87th Av
NE 89th
322nd St Pl

Cerveny Rd
NE 74th Av
31400

NE 69th Av
2

NE 322nd St

Mason   Creek
45°51'27"

45°51'01"

NE 72nd Av
8200
NE 316th St
NE 314th St 11300

NE MASON CREEK RD
NE 95th Av
NE 98th Av
NE 101st Ct
NE 104th Av
NE 311th St
NE 112th Av

8
NE 87th Av
NE 306th St
10000
NE Harrison Rd

NE 75th Pl
9
10

NE JR Anderson Rd
8200

NE 92nd Av
NE 98th Av
NE 103rd Av
NE 104th Av
NE 108th Av
NE Wilde Rd
10800
FS
NE Harrison Rd

NE 299th St
29900
NE 299th St
9800
NE 299th St 10800
NE 112th Av
29900
SEE
418
MAP

NE 296th St
NE 99th Av
45°50'09"

NE 294th St

NE 293rd St
NE 293rd St

NE 82ND AV
28900
NE 289th St
NE 88th Av
16
NE 112th Av
28500
15

NE 289th Cir
17

NE 74th Ct
NE 285th St
98604
NE 285th St
45°49'43"

NE 72nd Av

NE 280th Cir
91st Av
Goheen Airport
NE 96th Av
Terminal

NE 279th St
NE 279th St
NE 279th St
Charter Oak Rd
6

NE 73rd Av
NE 276th St
8200
NE 92nd Av
NE 97th Av
NE 102nd Av

NE 275th St
NE 82ND AV
NE 83rd Ct
NE 85th Ct
27200
A 1 NE 275th St
A 1 NE 87th Av
NE 272nd St
10600
45°49'17"

NE 69th Av
20
NE 8400 272nd St
NE 90th Av
21
NE 103rd Av
NE 105th Av
26900
NE 109th Av
22

NE 269th St
NE 72nd Av
NE 77th Av
NE McKenzie Rd
26600
NE DAYBREAK RD
NE WYATT RD
NE 269th St
NE 269th St
NE 96th Ct
26600
NE 97th Av
NE 102nd Av
NE 269th St
NE 105th Av
NE 112th Av
NE 266th St

East Fork   Lewis   River
DAYBREAK PARK

RAND M°NALLY

E   F   G   H   J

SEE **447** MAP

45°51'53"
1
3
45°51'27"
2
45°51'01"
3
45°50'35"
4
45°50'09"
5
45°49'43"
6
45°49'17"
7
45°48'51"

122°35'50"   122°35'13"   122°34'35"   122°33'58"   122°33'21"

MAP
418

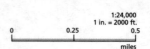

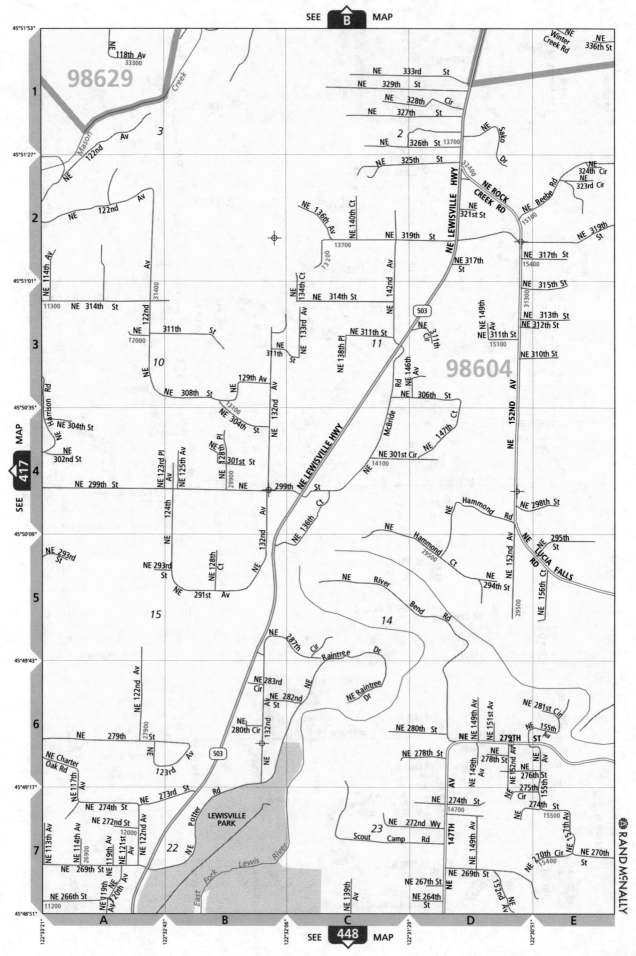

98629

98604

NE Winter Creek Rd
NE 336th St
NE 118th Av
33300
NE 333rd St
NE 329th St
NE 328th Cir
NE 327th St
NE 326th St 13700
NE 325th St
Mason Av
NE 122nd Av
NE Sako Dr
NE 324th Cir
NE 323rd Cir
NE 122nd Av
NE 136th Av
NE 140th Ct
NE 319th St
NE 321st St
NE 317th St
NE 317th St
15400
NE 114th Av
13700
13200
NE 134th Ct
NE 314th St
NE 142nd Av
NE 315th St
Av
31400
NE 313th St
NE 312th St
NE 314th St
11300
NE 149th Av
NE 311th St
15100
NE 122nd Av
NE 133rd Av
NE 311th St
503
NE 311th Cir
NE 310th St
311th St
12000
NE 311th St
Harrison Rd
NE 138th Pl
11
NE 132nd Av
129th Av
NE 146th Rd
NE 308th St
13100
NE 306th St
152ND AV
NE 304th St
31300
NE 302nd St
NE 304th St
McBride Ct
NE 147th Ct
NE 301st Cir
14100
NE 123rd Pl
NE 125th Av
NE 128th Pl
301st St
NE 299th St
29900
NE 299th St
Hammond Rd
NE 298th St
124th Av
NE 136th St
NE Hammond Ct
NE 295th St
NE 293rd St
NE 293rd St
132nd Av
29500
NE 152nd Av
NE Lucia Falls Rd
NE 128th Ct
NE River Bend Rd
NE 294th St
NE 156th Ct
15
NE 291st Av
29500
14
NE 287th Cir
Raintree Dr
NE 122nd Av
27900
NE 283rd Cir
NE 282nd St
NE Raintree Dr
NE 281st Cir
NE 280th Cir
132nd Av
NE 280th St
NE 149th Av
NE 151st Av
NE 155th Av
503
NE 279th St
123rd Av
NE 279TH ST
NE Charter Oak Rd
NE 278th St
NE 149th Av
NE 152nd Av
NE 276th Cir
NE 117th Av
NE 273rd St
Potter Rd
NE 274th St
14700
NE 275th Cir
NE 155th Av
NE 274th St
15500
NE 113th Av
NE 274th St
NE 272nd St
NE 122nd Av
LEWISVILLE PARK
23
NE 272nd Wy
147TH AV
NE 157th Av
22
Scout Camp Rd
NE 114th Av
NE 119th Av
NE 121st Av
12000
NE 149th Av
NE 270th Cir
15400
NE 270th St
26900
NE 269th St
East Fork Lewis River
NE 139th Av
NE 269th St
NE 266th St
NE 119th Av
NE 120th Av
11200
NE 267th St
152nd Av
NE 264th St

A   B   C   D   E

MAP
418

1:24,000
1 in. = 2000 ft.

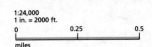

0   0.25   0.5

miles

SEE **B** MAP

NE 336th Av
NE 159th Av
NE 165th Av
NE 171st Av
NE 332nd St
33400
NE 171st Av

NE 335th Cir
NE 335th Cir
RD 33500
NE 335th Cir
NE Yacolt Mountain Rd

1

NE 176th Av
NE Kelly Rd
32500
NE KELLY
NE

1
NE Beebe Rd

6

5

NE 324th Cir
NE 323rd Cir

45°51'33"

NE 319th St

2

NE 319th St

NE 317th St
Southview Dr
NE Southview Ct 31100
Dr

45°51'07"

12

NE Spring Hill Rd

98675

Silvan

NE Brickle Creek Dr

3

7
NE 308th St Dr

8

45°50'41"

R2E
R3E

NE 171st Av
NE 172nd Av
NE 181st Av
NE 182nd Av
NE 182nd Av
NE Coyote Cir
NE Coyote Dr

Brickle Creek Dr

SEE
419
MAP

4

16900
17200
NE 299th St

NE 194th Av
31000

45°50'15"

NE 297th St
NE 169th Av

NE 182nd Ct

NE KELLY RD

NE LUCIA FALLS RD
18200

5

17400
NE 190th St
NE Cole Witter Rd

17

NE Basket Flat Rd
19700

13

NE 164th Av
NE 289th Cir

18

NE 288th Cir
NE 287th St

45°49'49"

Zinger Rd
East Fork Lewis River

NE 194th Av
28300
NE 201st Av
283rd NE St
NE 197th St

6

NE HEISSON RD

NE 176th Av
NE 176th Pl
NE 280th Av St
174th
NE 182nd Av

NE 279th St
NE 192nd Av
NE 280th St
NE 280th St
19700
NE 279th St

16200

45°49'23"

NE 162nd Av

NE HEISSON RD

27400
NE 200th Av
NE 272nd St
NE 202nd Av
NE 276th St

NE 274th St

24

19

20

NE 273rd St

NE 270th St

NE 194th Av
25900
NE 272nd St
NE 269th St

7

NE 267th St

E   F   G   H   J

122°30'14"
122°29'37"
122°29'00"
122°28'22"
122°27'45"

45°51'59"

45°48'56"

RAND MCNALLY

MAP
419

1:24,000
1 in. = 2000 ft.

0   0.25   0.5
miles

N

SEE B MAP

NE Wh T Garner Rd

NE Yacolt Mountain Rd

NE 207th Pl

NE Mystic Cir

NE Mystic Dr

NE Mystic Dr

NE Mystic Dr

45°51'59"

1

5

4

3

45°51'33"

30500

2

NE CC Landon Rd CC

NE CC Landon Rd

98675

24400

Cascara Ln

NE 312th St

45°51'07"

3

8

9

10

NE 309th St

NE 245th Av

NE 247th Av

NE

45°50'41"

MAP
418
SEE

4

NE Hantwick

NE LUCIA FALLS RD

NE LUCIA FALLS RD

LUCIA
FALLS SOUTH PARK

Rd

East Fork Lewis River

NE Steelhead Ln

45°50'15"

NE 228th Ct

Lucia

NE

Hantwick Rd

NE Basket Flat Rd

45°50'15"

19700

5

17

16

15

NE 236th Av

NE Hantwick Rd

45°49'49"

98604

6

YAKOLT BURN
STATE FOREST

45°49'23"

NE 279th St

NE 276th Wy

NE 212th Av

20

NE 273rd St

NE 269th St

7

27100

NE 271st St

Rock Creek

NE 214th Av

NE 220th Av

21

22

21200

NE 269th St

NE 267th St

45°48'56"

12°27'45"   12°27'08"   12°26'30"   12°25'53"   12°25'16"

1:24,000
1 in. = 2000 ft.

0   0.25   0.5
miles

 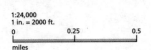
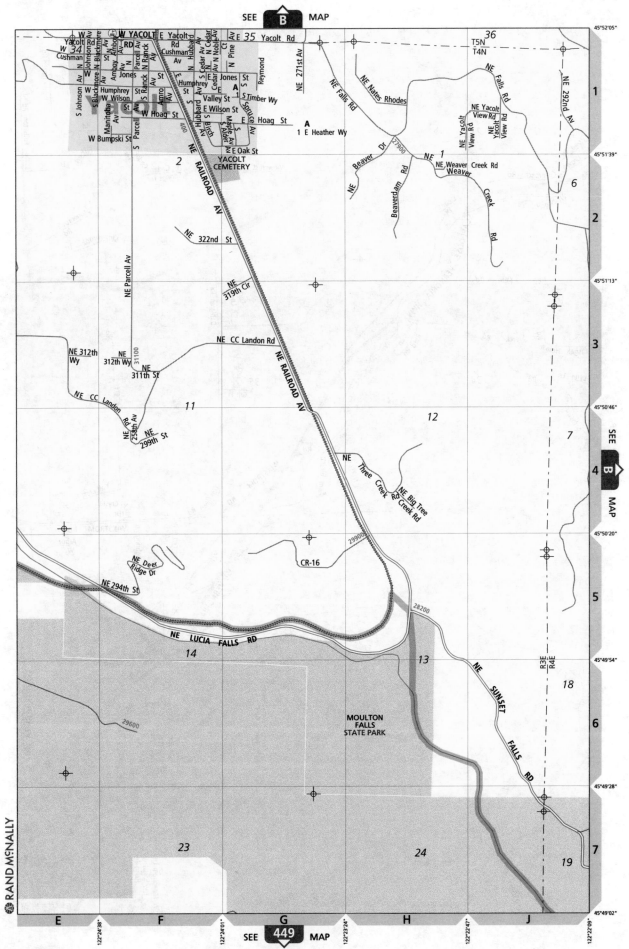

W Yacolt Rd   E 35 Yacolt Rd   36

W Yacolt

W 34

Yacolt

YACOLT CEMETERY

NE RAILROAD AV

NE 322nd St

NE Parcell Av

NE 319th Cir

NE CC Landon Rd

NE 312th Wy
NE 312th Wy
NE 311th St

NE CC Landon Rd

NE 255th Av
NE 299th St

11   12

NE Three Creek Rd
NE Big Tree Creek Rd

NE Deer Ridge Dr

NE 294th St

CR-16

NE LUCIA FALLS RD

14   13

23   24

MOULTON FALLS STATE PARK

NE SUNSET FALLS RD

18

19

NE Falls Rd
NE Nates Rhodes
NE Yacolt View Rd
NE Yacolt View Rd
NE Weaver Creek Rd
Weaver
Beaver Dr
Beaverdam Rd
Creek Rd

A
1 E Heather Wy

NE 271st Av

NE 292nd Av

T5N
T4N

R3E
R4E

1

6

2

3

4

5

6

7

7

E   F   G   H   J

45°52'05"
45°51'39"
45°51'13"
45°50'46"
45°50'20"
45°49'54"
45°49'28"
45°49'02"

122°24'38"   122°24'01"   122°23'24"   122°22'47"   122°22'09"

MAP
444

1:24,000
1 in. = 2000 ft.

0   0.25   0.5

miles

SEE 414 MAP

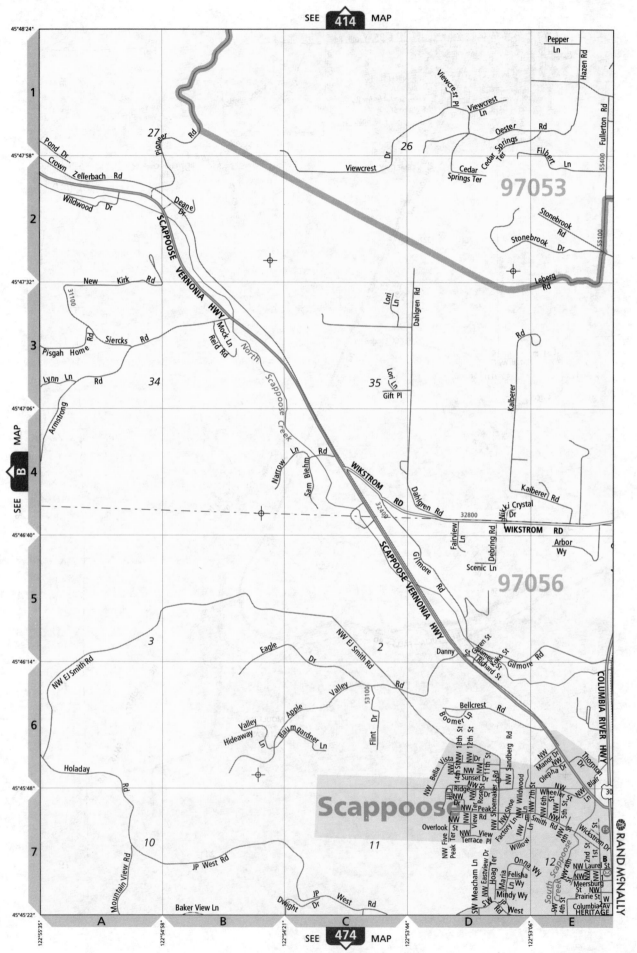

SEE 474 MAP

97053

97056

Scappoose

RAND MCNALLY

HERITAGE

MAP
444

1:24,000
1 in. = 2000 ft.

0   0.25   0.5

miles

SEE 414 MAP

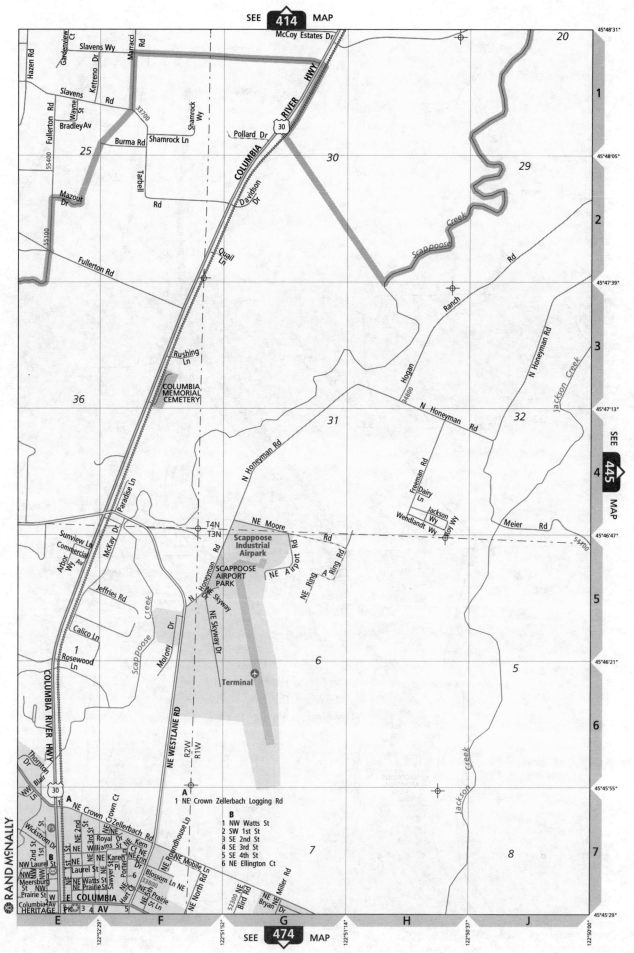

McCoy Estates Dr

20

Gardenview Ct
Hazen Rd
Slavens Wy
Marracci Rd
Ketreno Dr
Fullerton Rd
Slavens Rd
Wayne St
Bradley Av
55400
Burma Rd
Shamrock Ln
Shamrock Wy
33700
Tarbell Rd
Mazout Dr
55400
55550
Fullerton Rd

COLUMBIA RIVER HWY
30
Pollard Dr
Davidson Dr
Quail Ln

25

30

29

Scappoose Creek

Rd

Ranch

1

2

45°48'31"

45°48'05"

45°47'39"

Rushing Ln

COLUMBIA MEMORIAL CEMETERY

36

31

N Honeyman Rd

34800

Hogan

N Honeyman Rd

32

Jackson Creek

N Honeyman Rd

3

45°47'13"

SEE 445 MAP

Paradise Ln

McKay Dr

Sunview Ln
Commercial Av
Arbor Wy

T4N
T3N

NE Moore

Scappoose Industrial Airpark

Rd

NE Airport Rd

NE Ring Rd

Ring Rd

Freeman Rd
Dairy Ln
Jackson Wy
Wendlandt Wy
Roy Wy

Meier Rd

54100

4

45°46'47"

Jeffries Rd

SCAPPOOSE AIRPORT PARK

N Honeyman Dr
NE Skyway

NE Skyway Dr

Calico Ln
Rosewood Ln
1

Molony Dr

Scappoose Creek

6

Terminal

5

45°46'21"

5

COLUMBIA RIVER HWY

NE WESTLANE RD
R2W
R1W

Jackson Creek

6

45°45'55"

Thornton Dr
Blair
30
NW Ln
A
NE Crown Ct
NE Crown Zellerbach Rd

A
1 NE Crown Zellerbach Logging Rd

7

8

7

45°45'29"

Wickstrom Dr
NW 2nd St
NW 1st St
B
NW Laurel St
NW Meersburg St NW
Prairie St NW
Columbia Av
HERITAGE

NE 2nd St
NE 3rd St
NE Williams St
NE Royal St
NE Erin Ct
NE Kern Dr
NE Karen Pl
NE Sawyer St
NE Porter Dr
6
Hart Ct
Blossom Ln NE
33800
NE Prairie St NE

Laurel St NE
NE Watts St
NE Prairie St

E COLUMBIA AV
PK 3 4 5

NE Roundhouse Ln
NE Mobile St
NE North Rd

52300
NE Bird Rd
NE Bryan Dr
NE Miller Rd

B
1 NW Watts St
2 SW 1st St
3 SE 2nd St
4 SE 3rd St
5 SE 4th St
6 NE Ellington Ct

E   F   G   H   J

SEE 474 MAP

122°52'29"   122°51'52"   122°51'14"   122°50'37"   122°50'00"

MAP
445

1:24,000
1 in. = 2000 ft.

0   0.25   0.5

miles

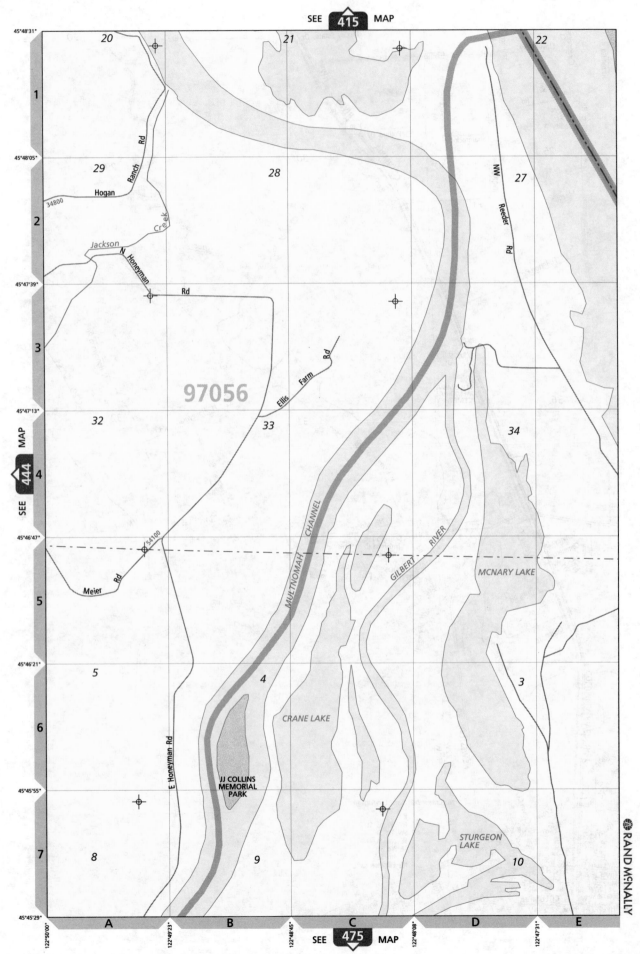

SEE 415 MAP

45°48'31"

20

21

22

1

45°48'05"

29

Ranch Rd

28

NW

27

Hogan

2

34800

Creek

Jackson

N Honeyman

Reeder Rd

45°47'39"

Rd

3

MAP
444
SEE

97056

Ellis Farm Rd

45°47'13"

32

33

34

4

54100

MULTNOMAH CHANNEL

GILBERT RIVER

45°46'47"

Meier Rd

MCNARY LAKE

5

45°46'21"

5

4

3

CRANE LAKE

6

E Honeyman Rd

JJ COLLINS MEMORIAL PARK

45°45'55"

STURGEON LAKE

7

8

9

10

45°45'29"

A   B   C   D   E

122°50'00"   122°49'23"   122°48'45"   122°48'08"   122°47'31"

SEE 475 MAP

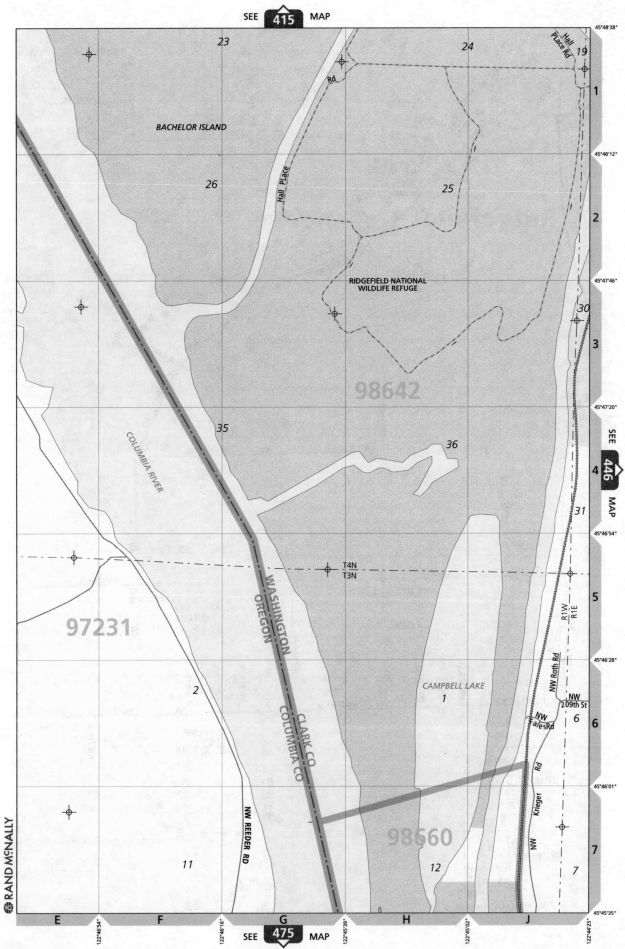

MAP
445

1:24,000
1 in. = 2000 ft.

0   0.25   0.5
miles

Hall Place Rd

23   24   19

Rd   1

BACHELOR ISLAND

45°48'38"

45°48'12"

26   25   2

45°47'46"

Hall Place

RIDGEFIELD NATIONAL
WILDLIFE REFUGE

30   45°47'20"

3

98642

SEE 446 MAP

35   36   4

COLUMBIA RIVER   31

45°46'54"

T4N
T3N

5

WASHINGTON
OREGON

R1W
R1E

45°46'28"

97231   NW Roth Rd

CAMPBELL LAKE

2   1   NW
209th St

NW
Fa/esRd   6   45°46'01"

CLARK CO
COLUMBIA CO

NW Krieger Rd

NW

98660   7

NW REEDER RD

11   12   7

E   F   G   H   J

122°46'54"   122°46'16"   122°45'39"   122°45'02"   122°44'25"

45°45'35"

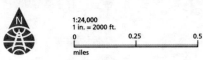

MAP
446

1:24,000
1 in. = 2000 ft.
0   0.25   0.5
miles

N

SEE 416 MAP

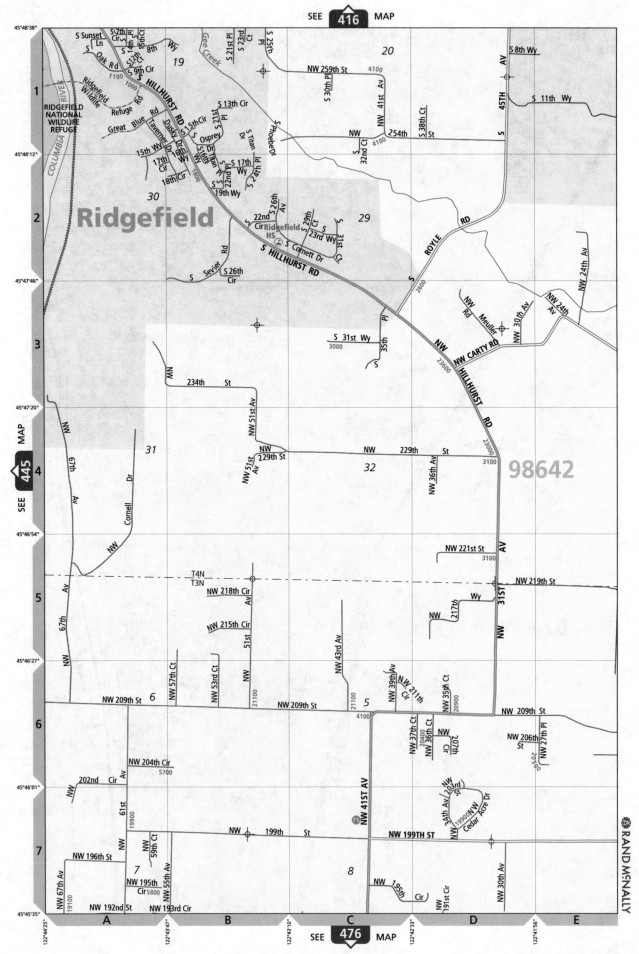

45°48'38"

S Sunset Ln
S 7th Pl
S 4th Ct
S 8th Wy
S 12th
Oak Rd
S 9th Cir
Ridgefield Wildlife Refuge Rd
1100
1000
HILLHURST RD
19
S 21st Pl
S 23rd Ct
S 25th Pl
NW 259th St
20
S 8th Wy
45 AV

RIDGEFIELD NATIONAL WILDLIFE REFUGE
Great Blue Rd
Taverner Dr
Dusky Dr
S 15th Cir
S 21st Pl
Osprey Dr
S 13th Cir
S Phoebe Dr
NW 41st Av
S 30th Pl
4100
NW 254th St
4100
S 38th Ct St
S 11th Wy

45°48'12"
15th Wy Dr
17th Cir
16th Wy
S Titan Dr
S 17th Pl
S 22nd Pl
S 24th Wy
S 26th Av
45TH S

18th Cir
19th Wy
30
Ridgefield
S 22nd Cir
Ridgefield HS
S 29th Ct
23rd Wy
S 31st Ct
29
ROYLE RD
NW 24th Av

45°47'46"
S Sevier Rd
S 26th Cir
S Cornett Dr
S HILLHURST RD
S 2600
NW Meuller Rd
NW 30th Av
NW 24th AV

S 31st Wy
3000
35th Pl
S
NW 23600
NW CARTY RD
HILLHURST RD

45°47'20"
NW 234th St
NW 51st Av
NW 51st Av
NW 229th St
NW 229th St
32
NW 36th Av
23000
3100
98642

SEE 445 MAP
31
Cornell Dr
NW 67th Av
NW NW 221st St
3100
31ST AV
NW 219th St

45°46'54"
T4N T3N
NW 218th Cir
217th Wy
NW 31ST
NW

45°46'27"
NW 215th Cir
51st Av
NW 43rd Av
NW 67th Av
NW 57th Ct
NW 53rd Ct
NW 39th Av
NW 211th Cir
NW 35th Ct
20900

NW 209th St 6
NW 209th St
21100
NW 209th St 5
4100
NW 37th Ct
20400
NW 36th Ct
207th Cir
NW 209th St
NW 206th St
NW 27th Pl
205000
NW 41ST AV

45°46'01"
NW 204th Cir
5700
NW 202nd Cir
NW 61st Av
19900
NW 203rd St
NW 33rd Av
19900 NW Cedar Acre Dr

NW 196th St
7
NW 59th Ct
NW 199th St
199th St
NW 199TH ST

45°45'35"
NW 67th Av
19100
NW 195th Cir 5800
NW 55th Av
NW 192nd St
NW 193rd Cir
8
NW 195th Cir
NW 191st Cir
NW 30th Av

A   B   C   D   E

122°44'25"   122°43'47"   122°43'10"   122°42'33"   122°41'56"

SEE 476 MAP

RAND McNALLY

MAP
446

1:24,000
1 in. = 2000 ft.
0   0.25   0.5
miles

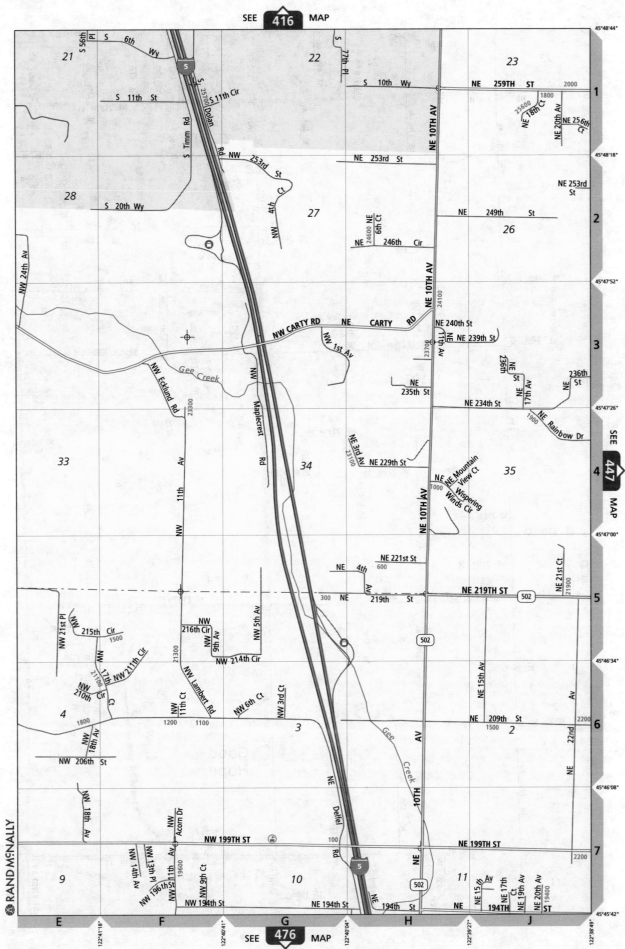

SEE 416 MAP

21
S 56th Pl
S 6th Wy
22
S 77th Pl
23
S 10th Wy
NE 259TH ST   2000
1
S 11th St
S 25700 Dolan   S 11th Cir
25600   1800
NE 18th Ct
NE 20th Av   NE 256th Ct
NE 10TH AV
NW 253rd St
NE 253rd St
NE 253rd St
28
4th Ct
S 20th Wy
27
NE 6th Ct
NE 249th St
26
2
NW 24600 NE
24600 NE   246th Cir
NW 24th Av
NE 10TH AV
24100
NW CARTY RD   NE CARTY RD
NE 240th St
3
NW 1st Av   23700   11th Av   NE 239th St
Gee Creek   NW   NE 236th
NW Ecklund Rd   23300   NE   236th St
NW Maplecrest Rd   NE 235th St   NE 17th Av   NE
NE 234th St   1900   NE Rainbow Dr
33   NW 3rd Av   23100   NE 229th St   NE Mountain View Ct   35   SEE 447 MAP
34   1000   Wispering Winds Cir
NW 11th Av
NE 10TH AV
NE 221st St
NE 4th   600   NE 21st Ct   21900
NW 21st Pl   215th Cir   NE 219th St   502
NW   1500   216th Cir   NW 5th Av   300 NE 219th St   502
NW 211th Cir   NW 9th Av
21300   NW 214th Cir   NE 15th Av
NW 17th Cir   21100
NW 210th Cir   NW Lambert Rd   NW 6th Ct   NW 3rd Ct   NE 209th St   22nd Av   2200
4   1800   NW 11th Ct   1200   1100   3   1500   2
NW 18th Av
NW 206th St   Gee Creek   NE 10TH AV   NE 22nd
NW 18th Av
NW Acorn Dr   NE Delfel Rd
NW 199TH ST   NE 199TH ST   2200
NW 14th Av   NW 13th Pl Av   19600   NW 9th Ct   NE 15th Av   NE 17th Av   NE 19th Av   NE 20th Av
9   NW 196th St   10   11   NE 17th Ct   19400
NW 194th St   NE 194th St   NE 194th St   NE 194TH

MAP
447

1:24,000
1 in. = 2000 ft.

0   0.25   0.5
miles

SEE 417 MAP

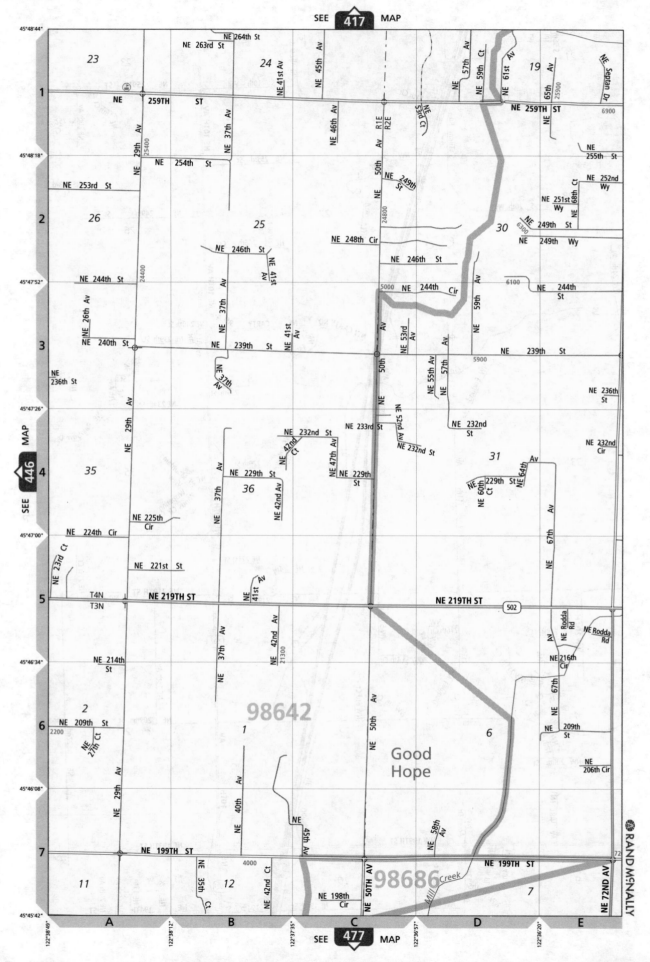

45°48'44"

23

NE 263rd St
NE 264th St

24

NE 41st Av

NE 45th Av

NE 57th Ct

NE 59th Ct

NE 61st Av

19

NE Septan Dr

NE 65th

25900

1

NE 259TH ST

NE 259th St

6900

NE 29th Av

25400

NE 37th Av

NE 46th Av

NE 50th Av

R1E R2E

NE 51st Ct

NE 255th St

45°48'18"

NE 254th St

NE 253rd St

NE 249th St

NE 252nd Wy

NE 251st Wy

NE 68th Ct

2

26

24800

25

NE 248th Cir

30

6900

NE 249th St

NE 249th Wy

NE 246th St

NE 246th St

45°47'52"

NE 244th St

24400

NE 41st Av

NE 244th Cir

5000

6100

NE 244th St

NE 26th Av

NE 37th Av

NE 53rd Av

NE 59th Av

NE 240th St

NE 239th St

NE 41st Av

NE 50th Av

NE 239th St

5900

NE 239th St

3

NE 236th St

NE 37th Av

NE 55th Av

NE 57th Av

NE 236th St

45°47'26"

NE 29th Av

NE 232nd St

NE 233rd St

NE 232nd St

NE 52nd Av

NE 232nd St

NE 232nd Cir

MAP

NE 232nd St

446

NE 42nd Ct

NE 229th St

NE 47th Av

NE 229th St

31

NE 64th Av

SEE

35

NE 37th Av

36

NE 42nd Av

NE 229th St

NE 60th Ct

NE 229th St

4

NE 225th Cir

NE 67th Av

NE 224th Cir

45°47'00"

NE 23rd Ct

NE 221st St

NE 41st Av

5

T4N

NE 219TH ST

NE 219TH ST

502

T3N

NE Rodda Rd

NE Rodda Rd

45°46'34"

NE 214th St

NE 37th Av

NE 42nd Av

21300

67th Av

NE 216th Cir

98642

67th Av

2

NE 50th Av

NE 209th St

45°46'08"

NE 209th St

2200

6

NE 27th Ct

1

6

NE 206th Cir

Good
Hope

NE 29th Av

NE 40th Av

NE 45th Av

NE 58th Av

7

NE 199TH ST

NE 199th St

NE 199TH ST

NE 72ND AV

72

45°45'42"

11

NE 35th Ct

12

NE 42nd Ct

NE 50TH AV

98686

Creek

7

NE 198th Cir

4000

Mill Creek

A   B   C   D   E

SEE 477 MAP

122°38'49"   122°38'12"   122°37'35"   122°36'57"   122°36'20"

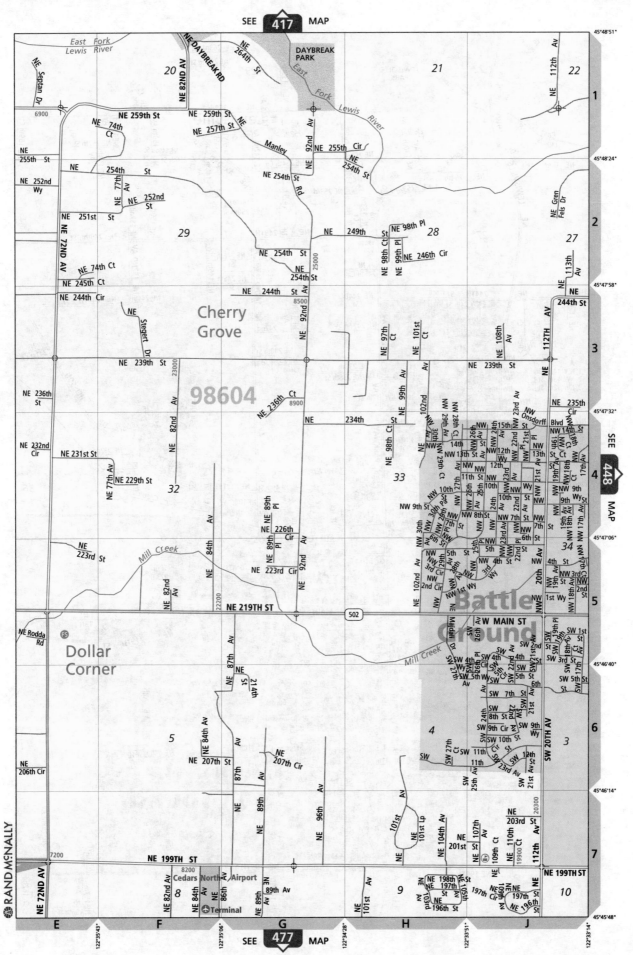

MAP
447

1:24,000
1 in. = 2000 ft.

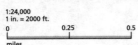

0   0.25   0.5
miles

SEE 417 MAP

45°48'51"

East Fork Lewis River

NE Septan Dr

NE 82ND AV

NE DAYBREAK RD

20

NE 264th St

DAYBREAK PARK

21

NE 112th Av

22

1

6900

NE 259th St

NE 74th Ct

NE 259th St

NE 257th St

Manley

NE 92nd Av

NE 255th Cir

NE 254th St

East Fork Lewis River

45°48'24"

NE 255th St

NE 252nd Wy

NE 77th Av

NE 254th St

NE 252nd St

NE 254th St Rd

NE Gren Fels Dr

NE 251st St

NE 72ND AV

29

NE 249th St

NE 98th Pl

28

27

2

NE 74th Ct

NE 254th St

NE 98th Ct

NE 99th Pl

NE 246th Cir

NE 113th Av

NE 245th Ct

NE 254th St

NE 244th Cir

NE 244th St Av

NE 92nd Av

8500

NE 112TH AV

NE 244th St

45°47'58"

NE

Cherry Grove

Stegert Dr

NE 97th Ct

NE 101st Ct

NE 108th Av

NE 239th St

NE 239th St

NE 235th Cir

3

45°47'32"

NE 236th St

82nd Av

23000

98604

NE 236th Ct

8900

NE 234th St

NE 99th Av

NE 102nd Av

NW 29th Ct

NW 28th Ct

NW 23rd Av

NW Onsdorff Blvd

NW 14th St

SEE 448 MAP

NE 232nd Cir

NE 231st St

NE 77th Av

NE 229th St

32

84th Av

NE 89th Pl

NE 226th Pl

NE 89th Pl Cir

92nd Av

NE 98th Ct

33

NW 30th

NW 29th

NW 14th

NW 13th St

NW 26th

NW 24th

NW 15th

NW 22nd

NW 12th Wy

NW 21st St

NW 19th St

NW 18th

NW 17th

NW 11th St

NW 27th

NW 26th

NW 25th

NW 10th

NW 23rd

NW 9th

4

NW 9th

NW 10th

NW 24th

NW 22nd

NW 7th St

NW 18th

NW 17th St

NW 8th St

NW 23rd

NW 30th

NW 27th Pl

NW 7th

NW 6th

45°47'06"

34

NE 223rd St

Mill Creek

NE 82nd Av

NE 223rd Cir

NW 30th

NW 5th

NW 29th

NW 28th

NW 23rd

NW 5th

NW 4th

NW 3rd

NW 4th St

NW 18th St

NW 3rd Cir

NW 2nd St

NW 102nd Av

NW 3rd Cir

NW 2nd Cir

NW 1st Wy

NW 20th

NW 19th St

NW 1st Wy

5

NE 219TH ST

22200

502

Mill Creek

W MAIN ST

SW 26th

Maidn Dr

SW 1st

SW 19th Pl

45°46'40"

NE Rodda Rd

Dollar Corner

NE 87th Av

SW 2nd

SW 4th Pl

SW 4th

SW 21st

SW 3rd Cir

SW 22nd

SW 18th

SW 17th St

SW 5th St

214th

NE 84th Av

5

NE 87th Av

NE 207th St

NE 207th Cir

SW 7th

4

SW 24th

SW 8th Av

SW 21st

SW 9th Cir

SW 20TH AV

3

6

NE 206th Cir

NE 89th Av

NE 96th Av

101st Av

NE 104th Av

NE 107th Ct

NE 110th Ct

NE 112th Av

NE 203rd Av

45°46'14"

20300

NE 199TH ST

8200

NE 199TH ST

7200

NE 72ND AV

Cedars North Airport

NE 82nd Av

NE 84th Av

NE 86th

NE 89th

89th Av

Terminal

NE 101st Av

9

NE 198th Av

NE 197th

NE 196th St

10

7

E   F   G   H   J

45°45'48"

SEE 477 MAP

MAP
448

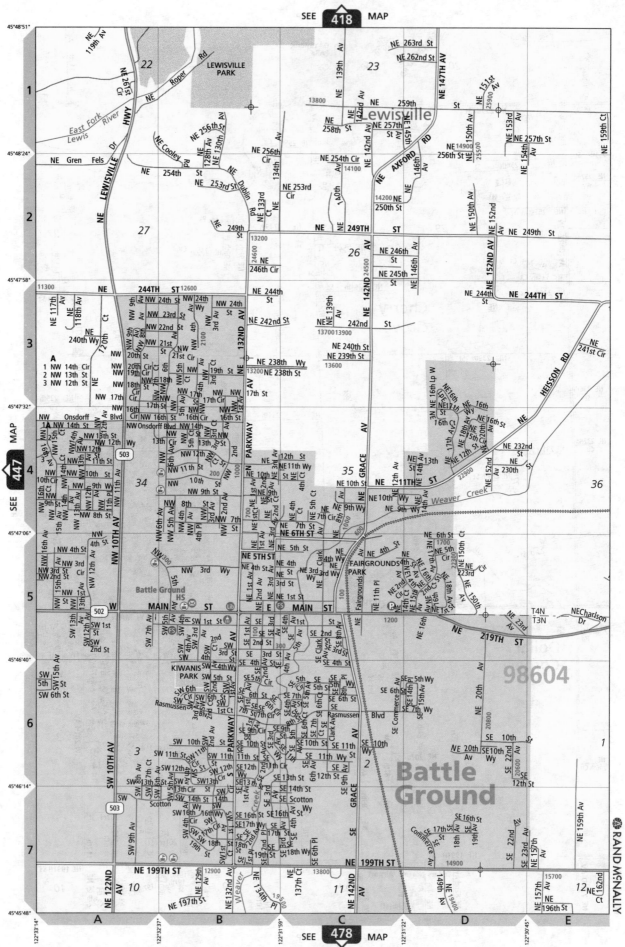

SEE [418] MAP

SEE [478] MAP

SEE [447] MAP

Battle Ground

Lewisville

98604

RAND MCNALLY

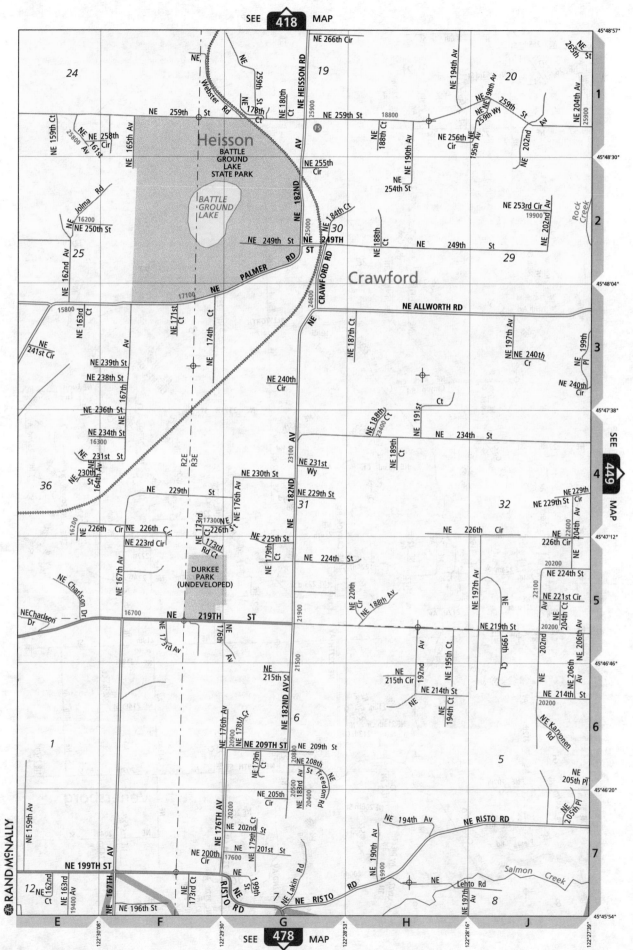

MAP
448

1:24,000
1 in. = 2000 ft.

0   0.25   0.5

miles

SEE 418 MAP

NE 266th Cir

24

NE 266th Cir

19

NE 194th Av

20

NE 265th

1

NE 259th St

NE 178th

NE 180th Ct

NE HEISSON RD

25900

NE 259th St

18800

NE 198th Av

259th Wy

259th St

NE 204th Av

25900

NE 259th

NE 159th Ct

NE 258th

NE 165th Av

25800

161st Cir

NE 256th Cir

195th

202nd Av

Heisson
BATTLE
GROUND
LAKE
STATE PARK

NE 255th Cir

NE 190th Av

NE 254th St

Jolma Rd

16200

NE 250th St

NE 182ND AV

BATTLE
GROUND
LAKE

NE 253rd Cir Av

19900

Rock Creek

2

25

NE 162nd Av

NE 249th St

NE 249TH ST

30

NE 184th Ct

NE 188th Ct

NE 249th St

29

25000

PALMER RD

24600

CRAWFORD RD

Crawford

15800

NE 163rd Ct

NE 171st Ct

NE 174th Ct

17100

NE ALLWORTH RD

NE 187th Ct

NE 197th Av

NE 199th Pl

3

NE 241st Cir

NE 167th Av

NE 240th Cr

NE 240th Cir

NE 239th St

NE 238th St

NE 240th Cir

NE 236th St

NE 188th Ct

23400

NE 191st Ct

NE 234th St

NE 234th St

16300

NE 182ND AV

23100

NE 189th Ct

NE 231st St

231st Wy

SEE 449 MAP

4

NE 230th

164th Av

R2E R3E

NE 230th St

NE 176th Av

NE 229th St

NE 229th St Cir

36

NE 229th St

31

32

NE 229th St

NE 226th Cir

16200

NE 226th Cir

NE 226th Ct

17300

226th Ct

NE 173rd Rd Ct

NE 225th St

NE 226th Cir

22600

204th Av

226th Cir

NE 223rd Cir

NE 179th Ct

NE 224th St

20200

NE 224th St

22100

NE Charlson Dr

NE 167th Av

DURKEE PARK (UNDEVELOPED)

NE 220th Cir

NE 188th Av

NE 197th Av

NE 221st Cir

5

NE Charlson Dr

16700

NE 219TH ST

173rd Av

176th Av

21900

NE 219th St

202nd Av

204th Ct

206th Av

21500

NE 215th St

NE 215th Cir

192nd Av

NE 195th Ct

20200

6

20900

178th Ct

21500

NE 214th St

194th Ct

NE 214th St

20200

NE Karvonen Rd

1

NE 176th Av

NE 209TH ST

NE 209th St

NE 205th Pl

5

NE 179th Ct

20800

NE 208th

Freeman Rd

20500

NE 183rd Av

20400

NE 205th Cir

NE 205th Pl

NE 159th Av

NE 176TH AV

20200

NE 202nd Ct

NE 179th St

201st St

17600

NE 200th Cir

NE 194th Av

NE RISTO RD

7

NE 199TH ST

NE 173rd Ct

RISTO RD

NE 196th St

NE 190th Av

19900

NE 197th Av

Salmon Creek

12

NE 162nd Ct

NE 163rd Av

19400 Av

NE 167TH AV

NE 196th St

RISTO RD

7

NE Lakin Rd

NE RISTO RD

Lehto Rd

8

RAND McNALLY

E   F   G   H   J

SEE 478 MAP

45°48'57"
45°48'30"
45°48'04"
45°47'38"
45°47'12"
45°46'46"
45°46'20"
45°45'54"

122°30'08"
122°29'30"
122°28'53"
122°28'16"
122°27'39"

MAP
449

1:24,000
1 in. = 2000 ft.

0   0.25   0.5
miles

SEE 419 MAP

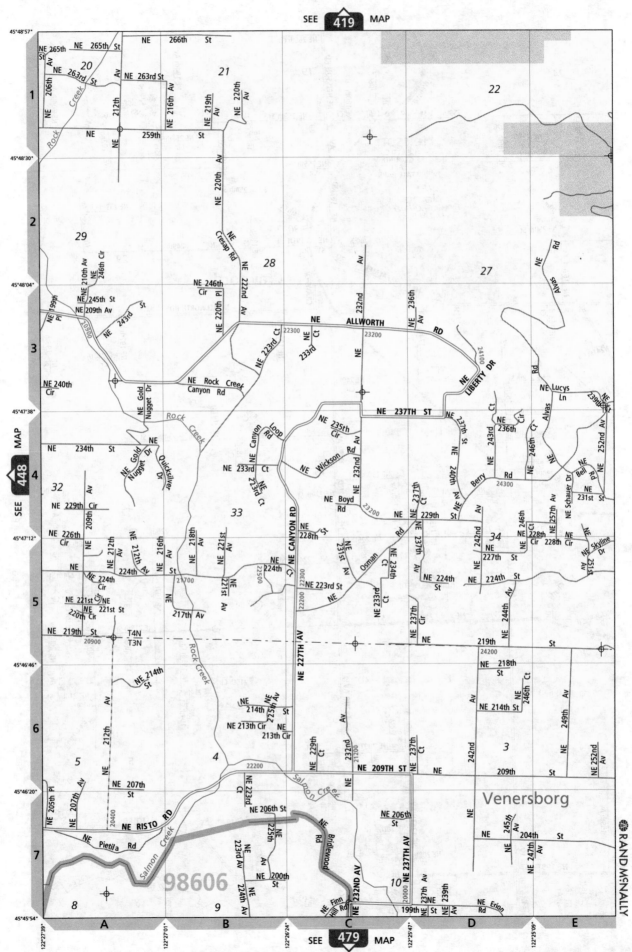

45°48'57"

NE 265th St
NE 265th St
NE 266th St
20
NE 263rd St
NE 263rd St
NE 206th
212th Av
21
22
1
Rock Creek
NE 259th St

45°48'30"

NE 220th Av
NE 216th Av
NE 219th Av
NE 220th Av

29
NE 246th Cir
NE 210th Av
28
NE 220th Pl
27
2
Cresap Rd

45°48'04"

NE 199th Pl
NE 245th St
NE 246th Cir
NE 232nd
NE 236th Av
NE 222nd Av
Alvas Rd
NE 209th Av
NE 243rd St
NE ALLWORTH RD
22300
23200
24100
NE 223rd Ct
233rd Ct
3
NE 240th Cir
NE Rock Creek Canyon Rd
NE LIBERTY DR
NE Lucys Ln
NE Gold Nugget Dr
Rock Creek
NE 237TH ST
NE 235th Cir
NE 237th St
236th Ct
252nd Av

45°47'38"

NE 234th St
NE Canyon Loop Rd
243rd Ct
NE 246th Ct
NE Gold Nugget Dr
Quicksilver Dr
NE 233rd Ct
NE Wickson Rd
232nd Av
240th Av
Berry Rd
231st St
NE Schauer Dr
4
32
NE 229th Cir
209th Av
213rd Ct
NE Boyd Rd
23200
NE 237th Ct
NE 229th St
242nd Av
NE 246th Ct
228th Cir
NE Skyline Dr
24300
33
NE 228th Cir
257th Av

45°47'12"

NE 226th Cir
NE 212th
NE 216th St
NE 218th Av
NE 221st Av
228th St
231st Av
Osman Rd
NE 234th Ct
NE 227th St
224th St
NE 224th Cir
NE 224th St
NE 224th
224th Av
5
NE 221st St
NE 221st Cir
217th Av
NE
NE 223rd St
22300
NE 237th Cir
244th Av
NE 220th Cir
21700
22500
22200
NE 219th St
20900
T4N
T3N
219th St
24200

45°46'46"

NE 214th St
NE 218th St
6
212th Av
Rock Creek
225th Av
NE 246th Ct
242nd Av
249th Av
NE 214th St
NE 214th St
NE 213th Cir
NE 213th Cir
NE 229th Ct
232nd Av
237th Ct
3
NE 227TH AV
NE 209TH ST
21200
5
4
22200
NE 207th St
Venersborg
NE 205th Pl
NE 207th Av
NE 232nd Ct
NE 206th St
NE 206th St
NE 245th Av
204th St

45°46'20"

NE RISTO RD
20400
Salmon Creek
225th Av
NE Bridlewood Rd
NE 247th Av
98606
NE Pietila Rd
223rd Av
NE 237TH AV
NE 237th Av
7
NE 200th
10
20000
NE Finn Hill Rd
232ND AV
NE 239th
NE Erion Rd
8
9
199th St
D

45°45'54"

A   B   C   D   E

SEE 479 MAP

122°27'39"
122°27'01"
122°26'24"
122°25'47"
122°25'09"

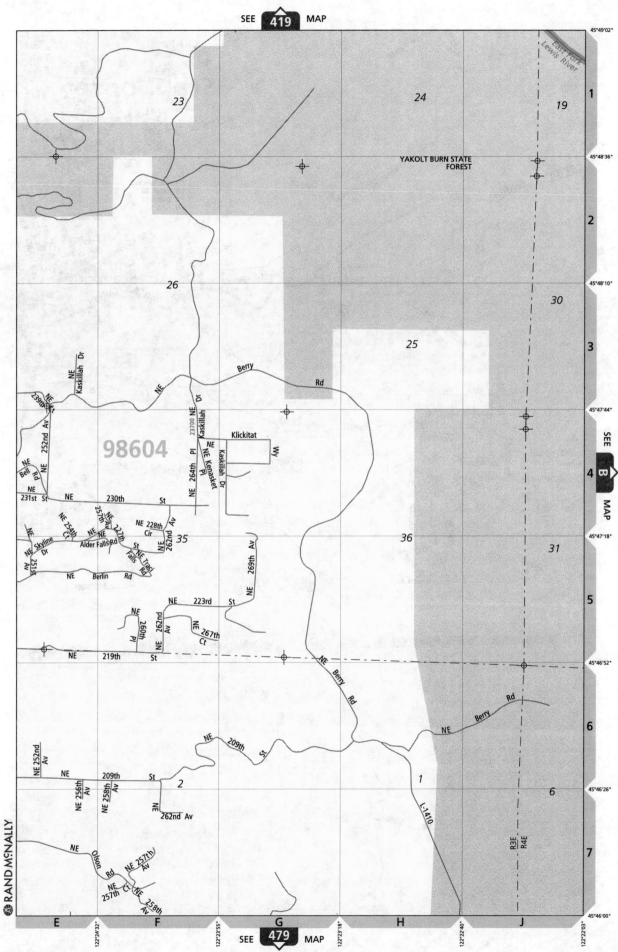

MAP
449

1:24,000
1 in. = 2000 ft.

0   0.25   0.5
miles

SEE 419 MAP

45°49'02"

23

24

19

1

YAKOLT BURN STATE
FOREST

45°48'36"

2

26

45°48'10"

30

25

3

NE Kaskillah Dr

NE

Berry

Rd

45°47'44"

NE 239th Ct

NE 252nd Av

23700 NE

NE Kaskillah Pl

NE 264th Pl

NE Kenasket

Kaskillah Dr

Klickitat

Wy

SEE

B

MAP

98604

4

NE Bell Rd

NE 231st St

NE 230th St

NE 257th Av

NE 254th Ct

NE 227th

NE 228th Cir

NE 262nd Av

35

NE Skyline Dr

Alder Falls Rd

NE 251st Av

NE Berlin Rd

St NE Falls Rd

NE Traci

NE 269th Av

36

45°47'18"

31

NE 223rd St

NE 262nd Av

NE 267th Ct

5

NE 290th Pl

NE 219th St

45°46'52"

NE Berry Rd

6

NE Berry Rd

NE Berry Rd

NE 252nd Av

NE 209th St

NE 209th St

2

NE 256th Av

NE 258th Av

NE 262nd Av

1

L-1410

R3E R4E

45°46'26"

6

7

NE Olson Rd

NE 257th Av

NE 257th Ct NE 258th Av

E   F   G   H   J

SEE 479 MAP

122°24'32"   122°23'55"   122°23'18"   122°22'40"   122°22'03"

45°46'00"

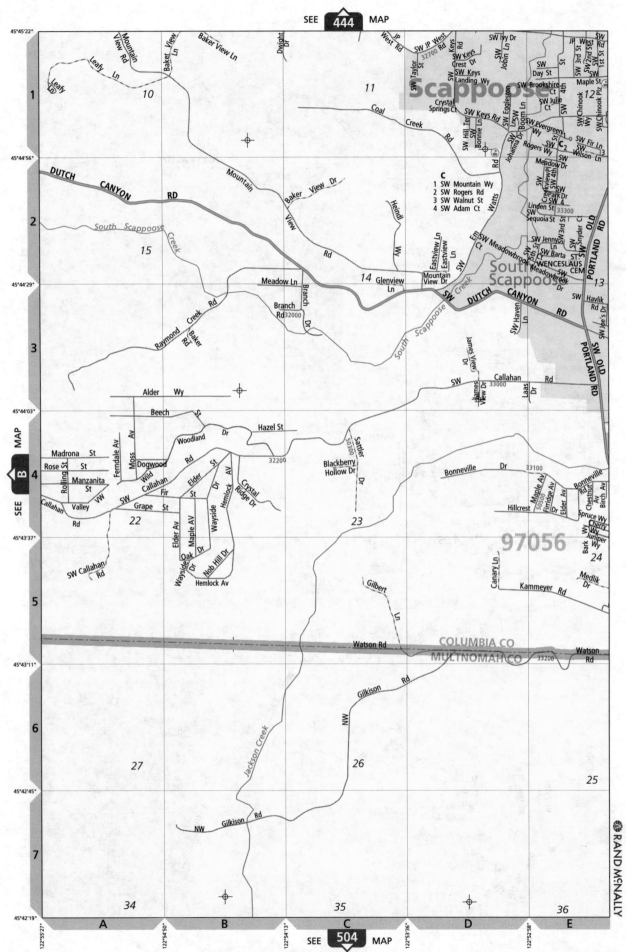

MAP
474

1:24,000
1 in. = 2000 ft.

0   0.25   0.5
miles

SEE ◇ **444** MAP

Scappoose

45°45'22"

Leafy Ln
Mountain View Rd
Baker View Ln
Baker View Ln
Dwight Dr
West Rd
West JP
SW JP West
32700
SW Taylor
SW Keys Crest Dr
Jobin St
SW Ivy Dr
SW 3rd St
JP West
1st St
SW 3rd St
SW 1st St

1

Leafy

10

11

Coal

Creek

Rd

SW Keys Landing Wy
Crystal Springs Ct
SW Keys Rd
SW Hill Ter
Bonnie
SW Johanna Dr
Rogers Wy
SW Boom Ln
SW Eggleston
SW Evergreen
SW Wilson Ln
SW Fir St
SW Day St
Maple St
SW Brookshire Ct
SW 4th
Chinook
SW Chinook Plz
SW Julie Ct

12

C
1 SW Mountain Wy
2 SW Rogers Rd
3 SW Walnut St
4 SW Adam Ct

45°44'56"

DUTCH CANYON RD

Mountain

Baker View Dr

View

Rd

Heindl Wy

Watts Rd

SW Meadow Dr
Creekview Pl
SW Park Dr
SW 4
Linden St
33300
SW Sequoia St
SW Jenny Ln
SW 3rd St
SW Snyder St
SW Barta St
C₂
SW Meadowbrook
WENCESLAUS
CEM
SW Meadowbrook Dr

C

South Scappoose

2

South Scappoose Creek

15

Meadow Ln

14 Glenview Ln

Eastview Ln
Eastview Ln
Mountain View Ln
ESW Meadowbrook Ct

South Scappoose

Scappoose

45°44'29"

Raymond Creek Rd
Baker Rd
Branch Dr
Branch Rd 32000

SW Dutch

DUTCH CANYON RD

SW Haven Ln

SW Havlik Rd
SW Joe's Rd

PORTLAND OLD RD

3

James View Dr

SW Callahan Dr

Callahan Rd

SW James View Dr
33000

Laas Dr

SW OLD PORTLAND RD

Alder Wy

45°44'03"

MAP

Beech St

Hazel St

Madrona St
Rose St
Ferndale Av
Moss Av
Woodland Dr
Dogwood Rd
Wild Callahan St
Elder St
Hemlock Av
Crystal Ridge Dr
32200
Blackberry Hollow Dr
Satler Dr
50300

Bonneville Dr
33100

Maple Av
Bonneville Av
Chestnut Av
Birch Av
Ferndale Av
Elder Av
Spruce Wy
Cherry Wy
Juniper Wy

B

4

Manzanita St
Rolling St
Fir St
Wayside Dr
Grape St
Elder Av
Maple AV
Oak Dr
Nob Hill Dr
Hemlock Av
Wayside Dr

22

23

97056

50500
Hillcrest Wy
Bark Wy

24

Medlik Dr

SEE

45°43'37"

SW Callahan Rd

Gilbert Ln

Canary Ln

Kammeyer Rd

5

Watson Rd

COLUMBIA CO
MULTNOMAH CO

Watson Rd
33200

45°43'11"

Gilkison Rd
NW

6

Jackson Creek

27

26

25

45°42'45"

NW Gilkison Rd

7

34

35

36

45°42'19"

122°55'27" A 122°54'50" B 122°54'13" C 122°53'36" D 122°52'58" E 122°52'58"

SEE ◇ **504** MAP

RAND McNALLY

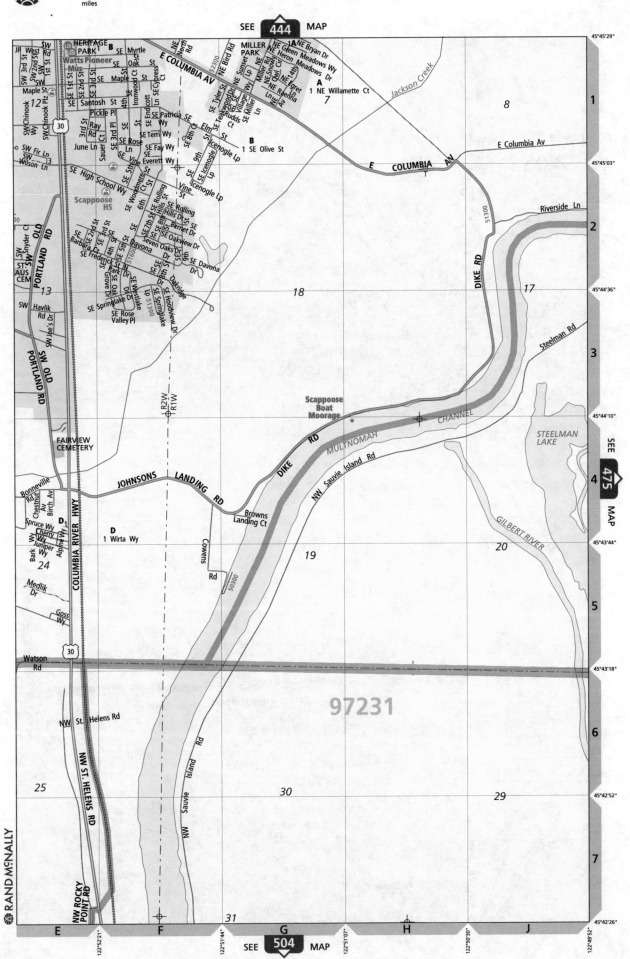

MAP
474

1:24,000
1 in. = 2000 ft.

0   0.25   0.5
miles

SEE 444 MAP

HERITAGE PARK
Watts Pioneer Mus

MILLER PARK

JP West St
SW 3rd St
SW 2nd St
SW 1st St
SW Rd

Maple St

SW Chinook Plz

SW Chinook Wy

12

SE 1st St
SE 2nd St
SE 3rd St

Santosh St

Pickle Pl

3rd St
Ray Rd

June Ln

Sauer St
3rd St

SW Fir Ln
SW Wilson Ln

13

SE High School Wy

Scappoose HS

SW Snyder Ct
SW ST. AUS CEM

SW Havlik Rd
SW Joe's Dr

SW OLD PORTLAND RD

OLD PORTLAND RD

SE Myrtle St
SE Oak St
SE Maple St
Ironwood Ct
SE Cypress

SE Endicott Ln
SE Patricia Wy
SE Terri Wy
SE Rose
SE Fay Wy
SE Everett Wy
SE Vine

SE 5th
SE Woodmere Ct
6th

SE 2nd St
SE 3rd St
SE 4th
Barbara Ct
SE Frederick St

E COLUMBIA AV

NE North Rd
NE Bird Rd
52300
NE Sunset Wy
SE Tyler St
SE Featherwood Ln
Rudds Ct
SE 8th St
SE Elm
SE 9th St
SE Icenogle Lp
Vine
SE Icenogle Lp
SE Icenogle Lp

SE Rolling Hills Dr
SE Rolling Hills Dr
Bernet Dr
SE Oakview Dr
Seven Oaks Dr
SE Davona Dr
SE Davona Dr
Park Dr
SE 8th Dr
9th
SE Westlake
SE Hoodview Dr
Oakridge
SE Springlake Dr
SE Springlake Dr
SE Springlake
SE Rose Valley Pl

NE Green Meadows Dr
NE Heron Meadows Dr
NE Snowy Owl Ct
NE Egret
Miller Rd
NE Raenna
NE Ln
Village Lp
SE Miller Ln
SE Olive St

1 NE Bryan Dr Wy
1A
A
1 NE Willamette Ct
7

1 SE Olive St

E COLUMBIA AV

E Columbia Av

8

Jackson Creek

51300

DIKE RD

Riverside Ln

17

Steelman Rd

18

R2W
R1W

Scappoose Boat Moorage

CHANNEL

MULTNOMAH

DIKE RD

NW Sauvie Island Rd

STEELMAN LAKE

GILBERT RIVER

SEE 475 MAP

FAIRVIEW CEMETERY

JOHNSONS LANDING RD

Bonneville Rd
Chestnut Av
Birch Av
Spruce Wy
Cherry Wy
Juniper Wy
Bark Wy
Alpine Wy

COLUMBIA RIVER HWY

D 1
D
1 Wirta Wy

Browns Landing Ct

Cowens Rd

50300

19

20

24

Medlik Dr

Goss Wy

Watson Rd

NW St. Helens Rd

25

NW ST. HELENS RD

NW ROCKY POINT RD

97231

30

29

31

SEE 504 MAP

RAND MCNALLY

45°45'29"
45°45'03"
45°44'36"
45°44'10"
45°43'44"
45°43'18"
45°42'52"
45°42'26"

122°52'22"
122°51'44"
122°51'07"
122°50'30"
122°49'52"

E   F   G   H   J

1   2   3   4   5   6   7

MAP
475

1:24,000
1 in. = 2000 ft.

0   0.25   0.5
miles

SEE **445** MAP

45°45'29"

1

8

E Honeyman Rd

9

Gilbert River

NW Rentenaar Rd

NW Rentenaar Rd

10

E Columbia
Av

45°45'03"

97056

GRASSY
LAKE

Riverside Ln

Steelman Rd

SEAL
LAKE

MULTNOMAH CHANNEL

2

MARTIN
LAKE

WILLOW
HOLE

45°44'36"

17

GILBERT RIVER

16

15

ROUND
LAKE

MUD LAKE

3

45°44'10"

SEE **474** MAP

4

97231

STEELMAN
LAKE

45°43'44"

20

21

22

5

45°43'18"

STURGEON LAKE

DAIRY CREEK

6

WAGONWHEEL
HOLE

45°42'52"

28

27

GILBERT RIVER

7

29

Gilbert
River

NW Oak Island Rd

HALDEMAN
POND

45°42'26"

A   B   C   D   E

122°49'52"   122°49'15"   122°48'38"   122°48'01"   122°47'23"

SEE **505** MAP

MAP
475

1:24,000
1 in. = 2000 ft.
0   0.25   0.5
miles

SEE ⌃ **445** MAP

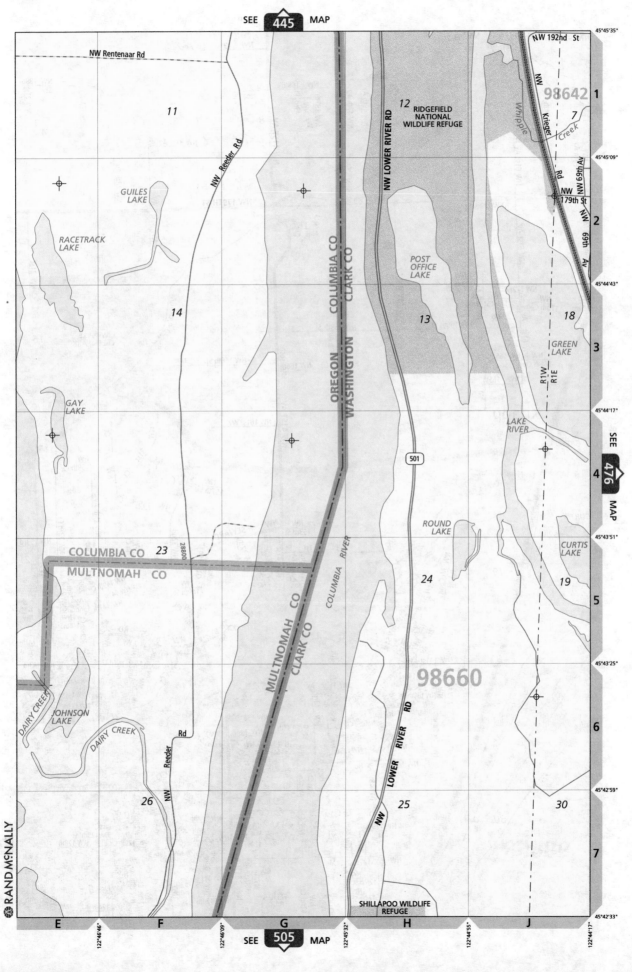

NW 192nd St
45°45'35"
NW 98642
Krieger Rd
Whipple Creek
7
1

RIDGEFIELD
NATIONAL
WILDLIFE REFUGE
12

NW Rentenaar Rd

11

GUILES
LAKE

RACETRACK
LAKE

NW Reeder Rd

NW LOWER RIVER RD

45°45'09"

NW 179th St
NW 69th Av
NW 69th Av
2

POST
OFFICE
LAKE

45°44'43"

14

13

18

GREEN
LAKE

R1W
R1E

3

45°44'17"

GAY
LAKE

SEE ⌃ **476** MAP

LAKE
RIVER

501

4

45°43'51"

ROUND
LAKE

CURTIS
LAKE

COLUMBIA CO
MULTNOMAH CO
23

COLUMBIA RIVER

24

19

45°43'25"

98660

5

MULTNOMAH CO
CLARK CO

JOHNSON
LAKE

DAIRY CREEK

DAIRY CREEK

Reeder Rd

LOWER RIVER RD

45°42'59"

6

26

NW Reeder Rd

25

30

7

SHILLAPOO WILDLIFE
REFUGE
45°42'33"

E   F   G   H   J

122°46'46"   122°46'09"   122°45'32"   122°44'55"   122°44'17"

COLUMBIA CO
CLARK CO
OREGON
WASHINGTON

SEE ⌃ **505** MAP

MAP
476

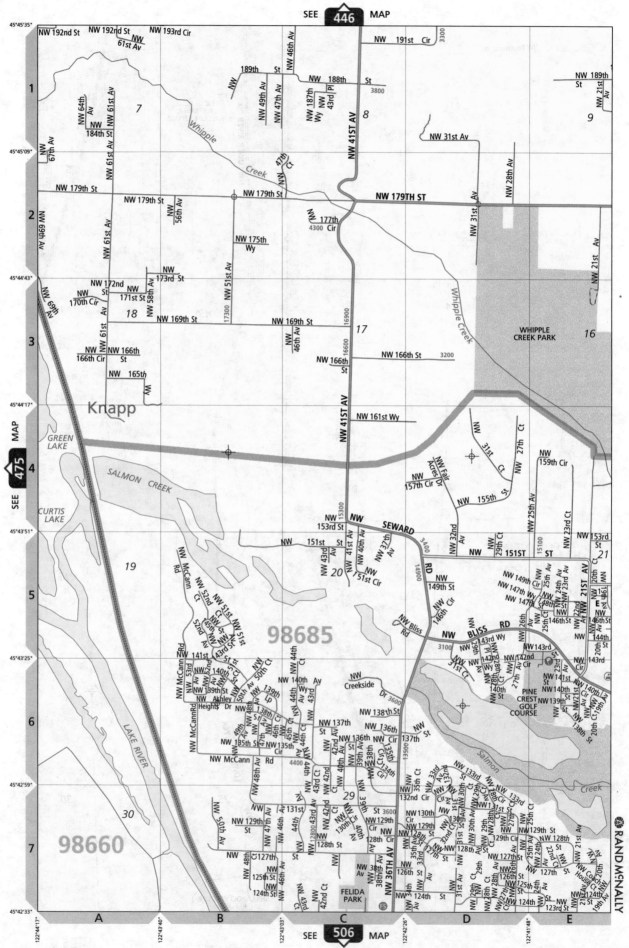

SEE 446 MAP

NW 192nd St   NW 192nd St   NW 193rd Cir
NW 61st Av
NW 191st Cir

NW 46th Av
NW 189th St
NW 188th St
NW 189th St
NW 49th Av   NW 47th Av
NW 187th Wy   43rd Pl   3800   NW 21st Av

7   8   9

NW 64th Av   NW 61st Av
NW 184th St   47th Ct
NW 67th Av

NW 31st Av

NW 28th Av

NW 179th St   NW 179th St   NW 179th St   NW 179TH ST   NW 31st Av

NW 56th Av
NW 61st Av   NW 177th Cir   4300
NW 69th Av   NW 175th Wy   NW 31st Av

NW 173rd St   NW 21st Av
NW 172nd St   NW 51st Av
NW 171st St   NW 58th Av
170th Cir
NW 61st Av   NW 169th St   NW 169th St   17   Whipple Creek   WHIPPLE CREEK PARK   16
18   16900
NW 46th Av   16600
NW 166th   NW 166th St   3200
166th Cir   St
NW 165th

Knapp

NW 161st Wy

GREEN LAKE   NW Fair Acres Dr   31st Ct   NW 27th Ct   NW 159th Cir
SALMON CREEK   157th Cir   NW 25th Av   NW 23rd Ct
SEE 475 MAP   NW 155th St
CURTIS LAKE   NW 153rd St   NW SEWARD   NW 153rd St   21
15300   3400   NW 32nd Av   NW 29th Ct   15100   NW 151ST ST
151st St   RD   NW 151st   14900   NW 149th St   NW 149th Cir   NW 24th Av   NW 23rd Av   21ST AV
19   NW 43rd St   NW 41st Av   NW 37th Av   NW 147th Cir   NW 146th St
NW 151st Cir   NW 147th
98685   20   NW 149th St   NW 148th   NW 146th St
NW McCann Rd   146th Cir   NW 25th Ct
NW 52nd Ct   NW 51st   NW Bliss Rd   NW 26th   NW 144th
45th   NW 51st   NW BLISS RD   NW 29th Pl   NW 143rd Wy   NW 143rd
52nd Av   43rd St   3100   142nd   NW 143rd   PINE
NW 141st   NW 53rd   NW 140th   31st Ct   27th   CREST
NW McCann Rd   140th   NW 141st   140th   GOLF
NW 139th St   50th Av   139th   NW Creekside Dr 3600   140th   NW 139th   COURSE
Ashley   Lp   138th   NW 138th St   137th   Salmon
Heights Dr   38th   44th Wy   43rd   NW 138th St   137th
49th   46th Ct   45th   137th   NW 137th   NW 136th   NW 136th St   135th
NW 48th   44th   NW 136th   Creek
NW McCann Rd   NW 185th St   NW 135th   NW 134th St
4400   NW 133rd Ct   NW 133rd
19th   43rd Ct   42nd   40th   132nd Cir   NW 35th Ct   NW 30th
131st   39th   NW 131st   St 3600   132nd Cir   NW 130th   NW 129th
30   NW 129th   NW 47th   44th   12800   NW 129th   NW 130th Cir   NW 128th
50th Av   46th   43rd Pl   40th   130th Cir   129th Cir
98660   NW 128th St   NW   NW   NW 128th
NW 48th Ct   127th   NW 127th   35th   NW 127th
125th St   46th St   NW 38th Av   31st St   NW 127th   NW 24th Av   Coach House Ct
124th   42nd Ct   126th   NW 124th
FELIDA   NW 3rd St   124th   NW 36TH AV   NW 124th
PARK   31st St   19th
NW 123rd St

A   B   C   D   E

1   2   3   4   5   6   7

45°45'35"
45°45'09"
45°44'43"
45°44'17"
45°43'51"
45°43'25"
45°42'59"
45°42'33"

122°44'17"   122°43'40"   122°43'03"   122°42'26"   122°41'48"

SEE 506 MAP

RAND McNALLY

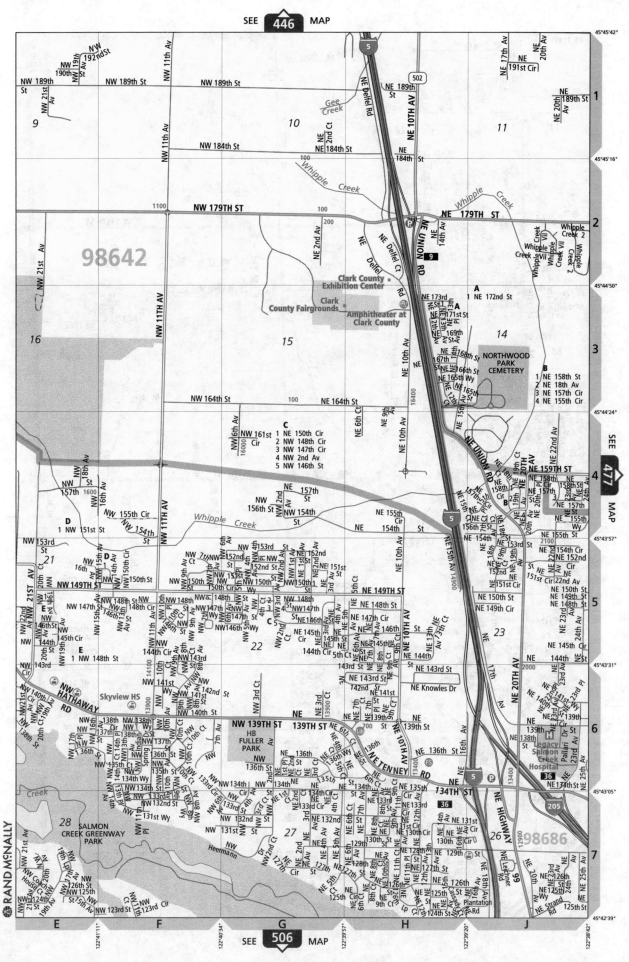

MAP
476

1:24,000
1 in. = 2000 ft.

0   0.25   0.5

miles

SEE 446 MAP

SEE 477 MAP

SEE 506 MAP

RAND MCNALLY

MAP
477

1:24,000
1 in. = 2000 ft.

0   0.25   0.5
miles

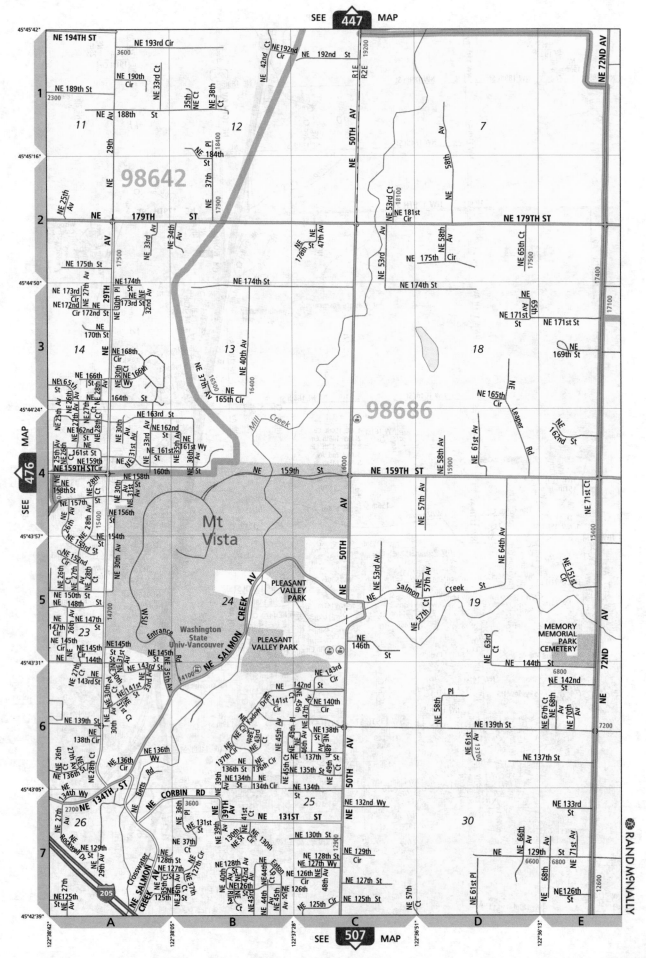

SEE **447** MAP

NE 194TH ST
NE 193rd Cir
NE 192nd St
NE 42nd Ct
NE 192nd St

NE 72ND AV

3600

NE 190th Cir
NE 33rd Ct
NE 189th St
35th St
NE 38th Ct

1

2300
NE 188th St
NE Av

29th
NE PI
NE 184th St
NE 50TH AV
58th Av
NE Av

7

98642

NE 25th Av
NE 37th St
17900
18400
NE 53rd Ct
18100
NE 181st Cir
19200
R1E R2E

NE 179TH ST

2

NE 179TH ST
NE 33rd Av
NE 34th Av
NE 178th St
NE 47th Av
53rd Av
NE 58th Av
NE 65th Ct
17500
17400

NE 175th St
AV
NE 175th Cir

17500

NE 173rd Cir
NE 27th
29TH
NE 174th St
NE 174th St

NE 171st St
459
NE Av

NE172nd Cir
172nd St
NE 30th PI
32nd Av
173rd Ct
NE 171st St

17100

NE 170th St
NE

3

14
NE 168th Cir
NE 30th Ct
30th
13
NE 40th Av
18
NE 169th St

NE 166th
NE 166th Wy
16500
NE 165th Cir

NE 165th Cir

NE 45th Av
NE 28th
164th St
16400

NE165th Av
NE 26th
NE 27th Ct
45°44'24"
NE 163rd St
NE 162nd
NE 58th Av
61st Av
NE 162nd

NE23rd Av
NE 28th Ct
NE 30th
33rd Av
NE 161st
161st Wy
Mill Creek
98686
NE Leaper Rd

NE25th Av
NE 26th
NE 31st St
36th Av
NE 159th Cir
160th
NE 159TH ST
NE 159th St
NE 159TH ST
57th Av
59th Av
NE 71st Ct

4

NE 158th St
NE 30th Av
NE Av

15400

NE157th
157th
NE 57th Av
15900

NE156th
64th Av
15400

Mt Vista
154th
NE 30th Av

NE 153rd St
NE 152nd
NE 26th
NE 27th
NE 28th Ct
24
NE SALMON CREEK AV
PLEASANT VALLEY PARK
NE 50TH
NE 53rd Av
NE 57th Av
Salmon Creek St
19
NE 151st Cir

5

NE 150th St
14700
WSU
NE 148th St
NE 57th Av

NE 147th St
Entrance
Washington State Univ-Vancouver
PLEASANT VALLEY PARK
NE 63rd Ct
MEMORY MEMORIAL PARK CEMETERY

NE26th
147th Cir
23
NE 146th St
NE 144th St
6800

NE 145th
NE145th
NE 143rd St
NE 142nd
NE 27th
143rd St
NE SALMON CREEK AV
NE 143rd Cir
NE 61st Av
NE 67th Ct
NE 68th Av
NE 70th Av
NE 72ND AV
7200

NE141st
35th Av
NE 142nd
NE Kadow Dr
141st Cir
NE 143rd
NE 58th PI
NE 142nd

6

NE 139th St
NE 138th
NE 45th
NE 47th
46th Av
NE 138th
NE 139th St
NE 61st Av
13700
NE 137th St
7200

NE 138th Cir
NE 48th Ct
43rd Ct
NE 45th Av
49th St
NE 137th

NE26th Ct
NE 137th Cir
NE 45th Av
NE 135th St
13000

NE 136th St
NE 28th Ct
NE 136th
Wy
NE 39th Av
136th St
NE 136th Cir
NE 134th

NE 136th St
134th Wy
NE 134TH ST
NE 39th Av
134th St
NE 134th Cir
25
NE 134th St
NE 133rd St

7

2700
NE 134TH ST
CORBIN RD
3600
NE39TH AV
41st
NE 131ST ST
NE 132nd Wy
30

26
NE 27th
NE 36th PI
NE 131st
NE 39th
NE 130th
NE 130th St
NE 66th Av
NE 71st Av

NE 129th
NE 37th Ct
NE 127th Cir
NE 128th
NE 129th Cir
NE 129th St
6600
6800

NE 128th St
NE 127th
Rockwell Dr
Crosswater
NE SALMON CREEK
NE 40th
NE 44th
NE 127th Wy
NE 128th
NE 68th Av
NE126th

NE 27th Av
NE 29th Av
NE 36th Av
125th St
NE 44th
NE45th
NE 126th
48th Av
NE 127th
NE 57th Ct
NE 61st PI
NE126th St

NE 125th Av
NE 43rd
NE 125th St
NE 125th Cir

205

12600

A   B   C   D   E

SEE **507** MAP

45°45'42"
45°45'16"
45°44'50"
45°43'57"
45°43'31"
45°43'05"
45°42'39"

122°38'42"
122°38'05"
122°37'28"
122°36'51"
122°36'13"

SEE 476 MAP

RAND MCNALLY

MAP
477

1:24,000
1 in. = 2000 ft.

0   0.25   0.5
miles

SEE 447 MAP

45°45'48"

NE 72ND AV
NE 75th Wy
NE 192nd
NE 74th Ct
NE 80th Ct
NE 82nd Av
NE 84th Av
NE 86th Av
NE 89th Av
19100
NE 191st St
NE 101st St
19100
NE 102nd Av
Av
NE 109th
NE 112TH AV
NE 193rd Av
NE 113th Cir
NE 191st
1

Columbia Adventist
NE 105th Ct
NE 189th St

Meadow Glade

8
NE 185th St
NE 92nd Av
NE 99th
NE 184th
NE 187th St
CRAMER RD
NE 189th Av
9
NE 187th St
NE 109th Av
10
NE 186th Cir
NE 185th St

45°45'22"

NE 185th St
NE 81st Av
NE 82nd Av
NE 84th Av
NE 85th Av
NE 86th Av
98604
NE 85th Av
CRAMER
18300
NE 183rd St
NE 111th Av
NE 182nd

NE 77th Ct
NE 180th Wy
99th Av
NE 181st St
18100
NE 181st Cir
NE 113th Cir

NE 179TH ST
9700
NE 180th Cir
105thCt
NE 179th St
17800
NE 182nd
NE 179th Cir

7700   7900
17400
NE 77th Av
94th Av
9400
96th Av
NE 97th
NE 99th
100th
NE 178th
178th Cir
NE 110th
178th
NE 177th Cir
17600
177th St
95th Av
176th
176th Cir

45°44'56"

NE 174th St
17100
173rd St

NE 92nd Av
NE 170th St

NE 169th St
17
16
NE 169th St
10200
15
NE 107th Av

45°44'30"

NE 166th Cir
NE 163rd
NE 163rd Cir

SEE 478 MAP

NE 164th St
NE 164th Cir
NE 164th St
112th
NE 75th Ct
NE 82nd Av
16200
94th Av
NE 163rd Cir
NE 159th St

NE 162nd St
NE 161st St

NE 71st Ct
NE 159TH ST
NE 92ND AV
NE 159th St
NE 81st Av
8100   8600
10200
NE 112TH AV
NE 117th Av

15400
NE 154th St
88th Av
NE 154th Cir
8300
NE 154TH ST
NE 116th Ct

45°44'04"

NE 151st Cir
98606
NE 149th St
5

20
21
NE 72ND AV
NE 148th St
100th St
NE 112th Ct
114th Ct
NE 115th Ct
NE 146th Wy
22

101st Pl
NE 144th Cir
14600
98662
LORETTA NORENE FOREST PRESERVE
NE 145th St
143rd Cir
NE 76th Av
82nd
NE 88th
NE
NE 141st St

45°43'38"

7200
NE 139th St
8200
NE 139th St
NE 97th Av
10500
Laurin Rd
6

Curtin Creek
NE 134th St
28
27
NE 132nd Av
NE 80th Av
131st Wy
9000
NE 90th Ct
90th Av
NE 108th
NE 110th Av
NE 131st St
29
NE 77th Av
NE 87th Av
NE 92nd Av
93rd
NE 130th Cir
NE 129th St
NE 117TH AV

45°43'12"

12600
11900
NE 126th Wy
12500
NE 105th Ct
NE 109th Av
7

45°42'45"

E   F   G   H   J

122°35'36"   122°34'59"   122°34'22"   122°33'44"   122°33'07"

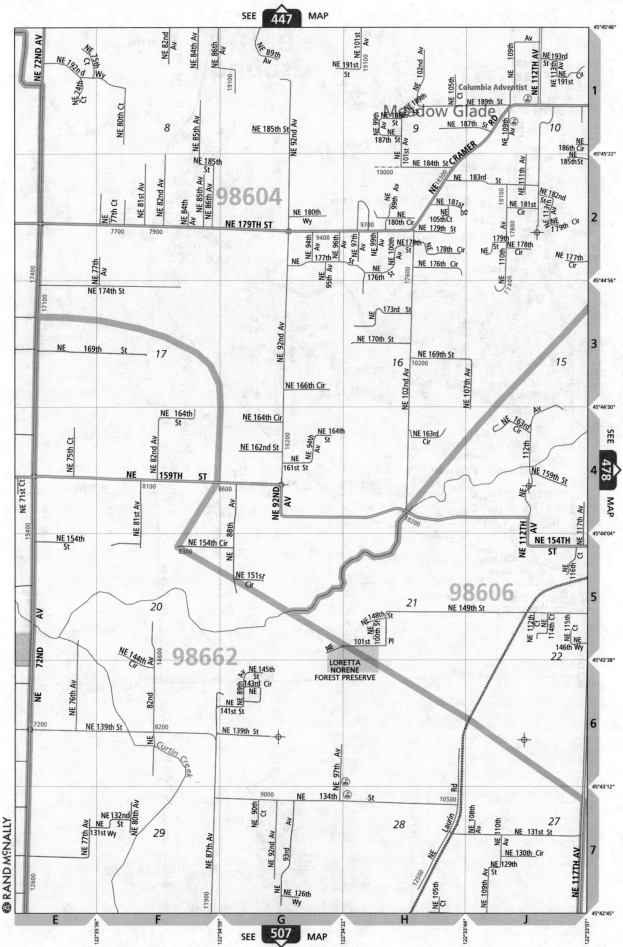

MAP
478

1:24,000
1 in. = 2000 ft.

0   0.25   0.5
miles

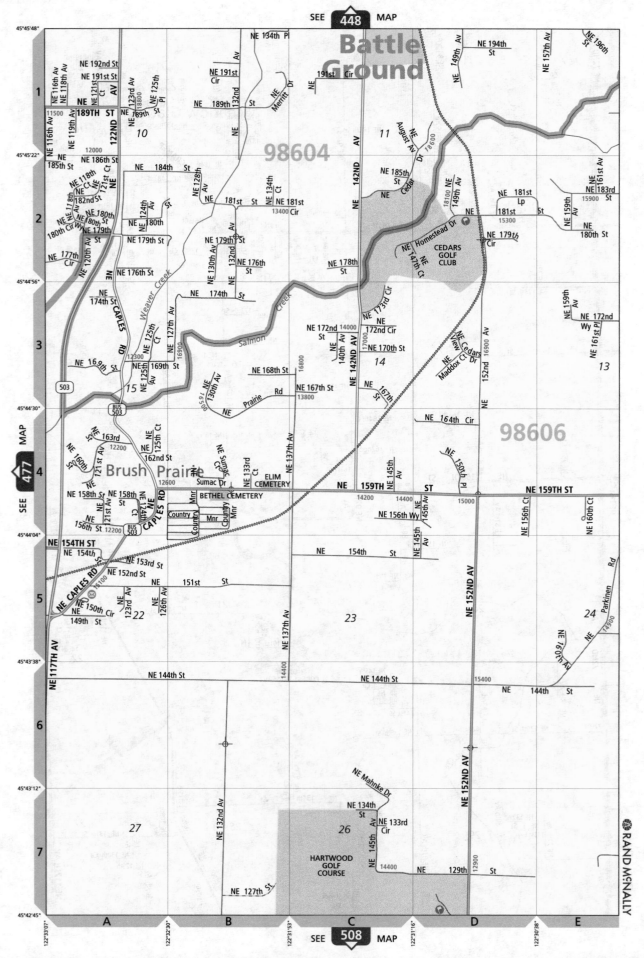

SEE **448** MAP

Battle Ground

98604

CEDARS GOLF CLUB

98606

NE 189TH ST

122ND AV

NE 142ND AV

NE 159TH ST

NE 152ND AV

NE 117TH AV

NE CAPLES RD

Brush Prairie

ELIM CEMETERY

BETHEL CEMETERY

NE 154TH ST

HARTWOOD GOLF COURSE

MAP **477** SEE

SEE **508** MAP

RAND M^cNALLY

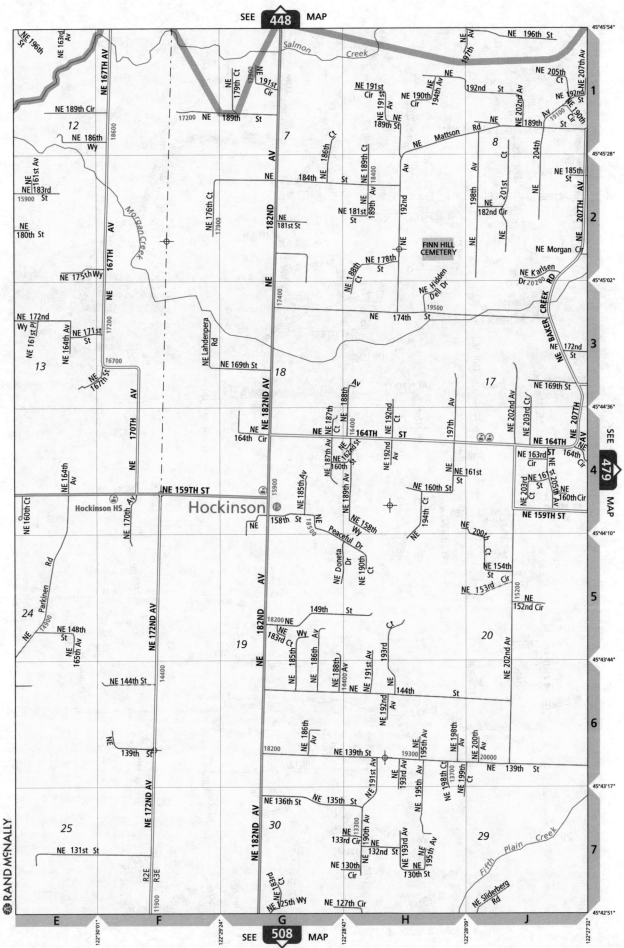

MAP
478

SEE 448 MAP

1:24,000
1 in. = 2000 ft.
0   0.25   0.5
miles

SEE 508 MAP

SEE 479 MAP

Hockinson

FINN HILL CEMETERY

Hockinson HS

MAP
479

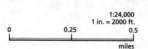

1:24,000
1 in. = 2000 ft.

0   0.25   0.5
miles

SEE **449** MAP

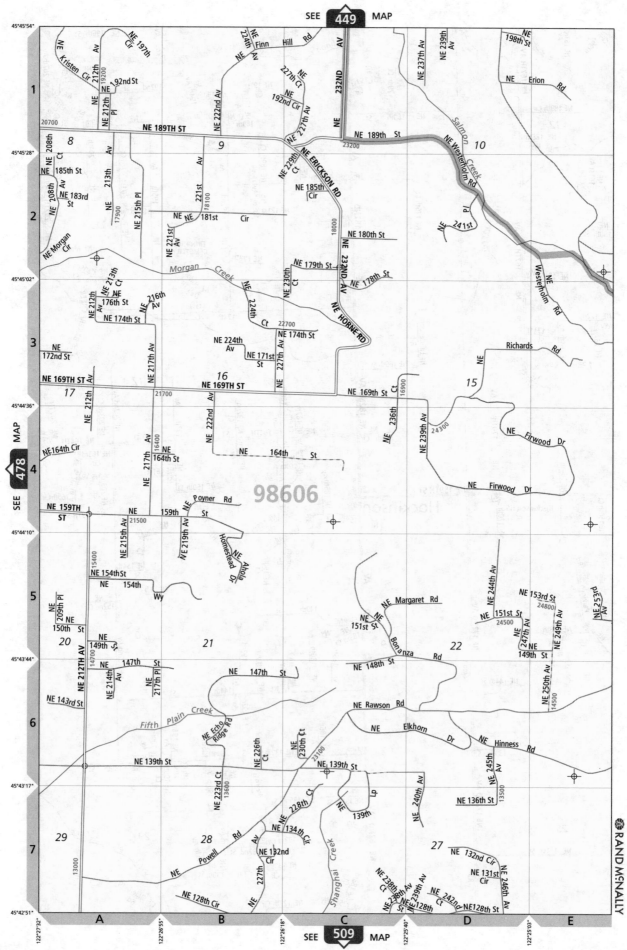

NE 197th Cir
NE 212th Av
Kristen Cir
19200
NE 192nd St
NE 212th Pl
20700
NE 224th Av
Finn Hill Rd
227th Ct
NE 232ND AV
192nd Cir
NE 198th St
NE 237th Av
NE 239th Av
NE Erion Rd

NE 189TH ST
NE 222nd Av
NE 189th St
23200
NE Westerholm Rd
Salmon Creek

8   9   10

45°45'28"
NE 208th Ct
NE 208th Av
NE 185th St
NE 213th Av
NE 183rd St
17900
NE 215th Pl
18100
NE 221st Av
221st Av
NE NE 181st Cir
NE 229th Ct
NE ERICKSON RD
NE 185th Cir
18000
NE 180th St
241st Pl

2

45°45'02"
NE Morgan Cir
Morgan Creek
NE 213th Ct
NE 212th Av
NE 176th St
216th Av
NE 174th St
224th Ct
22700
NE 179th St
NE 230th Ct
NE 232ND AV
NE 178th St
NE HORNE RD
Westerholm Rd

3
NE 172nd St
NE 217th Av
NE 224th Av
NE 171st St
NE 174th St
NE 227th Av
Richards Rd

NE 169TH ST Av
NE 212th Av
NE 169TH ST
16
21700
NE 222nd Av
NE 169th St Ct
16900
NE 236th Ct
NE 239th Av
24300
15

17
NE164th Cir
NE 217th Av
16400
NE 164th St
NE 164th St
NE Firwood Dr

4

45°44'36"
98606
NE Firwood Dr

NE 159TH ST
NE 215th Av
21500
159th St
Poyner Rd
NE 219th Av
Ahola
Homestead Dr

45°44'10"
15400
NE 154th St
NE 154th Wy
154th

5
NE 209th Pl
NE 150th St
NE Margaret Rd
NE 244th Av
NE 153rd St
24800
NE 253rd Av
NE 151st St
151st St
24500
NE 249th Av
NE 247th Av

20
NE 212TH AV
14700
NE 149th St
21
22
NE 149th St
NE 250th Av
14500

45°43'44"
NE 214th Av
NE 147th St
NE 217th Pl
NE 147th St
NE 148th St
Bonanza Rd

NE 143rd St
Fifth Plain Creek
NE Rawson Rd
NE Elkhorn Dr
NE Hinness Rd

6
NE Echo Ridge Rd
NE 226th Ct
NE 230th Ct
23100
NE 245th Av
13500
NE 139th St
NE 139th St
NE 240th Av
NE 136th St
13500

45°43'17"
13000
NE 223rd Ct
13600
NE 228th Ct
139th Lp
NE 132nd Cir
NE 131st Cir
NE 246th Av

29
28
NE Powell Rd
NE 134th Cir
NE 132nd Cir
27
NE 132nd Cir
NE 227th Av
Shanghai Creek
NE 238th Ct
NE 239th Av
NE 242nd Ct
NE128th St
NE 128th Cir
NE 128th St
NE 128th

45°42'51"

A   B   C   D   E

SEE **509** MAP

45°45'54"
122°27'32"   122°26'55"   122°26'18"   122°25'40"   122°25'03"

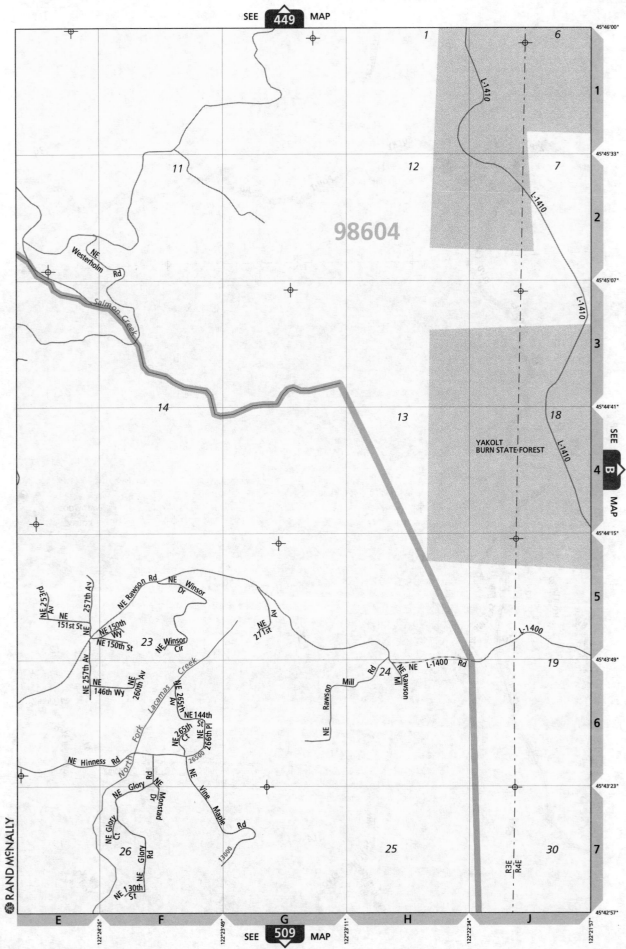

MAP
504

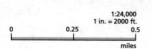

1:24,000
1 in. = 2000 ft.
0   0.25   0.5
miles

N

SEE 474 MAP

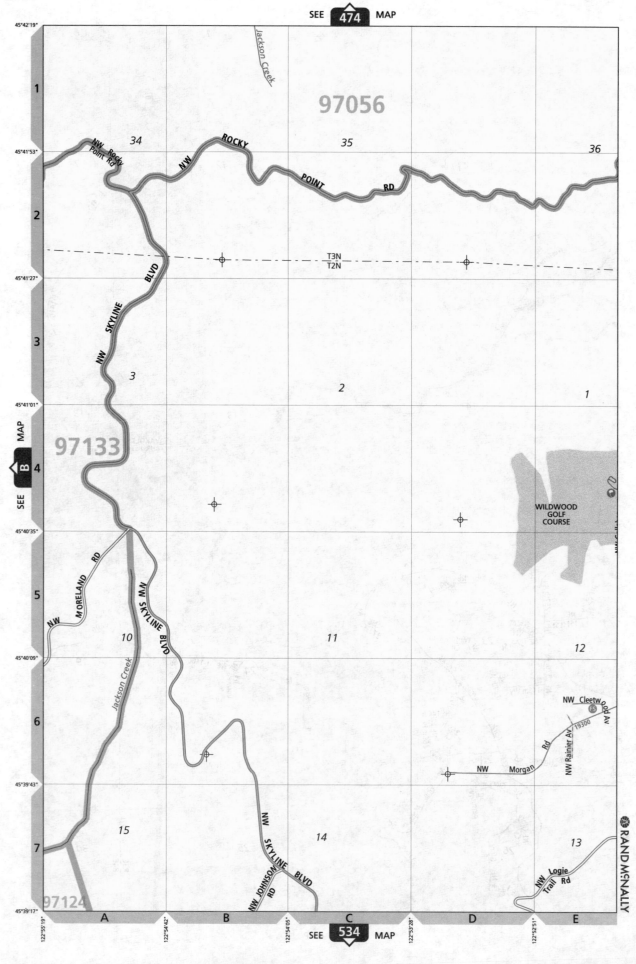

97056

34   NW Rocky   ROCKY
      Point Rd
            NW   POINT   RD
                              35   36

NW SKYLINE BLVD

T3N
T2N

45°42'19"
45°41'53"
45°41'27"
45°41'01"
45°40'35"
45°40'09"
45°39'43"
45°39'17"

1
2
3

SEE MAP
B

97133

3   2   1

WILDWOOD
GOLF
COURSE

4

NW MORELAND RD

NW SKYLINE BLVD

NW

Jackson Creek

10   11   12

5

6

NW Cleetwood Av
19300
NW Rainier Av
NW Morgan Rd

NW SKYLINE BLVD

NW JOHNSON RD

15   14   13

7

NW Logie
Trail Rd

97124

122°55'19" 122°54'42" 122°54'05" 122°53'28" 122°52'51"

A   B   C   D   E

SEE 534 MAP

RAND McNALLY

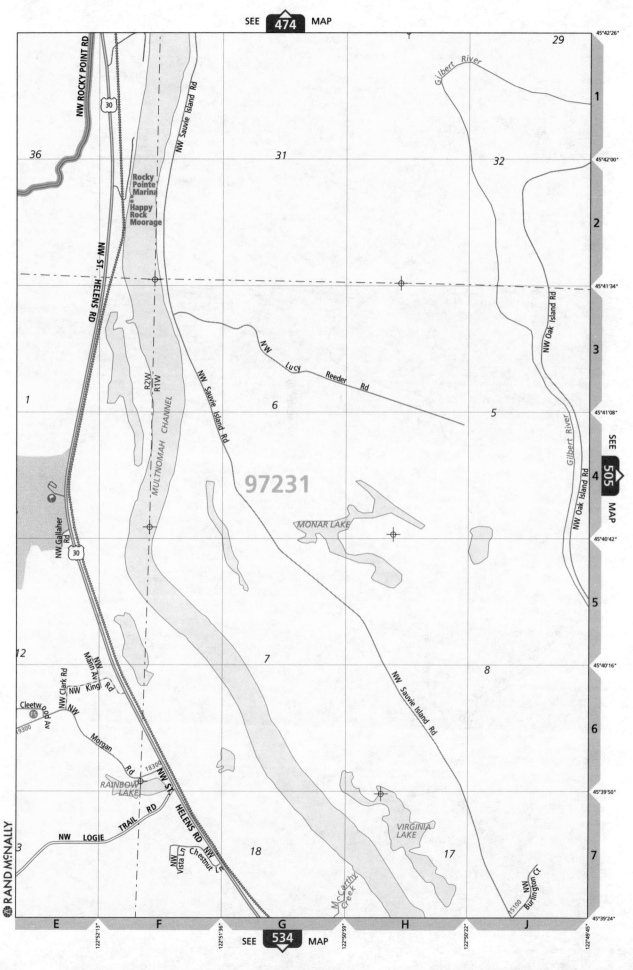

MAP
504

1:24,000
1 in. = 2000 ft.

0   0.25   0.5

miles

SEE 474 MAP

45°42'26"

29

1

NW ROCKY POINT RD

Gilbert River

36

31

32

45°42'00"

NW 30

NW Sauvie Island Rd

Rocky
Pointe
Marina

Happy
Rock
Moorage

2

NW ST. HELENS RD

45°41'34"

NW Oak Island Rd

R2W R1W

MULTNOMAH CHANNEL

NW Lucy Reeder Rd

3

NW Sauvie Island Rd

1

6

5

45°41'08"

Gilbert River

SEE 505 MAP

4

97231

MONAR LAKE

NW Gallaher Rd

NW 30

NW Oak Island Rd

5

45°40'42"

12

7

8

45°40'16"

NW Mann Av

NW Clark Rd

NW King Rd

Cleetwood Av

FS 9300

NW

NW

Morgan

6

Rd 18300

RAINBOW LAKE

NW ST.

NW Sauvie Island Rd

45°39'50"

NW TRAIL RD

VIRGINIA LAKE

HELENS RD

3

NW LOGIE

17

7

NW Vista Ln

NW Chestnut Ln

18

McCarthy Creek

15100 NW Burlington Ct

45°39'24"

E   F   G   H   J

SEE 534 MAP

122°52'13"   122°51'36"   122°50'59"   122°50'22"   122°49'45"

RAND McNALLY

MAP
505

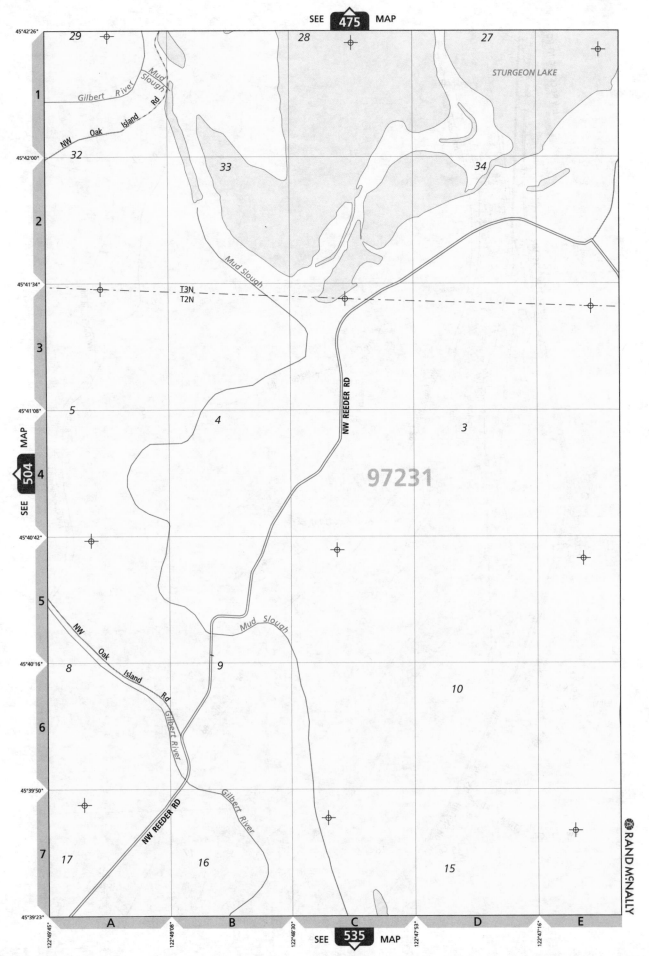

1:24,000
1 in. = 2000 ft.
0 0.25 0.5
miles

STURGEON LAKE

Gilbert River
Mud Slough
NW Oak Island Rd

29 28 27
32 33 34

Mud Slough

T3N
T2N

NW REEDER RD

5 4 3

97231

NW Oak Island Rd
Gilbert River

Mud Slough

8 9 10

Gilbert River

NW REEDER RD

17 16 15

A B C D E

RAND McNALLY

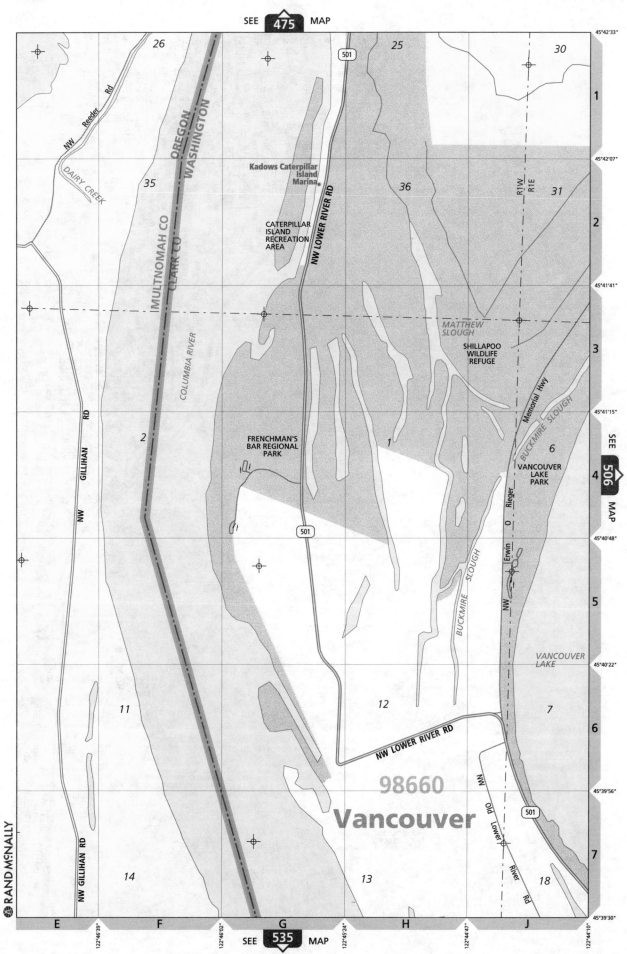

MAP
505

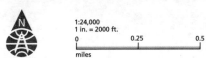

1:24,000
1 in. = 2000 ft.

0   0.25   0.5
miles

SEE ⬡ 475 MAP

26
25
30

501

45°42'33"

1

NW Reeder Rd

OREGON
WASHINGTON

45°42'07"

35

Kadows Caterpillar
Island
Marina

36

R1W | R1E

31

DAIRY CREEK

MULTNOMAH CO
CLARK CO

NW LOWER RIVER RD

CATERPILLAR
ISLAND
RECREATION
AREA

45°41'41"

2

COLUMBIA RIVER

MATTHEW
SLOUGH

SHILLAPOO
WILDLIFE
REFUGE

45°41'15"

3

NW GILLIHAN RD

2

FRENCHMAN'S
BAR REGIONAL
PARK

1

Memorial Hwy

BUCKMIRE SLOUGH

6

VANCOUVER
LAKE PARK

SEE ⬡ 506 MAP

4

501

NW O Rieger

45°40'48"

BUCKMIRE SLOUGH

Erwin

5

VANCOUVER
LAKE

45°40'22"

11

12

NW

7

6

NW LOWER RIVER RD

98660

Vancouver

Old Lower

501

NW

45°39'56"

RAND MᶜNALLY

14

13

River Rd

18

7

45°39'30"

E   F   G   H   J

122°46'39"   122°46'02"   122°45'24"   122°44'47"   122°44'10"

SEE ⬡ 535 MAP

MAP
506

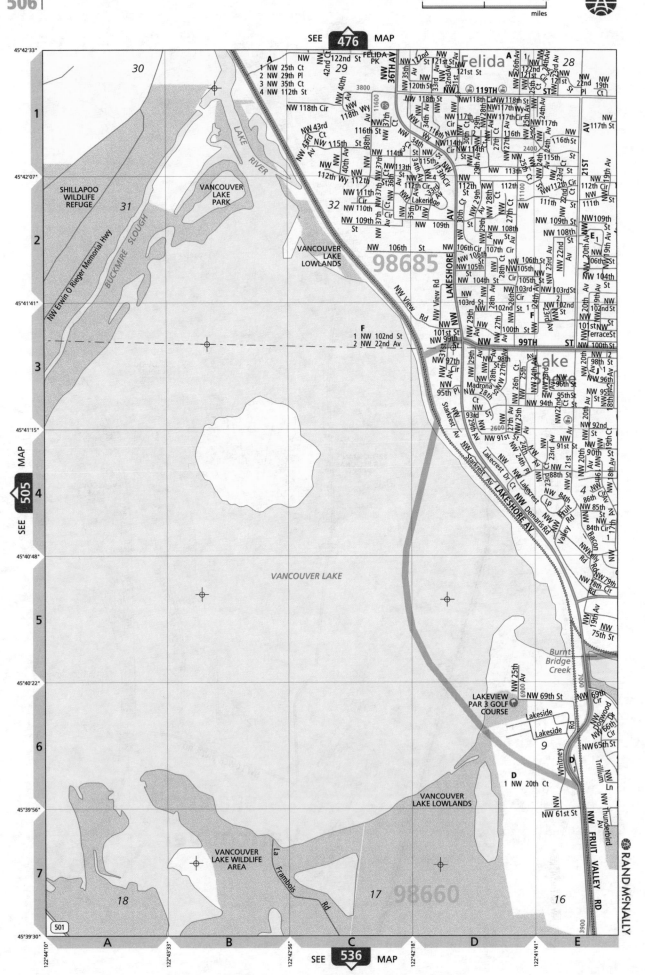

SEE [476] MAP

SHILLAPOO
WILDLIFE
REFUGE

VANCOUVER
LAKE
PARK

VANCOUVER
LAKE
LOWLANDS

98685

Felida

119TH

99TH ST

Lake Shore

98660

98660

VANCOUVER LAKE

VANCOUVER
LAKE
LOWLANDS

LAKEVIEW PAR 3 GOLF
COURSE

Lakeside
Lakeside

Burnt
Bridge
Creek

VANCOUVER
LAKE WILDLIFE
AREA

LAKESHORE AV

NW FRUIT VALLEY RD

SEE [536] MAP

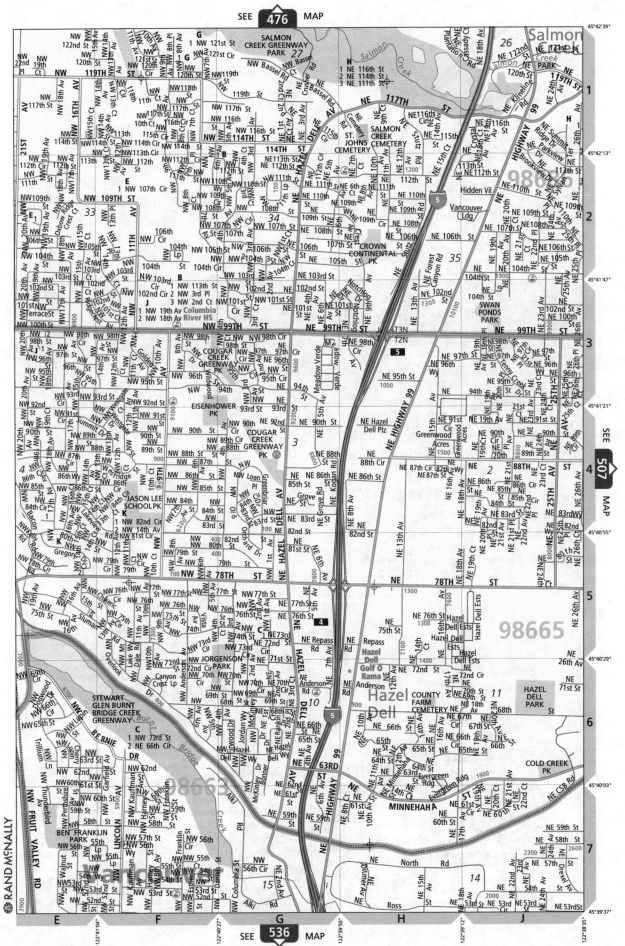

MAP
506

1:24,000
1 in. = 2000 ft.

0   0.25   0.5
miles

SEE 476 MAP

SEE 507 MAP

SEE 536 MAP

MAP
507

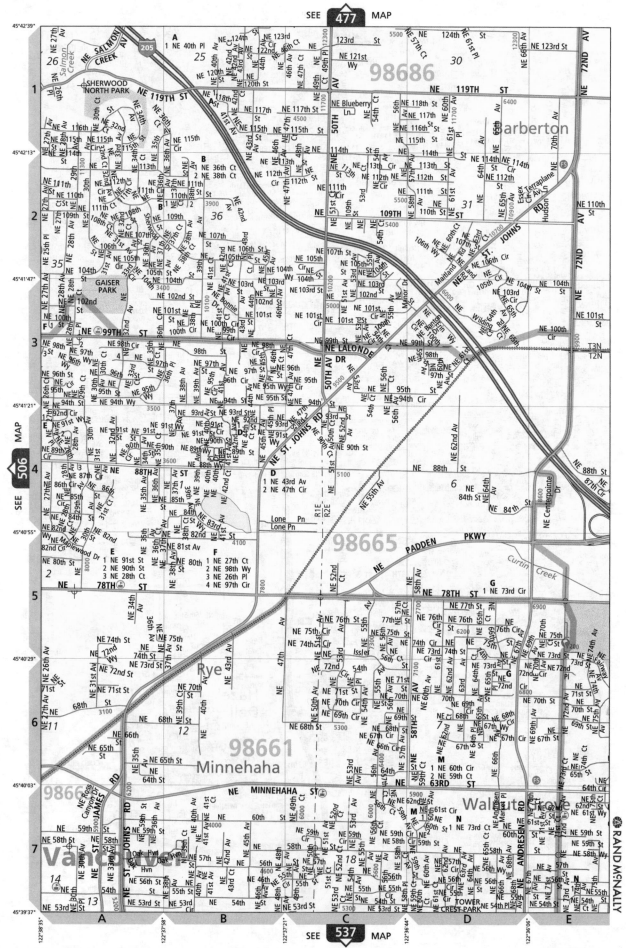

SEE ◇ 477 MAP

SEE ◇ 537 MAP

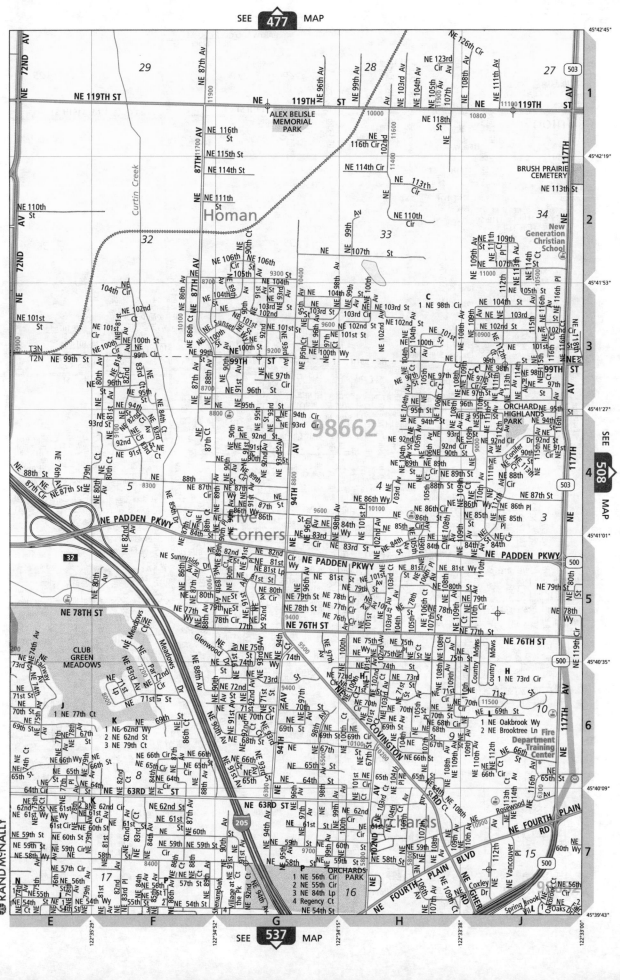

MAP
507

1:24,000
1 in. = 2000 ft.
0   0.25   0.5
miles

SEE 477 MAP

SEE 508 MAP

SEE 537 MAP

RAND McNALLY

MAP
508

1:24,000
1 in. = 2000 ft.

0   0.25   0.5
miles

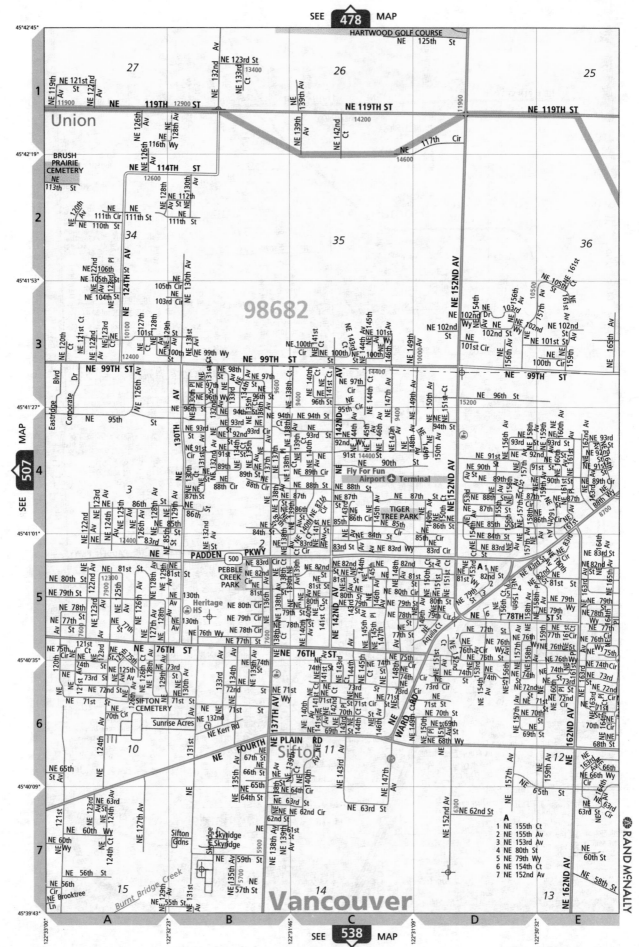

SEE **478** MAP

HARTWOOD GOLF COURSE

NE 125th St

27   26   25

NE 123rd St   13400

NE 119th
St   NE 121st NE 122nd
St   Av
11900   NE **119TH** 12900 **ST**   NE 139th Av   NE **119TH ST**   NE **119TH ST**

Union

NE 119TH ST   14200

NE 126th
Av   NE 128th Av   NE 142nd
NE 126th   116th   NE 139th   Ct
Wy   Av   NE 117th Cir
14600

45°42'19"

BRUSH
PRAIRIE
CEMETERY
NE   NE **114TH** **ST**
113th St   12600

NE 120th
Av   NE 112th
NE 128th 130th   St
NE   111th Cir 111th St   NE
110th Av   111th
NE   St
34   35   36

45°41'53"

NE 122nd 106th
NE 105th 123rd
NE 104th St   105th Cir   NE 130th Av   NE 161st
St   103rd St   NE 156th   St
98682   NE 105th
102nd   103rd   Ct
NE 120th   NE 121st   NE 123rd   NE 127th 128th   NE 154th   Dr   NE 102nd   NE 102nd
Ct   Ct   Ct   St NE 101st 131st   NE 100th 141st   NE 101st   Wy   102nd   NE 102nd   NE 101st
12400   100th NE 99th Wy   NE 144th 101st   102nd   NE
NE **99TH ST**   NE **99TH** **ST** Cir   NE 100th   146th   156th   100th   159th   NE 165th   St
101st Cir

45°41'27"   NE **99TH ST**   NE 98th   NE 140th 97th   NE 97th   NE **99TH**   **ST**
Eastridge Blvd   NE 126th   97th   Av   133rd   Cir   NE 96th   St
Corporate Dr   Av   96th   132nd   136th   9400   NE 147th Av   15200
95th   St   96th NE 94th   95th 144th   NE 150th Av   NE 93rd   NE 58th   NE 93rd
130TH   NE 93rd   93rd   138th   Ct 142ND   145th   NE 147th Av   151st Ct   93rd   159th   162nd   NE 93rd
NE   NE 91st 92nd 134th 135th   139th   93rd   AV   146th NE 148th Av   NE 91st 157th   60th   92nd   91st
507   AV   Cir   137th   92nd Wy   150th Av   Av   St   161st   91st Cir
89th   91st   91st 14400 St   Av   St
4   St   NE   89th 138th 139th   89th   Fly For Fun   NE 90th   NE 89th   89th Cir
88th Cir   88th   NE   NE 89th St   Airport ✈ Terminal   NE 89th Av
NE 122nd   NE 87th St   NE 88th   NE 88th St   NE152ND AV
3   86th   NE 128th 129th   87th   138th 141st   143rd   NE 87th   153rd   88th   NE 87th
NE 124th Av   126th 85th   86th   NE 132nd   139th   145th   TIGER   87th   155th   86th Cir
NE 85th   84th   NE   TREE PARK   149th   NE 85th
84th St   83rd   85th 86th   85th
12400 83rd   2   83rd Wy   83rd Cir   83rd Cir

45°41'01"   NE **PADDEN** **PKWY**   NE 83rd   82nd 84th   148th   81st 82nd   NE 82nd
500   NE 83rd Cir   148th   153rd   82nd   NE 83rd   NE 83rd Av
NE 80th 81st   PEBBLE   NE 82nd   82nd Ct   151st   **A**1   82nd Cir   NE 82nd
NE 81st Av   CREEK   Cir   81st   150th 151st 81st   153rd   81st   NE 81st
NE 80th   PARK   81st St   80th   149th   79th   Ct   158th Av   79th
St   130th   NE 80th 136th 138th   140th Ct   80th   NE   Wy   80th   Av   NE 79th
5   Heritage   79th Cir   141st   78th   78th   **6** ST   Wy
NE 78th   HS   NE 79th Cir   St   Aquila Ct 79th Cir   NE **78TH**
NE 123rd   130th   76th Wy   77th   77th   76th   76th Cir   79th   75th
NE 77th   NE 78th St   78th St   NE 76th   76th Cir   Wy   74th   75th
7600   7600 St   141st   148th   74th Cir   75th   73rd
NE 75th 121st 123rd   NE **76TH** **ST**   NE **76TH** **ST**   143rd   NE 74th   73rd
120th   74th   125th   133rd 134th   71st   144th 145th   74th   74th Cir   74th
NE 73rd St   128th   129th   72nd   141st   73rd   73rd Cir   72nd   NE 72nd
NE 72nd St   SIFTON   130th   NE 71st Wy   140th   NE   71st Cir   71st St   71st
NE 71st   CEMETERY   NE 132nd   Av   141st 143rd   NE   70th St   70th
70th Cir   Sunrise Acres   70th   NE   69th St   68th St
6   NE Kerr Rd   69th   150th   68th Wy
124th   10   131st   NE **PLAIN RD**   WARD RD   68th St
NE **FOURTH** Av   **Sifton** 11   NE 147th   **12**
NE 65th   67th   NE   NE 143rd   157th   159th NE 66th Wy
St   135th Av   66th   64th Cir   65th   Cir
64th   65th   63rd St   65th 63rd
62nd St   63rd   A   NE 63rd
NE 63rd   NE 123rd   127th Av   NE 63rd St   NE 62nd St   6300   NE 62nd St   1 NE 155th Ct   NE
Av   62nd   61st   2 NE 155th Av   63rd Cir
60th Wy   Sifton   Skyridge   3 NE 153rd Av
7   Gdns   NE 138th   NE 152nd Av   4 NE 80th St   NE
60th   124th   Skyridge   130th   5 NE 79th Wy   60th St
56th   61st   6 NE 154th St
Brooktree   NE 135th   59th   5900   7 NE 152nd Av
15   NE 55th 129th 131st   St   5700   NE **162ND AV**   NE 58th St
45°39'43"   Burnt Bridge Creek   57th   14   13
          Vancouver

A   B   C   D   E

SEE **538** MAP

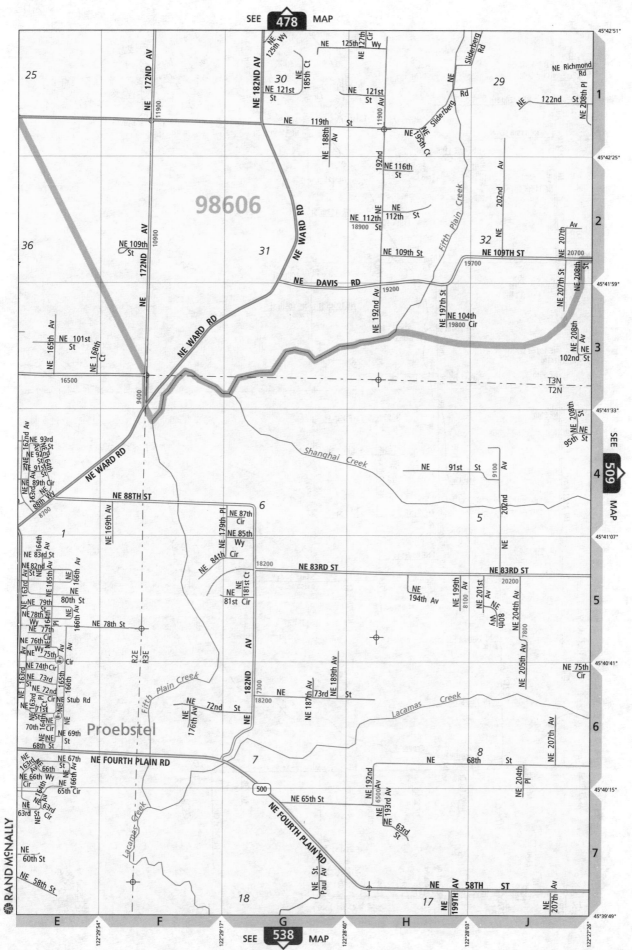

MAP
508

RAND McNALLY

1:24,000
1 in. = 2000 ft.

0   0.25   0.5
miles

SEE 478 MAP

25

30

NE 125th Wy

NE 125th 127th Wy
Cir

NE Richmond
Rd

29

NE 121st
St

NE 185th Ct

NE 121st
St

NE Sliderberg Rd

NE 122nd St 208th Pl

1

98606

NE 182ND AV

NE 119th St

NE 188th Av

NE 195th Ct

45°42'51"

45°42'25"

NE 116th
St

NE 192nd

NE 112th St
18900

NE 112th St

NE 202nd Av

NE 207th Av

2

31

NE WARD RD

NE 172ND AV

11900

10900

NE 109th St

NE 109th ST
19700

NE 207th
20700

36

NE 109th St

NE 172ND AV

NE DAVIS RD

NE 192nd Av
19200

NE 197th St

NE 104th Cir
19800

NE 208th Av

45°41'59"

3

NE 165th Av

NE 101st St

NE 168th Ct

16500

NE 207th Av

NE 208th Av

NE 102nd St

T3N
T2N

45°41'33"

NE WARD RD

9400

Shanghai Creek

NE 91st St
9100

NE 208th St

NE 95th St

SEE 509 MAP

4

NE 162nd Av NE 93rd St
NE 92nd St
NE 91st

NE 89th Cir
NE 88th Wy
8700

NE 88TH ST

NE 169th Av

NE 87th Cir

NE 85th Wy Cir

NE 84th Cir

6

NE 202nd

45°41'07"

1

NE 164th Av

NE 83rd St

NE 82nd Av

NE 166th Av

NE 163rd

NE 165th

NE 80th St

NE 79th

NE 78th
Wy

NE 164th

NE 166th Av

NE 77th

NE 76th Cir

NE 75th Wy Cir

NE 74th Cir

NE 73rd

NE 72nd Cir

NE 71st

NE 164th

NE 70th St

NE 69th

NE 68th St

NE 67th St

NE 66th St

NE 66th Wy Cir

NE 65th Cir

NE 63rd

63rd St Cir

NE 60th St

NE 58th St

NE 179th Pl Cir

NE 84th Cir

NE 181st Ct

NE 181st Cir

NE 78th St

R2E R3E

NE 182ND AV

Fifth Plain Creek

NE Stub Rd

Proebstel

NE 176th Av

NE FOURTH PLAIN RD

500

Lacamas Creek

NE 65th St

NE FOURTH PLAIN RD

NE St Paul Av

NE 18200 83RD ST

NE 194th Av

NE 83RD ST

NE 199th Av

NE 201st Av
8100

20200

NE 204th Av

NE 204th Wy
7800

NE 205th Av

NE 75th Cir

5

45°40'41"

NE 182ND 7300 AV

18200

NE 187th Av

NE 189th Av

NE 73rd St

Lacamas Creek

NE 207th Av

6

8

NE 68th St

NE 192nd Av

NE 204th Pl

NE 193rd Av

NE 63rd

6500

NE 58TH ST

NE 199TH AV

NE 207th Av

45°40'15"

7

17

18

7

SEE 538 MAP

45°39'49"

E   F   G   H   J

122°29'54"   122°29'17"   122°28'40"   122°28'03"   122°27'26"

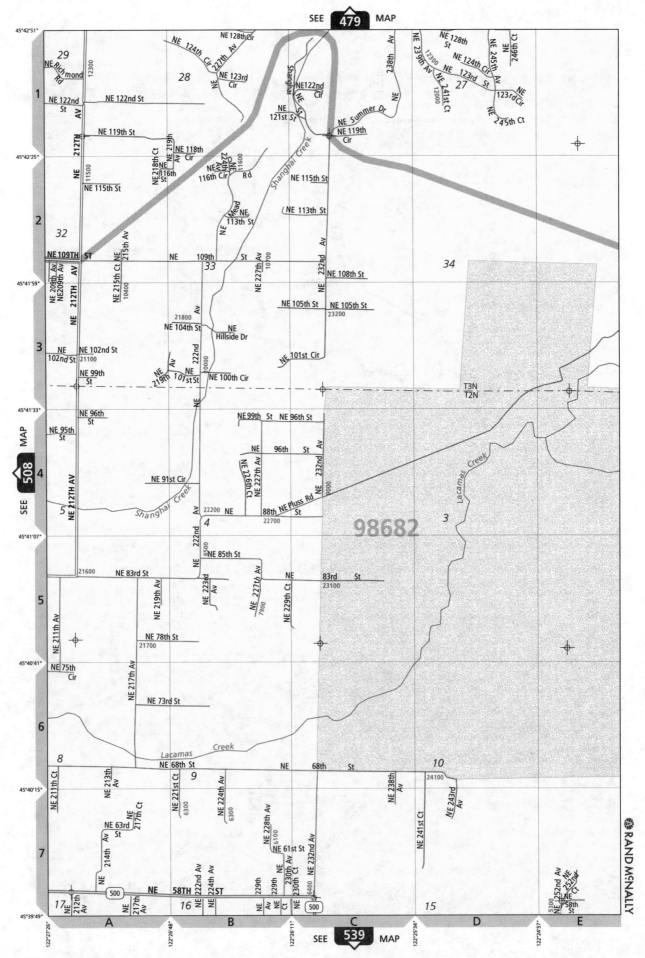

MAP
509

1:24,000
1 in. = 2000 ft.

0   0.25   0.5
miles

SEE 479 MAP

45°42'51"

29
NE Richmond Rd
12300
28
NE 124th Cir
NE 227th Av
NE 128th Cir
NE 123rd Cir
NE 128th St
NE 239th Av
12300
NE 124th Cir
NE 245th Av
NE 246th Ct
27
NE 123rd St
123rd Cir
NE 245th Ct
12000
NE 241st Ct

1
NE 122nd St
NE 122nd St
NE 119th St
NE 212TH AV
NE 219th Ct
NE 118th Cir
NE 218th Ct
NE 116th St
116th Cir
NE 224th Av
11600
11500
Rd
Shanghai St
NE 122nd Cir
NE 121st St
NE Summer Dr
NE 119th Cir

45°42'25"

NE 115th St
NE 113th St
NE Mead
NE 113th St
NE 115th St
Shanghai Creek

2
32
NE 109TH ST
215th Av
NE 215th Ct
10400
NE 109th St
NE 227th Av
10700
33
NE 232nd Av
NE 108th St
34

45°41'59"
NE 209th Av
NE 209th Av
NE 212TH AV
NE 105th St
NE 105th St
23200

NE 104th St
21800
NE Hillside Dr
NE 222nd Av
10000
NE 101st Cir

3
NE 102nd St
NE 102nd St
21100
NE 99th St
NE 219th Av
NE 101st St
NE 100th Cir

45°41'33"
NE 96th St
NE 95th St
NE 99th St
NE 96th St
T3N
T2N

4
NE 212TH AV
NE 91st Cir
NE 96th
St
NE 227th Av
NE 236th Ct
NE 232nd Av
96682
Lacamas Creek
98682

45°41'07"
5
Shanghai Creek
NE 222nd Av
22200 NE
4
88th NE Pluss Rd St
22700
9000
NE 232nd Av
3

NE 222nd Av
8500
NE 85th St
21600
NE 83rd St
NE 223rd
NE 227th Av
NE 83rd St
23100

5
NE 211th Av
NE 219th Av
NE 229th Av
7900

NE 78th St
21700

45°40'41"
NE 75th Cir
NE 217th Av
NE 73rd St

6
Lacamas Creek

8
NE 68th St
NE 68th St
10
24100

45°40'15"
NE 211th Ct
NE 213th Av
9
NE 221st Ct
6300
NE 224th Av
6300
NE 238th Av
NE 243rd Av

NE 63rd Av
NE 217th Ct
NE 228th Av
6100
NE 61st St
NE 241st Ct

7
NE 214th Av
NE 222nd Av
NE 224th Av
NE 229th Av
NE 229th Ct
NE 230th Ct
NE 230th Av
NE 232nd Av
6400
NE 252nd Av
NE 252nd Ct
5300
NE 58th St

17
NE 212th Av
NE 217th Av
NE 58TH ST
500
16
NE Av NE Ct
229th
500
15

45°39'49"

A   B   C   D   E

SEE 539 MAP

122°27'26"   122°26'48"   122°26'11"   122°25'34"   122°24'57"

RAND McNALLY

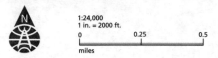

1:24,000
1 in. = 2000 ft.

0   0.25   0.5
miles

MAP
509

SEE 479 MAP

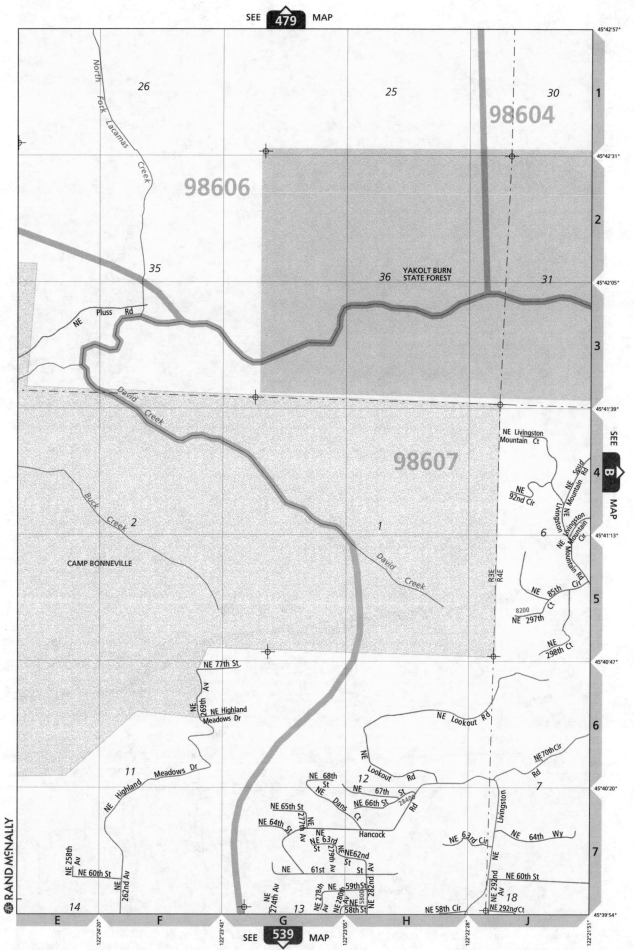

98604

26

25

30

1

45°42'57"

45°42'31"

98606

35

36   YAKOLT BURN
STATE FOREST

31

45°42'05"

2

NE   Pluss   Rd

NE

3

David   Creek

45°41'39"

NE Livingston
Mountain Ct

98607

NE Spud Mountain Rd

Buck Creek

2

1

NE
92nd Cir

NE Mountain Rd Livingston

Livingston Mountain Cir

4

SEE
B
MAP

CAMP BONNEVILLE

6

45°41'13"

David   Creek

R3E
R4E

NE Mountain Rd

NE 85th Ct Cir

8200

NE 297th

NE
298th Ct

5

45°40'47"

NE 77th St

NE 269th Av

NE Highland
Meadows Dr

NE Lookout Rd

NE 70th Cir

6

11   Meadows Dr

NE Highland

NE Lookout Rd

Rd

12

NE Lookout Rd

Livingston Rd

7

45°40'20"

NE 68th St

NE 67th St

NE 66th St

28400 Rd

NE 65th St

NE 277th Av

NE 64th St

Dans Ct

Hancock

NE 63rd Cir

NE 64th Wy

NE 63rd St

279th Av

NE62nd St

NE 292nd Av

NE 60th St

7

NE 258th Av

NE 60th St

262nd Av

NE 61st Av

NE 274th Av

NE 278th Av

NE 280th Av

5800

59th St

NE 282nd

58th St

NE 58th Cir

18

NE 292nd Ct

14

13

H

J

45°39'54"

E   F   G   H   J

122°24'20"   122°23'43"   122°23'05"   122°22'28"   122°21'51"

MAP
531

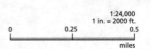

1:24,000
1 in. = 2000 ft.

0   0.25   0.5
miles

SEE B MAP

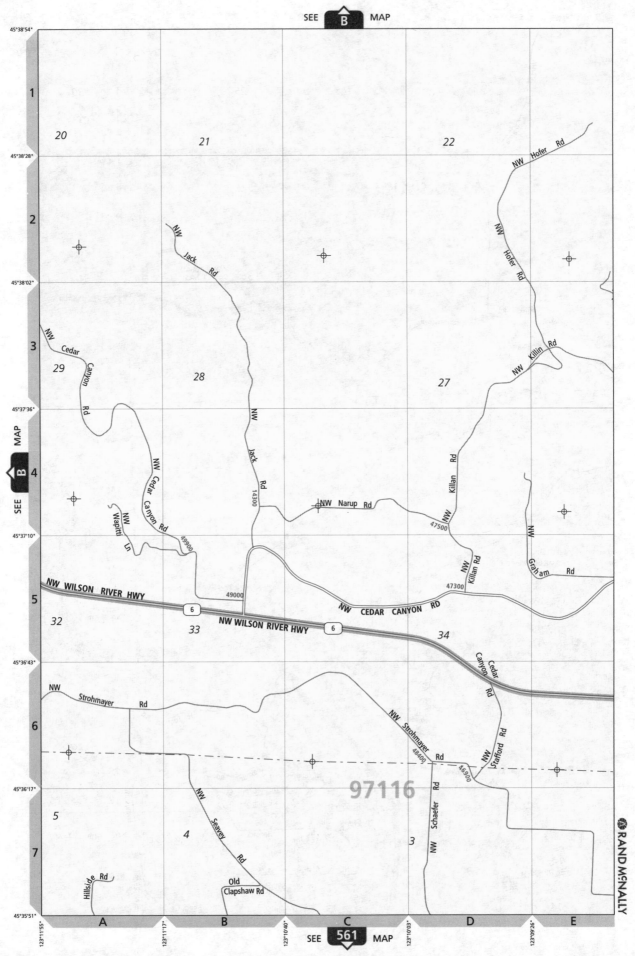

20

21

22

NW Hofer Rd

1

45°38'54"

45°38'28"

NW Hofer Rd

2

NW Jack Rd

45°38'02"

NW Cedar Canyon Rd

29

3

28

27

NW Killin Rd

45°37'36"

MAP
B 4
SEE

NW Cedar Canyon Rd

NW Wapitti Ln

NW Jack Rd
14300

NW Narup Rd

NW Killan Rd

NW 47500

NW Graham Rd

45°37'10"

49900

NW Killan Rd
47300

5

NW WILSON RIVER HWY

49000

6

NW WILSON RIVER HWY   6

NW CEDAR CANYON RD

32

33

34

Cedar Canyon Rd

45°36'43"

NW Strohmayer Rd

6

NW Strohmayer Rd
48400

NW Stafford Rd

46900

97116

45°36'17"

5

4

NW Seavey Rd

3

NW Schaefer Rd

7

Hillside Rd

Old Clapshaw Rd

45°35'51"

A   B   C   D   E

123°11'55"   123°11'??"   123°10'40"   123°10'03"   123°09'26"

SEE 561 MAP

RAND McNALLY

MAP
531

MAP
532

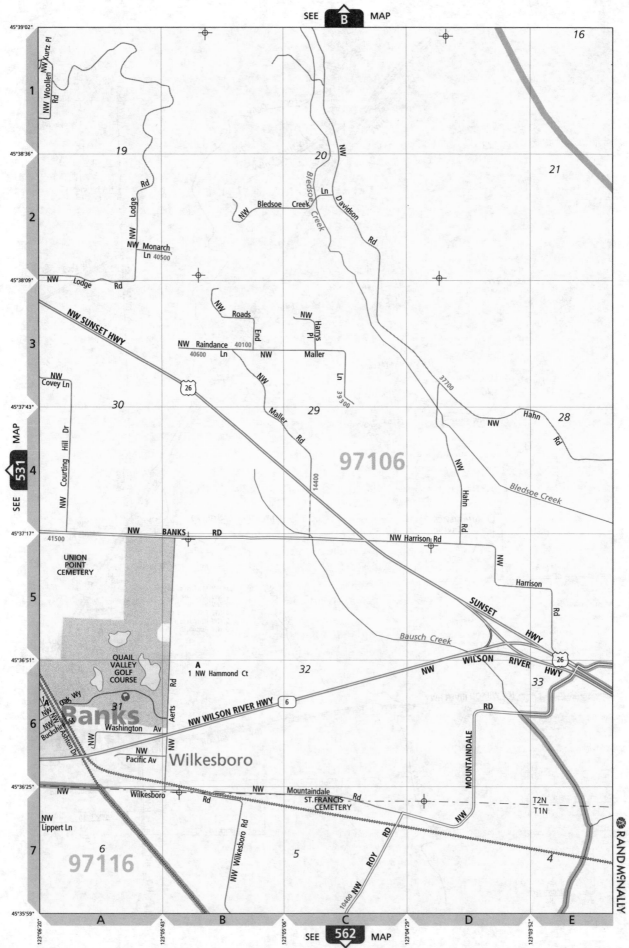

1:24,000
1 in. = 2000 ft.

0   0.25   0.5
miles

SEE **B** MAP

45°39'02"

16

NW Woollen
NW Kurtz Pl
NW Rd

1

19

20

NW

21

Bledsoe Creek

45°38'36"

NW Lodge Rd

NW Bledsoe Creek

Ln

Davidson Rd

2

NW Lodge

NW Monarch
Ln 40500

45°38'09"   NW   Lodge   Rd

NW SUNSET HWY

NW Roads

NW Harrys Pl

NW Raindance   40100
40600   Ln   NW   Maller

3

NW

Maller Ln 39300

26

37700

NW
Covey Ln

45°37'43"   30

29

NW Hahn
Rd   28

SEE **531** MAP

NW Courting Hill Dr

97106

14400

NW Hahn Rd

Bledsoe Creek

4

45°37'17"   41500   NW   BANKS   RD

NW Harrison Rd

UNION
POINT
CEMETERY

NN

Harrison

5

SUNSET

HWY

Rd

45°36'51"

QUAIL
VALLEY
GOLF
COURSE

A
1 NW Hammond Ct

32

Bausch Creek

NW   WILSON   RIVER

HWY

26

33

31

Aerts Rd

NW WILSON RIVER HWY   6

RD

MOUNTAINDALE

6

NW oak Wy

Banks

NW
NW Buckshire
NW Ashton Dr
Washington Av

NW

NW
Pacific Av   Wilkesboro

45°36'25"   NW

NW   Mountaindale   Rd

T2N

7

NW
Lippert Ln

Wilkesboro   Rd

ST. FRANCIS
CEMETERY

T1N

6

97116

5

NW   Wilkesboro   Rd

NW   ROY   RD

4

10400 NW

45°35'59"

A   B   C   D   E

123°06'20"   123°05'43"   123°05'06"   123°04'29"   123°03'52"

SEE **562** MAP

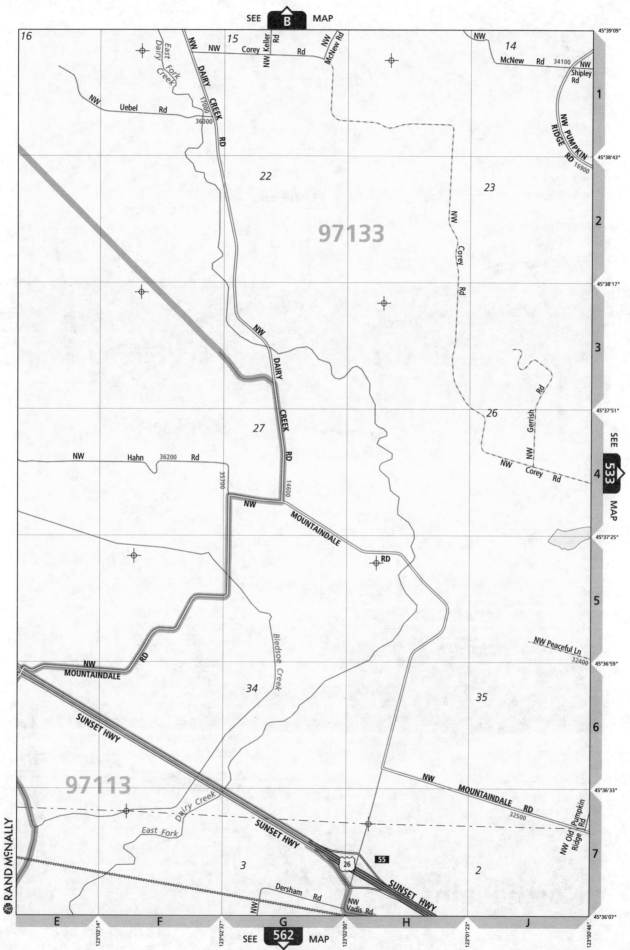

MAP
532

1:24,000
1 in. = 2000 ft.

0   0.25   0.5
miles

SEE **B** MAP

16

15   Corey   Rd

14   McNew   Rd   34100

NW   NW

NW Keller Rd

NW McNew Rd

NW Shipley Rd

East Fork Dairy Creek

NW   Uebel   Rd

DAIRY CREEK RD

11000

36300

NW PUMPKIN RIDGE RD 16900

45°39'09"

1

45°38'43"

22

97133

23

NW Corey Rd

2

45°38'17"

3

45°37'51"

DAIRY   CREEK   RD   14600

NW

27

26

Gerrish Rd

NW   Hahn   36200   Rd

35700

NW   Corey   Rd

SEE 533 MAP

4

45°37'25"

NW

MOUNTAINDALE

RD

5

Bledsoe Creek

RD

NW   MOUNTAINDALE

34

NW Peaceful Ln 32400

45°36'59"

35

6

97113

SUNSET HWY

NW   MOUNTAINDALE   RD   32500

45°36'33"

NW Old Pumpkin Ridge Rd

Dairy Creek

East Fork

SUNSET HWY

7

3

2

26 55

SUNSET HWY

Dersham   Rd

NW Vadis Rd

NW

RAND McNALLY

E   F   G   H   J

SEE 562 MAP

45°36'07"

123°03'14"   123°02'37"   123°02'00"   123°01'23"   123°00'46"

MAP
533

1:24,000
1 in. = 2000 ft.

0   0.25   0.5
miles

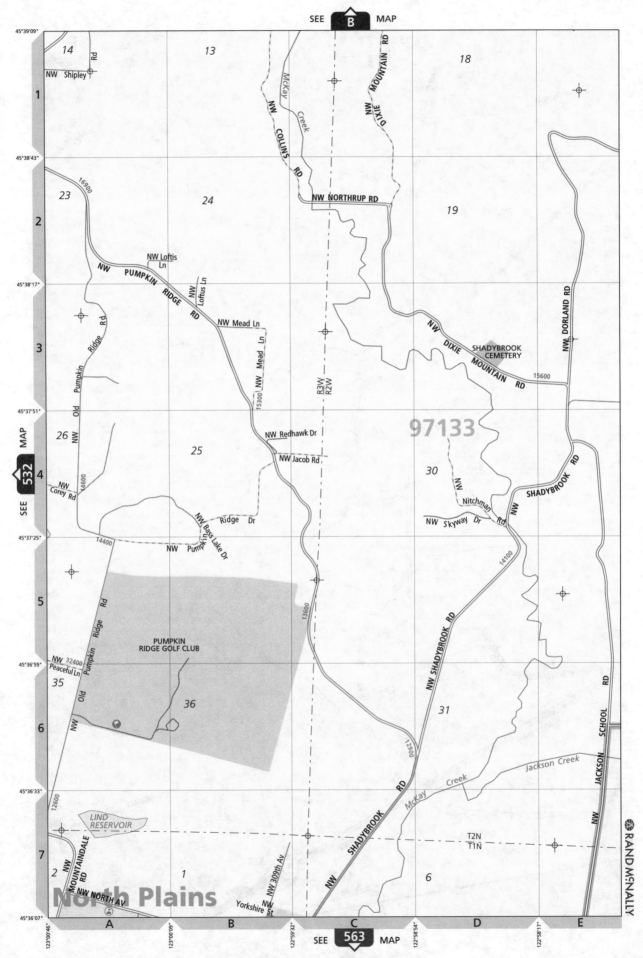

45°39'09"

14

NW Shipley Rd

13

NW COLLINS RD

McKay Creek

NW DIXIE MOUNTAIN RD

18

1

45°38'43"

23

16900

24

NW NORTHRUP RD

19

2

45°38'17"

NW Loftis Ln

NW PUMPKIN RIDGE RD

NW Loftus Ln

NW Mead Ln

NW DIXIE MOUNTAIN RD

SHADYBROOK CEMETERY

NW DORLAND RD

15600

3

Pumpkin Ridge Rd

NW Mead Ln

15300

R3W R2W

97133

45°37'51"

26

Old Pumpkin Ridge Rd

NW

25

NW Redhawk Dr

NW Jacob Rd

30

SHADYBROOK RD

14600

NW Corey Rd

NW Nitchman Rd

NW SHADYBROOK RD

4

45°37'25"

14400

NW Bass Lake Dr

Ridge Dr

NW Pumpkin

NW Skyway Dr

14100

13600

PUMPKIN RIDGE GOLF CLUB

Old Pumpkin Ridge Rd

5

45°36'59"

NW 32400
Peaceful Ln

35

36

31

NW SHADYBROOK RD

12900

JACKSON SCHOOL RD

6

NW Old Pumpkin Ridge Rd

Jackson Creek

45°36'33"

12600

LIND RESERVOIR

NW SHADYBROOK RD

McKay Creek

T2N
T1N

NW JACKSON

7

2

NW MOUNTAINDALE RD

1

NW 309th Av

6

North Plains

NW NORTH AV

NW Yorkshire St

45°36'07"

123°00'46"   A   123°00'09"   B   122°59'32"   C   122°58'54"   D   122°58'17"   E

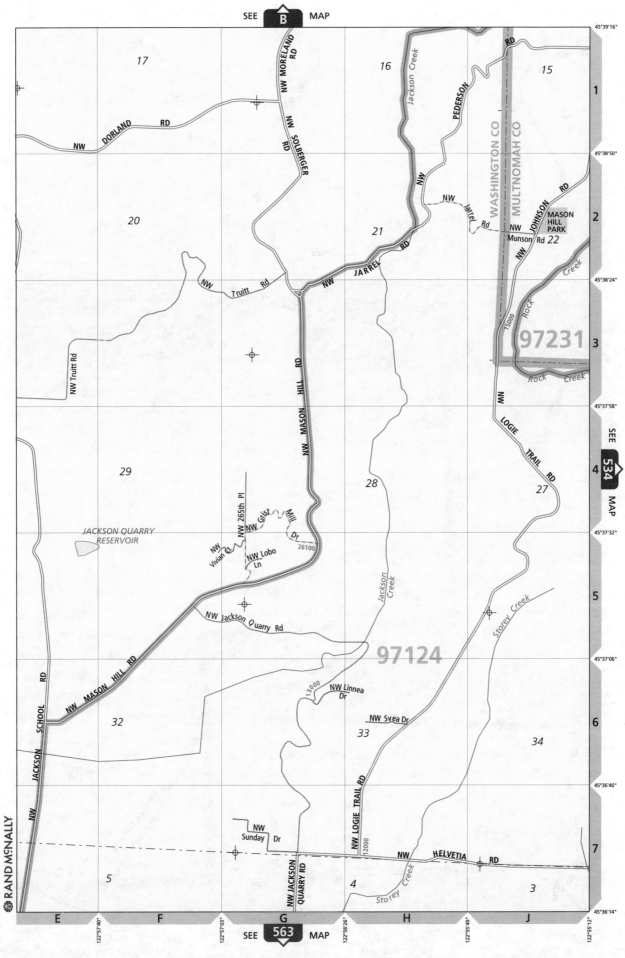

MAP
533

1:24,000
1 in. = 2000 ft.

0   0.25   0.5
miles

SEE **B** MAP

45°39'16"

17

16

15

NW MORELAND RD

Jackson Creek

PEDERSON

1

NW DORLAND RD

NW SOLBERGER RD

NW

45°38'50"

WASHINGTON CO
MULTNOMAH CO

NW JOHNSON RD

MASON HILL PARK

2

20

21

Jarrel Rd

NW

NW Munson Rd 22

NW Truitt Rd

NW JARREL RD

NW

Rock Creek

45°38'24"

NW Truitt Rd

15000

97231

3

Rock Creek

45°37'58"

NW

LOGIE

SEE **534** MAP

29

28

27

TRAIL RD

4

NW 265th Pl

NW Grist Mill Dr

JACKSON QUARRY RESERVOIR

NW MASON HILL RD

NW Vivian Ct

26100

NW Lobo Ln

45°37'32"

Jackson Creek

Storey Creek

45°37'06"

NW Jackson Quarry Rd

97124

5

13000

NW Linnea Dr

NW SCHOOL RD

NW MASON HILL RD

32

NW Svea Dr

33

34

6

45°36'40"

NW JACKSON

NW

Sunday Dr

NW LOGIE TRAIL RD

12000

45°36'14"

7

RAND M⁹NALLY

5

NW JACKSON QUARRY RD

4

NW HELVETIA RD

Storey Creek

3

Storey Creek

45°36'14"

E

F

G

H

J

122°57'40"

122°57'03"

122°56'26"

122°55'49"

122°55'12"

SEE **563** MAP

MAP
534

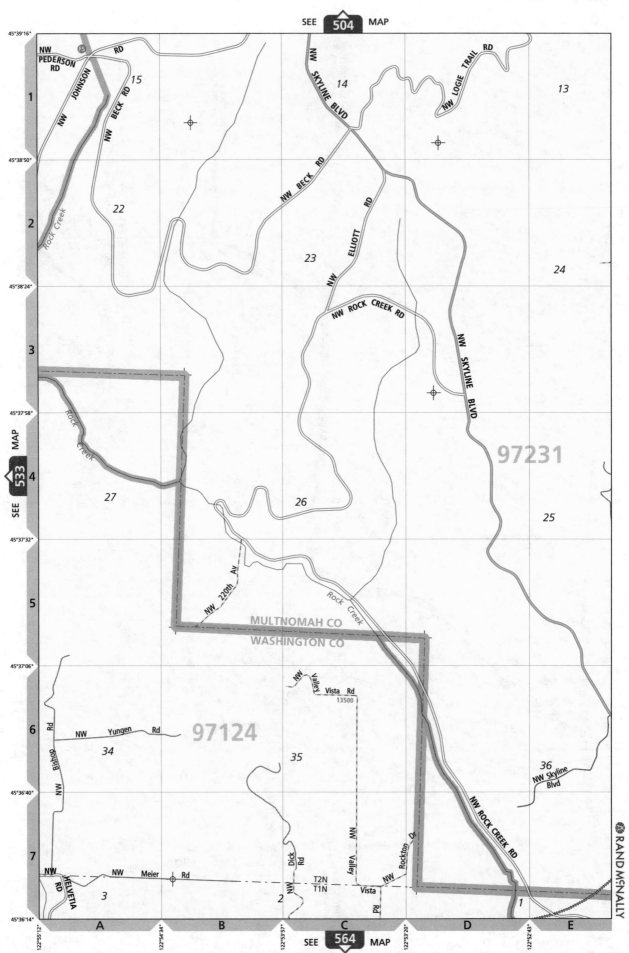

 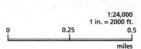

1:24,000
1 in. = 2000 ft.

0   0.25   0.5

miles

NW PEDERSON RD
FS
NW JOHNSON RD
NW BECK RD
RD
15
1
Rock Creek
22
2
45°39'16"
45°38'50"
45°38'24"

NW SKYLINE BLVD
14
NW LOGIE TRAIL RD
13

NW BECK RD
NW ELLIOTT RD
23
NW ROCK CREEK RD
24

NW SKYLINE BLVD
97231

45°37'58"
45°37'32"

MAP
533
SEE

Rock Creek
27
26
25
3
4

NW 220th Av
MULTNOMAH CO
WASHINGTON CO
Rock Creek

45°37'06"

NW Valley Vista Rd
13500

5

97124

NW Bishop Rd
NW Yungen Rd
34
35
NW Valley
NW Rockton Dr
36
NW Skyline Blvd
NW ROCK CREEK RD

45°36'40"

6

7

NW HELVETIA RD
NW Meier Rd
3
NW Dick Rd
2
T2N
T1N
NW Vista
Vista Rd
1

45°36'14"

A   B   C   D   E

RAND M^{c}NALLY

122°55'12"   122°54'34"   122°53'57"   122°53'20"   122°52'43"

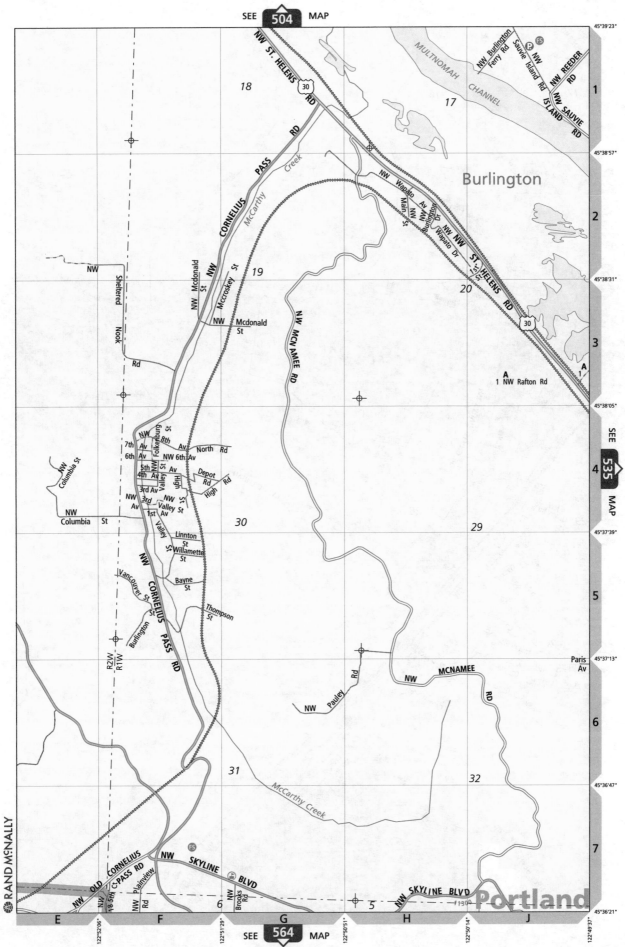

MAP
534

1:24,000
1 in. = 2000 ft.

0   0.25   0.5
miles

SEE 504 MAP

45°39'23"

NW ST. HELENS RD
30

18

MULTNOMAH CHANNEL

NW Burlington Ferry Rd
FS
NW Sauvie Island Rd
NW REEDER RD
NW SAUVIE ISLAND RD

17

1

45°38'57"

CORNELIUS PASS RD
McCarthy Creek

NW Wapato Av
NW Main St
NW Burlington Dr
NW Wapato Dr

Burlington

NW ST. HELENS RD

2

45°38'31"

NW Mcdonald St
Mccroskey St

19

NW Mcdonald St

20

NW MCNAMEE RD

30

3

45°38'05"

Sheltered Nook Rd

NW Columbia St

7th Av
6th Av
5th Av
4th Av
3rd Av
NW Folkenburg St
NW 8th Av
North Rd
NW 6th Av
Depot Rd
High Rd
High St
NW Valley St
NW 3rd Av
NW Valley St
1st Av
Valley St

A
1 NW Rafton Rd

SEE 535 MAP

A

4

45°37'39"

NW Columbia St

Linnton St
Willamette St
Bayne St

30

29

5

Vancouver St
Burlington
NW CORNELIUS PASS RD
Thompson St

R2W R1W

45°37'13"
Paris Av

NW MCNAMEE RD

NW Pauley Rd

6

45°36'47"

31

McCarthy Creek

32

NW MCNAMEE RD

7

RAND McNALLY

NW OLD CORNELIUS PASS RD
NW 5th Ct
FS
NW Plainview Rd
NW SKYLINE BLVD
NW Brooks Rd
6
5
NW SKYLINE BLVD
11300
Portland

45°36'21"

E   F   G   H   J

SEE 564 MAP

122°52'06"   122°51'29"   122°50'51"   122°50'14"   122°49'37"

MAP
535

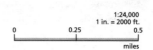

1:24,000
1 in. = 2000 ft.

0   0.25   0.5

miles

SEE 505 MAP

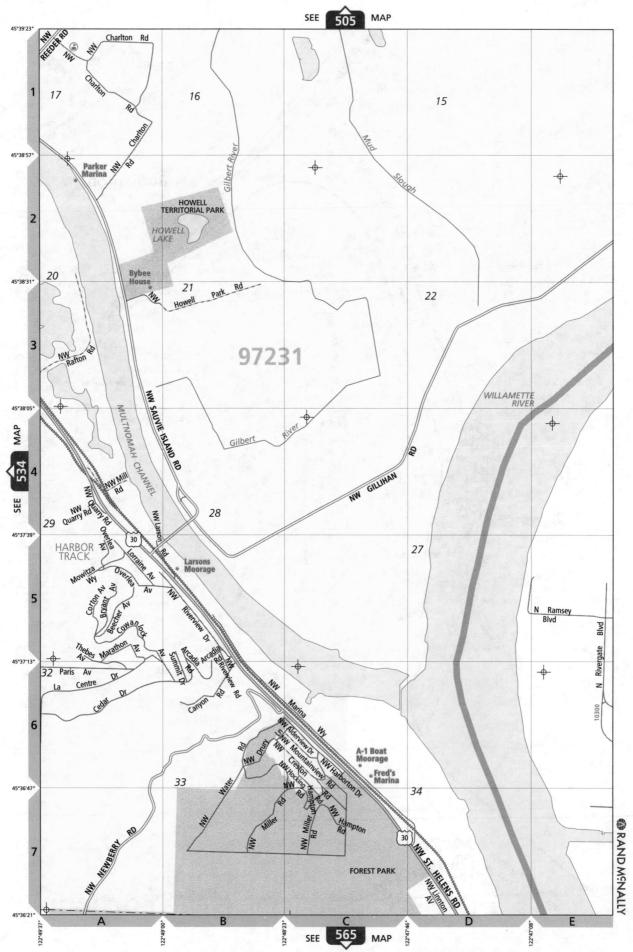

SEE 534 MAP

SEE 565 MAP

RAND M9NALLY

MAP
535

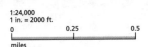

1:24,000
1 in. = 2000 ft.

0   0.25   0.5

miles

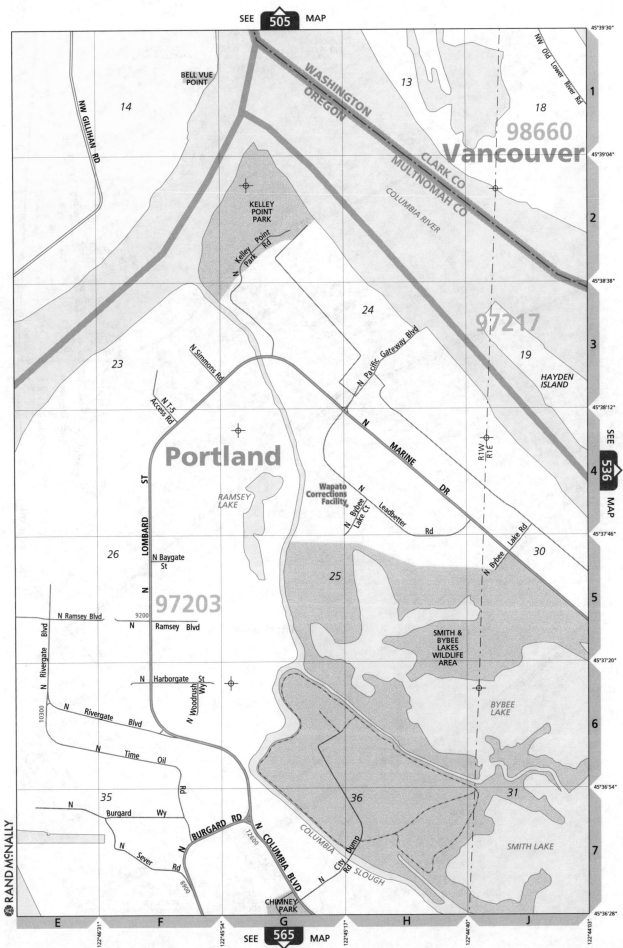

SEE 505 MAP

WASHINGTON
OREGON

13

NW Old Lower River Rd

1

BELL VUE
POINT

14

18

98660
Vancouver

NW GILLIHAN RD

CLARK CO
MULTNOMAH CO

45°39'30"

45°39'04"

KELLEY
POINT
PARK

COLUMBIA RIVER

2

45°38'38"

Kelley Point Park Rd

N

24

97217

N Simmons Rd

23

N Pacific Gateway Blvd

19

HAYDEN
ISLAND

3

45°38'12"

N T-5
Access Rd

Portland

RAMSEY
LAKE

N MARINE DR

R1W R1E

SEE
536
MAP

4

Wapato
Corrections
Facility

N Bybee Lake Ct

N Leadbetter Rd

N Bybee Lake Rd

30

LOMBARD ST

N Baygate
St

97203

25

45°37'46"

N Ramsey Blvd

9200
N   Ramsey   Blvd

SMITH &
BYBEE
LAKES
WILDLIFE
AREA

5

Rivergate Blvd

N Harborgate   St

N Woodrush Wy

45°37'20"

10300
N   Rivergate   Blvd

BYBEE
LAKE

6

N   Time   Oil

Rd

35

36

31

45°36'54"

N   Burgard   Wy

N COLUMBIA BLVD

COLUMBIA

SLOUGH

City Dump Rd

SMITH LAKE

7

N   Sever   Rd

BURGARD RD

12600

8900

CHIMNEY
PARK

E   F   G   H   J

122°46'31"   122°45'54"   122°45'17"   122°44'40"   122°44'03"

45°36'28"

SEE 565 MAP

MAP
536

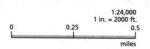

1:24,000
1 in. = 2000 ft.
0   0.25   0.5
miles

SEE 506 MAP

VANCOUVER
LAKE PARK

501

VANCOUVER
LAKE WILDLIFE
AREA

VANCOUVER
LAKE LOWLANDS

NW Old
Lower River Rd

NW LOWER RIVER RD

1

18

VANCOUVER
LAKE

17

La Frambois Rd

W Firestone Ln

16

NW FRUIT VALLEY RD

3900

NW Gateway Av

NW LOWER RIVER RD

2200

W 37th St
W 36th St

Thompson Av

W 34th St

2

19

FRUIT VALLEY
PARK

Yeoman
Xavier Av
Av

NW Uriander Av

NW Harborside Dr

98660
Vancouver

Weigel
Van A Illman Av

W 31st St

2100

NW Harborside Dr

NW Harborside Dr 20

NW Harborside Dr

W 28th St

21

Walnut St

3

W 28th St
W 27th St

W 27th St

2600

W 26th Av

St. Francys Ln

501

Kotobuki Wy

Thompson Av

24th Av
Roosevelt

45°38'12"

W 22nd St

W 20TH ST

SIMPSON AV

THOMPSON AV

4

28

W 16th St
Elevator Wy

Simpson Av

PORT WY

45°37'46"

29

HAYDEN ISLAND

N Hayden Island Dr

5

30

97217

N MARINE DR

BYBEE
LAKE

N Menzies Ct

N Menzies

6

SMITH
& BYBEE
LAKES
31 WILDLIFE
AREA

97203

5100

N Marine Dr

N Image Dr
N Canoe
N Broughton Dr
N Scouler Av

Broughton Ct

N Fir Av
N Elm Av

N Scouler Av

N Driftwood Av
N Cypress Av

45°36'54"

32

N Surtle Rd

33 N Westshore Dr
N West Middle
Shore St Shore Av South

N Jantzen St
N Jantzen Beach Ctr

7

SMITH
LAKE

PORTLAND RD

12100

N MARINE DR

N Force Av

11500 N

Portland

HERON
LAKES GOLF
COURSE

PORTLAND
METROPOLITAN EXPO CENTER

A   B   C   D   E

SEE 566 MAP

45°39'30"
45°39'04"
45°38'38"
45°38'12"
45°37'46"
45°37'20"
45°36'54"
45°36'28"

122°44'03"
122°43'26"
122°42'48"
122°42'11"
122°41'34"

SEE 535 MAP

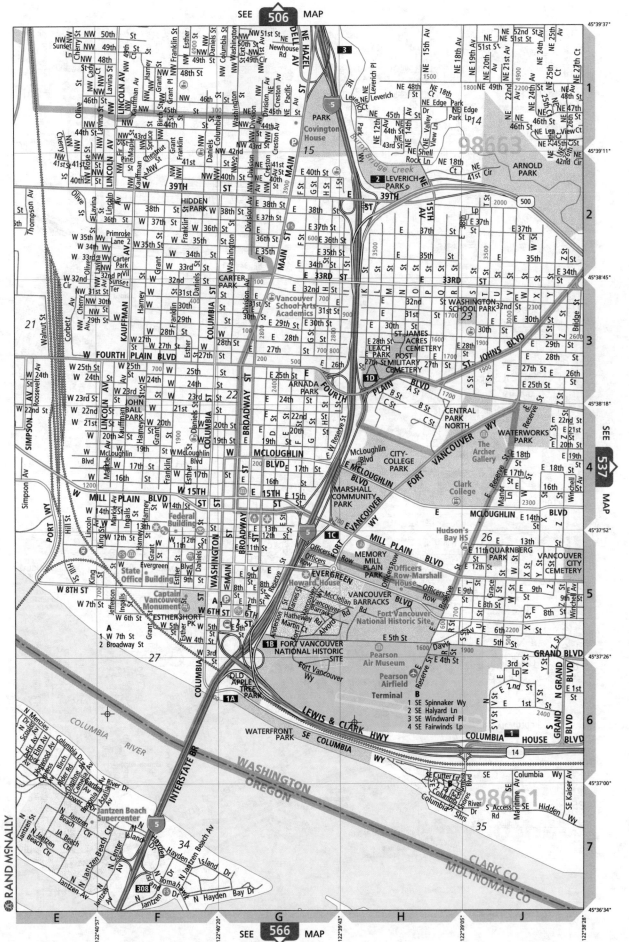

MAP
536

1:24,000
1 in. = 2000 ft.
0   0.25   0.5
miles

98663

ARNOLD PARK

Covington House

LEVERICH PARK

Burnt Bridge Creek

WASHINGTON SCHOOL PARK

Vancouver School Arts Academics

CARTER PARK

HIDDEN PARK

ST. JAMES ACRES

LEACH PARK

MILITARY CEMETERY

ST. JOHNS BLVD

ARNADA PARK

JOHN BALL PARK

CENTRAL PARK NORTH

WATERWORKS PARK

The Archer Gallery

Clark College

MCLOUGHLIN BLVD

CITY-COLLEGE PARK

MARSHALL COMMUNITY PARK

W 15TH ST

Federal Building

State Office Building

Captain Vancouver Monument

ESTHERSHORT PK

A
1 W 7th St
2 Broadway St

Howard House

Evergreen

McClellan

VANCOUVER BARRACKS

Officers Row

Officers Row-Marshall House

Hudson's Bay HS

QUARNBERG PARK

VANCOUVER CITY CEMETERY

MEMORY MILL PLAIN PARK

MILL PLAIN BLVD

FORT VANCOUVER NATIONAL HISTORIC SITE

Fort Vancouver Wy

Pearson Air Museum

Pearson Airfield Terminal

GRAND BLVD

N GRAND BLVD

OLD APPLE TREE PARK

B
1 SE Spinnaker Wy
2 SE Halyard Ln
3 SE Windward Pl
4 SE Fairwinds Lp

WATERFRONT PARK

LEWIS & CLARK HWY

SE COLUMBIA

COLUMBIA HOUSE

COLUMBIA RIVER

WASHINGTON
OREGON

98661

Jantzen Beach Supercenter

CLARK CO
MULTNOMAH CO

45°39'37"
45°39'11"
45°38'45"
45°38'18"
45°37'52"
45°37'26"
45°37'00"
45°36'34"

122°40'57"   122°40'20"   122°39'43"   122°39'05"   122°38'28"

E   F   G   H   J

1   2   3   4   5   6   7

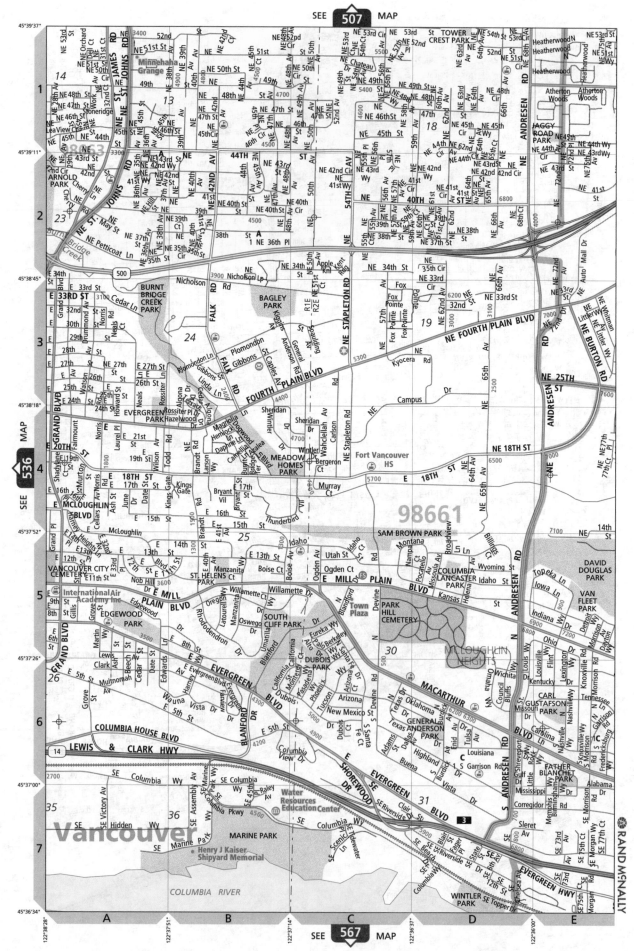

MAP
537

SEE 507 MAP

1:24,000
1 in. = 2000 ft.
0   0.25   0.5
miles

98661

Vancouver

COLUMBIA RIVER

RAND McNALLY

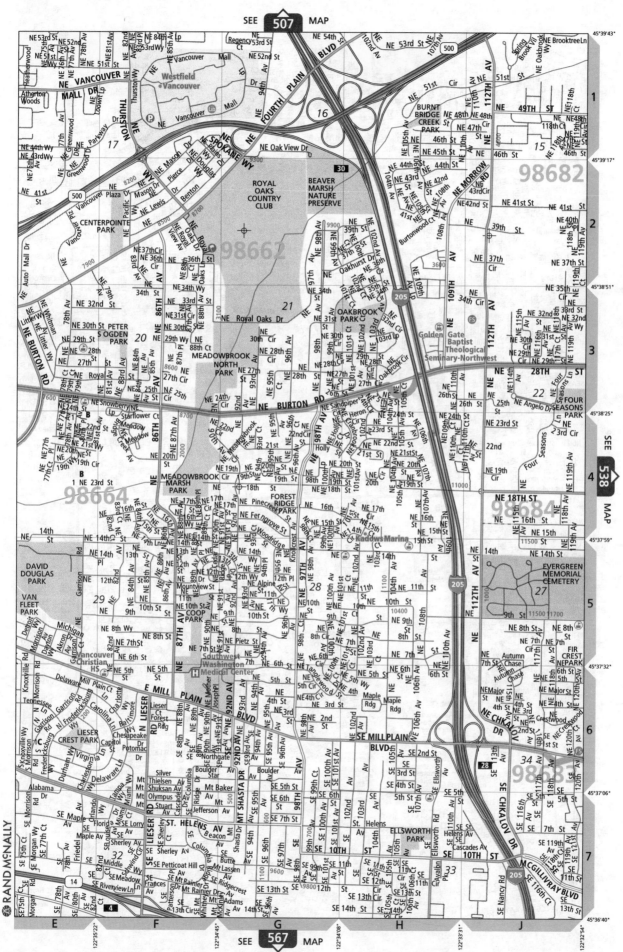

MAP
537

1:24,000
1 in. = 2000 ft.
0   0.25   0.5
miles

SEE **507** MAP

SEE **538** MAP

SEE **567** MAP

RAND M*NALLY

MAP
538

1:24,000
1 in. = 2000 ft.
0   0.25   0.5
miles

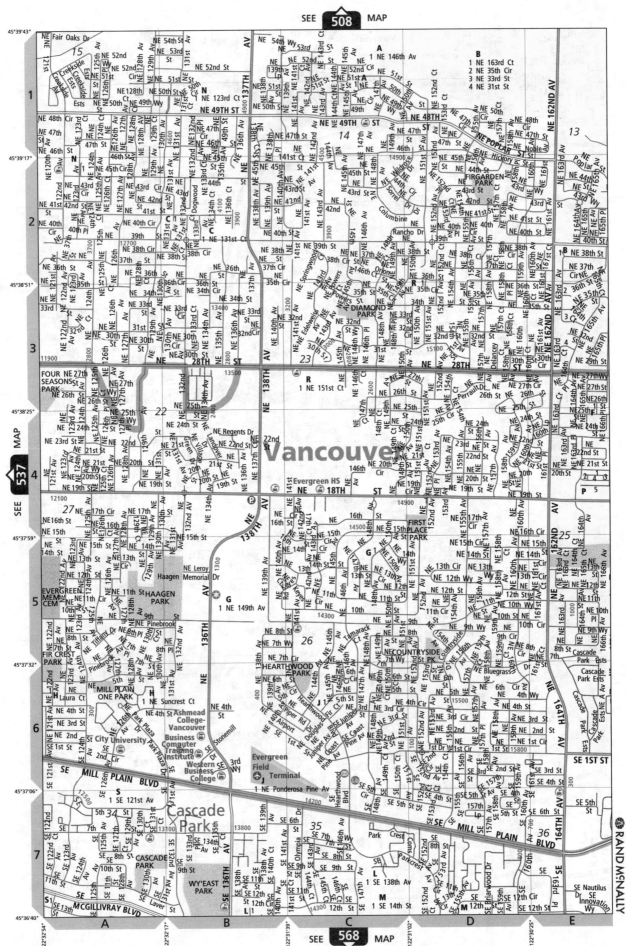

Vancouver

SEE 537 MAP

RAND McNALLY

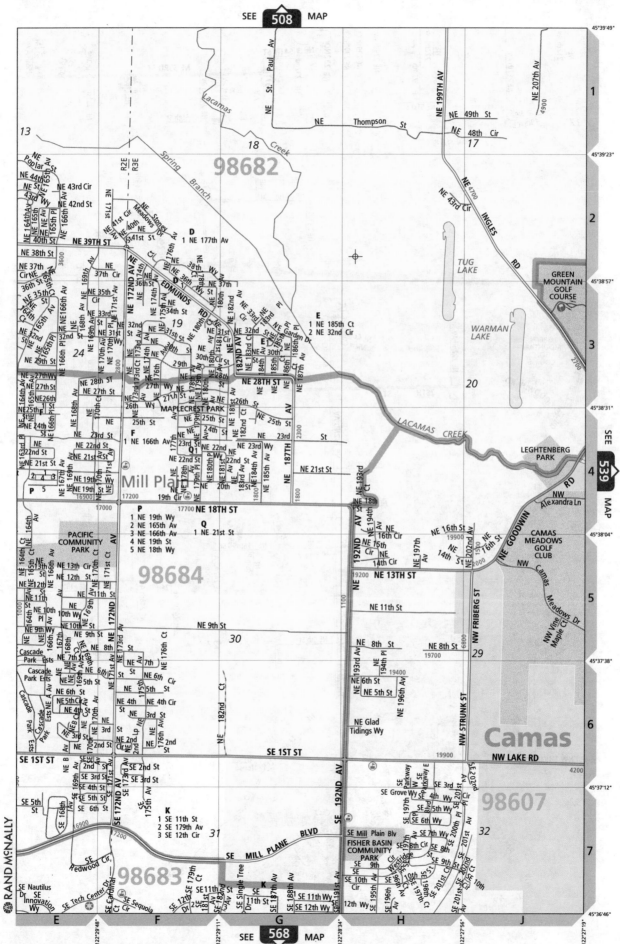

MAP
538

1:24,000
1 in. = 2000 ft.
0   0.25   0.5
miles

SEE 508 MAP

98682

98684

98683

98607

Camas

Mill Plain

Pacific Community Park

Maplecrest Park

Fisher Basin Community Park

Camas Meadows Golf Club

Green Mountain Golf Course

Leghtenberg Park

Tug Lake

Warman Lake

SEE 539 MAP

SEE 568 MAP

MAP
539

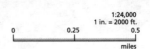

1:24,000
1 in. = 2000 ft.

0   0.25   0.5
miles

SEE 509 MAP

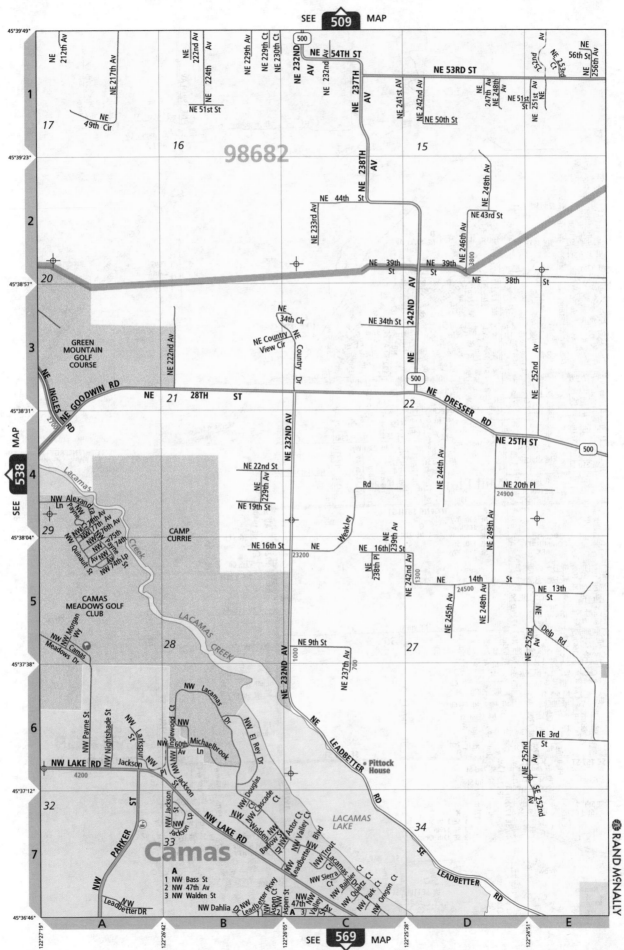

45°39'49"
45°39'23"
45°38'57"
45°38'31"
45°38'04"
45°37'38"
45°37'12"
45°36'46"

122°27'19"   122°26'42"   122°26'05"   122°25'28"   122°24'51"

NE 212th Av
NE 217th Av
NE 49th Cir
NE 222nd Av
NE 224th Av
NE 51st St
NE 229th Av
NE 229th Ct
NE 230th Ct
NE 232ND AV
500
NE 54TH ST
NE 237TH AV
NE 232nd Av
NE 53RD ST
NE 241st AV
NE 242nd AV
NE 50th St
NE 247th Av
NE 248th Av
NE 51st St
NE 251st St
NE 252nd Ct
NE 253rd
NE 56th Av
NE 256th Av

17
16
98682
15

NE 238TH AV
NE 44th St
NE 233rd Av
NE 248th Av
NE 43rd St
NE 246th Av
3800

20
NE 39th St
NE 39th St
NE 38th St

NE 34th Cir
NE Country View Cir
NE 34th St
NE 242ND AV
NE 252nd Av

GREEN MOUNTAIN GOLF COURSE
NE 222nd Av
NE Country Dr
500

NE INGLES RD
NE GOODWIN RD
NE 21 28TH ST
22
NE DRESSER RD
NE 25TH ST
500

538
MAP
SEE
2700

NE 232ND AV
NE 22nd St
NE 229th Av
NE 19th St
Rd
NE 244th Av
NE 20th Pl
24900

Lacamas
NW Alexandra Ln
NW Payne
NW 78th Av
NW 77th Av
NW 76th Av
NW 75th Av
NW Quinault St
NW 74th Av
NW 74th Lp
NW 74th St
CAMP CURRIE
NE 16th St
23200
NE Weakley Rd
NE 238th Pl
NE 16th St
NE 239th Av
NE 242nd Av
1300
NE 249th Av
NE 14th St
24500
NE 245th Av
NE 248th Av
NE 13th St
NE 252nd Av

29
Creek
28
LACAMAS CREEK
CAMAS MEADOWS GOLF CLUB
NW Morgan Wy
NW Camas Meadows Dr
NE 9th St
1000
NE 237th Av
700
27
NE Delp Rd
NE 252nd Av
SE 252nd Av

NW Lacamas Dr
NW El Rey Dr
NE LEADBETTER RD
Pittock House
NE 3rd St
NE 252nd Av

NW Payne St
NW Nightshade St
NW Larkspur St
NW Inglewood Ct
NW 60th Av
NW Michaelbrook Ln
NW LAKE RD
Jackson
NW Jackson Pl
4200

32
NW PARKER ST
NW Jackson St
NW Jackson Ct
NW LAKE RD
NW Walden Ln
NW Douglas Ct
NW Cascade Ct
NW Astor Ct
NW Valley Blvd
LACAMAS LAKE
34
SE LEADBETTER RD

7
Camas
A
1 NW Bass St
2 NW 47th Av
3 NW Walden St
NW Leadbetter DR
NW Dahlia
NW Leadbetter Pkwy
NW Aspen St
NW 47th Av
A 3
NW Trout Ct
NW Lacamas Ct
NW Sierra Ct
NW Rainier Ct
NW Quartz Ct
NW Park Ct
NW Oregon Ct

SEE 569 MAP

RAND McNALLY

A   B   C   D   E

MAP
539

1:24,000
1 in. = 2000 ft.
0   0.25   0.5
miles

SEE ⬆ 509 MAP

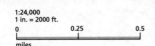

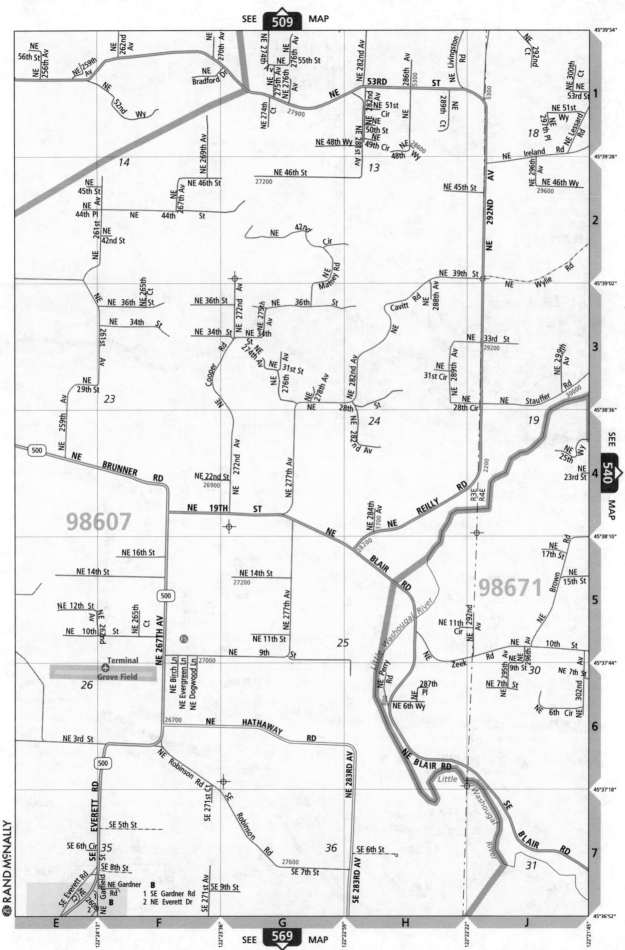

45°39'54"
45°39'28"
45°39'02"
45°38'36"
45°38'10"
45°37'44"
45°37'18"
45°36'52"

1
2
3
4
5
6
7

SEE 540 MAP

NE 56th Av
NE 256th Av
NE 259th Av
NE 262nd Av
NE 270th Av
NE 274th Av
NE 275th Av
NE 276th Av
NE 255th St
NE 282nd Av
53RD ST
286th Av
Livingston Rd
NE 292nd Av
NE 300th Ct
Bradford Dr
NE 52nd Wy
NE 274th Ct
27900
53RD
NE 282nd Av
282nd Av
51st Cir
289th Ct
53rd St
NE 51st Wy
NE 297th Pl
NE Lessard Rd
18
NE 50th St
NE 49th Cir
48th Wy
28600
NE Ireland Rd
NE 296th Pl
29600
NE 46th Wy
14
NE 269th Av
NE 48th Wy
NE 281st Av
13
NE 46th St
27200
NE 45th St
NE 45th St
NE 267th Av
NE 46th St
NE 261st
NE 42nd St
NE 44th Pl
NE 44th St
NE 42nd Cir
Marney Rd
NE 39th St
Wylie Rd
NE 265th Ct
NE 272nd Av
NE 275th Av
36th St
Cavitt Rd
288th Av
NE 36th St
NE 34th St
NE 261st Av
NE 34th St
NE 34th St
Cooper Rd
NE 274th Av
NE 31st St
276th Av
278th Av
NE 282nd Av
33rd St
29200
31st Cir
NE 289th Av
NE 299th Av
NE 29th St
23
28th St
NE 28th
24
28th Cir
Stauffer Rd
30000
19
NE 259th Av
NE 282nd Av
NE 25th Wy
NE 23rd St
2200
500
NE BRUNNER RD
NE 272nd Av
NE 22nd St
26900
NE 277th Av
NE 284th Av
1700
NE REILLY RD
R3E R4E
98607
NE 19TH ST
BLAIR RD
23200
98671
NE 17th St
NE 16th St
NE 14th St
NE 14th St
27200
NE 277th Av
Little Washougal River
NE 15th St
Brown Rd
500
NE 12th St
NE 262nd Av
NE 265th Ct
NE 11th St
25
NE 11th Cir
NE 292nd Av
10th St
NE 296th Av
FS
NE 9th St
Zeek Rd
NE 295th Av
9th St
30
NE 7th St
NE 267th AV
Terminal
Grove Field
26
NE Birch Ln
NE Evergreen Ln
NE Dogwood Ln
27000
NE Perry Rd
287th Pl
NE 6th Wy
800
NE 7th St
302nd
NE 6th Cir
26700
NE HATHAWAY RD
NE 3rd St
NE Robinson Rd
NE 283RD AV
NE BLAIR RD
Little Washougal River
SE BLAIR RD
EVERETT RD
500
SE 271st Ct
SE Robinson Rd
SE 5th St
SE 6th Cir
35
SE 8th St
SE 283RD AV
36
SE 6th St
SE 7th St
27600
31
SE Everett Rd
NE Garfield Rd
SE 271st Av
SE 9th St
NE Gardner Rd
B
1 SE Gardner Rd
2 NE Everett Dr
260th
B
2

⬇ RAND MᶜNALLY
12°24'13"
12°23'36"
12°22'59"
12°22'22"
12°21'45"
E   F   G   H   J
SEE 569 MAP

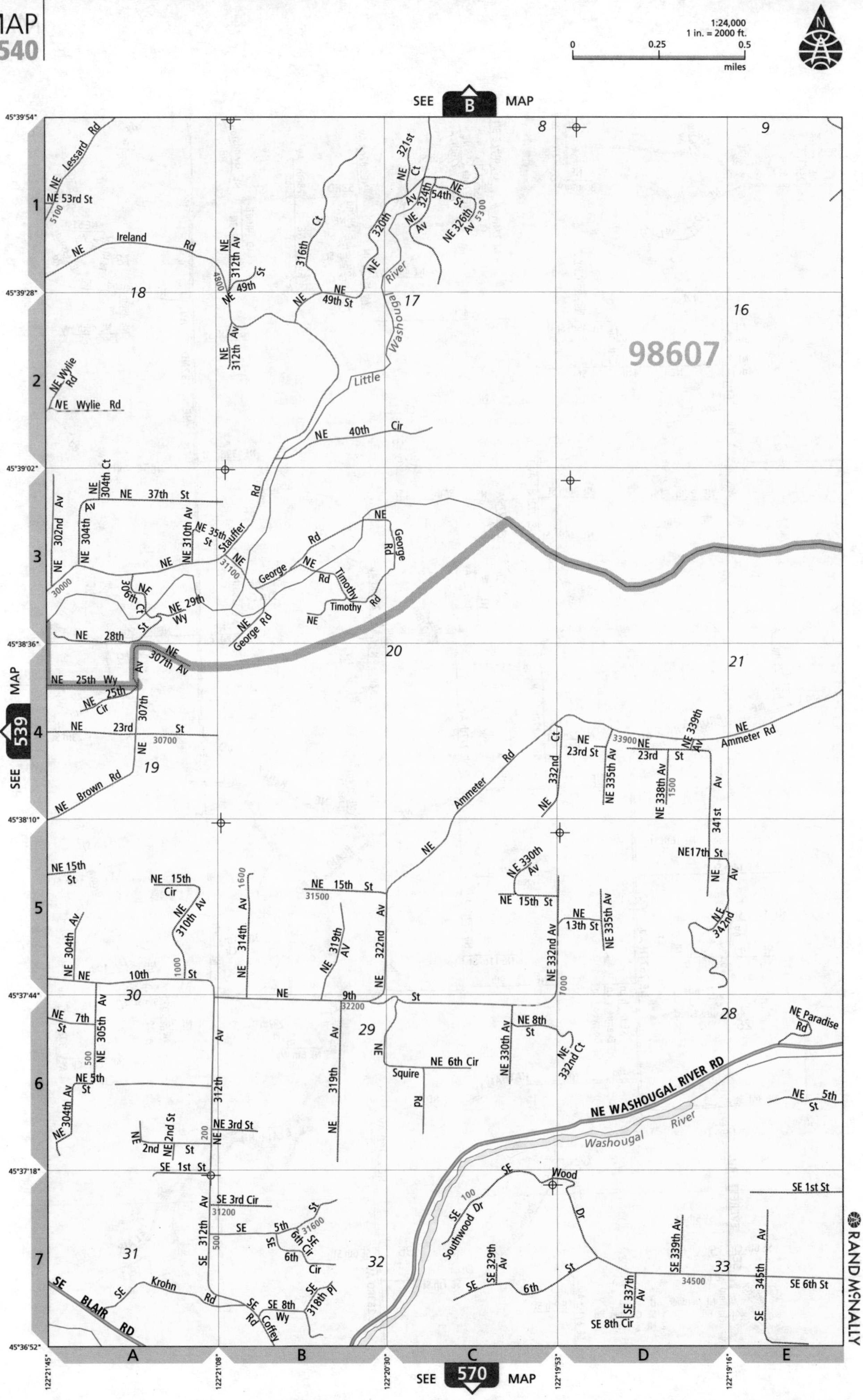

MAP
540

1:24,000
1 in. = 2000 ft.

0   0.25   0.5
miles

N

SEE **B** MAP

45°39'54"

8

9

NE Lessard Rd

NE 53rd St
5100

NE Ireland Rd

NE 312th Av

316th Ct

NE 321st Ct

NE 320th Av

NE 322nd Av

NE 54th St

NE 326th Av 5300

45°39'28"

18

NE 49th

4800

NE 49th St

17

Washougal River

16

98607

NE Wylie Rd

NE Wylie Rd

Little

NE 40th Cir

2

45°39'02"

NE 304th Ct

NE 37th St

NE 302nd Av

NE 304th Av

NE 310th Av

NE 35th St

NE Stauffer Rd

George Rd

NE George Rd

3

30000

NE 307th Ct

NE 29th Wy

31100

George Rd

NE George Rd

Timothy Rd

Timothy Rd

45°38'36"

NE 28th

NE 307th Av

20

21

MAP

SEE **539** MAP

NE 25th Wy

NE 25th Cir

NE 307th Av

NE 23rd St

30700

4

NE Ammeter Rd

NE 332nd Ct

NE 23rd St

NE 335th Av

NE 23rd St

NE 338th Av

33900

NE 339th

1500

NE 341st Av

NE Brown Rd

19

45°38'10"

NE Ammeter Rd

NE 330th Av

NE17th NE 342nd

NE 15th St

NE 15th Cir

NE 310th Av

NE 314th Av

1600

NE 15th St

31500

NE 319th Av

NE 322nd Av

NE 15th St

NE 13th Av

NE 335th Av

NE 332nd Av

5

NE 304th Av

NE 10th St

1000

NE 9th St

1000

45°37'44"

30

NE

32200

29

28

NE Paradise Rd

NE 7th St

NE 305th Av

500

NE 312th Av

NE 319th Av

NE 8th St

NE 330th Av

NE 332nd Ct

6

NE 5th St

NE 304th Av

NE 2nd St

200

NE 3rd St

NE 6th Cir

Squire Rd

NE WASHOUGAL RIVER RD

Washougal River

NE 5th St

45°37'18"

SE 1st St

2nd St

SE 3rd Cir

31200

SE 312th Av

500

SE 5th St

31600

SE 6th Cir

Wood

SE

Southwood Dr

100

SE Dr

SE 329th Av

SE 339th Av

SE 1st St

7

31

Krohn Rd

SE 6th Cir

SE 8th Wy

Coffey Rd

SE 318th Pl

32

SE 6th

SE 337th Av

SE 8th Cir

34500

345th Av

SE 6th St

33

SE BLAIR RD

45°36'52"

A   B   C   D   E

SEE **570** MAP

RAND McNALLY

12°21'45"   12°21'08"   12°20'30"   12°19'53"   12°19'16"

MAP
540

1:24,000
1 in. = 2000 ft.

miles

SEE **B** MAP

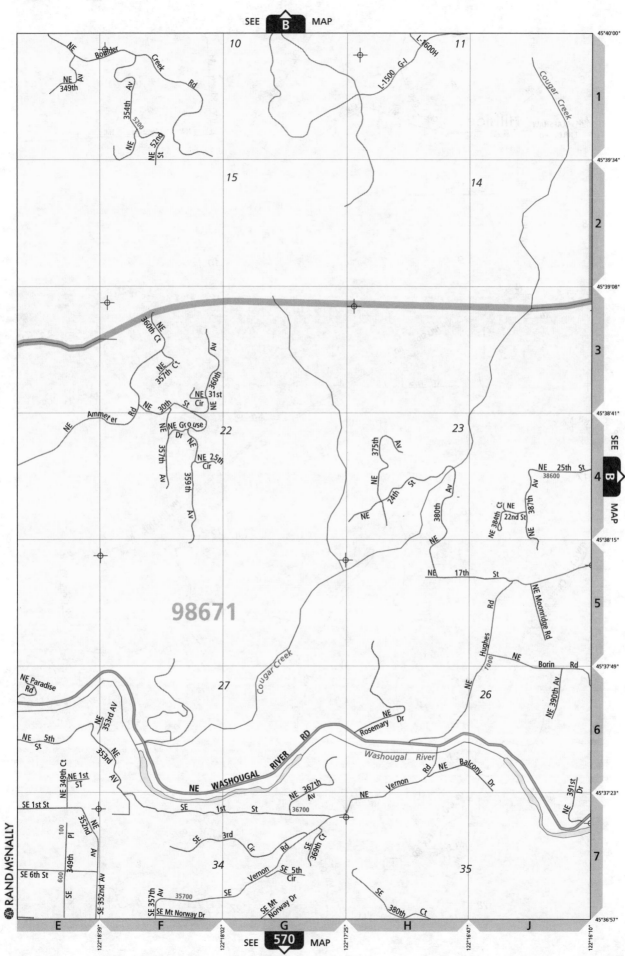

45°40'00"

10

11

L-1600H

L-1500 G-1

Cougar Creek

NE
Boulder
Creek
Rd

NE Av
NE
349th

NE 354th Av

5700

NE 52nd St

1

45°39'34"

15

14

2

45°39'08"

NE 360th Ct

NE 357th Ct

Av

NE 360th

NE 30th St

NE 31st Cir

NE

Ammeter Rd

NE

NE Grouse Dr

NE

22

23

NE 357th Av

NE 25th Cir

359th Av

NE 375th

Av

NE 24th St

NE

NE 380th

Av

NE 25th St

38600

NE 384th Ct

NE 387th Av

NE 22nd St

SEE **B** MAP

3

45°38'41"

4

45°38'15"

NE 17th St

NE Moonridge Rd

Rd

5

45°37'49"

98671

Cougar Creek

Hughes

1000

NE

Borin Rd

NE

26

NE 390th Av

NE Paradise Rd

NE 353rd AV

NE Rosemary Dr

27

NE

NE

353rd

AV

NE WASHOUGAL RIVER RD

Washougal River

Rd NE Balcony Dr

NE 391st Dr

6

45°37'23"

NE 5th St

NE 349th Ct

NE 1st ST

SE 1st St

NE 367th Av

SE 1st St

36700

NE Vernon

NE

7

NE 352nd Av

100

SE 349th Pl

600

SE 6th St

SE 3rd Cir

Rd

SE 369th Ct

SE 5th Cir

Vernon

SE

SE 357th Av

35700

SE Mt Norway Dr

SE

SE Mt Norway Dr

SE 380th Ct

34

35

E F G H J

122°18'39" 122°18'02" 122°17'25" 122°16'47" 122°1

45°36'57"

SEE **570** MAP

MAP
561

1:24,000
1 in. = 2000 ft.
0   0.25   0.5
miles

SEE 531 MAP

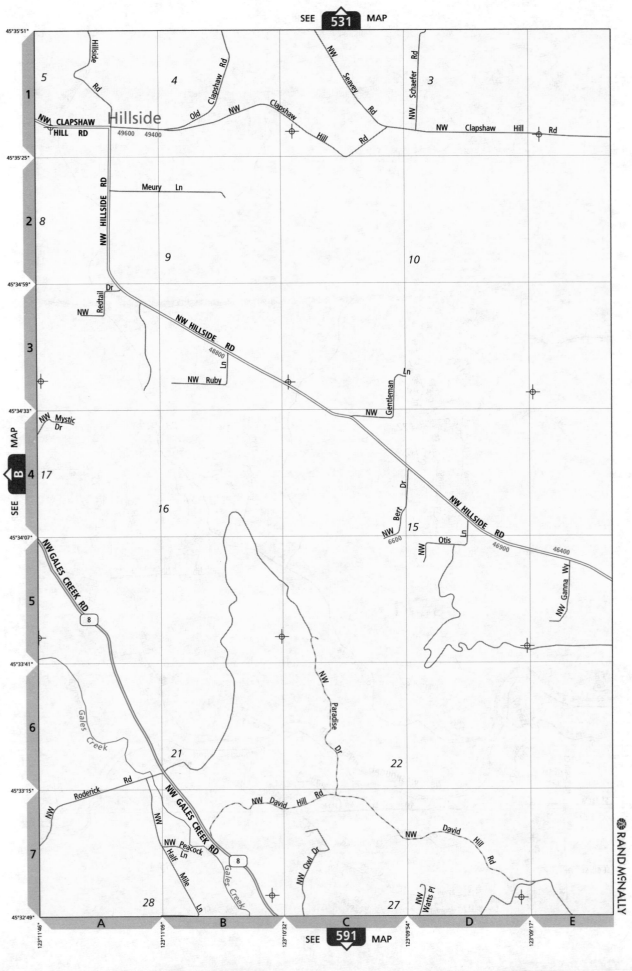

45°35'51"

5   4   NW Seavey Rd   NW Schaefer Rd   3

Hillside Rd

Old Clapshaw Rd

1

NW CLAPSHAW HILL RD   49600   49400   NW Clapshaw Hill Rd   NW Clapshaw Hill Rd

Hillside

45°35'25"

2   8   Meury   Ln

NW HILLSIDE RD

9   10

45°34'59"

Redtail Dr

NW

3   NW HILLSIDE RD
48800
Ln
NW Ruby   Ln
                        NW Gentleman

45°34'33"

NW Mystic Dr

MAP

B

4   17   Bert Dr   NW HILLSIDE RD

SEE

45°34'07"

16   NW 6600   15
                                        NW Otis Ln   46900   46400
NW GALES CREEK RD

5   8   NW Gamna Wy

45°33'41"

6   Gales Creek   NW Paradise Dr

21   22

45°33'15"

Roderick Rd   NW David Hill Rd
NW   NW GALES CREEK RD   NW David Hill Rd
NW
7   NW Peacock Ln   NW Owl Dr
        Half Mile Ln   8   NW Watts Pl
        28   Gales Creek   27

45°32'49"

A   B   C   D   E

123°11'46"   123°11'09"   123°10'32"   123°09'54"   123°09'17"

SEE 591 MAP

RAND McNALLY

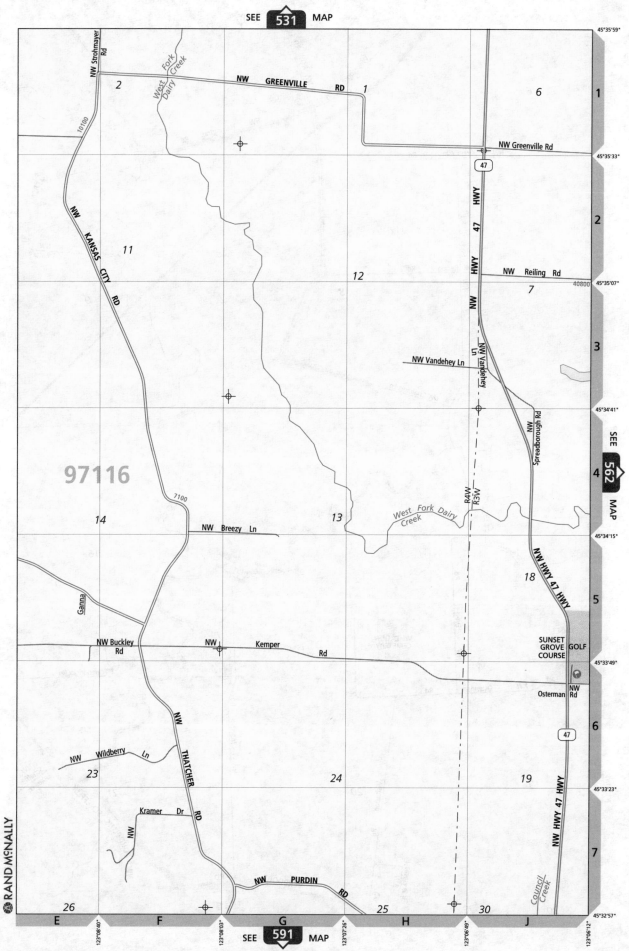

MAP
561

1:24,000
1 in. = 2000 ft.

0   0.25   0.5

miles

SEE 531 MAP

NW Strohmayer Rd

West Fork Dairy Creek

2

NW GREENVILLE RD

1

6

1

10100

NW Greenville Rd

47

NW KANSAS CITY RD

HWY 47 HWY

2

11

12

NW Reiling Rd

7

40800

NW

3

NW Vandehey Ln

NW Vandehey Ln

97116

Spreadborough Rd

SEE 562 MAP

4

7100

R4W R3W

West Fork Dairy Creek

14

13

NW Breezy Ln

18

Ganna

NW HWY 47 HWY

5

NW Buckley Rd

NW Kemper Rd

SUNSET GROVE GOLF COURSE

Osterman Rd

NW Rd

6

NW THATCHER RD

47

NW Wildberry Ln

23

24

19

NW HWY 47 HWY

7

Kramer Dr

NW

Council Creek

26

NW PURDIN RD

25

30

E   F   G   H   J

SEE 591 MAP

45°35'59"
45°35'33"
45°35'07"
45°34'41"
45°34'15"
45°33'49"
45°33'23"
45°32'57"

123°08'40"
123°08'03"
123°07'26"
123°06'49"
123°06'12"

MAP
562

1:24,000
1 in. = 2000 ft.
0   0.25   0.5
miles

SEE 532 MAP

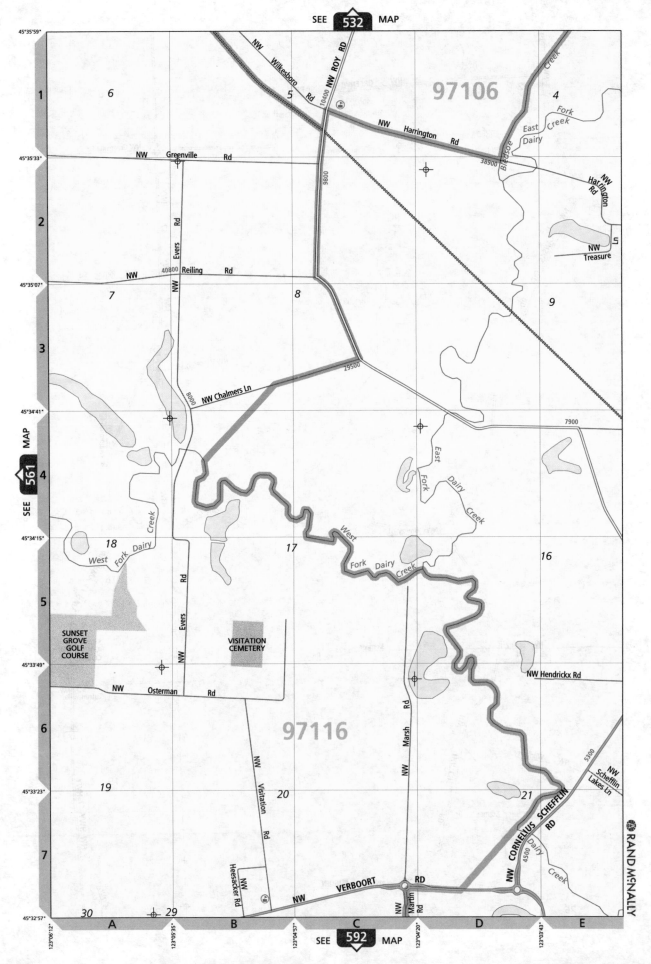

97106

97116

SUNSET
GROVE
GOLF
COURSE

VISITATION
CEMETERY

6

1

5

4

2

7

8

9

3

NW Wilkesboro Rd

10400 NW ROY RD

9800

NW Harrington Rd

NW Greenville Rd

Evers Rd

NW 40800 Reiling Rd

NW Chalmers Ln

8000

29500

38900

Bledsoe Creek

East Fork Dairy Creek

NW Harrington Rd

NW Treasure Ln

7900

4

West Fork Dairy Creek

East Fork Dairy Creek

West Fork Dairy Creek

18

17

16

19

20

21

NW Evers Rd

NW Osterman Rd

NW Visitation Rd

NW Marsh Rd

NW Hendrickx Rd

5300

NW Schefflin Lakes Ln

Heesacker Rd

NW

VERBOORT RD

NW Martin Rd

NW CORNELIUS SCHEFFLIN RD

4500 Dairy Creek

30

29

5

6

7

SEE 592 MAP

45°35'59"
45°35'33"
45°35'07"
45°34'41"
45°34'15"
45°33'49"
45°33'23"
45°32'57"

SEE 561 MAP

123°06'12"
123°05'35"
123°04'57"
123°04'20"
123°03'43"

A   B   C   D   E

RAND McNALLY

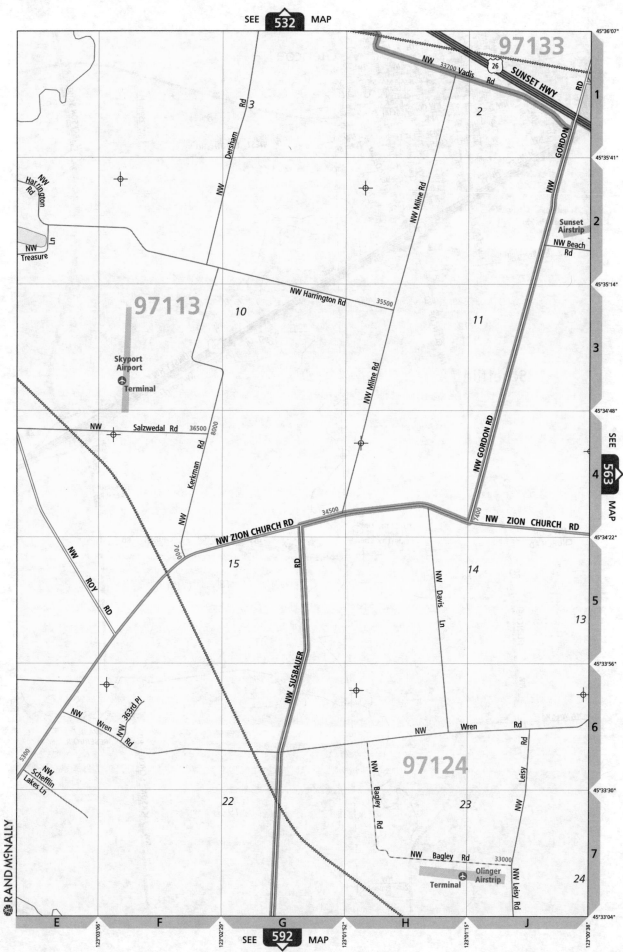

MAP
562

1:24,000
1 in. = 2000 ft.
0   0.25   0.5
miles

SEE 532 MAP

45°36'07"

97133

NW 33700 Vadis Rd
26 SUNSET HWY
GORDON RD

1

NW Harrington Rd

NW Dersham Rd 3

2

45°35'41"

NW Milne Rd

NW Harrington Rd

Sunset Airstrip

NW Beach Rd

2

NW Treasure Ln

45°35'14"

97113

NW Harrington Rd   35500

10

11

Skyport Airport

Terminal

3

45°34'48"

NW Milne Rd

NW Gordon Rd

SEE 563 MAP

NW Salzwedal Rd   36500

NW Kerkman Rd   8000

4

34500

7400   NW ZION CHURCH RD

45°34'22"

NW ZION CHURCH RD

NW ROY RD

15

NW Susbauer Rd

NW Davis Ln

14

13

5

45°33'56"

NW Wren Rd

NW 363rd Pl

NW Wren Rd

Leisy Rd

6

5300

NW Schefflin Lakes Ln

97124

NW Bagley Rd

45°33'30"

22

23

NW Leisy Rd

NW Bagley Rd   33000

Olinger Airstrip

Terminal

7

24

45°33'04"

E   F   G   H   J

123°03'06"   123°02'29"   123°01'52"   123°01'15"   123°00'38"

SEE 592 MAP

RAND McNALLY

MAP
563

1:24,000
1 in. = 2000 ft.

0   0.25   0.5
miles

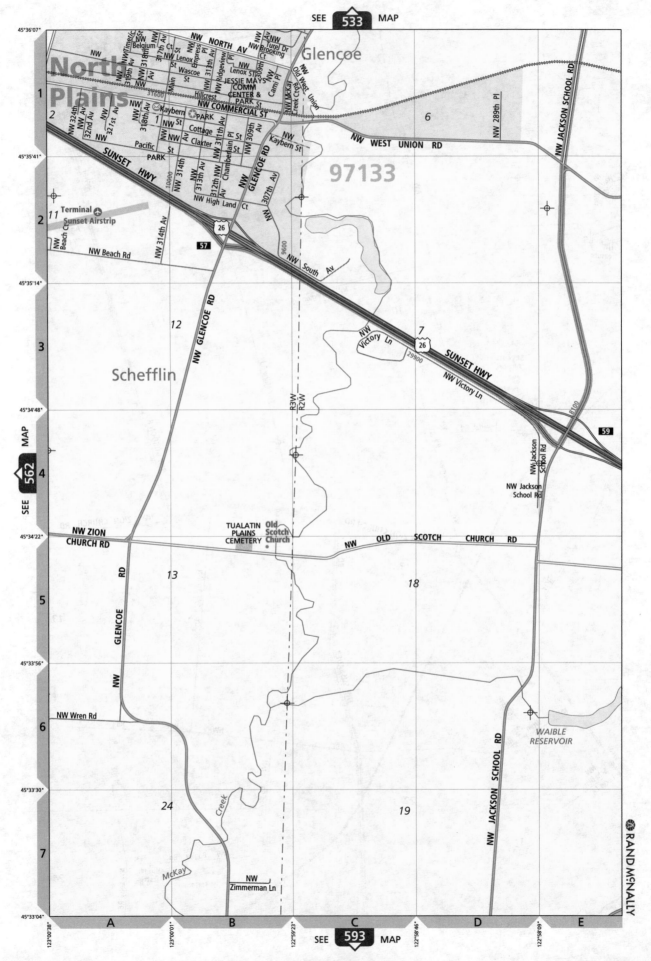

SEE 533 MAP

Glencoe

North Plains

45°36'07"

NW NORTH AV
NW Belgium Av
NW 319th Ct
NW Empress Av
NW Lenox St
NW Wascoe St
NW Main St
NW Ridgeview Pl
NW 309th St
Lenox St
NW Turel Dr
NW Brooking
NW Cami Pl
Cami Pl

NW 324th Av
NW 32nd Av
NW 321st Av
NW 318th Av
NW 314th Av
NW 313th Av
NW 312th Av
NW 311th Pl
NW Chamberlain Pl

JESSIE MAYS COMM CENTER & PARK
NW COMMERCIAL ST
Kaybern
1
PARK
Cottage
Clakter

Hillcrest
31600

Pacific
PARK
NW Glencoe Rd
NW 307th Av
NW High Land Ct
Kaybern St

2

45°35'41"

97133

NW WEST UNION RD

NW McKay Creek Ct
Old West Union
NW 289th Pl

6

NW Jackson School Rd

11 Terminal
Sunset Airstrip

2

NW Beach Ct
NW Beach Rd
NW 314th Av

26
57

9600
NW South Av

45°35'14"

12

Schefflin

NW GLENCOE RD

R3W R2W
9900

NW Victory Ln
7
26
SUNSET HWY
NW Victory Ln

8100

45°34'48"

59

3

NW Jackson School Rd
NW Jackson School Rd

45°34'22"

NW ZION CHURCH RD
GLENCOE RD

13

TUALATIN PLAINS CEMETERY
Old Scotch Church

NW OLD SCOTCH CHURCH RD

18

4

5

NW Wren Rd

NW GLENCOE RD
NW

45°33'56"

NW JACKSON SCHOOL RD

WAIBLE RESERVOIR

6

24
Creek

19

45°33'30"

McKay
NW Zimmerman Ln

7

SEE 562 MAP

45°33'04"

A   B   C   D   E

123°00'38"
123°00'01"
122°59'23"
122°58'46"
122°58'09"

SUNSET HWY
10000

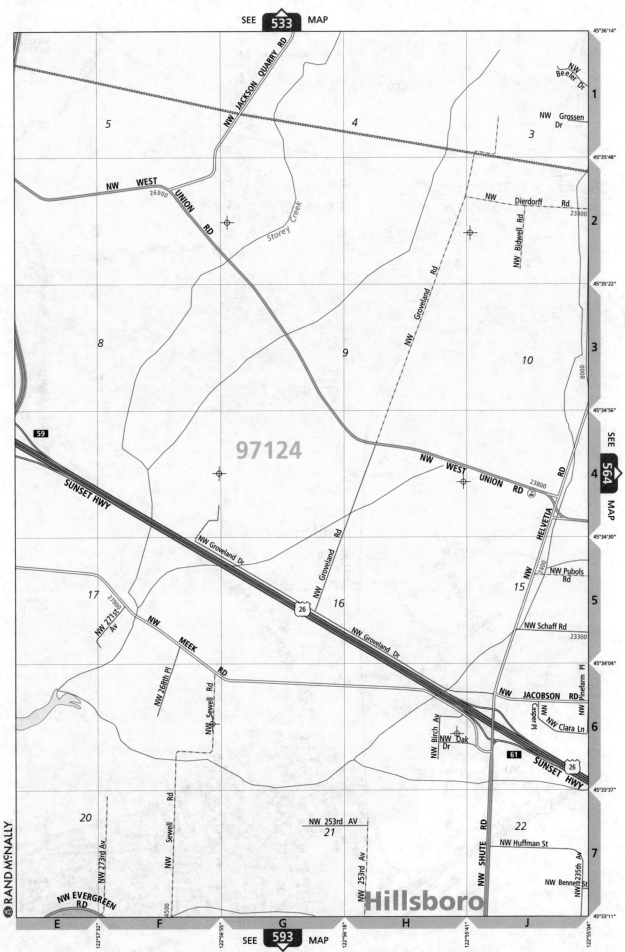

MAP
563

1:24,000
1 in. = 2000 ft.

SEE **533** MAP

45°36'14"

NW Beeler Dr

NW Grossen Dr

1

5

4

3

45°35'48"

NW WEST

26900

NW Dierdorff Rd

23800

Storey Creek

NW Bidwell Rd

2

UNION RD

45°35'22"

NW Groveland Rd

8

9

10

3

8000

45°34'56"

59

SEE **564** MAP

97124

NW WEST UNION RD

23800

4

SUNSET HWY

HELVETIA RD

45°34'30"

NW Groveland Dr

NW Groveland Rd

NW Pubols Rd

2400

17

15

5

NW 271st AV

27000

NW

16

NW

MEEK

NW Schaff Rd

23300

NW 268th Pl

RD

NW Groveland Dr

45°34'04"

NW Sewell Rd

Pinefarm Pl

NW JACOBSON RD

NW Casper Pl

NW Clara Ln

6

NW Birch Av

NW Oak Dr

61

SUNSET HWY

26

45°33'37"

NW Sewell Rd

20

NW 253rd AV

21

22

NW Shute RD

NW 253rd Av

NW Huffman St

7

NW 273rd Av

NW 235th Av

NW Bennett St

4500

NW EVERGREEN RD

Hillsboro

E   F   G   H   J

122°57'32"   122°56'55"   122°56'18"   122°55'41"   122°55'04"

SEE **593** MAP

45°33'11"

MAP
564

1:24,000
1 in. = 2000 ft.
0   0.25   0.5
miles

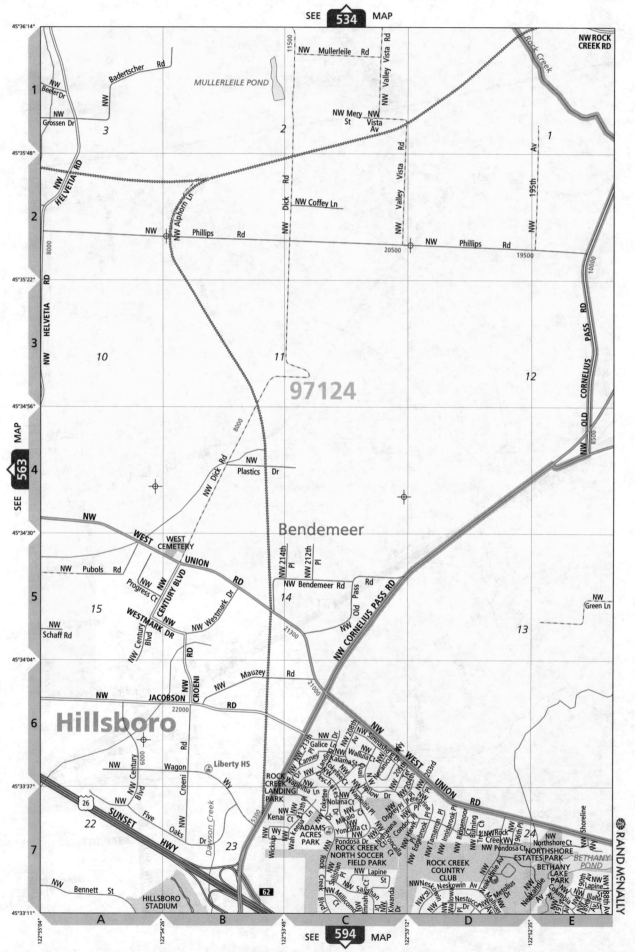

NW ROCK CREEK RD

SEE 534 MAP

NW Beeler Dr
NW Grossen Dr
Badertscher Rd
NW
3
MULLERLEILE POND
NW Mullerleile Rd
11500
NW Valley Vista Rd
NW Mery St
NW Vista Av
2
NW Valley Vista Rd
1

HELVETIA RD
NW Alphorn Ln
NW Phillips Rd
NW Dick Rd
NW Coffey Ln
8000
NW Valley Vista Rd
20500
NW Phillips Rd
19500
NW 195th Av
10000

HELVETIA RD
10
11
97124
12
NW OLD CORNELIUS PASS RD
8500

SEE 563 MAP

NW Dick Rd
8000
NW Plastics Dr
Bendemeer

NW WEST
WEST CEMETERY
UNION RD
NW Pubols Rd
NW Progress Ct
NW CENTURY BLVD
NW Century Blvd
WESTMARK DR
NW Westmark Dr
NW Schaff Rd
NW 214th
NW 212th Pl
NW Bendemeer Rd
Pass Rd
14
Old
21300
NW CORNELIUS PASS RD
13
NW Green Ln

NW CROENI RD
NW Mauzey Rd
21000
NW JACOBSON RD
22000
Hillsboro
NW Century Blvd
6000
Wagon Wy
Liberty HS
Croeni Rd
5300
NW West Union Rd
26
22
SUNSET HWY
Five Oaks
Dawson Creek
23
62
HILLSBORO STADIUM
NW Bennett St

NW 208th
NW 213th
NW Simnasho Dr
NW 204th Av
NW 203rd Av
Galice Ln
Cannes Dr
Kalama St
Necanicum Dr
Wallula
ROCK CREEK LANDING PARK
Wapinitia Ln
Toketee Dr
Yellow
Osprey Pl
Peregrine Dr
NW Tamarron Dr
Ridgemoor
NW Burning Tree Ct
NW Rock Creek Blvd
NW 196th Pl
24
NW Shoreline
Nolana Ct
Mikalo Ct
Yoncalla Ct
Indwana
Condor
Edgebrook
Innisbrook Pl
NW Pondosa Ct
NW Northshore Ct
NORTHSHORE ESTATES PARK
BETHANY POND
Kenai Ct
NW Wah Keena
NW 13th Pl
Pondosa Dr
Wickiup
ADAMS ACRES PARK
ROCK CREEK NORTH SOCCER FIELD PARK
NW Lapine St
ROCK CREEK COUNTRY CLUB
Neskowin Av
BETHANY LAKE PARK
NW Lapine
Salishan
NW Salishan
Millicoma
Kiwanda Dr
Nestucca
NW Metolius Dr
NW Neahkahnie Av
Columbia
NW 188th Av
NW Illahe
NW 190th
RAND McNALLY

SEE 594 MAP

MAP
564

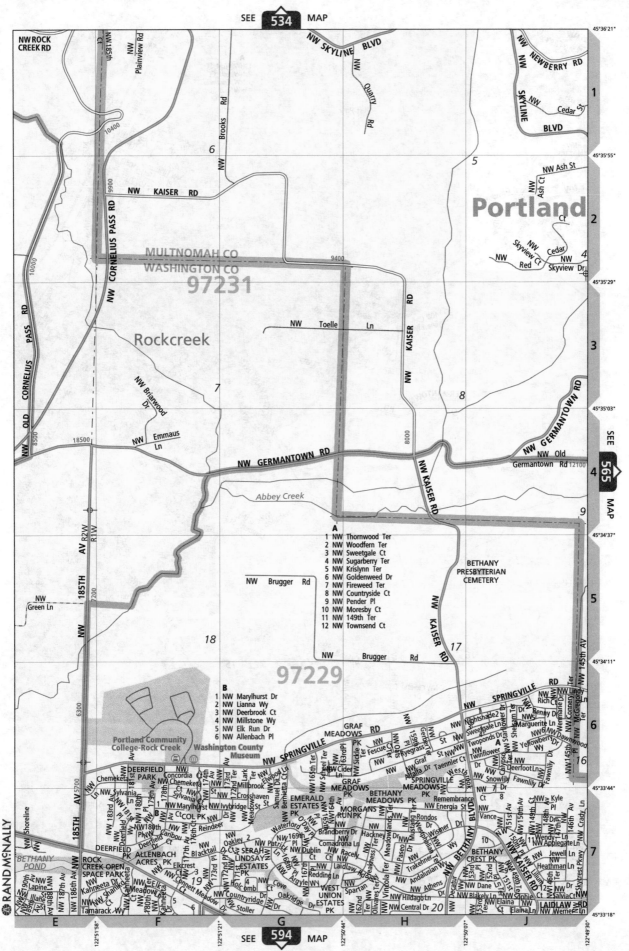

1:24,000
1 in. = 2000 ft.

0   0.25   0.5

miles

NW ROCK
CREEK RD

NW SKYLINE BLVD

NW
Plainview Rd

NW NEWBERRY RD

NW SKYLINE BLVD

NW Cedar St

NW Quarry Rd

Brooks Rd

1

NW KAISER RD

NW Ash St

NW Ash Ct

Portland

2

NW Skyview Ct

NW Cedar Ct

NW Red

NW Skyview Dr

NW CORNELIUS PASS RD

MULTNOMAH CO
WASHINGTON CO
97231

NW KAISER RD

NW Toelle Ln

Rockcreek

3

NW Brianwood Dr

NW GERMANTOWN RD

8

NW OLD CORNELIUS PASS RD

NW Emmaus Ln

NW GERMANTOWN RD

NW Old
Germantown Rd 12100

SEE ⊳ **565** MAP

Abbey Creek

NW KAISER RD

9

A
1 NW Thornwood Ter
2 NW Woodfern Ter
3 NW Sweetgale Ct
4 NW Sugarberry Ter
5 NW Krislynn Ter
6 NW Goldenweed Dr
7 NW Fireweed Ter
8 NW Countryside Ct
9 NW Pender Pl
10 NW Moresby Ct
11 NW 149th Ter
12 NW Townsend Ct

BETHANY
PRESBYTERIAN
CEMETERY

NW Green Ln

AV R2W R1W

185TH AV

NW Brugger Rd

5

NW 185TH AV

18

NW KAISER RD

17

NW Brugger Rd

97229

B
1 NW Marylhurst Dr
2 NW Lianna Wy
3 NW Deerbrook Ct
4 NW Millstone Wy
5 NW Elk Run Dr
6 NW Allenbach Pl

SPRINGVILLE RD

NW Lindy

NW Rich

NW Benny Dr

GRAF MEADOWS RD

NW Nightshade

NW Sweetgale Ln

NW Marguerite Ln

16

Portland Community
College-Rock Creek

Washington County
Museum

NW SPRINGVILLE RD

NW Twoponds Dr

NW Starflower

NW 145th AV

NW Yellowberry Wy

NW Deerfoot Ln

DEERFIELD
PARK

NW Concordia

NW Chemeketa Ct

NW 174th

NW 173rd

NW Cider

GRAF St

SPRINGVILLE MEADOWS PK

NW Snowlily

NW Fawnlily Dr

NW Chemeketa

NW Sylvania

NW Millbrook

NW Lark Ter

GRAF MEADOWS PK

BETHANY MEADOWS PK

NW 7

NW Kyle Pl

NW Marylhurst

COL PK

NW Crosshaven Dr

NW Ivybridge

NW Samuel Dr

NW Elwood Ln

NW Berhetta Ct

EMERALD ESTATES

Remembrance
NW Energia St

NW Vance

NW 151st Av

NW 150th

NW Applegate Ln

DEERFIELD PARK

NW 180th

NW Caribou Dr

NW Reindeer

NW Oakley

MORGANS RUN PK

NW Mustang Ter

NW Wistner

NW Jewell Ln

NW Heathman

ALLENBACH ACRES

NW Elkcrest

NW Patrick

NW Dublin

NW Brandberry Dr

NW Comadrona Ln

NW Racely

BETHANY CREST PK

NW Kyle

NW Kahneeta

NW Connett Meadow

NW Redding Ln

NW Argyle

NW Vinzola Ter

NW Paseo

NW Trakehner

NW Andalusian Dr

BETHANY BLVD

NW 152nd

NW Blakely Ln

NW Elaina

WEST UNION ESTATES PK

NW Spartan

NW Athens

NW Dane

NW Sophie

RAND M?NALLY

BETHANY POND

ROCK CREEK OPEN SPACE PARK

NW 186th Av

NW 187th Av

NW Lapine

NW Illahe

NW Shalial

NW Meadow Ln

NW Countryridge

NW Oakridge

NW Stoller

NW Cove

NW 162nd Ter

NW Central Dr

NW Werner

NW Elaina Ln

LAIDLAW RD

Tamarack Wy

E   F   G   H   J

7

MAP
565

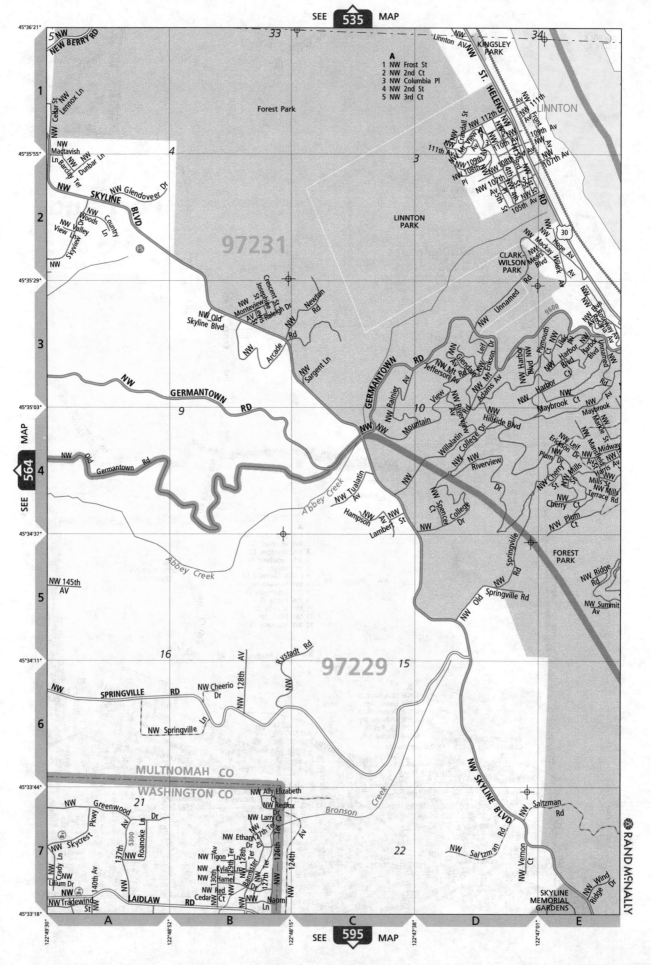

1:24,000
1 in. = 2000 ft.

0   0.25   0.5

miles

N

A
1 NW Frost St
2 NW 2nd Ct
3 NW Columbia Pl
4 NW 2nd St
5 NW 3rd Ct

Forest Park

NEW BERRY RD

NW Cedar St
NW Lennox Ln

NW Magtavish Ln
NW Barclay Ter
NW Dunbar Ln

NW SKYLINE BLVD

NW Glendoveer Dr

LINNTON
PARK

KINGSLEY
PARK

Linnton Av NW

ST. HELENS RD

LINNTON

NW Front St

NW 112th
NW Crandall St
NW M View
NW 111th
111th Av
NW 110th
NW 109th
NW 108th
NW 107th Av
NW 105th Av

97231

NW Woods Dr
NW Valley View Ln
Skyview
Country Ln

FS

NW Old
Skyline Blvd

Crescent St
Josephine Av
NW Monteview
Raleigh Dr
Newton Rd
NW Arcade Rd

NW Sargent Ln

CLARK-
WILSON
PARK

NW Mackay Av
NW Mears Av
NW Hoge Av
NW Wilark Av

NW BLVD
NW Unnamed Rd

30

9600

Glendale
Leif
NW Erikson Dr
Plymouth
Lilac
Harbor Ct NW
Harbor Blvd
Harbor Blvd
Unnamed

NW GERMANTOWN RD

GERMANTOWN RD

9

NW Rainier Av

NW Mountain

NW Jefferson Av
NW Mt Rd
NW View Av
NW Adams Av

NW Harbor
NW Harbor Ct

Maybrook Ct
Maybrook
Markle St

10

NW Old Germantown Rd

NW College Dr
Willalatin
Hillside Blvd
Riverview

Riverview Dr

NW Leif
Erickson Dr
NW Plum Dr
NW Cherry St
NW Mansfield Av
Midway
Harris Av
Mills St
NW Mills
Terrace Rd

SEE 564 MAP

Abbey Creek

NW Tualatin Av

Hampson
Lambert St

NW Spence Ct
NW College Dr

NW Cherry Ct
NW Plum Ct

Abbey Creek

NW 145th AV

Springville Rd

NW Old Springville Rd

FOREST
PARK

NW Ridge Rd
NW Summit Av

97229

RYstadt Rd
NW 128th AV

16

15

NW SPRINGVILLE RD

NW Cheerio Dr

NW Springville Ln

NW Springville

MULTNOMAH CO
WASHINGTON CO

NW Greenwood Dr

21

NW Ally Elizabeth Ct
NW Redfox Dr
NW Larry Ct
NW Ethan Dr

Bronson Creek

NW SKYLINE BLVD

NW Saltzman Rd

NW Skycrest Pkwy
137th Av
5300
NW Roanoke Ln

NW Tigon Ter
NW Kyla Ter
NW 130th
NW Bannister Ter
127th Ter
128th Ter
127th Ter
126th Ter
124th Av

22

NW Saltzman Rd
NW Vernon Ct

NW Crady Ln
NW Lilium Dr
NW Hamel
NW Red Cedar Ct
NW Naomi Ln

NW Wind Ridge Dr

140th Av

NW Tradewind St

LAIDLAW RD

SKYLINE
MEMORIAL
GARDENS

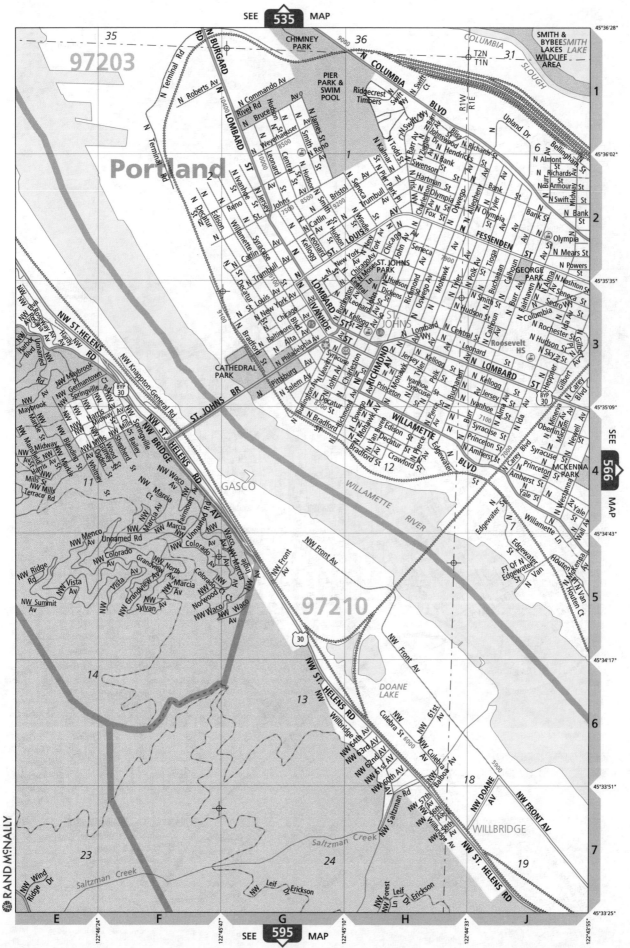

MAP
565

1:24,000
1 in. = 2000 ft.

0   0.25   0.5
miles

SEE **535** MAP

97203

Portland

COLUMBIA   SLOUGH

SMITH & BYBEE LAKES WILDLIFE AREA   SMITH LAKE

CHIMNEY PARK

PIER PARK & SWIM POOL

N COLUMBIA BLVD

FESSENDEN ST

GEORGE PARK

ST. JOHNS PARK

Roosevelt HS

N LOMBARD ST

CATHEDRAL PARK

ST. JOHNS BR

WILLAMETTE BLVD

MCKENNA PARK

NW ST. HELENS RD

NW BRIDGE AV

GASCO

WILLAMETTE RIVER

SEE **566** MAP

97210

DOANE LAKE

NW FRONT AV

NW ST. HELENS RD

NW DOANE AV

NW FRONT AV

WILLBRIDGE

Saltzman Creek

SEE **595** MAP

E   F   G   H   J

MAP
566

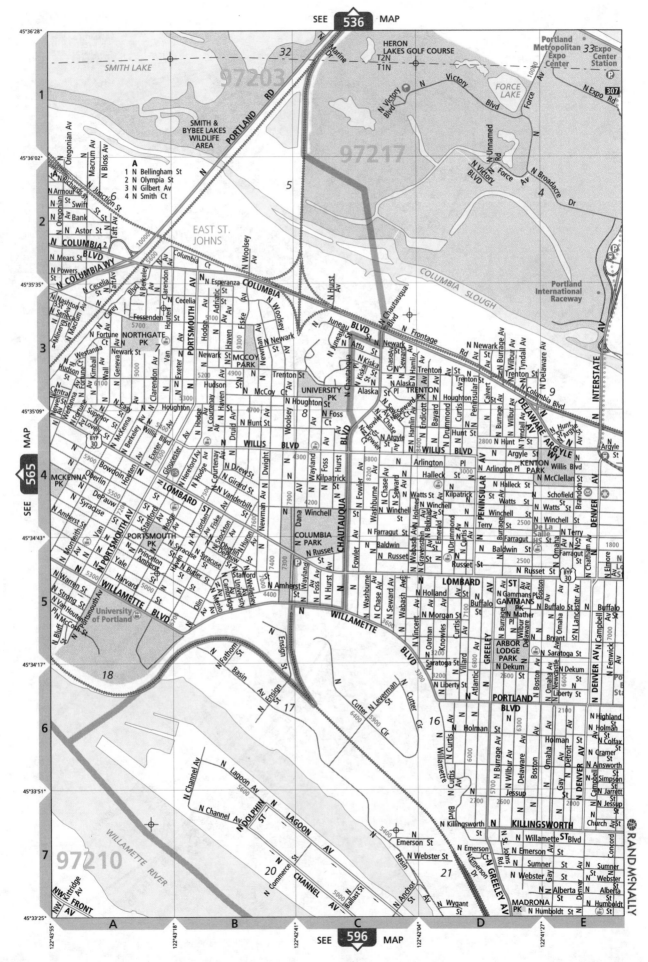

1:24,000
1 in. = 2000 ft.
0   0.25   0.5
miles

SEE 536 MAP

A
1 N Bellingham St
2 N Olympia St
3 N Gilbert Av
4 N Smith Ct

SEE 565 MAP

SEE 596 MAP

RAND M℠NALLY

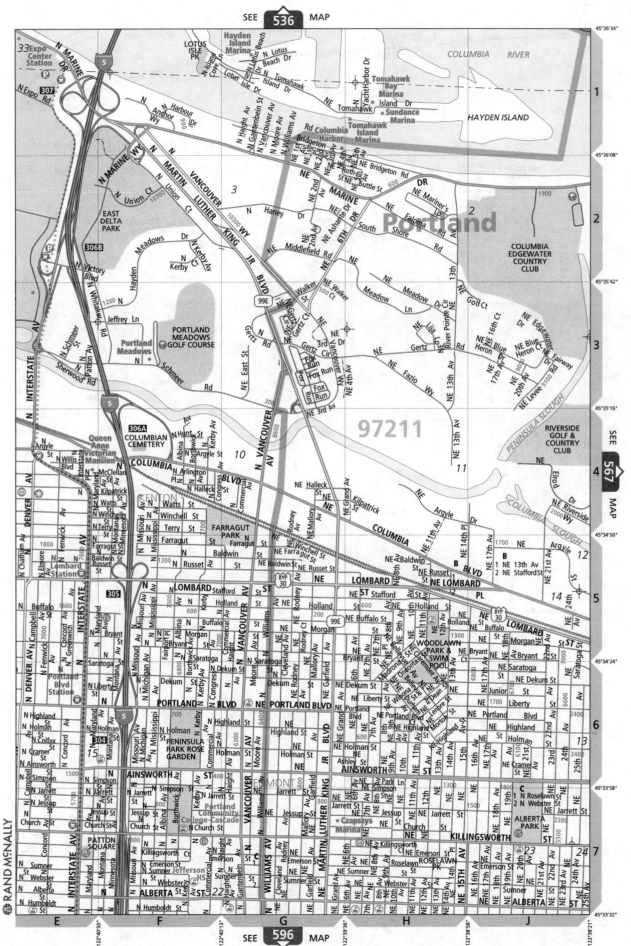

MAP
566

1:24,000
1 in. = 2000 ft.

0   0.25   0.5

miles

SEE 536 MAP

COLUMBIA   RIVER

HAYDEN ISLAND

Portland

COLUMBIA EDGEWATER COUNTRY CLUB

97211

RIVERSIDE GOLF & COUNTRY CLUB

SEE 567 MAP

PORTLAND MEADOWS GOLF COURSE

EAST DELTA PARK

FARRAGUT PARK

PENINSULA PARK ROSE GARDEN

WOODLAWN PARK & SWIM POOL

ALBERTA PARK

45°36'34"
45°36'08"
45°35'42"
45°35'16"
45°34'50"
45°34'24"
45°33'58"
45°33'32"

122°40'50"   122°40'13"   122°39'36"   122°38'58"   122°38'21"

SEE 596 MAP

MAP
567

1:24,000
1 in. = 2000 ft.

0   0.25   0.5

miles

SEE 537 MAP

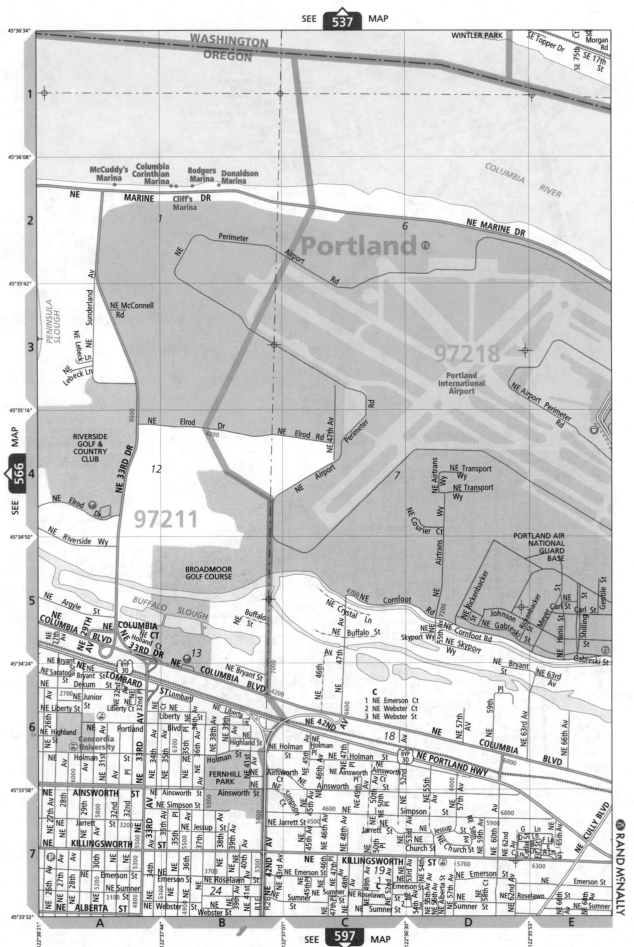

WASHINGTON
OREGON

WINTLER PARK

SE Topper Dr

SE 75th Ct

SE Morgan Rd

SE 17th St

45°36'34"

1

45°36'08"

COLUMBIA   RIVER

McCuddy's Marina   Columbia Corinthian Marina   Rodgers Marina   Donaldson Marina

NE   MARINE   DR   Cliff's Marina

NE MARINE DR

2

45°35'42"

Portland

Perimeter Airport Rd

6

NE

NE McConnell Rd

Sunderland Av

PENINSULA SLOUGH

NE Lebeck Ln

NE Lebeck Ln

3

45°35'42"

97218

MAP
566
SEE

Portland International Airport

NE Airport Perimeter Rd

45°35'16"

NE   Elrod   Dr
4200

NE Elrod Rd

NE 47th Av

Perimeter Rd

RIVERSIDE GOLF & COUNTRY CLUB

9000

NE 33RD DR

12

NE Airport

NE Airtrans Wy

NE Transport Wy

NE Transport Wy

7

4

NE Elrod Dr

97211

NE Courier Ct

Airtrans Wy

PORTLAND AIR NATIONAL GUARD BASE

45°34'50"

NE Riverside Wy

BROADMOOR GOLF COURSE

4700 NE

NE Cornfoot

Gentile St

Rickenbacker St

NE Argyle St

BUFFALO   SLOUGH

NE Buffalo St

NE Crystal Ln

Cornfoot Rd

7200

NE Rickenbacker

St

Johnson St

NE Gabreski

Rickenbacker St

Meyer St

Carl St

NE Carl St

Shilling

5

NE COLUMBIA BLVD

NE 29th Av

NE 27th Av

COLUMBIA NE CT

NE Holland Ct

NE 33RD DR

NE Buffalo St

Av

47th

46th

Skyport Wy

55th

NE Cornfoot Rd

NE Skyport Wy

Hanis St

Gabreski St

FS

13

NE COLUMBIA BLVD

NE Bryant St

NE Bryant St

7000

4200

NE Bryant St

NE 63rd Av

45°34'24"

NE Bryant St

NE Saratoga St

NE Dekum St

BYP 30

LOMBARD

C

1 NE Emerson Ct
2 NE Webster Ct
3 NE Webster St

Pl

59th

2700 NE Junior St

NE 32nd St

Liberty Ct

32nd Av

NE Liberty St

NE ST Lombard

Liberty

NE Liberty

NE 42ND

6

NE 26th

NE Highland

NE Av

Portland

Blvd

33rd

34th

35th

36th

38th

39th

Highland St

NE Holman

NE Holman

Holman St

18 Av

NE

COLUMBIA

63rd Av

66th Av

Concordia University

NE Holman St

31st

33RD

34th

35th

36th

41st

Holman St

NE 45th

46th

47th

NE Holman St

BYP 30

NE PORTLAND HWY

6000

FERNHILL PARK

NE

45°33'58"

NE 28th

AINSWORTH ST

NE Ainsworth St

Ainsworth St

NE Ainsworth

45th

46th

47th

Ainsworth

49th

50th

55th

57th

Simpson

NE CULLY BLVD

RAND MCNALLY

29th

32nd

NE Simpson St

Simpson

Ct

4600

NE

50th

Pl

NE

57th

Av

5900

6000

Jarrett St

35th

35th

38th

NE Jessup

NE Jarrett St 4500

NE Jarrett St

50th

Jessup

53rd

59th

60th

62nd

Church St

Cedar St

G Ln

KILLINGSWORTH ST

30th

34th

36th

NE 42ND AV

43rd

NE Killingsworth ST

19 Av

54th

5700

6300

7

45°33'32"

NE 26th

27th

28th

Emerson St

NE Sumner St

3100 St

Emerson St

3700

NE Roselawn St

NE R2

NE

St

24

NE Webster St

NE Webster St

R1E

NE

44th

45th

46th

47th 48th

NE Emerson St

Sumner St

49th

50th

52nd

Emerson St

Sumner

54th 55th

56th

57th

NE Emerson

58th

62nd

Roselawn

NE Sumner

66th

Emerson St

66th

NE Sumner

ALBERTA   ST

A   B   C   D   E

45°33'32"

122°38'21"   122°37'44"   122°37'07"   122°36'30"   122°35'53"

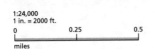
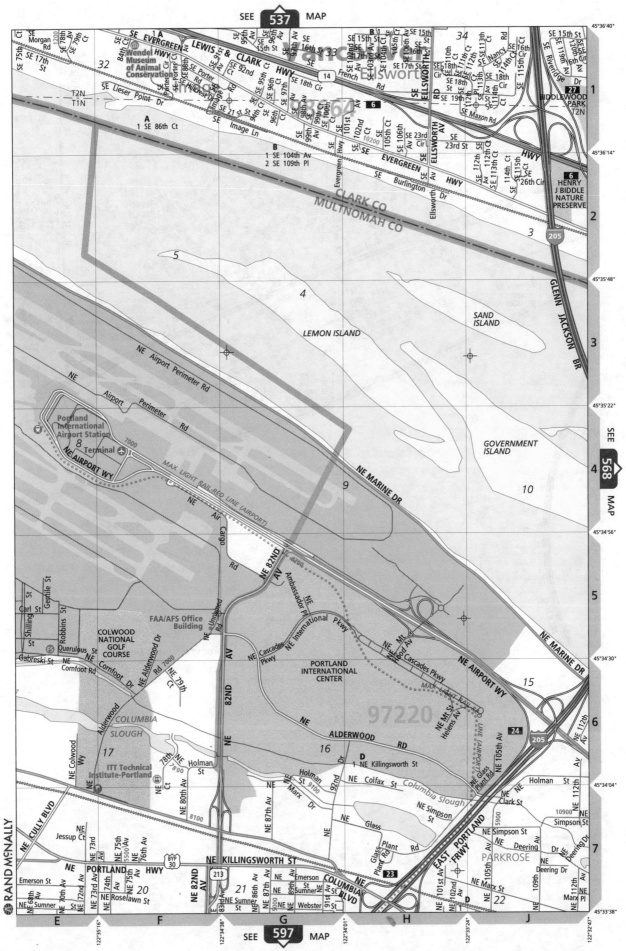

MAP 567

MAP
568

1:24,000
1 in. = 2000 ft.
0   0.25   0.5
miles

SEE 538 MAP

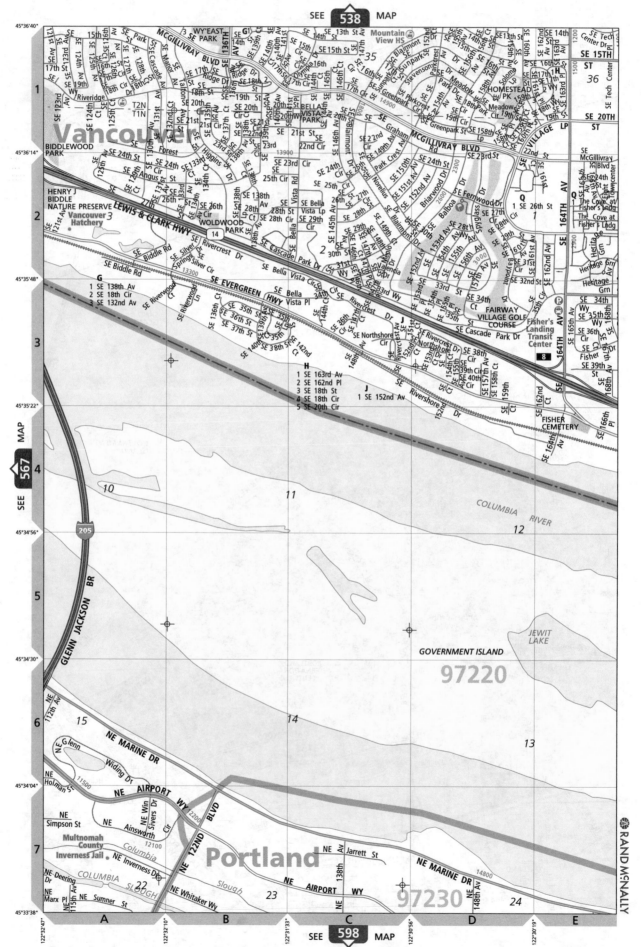

Vancouver

Portland

COLUMBIA RIVER

GOVERNMENT ISLAND

97220

JEWIT LAKE

GLENN JACKSON BR

NE MARINE DR

NE AIRPORT WY

NE 122ND BLVD

Multnomah County Inverness Jail

COLUMBIA SLOUGH

97230

SEE 567 MAP

SEE 598 MAP

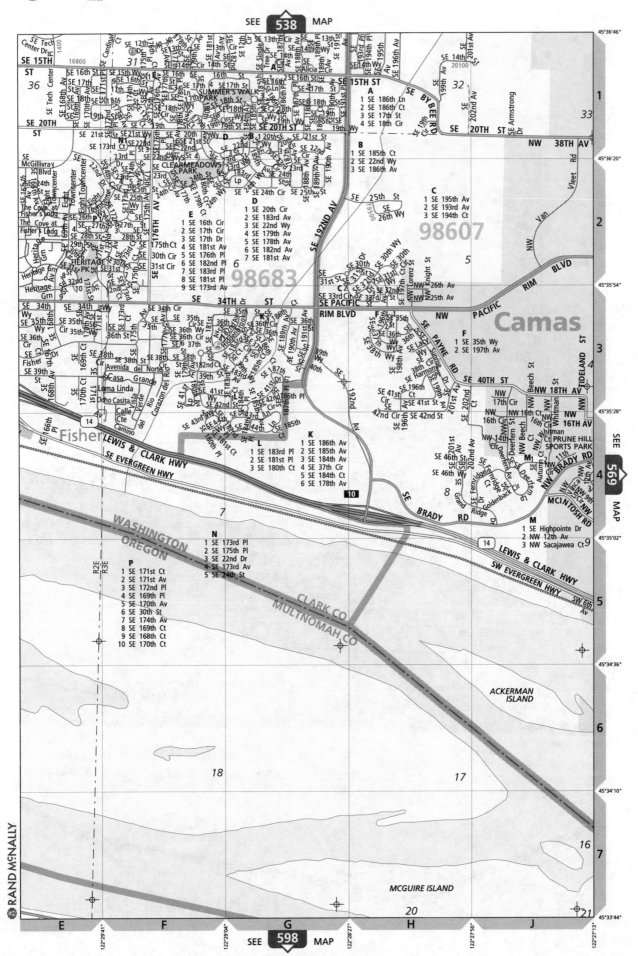

MAP
568

SEE 538 MAP
SEE 569 MAP
SEE 598 MAP

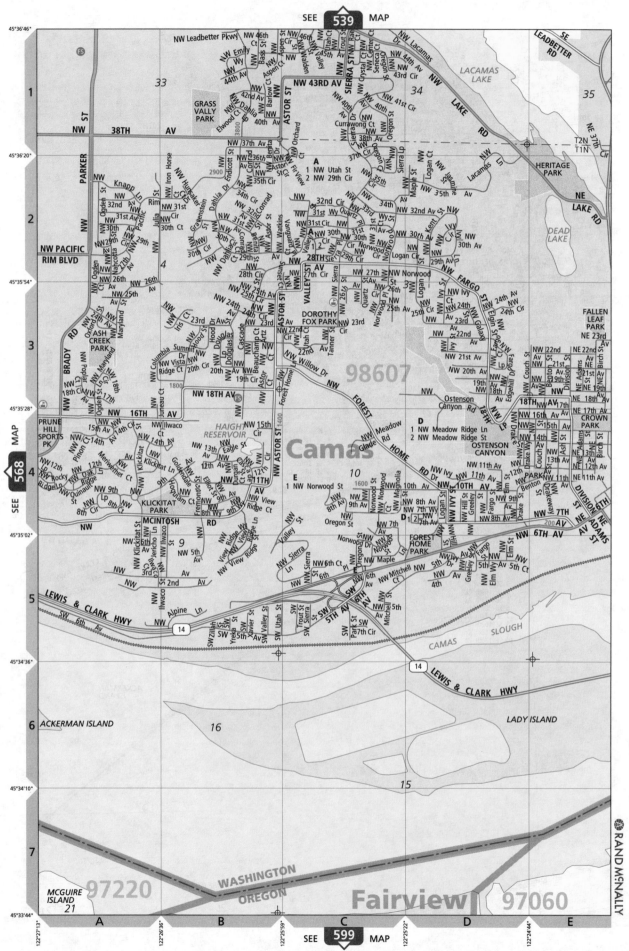

MAP
569

1:24,000
1 in. = 2000 ft.

0   0.25   0.5

miles

N

SEE 539 MAP

45°36'46"

NW Leadbetter Pkwy   NW 46th
NW Emily   NW 46th
NW Wy   NW 44th Av   Bass St   Aspen St

33

GRASS VALLEY PARK

34

35

LEADBETTER RD

LACAMAS LAKE

NW 43RD AV

NW 41st Cir

SIERRA ST

NW LAKE RD

1

NW 38TH   AV

45°36'20"

PARKER ST

NW

Knapp Ln

NW 37th Av

NW Utah St
NW 29th Cir

Currawong Ct

HERITAGE PARK

T2N
T1N

NE 37th Cir

2

NW PACIFIC RIM BLVD

NW

NW 32nd

32nd Cir   34th

NE LAKE RD

DEAD LAKE

45°35'54"

BRADY RD

ASH CREEK PARK

NW 28TH AV   VALLEY ST

NW 27th

NW Norwood

NW Fargo St

FALLEN LEAF PARK   NE 23rd

3

NW 24th

DOROTHY FOX PARK

98607

NE 22nd

NE 21st

CROWN PARK

NW 18TH AV

NW

Ostenson Canyon Rd

18TH AV   17th

45°35'28"

PRUNE HILL SPORTS PK

NW 16TH   AV

HAIGHT RESERVOIR

NW 15th Cir

Camas

Meadow Glade Rd

FOREST HOME RD

D
1 NW Meadow Ridge Ln
2 NW Meadow Ridge Ln

OSTENSON CANYON

NE 16th

4

KLICKITAT PARK

NW 11TH AV

E
1 NW Norwood St

10

1600

NW 10TH AV

PARK

NE 11th

MCINTOSH   RD

9

45°35'02"

NW

NW 5th

FOREST HOME PARK

NW 6TH AV

200

NE ADAMS ST

NE 6TH

5

LEWIS & CLARK HWY

SW 6th Av

14

Alpine Ln

5TH AV   6TH AV

CAMAS SLOUGH

45°34'36"

14   LEWIS & CLARK HWY

6

ACKERMAN ISLAND

16

LADY ISLAND

45°34'10"

15

7

MCGUIRE ISLAND
21

97220

WASHINGTON
OREGON

Fairview   97060

45°33'44"

A   B   C   D   E

12°27'13"   12°26'36"   12°25'59"   12°25'22"   12°24'44"

SEE 599 MAP

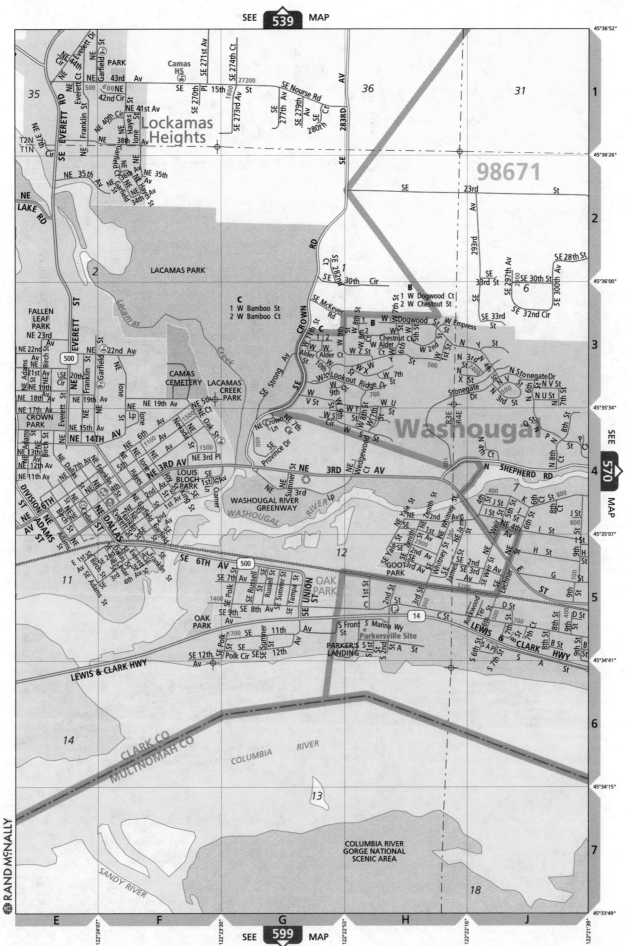

MAP
569

SEE ◇ **539** ◇ MAP

1:24,000
1 in. = 2000 ft.

0   0.25   0.5
miles

45°36'52"
45°36'26"
45°36'00"
45°35'34"
45°35'07"
45°34'41"
45°34'15"
45°33'49"

SEE **570** MAP

98671

Washougal

Lockamas Heights

LACAMAS PARK

FALLEN LEAF PARK

CAMAS CEMETERY

LACAMAS CREEK PARK

CROWN PARK

LOUIS BLOCH PARK

WASHOUGAL RIVER GREENWAY

OAK PARK

OAK PARK

GOOT PARK

Parkersville Site
PARKER'S LANDING

LEWIS & CLARK HWY

CLARK CO
MULTNOMAH CO

COLUMBIA RIVER

SANDY RIVER

COLUMBIA RIVER GORGE NATIONAL SCENIC AREA

C
1 W Bamboo St
2 W Bamboo Ct

B
1 W Dogwood Ct
2 W Chestnut St

35   36   31   1

2

6

3

7   4

11   12   5

14   6

13

18

◉ **RAND M**c**NALLY**

SEE ◇ **599** ◇ MAP

E   F   G   H   J

122°24'07"   122°23'30"   122°22'53"   122°22'16"   122°21'39"

MAP
570

1:24,000
1 in. = 2000 ft.

0   0.25   0.5

miles

SEE **540** MAP

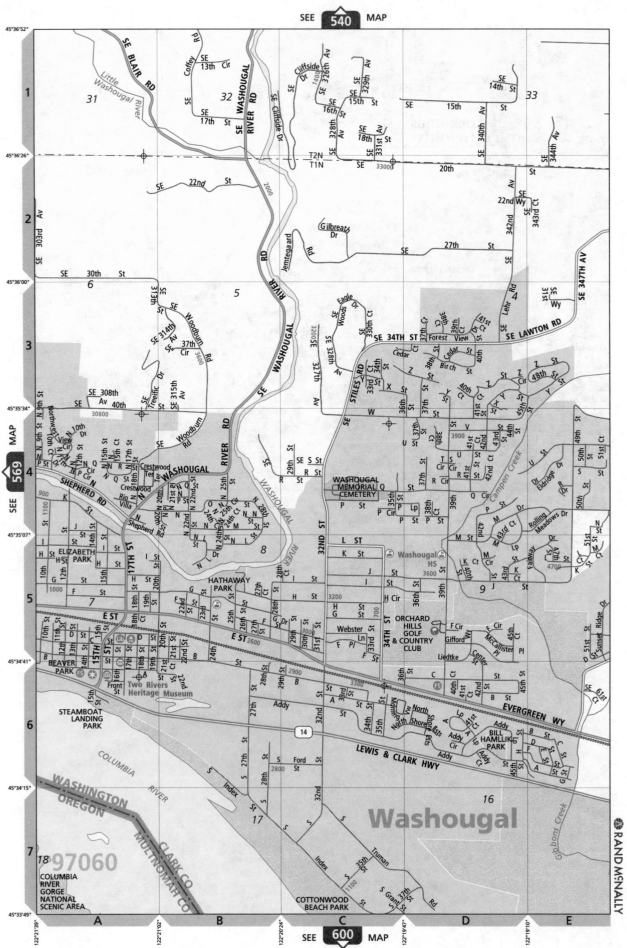

SEE **569** MAP

RAND M°NALLY

SEE **600** MAP

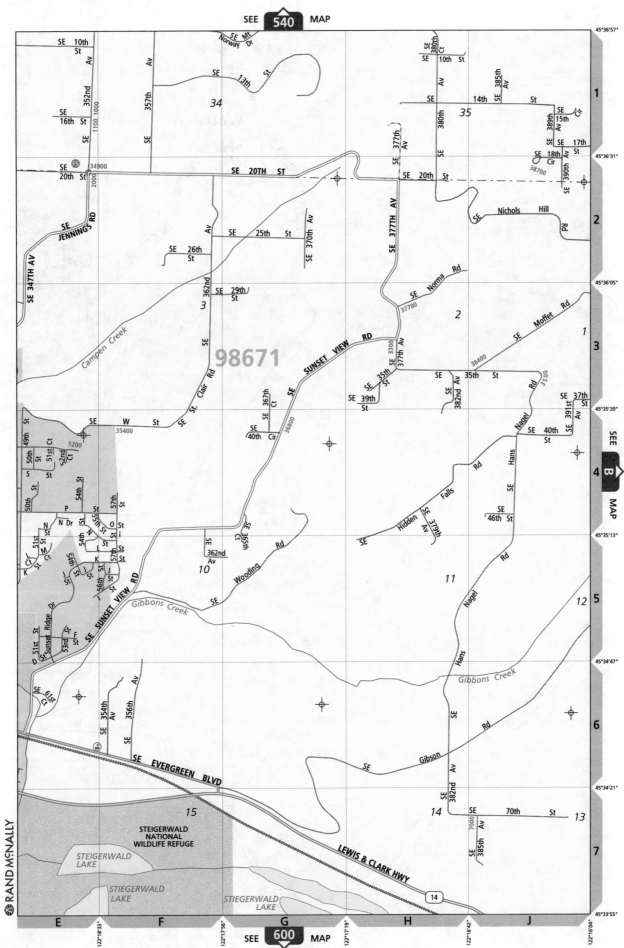

MAP
570

1:24,000
1 in. = 2000 ft.

0   0.25   0.5

miles

SEE 540 MAP

N

SE 10th St
SE 352nd Av
SE 16th St
357th Av
SE 13th St
SE Mt Norway Dr

34

SE 380th Ct
SE 10th St
SE 385th Av
385th Av
SE 14th St
35
380th Av
377th Av
SE 389th Av
15th Cir
SE 17th St
SE 18th Cir
390th Av
38700

SE 347TH AV
SE JENNINGS RD
SE 20th St
34900
2000

SE 20TH ST
SE 20th St
SE 377TH AV
Nichols Hill Pl

SE 25th St
SE 370th Av
SE 26th St

3
Campen Creek
362nd Av
SE 29th St

SE Norma Rd
37700

2
1
SE Moffet Rd
38400

98671

SE SUNSET VIEW RD
SE 3300
377th Av
SE 35th St
35th St
SE 382nd Av
Nagel Rd
3500
SE 37th Av
SE 391st Av

SE 367th Ct
SE 39th St
SE St. Clair Rd
36800
SE W St
35400
SE 40th Cir

SE 49th St
50th St
51st Ct
52nd Ct
5200
54th St
S St
50th St
P
N Dr
N St
55th St
O St
57th St
SE 365th Ct
SE 362nd Av
Wooding Rd
SE
10

40th St
SE 46th St
SE 319th Av
Hidden
Falls Rd
Hans Rd
Nagel Rd

11
12
5

51st St
M St
54th St
57th St
K J St
56th St
SE SUNSET VIEW RD
Gibbons Creek
SE

Sunset Ridge Dr
53rd St
F
D St
51st St

SE 61st Ct
SE 354th Av
356th Av
SE Evergreen Blvd

15
STEIGERWALD
NATIONAL
WILDLIFE REFUGE

STEIGERWALD LAKE
STEIGERWALD LAKE
STEIGERWALD LAKE

Gibbons Creek
SE Hans Rd
SE Gibson Rd

14
SE 382nd Av
SE 70th St
7000
SE 385th Av

13

LEWIS & CLARK HWY
14

RAND MCNALLY

SEE B MAP

SEE 600 MAP

45°36'57"
45°36'31"
45°36'05"
45°35'39"
45°35'13"
45°34'47"
45°34'21"
45°33'55"

122°18'33"
122°17'56"
122°17'19"
122°16'42"
122°16'04"

E   F   G   H   J

1 2 3 4 5 6 7

MAP
591

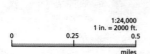

N

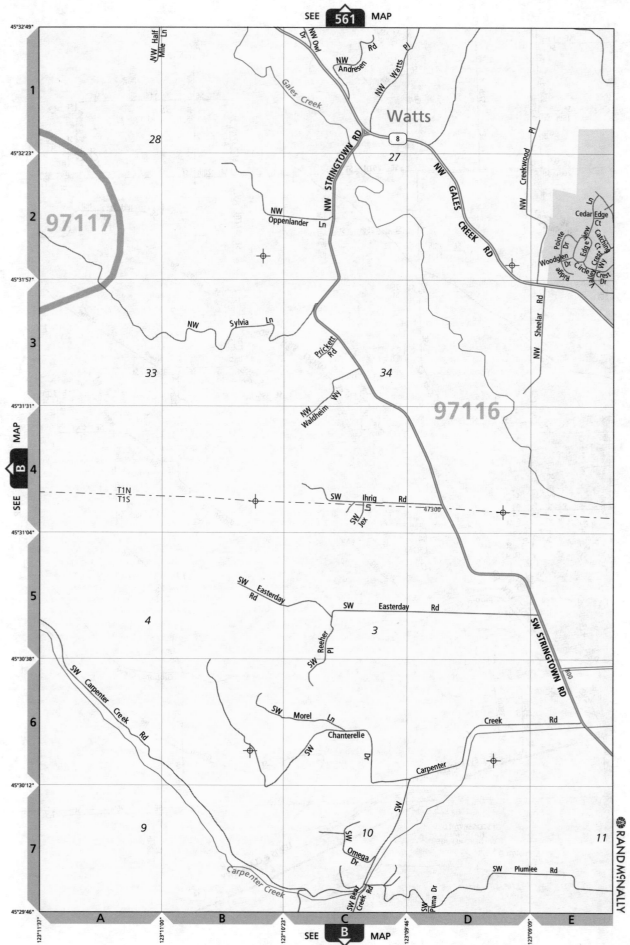

SEE 561 MAP

45°32'49"

NW Half Mile Ln

NW Owl Dr

NW Andresen Rd

NW Watts Pl

Gales Creek

Watts

8

28

45°32'23"

27

NW STRINGTOWN RD

NW Creekwood Pl

NW GALES CREEK RD

2

97117

NW Oppenlander Ln

Cedar Edge Ln

Cedar Edge Ct

Pointe Dr

Edge View Ct

Catching Crest Ct

NW Crest Dr

Woodglen Dr

Ridge

Circle

Valley

45°31'57"

NW Sylvia Ln

NW Sheelar Rd

3

Prickett Rd

33

34

45°31'31"

97116

NW Waldheim Wy

SEE B MAP

4

T1N
T1S

SW Ihrig Rd

47300

SW Jex Ln

45°31'04"

5

SW Easterday Rd

SW Easterday Rd

3

SW STRINGTOWN RD

SW Reeher Pl

4

45°30'38"

SW Carpenter Creek Rd

6

SW Morel Ln

Creek Rd

800

Chanterelle Dr

SW

Carpenter

45°30'12"

9

SW

10

SW Omega Dr

11

7

Carpenter Creek

SW Plumlee Rd

SW Bear Creek Rd

SW Puma Dr

45°29'46"

A   B   C   D   E

123°11'37"   123°11'00"   123°10'23"   123°09'46"   123°09'09"

SEE B MAP

RAND McNALLY

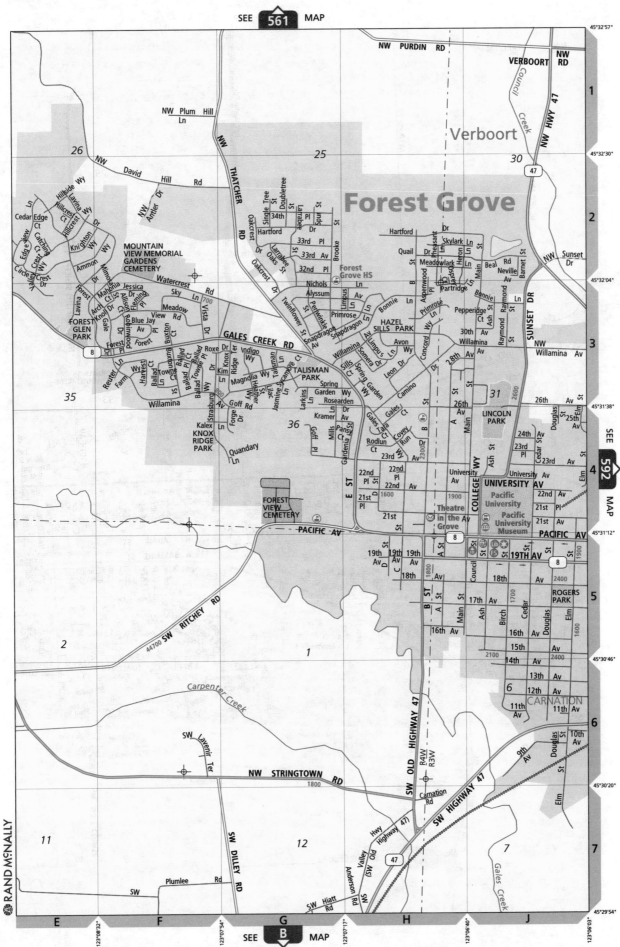

MAP
591

1:24,000
1 in. = 2000 ft.
0   0.25   0.5
miles

NW PURDIN RD

VERBOORT
NW RD

NW Plum Hill Ln

Verboort

26   NW David Hill Rd   25   30   47

Forest Grove

MOUNTAIN VIEW MEMORIAL GARDENS CEMETERY

Single Tree St   34th St   Doubletree St   Latrabee Pl   Spur St
Hartford   33rd Pl   Brooke   Hartford   Skylark Ct
Larrabee St   33rd Av   Oaks St   32nd Pl   Quail   Meadowlark Pl   Heron St   Neville   Barnet St   NW Sunset Dr
Nichols   Forest Grove HS   Ln   B   Partridge   Beal Rd
Alyssum   Limbus   Av   Aspenwood Pl   Primrose
Watercrest   Rd   Twinflower St   Periwinkle   Primrose   Av   Bonnie Ln   Pepperidge Ct   Bonnie   Raymond
FOREST GLEN PARK   Sky   Snapdragon Av   Snapdragon   HAZEL SILLS PARK   Avon Wy   30th   Willamina
GALES CREEK RD   Willamina   Sills Ct   Somera   Limbus Ln   Leon Dr   Concord   28th   NW Willamina Av
Willamina   Spring Garden   Camino   26th   31   26th Av   25th Av
Spring   Garden   Rosearden   Gales Ct   A St   LINCOLN PARK   24th Av
Kramer   Pansy   Dr   Av   Talo   Main St   23rd Pl   Cedar St   23rd
KALEX KNOX RIDGE PARK   Gardenia   Goff   Rodlun Ct   Covey Run   University Av   24th
Quandary   36   Goff Pl   Mills   23rd   University Av   22nd Av
FOREST VIEW CEMETERY   22nd Pl   22nd   **UNIVERSITY AV**   Pacific University   21st Av
E ST   21st Pl   22nd   University Av   Pacific University Museum   21st Av
Theatre in the Grove   8   A St   21st
PACIFIC AV   21st   Av   **PACIFIC AV**   8
19th Av   19th Av   19th Av   **19TH AV**   8
18th   18th Av   ROGERS PARK
B ST   17th Av   18th Av
SW RITCHEY RD   16th   Main St   17th Av   Ash   Birch   Cedar   Elm
2   44700   16th Av   16th Av
1   15th Av   14th Av   Av
Carpenter Creek   13th Av   6   12th Av   **Carnation**
SW Lavenir Ter   11th Av   11th Av
NW STRINGTOWN RD   10th Av   Douglas St   9th Av   Elm
SW OLD HIGHWAY 47   SW HIGHWAY 47   7
11   SW DILLEY RD   12   Carnation Rd   47   Gales Creek
Plumlee Rd   SW   Anderson Rd   SW Hiatt Rd   47

E   F   G   H   J

MAP
592

1:24,000
1 in. = 2000 ft.
0   0.25   0.5
miles

SEE 562 MAP

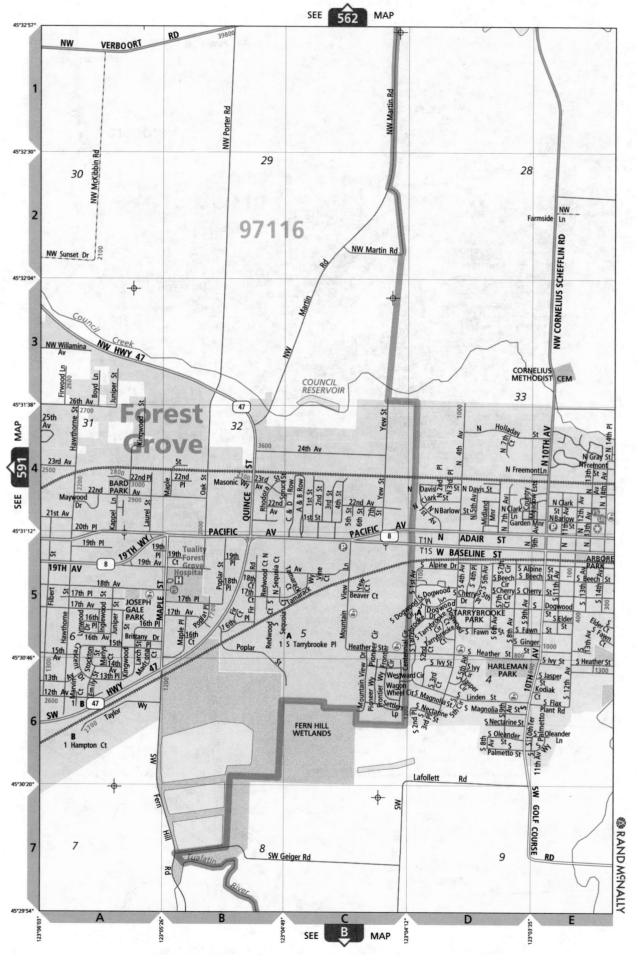

97116

Forest Grove

COUNCIL RESERVOIR

FERN HILL WETLANDS

CORNELIUS METHODIST CEM

RAND McNALLY

SEE 591 MAP

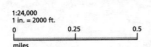

1:24,000
1 in. = 2000 ft.
0   0.25   0.5
miles

MAP
592

SEE **562** MAP

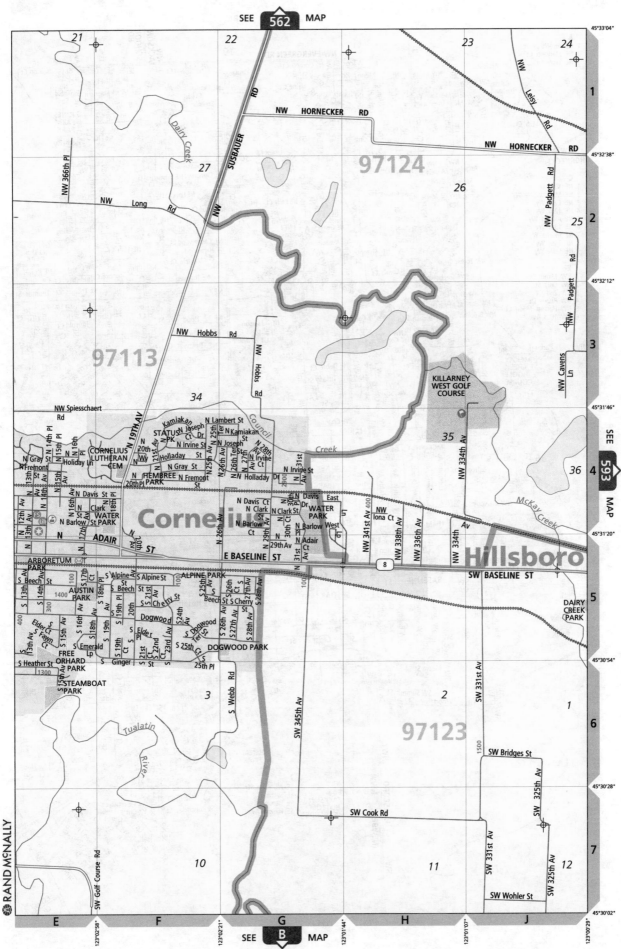

21   22   23   24

NW Leisy Rd

1

NW HORNECKER RD

NW HORNECKER RD

45°33'04"

45°32'38"

97124

27   26   25

NW Padgett Rd

NW Long Rd

NW SUSBAUER RD

2

45°32'12"

NW Hobbs Rd

NW Padgett Rd

NW Cavens Ln

97113

34

NW Hobbs Rd

Council

KILLARNEY WEST GOLF COURSE

3

45°31'46"

NW Spiesschaert Rd

Creek

35   36

SEE **593** MAP

NW 14th Pl
NW 15th Pl
NW 6th
Kamiakan
STATUS PK
N Joseph Ct Dr
N Lambert St
N 25th
N Kamiakan Ter
N 28th
N Joseph
NW 19th AV
20th Wy
21st Ct
N Irvine St
Holladay St
N 27th
N 31st
N Irvine Ct
McKay Creek
4
N Gray St
N Fremont
CORNELIUS LUTHERAN CEM
Holiday Ln
N Gray St
N 25th
N 26th Ter
N 27th
N Irvine St
N 34th Av
NW 334th Av
45°31'46"

N 13th St
N 15th St
20th Pl
N Fremont
HEMBREE PARK
N Fremont St
N Holladay Dr
N Irvine St
N Holladay
NW 334th Av

N 12th Av
N 16th St
N Davis St
N Davis Ct
N Davis East
WATER PARK
NW 341st Av
NW Iona Ct
NW 338th Av
NW 336th Av
NW 334th Av
45°31'20"
N 13th Av
N 16th
N Clark
N Clark St
N Clark St
N Barlow West
N Barlow
WATER PARK
N Barlow St
N 26th St
N Barlow Ct
N 29th
N Adair
29th Av
N Adair
31st
400

Cornelius

N ADAIR ST
12th
20th
E BASELINE ST
31st
8
SW BASELINE ST
Hillsboro

ARBORETUM PARK
S 13th St
S 14th St
100
S 17th Ct
Alpine St
S Alpine Av
ALPINE PARK
S 25th
S 26th
S 28th St
DAIRY CREEK PARK
5
45°31'20"

AUSTIN PARK
1400
S 18th St
S Beech
S 21st St
S Beech
S Cherry
S 27th Ct
S 28th

S 13th Av
S 14th Av
300
S 15th Av
S 16th Av
S 18th
S 19th
20th
S 24th
Dogwood
S 26th Av
Beech Av
S 27th Av

Elder Ct
S Fawn Ct
S 13th Av
400
S 16th St
S 19th Ct
S 19th
Elder Pl
S 23rd St
S Dogwood
DOGWOOD PARK
45°30'54"

FREE ORHARD PARK
Emerald Lp
S 21st St
S 22nd St
S 25th Ct
S Heather St
1300
S Ginger
25th Pl

STEAMBOAT PARK

3   2   1

SW 331st Av

6
45°30'54"

Tualatin River

97123

SW Bridges St

1500

SW 325th Av

45°30'28"

SW Cook Rd

SW 331st Av

7

SW Golf Course Rd
10   11   12
SW 325th Av
SW Wohler St

45°30'02"

E   F   G   H   J

123°02'58"   123°02'21"   123°01'44"   123°01'07"   123°00'29"

SEE **B** MAP

MAP
593

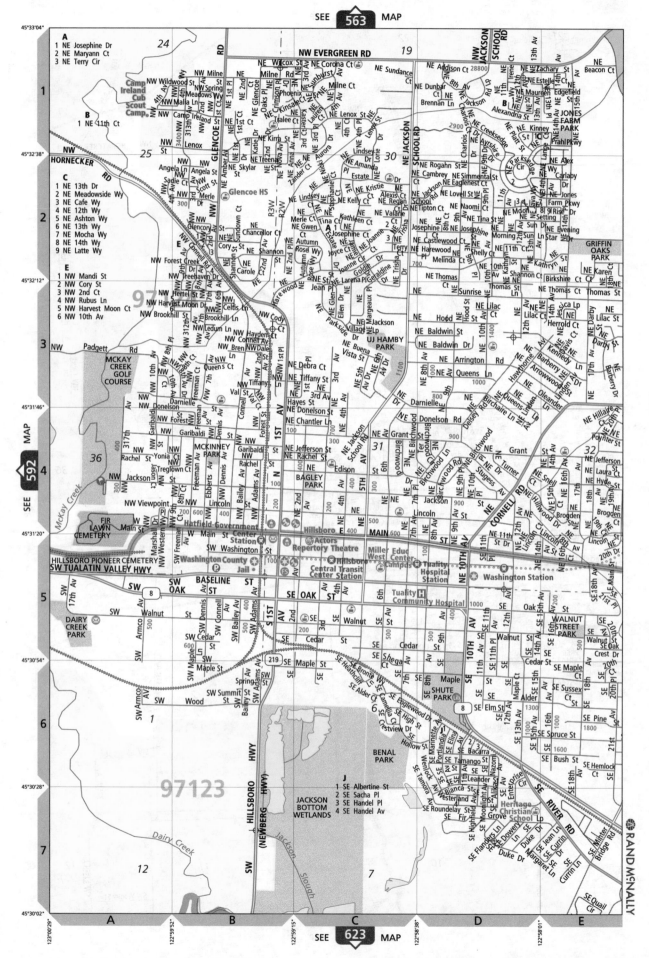

SEE 563 MAP

A
1 NE Josephine Dr
2 NE Maryann Ct
3 NE Terry Cir

B
1 NE 11th Ct

C
1 NE 13th Dr
2 NE Meadowside Wy
3 NE Cafe Wy
4 NE 12th Wy
5 NE Ashton Wy
6 NE 13th Wy
7 NE Mocha Wy
8 NE 14th Wy
9 NE Latte Wy

E
1 NW Mandi St
2 NW Cory St
3 NW 2nd Ct
4 NW Rubus Ln
5 NW Harvest Moon Ct
6 NW 10th Av

J
1 SE Albertine St
2 SE Sacha Pl
3 SE Handel Pl
4 SE Handel Av

SEE 592 MAP

SEE 623 MAP

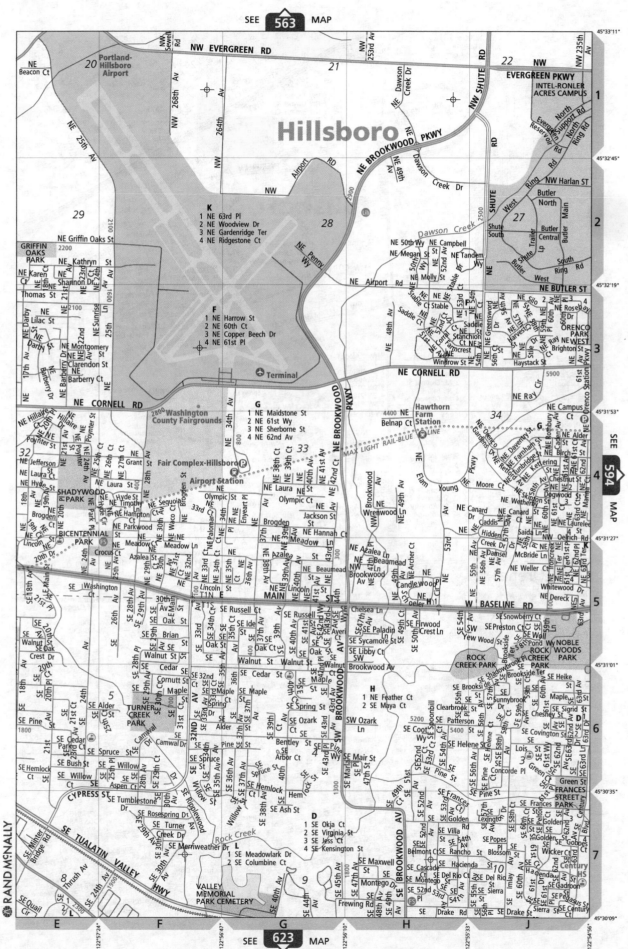

MAP
593

1:24,000
1 in. = 2000 ft.

0   0.25   0.5
miles

SEE ◇ 563 MAP

45°33'11"

NW EVERGREEN RD

NE Beacon Ct

Portland-Hillsboro Airport

20   21   NW 253rd Av

22   NW
EVERGREEN PKWY
INTEL-RONLER
ACRES CAMPUS

1

NE 235th Av

NW Seweli Rd

NW Shute Rd

NW 268th Av

NE 25th Av

NW 264th

Hillsboro

NE Brookwood Pkwy

NW Dawson Creek Dr

NW Harlan St

45°32'45"

29   28

Airport Rd

NW

Shute Rd

West Ring Rd

Evergreen Support Rd

North Reservoir Rd

North Ring Rd

27   Butler North

Butler Main

2

K
1 NE 63rd Pl
2 NE Woodview Dr
3 NE Gardenridge Ter
4 NE Ridgestone Ct

NE Griffin Oaks St

GRIFFIN OAKS PARK

NE Kathryn St

NE Karen St

NE 23rd Av

Dawson Creek

NE 50th Wy NE Campbell

NE Megan Av

NE Tandem Wy

Butler Trailer Lp

Butler Central

Butler South

West Ring Rd

45°32'19"

NE BUTLER ST

NE Penny Wy

NE Airport Rd

NE Stable Ct

NE 53rd

Silo

Roseball Dr

ORENCO PARK

NE WEST Brighton St

3

NE Thomas St

NE Lilac St

NE Darby St

NE Darby St

NE Montgomery Dr

NE Clarendon St

NE Barberry Ct

NE Sunrise Ln

NE 25th

NE 22nd Av

F
1 NE Harrow St
2 NE 60th Ct
3 NE Copper Beech Dr
4 NE 61st Pl

NE 48th Av

Saddle Ct Stable Ct

NE Stanchion

NE Farmcrest Ct

Winthrow St

Haystack St

NE Greensword

NE Harvest

NE Ray

45°31'53"

NE CORNELL RD

Terminal

NE CORNELL RD

NE Ray Cir

NE Campus Av

Orenco Station Pkwy

5900

NE CORNELL RD

G
1 NE Maidstone St
2 NE 61st Wy
3 NE Sherborne St
4 NE 62nd Av

Washington County Fairgrounds

34th Av

Hawthorn Farm Station

Belnap Ct

4400 NE

G
NE Alder St
NE Birch St

NE Rothbury Av

NE Orenco Gardens Dr

NE Daventry St

NE Farnham

NE Brunbridge Av

NE Kettering

NE Chestnut

45°31'53"

4

SEE ◇ 594 MAP

Fair Complex-Hillsboro

MAX LIGHT RAIL-BLUE LINE

Airport Station

SHADYWOOD PARK

NE Jefferson St

NE Laura St

NE Hyde St

NE Poynter St

NE Hillaire Ct

NE Brogden St

Olympic St

Olympic Ct

NE Laura St

NE Hampton

NE Timothy

NE Sequoia

Enyeart Pl

Jackson St

NE Hannah St

Brookwood Av

Wrenwood

NE Canard Dr

NE Moore Ct

NE Wetherlay

NE Canard Av

NE Skipton Ct

NE Dogwood

NE Laurelee

45°31'27"

BICENTENNIAL PARK

Lincoln St

Crocus St

Meadow Ct

Meadow Ln

Azalea Ln

Beaumead

NE Azalea Ln

NE Archer Ct

Saida Ln

McBride Ln

NE Weller St

NE Dereck Ln

Whitewood Dr

NW Oelrich Rd

Hidden

Creek Dr

Damsel

45°31'27"

Parkwood

Brogden St

NE Meadow Ln

NW Brookwood Av

Candlewood

NE Beaumead

W BASELINE RD

H
1

45°31'27"

SE Washington Ct

SE Russell St

SE Russell St

Chelsea Ln

SE Snowberry Ln

SE Preston Ct

SE Firwood Crest Ln

NOBLE WOODS PARK

ROCK CREEK PARK

45°31'01"

5

SE Oak St

SE Brian St

SE Ide St

SE Paladin

SE Sycamore St

SE Libby Ct

Brookwood Av

SW Ozark Ln

Yew Wood

SE Wolf

Pond Wy

SE Heike

ROCK CREEK PARK

SE 29th

SE Oak St

SE Cedar St

SE Maple

SE Maple

SE Brooks Side

Brookside Pl

SE Brookside Ter

SE Maple

63rd

SE Walnut St

Walnut St

SE Maple

H
1 NE Feather Ct
2 SE Maya Ct

SE Brookside

Sunnybrook

SE Chesney St

SE Sigrid

SE 63rd

6

TURNER CREEK PARK

SE Alder St

Cornutt St

SE Maple

Camwal Dr

SE Spring St

SE Ozark Ln

5200

Clearbrook

SE Patterson St

SE Helene Av

SE Covington St

SE Pine

SE Cedar Park Ct

SE Spruce St

SE Bush St

SE Willow St

Alder

SE Pine Av

Bentley St

SE Arbor Ct

SE Mair St

SE Pine St

SE Helene Av

Lois

SE Concorde Pl

Green

FRANCES STREET PARK

45°30'35"

SE Pine St

SE Hemlock Ct

SE Willow Ct

SE Spruce St

SE Hemlock St

SE Ash St

D
1 SE Okja Ct
2 SE Virginia St
3 SE Jessica St
4 SE Kensington St

SE Frances Ct

SE Villa

SE Golden

SE Frances Ct

SE Belmont St

Wicker Ct

FRANCES STREET PARK

Green Century Blvd

7

CYPRESS ST

SE Tumblestone Dr

SE Rosespring Dr

SE Turner Creek Dr

SE Merriweather Dr

Rock Creek

L
1 SE Meadowlark Dr
2 SE Columbine Ct

SE Maxwell St

SE Montego

SE Cascade St

SE Rancho

SE Hacienda St

Del Rio Ct

SE Imlay

Wicker Ct

Century HS

SE TUALATIN VALLEY HWY

SE Minter Bridge Rd

Thrush Av

SE 24th Av

VALLEY MEMORIAL PARK CEMETERY

Frewing Rd

SE Montego

SE Sierra

Drake Rd

SE Gadron

SE Century

SE Quail Cir

45°30'09"

E   F   G   H   J

SEE ◇ 623 MAP

RAND MCNALLY

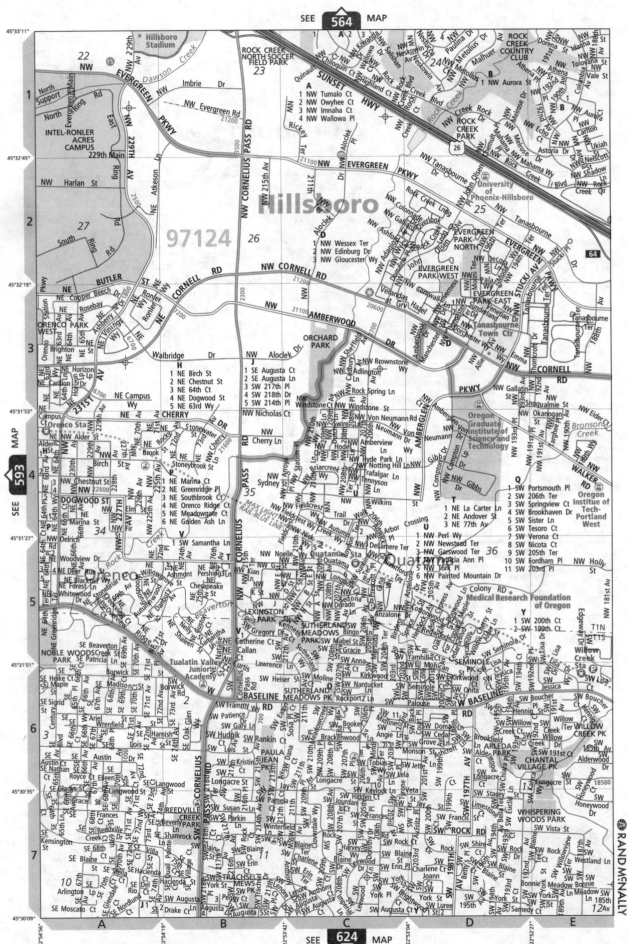

MAP
594

1:24,000
1 in. = 2000 ft.
0   0.25   0.5
miles

RAND MCNALLY

MAP
594

1:24,000
1 in. = 2000 ft.
0   0.25   0.5
miles

SEE 564 MAP

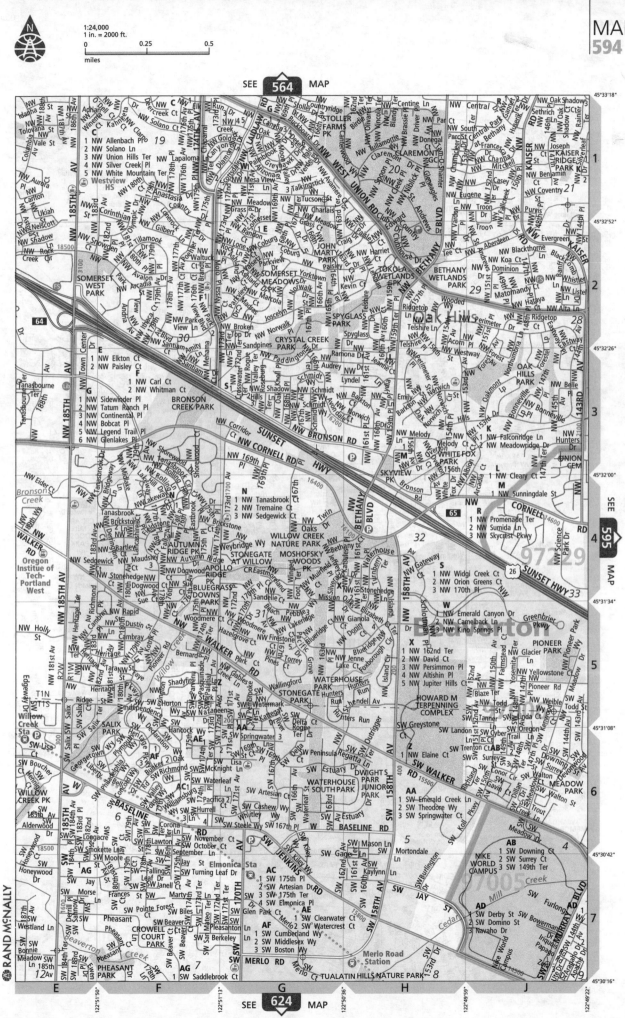

SEE 595 MAP

SEE 624 MAP

RAND MCNALLY

MAP
595

1:24,000
1 in. = 2000 ft.

0   0.25   0.5
miles

SEE 565 MAP

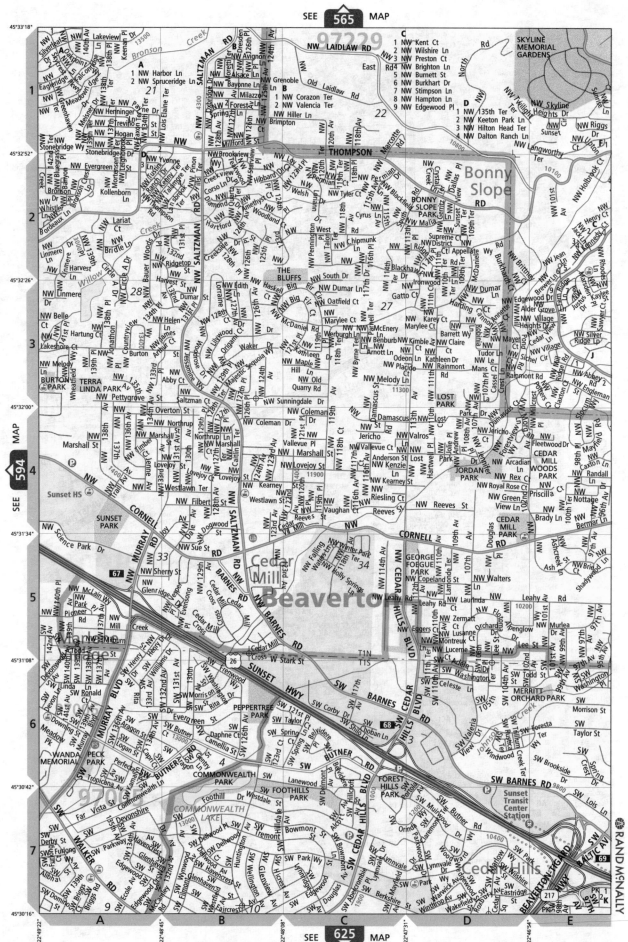

97229

Bonny Slope

THE BLUFFS

Beaverton

Cedar Mill

97005

97006

Cedar Hills

SEE 594 MAP

SEE 625 MAP

RAND M9NALLY

A   B   C   D   E

A
1 NW Harbor Ln
2 NW Spruceridge Ln

B
1 NW Corazon Ter
2 NW Valencia Ter

C
1 NW Kent Ct
2 NW Wilshire Ct
3 NW Preston Ct
4 NW Brighton St
5 NW Burnett St
6 NW Burkhart Dr
7 NW Stimpson Ln
8 NW Hampton Ln
9 NW Edgewood Pl

D
1 NW 135th Ter
2 NW Keeton Park Ln
3 NW Hilton Head Ter
4 NW Dalton Ranch Ln

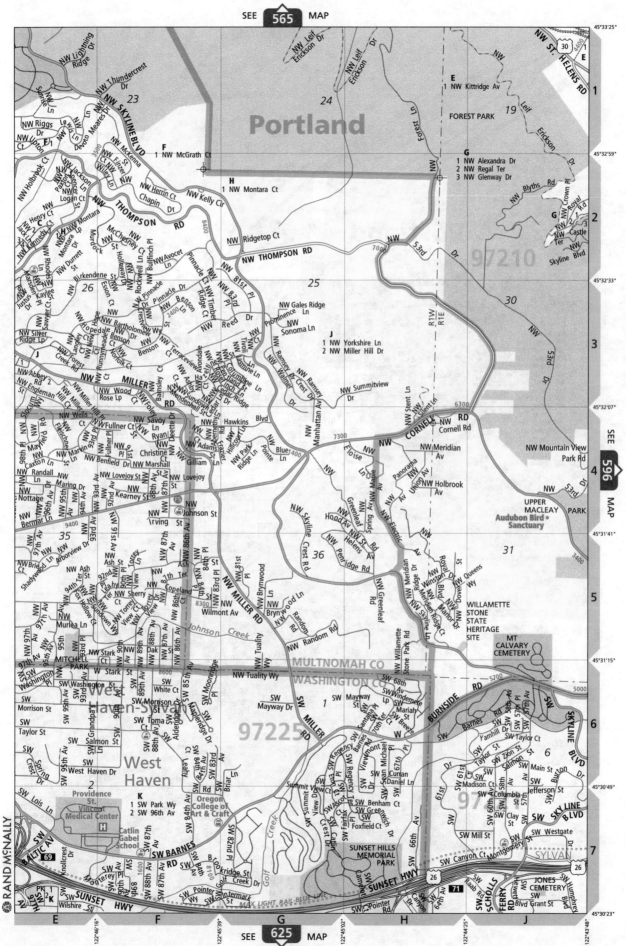

MAP
595

1:24,000
1 in. = 2000 ft.

0   0.25   0.5
miles

SEE ◇ **565** ◇ MAP

45°33'25"

NW Lightning Ridge Dr

NW ST. HELENS RD

30

E

NW Leif Erickson Dr
NW Leif Erickson Dr
NW Leif Erickson Dr

NW Thundercrest Dr

23

NW SKYLINE BLVD

Portland

24

E
1 NW Kittridge Av

FOREST PARK

19

45°32'59"

NW Riggs Dr
NW Upton Ct
F

NW McKenna
NW Finzer
NW Willey Ct

F
1 NW McGrath Ct

G
1 NW Alexandra Dr
2 NW Regal Ter
3 NW Glenway Dr

NW Blyths Rd

NW Crown Rd

NW Royal Rd

NW THOMPSON RD

H
1 NW Montara Ct

NW Herrin Ct
NW Kelly Cir
Chapin Dr

G

NW Castle Ter

45°32'33"

97210

NW Skyline Blvd

NW Ridgetop Ct

NW THOMPSON RD

25

30

53rd Dr

45°32'07"

26

NW Gales Ridge Ln
NW Sonoma Ln

J
1 NW Yorkshire Ln
2 NW Miller Hill Dr

R1W R1E

NW MILLER RD

NW Summitview Dr

NW Stent Ln
NW Silent Ln

6300

NW CORNELL RD

NW Cornell Rd

NW Meridian Av

NW Mountain View Park Rd

NW Wells
NW Savoy Ln
NW Fullner Ct

Hawkins Blvd

7300

NW Eloise

NW Holbrook Av

UPPER MACLEAY PARK

Audubon Bird Sanctuary

45°31'41"

35

NW Lovejoy St

NW Johnson St
NW Irving

36

NW Skyline Crest Rd

NW Hood Av
NW Helens Av
NW Penridge Rd

31

WILLAMETTE STONE STATE HERITAGE SITE

MT CALVARY CEMETERY

45°31'15"

MITCHELL PARK

Johnson Creek

NW MILLER RD

NW Tuality Wy

MULTNOMAH CO
WASHINGTON CO

BURNSIDE RD

5000

SKYLINE BLVD

West Haven-Sylvan

97225

1 SW Mayway St

6

West Haven

K
1 SW Park Wy
2 SW 96th Av

Oregon College of Art & Craft

SUNSET HILLS MEMORIAL PARK

SW SKY LINE BLVD

45°30'49"

Providence St. Vincent Medical Center

Catlin Gabel School

SW BARNES RD

SYLVAN

7

SUNSET HWY

SUNSET HWY

MAX LIGHT RAIL-BLUE LINE

JONES CEMETERY

SW SCHOLLS FERRY RD

45°30'23"

E   F   G   H   J

SEE ◇ **625** ◇ MAP

MAP
596

1:24,000
1 in. = 2000 ft.

0   0.25   0.5
miles

SEE **566** MAP

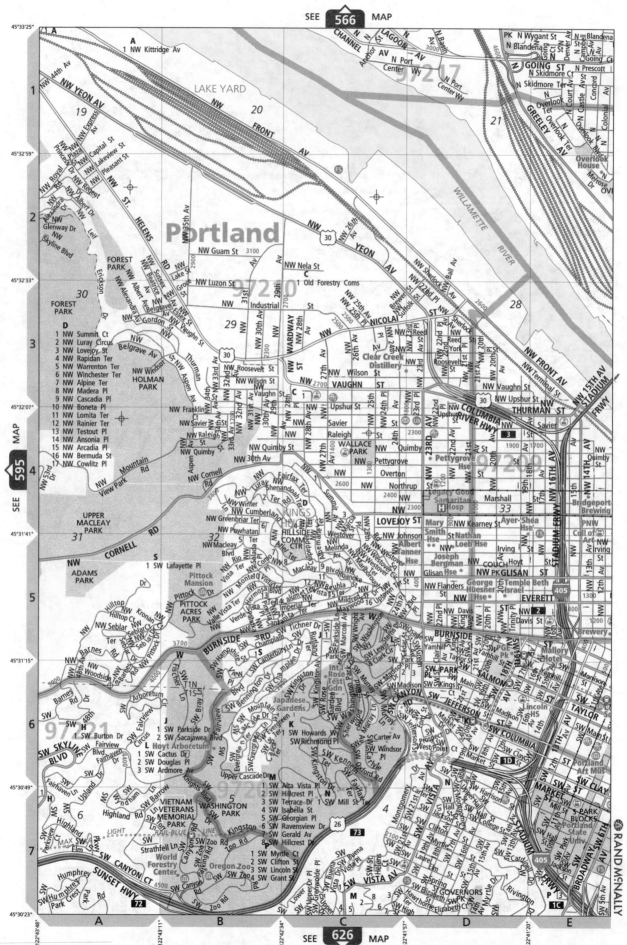

SEE **595** MAP

SEE **626** MAP

LAKE YARD

Portland

FOREST PARK

30

FOREST PARK
D
1 NW Summit Ct
2 NW Luray Circus
3 NW Lovejoy St
4 NW Rapidan Ter
5 NW Warrenton Ter
6 NW Winchester Ter
7 NW Alpine Ter
8 NW Madera Pl
9 NW Cascadia Pl
10 NW Boneta Pl
11 NW Lomita Ter
12 NW Rainier Ter
13 NW Testout Pl
14 NW Ansonia Pl
15 NW Arcadia Pl
16 NW Bermuda St
17 NW Cowlitz Pl

UPPER MACLEAY PARK
31

ADAMS PARK

Pittock Mansion
PITTOCK ACRES PARK

WASHINGTON PARK

VIETNAM VETERANS MEMORIAL PARK

World Forestry Center

Oregon Zoo

Hoyt Arboretum
L
1 SW Cactus Dr
2 SW Douglas Pl
3 SW Ardmore Av

M
1 SW Alta Vista Pl
2 SW Hillcrest Pl
3 SW Terrace Dr
4 SW Isabella St
5 SW Georgian Pl
6 SW Ravensview Dr
7 SW Gerald Av
8 SW Hillcrest Dr

N
1 SW Mill St Ter

J
1 SW Parkside Dr
2 SW Sacajawea Blvd

K
1 SW Howards Wy

RAND McNALLY

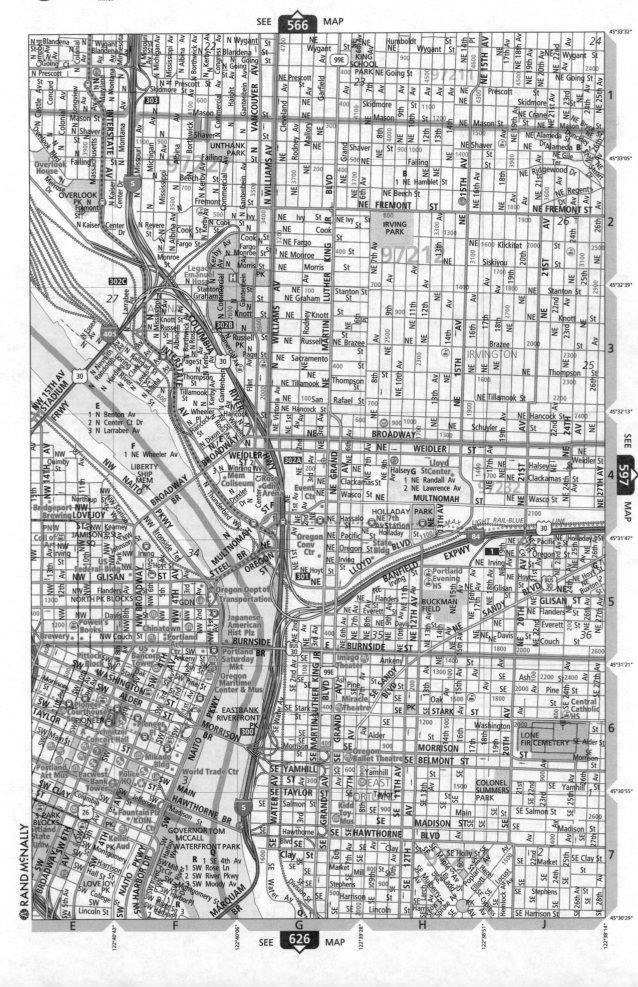

MAP
596

1:24,000
1 in. = 2000 ft.

0   0.25   0.5
miles

SEE **566** MAP

SEE **597** MAP

SEE **626** MAP

RAND M^cNALLY

MAP
597

1:24,000
1 in. = 2000 ft.

0   0.25   0.5
miles

N

SEE 567 MAP

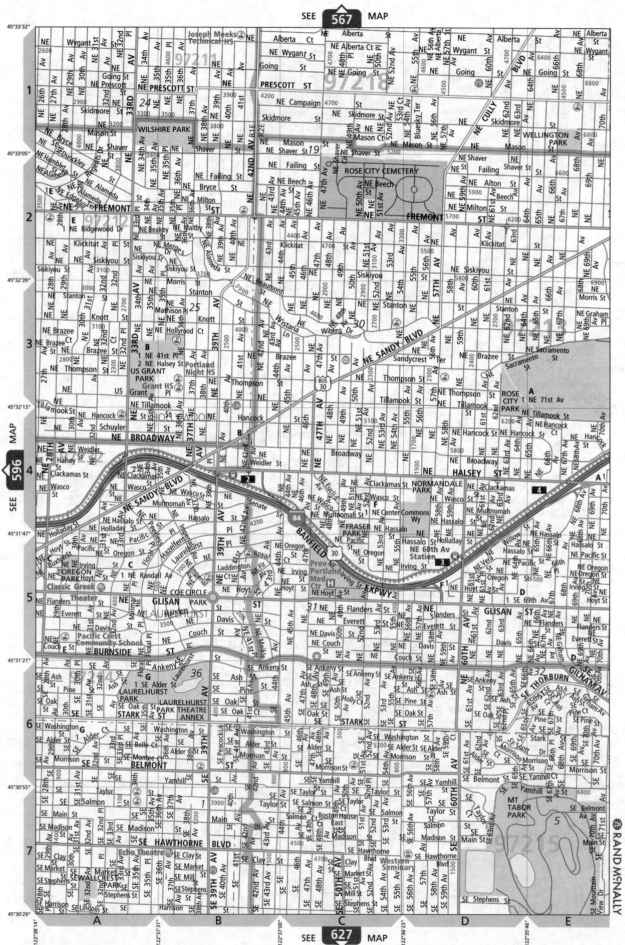

SEE 596 MAP

SEE 627 MAP

RAND McNALLY

MAP
597

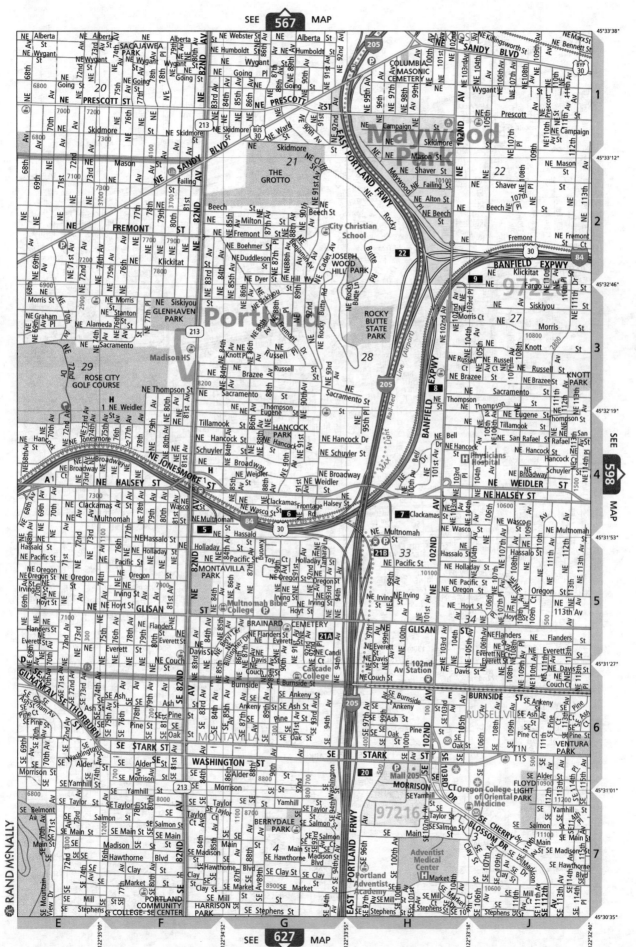

SEE 567 MAP

SEE 598 MAP

SEE 627 MAP

1:24,000
1 in. = 2000 ft.

0   0.25   0.5
miles

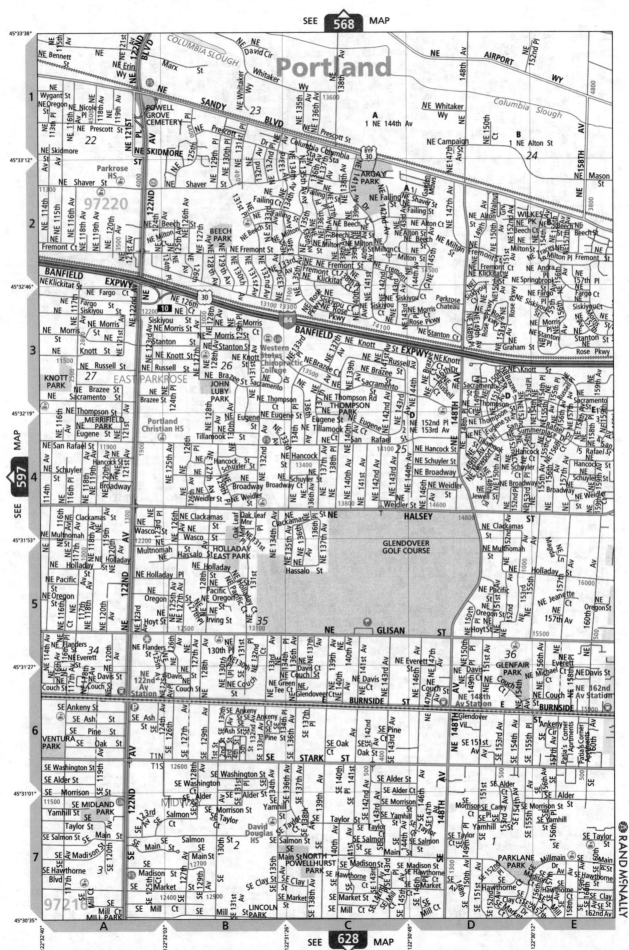

MAP
598

1:24,000
1 in. = 2000 ft.

0   0.25   0.5
miles

SEE 568 MAP

Portland

SEE 628 MAP

RAND McNALLY

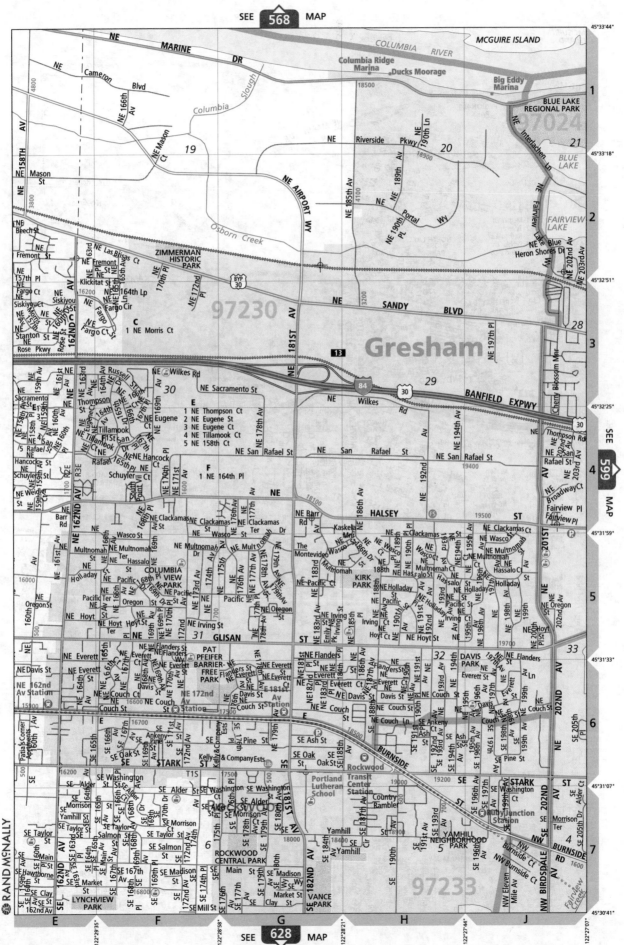

MAP
598

1:24,000
1 in. = 2000 ft.

0   0.25   0.5

miles

SEE 568 MAP

COLUMBIA RIVER   *MCGUIRE ISLAND*

NE MARINE DR

NE Cameron Blvd

Columbia Ridge Marina

Ducks Moorage

Big Eddy Marina

97024

BLUE LAKE REGIONAL PARK

BLUE LAKE

NE Riverside Pkwy

19

20

21

FAIRVIEW LAKE

NE AIRPORT WY

Osborn Creek

ZIMMERMAN HISTORIC PARK

BYP 30

NE SANDY BLVD

97230

Gresham

13

I-84

BANFIELD EXPWY

29

30

NE HALSEY ST

NE San Rafael St

SEE 599 MAP

COLUMBIA VIEW PARK

KIRK PARK

NE GLISAN ST

31

PAT PFEIFER BARRIER-FREE PARK

32

33

DAVIS PARK

SE STARK ST

SE BURNSIDE

Portland Lutheran School

Rockwood Transit Center Station

Country Rambler

Ruby Junction Station

Yamhill Neighborhood Park

ROCKWOOD CENTRAL PARK

VANCE PARK

LYNCHVIEW PARK

97233

NW BURNSIDE RD

Fairview Creek

E   F   G   H   J

SEE 628 MAP

45°33'44"
45°33'18"
45°32'51"
45°32'25"
45°31'59"
45°31'33"
45°31'07"
45°30'41"

122°29'35"   122°28'58"   122°28'21"   122°27'44"   122°27'07"

MAP

599

1:24,000
1 in. = 2000 ft.

0   0.25   0.5

miles

SEE 569 MAP

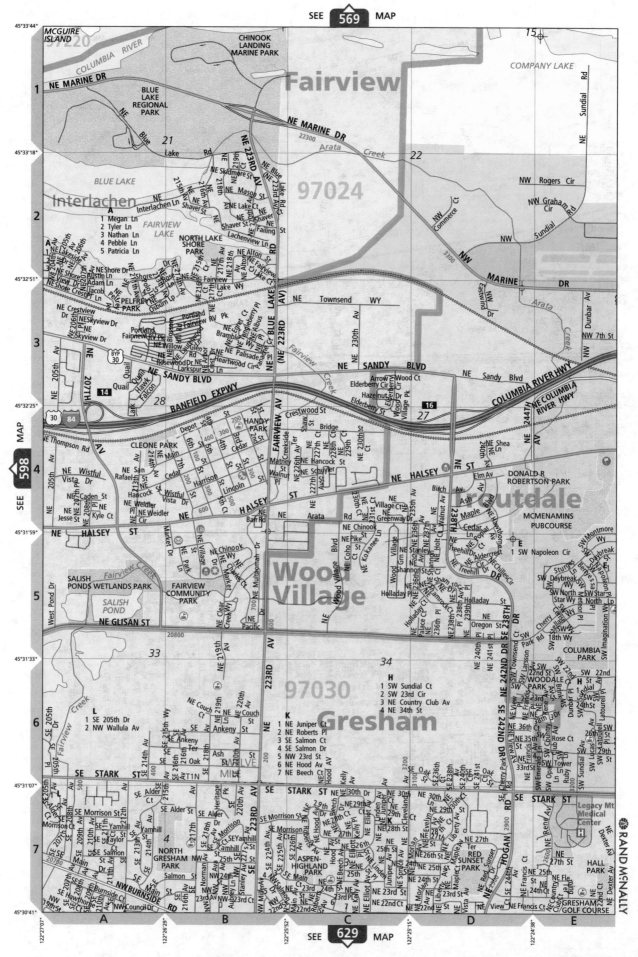

SEE 598 MAP

SEE 629 MAP

RAND MCNALLY

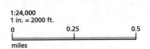

MAP
599

1:24,000
1 in. = 2000 ft.
0   0.25   0.5
miles

SEE 569 MAP

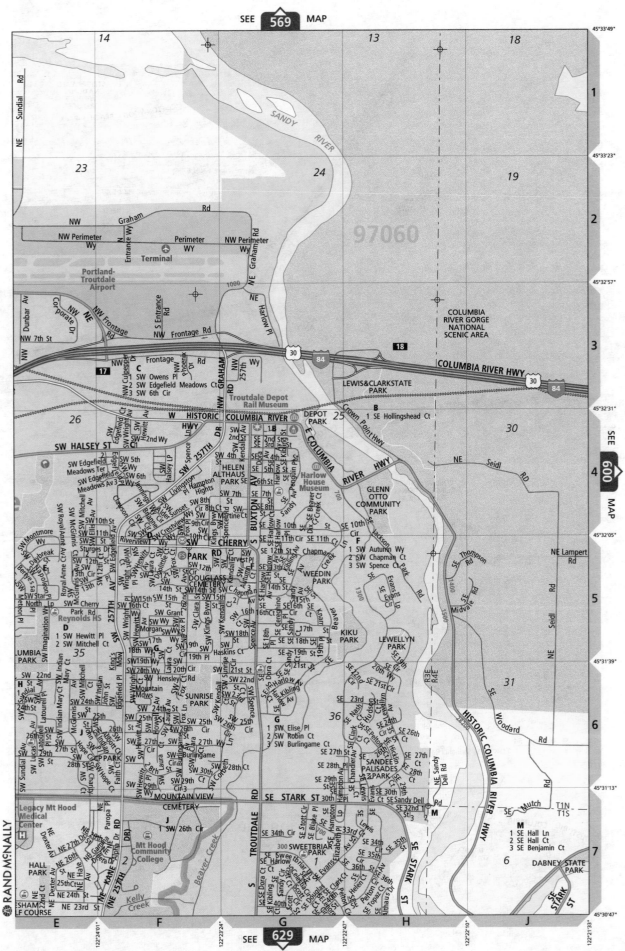

14   13   18

45°33'49"

1

NE Sundial Rd

45°33'23"

23   24   19

SANDY RIVER

2

97060

NW Graham Rd
NW Perimeter Wy
NW Perimeter Wy   NW Perimeter Wy
N Entrance Wy
Terminal

Portland-
Troutdale
Airport

45°32'57"

COLUMBIA
RIVER GORGE
NATIONAL
SCENIC AREA

NE Dunbar Av
Corporate Dr
NW 7th St
NE NW Frontage Rd
S Entrance Rd
NW Frontage Rd

3

NW Frontage
C 1 SW Owens Pl
2 SW Edgefield Meadows Ct
3 SW 6th Cir
17

NW Graham Rd
NW 257th
Phoenix Dr
NW Culpepper

30   84
18
COLUMBIA RIVER HWY   30
84

LEWIS & CLARK STATE
PARK

Troutdale Depot
Rail Museum

45°32'31"

26   W HISTORIC COLUMBIA RIVER   25   30
HWY   DEPOT
PARK   B 1 SE Hollingshead Ct

SW HALSEY ST
SW Edgefield
Meadows Ter
SW Edgefield
Meadows Av 3

C
SW 257TH
SW Hewitt
SW Wright Ct
SW 2nd Wy
SW 5th
SW 6th
Halsey LP

E COLUMBIA RIVER HWY

NE Seidl Rd

45°32'05"

HELEN
ALTHAUS
PARK
Harlow
House
Museum

GLENN
OTTO
COMMUNITY
PARK

F 1 SW Autumn Wy
2 SW Chapman Ct
3 SW Spence Ct

NE Lampert Rd

4

SW Montmore
Wy
Dalbreak
St
SW 10th
SW 11th
SW Mitchell
McGinnis
SW Royal Anne Av
Sturges Dr
SW 12th
SW 13th Cir

SW Livingston
Pl Hampton
Hights
SW 8th
SW 9th Cir
Cir 8th Ct
SW Cherry
SW Sunset

Clawson

SE Harlow
Buxton Av

SE Beaver
Creek
Dix Ct
Sandy Av
SE 10th
SE 11th Cir
SE 11th Ct
Jackson

45°32'05"

F
5

SW Star
North Lp

D
SW Crestview
Riverview
SW
PARK
CHERRY
SW 12th
Cir
Harvest Pl
SW Autumn

Chapman
WEEDIN
PARK

SE
SE Evans Lp
SE Evans
Cir

SE Thompson
Rd
Midvale Rd

REYNOLDS HS
Park Rd
Imagination

SW 15th
SW 15th
SW Clara
SW Kendall

SW 16th
Cir
16th Ct
Beaver
Creek

KIKU
PARK

LEWELLYN
PARK

45°31'39"

31

45°31'39"

6
COLUMBIA
PARK
D 1 SW Hewitt Pl
2 SW Mitchell Ct
35

SW Indian
Mary Ct
King's
Mary
SW 17th
18th Wy
SW 19th Wy

SW Laura
SW Fox
Morgan

SE 17th
SE 18th
SE 18th St
SE 19th
SE 19th Cir

20th Wy
SE 21st Cir

R3E R4E

SW 22nd
H 1 SW Sundial
St
SW Indian
Mdws
SUNRISE
PARK
SW 22nd
SW Kendall
21st St
SE Harlow
SE Kibling

SE 23rd
Woodard
Rd

SW Indian Mary Ct
McGinnis
Av
Latourell
Latourell Pl

SW Indian
John Ct
Edgefield Rd

SW Hensley
Rd

G 1 SW Elise Pl
2 SW Robin Ct
3 SW Burlingame

SE Clark
SE Pelton
SE Lewellyn
SE 24th
SE 26th

HISTORIC COLUMBIA RIVER HWY

SW 24th
SW 25th
SW 26th
SW 25th
SW 25th
SW 25th
Burlingame

SE 27th
SE 28th

SANDEE
PALISADES
PARK

6

SW Lucas
Hope Ct
SW Faith
St
SW Hope Ct

J CT PARK

SW Laura
Cir
SW Burlingame
SW 30th

SE 28th Ct
SE 29th

NE Sandy
Del Rd

M
M 1 SE Hall Ln
2 SE Hall Ct
3 SE Benjamin Ct

45°31'13"

Legacy Mt Hood
Medical
Center

MOUNTAIN VIEW
CEMETERY
SW 29th
J 1 SW 26th Cir

SE STARK ST
SW Conbeth

SE 30th
Rd
SE Sandy Dell

SE Mutch

T1N
T1S

7
HALL
PARK

NE 27th
NE 26th
NE Dexter Av
NE Hale

Mt Hood
Community
College

SWEETBRIAR
PARK

300

SE 34th Cir
SE Harlow

SE 33rd
SE Blake Pl

SE 34th
SE 35th
SE 36th

6
DABNEY STATE
PARK

SHAMROCK
GOLF COURSE
NE 25th St
NE 24th St
NE 23rd
Kelly
Creek

TROUTDALE RD
SE Kibling
SE 40th
SE Dora
SE Scott
SE Douglas
SE Clark Ct
SE Helen Ct
SE Topaz Ct
SE 36th

SE STARK ST

E   F   G   H   J

45°30'47"

SEE 629 MAP

RAND MCNALLY

MAP
600

1:24,000
1 in. = 2000 ft.

0   0.25   0.5
miles

SEE 570 MAP

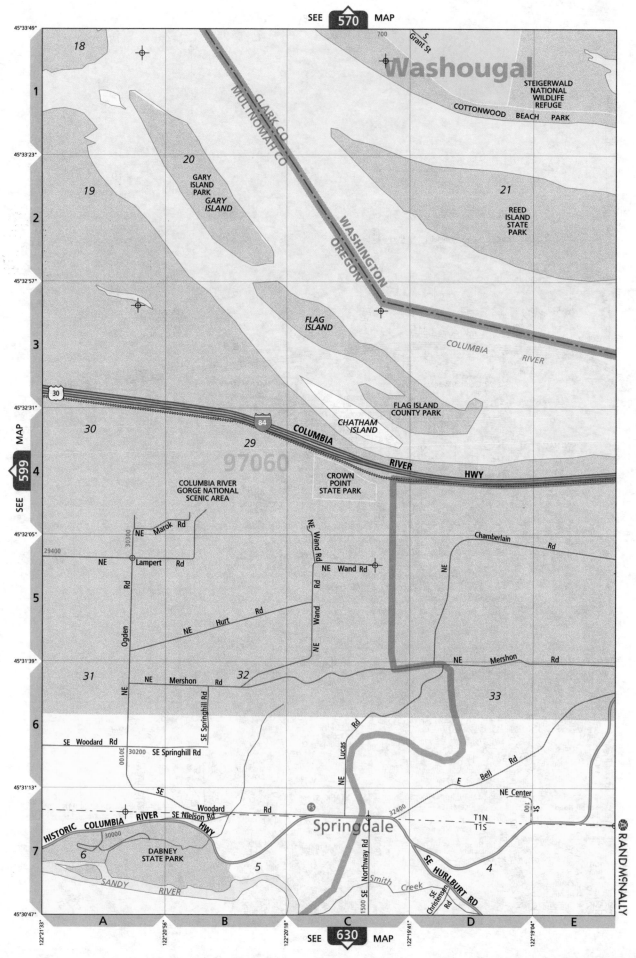

18

20

GARY
ISLAND
PARK

GARY
ISLAND

19

21

REED
ISLAND
STATE
PARK

Washougal

STEIGERWALD
NATIONAL
WILDLIFE
REFUGE

COTTONWOOD   BEACH   PARK

CLARK CO
MULTNOMAH CO

WASHINGTON
OREGON

S Grant St

700

FLAG
ISLAND

COLUMBIA   RIVER

CHATHAM
ISLAND

FLAG ISLAND
COUNTY PARK

30

84

COLUMBIA

30

29

97060

COLUMBIA RIVER
GORGE NATIONAL
SCENIC AREA

CROWN
POINT
STATE PARK

RIVER   HWY

MAP
599
SEE

NE Marok Rd
NE
NE   Lampert   Rd
Ogden Rd
NE
29400
30300

NE Wand Rd
NE Wand Rd
NE Wand Rd

Chamberlain   Rd

NE

NE Hurt   Rd

NE   Mershon   Rd

NE Mershon Rd

31

NE   Mershon   Rd

32

33

SE Springhill Rd

SE Woodard Rd

30200 SE Springhill Rd
30100

Lucas Rd

E   Bell   Rd

NE Center

SE

NE Center St
100

32400

T1N
T1S

HISTORIC COLUMBIA RIVER HWY

SE Nielson Rd
Woodard   Rd

FS

Springdale

30000

6

DABNEY
STATE PARK

SANDY   RIVER

5

Smith Creek

SE Northway Rd

SE Christensen Rd

SE HURLBURT RD

4

1500 SE

RAND McNALLY

SEE 630 MAP

45°33'49"
45°33'23"
45°32'57"
45°32'31"
45°32'05"
45°31'39"
45°31'13"
45°30'47"

122°21'33"
122°20'56"
122°20'18"
122°19'41"
122°19'04"

A   B   C   D   E

1   2   3   4   5   6   7

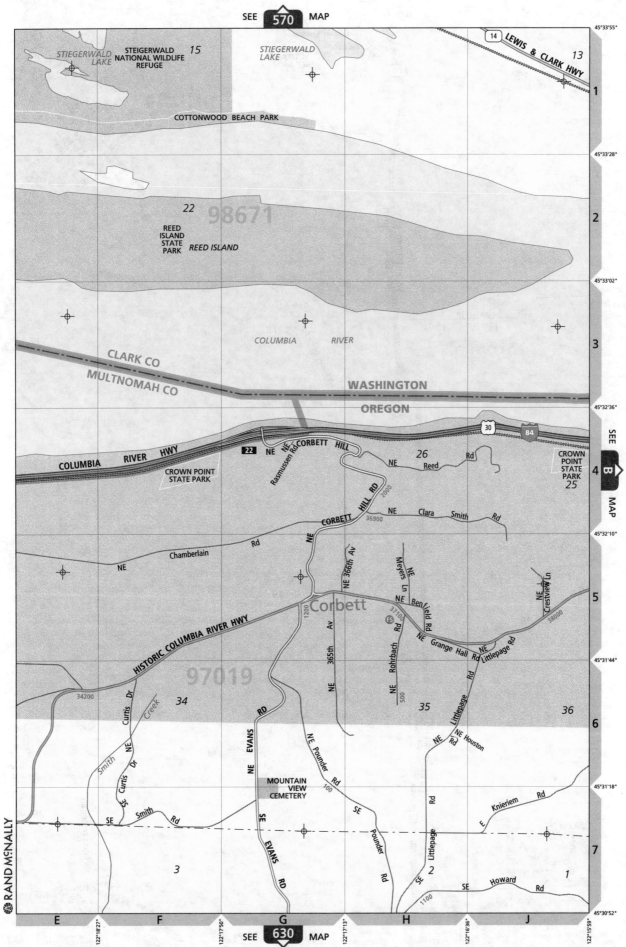

MAP
600

1:24,000
1 in. = 2000 ft.

0   0.25   0.5

miles

SEE 570 MAP

14 LEWIS & CLARK HWY

13

STIEGERWALD
LAKE

STEIGERWALD
NATIONAL WILDLIFE
REFUGE

15

STIEGERWALD
LAKE

1

COTTONWOOD BEACH PARK

22

98671

REED
ISLAND
STATE
PARK   REED ISLAND

2

COLUMBIA   RIVER

3

CLARK CO

MULTNOMAH CO

WASHINGTON

OREGON

30   84   SEE B MAP

COLUMBIA   RIVER   HWY

22   NE   NE CORBETT HILL

Rasmussen Rd

CROWN POINT
STATE PARK

26   Rd

NE   Reed

CROWN
POINT
STATE
PARK

25

4

CORBETT   HILL   RD

NE   Clara   Smith   Rd
36900

2000

Rd

Chamberlain   Rd

NE

NE 366th Av

Meyers Ln

NE

NE Crestview Ln

5

Corbett

Av
1200

37100

Benfield Rd

NE   Grange Hall Rd

Littlepage Rd

38000

HISTORIC COLUMBIA RIVER HWY

97019

34200

Curtis Dr

Creek

34

NE EVANS RD

NE   365th

NE Pounder Rd

NE
Rohrbach
Rd

500

35

NE   Littlepage   Rd

Littlepage

Rd

NE   NE Houston

36

6

Smith

SE Curtis Dr

NE

MOUNTAIN
VIEW
CEMETERY

100

SE

Knieriem   Rd

E

SE   Smith   Rd

SE

SE
EVANS
RD

Pounder
Rd

Littlepage

1100

SE Howard   Rd

7

3

2

1

SEE 630 MAP

E   F   G   H   J

122°18'27"   122°17'50"   122°17'13"   122°16'36"   122°15'59"

45°33'55"

45°33'28"

45°33'02"

45°32'36"

45°32'10"

45°31'44"

45°31'18"

45°30'52"

MAP
623

1:24,000
1 in. = 2000 ft.

0   0.25   0.5
miles

SEE 593 MAP

Clean Water Services
Jackson Bottom Wetlands

JACKSON BOTTOM WETLANDS

219

45°30'02"

1

12

7

A
1 SE Quail Cir
2 SE Hollyhock Ct
3 SE Sunflower Ct

B
1 SE Purplelily Av
2 SE Blackwell Wy
3 SE Harwell Wy

SE Quail Ct
SE Tanager Ct
SE Laurel Ln
SE Thistle Ct
SE Mariposa

SE Mel Ct
SE Primrose Ct
SE Clematis
SE Brodiaea

SE 12th
SE 13th
SE 13th Dr
Jacquelin

Anthony Ct
SE Gail

SE Blanchard St
SE Gerhard

SE Yellowbird Av
SE San
SE Marino Av
SE Sweetbay St
SE Yulan Wy
SE Kabus Wy
SE Boren

SE Royalsilk Dr
SE Hanover
SE Doren

SW Minter Bridge Rd
SE Galaxy
SE Morgan Rd
SE Paul Jr

SE Larson Ct

SE Hanover Ct

SW Morilon Ln

45°29'35"

2

Jackson Slough

SE Noland St

3800

45°29'09"

SW Tongue Ln

13

97113

TUALATIN

18

17

3

RIVER

SW Minter Bridge Rd

SW Grabel Rd

SW Hillecke Rd

45°28'43"

R3W R2W

4

MAP
SEE B

Davis Creek

45°28'17"

SW Johnson School Rd

24

SW
Enschede
Dr

19

20

5

SW Trinity Pl

31400 31600

SW Simpson Rd

Davis Creek

45°27'51"

SW Riedwig Rd

SW Burkhalter Rd

BURKHALTER RESERVOIR

SW Burkhalter Rd

6

SW

45°27'25"

25

30

29

7

SW Line Dr
SW Link Dr
SW Par Dr
SW 313th Av
SW 310th Av

SW Link St
SW Birdie Dr
SW Three
SW Bogey Ct

SW ROOD BRIDGE RD

SW Heikes Dr

9100

SW Unger Rd

SW FARMINGTON RD

10

45°26'59"

RAND M\cNALLY

219

123°00'21"   122°59'44"   122°59'07"   122°58'30"   122°57'53"

A   B   C   D   E

SEE 653 MAP

MAP
623

1:24,000
1 in. = 2000 ft.

0   0.25   0.5

miles

SEE 593 MAP

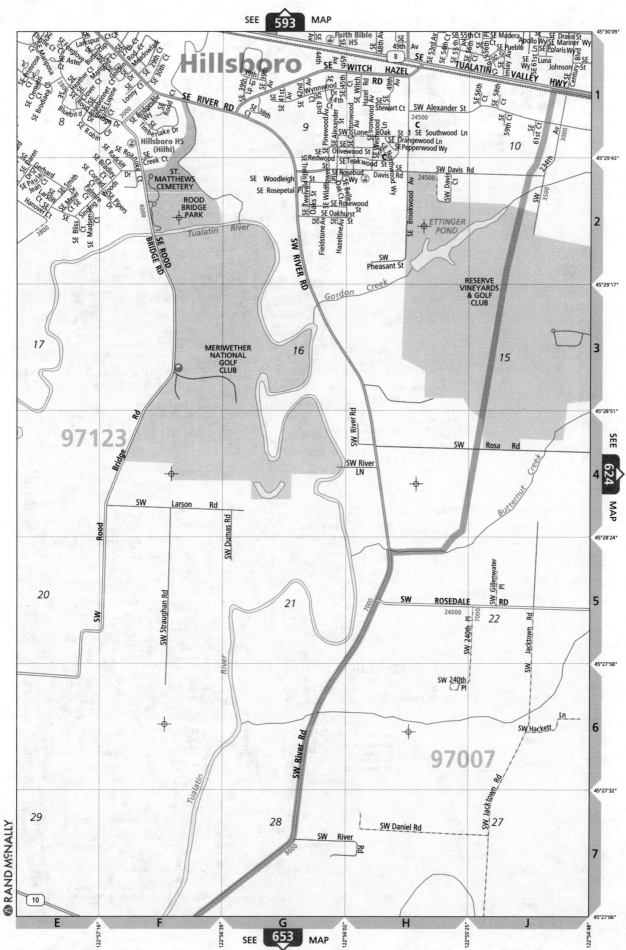

SEE 624 MAP

SEE 653 MAP

MAP
624

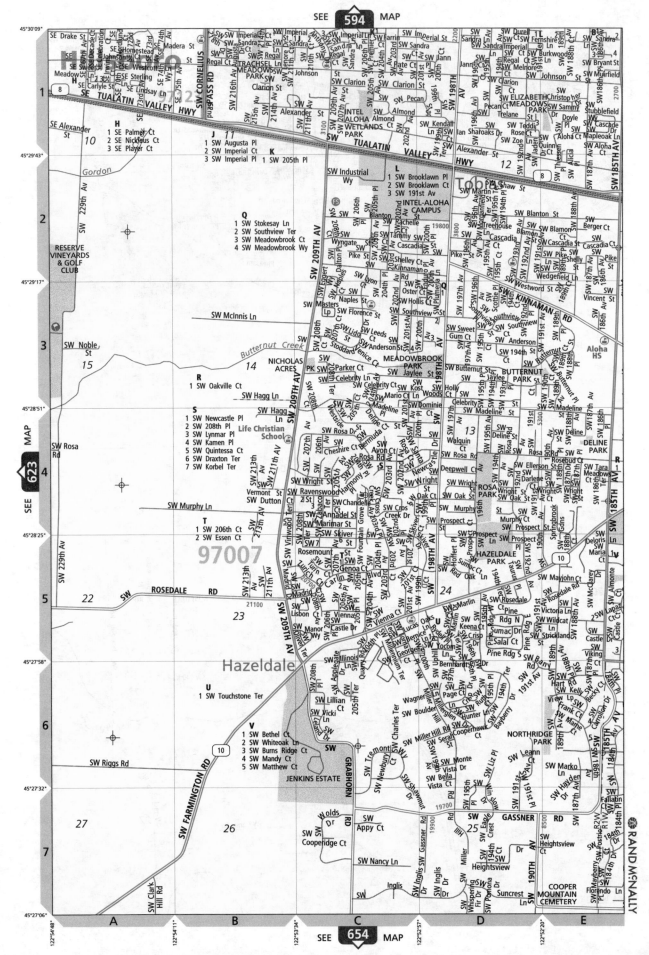

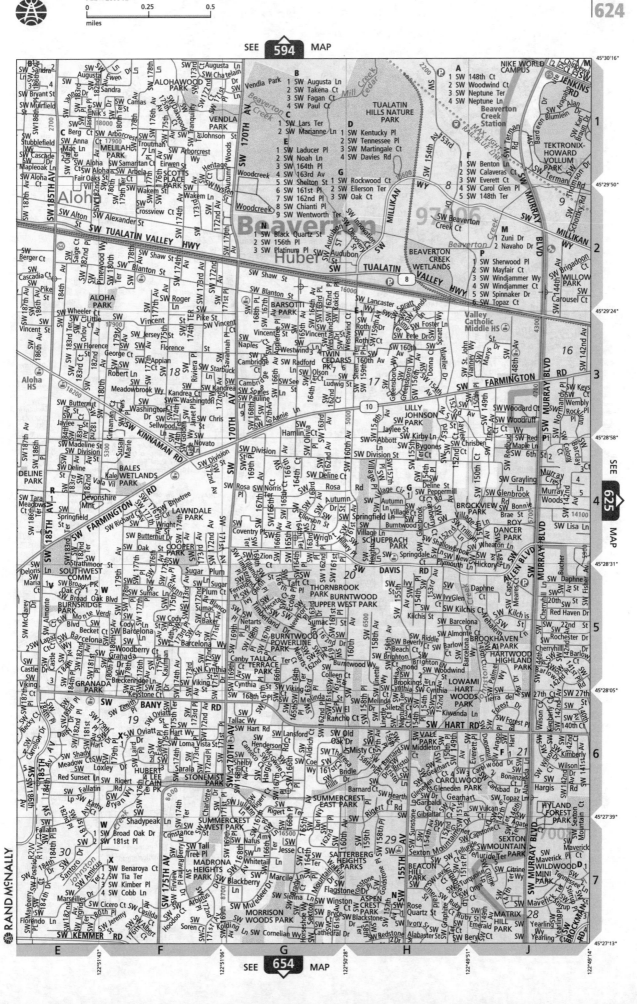

MAP
625

1:24,000
1 in. = 2000 ft.

SEE 595 MAP

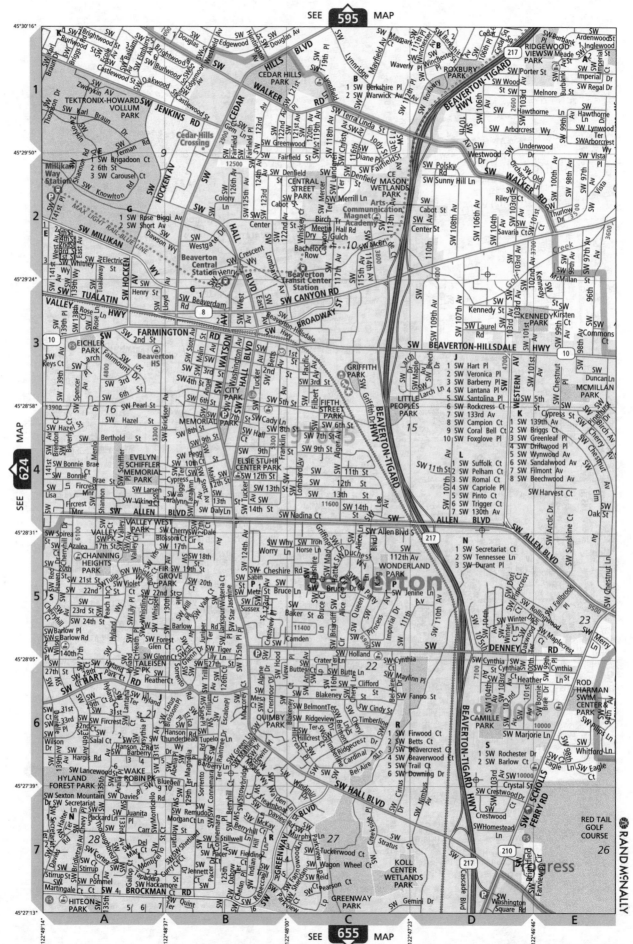

MAP
624
SEE

SEE 655 MAP

RAND McNALLY

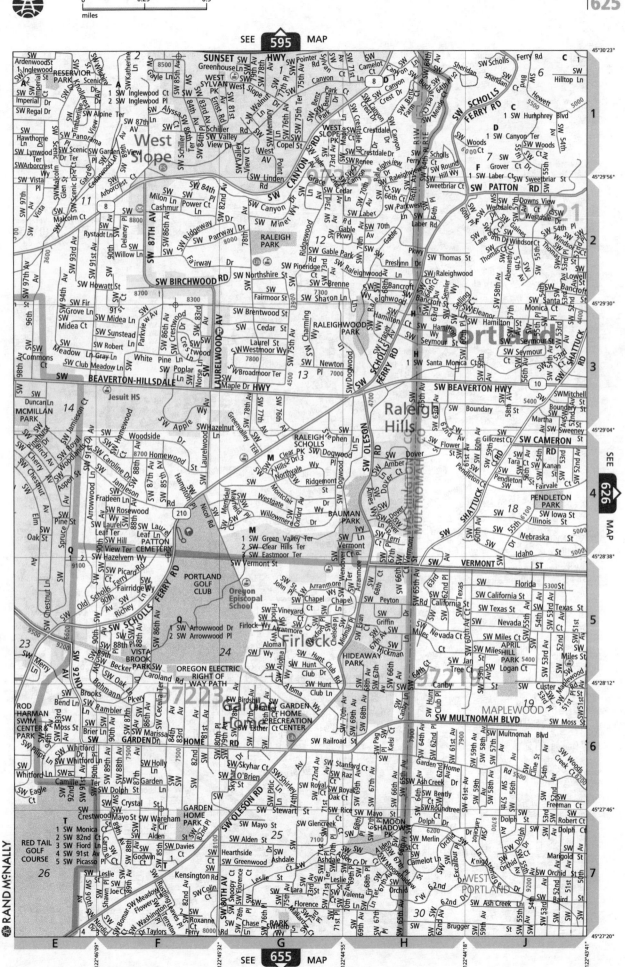

MAP
625

1:24,000
1 in. = 2000 ft.

0   0.25   0.5
miles

SEE 595 MAP

SEE 626 MAP

SEE 655 MAP

RAND M?NALLY

MAP
626

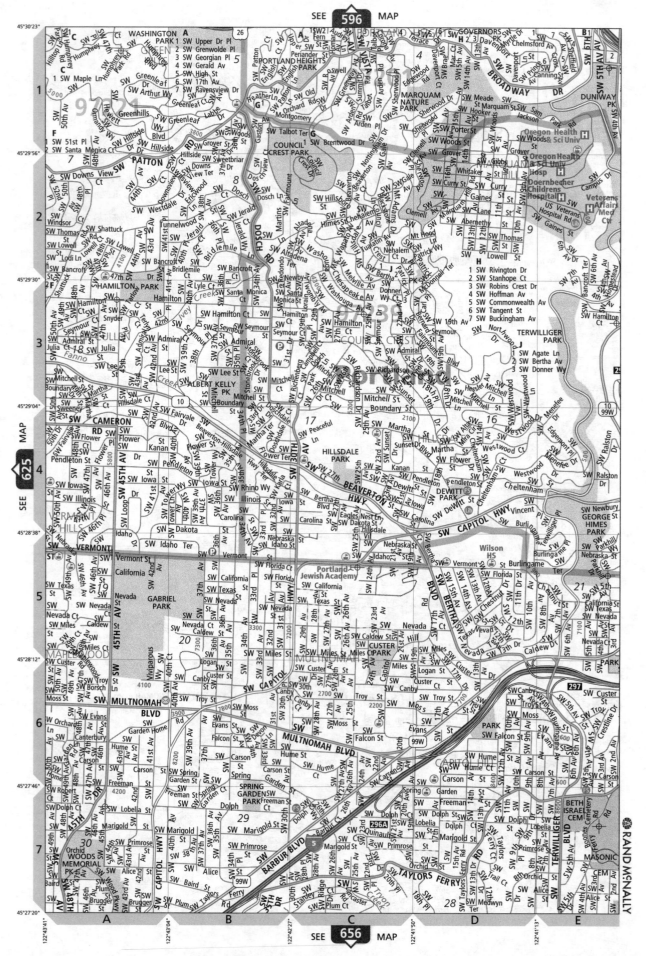

1:24,000
1 in. = 2000 ft.
0   0.25   0.5
miles

RAND McNALLY

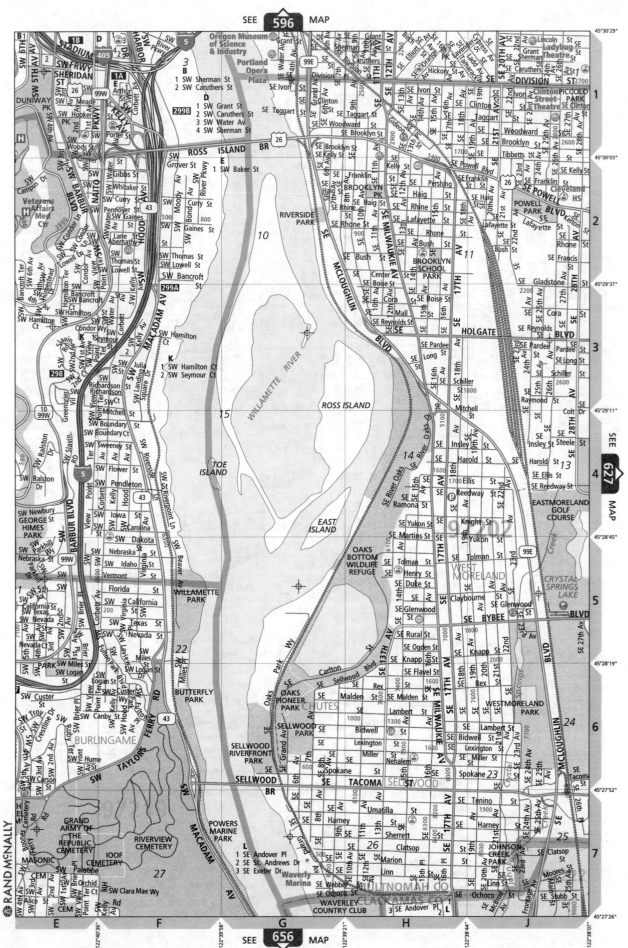

MAP
626

1:24,000
1 in. = 2000 ft.

0   0.25   0.5
miles

SEE 596 MAP

SEE 627 MAP

SEE 656 MAP

RAND M⁹NALLY

MAP
627

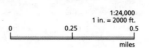

1:24,000
1 in. = 2000 ft.

0   0.25   0.5
miles

SEE 597 MAP

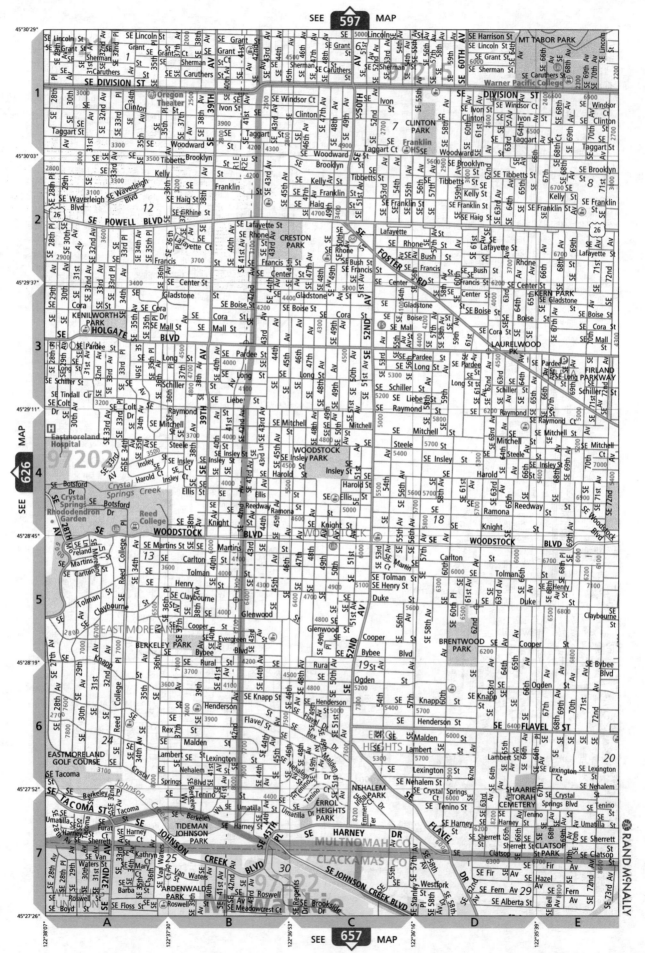

SEE 657 MAP

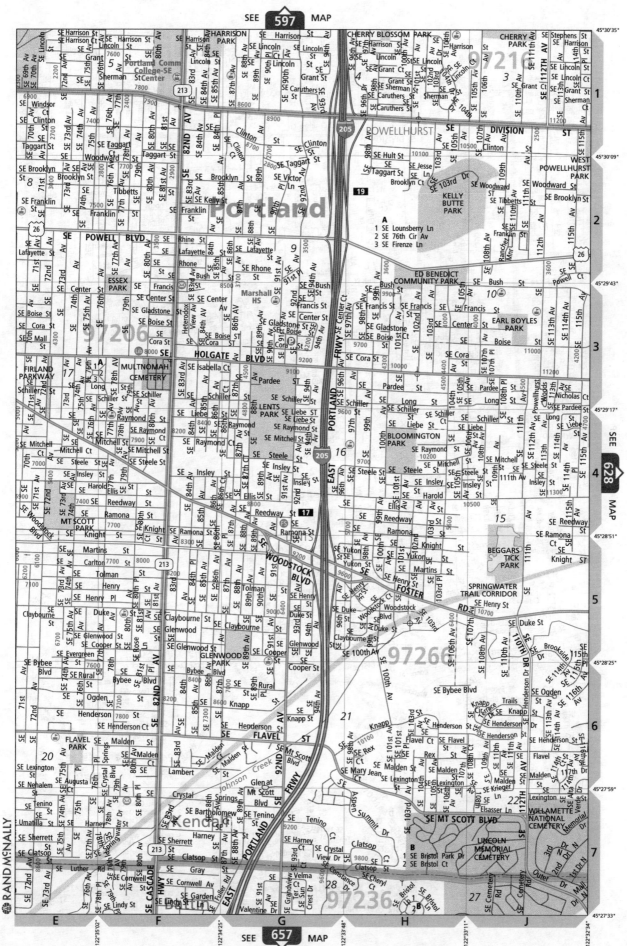

MAP
627

1:24,000
1 in. = 2000 ft.
0   0.25   0.5
miles

SEE 628 MAP

RAND McNALLY

97216
97206
97266
97236

MAP
628

1:24,000
1 in. = 2000 ft.

0   0.25   0.5
miles

SEE 598 MAP

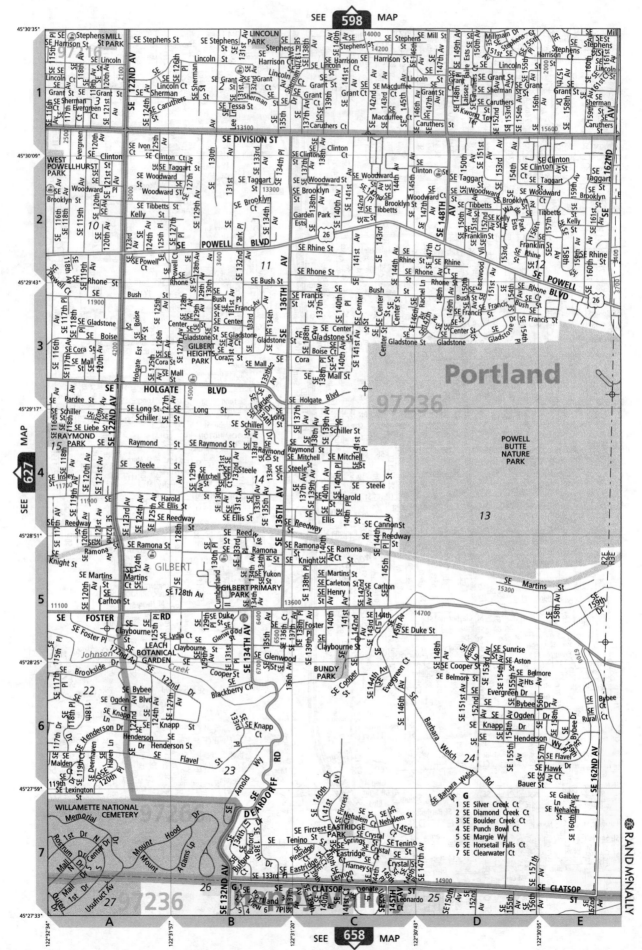

Portland
97236

POWELL BUTTE NATURE PARK

GILBERT HEIGHTS PARK

GILBERT PRIMARY PARK

LEACH BOTANICAL GARDEN

BUNDY PARK

EASTRIDGE PARK

WILLAMETTE NATIONAL CEMETERY

WEST POWELLHURST PARK

RAYMOND PARK

G
1 SE Silver Creek Ct
2 SE Diamond Creek Ct
3 SE Boulder Creek Ct
4 SE Punch Bowl Ct
5 SE Margie Wy
6 SE Horsetail Falls Ct
7 SE Clearwater Ct

SEE 627 MAP

SEE 658 MAP

RAND McNALLY

A   B   C   D   E
1   2   3   4   5   6   7

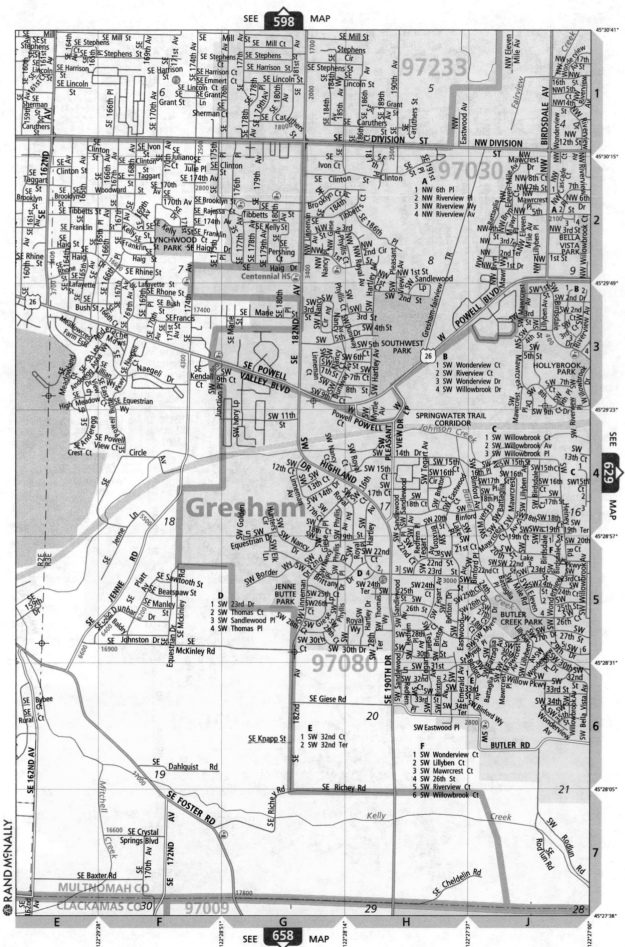

MAP
628

1:24,000
1 in. = 2000 ft.
0   0.25   0.5
miles

RAND MCNALLY

MAP
629

1:24,000
1 in. = 2000 ft.

0   0.25   0.5
miles

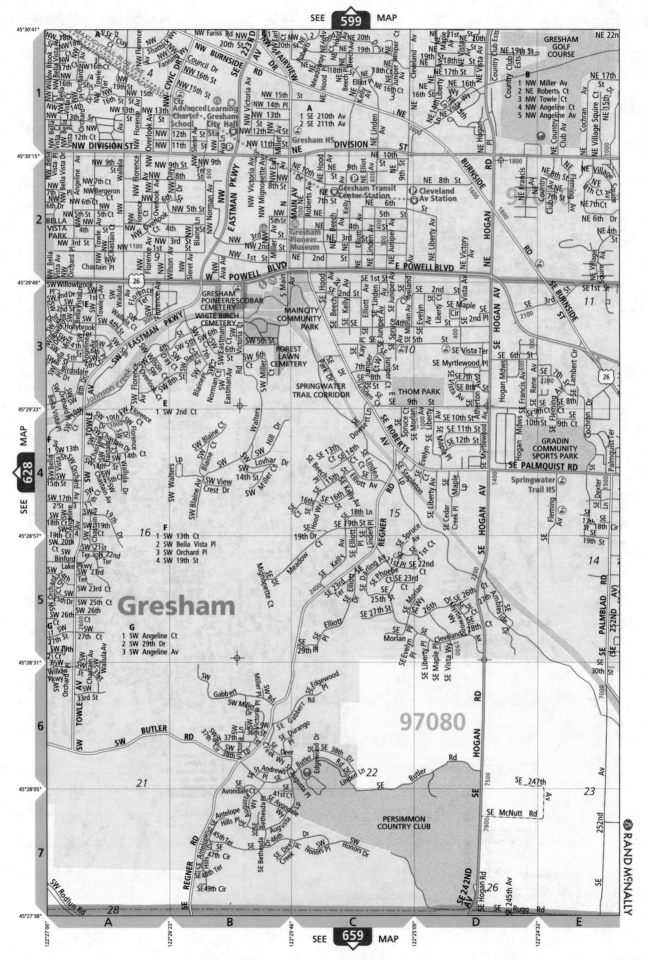

B
1 NW Miller Av
2 NE Roberts Ct
3 NW Towle Ct
4 NW Angeline Ct
5 NW Angeline Av

A
1 SE 210th Av
2 SE 211th Av

F
1 SW 13th Ct
2 SW Bella Vista Pl
3 SW Orchard Pl
4 SW 19th St

G
1 SW Angeline Ct
2 SW 29th Dr
3 SW Angeline Av

Gresham

97080

GRESHAM
GOLF
COURSE

PERSIMMON
COUNTRY CLUB

MAP 628
SEE

MAP
629

1:24,000
1 in. = 2000 ft.

0   0.25   0.5
miles

SEE 599 MAP

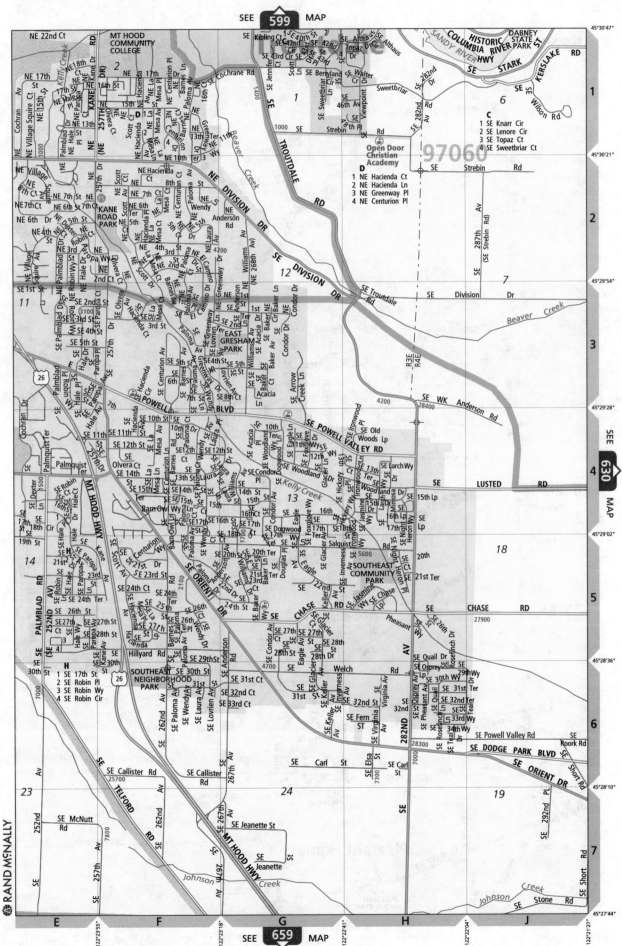

97060

C
1 SE Knarr Cir
2 SE Lenore Cir
3 SE Topaz Ct
4 SE Sweetbriar Ct

D
1 NE Hacienda Ct
2 NE Hacienda Ln
3 NE Greenway Pl
4 NE Centurion Pl

H
1 SE 17th St
2 SE Robin Pl
3 SE Robin Wy
4 SE Robin Cir

SEE 630 MAP

E   F   G   H   J

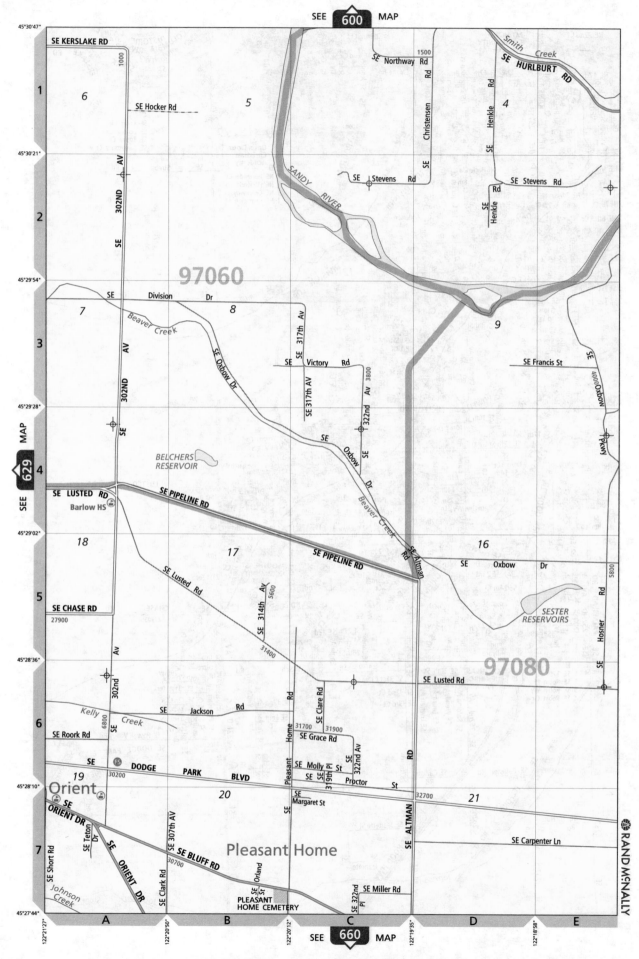

MAP
630

1:24,000
1 in. = 2000 ft.

0   0.25   0.5
miles

N

SEE 600 MAP

SE KERSLAKE RD

SE Northway Rd   1500

Smith Creek

SE HURLBURT RD

1000

6   SE Hocker Rd   5   Christensen Rd   SE Henkle Rd   4

SE 302ND AV

SANDY RIVER   SE Stevens Rd   SE Henkle Rd   SE Stevens Rd

97060

SE Henkle Rd

7   SE Division Dr   8   SE 317th Av   9

Beaver Creek

SE Oxbow Dr   SE Victory Rd   SE Francis St

SE 302ND AV   SE 317th AV   SE 322nd Av   3800   SE Oxbow Pkwy   4000

MAP 629   SE   SE Oxbow Dr   SE Oxbow Dr

BELCHERS RESERVOIR   Beaver Creek   SE Altman Rd

SE LUSTED RD   SE PIPELINE RD

Barlow HS

18   17   SE PIPELINE RD   16

SE Lusted Rd   SE Altman Rd   SE Oxbow Dr

SE 314th Av   5600   Hosner Rd   5800

SE CHASE RD   27900   31400   SESTER RESERVOIRS

302nd Av   97080

Kelly Creek   SE Jackson Rd   Home Rd   SE Lusted Rd

6   SE Roork Rd   6800   31700   SE Clare Rd   31900   SE Grace Rd   322nd Av   RD

19   SE DODGE PARK BLVD   30200   Pleasant   SE Molly Pl   SE Proctor St   32nd Av

Orient   20   SE Margaret St   32700   21

SE ORIENT DR   SE Teton Dr   SE 307th AV   SE BLUFF RD   Pleasant Home   SE ALTMAN RD   SE Carpenter Ln

7   SE Short Rd   SE Clark Rd   30700   SE Orland St   SE 322nd Pl   SE Miller Rd   RAND McNALLY

Johnson Creek   PLEASANT HOME CEMETERY

A   B   C   D   E

SEE 660 MAP

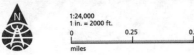

1:24,000
1 in. = 2000 ft.

0   0.25   0.5
miles

MAP
630

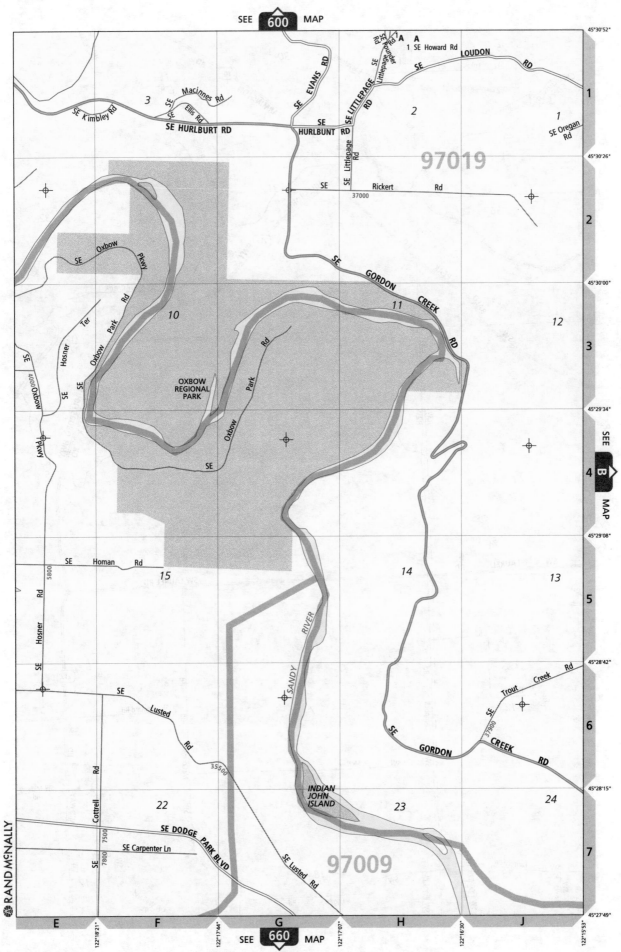

SEE 600 MAP

45°30'52"

A 1 SE Howard Rd
A

SE Evans Rd

SE Pounder Rd

SE LITTLEPAGE RD

SE Littlepage Rd

SE LOUDON RD

Macinnes Rd

3

SE Kimbley Rd

SE Ellis Rd

SE HURLBURT RD

HURLBUNT RD

2

1

SE Oregan Rd

1

97019

45°30'26"

SE Rickert Rd

37000

2

SE Oxbow Pkwy

Oxbow Park Rd

SE GORDON CREEK RD

10

11

12

45°30'00"

3

Hosner Ter

4000 Oxbow

SE

OXBOW
REGIONAL
PARK

Oxbow Park Rd

SE

45°29'34"

SEE B MAP

Pkwy

4

45°29'08"

SE Homan Rd

5800

15

14

13

5

Hosner Rd

SANDY RIVER

45°28'42"

SE Trout Creek Rd

37000

SE

SE Lusted Rd

6

SE GORDON CREEK RD

355.00

Cottrell Rd

22

INDIAN
JOHN
ISLAND

23

24

45°28'15"

SE DODGE PARK BLVD

7500

7800

SE Carpenter Ln

SE Lusted Rd

97009

7

45°27'49"

RAND McNALLY

E   F   G   H   J

122°18'21"

122°17'44"

SEE 660 MAP

122°17'07"

122°16'30"

122°15'53"

MAP
653

1:24,000
1 in. = 2000 ft.

0   0.25   0.5
miles

SEE 623 MAP

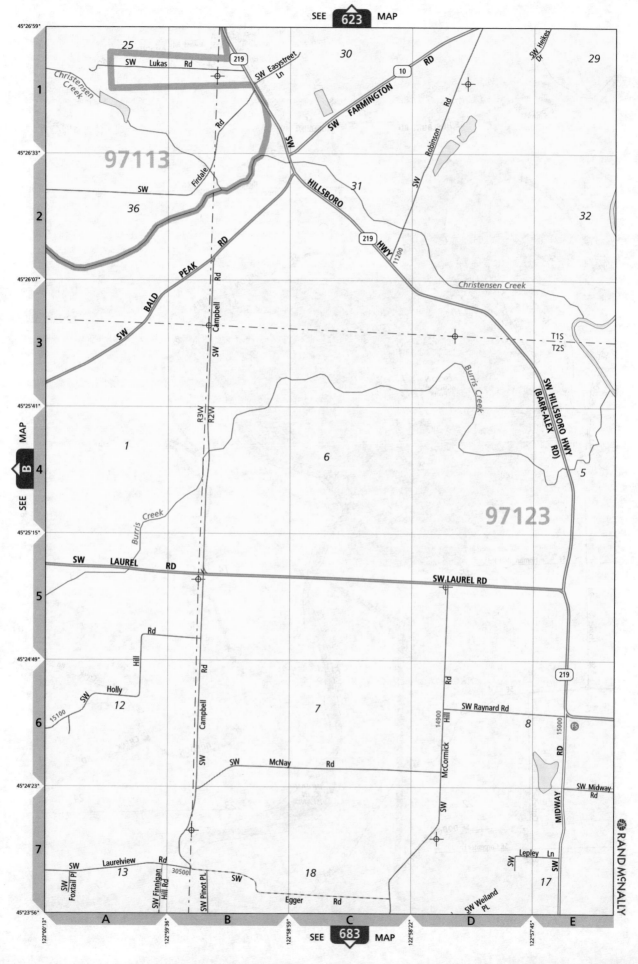

45°26'59"

25

SW Lukas Rd

219

SW Easystreet Ln

30

SW Heikes Dr

29

Christensen Creek

10

RD

SW FARMINGTON

1

Rd

Robinson

45°26'33"

97113

Firdale

SW

36

Rd

HILLSBORO

31

SW

32

2

RD

PEAK

219

HWY

11200

Christensen Creek

45°26'07"

BALD

Rd

Campbell

SW

T1S

3

SW

SW

Burris Creek

T2S

R3W
R2W

SW HILLSBORO HWY

45°25'41"

Burris Creek

1

6

(BARR-ALEX RD)

SEE B 4 MAP

5

97123

45°25'15"

SW   LAUREL   RD

SW LAUREL RD

5

45°24'49"

Rd

Hill

Rd

Campbell

SW

Rd

Hill

McCormick

219

Holly

SW Raynard Rd

45°24'23"

15100

SW

12

SW

7

14900

8

15000

RD

FS

6

SW McNay   Rd

SW

Midway

SW Midway Rd

45°24'23"

MIDWAY

7

Lepley   Ln

45°23'56"

SW   Laurelview   Rd

SW

13

18

17

SW Foxtail Pl

SW Finnigan Hill Rd

SW Pinot Pl

30500

SW

Egger   Rd

SW Weiland Pl

SW

RAND McNALLY

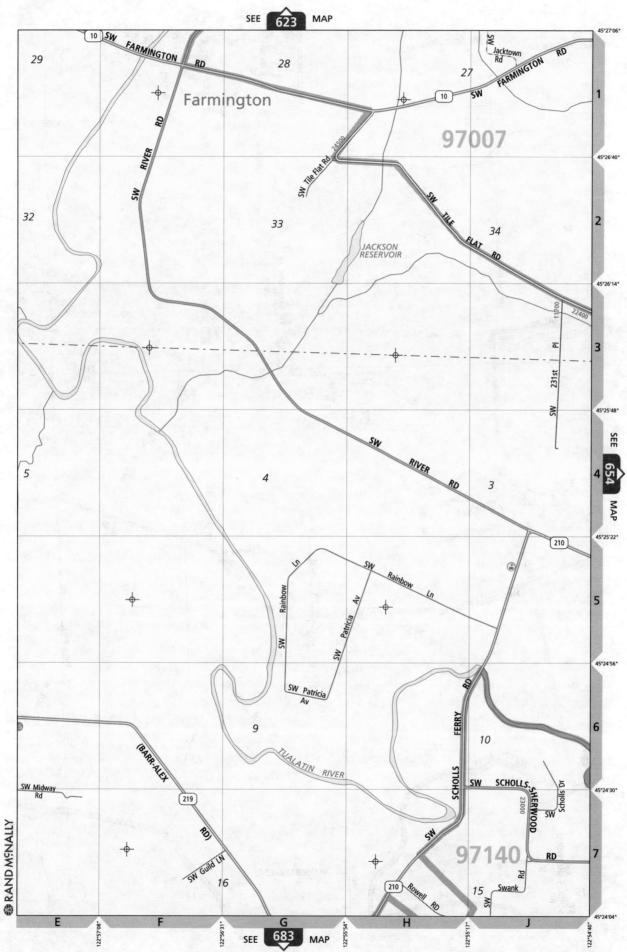

MAP
653

1:24,000
1 in. = 2000 ft.
0   0.25   0.5
miles

SEE 623 MAP

29

28

27

SW FARMINGTON RD

10

Jacktown Rd

SW FARMINGTON RD

10

SW

Farmington

97007

SW Tile Flat Rd 24500

SW RIVER RD

32

33

34

SW TILE FLAT RD

JACKSON RESERVOIR

45°27'06"

1

45°26'40"

2

45°26'14"

11700 22400

231st Pl

SW

3

45°25'48"

SEE 654 MAP

5

4

3

SW RIVER RD

210

45°25'22"

Rainbow Ln

SW Rainbow Ln

SW Patricia Av

SW Rainbow Ln

SW Patricia Av

5

45°24'56"

SCHOLLS FERRY RD

9

10

TUALATIN RIVER

SW Patricia Av

6

SW Midway Rd

(BARR-ALEX

219

RD)

SW SCHOLLS-SHERWOOD

SW SCHOLLS

Scholls Dr

SW

23000

97140

45°24'30"

RD

7

SW Guild LN

16

15

210

Rowell RD

Swank

Rd

SW

45°24'04"

E   F   G   H   J

122°57'08"   122°56'31"   122°55'54"   122°55'17"   122°54'40"

SEE 683 MAP

MAP
654

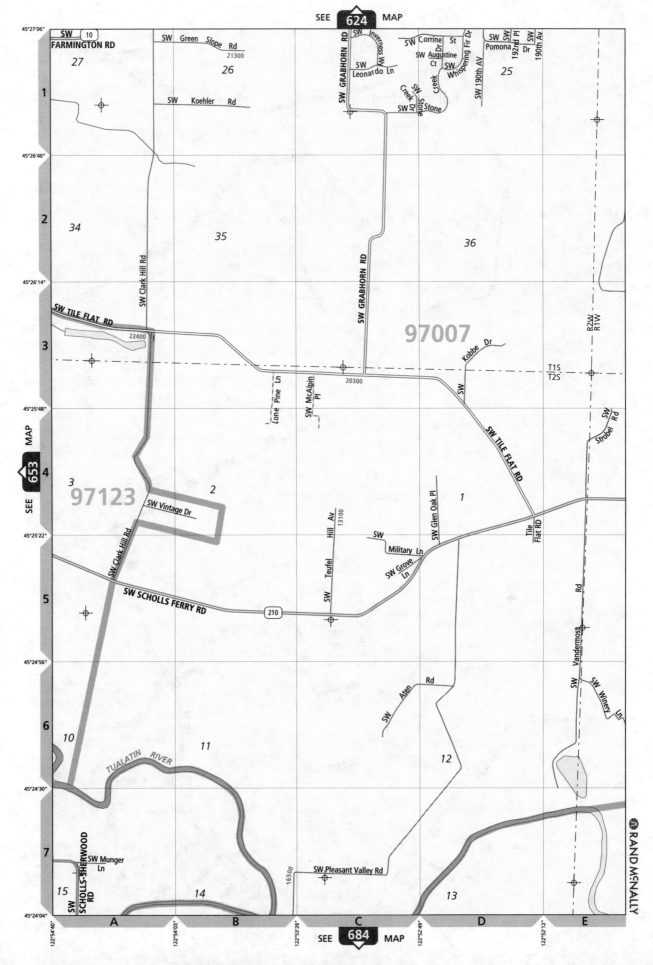

1:24,000
1 in. = 2000 ft.

0   0.25   0.5
miles

45°27'06"
SW 10
FARMINGTON RD

SW Green Slope Rd
21300

27

26

SW Koehler Rd

45°26'40"

SW GRABHORN RD
SW Inverness Wy
SW Leonardo Ln

SW Corrine St
Dr
SW Augustine
Ct
SW

SW Whispering Fir Dr
Creek
SW Stone
Creek Dr
SW Stone Dr

SW Pomona
SW 192nd Pl
Dr
SW 190th Av

SW 190th AV

25

1

2

34

35

36

45°26'14"

SW Clark Hill Rd

SW TILE FLAT RD
22400

SW GRABHORN RD

97007

Kobbe Dr

R2W R1W

3

45°25'48"

Lone Pine Ln

SW McAlpin Pl

20300

SW

SW TILE FLAT RD

T1S
T2S

SW Strobel Rd

45°25'22"

MAP
653

SEE

4

3

97123

SW Vintage Dr

2

SW Glen Oak Pl

1

Tile
Flat RD

SW Clark Hill Rd

SW Teufel Hill Av
13100

SW
Military Ln

SW Grove
Ln

45°25'22"

SW SCHOLLS FERRY RD

210

SW

5

Vandermost Rd

SW
SW Winery
Ln

45°24'56"

SW Aten Rd

6

10

11

12

TUALATIN RIVER

45°24'30"

7

SW SCHOLLS-SHERWOOD RD

SW Munger
Ln

SW Pleasant Valley Rd

16500

15

14

13

45°24'04"

A   B   C   D   E

122°55'40"   122°54'03"   122°53'26"   122°52'49"   122°52'12"

MAP
654

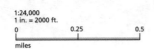

1:24,000
1 in. = 2000 ft.

0   0.25   0.5

miles

SEE **624** MAP

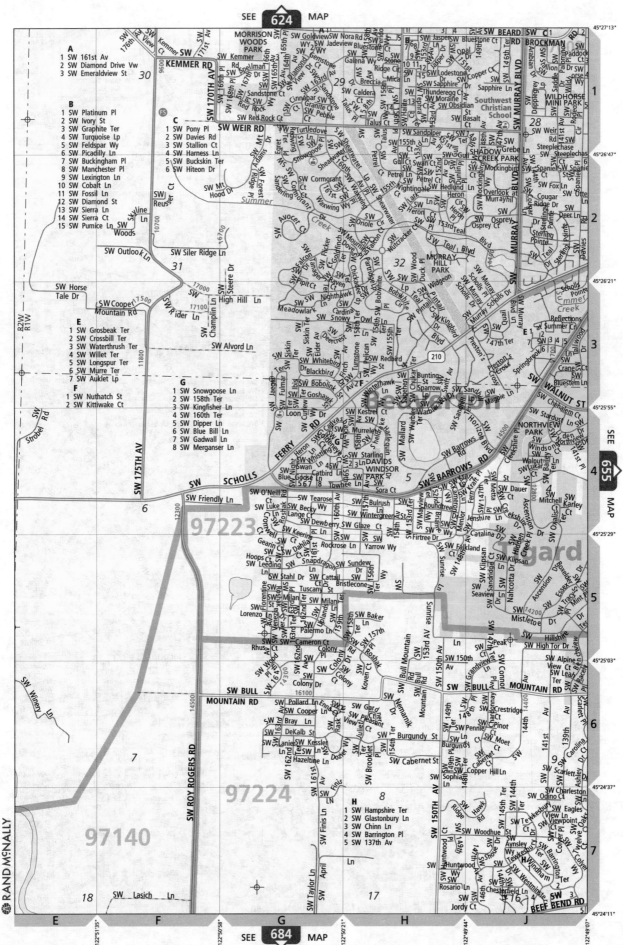

A
1 SW 161st Av
2 SW Diamond Drive Vw
3 SW Emeraldview St

B
1 SW Platinum Pl
2 SW Ivory St
3 SW Graphite Ter
4 SW Turquoise Lp
5 SW Feldspar Wy
6 SW Picadilly Ln
7 SW Buckingham Pl
8 SW Manchester Pl
9 SW Lexington Ln
10 SW Cobalt Ln
11 SW Fossil Ln
12 SW Diamond St
13 SW Sierra Ln
14 SW Sierra Ct
15 SW Pumice Ln

C
1 SW Pony Pl
2 SW Davies Rd
3 SW Stallion Ct
4 SW Harness Ln
5 SW Buckskin Ter
6 SW Hiteon Dr

E
1 SW Grosbeak Ter
2 SW Crossbill Ter
3 SW Waterthrush Ter
4 SW Willet Ter
5 SW Longspur Ter
6 SW Murre Ter
7 SW Auklet Lp

F
1 SW Nuthatch St
2 SW Kittiwake Ct

G
1 SW Snowgoose Ln
2 SW 158th Ter
3 SW Kingfisher Ln
4 SW 160th Ter
5 SW Dipper Ln
6 SW Blue Bill Ln
7 SW Gadwall Ln
8 SW Merganser Ln

H
1 SW Hampshire Ter
2 SW Glastonbury Ln
3 SW Chinn Ln
4 SW Barrington Pl
5 SW 137th Av

SEE **655** MAP

SEE **684** MAP

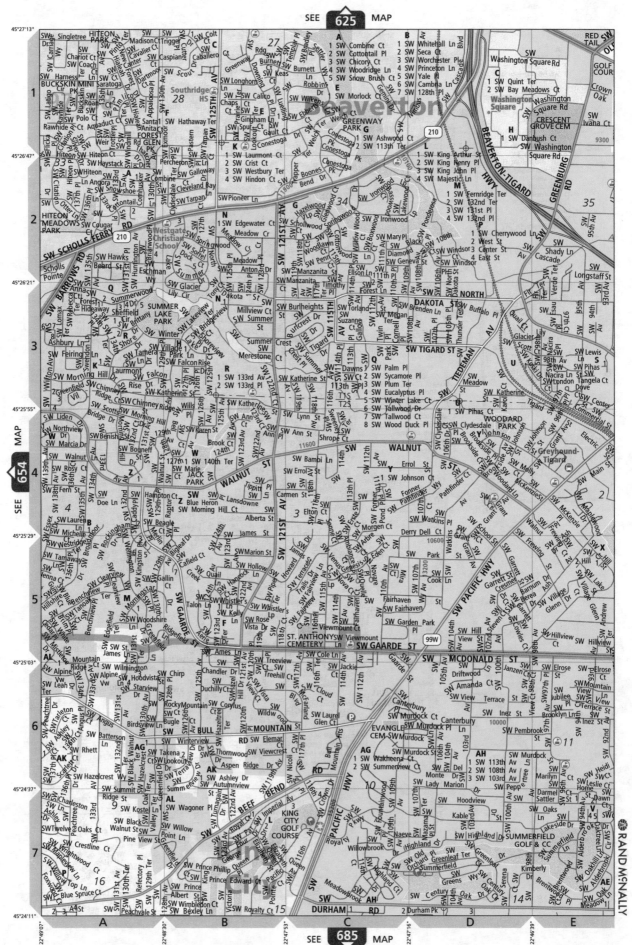

MAP
655

1:24,000
1 in. = 2000 ft.
0   0.25   0.5
miles

SEE 625 MAP

RAND McNALLY

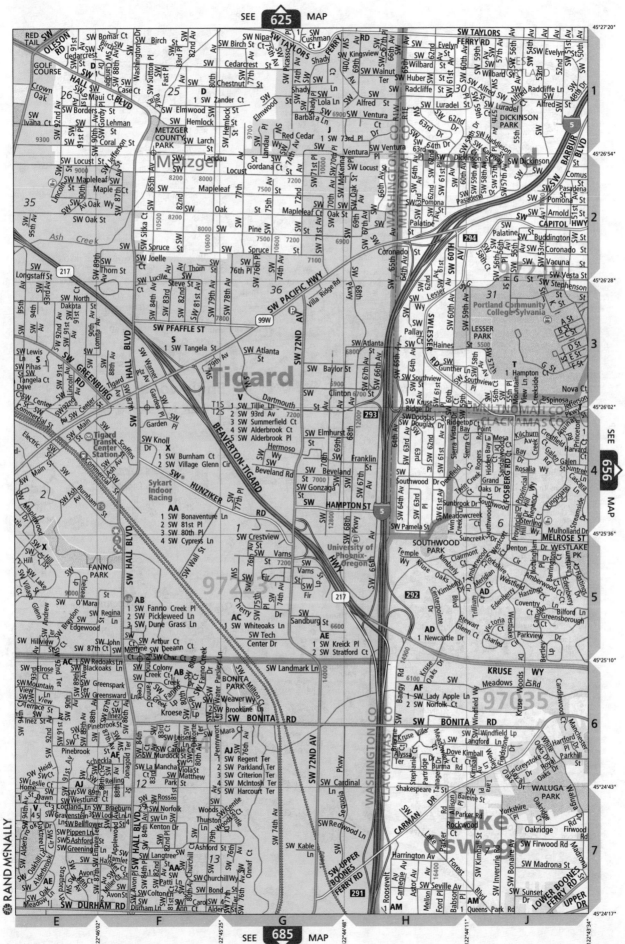

MAP
655

1:24,000
1 in. = 2000 ft.

0   0.25   0.5
miles

SEE 625 MAP

RAND MC NALLY

Metzger

Tigard

FANNO PARK

SW PFAFFLE ST

SW PACIFIC HWY

SW HALL BLVD

SW GREENBURG RD

BEAVERTON-TIGARD HWY

SW HUNZIKER RD

Portland Community College-Sylvania

LESSER PARK

University of Phoenix-Oregon

SOUTHWOOD PARK

MELROSE ST

KRUSE WY

SW BONITA RD

WALUGA PARK

Lake Oswego

SW DURHAM RD

SEE 656 MAP

MAP
656

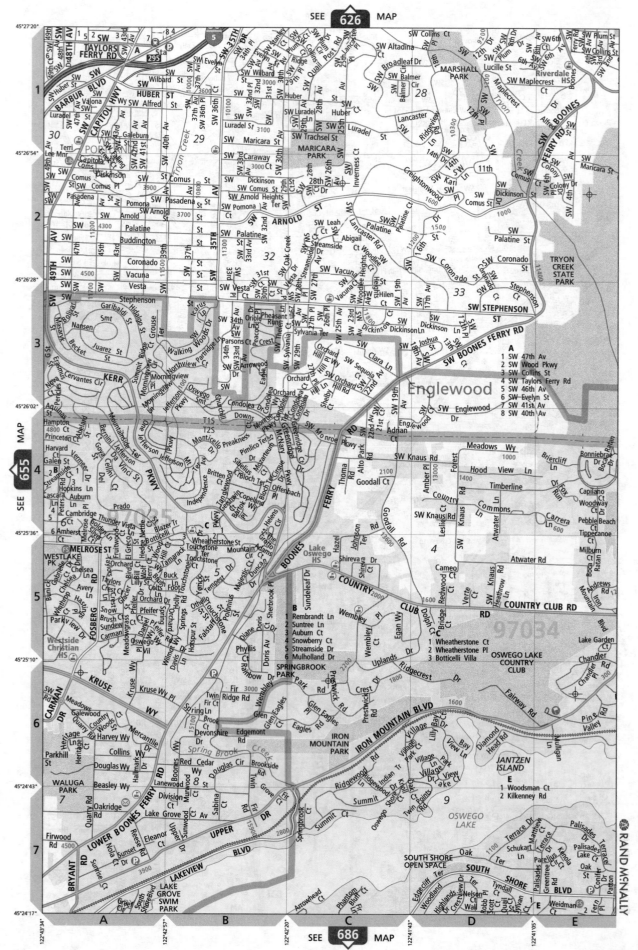

1:24,000
1 in. = 2000 ft.

0   0.25   0.5
miles

RAND McNALLY

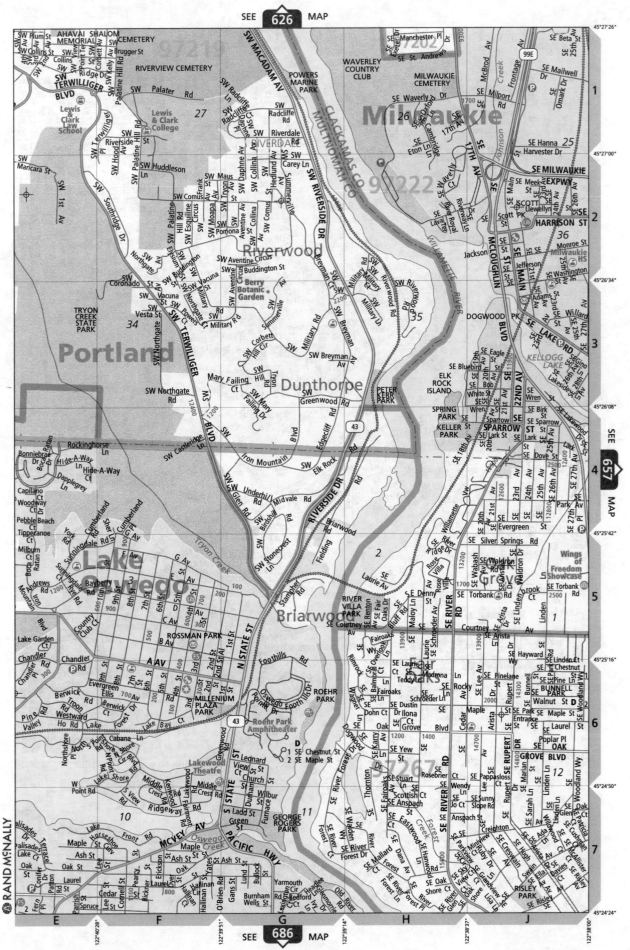

MAP
656

1:24,000
1 in. = 2000 ft.

0   0.25   0.5
miles

SEE 657 MAP

MAP
657

SEE 627 MAP

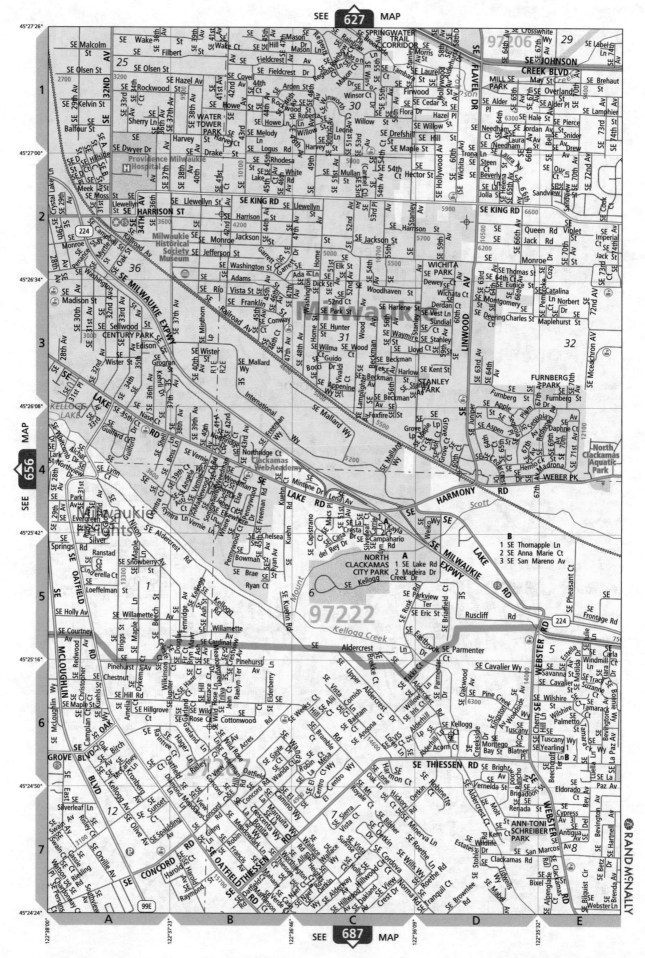

SEE 656 MAP

SEE 687 MAP

RAND MCNALLY

MAP
657

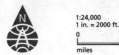

1:24,000
1 in. = 2000 ft.
0   0.25   0.5
miles

SEE 627 MAP

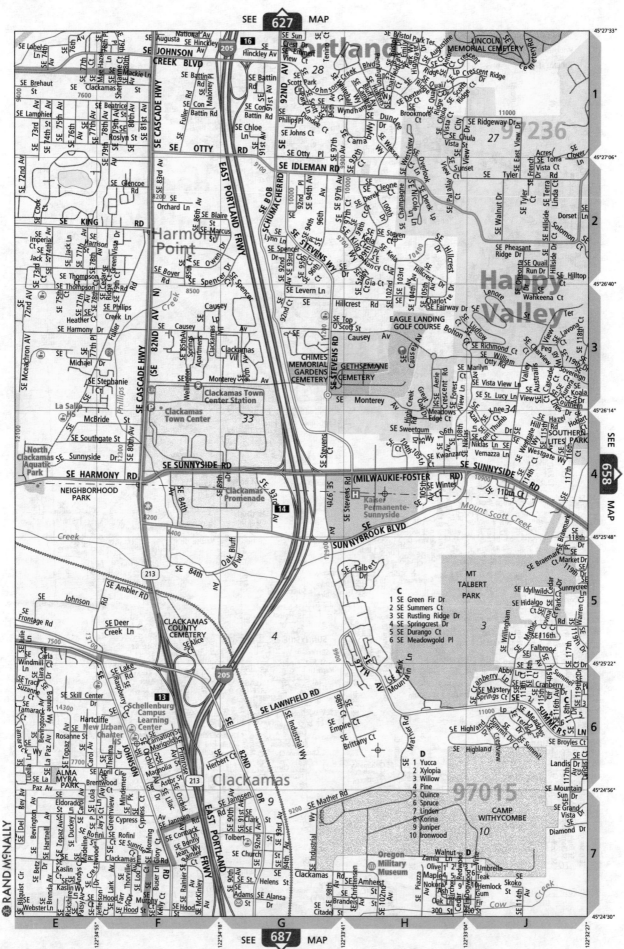

SEE 658 MAP

SEE 687 MAP

RAND MƆNALLY

MAP
658

1:24,000
1 in. = 2000 ft.

0   0.25   0.5
miles

SEE 628 MAP

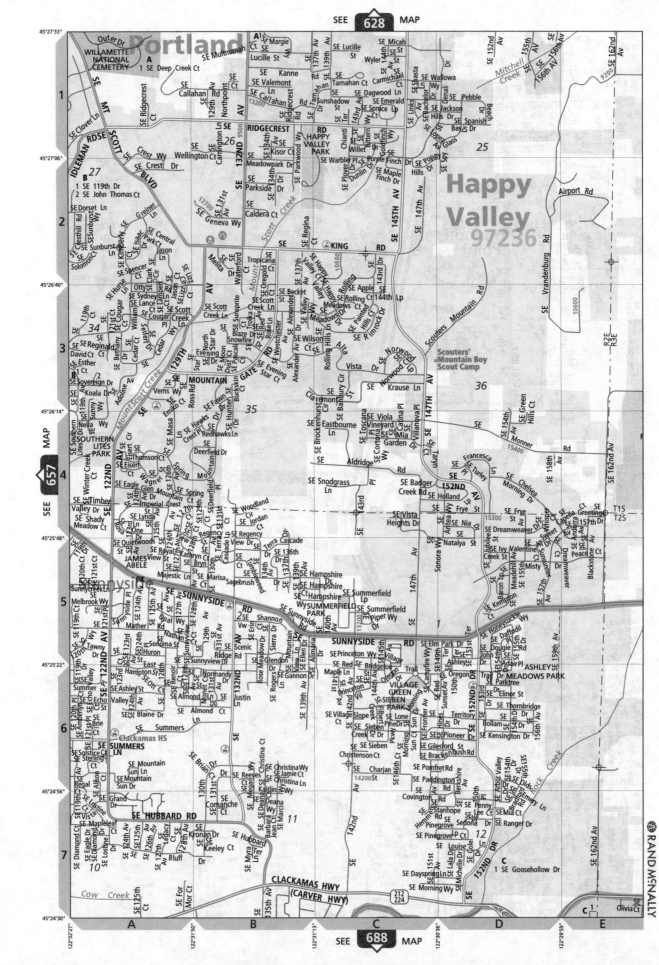

Portland

Happy Valley 97236

WILLAMETTE NATIONAL CEMETERY

HAPPY VALLEY PARK

Scouters' Mountain Boy Scout Camp

SOUTHERN LITES PARK

Sunnyside

MEADOWS PARK

ASHLEY

VILLAGE GREEN SIEBEN PARK

WYSUMMERFIELD PARK

JAMES ABELE

Clackamas HS

SE HUBBARD RD

SEE 657 MAP

CLACKAMAS HWY (CARVER HWY)
212 224

SEE 688 MAP

45°27'33"
45°27'06"
45°26'40"
45°26'14"
45°25'48"
45°25'22"
45°24'56"
45°24'30"

122°32'27"
122°31'50"
122°31'13"
122°30'36"
122°29'59"

A   B   C   D   E

RAND McNALLY

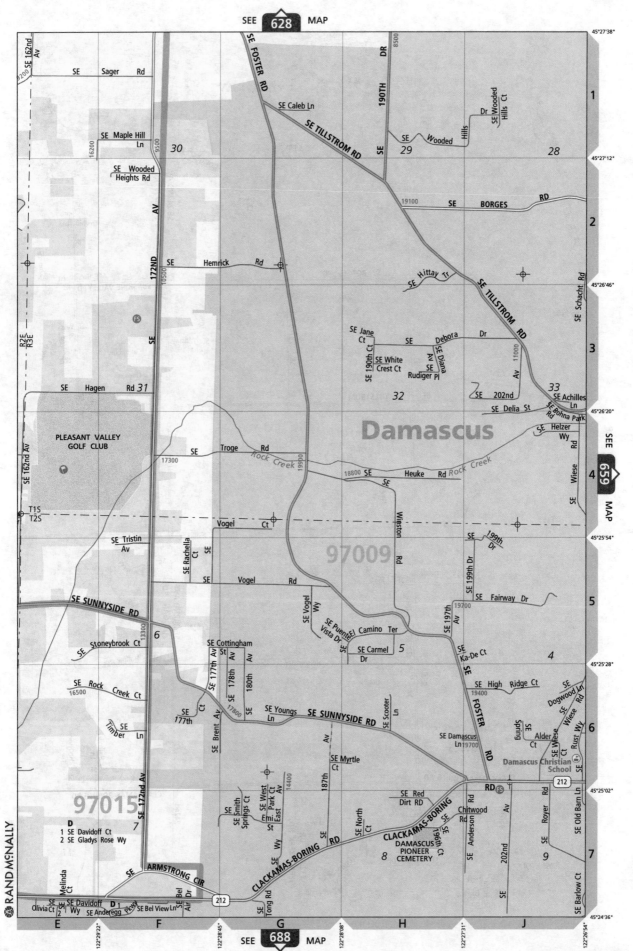

MAP
658

1:24,000
1 in. = 2000 ft.

0   0.25   0.5

miles

SEE 628 MAP

SE 162nd Av

9200

SE Sager Rd

SE Maple Hill Ln

16200

9500

SE 172ND AV

SE Wooded Heights Rd

SE FOSTER RD

SE Caleb Ln

SE TILLSTROM RD

SE 190TH DR

8500

30

SE 29 Wooded Hills

Dr

SE Wooded Hills Ct

28

1

SE BORGES RD

19100

2

10500

SE Hemrick Rd

R2E
R3E

FS

SE Hittay Tr

SE TILLSTROM RD

SE Schacht Rd

3

SE Jane Ct

SE White Crest Ct

SE 190th Ct

Debora Dr

SE Diana Av

Rudiger Pl

11000

SE 202nd

33

SE Achilles Ln

SE Hagen Rd 31

32

Damascus

SE Delia St

SE Bohna Park Rd

SE 162nd Av

PLEASANT VALLEY GOLF CLUB

SE Troge Rd

Rock Creek

17300

19900

18800 SE Heuke Rd Rock Creek

SE

SE Helzer Wy

Rd

4

T1S
T2S

Vogel Ct

Winston Rd

97009

SE 199th Dr

199th Dr

SE Wiese Rd

SEE 659 MAP

SE Tristin Av

SE Rachella Ct

SE

SE

Vogel Rd

SE 199th Dr

SE Fairway Dr

19700

5

SE SUNNYSIDE RD

13300

6

Stoneybrook Ct

SE

SE Cottingham St

SE Vogel Wy

SE Puente
El Vista Dr

El Camino Ter

SE Carmel Dr

5

SE 197th Av

SE Ka-De Ct

4

SE Rock Creek Ct

16500

SE 177th Av

SE 178th Av

180th

SE Youngs Ln

SE SUNNYSIDE RD

SE Scooter Ln

SE High Ridge Ct

19400

SE Dogwood Rd

SE Wiese Rd

SE

6

SE 177th Ct

17800

SE Brent Av

SE Timber Ln

SE Damascus Ln 19700

Buuds Ct

SE Wiese Ct

Alder Ct

Rust Wy

Damascus Christian School

FS

97015

7

D
1 SE Davidoff Ct
2 SE Gladys Rose Wy

SE West Park Ct

SE Smith Springs Ct

SE Emi East St

14400

187th Av

SE Myrtle Ct

SE North Ct

SE Red Dirt RD

CLACKAMAS-BORING RD

FS

212

45°25'02"

Chitwood Rd

SE Anderson Rd

190th Av

SE Royer Rd

SE Old Barn Ln

9

7

D 1

Melinda Ct

Olivia Ct

SE Davidoff Wy

2

SE Anderegg Pkwy

SE Bel View Ln

SE Bel Air Dr

ARMSTRONG CIR

212

SE Tong Rd

CLACKAMAS-BORING RD

DAMASCUS PIONEER CEMETERY

8

SE 202nd

SE Barlow Ct

SEE 688 MAP

RAND M?NALLY

E   F   G   H   J

45°27'38"
45°27'12"
45°26'46"
45°26'20"
45°25'54"
45°25'28"
45°25'02"
45°24'36"

122°29'22"   122°28'45"   122°28'08"   122°27'31"   122°26'54"

MAP
659

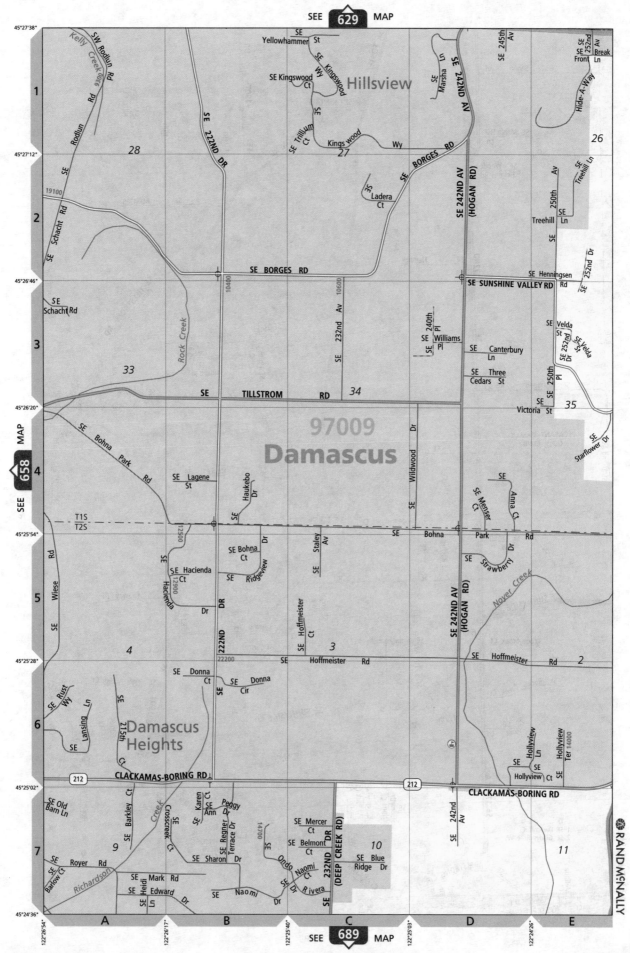

1:24,000
1 in. = 2000 ft.
0   0.25   0.5
miles

N

45°27'38"

SE Rodlun Rd
SW Rodlun Rd
Kelly Creek

SE 222ND DR

SE Yellowhammer St

SE Kingswood Wy
SE Kingswood Ct

SE Trillium Ct

Hillsview

Kings wood Wy

SE Marsha Ln

SE 242ND AV

SE 245th Av

SE 252nd Av
SE Front Ln
SE Break Ln

Hide-A-Way

1

26

45°27'12"

28

27

19100

SE Schacht Rd

SE Borges Rd

SE Ladera Ct

SE 242ND AV (HOGAN RD)

SE Treehill Ln

250th Av

SE Treehill Ln

2

45°26'46"

SE Schacht Rd

Rock Creek

10400

SE BORGES RD

10600

SE 232nd Av

SE Sunshine Valley Rd

SE Henningsen Rd

SE 252nd Dr

SE Velda St
SE 252nd Dr
SE Velda St

SE Williams Pl

SE 240th Pl

SE Canterbury Ln

SE Three Cedars St

SE 250th Pl

SE 250th Pl

Victoria St

3

33

34

35

45°26'20"

SE TILLSTROM RD

97009
Damascus

Wildwood Dr

Starflower Dr

MAP 658

SE Bohna Park Rd

SE Lagene St

SE Haukebo Dr

SE Menser Ct

SE Anna Ct

4

SEE

T1S
T2S

SE Bohna Park Rd

45°25'54"

12500

SE Bohna Ct

SE Ridgeview Dr

SE Staley Av

SE Strawberry Dr

Nover Creek

SE Wiese Rd

SE Hacienda Ct
SE Hacienda Dr

12900

SE 222ND DR

SE Hoffmeister Ct

SE 242ND AV (HOGAN RD)

5

4

22200

3

SE Hoffmeister Rd

SE Hoffmeister Rd

2

45°25'28"

SE Donna Ct

SE Donna Cir

45°25'02"

SE Rust Wy
SE Lansing Ln

Damascus
Heights

SE 215th Ct

6

SE 242nd Av

SE Hollyview Ter

SE Hollyview Ct

14000

212

CLACKAMAS-BORING RD

212

CLACKAMAS-BORING RD

SE Old Barn Ln

SE Barkley Ct

Crosscreek

SE Karen Ct
SE Ann Ct

SE Peggy Dr

SE Regner Terrace Dr

SE Mercer Ct

SE Belmont Ct

SE 232ND DR (DEEP CREEK RD)

SE Blue Ridge Dr

7

9

SE Royer Rd

SE Sharon Dr

SE Ondo Dr

SE Naomi Ct

10

11

SE Barlow Ct

SE Heidi Ln

SE Mark Rd

SE Edward Dr

SE Naomi Dr

SE Rivera Dr

Richardson Creek

RAND McNALLY

45°24'36"

A   B   C   D   E

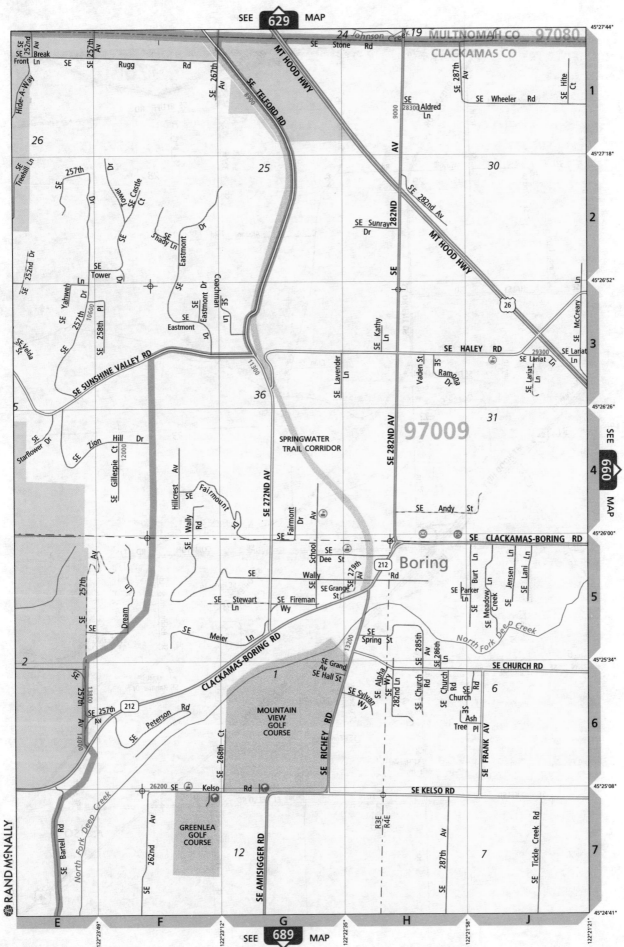

MAP
659

1:24,000
1 in. = 2000 ft.

0   0.25   0.5

miles

SEE 629 MAP

24 Johnson Creek 19   **MULTNOMAH CO** **97080**
SE Stone Rd   **CLACKAMAS CO**

SE SE 252nd
SE Break
Front Ln   SE   SE 257th Av   SE Rugg   Rd

Hide-A-Way

26

SE 267th Av

SE TELFORD RD

MT HOOD HWY

SE 287th Av   SE Hite Ct

SE Wheeler Rd

1

SE Treehill Ln

SE 257th

257th Dr

Tower Dr

SE Castle Ct

Dr   SE Shady Ln

Eastmont

Coachman

25

30

SE 28300 Aldred Ln

SE 282nd Av

SE Sunray Dr

MT HOOD HWY

2

SE 252nd Dr

SE Yahweh Dr

SE 257th Pl

10600

SE Tower Ln

SE 258th Dr

Eastmont

Eastmont Dr

SE 282ND AV

26

SE Velda St

SE SUNSHINE VALLEY RD

11300

SE Kathy Ln

SE Haley Rd

Vaden St

Ramona Dr

SE 29300 Lariat Ln

SE McCreary

SE Lariat Ln

SE Lariat Ln

3

SE Lavender Ln

SE 282ND AV

36

97009

31

45°26'26"

SE Starflower Dr

SE Zion Hill Dr

SE Gillespie Ct

12000

SPRINGWATER TRAIL CORRIDOR

SEE 660 MAP

4

Hillcrest Av

SE Fairmount Dr

SE 272ND AV

Fairmount Dr

Av

SE Andy St

SE CLACKAMAS-BORING RD

SE Wally Rd

SE Fairmont Dr

Boring

212

School St

SE Dee St

SE Wally Rd

SE 279th Rd

SE Grange Av

SE Burt Ln

SE Parker Ln

SE Meadow Ln

North Fork Deep Creek

SE Jensen Ln

SE Lani Ln

5

SE 257th Av

Dream Ln

SE

SE Stewart Ln

SE Fireman Wy

SE Meier Ln

CLACKAMAS-BORING RD

13200

SE Spring St

SE 285th Av

SE 286th Av

SE CHURCH RD

2

1

SE Grand Av

SE Hall St

SE Alpha Wy

SE Sylvan Wy

SE 282nd Ln

SE Church Rd

SE Church Rd

SE Church Rd

Church Pl

SE Church Rd

6

SE 257th Av

13800

257th

212

SE Peterson Rd

MOUNTAIN VIEW GOLF COURSE

SE RICHEY RD

SE Ash Tree Pl

SE FRANK AV

6

SE Bartell Rd

North Fork Deep Creek

26200 SE

Kelso Rd

SE 268th Ct

SE Kelso Rd

R3E R4E

GREENLEA GOLF COURSE

12

SE 262nd Av

SE AMISIGGER RD

7

SE 287th Av

SE Tickle Creek Rd

7

E   F   G   H   J

SEE 689 MAP

MAP
660

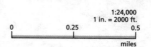

1:24,000
1 in. = 2000 ft.

0   0.25   0.5

miles

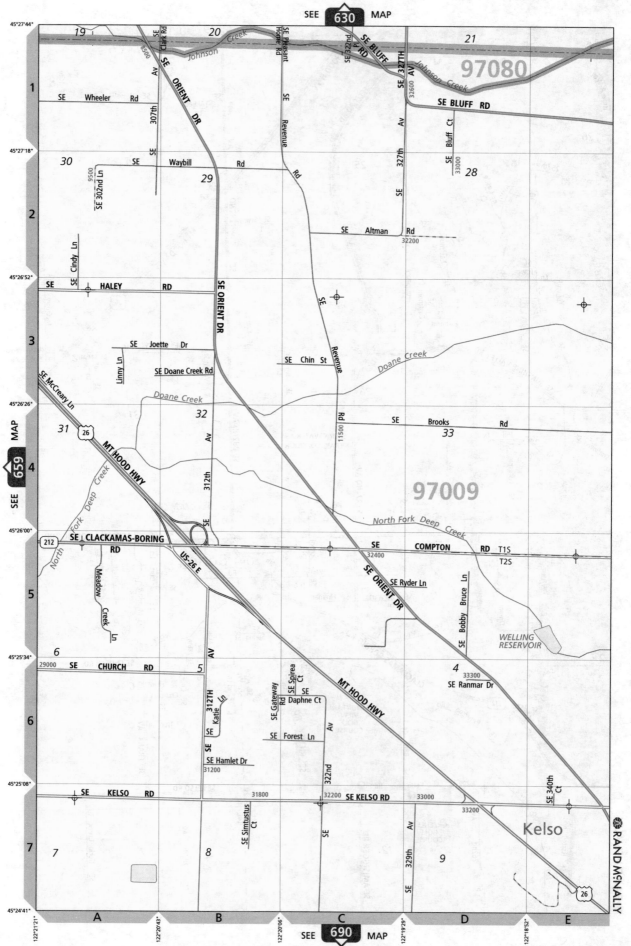

SEE 630 MAP

45°27'44"

19   20   21

97080

SE Clark Rd

Johnson Creek

SE Pleasant Home Rd

SE 322nd Pl

SE BLUFF RD

SE 327TH

Johnson Creek

32600 AV

1

SE Wheeler Rd

SE ORIENT DR

SE Revenue

SE 327th

SE Bluff Ct

SE BLUFF RD

SE 307th Av

8500

33000

45°27'18"

30   29   28

SE Waybill Rd

SE 302nd Ln

9500

2

SE Altman Rd

32200

SE Cindy Ln

45°26'52"

SE HALEY RD

SE Revenue

3

SE Joette Dr

SE Chin St

Doane Creek

Linny Ln

SE Doane Creek Rd

Revenue

SE McCreany Ln

Doane Creek

45°26'26"

32   33

SE Brooks Rd

11500 Rd

31

US 26

97009

SE 312th Av

MAP
659
SEE

MT HOOD HWY

North Fork Deep Creek

45°26'00"

North Fork Deep Creek

212

SE CLACKAMAS-BORING RD

SE COMPTON RD

T1S
T2S

32400

US-26 E

SE ORIENT DR

SE Ryder Ln

5

Meadow Creek Ln

SE Bobby Bruce Ln

WELLING RESERVOIR

45°25'34"

6   5   4

29000

SE CHURCH RD

SE Ranmar Dr

33300

312TH

AV

6

SE Spirea Ct

SE Gateway Rd

SE Daphne Ct

SE Katie Ln

SE 322nd Av

SE Forest Ln

MT HOOD HWY

SE Hamlet Dr

31200

45°25'08"

SE KELSO RD

31800   32200 SE KELSO RD   33000

SE 340th Ct

33200

SE Simtustus Ct

Kelso

7

7   8   9

SE 329th Av

SE 322nd

26

45°24'41"

A   B   C   D   E

122°21'21"   122°20'43"   122°20'06"   SEE 690 MAP   122°19'29"   122°18'52"

MAP
660

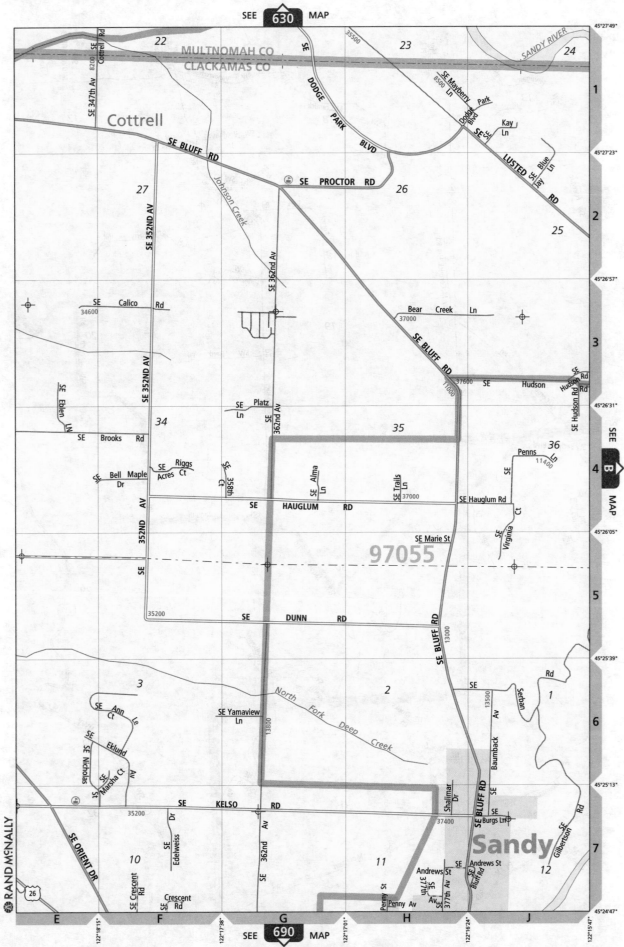

SEE 630 MAP

1:24,000
1 in. = 2000 ft.

0   0.25   0.5
miles

MULTNOMAH CO
CLACKAMAS CO

Cottrell

SE 347th Av
SE Cottrell Rd
8200

22

35500

23

SANDY RIVER

24

SE Mayberry Ln
8500

Dodge Park

DODGE PARK BLVD

Dodge Blvd

SE Kay Ln

SE LUSTED RD

SE Blue Jay Ln

SE BLUFF RD

Johnson Creek

SE PROCTOR RD

27

26

25

SE 352ND AV

SE 362nd Av

SE Calico Rd
34600

Bear Creek Ln
37000

SE BLUFF RD

SE Hudson Rd
37600   11000

SE Hudson Rd

SE Hudson Rd Rd

3

SE 352ND AV

SE Eblen LN

SE Platz Ln

34

SE 362nd Av

SE Brooks Rd

35

36

Penns Ln
11400

SEE B MAP

SE Riggs Ct
SE Acres

SE Bell Maple Dr

SE 358th Ct

SE Alma Ln

SE Trails Ln
37000

SE Virginia Ct

SE Hauglum Rd

4

SE 352ND AV

SE HAUGLUM RD

SE Marie St

97055

SE

35200

SE DUNN RD

SE BLUFF RD
13000

5

3

2

1

North Fork Deep Creek

SE Ann Ct

SE Yamaview Ln

13800

SE Serban Rd

SE Baumback Av
13500

6

SE Eklund

SE Nicholas

SE Marsha Ct

SE KELSO RD
35200

SE 362nd Av

Shalimar Dr

SE BLUFF RD
37400

SE Burgs Ln

SE Gilbertson Rd

Sandy

10

SE Dr

SE Edelweiss

SE Crescent Rd

Crescent Rd

11

Penny St
Penny Av

Andrews St

SE 377th Av

SE Andrews St

SE Bluff Rd

SE 377th Av

12

SE ORIENT DR

26

E   F   G   H   J

SEE 690 MAP

45°27'49"
45°27'23"
45°26'57"
45°26'31"
45°26'05"
45°25'39"
45°25'13"
45°24'47"

122°18'15"
122°17'38"
122°17'01"
122°16'24"
122°15'47"

MAP
683

1:24,000
1 in. = 2000 ft.
0   0.25   0.5
miles

N

SEE 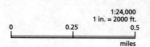 653 MAP

45°23'56"

SW Pinot Pl

SW Finnigan Hill Rd

13

SW

1

45°23'30"

SW Finnigan Hill Rd

SW Finnigan

Hill Rd

2

45°23'04"

SW McCormick Hill Rd

R3W
R2W

97123

24

3

McCormick Hill Rd

45°22'38"

SW

MAP

SW Bachelor Blvd

B

SEE

4

SW McCormick Rd Hill

45°22'12"

Shine Dr

25

45°21'46"

SW Weaver Dr

30

5

SW McCormick

18

SW Hill

SW Vanderschuere Rd
28300

SW McCormick

Rd

SW Wildhaven Ln

SW Bryanna Ct

Fernhollow Ln

SW Neugebauer

Park Rd

SW Forest

18300

SW Hideaway Ln

19

SW Herd Ln

Neugebauer Rd

Rd

Buckhaven Rd

SW Jaquith Rd

SW Jaquith Rd

SW Jaquith Rd

Mannsland Pl
Weiland Pl
SW

SW Lazy River Pl
SW MIDWAY RD
SW 247th Pl
27400

17

SW Strawberry Hill Dr

20

SW Jaquith Rd

29

219

6

45°21'20"

NE Brooks Ln

NE Ellis Ln
19500

NE Brooks

Ln

NE Mountain Top Rd

36

7

45°20'54"

NE BALD
NE Chehalem Dr

PEAK
RD
18000

NE

NE Jaquith Rd

31

NE Mountain Top Rd

YAMHILL CO
WASHINGTON CO

SW Wildflower Dr

SW HILLSBORO HWY

219

32

123°00'05"   A   122°59'28"   B   122°58'51"   C   122°58'14"   D   122°57'37"   E

RAND McNALLY

MAP
683

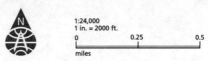

1:24,000
1 in. = 2000 ft.

0   0.25   0.5
miles

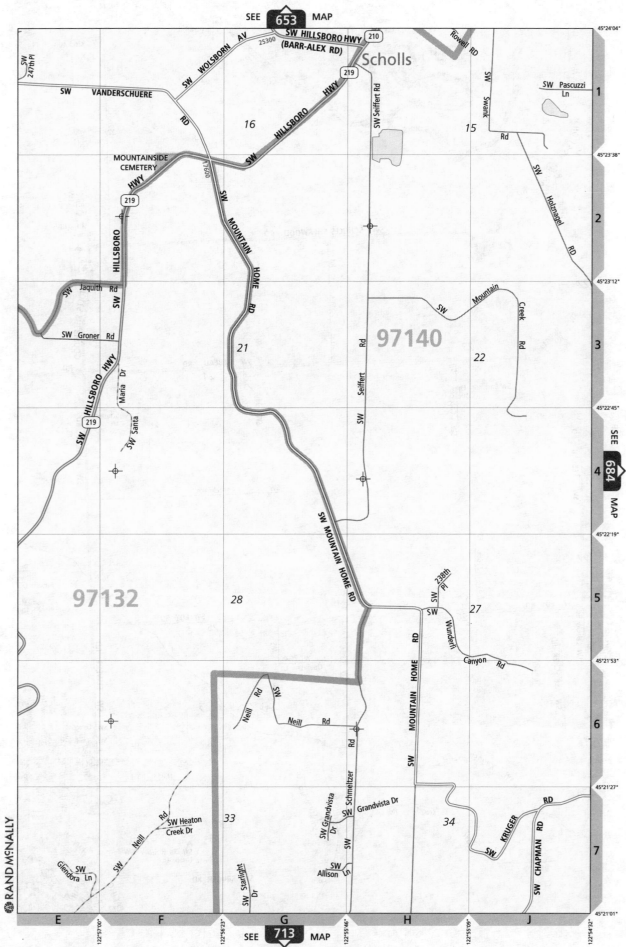

SEE **653** MAP

SW Hillsboro Hwy
(BARR-ALEX RD)
25300
210

SW WOLSBORN AV

SW 247th Pl

SW VANDERSCHUERE

SW HILLSBORO HWY

219

Scholls

SW Seiffert Rd

Rowell RD

SW Swank Rd

SW Pascuzzi Ln

1

16

15

MOUNTAINSIDE CEMETERY

HWY

219

17600

SW MOUNTAIN HOME RD

45°23'38"

SW Holznagel RD

2

SW Hillsboro

SW Jaquith Rd

SW Groner Rd

219

Maria Dr

SW Santa

45°23'12"

97140

SW Mountain Creek Rd

SW Seiffert Rd

21

3

22

45°22'45"

SEE **684** MAP

SW HILLSBORO HWY

4

45°22'19"

SW MOUNTAIN HOME RD

97132

28

SW 238th Pl

SW Wunderli Canyon Rd

27

5

45°21'53"

SW MOUNTAIN HOME RD

Neill Rd

SW

Neill Rd

SW Schmeltzer Rd

6

45°21'27"

SW Neill Rd

SW Heaton Creek Dr

33

SW Grandvista Dr

SW Grandvista Dr

SW Schmeltzer Rd

KRUGER RD

34

SW CHAPMAN RD

SW Glendora Ln

SW

SW Starlight Dr

SW Allison Ln

7

45°21'01"

E   F   G   H   J

122°57'00"   122°56'23"   122°55'46"   122°55'09"   122°54'32"

SEE **713** MAP

45°24'04"

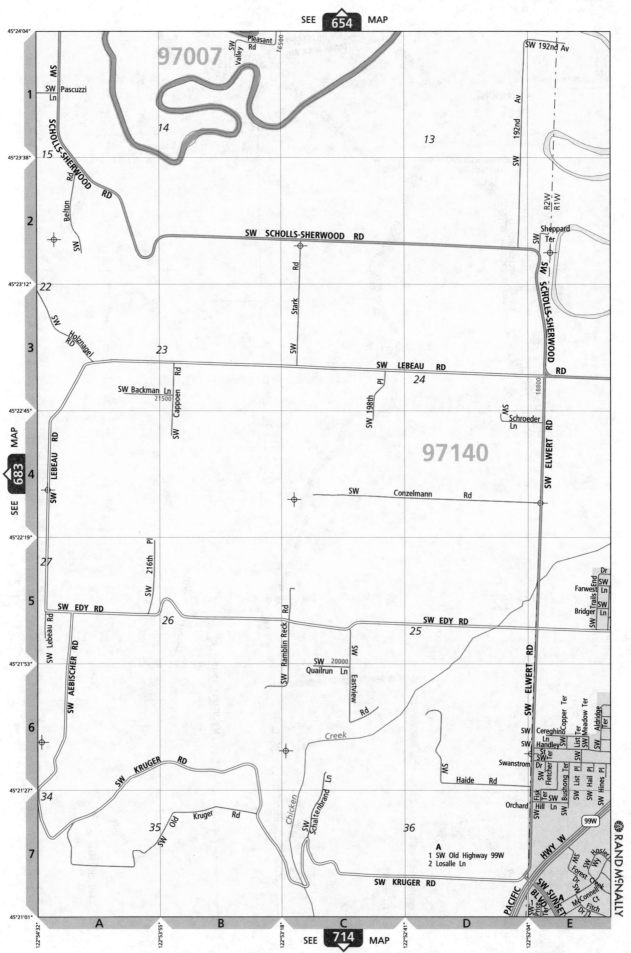

MAP
684

1:24,000
1 in. = 2000 ft.

0   0.25   0.5
miles

SEE 654 MAP

SEE 683 MAP

SEE 714 MAP

RAND M℃NALLY

97007

97140

SW Pascuzzi Ln

SW 192nd Av

SW 192nd Av

SW Valley Pleasant Rd

14

13

SCHOLLS-SHERWOOD RD

Belton

SW SCHOLLS-SHERWOOD RD

SW

15

R2W
R1W

Sheppard Ter

SW SCHOLLS-SHERWOOD

Stark Rd

22

SW Holznagel Rd

23

SW LEBEAU RD

24

SW Backman Ln
21500

SW Cappoen Rd

SW 198th Pl

Schroeder Ln

SW LEBEAU RD

SW ELWERT RD

27

SW 216th Pl

SW Conzelmann Rd

Farwest End Dr
SW Ln
SW Trails End
Bridger SW Ln

SW EDY RD

26

SW EDY RD

25

SW Lebeau Rd

SW AEBISCHER RD

SW Ramblin Reck Rd

SW 20000
Quailrun Ln

SW Eastview Rd

SW Cereghino Ln
SW Handley Ter
SW Copper Ter
SW List Ter
SW Meadow Ter
SW Aldridge Ter

Creek

Swanstrom Dr

SW Fletcher
SW Bushong Ter
SW Hail Pl
SW Hines Pl

SW KRUGER RD

Haide Rd

SW Fisk Ter
SW List Pl

Orchard Hill
SW Price Ter

34

35

SW Old Kruger Rd

SW Schaltenbrand Ln

Chicken

36

A
1 SW Old Highway 99W
2 Losalle Ln

99W

Hosler

Forest Creek Dr

SW McConnell Ct
Fitch Dr

PACIFIC HWY W

SW SUNSET BLVD

SW KRUGER RD

MAP
684

1:24,000
1 in. = 2000 ft.

0   0.25   0.5

miles

SEE  654 MAP

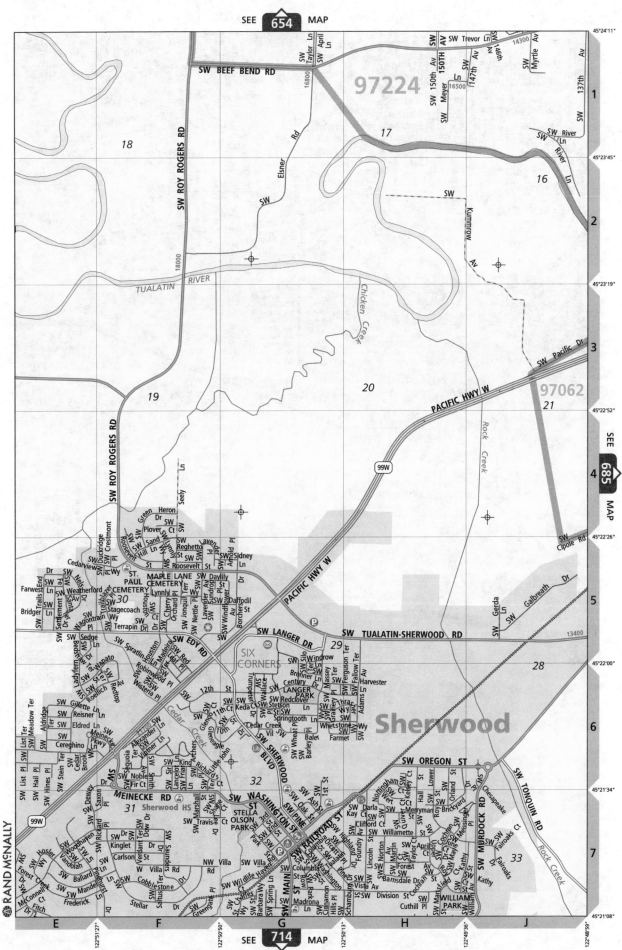

SW Trevor Ln

SW BEEF BEND RD

SW ROY ROGERS RD

97224

18

17

16

SW River Ln

River Ln

SW

Kummrow Av

TUALATIN RIVER

Chicken Creek

SW Pacific Dr

3

20

97062

PACIFIC HWY W

19

21

99W

Rock Creek

SEE
685
MAP

4

SW Cipole Rd

45°24'11"

1

45°23'45"

45°23'19"

2

45°22'52"

45°22'26"

SW ROY ROGERS RD

Seely Ln

Heron Dr
Green Dr
SW Plover Ct
SW Crestmont
SW Duckridge
Roosevelt Hill Ln
Sand Ct
Reghetto
Lavender Pl
SW Roosevelt St
Arnold
Sidney Ln

Gerda Dr
SW Galbreath Dr

5

Cedarview
Farwest Ln
Trails End
Bridger
Weatherford Dr
Nelson Dr
SW Settlement Dr
Stagecoach
Nagontrain Dr
Terrapin Dr

ST. PAUL CEMETERY
MAPLE LANE CEMETERY
30
Lynnly
Cherry Orchard
Jonquil Terr
Nettle
Windfield
Borcher St
Daffodil
Dayliily
Sundrop

SW Sedge
Ladyfern Aspen
SW Wapato
Roellich Av
Reltop Av

SW EDY RD
Spratlin Ln
Houston
Madera
Red
Robinwood Pl
Wisteria Pl

SW LANGER DR
SIX CORNERS
29
Silo
Windrow
Branner Ter
Massey
Ferguson Ter
Fallow Ter

SW TUALATIN-SHERWOOD RD

13400

28

6

SW Gillette Ln
SW Reisner Ln
SW Eldred Ln
Aldridge
Cereghino

Cedar Creek

12th
St
Keda Ct
11th St
70th
Glenn
Glenn Ct
Glaneagle
Cedar Creek Vil

Century Pl
LANGER PARK
Redclover
Stetson
Springtooth Ln
Whetstone
Barley
Balet
Farmer

Granery Pl
Adams Av
Harvester

Sherwood

SW List Ter
SW List Pl
Meadow Ter
SW Hall Pl
SW Hines Pl

Sequoia
Cedar Brook
Vintner Ln
King Richards
SW Noble Ln
Alexander
Archers
Lancelot
SW Friar
Smith
Little John

SW Wheat St
SW Barley

SW OREGON ST

SW TONQUIN RD
SW MURDOCK RD

45°22'00"

45°21'34"

7

99W

MEINECKE RD
31
Sherwood HS
STELLA OLSON PARK

Saxon
Dewey Ct
Meinecke Pkwy
Stein Ter

32

SW WASHINGTON ST

SW Oak St
SW Ash St

SW Pine St
SW Main St
SW RAILROAD ST

Nottingham
Kelkay
Hall
Lower
Orland
Brickyard
Cheapeake
Fairoaks Ct
Fairoaks

33

WILLIAM PARK

Rock Creek

Hosler
Woodhaven
Vandolah
Ballard
Mandel
Frederick
Fitch
McConnell Ct
Forest Creek Ter

Rickard
Kinglet
Carlson
Verdant Ter
Dow Dr
W Villa Rd
NW Villa
SW Villa Rd
Cobblestone Dr
Stellar Dr
Saltus Dr
Greengate Pl
Wildlife Haven Rd

SW Travis Ct
Marshall
Change
Park
2nd
3rd
Columbia
Pine Dr
Highland Dr
Willamette
Lincoln
Norton
Forest
Barnsdale Dr
Division St
Cuthill Pl
Willow
Kathy
Messinger
April
Cochran
Maple
Kathy

Darla
Kay Ct
Clifford Ct
Merryman
Taylor Ct
Vista Av
Schamburg

45°21'08"

E   F   G   H   J

122°51'27"   122°50'50"   122°50'13"   122°49'36"   122°48'59"

SEE 714 MAP

MAP
685

1:24,000
1 in. = 2000 ft.
0   0.25   0.5
miles

SEE 655 MAP

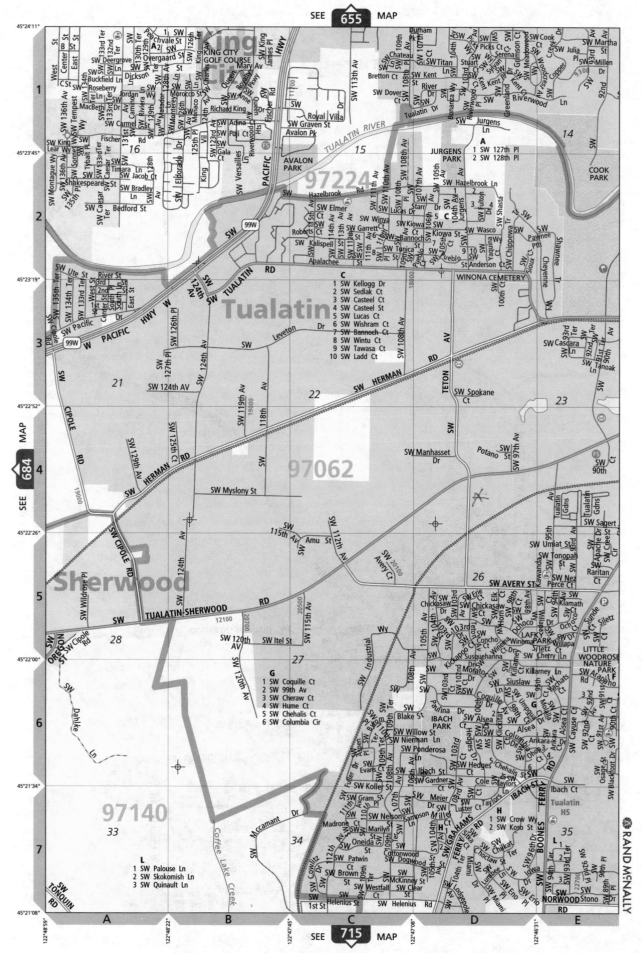

King City

KING CITY GOLF COURSE

AVALON PARK

97224

Tualatin

TUALATIN RIVER

JURGENS PARK

COOK PARK

WINONA CEMETERY

C
1 SW Kellogg Dr
2 SW Sedlak Ct
3 SW Casteel Ct
4 SW Casteel St
5 SW Lucas Ct
6 SW Wishram Ct
7 SW Bannoch Ct
8 SW Wintu Ct
9 SW Tawasa Ct
10 SW Ladd Ct

SW HERMAN RD

SW Spokane Ct

SW Manhasset Dr

97062

SW Myslony St

SW CIPOLE RD

Sherwood

TUALATIN-SHERWOOD RD

G
1 SW Coquille Ct
2 SW 99th Av
3 SW Cheraw Ct
4 SW Hume Ct
5 SW Chehalis Ct
6 SW Columbia Cir

IBACH PARK

LAFKY PARK

LITTLE WOODROSE NATURE PARK

Tualatin HS

97140

33

L
1 SW Palouse Ln
2 SW Skokomish Ln
3 SW Quinault Ln

SW TONQUIN RD

Coffee Lake Creek

H
1 SW Crow Wy
2 SW Koso St

NORWOOD RD

SEE 715 MAP

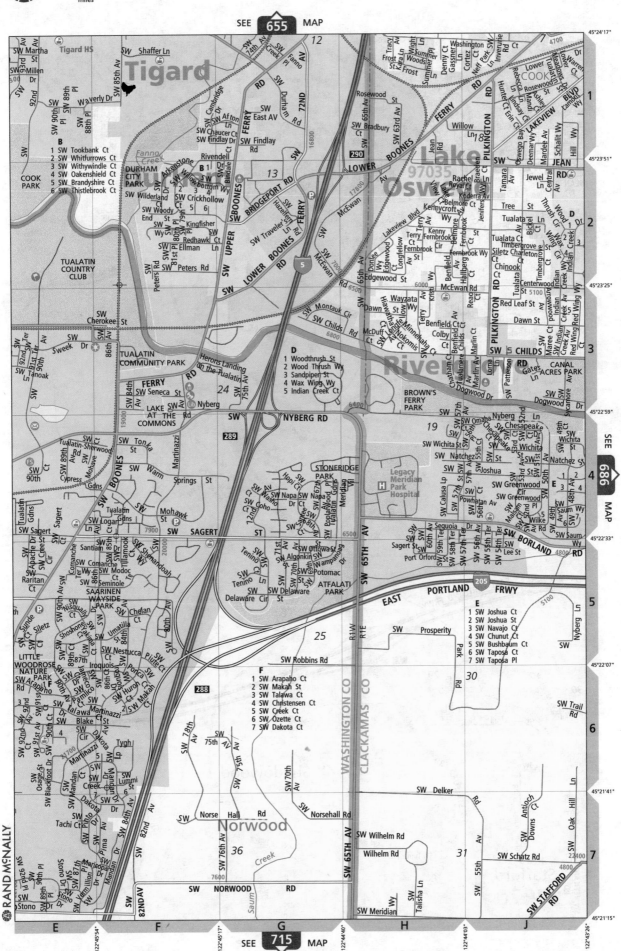

MAP
685

1:24,000
1 in. = 2000 ft.
0   0.25   0.5
miles

SEE 655 MAP

45°24'17"
45°23'51"
45°23'25"
45°22'59"
45°22'33"
45°22'07"
45°21'41"
45°21'15"

Tigard
Tigard HS
SW Shaffer Ln
SW 85th Av
SW Martha
SW 93rd Av
SW Millen Dr
SW 92nd
SW 90th Pl
SW 89th
SW 88th Ct
SW Waverly Dr

COOK

Lake Oswego
97035

Riverdale

COOK

B
1 SW Tookbank Ct
2 SW Whitfurrows Ct
3 SW Withywindle Ct
4 SW Oakenshield Ct
5 SW Brandyshire Ct
6 SW Thistlebrook Ct

COOK
PARK

DURHAM
CITY
PARK

TUALATIN
COUNTRY
CLUB

TUALATIN
COMMUNITY PARK

FERRY

LAKE
AT THE
COMMONS

D
1 Woodthrush St
2 Wood Thrush Wy
3 Sandpiper St
4 Wax Wing Wy
5 Indian Creek Ct

BROWN'S
FERRY
PARK

CANAL
ACRES PARK

Legacy
Meridian
Park
Hospital

STONERIDGE
PARK

SW SAGERT ST

SAARINEN
WAYSIDE
PARK

ATFALATI
PARK

EAST PORTLAND FRWY

E
1 SW Joshua Ct
2 SW Joshua St
3 SW Navajo Ct
4 SW Chunut Ct
5 SW Bushbaum Ct
6 SW Taposa Ct
7 SW Taposa Pl

F
1 SW Arapaho Ct
2 SW Makah St
3 SW Talawa St
4 SW Christensen Ct
5 SW Creek Ct
6 SW Ozette Ct
7 SW Dakota Ct

LITTLE
WOODROSE
NATURE
PARK

SW Robbins Rd

WASHINGTON CO
CLACKAMAS CO

Norwood

SW Norsehall Rd
Norse Hall Rd

SW Wilhelm Rd
Wilhelm Rd

SW Delker

SW NORWOOD RD

SW Schatz Rd

SW STAFFORD RD

SW Meridian

SEE 686 MAP

SEE 715 MAP

E   F   G   H   J

122°45'54"   122°45'17"   122°44'40"   122°44'03"   122°43'26"

MAP
686

1:24,000
1 in. = 2000 ft.

0   0.25   0.5
miles

N

SEE 656 MAP

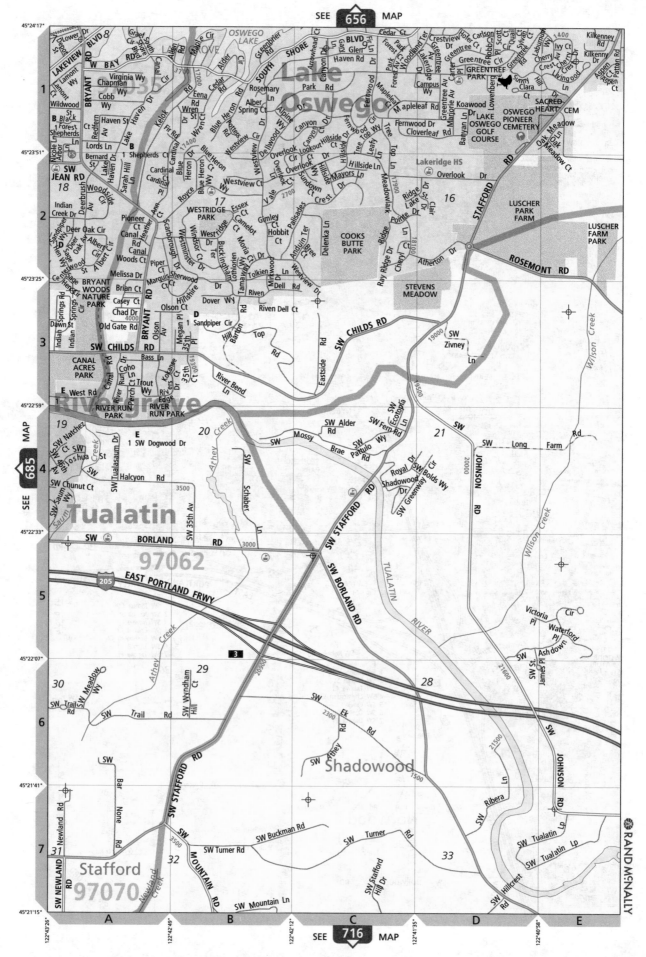

Lake Oswego

OSWEGO LAKE

SOUTH SHORE BLVD

GREENTREE PARK

OSWEGO PIONEER CEMETERY

SACRED HEART CEM

LAKE OSWEGO GOLF COURSE

Lakeridge HS

STAFFORD RD

LUSCHER PARK FARM

LUSCHER FARM PARK

ROSEMONT RD

COOKS BUTTE PARK

STEVENS MEADOW

SW CHILDS RD

WESTRIDGE PARK

BRYANT WOODS NATURE PARK

SW CHILDS RD

CANAL ACRES PARK

SW ZIVNEY LN

JOHNSON RD

Wilson Creek

RIVER RUN PARK

Rivergrove

SEE 685 MAP

Tualatin

97062

SW BORLAND RD

SW STAFFORD RD

SW BORLAND RD

TUALATIN RIVER

205 EAST PORTLAND FRWY

Wilson Creek

Victoria Pl

Waterford Pl

Ashdown

SW St James Pl

Athey Creek

Shadowood

SW JOHNSON RD

SW Ribera

SW Tualatin

SW Tualatin Lp

Stafford
97070

SW NEWLAND RD

SW MOUNTAIN RD

SW Turner Rd

SW Buckman Rd

SW Turner Rd

SW Mountain Ln

SW Hillcrest Rd

Newland Creek

SEE 716 MAP

RAND McNALLY

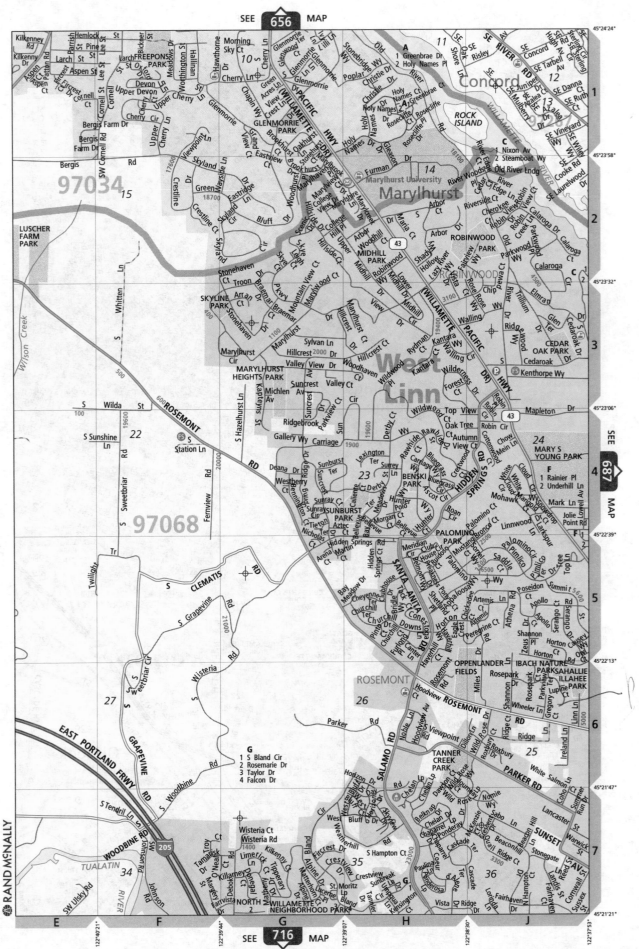

MAP
686

1:24,000
1 in. = 2000 ft.

0   0.25   0.5
miles

45°24'24"

Concord

97222

ROCK ISLAND

1

97034
15

LUSCHER
FARM
PARK

45°23'58"

Marylhurst University

Marylhurst

2

45°23'32"

ROBINWOOD
PARK

SKYLINE
PARK

West
Linn

3

CEDAR
OAK PARK

45°23'06"

MARYLHURST
HEIGHTS PARK

Kenthorpe Wy

SEE 687 MAP

24
MARY S
YOUNG PARK

ROSEMONT RD

97068

BENSKI
PARK

4

45°22'39"

22

23

SUNBURST
PARK

PALOMINO
PARK

45°22'13"

CLEMATIS RD

OPPENLANDER
FIELDS

IBACH NATURE
PARK SAHALLIE
ILLAHEE
PARK

ROSEMONT

26

ROSEMONT RD

5

45°22'13"

27

Parker Rd

TANNER
CREEK
PARK

25

PARKER RD

6

45°21'47"

G
1 S Bland Cir
2 Rosemarie Dr
3 Taylor Dr
4 Falcon Dr

EAST PORTLAND FRWY

GRAPEVINE RD

WOODBINE RD

205

SUNSET AV

TUALATIN
34

NORTH
2
WILLAMETTE
NEIGHBORHOOD PARK

35

36

7

45°21'21"

E   F   G   H   J

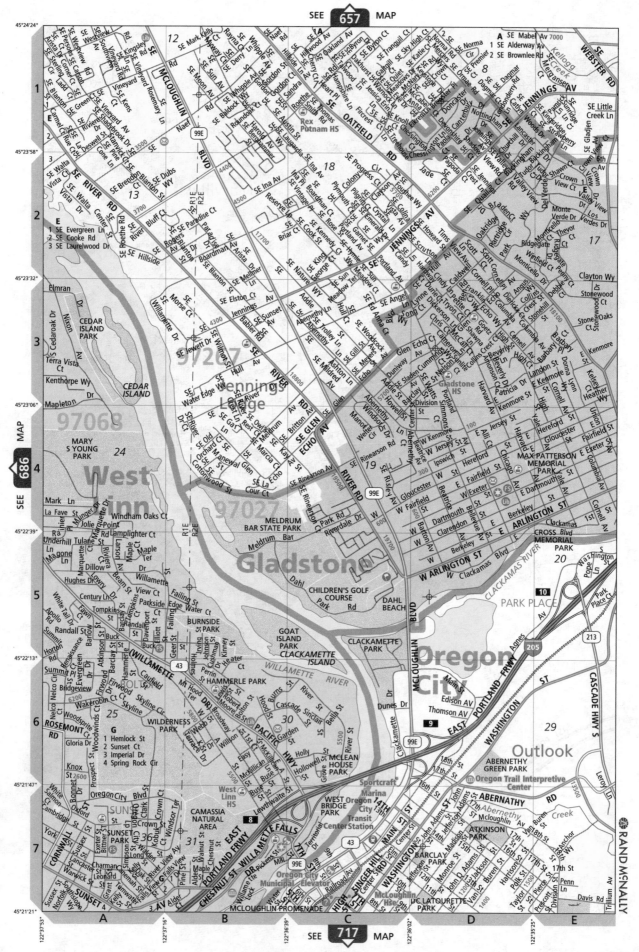

MAP
687

1:24,000
1 in. = 2000 ft.
0   0.25   0.5
miles

SEE [657] MAP

MAP [686] SEE

SEE [717] MAP

RAND M�C NALLY

West Linn

Gladstone

Oregon City

Outlook

Park Place

97267

97068

97027

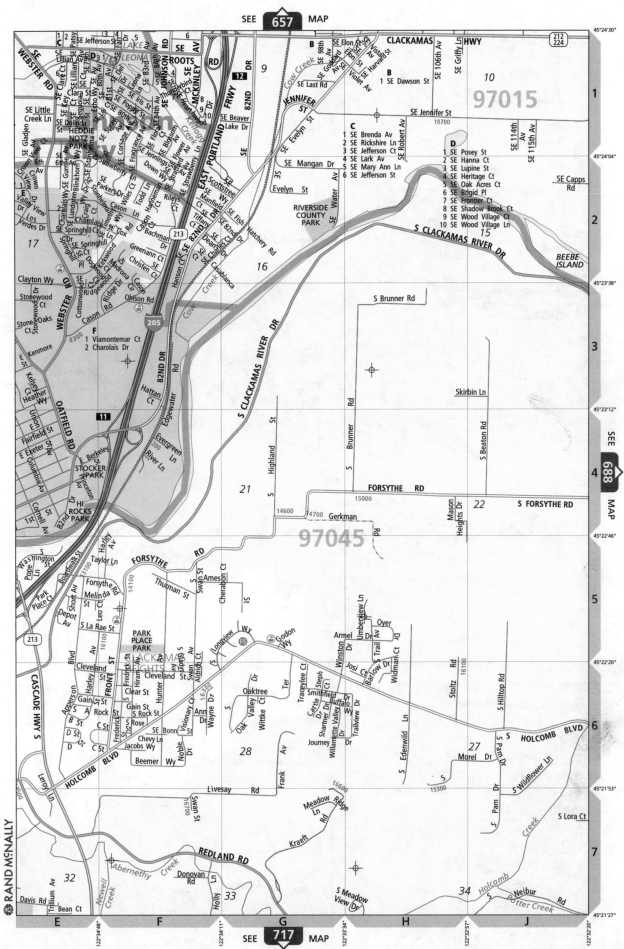

MAP
687

1:24,000
1 in. = 2000 ft.
0   0.25   0.5
miles

SEE **657** MAP

97015

97045

SEE **688** MAP

RIVERSIDE
COUNTY
PARK

BEEBE
ISLAND

PARK
PLACE
PARK

STOCKER
PARK

HI
ROCKS
PARK

HEDDIE
NOTZ
PARK

C
1 SE Brenda Av
2 SE Rickshire Ln
3 SE Jefferson Ct
4 SE Lark Av
5 SE Mary Ann Ln
6 SE Jefferson St

D
1 SE Posey St
2 SE Hanna Ct
3 SE Lupine St
4 SE Heritage Ct
5 SE Oak Acres Ct
6 SE Brigid Pl
7 SE Frontier Ct
8 SE Shadow Brook Ct
9 SE Wood Village Ct
10 SE Wood Village Ln

F
1 Viamontemar Ct
2 Charolais Dr

SEE **717** MAP

45°24'30"
45°24'04"
45°23'38"
45°23'12"
45°22'46"
45°22'20"
45°21'53"
45°21'27"

122°34'48"
122°34'11"
122°33'34"
122°32'57"
122°32'20"

E F G H J
1 2 3 4 5 6 7

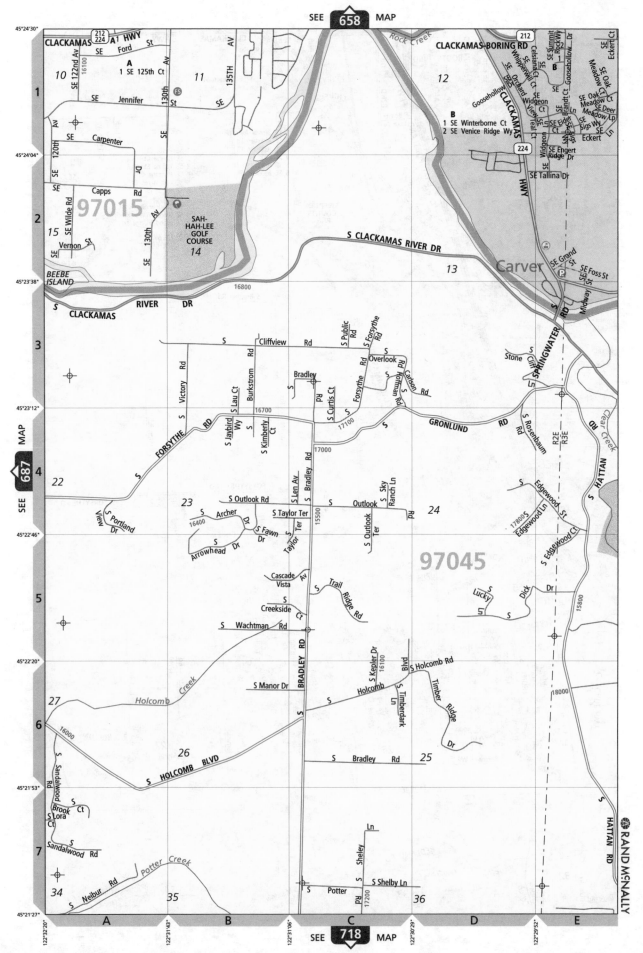

MAP
688

SEE 658 MAP

45°24'30"

CLACKAMAS A¹ HWY
212 224
SE Ford St
A
1 SE 125th Ct

10 SE 122nd Av 16100

SE 130th St F5

1   SE Jennifer

135TH AV

11

SE

CLACKAMAS-BORING RD 212

Celsiana Ct
SE Whipparwil Ct
SE Orchard View Ln Goosehollow Dr
Summit Rock Wy
Eckert Ct SE
SE Oak Meadow Wy Goosehollow
B
SE Oak Meadow Ct
SE Deer Meadow Ln
Widgeon Ct

12

B
SE Winterborne Ct
SE Venice Ridge Wy

SE Eider Ct SE Sigs Wy SE Ln
SE Teal Ct Widgeon Eckert

SE Engert Ridge Dr

224

45°24'04"

SE Carpenter Dr
120th
Av
SE 120th

SE Capps Rd

SE Wilde Rd

97015

15 SE 130th Av

SE Vernon St

SE Tallina Dr

CLACKAMAS HWY

2

SAH-HAH-LEE GOLF COURSE
14

S CLACKAMAS RIVER DR

13

Carver

SE Grand St
SE Foss St
SE Water St
Midway

45°23'38"

BEEBE ISLAND

S CLACKAMAS RIVER DR

16800

S SPRINGWATER RD

3

S Victory Rd
Cliffview Rd
S Public Rd
S Forsythe Rd

S Burkstrom Rd
Bradley
S Lau Ct
S Curtis Ct
Pl

Overlook Rd
Forsythe Rd
Hoffman Rd
Carlson Rd

Stone
S Cliff Ln
SPRINGWATER

Clear Creek

45°23'12"

16700

S Jaybird Wy
S Kimberly Ct
17100

GRONLUND RD
S Rosenbaum Rd

R2E R3E

4 FORSYTHE RD

17000

S Bradley Rd

S Len Av

22

S Outlook Rd
23
S Archer Dr
16400
S Fawn Dr
S Taylor Ter
15500
S Taylor Ter

Outlook Rd
Sky Ranch Ln

24

S Edgewood Ln
17800 S Edgewood St
S Edgewood Ct

HATTAN RD

45°22'46"

S View Dr S Portland Dr

S Arrowhead Dr

Cascade Vista Av

S Outlook Ter

97045

5

S Trail Ridge Rd

Lucky
S Dick Dr
15800

Creekside Ct

S Wachtman Rd

45°22'20"

BRADLEY RD

Holcomb Creek

S Manor Dr

S Kepler Dr
16100
Holcomb
S Holcomb Rd
S Timberdark Ln
Timber Ridge Dr

18000

6 16000

27

26

HOLCOMB BLVD

S Bradley Rd
25

45°21'53"

S Sandalwood Rd
Brook Ct
S Lora Ct

7 S Sandalwood Rd

Potter Creek

Ln
S Sheley Pl

S Shelby Ln

HATTAN RD

RAND MCNALLY

45°21'27"

34 S Neibur Rd
35
S Potter Pl 17200
36

A   B   C   D   E

SEE 718 MAP

122°33'20" 122°31'43" 122°31'06" 122°30'29" 122°29'52"

1:24,000
1 in. = 2000 ft.

0   0.25   0.5
miles

MAP
688

SEE 658 MAP

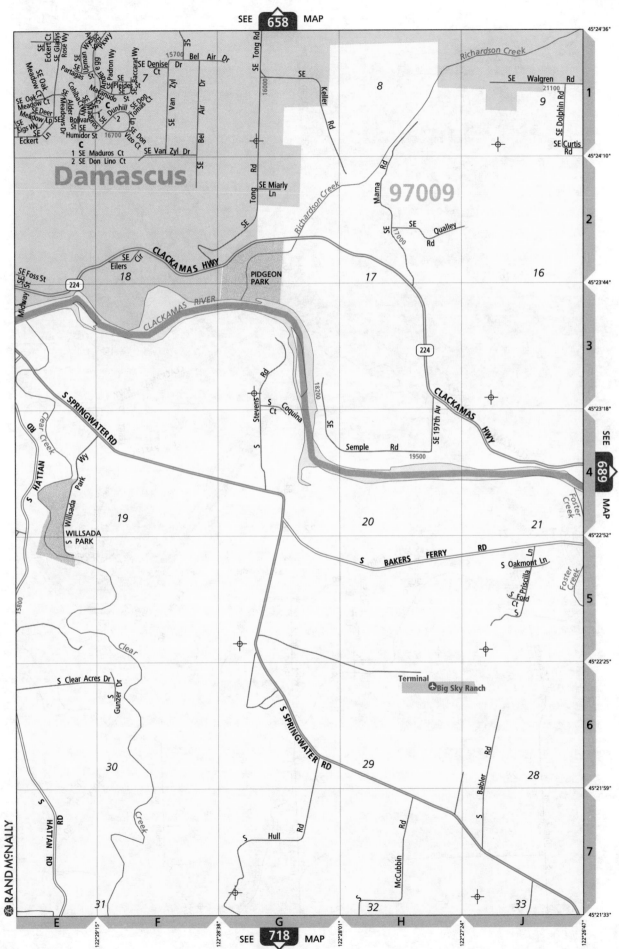

45°24'36"

Richardson Creek

SE Walgren Rd
21100
SE Dolphin Rd

8

9

1

SE Curtis Rd

45°24'10"

SE Tong Rd

SE

Keller Rd

Marna Rd

97009

SE Qualley Rd
17000

2

SE Miarly Ln

Richardson Creek

SE Eilers Cir

CLACKAMAS HWY

PIDGEON PARK

17

16

45°23'44"

SE Foss St

224

18

CLACKAMAS RIVER

224

3

Midway

Stevens Rd

S Coquina Ct

18200

SE

CLACKAMAS HWY

SE 197th Av

45°23'18"

S SPRINGWATER RD

Clear Creek

Semple Rd
19500

Foster Creek

SEE 689 MAP

4

HATTAN RD

Willsada Park Wy

19

20

21

45°22'52"

WILLSADA PARK

S BAKERS FERRY RD

S Oakmont Ln

S Priscilla Ln

Foster Creek

5

S Ford Ct

15800

Clear

45°22'25"

S Clear Acres Dr

S Gunzer Dr

Terminal
Big Sky Ranch

Babler Rd

6

S SPRINGWATER RD

30

29

28

45°21'59"

S HATTAN RD

Creek

S Hull Rd

McCubbin Rd

7

31

32

33

45°21'33"

E   F   G   H   J

12°29'15"   12°28'38"   12°28'01"   12°27'24"   12°26'47"

SEE 718 MAP

Damascus

C
1 SE Maduros Ct
2 SE Don Lino Ct

MAP
689

1:24,000
1 in. = 2000 ft.
0   0.25   0.5
miles

SEE 659 MAP

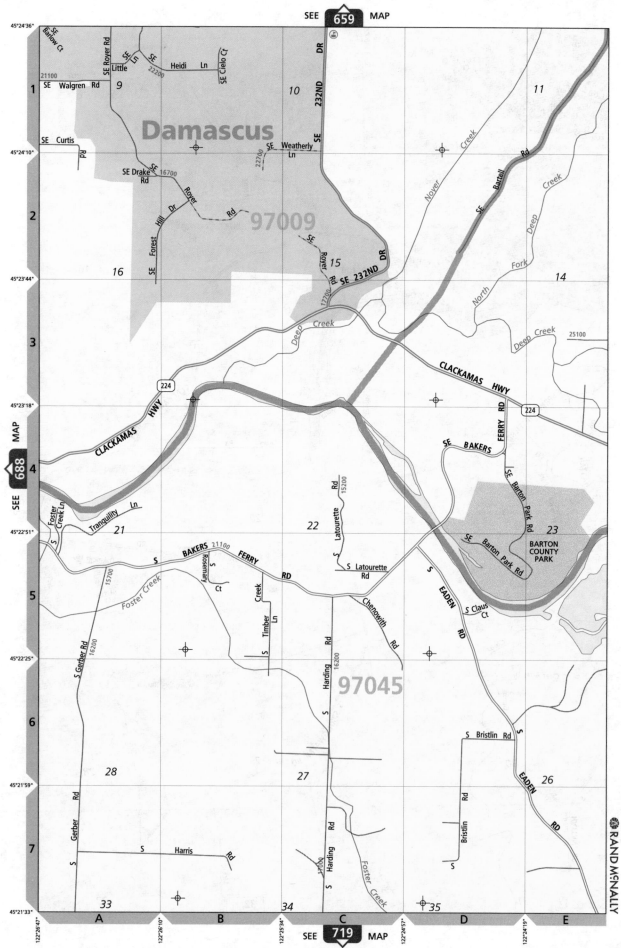

SE Bartow Ct
SE Royer Rd
21100
SE Walgren Rd
SE Little Ln
SE 22200
Heidi Ln
SE Cielo Ct
9
10
SE 232ND DR
11

Damascus

SE Curtis Rd
SE Weatherly Ln
22700
SE Drake Rd
SE 16700
Royer Rd
SE Forest Hill Dr
97009
SE Royer Rd
16
15
14
17700
SE 232ND DR
Nover Creek
SE Bartell Rd
North Fork
Deep Creek

Deep Creek
25100
CLACKAMAS HWY
Deep Creek
224
3

CLACKAMAS HWY
224
MAP 688
SEE
FERRY RD
SE BAKERS
SE Barton Park Rd
Latourette Rd
15200
Foster Creek Ln
Tranquility Ln
21
22
SE Barton Park Rd
23
BARTON COUNTY PARK

S
BAKERS 21100 FERRY RD
Rosemary Ct
Timber Ln
Creek
S Latourette Rd
S
EADEN RD
S Claus Ct
15700
Foster Creek
S
Chenowith Rd
5

S Gerber Rd
16200
Harding Rd
16200
97045
S Bristlin Rd
S
28
27
26
EADEN RD

Gerber Rd
S
S Harris Rd
Harding Rd
17000
Bristlin Rd
S
RAND M?NALLY
33
34
35

A   B   C   D   E

45°24'36"
45°24'10"
45°23'44"
45°23'18"
45°22'51"
45°22'25"
45°21'59"
45°21'33"

122°26'47"
122°26'10"
122°25'34"
122°24'57"
122°24'19"

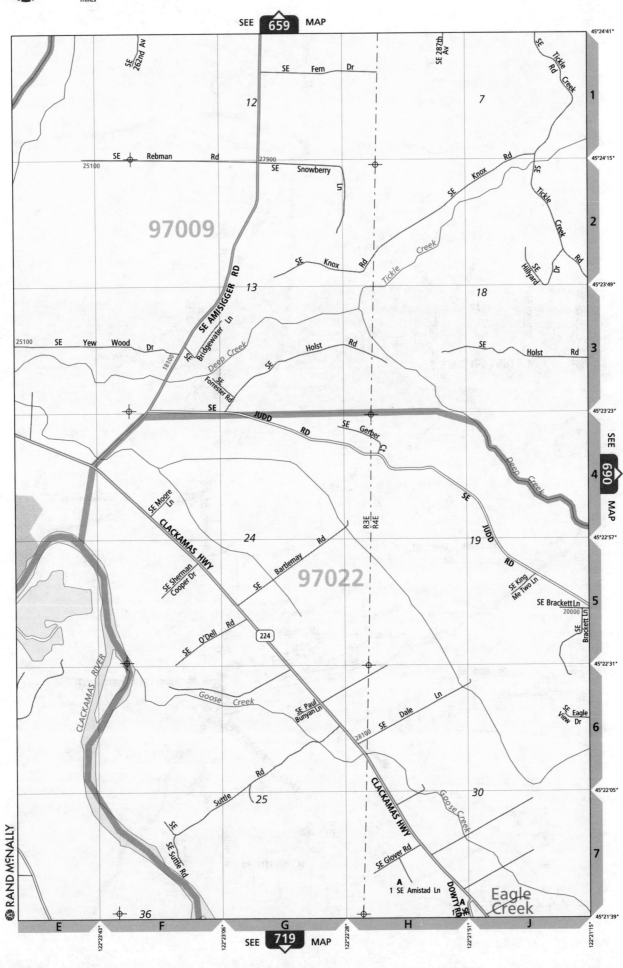

MAP
689

1:24,000
1 in. = 2000 ft.

0   0.25   0.5

miles

SEE **659** MAP

SE 262nd Av

SE Fern Dr

SE 287th Av

SE Tickle Rd Creek

45°24'41"

12

7

1

SE Rebman Rd

25100   27900

SE Snowberry

Ln

SE Knox Rd

SE Tickle Creek Rd

45°24'15"

97009

2

SE Knox Rd

Tickle Creek

SE Hillyard

Dr

45°23'49"

13

18

SE AMISIGGER RD

25100   SE Yew Wood Dr

18100

SE Bridgewater Ln

Deep Creek

SE Holst Rd

SE Holst Rd

3

SE Forrester Rd

SE

SE

JUDD RD

SE Gerber

45°23'23"

Ct

SEE **690** MAP

SE Moore Ln

CLACKAMAS HWY

Deep Creek

R3E R4E

SE

JUDD RD

4

45°22'57"

24

SE Sherman Cooper Dr

Bartlemay Rd

SE

97022

19

SE King Me Two Ln

SE Brackett Ln

20000

SE O'Dell Rd

224

SE Brackett Ln

5

45°22'31"

CLACKAMAS RIVER

Goose Creek

SE Paul Bunyan Ln

28100

SE Dale Ln

SE Eagle View Dr

6

45°22'05"

Rd

CLACKAMAS HWY

Goose Creek

30

Suttle

25

SE

SE Suttle Rd

SE Glover Rd

DOWTY RD

7

A

1 SE Amistad Ln

A SE

Eagle Creek

45°21'39"

RAND McNALLY

36

E   F   G   H   J

122°23'43"   122°23'06"   122°22'28"   122°21'51"   122°21'15"

MAP
690

1:24,000
1 in. = 2000 ft.

0   0.25   0.5
miles

SEE **660** MAP

45°24'41"

1 7   8   SE 312th Av   SE 322nd Av   SE 329th Av   9

45°24'15"

Tickle Creek

2   SE Waybill Rd   SE Colorado Rd   SE 329th Pl

SE Fosberg Rd   Fosberg Rd

45°23'49"

3 18   SE Decker Rd   17   16
SE Tickle Creek Rd   SE Colorado Rd

SE Holst Rd   SE Tickle Creek Rd   18200   SE Fosberg Rd

97009

Moonbeam Dr   Twilight Ln

45°23'23"

SEE MAP **689**

4   SE Tickle Creek Rd   Gunderson Rd   SE Gunderson Rd   18600 Autumn Wy

45°22'57"

5 19   SE Tickle Creek Ct   20   21
Deep Creek
SE Tickle Creek

Becky Ct   Debra Ct   Debra Ln
Becky Ct   Becky Ct   Charles Av   Albert Av   SE Leewood Ln Rd
SE Tara Lara Ln   Alice   Becky Ln Brian Av   SE Leewood Ln

45°22'31"

SE Eagle View Dr   **SE JUDD RD**   SE Leinan Rd   SE Norse Rd   SE Leewood Ln

6 30   SE Leavenworth Ct   SE Tear Ln   SE Idlewine Rd   SE Spitzenberg Ln   32000   EAGLE CREEK-SANDY HWY   SE Ln Sofich

45°22'05"

7 29   SE Happiness Hill Ln   SE Fernwood Dr   **97022**   28   SE Smokey Ln   Shadow Rd
SE Coop Rd   211   SE Judd Rd
SE HOWLETT RD

SE Jackknife Rd   SE Filbert Rd   SE Van Curen Rd

45°21'39"

A   B   C   D   E
12°22'1'15"   12°22'0'38"   12°22'0'00"   12°21'9'23"   12°22'18'46"

SEE **720** MAP

MAP
690

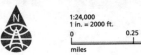

1:24,000
1 in. = 2000 ft.

0   0.25   0.5

miles

SEE 660 MAP

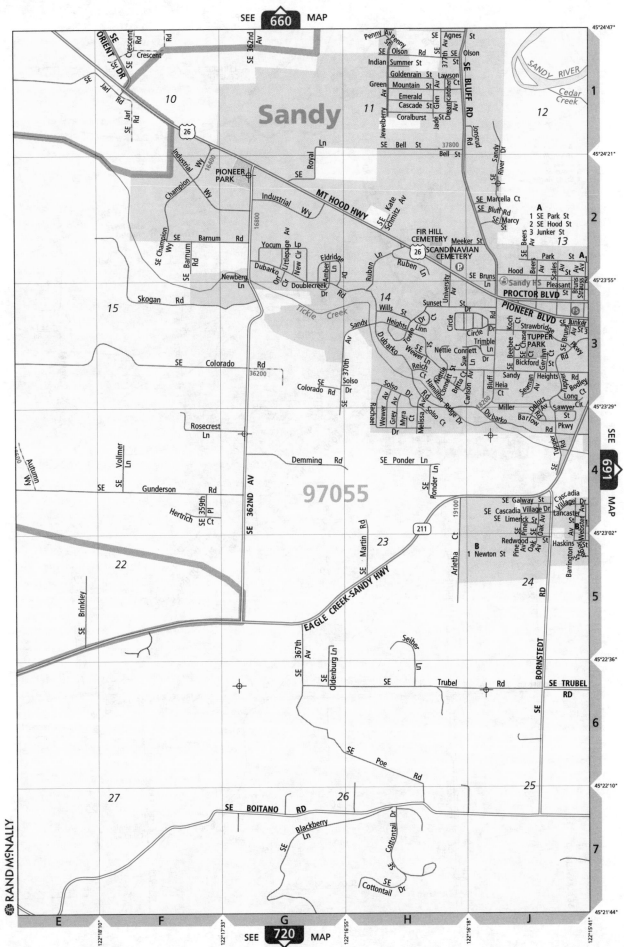

Sandy

Sandy River

Cedar Creek

45°24'47"

SE ORIENT DR
SE Crescent Rd
SE Crescent Rd
Crescent
SE 362nd Av

Penny Av Penny
SE Agnes St
377th Av
SE Olson Rd
SE Olson St
Indian Summer St
Goldenrain St Lawson
Green Mountain St Ct
Emerald Glen
Cascade St
Coralburst
Jewelberry Ln
SE Bell St
Bell St
37800
Johnsrud Rd
SE BLUFF RD
Sandy River Dr

1

SE Jarl Rd
10
26

45°24'21"

Industrial Wy
16400
PIONEER PARK
SE Royal Ln
MT HOOD HWY
SE Kate
Schmitz Av
Industrial Wy
16800
SE Marcella Ct
SE Bluff Rd
SE Marcy St

A
1 SE Park St
2 SE Hood St
3 Junker St
13

2

45°23'55"

Champion Wy
SE Champion Wy
SE Barnum Rd
Barnum Rd
SE Barnum Rd
Newberg Ln
Yocum Av
Littlepage Lp
New Cir
Dubarko Dr
Cir
Doublecreek Dr
Eldridge Ln
Amber Ln
Ruben Rd
Ruben Ln
FIR HILL CEMETERY
26
Meeker St
SCANDINAVIAN CEMETERY
P
SE Bruns St
University St
Sandy HS
PROCTOR BLVD
PIONEER BLVD
SE Beers Av
Beers Av
Park St
Hood
Beers Av
Scales Av
Pleasant St
Bruns Strauss
A

Skogan Rd
15
14
Wills St
Sunset
Circle Dr
Circle
Koch
Strawbridge
TUPPER PARK
SE Junker St 3
Bruns Pkwy

3

45°23'29"

SE Colorado Rd
36200
SE 370th Av
SE Solso Dr
Colorado Rd
SE Colorado Rd
Sandy Av
Dubarko
Heights
Towle
Linn
Trimble
Wewer Ln
Nettie Connett
Reich
Nettie
Connett St
Sue Ct
Britta Ct
Carlson Av
Bluff
Sandy Heights
Heia Ct
Seaman Av
Tupper Rd
Bodley
Long Cir
Delors Rd
Sawyer Av
Beebee
Gerlyn Ct
Bickford
Miller
Barlow
Dubarko Rd
18200

Solso Av
Wewer Av
Grey Ct
Myra Ct
Melissa Ct
Rachael Dr
Hamilton Ridge Dr
Solso Ct
Tupper Rd Pkwy

45°23'02"

Rosecrest Ln

SE Demming Rd
SE Ponder Ln
SE Ponder Ln

SEE 691 MAP

4

SE Vollmer Ln
SE Autumn Wy
SE Gunderson Rd
SE 359th Pl
SE 362ND AV
SE 367th Av
Hertrich Ct

97055

SE Galway St
SE Cascadia Village Dr
SE Limerick St
Cascadia Village
Lancaster
Pine Av
Oak St
Redwood Dr
Oak Av
Haskins St
Webster Av
Barrington
B

45°23'02"

22
Martin Rd
23
211
Arletha Ct
19100
B
1 Newton St
24
BORNSTEDT RD

5

45°22'36"

SE Brinkley
EAGLE CREEK-SANDY HWY
SE Oldenburg Ln
Seiber Ln
Trubel Rd
SE TRUBEL RD

6

45°22'10"

SE Poe Rd

7

27
SE BOITANO RD
26
Blackberry Ln
Cottontail Dr
25
SE Cottontail Dr

45°21'44"

E   F   G   H   J

SEE 720 MAP

122°18'10"   122°17'33"   122°16'55"   122°16'18"   122°15'41"

MAP 691

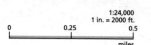

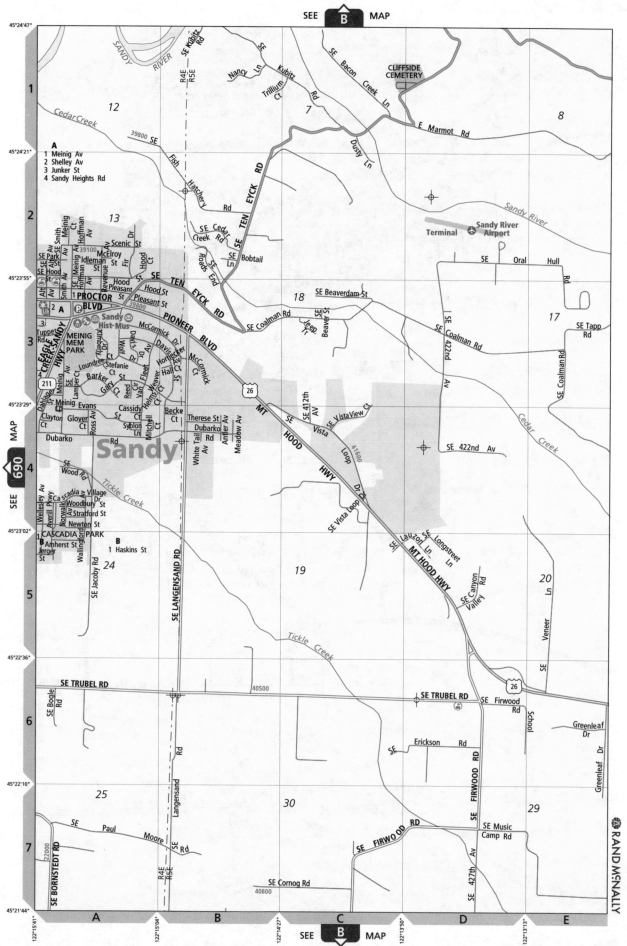

MAP
691

1:24,000
1 in. = 2000 ft.
0   0.25   0.5
miles

SEE B MAP

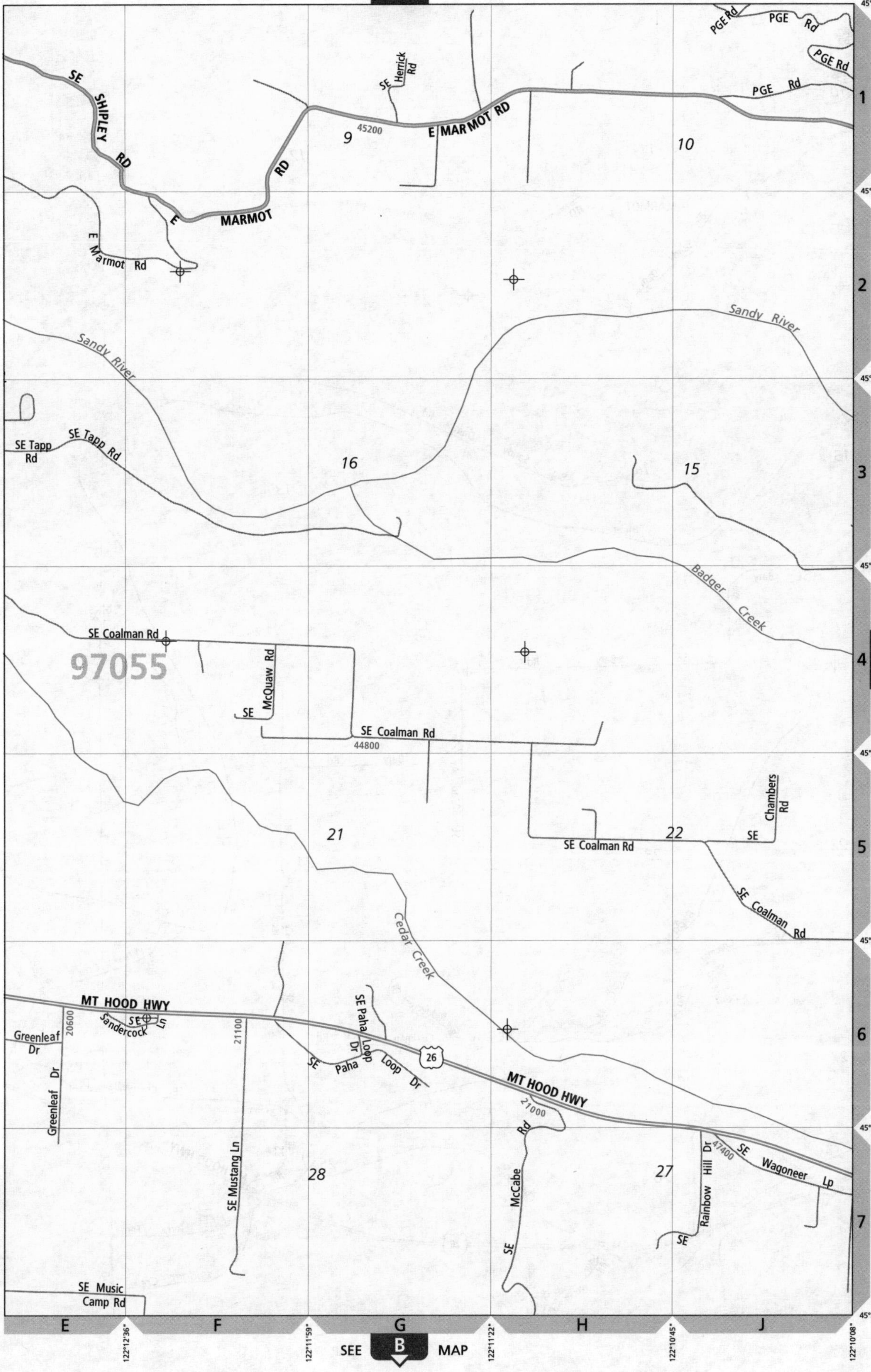

PGE Rd
PGE Rd
PGE Rd
PGE Rd

SE SHIPLEY RD

SE Herrick Rd

E MARMOT RD

45°24'52"
1

9 45200

10

E Marmot Rd
E Marmot Rd
MARMOT RD

45°24'26"
2

Sandy River

Sandy River

45°24'00"

SE Tapp Rd
SE Tapp Rd

16

15

3

45°23'34"

Badger Creek

SEE 692 MAP

SE Coalman Rd

97055

McQuaw Rd
SE

SE Coalman Rd
44800

4

45°23'08"

21

22

Chambers Rd

SE Coalman Rd   SE

5

SE Coalman Rd

45°22'41"

Cedar Creek

MT HOOD HWY

SE Paha Loop Dr
SE Paha Loop Dr

26

Greenleaf Dr
Sandercock
SE Ln
20600
21100

Greenleaf Dr

MT HOOD HWY
21000

6

45°22'15"

SE Mustang Ln

28

McCabe Rd
SE

27

Rainbow Hill Dr
47400
SE Wagoneer Lp
SE

7

SE Music Camp Rd

45°21'49"

E   F   G   H   J

RAND M?NALLY

122°12'36"   122°11'59"   122°11'22"   122°10'45"   122°10'08"

MAP
692

SEE B MAP

1:24,000
1 in. = 2000 ft.

0   0.25   0.5
miles

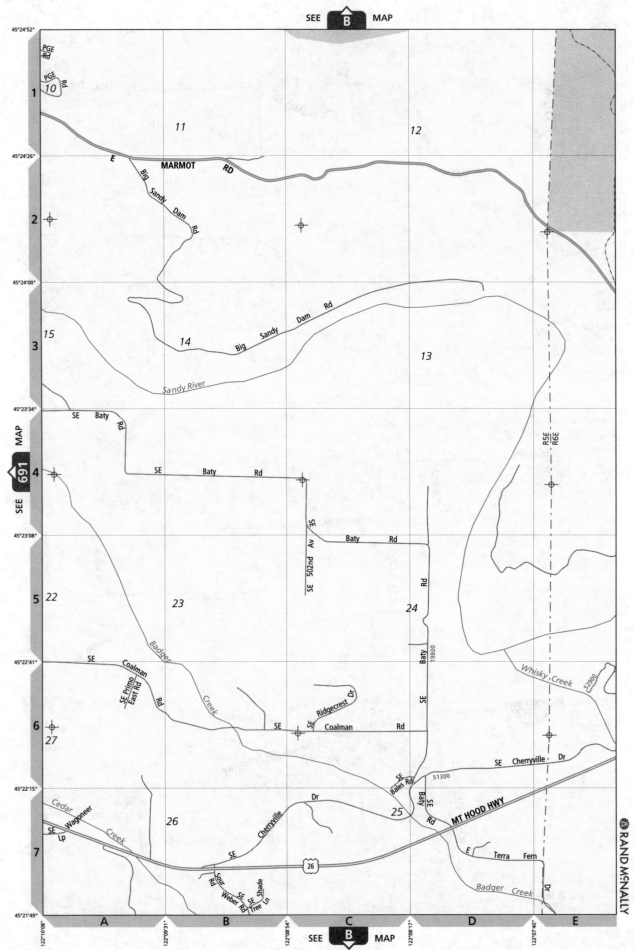

PGE Rd

PGE Rd
10

45°24'52"

11   12

45°24'26"
E
MARMOT RD
Big Sandy Dam Rd

45°24'00"

15   14   Big Sandy Dam Rd
13

Sandy River

45°23'34"
SE Baty Rd

MAP SEE 691

SE   Baty   Rd

45°23'08"
SE Fairom Dr
Baty Rd

R5E R6E

SE 502nd Av

22   23   24

Baty Rd

45°22'41"
SE Coalman
Badger
SE Primo East Rd
Rd
Creek
SE Ridgecrest Dr
SE SE Coalman Rd

19800
SE Baty

Whisky Creek
52900

45°22'15"
27
SE Bales Rd
51300
SE Cherryville Dr

Cedar Wagoneer
SE Lp
Creek
26
Cherryville
Dr
SE
25
Baty Rd
MT HOOD HWY

SE
26
E
Terra Fern

Scur Rd
SE Weber Rd
SE Tree Ln
SE Shade
Badger Creek
Dr

45°21'49"

A   B   C   D   E

SEE B MAP

122°10'08"   122°09'31"   122°08'54"   122°08'17"   122°07'40"

RAND McNALLY

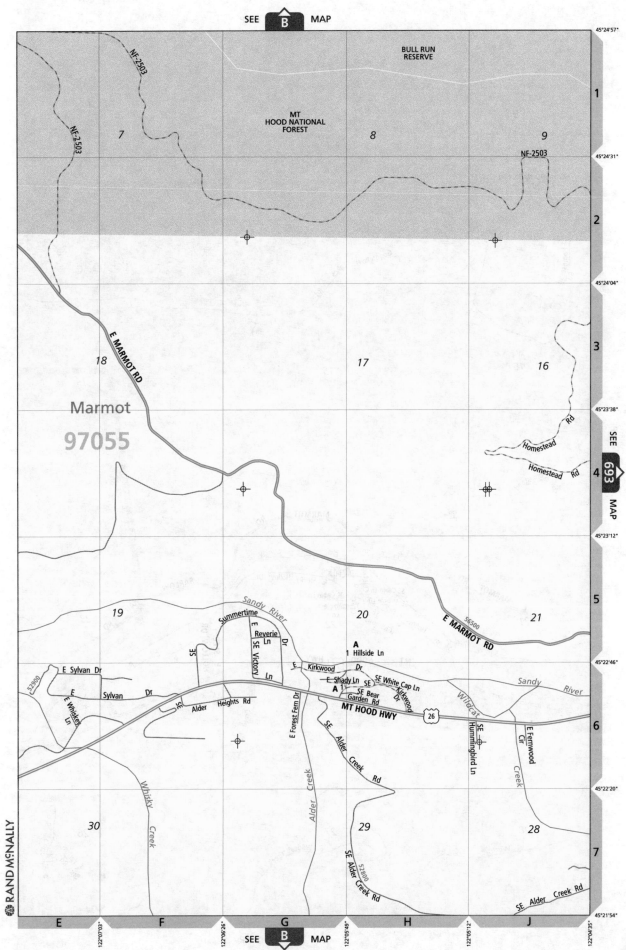

MAP
692

1:24,000
1 in. = 2000 ft.

0   0.25   0.5
miles

SEE **B** MAP

45°24'57"

NF-2503

BULL RUN
RESERVE

1

NF-2503

MT
HOOD NATIONAL
FOREST

7   8   9

NF-2503

45°24'31"

2

45°24'04"

E MARMOT RD

18   17   16

3

45°23'38"

Marmot

97055

Homestead Rd

Homestead Rd

SEE **693** MAP

4

45°23'12"

Sandy River

E MARMOT RD

5

19   Summertime   20   5 6500   21

E Reverie Ln

SE Victory Ln

SE

A
1 Hillside Ln

E Sylvan Dr   E Kirkwood Dr

SE White Cap Ln

E Shady Ln   SE   Sandy   River
52900

E   A 1   SE Kirkwood Dr
Sylvan   Dr   SE Bear
E Whiskey Ln   SE   Alder Heights Rd   Garden Rd

Wildcat

MT HOOD HWY   26

SE   E Fernwood
Hummingbird Ln   Cir

45°22'46"

E Forest Fern Dr

SE Alder Creek Rd

Creek

6

45°22'20"

30   Whisky   29   28

Creek

7

SE
52800

Alder Creek Rd

SE Alder Creek Rd

45°21'54"

E   F   G   H   J

122°07'03"   122°06'26"   122°05'49"   122°05'12"   122°04'35"

SEE **B** MAP

MAP
693

1:24,000
1 in. = 2000 ft.

0   0.25   0.5
miles

SEE **B** MAP

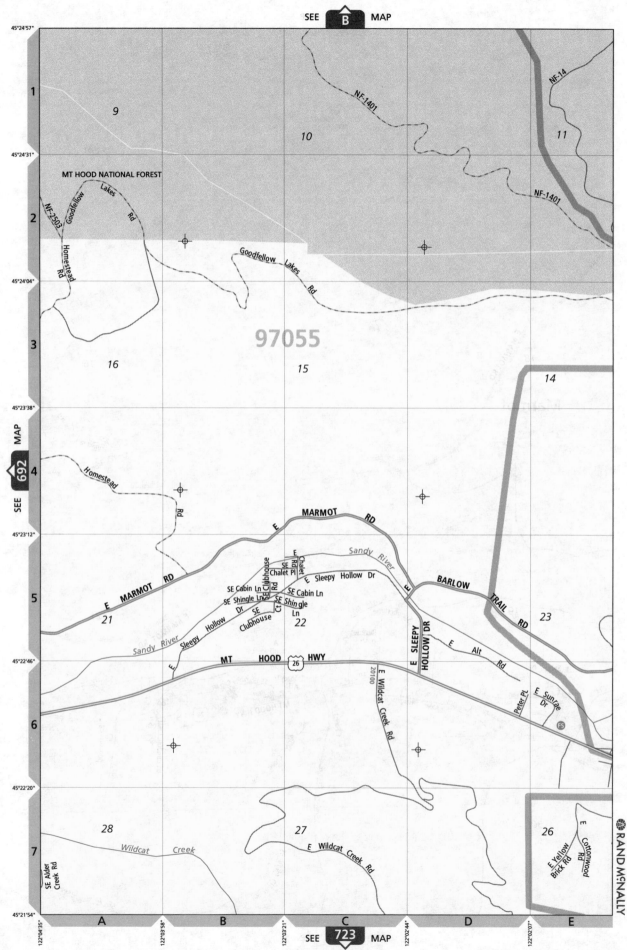

45°24'57"

1

9

10

11

NF-1401

NF-14

45°24'31"

MT HOOD NATIONAL FOREST

Goodfellow Lakes Rd

NF-2503

2

Homestead Rd

Goodfellow Lakes Rd

NF-1401

45°24'04"

97055

45°23'38"

3

16

15

14

SEE **692** MAP

4

Homestead Rd

45°23'12"

E MARMOT RD

Sandy River

E

45°23'12"

E MARMOT RD

5

21

SE Cabin Ln
SE Clubhouse Rd
Chalet Pl
SE Chalet Rd
E Sleepy Hollow Dr
SE Cabin Ln
SE Shingle Ln
SE Clubhouse Ct
SE Shingle Ln

22

BARLOW TRAIL RD

23

E

Sandy River
Sleepy Hollow Dr

E Sleepy Hollow Dr

E Alt Rd

45°22'46"

MT HOOD HWY (26)

E

E Wildcat Creek Rd
20100

Peter Pl
E Sunrae Dr

F5

6

45°22'20"

28

27

26

E Yellow Brick Rd
E Cottonwood Rd

7

Wildcat Creek

SE Alder Creek Rd

E Wildcat Creek Rd

45°21'54"

A   B   C   D   E

122°04'35"   122°03'58"   122°03'21"   122°02'44"   122°02'07"

SEE **723** MAP

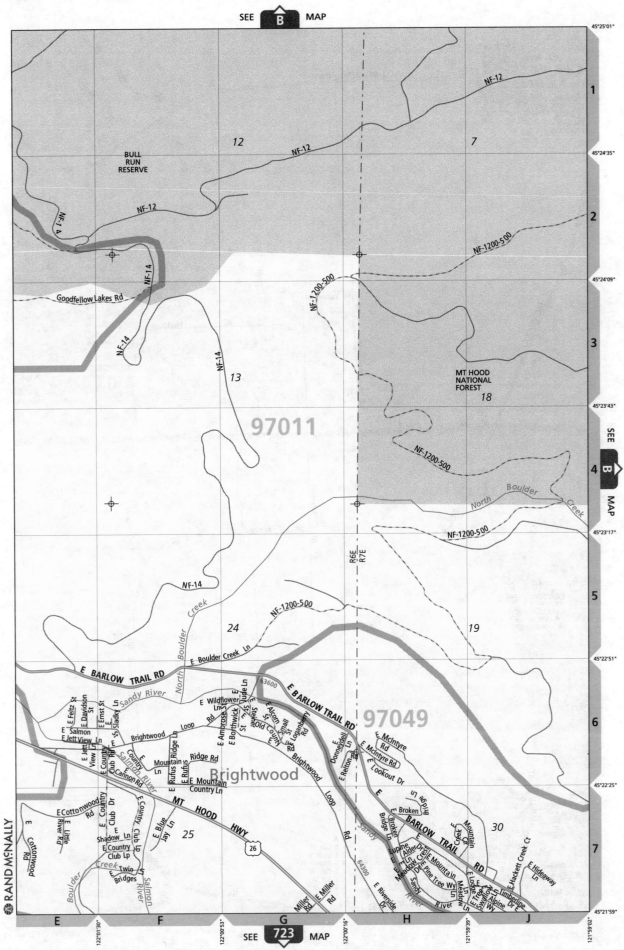

MAP
693

1:24,000
1 in. = 2000 ft.

0   0.25   0.5

miles

N

NF-12

1

12   NF-12   7

BULL
RUN
RESERVE

NF-12

NF-1

2

NF-14   NF-1200-500

Goodfellow Lakes Rd

NF-1200-500

45°25'01"

45°24'35"

45°24'09"

NF-14

3

NF-14   13

MT HOOD
NATIONAL
FOREST
18

45°23'43"

97011

4

NF-1200-500

North   Boulder   Creek

NF-1200-500

45°23'17"

R6E
R7E

NF-14

5

North Boulder Creek   NF-1200-500

24   19

45°22'51"

E BARLOW TRAIL RD

E Boulder Creek Ln

E BARLOW TRAIL RD

Sandy River

63600

97049

E Wildflower
Ln
E Jude Ln

6

E Feltz St
E Davidson
St
E Ernst St
SS Sladky
Ln

E Salmon
E Jett View Ln

Brightwood
Loop

Country Rd
Salmon River Rd
Club Rd
E Cannon Rd

Mountain
Ridge Ln
E Rufus
Ridge Rd

Rufus
E Mountain
Country Ln

Brightwood

E Ambrose St
E Borthwick St
E Steiner St
E Alcorn St
E Small St
Old Country
Rd
E Loganberry
Rd

Brightwood
Loop

Sandy

E Donner
Dell Ln
E Felton Ln

E McIntyre
Rd
E McIntyre Rd
E Lookout Dr

45°22'25"

E Cottonwood
Rd
E Country
Club Dr
E Country Club Lp

E Little
River Rd

E Blue
Jay Ln

E Shadow Ln

E Country
Club Lp

25

MT HOOD HWY

26

Miller
Rd

E Broken
Bridge Ln

E Broken
Bridge Ln

BARLOW
TRAIL
RD

Mountain
View Ln

E Hackett Creek Ct

E Hideaway
Ln

30

7

Boulder
Creek

E Twin
Bridges

Salmon
River

E Miller
Rd

64300

Sandy

E Riverside
Dr

River

Sandy
River

E Lupine
Ln
E Meadow Dr
E Alder Dr
E Pine Tree Wy
E Mountain
E Lodge
E Meadow
Wy
E Swallow
E Alpine Dr
E Timberline

45°21'59"

E   F   G   H   J

RAND MᶜNALLY

122°01'30"   122°00'53"   122°00'16"   121°59'39"   121°59'02"

MAP
711

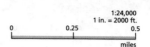

1:24,000
1 in. = 2000 ft.

0   0.25   0.5
miles

N

SEE B MAP

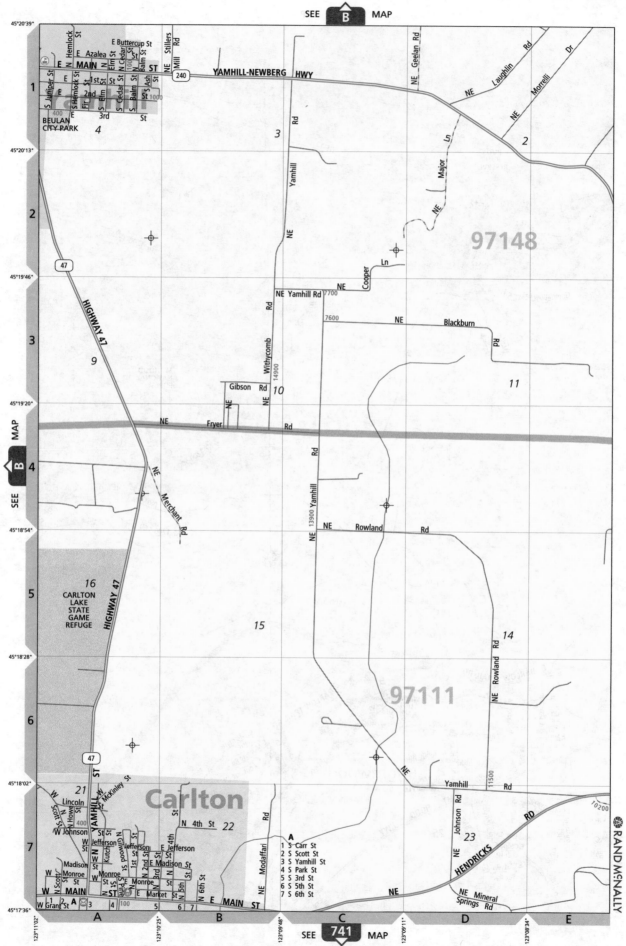

45°20'39"

E Hemlock St
E Azalea St
E Buttercup St
E N MAIN ST
E Elm St
N Cedar St
E N Balm St
S Ash St
Stillers Rd
NE Mill Rd

YARHILL

240

YAMHILL-NEWBERG HWY

NE Geelan Rd

Rd

NE Laughlin

Dr

NE Morelli

S Juniper St
S Hemlock St
1st St
2nd St
E Fir St
S Elm St
E S Cedar St
S Balm St

1
400
1000

400
E 3rd St

BEULAN
CITY PARK   4

3

Yamhill   Rd

NE Major   Ln

2

45°20'13"

NE

97148

2

47

45°19'46"

HIGHWAY 47

9

NE

Cooper   Ln

NE

NE Yamhill Rd   7700

3

Withycomb   Rd

14900

7600

NE   Blackburn

Rd

11

45°19'20"

Gibson   Rd

NE

NE

10

MAP
B
SEE

NE   Fryer   Rd

4

NE Merchant   Rd

13900 Yamhill   Rd

NE

NE   Rowland   Rd

45°18'54"

45°18'28"

16
CARLTON
LAKE
STATE
GAME
REFUGE

HIGHWAY 47

15

14

NE Rowland Rd

97111

45°18'02"

6

47

NE

1500

Yamhill   Rd

10200

HENDRICKS   RD

21

YAMHILL   ST

W Lincoln St

W Mckinley St

Carlton

N 4th St   22

NE Johnson Rd

23

W Scott St
W Howe St

W Johnson

St

W Jefferson St

N Kutch St
N Spoon St
Jefferson
E Jefferson St

4th St

NE Modaffari   Rd

NE

7

Madison
W Monroe St

W Scott St

Monroe
N 1st St
N 2nd St
3rd St
E S Monroe
N 5th St
E Market St
N 6th St

E   MAIN   ST

A
1 S Carr St
2 S Scott St
3 S Yamhill St
4 S Park St
5 S 3rd St
6 S 5th St
7 S 6th St

HENDRICKS

NE   Mineral
Springs Rd

RAND MCNALLY

W   MAIN   ST

W Grant St   A

45°17'36"

A   B   C   D   E

123°11'02"   123°10'25"   123°09'48"   123°09'11"   123°08'34"

SEE 741 MAP

MAP
711

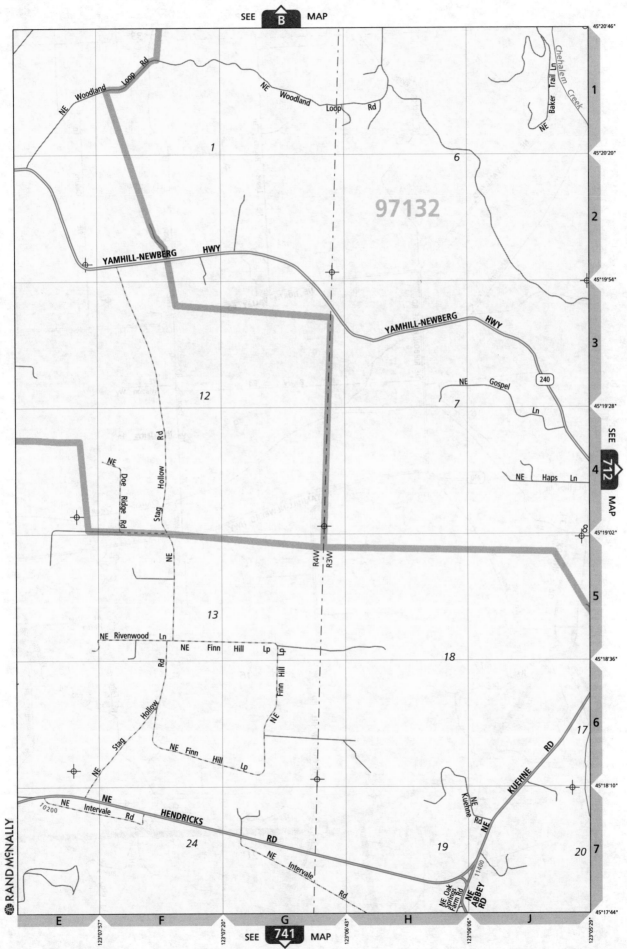

SEE B MAP

1:24,000
1 in. = 2000 ft.
0   0.25   0.5
miles

N

NE Woodland Loop Rd

NE Woodland Loop Rd

NE Baker Trail Ln

Chehalem Creek

1

6

97132

YAMHILL-NEWBERG HWY

YAMHILL-NEWBERG HWY

NE Gospel Ln

240

12

7

SEE 712 MAP

NE Doe Ridge Rd

NE Stag Hollow Rd

NE

NE Haps Ln

R4W R3W

13

18

NE Rivenwood Ln

NE Finn Hill Lp

NE Finn Hill Lp

Rd

NE Stag Hollow

NE Finn Hill Lp

17

KUEHNE RD

NE Kuehne Rd

NE 70200

NE Intervale Rd

HENDRICKS RD

NE Intervale Rd

24

19

20

NE Oak Springs Farm Rd

11400

NE ABBEY RD

E   F   G   H   J

SEE 741 MAP

45°20'46"
45°20'20"
45°19'54"
45°19'28"
45°19'02"
45°18'36"
45°18'10"
45°17'44"

1
2
3
4
5
6
7

123°07'57"
123°07'20"
123°06'43"
123°06'06"
123°05'29"

MAP
712

1:24,000
1 in. = 2000 ft.

0   0.25   0.5

miles

SEE **B** MAP

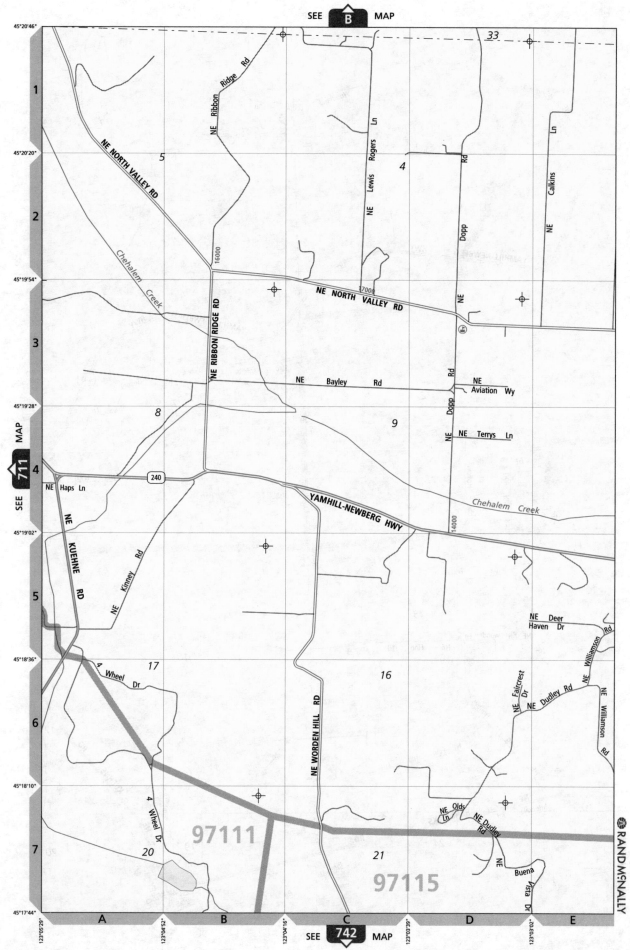

45°20'46"

33

NE Ribbon Ridge Rd

1

NE NORTH VALLEY RD

45°20'20"

5

NE Lewis

NE Rogers Ln

4

NE Dopp Rd

NE Calkins Ln

2

Chehalem Creek

45°19'54"

16000

NE RIBBON RIDGE RD

NE NORTH VALLEY RD

17000

NE Dopp

3

NE Bayley Rd

NE Dopp Rd

NE Aviation Wy

45°19'28"

8

9

NE Terrys Ln

MAP

711

SEE

4

240

NE Haps Ln

YAMHILL-NEWBERG HWY

Chehalem Creek

14000

45°19'02"

NE KUEHNE RD

NE Kinney Rd

5

NE Deer Haven Dr

NE Williamson Rd

45°18'36"

4 Wheel Dr

17

16

NE Fairrcrest Dr

NE Dudley Rd

NE Williamson Rd

6

NE WORDEN HILL RD

45°18'10"

NE Olds Ln

NE Dudley Rd

97111

7

4 Wheel Dr

20

21

97115

NE Buena

Vista Dr

45°17'44"

A   B   C   D   E

SEE **742** MAP

45°05'29"   123°04'52"   123°04'16"   123°03'39"   123°03'02"

RAND McNALLY

MAP
712

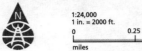

1:24,000
1 in. = 2000 ft.

0   0.25   0.5

miles

SEE **B** MAP

34

35

36

NE Chehalem Dr

T2S
T3S

NE Hillside Dr

NE Hillside Dr

1

45°20'54"

45°20'28"

3

NE Sullivan Ln

2

NE Hillside Dr

1

2

45°20'02"

NE Nelson Rd

NE Kings Grade

NE Hillside Dr

20800   **NE NORTH VALLEY RD**

3

NE Stone Rd

NE Flying Feather Ln

45°19'36"

10

97132

11

12

NE TANGEN RD

SEE
713
MAP

4

NE Trinity Ln

14400

45°19'10"

NE Tranquil Ln

Chehalem Creek

13500

240

NE Rainbow Ln

NE Williamson Rd

NE Berry Ln

NE Whitlow Ln

NE Fox Hollow Ln

Mindy Ln

YAMHILL-NEWBERG HWY

240

NE Old Yamhill Rd

5

45°18'44"

15

NE Williamson Rd

NE Herring Ln

14

Red Hills Rd

13

45°18'17"

NE Richlands Ln

Ln

Richlands

NE Red Hills Rd

12300

NE Larkins Rd

6

NE Dillon Rd

NE Williamson Rd

NE Hughes Ln

NE Sunnycrest Rd

NE Sunnycrest Rd

7

22

23

24

NE Big Fir Ln

NE Red Hills Rd

NE Fox Farm Rd

NE Hidden Springs Rd

45°17'51"

E   F   G   H   J

123°02'25"   123°01'48"   123°01'11"   123°00'34"   122°59'57"

SEE **742** MAP

RAND McNALLY

MAP
713

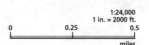

1:24,000
1 in. = 2000 ft.

0   0.25   0.5

miles

SEE 683 MAP

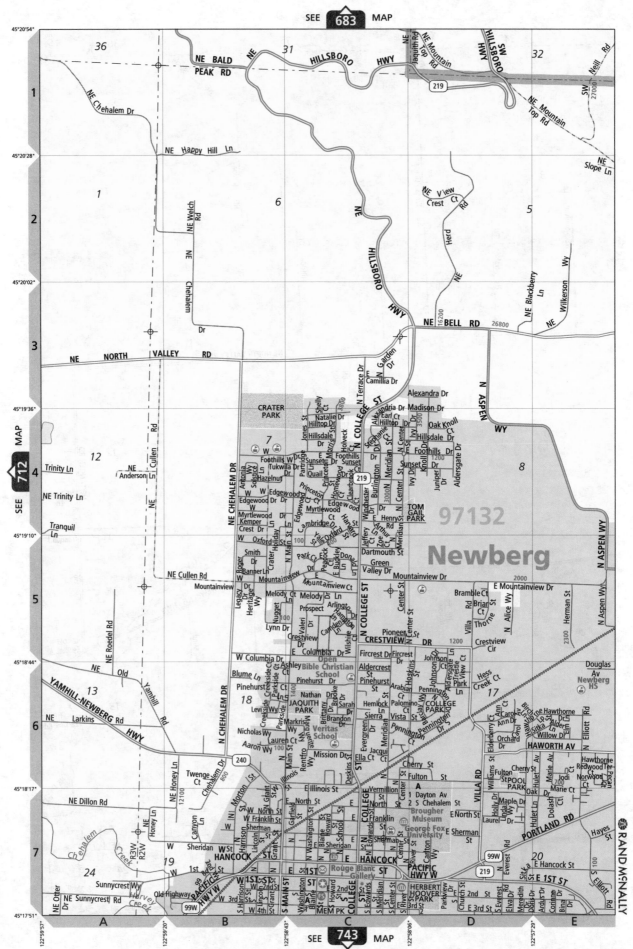

SEE 712 MAP

SEE 743 MAP

RAND MCNALLY

MAP
713

1:24,000
1 in. = 2000 ft.
0   0.25   0.5
miles

SEE **683** MAP

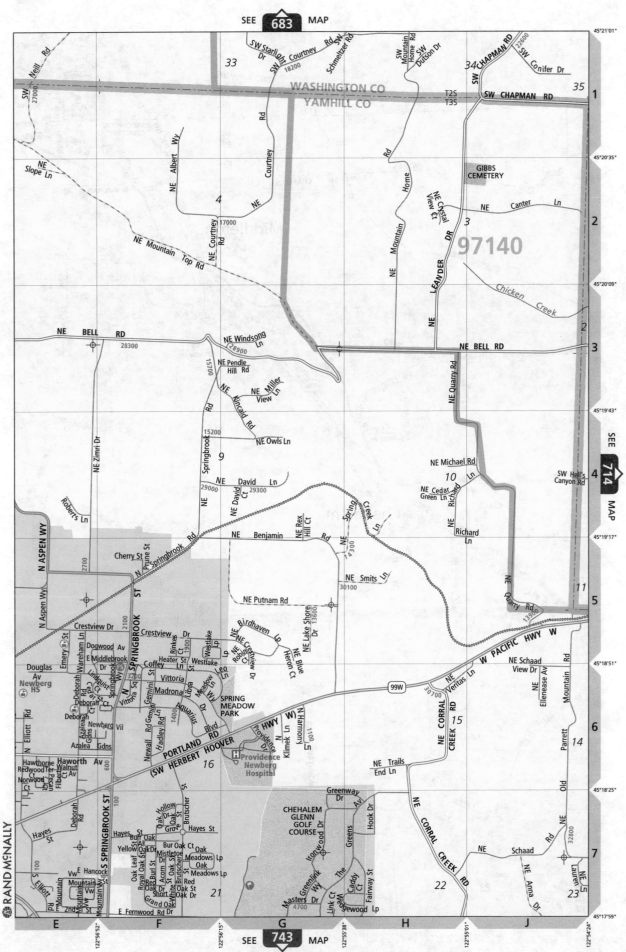

45°21'01"
45°20'35"
45°20'09"
45°19'43"
45°19'17"
45°18'51"
45°18'25"
45°17'59"

SEE **714** MAP

SEE **743** MAP

E   F   G   H   J

122°56'52"   122°56'15"   122°55'38"   122°55'01"   122°54'24"

WASHINGTON CO
YAMHILL CO
T2S
T3S

97140

GIBBS CEMETERY

Chicken Creek

CHEHALEM GLENN GOLF COURSE

SPRING MEADOW PARK

Providence Newberg Hospital

Newberg HS

RAND McNALLY

MAP
714

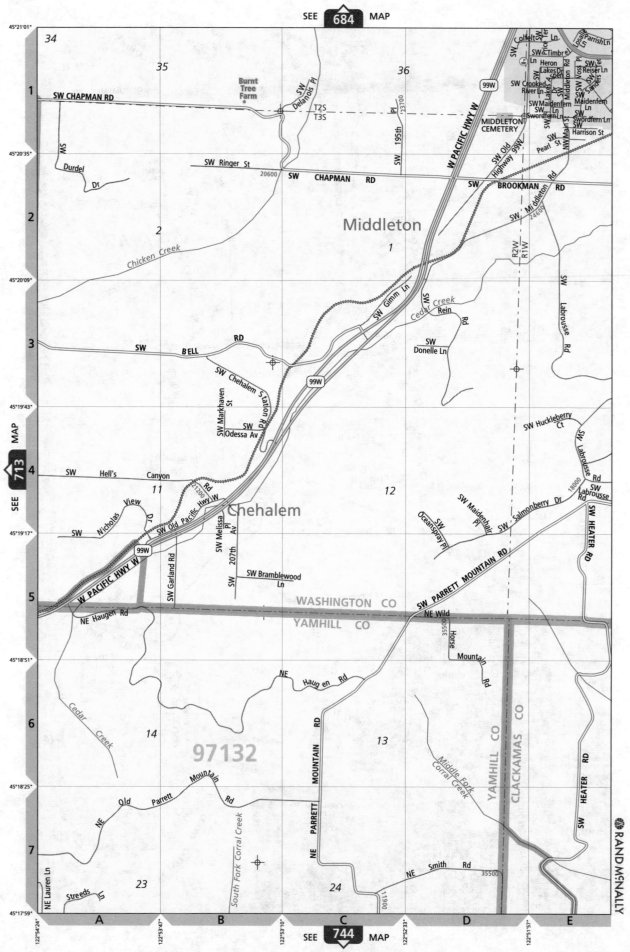

SEE ◆ **684** ◆ MAP

45°21'01"

34

35

36

SW CHAPMAN RD

SW Chapman Rd

Burnt Tree Farm

SW Delanois Pl

T2S
T3S

99W

SW Colfelt Ln
SW Timbre
SW Price Ter
Losalle Ln
Parrish Ln

Heron
Lakes Dr
SW
Ln

SW Voss Pl

SW Reiser Ln

SW Canders Ln

SW Crooked
River Ln

SW Maidenfern
Ln

SW Maidenfern
Ln

SW
Swordfern Ln

SW Swordfern Ln

MIDDLETON CEMETERY

W PACIFIC HWY W

SW Old Highway 99W

Pearl St

NW Main St

Harrison St

45°20'35"

SW Durdel Dr

SW Ringer St

20600

SW CHAPMAN RD

SW 195th Pl

23700

SW BROOKMAN RD

SW Middleton Rd

24600

2

Middleton

2

Chicken Creek

1

R2W
R1W

SW Labrousse Rd

45°20'09"

45°19'43"

3

SW BELL RD

SW Chehalem Station Rd

SW Gimm Ln

Cedar Creek

Rein Rd

SW Donelle Ln

99W

SW Markhaven St

SW Odessa Av

SW Huckleberry Ct

SW Labrousse Rd

45°19'17"

SEE **713** MAP

4

SW Hell's Canyon Rd

21200

11

Nicholas View Dr

SW Old Pacific Hwy W

Chehalem

12

SW Maidenhair Pl

SW Salmonberry Dr

18000

SW Labrousse Rd

SW HEATER RD

SW Melissa Av

SW Oceanspray Pl

SW Nicholas

SW 207th Av

99W

SW Garland Rd

SW Bramblewood Ln

W PACIFIC HWY W

SW BRAMBLEWOOD

5

WASHINGTON CO

SW PARRETT MOUNTAIN RD

NE Wild

NE Haugen Rd

YAMHILL CO

35500

Horse Mountain Rd

45°18'51"

6

Cedar Creek

14

NE Haug en Rd

97132

13

PARRETT MOUNTAIN RD

Middle Fork Corral Creek

YAMHILL CO

CLACKAMAS CO

SW HEATER RD

45°18'25"

NE Old Parrett Mountain Rd

7

NE Lauren Ln

Stre eds

23

South Fork Corral Creek

NE PARRETT MOUNTAIN RD

24

11900

NE Smith Rd

35500

45°17'59"

122°54'24"

A

122°53'47"

B

122°53'10"

C

122°52'33"

D

122°51'57"

E

SEE ◆ **744** ◆ MAP

RAND M°NALLY

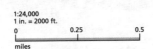
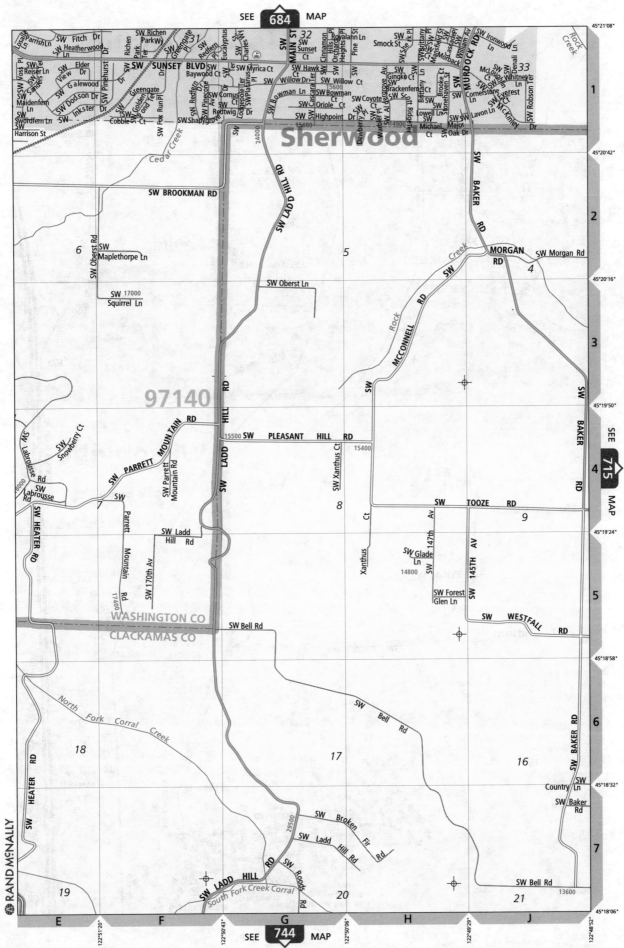

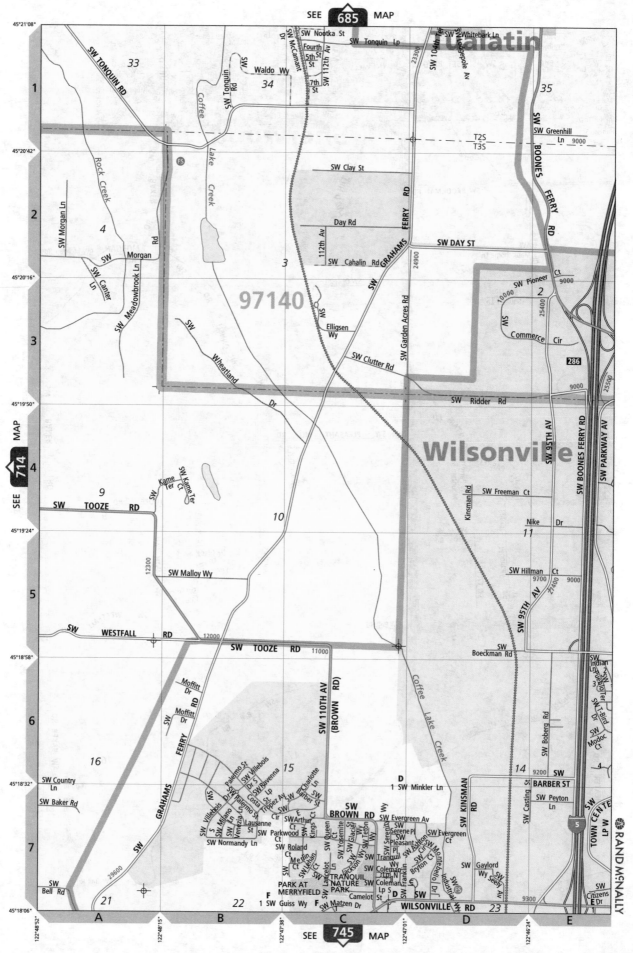

MAP
715

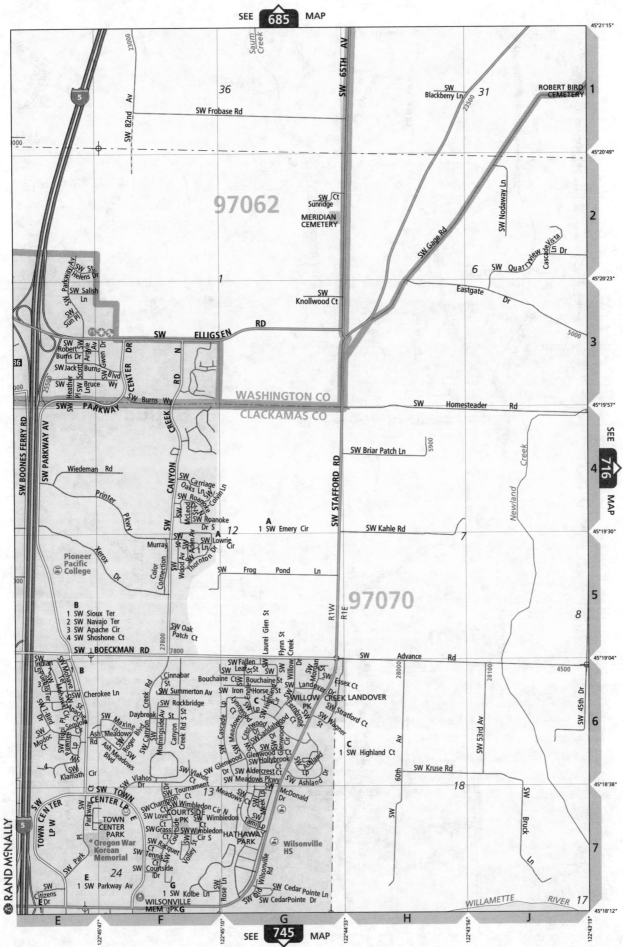

1:24,000
1 in. = 2000 ft.
0   0.25   0.5
miles

N

SEE 685 MAP

Saum Creek

SW 65th Av

45°21'15"

I-5

23000

36

SW 82nd Av

SW Frobase Rd

SW Blackberry Ln

31

ROBERT BIRD CEMETERY

1

45°20'49"

97062

SW Nodaway Ln

SW Ct Sunridge

MERIDIAN CEMETERY

SW Gage Rd

2

SW Quarryview Vista Ln Dr

Cascade Dr

6

SW Knollwood Ct

Eastgate Dr

45°20'23"

5000

3

SW ELLIGSEN RD

SW Robert Burns Dr

SW Helens Dr St Parkway Av

SW Salish Ln

SW Sun Pl

SW Jack Scott Argyle Av

SW Gwen Dr

Burns Blvd

Bruce Wy

SW Heather Pl

SW Burns Wy

N CENTER DR

SW CENTER RD

CREEK RD

WASHINGTON CO
CLACKAMAS CO

SW Homesteader Rd

45°19'57"

SW PARKWAY

SW BOONES FERRY RD

SW PARKWAY AV

SW Briar Patch Ln

5900

SEE 716 MAP

4

45°19'30"

Wiedeman Rd

Printer Pkwy

SW CANYON CREEK RD

SW Carriage Oaks Ln

SW Roanoke Colvin Ln

SW McLeod St

SW Roanoke Dr S

A
1 SW Emery Cir

SW Stafford Rd

SW Kahle Rd

Newland Creek

7

Xerox Dr

Murray St

SW Wood Av

SW Glen Dr

SW Thornton Dr

A Lowrie Cir

SW Frog Pond Ln

Pioneer Pacific College

Color Connection

B
1 SW Sioux Ter
2 SW Navajo Ter
3 SW Apache Cir
4 SW Shoshone Ct

97070

R1W R1E

5

8

SW Oak Patch Ct

27800

SW BOECKMAN RD

7800

SW Advance Rd

45°19'04"

28000

28100

4500

SW 45th Dr

SW Indian Ln

SW Mohave Ter

SW Apache Cir

SW Sequoia

SW Cherokee Ln

B
1
2
3

Cinnabar St

SW Summerton Av

SW Rockbridge

SW Fallen Leaf St

Bouchaine Ct

Bouchaine St

SW Iron Horse St

SW Willow St

SW Morgan Ct

SW Essex Ct

WILLOW CREEK LANDOVER

6

Daybreak St

SW Maxine Ln

Ash Meadows Rd

SW Roger Dr

SW Canyon Creek Rd S

SW Morningside Av

SW Meadows

SW Eastgate

SW Crestwood

SW Sandalwood

SW Highland

SW Fanbrook Ct

SW Stratford Ct

SW Wagner

C

SW 53rd Av

SW 45th Dr

Modoc Ct

Ash Meadows Blvd

SW Glenwood Dr

SW Glenwood

SW Hollybrook Dr

SW Glenwood Ct

SW Ashland Lp

C
1 SW Highland Ct

SW 60th Av

SW Klamath Cir

SW Vlahos Dr

SW Courtside

SW Aldercrest Ct

SW Meadows Pkwy

SW Ashland Dr

SW Kruse Rd

18

SW TOWN CENTER LP E

SW Town Center Lp W

SW Vlahos Dr

SW Tournament Ct

13 Meadows Ct

SW Champion Ct

SW Wimbledon Cir N

COURTSIDE PK

SW Wimbledon Ct

SW Meek Lp

McDonald Dr

45°18'38"

60th Av

SW Bruck Ln

7

TOWN CENTER PARK

Oregon War Korean Memorial

SW Park Pl

SW Love Ct

SW Grass Ct

SW Racquet Ct

SW Tennis Ct

SW Courtside Dr

SW Wimbledon Cir S

Valley Ct

SW Rose Ln

HATHAWAY PARK

Wilsonville HS

SW Old Wilsonville Rd

E
1 SW Parkway Av

E
24

SW Citizens Dr

G
1 SW Kolbe Ln

SW Cedar Pointe Ln

SW CedarPointe Dr

WILSONVILLE MEM PK

WILLAMETTE RIVER

17

45°18'12"

RAND McNALLY

I-5

E   F   G   H   J

122°45'47"   122°45'10"   122°44'33"   122°43'56"   122°43'19"

SEE 745 MAP

MAP
716

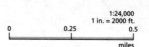

SEE 686 MAP

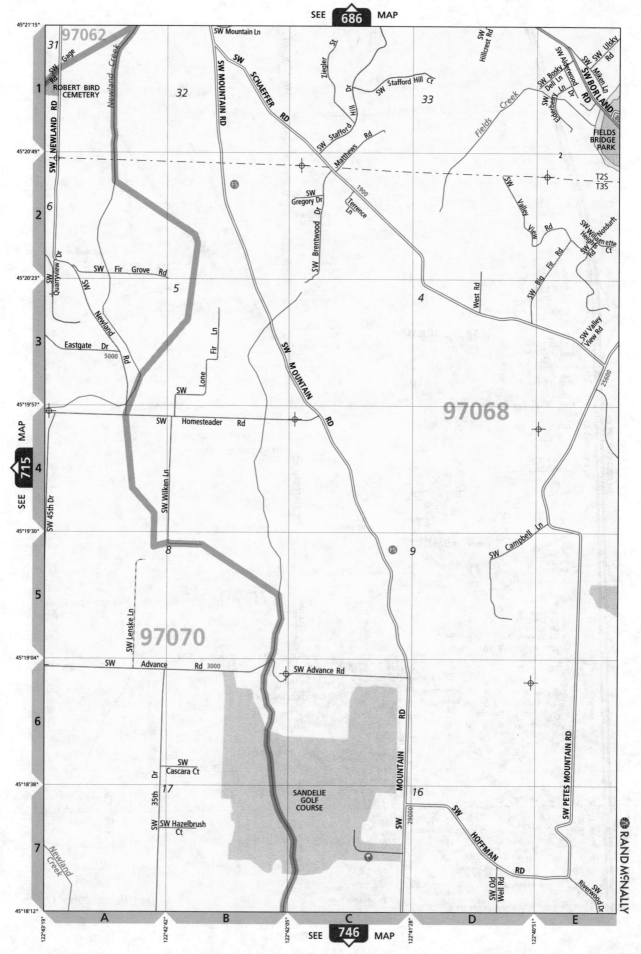

45°21'15"
97062
31
SW Gage Rd
ROBERT BIRD CEMETERY
Newland Creek
1
32
SW Mountain Ln
SW MOUNTAIN RD
SW SCHAEFFER RD
Ziegler St
Stafford Hill Dr
SW Stafford Hill Ct
33
SW Hillcrest Rd
SW Milken Ln
SW SW Ulsky Rd
SW Bosky Dell Ln
SW Alderwood Dr
SW BORLAND RD
SW Edgeberry Dr
45°20'49"
SW NEWLAND RD
FS
SW Stafford Rd
SW Matthews Rd
1900
Fields Creek
FIELDS BRIDGE PARK
2
T2S
T3S
6
2
SW Gregory Dr
SW Brentwood Dr
Terrence Ln
SW Valley View Rd
SW Willamette Heights Rd
SW Whitcotourft Ct
45°20'23"
SW Quarryview Dr
SW Fir Grove Rd
5
SW Newland Rd
4
West Rd
SW Big Fir Rd
3
Eastgate Dr
5000
Lone Fir Ln
SW
SW Valley View Dr
25600
45°19'57"
SW Homesteader Rd
SW MOUNTAIN RD
97068
MAP
715
SEE
4
SW 45th Dr
SW Wilken Ln
45°19'30"
SW Campbell Ln
FS 9
5
8
97070
SW Lenske Ln
45°19'04"
SW Advance Rd 3000
SW Advance Rd
6
MOUNTAIN RD
SW PETES MOUNTAIN RD
45°18'38"
SW 35th Dr
SW Cascara Ct
17
SANDELIE GOLF COURSE
16
29000
SW HOFFMAN RD
7
Newland Creek
SW SW Hazelbrush Ct
SW Old Well Rd
SW Riverwood Dr

45°18'12"
A   B   C   D   E

122°43'19"   122°42'42"   122°42'05"   122°41'28"   122°40'51"

SEE 746 MAP

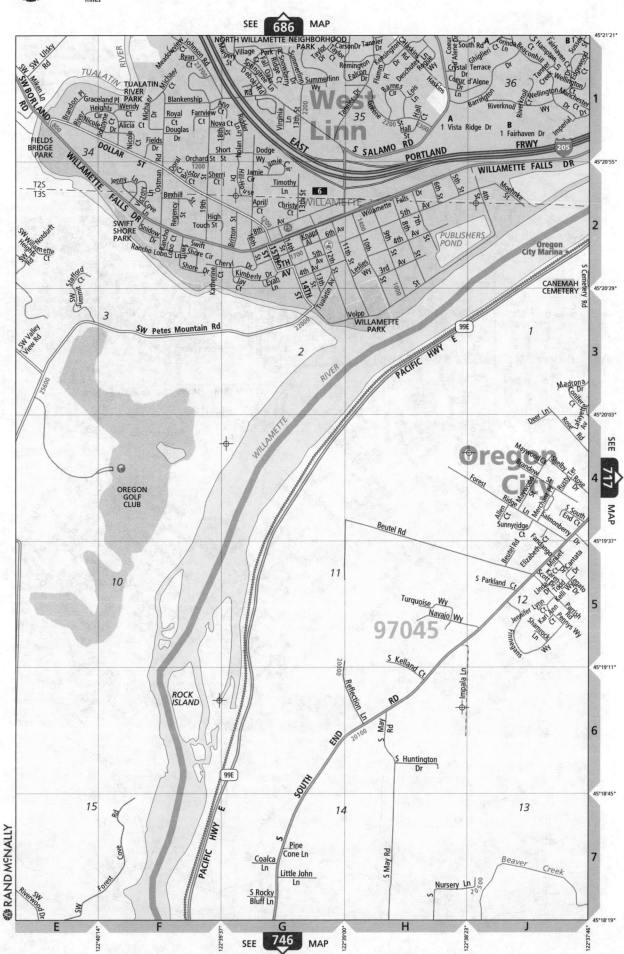

MAP
716

1:24,000
1 in. = 2000 ft.

0   0.25   0.5
miles

NORTH WILLAMETTE NEIGHBORHOOD PARK

West Linn

TUALATIN RIVER

SW Ulsky Rd
SW Miken Ln
SW Borland Rd

FIELDS BRIDGE PARK

DOLLAR ST

WILLAMETTE FALLS DR

SWIFT SHORE PARK

S SALAMO RD

EAST PORTLAND FRWY

205

WILLAMETTE FALLS DR

PUBLISHERS POND

Oregon City Marina

CANEMAH CEMETERY

S Cemetery Rd

WILLAMETTE PARK

WILLAMETTE RIVER

PACIFIC HWY E

99E

SW Petes Mountain Rd

SW Valley View Rd

OREGON GOLF CLUB

Madrona Dr

Deer Ln

Oregon City

Forest Ridge

Beutel Rd

Turquoise Wy
Navajo Wy

97045

S Parkland Ct

ROCK ISLAND

S Kelland Ct

Reflection Ln

SOUTH END RD

S May Rd

Impala Ln

S Huntington Dr

99E

PACIFIC HWY E

Beaver Creek

Pine Cone Ln

Coalca Ln

Little John Ln

S Rocky Bluff Ln

S May Rd

Nursery Ln

SW Forest Cove Rd

SW Riverwood Dr

RAND McNALLY

E   F   G   H   J

45°21'21"
45°20'55"
45°20'29"
45°20'03"
45°19'37"
45°19'11"
45°18'45"
45°18'19"

122°40'14" 122°39'37" 122°39'00" 122°38'23" 122°37'46"

MAP
717

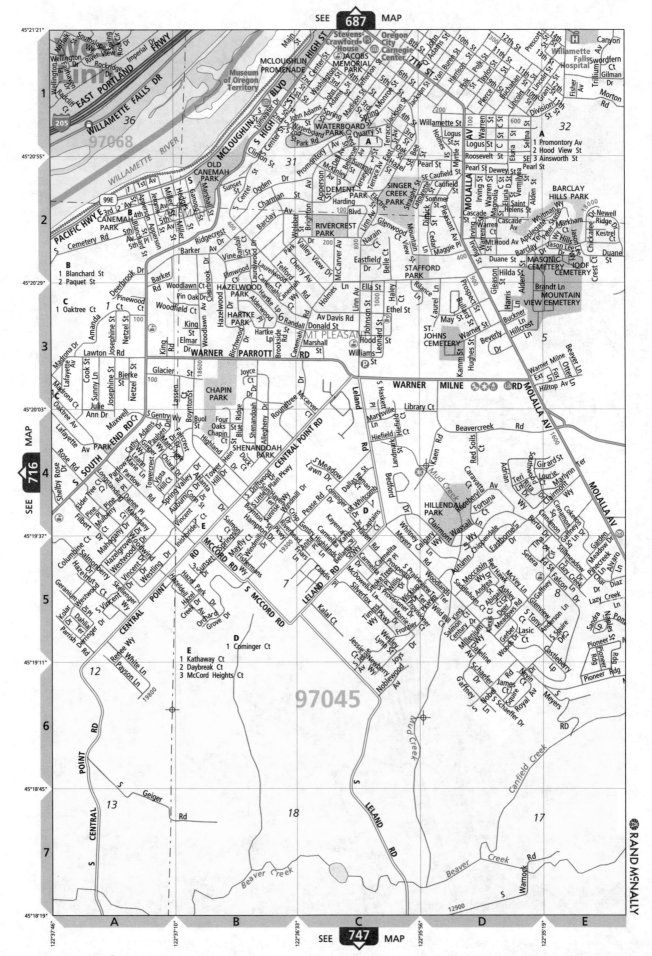

1:24,000
1 in. = 2000 ft.

0   0.25   0.5
miles

N

SEE 716 MAP

SEE 747 MAP

RAND McNALLY

97068

97045

MAP
717

1:24,000
1 in. = 2000 ft.
0   0.25   0.5
miles

SEE 687 MAP

45°21'27"

Canyon Ct
Swordfern Ct
Wake-Robin
Gilman Av
Trillium
Harriet Av
Morton Rd

Holly Crest Ln
Donovan Rd

REDLAND RD

S Meadow View Dr
Holcomb Creek
S Neibur Rd
REDLAND
S/Lost Horse Ln

S Garden Ln
S Hidden Lake Dr
S Unity Ln

1

BULL FROG RESERVOIR
Creek
Lakeside Ct
34
Lake Ridge Wy
S Hidden Lake Dr

45°21'01"

33
Morton Rd
14000

S Greenfield Dr 17600
S Joseph Dr
Grant Dr
Madeline Dr
Brookfield Dr
S Brown Dr
S Brookfield Dr
James Ct
Bayberry Dr
S Fox Pointe Dr
S Silverwood Dr
S Blue
S Plum
S Vista Dr
S Appleton Dr
S Treetop Dr
14900

Waldow Rd

Lake Ridge Wy

S Country Air Ct

2

S Fresh Air Ct

S Laurisa Ln

45°20'35"

213
Newell Creek

Holly Ln

Grove Cir
Quail Cir Ct
Village Ct
Heather Glen Dr
Heather Glen Dr
Nancy Marie Ln

S Waldow Rd
MAPLELANE RD
S Maple Ln Ests
Maple Ln Ests
Carrie Ct
S Hill Valley Ln

3

Abernethy Creek

3

45°20'09"

S Maple Ln Ct
BEAVERCREEK RD
3200
Ira Ln

THAYER RD
Thayer Ct
Coltrane St
Wynton Dr
Stitt Ct
Miles St
Rollins

S Forest
Grove Lp
S Forest
Grove Lp
15800

Grove
Grove

SEE 718 MAP

4

45°19'43"

MOLALLA AV
Fir St
Garden Meadow Dr
Pinecreek Dr
Char Dr
Alvaro Ln
Diaz
Lazy Creek Ln
Sandra
Venice
Sebastian
Pom Pel Dr
Pioneer Rdg
N Clackamas Christian School
Pioneer Rdg
Meyers Rd

CASCADE HWY S
Kingsberry Hts
Kingsberry
Kingsberry Hts
Kingsberry Hts
Inskeep Dr
Marjorie
Clairmont Dr

BEAVERCREEK RD

Douglas Lp
Grove Cir S
Clackamas Community College
Killdeer Rd
Douglas Loop
9

15000 Loder Rd
10
Loder Rd
S Nelson Ln
Thimble Creek Dr
Loder Rd

Fairways Airport

5

45°19'17"

19400

Pioneer Rdg
Meyers Rd

Oregon City HS

Oregon City

GLEN OAK RD

Caufield Rd
Current Dr
Candice Dr
Canyon Ridge Dr
Canyon Ridge Dr
Conway

Brittany
Quiet Oak
Russ Wilcox Wy
Talawa

213

Chanticleer Pl

Andrea Ter
Lynn Ter
Mossy Av
Tad Pl
Cambria Ter
Emily Pl
Helder Dr
Meadows
Kimberly Rose Dr
Turtle Bay Dr

Meyers Rd
Emmerson Dr
Sophia Ct
Connie Ct
Emmerson Ct
Torrey Pines Dr
Coguille St
Andrews Dr
Coquille Ct
Haida 1
Quinalt Dr
Torrey Pines Ct
Quinalt Ct
Woodglen Ct
Crystal

S Glendover
S Meadow
Hilton Head Dr
Augusta
Pebble Beach
Spyglass
Meriwether
S Meadow
Wood Pl
Canterwood
Glen Ct
Persimmon
View
Arborview Wy
Timbersky Wy
Glen Ct
Shady Glen St
Woodglen Wy
Homestead Glen Ct
Quiet Glen Ct
Patsy Dr

Terminal

OREGON CITY GOLF COURSE

Danny Ct

S Old Acres Ln
15
Saddle Ln

Danny
20400

6

45°18'51"

16
Bronco Ln

HENRICI RD

CASCADE HWY S

Shelly Scott Ln
Kelmsley Dr

S Quail Crest Ln
S Reeder Rd

F
1 St. Andrews Ct

Henrici

HENRICI RD

Wilshire Cir

7

45°18'25"

E   F   G   H   J

SEE 747 MAP

122°34'42"   122°34'05"   122°33'28"   122°32'51"   122°32'14"

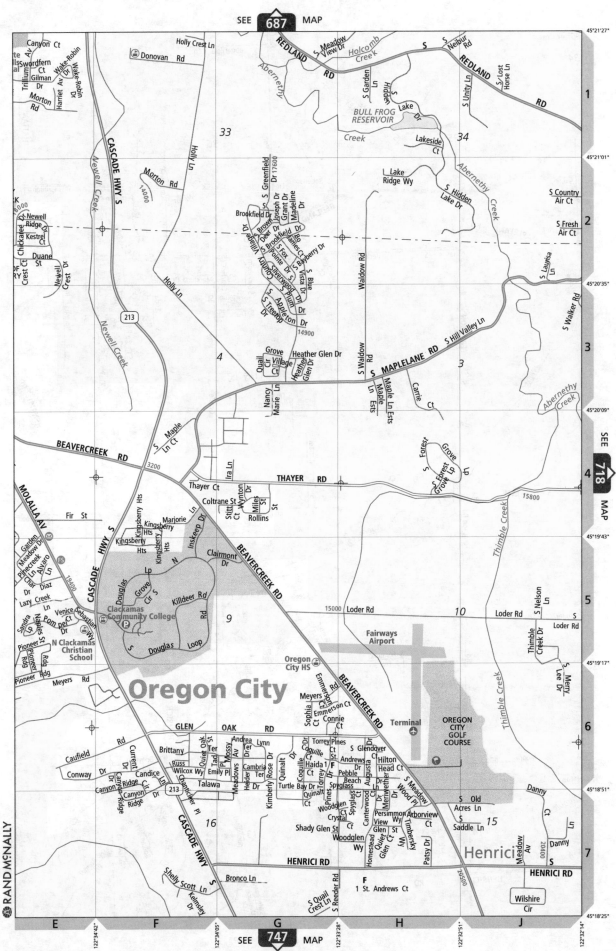

MAP
718

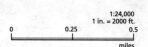

SEE **688** MAP

1:24,000
1 in. = 2000 ft.
0   0.25   0.5
miles

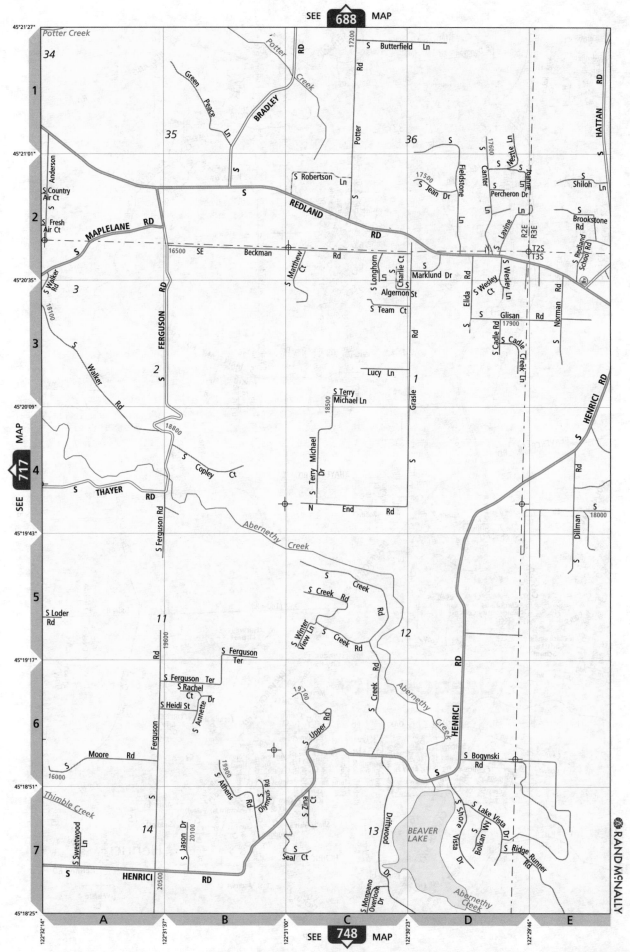

45°21'27"

Potter Creek

34

35

BRADLEY

Green Peace Ln

Potter Creek

Potter Rd

RD

17200

S Butterfield Ln

HATTAN RD

45°21'01"

1

S Anderson

S Country Air Ct

S Fresh Air Ct

MAPLELANE RD

FERGUSON RD

REDLAND RD

S Robertson Ln

36

S Jean Dr

17500

Fieldstone

17600

Canter

Nestle Ln

Joanne Ln

Lavine Ln

Percheron Dr

S

Shiloh Ln

Brookstone Rd

R2E R3E

S Redland School Rd

T2S T3S

2

3

Beckman

16500 SE

Rd

S Matthew Ct

S Longhorn Ln

Algernon St

Charlie Ct

S Team Ct

Marklund Dr

S Wesley Ct

S Wesley Ln

Elida Rd

Norman Rd

S Cadle Rd

17900

Glisan Rd

S Cadle Creek Ln

45°20'35"

S Walker Rd

3

2

18100

Walker Rd

Grasle Rd

Lucy Ln

1

45°20'09"

SEE **717** MAP

4

18800

S Copley Ct

S THAYER RD

S Ferguson Rd

S Terry Michael Ln

18500

S Terry Michael Dr

N   End   Rd

Henrici Rd

Dillman Rd

18000

45°19'43"

Abernethy Creek

5

S Loder Rd

11

19600 Rd

S Creek Rd

Creek Rd

Winter View Ln

S Creek Rd

Creek Rd

12

HENRICI RD

Abernethy Creek

45°19'17"

S Ferguson Ter

S Ferguson Ter

S Rachel Ct

S Heidi St

S Annette Dr

19700

Upper Rd

S Creek Rd

6

Ferguson Rd

Moore Rd

16000

S

45°18'51"

Thimble Creek

14

S Athens Rd

19900

Olympus Rd

S Zina Ct

S Bogynski Rd

Driftwood Dr

BEAVER LAKE

S Shore Vista Dr

S Lake Vista Dr

Bolkan Wy

S Ridge Runner Rd

13

7

S Sweetwood Ln

S Jason Dr

20100

Seal Ct

S Monpano Overlook Dr

Abernethy Creek

45°18'25"

HENRICI RD

20500

A   B   C   D   E

122°32'14"   122°31'37"   122°31'00"   122°30'23"   122°29'46"

SEE **748** MAP

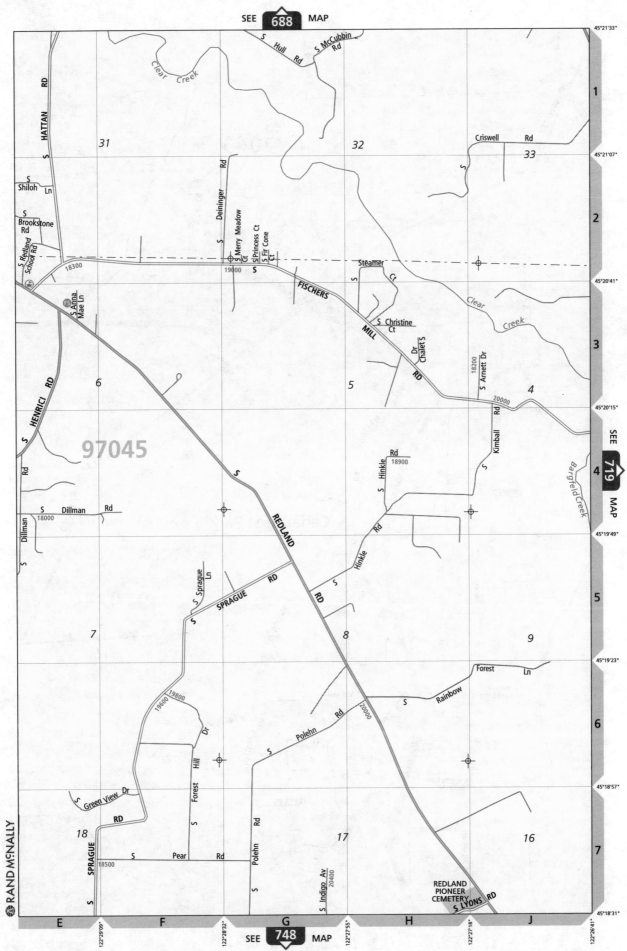

MAP
718

1:24,000
1 in. = 2000 ft.

0   0.25   0.5

miles

S Hull Rd   S McCubbin Rd

Clear Creek

31   32   Criswell   Rd

33

HATTAN   RD   S

45°21'33"

1

45°21'07"

Shiloh   Ln   S

Brookstone Rd

S Redland School Rd

18300

45°20'41"

Deininger   Rd   S

S Merry Meadow Ct
S Princess Ct
S Fir Cone Ct

19000   S

Steamer   Ct

FISCHERS

2

S Anna Mae Ln

S Christine Ct

MILL

Dr Chalet S

18200   S Arnett Dr

45°20'15"

HENRICI   RD   S

6   5   RD   20000

4

97045

Rd   S

18900

S Hinkle   Rd

Kimball   Rd   S

SEE 719 MAP

Bargfeld Creek

45°19'49"

3

4

Dillman   Rd   S

18000

Dillman   S

Hinkle   Rd

REDLAND

S Sprague Ln

SPRAGUE   RD

RD   S

S

RD

8

9

Forest   Ln

Rainbow   S

7   20000

45°19'23"

5

19600   19800

Polehn   Rd   S

45°18'57"

6

Forest Hill Dr

Green View   Dr   S

RD

18   17   16

SPRAGUE

Pear   Rd   S

18500

Polehn   Rd   S

S Indigo Av   20400

REDLAND PIONEER CEMETERY

S LYONS RD

45°18'31"

7

E   F   G   H   J

122°29'09"   122°28'32"   122°27'55"   122°27'18"   122°26'41"

MAP
719

1:24,000
1 in. = 2000 ft.

0   0.25   0.5
miles

SEE **689** MAP

45°21'33"
S Gerber Rd
SPRINGWATER RD
S Criswell Rd
21200
1
S Arthur Rd
S Harding Rd
33
34
97045
35
45°21'07"
S Rory Ct
22600
S Eaden Rd
17700
2
S Charriere Rd
S Harding Rd
S Strowbridge Rd
45°20'41"
T2S
SEADEN RD
Foster Creek
T3S
18000
FS
3
S FISCHERS MILL RD
21300
Bilyeu AV
S Strowbridge Rd
21100
Clear Creek
4
S FISCHERS MILL
20900
3
2
45°20'15"
S FISCHERS MILL RD
18700
18500
MATTOON RD
S SPRINGWATER RD
SEE **718** MAP
20000
Trout
Norton Rd
S Allen Ln
Cove St
Forest Glen Rd
S Kramer Rd
Horseshoe Ln
Cedarhurst Park
S RIDGE RD
19200
Sherwood
Av
Sylvan Av
45°19'49"
Sylvan Av
S Neil Rd
S Sylvan
S MATTOON RD
5
97023
9
10
S Spring Creek Rd
11
45°19'23"
Barafield Creek
Fantasy Trail
Wenzel Farm
S McKenzie Ln
Clear Creek
Rd
S Lost Mountain Rd
6
S Syth
Mija Ln
S MATTOON RD
45°18'57"
S Summit Ridge Ln
S Circle
S Patrick Wy
S RIDGE RD
S Ridgeway Ln
Diamond
Stormer Rd
7
16
15
14
S
S Bluebird Ln
45°18'31"
122°26'41"
A
122°26'04"
B
122°25'27"
C
122°24'50"
D
122°24'13"
E

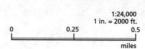
RAND McNALLY

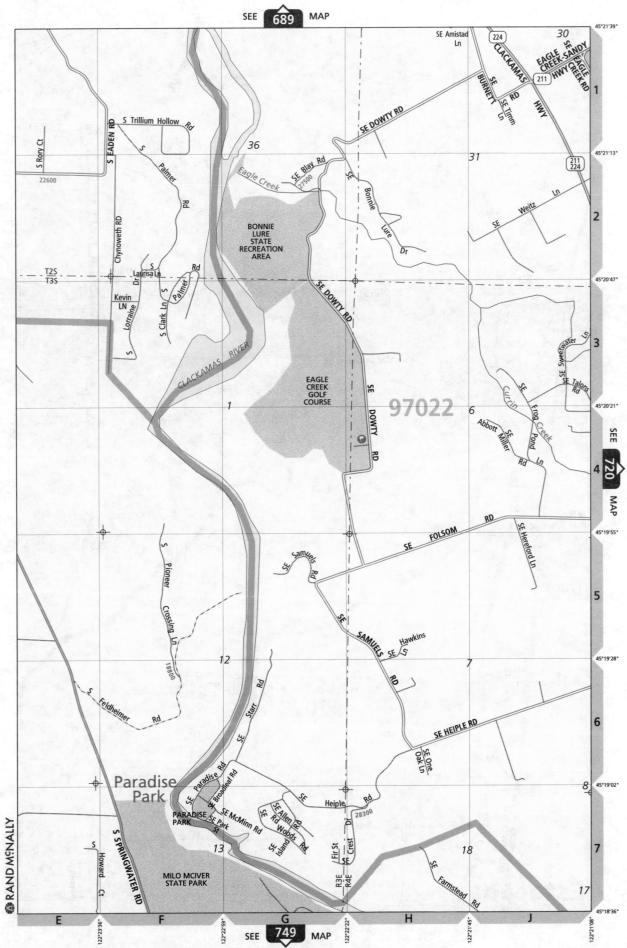

MAP
719

1:24,000
1 in. = 2000 ft.

0   0.25   0.5

miles

SEE **689** MAP

SE Amistad Ln

224

30

CLACKAMAS HWY

EAGLE CREEK-SANDY

EAGLE CREEK RD

211

1

SE BURNETT RD

SE Timm Ln

SE DOWTY RD

S EADEN RD

S Trillium Hollow Rd

45°21'39"

45°21'13"

211
224

36

SE Blay Rd

27500

SE

Bonnie Lure Dr

SE Weitz Ln

2

Eagle Creek

S Rory Ct

22600

S Palmer Rd

Chynoweth RD

BONNIE LURE STATE RECREATION AREA

45°20'47"

T2S
T3S

Laurisa Ln

S Rd

SE DOWTY RD

SE Sweetwater Ln

3

Kevin LN

Lorraine Dr

S Clark Ln

S Palmer Rd

SE Talons Rd

S

CLACKAMAS RIVER

EAGLE CREEK GOLF COURSE

Currin

SE Frog Pond Ln

45°20'21"

1

6

97022

Abbott Miller Rd

SE

4

SE DOWTY RD

SEE **720** MAP

45°19'55"

SE FOLSOM RD

SE Hereford Ln

SE Samuels Rd

5

S Pioneer Crossing Ln

18800

SE

SAMUELS RD

SE Ln

Hawkins

7

45°19'28"

12

SE Starr Rd

SE Heiple RD

6

S Feldheimer Rd

SE One Oak Ln

45°19'02"

8

Paradise Park

SE Paradise Rd

SE Broadleaf Rd

Heiple

SE Crest Dr

Rd

28300

18

7

PARADISE PARK

SE Park St

SE McMinn Rd

SE Allen Rd

SE Wobds Rd

SE Island Rd

SE Fir St

SE Crest Dr

R3E
R4E

SE Farmstead Rd

17

S Howard Ct

S SPRINGWATER RD

13

MILO MCIVER STATE PARK

E   F   G   H   J

45°18'36"

SEE **749** MAP

12°23'36"   12°22'59"   12°22'22"   12°21'45"   12°21'08"

MAP
720

1:24,000
1 in. = 2000 ft.

0   0.25   0.5
miles

N

SEE 690 MAP

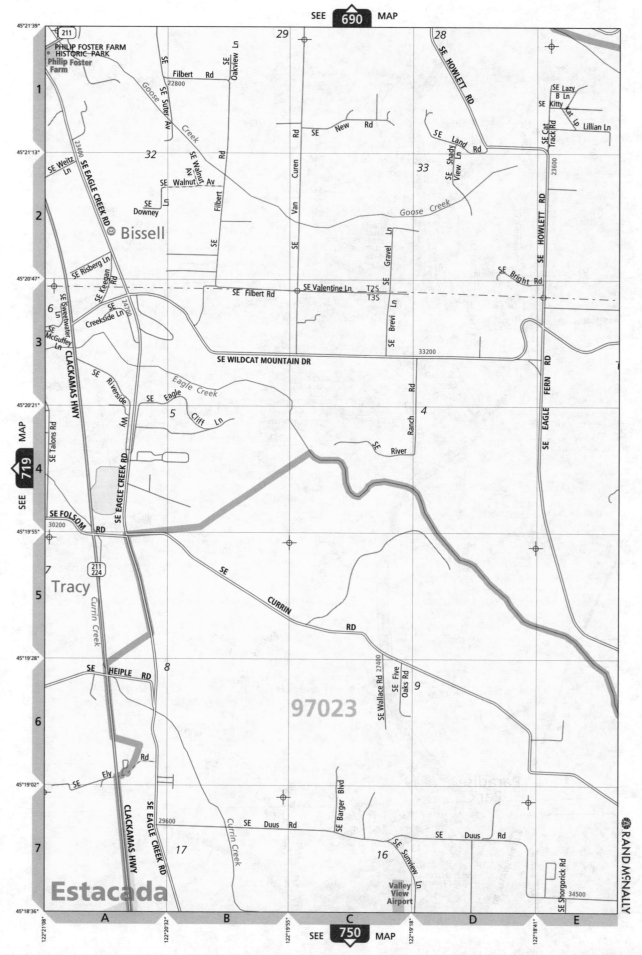

45°21'39"

211

PHILIP FOSTER FARM
HISTORIC PARK
Philip Foster
Farm

29   28

SE HOWLETT RD

SE
Filbert Rd

SE Oakview Ln

22800

1

SE Suter Av

SE Lazy
B Ln

SE Cat Track Lp

SE Kitty

Lillian Ln

Goose

23400

SE Weitz Ln

SE EAGLE CREEK RD

Creek

SE
Walnut
Rd

SE
New   Rd

SE Land
Rd

SE Cat Track Rd

23600

45°21'13"

32

SE Walnut
Av

Curen

SE Shady
View Ln

33

SE Walnut Av

Filbert

Van

SE

SE
Downey

2   Bissell

SE   Goose Creek

SE Risberg Ln

SE Keegan

Gravel

SE Howlett RD

SE Bright Rd

45°20'47"

24700

SE Filbert Rd

SE Valentine Ln

T2S

Ln

SE Sweetwater

T3S

6

Creekside Ln

SE Brevi

SE
McGuffey
Ln

3

33200

CLACKAMAS HWY

SE WILDCAT MOUNTAIN DR

SE Riverside

Eagle   Creek

Rd

SE Eagle

SE Talons Rd

Hwy

5   Cliff Ln

4

Ranch

45°20'21"

SE
River

SE EAGLE FERN RD

4

MAP

719

SE FOLSOM

30200   RD

45°19'55"

211
224

SE

Tracy

CURRIN

5

RD

Currin Creek

45°19'28"

SE HEIPLE RD

8

SE Wallace Rd

27400

SE Five
Oaks Rd

9

97023

6

Rd

SE Ely

45°19'02"

SE Barger Blvd

CLACKAMAS HWY

SE EAGLE CREEK RD

29600

Currin Creek

SE Duus Rd

SE Duus Rd

SE Sunview Ln

SE Shorgorick Rd

7   17   16

34500

Estacada

Valley
View
Airport

RAND McNALLY

45°18'36"

A   B   C   D   E

122°21'08"   122°20'32"   122°19'55"   122°19'18"   122°18'41"

SEE 750 MAP

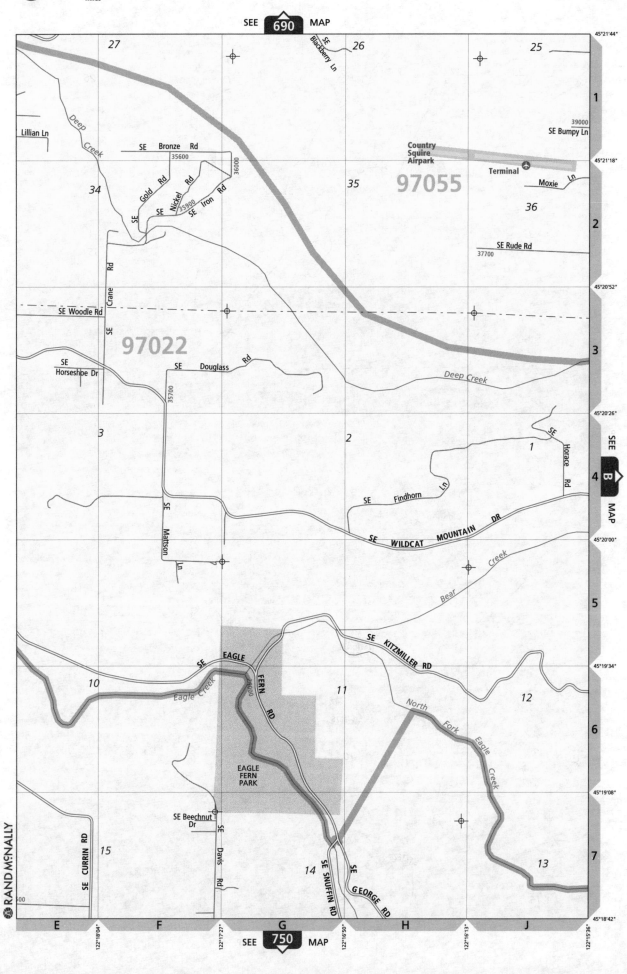

MAP
720

1:24,000
1 in. = 2000 ft.

0   0.25   0.5
miles

SEE 690 MAP

45°21'44"

27   26   25

1

Deep Creek

Lillian Ln   39000
                                                              SE Bumpy Ln
SE   Bronze   Rd
35600   Country
                                                  Squire
                    36000   Airpark
                                                              Terminal   Moxie   Ln
34   Gold Rd   97055
        Nickel Rd   36
        35900
        SE   Iron   Rd   35

45°21'18"

2

                                                              SE Rude Rd
Crane Rd   37700

45°20'52"

SE Woodle Rd   SEE
                                                                          B
97022   MAP

3

SE   SE   Douglass   Rd
Horseshoe Dr   Deep Creek
              35700

45°20'26"

3   2   1   SE

                                                              Horace Rd

B

SE Mattson Ln   SE   Findhorn   Ln

              SE   WILDCAT   MOUNTAIN   DR

45°20'00"

                                              Bear   Creek

5

                              SE   KITZMILLER   RD

SE   EAGLE   Creek
10   Eagle Creek   FERN 11   North   12
                              36000 RD

45°19'34"

6

                    EAGLE   Fork   Eagle Creek
                    FERN
                    PARK

45°19'08"

SE Beechnut
Dr

SE   CURRIN   RD   13
15   Davis Rd

7

        14 SE SNUFFIN RD
            SE   GEORGE   RD

45°18'42"

E   F   G   H   J

122°18'04"   122°17'27"   122°16'50"   122°16'13"   122°15'36"

SEE 750 MAP

MAP
723

1:24,000
1 in. = 2000 ft.

0   0.25   0.5
miles

SEE 693 MAP

45°21'54"

28   27   26

1

45°21'28"

Wildcat

2   33   34   Wildcat Creek Rd   35

45°21'02"

Creek

3

T2S
T3S

45°20'36"

MAP
B
4
SEE

4   3   97055   2

45°20'10"

5   Alder Creek   NF-3626

MT
HOOD
NATIONAL
FOREST

45°19'44"

6   9   NF-3626   10   11

SE Weber Rd

45°19'18"

Alder Creek

7   16   NF-3626   15   14

45°18'51"

A   122°03'53"   B   122°03'16"   C   122°02'39"   D   122°02'02"   E
122°04'30"

SEE B MAP

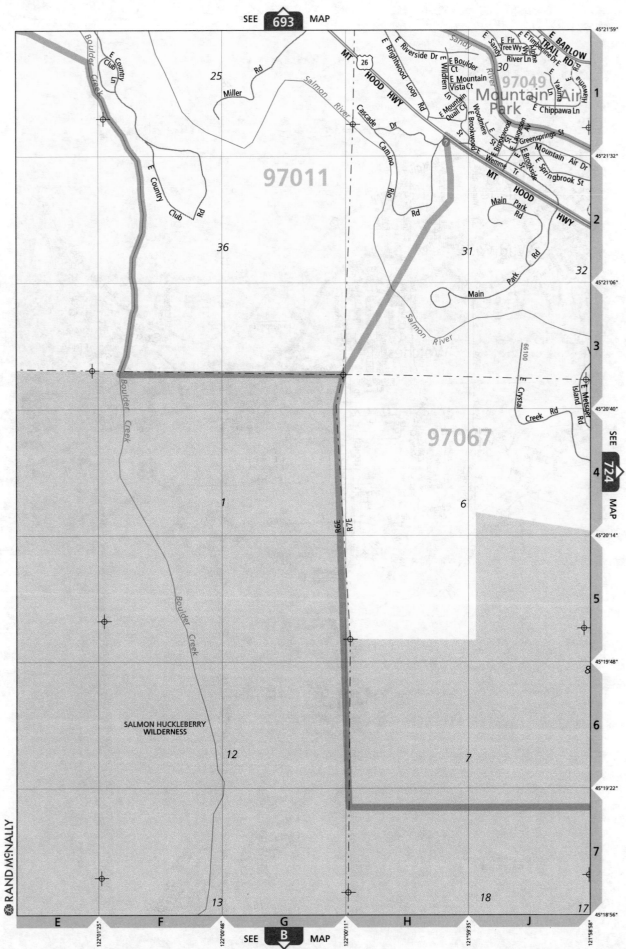

MAP
723

1:24,000
1 in. = 2000 ft.

0   0.25   0.5

miles

SEE 693 MAP

SEE 724 MAP

SEE B MAP

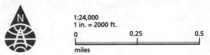

RAND McNALLY

45°21'59"

45°21'32"

45°21'06"

45°20'40"

45°20'14"

45°19'48"

45°19'22"

45°18'56"

E BARLOW TRAIL RD

MT HOOD HWY

26

Mountain Air Park

97049

97011

97067

SALMON HUCKLEBERRY WILDERNESS

Boulder Creek

Salmon River

E Country Club Ln

E Country Club Rd

Miller Rd

Salmon River

Cascade Camino Rio Rd

E Riverside Dr

E Brightwood Loop Rd

E Boulder Ct

E Widfern Ln

E Mountain Vista Ct

E Mountain Quail Ct

Woodmere St

E Brookwood St

E Brookwood St

E Laurelan St

E Brookside Ln

E Wemme Tr

E Fir Tree Wy

E Sandy River Ln

E Timberline Dr E

E Alpine Wy

E Yakima

E Chippawa Ln

Greensprings St

Mountain Air Dr

E Springbrook St

Sandy River

Main Park Rd

Main Park Rd

Main

E Crystal Creek Rd

E Metsger Island Rd

66100

R6E R7E

25

36

30

31

32

3

1

6

5

8

12

7

13

18

17

E   F   G   H   J

MAP
724

1:24,000
1 in. = 2000 ft.

0   0.25   0.5
miles

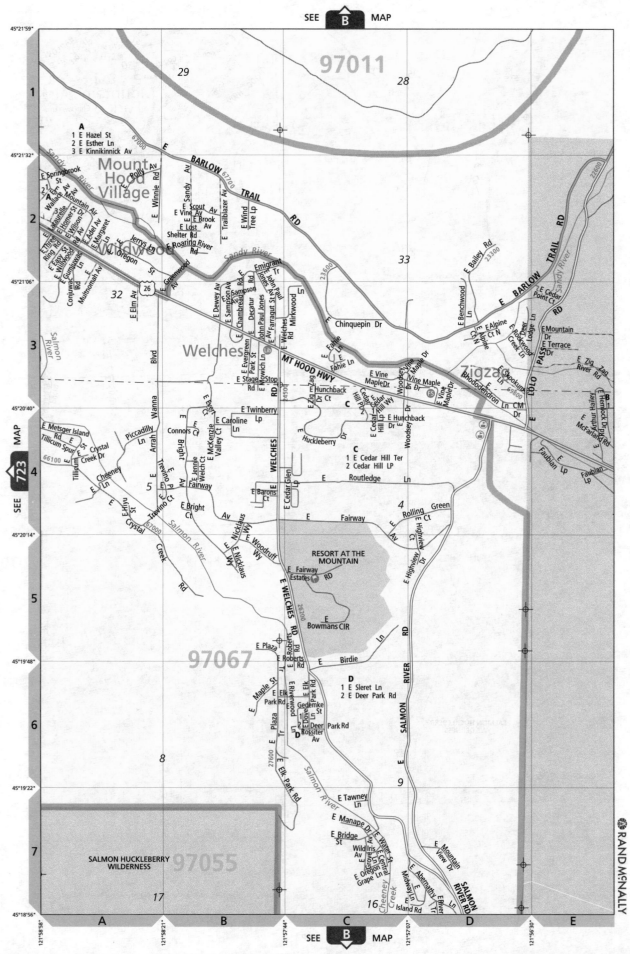

97011

29

28

A
1 E Hazel St
2 E Esther Ln
3 E Kinnikinnick Av

Mount
Hood
Village

E Springbrook
St
E Winnie Rd
Polly Av

BARLOW
TRAIL
RD

E Sandy Av
E Scout Av
E Vine Av
E Trailblazer Lp
E Wind Tree Lp

E Bailey Rd

E BARLOW TRAIL RD

Wildwood

E Lafayette
E Homer Dr
E Wilson Av
E Adel Av
E Margaret Ln

E Brook Av
E Last Av
Shelter Rd
E Roaring River Rd

Sandy River

33

E Benchwood

E Cedar Point Ct

Zigzag

E Alpine
E Alpine Ct N
CI N

E Rockwood
Creek Ln
Lodge Ln

E Mountain Dr
E Terrace Dr

E Zig Zag River Rd

E Three
Ring Rd
E Essy St
E Willwood
E Gurnumac Rd
Conjuwac
Rd
Multnomah Av

E Oregon St

E Greenwood Av

E Elm Av

26

32

Salmon River

Welches

Blvd

E Dewey Av
E Sampson Av
Chambreau Rd
Decatur
E Welches

Sampson Rd
John Paul Jones
E Av Farragut St
Mirkwood Ln

Emigrant Tr

Chinquepin Dr

E Fahie Ln
E Fahie Ln

MT HOOD HWY

E Vine Maple Dr
Vine Maple Dr
Woodsey Ln
E Vine Maple Dr

Rhododendron Ln CM Dr

E LOLO PASS RD

Okookum Dr

E Hemlock Dr
E Hemlock Halle
McFarland Rd

B

E Metsger Island Rd
E Crystal Ln
Tillicum Spur
Crystal Creek Dr

Piccadilly Ln
Arrah Ln
Connors Ln
Bright St
E McKenzie Ct
Caroline Ln
E Caroline Ln

E Evergreen Ln
Park St
E Mowich Ln
E Moe Stop
E Stage Rd
E Twinberry Lp
Huckleberry

E Zig Zag Hill Pl
Hunchback Dr Ct
E Cedar Hill Pl
Cedar Hill Wy
E Hunchback Ln

C

1 E Cedar Hill Ter
2 Cedar Hill LP

Woodsey Dr

66100

Cheeney

E Hiyu Ln
E Crystal

67000

Salmon River Creek

Trevino Ct
E Jennie Welch Ct
Trevino Av
E Fairway
E Bright Ct

E Barons Ct
E Cedar Glen
E Cedar Glen Ln

WELCHES

E Nicklaus Wy
E Nicklaus Wy
Woodruff Wy

E
Routledge Ln

Rolling Green

4

E Highview
E Highview Dr

Fairway Av

RESORT AT THE MOUNTAIN

E Fairway Estates
RD

E Bowmans CIR

26200

97067

E Plaza
E Roberts Rd
E Roberts Rd

Birdie

SALMON RIVER RD

Maple St
E Elk Park Rd
E Elk Park Rd
Gedemke St
E Dove Ln
E Deer Park Rd
E Plaza Tr
Rossiter Av

E Elk Park Rd

D

1 E Sleret Ln
2 E Deer Park Rd

27600

E Tawney Ln

E Manape Dr

E Bridge St

9

E Mountain View Dr

8

97055

SALMON HUCKLEBERRY WILDERNESS

17

Wild Iris Av
E Grove St
E Oregon Grape St
E Central St
E Water St
E Abernathy Rd
Midway Ln
Island Rd
E River

SALMON RIVER RD

16

Cheeney Creek

45°21'59"
45°21'32"
45°21'06"
45°20'40"
45°20'14"
45°19'48"
45°19'22"
45°18'56"

121°58'58"
121°58'21"
121°57'44"
121°57'07"
121°56'30"

MAP
723
SEE

A   B   C   D   E

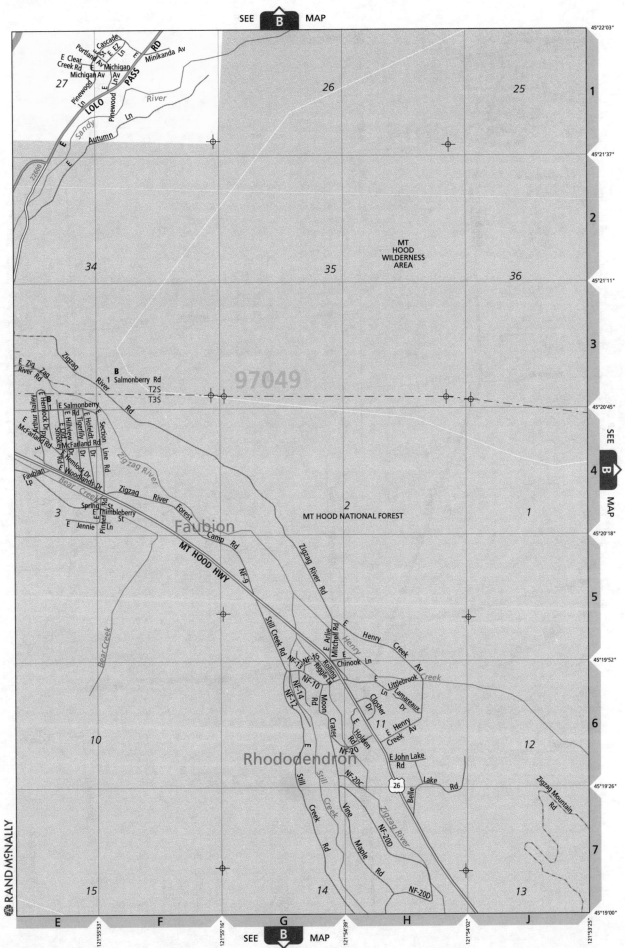

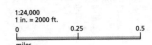

MAP
724

1:24,000
1 in. = 2000 ft.

0   0.25   0.5

miles

SEE B MAP

45°22'03"

1

27

LOLO PASS RD

E Cascade St
E EZ Ln
Portland Av
E Michigan Av
Michigan Av
E Clear Creek Rd
E Pinewood Ln
Pinewood Ln

Minikanda Av

Sandy River

Autumn

26

25

45°21'37"

2

34

35

MT HOOD WILDERNESS AREA

36

45°21'11"

3

E Zig Zag River Rd

Zigzag River

B 1 Salmonberry Rd
T2S
T3S

97049

45°20'45"

SEE B MAP

B
E Hemlock Dr
McFarland Rd
Mahar Hahar
E Salmonberry Rd
E Hofeldt
E Hillview Dr
E Tigerlily
E Olce
E Smoke
E Hemlock Dr
E McFarland Rd
E Section Line Rd

Zigzag River

4

Faubian Lp
Bear Creek
E Woodlands Dr
Spring St
E Thimbleberry St
E Primrose Ln
E Jennie Ln

Zigzag River Forest

2

MT HOOD NATIONAL FOREST

1

45°20'18"

Faubion

Camp Rd

NF-9

MT HOOD HWY

3

Bear Creek

Zigzag River Rd

5

Still Creek Rd
NF-15
NF-13
Riggle
NF-10
E Arlie
Mitchell Rd
E Henry
Henry Creek Av
E Chinook Ln

45°19'52"

NF-14
Moon
Rd
E Crater
NF-20
Littlebrook
Closher Dr
Lamareaux Dr

Creek

6

NF-12

Rhododendron

E Holden Rd
11
E Henry Creek Av
E John Lake Rd

12

45°19'26"

10

NF-20C
Still
Still Creek
Creek Rd
Vine
Maple Rd
NF-20D
NF-20D

26

Belle

Lake Rd

Zigzag River

Zigzag Mountain Rd

7

15

14

13

45°19'00"

E   F   G   H   J

SEE B MAP

121°55'53"   121°55'16"   121°54'39"   121°54'02"   121°53'25"

MAP
741

1:24,000
1 in. = 2000 ft.

0   0.25   0.5

miles

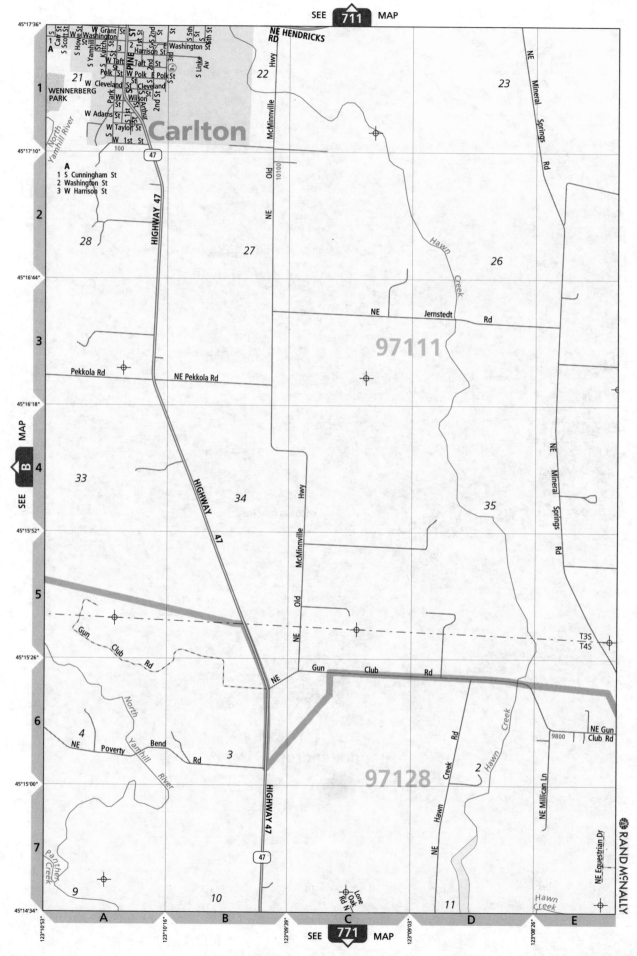

SEE 711 MAP

45°17'36"

NE HENDRICKS RD

W Grant St
W Washington St
S Car St
S Scott St
S Howe St
S Yamhill St
W Taft St
W Polk St
W Cleveland St
Park
W Wilson St
W Arthur St
S Pine St
E 1st St
S 2nd St
E Taft St
E Polk St
E Cleveland St
S 5th St
W Washington St
S Linke Av

21

22

23

NE Mineral Springs Rd

A

1

WENNERBERG
PARK

W Adams St

W Taylor St

W 1st St

Carlton

North Yamhill River

100

47

45°17'10"

A
1 S Cunningham St
2 Washington St
3 W Harrison St

28

27

NE Old McMinnville Hwy

10100

26

Hawn Creek

2

45°16'44"

HIGHWAY 47

NE Jernstedt Rd

3

97111

Pekkola Rd

NE Pekkola Rd

45°16'18"

SEE MAP B

33

34

NE Old McMinnville Hwy

35

NE Mineral Springs Rd

4

45°15'52"

HIGHWAY 47

5

45°15'26"

Gun Club Rd

T3S
T4S

NE Gun Club Rd

NE Old McMinnville

North Yamhill River

Gun Club Rd

6

4

NE Poverty Bend Rd

3

Hawn Creek

2

Creek Rd

9800

NE Gun Club Rd

NE Millican Ln

45°15'00"

97128

HIGHWAY 47

7

45°14'34"

Panther Creek

9

10

47

Lone Oak Rd N

11

NE Equestrian Dr

NE Hawn Creek

Hawn Creek

A   B   C   D   E

123°10'53"   123°10'16"   123°09'39"   123°09'03"   123°08'26"

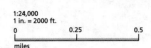
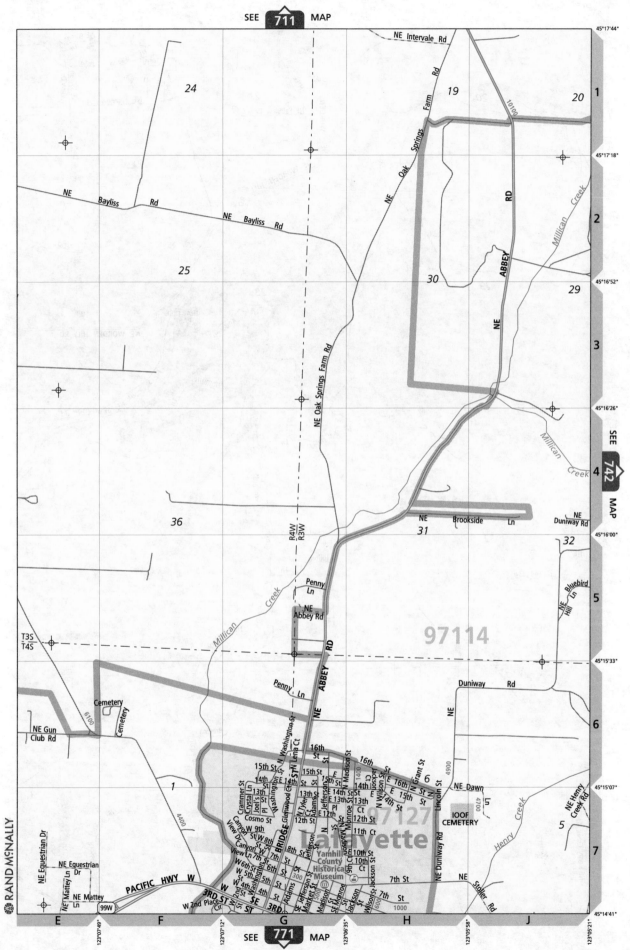

MAP 741

MAP
742

1:24,000
1 in. = 2000 ft.

0   0.25   0.5
miles

SEE 712 MAP

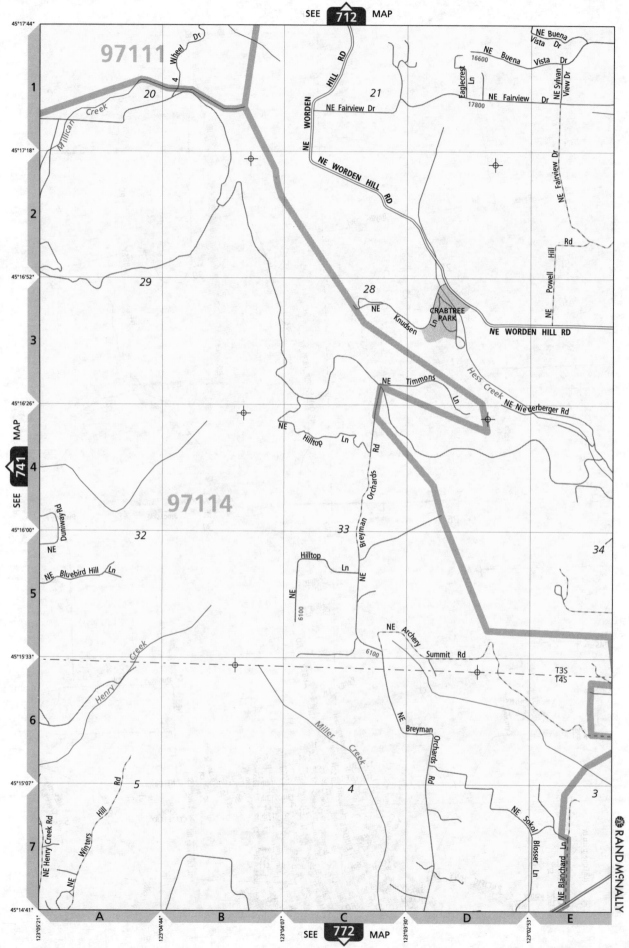

97111

NE Buena Vista Dr
NE Buena Vista Dr
16600

Wheel Dr

20

NE WORDEN HILL RD

NE Fairview Dr

21

Eaglecrest Ln
17800

NE Fairview Dr

NE Sylvan View Dr

Millican Creek

NE WORDEN HILL RD

NE Fairview Dr

45°17'44"
45°17'18"
45°16'52"
45°16'26"
45°16'00"
45°15'33"
45°15'07"
45°14'41"

1
2
3
4
5
6
7

29

28

NE Knudsen Ln

CRABTREE PARK

Powell Hill Rd

NE WORDEN HILL RD

NE Timmons Ln

Hess Creek NE Niederberger Rd

NE Hilltop Ln

Orchards Rd

97114

SEE 741 MAP

Duniway Rd

NE

32

33

34

Hilltop Ln

NE

Breyman

6100

NE Bluebird Hill Ln

NE Archery

Summit Rd

6100

T3S
T4S

NE Breyman

Henry Creek

Miller Creek

Orchards Rd

5

4

3

NE Henry Creek Rd

NE Winters Hill Rd

NE Sokol Blosser Ln

NE Blanchard Ln

RAND MCNALLY

A   B   C   D   E

123°05'21"
123°04'44"
123°04'07"
123°03'30"
123°02'53"

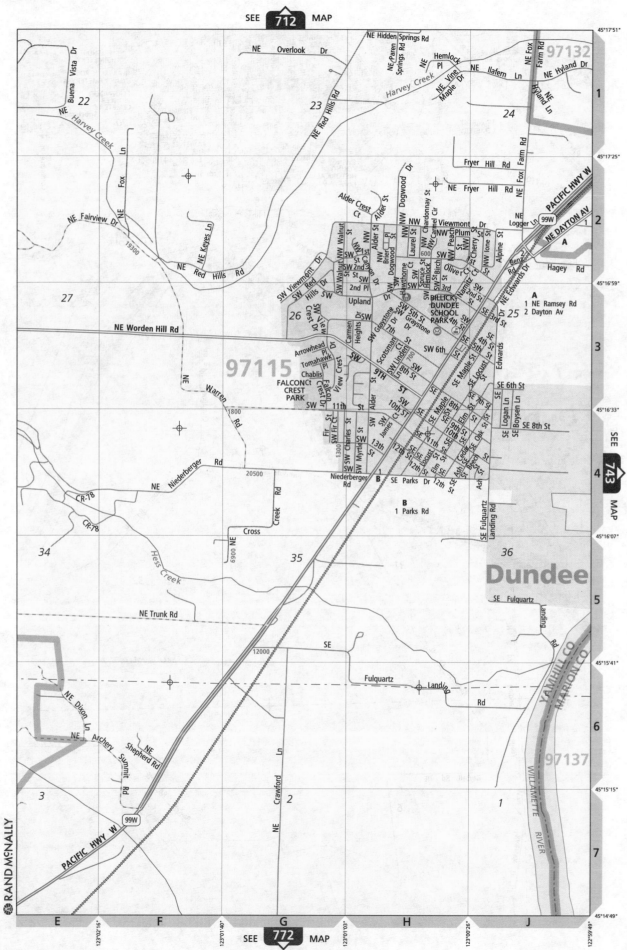

MAP
742

1:24,000
1 in. = 2000 ft.

0   0.25   0.5
miles

SEE 712 MAP

45°17'51"
45°17'25"
45°16'59"
45°16'33"
45°16'07"
45°15'41"
45°15'15"
45°14'49"

1
2
3
4
5
6
7

97132
97115
97137

Dundee

SEE 743 MAP

A
1 NE Ramsey Rd
2 Dayton Av

B
1 Parks Rd

NE Hidden Springs Rd
NE Overlook Dr
NE Praren Springs Rd
Hemlock Pl
NE Vine Maple Dr
NE Ilafern Ln
NE Fox Farm Rd
NE Hyland Dr
NE Hyland Ln
Harvey Creek

NE Buena Vista Dr
22
23
24

NE Harvey Creek
NE Red Hills Rd
Fryer Hill Rd
NE Fryer Hill Rd
NE Fox Farm Rd
PACIFIC HWY W

Ln
NE Fox
NE Fairview Dr
19300
NE Keyes Ln
NE Logger Ln
99W
NE DAYTON AV

Alder Crest Ct
Alder St
NW Dogwood
NW Chardonnay St
NW Carmel Cir
Viewmont Dr
NE Edwards Dr
A

NE Red Hills Rd
SW Viewmont Dr
Walnut St
NW Walnut
NW Alder St
Brier Pl
Laurel St
NW Peach
NW Plum
Cherry
NW Ione St
Alpine St
Benz Rd
Hagey Rd

27
SW Walnut St
SW 2nd St
SW Red Hills
1st Canyon Dr
NW Dogwood Pl
Hawthorne
Spruce St
Hemlock St
Oliver
Nimitz Ct
2nd St
600

SW Viewmont Dr
SW 2nd Pl
Upland
SW 3rd Dr
BILLICK DUNDEE SCHOOL PARK
SW 4th
25

26
SW View Crest Dr
Carmen Heights
SW Graystone Dr
SW Graystone Dr
SW 5th St
SE Maple Dr
SE 4th St
Edwards

NE Worden Hill Rd
Arrowhead Pl
Scotsman Ct
SW Linden Ln
SW 6th
SE Locust St
SE 6th St

Tomahawk Pl
SW 7th St
700
SE 5th

Chablis
View Crest
SW 8th St
SE Logan Ln
SE Boysen Ln

FALCON CREST PARK
FALCON Ct
Falcon Crest Dr
SW 9TH ST
SW Alder St
SW 10th St
SE Maple
8th
SE Elm
9th St
SE 10th
SE 8th St

1800
SW 11th St
SW Fir Ct
Fir St
SW James Ct
SE 11th St
SE Cedar St
SE Ash St
SE Beech St

SW Charles St
SW 13th St
SW Myrtle St
12th St
SE Locust
Elm St
Ash St
Oak St

NE Warren Rd
1300
SE Parks Dr
12th St
SE Fulquartz

NE Niederberger Rd
20500
Niederberger Rd
B

CR-78
NE
Creek Rd
NE Cross
6900 NE
12000
SE
SE Fulquartz Landing Rd
SE Fulquartz

CR-78
34
35
36
SE Fulquartz
Landing Rd

Hess Creek
NE Trunk Rd
Fulquartz
Landing
Rd
YAMHILL CO
MARION CO
WILLAMETTE RIVER

NE Dixon Ln
NE Archery Ln
NE Shepherd Rd
NE Summit Rd
NE Crawford Ln
3
2
1

99W
PACIFIC HWY W

E   F   G   H   J

123°02'16"   123°01'40"   123°01'03"   123°00'26"   122°59'49"

SEE 772 MAP

RAND MCNALLY

MAP
743

1:24,000
1 in. = 2000 ft.

0   0.25   0.5
miles

SEE 713 MAP

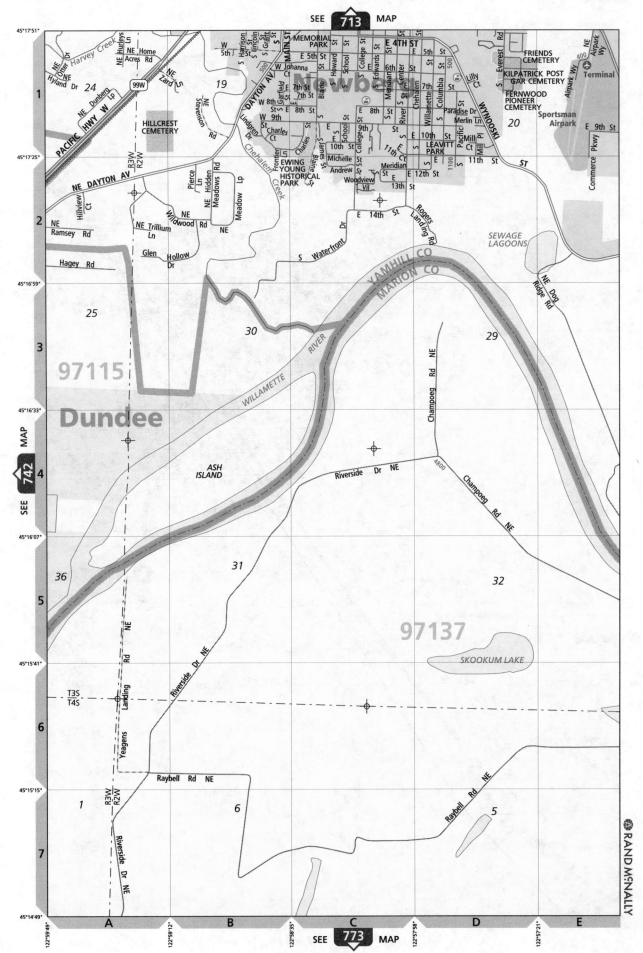

Harvey Creek

NE Otter Dr
NE Hurleys Ln
NE Home Acres Rd
NE
ONE
Hyland Dr   *24*
NE Dunberg
NE Zard Ln
99W
19
PACIFIC HWY W

NE Stevenson Rd

HILLCREST CEMETERY

NE DAYTON AV

Hillview Ct
NE Pierce Ln
NE Hidden Meadows Rd
NE Meadows Lp
NE Meadow Rd

NE Ramsey Rd
NE Wildwood Rd
NE Trillium Ln
NE

Glen Hollow Dr

Hagey Rd

Lindgren Dr
Charles Ct
Charles St
S James St
S Blaine St
Frontier St

Chehalem Creek

EWING YOUNG HISTORICAL PARK

W 5th
S Harrison St
S Grant St
S Lincoln St
MAIN ST
MEMORIAL PARK
E 4TH ST

W Johanna St
E 5th St
DAYTON AV
S 500
W 7th St
7th St
E Garfield St
W 8th St
8th St
E
W 9th St
9th
St
E
S School St
S Edwards St
S College St
S Meridian St
S Center St
S River St
S Willamette St
S Columbia St
Paradise Dr
Merlin Ln
Mill Pl
Mill Ct
S Pacific
1100
6th
7th
8th
9th
E 10th St
11th St
E 12th St
500
Lilly Ct
WYNOOSKI
LEAVITT PARK
ST

Newberg

Howard
Blaine
School

Michelle
Andrew
Meridian
E 13th St
Woodview Vil.

Dr
E 14th St
S Waterfront
Rogers Landing Rd

EVEREST Rd
NE
400
Airpark Wy NE
Airpark Wy
Terminal

FRIENDS CEMETERY
KILPATRICK POST GAR CEMETERY
FERNWOOD PIONEER CEMETERY
20
Sportsman Airpark
E 9th St
Commerce Pkwy

SEWAGE LAGOONS

YAMHILL CO
MARION CO

NE Dog Ridge Rd

25

97115

30

WILLAMETTE

RIVER

29

Champoeg Rd NE

Dundee

ASH ISLAND

Riverside Dr NE
4800
Champoeg Rd NE

SEE 742 MAP

36

31

32

97137

SKOOKUM LAKE

Riverside Dr NE

T3S
T4S

Landing Rd NE
Yeagens

R3W
R2W

Raybell Rd NE

1

6

Raybell Rd NE

5

Riverside Dr NE

45°17'51"
45°17'25"
45°16'59"
45°16'33"
45°16'07"
45°15'41"
45°15'15"
45°14'49"

1
2
3
4
5
6
7

A   B   C   D   E

122°59'49"
122°59'12"
122°58'35"
122°57'58"
122°57'21"

SEE 773 MAP

MAP
743

1:24,000
1 in. = 2000 ft.
0   0.25   0.5
miles

SEE **713** MAP

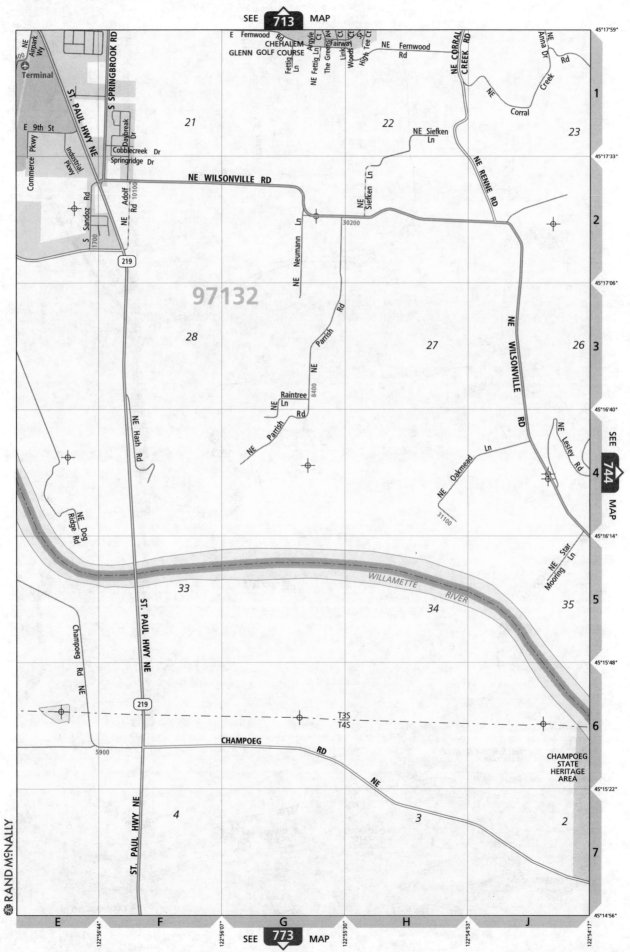

E Fernwood Rd
CHEHALEM
GLENN GOLF COURSE

NE Airpark Wy
Terminal

E 9th St

S SPRINGBROOK RD

Commerce Pkwy
Industrial Pkwy

ST. PAUL HWY NE

Daybreak Dr
Cobblecreek Dr
Springridge Dr

Sandoz Rd
S 1700

NE Adolf Rd 10100

21

Argyle Ln
Fettig Ln
NE Fettig Ln Ct
The Greens
Link Ct
Woods St
High Tee Ct
Fairway

NE Fernwood Rd

22

NE CORRAL CREEK RD

NE Anna Dr
Rd

NE Corral Creek

Corral

23

1

NE Siefken Ln

NE Siefken Ln

NE RENNE RD

45°17'33"

NE WILSONVILLE RD

NE Neumann Ln

30200

219

2

45°17'06"

97132

28

NE Parrish Rd

NE Parrish Rd
8400

27

NE WILSONVILLE RD

26

3

Raintree Ln

NE Parrish Rd

NE Hash Rd

45°16'40"

NE Oakmead Ln

NE Lesley Rd

31100

SEE **744** MAP

4

NE Dog Ridge Rd

WILLAMETTE RIVER

45°16'14"

NE Star Mooring Ln

33

34

35

5

ST. PAUL HWY NE

Champoeg Rd NE

45°15'48"

219

5900

CHAMPOEG

RD

NE

T3S
T4S

6

45°15'22"

CHAMPOEG STATE HERITAGE AREA

ST. PAUL HWY NE

4

3

2

7

E   F   G   H   J

122°56'44"   122°56'07"   122°55'30"   122°54'53"   122°54'17"

45°14'56"

SEE **773** MAP

MAP
744

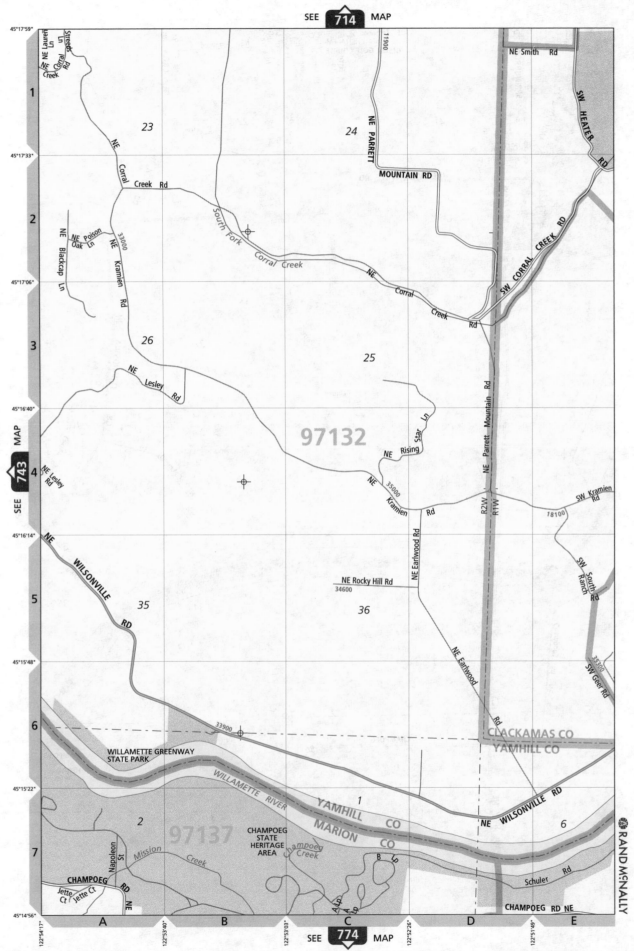

1:24,000
1 in. = 2000 ft.

0   0.25   0.5

miles

NE Lauren Ln

NE Streets

NE Corral Ln

NE Creek Rd

NE Smith Rd

SW HEATER RD

1

23

24

NE PARRETT

MOUNTAIN RD

NE Corral Creek Rd

NE Poison Oak Ln

NE Blackcap Ln

33000

NE Kramien Rd

South Fork Corral Creek

NE Corral

Creek Rd

SW CORRAL CREEK RD

11900

2

45°17'33"

45°17'06"

26

25

3

NE Lesley Rd

97132

NE Rising Star Ln

NE Parrett Mountain Rd

45°16'40"

MAP
743
SEE

NE Lesley Rd

35000

NE Kramien Rd

R2W
R1W

18100

SW Kramien Rd

SW South Ranch Rd

4

45°16'14"

NE WILSONVILLE RD

35

NE Rocky Hill Rd
34600

36

NE Earlwood Rd

NE Earlwood Rd

SW Geer Rd
33900

5

45°15'48"

33900

CLACKAMAS CO
YAMHILL CO

6

WILLAMETTE GREENWAY
STATE PARK

WILLAMETTE RIVER

YAMHILL CO

MARION CO

1

NE WILSONVILLE RD

6

RAND McNALLY

45°15'22"

97137

2

Napoleon St

Mission Creek

CHAMPOEG
STATE
HERITAGE
AREA

Champoeg Creek

B Lp

Schuler Rd

7

CHAMPOEG

Jette Ct   Jette Ct

CHAMPOEG RD NE

Al Lp

CHAMPOEG RD NE

45°14'56"

A   B   C   D   E

122°54'17"   122°53'40"   122°53'03"   122°52'26"   122°51'49"

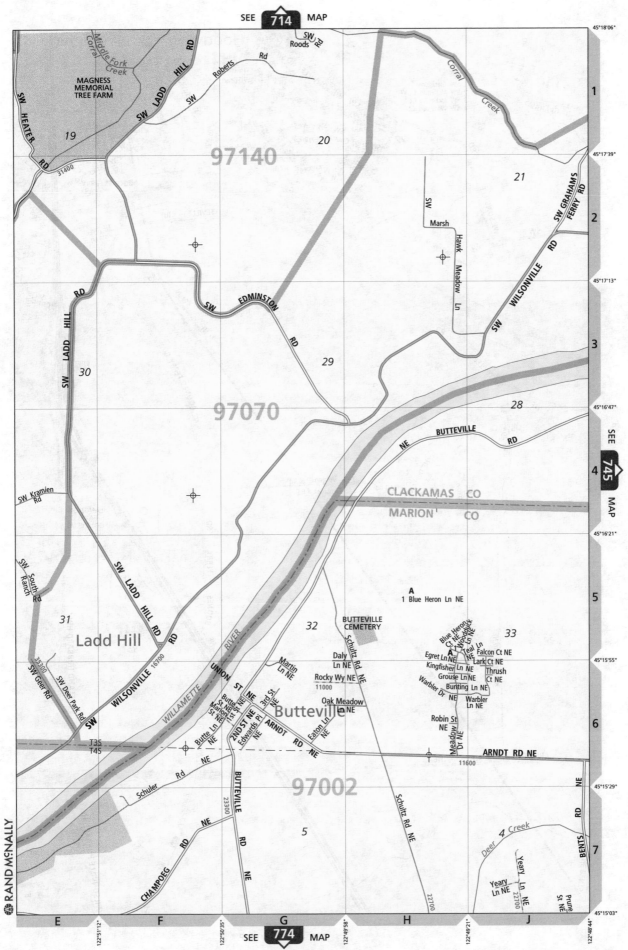

MAP
744

1:24,000
1 in. = 2000 ft.
0   0.25   0.5
miles

N

SEE 714 MAP

SW Roods Rd

Middle Fork Creek

Corral Creek

MAGNESS
MEMORIAL
TREE FARM

SW HEATER RD

SW LADD HILL RD

Roberts Rd

SW

19

20

97140

31400

21

SW Marsh

Hawk Meadow Ln

SW GRAHAMS FERRY RD

SW WILSONVILLE RD

1

45°18'06"

45°17'39"

2

45°17'13"

SW LADD HILL RD

SW EDMINSTON RD

30

29

97070

28

3

45°16'47"

NE BUTTEVILLE RD

SEE 745 MAP

4

SW Kramien Rd

CLACKAMAS CO
MARION CO

45°16'21"

SW South Ranch Rd

SW LADD HILL RD

31

Ladd Hill

SW Geer Rd

SW Deer Park Rd SW

35310

WILSONVILLE RD 16700

WILLAMETTE RIVER

UNION ST NE

Martin Ln NE

Schultz Rd NE

Daly Ln NE

Rocky Wy NE
11000

Oak Meadow Ln NE

32

BUTTEVILLE
CEMETERY

A
1 Blue Heron Ln NE

Blue Heron Ct NE

Woodduck Ln NE

Teal Ln

Egret Ln NE

A

Falcon Ct NE

Lark Ct NE

Kingfisher Ln NE

Grouse Ln NE

Thrush Ct NE

Bunting Ln NE

Warbler Dr NE

Warbler Ln NE

Robin St NE

33

5

45°15'55"

Butte St NE
Marion St NE

1st St NE

2ND ST NE

3rd St NE

Edwards Pl

ARNDT RD NE

Butteville

Butte Ln NE

Eaton Ln NE

Meadow Dr NE

ARNDT RD NE
11600

6

T3S
T4S

Schuler Rd

NE

BENTS RD NE

45°15'29"

BUTTEVILLE RD NE

23300

Schuler Rd

97002

5

Schultz Rd NE

22700

Deer Creek

4

Yeary Ln NE

Yeary Ln NE

22700

Prune St NE

7

45°15'03"

CHAMPOEG RD NE

RAND McNALLY

SEE 774 MAP

E   F   G   H   J

122°51'12"   122°50'35"   122°49'58"   122°49'21"   122°48'44"

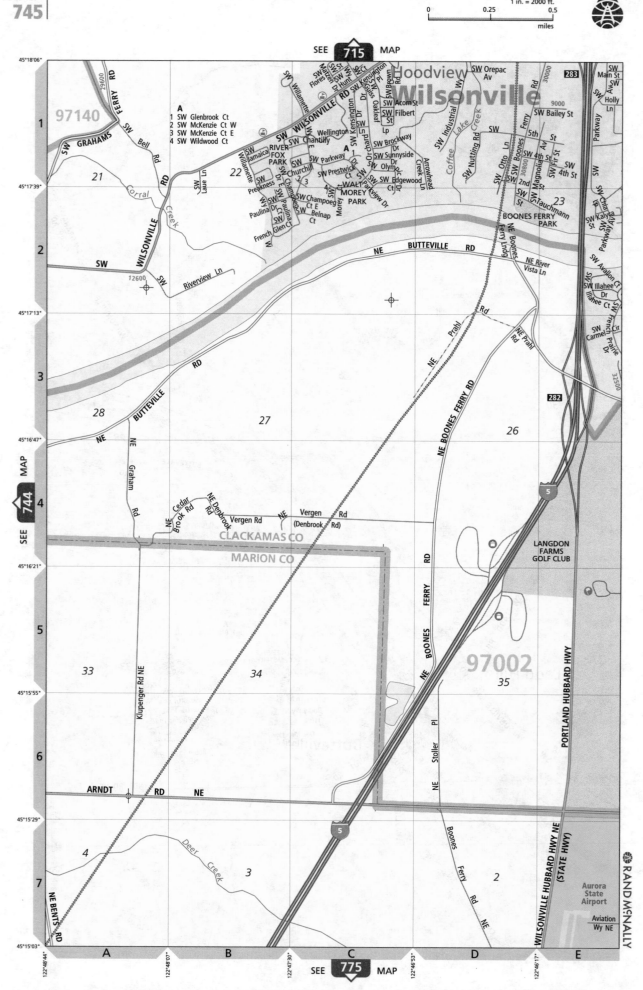

MAP
745

1:24,000
1 in. = 2000 ft.
0   0.25   0.5
miles

N

SEE [715] MAP

A
1 SW Glenbrook Ct
2 SW McKenzie Ct W
3 SW McKenzie Ct E
4 SW Wildwood Ct

Hoodview
Wilsonville

97140

SW GRAHAMS FERRY RD

SW Bell Rd

21

Corral Creek

WILSONVILLE RD

SW Laue Ln

22

SW WILSONVILLE RD

RIVER FOX PARK

SW Jamaica Dr

SW Willamette

SW Chantilly

Wellington

SW Parkway

SW Churchill Dr

SW Preakness

SW Champoeg Dr E

SW Paulina Dr

SW Champoeg Ct E

SW Paulina Ct

French Glen Ct

SW Belnap Ct

SW Morey

SW Prestwick

SW Champoeg

WALT MOREY PARK

SW Parkview Dr

SW Edgewood Ct

SW Olympic Dr

SW Sunnyside Dr

SW Brockway Dr

Arrowhead Creek Dr

Arrowhead Creek Ln

Coffee Lake Creek

SW Industrial

Acorn St

SW Filbert St

SW Orepac Av

SW 5th St

SW Bailey St

SW Nutting Rd

SW Boones Ferry Rd

SW Otto Ln

SW Magnolia

SW 2nd St

30800

30000

9240

9000

283

SW Main St

SW Holly Ln

SW 4th St

SW Fir St

SW 4th St

23

SW Stauchmann Ct

SW Chanay Av

SW Kalyca St

SW Avallon Ct

BOONES FERRY PARK

NE Boones Ferry Lndg

NE River Vista Ln

SW Illahee Dr

SW Illahee Ct

SW French Prairie Dr

SW Carmel St

SW

2

SW

Riverview Ln

12600

NE BUTTEVILLE RD

NE BUTTEVILLE RD

NE Prahl Rd

NE Prahl Rd

282

32500

3

28

27

26

5

NE Graham Rd

NE Cedar Brook Rd

NE Denbrook Rd

Vergen Rd

4

Vergen Rd
(Denbrook Rd)

NE Boones Ferry Rd

CLACKAMAS CO

MARION CO

LANGDON FARMS GOLF CLUB

5

33

34

35

NE Klupenger Rd NE

NE Boones Ferry Rd

97002

NE Stoller Pl

PORTLAND HUBBARD HWY

6

ARNDT RD NE

I-5

NE

Deer Creek

4

3

2

Boones Ferry Rd NE

7

WILSONVILLE HUBBARD HWY NE (STATE HWY)

Aurora State Airport

Aviation Wy NE

NE BENTS RD

A   B   C   D   E

SEE [775] MAP

RAND McNALLY

45°18'06"
45°17'39"
45°17'13"
45°16'47"
45°16'21"
45°15'55"
45°15'29"
45°15'03"

122°48'44"
122°48'07"
122°47'30"
122°46'53"
122°46'17"

SEE MAP 744

MAP
745

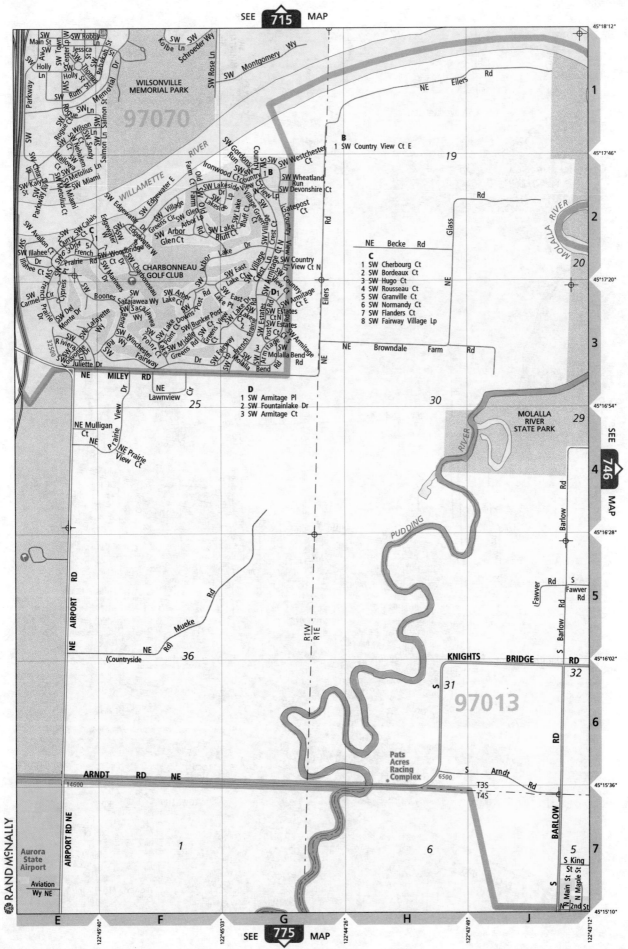

1:24,000
1 in. = 2000 ft.

0   0.25   0.5

miles

SEE 715 MAP

45°18'12"

45°17'46"

45°17'20"

45°16'54"

45°16'28"

45°16'02"

45°15'36"

45°15'10"

WILSONVILLE MEMORIAL PARK

97070

WILLAMETTE RIVER

CHARBONNEAU GOLF CLUB

MOLALLA RIVER

B
1 SW Country View Ct E

19

C
1 SW Cherbourg Ct
2 SW Bordeaux Ct
3 SW Hugo Ct
4 SW Rousseau Ct
5 SW Granville Ct
6 SW Normandy Ct
7 SW Flanders Ct
8 SW Fairway Village Lp

NE Becke Rd

NE Browndale Farm Rd

D
1 SW Armitage Pl
2 SW Fountainlake Dr
3 SW Armitage Ct

25

30

20

29

MOLALLA RIVER STATE PARK

SEE 746 MAP

PUDDING RIVER

KNIGHTS   BRIDGE   RD

31

32

97013

Pats
Acres
Racing
Complex

ARNDT   RD   NE

T3S
T4S

R1W
R1E

36

1

6

5

Aurora State Airport

Aviation
Wy NE

AIRPORT RD NE

NE AIRPORT RD

BARLOW RD

S King

N Main St
N Maple St
N 2nd St

RAND McNALLY

E   F   G   H   J

SEE 775 MAP

122°45'40"   122°45'03"   122°44'26"   122°43'49"   122°43'12"

1   2   3   4   5   6   7

MAP
746

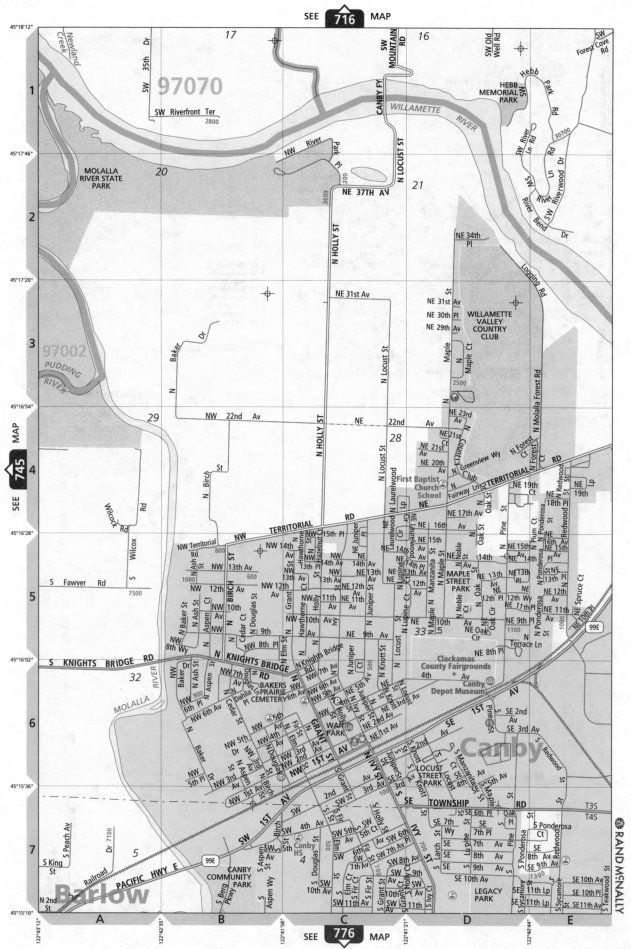

1:24,000
1 in. = 2000 ft.

0   0.25   0.5

miles

SEE 716 MAP

45°18'12"

Newland Creek

SW 35th Dr

17

16

SW MOUNTAIN RD

SW Old Well Rd

SW Forest Cove Rd

97070

CANBY FY

WILLAMETTE RIVER

HEBB MEMORIAL PARK

Hebb Park Rd

1

SW Riverfront Ter
2800

45°17'46"

NW River Park Pl

N LOCUST ST

SW River Ln Rd

30700

SW River Ln

SW Riverwood Dr

MOLALLA RIVER STATE PARK

20

200

NE 37TH AV

21

SW River Bend Dr

2

3600

45°17'20"

NE 31st Av

NE 31st Av

NE 30th Pl

NE 29th Av

Logging Rd

Baker Dr

N

N HOLLY ST

WILLAMETTE VALLEY COUNTRY CLUB

97002

PUDDING RIVER

N Locust St

Maple St

Maple Ct

3

2500

45°16'54"

29

NW 22nd Av

NE

22nd Av

NE 23rd Av

N Molalla Forest Rd

28

NE 21st Av

N Forest Ct

N Country Club

N Forest Ct

N Birch St

N Locust St

NE 21st Av

NE 20th Av

Greenview Wy

TERRITORIAL RD

N Redwood

NE 19th

4

First Baptist Church School

N Laurelwood Lp

NE

Fairway Ln

Oak St

NE 19th Ct

18th Pl

NE 19th St

NE Lp

S Wilcox Rd

Wilcox Rd

NE 17th Av

Pine St

45°16'28"

NW Territorial

TERRITORIAL RD

N Hawthorne St

15th Pl

NE Juniper St

NE 16th

Oak St

N Ponderosa

NE 15th

NE 16th Pl

NE 15th

NE 15th Pl

Wilcox Rd

NW Territorial Rd
800

NW 14th Av

NE Laurelwood

N Noble St

N Manzanita St

N Maple St

14th

Plum Ct

NE 14th Pl

S Fawver Rd

1000

N Ash St

BIRCH ST

NW 13th Av
600

13th Av

NE 14th Av

14th Av

NE 14th Av

NE Laurelwood Ct

12th Av

N Noble Ct

MAPLE STREET PARK

N Oak

NE 13th Av

NE 13th Pl

N Ponderosa

NE 13th Pl

NE 12th

5

7500

NW 12th Av

NW 12th Av

NE 12th Av

NE 11th Av

N Maple St

12th Wy

NE 11th Ct

NE 11th Ponderosa

NE 11th

Grant St

Holly St

1100

NE 9th Av

N Ponderosa

NE 1017 Pl

99E

N Baker St

N Ash Ct

NW 10th Av

Cedar Ct

N Douglas St

NW Hawthorne

11th Av

NE 11th Av

N Lupine Ct

N Maple St

N Noble Ct

NE Oak Cir

N Oak Cir

1000

NW 9th

NW 8th Pl

NE 9th St

N Locust

33

N Maple St

NE 8th Av

Terrace Ln

NW 8th Wy

KNIGHTS BRIDGE RD

N Knights Bridge Rd

N Juniper

N Knott St

Clackamas County Fairgrounds

NE 8th Av

45°16'02"

S KNIGHTS BRIDGE RD

32

N Baker Dr

N Ash Ct

NW 7th

Douglas Ln

N Knights Bridge Rd

N 7th Av

4th

Canby Depot Museum

MOLALLA RIVER

BAKERS PRAIRIE CEMETERY

Dahlia Pl

NW 6th Av

6th Av

N 6th Av

N 5th

NE 2nd

4th

SE 1st AV

SE 2nd Av

6

N Baker St

NW 900

6th Pl

N Cedar St

NW 6th Av

NW 5th Dr

N Elm St

N 5th

WAR PARK

N 3rd

NE 1st Av

Canby

SE 3rd Av

NW 5th

NW 4th

N Elm St

N 3rd

N 2nd

N 1st

NW 1st AV

SE 1st AV

1st Pl

SE Redwood

NW 5th Pl

NW 3rd Av

N Aspen St

N Birch St

NW 1st Av

2nd

S 2nd

S Knott St

N Knott St

LOCUST STREET PARK

SE Manzanita St

S Maple St

45°15'36"

SW 1st AV

1st Av

3rd St

S Grant St

S Holly St

100

S IVY ST

SE TOWNSHIP RD

T3S

T4S

Barlow

Railroad Dr 7100

PACIFIC HWY E

99E

SW 1st AV

Birch St

SW 2nd

5th Canby HS

S Douglas St

S Elm St

500

6th

SW 5th Av

7th

SE 6th Pl

Oak St

SE 7th Wy

7th Pl

S Ponderosa Ct

S Ponderosa

SE 10th Av

SE 10th Pl

7

5

S Peach Av

S King St

Dr

CANBY COMMUNITY PARK

S Berg Pkwy

S Aspen Wy

SW 4th

S Aspen

SW 5th Av

S Douglas St

6th St

SW 6th Av

SW 7th Av

SW 8th Av

S Larch St

SE Lupine

SE 7th Av

SE 8th Av

S Ponderosa

SE 9th Av

1300

SE 11th Lp

SE 11th Av

N 2nd St

45°15'10"

SW 1st Av

10th Av

S Elm Ct

S Fir Ct

S Fir St

SW 10th Av

SW 9th

S Grant St

SW 11th

S Grant Ct

S Holly St

S Ivy St

SW 11th Av

700

LEGACY PARK

S Sycamore St

SE 11th Lp

S Sycamore

SE Tealwood

SE 10th Pl

SE 11th Av

A   B   C   D   E

SEE 776 MAP

122°43'12"   122°42'35"   122°41'58"   122°41'21"   122°40'44"

MAP
746

1:24,000
1 in. = 2000 ft.
0   0.25   0.5
miles

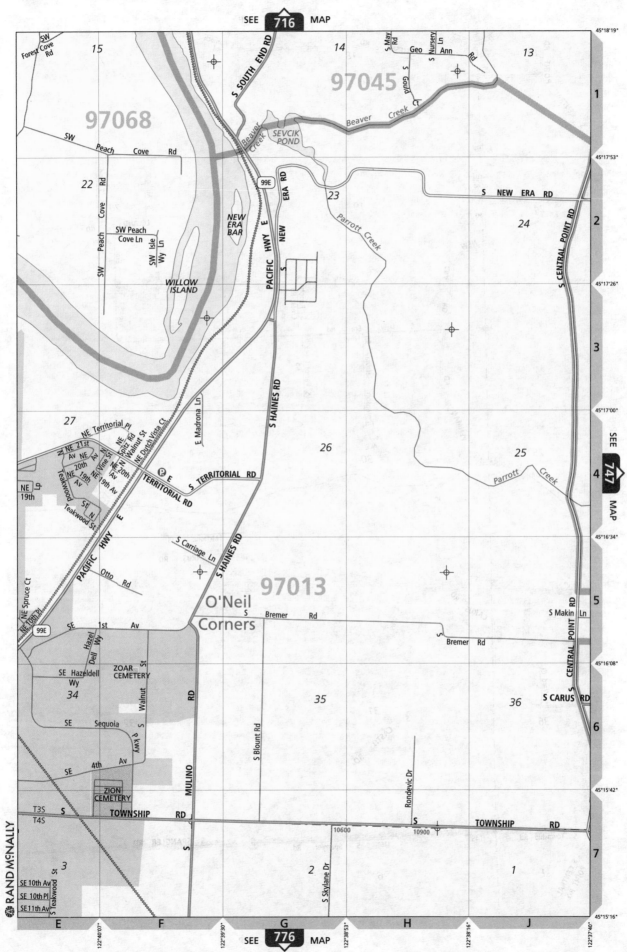

SW Forest Cove Rd

15

97068

SW Peach Cove Rd

22

SW Cove Rd

SW Peach Cove Ln

SW Peach Cove Ln

SW Isle Wy Ln

WILLOW ISLAND

NEW ERA BAR

PACIFIC HWY E

99E

NEW ERA RD

S SOUTH END RD

14

97045

S May Rd

S Gould Ct

Geo

S Nursery Ln

Ann Rd

13

Beaver Creek

SEVCIK POND

Beaver Creek

S NEW ERA RD

23

24

Parrott Creek

S CENTRAL POINT RD

1

2

3

27

NE Territorial Pl

NE 21st Av

NE 20th Av

NE Spitz Rd

NE Vine St

NE Walnut St

NE Dutch Vista Ct

NE 20th Av

NE 19th Av

NE Teakwood St

NE 19th Ct

Teakwood St N

Teakwood St

E Madrona Ln

S HAINES RD

P E TERRITORIAL RD

S TERRITORIAL RD

26

25

Parrott Creek

SEE 747 MAP

4

S Carriage Ln

S HAINES RD

97013

Otto Rd

PACIFIC HWY E

NE Spruce Ct

NE 10th Pl

99E

O'Neil Corners

S Bremer Rd

S Bremer Rd

S Makin Ln

S CENTRAL POINT RD

5

SE 1st Av

Hazel Dell Wy

SE Hazeldell Wy

ZOAR CEMETERY

34

SE Sequoia

Walnut St

S Walnut St

S Pkwy

SE 4th Av

MULINO RD

35

S Blount Rd

36

S CARUS RD

6

ZION CEMETERY

T3S
T4S

TOWNSHIP RD

Rondevic Dr

S TOWNSHIP RD

10600   10900

7

SE 10th Av

SE 10th Pl

SE 11th Av

3

SE Teakwood St

2

S Skylane Dr

1

E   F   G   H   J

45°18'19"
45°17'53"
45°17'26"
45°17'00"
45°16'34"
45°16'08"
45°15'42"
45°15'16"

122°40'07"   122°39'30"   122°38'53"   122°38'16"   122°37'40"

RAND McNALLY

MAP
747

1:24,000
1 in. = 2000 ft.
0   0.25   0.5
miles

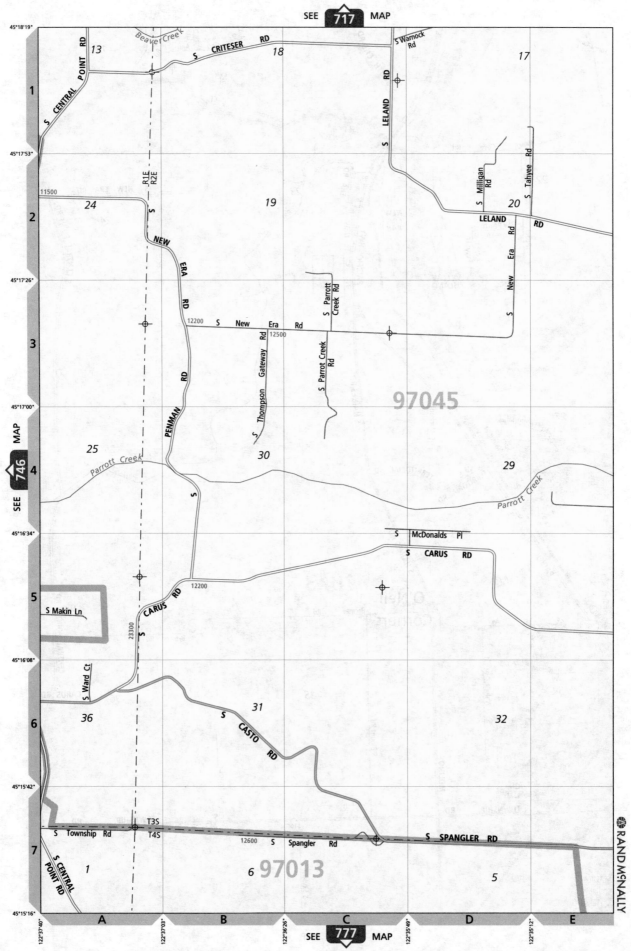

SEE 717 MAP

45°18'19"

S CENTRAL POINT RD

13   Beaver Creek   S CRITESER RD   18   S Warnock Rd   17

1

45°17'53"

11500   24   R1E R2E   19   S Milligan Rd   S Tahvee Rd   20

2   NEW   LELAND RD

S LELAND RD

45°17'26"

ERA RD   S Parrott Creek Rd   S New Era Rd

3   12200   S New Era Rd   12500   Thompson Gateway Rd   S Parrot Creek Rd   97045

PENMAN RD

45°17'00"

SEE 746 MAP   25   Parrott Creek   30   29

4   S   Parrott Creek

45°16'34"

S McDonalds Pl

S CARUS RD

5   S Makin Ln   12200   CARUS RD   S

23300   S

45°16'08"

S Ward Ct

6   36   S CASTO RD   31   32

45°15'42"

T3S

S Township Rd   T4S

7   S CENTRAL POINT RD   1   12600   S Spangler Rd   S SPANGLER RD   6   97013   5

45°15'16"

A   B   C   D   E

122°37'40"   122°37'03"   122°36'26"   122°35'49"   122°35'12"

SEE 777 MAP

RAND M^cNALLY

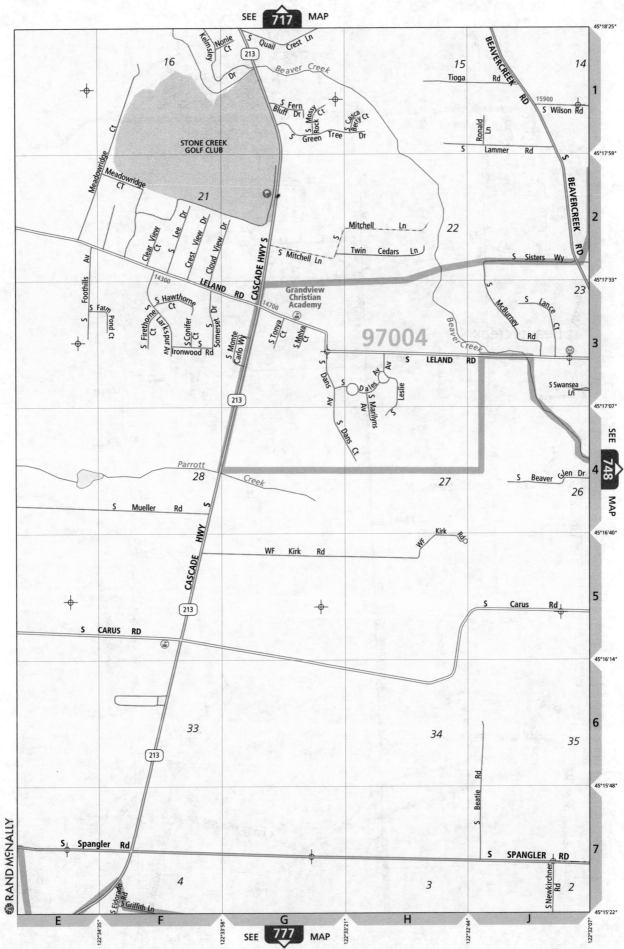

MAP
747

1:24,000
1 in. = 2000 ft.

0   0.25   0.5

miles

SEE 717 MAP

45°18'25"

Kelmsley
Nonie Ct
S Quail Crest Ln

213 Dr

Beaver Creek

16

15

14

BEAVERCREEK RD

Tioga   Rd

15900

S Wilson Rd

1

S Fern
Bluff Dr
S Mossy
Rock Ct
S Green Tree
S Casca
Berty Ct
Dr

Ronald
Ln

S   Lammer   Rd

45°17'59"

STONE CREEK
GOLF CLUB

Meadowridge Ct

Meadowridge
CT

21

22

Mitchell   Ln

BEAVERCREEK RD

2

S Sisters   Wy

45°17'33"

S Foothills Av

Clear View Ct

S Lee Dr

Crest View Dr

Cloud View Dr

CASCADE HWY S

S Mitchell Ln

Twin Cedars Ln

23

S McBurney Rd

S Lance Ct

14300

LELAND   RD

14700

Grandview
Christian
Academy

Beaver Creek

3

S Farm
Pond Ct

S Hawthorne
Ct

S Firethorne
Larkspur Av
S Conifer
Somerset Dr

Ironwood Rd

S Monte
Carlo Wy

S Tonya
Ct

S Melva
Ct

97004

S   Dans   Av

Dales Av

S Marilyns Av

Av

Leslie

S LELAND   RD

S Swansea
Ln

213

45°17'07"

S Dans Ct

Parrott

28

Creek

27

26

S Beaver Glen Dr

4

SEE 748 MAP

45°17'07"

S   Mueller   Rd

CASCADE HWY S

WF   Kirk   Rd

WF Kirk Rd

45°16'40"

213

S   Carus   Rd

5

S CARUS RD

45°16'14"

33

34

35

S Beatie Rd

6

213

45°15'48"

S Spangler Rd

S SPANGLER RD

7

4

3

S Newkirchner Rd

2

S Eldorado

S Griffith Ln

45°15'22"

E   F   G   H   J

SEE 777 MAP

122°34'35"   122°33'58"   122°33'21"   122°32'44"   122°32'07"

RAND MᶜNALLY

MAP
748

1:24,000
1 in. = 2000 ft.
0   0.25   0.5
miles

SEE 718 MAP

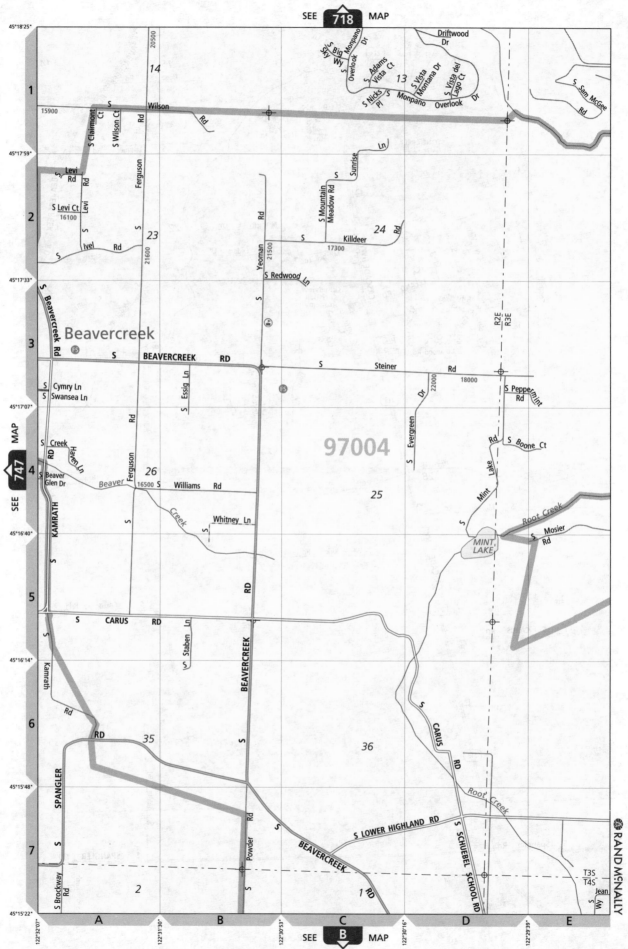

97004

Beavercreek

MINT LAKE

Root Creek

SEE 747 MAP

SEE B MAP

RAND M℠NALLY

MAP
748

1:24,000
1 in. = 2000 ft.
0   0.25   0.5
miles

SEE **718** MAP

S SPRAGUE RD

S Polehn Rd

S Badger Dr

S Indigo Av

S REDLAND RD

LYONS
VIEW
PARK

18

17

16

S Sam McGee Rd

1

S
LYONS RD

S

Abernethy

Creek

97045

2

45°18'31"

45°18'05"

19

20

21

45°17'38"

3

SEE **749** MAP

S Mosier Rd

S RIDGE RD

S Ridgeside Ln

45°17'12"

4

30

S Mosier Rd

29

28

Mosier Creek

45°16'46"

5

Bluhm Rd

S

Bluhm Rd

S

Abernethy Creek

S Alberta Rd

45°16'20"

S Alberta Rd

Ln

6

31

32

S Alberta Rd

33

Rutherford

23500

23200 S

45°15'54"

S LOWER HIGHLAND RD

Dr

S LOWER HIGHLAND RD

20400

7

Logan

S

S

S
RIDGE
RD

Mosier Creek

S Mosier Creek Ln

T3S
T4S

Jean Wy

Cate Ln

42200

6

5

4

45°15'28"

E

122°29'03"

F

122°28'26"

SEE **B** MAP

G

122°27'49"

H

122°27'12"

J

122°26'35"

MAP
749

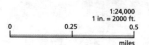

1:24,000
1 in. = 2000 ft.

0   0.25   0.5
miles

SEE **719** MAP

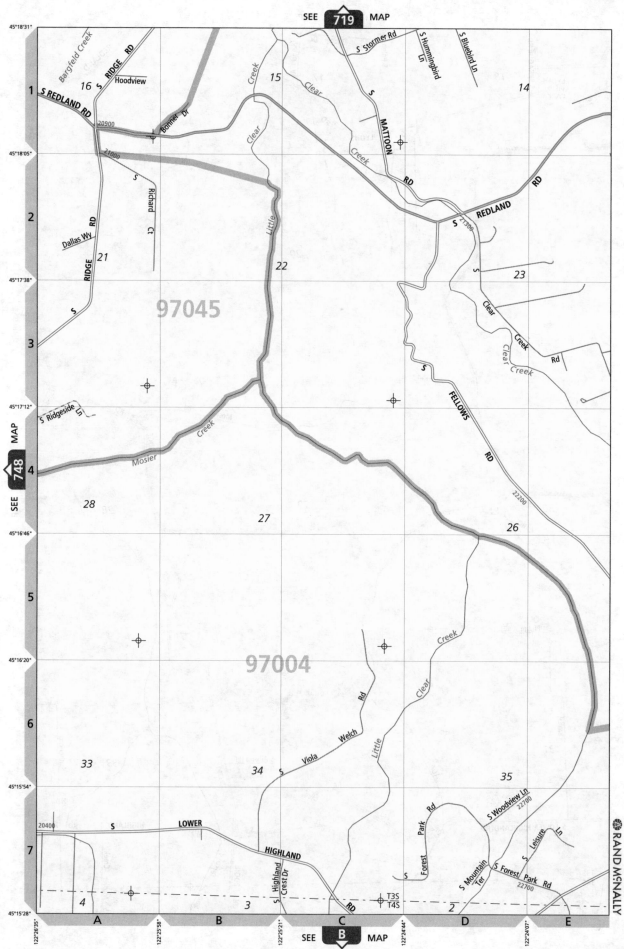

Bargfeld Creek

RIDGE RD

16 S Hoodview

S REDLAND RD

20900

Bonner Dr

21000

S

Richard Ct

Dallas Wy

RIDGE RD

21

S

S Ridgeside

Mosier Creek

97045

14

S Stormer Rd
S Hummingbird Ln
S Bluebird Ln

Clear

Clear

MATTOON RD

Creek

15

Little Creek

22

REDLAND RD

21300

S

S 23

Clear Creek

Clear Creek

Rd

S

FELLOWS RD

22200

SEE **748** MAP

28

27

26

Clear Creek

33

34

35

Little Creek

Rd

Welch Rd

S Viola

S

Park Rd

S Woodview Ln 22700

20400

S

LOWER

S Forest

S Mountain Ter

S Leisure Ln

HIGHLAND

S Highland Crest Dr

S Forest Park Rd 22700

T3S
T4S

4

3

RD

2

97004

A   B   C   D   E

SEE **B** MAP

45°18'31"
45°18'05"
45°17'38"
45°17'12"
45°16'46"
45°16'20"
45°15'54"
45°15'28"

122°26'35"
122°25'58"
122°25'21"
122°24'44"
122°24'07"

MAP
749

SEE 719 MAP

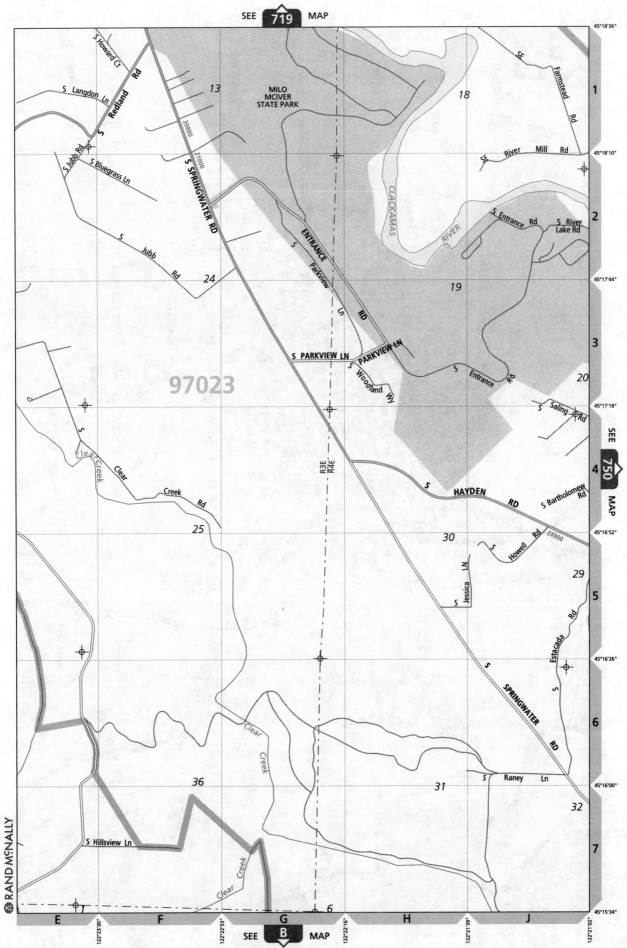

1:24,000
1 in. = 2000 ft.

0   0.25   0.5
miles

S Howard Ct

S Langdon Ln

S Redland Rd

13

MILO MCIVER STATE PARK

18

SE Farmstead Rd

45°18'36"

1

20800

S Jubb Rd

S Bluegrass Ln

21000

S SPRINGWATER RD

SE River Mill Rd

45°18'10"

S Entrance Rd

S River Lake Rd

CLACKAMAS

2

45°17'44"

S Jubb Rd

24

S Parkview Ln

ENTRANCE RD

RIVER

19

97023

S PARKVIEW LN   PARKVIEW LN

S Woodland Wy

S Entrance Rd

20

3

45°17'18"

SEE 750 MAP

S Clear Creek

Clear

Clear Creek Rd

25

R3E R4E

S Saling Rd

S HAYDEN RD

S Bartholomew Rd

30

4

45°16'52"

24900

S Howell Rd

S Jessica Ln

29

S Estacada Rd

5

45°16'26"

S SPRINGWATER RD

6

Clear

Creek

36

31

S Raney Ln

32

45°16'00"

RAND MCNALLY

S Hillsview Ln

7

Clear Creek

45°15'34"

E   F   G   H   J

122°23'30"   122°22'53"   122°22'16"   122°21'39"   122°21'02"

SEE B MAP

MAP
750

1:24,000
1 in. = 2000 ft.

0   0.25   0.5

miles

SEE 720 MAP

45°18'36"

97022

NW Park AV NW
NW Commerce Ct NW
Campus DR NW

1

CLACKAMAS HWY
211 224

17 Rd
EAGLE CREEK RD

SE River Mill
Kilowatt Ln
SE Strubhar
SE Hinman Av
NW Cazadero Ct
NW Broadway Ct
Wren Rd
Violet Av
Cemetery Rd
Currin Creek
Valley View Arpt

Terminal

SE Sunview Ln
16

SE Shorgorick Rd
29000

45°18'10"
30100

TIMBER PARK

Wade Creek

CLACKAMAS NW

Tulip Rd
NW Industrial Wy
Lakeshore Rd

NW 10th St
NW Carlton St
8th Av

600
Estacada HS
6TH AV
IOOF CEMETERY
Bunyard

Estacada

SE Woodland Rd
SE Lawrence

SE Lucky Ln

45°17'44"
20

MILO MCIVER STATE PARK

Gooseberry Rd
Aspen Rd
Serne Rd

6th Av
NW Wade St
NW 5th Av
NW 4th Av
NW 2nd Pl
SW Oak Rd
SW Nymph Rd
SW Maple Rd
SW Laurel Rd
SW Knox Rd
SW Juniper Rd
Clackamas Ln
NW Cliff Frontage Rd
NW Cary St
NW Standish St
NW 3rd Av
NW 2nd Av
NW 1st Av

5th Av
Zobrist St
NE 4th Av
NE Broadway
NE 2nd Av
NE 1st Av

NE Pierce
100
NE Carole
NE Carole
NE Shafford
NE Ginseng
Oakview
Westview

300
SE Stamp Rd
Edgehill
NE Foothill Dr
NE Glen Ct
NE Hill Wy

1 N Broadway St

SE Independence Av

21
SE Summer Rd

33700

Lawrence

SE Avalon Ct
Teeples Ln

3

45°17'18"

River Lake Rd
Dubois Creek

SW Grove Rd
SW Forest Rd
SW Cedar Rd
SW Ivy Rd
SW Elm Rd
SE Larch Rd
SE Cedar Rd

SE Main St
SE Currin
SE Broadway
SE 3rd Av
SE 2nd Av
SE 1st Av
SE Shafford
SE Pierce
Short

NE Main St
Wade
3rd Av
4th
5th

Ginseng Dr
SE Oak View Ln
SE Mountain View

SE Pineview Ct
SE Regan Hill Lp
Viewcrest
SE Regan Hill Lp
SE Filly Ln
SE Bryant Rd
SE Dance

33900
34300

SE MOSS HILL RD
Funny Farm Rd

4

MAP
749
SEE

Saling Rd
S Bartholomew Rd

Mirror Lake
S Fuchsia
S Endive Rd
S Canary
S Dandelion Rd
Begonia
Sand Rd
SW Dr

CLACKAMAS RIVER

Overlook Rd
Maranna Ct

SE Forest Glen Rd
SE Darrow Rd

SE 4th Av

28

B
1 SW Hawthorne Rd
2 SW Dogwood Rd
3 SW Clubhouse Rd

45°16'52"

HAYDEN RD
S Estacada Rd

WOODBURN-ESTACADA

29
Laura Ln
S Reid

Poplar Rd

CLACKAMAS HWY

Cadanau Rd

Clackamas River

Linglebeck Creek

SE Chrysler Ln
SE Chrysler RD

5

45°16'26"

211

Spring Creek
DAY HILL RD

Valley View Rd

224

SE SURFACE

6

S Reid Rd
Rd
S Tibbs Wy

WOODBURN-ESTACADA HWY
Dubois Creek

S Dubois Ln

FARADAY RD
CLACKAMAS HWY

45°16'00"
32

S Reid Rd

33

FARADAY LAKE

Clackamas River

Kelly Rd

7

SPRINGWATER RD
S Ester Ct

S DAY HILL RD

Day Ln
Bard Pl

45°15'34"

A   B   C   D   E

122°21'02" 122°20'26" 122°19'49" 122°19'12" 122°18'35"

SEE B MAP

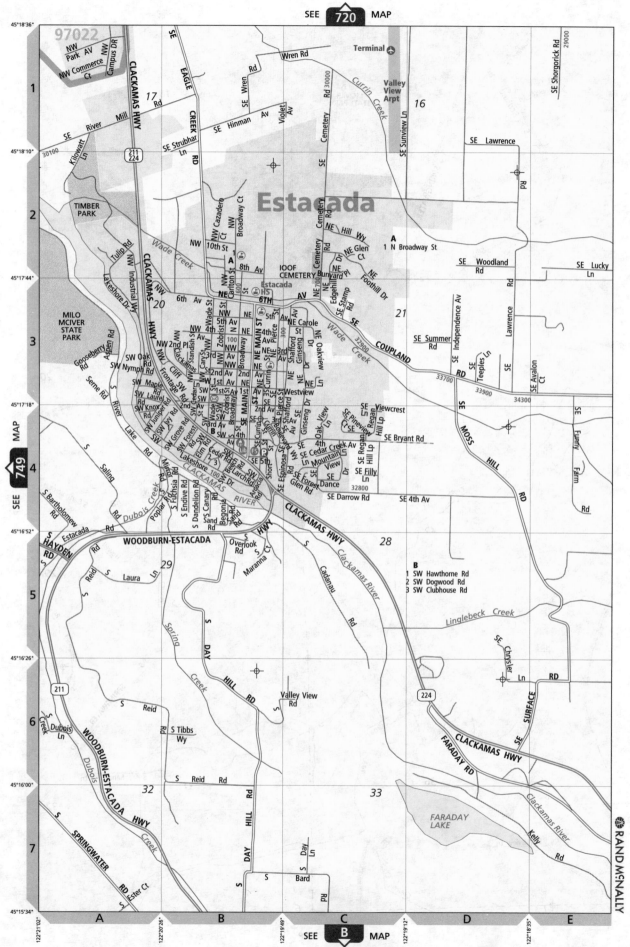

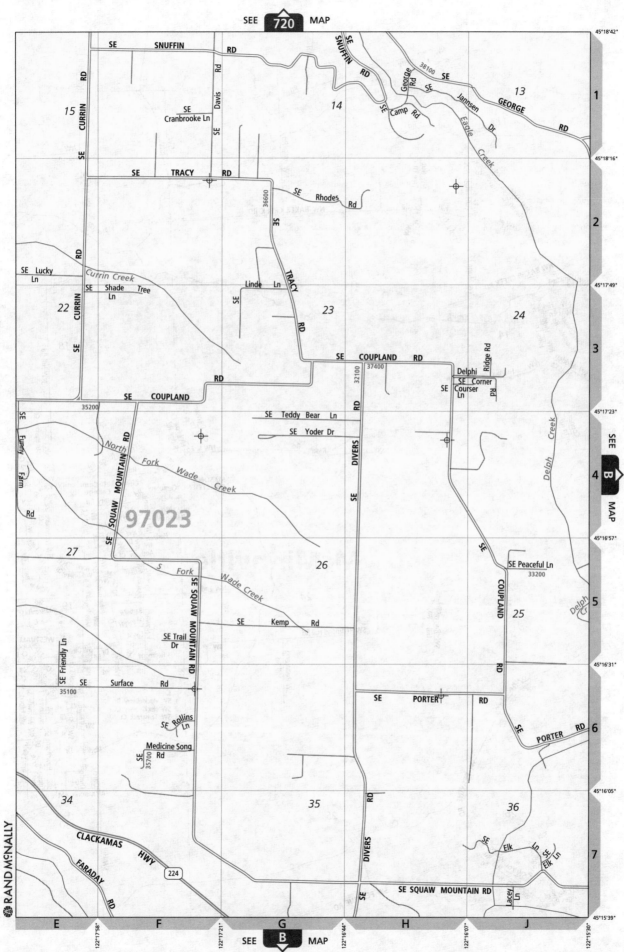

MAP
750

1:24,000
1 in. = 2000 ft.

0   0.25   0.5

miles

SEE 720 MAP

45°18'42"

SE   SNUFFIN   RD

SNUFFIN RD

38100   SE

George Rd

SE   Camp Rd

Jannsen Dr

13

GEORGE   RD

1

15

CURRIN RD

SE

SE
Cranbrooke Ln

Davis Rd

14

Eagle Creek

SE

45°18'16"

SE   TRACY   RD

36600

SE

SE   Rhodes   Rd

2

45°17'49"

SE   Lucky
Ln

Currin Creek

SE   Shade   Tree
Ln

Linde   Ln

TRACY

RD

23

24

3

22

CURRIN RD

SE

RD

SE   COUPLAND   RD

32100

37400

Delphi

SE   Corner
Courser
Ln

Ridge Rd

Rd

SE   COUPLAND   RD

35200

SE

SE   Teddy   Bear   Ln

SE   Yoder Dr

SE

DIVERS

RD

Delph Creek

45°17'23"

SEE
B
MAP

4

SE

Funny

Farm

Rd

North   Fork   Wade   Creek

SE SQUAW MOUNTAIN RD

97023

45°16'57"

27

S   Fork   Wade   Creek

SE SQUAW MOUNTAIN RD

26

SE

COUPLAND RD

25

SE Peaceful Ln

33200

Delph Cr

5

SE Friendly Ln

SE Trail
Dr

SE   Kemp   Rd

45°16'31"

35100

SE   Surface   Rd

SE Rollins
Ln

SE   PORTER   RD

SE   PORTER   RD

6

Medicine Song
Rd

SE
35700

45°16'05"

34

35

DIVERS RD

SE

36

7

CLACKAMAS   HWY

FARADAY   RD

224

SE

DIVERS

SE   Elk   Ln   SE
Elk   Ln

SE   SQUAW   MOUNTAIN   RD

Lacey
Ln

45°15'39"

E   F   G   H   J

122°17'58"   122°17'21"   122°16'44"   122°16'07"   122°15'30"

SEE B MAP

MAP
770

1:24,000
1 in. = 2000 ft.

0   0.25   0.5

miles

N

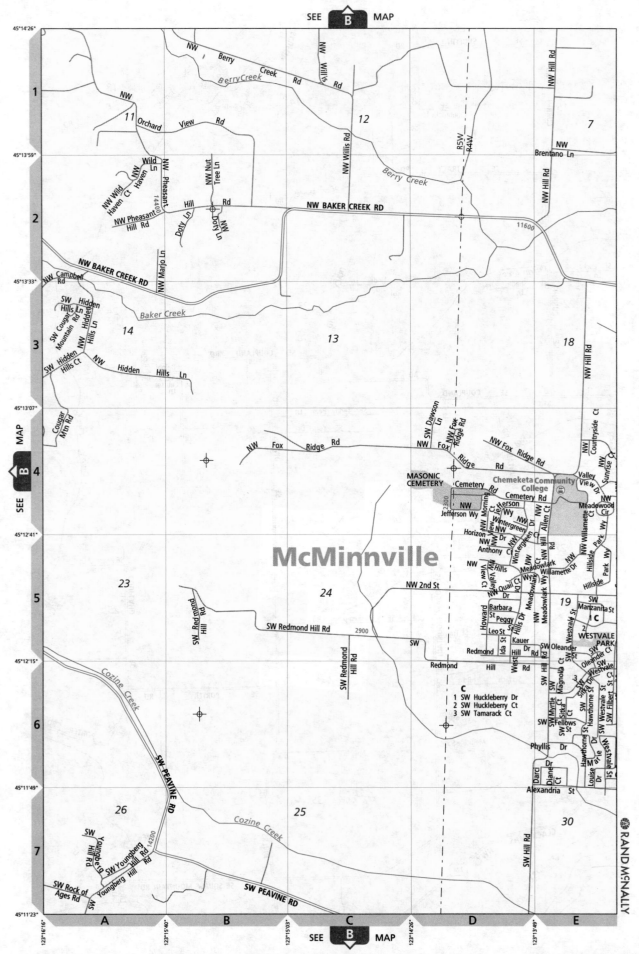

45°14'26"

SEE MAP B

1

NW Berry Creek Rd

NW Willis Rd

NW Hill Rd

11 NW Orchard View Rd

12

7

45°13'59"

NW Wild Haven Ln

NW Wild Haven Ct

NW Haven Ct

NW Pheasant Hill

14400

NW Nut Tree Ln

Hill Rd

Doty Ln

NW Doty Ln

NW Willis Rd

Berry Creek

R5W R4W

NW Brentano Ln

NW Hill Rd

2

NW Pheasant Hill Rd

NW BAKER CREEK RD

11600

45°13'33"

NW Campbell Rd

NW BAKER CREEK RD

NW Marjo Ln

SW Hidden Hills Ln

SW Cougar Mountain Rd

NW Hidden Hills Ln

Baker Creek

14

13

18

3

SW Hidden Hills Ct

NW Hidden Hills Ln

NW Hidden Hills Ln

NW Hill Rd

Cougar Mtn Rd

45°13'07"

SEE MAP B

4

NW Fox Ridge Rd

SW Dawson Ln

NW Fox Ridge Rd

NW Fox Ridge Rd

NW Fox Ridge Rd

Countryside Ct

Sunrise Ct

MASONIC CEMETERY

Cemetery Rd

Chemeketa Community College

Valley View Ct

Meadowood Cir

NW Jefferson Wy

2300

NW Jefferson Wy

Cemetery Rd

Jefferson Dr

NW Wintergreen

Allen Ct

NW Willamette

Park Wy

45°12'41"

Horizon

NW Wy

NW Wintergreen Dr

NW Willamette Dr

Hillside

Park

Hillside

Anthony Ct

NW

NW View Ct

McMinnville

NW Hills Dr

NW Quail Dr

NW 2nd St

NW Meadowlark Wy

Meadowlark Dr

Hillside

5

23

24

Howard

Barbara

Peggy St

Leo St

Manzanita St

C

SW Redmond Hill Rd

SW Redmond Hill Rd

2900

Ida St

SW Meadowlark Dr

SW Westvale Dr

WESTVALE PARK

45°12'15"

Cozine Creek

SW Redmond Hill Rd

SW

Kauer Dr

Redmond

Magnolia Ct

Oleander

SW Oleander St

SW Westvale

Redmond Hill Westvale Rd

SW Westvale

6

Cozine Creek

C
1 SW Huckleberry Dr
2 SW Huckleberry Ct
3 SW Tamarack Ct

SW Myrtle St

SW Sitka Ct

SW Hawthorne St

SW Filbert St

SW Fellows St

Phyllis Dr

Hawthorne Dr

Louise Marie

Westvale St

45°11'49"

SW PEAVINE RD

Darci Dr

Diane Ct

Alexandria St

26

25

30

7

SW Youngberg Hill Rd

14200

SW Youngberg Hill Rd

Cozine Creek

SW Hill Rd

SW Rock of Ages Rd

SW Youngberg Hill Rd

SW PEAVINE RD

45°11'23"

A   B   C   D   E

123°16'16"   123°15'40"   123°15'03"   123°14'26"   123°13'49"

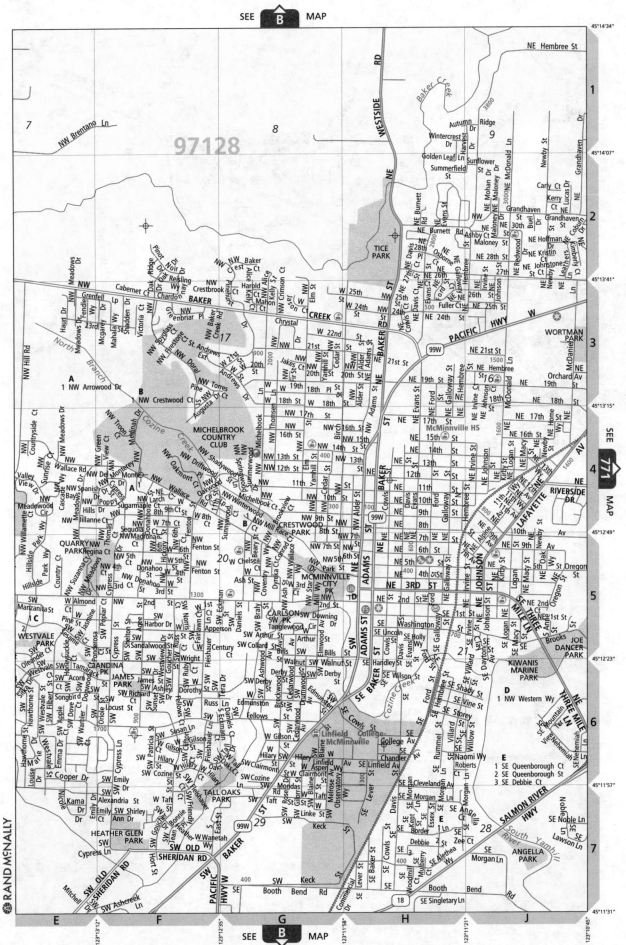

MAP
770

1:24,000
1 in. = 2000 ft.

0   0.25   0.5
miles

SEE ◆B◆ MAP

45°14'34"

NE Hembree St

WESTSIDE RD

Baker Creek

1

7   NW Brentano Ln   8   Autumn Ridge Dr   9

97128   Wintercrest Dr   Harvest

Golden Leaf Ln   Sunflower St   Newby St   Grandhaven Dr

Summerfield St   45°14'07"

2

NE Burnett Rd   NE 30th   Buel   Grandhaven St   Grandhaven Dr

NW Baker Crest   NE Burnett Rd   NE 28th   NE Hoffman

TICE PARK   NE 27th St   NE Redwood   NE Kristin   Newby

Cabernet Ct   NW Baker Creek Rd   NE 26th   NE 27th   NE Johnstone

BAKER   CREEK   W 25th St   NE 25th   45°13'41"

3

17   W 24th St   PACIFIC HWY   99W   WORTMAN PARK

NE 21st St   McDaniel

NW 20th   W 21st   21st   NE Hembree   16   Orchard Av   NE 19th   45°13'15"

NW 19th   18th Pl   NE 19th   McDonald

MICHELBROOK COUNTRY CLUB   NW 17th   NE 18th   NE 17th St

4

McMinnville HS   NE 15th   NE 16th St   SEE 771 MAP

NW 13th   NE 14th   NE 13th   RIVERSIDE DR

NW 12th   NE 13th   NE 11th   RE NE

QUARRY NW PARK   11th   11th   45°12'49"

CRESTWOOD PARK   NE 9th   8th   NE 10th   10th Av

5

McMINNVILLE CITY PK   NE 3RD ST   45°12'23"

WESTVALE PARK   CARLSON   Washington   JOE DANCER PARK

JANDINA PK   KIWANIS MARINE PARK

JAMES PARK   D 1 NW Western Wy

6

Linfield College-McMinnville   E

45°11'57"

TALL OAKS PARK   SALMON RIVER HWY   1 SE Queenborough Ct

2 SE Queenborough St

3 SE Debbie St

HEATHER GLEN PARK   28   ANGELLA PARK

7

SW OLD SHERIDAN RD   99W   29   South Yamhill River   45°11'31"

Booth Bend Rd   18   SE Singletary Ln

E   F   G   H   J

123°13'12"   123°12'35"   123°11'58"   123°11'21"   123°10'45"

SEE ◆B◆ MAP

◆ RAND McNALLY

MAP
771

1:24,000
1 in. = 2000 ft.

0   0.25   0.5
miles

SEE 741 MAP

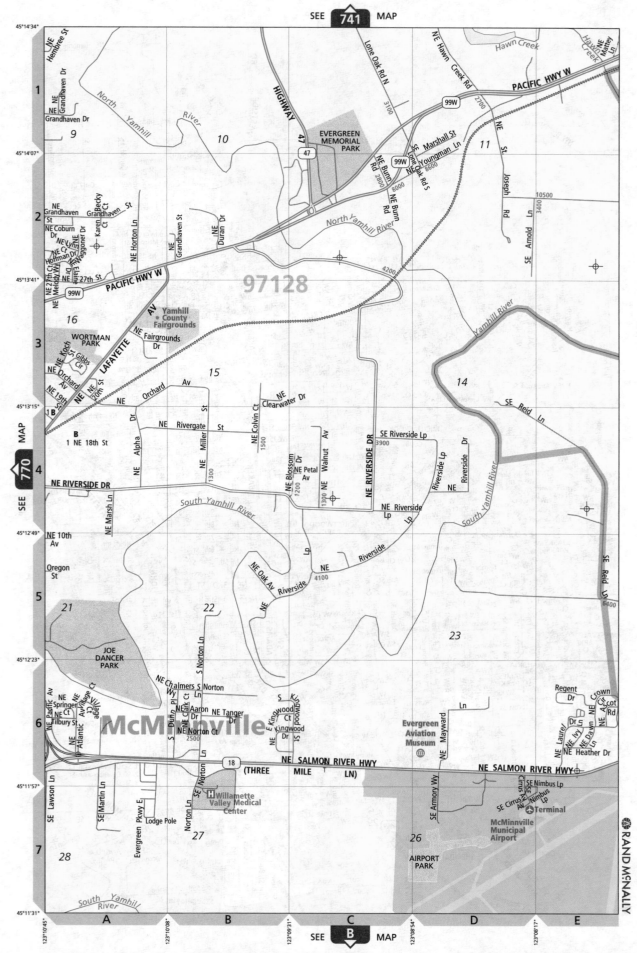

97128

McMinnville

RAND McNALLY

SEE 770 MAP

SEE B MAP

MAP
771

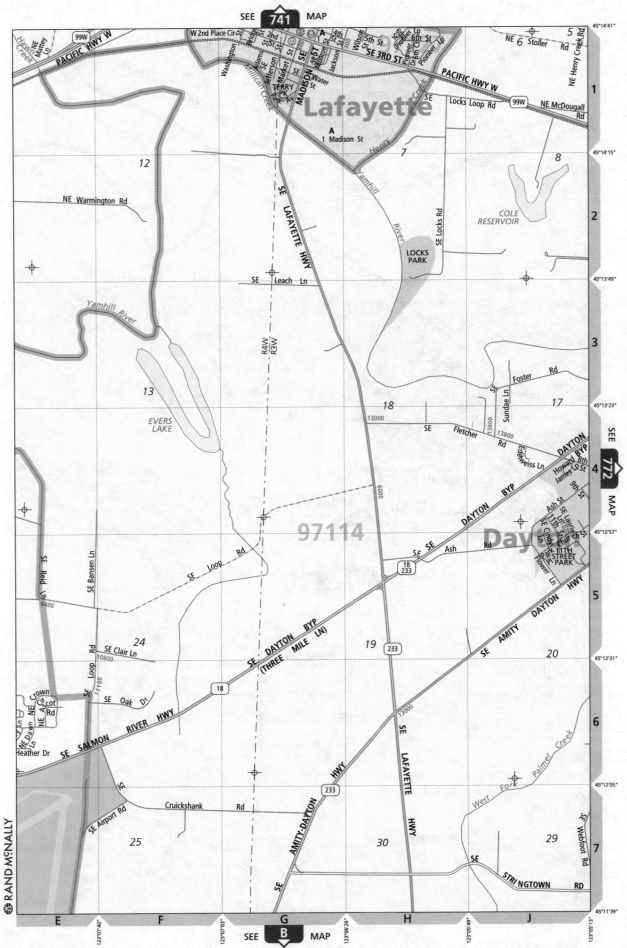

1:24,000
1 in. = 2000 ft.

0   0.25   0.5
miles

Lafayette

Dayton

97114

SEE 772 MAP

SEE B MAP

RAND McNALLY

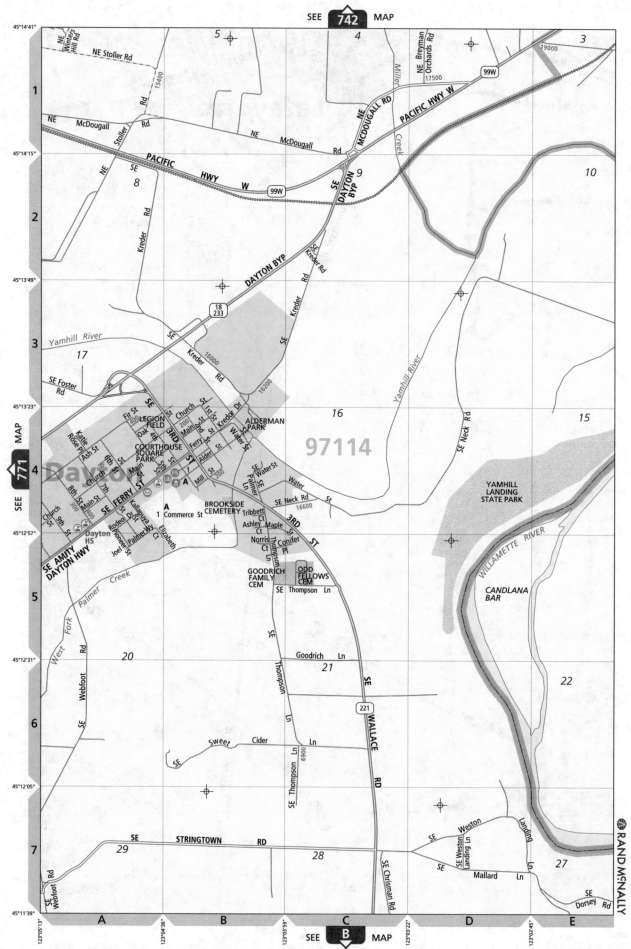

MAP
772

1:24,000
1 in. = 2000 ft.

0   0.25   0.5
miles

SEE **742** MAP

5   4   3

NE Winters Hill Rd

NE Stoller Rd

NE Breyman Orchards Rd

99W

19000

1

NE McDougall Rd

Stoller Rd

15400

NE McDougall Rd

NE MCDOUGALL RD

PACIFIC HWY W

17500

Miller Creek

PACIFIC HWY W

99W

8

NE

SE

SE DAYTON BYP

9

10

2

Kreder Rd

DAYTON BYP

SE Kreder Rd

SE Kreder Rd

18
233

Yamhill River

3

17

SE Kreder Rd

16000

SE Foster Rd

16200

Kreder Rd

16   15

Yamhill River

SE Neck Rd

97114

SEE **771** MAP

Dayton

Fir St
SE Church St
SE 3RD St
Main St
1st St
Kredor Dr
ALDERMAN PARK

LEGION FIELD

Oak
4th
Ferry St
Water St

200

Katle
Rose Pl
Ash St
COURTHOUSE SQUARE PARK
6th
5th
Alder St

SE Water St
SE Palmer Ct

Water St

YAMHILL LANDING STATE PARK

4

Church St
7th
Main St
SE FERRY ST
Mill St
200
SE Neck Rd
16600

8th St
Main St
300

SE

A
1 Commerce St
BROOKSIDE CEMETERY
Tribbett Ct
Ashley Maple Ct
3RD ST

Church St
9th

Dayton HS

Rodeo Dr
Kallapuya Ct
Joel St
Pioneer St
Palmer Wy
Elizabeth

Norris Ct
Conifer Pl
Thompson

Water St

WILLAMETTE RIVER

5

SE AMITY DAYTON HWY

Palmer Creek

GOODRICH FAMILY CEM
ODD FELLOWS CEM
SE Thompson Ln

CANDLANA BAR

West Fork

Webfoot Rd

20

SE Thompson Ln

Goodrich Ln

21

SE WALLACE RD

22

6

SE

221

Sweet   Cider   Ln
6900
SE Thompson Ln

7

SE Webfoot Rd

SE

29

SE STRINGTOWN RD

28

SE Chrisman Rd

SE Weston Landing Ln
Weston Landing Ln

Mallard Ln

27

SE Dorsey Rd

A   B   C   D   E

SEE **B** MAP

45°14'41"
45°14'15"
45°13'49"
45°13'23"
45°12'57"
45°12'31"
45°12'05"
45°11'39"

123°05'13"
123°04'36"
123°03'59"
123°03'22"
123°02'45"

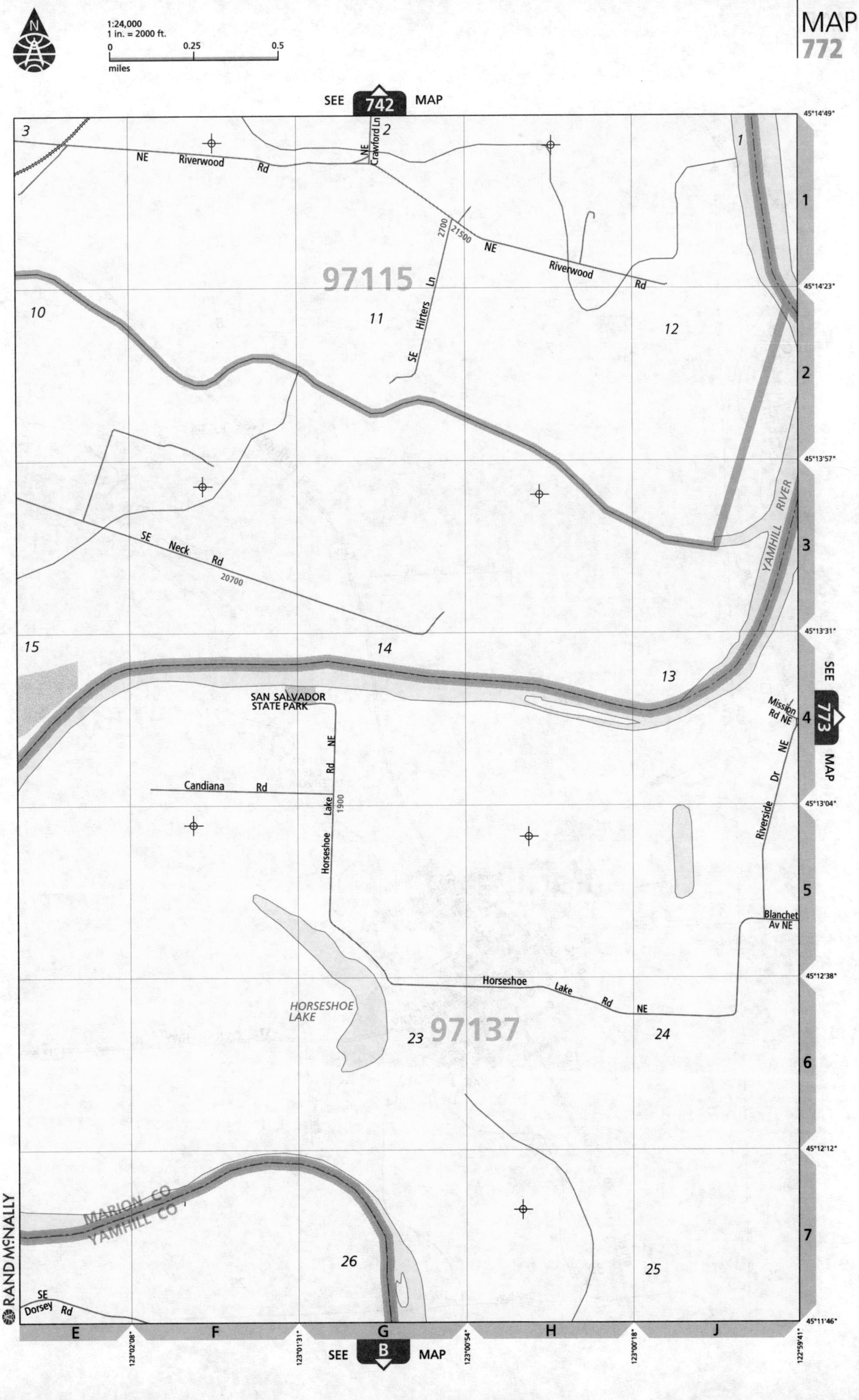

MAP
772

1:24,000
1 in. = 2000 ft.

0   0.25   0.5
miles

SEE 742 MAP

3

NE Riverwood Rd

NE Crawford Ln

2

1

97115

2700 21500

NE

Riverwood Rd

SE Hitters Ln

10

11

12

45°14'49"

45°14'23"

45°13'57"

YAMHILL RIVER

SE Neck Rd

20700

15

14

13

45°13'31"

SEE 773 MAP

SAN SALVADOR
STATE PARK

Horseshoe Lake Rd NE

1900

Mission Rd NE

Riverside Dr NE

Candiana Rd

45°13'04"

Blanchet Av NE

Horseshoe Lake Rd NE

HORSESHOE
LAKE

97137

23

24

45°12'38"

45°12'12"

MARION CO
YAMHILL CO

26

25

SE Dorsey Rd

RAND McNALLY

E   F   G   H   J

123°02'08"   123°01'31"   123°00'54"   123°00'18"   122°59'41"

45°11'46"

SEE B MAP

MAP
773

1:24,000
1 in. = 2000 ft.

0   0.25   0.5
miles

SEE [743] MAP

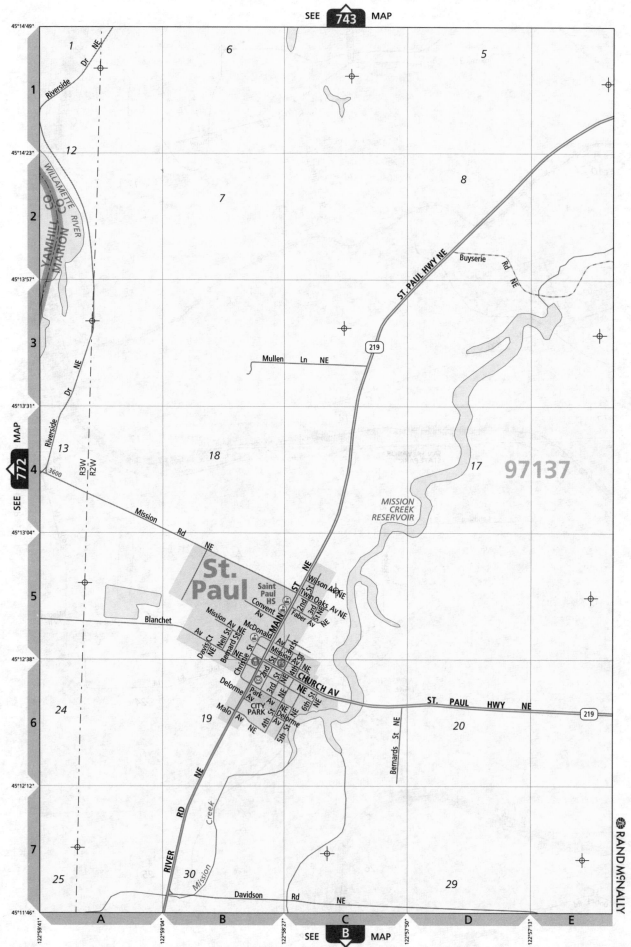

N

45°14'49"

1   6   5

45°14'23"   1

Riverside   Dr   NE

12

WILLAMETTE RIVER

YAMHILL CO
MARION CO

7   8

45°13'57"

St. Paul Hwy NE   Buyserie   Rd   NE

3   [219]

Mullen   Ln   NE

45°13'31"

MAP
[772]
SEE

13   18   17   97137

3600   R3W R2W

Mission   Rd   NE

45°13'04"

MISSION
CREEK
RESERVOIR

St.
Paul   Saint
Paul
Convent
Av

5   Wilson Av NE

Twin Oaks Av NE
Faber Av NE

Blanchet   Mission Av NE
McDonald

Davis Ct   Av   NE   Neil St
Bernard St NE
Christie St

45°12'38"

Delorme
Av   Park
Av
Malo Av
NE   CITY
PARK

24   19   20

45°12'12"

RIVER RD NE

Creek

45°11'46"

25   30   29

Davidson   Rd   NE

A   B   C   D   E

CHURCH AV
NE

St.   Paul   Hwy   NE   [219]

Bernards St NE

Mission

SEE [B] MAP

RAND M°NALLY

MAP
773

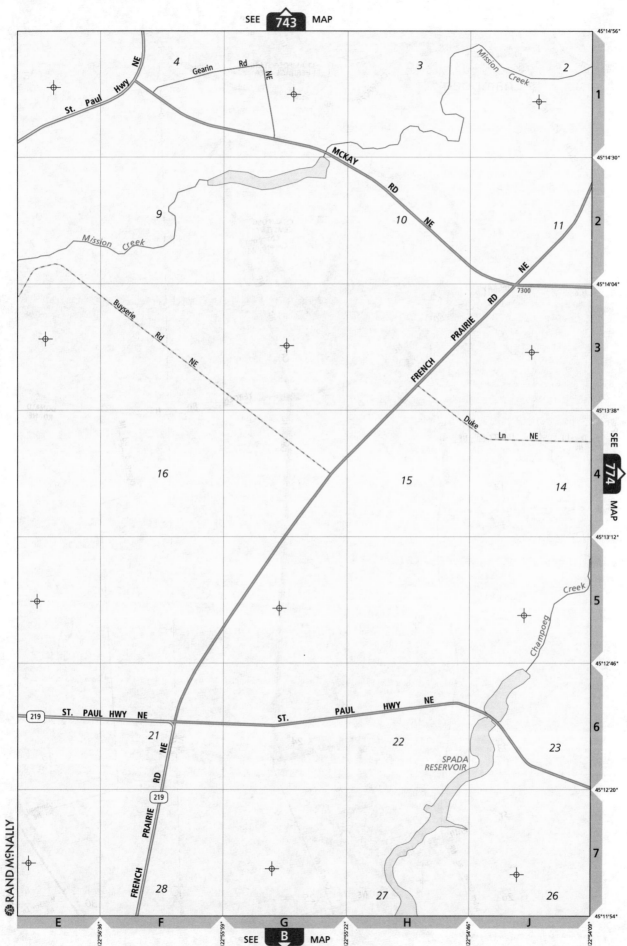

1:24,000
1 in. = 2000 ft.

0   0.25   0.5
miles

SEE 743 MAP

45°14'56"

4   Gearin   Rd   NE   3   Mission Creek   2

St. Paul Hwy   NE   1

MCKAY   45°14'30"

9   RD   NE   10   NE   11   2

Mission   Creek

NE   45°14'04"

7300

Buyserie   FRENCH   PRAIRIE   RD   3

Rd   NE

45°13'38"

Duke   Ln   NE

SEE 774 MAP

16   15   14   4

45°13'12"

Creek   5

Champoeg

45°12'46"

St.   PAUL   HWY   NE

219   ST.   PAUL HWY   NE   6

21   ST.   22   23

NE   SPADA
RESERVOIR

PRAIRIE   RD

219   45°12'20"

RAND McNALLY   FRENCH   28   27   26   7

45°11'54"

E   F   G   H   J

122°56'36"   122°55'59"   122°55'22"   122°54'46"   122°54'09"

SEE B MAP

MAP
774

1:24,000
1 in. = 2000 ft.

0   0.25   0.5
miles

N

SEE  744 MAP

45°14'56"

Newell
House Museum

8100

Pioneer
Mothers Memorial Cabin Museum

Mission Creek

2

Champoeg

CHAMPOEG STATE
HERITAGE AREA

A
C.

1

6

CHAMPOEG RD NE

8800

Creek

45°14'30"

FRENCH PRAIRIE RD NE

Champoeg

11

2

CHAMPOEG
CEMETERY
Champoeg
Cemetery Rd.

12

7

45°14'04"

MCKAY

7300

RD

NE

CASE RD NE

45°13'38"

YERGEN RD NE

9700

DONALD
RD NE

3

Duke Ln
NE

Pokorny Rd NE

Arbor Grove Rd NE

Champoeg

Creek

SEE MAP 773

14

97137

13

Case Rd NE

Olmstead Rd NE

18

45°13'12"

4

5

45°12'46"

R2W
R1W

6

23

24

19

45°12'20"

Olmstead
Rd NE

ST.
PAUL

8400

HWY

NE

Case Rd NE

7

Arbor Grove Rd NE

26

25

30

Wiseacre Ln
NE

45°11'53"

A

B

C

D

E

SEE B MAP

122°54'09"   122°53'32"   122°52'55"   122°52'18"   122°51'41"

RAND McNALLY

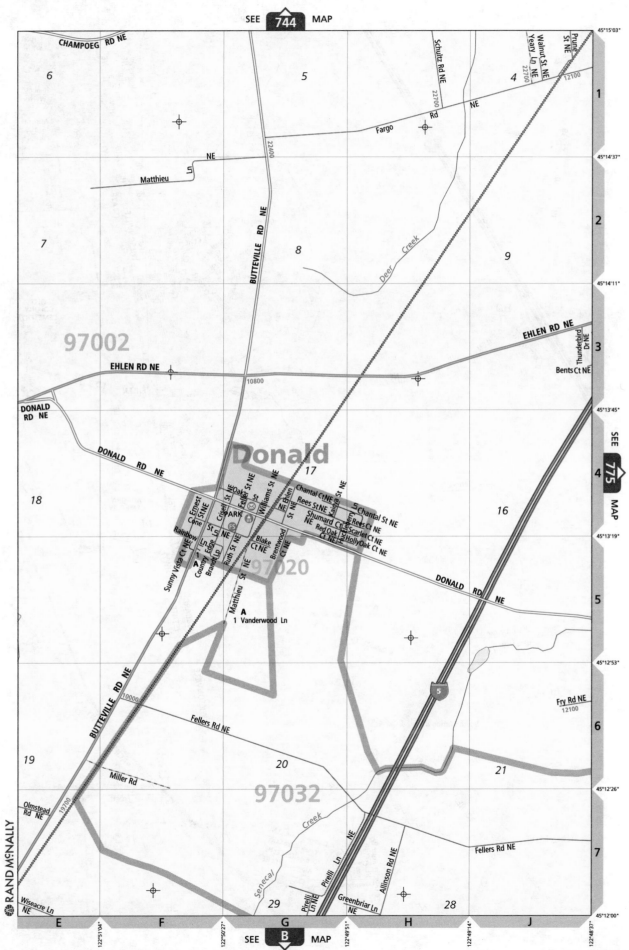

MAP
774

1:24,000
1 in. = 2000 ft.

0   0.25   0.5
miles

SEE 744 MAP

CHAMPOEG RD NE

6

5

4

1

45°15'03"

Schultz Rd NE

22700

Walnut St NE
Yeary Ln NE
Prune St NE

12100

NE

Fargo   Rd   NE

45°14'37"

22400

Matthieu   Ln   NE

BUTTEVILLE   RD   NE

7

8

9

2

Deer   Creek

45°14'11"

97002

EHLEN RD NE

EHLEN RD NE

3

Thunderbird Dr NE

10800

Bents Ct NE

45°13'45"

SEE 775 MAP

DONALD
RD NE

DONALD   RD   NE

Donald

18

17

16

4

Chantal Ct NE
Oak St NE
Feller St
Williams St NE
Ehlen St NE
Chantal St NE
Rees St NE
Kalona St NE
Rees Ct NE

Ernest St NE
Cone St
Crigell St NE
PARK

Shumard Ct NE
Scarlet Ct NE
Red Oak Ct NE
HollyOak Ct NE

45°13'19"

Rainbow Ln NE
Sunny Vista Ct NE
Country Edge Ln NE
Brandt Lp
Ruth St NE
Matthieu St NE
Blake Ct NE
Brentwood Ct NE

97020

A

DONALD   RD   NE

5

45°12'53"

BUTTEVILLE RD NE

10000

A
1 Vanderwood Ln

5

Fry Rd NE
12100

Fellers Rd NE

19

20

21

6

45°12'26"

19700

Miller Rd

97032

Olmstead
Rd NE

Senecal   Creek

Fellers Rd NE

7

Wiseacre Ln
NE

29

Pirelli Ln NE
Pirelli Ln NE
Greenbriar Ln

Allinson Rd NE

28

45°12'00"

E   F   G   H   J

122°51'04"   122°50'27"   122°49'51"   122°49'14"   122°48'37"

SEE B MAP

MAP
775

1:24,000
1 in. = 2000 ft.
0   0.25   0.5
miles

SEE 745 MAP

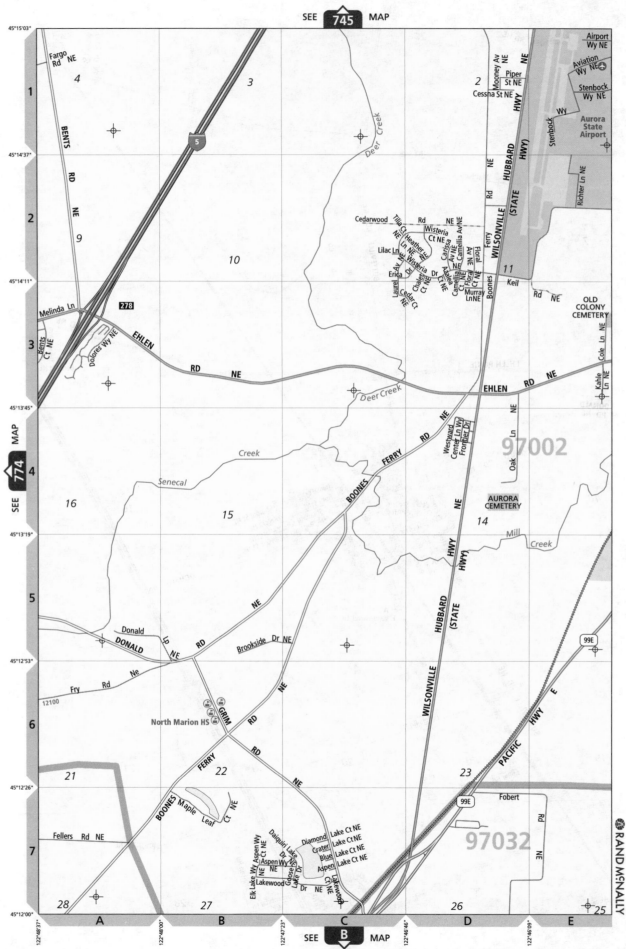

45°15'03"

Fargo Rd NE

4

3

2

Mooney Av NE
Piper St NE
Cessna St NE
HWY

Airport Wy NE
Aviation Wy NE
Stenbock Wy NE

Aurora State Airport

1

BENTS

45°14'37"

RD

NE

WILSONVILLE (STATE) HUBBARD

Stenbock Wy

2

9

Cedarwood Rd NE
Tilia Ct
Heather Ln NE
Wisteria Ct NE
Lilac Ln NE
Camellia Av NE
Camellia Av NE
Wisteria Dr NE
Carissa
Azalea
Camellia Ct NE
Erica Av NE
Floral
Floral
Floral
Cedar Ct NE
Murray Ln NE
Laurel Av NE
Ferry Rd
Boones

Richter Ln NE

10

11

Keil Rd NE

OLD COLONY CEMETERY

45°14'11"

Melinda Ln

278

Bents Ct NE

Dolores Wy NE

EHLEN   RD   NE

EHLEN   RD   NE

Cole Ln NE
Kahle Ln NE

3

45°13'45"

Deer Creek

SEE MAP 774

Creek

Senecal

Westyard
Center Ln Wy
Frontier Dr

97002

Oak Ln

NE

4

16

15

BOONES   FERRY   RD   NE

AURORA CEMETERY

14

Mill   Creek

45°13'19"

NE

HUBBARD (STATE) HWY)

99E

WILSONVILLE

Donald Ln NE
DONALD   RD   NE
Brookside Dr NE

5

45°12'53"

Fry   Rd   Ne

12100

GRIM   RD

North Marion HS

PACIFIC   HWY   E

6

FERRY   RD

99E

23

21

22

Fobert Rd

45°12'26"

BOONES   Maple Leaf Ct NE

97032

Fellers Rd NE

Diamond Lake Ct NE
Crater Lake Ct NE
Blue Lake Ct NE
Aspen Lake Ct NE
Daiquiri Lake Ct NE
Aspen Wy NE
Elk Lake Wy NE
Goose Lake Dr NE
Lakewood
Lakewood Ct NE

7

28

27

26

25

45°12'00"

45°12'37"
122°48'00"
122°47'23"
122°46'46"
122°46'09"

SEE B MAP

RAND McNALLY

MAP
775

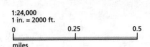

1:24,000
1 in. = 2000 ft.

0   0.25   0.5

miles

SEE **745** MAP

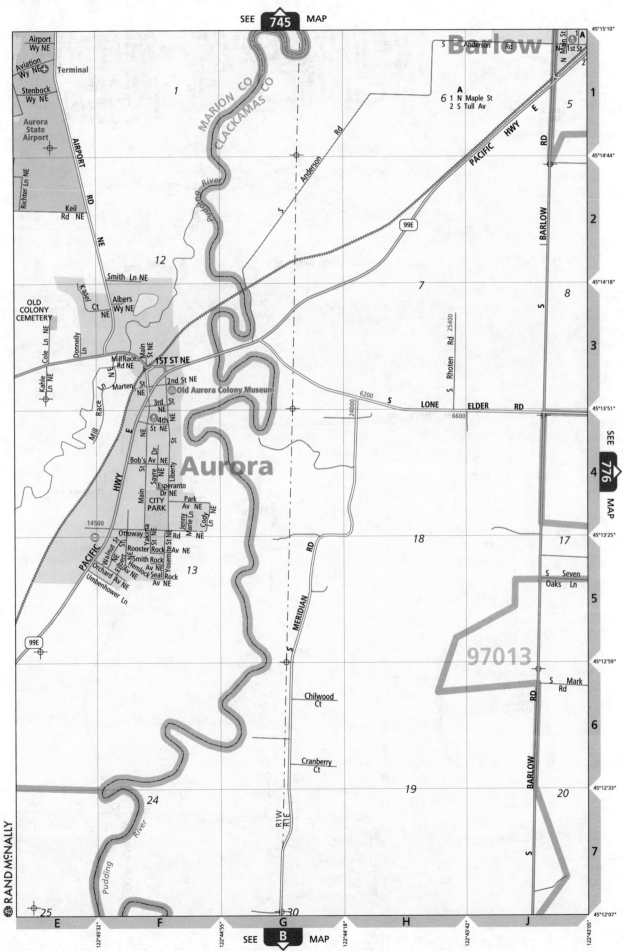

Airport Wy NE

Aviation Wy NE   Terminal

Stenbock Wy NE

Aurora State Airport

Richter Ln NE

AIRPORT   RD   NE

Keil Rd NE

MARION CO

CLACKAMAS CO

Pudding River

Barlow

S   Anderson   Rd

PACIFIC   HWY   E

BARLOW   RD

99E

A
6 1 N Maple St
2 S Tull Av

S   Barlow   Rd

N Main St
1st St

1 A

A

1

5

2

12

Smith Ln NE

Kasel Ct NE

Albers Wy NE

OLD COLONY CEMETERY

Cole Ln NE

Donnelly Ln

Kahle Ln NE

MillRace Rd NE

Main St NE

1ST ST NE

2nd St NE

Marten St NE

3rd St NE

🏛 Old Aurora Colony Museum

4th St NE

Mill Race Ln NE

Bob's Av NE

Sayre Dr NE

Esperanto Dr NE

Aurora

Liberty St NE

Main St NE

CITY PARK

Park Av NE

Cody Ln NE

Jenny Marie Ln NE

14500

Ottoway Rd NE

Yakima St NE

Rooster Rock Av NE

Walnut St NE

Elbert St NE

Smith Rock Av NE

Hemlock Av NE

Yosemite St NE

Seal Rock Av NE

Orchard Av NE

Umbenhower Ln

PACIFIC   HWY   E

13

7

8

3

S   Rhoten   Rd   25400

6200   S

24000

LONE   **ELDER**   **RD**

6600

SEE **776** MAP

4

18

17

S Seven Oaks Ln

5

97013

S   MERIDIAN   RD

Pudding River

Chilwood Ct

Cranberry Ct

S   Mark Rd

BARLOW   RD

6

19

20

24

Pudding River

R1W R1E

25

30

7

SEE **B** MAP

E   F   G   H   J

99E

99E

45°15'10"
45°14'44"
45°14'18"
45°13'51"
45°13'25"
45°12'59"
45°12'33"
45°12'07"

122°45'32"   122°44'55"   122°44'18"   122°43'42"   122°43'05"

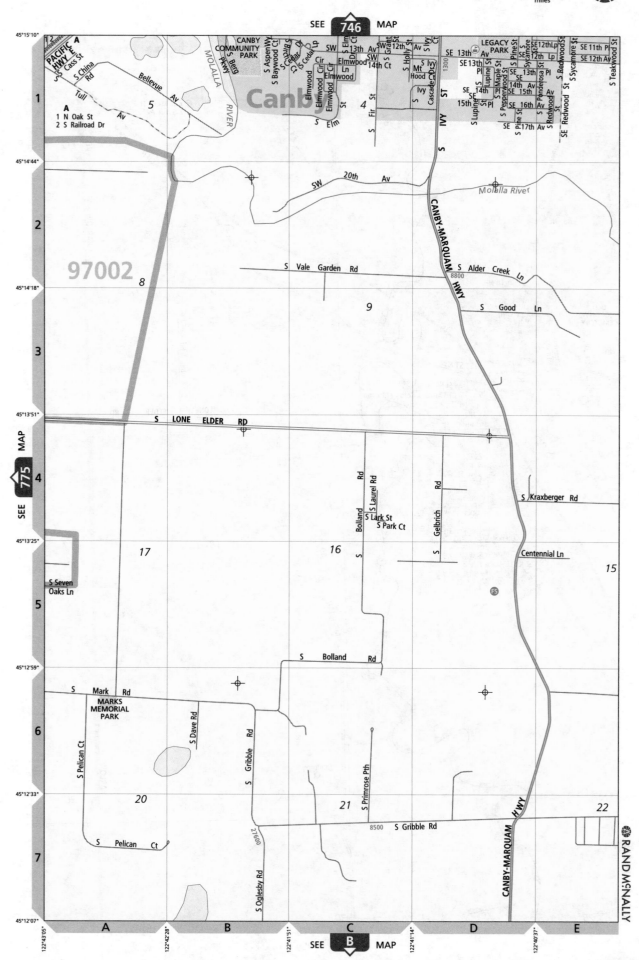

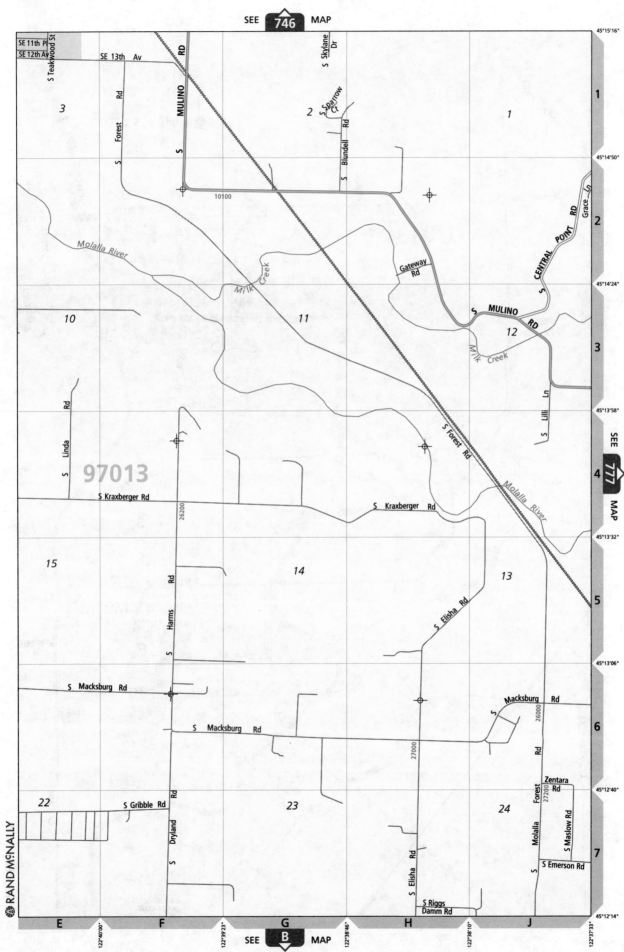

MAP
776

1:24,000
1 in. = 2000 ft.

0   0.25   0.5

miles

SEE 746 MAP

45°15'16"

SE 11th Pl
SE 12th Av
SE 13th Av

S Teakwood St

S MULINO RD

S Skylane Dr

S Barrow Cr

3

2

1

S Forest Rd

S Blundell Rd

45°14'50"

10100

Grace Ln

CENTRAL POINT RD

2

Molalla River

Milk Creek

Gateway Rd

S MULINO RD

10

11

12

S Lilli Ln

Milk Creek

3

45°14'24"

45°13'58"

S Linda Rd

97013

S Forest Rd

Molalla River

SEE 777 MAP

4

S Kraxberger Rd

26200

S Kraxberger Rd

45°13'32"

15

Harms Rd

14

13

S Elisha Rd

5

45°13'06"

S Macksburg Rd

Macksburg Rd

26000

6

S Macksburg Rd

27000

Forest Rd

S Macksburg Rd

Zentara Rd
27200

45°12'40"

22

S Gribble Rd

Dryland Rd

23

24

Molalla Forest Rd

S Maslow Rd

7

S Elisha Rd

S Emerson Rd

S Riggs Damm Rd

45°12'14"

E   F   G   H   J

122°40'00"   122°39'23"   122°38'46"   122°38'10"   122°37'33"

SEE B MAP

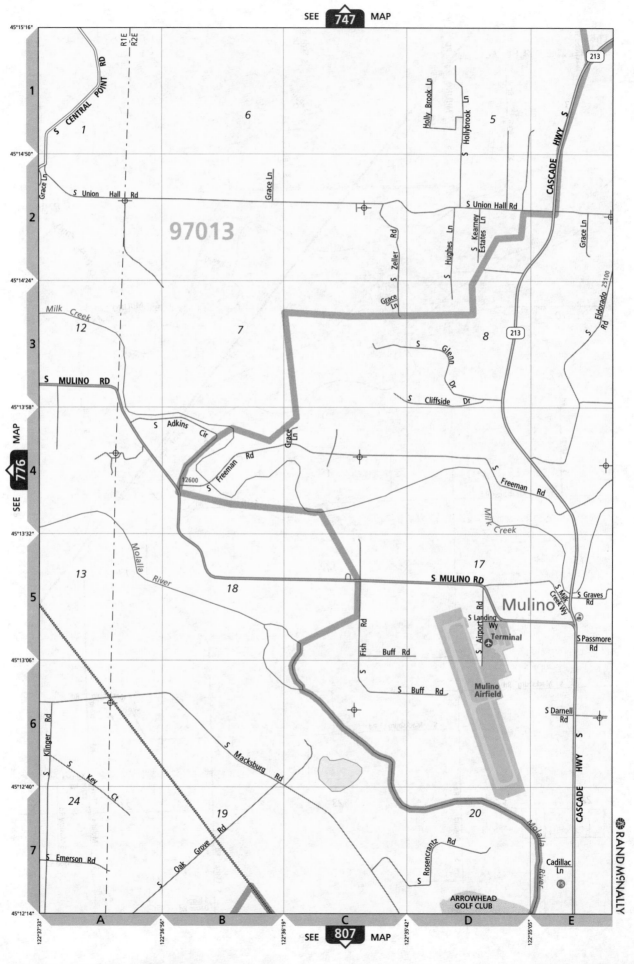

MAP
777

1:24,000
1 in. = 2000 ft.

0   0.25   0.5
miles

N

SEE ⬆ 747 MAP

45°15'16"

R1E
R2E

1

S CENTRAL POINT RD

6

Holly Brook Ln

Hollybrook Ln

5

213

CASCADE HWY S

45°14'50"

Grace Ln

1

S Union Hall Rd

Grace Ln

S Union Hall Rd

2

97013

S Zeller Rd

S Hughes Ln

S Kearney Estates Ln

Grace Ln

45°14'24"

Milk Creek

12

7

Grace Ln

8

213

Eldorado 25100 Rd

S

3

S Glenn Dr

S Cliffside Dr

MAP

S MULINO RD

45°13'58"

776

S Adkins Cir

Grace Ln

Freeman Rd

SEE

4

12600

S Freeman Rd

Freeman Rd

Milk Creek

45°13'32"

Molalla River

17

13

18

S MULINO RD

Mulino

S Milk Creek Wy

S Graves Rd

5

S Airport Rd

S Landing Wy

Terminal

S Passmore Rd

45°13'06"

Fish Rd

Buff Rd

S Buff Rd

Mulino Airfield

6

Klinger Rd

S

S Macksburg Rd

S Darnell Rd

S Key Ct

45°12'40"

24

19

20

Molalla River

7

S Emerson Rd

Oak Grove Rd

S

Rosencrantz Rd

S

Cadillac Ln

CASCADE HWY S

ARROWHEAD GOLF CLUB

45°12'14"

A   B   C   D   E

122°37'33"   122°36'56"   122°36'19"   122°35'42"   122°35'05"

SEE ⬇ 807 MAP

RAND M℠NALLY

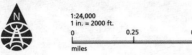

MAP
777

1:24,000
1 in. = 2000 ft.

0   0.25   0.5

miles

N

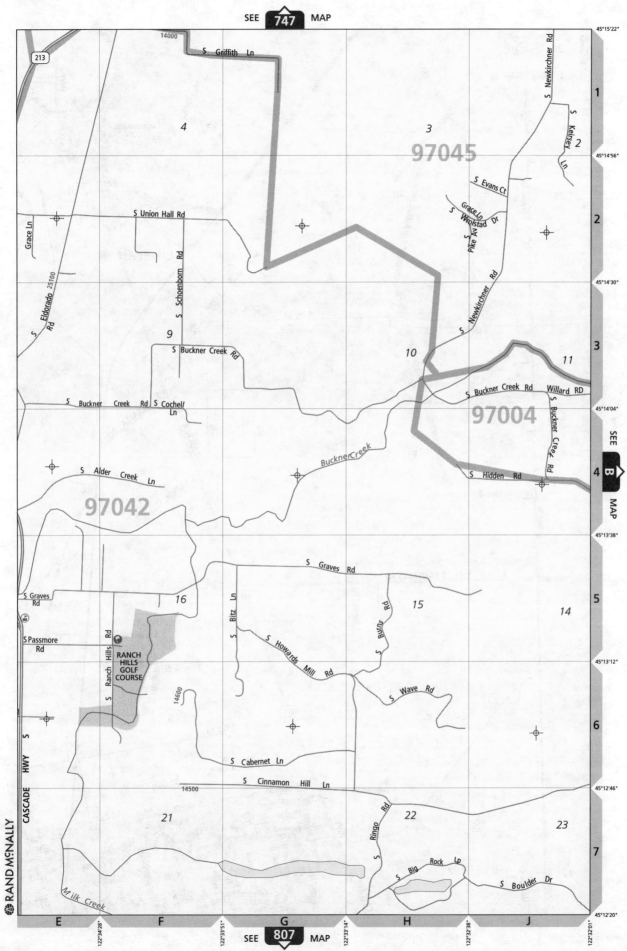

SEE **747** MAP

213

14000

S Griffith Ln

1

S Newkirchner Rd

45°15'22"

4

3

97045

2

S Keisey Ln

45°14'56"

S Evans Ct

Grace Ln

Grace Ln

S Union Hall Rd

2

S Wrolstad Dr

S Pike Av

45°14'30"

S Schoenborn Rd

S Newkirchner Rd

9

45°14'30"

S Buckner Creek Rd

10

11

3

45°14'04"

S Buckner Creek Rd   Willard RD

S Buckner Creek Rd S Cochell Ln

97004

S Eldorado 25100 Rd

S Buckner Creek Rd

SEE

B

45°14'04"

MAP

S Alder Creek Ln

Buckner Creek

S Hidden Rd

4

97042

45°13'38"

S Graves Rd

16

S Bitz Ln

15

S Burns Rd

14

5

S Graves Rd

S Howards Mill Rd

S Passmore Rd

Ranch Hills Rd

45°13'12"

RANCH
HILLS
GOLF
COURSE

S Wave Rd

14600

6

S Cabernet Ln

45°12'46"

S Cinnamon Hill Ln

14500

CASCADE HWY S

21

Ringo Rd

22

23

7

Milk Creek

S Big Rock Lp

S Boulder Dr

45°12'20"

RAND MᶜNALLY

E   F   G   H   J

122°34'28"   122°33'51"   122°33'14"   122°32'38"   122°32'01"

SEE **807** MAP

MAP
807

 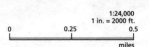

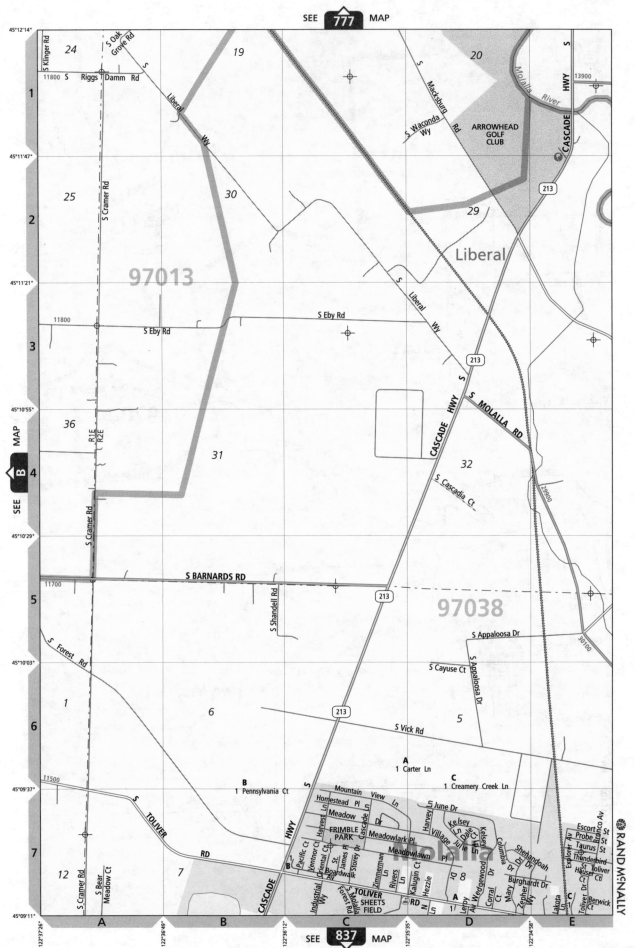

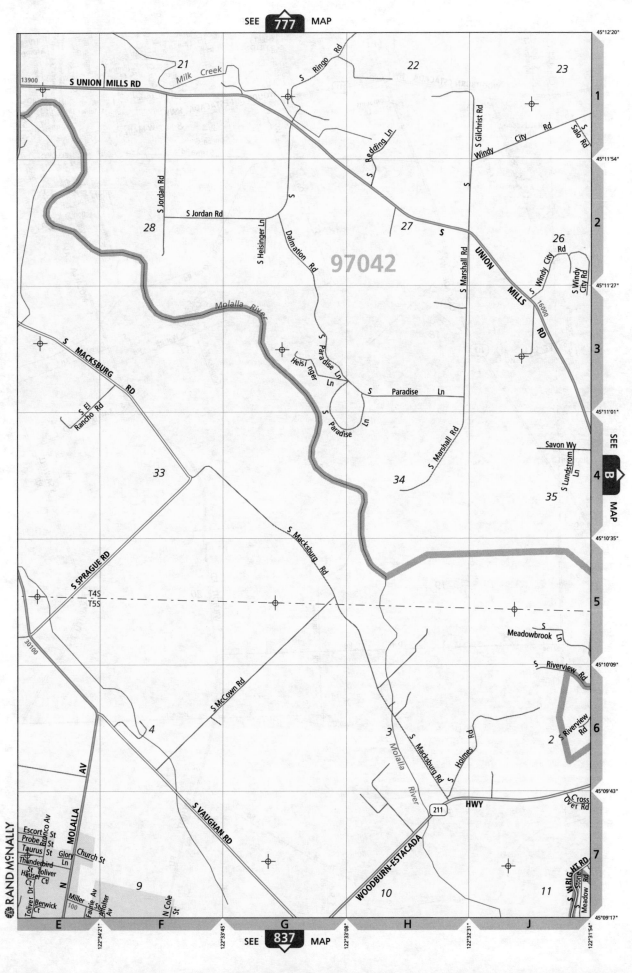

MAP
807

1:24,000
1 in. = 2000 ft.

0   0.25   0.5
miles

SEE 777 MAP

45°12'20"

21   Milk Creek   S Ringo Rd   22   23

13900   S UNION MILLS RD

1

Redding Ln

S Gilchrist Rd   Windy   City   Rd   S Salo Rd

45°11'54"

S Jordan Rd

S Jordan Rd   S Heisinger Ln   Dalmation Rd   27   S   UNION   26   S Windy City Rd   S Windy City Rd

28   2

97042

MILLS   16000   45°11'27"

Molalla River   S   S Marshall Rd   RD

S MACKSBURG   RD

S El Rancho Rd   Heisinger Ln   Paradise Ln   Ln   3   45°11'01"

Paradise   Ln

S Paradise   Ln   Paradise   Ln

S Marshall Rd   Savon Wy   SEE B MAP

33   34   35   S Lundstrom Ln   4

S Macksburg   Rd

45°10'35"

S SPRAGUE RD   T4S   T5S   5

30100   Meadowbrook   S

S Riverview   Rd   45°10'09"

S McCown Rd   S Riverview Rd

4   3   Molalla   S Macksburg Rd   S Holmes Rd   2   S Riverview Rd   6

MOLALLA   AV   River   45°09'43"

S VAUGHAN RD   211   HWY   Cross Over Rd

Escort St
Rancho Av
Probe St
Taurus St
Thunderbird St   Glory Ln   Church St   Toliver   Av   WOODBURN-ESTACADA   S WRIGHT RD   7
Hauser Ct
Toliver Dr   N   Miller Av   Shotter Av   9   N Cole St   10   11   Stone Rd   Meadow Rd
Berwick   Faurie Av
100

E   F   G   H   J   45°09'17"

SEE 837 MAP

122°34'21"   122°33'45"   122°33'08"   122°32'31"   122°31'54"

RAND MCNALLY

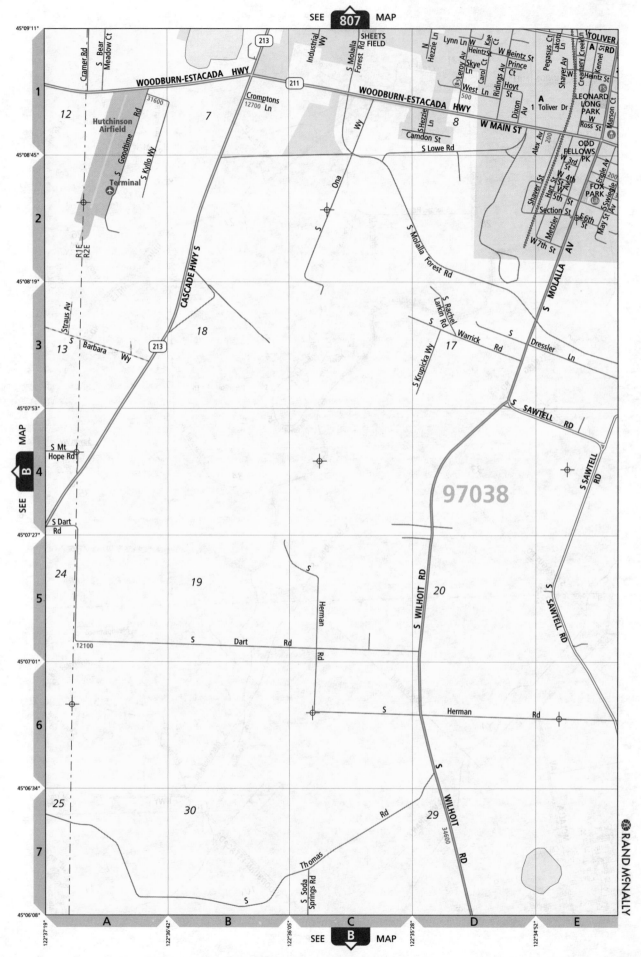

MAP
837

1:24,000
1 in. = 2000 ft.
0   0.25   0.5
miles

SEE 807 MAP

97038

RAND McNALLY

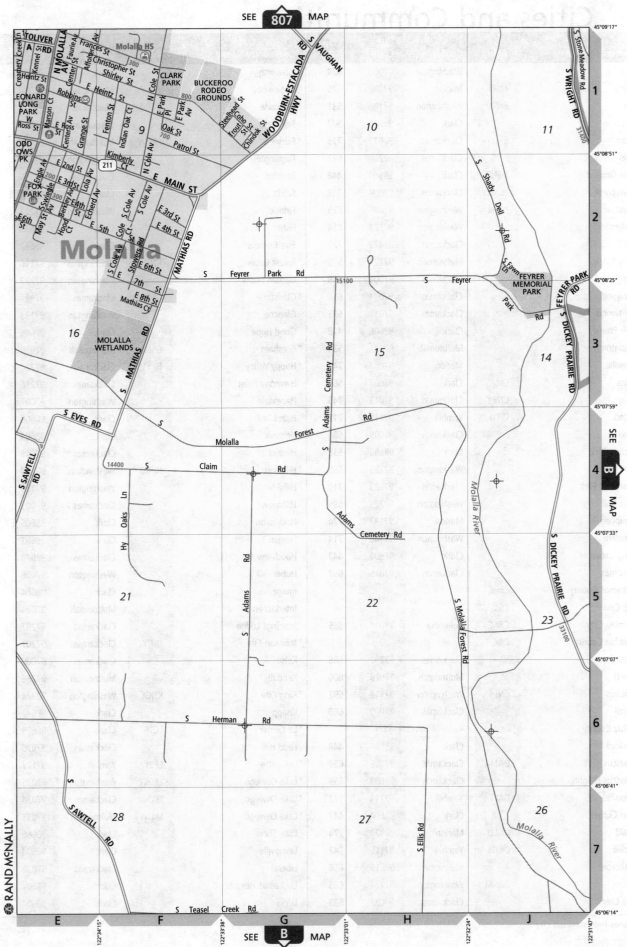

MAP
837

1:24,000
1 in. = 2000 ft.

0   0.25   0.5

miles

45°09'17"

TOLIVER RD

Creamery Creek Ln

Kennel St

Heintz St

Frances Av

Faurie Av

Christopher St

Shirley St

N MOLALLA AV

Center St

Afton St

Molalla HS

300

N Cole St

CLARK PARK

BUCKEROO RODEO GROUNDS

S VAUGHAN RD

WOODBURN-ESTACADA HWY

10

11

S STONE MEADOW RD

S WRIGHT RD

1

31400

LEONARD LONG PARK

Robbins St

E Heintz St

E Park St

Marson St

E Ross St

Grange St

Fenton St

Indian Oak Ct

E Park Pl

E Park Av

Oak St

800

45°08'51"

W Ross St

Engle Av

E 2nd St

Kimberly Ct

211

N Cole Av

E MAIN ST

Patrol St

700

9

Steelhead St

Coho St

Chinook St

Trout St

S Shady Dell Rd

2

45°08'25"

FOX PARK

E 6th St

E 5th St

E 4th St

S Cole Av

S Cole Av

S Cole Av

S Cole Ct

Echerd Av

Lola Av

Berkey Ct

Hood Av

Swiegle Ct

May St

E 3rd St

200

300

E 3rd St

E 4th St

MATHIAS RD

S Feyrer Park Rd

15100

S Feyrer

S Fawn Ln

Feyrer Park Rd

FEYRER MEMORIAL PARK

FEYRER PARK RD

S DICKEY PRAIRIE RD

Molalla

16

MOLALLA WETLANDS

MATHIAS RD

Stowers Rd

E 6th St

7th St

E 8th St

Mathias Ct

15

14

3

S Eves Rd

S EVES RD

Cemetery Rd

45°07'59"

S SAWTELL RD

S

Molalla Forest

Adams Rd

Molalla River

SEE B MAP

4

14400

Claim Rd

Hy Oaks Ln

Adams Cemetery Rd

45°07'33"

21

Adams Rd

22

23

S Molalla Forest Rd

S DICKEY PRAIRIE RD

33100

5

45°07'07"

Herman Rd

6

45°06'41"

28

SAWTELL RD

S SAWTELL RD

27

S Ellis Rd

26

Molalla River

7

S Teasel Creek Rd

45°06'14"

E   F   G   H   J

122°34'15"   122°33'38"   122°33'01"   122°32'24"   122°31'47"

RAND M^{c}NALLY

Cities and Communities

Community Name	Abbr.	County	ZIP Code	Map Page	Community Name	Abbr.	County	ZIP Code	Map Page
Aloha		Washington	97006	624	Ellsworth		Clark	98664	567
*Aurora	AURA	Marion	97002	775	Englewood		Multnomah	97034	656
*Banks	BNKS	Washington	97106	531	*Estacada	ECDA	Clackamas	97023	750
Barberton		Clark	98686	507	Fair Oaks		Clackamas	97267	656
*Barlow	BRLO	Clackamas	97013	775	*Fairview	FRVW	Multnomah	97024	599
Battin		Clackamas	97236	627	Farmington		Washington	97123	653
*Battle Ground	BGND	Clark	98604	448	Faubion		Clackamas	97049	724
Beavercreek		Clackamas	97004	748	Felida		Clark	98685	506
*Beaverton	BRTN	Washington	97005	625	Firlock		Washington	97223	625
Bendemeer		Washington	97124	564	Fisher		Clark	98683	568
Bissell		Clackamas	97022	720	Five Corners		Clark	98662	507
Bonny Slope		Multnomah	97229	595	*Forest Grove	FTGV	Washington	97116	591
Boring		Clackamas	97009	659	Garden Home		Washington	97223	625
Briarwood		Clackamas	97034	656	*Gladstone	GLDS	Clackamas	97027	687
Brightwood		Clackamas	97011	693	Glencoe		Washington	97133	563
Brush Prairie		Clark	98606	478	Good Hope		Clark	98686	447
Burlington		Multnomah	97231	534	*Gresham	GSHM	Multnomah	97030	629
Butteville		Marion	97002	744	*Happy Valley	HPYV	Clackamas	97236	658
*Camas	CMAS	Clark	98607	569	Harmony Point		Clackamas	97236	657
*Canby	CNBY	Clackamas	97013	746	Hazeldale		Washington	97007	624
*Carlton	CLTN	Yamhill	97111	711	Hazel Dell		Clark	98665	506
Carver		Clackamas	97009	688	Heisson		Clark	98604	448
Cascade Park		Clark	98683	538	Henrici		Clackamas	97045	717
Cedar Hills		Washington	97225	595	*Hillsboro	HBRO	Washington	97123	593
Cedarhurst Park		Clackamas	97023	719	Hillside		Washington	97116	561
Cedar Mill		Washington	97229	595	Hillsview		Clackamas	97009	659
Champoeg		Marion	97137	774	Hockinson		Clark	98606	478
Chehalem		Washington	97140	714	Homan		Clark	98662	507
Cherry Grove		Clark	98604	447	Hoodview		Clackamas	97070	745
Clackamas		Clackamas	97015	657	Huber		Washington	97006	624
--Clackamas County	CmsC				Image		Clark	98664	567
--Clark County	ClkC				Interlachen		Multnomah	97024	599
*Columbia City	CBAC	Columbia	97018	385	Jennings Lodge		Clackamas	97267	687
--Columbia County	ClbC				*Johnson City	JNCY	Clackamas	97267	687
Concord		Clackamas	97267	686	Kelso		Clackamas	97009	660
Corbett		Multnomah	97019	600	Kendall		Multnomah	97266	627
*Cornelius	CNLS	Washington	97113	592	*King City	KNGC	Washington	97224	655
Cottrell		Clackamas	97009	660	Knapp		Clark	98642	476
--Cowlitz County	CtzC				*La Center	LCTR	Clark	98629	386
Crawford		Clark	98604	448	Ladd Hill		Clackamas	97070	744
*Damascus	DAMA	Clackamas	97009	659	*Lafayette	LFYT	Yamhill	97127	771
Damascus Heights		Clackamas	97009	659	*Lake Oswego	LKOW	Washington	97035	685
*Dayton	DAYT	Yamhill	97114	772	*Lake Oswego	LKOW	Clackamas	97034	656
Dollar Corner		Clark	98604	447	*Lake Oswego	LKOW	Multnomah	97035	656
*Donald	DNLD	Marion	97020	774	Lake Shore		Clark	98665	506
*Dundee	DNDE	Yamhill	97115	742	Lewisville		Clark	98604	448
Dunthorpe		Multnomah	97219	656	Liberal		Clackamas	97038	807
*Durham	DRHM	Washington	97224	685	Lockamas Heights		Clark	98607	569
Eagle Creek		Clackamas	97022	689	Lucia		Clark	98604	419

*Indicates incorporated city

Cities and Communities

Community Name	Abbr.	County	ZIP Code	Map Page
--Marion County	MrnC			
Marlene Village		Washington	97005	595
Marmot		Clackamas	97055	692
Marylhurst		Clackamas	97034	686
*Maywood Park	MWDP	Multnomah	97220	597
*McMinnville	MCMV	Yamhill	97128	770
McNulty		Columbia	97051	414
Meadow Glade		Clark	98604	477
Metzger		Washington	97223	655
Middleton		Washington	97140	714
Mill Plain		Clark	98682	538
*Milwaukie	MWKE	Clackamas	97222	656
Milwaukie Heights		Clackamas	97222	657
Minnehaha		Clark	98661	507
*Molalla	MOLA	Clackamas	97038	837
Mountain Air Park		Clackamas	97011	723
Mount Hood Village		Clackamas	97011	724
Mt Vista		Clark	98686	477
Mulino		Clackamas	97042	777
--Multnomah County	MthC			
*Newberg	NWBG	Yamhill	97132	713
*North Plains	NPNS	Washington	97133	563
Norwood		Washington	97062	685
Oak Grove		Clackamas	97222	656
Oak Hills		Washington	97006	594
O'Neil Corners		Clackamas	97013	746
Orchards		Clark	98662	507
*Oregon City	ORCY	Clackamas	97045	717
Orenco		Washington	97124	594
Orient		Multnomah	97080	630
Outlook		Clackamas	97045	687
Paradise Park		Clackamas	97022	719
Pine Grove		Clark	98674	386
Pleasant Home		Multnomah	97080	630
*Portland	PTLD	Washington	97229	595
*Portland	PTLD	Clackamas	97236	658
*Portland	PTLD	Multnomah	97204	596
Proebstel		Clark	98682	508
Progress		Washington	97008	625
Quatama		Washington	97006	594
Raleigh Hills		Washington	97225	625
Rhododendron		Clackamas	97049	724
*Ridgefield	RDGF	Clark	98642	416
*Rivergrove	RVGR	Washington	97035	685
*Rivergrove	RVGR	Clackamas	97035	685
Riverwood		Multnomah	97219	656
Rockcreek		Washington	97231	564
Rockwood		Multnomah	97233	598
Rye		Clark	98661	507
*St. Helens	STHN	Columbia	97051	385
*St. Paul	STPL	Marion	97137	773
Salmon Creek		Clark	98686	506
*Sandy	SNDY	Clackamas	97055	691
*Scappoose	SPSE	Columbia	97056	444
Schefflin		Washington	97124	563
Scholls		Washington	97140	683
Shadowood		Clackamas	97068	686
*Sherwood	SRWD	Washington	97140	684
Sifton		Clark	98682	508
South Scappoose		Columbia	97056	474
Springdale		Multnomah	97019	600
Stafford		Clackamas	97062	686
Sunnyside		Clackamas	97015	658
*Tigard	TGRD	Washington	97223	655
Tobias		Washington	97007	624
Tracy		Clackamas	97022	720
*Troutdale	TDLE	Multnomah	97060	599
*Tualatin	TLTN	Clackamas	97062	685
*Tualatin	TLTN	Washington	97062	685
Union		Clark	98682	508
*Vancouver	VCVR	Clark	98660	536
Venersborg		Clark	98604	449
Verboort		Washington	97116	591
Walnut Grove		Clark	98661	507
Warren		Columbia	97053	414
--Washington County	WasC			
*Washougal	WHGL	Clark	98671	570
Watts		Washington	97116	591
Welches		Clackamas	97067	724
West Haven		Washington	97225	595
West Haven-Sylvan		Washington	97225	595
*West Linn	WLIN	Clackamas	97068	686
West Slope		Washington	97225	625
Wildwood		Clackamas	97011	724
Wilkesboro		Washington	97106	532
*Wilsonville	WNVL	Washington	97070	715
*Wilsonville	WNVL	Clackamas	97070	715
*Woodland	WDLD	Clark	98674	386
*Woodland	WDLD	Cowlitz	98674	385
*Wood Village	WDVL	Multnomah	97060	599
*Yacolt	YCLT	Clark	98675	419
*Yamhill	YMHL	Yamhill	97148	711
--Yamhill County	YmhC			
Zigzag		Clackamas	97049	724

*Indicates incorporated city

List of Abbreviations

Admin	Administration	Cto	Cut Off	Lp	Loop	Ste.	Sainte
Agri	Agricultural	Dept	Department	Mnr	Manor	Sci	Science
Ag	Agriculture	Dev	Development	Mkt	Market	Sci	Sciences
AFB	Air Force Base	Diag	Diagonal	Mdw	Meadow	Sci	Scientific
Arpt	Airport	Div	Division	Mdws	Meadows	Shop Ctr	Shopping Center
Al	Alley	Dr	Drive	Med	Medical	Shr	Shore
Amer	American	Drwy	Driveway	Mem	Memorial	Shrs	Shores
Anx	Annex	E	East	Metro	Metropolitan	Skwy	Skyway
Arc	Arcade	El	Elevation	Mw	Mews	S	South
Arch	Archaeological	Env	Environmental	Mil	Military	Spr	Spring
Aud	Auditorium	Est	Estate	Ml	Mill	Sprs	Springs
Avd	Avenida	Ests	Estates	Mls	Mills	Sq	Square
Av	Avenue	Exh	Exhibition	Mon	Monument	Stad	Stadium
Bfld	Battlefield	Expm	Experimental	Mtwy	Motorway	St For	State Forest
Bch	Beach	Expo	Exposition	Mnd	Mound	St Hist Site	State Historic Site
Bnd	Bend	Expwy	Expressway	Mnds	Mounds	St Nat Area	State Natural Area
Bio	Biological	Ext	Extension	Mt	Mount	St Pk	State Park
Blf	Bluff	Frgds	Fairgrounds	Mtn	Mountain	St Rec Area	State Recreation Area
Blvd	Boulevard	ft	Feet	Mtns	Mountains	Sta	Station
Brch	Branch	Fy	Ferry	Mun	Municipal	St	Street
Br	Bridge	Fld	Field	Mus	Museum	Smt	Summit
Brk	Brook	Flds	Fields	Nat'l	National	Sys	Systems
Bldg	Building	Flt	Flat	Nat'l For	National Forest	Tech	Technical
Bur	Bureau	Flts	Flats	Nat'l Hist Pk	National Historic Park	Tech	Technological
Byp	Bypass	For	Forest	Nat'l Hist Site	National Historic Site	Tech	Technology
Bywy	Byway	Fk	Fork	Nat'l Mon	National Monument	Ter	Terrace
Cl	Calle	Ft	Fort	Nat'l Park	National Park	Terr	Territory
Cljn	Callejon	Found	Foundation	Nat'l Rec Area	National Recreation Area	Theol	Theological
Cmto	Caminito	Frwy	Freeway	Nat'l Wld Ref	National Wildlife Refuge	Thwy	Throughway
Cm	Camino	Gdn	Garden	Nat	Natural	Toll Fy	Toll Ferry
Cap	Capitol	Gdns	Gardens	NAS	Naval Air Station	TIC	Tourist Information Center
Cath	Cathedral	Gen Hosp	General Hospital	Nk	Nook	Trc	Trace
Cswy	Causeway	Gln	Glen	N	North	Trfwy	Trafficway
Cem	Cemetery	GC	Golf Course	Orch	Orchard	Tr	Trail
Ctr	Center	Grn	Green	Ohwy	Outer Highway	Tun	Tunnel
Ctr	Centre	Grds	Grounds	Ovl	Oval	Tpk	Turnpike
Cir	Circle	Grv	Grove	Ovlk	Overlook	Unps	Underpass
Crlo	Circulo	Hbr	Harbor/Harbour	Ovps	Overpass	Univ	University
CH	City Hall	Hvn	Haven	Pk	Park	Vly	Valley
Clf	Cliff	HQs	Headquarters	Pkwy	Parkway	Vet	Veterans
Clfs	Cliffs	Ht	Height	Pas	Paseo	Vw	View
Clb	Club	Hts	Heights	Psg	Passage	Vil	Village
Cltr	Cluster	HS	High School	Pass	Passenger	Wk	Walk
Col	Coliseum	Hwy	Highway	Pth	Path	Wall	Wall
Coll	College	Hl	Hill	Pn	Pine	Wy	Way
Com	Common	Hls	Hills	Pns	Pines	W	West
Coms	Commons	Hist	Historical	Pl	Place	WMA	Wildlife Management Area
Comm	Community	Hllw	Hollow	Pln	Plain		
Co.	Company	Hosp	Hospital	Plns	Plains		
Cons	Conservation	Hse	House	Plgnd	Playground		
Conv & Vis Bur	Convention and Visitors Bureau	Ind Res	Indian Reservation	Plz	Plaza		
Cor	Corner	Info	Information	Pt	Point		
Cors	Corners	Inst	Institute	Pnd	Pond		
Corp	Corporation	Int'l	International	PO	Post Office		
Corr	Corridor	I	Island	Pres	Preserve		
Cte	Corte	Is	Islands	Prov	Provincial		
CC	Country Club	Isl	Isle	Rwy	Railway		
Co	County	Jct	Junction	Rec	Recreation		
Ct	Court	Knl	Knoll	Reg	Regional		
Ct Hse	Court House	Knls	Knolls	Res	Reservoir		
Cts	Courts	Lk	Lake	Rst	Rest		
Cr	Creek	Lndg	Landing	Rdg	Ridge		
Cres	Crescent	Ln	Lane	Rd	Road		
Cross	Crossing	Lib	Library	Rds	Roads		
Curv	Curve	Ldg	Lodge	St.	Saint		

Portland Street Index

STREET Block City ZIP Map# Grid

HIGHWAYS

ALT - Alternate Route
BUS - Business Route
CO - County Highway/Road
FM - Farm To Market Road
HIST - Historic Highway
I - Interstate Highway
LP - State Loop
P - Provincial Highway
PK - Park & Recreation Road
RTE - Other Route
SPR - State Spur
SR - State Route/Highway
US - United States Highway

CO-74
9600 YmhC 97115 742 J2
10400 YmhC 97132 742 J1
11100 YmhC 97115 712 J7
11100 YmhC 97132 712 J7
CO-74 Dayton Av
- YmhC 97115 742 J2
CO-74 NE Fox Farm Rd
9600 YmhC 97115 742 J2
10400 YmhC 97132 742 J1
11100 YmhC 97115 712 J7
11100 YmhC 97132 712 J7
I-5
- ClkC - 386 A2
- ClkC - 416 E4
- ClkC - 446 G2
- ClkC - 476 H1
- ClkC - 506 G6
- CmsC - 655 H7
- CmsC - 745 C7
- DRHM - 685 G3
- LKOW - 655 H5
- MrnC - 774 H6
- MrnC - 775 B1
- PTLD - 536 F7
- PTLD - 566 F6
- PTLD - 596 F1
- PTLD - 626 C7
- PTLD - 655 J2
- PTLD - 656 B1
- RDGF - 416 F6
- RDGF - 446 F1
- RVGR - 685 G3
- TGRD - 655 H6
- TGRD - 685 H1
- TLTN - 685 G3
- VCVR - 506 H2
- VCVR - 536 G1
- WasC - 685 G2
- WasC - 715 E1
- WDLD - 386 A2
- WNVL - 715 E7
- WNVL - 745 E1
I-5 TRK
- PTLD - 655 J2
I-5 Columbia River Hwy
- PTLD - 596 G4
I-5 Interstate Br
- PTLD - 536 F6
- VCVR - 536 F6
I-5 Marquam Br
- PTLD - 596 F7
- PTLD - 626 F1
I-84
- FRVW - 598 J4
- FRVW - 599 A4
- GSHM - 598 H3
- MthC - 599 J3
- MthC - 600 B4
- MWDP - 597 H2
- PTLD - 596 H5
- PTLD - 597 C4
- PTLD - 598 C3
- TDLE - 599 E3
- WDVL - 599 E3
I-84 Banfield Expwy
- FRVW - 598 J4
- FRVW - 599 A4
- GSHM - 598 H3
- MWDP - 597 H2
- PTLD - 596 H5
- PTLD - 597 C4
- PTLD - 598 B3
- TDLE - 599 E3
- WDVL - 599 E3
I-84 Columbia River Hwy
- MthC - 599 J3
- MthC - 600 J4
- TDLE - 599 G3
- WDVL - 599 E3
I-205
- ClkC - 476 J7
- ClkC - 477 A7
- ClkC - 507 A1
- ClkC - 537 G1
- CmsC - 627 G1
- CmsC - 657 G1
- CmsC - 685 J5
- CmsC - 686 B5
- CmsC - 687 F3
- GLDS - 687 F4
- MthC - 567 J2
- MthC - 568 A4
- MWDP - 597 H6
- ORCY - 687 F4
- PTLD - 567 J6
- PTLD - 568 A5
- PTLD - 597 G6
- PTLD - 627 G7
- TLTN - 685 J5
- VCVR - 507 G7
- VCVR - 537 G1
- VCVR - 567 J1
- WLIN - 686 F7
- WLIN - 687 C6
- WLIN - 716 J1
- WLIN - 717 A1
I-205 East Portland Frwy
- CmsC - 627 G1
- CmsC - 657 F6
- CmsC - 685 J5
- CmsC - 686 B5
- CmsC - 687 F3
- GLDS - 687 F4
- MWDP - 597 G6
- ORCY - 687 F4
- PTLD - 567 J6
- PTLD - 568 A5

I-205 East Portland Frwy
- PTLD - 597 G6
- PTLD - 627 G1
- TLTN - 685 J5
- WLIN - 686 F7
- WLIN - 687 C6
- WLIN - 716 J1
- WLIN - 717 A1
I-205 Glenn Jackson Br
- MthC - 567 J2
- MthC - 568 A4
- PTLD - 568 A5
- VCVR - 567 J2
I-405
- PTLD - 596 E7
- PTLD - 626 F1
I-405 Stadium Frwy
- PTLD - 596 E3
- PTLD - 626 E1
SR-6
- BNKS 97106 531 J6
- BNKS 97106 532 C6
- WasC 97106 531 J6
- WasC 97106 532 C6
50000 WasC 97116 531 B5
SR-6 NW Wilson River Hwy
- BNKS 97106 531 J6
- BNKS 97106 532 C6
- WasC 97106 532 C6
- WasC 97106 531 J6
50000 WasC 97106 531 B5
SR-8
100 FTGV 97116 592 C5
100 HBRO 97123 593 A5
1600 WasC 97116 591 C1
1800 FTGV 97116 591 H5
2200 CNLS 97113 592 H5
3100 CNLS 97123 592 G5
3600 HBRO 97123 623 H1
4000 WasC 97116 561 A5
5800 HBRO 97007 623 J1
6300 HBRO 97007 624 A1
6300 HBRO 97123 624 A1
6700 WasC 97123 624 A1
6800 BRTN 97225 625 H1
7500 HBRO 97006 624 B1
9500 WasC 97225 625 E2
9700 WasC 97005 625 E2
10700 BRTN 97005 625 B3
14200 BRTN 97005 624 J3
14400 BRTN 97006 624 J3
14400 HBRO 97007 624 J3
14500 WasC 97007 624 J2
18500 WasC 97006 624 E2
32200 HBRO 97123 592 J5
32300 WasC 97123 592 J5
32300 WasC 97124 592 J5
33600 CNLS 97124 592 H5
SR-8 SE 10th Av
300 HBRO 97123 593 D6
SR-8 19th Av
1800 FTGV 97116 591 H5
2500 FTGV 97116 592 A5
SR-8 19th Wy
- FTGV 97116 592 A5
SR-8 N Adair St
100 CNLS 97113 592 D4
100 FTGV 97116 592 D4
SR-8 B St
1900 FTGV 97116 591 J5
SR-8 E Baseline St
1200 CNLS 97113 592 H5
3100 CNLS 97113 592 G5
34300 WasC 97124 592 H5
SR-8 SE Baseline St
100 HBRO 97123 593 B5
SR-8 SW Baseline St
- CNLS 97113 592 H5
100 HBRO 97123 593 B5
32300 HBRO 97123 592 J5
32300 WasC 97123 592 J5
32300 WasC 97124 592 J5
33400 CNLS 97113 592 H5
33600 CNLS 97124 592 H5
SR-8 W Baseline St
100 CNLS 97113 592 D5
100 FTGV 97116 592 D5
SR-8 SW Canyon Rd
6800 BRTN 97225 625 H1
9500 WasC 97225 625 E2
9700 WasC 97005 625 E2
10700 BRTN 97005 625 D2
SR-8 E St
2000 FTGV 97116 591 H4
SR-8 Gales Creek Rd
1600 FTGV 97116 591 E3
1600 WasC 97116 591 E3
SR-8 NW Gales Creek Rd
1600 FTGV 97116 591 E3
1600 WasC 97116 591 C1
4000 WasC 97116 561 A5
SR-8 SE Oak St
100 HBRO 97123 593 B5
SR-8 SW Oak St
100 HBRO 97123 593 A5
SR-8 Pacific Av
1500 FTGV 97116 591 H5
4100 FTGV 97116 592 C5
4300 CNLS 97113 592 C5
SR-8 SE Tualatin Valley Hwy
900 HBRO 97123 593 D6
3600 HBRO 97123 623 H1
5800 HBRO 97123 623 J1
6300 HBRO 97007 624 A1
6300 HBRO 97123 624 A1
6700 WasC 97123 624 A1
7500 HBRO 97006 624 B1
SR-8 SW Tualatin Valley Hwy
13400 BRTN 97005 625 B3
14200 BRTN 97005 624 J3
14400 BRTN 97006 624 J3
14400 BRTN 97007 624 J3
14500 WasC 97007 624 J2
18500 WasC 97006 624 E2
21500 HBRO 97006 624 B1
21700 HBRO 97123 624 B1
32000 HBRO 97123 593 A5
32200 HBRO 97123 592 J5
SR-10
- PTLD 97221 626 B3
2600 PTLD 97201 626 F1
3900 PTLD 97239 626 E4
6500 PTLD 97221 625 H3

SR-10
6500 PTLD 97225 625 H3
6500 WasC 97225 625 H3
8100 BRTN 97225 625 F3
9500 BRTN 97005 625 A3
10300 WasC 97005 625 D3
14100 BRTN 97005 624 J3
14300 BRTN 97007 624 J3
18500 WasC 97007 624 B6
22500 WasC 97007 654 A1
22900 WasC 97007 653 E1
24600 WasC 97123 653 E1
26700 WasC 97123 623 E7
SR-10 SW Barbur Blvd
3900 PTLD 97239 626 F2
SR-10 SW Beaverton Hwy
- PTLD 97221 625 H3
- PTLD 97221 626 B3
- PTLD 97225 625 H3
- PTLD 97239 626 C4
- WasC 97225 625 H3
SR-10 SW Beaverton-Hillsdl Hwy
6500 PTLD 97221 625 H3
6500 PTLD 97225 625 H3
6500 WasC 97225 625 H3
8100 BRTN 97225 625 F3
9500 BRTN 97005 625 E3
10300 WasC 97005 625 D3
SR-10 SW Capitol Hwy
6000 PTLD 97239 626 E4
SR-10 SW Farmington Rd
12000 BRTN 97005 625 A3
14100 BRTN 97005 624 J3
14300 BRTN 97007 624 J3
18500 WasC 97007 624 B6
22500 WasC 97007 654 A1
22900 WasC 97007 653 E1
26700 WasC 97123 623 E7
28500 WasC 97123 653 C1
SR-10 SW Naito Pkwy
- PTLD 97239 626 E4
2600 PTLD 97201 626 F1
SR-14
- ClkC - 568 F4
- ClkC 98671 570 D6
- ClkC 98671 600 J1
- CMAS 98607 568 J5
- CMAS 98607 569 B5
- VCVR - 536 J6
- VCVR - 537 D7
- VCVR - 567 G1
- VCVR - 568 B2
- WHGL 98671 569 H5
- WHGL 98671 570 C6
SR-14 Lewis & Clark Hwy
- ClkC - 568 J5
- ClkC 98671 570 F7
- ClkC 98671 600 J1
- CMAS 98607 568 J5
- CMAS 98607 569 B5
- VCVR - 536 J6
- VCVR - 537 A6
- VCVR - 567 G1
- VCVR - 568 B2
- WHGL 98671 569 H5
- WHGL 98671 570 C6
SR-18
- DAYT 97114 772 A4
- MCMV 97128 770 H7
- YmhC 97128 770 H7
2100 MCMV 97128 771 B6
2100 YmhC 97128 771 B6
3000 YmhC 97114 772 C2
4100 YmhC 97114 771 H5
13400 DAYT 97114 771 J4
SR-18 Dayton Byp
- DAYT 97114 771 J4
- DAYT 97114 772 A4
- YmhC 97114 771 J4
- YmhC 97114 772 C2
SR-18 SE Dayton Byp
3000 YmhC 97114 772 C2
12200 YmhC 97114 771 H5
13400 DAYT 97114 771 J4
SR-18 Salmon River Hwy
- MCMV 97128 770 H7
- MCMV 97128 771 B6
- YmhC 97114 771 E6
- YmhC 97128 770 H7
- YmhC 97128 771 B6
SR-18 NE Salmon River Hwy
2100 MCMV 97128 771 A6
4100 YmhC 97114 771 E6
4100 YmhC 97128 771 E6
SR-18 SE Salmon River Hwy
100 YmhC 97114 771 F6
SR-18 Three Mile Ln
2100 MCMV 97128 771 A6
2100 YmhC 97128 771 A6
4100 YmhC 97114 771 E6
SR-18 E Three Mile Ln
4000 MCMV 97128 771 D6
SR-43
10 LKOW 97034 656 G6
500 ORCY 97045 687 C7
2900 PTLD 97201 626 F1
3300 PTLD 97239 626 F2
6600 PTLD 97219 626 F4
8900 MthC 97219 656 G6
8900 PTLD 97219 656 G6
12400 MthC 97034 656 H4
13100 LKOW 97219 656 G4
16400 LKOW 97034 686 H2
17700 WLIN 97068 686 H2
20600 WLIN 97068 687 B6
SR-43 7th St
- ORCY 97045 687 C7
- WLIN 97068 687 C7
SR-43 SW Hood Av
3300 PTLD 97239 626 F2
SR-43 SW Kelly Av
- PTLD 97239 626 F2
2900 PTLD 97201 626 F1
SR-43 SW Macadam Av
3300 PTLD 97239 626 F2
6600 PTLD 97219 626 F4
8900 MthC 97219 656 G1
8900 PTLD 97219 656 G1
SR-43 Main St
500 ORCY 97045 687 C7
SR-43 Pacific Hwy
15000 LKOW 97034 656 G7

SR-43 Pacific Hwy
16400 LKOW 97034 686 H2
17700 WLIN 97068 686 H2
20600 WLIN 97068 687 B6
SR-43 Riverside Dr
13000 CmsC 97034 656 G4
13000 CmsC 97219 656 G4
13100 LKOW 97034 656 G4
13100 LKOW 97219 656 G4
SR-43 SW Riverside Dr
9800 MthC 97219 656 G6
9800 PTLD 97219 656 G6
12400 CmsC 97034 656 H4
SR-43 N State St
- LKOW 97034 656 G5
10 LKOW 97034 656 G6
800 CmsC 97034 656 G5
800 CmsC 97219 656 G5
SR-43 S State St
10 LKOW 97034 656 G6
SR-43 Willamette Dr
16800 LKOW 97034 686 G1
17700 WLIN 97068 686 H2
20600 WLIN 97068 687 A5
SR-47
- WasC 97116 591 H7
- YmhC 97111 741 A1
- YmhC 97128 741 A2
- YmhC 97128 771 C2
- YmhC 97148 711 A2
- YMHL 97148 711 A2
100 BNKS 97106 531 J5
100 CLTN 97111 711 A7
200 CLTN 97111 741 A1
600 WasC 97116 531 J7
700 YmhC 97111 711 A6
2100 FTGV 97116 592 B4
2300 WasC 97116 592 B4
2400 FTGV 97116 591 J2
4500 WasC 97116 561 J6
45000 WasC 97116 531 F1
SR-47 Highway 47
- CLTN 97111 711 A6
- CLTN 97111 741 A1
- YmhC 97111 711 A4
- YmhC 97111 741 A1
- YmhC 97128 741 A2
- YmhC 97128 771 C2
- YmhC 97148 711 A2
- YMHL 97148 711 A2
SR-47 SW Highway 47
- FTGV 97116 591 J6
- FTGV 97116 592 A6
- WasC 97116 591 H7
SR-47 NW HWY 47
- BNKS 97106 531 J4
- FTGV 97116 592 B4
- WasC 97116 592 B4
2400 FTGV 97116 591 J2
2400 WasC 97116 591 J2
4500 WasC 97116 561 J6
10000 WasC 97116 531 J7
16500 WasC 97106 531 J6
SR-47 N Main St
100 BNKS 97106 531 J5
100 WasC 97106 531 J4
SR-47 S Main St
100 BNKS 97106 531 J5
500 WasC 97106 531 J6
600 WasC 97116 531 J6
SR-47 W Main St
100 CLTN 97111 711 A7
SR-47 S Pine St
200 CLTN 97111 741 A1
SR-47 Quince St
2100 FTGV 97116 592 B4
2300 WasC 97116 592 B4
SR-47 NW Sunset Hwy
45000 WasC 97106 531 F1
SR-47 N Yamhill St
100 CLTN 97111 711 A7
700 YmhC 97111 711 A6
SR-99E
- AURA 97002 775 F3
- BRLO 97013 746 A7
- BRLO 97013 775 J1
- BRLO 97013 776 A1
- CmsC 97002 775 J1
- CmsC 97013 775 J1
- CmsC 97013 776 A1
- CmsC 97045 716 H3
- CmsC 97045 746 F1
- MrnC 97032 775 D7
- ORCY 97045 716 J2
- ORCY 97045 717 A2
10 ORCY 97045 717 A2
10 PTLD 97214 596 G6
10 PTLD 97232 596 G5
100 CNBY 97013 746 B7
100 ORCY 97045 687 C7
700 CmsC 97045 717 A2
1100 CmsC 97013 746 B7
1600 PTLD 97212 596 G1
2000 PTLD 97214 626 G1
2700 PTLD 97202 626 G1
4000 PTLD 97211 596 G1
4900 PTLD 97211 566 G5
8300 MWKE 97202 626 J7
8300 MWKE 97222 626 J5
9000 PTLD 97217 566 G3
9100 MWKE 97222 656 J1
12300 CmsC 97222 656 J4
13200 CmsC 97222 657 A7
13800 CmsC 97267 657 A5
15800 CmsC 97267 687 B1
18500 GLDS 97267 687 C4
18800 GLDS 97027 687 C4
SR-99E SE 1st Av
100 CNBY 97013 746 C6
1300 CmsC 97013 746 E5
SR-99E SW 1st Av
100 CNBY 97013 746 B7
1100 CmsC 97013 746 B7
SR-99E 5th St
- ORCY 97045 717 A2
100 ORCY 97045 687 C7
SR-99E NE Grand Av
10 PTLD 97214 596 G5
10 PTLD 97232 596 G5
1600 PTLD 97212 596 G4
SR-99E SE Grand Av
10 PTLD 97214 596 G6
10 PTLD 97232 596 G5
2000 PTLD 97214 626 G1
2800 PTLD 97202 626 G1

SR-99E N Martin L King Jr Blvd
9200 PTLD 97211 566 G3
9200 PTLD 97217 566 G3
SR-99E NE ML King Jr Blvd
10 PTLD 97214 596 G5
10 PTLD 97232 596 G5
1900 PTLD 97212 596 G1
4000 PTLD 97211 596 G1
4900 PTLD 97211 566 G5
9000 PTLD 97217 566 G3
SR-99E SE ML King Jr Blvd
10 PTLD 97214 596 G5
10 PTLD 97232 596 G5
2100 PTLD 97214 626 G1
SR-99E McLoughlin Blvd
10 ORCY 97045 717 B1
500 ORCY 97045 687 D6
19100 CmsC 97027 687 C4
19100 CmsC 97267 687 C4
19100 GLDS 97027 687 C4
19100 GLDS 97267 687 C4
SR-99E S McLoughlin Blvd
100 ORCY 97045 717 B1
700 CmsC 97045 717 A2
SR-99E SE McLoughlin Blvd
2700 PTLD 97202 626 G1
8300 MWKE 97202 626 J7
8300 MWKE 97222 626 J5
9100 MWKE 97222 656 J1
12300 CmsC 97222 656 J4
13200 CmsC 97222 657 A7
13800 CmsC 97267 657 A5
15800 CmsC 97267 687 B1
18500 GLDS 97267 687 C3
18800 CmsC 97027 687 C3
18800 GLDS 97027 687 C4
SR-99E Pacific Hwy E
- AURA 97002 775 F3
- BRLO 97013 746 A7
- BRLO 97013 775 J1
- BRLO 97013 776 A1
- CmsC 97002 775 J1
- CmsC 97013 746 G2
- CmsC 97013 775 J1
- CmsC 97013 776 A1
- CmsC 97045 716 H3
- CmsC 97045 717 A2
- CmsC 97045 746 F1
- CNBY 97013 746 E5
- MrnC 97032 775 D7
- ORCY 97045 716 J2
- ORCY 97045 717 A2
SR-99W
- MCMV 97128 771 A3
- NWBG 97132 713 B7
- NWBG 97132 743 B1
- WasC 97132 714 A5
- WasC 97140 714 A5
- YmhC 97115 742 J2
- YmhC 97115 743 A2
- YmhC 97132 713 B7
- YmhC 97132 743 A1
100 LFYT 97127 741 G7
100 MCMV 97128 770 H4
100 YmhC 97128 741 F7
300 LFYT 97127 771 J1
1200 LFYT 97114 771 H1
1200 YmhC 97114 771 H1
1200 YmhC 97127 771 H1
1300 DNDE 97115 742 H4
2400 PTLD 97201 626 F1
4200 PTLD 97239 626 E5
7200 PTLD 97219 626 B7
7800 YmhC 97128 771 C2
9400 PTLD 97219 656 B1
10400 PTLD 97219 655 G3
12000 TGRD 97223 655 E4
14300 TGRD 97224 655 D5
15000 KNGC 97224 655 C7
15500 WasC 97224 655 D5
16000 TGRD 97224 685 C1
16100 KNGC 97224 685 B1
16100 WasC 97224 685 B1
17500 TLTN 97062 685 A3
17500 TLTN 97224 685 B2
18200 WasC 97062 685 A3
18600 YmhC 97114 772 B2
18600 YmhC 97115 772 E1
18700 WasC 97062 684 J3
18800 YmhC 97114 742 E7
20200 SRWD 97140 684 E7
22000 WasC 97140 684 E7
23000 SRWD 97140 714 D1
SR-99W E 1st St
100 NWBG 97132 713 C7
SR-99W W 1st St
100 NWBG 97132 713 B7
SR-99W SE 3rd St
100 LFYT 97127 741 G7
300 LFYT 97127 771 J1
1200 LFYT 97114 771 H1
1200 YmhC 97114 771 H1
1200 YmhC 97127 771 H1
SR-99W W 3rd St
100 LFYT 97127 741 G7
100 YmhC 97128 741 F7
SR-99W NE Adams St
100 MCMV 97128 770 H5
SR-99W SW Adams St
100 MCMV 97128 770 H5
SR-99W NE Baker St
100 MCMV 97128 770 H5
SR-99W SE Baker St
100 MCMV 97128 770 H5
SR-99W SW Baker St
700 MCMV 97128 770 H4
SR-99W SW Barbur Blvd
3900 PTLD 97239 626 E5
7200 PTLD 97219 626 B7
9400 PTLD 97219 656 B1
10400 PTLD 97219 655 G3
11400 TGRD 97223 655 H2
SR-99W E Hancock St
100 NWBG 97132 713 C7
SR-99W W Hancock St
100 NWBG 97132 713 B7
SR-99W SW Herber Hoover Hwy W
4200 NWBG 97132 713 G6
30200 YmhC 97132 713 H6

SR-99W Herbert Hoover Hwy W
1400 NWBG 97132 713 D7
SR-99W SW Herbert Hoover Hwy W
3200 NWBG 97132 713 F6
4300 YmhC 97132 713 G6
SR-99W SW Naito Pkwy
- PTLD 97239 626 E4
2400 PTLD 97201 626 E1
SR-99W Pacific Hwy W
- LFYT 97114 771 H1
- LFYT 97127 771 H1
- MCMV 97128 770 G7
- MCMV 97128 771 A3
- NWBG 97132 713 B7
- NWBG 97132 743 B1
- WasC 97132 714 A5
- WasC 97140 714 A5
- YmhC 97114 771 J1
- YmhC 97115 742 J2
- YmhC 97115 743 A1
- YmhC 97127 771 H1
- YmhC 97132 713 B7
- YmhC 97132 743 A1
1300 DNDE 97115 742 H4
7800 YmhC 97128 771 C2
10900 YmhC 97128 741 F7
11300 LFYT 97127 741 F7
17500 KNGC 97224 685 B2
17500 TLTN 97062 685 A3
17500 TLTN 97224 685 B2
17500 WasC 97224 685 B2
18200 WasC 97062 685 A3
18600 YmhC 97114 772 B2
18600 YmhC 97115 772 E1
18700 WasC 97062 684 J3
18800 YmhC 97114 742 E7
20200 SRWD 97140 684 E7
22000 SRWD 97140 684 E7
23000 SRWD 97140 714 D1
SR-99W SW Pacific Hwy
11400 PTLD 97219 655 H2
12000 TGRD 97223 655 E4
14300 TGRD 97224 655 D5
15000 KNGC 97224 655 C7
15500 WasC 97224 655 D5
16000 TGRD 97224 685 C1
16000 WasC 97224 685 C1
16100 KNGC 97224 685 B1
SR-99W Portland Rd
1400 NWBG 97132 713 D7
4300 YmhC 97132 713 G6
SR-210
4700 WasC 97225 625 G3
5400 BRTN 97225 625 F4
5800 WasC 97223 625 F4
6500 WasC 97223 625 E5
6700 BRTN 97005 625 E5
6700 BRTN 97008 625 D7
6700 WasC 97008 625 E5
8500 BRTN 97223 625 D7
8700 TGRD 97008 625 D7
8700 TGRD 97223 625 D7
9400 BRTN 97008 655 A2
9400 BRTN 97223 655 D1
9400 TGRD 97223 655 D1
11800 TGRD 97008 655 B2
13500 BRTN 97008 655 A2
13500 TGRD 97007 655 A2
14000 BRTN 97007 654 J2
14000 BRTN 97008 654 J2
17500 WasC 97007 654 B5
20300 WasC 97123 654 B5
22600 WasC 97123 653 H7
23600 WasC 97140 653 H7
24100 WasC 97123 683 H1
24100 WasC 97140 683 H1
SR-210 SW Scholls Ferry Rd
4700 WasC 97225 625 G3
5400 BRTN 97225 625 F4
5800 WasC 97223 625 F4
6500 WasC 97223 625 E5
6700 BRTN 97005 625 E5
6700 BRTN 97008 625 D7
6700 WasC 97008 625 E5
8500 BRTN 97223 625 D7
8700 TGRD 97008 625 D7
8700 TGRD 97223 625 D7
9400 BRTN 97008 655 A2
9400 BRTN 97223 655 D1
9400 TGRD 97223 655 D1
11800 TGRD 97008 655 B2
13500 BRTN 97007 655 A2
13500 TGRD 97007 655 A2
14000 BRTN 97007 654 J2
14000 BRTN 97008 654 J2
17500 WasC 97007 654 B5
20300 WasC 97123 654 B5
22600 WasC 97123 653 H7
23600 WasC 97140 653 H7
24100 WasC 97123 683 H1
24100 WasC 97140 683 H1
SR-211
- CmsC 97009 690 E6
- CmsC 97022 690 C7
- CmsC 97022 719 J1
- CmsC 97022 720 A1
- CmsC 97023 720 A6
- CmsC 97023 750 A6
- CmsC 97038 807 H7
- CmsC 97055 690 J4
- ECDA 97022 720 A7
- ECDA 97022 750 A1
- ECDA 97023 720 A7
- ECDA 97023 750 A2
- SNDY 97055 690 J4
100 MOLA 97038 837 C1
800 CmsC 97038 837 C1
17400 SNDY 97055 691 A3
SR-211 Clackamas Hwy
- CmsC 97022 719 J2
- CmsC 97022 720 A5
- CmsC 97023 720 A6
- CmsC 97023 750 A1
- ECDA 97022 720 A7
- ECDA 97022 750 A1
- ECDA 97023 720 A7
- ECDA 97023 750 A2
SR-211 Eagle Creek-Sandy Hwy
- CmsC 97009 690 E6
- CmsC 97022 690 C7
- CmsC 97022 719 J1

SR-211 Eagle Creek-Sandy Hwy
- CmsC 97022 720 A1
- CmsC 97055 690 J4
- SNDY 97055 690 J4
- SNDY 97055 691 A3
SR-211 E Main St
100 MOLA 97038 837 E1
SR-211 W Main St
100 MOLA 97038 837 E1
800 CmsC 97038 837 D1
SR-211 Meinig Av
17400 SNDY 97055 691 A3
SR-211 Woodburn-Estacada Hwy
- CmsC 97023 750 A6
- CmsC 97038 807 H7
- CmsC 97038 837 C1
- ECDA 97023 750 B4
- MOLA 97038 837 C1
SR-212
- CmsC 97009 658 E7
- CmsC 97009 688 D1
- CmsC 97015 658 C7
- CmsC 97015 687 J1
- CmsC 97015 688 A1
- DAMA 97009 658 D7
- DAMA 97009 659 A6
- DAMA 97009 688 D1
- DAMA 97015 658 F7
- HPYV 97009 658 E7
- HPYV 97015 658 F7
12500 CmsC 97009 659 H5
29300 CmsC 97009 660 A5
SR-212 Carver Hwy
- CmsC 97009 658 D7
- CmsC 97015 658 B7
- DAMA 97009 658 D7
- DAMA 97015 658 D7
- HPYV 97015 658 D7
SR-212 Clackamas Hwy
- CmsC 97009 658 D7
- CmsC 97015 658 C7
- CmsC 97015 687 J1
- CmsC 97015 688 A1
- DAMA 97009 658 D7
- DAMA 97015 658 D7
- HPYV 97015 658 D7
SR-212 Clackamas-Boring Rd
- CmsC 97009 658 E7
- CmsC 97009 659 C6
- CmsC 97009 688 D1
- CmsC 97015 658 D7
- CmsC 97015 688 D1
- DAMA 97009 658 E7
- DAMA 97009 659 A6
- DAMA 97009 688 D1
- DAMA 97015 658 D7
- HPYV 97009 658 E7
- HPYV 97015 658 F7
SR-212 SE Clackamas-Boring Rd
28300 CmsC 97009 659 H5
29300 CmsC 97009 660 A5
SR-212 Clackamas-Boring Rdg
- CmsC 97009 659 H5
SR-212 SE Clackamas-Boring Rdg
12500 CmsC 97009 659 H5
SR-213
- CmsC - 657 F7
- CmsC - 687 F2
- CmsC 97004 747 G3
- CmsC 97013 777 E1
- CmsC 97038 807 C6
- CmsC 97038 837 A3
- CmsC 97042 747 F7
- CmsC 97042 777 E1
- CmsC 97042 807 C6
- CmsC 97045 687 E6
- CmsC 97045 717 F7
- CmsC 97045 747 F6
- CmsC 97045 777 E1
- GLDS - 687 F4
- MOLA 97038 807 C6
- MOLA 97038 837 B1
- ORCY 97045 687 E5
10 PTLD 97213 597 F6
10 PTLD 97215 597 F6
10 PTLD 97216 597 F6
10 PTLD 97220 597 F1
2000 PTLD 97206 627 F7
2000 PTLD 97215 627 F1
2000 PTLD 97216 627 F1
2000 PTLD 97266 627 F7
3900 PTLD 97218 597 F1
5200 PTLD 97218 567 F7
5200 PTLD 97220 567 F7
8400 CmsC 97206 627 F7
8400 CmsC 97236 627 F7
9000 CmsC 97206 657 F1
9000 CmsC 97236 657 F5
9200 CmsC 97222 657 F5
19600 ORCY 97045 717 F3
SR-213 NE 82nd Av
10 PTLD 97213 597 F6
10 PTLD 97215 597 F6
10 PTLD 97216 597 F6
10 PTLD 97220 597 F1
3900 PTLD 97218 597 F1
5200 PTLD 97218 567 F7
5200 PTLD 97220 567 F7
SR-213 SE 82nd Av
- CmsC - 657 F5
- CmsC 97015 657 F5
10 PTLD 97213 597 F6
10 PTLD 97215 597 F6
10 PTLD 97216 597 F6
10 PTLD 97220 597 F6
2000 PTLD 97206 627 F7
2000 PTLD 97215 627 F1
2000 PTLD 97216 627 F1
2000 PTLD 97266 627 F7
8400 CmsC 97206 627 F7
8400 CmsC 97236 627 F7
SR-213 SE 82nd Av N
8500 CmsC 97206 627 F7
8500 CmsC 97236 627 F7
8500 PTLD 97266 627 F7
9000 CmsC 97206 657 F1
9000 CmsC 97236 657 F1
9200 CmsC 97222 657 F1
12500 CmsC 97015 657 F4

STREET Block City ZIP Map# Grid

SR-213 Cascade Hwy S
- CmsC 97004 747 G3
- CmsC 97013 777 E1
- CmsC 97038 807 C6
- CmsC 97038 837 A3
- CmsC 97042 747 F7
- CmsC 97042 777 E1
- CmsC 97042 807 C6
- CmsC 97045 687 E6
- CmsC 97045 717 F7
- CmsC 97045 747 F6
- CmsC 97045 777 E1
- MOLA 97038 807 C6
- MOLA 97038 837 B1
- ORCY 97045 687 E5
19600 ORCY 97045 717 F3
SR-213 SE Cascade Hwy
8500 CmsC 97206 627 F7
8500 CmsC 97236 627 F7
8500 PTLD 97266 627 F7
9000 CmsC 97206 657 F1
9000 CmsC 97236 657 F5
9200 CmsC 97222 657 F5
12500 CmsC 97015 657 F4
SR-213 SE Cascade Hwy N
- CmsC - 657 F5
- CmsC 97222 657 F5
SR-213 East Portland Frwy
- CmsC - 657 F6
- CmsC - 687 F2
- GLDS - 687 F2
- ORCY - 687 F4
SR-217
- BRTN - 595 E7
- BRTN - 625 D5
- BRTN - 655 D1
- LKOW - 655 H5
- TGRD - 655 E2
- WasC - 595 E7
- WasC - 625 D1
SR-217 Beaverton-Tigard Hwy
- BRTN - 595 E7
- BRTN - 625 D1
- BRTN - 655 D1
- LKOW - 655 H5
- TGRD - 655 E2
- WasC - 595 E7
- WasC - 625 D1
SR-219
100 NWBG 97132 713 D7
300 HBRO 97123 593 B6
900 NWBG 97132 743 F2
900 YmhC 97132 743 F2
2400 WasC 97123 593 B6
2500 HBRO 97123 623 B1
2500 WasC 97113 623 B1
2500 WasC 97123 623 B1
4100 STPL 97137 773 B6
4700 MrnC 97137 773 F7
8400 MrnC 97137 743 F5
9600 WasC 97113 653 B1
9600 WasC 97123 653 B1
16200 WasC 97123 683 E4
16300 WasC 97140 683 H1
17400 WasC 97132 683 F2
17600 WasC 97132 713 D1
SR-219 S 1st Av
300 HBRO 97123 593 B5
SR-219 E 1st St
700 NWBG 97132 713 C7
1700 YmhC 97132 713 E7
SR-219 Barr-Alex Rd
10900 WasC 97123 653 C2
16200 WasC 97123 683 G1
16300 WasC 97140 683 H1
SR-219 Church Av NE
4100 STPL 97137 773 B6
4300 MrnC 97137 773 C6
SR-219 N College St
100 NWBG 97132 713 C7
3100 YmhC 97132 713 C4
SR-219 French Prairie Rd NE
19100 MrnC 97137 773 F7
SR-219 E Hancock St
700 NWBG 97132 713 C7
SR-219 Herbert Hoover Hwy W
1400 NWBG 97132 713 D7
SR-219 NE Hillsboro Hwy
17600 WasC 97132 713 D1
SR-219 SW Hillsboro Hwy
2400 HBRO 97123 593 B6
2400 WasC 97123 593 B6
2500 HBRO 97123 623 B1
2500 WasC 97113 623 B1
2500 WasC 97123 623 B1
9600 WasC 97113 653 B1
9600 WasC 97123 653 B1
16200 WasC 97123 683 E4
16300 WasC 97140 683 H1
20100 WasC 97132 683 E4
23600 WasC 97132 713 D1
SR-219 Main St NE
20200 STPL 97137 773 B5
20400 MrnC 97137 773 C5
SR-219 Newberg Hwy
2400 HBRO 97123 593 B7
2400 WasC 97123 593 B7
2500 HBRO 97123 623 B1
2500 WasC 97113 623 B1
2500 WasC 97123 623 B1
SR-219 Pacific Hwy W
- NWBG 97132 713 C7
SR-219 Portland Rd
1400 NWBG 97132 713 D7
SR-219 St. Paul Hwy NE
900 NWBG 97132 743 F2
900 YmhC 97132 743 F2
8400 MrnC 97137 743 F5
20400 STPL 97137 773 C5
21800 MrnC 97137 773 E1
SR-219 Villa Rd
100 NWBG 97132 713 D7
SR-221
100 DAYT 97114 772 C6
700 YmhC 97114 772 C6
SR-221 3rd St
700 DAYT 97114 772 C4
700 YmhC 97114 772 C4
SR-221 SE 3rd St
100 DAYT 97114 772 A3
700 YmhC 97114 772 B4

SR-221 Salem-Dayton Hwy
- DAYT 97114 772 C6
- YmhC 97114 772 C6
SR-221 SE Wallace Rd
6000 DAYT 97114 772 C5
6000 YmhC 97114 772 C5
SR-224
- CmsC 97009 658 D7
- CmsC 97009 688 D1
- CmsC 97009 689 B3
- CmsC 97015 658 C7
- CmsC 97015 687 J1
- CmsC 97015 688 A1
- CmsC 97022 689 E4
- CmsC 97022 719 J2
- CmsC 97022 720 A5
- CmsC 97023 720 A6
- CmsC 97023 750 D6
- CmsC 97222 657 E5
- CmsC 97267 657 F5
- DAMA 97009 658 D7
- DAMA 97009 688 D1
- DAMA 97009 689 C3
- DAMA 97015 658 D7
- ECDA 97022 720 A7
- ECDA 97022 750 A1
- ECDA 97023 720 A7
- ECDA 97023 750 D6
- HPYV 97015 658 D7
- MWKE 97222 656 J2
- MWKE 97222 657 A2
14200 CmsC 97015 657 F6
SR-224 SE 82nd Dr
14200 CmsC 97015 657 F6
SR-224 Carver Hwy
- CmsC 97009 658 D7
- CmsC 97015 658 B7
- DAMA 97009 658 D7
- DAMA 97015 658 D7
- HPYV 97015 658 D7
SR-224 Clackamas Hwy
- CmsC 97009 658 D7
- CmsC 97009 688 D1
- CmsC 97009 689 A3
- CmsC 97015 658 C7
- CmsC 97015 687 J1
- CmsC 97015 688 A1
- CmsC 97022 689 E4
- CmsC 97022 719 J2
- CmsC 97022 720 A5
- CmsC 97023 720 A6
- CmsC 97023 750 D6
- DAMA 97009 658 D7
- DAMA 97009 688 D1
- DAMA 97009 689 C3
- DAMA 97015 658 D7
- ECDA 97022 720 A7
- ECDA 97022 750 A1
- ECDA 97023 720 A7
- ECDA 97023 750 D6
- HPYV 97015 658 D7
SR-224 SE Milwaukie Expwy
- CmsC 97015 657 F6
- CmsC 97222 657 D5
- CmsC 97267 657 F5
- MWKE 97222 656 J2
- MWKE 97222 657 A2
SR-233
- DAYT 97114 772 A4
3000 YmhC 97114 772 C2
6500 YmhC 97114 771 G7
13400 DAYT 97114 771 J4
SR-233 SE Amity-Dayton Hwy
10600 YmhC 97114 771 G7
SR-233 Dayton Byp
- DAYT 97114 771 J4
- DAYT 97114 772 A4
- YmhC 97114 771 J4
- YmhC 97114 772 C2
SR-233 SE Dayton Byp
3000 YmhC 97114 772 C2
12700 YmhC 97114 771 H5
13400 DAYT 97114 771 J4
SR-233 SE Lafayette Hwy
6500 YmhC 97114 771 G7
SR-240
- YmhC 97132 711 G2
- YmhC 97148 711 E1
100 NWBG 97132 713 B7
300 YMHL 97148 711 B1
23000 YmhC 97132 712 F5
23000 YmhC 97132 713 B6
SR-240 E Main St
300 YMHL 97148 711 B1
1000 YmhC 97148 711 B1
SR-240 N Main St
100 NWBG 97132 713 B7
SR-240 Yamhill-Newberg Hwy
- NWBG 97132 713 B6
- YmhC 97132 711 G2
- YmhC 97132 712 A4
- YmhC 97148 711 E2
23000 YmhC 97132 713 B6
SR-500
- ClkC - 507 J7
- ClkC - 537 H1
- ClkC 98661 537 C2
- ClkC 98682 507 J5
- VCVR - 507 J7
- VCVR - 537 H1
- VCVR 98663 536 G4
- VCVR 98663 537 A2
200 CMAS 98607 569 G5
800 CMAS 98607 539 E7
2800 ClkC 98607 539 D3
3400 ClkC 98682 539 C1
5300 ClkC 98682 509 C7
7000 ClkC 98682 508 B5
SR-500 NE 3rd Av
500 CMAS 98607 569 F4
SR-500 NE 3rd St
26300 ClkC 98607 539 F6
SR-500 SE 6th Av
500 CMAS 98607 569 G5
SR-500 NE 14th Av
600 CMAS 98607 569 E4
SR-500 NE 25th St
400 ClkC 98607 539 D4
SR-500 NE 44th St
23800 ClkC 98682 539 C2
SR-500 NE 54th St
23200 ClkC 98682 539 C1

SR-500 NE 58th St
19100 ClkC 98682 508 H7
20700 ClkC 98682 509 C7
SR-500 NE 117th Av
- VCVR 98682 507 J7
6300 ClkC 98662 507 J6
6300 ClkC 98682 507 J6
SR-500 NE 162nd Av
7000 ClkC 98682 508 E6
SR-500 NE 232nd Av
5300 ClkC 98682 509 C7
5300 ClkC 98682 539 C1
SR-500 NE 237th Av
4800 ClkC 98682 539 C1
SR-500 NE 238th Av
4400 ClkC 98682 539 C2
SR-500 NE 242nd Av
2800 ClkC 98607 539 D3
3400 ClkC 98682 539 D2
SR-500 NE 267th Av
300 ClkC 98607 539 F6
SR-500 NE Brunner Rd
25200 ClkC 98607 539 E4
SR-500 NE Dallas St
200 CMAS 98607 569 F4
SR-500 NE Dresser Rd
24200 ClkC 98607 539 D3
SR-500 SE Everett Rd
100 ClkC 98607 539 F6
800 CMAS 98607 539 E7
1000 CMAS 98607 569 E1
SR-500 NE Everett St
1400 CMAS 98607 569 E3
SR-500 NE Fourth Plain Rd
16200 ClkC 98682 508 G7
SR-500 NE Garfield St
300 CMAS 98607 569 F4
SR-500 NE Padden Pkwy
- ClkC 98662 507 J5
- ClkC 98682 507 J5
- ClkC 98682 508 B5
SR-500 SE Union St
600 CMAS 98607 569 G5
SR-500 NE Ward Rd
8300 ClkC 98682 508 E5
SR-501
200 RDGF 98642 415 J7
600 VCVR 98663 536 G4
700 RDGF 98642 416 B7
2000 VCVR 98660 536 A1
5200 ClkC 98660 536 A1
6300 ClkC 98660 505 G1
6300 ClkC 98660 506 A7
6300 VCVR 98660 505 J7
6300 VCVR 98660 506 A7
10000 ClkC 98660 475 H4
SR-501 E 15th St
100 VCVR 98660 536 G4
100 VCVR 98663 536 G4
SR-501 W 15th St
100 VCVR 98660 536 G4
100 VCVR 98663 536 G4
SR-501 NW Lower River Rd
2000 VCVR 98660 536 A1
5200 ClkC 98660 536 A1
6300 ClkC 98660 505 G1
6300 ClkC 98660 506 A7
6300 VCVR 98660 505 J7
6300 VCVR 98660 506 A7
10000 ClkC 98660 475 H4
SR-501 E Mill Plain Blvd
100 VCVR 98660 536 G4
100 VCVR 98663 536 G4
SR-501 W Mill Plain Blvd
1000 VCVR 98663 536 G4
2300 VCVR 98660 536 D3
SR-501 Pioneer St
200 RDGF 98642 415 J7
700 RDGF 98642 416 B7
SR-502
10000 BGND 98604 448 A5
1000 ClkC 98642 446 H7
1500 BGND 98604 447 J5
2200 ClkC 98642 447 D5
2900 ClkC 98604 447 H5
17900 ClkC 98604 476 H1
SR-502 NE 10th Av
17900 ClkC 98642 476 H1
19400 ClkC 98642 446 H7
SR-502 NE 219th St
1000 ClkC 98642 446 J5
2200 ClkC 98642 447 D5
4200 ClkC 98604 447 C5
9200 BGND 98604 447 H5
SR-502 W Main St
1000 BGND 98604 448 A5
1500 BGND 98604 447 J5
2900 ClkC 98604 447 H5
SR-503
- VCVR 98682 507 J7
10 BGND 98604 448 A6
10 ClkC 98604 448 A7
1000 WDLD 98674 386 A1
6300 ClkC 98662 507 J4
6300 ClkC 98682 507 J4
11700 ClkC 98606 507 J1
11900 ClkC 98606 477 J7
11900 ClkC 98662 477 J7
13100 ClkC 98606 478 A3
17900 ClkC 98604 478 A2
26200 ClkC 98604 418 B6
32900 ClkC 98675 418 D1
SR-503 BUS
14800 ClkC 98606 478 A4
16700 ClkC 98604 478 A3
SR-503 NW 10th Av
12200 BGND 98604 448 A4
12200 ClkC 98604 448 A4
SR-503 SW 10th Av
10 BGND 98604 448 A6
10 ClkC 98604 448 A7
SR-503 NE 117th Av
- VCVR 98682 507 J7
6300 ClkC 98662 507 J4
6300 ClkC 98682 507 J4
11700 ClkC 98606 507 J1
11900 ClkC 98606 477 J7
11900 ClkC 98662 477 J7
13100 ClkC 98606 478 A3
SR-503 NE 122nd Av
13300 BGND 98604 448 A3
17900 ClkC 98604 478 A2
17900 ClkC 98606 478 A2
19200 ClkC 98604 448 A7

SR-503 BUS NE Caples Rd
14800 ClkC 98606 478 A4
16700 ClkC 98604 478 A3
SR-503 Lewis River Rd
1000 WDLD 98674 386 A1
SR-503 NE Lewisville Hwy
24400 BGND 98604 448 A3
24400 ClkC 98604 448 A7
26200 ClkC 98604 418 B6
32900 ClkC 98675 418 D1
US-26
- BRTN - 594 F3
- BRTN - 595 J7
- BRTN - 625 G1
- CmsC 97009 659 G1
- CmsC 97009 660 A4
- CmsC 97009 690 F1
- CmsC 97011 693 E6
- CmsC 97011 723 H1
- CmsC 97011 724 A3
- CmsC 97049 724 D4
- CmsC 97055 690 F1
- CmsC 97055 693 C6
- CmsC 97067 723 H1
- CmsC 97067 724 A3
- DAMA 97009 659 G1
- HBRO - 563 J6
- HBRO - 564 B7
- HBRO - 594 D1
- MthC - 595 H7
- MthC - 596 A7
- MthC 97080 629 F6
- MthC 97080 659 J3
- NPNS - 562 J1
- NPNS - 563 B2
- PTLD - 595 J7
- PTLD - 596 C7
- PTLD - 626 B1
- PTLD 97239 626 G1
- WasC - 562 J1
- WasC - 563 E4
- WasC - 594 D1
- WasC - 595 B6
- WasC 97106 532 E6
- WasC 97113 532 E6
- WasC 97133 532 G7
10 GSHM 97030 629 A3
10 GSHM 97080 629 A3
10 PTLD 97201 626 E1
500 PTLD 97202 626 J2
1900 GSHM 97030 628 J2
1900 GSHM 97080 628 J2
2800 PTLD 97202 627 A2
4900 GSHM 97236 628 F3
6900 PTLD 97206 627 J2
8000 PTLD 97266 627 J2
11500 PTLD 97266 628 C2
12000 PTLD 97236 628 A2
38200 SNDY 97055 690 H2
39000 SNDY 97055 691 B3
39700 CmsC 97055 691 B3
39700 WasC 97106 531 H2
47300 CmsC 97055 692 C7
US-26 SW 3rd Av
2400 PTLD 97201 626 E1
US-26 SW 5th Av
2300 PTLD 97201 626 E1
US-26 SW Arthur St
10 PTLD 97201 626 F1
US-26 SW Caruthers St
300 PTLD 97201 626 E1
US-26 SW Clay St
700 PTLD 97201 596 E7
US-26 SW Corbett Av
2900 PTLD 97201 626 F1
US-26 SW Kelly Av
2700 PTLD 97201 626 F1
US-26 SW Market St
700 PTLD 97201 596 E7
US-26 Mt Hood Hwy
- CmsC 97009 659 H1
- CmsC 97009 660 A4
- CmsC 97009 690 F1
- CmsC 97011 693 E6
- CmsC 97011 723 H1
- CmsC 97011 724 A3
- CmsC 97049 724 D4
- CmsC 97055 690 F1
- CmsC 97055 693 C6
- CmsC 97067 723 H1
- CmsC 97067 724 A3
- DAMA 97009 659 G1
- GSHM 97080 629 F6
- MthC 97080 629 F6
- MthC 97080 659 J3
- SNDY 97055 690 H2
41600 CmsC 97055 691 C4
41600 SNDY 97055 691 C4
47300 CmsC 97055 692 C7
US-26 Pioneer Blvd
38200 SNDY 97055 690 J3
38900 SNDY 97055 691 B3
39700 CmsC 97055 691 B3
US-26 E Powell Blvd
- GSHM 97030 629 E3
10 GSHM 97030 629 C2
US-26 SE Powell Blvd
500 PTLD 97202 626 J2
2800 PTLD 97202 627 A2
6900 PTLD 97206 627 J2
8000 PTLD 97266 627 J2
11500 PTLD 97266 628 C2
12000 PTLD 97236 628 A2
17400 GSHM 97030 628 F3
17400 GSHM 97080 628 F3
17400 GSHM 97236 628 F3
US-26 W Powell Blvd
10 GSHM 97030 629 A3
10 GSHM 97080 629 A3
1900 GSHM 97030 628 J2
1900 GSHM 97080 628 J2
US-26 SE Powell Valley Blvd
4200 GSHM 97030 628 G3
4200 GSHM 97080 628 G3
4900 GSHM 97236 628 F3
4900 PTLD 97236 628 F3
US-26 Proctor Blvd
38200 SNDY 97055 690 J3
39000 SNDY 97055 691 A3
US-26 Ross Island Br
- PTLD 97201 626 F1
- PTLD 97202 626 G1
- PTLD 97239 626 F1

US-26 SW Sheridan St
300 PTLD 97201 626 E1
US-26 Sunset Hwy
- BRTN - 594 F3
- BRTN - 595 H7
- BRTN - 625 G1
- HBRO - 563 J6
- HBRO - 564 B7
- HBRO - 594 D1
- MthC - 595 H7
- MthC - 596 A7
- NPNS - 562 J1
- NPNS - 563 B2
- PTLD - 595 J7
- PTLD - 596 B7
- PTLD - 626 B1
- WasC - 562 J1
- WasC - 563 B2
- WasC - 594 D1
- WasC - 595 B6
- WasC 97106 532 E6
- WasC 97113 532 G7
- WasC 97133 532 E6
US-26 NW Sunset Hwy
39500 WasC 97106 532 B3
39700 WasC 97106 531 H2
US-30
- FRVW - 598 J4
- FRVW - 599 C3
- GSHM - 598 J4
- MthC - 599 J3
- MthC - 600 A3
- MWDP - 597 H2
- PTLD - 596 G4
- PTLD - 597 G4
- PTLD - 598 B3
- TDLE - 599 G3
- WDVL - 599 E3
10 STHN 97051 415 A2
100 STHN 97051 385 B7
700 ClbC 97051 385 C6
2200 PTLD 97210 596 B3
4400 PTLD 97210 595 J1
4600 PTLD 97210 565 G5
7500 PTLD 97231 565 G5
11600 PTLD 97231 535 D7
12300 MthC 97231 535 A5
15000 MthC 97231 534 J3
17700 MthC 97231 504 F1
25200 MthC 97231 474 F7
27200 ClbC 97056 474 E5
50600 SPSE 97056 474 E1
52600 SPSE 97056 444 E7
52700 ClbC 97056 444 E7
55600 ClbC 97053 444 G1
56000 ClbC 97053 414 H7
57800 ClbC 97051 414 J4
58100 ClbC 97051 415 A2
61100 CBAC 97018 385 C4
61100 ClbC 97018 385 C4
62900 ClbC 97054 385 C6
US-30 BUS
10 PTLD 97214 596 J5
10 PTLD 97232 596 J5
2700 PTLD 97232 597 C3
3900 PTLD 97212 597 B4
6800 PTLD 97213 597 G1
8100 PTLD 97218 597 G1
8100 PTLD 97220 597 G1
9100 MWDP 97220 597 G1
US-30 BYP
- PTLD 97210 565 F4
10 PTLD 97211 566 J5
1700 PTLD 97217 566 E5
2200 PTLD 97211 567 C6
3900 PTLD 97203 566 A4
4000 PTLD 97218 567 B6
6500 PTLD 97203 565 J3
7600 PTLD 97220 567 F7
8700 PTLD 97231 565 F3
9600 PTLD 97220 597 J1
11300 PTLD 97220 598 C2
11900 PTLD 97230 598 A1
16500 GSHM 97230 598 F2
19700 GSHM 97024 598 J3
20100 FRVW 97024 598 J3
20400 FRVW 97024 599 A3
US-30 Banfield Expwy
- FRVW - 598 J4
- FRVW - 599 C3
- GSHM - 598 H3
- MWDP - 597 H2
- PTLD - 596 J4
- PTLD - 597 J2
- PTLD - 598 B3
- TDLE - 599 E3
- WDVL - 599 E3
US-30 BYP NW Bridge Av
- PTLD 97210 565 F4
8700 PTLD 97231 565 F3
US-30 BUS E Burnside St
10 PTLD 97214 596 J5
10 PTLD 97232 596 J5
US-30 BYP NE Columbia Blvd
9200 PTLD 97220 567 H7
9600 PTLD 97220 597 J1
US-30 Columbia River Hwy
- MthC - 599 J3
- MthC - 600 A3
- PTLD - 596 G3
- PTLD 97210 596 D3
- TDLE - 599 G3
- WDVL - 599 E3
50000 ClbC 97056 474 E5
50600 SPSE 97056 474 E1
52400 SPSE 97056 444 E7
52700 ClbC 97056 444 E7
55600 ClbC 97053 444 G1
56000 ClbC 97053 414 H7
57800 ClbC 97051 414 J4
58100 ClbC 97051 415 A2
58300 STHN 97051 415 A2
60700 ClbC 97051 385 C6
61100 CBAC 97018 385 C4
61100 ClbC 97018 385 C4
62900 ClbC 97054 385 C6
US-30 N Columbia River Hwy
200 STHN 97051 385 B7
700 ClbC 97051 385 C6
US-30 S Columbia River Hwy
100 STHN 97051 415 B1

US-30 BYP N Ivanhoe St
8200 PTLD 97203 565 H3
US-30 BYP NE Killingsworth St
7200 PTLD 97218 567 E7
7600 PTLD 97220 567 F7
US-30 BYP N Lombard St
10 PTLD 97211 566 G5
1700 PTLD 97217 566 E5
3900 PTLD 97203 566 A4
6500 PTLD 97203 565 J4
US-30 BYP NE Lombard St
10 PTLD 97211 566 J5
10 PTLD 97217 566 G5
2200 PTLD 97211 567 C6
4000 PTLD 97218 567 B6
US-30 N Lwr Columbia River Hwy
100 STHN 97051 385 B7
US-30 S Lwr Columbia River Hwy
10 STHN 97051 415 B1
US-30 BYP N Philadelphia Av
7200 PTLD 97203 565 J3
US-30 BYP NE Portland Hwy
4200 PTLD 97211 567 C6
4200 PTLD 97218 567 C6
US-30 BYP NE Richmond Av
7300 PTLD 97203 565 H3
US-30 NW St. Helens Rd
2200 PTLD 97210 596 B3
4500 PTLD 97210 595 J1
4600 PTLD 97210 565 G5
7500 PTLD 97231 565 G5
11600 PTLD 97231 535 D7
12300 MthC 97231 535 A5
15000 MthC 97231 534 J3
17700 MthC 97231 504 F1
25200 MthC 97231 474 F7
27200 ClbC 97056 474 E5
US-30 BYP St. Johns Br
- PTLD 97203 565 G3
- PTLD 97210 565 F4
- PTLD 97231 565 F4
US-30 BUS NE Sandy Blvd
1200 PTLD 97214 596 H5
1200 PTLD 97232 596 H5
2700 PTLD 97232 597 C3
3900 PTLD 97212 597 B4
6800 PTLD 97213 597 G1
8100 PTLD 97218 597 G1
8100 PTLD 97220 597 G1
9100 MWDP 97220 597 G1
US-30 BYP NE Sandy Blvd
9900 PTLD 97220 597 H1
11300 PTLD 97220 598 C2
11900 PTLD 97230 598 A1
16500 GSHM 97230 598 F2
19700 GSHM 97024 598 J3
20100 FRVW 97024 598 J3
20400 FRVW 97024 599 A3
US-30 Stadium Frwy
- PTLD - 596 E3
US-30 NW Yeon Av
2500 PTLD 97210 596 C2
4400 PTLD 97210 595 J1

A

A Av
10 LKOW 97034 656 F6
NE A Av
- ClkC 98684 538 E6
W A Av
- ClkC 98629 386 G6
200 LCTR 98629 386 G7
A Ln
- PTLD 97218 567 E7
A Lp
- MrnC 97137 744 C7
- MrnC 97137 774 C1
4000 WHGL 98671 570 D6
S A Pl
600 WHGL 98671 569 J5
A St
- PTLD 97219 655 J3
- VCVR 98661 536 H3
- WasC 97224 655 A7
300 CBAC 97018 385 C2
1000 WDLD 98674 386 A1
1000 WHGL 98671 570 A6
1900 FTGV 97116 591 H5
E A St
5200 WLIN 97068 687 B6
NW A St
- WasC 97006 594 C5
S A St
10 WHGL 98671 569 H5
500 ORCY 97045 687 E6
SE A St
10000 MWKE 97222 657 A1
W A St
5200 WLIN 97068 687 B6
A & B Row
- FTGV 97116 592 C4
NE Aaron Dr
2500 MCMV 97128 771 B6
Aaron Wy
100 NWBG 97132 713 B6
SW Abagail Ct
2500 PTLD 97219 656 C2
NE Abbey Rd
5400 LFYT 97127 741 G6
5400 YmhC 97114 741 G6
5400 YmhC 97128 741 G6
6000 YmhC 97111 741 G5
10800 YmhC 97111 711 J7
NW Abbey Rd
9900 PTLD 97229 595 E3
SW Abbott Ct
2600 TDLE 97060 599 F6
SW Abbott Ln
15800 WasC 97007 624 H4
SE Abbott Miller Rd
29300 CmsC 97022 719 J4
NW Abby Ct
13000 WasC 97229 595 B3
SE Abby Ln
11300 CmsC 97015 657 J6
Abelard St
10 LKOW 97035 656 A4
SW Abelia Pl
7900 BRTN 97008 625 B6

SW Abercrombie Pl
1900 BRTN 97225 595 C7
1900 WasC 97225 595 C7
NW Aberdeen Dr
15000 WasC 97229 594 J2
SW Abernathy Ct
5700 MthC 97221 625 J2
E Abernathy Ln
28100 CmsC 97067 724 D7
Abernathy Rd
500 ORCY 97045 687 D7
SW Abernathy St
500 PTLD 97239 626 F2
Abernethy Ct
5400 GLDS 97027 687 C4
Abernethy Ln
18900 CmsC 97267 687 C3
18900 GLDS 97027 687 C3
18900 GLDS 97267 687 C3
SE Abernethy Ln
18300 CmsC 97267 687 C3
18800 GLDS 97027 687 C3
18800 GLDS 97267 687 C3
NW Abernethy Rd
1300 PTLD 97229 595 F4
SW Abernethy St
- PTLD 97239 626 D2
Abigail Ct
13300 CmsC 97045 717 D5
13300 ORCY 97045 717 D5
SW Abigail Ct
- PTLD 97219 656 C2
N Abrams Park Rd
400 RDGF 98642 416 A6
SE Acacia Dr
100 GSHM 97080 629 G3
SE Acacia Ln
600 GSHM 97080 629 G3
SE Acacia Pl
1000 GSHM 97080 629 G4
S Access Rd
1700 VCVR 98661 536 J7
Achilles Ln
- ClbC 97053 414 H4
SE Achilles Ln
20100 DAMA 97009 658 J3
Achilles Rd
34700 ClbC 97053 414 J4
Achillies
- ClbC 97053 414 J4
SE Acorn Ct
6100 CmsC 97267 657 D6
SW Acorn Ct
1800 MCMV 97128 770 E6
NW Acorn Dr
19900 ClkC 98642 446 F7
NW Acorn Pl
15200 WasC 97006 594 H2
Acorn St
200 NWBG 97132 713 F7
SW Acorn St
- WNVL 97070 745 C1
SE Ada Ln
2300 CmsC 97267 656 J7
4600 MWKE 97222 657 C2
NW Adagio Wy
2800 HBRO 97124 594 C2
N Adair Ct
3000 CNLS 97113 592 G5
SE Adair Pl
15400 CmsC 97015 658 D6
N Adair St
100 FTGV 97116 592 D4
1200 CNLS 97113 592 F5
N Adair St SR-8
100 CNLS 97113 592 D5
100 FTGV 97116 592 D4
SW Adam Ct
33300 SPSE 97056 474 D2
Adam Ln
20700 FRVW 97024 599 A3
NW Adams Av
100 HBRO 97123 593 B4
100 HBRO 97124 593 B4
SW Adams Av
- SRWD 97140 684 H6
100 HBRO 97124 593 B4
700 HBRO 97123 593 B6
Adams Ct
10 LKOW 97035 656 B5
S Adams Rd
33000 CmsC 97038 837 G5
Adams St
100 LFYT 97127 771 G1
100 VCVR 98661 537 C6
1100 LFYT 97127 741 G7
NE Adams St
1900 CMAS 98607 569 E3
1900 MCMV 97128 770 H3
NE Adams St SR-99W
100 MCMV 97128 770 H5
NW Adams St
1500 MCMV 97128 770 H4
8300 PTLD 97229 595 F4
SE Adams St
100 CMAS 98607 569 E5
2000 MWKE 97222 656 J3
3700 MWKE 97222 657 B3
9000 CmsC 97015 657 G7
SW Adams St
100 MCMV 97128 770 H5
SW Adams St SR-99W
100 MCMV 97128 770 H5
W Adams St
100 CLTN 97111 741 A1
Adams Cemetery Rd
33000 CmsC 97038 837 G4
S Adams Cemetery Rd
32100 CmsC 97038 837 G4
S Adams Vista Ct
20500 CmsC 97045 748 C1
Adaptive Storage Ct
34700 ClbC 97053 414 H7
Addie St
18900 CmsC 97027 687 C3
18900 CmsC 97267 687 C3
18900 GLDS 97027 687 C3
18900 GLDS 97267 687 C3
SE Addie St
17700 CmsC 97267 687 C3
18600 CmsC 97027 687 C3
18600 GLDS 97027 687 C3
18600 GLDS 97267 687 C3
NE Addison Ct
800 HBRO 97124 593 D1

Portland Street Index

STREET Block City ZIP Map# Grid

Addy Cir
3800 WHGL 98671 570 D6
Addy Ct
4100 WHGL 98671 570 D6
Addy Lp
4000 WHGL 98671 570 D6
Addy St
2700 WHGL 98671 570 D6
E Adel Av
23300 CmsC 97011 724 A2
SW Adele Dr
10600 WasC 97225 595 D6
10600 WasC 97229 595 D6
11000 BRTN 97225 595 D6
SW Aden Av
27100 WNVL 97070 715 F5
SW Adina Ct
12200 WasC 97224 685 B1
S Adkins Cir
12100 CmsC 97013 777 B4
12100 CmsC 97042 777 B4
NW Adlington Ln
20700 HBRO 97006 594 C3
SW Admiral Ct
4200 PTLD 97221 626 A3
SW Admiral St
- PTLD 97239 626 C3
4700 PTLD 97221 626 A3
NE Adolf Rd
9600 YmhC 97132 743 F2
SE Adoline Av
11400 CmsC 97236 658 A3
11400 HPYV 97236 658 A3
Adrian Ct
12600 CmsC 97034 656 C4
12600 LKOW 97034 656 C4
12600 PTLD 97034 656 C4
NW Adrian St
18500 WasC 97229 594 E1
Adrian Wy
- ORCY 97045 717 D4
N Adriatic Av
9100 PTLD 97203 566 B3
SW Advance Rd
1600 CmsC 97068 716 C6
1600 CmsC 97070 716 C6
3700 CmsC 97070 715 H5
6000 WNVL 97070 715 H5
NW Adwick Dr
- HBRO 97006 594 C4
SW Aebischer Rd
21200 WasC 97140 684 A6
SW Aerie Dr
13500 TGRD 97223 655 B5
SE Aerie Crescent Rd
11500 HPYV 97236 657 H3
NW Aerts Rd
12100 WasC 97106 532 B6
Affolter Av
700 MOLA 97038 807 F7
700 MOLA 97038 837 E1
SW Afton Ln
7500 DRHM 97224 685 G1
SW Agate Ct
14500 BRTN 97007 624 J7
SW Agate Ln
4100 PTLD 97239 626 D3
SW Agee St
100 MCMV 97128 770 F5
Agnes Av
15900 ORCY 97045 687 D5
SE Agnes St
37700 CmsC 97055 690 H1
37700 SNDY 97055 690 H1
NE Ahola Homestead Dr
15200 ClkC 98606 479 B5
NE Ainsworth Cir
11500 PTLD 97220 568 A7
12100 PTLD 97230 568 A7
NE Ainsworth Ct
4100 PTLD 97211 567 B6
5000 PTLD 97218 567 C6
NE Ainsworth Pl
- PTLD 97218 567 C6
Ainsworth St
300 ORCY 97045 717 E2
N Ainsworth St
10 PTLD 97211 566 G6
10 PTLD 97217 566 F6
NE Ainsworth St
10 PTLD 97211 566 H6
10 PTLD 97217 566 G6
4100 PTLD 97218 567 B7
4200 PTLD 97211 567 C6
NE Air Cargo Rd
- PTLD 97220 567 G5
7700 PTLD 97218 567 F4
Airpark Wy
- YmhC 97132 743 E1
NE Airpark Wy
300 YmhC 97132 743 E1
NE Airport Dr
13800 VCVR 98684 538 B6
Airport Rd
- CmsC 97236 658 E2
- HPYV 97236 658 D2
Airport Rd NE
21000 AURA 97002 775 E1
21000 MrnC 97002 775 E1
22800 MrnC 97002 745 E7
NE Airport Rd
- WNVL 97070 745 E5
4400 HBRO 97124 593 H2
23700 CmsC 97002 745 E5
53600 ClbC 97056 444 G5
53600 SPSE 97056 444 G5
NW Airport Rd
- HBRO 97124 593 G2
S Airport Rd
26500 CmsC 97042 777 D5
SE Airport Rd
9800 MCMV 97128 771 E7
9800 YmhC 97114 771 E7
9800 YmhC 97128 771 E7
Airport Wy NE
- MrnC 97002 775 E1
NE Airport Wy
7300 PTLD 97218 567 E4
8200 PTLD 97220 567 J6
11300 PTLD 97220 568 A7
12500 PTLD 97230 568 C7
15300 PTLD 97230 598 E2
17200 GSHM 97230 598 G2
NE Airport Perimeter Rd
- PTLD 97211 567 B2
- PTLD 97218 567 C2
- PTLD 97220 567 H4
NE Airtrans Wy
8200 PTLD 97218 567 D4
Akron Av
600 VCVR 98664 537 E5
Alabama Dr
7300 VCVR 98664 537 E6
SW Alabama St
- TLTN 97062 685 D7
SW Alabaster St
15300 BRTN 97007 624 H7
NE Alameda Dr
2000 PTLD 97211 596 J1
2000 PTLD 97212 596 J1
SW Alameda Ln
7700 BRTN 97007 624 J6
NE Alameda St
1800 PTLD 97212 596 J1
2800 PTLD 97212 597 A2
7200 PTLD 97213 597 E3
NE Alameda Ter
3000 PTLD 97212 597 A2
SW Alan Blumlein Dr
- WasC 97005 624 J1
SE Alansa Dr
9300 CmsC 97015 657 G7
N Alaska Pl
3500 PTLD 97217 566 C3
N Alaska St
3600 PTLD 97217 566 C3
3800 PTLD 97203 566 C3
NW Albemarle Ter
300 PTLD 97210 596 C5
Albers Wy NE
14700 AURA 97002 775 F3
Alber Spring Ct
3100 LKOW 97034 686 B1
Albert Av
- CmsC 97009 690 C5
- CmsC 97022 690 C5
NW Albert Av
- PTLD 97210 596 A3
Albert Cir
4200 LKOW 97035 686 A2
SW Albert Ct
17500 WasC 97007 624 F7
NW Albert Dr
- PTLD 97210 596 A2
NE Albert Wy
17000 YmhC 97132 713 F2
NE Alberta Ct
3300 PTLD 97211 597 B1
4700 PTLD 97218 597 C1
S Alberta Rd
19400 CmsC 97004 748 H6
N Alberta St
10 PTLD 97211 566 G7
1500 PTLD 97217 566 E7
NE Alberta St
10 PTLD 97211 566 J7
10 PTLD 97217 566 G7
2600 PTLD 97211 567 A7
4200 PTLD 97211 597 B1
4200 PTLD 97218 597 D1
5600 PTLD 97218 567 D7
8700 PTLD 97220 597 G1
SE Alberta St
6200 CmsC 97206 627 D7
6200 MWKE 97206 627 D7
SW Alberta St
12100 TGRD 97223 655 B4
SE Albertine St
900 HBRO 97123 593 C7
N Albina Av
2600 PTLD 97227 596 F3
4500 PTLD 97217 596 F1
8300 PTLD 97217 566 F4
NW Albion Ct
1800 WasC 97006 594 J3
NE Albus Ct
3000 FRVW 97024 599 B3
SE Alchar Dr
12400 CmsC 97222 657 A4
E Alcorn St
20100 CmsC 97011 693 G6
SW Alcott Av
1200 WasC 97225 595 C7
SW Alden Ct
6900 WasC 97223 625 G7
Alden St
- CmsC 97045 717 D2
17800 ORCY 97045 717 D3
SW Alden St
6500 PTLD 97219 625 H7
6500 PTLD 97223 625 H7
8100 WasC 97223 625 F7
S Alder Av
- YCLT 98675 419 G1
Alder Cir
16700 LKOW 97034 686 B1
SW Alder Cir
800 TDLE 97060 599 F4
Alder Ct
5500 WLIN 97068 687 B7
SE Alder Ct
500 HBRO 97123 593 C6
3000 PTLD 97214 597 A6
15300 PTLD 97233 598 D6
20400 GSHM 97030 598 J7
21300 GSHM 97030 599 A7
W Alder Ct
600 WHGL 98671 569 H3
SE Alder Dr
21700 GSHM 97030 599 B7
Alder Ln
- WasC 97006 594 D5
2300 NWBG 97132 713 E6
E Alder Ln
21300 CmsC 97049 693 H7
SE Alder Pl
5700 PTLD 97215 597 D6
6200 CmsC 97222 657 D1
Alder Rd
- PTLD 97217 536 E6
SW Alder Rd
2200 CmsC 97068 686 C4
Alder St
- DNDE 97115 742 H2
- YmhC 97114 772 B4
- YmhC 97115 742 H2
10 DAYT 97114 772 B4
4600 WLIN 97068 687 B7
35100 ClbC 97051 414 J2
NE Alder St
5800 HBRO 97124 593 J4
6200 HBRO 97124 594 A4
NW Alder St
100 DNDE 97115 742 H2
100 YmhC 97115 742 H2
2000 MCMV 97128 770 H3
22700 HBRO 97124 594 A4
22700 WasC 97124 594 A4
SE Alder St
10 PTLD 97214 596 H6
1100 HBRO 97123 593 D6
3200 PTLD 97214 597 B6
4100 PTLD 97215 597 B6
10900 PTLD 97216 597 J6
11500 PTLD 97216 598 A6
14200 PTLD 97233 598 C6
17600 GSHM 97233 598 G7
21300 GSHM 97030 599 B7
SW Alder St
- PTLD 97209 596 D5
100 DNDE 97115 742 H3
100 PTLD 97204 596 F6
500 PTLD 97205 596 F6
1300 YmhC 97115 742 H4
7600 TGRD 97224 655 F7
W Alder St
- WHGL 98671 569 G3
Alder Wy
- ClbC 97056 474 A3
SW Alderbrook Cir
15300 TGRD 97224 655 E7
SW Alderbrook Ct
15200 TGRD 97224 655 G4
SW Alderbrook Dr
15200 TGRD 97224 655 E7
SW Alderbrook Pl
15200 TGRD 97224 655 G4
S Alder Creek Ln
8800 CmsC 97013 776 D2
13800 CmsC 97042 777 E4
SE Alder Creek Rd
20000 CmsC 97055 692 H7
52800 CmsC 97055 693 A7
NE Aldercrest Cir
23900 WDVL 97060 599 D5
Alder Crest Ct
- YmhC 97115 742 G2
SE Aldercrest Ct
6300 CmsC 97267 657 D7
SW Aldercrest Ct
6700 WNVL 97070 715 G6
SE Aldercrest Ln
5500 CmsC 97222 657 C5
SE Aldercrest Rd
3200 CmsC 97222 657 B5
5900 CmsC 97267 657 C6
Aldercrest St
700 NWBG 97132 713 C6
NE Alder Falls Rd
22500 ClkC 98604 449 E5
SW Aldergrove Av
23500 SRWD 97140 714 H1
NW Alder Grove Ln
10200 PTLD 97229 595 D3
SE Alder Heights Dr
54000 CmsC 97055 692 G6
SE Alder Heights Rd
53700 CmsC 97055 692 F6
SE Alderhill Lp
6000 CmsC 97267 657 D6
SE Alderhurst Dr
- CmsC 97222 657 D1
- MWKE 97206 657 D1
- MWKE 97222 657 D1
SW Alderidge Dr
200 WasC 97225 595 F6
SE Alder Meadows Dr
16100 DAMA 97009 688 E1
Aldersgate Dr
3200 NWBG 97132 713 D4
Aldersgate Ln
1500 NWBG 97132 713 D6
SE Alder Spring Ct
20000 DAMA 97009 658 J6
NW Alderview Dr
12400 MthC 97231 535 C6
SE Alderway Av
5100 CmsC 97267 657 C7
5100 CmsC 97267 687 D1
Alderwood Ct
59300 STHN 97051 415 B1
SW Alderwood Ct
19500 WasC 97006 594 D6
Alderwood Dr
35500 STHN 97051 415 A1
NE Alderwood Dr
- PTLD 97218 567 F6
SW Alderwood Dr
400 CmsC 97068 716 E1
18500 WasC 97006 594 E6
Alderwood Pl
300 ORCY 97045 717 B3
NE Alderwood Rd
6000 PTLD 97218 567 F6
7000 PTLD 97220 567 G6
SE Aldred Ln
28300 CmsC 97009 659 H1
Aldrich Ct
10 ORCY 97045 687 F6
SW Aldrich Ct
7600 WasC 97007 624 G6
SE Aldridge Rd
13700 CmsC 97236 658 C4
14200 HPYV 97236 658 C4
SW Aldridge Ter
21600 SRWD 97140 684 E6
SE Alethea Wy
400 MCMV 97128 770 H7
Alex Av
200 MOLA 97038 837 E1
NE Alex Wy
1300 HBRO 97124 593 E2
SE Alexander Av
11000 HPYV 97236 658 B3
SE Alexander Dr
10700 HPYV 97236 658 B3
SW Alexander Ln
21700 SRWD 97140 684 F6
SE Alexander St
3300 HBRO 97123 623 G1
5100 WasC 97123 623 H1
6100 HBRO 97123 623 J1
6200 HBRO 97007 624 A1
6200 WasC 97007 624 A1
SW Alexander St
- BRTN 97006 624 G2
20900 WasC 97006 624 B1
24500 HBRO 97123 623 H1
24500 WasC 97123 623 H1
NW Alexandra Av
2600 PTLD 97210 596 A3
Alexandra Dr
1000 NWBG 97132 713 D3
NW Alexandra Dr
- PTLD 97210 595 J2
- PTLD 97210 596 A2
Alexandra Ln
58900 STHN 97051 414 J2
NW Alexandra Ln
- ClkC 98607 538 J4
- CMAS 98607 538 J4
- CMAS 98607 539 A4
Alexandria Dr
- YmhC 97132 713 C4
700 NWBG 97132 713 C4
Alexandria St
- MCMV 97128 770 E7
- YmhC 97128 770 E6
NE Alexandria St
1100 HBRO 97124 593 D1
SW Alexandria St
1400 MCMV 97128 770 F7
Alexis Ct
19500 ORCY 97045 717 D5
NE Alexis Ct
600 HBRO 97124 593 C2
NW Alfalfa Dr
5900 WasC 97229 564 H6
SW Alfred Ct
5500 PTLD 97219 655 J1
SW Alfred St
3800 PTLD 97219 656 A1
5700 PTLD 97219 655 J1
6200 TGRD 97223 655 H1
SW Alger Av
5100 BRTN 97005 625 C4
5900 BRTN 97008 625 C4
S Algernon St
17400 CmsC 97045 718 C3
Algona Dr
2300 VCVR 98661 537 B4
SW Algonkin St
7000 TLTN 97062 685 G5
SW Alibhai St
13900 WasC 97005 595 A7
Alice Av
- CmsC 97009 690 C5
- CmsC 97022 690 B5
SE Alice Ct
8500 CmsC 97015 657 F5
SW Alice Ct
6600 BRTN 97008 625 C5
SW Alice Ln
6000 BRTN 97005 625 C4
6000 BRTN 97008 625 C5
SW Alice St
3300 PTLD 97219 626 B7
N Alice Wy
2000 NWBG 97132 713 D5
2200 YmhC 97132 713 D5
Alice Kelly Ct
- MCMV 97128 770 G2
NW Alice Kelly St
2300 MCMV 97128 770 G3
2300 YmhC 97128 770 G3
SE Alicia Cir
18800 VCVR 98683 568 G1
Alicia Ct
800 WLIN 97068 716 F1
SW Alicia Pl
3200 WasC 97006 624 E2
SE Alii Ct
5000 CmsC 97267 657 C6
SE Alika Av
1000 HBRO 97123 593 D7
SE Alimaria Dr
13800 CmsC 97015 658 C5
SE Alison Ct
14600 CmsC 97015 658 A6
Alki Rd
100 ClkC 98663 506 G7
3200 VCVR 98663 506 G7
SE Allan Rd
4600 CmsC 97267 657 C7
N Allegheny Av
8500 PTLD 97203 565 J2
Allegheny Dr
18600 ORCY 97045 717 B4
SW Allen Blvd
9200 BRTN 97223 625 E5
9200 WasC 97223 625 E5
9500 BRTN 97005 625 A4
9500 BRTN 97008 625 A4
14100 BRTN 97005 624 J4
14100 BRTN 97008 624 J4
14300 BRTN 97007 624 J5
SW Allen Blvd S
- BRTN 97008 625 C5
Allen Ct
11100 CmsC 97045 716 J4
NW Allen Ct
600 MCMV 97128 770 E4
S Allen Ln
20700 CmsC 97045 719 A4
Allen Rd
16800 LKOW 97035 686 B1
SE Allen Rd
28600 CmsC 97022 719 G7
NW Allenbach Pl
4700 WasC 97229 564 G5
4700 WasC 97229 594 F1
NW Allen Canyon Rd
31000 ClkC 98642 416 C2
N Allen Creek Dr
- RDGF 98642 416 D6
Allendale Ct
200 STHN 97051 385 A7
Allendale Dr
100 STHN 97051 385 A7
Alli Ct
100 GLDS 97027 687 D4
NW Allie Av
2000 HBRO 97124 594 D3
Allinson Rd NE
19300 MrnC 97032 774 H7
Allison Ct
200 FTGV 97116 591 F3
SW Allison Ln
24600 WasC 97140 683 G7
Allison Pl
- CmsC 97035 655 H7
- LKOW 97035 655 H7
NE Allworth Rd
18300 ClkC 98604 448 H3
19700 ClkC 98604 449 C3
NW Ally Elizabeth Ct
12600 WasC 97229 565 B7
N Alma Av
9400 PTLD 97203 565 J3
SE Alma Ln
11700 CmsC 97055 660 G4
SE Almond Ct
12700 CmsC 97015 658 B6
SW Almond Ct
20300 WasC 97006 624 C1
W Almond Ct
1700 MCMV 97128 770 E5
SE Almond Ln
12900 CmsC 97015 658 A6
SW Almond St
19800 WasC 97006 624 C1
N Almont St
- PTLD 97203 565 J2
SW Almonte Ct
15100 BRTN 97007 624 H5
18300 WasC 97007 624 E5
NW Aloclek Dr
2500 HBRO 97124 594 C2
NW Aloclek Pl
3600 HBRO 97124 594 C1
SW Aloha Ct
18700 WasC 97006 624 E1
SW Aloha St
18000 WasC 97006 624 E1
SW Aloma Wy
7400 PTLD 97223 625 G6
7400 WasC 97223 625 G6
SE Alpenglade Ct
15800 CmsC 97267 657 E7
15800 CmsC 97267 687 E1
NW Alpenglow Wy
10100 WasC 97229 595 D5
NE Alpha Dr
1200 MCMV 97128 771 A4
3300 GSHM 97030 599 F7
SE Alpha Wy
13500 CmsC 97009 659 H6
NW Alphorn Ln
10100 WasC 97124 564 B2
Alpine Av
34500 STHN 97051 414 H1
NE Alpine Av
700 MCMV 97128 770 J5
E Alpine Ct N
69800 CmsC 97049 724 D3
Alpine Dr
2000 WLIN 97068 686 G7
S Alpine Dr
200 CNLS 97113 592 D5
SW Alpine Dr
7200 BRTN 97008 625 B6
NW Alpine Ln
2800 CMAS 98607 569 B5
Alpine St
100 DNDE 97115 742 J2
100 YmhC 97115 742 J2
NE Alpine St
9200 VCVR 98664 537 G5
S Alpine St
400 CNLS 97113 592 D5
2800 WasC 97123 592 G5
NW Alpine Ter
500 PTLD 97210 596 A3
SW Alpine Ter
9100 WasC 97225 625 F1
SW Alpine Vw
13500 TGRD 97224 655 A6
13800 TGRD 97224 654 J6
Alpine Wy
17300 LKOW 97034 686 B1
50500 ClbC 97056 474 E5
E Alpine Wy
65200 CmsC 97049 693 J7
65400 CmsC 97049 723 J1
SW Alpine View Ct
13800 TGRD 97224 654 J6
NW Alsace Ln
12500 WasC 97229 595 B1
SW Alsea Ct
21400 TLTN 97062 685 E6
SW Alsea Dr
9400 TLTN 97062 685 D6
Alt Av
17300 SNDY 97055 691 A3
SE Alt Av
17100 SNDY 97055 691 A2
E Alt Rd
60200 CmsC 97055 693 D5
N Alta Av
6700 PTLD 97203 565 G3
NW Alta Ln
14400 WasC 97229 594 J2
SW Altadena Av
3900 PTLD 97239 626 C2
SW Altadena Ter
3100 PTLD 97239 626 B2
SW Altadina Ct
2100 PTLD 97219 656 C1
SW Alta Mira Cir
5400 PTLD 97239 626 D4
SE Alta Verde Dr
7800 PTLD 97266 627 J7
SE Alta Vista Dr
13600 HPYV 97236 658 C3
14600 CmsC 97236 658 C3
SW Alta Vista Pl
2600 PTLD 97201 596 C6
SE Althaus Cir
4200 TDLE 97060 629 H1
SE Althaus Dr
900 TDLE 97060 629 H1
1200 MthC 97060 599 H7
1200 TDLE 97060 599 H7
NW Altishin Pl
600 BRTN 97006 594 H5
SE Altman Rd
5400 MthC 97060 630 D5
5400 MthC 97080 630 C7
8200 CmsC 97080 660 C1
9000 CmsC 97009 660 C2
NE Alton Ct
3600 FRVW 97024 599 B2
14100 PTLD 97230 598 D2
NE Alton St
5700 PTLD 97213 597 D2
9900 MWDP 97220 597 H2
9900 PTLD 97220 597 H2
15400 PTLD 97230 598 E1
21800 FRVW 97024 599 B2
SW Alton St
18200 WasC 97006 624 E2
Alto Park Rd
12600 CmsC 97034 656 C4
12600 LKOW 97034 656 C4
12600 PTLD 97034 656 C4
Alvaro Ln
19300 ORCY 97045 717 E5
NE Alvas Rd
23300 ClkC 98604 449 E4
SW Alvord Ln
16500 WasC 97007 654 G3
Alvord Rd
- VCVR 98661 536 G5
SW Alyssa Ln
8500 WasC 97225 625 F1
Alyssa Ter
6200 CmsC 97035 655 H6
6200 LKOW 97035 655 H6
Alyssum Av
1100 FTGV 97116 591 G3
Amanda Ct
100 ORCY 97045 717 A3
SW Amanda Ct
10300 TGRD 97224 655 D6
NE Amanda Pl
500 HBRO 97124 593 C2
NE Ambassador Pl
7500 PTLD 97220 567 G5
NE Amber Av
2500 HBRO 97124 593 B2
Amber Ln
17100 SNDY 97055 690 G2
SW Amber Ln
6600 BRTN 97225 625 H4
6600 WasC 97225 625 H4
Amber Pl
13000 CmsC 97034 656 D4
13000 LKOW 97034 656 D4
NW Amberbrook Dr
2100 HBRO 97006 594 D3
2100 HBRO 97124 594 D3
NW Amberglen Ct
1500 HBRO 97006 594 D3
NW Amberglen Pkwy
1100 HBRO 97006 594 D4
1500 HBRO 97124 594 D4
SE Amberlyn Ct
14300 CmsC 97015 658 A6
NW Amberview Ln
20700 HBRO 97006 594 C4
Amberwood Cir
13800 LKOW 97035 655 J5
Amberwood Ct
5200 LKOW 97035 655 J5
NW Amberwood Dr
19400 HBRO 97006 594 C3
19400 HBRO 97124 594 C3
SW Ambiance Ct
11300 TGRD 97223 655 C5
SE Ambler Rd
- CmsC 97015 657 F5
- CmsC 97222 657 F5
SE Ambleside Dr
2400 GSHM 97080 629 D5
Amboy Av
100 YCLT 98675 419 F1
N Amboy Av
200 YCLT 98675 419 F1
E Ambrose St
20100 CmsC 97011 693 G6
SE Amelia Ct
14300 CmsC 97267 657 A6
SW Ames Ln
12100 TGRD 97224 655 B5
Ames St
14300 ORCY 97045 687 F5
SW Ames Wy
5400 BRTN 97225 625 H4
5400 WasC 97225 625 H4
NW Amethyst Ct
12500 WasC 97229 595 B2
Amherst Ct
4700 LKOW 97035 656 A5
Amherst St
39100 SNDY 97055 691 A5
N Amherst St
5700 PTLD 97203 566 A4
6900 PTLD 97203 565 J4
SE Amherst St
9800 CmsC 97015 657 H7
SW Amicus Ter
8600 WasC 97007 624 E7
NW Amidon Rd
6000 ClkC 98674 386 B1
SE Amisigger Rd
14900 CmsC 97009 659 G7
14900 CmsC 97009 689 F3
18500 CmsC 97022 689 F4
SE Amistad Ln
28800 CmsC 97022 689 H7
28800 CmsC 97022 719 H1
Amity Ln
32800 ClbC 97051 414 D1
NW Amity Ln
2700 WasC 97229 594 F3
SE Amity Dayton Hwy
800 DAYT 97114 772 A5
800 YmhC 97114 772 A5
1000 DAYT 97114 771 J5
1000 YmhC 97114 771 J5
SE Amity-Dayton Hwy
10600 YmhC 97114 771 G7
SE Amity-Dayton Hwy SR-233
10600 YmhC 97114 771 G7
NE Ammeter Rd
34200 ClkC 98671 540 E4
Ammon Wy
3200 FTGV 97116 591 E2
Amonson Ct
1600 GLDS 97027 687 D3
Amro Av
200 YCLT 98675 419 F1
SW Amu St
11200 TLTN 97062 685 C5
SW Amy Ln
16500 WasC 97007 624 G7
NW Anastasia Dr
17400 WasC 97006 594 F1
17400 WasC 97229 594 F1
N Anchor St
- PTLD 97217 596 C1
3400 PTLD 97217 566 C7
Anchor Wy
17000 CmsC 97045 687 E7
17000 ORCY 97045 687 E7
N Anchor Wy
900 PTLD 97217 566 F1
SE Ancona Ct
5500 CmsC 97267 657 C6
NW Andalusian Wy
15300 WasC 97229 564 H7
Anderache Mdws
- PTLD 97236 628 F3
SE Anderegg Dr
4100 PTLD 97236 628 E3
SE Anderegg Lp
4200 PTLD 97236 628 E4
SE Anderegg Pkwy
15500 DAMA 97009 658 E7
15500 DAMA 97015 658 F7
15500 HPYV 97015 658 F7
15600 DAMA 97009 688 F1
NW Anderson Av
6800 ClkC 98665 506 F6
SE Anderson Av
1900 GSHM 97080 629 F5
SW Anderson Ct
10200 TLTN 97062 685 D2
Anderson Ln
13400 CmsC 97045 717 E5
13400 ORCY 97045 717 D5
NE Anderson Ln
23700 YmhC 97132 713 A4
SE Anderson Ln
100 GSHM 97080 629 G3
Anderson Rd
60000 ClbC 97051 384 C6
NE Anderson Rd
500 GSHM 97030 629 F2
700 ClkC 98665 506 H6
S Anderson Rd
5600 BRLO 97002 775 H1
5600 BRLO 97013 775 H1
5600 CmsC 97002 775 J1
17600 CmsC 97045 718 A2
SE Anderson Rd
- MthC 97080 629 G6
2800 GSHM 97080 629 G6
14500 DAMA 97009 658 J7
SW Anderson Rd
3100 WasC 97116 591 H7
Anderson St
700 VCVR 98661 536 G5
NW Anderson St
11200 WasC 97229 595 C4
SW Anderson St
19100 WasC 97007 624 D3
SE Andorra Av
12400 HPYV 97236 658 E4
SE Andover Pl
500 PTLD 97202 626 H7
NE Andover St
7500 HBRO 97124 594 D4
NE Andra Pl
15400 PTLD 97230 598 E2
Andrea St
13200 CmsC 97045 717 D5
13200 ORCY 97045 717 D5
Andrea Lynn Ter
14400 ORCY 97045 717 G6
N Andresen Rd
100 VCVR 98661 537 D5
100 VCVR 98664 537 D5
NE Andresen Rd
1700 VCVR 98661 537 E4
1700 VCVR 98664 537 E4
1800 VCVR 98662 537 E4
4100 ClkC 98661 537 D1
5100 ClkC 98661 507 D7
6300 ClkC 98665 507 D7
8500 ClkC 98662 507 D7
NW Andresen Rd
3600 WasC 97116 591 C1
S Andresen Rd
100 VCVR 98661 537 D7
100 VCVR 98664 537 D7
NE Andresen Market Pl
- ClkC 98661 507 D7
NW Andrew Pl
1600 WasC 97229 595 D4
Andrew St
500 NWBG 97132 743 C2
SW Andrew Ter
- TGRD 97223 655 E5
Andrews Rd
1200 LKOW 97034 656 E5
Andrews St
37000 SNDY 97055 660 H7
SE Andrews St
37700 CmsC 97055 660 J7
37700 SNDY 97055 660 J7
NW Andria Av
17900 WasC 97229 594 F2
Anduin Ter
18100 LKOW 97034 686 C2
SE Andy St
28200 CmsC 97009 659 H4
SE Andys Ct
15600 CmsC 97267 657 E7
SW Angel Av
4500 BRTN 97005 625 B3
SE Angel Ln
5800 CmsC 97267 687 C3
5800 GLDS 97027 687 C3
NW Angela Ln
300 HBRO 97124 593 A2
NW Angela St
200 HBRO 97124 593 B2
Angela Wy
35200 ClbC 97051 414 J4
35200 ClbC 97053 414 J4
SE Angela Wy
3800 MWKE 97222 657 B4
NW Angeline Av
1500 GSHM 97030 629 E1
SW Angeline Av
300 GSHM 97080 629 A3
NW Angeline Ct
1600 GSHM 97030 629 E1
SW Angeline Ct
2700 GSHM 97080 629 A5

Portland Street Index

STREET
Block City ZIP Map# Grid

SE Angella Ct
900 MCMV 97128 770 H7
NE Angelo Dr
11400 VCVR 98684 537 J3
SW Angie Ln
20200 WasC 97006 594 C6
SW Angora Ln
13200 BRTN 97008 655 A2
SW Angus Ct
- TGRD 97224 655 A6
- WasC 97224 655 A6
SW Angus Pl
- TGRD 97224 655 A6
- WasC 97224 655 A6
SE Angus St
12500 VCVR 98683 568 A2
Angus Wy
6800 GLDS 97027 687 D3
Anita Pl
12500 CmsC 97045 717 C5
12500 ORCY 97045 717 C5
SE Ankeny Cir
100 PTLD 97233 598 E6
SE Ankeny Ct
13200 PTLD 97233 598 B6
19000 GSHM 97230 598 H6
19000 GSHM 97233 598 H6
SE Ankeny St
100 PTLD 97214 596 H5
4100 PTLD 97214 597 B6
4100 PTLD 97215 597 B6
9000 PTLD 97216 597 G6
11700 PTLD 97216 598 A6
13000 PTLD 97233 598 B6
16500 GSHM 97233 598 F6
21400 GSHM 97030 599 B6
SW Ankeny St
10 PTLD 97204 596 F5
700 PTLD 97205 596 F5
SE Ankeny Ter
21500 GSHM 97030 599 B6
Ann Ct
1300 WLIN 97068 716 G1
1800 NWBG 97132 713 D6
SW Ann Ct
12200 TGRD 97223 655 B4
Ann Dr
14300 ORCY 97045 687 F6
SW Ann Pl
12100 TGRD 97223 655 B4
SW Ann St
11500 TGRD 97223 655 C4
NE Anna Av
2500 HBRO 97124 593 B2
SE Anna Ct
12000 DAMA 97009 659 D4
SW Anna Ct
- BRTN 97007 655 A3
- TGRD 97223 655 A3
20500 WasC 97006 594 C5
NE Anna Dr
11400 YmhC 97132 713 J7
11400 YmhC 97132 743 J1
SW Annadel St
20400 WasC 97007 624 C4
SE Anna Eve Dr
16500 CmsC 97267 687 C1
S Anna Mae Ln
18100 CmsC 97045 718 E3
SW Anna Mae Ln
18400 WasC 97006 624 E1
SE Anna Marie Ct
14500 CmsC 97267 657 D5
SW Anne Av
7000 BRTN 97008 625 C6
S Anne St
100 MCMV 97128 770 J5
NW Annette Ct
10600 WasC 97229 595 D3
S Annette Dr
16600 CmsC 97045 718 B6
SW Annie Ln
16500 WasC 97007 624 G3
NW Ansonia Pl
10 PTLD 97210 596 A4
SE Anspach St
1300 CmsC 97267 656 H7
SE Antea Wy
12200 HPYV 97236 658 D4
SE Antelope Hills Dr
4500 GSHM 97080 629 B7
SE Antelope Hills Pl
4400 GSHM 97080 629 B7
NW Anthony Ct
2300 MCMV 97128 770 D5
SW Anthony Ct
20900 WasC 97006 594 C7
SW Anthony Dr
1600 WasC 97006 594 C7
2300 WasC 97006 624 C1
SE Anthony St
1400 HBRO 97123 623 D1
SE Antigua Av
7100 CmsC 97267 657 E7
SW Antioch Downs Ct
22100 CmsC 97062 685 J7
Antler Av
- CmsC 97055 691 B4
- SNDY 97055 691 B4
NW Antler Dr
2300 FTGV 97116 591 F2
2300 WasC 97116 591 F2
SE Anton Ct
9100 CmsC 97236 657 H1
SW Anton Dr
11900 TGRD 97223 655 B2
Antonia Wy
3200 NWBG 97132 713 B4
NW Anzalone Dr
20200 HBRO 97006 594 D5
20200 WasC 97006 594 D5
SW Apache Cir
8500 WNVL 97070 715 E5
SE Apache Ct
8500 WNVL 97070 715 E6
Apache Dr
- WasC 97005 594 J7
- WasC 97005 624 J1
SW Apache Dr
9000 TLTN 97062 685 E5
SW Apalachee St
11100 TLTN 97062 685 C2
Apollo Ct
21000 WLIN 97068 686 J5
Apollo Rd
6500 WLIN 97068 686 J5
6800 WLIN 97068 687 A5
SE Apollo Wy
6100 HBRO 97123 623 J1
S Appaloosa Dr
30200 CmsC 97038 807 D5
SW Appaloosa Pl
9700 BRTN 97008 655 A1
Appaloosa Wy
2200 WLIN 97068 686 H5
NW Appellate Wy
10800 WasC 97229 595 D2
SE Appenine Wy
5000 MWKE 97222 657 C3
Apperson Blvd
15800 ORCY 97045 687 E6
Apperson St
100 ORCY 97045 717 A2
W Apperson St
1200 MCMV 97128 770 F5
SW Appian Ct
17700 WasC 97007 624 F3
SE Apple Ct
14100 HPYV 97236 658 C3
SW Apple Ct
900 MCMV 97128 770 E6
Apple Knl
- VCVR 98661 537 C2
SE Apple St
6300 MWKE 97222 657 D3
SW Apple Wy
8200 BRTN 97225 625 F3
8200 WasC 97225 625 F3
SW Applegate Dr
6600 WasC 97007 624 C6
NW Applegate Ln
14600 WasC 97229 564 J7
Applegate Ter
13400 ORCY 97045 717 D2
S Appleton Dr
14700 CmsC 97045 717 G3
SW Appletree Pl
4400 WasC 97007 624 G3
Apple Valley Rd
32000 ClbC 97056 444 C6
SW Applewood Av
15200 TGRD 97224 655 F7
SW Appy Ct
20200 WasC 97007 624 C7
SE April Cir
7900 CmsC 97267 657 F6
April Ct
1600 WLIN 97068 716 G2
SW April Ct
14900 SRWD 97140 684 H7
SW April Ln
- WasC 97140 684 G1
- WasC 97224 684 G1
15500 WasC 97224 654 G7
SW Aquaduct Ct
13200 BRTN 97008 655 A1
Aquarius Blvd
3200 NWBG 97132 713 F6
NE Aquila Ct
7600 ClkC 98682 508 D5
Aquinas St
10 LKOW 97035 655 J4
10 LKOW 97035 656 A4
Arabian Ct
1400 NWBG 97132 713 C6
SW Arabian Dr
14300 BRTN 97008 654 J1
SW Arago Pl
7500 BRTN 97007 624 J6
SW Aragon St
13400 WasC 97005 595 A6
SW Aralia Pl
8100 BRTN 97008 625 A7
SW Arapaho Ct
21100 TLTN 97062 685 G6
Arapaho Dr
- WasC 97005 594 J7
- WasC 97005 624 J1
SW Arapaho Rd
8800 TLTN 97062 685 E6
NE Arata Rd
22400 FRVW 97024 599 C4
22400 WDVL 97024 599 C4
22400 WDVL 97060 599 C4
SW Arbela Ct
17800 WasC 97006 624 F1
Arbor Av
- PTLD 97217 536 E6
Arbor Ct
18100 WLIN 97068 686 H2
SE Arbor Ct
3900 HBRO 97123 593 G6
Arbor Dr
2200 WLIN 97068 686 H2
S Arbor Dr
2600 WLIN 97068 686 H2
Arbor Ln
17600 LKOW 97035 686 A2
Arbor Wy
53500 ClbC 97056 444 E5
SW Arborcrest Ct
8900 WasC 97225 625 F2
17900 WasC 97006 624 F1
NE Arbor Crest Dr
2800 FRVW 97024 599 B3
SW Arborcrest Wy
9900 WasC 97225 625 D1
17400 WasC 97006 624 F1
NW Arbor Crossing Pl
- HBRO 97006 594 C4
SW Arboretum Cir
600 PTLD 97210 596 A6
600 PTLD 97221 596 A6
SW Arbor Glen Ct
7500 WNVL 97070 745 F2
SW Arbor Glen Lp
31400 WNVL 97070 745 F2
Arbor Grove Rd NE
19000 MrnC 97137 774 B4
20900 MrnC 97002 774 B3
SW Arbor Lake Ct
7600 WNVL 97070 745 F3
SW Arbor Lake Dr
6800 WNVL 97070 745 F2
NW Arborpark Lp
12600 BNKS 97106 531 H5
SE Arbor Valley Dr
14500 CmsC 97015 658 D6
Arborview Ct
15300 CmsC 97045 717 H7
NW Arborview Dr
9500 WasC 97229 595 E5
SW Arbre Ct
11200 TGRD 97223 655 C5
SW Arbutus Dr
16900 WasC 97007 624 F7
Arcacia Rd
- ECDA 97023 750 B4
NW Arcade Rd
- MthC 97231 565 B3
- PTLD 97231 565 B3
NW Arcadia Ct
1700 WasC 97006 594 J4
NW Arcadia Pl
- PTLD 97210 596 A4
Arcadia Rd
- MthC 97231 535 B5
NW Arcadia St
17800 WasC 97229 594 F2
NW Arcadian Ln
10200 WasC 97229 595 D4
Archer Ct
59100 STHN 97051 414 J1
NE Archer Ct
100 HBRO 97124 593 H5
Archer Dr
35000 STHN 97051 414 J1
S Archer Dr
16400 CmsC 97045 688 B4
SW Archers Pl
22100 SRWD 97140 684 F6
NE Archery Summit Rd
18000 YmhC 97114 742 E6
18000 YmhC 97115 742 E6
Arch Knoll Dr
3200 FTGV 97116 591 F3
SW Arctic Dr
5500 BRTN 97005 625 E4
6100 BRTN 97008 625 E4
SW Arden Pl
2500 PTLD 97201 626 C1
SW Arden Rd
2400 PTLD 97201 626 C1
SE Arden St
4500 MWKE 97222 657 B1
SW Ardenwood St
9400 WasC 97225 625 E1
9900 BRTN 97225 625 E1
SW Ardmore Av
1000 PTLD 97205 596 B6
Ardus Dr
200 NWBG 97132 713 E7
200 YmhC 97132 713 E7
Arena Ct
1900 WLIN 97068 686 G5
SW Argyle Av
25600 WNVL 97070 715 E3
Argyle Ct
100 NWBG 97132 743 G1
NE Argyle Dr
1400 PTLD 97211 566 H4
N Argyle St
3600 PTLD 97217 566 C4
NE Argyle St
1700 PTLD 97211 566 J5
2100 PTLD 97211 567 A5
N Argyle Wy
8500 PTLD 97217 566 E4
NW Argyle Wy
16400 WasC 97229 564 G7
SE Ariel St
6500 HBRO 97123 594 A6
NW Ariel Ter
2700 PTLD 97210 596 B5
SW Arikara Ct
21700 TLTN 97062 685 E6
SW Arikara Dr
9500 TLTN 97062 685 D6
SE Arista Dr
13700 CmsC 97267 656 J5
13900 CmsC 97222 656 J6
16200 CmsC 97267 686 J1
16200 CmsC 97267 687 A1
SE Arista Ln
2100 CmsC 97267 656 J5
Arizona Ct
300 VCVR 98661 537 C6
Arizona Dr
5200 VCVR 98661 537 C6
NW Arizona Dr
16600 WasC 97006 594 G1
SW Arkenstone Dr
17000 DRHM 97224 685 F2
Arletha Ct
19100 CmsC 97055 690 H5
19100 SNDY 97055 690 H5
E Arlie Mitchell Rd
26700 CmsC 97049 724 G5
Arlington Dr
600 NWBG 97132 713 C5
SE Arlington Lp
2000 HBRO 97123 594 A7
N Arlington Pl
700 PTLD 97217 566 F4
E Arlington St
100 GLDS 97027 687 D4
W Arlington St
100 GLDS 97027 687 D5
SW Armco Av
400 HBRO 97123 593 A5
Armel Dr
14100 CmsC 97045 687 G5
14100 ORCY 97045 687 G5
SW Armitage Cir
7000 WNVL 97070 745 G4
SW Armitage Ct E
32200 WNVL 97070 745 G3
SW Armitage Ct N
32100 WNVL 97070 745 G2
SW Armitage Ct S
32400 WNVL 97070 745 G3
SW Armitage Pl
32200 WNVL 97070 745 G3
SW Armitage Rd
32100 WNVL 97070 745 G3
SE Armory Wy
100 MCMV 97128 771 D7
N Armour St
- PTLD 97203 566 A2
6800 PTLD 97203 565 J2
SE Armstrong Cir
17200 CmsC 97015 658 F7
17200 DAMA 97009 658 F7
SE Armstrong Cir
17200 DAMA 97015 658 F7
17200 HPYV 97015 658 F7
SE Armstrong Dr
1900 ClkC 98607 568 J1
1900 CMAS 98607 568 J1
Armstrong Rd
54100 ClbC 97056 444 A4
Arndt Rd NE
- CmsC 97013 745 E6
10700 MrnC 97002 744 J6
14400 CmsC 97002 745 E6
S Arndt Rd
6200 CmsC 97002 745 H7
6200 CmsC 97013 745 J6
S Arnett Dr
18200 CmsC 97045 718 J3
Arnold Dr
100 STHN 97051 385 B6
SE Arnold Ln
3400 YmhC 97128 771 D2
SW Arnold Pl
20400 SRWD 97140 684 G5
SW Arnold St
800 PTLD 97219 656 B2
5100 PTLD 97219 655 J2
SE Arnold Wy
- PTLD 97266 628 B7
7500 PTLD 97236 628 B7
SW Arnold Heights Ter
3300 PTLD 97219 656 B2
NW Arnott Ln
- WasC 97229 595 C3
E Arrah Wanna Blvd
23800 CmsC 97011 724 A3
23800 CmsC 97067 724 A4
Arran Ct
1600 WLIN 97068 686 G3
SW Arranmore Ct
6400 WasC 97223 625 G5
SW Arranmore Pl
6200 WasC 97223 625 H5
SW Arranmore Wy
- BRTN 97223 625 H5
9600 WasC 97223 625 G5
NE Arrington Rd
700 HBRO 97124 593 D3
SE Arrow Creek Ln
300 GSHM 97080 629 G3
300 MthC 97080 629 G4
Arrowhead Ct
2700 LKOW 97034 656 C7
2700 LKOW 97034 686 C1
S Arrowhead Dr
16400 CmsC 97045 688 B5
Arrowhead Pl
- DNDE 97115 742 G3
Arrowhead Creek Ln
- WNVL 97070 745 D1
NW Arrowood Dr
900 MCMV 97128 770 E3
SW Arrowood Dr
3200 PTLD 97219 656 B3
Arrowwood Av
18800 CmsC 97035 685 J3
Arrow Wood Ct
- WDVL 97060 599 C3
SW Arrowwood Dr
9200 BRTN 97005 625 F5
9200 WasC 97223 625 F5
SW Arrowwood Ln
5300 WasC 97223 625 E4
5300 WasC 97225 625 E4
SW Arrowwood Pl
9100 WasC 97223 625 F5
NE Arrowwood St
1800 HBRO 97124 593 D3
NW Arroyo Pl
1000 HBRO 97006 594 C4
Artemis Ct
6500 WLIN 97068 686 J5
Artemis Ln
6500 WLIN 97068 686 J5
SW Artesian Ct
16700 BRTN 97006 594 G6
SW Artesian Dr
17100 BRTN 97006 594 G7
17100 WasC 97006 594 G7
SW Arthur Ct
8300 TGRD 97223 655 F5
10800 CmsC 97070 715 C7
10800 WNVL 97070 715 C7
NE Arthur Dr
- HBRO 97124 594 A5
Arthur Ln
2700 NWBG 97132 713 C4
S Arthur Rd
21200 CmsC 97045 719 B1
S Arthur St
600 CLTN 97111 741 A1
SW Arthur St
10 PTLD 97201 626 F1
800 MCMV 97128 770 G5
SW Arthur St US-26
10 PTLD 97201 626 F1
W Arthur St
500 MCMV 97128 770 G5
SW Arthur Wy
4100 PTLD 97221 626 A1
E Arthur Hailey Rd
24600 CmsC 97049 724 E4
NW Artz Ct
- CMAS 98607 569 B3
SW Ascension Dr
12600 TGRD 97223 654 J4
13600 WasC 97223 654 J4
Ascot Cir
2900 WLIN 97068 686 H4
SW Ascot Ct
7100 WasC 97225 595 G7
NE Ascot Rd
- MCMV 97128 771 E6
Ash
- CmsC 97015 657 H7
- WasC 97006 594 D5
Ash Av
100 WDVL 97060 599 D4
SE Ash Av
13900 CmsC 97267 657 B5
SW Ash Av
12400 TGRD 97223 655 F4
NW Ash Ct
- PTLD 97231 564 J2
SE Ash Ct
6300 PTLD 97215 597 E6
SE Ash Ct
11300 PTLD 97216 597 J6
11300 PTLD 97216 598 A6
12300 MWKE 97222 657 D4
SW Ash Dr
13100 TGRD 97223 655 E5
SE Ash Pl
6700 PTLD 97215 597 E6
SE Ash Rd
13400 YmhC 97114 771 H5
14100 DAYT 97114 771 H5
Ash St
- DNDE 97115 742 J4
- GSHM 97233 598 H6
- YmhC 97115 742 J4
10 RDGF 98642 415 J6
500 DAYT 97114 772 A4
900 DAYT 97114 771 J4
900 YmhC 97114 771 J4
1000 LKOW 97034 656 E7
1500 VCVR 98661 537 A4
3000 FTGV 97116 591 J3
N Ash St
1300 CNBY 97013 746 B5
NW Ash St
200 MCMV 97128 770 G5
1100 CMAS 98607 569 E4
9600 WasC 97229 595 E5
14600 PTLD 97231 564 J2
S Ash St
100 YMHL 97148 711 A1
SE Ash St
- CmsC 97222 657 B5
100 PTLD 97214 596 J6
1000 DNDE 97115 742 H4
1000 YmhC 97115 742 H4
3800 HBRO 97123 593 G7
3900 PTLD 97214 597 B6
5500 PTLD 97215 597 D6
9000 PTLD 97216 597 G6
12200 PTLD 97216 598 A6
13000 PTLD 97233 598 B6
18100 GSHM 97233 598 G6
21400 GSHM 97030 599 B6
SW Ash St
10 PTLD 97204 596 F6
22400 SRWD 97140 684 G7
W Ash St
300 MCMV 97128 770 G5
NE Ashante Dr
10500 PTLD 97211 566 G2
NE Ashberry Dr
1500 HBRO 97124 594 A3
SW Ashbury Ln
13500 TGRD 97223 655 A3
NE Ashby Ct
800 MCMV 97128 770 J2
NW Ashby Ct
1700 PTLD 97229 595 F3
SW Ash Creek Dr
6200 PTLD 97219 625 H6
NW Ashcreek Ln
800 WasC 97229 595 E5
SW Ash Creek Ln
- PTLD 97219 625 J7
SW Ashcreek Ln
2100 MCMV 97128 770 F7
2100 YmhC 97128 770 F7
SW Ashcroft Ln
19700 WasC 97006 594 D6
SW Ashdale Ct
7400 WasC 97223 625 G7
SW Ashdale Dr
6700 WasC 97223 625 G7
SW Ashdown Cir
200 CmsC 97068 686 E5
NW Ashford Cir
3000 HBRO 97124 594 C2
SW Ashford St
7400 TGRD 97224 655 F7
NW Ashland Dr
3000 WasC 97006 594 G2
3400 WasC 97229 594 F2
SW Ashland Dr
28400 WNVL 97070 715 G6
SW Ashland Lp
28500 WNVL 97070 715 G6
NW Ashland Pl
3500 WasC 97006 594 G2
Ashley Ct
- DAYT 97114 772 B4
100 NWBG 97132 713 B6
17300 LKOW 97035 685 J1
SW Ashley Ct
13600 WasC 97224 655 A6
Ashley Dr
19400 CmsC 97045 717 D5
19400 ORCY 97045 717 D5
SW Ashley Dr
1500 MCMV 97128 770 F6
14800 WasC 97224 654 J6
14800 WasC 97224 655 B6
NE Ashley St
400 PTLD 97211 566 G6
SE Ashley St
12200 CmsC 97015 658 A6
NW Ashley Heights Dr
4500 ClkC 98685 476 B6
SW Ash Meadows Blvd
28500 WNVL 97070 715 F6
Ash Meadows Rd
8300 WNVL 97070 715 E6
NE Ashmont St
7100 HBRO 97124 594 B5
SW Ashton Cir
10200 WNVL 97070 715 D7
NW Ashton Dr
12400 BNKS 97106 532 A6
12700 BNKS 97106 531 H5
SE Ashton Ln
18400 CmsC 97267 687 C3
18600 GLDS 97027 687 C3
18600 GLDS 97267 687 C3
NE Ashton Wy
2300 HBRO 97124 593 A2
SE Ash Tree Pl
28600 CmsC 97009 659 J6
SW Ashwood Av
400 MCMV 97128 770 G6
Ashwood Ct
59100 STHN 97051 414 J1
SW Ashwood Ct
11600 TGRD 97223 655 C1
Aspen Av
300 LCTR 98629 416 H1
Aspen Av
500 LCTR 98629 386 H7
1500 ClkC 98629 386 H6
NW Aspen Av
1600 PTLD 97210 596 B3
Aspen Ct
1700 LKOW 97034 686 E1
N Aspen Ct
800 CNBY 97013 746 B5
NW Aspen Ct
4400 CMAS 98607 569 B1
4700 CMAS 98607 539 B7
SE Aspen Ct
2600 HBRO 97123 593 F6
SW Aspen Pl
21600 TLTN 97062 685 C6
W Aspen Pl
- ClkC 98629 386 G6
- LCTR 98629 386 G7
Aspen Rd
- CmsC 97023 750 A3
Aspen St
1400 LKOW 97034 686 E1
N Aspen St
600 CNBY 97013 746 B6
NW Aspen St
4500 CMAS 98607 539 C7
4500 CMAS 98607 569 C1
S Aspen St
400 CNBY 97013 746 B7
SE Aspen St
6200 MWKE 97222 657 D4
SW Aspen St
9300 BRTN 97005 625 E4
Aspen Wy NE
13100 MrnC 97002 775 B7
N Aspen Wy
2300 NWBG 97132 713 E5
2900 YmhC 97132 713 E5
S Aspen Wy
1100 CNBY 97013 746 B7
1100 CNBY 97013 776 B1
W Aspen Wy
400 MCMV 97128 770 G6
Aspen Lake Ct NE
13400 MrnC 97002 775 C7
SW Aspen Lakes Dr
23700 SRWD 97140 714 E1
23800 WasC 97140 714 E1
SW Aspen Ridge Dr
11800 WasC 97224 655 B6
12200 TGRD 97224 655 B6
SE Aspen Summit Dr
7700 PTLD 97266 627 H7
Aspenwood Pl
3200 FTGV 97116 591 H3
Aspen Wy Ct NE
19600 MrnC 97002 775 B7
SE Assembly Av
600 VCVR 98661 537 B7
SE Aster Ct
- HBRO 97123 623 E1
SE Asti Ct
4000 MWKE 97222 657 B4
SE Aston Lp
15100 PTLD 97236 628 D5
SE Aston St
- PTLD 97236 628 D6
Astor Av
16600 CmsC 97035 655 H7
NW Astor Ct
- CMAS 98607 569 B3
5100 CMAS 98607 539 C7
N Astor St
6200 PTLD 97203 566 A2
6800 PTLD 97203 565 J2
NW Astor St
3500 CMAS 98607 569 B2
SE Astor St
8200 CmsC 97267 657 F6
NW Astoria Dr
18700 WasC 97229 594 E1
SW Aten Rd
19800 WasC 97007 654 C6
NW Athena Pl
19200 WasC 97229 594 D1
Athena Rd
2300 WLIN 97068 686 J5
NW Athena St
18800 WasC 97229 594 E1
NW Athens Dr
15500 WasC 97229 564 H7
S Athens Rd
19900 CmsC 97045 718 B6
SE Atherton Av
700 GSHM 97080 629 D4
Atherton Dr
1700 CmsC 97034 686 D2
1700 LKOW 97034 686 D2
Atherton Woods
- VCVR 98661 537 E1
- VCVR 98662 537 E1
SW Athey Rd
21000 CmsC 97068 686 C6
NE Atkeson Ln
- HBRO 97124 594 A2
Atkinson St
6100 WLIN 97068 687 A6
Atlanta Dr
18800 ORCY 97045 717 B4
SW Atlanta St
6500 PTLD 97219 655 H3
6500 TGRD 97223 655 H3
N Atlantic Av
5500 PTLD 97217 566 D6
NE Atlantic Av
100 MCMV 97128 771 A6
100 YmhC 97128 771 A6
Atlantic St
- WDLD 98674 386 A1
N Attu St
3800 PTLD 97203 566 C3
3800 PTLD 97217 566 C3
NW Atwater Ct
42000 BNKS 97106 531 J6
Atwater Ln
13300 LKOW 97034 656 D5
13300 LKOW 97034 656 D5
Atwater Rd
500 LKOW 97034 656 D5
600 CmsC 97034 656 D5
NW Aubrey Ln
2300 GSHM 97030 599 B7
Aubuchon Dr
35100 STHN 97051 414 J1
E Aubuchon Dr
35200 STHN 97051 414 J1
Auburn Ct
13300 LKOW 97035 656 C5
Auburn Dr
19300 ORCY 97045 717 B4
Auburn Ln
4500 LKOW 97035 656 A4
NW Audrey Dr
15900 WasC 97006 594 G3
SW Audrey Ln
2500 PTLD 97201 626 C1
SW Audubon St
16000 BRTN 97006 624 G2
NE August Av
18500 ClkC 98604 478 C1
SE Augusta Ct
7300 HBRO 97123 594 B3
7400 PTLD 97206 627 E6
SW Augusta Ct
20100 WasC 97006 594 C7
Augusta Dr
20000 ORCY 97045 717 H6
NW Augusta Dr
1200 MCMV 97128 770 F4
SW Augusta Dr
2100 WasC 97006 594 B7
2100 WasC 97123 594 B7
2300 WasC 97006 624 B1
SE Augusta Ln
7400 HBRO 97123 594 B3
7400 WasC 97123 594 B3
SW Augusta Ln
17000 BRTN 97006 624 G1
17000 WasC 97006 624 F1
21900 HBRO 97123 594 B7
21900 WasC 97006 594 B7
21900 WasC 97123 594 B7
SE Augusta Lp
3900 GSHM 97080 629 B7
SE Augusta Pl
3800 GSHM 97080 629 C6
SW Augusta Pl
2200 WasC 97006 594 C7
2200 WasC 97006 624 B1
SW Augusta St
21200 WasC 97006 594 B7
SE Augusta Wy
4000 GSHM 97080 629 B7
SE Augusta National Av
- CmsC 97206 657 F1
- CmsC 97236 657 F1
SE Augustine Ct
9000 CmsC 97236 657 H1
SW Augustine Ct
19800 WasC 97007 654 D1
SW Auklet Lp
11600 BRTN 97007 654 E3
SE Aurora Ct
11600 CmsC 97236 657 J3
NE Aurora Dr
2600 HBRO 97124 593 C1
NW Aurora Pl
18800 WasC 97229 594 E1
NW Aurora St
18900 WasC 97229 594 D1
SE Austin Ct
6300 HBRO 97123 594 A6
SE Austin Dr
6500 HBRO 97123 594 A6
Austin Ln
20700 FRVW 97024 599 A2
SE Austin St
16600 CmsC 97267 687 B1
SE Austrailis Ct
11300 CmsC 97236 657 J3
NE Auto Mall Dr
3200 VCVR 98662 537 E2
SE Autumn Ct
4600 ClkC 98607 568 J4
SW Autumn Ct
1200 TDLE 97060 599 G5
SW Autumn Dr
16000 BRTN 97007 624 G4
16000 WasC 97007 624 G4
Autumn Ln
13100 ORCY 97045 717 D5
E Autumn Ln
21000 CmsC 97049 724 E1
SW Autumn Ln
15600 BRTN 97007 624 H4
Autumn Wy
18600 CmsC 97055 690 E4
SW Autumn Wy
1100 TDLE 97060 599 H5
Autumn Chase
- VCVR 98684 537 J5
NW Autumn Creek Wy
600 HBRO 97006 594 C4
Autumn Ridge Dr
- MCMV 97128 770 H1
- YmhC 97128 770 J1
NW Autumn Ridge Dr
17300 BRTN 97006 594 F4
NE Autumn Rose Wy
300 HBRO 97124 593 C2
Autumn View Ct
3100 WLIN 97068 686 H4
SW Autumnview St
- TGRD 97224 655 B6
- WasC 97224 655 B6
NE Autumnwood Ter
100 HBRO 97124 594 A5
100 WasC 97124 594 A5
Autumn Woods
- WasC 97006 624 G2
NW Ava Av
10 GSHM 97030 629 B2
10 GSHM 97080 629 B2
2300 GSHM 97030 599 B7
Ava Ct
- STHN 97051 385 A7
NW Ava Ln
1000 GSHM 97030 629 B1
SW Avallon Ct
- WNVL 97070 745 E2
SE Avalon Ct
32000 CmsC 97023 750 E3
NW Avalon Dr
17800 WasC 97229 594 F2
Avalon Pk
- KNGC 97224 685 B1
- VCVR 98664 537 H7
- WasC 97224 685 B1

STREET Block	City	ZIP	Map#	Grid
NW Avamere Ct				
16300	WasC	97006	594	G1
16300	WasC	97229	594	G1
Av Davis Rd				
100	ORCY	97045	717	C3
Avenida del Norte				
-	VCVR	98683	568	F3
SW Aventine Av				
10900	MthC	97219	656	G2
SW Aventine Circus				
11300	MthC	97219	656	G2
SE Averi Ct				
4100	HBRO	97123	593	G5
Averill Pkwy				
19000	SNDY	97055	691	A4
SW Avery Ct				
20100	TLTN	97062	685	C5
Avery Ln				
4600	LKOW	97035	656	A5
SW Avery St				
8900	TLTN	97062	685	D5
Aviation Wy NE				
-	MrnC	97002	775	E1
22700	MrnC	97002	745	E7
NE Aviation Wy				
14900	YmhC	97132	712	D3
NW Avignon Ln				
12500	WasC	97229	595	B1
SE Avo St				
16800	DAMA	97009	688	E1
SW Avocet Ct				
10700	BRTN	97007	654	G2
NW Avocet Ln				
2700	PTLD	97229	595	F2
SW Avon Ct				
8800	TGRD	97224	655	E7
20300	WasC	97007	624	C4
SW Avon Pl				
15800	TGRD	97224	655	F7
SW Avon St				
8500	TGRD	97224	655	F7
Avon Wy				
1600	FTGV	97116	591	H3
NW Avondale Ct				
1700	PTLD	97229	595	F3
SE Avondale Ct				
10	GSHM	97080	629	B7
NW Avondale Dr				
15800	WasC	97006	594	G3
SE Avondale Wy				
100	GSHM	97080	629	B7
Axel Rd				
62000	ClbC	97051	384	E2
NE Axford Rd				
14200	ClkC	98604	448	C2
SW Aynsley Wy				
14200	WasC	97224	654	J7
NE Ayrshire Dr				
900	HBRO	97124	593	D1
Azalea Ct NE				
21900	MrnC	97002	775	D2
SE Azalea Ct				
2400	CmsC	97267	686	J1
SW Azalea Ct				
13900	BRTN	97008	625	A5
SE Azalea Dr				
16600	CmsC	97267	686	J1
Azalea Gdns				
-	NWBG	97132	713	E6
Azalea Ln				
4300	VCVR	98661	537	B4
NE Azalea Ln				
4600	HBRO	97124	593	H5
4600	WasC	97124	593	H5
E Azalea St				
500	YMHL	97148	711	A1
800	YmhC	97148	711	A1
NE Azalea St				
2800	HBRO	97124	593	F5
Azalia Av				
-	PTLD	97217	536	F7
SE Azar Dr				
10800	CmsC	97236	657	J4
Aztec Ct				
1900	WLIN	97068	686	G4
B				
B Av				
10	LKOW	97034	656	F5
NE B Av				
-	ClkC	98684	538	E6
-	VCVR	98684	538	E6
W B Av				
100	LCTR	98629	386	G7
NE B Ct				
-	ClkC	98684	538	E6
B Ln				
-	PTLD	97218	567	E7
B Lp				
-	MrnC	97137	744	C7
B St				
-	PTLD	97219	655	J3
-	VCVR	98661	536	H3
-	WasC	97224	685	A1
100	CBAC	97018	385	C3
500	ORCY	97045	687	E6
700	WHGL	98671	569	J5
900	WHGL	98671	570	C6
1000	WDLD	98674	386	A1
1500	FTGV	97116	591	H5
1500	WasC	97116	591	H5
B St SR-8				
1900	FTGV	97116	591	H5
NW B St				
-	WasC	97006	594	C5
SE B St				
10000	MWKE	97222	657	A2
S Babler Rd				
16200	CmsC	97045	688	J7
SE Babler Rd				
18300	CmsC	97267	687	B3
Babson Pl				
16600	CmsC	97035	655	H7
SE Bacarra St				
1000	HBRO	97123	593	D6
SE Baccarat Wy				
16000	DAMA	97009	688	F1
SW Bachelor Blvd				
21300	YmhC	97123	683	A4
21300	YmhC	97132	683	A4
SE Bachelor Dr				
9200	HPYV	97236	658	C1
Bachelor Row				
-	BRTN	97005	625	C2

STREET Block	City	ZIP	Map#	Grid
Bachelor Flat Rd				
34000	ClbC	97051	414	G2
34000	ClbC	97053	414	G2
34000	STHN	97051	414	G2
S Bachelor Flat Rd				
57700	ClbC	97053	414	G3
58600	ClbC	97051	414	G2
Bachman Dr				
8400	CmsC	97027	687	F2
SW Back Court Pl				
700	WasC	97006	594	D6
SW Backman Ln				
21500	WasC	97140	684	A3
NW Bacon Rd				
7800	ClkC	98665	506	E4
SE Bacon Creek Ln				
41200	CmsC	97055	691	C1
NW Badertscher Rd				
22500	WasC	97124	564	A1
S Badger Dr				
19100	CmsC	97045	748	G1
SE Badger Creek Rd				
14700	CmsC	97236	658	C4
14700	HPYV	97236	658	C4
NW Bagley Rd				
33000	WasC	97124	562	H7
NW Bailey Av				
100	HBRO	97123	593	B4
100	HBRO	97124	593	B4
SW Bailey Av				
400	HBRO	97123	593	B5
E Bailey Rd				
23300	CmsC	97049	724	D2
NW Bailey St				
-	PTLD	97231	565	F4
SW Bailey St				
9000	WNVL	97070	745	E1
SW Bailey Ter				
12600	TGRD	97223	654	J4
SW Baird St				
3600	PTLD	97219	626	B7
4900	PTLD	97219	625	J7
SE Baker Av				
400	GSHM	97080	629	G3
SE Baker Cir				
100	GSHM	97080	629	G3
SE Baker Ct				
500	GSHM	97080	629	G3
N Baker Dr				
300	CNBY	97013	746	B6
2200	CmsC	97013	746	B3
NW Baker Dr				
600	CNBY	97013	746	B6
NE Baker Ln				
10	GSHM	97080	629	G3
SE Baker Ln				
2000	GSHM	97080	629	G5
SW Baker Ln				
15500	WasC	97224	654	H5
Baker Rd				
-	ClbC	97056	474	B3
SW Baker Rd				
24000	CmsC	97140	714	J2
24000	SRWD	97140	714	J2
29300	CmsC	97140	715	A7
N Baker St				
800	CNBY	97013	746	B5
NE Baker St				
100	MCMV	97128	770	H3
NE Baker St SR-99W				
100	MCMV	97128	770	H4
SE Baker St				
100	MCMV	97128	770	H6
SE Baker St SR-99W				
100	MCMV	97128	770	H6
SW Baker St				
100	PTLD	97201	626	G2
700	MCMV	97128	770	G7
11500	BRTN	97008	625	C5
17000	WasC	97007	624	F5
SW Baker St SR-99W				
700	MCMV	97128	770	G7
SE Baker Wy				
2300	GSHM	97080	629	G5
NE Baker Creek Rd				
16900	ClkC	98606	478	J3
NW Baker Creek Rd				
1100	MCMV	97128	770	F3
1800	YmhC	97128	770	E3
NW Baker Crest Ct				
1000	MCMV	97128	770	G2
S Bakers Ferry Rd				
19100	CmsC	97045	688	H5
20100	CmsC	97045	689	B5
21800	CmsC	97009	689	D4
SE Bakers Ferry Rd				
18500	CmsC	97009	689	D4
18500	CmsC	97045	689	D4
NE Baker Trail Ln				
15100	YmhC	97132	711	J1
Baker View Dr				
32200	ClbC	97056	474	C2
Baker View Ln				
32200	ClbC	97056	444	B7
32200	ClbC	97056	474	B1
NW Balboa Av				
5800	PTLD	97210	565	H6
SE Balboa Dr				
2200	VCVR	98683	568	D2
NE Balcony Dr				
38400	ClkC	98671	540	H6
SE Baldock Wy				
4500	CmsC	97267	687	B1
NE Bald Peak Rd				
18000	YmhC	97132	683	A7
18000	YmhC	97132	713	B1
SW Bald Peak Rd				
29900	WasC	97123	653	A3
SW Baldry St				
16700	MthC	97236	628	F5
16700	PTLD	97236	628	F5
NE Baldwin Dr				
700	HBRO	97124	593	D3
N Baldwin St				
10	PTLD	97211	566	F5
3800	PTLD	97217	566	C5
3900	PTLD	97203	566	C5
NE Baldwin St				
10	PTLD	97211	566	G5
10	PTLD	97217	566	G5
700	HBRO	97124	593	D3
SW Baleine St				
5700	CmsC	97035	655	H7
5700	LKOW	97035	655	H7

STREET Block	City	ZIP	Map#	Grid
SW Baler Wy				
15700	SRWD	97140	684	G6
SE Bales Rd				
50800	CmsC	97055	692	C7
SE Balfour St				
2800	MWKE	97222	657	A1
NW Ball Av				
-	PTLD	97210	596	D2
Ballad Ct				
2800	FTGV	97116	591	F3
Ballad Ln				
500	FTGV	97116	591	F3
Ballad Pl				
2700	FTGV	97116	591	F3
Ballad Wy				
500	FTGV	97116	591	F3
Ballad Towne Pl				
2800	FTGV	97116	591	F3
SW Ballard Ln				
17600	SRWD	97140	684	E7
N Ballast St				
3800	PTLD	97217	566	C7
N Balm St				
100	YmhC	97148	711	A1
100	YMHL	97148	711	A1
S Balm St				
100	YMHL	97148	711	A1
300	YmhC	97148	711	A1
SW Balmer Cir				
10000	PTLD	97219	656	C1
SE Balmoral Ct				
14300	CmsC	97267	656	H6
SW Balsam Av				
2200	WasC	97005	625	A1
SW Baltic Av				
800	WasC	97225	595	E7
N Baltimore Av				
6600	PTLD	97203	565	G3
Baltimore Wy				
100	VCVR	98664	537	F6
SW Bambi Ln				
11500	TGRD	97223	655	C4
W Bamboo Ct				
-	WHGL	98671	569	G3
W Bamboo St				
-	WHGL	98671	569	G3
SE Banbury Cir				
11600	HPYV	97236	658	C3
SW Bancroft Ct				
100	PTLD	97239	626	E3
3500	PTLD	97221	626	B2
SW Bancroft St				
500	PTLD	97239	626	F2
4000	PTLD	97221	626	A2
6200	PTLD	97221	625	H2
6400	PTLD	97225	625	H2
SW Bancroft Ter				
700	PTLD	97239	626	E3
SW Bancroft Wy				
6600	WasC	97225	625	H2
NW Bandon Ct				
17100	WasC	97006	594	G2
NW Banff Dr				
3200	WasC	97229	594	J2
Banfield Expwy				
-	FRVW	-	598	J4
-	FRVW	-	599	B4
-	GSHM	-	598	J3
-	GSHM	-	599	B4
-	MWDP	-	597	H2
-	PTLD	-	596	H5
-	PTLD	-	597	C5
-	PTLD	-	598	C3
-	TDLE	-	599	E3
-	WDVL	-	599	B4
Banfield Expwy I-84				
-	FRVW	-	598	J4
-	FRVW	-	599	B4
-	GSHM	-	598	H3
-	GSHM	-	599	B4
-	MWDP	-	597	H2
-	PTLD	-	596	H5
-	PTLD	-	597	J2
-	PTLD	-	598	C3
-	TDLE	-	599	E3
-	WDVL	-	599	B4
Banfield Expwy US-30				
-	FRVW	-	598	J4
-	FRVW	-	599	B4
-	GSHM	-	598	J3
-	MWDP	-	597	H2
-	PTLD	-	596	H5
-	PTLD	-	597	C4
-	PTLD	-	598	C3
-	TDLE	-	599	E3
-	WDVL	-	599	B4
SW Bangy Rd				
14900	CmsC	97035	655	H6
14900	LKOW	97035	655	H6
N Bank St				
6200	PTLD	97203	566	A2
8300	PTLD	97203	565	H2
NW Banks Rd				
39100	WasC	97106	532	B5
41500	BNKS	97106	531	J5
41500	WasC	97106	531	J5
Banner Ln				
300	NWBG	97132	713	B5
NW Bannister Dr				
5000	WasC	97229	565	B7
SW Bannoch Ct				
10500	TLTN	97062	685	C3
SW Bannoch St				
10600	TLTN	97062	685	C2
SE Bansen Ln				
5800	YmhC	97114	771	E5
SE Bantam Ct				
5400	CmsC	97267	657	C6
NE Banton Dr				
9900	ClkC	98686	507	D3
SW Bany Rd				
-	BRTN	97007	624	G6
18900	WasC	97007	624	D6
Banyan Ln				
17300	LKOW	97034	686	D1
NW Banyon Pl				
3400	WasC	97229	595	A2
SE Barba St				
3300	MWKE	97222	627	A7
3500	PTLD	97222	627	A7
SE Barbara Ct				
33600	SPSE	97056	474	E2
SW Barbara Ln				
6900	TGRD	97223	655	G1
Barbara St				
-	MCMV	97128	770	D5

STREET Block	City	ZIP	Map#	Grid
S Barbara Wy				
11700	CmsC	97038	837	A3
SE Barbara Jean Ct				
13500	CmsC	97015	658	B7
SE Barbara Welch Ln				
-	MthC	97236	628	D7
14800	PTLD	97236	628	D7
SE Barbara Welch Rd				
6400	PTLD	97236	628	D6
7800	CmsC	97236	628	D7
7800	HPYV	97236	628	D7
Barbary Ct				
600	GLDS	97027	687	E3
Barbary Pl				
500	GLDS	97027	687	E3
SW Barber St				
-	CmsC	97070	715	C7
9000	WNVL	97070	715	E6
NE Barberry Ct				
2100	HBRO	97124	593	E3
NE Barberry Dr				
2000	HBRO	97124	593	E3
SW Barberry Dr				
12700	BRTN	97008	625	A6
SW Barberry Ln				
12500	BRTN	97008	625	B6
SW Barberry Pl				
7900	BRTN	97008	625	D3
SW Barbur Blvd				
2500	PTLD	97201	626	E1
3200	PTLD	97239	626	E5
7200	PTLD	97219	626	B7
9400	PTLD	97219	656	A1
10400	PTLD	97219	655	J2
11400	TGRD	97223	655	H2
SW Barbur Blvd SR-10				
3900	PTLD	97239	626	E5
SW Barbur Blvd SR-99W				
3900	PTLD	97239	626	E5
7200	PTLD	97219	626	B7
9400	PTLD	97219	656	A1
10400	PTLD	97219	655	J2
11400	TGRD	97223	655	H2
SW Barbur Ct				
8700	PTLD	97219	626	C7
SW Barcelona Ct				
15200	BRTN	97007	624	H5
SW Barcelona Ln				
-	WasC	97007	624	F5
SW Barcelona Wy				
15000	BRTN	97007	624	H5
17000	WasC	97007	624	F5
Barclay Av				
100	ORCY	97045	717	B2
SW Barclay Ct				
5100	BRTN	97005	624	J4
Barclay St				
5700	GLDS	97027	687	C3
6000	WLIN	97068	687	A6
NW Barclay Ter				
10300	PTLD	97231	565	A2
Barclay Wy				
1300	NWBG	97132	713	D6
Barclay Hills Dr				
400	ORCY	97045	717	D2
S Bard Rd				
23600	CmsC	97023	750	C7
SW Bardeen Dr				
-	BRTN	97005	624	J1
-	WasC	97005	624	J1
SE Barger Blvd				
28600	CmsC	97023	720	C7
Barger Rd				
61000	ClbC	97051	384	E4
Bark Wy				
50500	ClbC	97056	474	E5
Barker Av				
100	ORCY	97045	717	B2
Barker Ct				
39200	SNDY	97055	691	A3
Barker Rd				
100	ORCY	97045	717	A2
SE Barkley Ct				
14500	DAMA	97009	659	A7
NW Barkton Ct				
16100	WasC	97006	594	H3
NW Barkton St				
15400	WasC	97006	594	H3
SW Barley Pl				
21700	SRWD	97140	684	G6
N Barlow Ct				
2700	CNLS	97113	592	G4
NW Barlow Ct				
3900	CMAS	98607	569	B1
SE Barlow Ct				
15300	DAMA	97009	658	J7
15300	DAMA	97009	659	A7
15300	DAMA	97009	689	A1
SW Barlow Ct				
13900	BRTN	97008	624	J5
13900	BRTN	97008	625	A5
15100	BRTN	97007	624	H5
Barlow Dr				
16200	CmsC	97045	687	H6
16200	ORCY	97045	687	H6
Barlow Pkwy				
38300	SNDY	97055	690	J4
N Barlow Pl				
3000	CNLS	97113	592	G4
SW Barlow Pl				
13800	BRTN	97008	625	A5
Barlow Rd				
-	CmsC	97013	745	J4
S Barlow Rd				
23400	CmsC	97013	745	J7
24300	BRLO	97013	745	J7
24400	BRLO	97002	745	J7
24500	BRLO	97002	775	J7
24500	BRLO	97013	775	J7
24500	CmsC	97002	775	J6
24800	CmsC	97013	775	J1
SW Barlow Rd				
12600	BRTN	97008	625	B5
14000	BRTN	97008	624	J5
14400	BRTN	97007	624	J5
Barlow St				
6100	WLIN	97068	687	A5
N Barlow St				
1600	CNLS	97113	592	E4
NW Barlow St				
5200	CMAS	98607	539	B7
E Barlow Trail Rd				
60100	CmsC	97055	693	D5
60700	CmsC	97011	693	G6
63100	CmsC	97049	693	H7

STREET Block	City	ZIP	Map#	Grid
E Barlow Trail Rd				
65600	CmsC	97049	723	J1
66100	CmsC	97049	724	D3
SW Barnard Ct				
15700	BRTN	97007	624	H6
SW Barnard Dr				
7600	BRTN	97007	624	H6
S Barnards Rd				
11700	CmsC	97013	807	A5
11700	CmsC	97038	807	B5
NE Barnes Av				
10	GSHM	97030	629	F2
10	GSHM	97080	629	F2
SE Barnes Av				
300	GSHM	97080	629	F3
Barnes Cir				
1800	WLIN	97068	716	H1
NE Barnes Ct				
1200	GSHM	97030	629	F1
NE Barnes Ln				
1500	GSHM	97030	629	F1
NW Barnes Rd				
4200	PTLD	97210	596	A5
4200	PTLD	97221	596	A6
12000	BRTN	97225	595	C5
12000	BRTN	97229	595	B5
12000	WasC	97229	595	B5
SE Barnes Rd				
900	GSHM	97080	629	F4
3000	MthC	97080	629	F6
SW Barnes Rd				
-	WasC	97225	595	C6
4900	PTLD	97210	596	A6
4900	PTLD	97221	596	A6
5300	MthC	97221	595	J6
5300	PTLD	97221	595	J6
6300	PTLD	97225	595	H6
9700	BRTN	97225	595	E7
11900	BRTN	97229	595	C5
Barnes St				
600	VCVR	98661	536	G5
Barnet St				
3200	FTGV	97116	591	J2
SW Bar None Rd				
21200	CmsC	97062	686	A6
SE Barn Owl Ln				
1600	GSHM	97080	629	F5
SE Barn Owl Wy				
1400	GSHM	97080	629	F4
SW Barnsdale Dr				
15000	SRWD	97140	684	H7
NW Barnsley Ct				
1600	PTLD	97229	595	F3
SW Barnum Dr				
13400	TGRD	97223	655	D5
SE Barnum Rd				
-	CmsC	97055	690	F2
35400	SNDY	97055	690	F2
SE Baron Lp				
15200	HPYV	97236	658	D5
E Barons Ct				
68100	CmsC	97067	724	B4
Barr Av				
59200	ClbC	97051	414	J1
59200	STHN	97051	414	J1
59600	ClbC	97051	384	J7
59600	STHN	97051	384	J7
N Barr Av				
10300	PTLD	97203	565	H1
NE Barr Rd				
-	GSHM	97230	598	E4
-	PTLD	97230	598	E4
22200	FRVW	97024	599	B4
Barrack Rd				
60100	ClbC	97051	385	A6
60100	STHN	97051	385	A6
Barr-Alex Rd				
10900	WasC	97123	653	D3
16300	WasC	97123	683	G1
16300	WasC	97140	683	G1
Barr-Alex Rd SR-219				
10900	WasC	97123	653	D3
16300	WasC	97123	683	G1
16300	WasC	97140	683	G1
NW Barrett Wy				
10900	WasC	97229	595	D3
Barrington Av				
18900	CmsC	97055	690	J5
18900	SNDY	97055	690	J5
Barrington Ct				
14000	LKOW	97035	655	J5
Barrington Dr				
3300	CmsC	97068	716	J1
3300	WLIN	97068	716	H1
SW Barrington Pl				
16000	WasC	97224	654	H7
SW Barrington Ter				
15600	WasC	97224	654	J7
SW Barrow Ln				
1300	MthC	97221	596	A7
1300	PTLD	97221	596	A7
SW Barrows Rd				
-	WasC	97223	654	H4
13600	BRTN	97007	655	A3
13600	BRTN	97008	655	A2
13600	TGRD	97007	655	A2
13600	TGRD	97008	655	A2
13600	TGRD	97223	655	A3
13800	BRTN	97007	654	H4
13800	TGRD	97223	654	H4
14000	BRTN	97008	654	J3
14600	BRTN	97223	654	H4
SW Barta Ct				
33200	SPSE	97056	474	E2
SE Bartell Rd				
14600	CmsC	97009	659	E7
14600	DAMA	97009	659	E7
14700	CmsC	97009	689	D2
SE Bartholomew Ct				
8700	PTLD	97266	627	F7
NW Bartholomew Dr				
7700	PTLD	97229	595	F3
S Bartholomew Rd				
22200	CmsC	97023	749	J4
22200	CmsC	97023	750	A4
SE Bartlemay Rd				
27100	CmsC	97022	689	G5
E Bartlett Ct				
-	ClkC	98629	386	H6
NW Bartley Ct				
17900	BRTN	97006	594	F4
Bartok Pl				
10	LKOW	97035	656	B4
Barton Av				
100	GLDS	97027	687	D4

STREET Block	City	ZIP	Map#	Grid
NW Barton Ct				
42000	BNKS	97106	531	J6
Barton Rd				
18800	CmsC	97034	686	B3
18800	LKOW	97034	686	B3
SE Barton Park Rd				
19000	CmsC	97009	689	D4
SW Basalt Ct				
15100	BRTN	97007	654	H1
W Baseline Rd				
7200	HBRO	97123	594	B6
7200	HBRO	97124	594	B6
7200	WasC	97124	594	B6
7300	WasC	97123	594	B6
15800	BRTN	97006	594	G6
15800	WasC	97006	594	F6
18400	HBRO	97006	594	E6
23300	HBRO	97123	593	J5
23300	HBRO	97124	593	J5
23700	WasC	97123	593	J5
24300	WasC	97124	593	H5
E Baseline St				
1200	CNLS	97113	592	G5
3100	CNLS	97123	592	G5
34300	WasC	97124	592	H5
E Baseline St SR-8				
1200	CNLS	97113	592	G5
3100	CNLS	97123	592	G5
34300	WasC	97124	592	H5
SE Baseline St				
100	HBRO	97123	593	B5
SE Baseline St SR-8				
100	HBRO	97123	593	B5
SW Baseline St				
-	CNLS	97113	592	H5
100	HBRO	97123	593	B5
32300	HBRO	97123	592	J5
32300	WasC	97123	592	J5
32300	WasC	97124	592	J5
33400	CNLS	97123	592	J5
33600	CNLS	97124	592	J5
SW Baseline St SR-8				
-	CNLS	97113	592	H5
100	HBRO	97123	593	B5
32300	HBRO	97123	592	J5
32300	WasC	97123	592	J5
32300	WasC	97124	592	J5
33400	CNLS	97123	592	J5
33600	CNLS	97124	592	J5
W Baseline St				
100	CNLS	97113	592	D5
100	FTGV	97116	592	D5
W Baseline St SR-8				
100	CNLS	97113	592	D5
100	FTGV	97116	592	D5
N Basin Av				
4500	PTLD	97217	596	D1
4800	PTLD	97217	566	B6
NE Basket Flat Rd				
19700	ClkC	98604	418	J5
19700	ClkC	98604	419	A5
Bass Ln				
3800	LKOW	97034	686	A3
NW Bass St				
4400	CMAS	98607	569	B1
4700	CMAS	98607	539	B7
NW Bassel Ct				
12000	ClkC	98685	506	G1
NE Bassel Rd				
100	ClkC	98685	506	G1
NW Bassel Rd				
100	ClkC	98685	506	G1
NW Bass Lake Dr				
31600	WasC	97133	533	B4
SW Basswood Ct				
11300	TGRD	97223	655	C2
NW Battaglia Av				
100	GSHM	97030	628	J2
SW Battaglia Av				
1400	GSHM	97080	628	J4
SW Battaglia Pl				
2200	GSHM	97080	628	J5
SW Batterson Ln				
-	TGRD	97224	655	A6
-	WasC	97224	655	A6
SE Battin Rd				
8500	CmsC	97236	657	F1
Battlemountain Rd				
59800	ClbC	97051	384	J7
SE Baty Rd				
19000	CmsC	97055	692	A4
SE Bauer St				
15600	PTLD	97236	628	D6
NW Bauer Woods Dr				
2600	WasC	97229	595	A2
SE Baumback Av				
13500	CmsC	97055	660	J6
13500	SNDY	97055	660	J6
Baumgardner Ln				
32000	ClbC	97056	444	C6
SE Baxter Rd				
16200	MthC	97236	628	E7
W Bay Rd				
4000	LKOW	97035	686	A1
N Bayard Av				
8400	PTLD	97217	566	D4
S Bayberry Dr				
14900	CmsC	97045	717	G2
SW Bayberry Dr				
7300	WasC	97007	624	D6
Bayberry Rd				
1000	LKOW	97034	656	E5
Bay Creek Dr				
5400	LKOW	97035	655	J4
N Baygate St				
-	PTLD	97203	535	F5
Bay Hill Ln				
34900	ClbC	97053	414	H5
NE Bayley Rd				
-	YmhC	97132	712	C3
NE Bayliss Rd				
9600	YmhC	97111	741	G2
SW Baylor St				
6800	TGRD	97223	655	G3
Bay Meadow Dr				
1800	CmsC	97068	686	G5
1800	WLIN	97068	686	G5
SW Bay Meadows Ct				
13200	BRTN	97008	655	D1
Bay Meadows Dr				
1900	WLIN	97068	686	H4
Bayne St				
-	MthC	97231	534	F5
NW Bayonne Ln				
12500	WasC	97229	595	B1

STREET Block	City	ZIP	Map#	Grid
Bay Point Dr				
5700	LKOW	97035	655	H4
SE Baypoint Dr				
2300	VCVR	98683	568	D2
Bayport Marina Ln				
-	ClbC	97053	414	J5
NW Bays Dr				
14200	WasC	97106	531	G4
Bay View Dr				
57600	ClbC	97053	415	A4
Bay View Ln				
1500	LKOW	97034	656	D6
Bay View Rd				
57300	ClbC	97053	414	J5
S Baywood Ct				
1300	CNBY	97013	776	B1
SW Baywood Ct				
16600	SRWD	97140	714	F1
NW Beach Ct				
9600	WasC	97124	563	A2
JA Beach Ctr				
-	PTLD	97217	536	E7
SE Beach Dr				
6000	VCVR	98661	537	D7
NW Beach Rd				
31300	WasC	97124	563	A2
32600	WasC	97113	562	J2
32600	WasC	97124	562	J2
Beacon Av				
8800	VCVR	98664	537	F7
NE Beacon Ct				
1800	HBRO	97124	593	E1
Beaconhill Dr				
2500	WLIN	97068	686	J7
2700	WLIN	97068	716	J1
Beacon Hill Ln				
-	CmsC	97068	686	J7
-	WLIN	97068	686	J7
SW Beagle Ct				
12800	TGRD	97223	655	A4
NE Beakey St				
3300	PTLD	97212	597	A2
Beal Rd				
-	FTGV	97116	591	J2
Beam St				
6500	WLIN	97068	687	A5
Bean Ct				
13700	ORCY	97045	687	E7
Bear Creek Ln				
37000	CmsC	97009	660	H3
SW Bear Creek Rd				
3200	WasC	97116	591	C7
SW Beard Rd				
14500	BRTN	97007	654	J1
14500	BRTN	97008	654	J1
SE Bear Garden Rd				
55100	CmsC	97055	692	H6
S Bear Meadow Ct				
31100	CmsC	97038	807	A7
31100	CmsC	97038	837	A1
SE Bearspaw St				
17100	PTLD	97236	628	F5
NW Beary St				
500	MCMV	97128	770	G5
NE Beasley Rd				
2800	ClkC	98629	417	B3
Beasley Wy				
4300	LKOW	97035	656	A7
S Beatie Rd				
23000	CmsC	97045	747	J7
S Beaton Rd				
14800	CmsC	97045	687	J4
Beatrice Av				
1000	GLDS	97027	687	D4
NW Beatrice Av				
-	PTLD	97210	596	A2
SE Beatrice St				
7900	CmsC	97222	657	F1
NW Beauchamp Ct				
-	CMAS	98607	569	B3
NE Beaumead Ln				
4600	HBRO	97124	593	H5
NE Beaumead St				
4000	HBRO	97124	593	G5
NE Beaumont St				
4100	PTLD	97212	597	B3
4100	PTLD	97213	597	B3
SW Beaver Av				
6300	PTLD	97239	626	F5
Beaver Ct				
4100	FTGV	97116	592	C5
SW Beaver Ct				
17300	WasC	97006	594	F7
NE Beaver Dr				
-	ClkC	98675	419	H2
Beaver Ln				
1300	ORCY	97045	717	E3
SE Beaver St				
-	CmsC	97055	691	C3
SE Beaver Creek Ct				
600	TDLE	97060	599	G4
SE Beaver Creek Ln				
400	TDLE	97060	599	G5
Beavercreek Rd				
200	ORCY	97045	717	D4
13500	CmsC	97045	717	H6
20500	CmsC	97045	747	J1
S Beavercreek Rd				
21000	CmsC	97045	747	J2
21200	CmsC	97004	747	J2
21600	CmsC	97004	748	C7
SW Beavercrest Ct				
11900	BRTN	97008	625	D6
Beaverdam Rd				
32300	ClkC	98675	419	H2
SW Beaverdam Rd				
12600	BRTN	97005	625	B3
SE Beaverdam St				
41200	CmsC	97055	691	C3
S Beaver Glen Dr				
15500	CmsC	97004	748	A4
15500	CmsC	97045	747	J4
15500	CmsC	97045	748	A4
SE Beaver Lake Dr				
8900	CmsC	97015	687	G1
SW Beaverton Av				
3500	PTLD	97239	626	C2
SW Beaverton Ct				
3500	PTLD	97239	626	C2
SW Beaverton Hwy				
-	PTLD	97221	625	H3
-	PTLD	97221	626	A3
-	PTLD	97225	625	H3
-	PTLD	97239	626	C4
-	WasC	97225	625	H3

STREET
Block City ZIP Map# Grid

SW Beaverton Hwy SR-10
- PTLD 97221 625 H3
- PTLD 97221 626 A3
- PTLD 97225 625 H3
- PTLD 97239 626 C4
- WasC 97225 625 H3
SW Beaverton Creek Ct
15300 BRTN 97006 624 H2
SE Beaverton Creek St
- HBRO 97123 594 A5
SW Beaverton-Hillsdale Hwy
3300 PTLD 97221 626 B4
3300 PTLD 97239 626 B4
6500 PTLD 97221 625 H3
6500 PTLD 97225 625 H3
6500 WasC 97225 625 H3
8100 BRTN 97225 625 F3
9100 WasC 97005 625 E3
9500 BRTN 97005 625 D3
SW Beaverton-Hillsdl Hwy SR-10
6500 PTLD 97221 625 H3
6500 PTLD 97225 625 H3
6500 WasC 97225 625 H3
8100 BRTN 97225 625 F3
9100 WasC 97005 625 E3
9500 BRTN 97005 625 D3
Beaverton-Tigard Hwy
- BRTN - 595 E7
- BRTN - 625 D6
- BRTN - 655 D1
- LKOW - 655 F4
- TGRD - 655 D1
- WasC - 595 E7
- WasC - 625 E1
Beaverton-Tigard Hwy SR-217
- BRTN - 595 E7
- BRTN - 625 E1
- BRTN - 655 D1
- LKOW - 655 F4
- TGRD - 655 F4
- WasC - 595 E7
- WasC - 625 E1
SW Beaverwood Ct
11900 BRTN 97008 625 D6
NW Beck Rd
21500 MthC 97124 534 A1
21500 MthC 97231 534 A1
Becke Ct
40100 SNDY 97055 691 B4
NE Becke Rd
15600 CmsC 97002 745 H2
SW Becker Dr
8700 WasC 97223 625 F5
SW Becket Ct
6700 WasC 97007 624 E5
Becket St
10 LKOW 97035 656 A3
SE Becket St
13400 HPYV 97236 658 B3
SE Beckman Av
11300 MWKE 97222 657 C3
SE Beckman Rd
16500 CmsC 97045 718 B2
SE Beckman Ter
5500 MWKE 97222 657 C3
Becky Av
- CmsC 97022 690 B5
Becky Ct
- CmsC 97022 690 B5
- MCMV 97128 771 A2
SW Becky Ct
7500 WasC 97007 624 E6
Becky Ln
- CmsC 97022 690 B5
57300 ClbC 97053 414 J4
SW Becky Lange Ct
16200 WasC 97223 654 G4
Bedford Ct
1500 LKOW 97034 656 G7
Bedford Dr
19000 ORCY 97045 717 C4
SW Bedford St
12800 KNGC 97224 685 A2
12800 WasC 97224 685 A2
SW Bedstraw Ter
21000 SRWD 97140 684 E5
SE Bee St
- ORCY 97045 717 C1
NE Beebe Rd
15100 ClkC 98604 418 E2
SE Beebee Ct
17700 SNDY 97055 690 J3
NE Beech Av
1800 GSHM 97030 629 C1
2400 GSHM 97030 599 C7
SE Beech Av
100 GSHM 97080 629 C3
S Beech Cir
600 CNLS 97113 592 D5
NE Beech Ct
2200 GSHM 97030 599 C6
13700 PTLD 97230 598 C2
NW Beech Ct
1300 CMAS 98607 568 J4
NE Beech Dr
2600 GSHM 97030 599 C7
SW Beech Dr
4600 BRTN 97005 625 D3
NE Beech Pl
1700 GSHM 97030 629 C1
SE Beech Pl
1400 GSHM 97080 629 C4
SW Beech Rd
500 ECDA 97023 750 B4
Beech St
- ClbC 97056 474 A4
300 VCVR 98661 537 A6
N Beech St
10 PTLD 97212 596 G2
10 PTLD 97227 596 F2
NE Beech St
10 PTLD 97212 596 H2
10 PTLD 97227 596 G2
4200 PTLD 97212 597 B2
5000 PTLD 97213 597 C2
9900 MWDP 97220 597 H2
9900 PTLD 97220 597 H2
12200 PTLD 97220 598 A2
15700 PTLD 97230 598 E2
NW Beech St
1500 CMAS 98607 568 J3

S Beech St
1200 CNLS 97113 592 E5
SE Beech St
1000 DNDE 97115 742 J4
13300 CmsC 97222 657 A5
SE Beechcroft Ter
- CmsC 97267 657 E6
Beecher Av
- MthC 97231 535 A5
SE Beechnut Dr
35900 CmsC 97023 720 F7
SW Beechwood Av
2300 WasC 97005 625 E4
2300 WasC 97225 625 D4
Beechwood St
400 WDLD 98674 385 J1
400 WDLD 98674 386 A1
SW Beef Bend Rd
11400 KNGC 97224 655 B7
11400 TGRD 97224 655 B7
11600 WasC 97224 655 B7
13700 WasC 97224 654 J7
14300 WasC 97224 684 F1
15700 WasC 97140 684 G1
NW Beeler Dr
23500 WasC 97124 563 J1
23500 WasC 97124 564 A1
Beemer Wy
14000 ORCY 97045 687 F6
Beers Av
17100 SNDY 97055 690 J2
SE Beers Av
17000 CmsC 97055 690 J2
17000 SNDY 97055 690 J2
Begonia Av
- PTLD 97217 536 E7
Begonia Rd
- CmsC 97023 750 B4
SE Bel Air Dr
15600 DAMA 97009 658 F7
15600 DAMA 97009 688 F1
15600 DAMA 97015 658 F7
15600 HPYV 97015 658 F7
SW Bel-Aire Dr
7000 BRTN 97008 625 C6
SW Bel-Aire Ln
11100 BRTN 97008 625 C6
NW Belgium Ct
31800 NPNS 97133 563 A1
NW Belgrave Av
- PTLD 97210 596 A3
N Belknap Av
7800 PTLD 97217 566 D4
Belknap Dr
3400 WLIN 97068 686 H7
SE Bell Av
9100 CmsC 97206 627 E7
9100 CmsC 97206 657 E1
9100 CmsC 97222 657 E1
SW Bell Ct
12200 TGRD 97223 655 B4
NE Bell Dr
1900 PTLD 97220 597 H4
E Bell Rd
32400 MthC 97019 600 D6
NE Bell Rd
24900 ClkC 98604 449 E4
26100 YmhC 97132 713 D3
28900 YmhC 97140 713 G3
SW Bell Rd
12500 CmsC 97070 745 A1
12500 CmsC 97140 745 A1
12900 CmsC 97070 715 A7
12900 CmsC 97140 714 J7
12900 CmsC 97140 715 A7
Bell St
37800 SNDY 97055 690 H1
SE Bell St
37800 CmsC 97055 690 H1
37800 SNDY 97055 690 H1
Bella St
1400 WLIN 97068 687 C6
SW Bella Ter
1300 WasC 97006 594 D7
Bellamy Wy
12700 ORCY 97045 717 C5
NW Bella Vista Av
10 GSHM 97080 629 A2
1600 GSHM 97030 629 A1
SE Bella Vista Av
- VCVR 98683 568 C2
SW Bella Vista Av
1300 GSHM 97080 629 A4
3200 GSHM 97080 628 J6
SE Bella Vista Cir
14000 VCVR 98683 568 B2
NW Bella Vista Ct
1500 GSHM 97030 629 A1
SW Bella Vista Ct
19700 WasC 97007 624 D6
NW Bella Vista Dr
400 GSHM 97030 629 A2
32700 SPSE 97056 444 D6
SW Bella Vista Ln
200 GSHM 97080 629 A3
SE Bella Vista Lp
2600 VCVR 98683 568 C2
NW Bella Vista Pl
800 GSHM 97030 628 J2
800 GSHM 97030 629 A2
SE Bella Vista Pl
3300 VCVR 98683 568 C3
SW Bella Vista Pl
600 GSHM 97080 629 A3
SE Bella Vista Rd
1900 VCVR 98683 568 C2
Bellcrest Rd
32700 ClbC 97056 444 D6
Belle Ct
100 ORCY 97045 717 C2
400 CBAC 97018 385 C3
NW Belle Ct
14100 WasC 97229 595 A3
SE Belle Ct
3300 PTLD 97214 597 A6
NW Belle Pl
14300 WasC 97006 594 J3
Belle Lake Rd
- CmsC 97049 724 H7
SE Belle Oak Av
3800 HBRO 97123 623 G2
SE Belle Oak Ct
3700 HBRO 97123 623 G2
Bellevue Av
- CmsC 97013 776 A1

Bellevue Av
100 GLDS 97027 687 D4
100 ORCY 97045 717 C2
NE Bellevue Av
6800 PTLD 97211 566 H5
Bellevue Ct
2900 WLIN 97068 686 H4
Bellevue Ter
2400 WLIN 97068 686 H5
Bellevue Wy
19700 WLIN 97068 686 H4
SW Bellflower St
8500 TGRD 97224 655 E7
NW Bellingham Ct
41700 BNKS 97106 531 H5
N Bellingham St
- PTLD 97203 565 J1
- PTLD 97203 566 A2
SE Bell Maple Dr
34800 CmsC 97009 660 F4
SE Belmont Av
- PTLD 97215 597 E7
SE Belmont Ct
5000 HBRO 97123 593 H7
22800 DAMA 97009 659 C7
SW Belmont Dr
7500 BRTN 97008 625 C6
SE Belmont St
500 PTLD 97214 596 H6
2800 PTLD 97214 597 A6
4000 PTLD 97215 597 D6
SW Belmont Ter
11600 BRTN 97008 625 C6
Belmont Wy
6200 WLIN 97068 686 H5
Belmore Av
17900 CmsC 97035 685 H2
17900 LKOW 97035 685 J2
Belmore Ct
18000 CmsC 97035 685 H2
SE Belmore Hts
15400 PTLD 97236 628 D6
SE Belmore St
15000 PTLD 97236 628 D6
NE Belnap Ct
4400 HBRO 97124 593 H4
SE Belnap Ct
11100 WNVL 97070 745 C2
Belton Rd
10 STHN 97051 385 D5
SW Belton Rd
17400 WasC 97140 684 A2
SW Belvidere Pl
11800 WasC 97225 595 C6
SE Bel View Ln
17300 DAMA 97009 658 F7
17300 DAMA 97015 658 F7
17300 HPYV 97015 658 F7
Ben Ct
6200 GLDS 97027 687 D3
SW Benaroya Ct
17800 WasC 97007 624 F7
NW Benburb Ln
11600 WasC 97229 595 C3
SW Benchview Pl
13600 TGRD 97223 655 A5
SW Benchview Ter
13200 TGRD 97223 655 A5
13800 TGRD 97223 654 J6
13900 TGRD 97224 654 J5
14200 WasC 97224 654 J6
E Benchwood Ln
23700 CmsC 97049 724 D3
NW Bendemeer Rd
20800 WasC 97124 564 C5
21400 HBRO 97124 564 B5
Benfield Av
18200 CmsC 97035 685 H2
19000 LKOW 97035 685 H3
19200 RVGR 97035 685 H3
Benfield Ct
5800 CmsC 97035 685 H3
NW Benfield Dr
1200 WasC 97229 595 F4
1500 PTLD 97229 595 E4
NE Benfield Rd
37000 MthC 97019 600 H5
SW Benham Ct
6800 WasC 97225 595 H7
SW Benish St
13400 TGRD 97223 655 A4
NW Benita Dr
3600 CMAS 98607 569 B1
NW Benita St
2900 CMAS 98607 569 B2
NE Benjamin Av
8900 PTLD 97220 597 G2
NW Benjamin Ct
14600 WasC 97229 594 J1
SE Benjamin Ct
3200 TDLE 97060 599 J7
Benjamin Ln
59300 ClbC 97051 414 H1
NE Benjamin Rd
29000 YmhC 97132 713 G5
Bennett Rd
33500 ClbC 97053 414 F4
NE Bennett Rd
26900 ClkC 98604 417 D7
NE Bennett St
10 PTLD 97220 597 J1
11200 PTLD 97220 598 A1
NW Bennett St
22800 HBRO 97124 563 J7
22800 HBRO 97124 564 A7
Bennington Ct
19700 WLIN 97068 686 G4
SW Bennington Dr
2900 PTLD 97205 596 B6
NW Benny Dr
14600 WasC 97229 564 J6
NW Benson Ct
9100 PTLD 97229 595 F3
NW Benson Ln
2400 PTLD 97229 595 F3
NW Benson St
8700 PTLD 97229 595 F3
SE Bentley St
3200 HBRO 97123 593 G6
4300 WasC 97123 593 G6
SW Bently Ct
6300 PTLD 97219 625 H6
N Benton Av
1500 PTLD 97227 596 E4

NE Benton Dr
8300 VCVR 98662 537 F2
SW Benton Ln
7600 BRTN 97007 624 J1
NW Benton St
1600 CMAS 98607 569 E3
Bents Ct NE
21500 MrnC 97002 774 J3
21500 MrnC 97002 775 A3
Bents Rd NE
21800 MrnC 97002 775 A1
22700 MrnC 97002 745 A7
23000 MrnC 97002 744 J7
Benz Rd
200 DNDE 97115 742 J2
200 YmhC 97115 742 J2
SW Benz Farm Ct
2200 WasC 97225 625 H1
SW Benz Park Ct
7200 BRTN 97225 625 G1
SW Benz Park Dr
7100 BRTN 97225 625 G1
7100 WasC 97225 625 G1
SW Berea Dr
13600 TGRD 97223 655 D5
SW Berg Ct
18200 WasC 97006 624 E1
S Berg Pkwy
100 CNBY 97013 746 B7
1100 CNBY 97013 776 B1
Berg Rd
33500 ClbC 97053 414 F7
Bergan St
34300 ClbC 97053 414 G7
SW Berger Ct
18700 WasC 97007 624 E2
Bergeron Ct
1800 VCVR 98661 537 C4
NW Bergeron Ct
1400 GSHM 97030 629 A2
SE Berghammer St
16700 CmsC 97267 687 B1
Bergis Rd
300 CmsC 97034 686 E2
300 LKOW 97034 686 E2
Bergis Farm Dr
17300 CmsC 97034 686 F1
17300 LKOW 97034 686 F1
N Berkeley Av
9500 PTLD 97203 566 A3
SW Berkeley Ln
17000 BRTN 97006 594 G7
17000 WasC 97006 594 F7
SE Berkeley Pl
2800 PTLD 97202 627 A7
E Berkeley St
800 GLDS 97027 687 E4
W Berkeley St
100 GLDS 97027 687 D5
Berkeley Wy
5100 VCVR 98661 537 C5
SE Berkeley Wy
- PTLD 97202 627 B7
- PTLD 97222 627 B7
Berkley Av
100 MOLA 97038 837 E2
SE Berkshire Av
14500 CmsC 97015 658 D7
SW Berkshire Pl
10900 WasC 97225 625 C1
SW Berkshire St
10700 BRTN 97225 625 D1
10700 WasC 97225 625 D1
11000 BRTN 97225 595 C7
11000 WasC 97225 595 C7
NE Berlin Rd
24500 ClkC 98604 449 E5
NW Bermar Ln
9600 WasC 97229 595 E4
SW Bermuda Ct
20400 WasC 97007 624 C4
NW Bermuda St
- PTLD 97210 596 A4
SW Bernard Dr
4300 PTLD 97239 626 D3
NW Bernard Pl
17300 BRTN 97006 594 F5
Bernard St
4200 LKOW 97035 686 A2
20200 STPL 97137 773 B6
Bernards St NE
19600 MrnC 97137 773 C6
SE Bernet Dr
33800 SPSE 97056 474 F2
SW Bernhardt Dr
19500 WasC 97007 624 D6
SW Bernice Ln
20100 WasC 97007 624 C5
NW Bernie Dr
5900 VCVR 98663 506 E6
6700 VCVR 98665 506 E6
NW Bernietta Ct
16800 WasC 97229 564 G7
Bernini Ct
10 LKOW 97035 656 A4
NE Berry Ln
19100 YmhC 97132 712 E5
SW Berry Ln
8500 WasC 97007 624 F7
NE Berry Rd
23900 ClkC 98604 449 D4
NW Berry Creek Rd
13200 YmhC 97128 770 B1
SW Berryessa Pl
12200 TDLE 97060 599 E5
SW Berryhill Ct
8000 BRTN 97008 625 B7
SW Berryhill Ln
8300 BRTN 97008 625 B7
SE Berryland Cir
900 TDLE 97060 629 G1
NW Bert Dr
6600 WasC 97116 561 C4
Berta Dr
13000 ORCY 97045 717 D4
SW Bertha Av
4100 PTLD 97239 626 C2
SW Bertha Blvd
1000 PTLD 97219 626 D5
2200 PTLD 97239 626 C4
SW Bertha Ct
6300 PTLD 97219 626 D5
6300 PTLD 97239 626 D5
SW Berthold St
13100 BRTN 97005 625 A4

Bertley Lp
- LKOW 97035 655 J5
S Bertsinger Rd
2100 RDGF 98642 416 B7
Berwick Ct
10 MOLA 97038 807 E7
700 LKOW 97034 656 F6
Berwick Rd
10 LKOW 97034 656 E6
SW Beryl Ct
15000 BRTN 97007 624 H7
NE Beryl Ter
100 PTLD 97220 597 G5
NE Beta Dr
- GSHM 97030 599 F7
SE Beta St
2300 MWKE 97222 656 J1
NW Bethany Blvd
1500 BRTN 97006 594 H4
1500 WasC 97006 594 H4
3000 WasC 97229 594 H2
4800 WasC 97229 564 H7
NW Bethany Ct
16200 BRTN 97006 594 G4
16200 WasC 97006 594 G4
SE Bethany Dr
11200 HPYV 97236 658 A3
SW Bethel Ct
18400 WasC 97007 624 B6
SE Bethesda Dr
4500 GSHM 97080 629 B7
SE Bethesda Pl
4100 GSHM 97080 629 B7
SW Betts Av
4500 BRTN 97005 625 B3
SW Betts Ct
12100 BRTN 97008 625 D6
NE Betts Rd
13100 ClkC 98686 477 A7
SW Betty's Pl
- WasC 97006 594 D7
SE Betz Dr
7400 CmsC 97267 657 E7
NW Beuhla Vista Ter
2600 PTLD 97210 596 C5
Beutel Rd
10400 CmsC 97045 716 J5
11200 ORCY 97045 716 H4
SW Beveland Rd
7300 TGRD 97223 655 G4
SW Beveland St
6900 TGRD 97223 655 G4
SW Beverly Ct
5400 BRTN 97005 625 A4
Beverly Dr
100 ORCY 97045 717 D3
1300 GLDS 97027 687 D3
Beverly Ln
300 GLDS 97027 687 D3
SE Beverly Ln
6200 CmsC 97222 657 D2
7400 HBRO 97123 594 B7
7400 WasC 97123 594 B7
SW Beverly Beach Ct
15500 BRTN 97007 624 H5
NE Bevin Rd
28100 ClkC 98604 417 D6
SE Bevington Av
14300 CmsC 97267 657 E6
Bexhill St
1100 WLIN 97068 716 F2
SW Bexley Ln
12500 WasC 97224 655 B7
SE Bianca St
1000 HBRO 97123 593 D7
Bickel Ct
18200 LKOW 97035 685 J2
Bickford St
38300 SNDY 97055 690 J3
Bickner St
800 LKOW 97034 656 F7
1300 LKOW 97034 686 F1
SE Biddle Rd
3200 VCVR 98683 568 A2
NW Bidwell Rd
9700 WasC 97124 563 J2
SE Bidwell St
700 PTLD 97202 626 H6
NW Big Fir Cir
11900 WasC 97229 595 C3
NW Big Fir Ct
12100 WasC 97229 595 C3
NE Big Fir Ln
20800 YmhC 97115 712 G7
SW Big Fir Rd
24700 CmsC 97068 716 E3
SW Biggi Ter
5600 BRTN 97005 625 B4
SW Bigleaf Dr
13200 TGRD 97223 655 B5
S Big Rock Lp
15000 CmsC 97042 777 H7
Big Sandy Dam Rd
- CmsC 97055 692 B3
S Big Sky Wy
17400 CmsC 97045 748 C1
NE Big Tree Creek Rd
30200 ClkC 98675 419 H4
SW Biles Ln
11700 WasC 97006 594 F7
Bilford Ln
4900 LKOW 97035 655 J5
NE Billingher Dr
10 PTLD 97220 597 G5
Billings Ct
1200 VCVR 98661 537 D5
Bills St
800 MCMV 97128 770 G5
SW Bills St
200 MCMV 97128 770 G5
SE Bilquist Cir
15900 CmsC 97267 657 E7
SE Bilsher Ct
15200 CmsC 97267 657 C7
Bilyeu Av
- CmsC 97023 719 C3
Bina Dr
200 NWBG 97132 713 E7
200 YmhC 97132 713 E7
SW Bindale Ct
17000 DRHM 97224 685 G2
SW Binford Av
1500 GSHM 97080 628 J4
SW Binford Pl
2300 GSHM 97080 628 J5

SW Binford Wy
3200 GSHM 97080 628 J6
SW Binford Lake Pkwy
1300 GSHM 97080 629 A5
1500 GSHM 97080 628 H4
SW Bingo Ln
20600 WasC 97006 594 C5
Birch
- CmsC 97015 657 H7
Birch Av
- PTLD 97217 536 E6
100 WDVL 97060 599 D4
50600 ClbC 97056 474 E4
E Birch Av
400 LCTR 98629 386 H7
NW Birch Av
5400 HBRO 97124 563 H6
5400 WasC 97124 563 H6
S Birch Av
- YCLT 98675 419 F1
SE Birch Av
3100 CmsC 97267 657 A6
SW Birch Av
5200 BRTN 97005 625 E4
S Birch Ct
1300 CNBY 97013 776 C1
Birch Ln
1900 NWBG 97132 713 D6
NE Birch Ln
- ClkC 98607 539 F6
Birch St
- WasC 97006 594 C5
1000 FTGV 97116 591 J5
3700 WHGL 98671 570 D3
N Birch St
800 CNBY 97013 746 B5
1500 CmsC 97013 746 B4
NE Birch St
1900 CMAS 98607 569 E3
6000 HBRO 97124 593 J4
6200 HBRO 97124 594 B3
6400 WasC 97124 594 A4
NW Birch St
500 MCMV 97128 770 G4
4300 VCVR 98660 536 F1
22100 HBRO 97124 594 A4
22100 WasC 97124 594 A4
S Birch St
400 CNBY 97013 746 B7
SE Birch St
100 CMAS 98607 569 E5
1300 PTLD 97214 626 H1
SW Birch St
100 DNDE 97115 742 H2
8500 WasC 97223 655 F1
Birch Tr
- BRTN 97005 625 C2
NE Birchaire Ln
800 HBRO 97124 593 D3
NE Birchwood Cir
500 HBRO 97124 593 D4
Birchwood Dr
1000 ORCY 97045 717 B3
NE Birchwood Dr
400 HBRO 97124 593 C4
NE Birchwood Ln
400 HBRO 97124 593 D4
NE Birchwood Pl
500 HBRO 97124 593 D4
NE Birchwood Rd
300 HBRO 97124 593 D4
SW Birchwood Rd
8000 BRTN 97225 625 F2
8000 WasC 97225 625 G2
NE Birchwood Ter
400 HBRO 97124 593 C4
NE Bird Rd
52300 ClbC 97056 444 G7
52300 ClbC 97056 474 G1
52300 SPSE 97056 474 G1
Bird Bill Ct
4100 LKOW 97035 656 A5
NE Birdhaven Lp
4200 YmhC 97132 713 G5
SW Birdie Dr
9000 WasC 97113 623 A7
E Birdie Ln
68500 CmsC 97067 724 C6
NW Birdie Ln
16000 WasC 97229 594 H1
NW Birdsdale Av
10 GSHM 97030 628 J1
10 GSHM 97080 628 J2
1600 GSHM 97030 598 J7
SW Birdsdale Ct
1400 GSHM 97080 628 J4
SW Birdsdale Dr
10 GSHM 97030 628 J2
10 GSHM 97080 628 J3
600 GSHM 97080 629 A3
SW Birdsdale Pl
1900 GSHM 97080 628 J5
SW Birdshill Ct
7800 WasC 97223 625 G6
SW Birdshill Rd
100 CmsC 97219 656 G4
Bird Song Wy
5800 CmsC 97267 687 C3
5800 GLDS 97027 687 C3
SW Birdsview Ln
12800 TGRD 97224 655 A6
SE Birk St
2300 MWKE 97222 656 J4
NW Birkendene St
2200 PTLD 97229 595 E2
NE Birkshire Ct
1200 HBRO 97124 593 E2
Birmingham Wy
300 VCVR 98664 537 E7
NW Bishop Rd
12000 WasC 97124 534 A6
SE Bittern Wy
9500 HPYV 97236 658 C1
Bittner St
4600 WLIN 97068 687 A7
S Bitz Ln
26700 CmsC 97042 777 G5
SE Bixel St
6800 CmsC 97267 657 D7
Bjerke St
- ORCY 97045 717 A3
NE Bjur Rd
3500 ClkC 98642 417 B7
SE Blackberry Cir
13100 PTLD 97236 628 B6

NE Blackberry Ln
27000 YmhC 97132 713 D3
SE Blackberry Ln
36300 CmsC 97055 690 G7
36300 CmsC 97055 720 G1
SW Blackberry Ln
5600 CmsC 97062 715 H1
16700 WasC 97007 624 G7
Blackberry Hollow Dr
32300 ClbC 97056 474 C4
SW Blackbird Dr
15800 BRTN 97007 654 G3
NE Blackburn Rd
7600 YmhC 97148 711 D3
NE Blackcap Ln
9200 YmhC 97132 744 A2
NW Blackcomb Dr
3200 WasC 97229 594 J2
SW Black Diamond Wy
10600 TGRD 97223 655 D2
NW Blackfield Ln
11400 WasC 97229 595 C2
SW Blackfoot Dr
21700 TLTN 97062 685 E6
Black Forest Ct
4500 LKOW 97035 686 A1
NW Blackhawk Dr
11200 WasC 97229 595 C2
N Blackmore Av
100 YCLT 98675 419 F1
S Blackmore Av
100 YCLT 98675 419 F1
SW Blackoaks Ln
8900 TGRD 97224 655 E6
SW Black Quartz St
15500 BRTN 97007 624 G2
SE Blackstone Av
12500 HPYV 97236 658 E5
SW Blackstone Dr
15700 BRTN 97007 624 H7
SW Blackstone Ln
3500 PTLD 97239 626 C2
Blackstone Wy
34400 STHN 97051 414 H2
NW Blacktail Dr
17100 WasC 97229 564 F7
NE Blacktail Wy
6600 WasC 97124 594 A5
NW Blackthorne Ln
14600 WasC 97229 594 J2
SW Black Walnut St
12900 TGRD 97223 655 A7
12900 WasC 97224 655 A7
SW Black Walnut Ter
14900 TGRD 97224 655 A6
SE Blackwell Wy
1700 HBRO 97123 623 D1
Blaha Rd
33300 ClbC 97053 414 F3
SW Blaine Av
1400 GSHM 97080 629 B4
SW Blaine Ct
1100 GSHM 97080 629 B4
21500 WasC 97006 594 B7
SE Blaine Dr
12200 CmsC 97015 658 A6
SW Blaine Dr
1600 WasC 97006 594 C7
NW Blaine Ln
200 GSHM 97030 629 B2
SW Blaine Pl
600 GSHM 97080 629 B3
N Blaine St
100 NWBG 97132 713 C7
S Blaine St
100 NWBG 97132 713 C7
300 NWBG 97132 743 C1
900 YmhC 97132 743 C1
SE Blaine St
6700 HBRO 97123 594 A7
SW Blaine St
800 MCMV 97128 770 G6
20300 WasC 97006 594 C7
21700 HBRO 97123 594 B7
SW Blaine Ter
19000 WasC 97006 594 E7
NW Blair Ln
33000 SPSE 97056 444 E6
NE Blair Rd
10 ClkC 98671 539 H6
1100 ClkC 98607 539 H5
SE Blair Rd
10 ClkC 98671 539 J7
10 ClkC 98671 540 A7
900 ClkC 98671 570 A1
SE Blair St
800 VCVR 98661 537 D7
SE Blaire St
8600 CmsC 97236 657 F2
SE Blairmont Dr
1400 VCVR 98683 568 C1
Blake Ct NE
10800 DNLD 97020 774 G5
SE Blake Pl
3300 TDLE 97060 599 G7
SW Blake St
8200 TLTN 97062 685 E6
10600 WasC 97062 685 C6
NW Blakely Ln
15000 WasC 97229 564 J7
SW Blakeney Ct
11900 BRTN 97008 625 C6
SW Blakeney St
11100 BRTN 97008 625 C6
SW Blamon Ct
18800 WasC 97007 624 E2
SW Blamon St
19100 WasC 97007 624 D2
NE Blanchard Ln
4200 YmhC 97114 742 E7
4200 YmhC 97115 742 E7
Blanchard St
300 ORCY 97045 717 A2
SE Blanchard St
1400 HBRO 97123 623 D1
Blanchet Av NE
3300 MrnC 97137 772 J5
3300 MrnC 97137 773 A5
3300 STPL 97137 773 A5
SW Blanco Pl
16900 BRTN 97007 624 F5
Bland Cir
22800 WLIN 97068 686 G7
23000 CmsC 97068 686 G7

Portland Street Index

STREET
Block City ZIP Map# Grid

Bland Cir
- WLIN 97068 686 G7
Blandena St
10 PTLD 97211 596 G1
200 PTLD 97217 596 F1
Blandford Dr
- VCVR 98661 537 C5
NW Blanding St
- PTLD 97231 565 E4
NW Blandy Ter
- WasC 97229 594 H1
Blanford Dr
100 VCVR 98661 537 B6
Blankenship Rd
1100 WLIN 97068 716 F1
SE Blanton St
16600 CmsC 97267 687 A1
SW Blanton St
18500 WasC 97007 624 D2
SE Blatner Pl
6700 CmsC 97267 657 D6
SE Blay Rd
27500 CmsC 97022 719 G2
SE Blaze Dr
13300 HPYV 97236 658 B3
NW Blaze Ter
15000 WasC 97006 594 J5
Blazer Tr
13500 LKOW 97035 656 A4
NW Bledsoe Creek Ln
39400 WasC 97106 532 B2
Blinkhorn Wy
7700 CmsC 97027 687 E2
SE Bliss Ct
3800 HBRO 97123 623 E2
NW Bliss Rd
1800 ClkC 98685 476 D5
N Bliss St
8200 PTLD 97203 565 H1
Bloch Ter
10 LKOW 97035 656 B4
N Bloss Av
10400 PTLD 97203 566 A2
SE Blossom Av
16600 CmsC 97267 687 F1
NE Blossom Dr
1200 MCMV 97128 771 C4
1200 YmhC 97128 771 C4
NE Blossom Ln
33800 SPSE 97056 444 F7
NW Blossom Ln
42100 WasC 97106 531 J1
SE Blossom St
5800 HBRO 97123 593 J7
NE Blossom Hill Rd
- FRVW 97024 599 B3
S Blount Rd
23200 CmsC 97013 746 G6
SW Bluebell Ln
12800 BRTN 97008 625 A6
Blueberry Ln
59300 ClbC 97051 414 C1
59300 ClbC 97053 414 C1
NE Blueberry Ln
5000 ClkC 98686 507 C1
SW Blue Bill Ln
12800 BRTN 97007 654 F4
SE Bluebird Dr
2900 HBRO 97123 623 E1
S Bluebird Ln
20500 CmsC 97023 719 D7
20500 CmsC 97023 749 D1
SE Blue Bird St
- MWKE 97222 656 J3
SE Bluebird St
1900 MWKE 97222 656 H3
NE Bluebird Hill Ln
14200 YmhC 97114 741 J5
14200 YmhC 97114 742 A5
SE Bluebonnet Ct
2500 HBRO 97123 623 E1
SW Blue Goose Ln
16100 BRTN 97007 654 G4
Bluegrass Cir
19900 WLIN 97068 686 H4
NE Bluegrass Dr
15500 VCVR 98684 538 D6
S Bluegrass Ln
23000 CmsC 97023 749 F2
NW Bluegrass Pl
3600 WasC 97229 595 A2
Bluegrass Wy
2900 WLIN 97068 686 H4
SW Blue Gum Ct
13600 TGRD 97223 655 A5
Blue Heron Ct
17500 LKOW 97034 686 B1
Blue Heron Ct NE
23900 MrnC 97002 744 H5
NE Blue Heron Ct
4500 YmhC 97132 713 G5
9400 PTLD 97211 566 J3
Blue Heron Dr
17400 LKOW 97034 686 B2
NE Blue Heron Dr
1500 PTLD 97211 566 J3
Blue Heron Ln NE
11500 MrnC 97002 744 H5
SW Blue Heron Pl
12700 TGRD 97223 655 B4
Blue Heron Rd
17100 LKOW 97034 686 B1
Blue Heron Wy
17500 LKOW 97034 686 B2
NE Blue Heron Shores Dr
20100 FRVW 97024 598 J2
20100 FRVW 97230 598 J2
Blue Jay Av
200 FTGV 97116 591 F3
Blue Jay Ln
59600 ClbC 97051 384 G7
E Blue Jay Ln
21200 CmsC 97011 693 F7
SE Blue Jay Ln
9100 CmsC 97009 660 J2
Blue Lake Ct NE
13400 MrnC 97002 775 C7
NE Blue Lake Rd
3200 TDLE 97060 599 B3
4000 FRVW 97024 599 B2
NW Blue Pointe Ln
7600 PTLD 97229 595 G4
NW Blueridge Ct
500 BRTN 97006 594 G5
Blue Ridge Dr
12200 ORCY 97045 717 B4
NW Blueridge Dr
15600 BRTN 97006 594 H5
SE Blue Ridge Dr
23200 DAMA 97009 659 C7
Bluesky Ter
- PTLD 97218 597 D1
SW Blue Spruce Ct
13600 WasC 97224 655 A7
SW Bluestem Ln
13900 TGRD 97223 654 J3
SW Bluestone Ct
15000 BRTN 97007 654 H1
S Blue Vista Dr
14900 CmsC 97045 717 G2
SE Bluff Ct
33000 CmsC 97009 660 D1
SE Bluff Dr
12000 CmsC 97015 658 A7
Bluff Rd
17500 SNDY 97055 690 J3
SE Bluff Rd
11000 CmsC 97055 660 H4
13500 SNDY 97055 660 J7
13700 CmsC 97222 656 H5
13700 CmsC 97267 656 H5
15000 SNDY 97055 690 J2
30100 MthC 97080 630 B7
31700 MthC 97080 660 C1
32300 CmsC 97009 660 D1
N Bluff St
5300 PTLD 97203 566 A5
S Bluff St
100 ORCY 97045 717 B1
S Bluhm Rd
22900 CmsC 97004 748 E6
Blume Ln
400 YmhC 97132 713 B6
S Blundell Rd
24600 CmsC 97013 776 G2
NW Blyths Rd
- PTLD 97210 595 J2
SE Boardman Av
4000 CmsC 97267 687 B2
SE Boardman Ct
17400 CmsC 97267 687 C2
Boardwalk Av
1200 MOLA 97038 807 C7
Boardwalk St
15700 ORCY 97045 687 E5
SE Bobby Bruce Ln
12600 CmsC 97009 660 D5
NW Bobcat Pl
4500 WasC 97006 594 F3
SW Boberg Rd
28000 WNVL 97070 715 E6
SW Bobolink St
15900 BRTN 97007 654 G3
Bob's Av NE
14800 AURA 97002 775 F4
SE Bob Schumacher Rd
- CmsC 97236 657 G2
- HPYV 97236 657 G4
SE Bobtail Ln
40400 CmsC 97055 691 B2
SW Bobwhite Cir
15400 BRTN 97007 654 H3
SW Bobwhite Pl
11300 BRTN 97007 654 H3
SE Bob White St
1900 MWKE 97222 656 J3
Boca Ratan Dr
1100 LKOW 97034 656 E5
Bodley Ct
18000 SNDY 97055 690 J3
SW Boeckman Rd
6600 CmsC 97070 715 G5
8500 WNVL 97070 715 D5
NE Boehmer St
8400 PTLD 97220 597 G2
SW Bogey Ct
31500 WasC 97113 623 A7
SE Bogle Rd
20700 CmsC 97055 691 A6
S Bogynski Rd
17800 CmsC 97045 718 D6
SW Bohmann Pkwy
8400 WasC 97223 625 E6
SE Bohna Ct
22300 DAMA 97009 659 B5
SE Bohna Park Rd
20800 DAMA 97009 658 J3
20800 DAMA 97009 659 A4
Boise Av
1100 VCVR 98661 537 C5
Boise Ct
4400 VCVR 98661 537 B5
SE Boise Ct
13800 PTLD 97236 628 C3
SE Boise St
800 PTLD 97202 626 H3
3900 PTLD 97202 627 B3
4200 PTLD 97206 627 C3
8000 PTLD 97266 627 F3
11500 PTLD 97266 628 A3
12300 PTLD 97236 628 A3
SE Boitano Rd
36100 CmsC 97055 690 G7
Bo James Ct
18000 CmsC 97045 717 G2
SW Bolds Wy
19600 CmsC 97068 686 D4
NE Bolen St
1500 ClkC 98629 386 F6
NW Bolen St
900 ClkC 98629 386 F6
Bolivar St
10 LKOW 97035 656 A3
10 PTLD 97219 656 A3
SE Bolivar St
16700 DAMA 97009 688 E1
S Bolkan Wy
20200 CmsC 97045 718 D7
SE Bollam Dr
15200 CmsC 97015 658 D6
S Bolland Rd
26000 CmsC 97013 776 C4
SE Bolton Ct
11200 CmsC 97236 657 H3
11200 HPYV 97236 657 H3
Bolton St
1500 WLIN 97068 687 B6
SW Bomar Ct
8700 WasC 97223 625 F7
SW Bomar Ct
8700 WasC 97223 655 F1
SW Bonaire Av
16000 CmsC 97035 655 J7
16000 LKOW 97035 655 J7
SW Bonanza Ct
14600 BRTN 97007 624 J6
NE Bonanza Rd
14000 ClkC 98606 479 C5
SW Bonanza Wy
10300 TGRD 97224 685 D1
SW Bonaventure Ln
8200 TGRD 97224 655 F4
SW Bond Av
3300 PTLD 97239 626 F2
SW Bond St
7600 TGRD 97224 655 F7
NW Boneta Pl
- PTLD 97210 596 A4
Bonita Rd
- TGRD 97224 655 H6
5100 LKOW 97035 655 J6
6100 CmsC 97035 655 H6
SW Bonita Rd
5200 CmsC 97035 655 H6
5200 LKOW 97035 655 J6
6500 TGRD 97224 655 G6
Bonn St
14100 ORCY 97045 687 F6
Bonner Dr
- CmsC 97023 749 B1
- CmsC 97045 749 B1
6000 ClkC 98665 506 G6
Bonnet Dr
4800 WLIN 97068 687 A7
Bonneville Dr
- ClbC 97056 474 D4
NW Bonneville Lp
14600 WasC 97006 594 J3
NW Bonneville Pl
14700 WasC 97006 594 J3
Bonneville Rd
33100 ClbC 97056 474 E4
Bonney Ln
59900 ClbC 97051 385 A7
59900 STHN 97051 385 A7
NE Bonnie Dr
4100 ClkC 98686 507 B3
Bonnie Ln
1400 FTGV 97116 591 H3
2000 WasC 97116 591 J3
SW Bonnie Ln
51900 ClbC 97056 474 D1
51900 SPSE 97056 474 D1
SE Bonnie Wy
14100 CmsC 97267 657 E6
SW Bonnie Brae Ct
13700 BRTN 97005 625 A4
Bonniebrae Dr
1300 LKOW 97034 656 E4
SW Bonnie Brae Dr
9800 BRTN 97008 625 E6
9800 WasC 97008 625 E6
SW Bonnie Brae St
13400 BRTN 97005 625 A4
14100 BRTN 97005 624 J4
14400 BRTN 97007 624 J4
SW Bonnie Jean Pl
1600 MCMV 97128 770 F7
SE Bonnie Lure Dr
23600 CmsC 97022 719 H2
SW Bonnie Meadow Ln
18600 WasC 97006 594 E7
SE Bonny Jean Wy
8500 CmsC 97015 657 F7
SW Booker Ct
- WasC 97006 594 C6
SW Boom Ln
52000 SPSE 97056 474 D1
Boomer Lp
32700 ClbC 97056 444 D6
S Boone Ct
18000 CmsC 97004 748 D4
Boones Wy
14900 LKOW 97035 656 B6
SW Boones Bend Dr
11600 BRTN 97008 655 C2
11900 TGRD 97008 655 B2
11900 TGRD 97223 655 B2
SW Boones Bend Rd
31000 WNVL 97070 745 F3
NE Boones Ferry Lndg
26100 CmsC 97002 745 D2
Boones Ferry Rd
12300 MthC 97219 656 C3
12300 PTLD 97034 656 C3
12300 PTLD 97035 656 C3
12300 PTLD 97219 656 C3
12700 LKOW 97034 656 B5
12700 LKOW 97035 656 B5
12900 CmsC 97034 656 C5
Boones Ferry Rd NE
- CmsC 97002 745 D7
19200 MrnC 97002 775 C4
19200 MrnC 97032 775 C4
NE Boones Ferry Rd
23500 CmsC 97002 745 D3
SW Boones Ferry Rd
8500 PTLD 97219 626 E7
9200 PTLD 97219 656 E1
12200 MthC 97034 656 D3
12200 MthC 97219 656 D3
12200 PTLD 97034 656 D3
12200 PTLD 97035 656 D3
18000 DRHM 97224 685 F3
18000 TLTN 97224 685 F3
20300 TLTN 97062 685 E7
22000 WasC 97062 685 E7
23000 TLTN 97062 715 E1
23000 WasC 97062 715 E1
24400 WasC 97140 715 E2
24400 WNVL 97140 715 E2
25400 WNVL 97070 715 E4
30000 WNVL 97070 745 D1
SE Booth Bend Rd
300 YmhC 97128 770 H7
500 MCMV 97128 770 G7
W Booth Bend Rd
100 MCMV 97128 770 H7
SW Borchers Dr
- WasC 97140 684 G5
20400 SRWD 97140 684 G5
SW Bordeaux Ct
- WNVL 97070 745 H2
NW Bordeaux Ln
14200 WasC 97229 595 A2
SE Border Ln
400 MCMV 97128 770 H7
SW Border Wy
2300 GSHM 97080 628 G5
SW Borders St
8700 WasC 97223 655 E1
SE Borges Rd
19100 DAMA 97009 658 J2
19100 DAMA 97009 659 B2
NE Borin Rd
38400 ClkC 98671 540 J6
SW Borland Rd
- WLIN 97068 716 E1
400 CmsC 97068 686 D7
400 CmsC 97068 716 E1
1500 CmsC 97062 686 A5
3600 TLTN 97062 686 A5
4500 CmsC 97062 685 J5
4500 TLTN 97062 685 J5
SE Bornstedt Rd
18900 CmsC 97055 690 J6
18900 SNDY 97055 690 J6
21700 CmsC 97055 691 A7
SW Borsch Ln
4700 PTLD 97219 626 A6
N Borthwick Av
3100 PTLD 97227 596 F1
4500 PTLD 97217 596 F1
8200 PTLD 97217 566 F4
E Borthwick St
20100 CmsC 97011 693 G6
SW Borwick Rd
7300 HBRO 97123 594 A6
7300 HBRO 97124 594 A6
7300 WasC 97124 594 B6
SE Borwick St
6500 HBRO 97123 594 A6
SW Bosky Dell Ln
23100 CmsC 97068 716 E1
SE Boss Ln
12400 MWKE 97222 657 B4
N Boston Av
7000 PTLD 97217 566 E5
SW Boston Wy
400 WasC 97006 594 G7
Boston House East
- PTLD 97215 597 C7
SE Botsford Dr
- PTLD 97202 627 A4
Botticelli St
3800 LKOW 97035 656 A5
Botticelli Villa
10 LKOW 97035 656 D5
SW Bouchaine Ct
7200 WNVL 97070 715 F6
SW Bouchaine St
7000 WNVL 97070 715 G6
SW Boucher Ct
18800 WasC 97006 594 E6
SW Boucher Pl
19200 WasC 97006 594 E6
Boulder Av
9400 VCVR 98664 537 G6
Boulder Ct
34600 STHN 97051 414 H2
E Boulder Ct
65000 CmsC 97011 723 H1
S Boulder Dr
15600 CmsC 97042 777 J7
SW Boulder Ln
19500 WasC 97007 624 C6
SE Boulder Creek Ct
8500 HPYV 97236 628 D7
E Boulder Creek Ln
62800 CmsC 97011 693 F6
NE Boulder Creek Rd
4800 ClkC 98607 540 F1
SE Boulevard Wy
200 ECDA 97023 750 B4
SW Boundary Ct
10 PTLD 97239 626 F4
SW Boundary St
1800 PTLD 97239 626 C4
4800 PTLD 97221 626 A3
5400 PTLD 97221 625 J3
6300 WasC 97225 625 H3
SW Bouneff St
13000 TGRD 97223 655 A4
N Bowdoin St
5000 PTLD 97203 566 A4
SW Bowerman Dr
10 WasC 97005 594 J7
Bowling Alley Ln
- STHN 97051 415 A2
SW Bowman Ct
15500 SRWD 97140 714 G1
SW Bowman Ln
15800 SRWD 97140 714 G1
SE Bowman St
4200 CmsC 97222 657 B5
4200 MWKE 97222 657 B5
E Bowmans Cir
- CmsC 97067 724 C5
SW Bowmont Ln
11600 BRTN 97225 595 C7
11600 WasC 97225 595 C7
SW Bowmont St
11600 WasC 97225 595 C7
SW Boxelder St
13800 TGRD 97223 654 J5
SW Boxwood Ct
11100 TGRD 97223 655 C2
Boyd Ln
2600 FTGV 97116 592 A3
2600 WasC 97116 592 A3
NE Boyd Rd
22800 ClkC 98604 449 C4
SE Boyd St
2700 MWKE 97222 627 A7
SE Boyer Rd
8200 CmsC 97222 657 F2
8200 CmsC 97236 657 F2
Boynton St
12200 ORCY 97045 717 B4
SE Boysen Ln
600 DNDE 97115 742 J4
Bozarth Av
10 WDLD 98674 385 J2
SE Brackenbush Rd
14700 CmsC 97015 658 C6
SW Brackenfern Ct
15100 SRWD 97140 714 H1
SW Brackenwood Ln
20400 WasC 97006 594 C6
SE Brackett Ln
20000 CmsC 97022 689 J5
SW Bradbury Ct
6500 TGRD 97224 685 H1
6500 TLTN 97035 685 H1
6500 TLTN 97224 685 H1
Braden Ct
17400 GLDS 97027 687 D2
NE Bradford Dr
26700 ClkC 98682 539 F1
NE Bradford Rd
25900 ClkC 98682 539 E1
27000 ClkC 98607 539 G1
SE Bradford Rd
14900 CmsC 97015 658 D7
N Bradford St
8600 PTLD 97203 565 G3
Bradley Av
33300 ClbC 97053 444 E1
SE Bradley Ct
3500 HBRO 97123 623 F2
SW Bradley Ln
12800 KNGC 97224 685 A2
12800 WasC 97224 685 A2
SW Bradley Pl
9200 BRTN 97008 655 C1
S Bradley Rd
14900 CmsC 97045 688 C6
17000 CmsC 97045 718 B1
Bradley St
100 STHN 97051 385 B7
N Bradley St
- STHN 97051 415 B1
SW Brady Ct
8700 BRTN 97007 624 G7
NW Brady Ln
10000 WasC 97229 595 E4
NW Brady Rd
1100 ClkC 98607 568 J4
1100 CMAS 98607 568 J4
1200 CMAS 98607 569 A3
SE Brady Rd
19200 ClkC 98607 568 H4
SE Brae St
4200 CmsC 97222 657 B5
4200 MWKE 97222 657 B5
SW Braeburn Ln
8500 TGRD 97224 655 F7
Braeden Ct
- LKOW 97035 685 J2
Braemar Ct
1500 WLIN 97068 686 G3
SW Brae Mar Ct
2600 PTLD 97201 626 D1
Braemar Dr
1400 WLIN 97068 686 G3
SE Braemark Ct
11600 CmsC 97015 657 J5
SE Braemark Pl
12800 CmsC 97015 657 J5
SW Braly St
100 MCMV 97128 770 G5
Bramble Ct
1600 NWBG 97132 713 D5
1600 YmhC 97132 713 D5
SE Bramble Ct
14500 CmsC 97267 657 C6
NE Bramble Wy
21600 FRVW 97024 599 B3
SW Bramblewood Ln
20400 WasC 97140 714 B5
Branch Dr
51100 ClbC 97056 474 C3
Branch Rd
32000 ClbC 97056 474 B3
NW Brandberry Dr
16200 WasC 97229 564 G7
SE Brandeis St
9800 CmsC 97015 657 G7
N Brandon Av
7500 PTLD 97217 566 E4
Brandon Dr
400 NWBG 97132 713 C6
Brandon Pl
2100 WLIN 97068 716 E1
Brandow St
11200 ORCY 97045 716 J4
SE Brandt Ct
16400 DAMA 97009 688 E1
Brandt Ln
- ORCY 97045 717 D3
Brandt Lp
- DNLD 97020 774 F5
NW Brandt Pl
3300 WasC 97229 594 F2
Brandt Rd
1000 VCVR 98661 537 B5
NE Brandt Rd
1800 VCVR 98661 537 B4
SW Brandyshire Ct
17300 DRHM 97224 685 E2
NW Brassie Pl
4600 WasC 97229 594 H1
NW Bratton Rd
2900 ClkC 98674 386 C3
SW Bray Ln
- PTLD 97221 596 B6
16100 WasC 97224 654 G6
SW Braydon Ct
- TGRD 97223 655 E5
NE Brazee Ct
2700 PTLD 97212 597 A3
13500 PTLD 97230 598 C3
NE Brazee St
700 PTLD 97212 596 J3
2600 PTLD 97212 597 A3
4100 PTLD 97213 597 B3
8200 PTLD 97220 597 G3
11700 PTLD 97220 598 A3
12200 PTLD 97230 598 A3
SE Break Front Ln
25100 CmsC 97009 659 E1
25100 DAMA 97009 659 E1
SW Breccia Dr
15500 BRTN 97007 654 H1
SW Breckenridge Ln
17600 WasC 97007 624 F5
Bree Ct
2500 LKOW 97034 686 C2
SW Breeze Ct
300 WasC 97225 595 H6
NW Breezy Ln
44000 WasC 97116 561 G4
SE Brehaut St
6800 CmsC 97222 657 E1
SE Brekke Ct
14000 CmsC 97222 657 C5
S Bremer Rd
10000 CmsC 97013 746 G5
10200 CmsC 97045 746 J5
NW Bren Ln
- HBRO 97124 593 B3
SE Brenda Av
15800 CmsC 97267 657 E7
15900 CmsC 97267 687 H1
SW Brenden Ln
- TGRD 97223 655 D3
SE Brendon Ct
3600 CmsC 97267 687 A2
SW Brendon Ct
5400 BRTN 97005 625 A4
NE Brennan Ln
700 HBRO 97124 593 D1
SW Brenne Ln
7000 WasC 97225 625 G2
SE Brent Av
14000 DAMA 97009 658 F6
SE Brent St
2700 HBRO 97123 623 E1
NW Brentano Ln
10200 YmhC 97128 770 E1
NW Brentford Ter
- HBRO 97006 594 C5
Brentwood Ct NE
- DNLD 97020 774 G5
SE Brentwood Ct
7900 CmsC 97267 657 E6
SW Brentwood Ct
15900 TGRD 97224 655 E7
SW Brentwood Dr
3400 PTLD 97201 626 C1
3400 PTLD 97239 626 C1
24000 CmsC 97068 716 C2
SW Brentwood Pl
9400 TGRD 97224 655 E7
SW Brentwood St
7400 WasC 97225 625 G3
7800 BRTN 97225 625 G3
SW Bretton Ct
10800 TGRD 97224 685 C1
SE Brevi Ln
24600 CmsC 97022 720 C3
NW Brewer Ln
2300 PTLD 97229 595 E3
NW Brewer St
2200 PTLD 97210 596 C3
SE Brewster Pl
5900 CmsC 97267 687 D1
SW Breyman Av
11300 MthC 97219 656 G3
SW Breyman Ct
11400 MthC 97219 656 G2
NE Breyman Orchards Rd
- YmhC 97115 742 C3
3700 YmhC 97114 772 D1
4100 YmhC 97114 742 D6
Brian Ct
4000 LKOW 97034 686 A3
SE Brian Ct
12900 CmsC 97015 658 B6
Brian Ln
- CmsC 97022 690 C5
SE Brian St
2800 HBRO 97123 593 F5
SW Brianne Cir
900 TDLE 97060 599 F4
Brianne Ct
15400 LKOW 97035 655 H6
SW Brianne Wy
13000 WasC 97223 654 H4
Briar Ct
1600 NWBG 97132 713 D5
SE Briar Ct
- CmsC 97267 687 B2
SW Briar Ln
500 WasC 97225 595 G7
SW Briarcliff Cir
6700 BRTN 97008 625 C5
NW Briarcreek Wy
1000 HBRO 97006 594 C4
SE Briarfield Ct
13500 CmsC 97222 657 D5
SW Briar Patch Ln
5900 CmsC 97070 715 H4
NW Briarwood Dr
8600 WasC 97231 564 F3
SE Briarwood Dr
- VCVR 98683 538 D7
1300 VCVR 98683 568 D2
SW Briarwood Pl
10800 TGRD 97223 655 A2
Briarwood Rd
10 CmsC 97034 656 G4
10 CmsC 97219 656 G4
10 LKOW 97034 656 G4
10 LKOW 97219 656 G4
NE Brickie Creek Dr
30400 ClkC 98675 418 H3
Brickle Creek Dr
31000 ClkC 98675 418 J4
NW Brickstone Ct
17300 BRTN 97006 594 F4
NW Brickstone Ln
17900 BRTN 97006 594 F4
SW Brickyard Dr
- SRWD 97140 684 H7
NW Bridge Av
- PTLD 97210 565 F4
8700 PTLD 97231 565 F4
NW Bridge Av US-30 BYP
- PTLD 97210 565 F4
8700 PTLD 97231 565 F4
Bridge Ct
14200 LKOW 97034 656 D5
Bridge St
10 FRVW 97024 599 C4
100 LFYT 97127 771 G1
200 LFYT 97127 741 G7
1500 YmhC 97128 741 G6
2900 VCVR 98661 536 J3
E Bridge St
27900 CmsC 97067 724 C7
NE Bridge Creek Av
1900 VCVR 98664 537 F4
2300 VCVR 98662 537 F4
SW Bridgeport Rd
7200 TLTN 97224 685 G2
7400 DRHM 97224 685 G2
SW Bridger Ln
17900 SRWD 97140 684 E5
SW Bridges St
32000 WasC 97123 592 J6
SE Bridgeside Wy
2900 HBRO 97123 623 F1
N Bridgeton Rd
10 PTLD 97211 566 G1
10 PTLD 97217 566 G1
NE Bridgeton Rd
10 PTLD 97211 566 H2
10 PTLD 97217 566 H2
SE Bridgeton St
14200 CmsC 97015 658 C6
SW Bridgeview Ct
12500 TGRD 97223 655 B3
Bridge View Dr
- WLIN 97068 687 A6
Bridgeview Dr
6200 WLIN 97068 687 A6
SE Bridgewater Ln
26600 CmsC 97009 689 F3
NW Bridgeway Ln
1500 WasC 97006 594 F4
NW Bridle Ln
13600 WasC 97229 595 A2
Bridle Wy
2100 WLIN 97068 686 H5
SW Bridle Hills Dr
15500 BRTN 97007 624 G6
16000 WasC 97007 624 G6
SW Bridlemile Ct
3900 PTLD 97221 626 B2
SW Bridlemile Ln
3400 PTLD 97221 626 B2
3400 PTLD 97239 626 B2
SW Bridletrail Av
8500 BRTN 97008 625 A7
NE Bridlewood Rd
19900 ClkC 98604 449 C7
19900 ClkC 98606 449 C7
NW Brie Ct
9800 WasC 97229 595 E5
SE Brie Ct
12000 CmsC 97015 658 A6
SW Brier Ln
9000 WasC 97223 625 E6
NW Brier Pl
200 DNDE 97115 742 H2
200 YmhC 97115 742 H2
SW Brier Pl
- PTLD 97239 626 E5
9200 PTLD 97219 626 E7
Briercliff Ln
700 LKOW 97034 656 E4
SW Brigadoon Ct
14100 BRTN 97005 624 J2
14100 BRTN 97005 625 A2
SE Brigadoon St
6700 CmsC 97267 657 D7
SW Briggs Ct
1900 WasC 97005 595 A7
1900 WasC 97005 625 D4
SW Briggs Rd
1900 WasC 97005 595 A7
2100 WasC 97005 625 A1
SE Briggs St
12900 CmsC 97222 657 A5
13700 CmsC 97267 657 A5
E Bright Av
24500 CmsC 97067 724 B4
E Bright Ct
67400 CmsC 97067 724 B4
SE Bright Rd
34100 CmsC 97022 720 D2
SW Brightfield Cir
8500 BRTN 97008 625 D7
8500 WasC 97008 625 D7
Brighton Av
400 ORCY 97045 717 C2
SW Brighton Ct
15500 BRTN 97007 624 H5
NW Brighton Ln
10000 PTLD 97229 595 D1
SW Brighton Ln
- BRTN 97007 624 H5
NE Brighton St
6000 HBRO 97124 593 J3
6000 WasC 97124 593 J3
6100 HBRO 97124 594 A3
SE Brightwood Av
14500 CmsC 97267 657 D6
SW Brightwood Ct
20200 WasC 97006 594 C7
SW Brightwood St
12900 WasC 97005 625 A1
E Brightwood Bridge Rd
- CmsC 97049 693 G6
62900 CmsC 97011 693 F6
E Brightwood Loop Rd
- CmsC 97055 693 E6
61800 CmsC 97011 693 G6
64300 CmsC 97011 723 H1
SE Brigid Pl
7500 CmsC 97267 687 H2
SW Brim Pl
13500 TGRD 97223 655 A5
13500 TGRD 97224 655 A5
NW Brimpton Ct
12500 MthC 97229 595 B1
SW Brink Av
2200 TDLE 97060 599 E6
SE Brinkley
- CmsC 97009 690 E5
- CmsC 97055 690 E5
Brinn Rd
31000 ClbC 97051 384 D6
Brisbane Wy
57500 ClbC 97053 414 F4
SW Bristlecone Wy
15500 WasC 97223 654 G5
S Bristlin Rd
16400 CmsC 97045 689 D6
N Bristol Av
8500 PTLD 97203 565 G2
Bristol Ct
1900 WLIN 97068 716 F2
SE Bristol Ct
10200 CmsC 97236 627 H7
SW Bristol Ct
7700 BRTN 97007 624 H6
SE Bristol Ln
10200 CmsC 97236 627 H7
SW Bristol Ln
15500 BRTN 97007 624 H6

STREET
Block City ZIP Map# Grid

SE Bristol Lp
10000 CmsC 97236 627 H7
SE Bristol Park Dr
8500 CmsC 97236 627 H7
8700 CmsC 97236 657 H1
SE Bristol Park Ter
10100 CmsC 97236 657 H1
SW Britetree Cir
17400 WasC 97007 624 F4
Britta Ct
- SNDY 97055 690 H3
SE Brittany Ct
10100 CmsC 97015 657 H6
Brittany Dr
1300 NWBG 97132 713 C6
3000 FTGV 97116 592 A5
SW Brittany Dr
3600 GSHM 97080 628 G5
13200 TGRD 97223 655 A3
SW Brittany Ln
23300 SRWD 97140 714 H1
SW Brittany Pl
23200 SRWD 97140 714 H1
Brittany Ter
14200 ORCY 97045 717 F6
Britten Ct
10 LKOW 97035 656 B4
NW Brittney Ct
10400 PTLD 97229 595 D2
SE Britton Av
4900 CmsC 97267 687 C4
Britton St
1600 WLIN 97068 716 G2
SW Brixton Av
3200 GSHM 97080 628 H6
SW Brixton Ct
1500 GSHM 97080 628 H4
SW Brixton Dr
2500 GSHM 97080 628 H5
SW Brixton Pl
2000 GSHM 97080 628 H4
N Broadacre Dr
- PTLD 97217 566 D2
SW Broadleaf Dr
1800 PTLD 97219 656 C1
SE Broadleaf Rd
28300 CmsC 97022 719 F7
SW Broadmoor Pl
13000 TGRD 97223 655 A5
SW Broadmoor Ter
7500 WasC 97225 625 G3
SW Broad Oak Blvd
17900 WasC 97007 624 E5
SW Broad Oak Ct
18200 WasC 97007 624 E5
SW Broad Oak Dr
6300 WasC 97007 624 F7
NW Broadshire Ln
41800 BNKS 97106 531 J6
Broadview Ln
6100 VCVR 98661 537 D5
N Broadway
10 PTLD 97212 596 G4
10 PTLD 97227 596 F4
10 PTLD 97232 596 G4
NE Broadway
10 PTLD 97212 596 H4
10 PTLD 97227 596 G4
10 PTLD 97232 596 H4
2700 PTLD 97212 597 A4
4000 PTLD 97232 597 C4
4100 PTLD 97213 597 C4
10800 PTLD 97220 597 J4
12000 PTLD 97220 598 A4
15700 PTLD 97230 598 E4
NW Broadway
10 PTLD 97205 596 F5
10 PTLD 97209 596 F5
SW Broadway
- PTLD 97201 626 E1
100 PTLD 97205 596 F5
100 PTLD 97209 596 F5
1500 PTLD 97201 596 E7
Broadway Br
- PTLD 97209 596 F4
- PTLD 97227 596 F4
NE Broadway Ct
7000 PTLD 97213 597 E4
13300 PTLD 97230 598 B4
20100 FRVW 97024 598 J4
20100 GSHM 97230 598 J4
NW Broadway Ct
900 ECDA 97023 750 B2
SW Broadway Dr
600 PTLD 97201 596 E7
600 PTLD 97201 626 D1
Broadway St
600 VCVR 98660 536 G5
1300 VCVR 98663 536 G4
4900 WLIN 97068 687 B6
N Broadway St
800 ECDA 97023 750 C2
S Broadway St
100 ECDA 97023 750 B4
SW Broadway St
11900 BRTN 97005 625 C3
SE Brockenhurst Cir
11600 HPYV 97236 658 C4
SW Brockman Rd
12600 BRTN 97008 625 A7
13700 BRTN 97008 624 J7
14000 BRTN 97008 654 J1
14300 BRTN 97007 654 J1
SW Brockway Dr
10500 WNVL 97070 745 C1
S Brockway Rd
24000 CmsC 97045 748 A7
SW Brockwood Av
200 MCMV 97128 770 G6
SE Brodiaea Ct
2800 HBRO 97123 623 E1
NE Brogden Ct
1900 HBRO 97124 593 E4
NE Brogden St
2800 HBRO 97124 593 F4
Broken Bridge Ln
- CmsC 97049 693 H7
E Broken Bridge Ln
64400 CmsC 97049 693 H7
SW Broken Fir Rd
15000 CmsC 97140 714 G7
NW Broken Top Dr
17000 WasC 97006 594 G2
Bronco Av
700 MOLA 97038 807 E7

Bronco Ct
2500 WLIN 97068 686 J5
Bronco Ln
14600 CmsC 97045 717 G7
SW Bronner Ln
15800 SRWD 97140 684 G6
NW Bronson Rd
15600 WasC 97006 594 H4
16800 BRTN 97006 594 G3
17200 WasC 97229 594 F3
NW Bronson Creek Dr
13900 WasC 97229 595 A2
NW Bronson Crest Lp
3500 WasC 97229 595 A2
SE Bronte Wy
500 HBRO 97123 593 C6
SE Bronze Rd
35200 CmsC 97022 720 F1
E Brook Av
67500 CmsC 97049 724 B2
Brook Ct
15100 LKOW 97035 656 B6
S Brook Ct
15900 CmsC 97045 688 A7
SW Brook Ct
12400 TGRD 97223 655 B4
SW Brooke Ct
14600 SRWD 97140 714 H1
Brooke Dr
1300 NWBG 97132 713 C6
Brooke St
2900 FTGV 97116 591 G2
S Brookfield Dr
- CmsC 97045 717 G2
SW Brookfield Ln
19700 WasC 97006 594 D6
SW Brookhaven Dr
20700 WasC 97006 594 E4
NW Brookhill Ln
600 HBRO 97124 593 B3
NW Brookhill St
800 HBRO 97124 593 A3
Brookhurst Ct
17400 LKOW 97034 686 G1
Brookhurst Dr
17300 LKOW 97034 686 G2
NW Brooking Ct
30700 NPNS 97133 563 B1
30700 WasC 97133 563 B1
SW Brookings Ln
- BRTN 97007 624 H5
SW Brooklawn Ct
18900 WasC 97006 624 C2
SW Brooklawn Pl
19000 WasC 97006 624 C2
SW Brooklet Pl
14800 WasC 97224 654 H6
SW Brookline Ln
7800 TGRD 97224 655 G6
SE Brooklyn Ct
10100 PTLD 97266 627 H2
13200 PTLD 97236 628 B2
18200 GSHM 97030 628 G2
18200 GSHM 97236 628 G2
SW Brooklyn Ln
9400 TGRD 97224 655 E6
SE Brooklyn Pl
18300 GSHM 97030 628 G2
SE Brooklyn St
1000 PTLD 97202 626 H1
2800 PTLD 97202 627 B2
7100 PTLD 97206 627 E2
8200 PTLD 97266 627 F2
11500 PTLD 97266 628 A2
15300 PTLD 97236 628 D2
17500 GSHM 97236 628 G2
17900 GSHM 97030 628 G2
SW Brookman Rd
16200 SRWD 97140 714 G1
17500 WasC 97140 714 D2
SE Brookmore Ct
10200 CmsC 97236 657 H1
SW Brookridge St
8000 WasC 97225 595 F7
NE Brooks Ln
19000 YmhC 97132 683 B7
Brooks Rd
30800 ClbC 97051 414 A2
31900 ClbC 97053 414 A2
NW Brooks Rd
10500 MthC 97231 534 G7
10500 MthC 97231 564 G1
SE Brooks Rd
32100 CmsC 97009 660 D4
SE Brooks St
900 MCMV 97128 770 J5
1600 YmhC 97128 770 J5
SW Brooks Bend Ln
9200 WasC 97223 625 E6
SW Brookshire Ct
33200 SPSE 97056 474 E1
SW Brookside Av
12300 TGRD 97223 655 D4
SW Brookside Ct
10200 TGRD 97223 655 D4
Brookside Dr NE
13000 MrnC 97002 775 B5
SE Brookside Dr
4500 MWKE 97222 627 C7
4800 MWKE 97222 657 C1
11200 PTLD 97266 627 J5
11500 PTLD 97266 628 A6
11700 PTLD 97236 628 A6
SW Brookside Dr
9700 WasC 97225 595 E6
NE Brookside Ln
12900 YmhC 97111 741 H4
12900 YmhC 97114 741 H4
SW Brookside Pl
10100 TGRD 97223 655 D4
Brookside Rd
- ORCY 97045 717 B3
2800 LKOW 97035 656 B6
E Brookside St
65600 CmsC 97011 723 J2
SE Brookside St
5400 HBRO 97123 593 H6
SE Brookside Ter
500 HBRO 97123 593 J5
S Brookstone Rd
18100 CmsC 97045 718 E2
NE Brooktree Ln
- VCVR 98682 507 J6
- VCVR 98682 508 A7
- VCVR 98682 537 J1

NW Brookview Ct
600 MCMV 97128 770 G4
NE Brookview Dr
2100 ClkC 98686 506 J2
NW Brookview Wy
3800 WasC 97229 595 B2
NW Brookwood Av
300 HBRO 97124 593 H5
300 WasC 97124 593 H5
SE Brookwood Av
1400 HBRO 97123 593 H7
2800 HBRO 97123 623 H2
2800 WasC 97123 623 H2
SW Brookwood Av
100 HBRO 97123 593 H6
100 HBRO 97124 593 H5
300 WasC 97123 593 H5
NE Brookwood Pkwy
- HBRO 97123 593 H5
- WasC 97124 593 H5
2300 HBRO 97124 593 H2
E Brookwood St
22500 CmsC 97011 723 J1
N Broughton Ct
2200 PTLD 97217 536 D6
N Broughton Dr
2200 PTLD 97217 536 E6
NW Brown Dr
39000 ClkC 98674 386 B1
Brown Rd
10700 CmsC 97070 715 C6
10700 WNVL 97070 715 C6
NE Brown Rd
1100 ClkC 98671 539 J5
29000 ClkC 98671 540 A4
SW Brown Rd
29400 CmsC 97070 715 C7
29400 WNVL 97070 715 C7
30000 WNVL 97070 745 C1
SW Brown St
10800 TLTN 97062 685 C7
NE Browndale Farm Rd
15600 CmsC 97002 745 H3
S Brown Deer Dr
14600 CmsC 97045 717 G2
SE Brownlee Rd
6100 CmsC 97267 657 D7
6100 CmsC 97267 687 D1
Browns Pl
200 STHN 97051 415 A1
Browns Landing Ct
34300 ClbC 97056 474 G4
NW Brownstone Wy
- HBRO 97006 594 C3
SE Broyles Ct
11700 CmsC 97015 657 J6
N Bruce Av
7500 PTLD 97203 565 G1
SW Bruce Ct
11700 BRTN 97008 625 C5
SW Bruce Dr
11400 BRTN 97008 625 C5
SW Bruce Ln
12000 BRTN 97008 625 B5
SW Bruce Wy
- WNVL 97070 715 E3
SW Bruck Ln
28800 CmsC 97070 715 J7
NW Brugger Rd
15700 WasC 97229 564 H5
SW Brugger St
10 PTLD 97219 656 F1
4400 PTLD 97219 626 A7
5500 PTLD 97219 625 H7
6200 WasC 97223 625 H7
NE Brunner Rd
25200 ClkC 98607 539 F4
NE Brunner Rd SR-500
25200 ClkC 98607 539 F4
S Brunner Rd
14500 CmsC 97045 687 H3
Bruns Av
17200 SNDY 97055 690 J3
SE Bruns Av
17600 SNDY 97055 690 J3
SE Bruns Ln
38000 SNDY 97055 690 J2
Brutscher St
- YmhC 97132 713 F7
800 NWBG 97132 713 F7
NE Bryan Dr
34300 SPSE 97056 444 G7
34300 SPSE 97056 474 G1
SW Bryan Wy
17800 WasC 97007 624 F6
SW Bryanna Ct
28200 WasC 97123 683 D1
Bryant Av
- MthC 97231 535 A5
NE Bryant Ct
1300 PTLD 97211 566 J5
Bryant Rd
16200 LKOW 97035 656 A7
16400 CmsC 97035 656 A7
16600 LKOW 97035 686 A3
18000 LKOW 97034 686 A2
18800 CmsC 97034 686 A3
SE Bryant Rd
33100 CmsC 97023 750 C4
33100 ECDA 97023 750 C4
Bryant St
1500 VCVR 98661 537 B4
N Bryant St
10 PTLD 97211 566 G5
1200 PTLD 97217 566 F5
NE Bryant St
10 PTLD 97211 566 H5
10 PTLD 97217 566 G5
2700 PTLD 97211 567 A6
3900 PTLD 97218 567 B6
SW Bryant St
18600 WasC 97006 624 E1
Bryant Vil
- VCVR 98661 537 B4
SW Bryce Ct
16100 BRTN 97007 624 G7
16100 WasC 97007 624 G7
NE Bryce St
2600 PTLD 97211 596 J1
2600 PTLD 97211 597 A1
2600 PTLD 97212 596 J1
2600 PTLD 97212 597 B2
3900 PTLD 97213 597 B2
SE Bryn St
12800 CmsC 97236 658 B5

SE Bryn Mawr Ct
14100 CmsC 97267 657 B6
NW Bryn Mawr Pl
400 GSHM 97030 628 J2
NW Bryn Mawr Wy
- GSHM 97030 628 J2
NW Brynwood Ln
300 MthC 97229 595 G5
SW Bryton Ct
10100 WNVL 97070 715 D7
N Buchanan Av
8500 PTLD 97203 565 J3
Buchanan St
1300 ORCY 97045 717 D1
SW Bucharest Ct
2600 WasC 97225 625 H1
SW Bucher Av
6400 BRTN 97008 624 J5
Buck St
2100 WLIN 97068 687 A5
NW Buckboard Dr
4600 WasC 97229 594 G1
Buck Brush Ln
4000 LKOW 97035 656 B5
Buckeye St
100 WDLD 98674 386 A1
200 WDLD 98674 385 J1
SW Buckfield Ln
13100 WasC 97224 685 A1
SW Buckhaven Rd
29700 WasC 97123 683 B4
30500 YmhC 97132 683 A4
SW Buckingham Av
2500 PTLD 97201 626 D3
Buckingham Ct
6700 GLDS 97027 687 D2
Buckingham Dr
6600 CmsC 97267 687 D2
6600 GLDS 97027 687 D2
SW Buckingham Pl
9200 BRTN 97007 654 E2
Buckingham Ter
10 LKOW 97034 686 B2
E Buckley Ln
500 NWBG 97132 713 C5
NW Buckley Rd
45200 WasC 97116 561 F5
SW Buckman Rd
2300 CmsC 97068 686 B7
Buckner Ln
400 ORCY 97045 717 D3
S Buckner Creek Rd
13900 CmsC 97042 777 J3
14600 CmsC 97004 777 J3
NW Buckshire St
41600 BNKS 97106 531 J6
41600 BNKS 97106 532 A6
SE Buckskin Ct
11600 HPYV 97236 658 B3
SW Buckskin Ter
9200 BRTN 97008 655 A1
9900 BRTN 97008 654 F2
SW Buddington St
1500 MthC 97219 656 G2
3500 PTLD 97219 656 A2
5100 PTLD 97219 655 J2
Buel Dr
- MCMV 97128 770 J2
Buena Vista Dr
5600 VCVR 98661 537 C6
6100 VCVR 98664 537 D7
NE Buena Vista Dr
18000 YmhC 97115 742 E1
18400 YmhC 97115 712 D7
18400 YmhC 97132 712 D7
SW Buena Vista Dr
2600 PTLD 97201 596 C7
SW Buena Vista Pl
2600 PTLD 97201 596 C7
NE Buena Vista St
400 HBRO 97124 593 C3
Buff Rd
- CmsC 97042 777 C5
S Buff Rd
13000 CmsC 97042 777 D6
SW Buffalo Pl
11200 TGRD 97223 655 D3
N Buffalo St
10 PTLD 97211 566 G5
2700 PTLD 97217 566 D5
NE Buffalo St
10 PTLD 97211 566 H5
10 PTLD 97217 566 G5
3700 PTLD 97211 567 B5
3700 PTLD 97218 567 B5
Buffalo Wy
14900 ORCY 97045 687 G6
SE Buford Ct
13200 PTLD 97236 628 B7
SE Buford Ln
8100 PTLD 97236 628 B7
SW Bugle Ct
12700 TGRD 97224 655 B6
Bullard St
1000 ORCY 97045 717 D3
NW Bullfinch Pl
2700 PTLD 97229 595 F2
Bull Mountain Hts
- TGRD 97224 655 C6
SW Bull Mountain Rd
11200 TGRD 97224 655 B6
11800 WasC 97224 655 B6
13700 TGRD 97224 654 J6
13700 WasC 97224 654 J6
16300 WasC 97140 654 F6
17000 WasC 97007 654 F6
Bullock St
800 LKOW 97034 656 G7
SW Bulrush Ln
15500 WasC 97223 654 H4
W Bumpski St
300 YCLT 98675 419 F1
SE Bumpy Ln
39000 CmsC 97055 720 J1
Bunick Dr
- LKOW 97035 656 A5
SW Bunker Oak Rd
17600 WasC 97006 594 F6
SW Bunker Post Ct
7400 WNVL 97070 745 F3
NE Bunn Rd
2800 YmhC 97128 771 C2
SE Bunnell St
14200 CmsC 97267 656 J6

Bunting Ln NE
11500 MrnC 97002 744 H6
SW Bunting St
- BRTN 97007 654 H3
NE Bunyard Pl
700 ECDA 97023 750 C2
Buol St
- ORCY 97045 717 B4
SW Burbank Av
2300 WasC 97225 625 E1
SW Burbank Pl
2100 WasC 97225 625 E1
N Burdick Av
100 VCVR 98661 537 D6
S Burdick Av
100 VCVR 98661 537 D6
N Burgard Rd
11600 PTLD 97203 535 F7
11600 PTLD 97203 565 F1
N Burgard Wy
9000 PTLD 97203 535 F7
Burghardt Dr
600 MOLA 97038 807 D7
SE Burgs Ln
38100 SNDY 97055 660 J7
38200 CmsC 97055 660 J7
SW Burgundy Ct
14700 WasC 97224 654 H6
SW Burgundy St
15000 WasC 97224 654 H6
SW Burkhalter Rd
27800 WasC 97123 623 B6
30200 WasC 97113 623 B6
NW Burkhardt Ct
10300 PTLD 97229 595 D2
NW Burkhart Dr
2300 PTLD 97229 595 D1
S Burkstrom Rd
14700 CmsC 97045 688 B3
SW Burkwood Ln
19000 WasC 97006 624 E1
Burl St
100 NWBG 97132 713 F7
SW Burlcrest Dr
11500 TGRD 97223 655 C3
SW Burlheights St
11900 TGRD 97223 655 C3
SW Burlingame Av
2700 TDLE 97060 599 F6
6200 PTLD 97239 626 D4
7700 PTLD 97219 626 E6
SW Burlingame Cir
600 TDLE 97060 599 F6
SW Burlingame Ct
2800 TDLE 97060 599 G6
SW Burlingame Pl
6400 PTLD 97239 626 D5
SW Burlingame Ter
600 PTLD 97239 626 D5
N Burlington Av
7400 PTLD 97203 565 G3
NW Burlington Ct
15100 MthC 97231 504 J7
Burlington Dr
2800 NWBG 97132 713 C4
3000 YmhC 97132 713 C4
NW Burlington Dr
16500 MthC 97231 534 H2
SE Burlington Dr
10300 VCVR 98664 567 H2
SW Burlington Dr
1100 BRTN 97006 594 H7
1100 WasC 97006 594 H7
Burlington St
- MthC 97231 534 F5
NW Burlington Ferry Rd
15400 MthC 97231 534 J1
SW Burlwood St
13500 WasC 97005 625 A1
Burma Rd
5600 CmsC 97035 655 H6
5600 LKOW 97035 655 J6
33500 ClbC 97053 444 F1
33500 ClbC 97056 444 F1
SW Burnett Ct
12000 BRTN 97008 655 B1
SW Burnett Ln
11700 BRTN 97008 655 C1
NE Burnett Rd
300 YmhC 97128 770 H2
400 MCMV 97128 770 H2
SE Burnett Rd
29200 CmsC 97022 719 J1
NW Burnett St
2400 PTLD 97229 595 D1
SW Burnham Ct
13200 TGRD 97223 655 F4
Burnham Rd
100 LKOW 97034 656 G7
SW Burnham St
8700 TGRD 97223 655 E4
NW Burning Tree Ct
5400 WasC 97229 564 D7
S Burns Rd
26400 CmsC 97042 777 H5
Burns St
1400 WLIN 97068 687 B6
SW Burns Wy
7900 WNVL 97070 715 F3
Burnside Br
- PTLD 97204 596 G5
- PTLD 97209 596 F5
- PTLD 97214 596 F5
- PTLD 97232 596 F5
NW Burnside Ct
- GSHM 97233 598 J7
2400 GSHM 97030 598 J7
SE Burnside Ct
9900 PTLD 97216 597 H6
20600 GSHM 97030 599 A7
E Burnside Rd
19000 GSHM 97233 598 H6
19700 GSHM 97030 598 J7
NE Burnside Rd
500 GSHM 97030 629 D2
1800 GSHM 97080 629 D2
NW Burnside Rd
10 GSHM 97030 629 B1
700 GSHM 97030 599 A7
1600 GSHM 97030 598 J7
1600 GSHM 97233 598 J7
W Burnside Rd
2900 PTLD 97205 596 B5
2900 PTLD 97210 596 B5
3200 PTLD 97221 596 B5

W Burnside Rd
5000 PTLD 97210 595 H6
5000 PTLD 97221 595 H6
6400 PTLD 97225 595 H6
6400 WasC 97225 595 H6
E Burnside St
10 PTLD 97214 596 G5
10 PTLD 97232 596 G5
2800 PTLD 97214 597 A5
2800 PTLD 97232 597 A5
3900 PTLD 97215 597 A5
4100 PTLD 97213 597 A5
8100 PTLD 97216 597 G6
9000 PTLD 97220 597 G6
11400 PTLD 97216 598 A6
11400 PTLD 97220 598 A6
12000 PTLD 97230 598 E6
15800 PTLD 97233 598 H6
16000 GSHM 97230 598 E6
16000 GSHM 97233 598 H6
E Burnside St US-30 BUS
10 PTLD 97214 596 G5
10 PTLD 97232 596 G5
SE Burnside St
2300 GSHM 97030 629 E2
2700 GSHM 97080 629 E3
W Burnside St
10 PTLD 97204 596 F5
1200 PTLD 97205 596 D5
1200 PTLD 97209 596 D5
2000 PTLD 97210 596 D5
SW Burns Ridge Ct
18300 WasC 97007 624 B6
Burnt Bridge Ter
- VCVR 98661 537 B4
SW Burntwood Ct
15500 BRTN 97007 624 H4
SW Burntwood Wy
15800 BRTN 97007 624 G5
Bur Oak Ct
3600 NWBG 97132 713 F7
N Burr Av
8500 PTLD 97203 565 J3
N Burrage Av
9000 PTLD 97217 566 D3
Burr Oak Al
3500 NWBG 97132 713 F7
Burt Ct
34800 STHN 97051 414 J1
SE Burt Ln
12700 CmsC 97009 659 J5
Burt Rd
34800 STHN 97051 414 J1
35100 ClbC 97051 414 J1
SW Burton Dr
5100 PTLD 97221 595 J6
5100 PTLD 97221 596 A6
NE Burton Rd
2500 VCVR 98661 537 E3
2500 VCVR 98662 537 G3
2500 VCVR 98664 537 G3
10700 VCVR 98682 537 H3
10700 VCVR 98684 537 H3
NW Burton St
13100 WasC 97229 595 A3
NE Burtonwood Ct
3900 VCVR 98682 537 H2
Buse St
1700 WLIN 97068 687 B6
SE Buser Ln
15500 CmsC 97015 657 F7
15500 CmsC 97267 657 F7
SE Bush Pl
13000 PTLD 97236 628 B3
NW Bush St
- PTLD 97231 565 F4
SE Bush St
2000 PTLD 97202 626 J2
2100 HBRO 97123 593 E6
8000 PTLD 97206 627 F2
8000 PTLD 97266 627 F2
11500 PTLD 97266 628 A3
16500 PTLD 97236 628 E3
SW Bushbaum Ct
5200 TLTN 97062 685 J5
SW Bushong Ter
22000 SRWD 97140 684 E7
SE Butler Rd
500 GSHM 97080 629 C6
700 MthC 97080 629 D6
SW Butler Rd
1300 GSHM 97080 629 A6
1700 GSHM 97080 628 J6
2200 MthC 97080 628 J6
N Butler St
4700 PTLD 97203 566 B5
NE Butler St
- HBRO 97124 593 J3
6900 HBRO 97124 594 A3
Butler Central
- HBRO 97124 593 J2
Butler Main
- HBRO 97124 593 J2
Butler North
- HBRO 97124 593 J2
Butler West
- HBRO 97124 593 J2
SW Butner Ct
13000 WasC 97005 595 B6
SW Butner Rd
10400 WasC 97225 595 D7
12300 WasC 97005 595 A6
13600 WasC 97006 595 A6
SE Butte Av
8900 VCVR 98664 537 G7
SW Butte Ct
- BRTN 97008 625 C6
Butte Ln NE
23500 MrnC 97002 744 F6
SW Butte Ln
11500 BRTN 97008 625 C6
Butte St NE
10700 MrnC 97002 744 G6
SE Buttercup Ct
2500 HBRO 97123 623 E1
E Buttercup St
700 YmhC 97148 711 A1
700 YMHL 97148 711 A1
S Butterfield Ln
17400 CmsC 97045 718 C1
SW Butternut Dr
17500 WasC 97007 624 F4
SW Butternut Pl
4900 WasC 97007 624 E3

SW Butternut St
19200 WasC 97007 624 D3
Butteville Rd NE
19400 MrnC 97002 774 G2
20200 DNLD 97020 774 E6
20900 MrnC 97020 774 F4
22500 MrnC 97002 744 G6
NE Butteville Rd
24500 CmsC 97002 744 H4
24500 CmsC 97002 745 C2
NE Button Dr
32500 ClkC 98629 417 E1
S Buxton Av
100 TDLE 97060 599 G4
Buxton Ct
2900 FTGV 97116 591 F3
Buxton St
2600 FTGV 97116 591 F3
NE Buxton St
2600 PTLD 97232 596 J5
2700 PTLD 97232 597 A5
Buyserie Rd NE
5100 MrnC 97137 773 F3
SE Bybee Blvd
- PTLD 97266 627 H6
1400 PTLD 97202 626 J5
2700 PTLD 97202 627 B5
7200 PTLD 97206 627 E6
12200 PTLD 97236 628 A6
12200 PTLD 97266 628 A6
SE Bybee Ct
16000 PTLD 97236 628 E6
SE Bybee Dr
15200 PTLD 97236 628 D6
SE Bybee Rd
1800 ClkC 98607 568 H1
19600 VCVR 98607 568 H1
N Bybee Lake Ct
14300 PTLD 97203 535 H4
N Bybee Lake Rd
14300 PTLD 97203 535 J5
SW Bygones Ct
15400 WasC 97007 624 H4
NW Byrne Ter
2300 WasC 97229 595 C3
SW Byrom Ter
10900 TLTN 97062 685 C6
SE Byron Ct
5600 CmsC 97267 687 C1
SE Byron Dr
5300 CmsC 97267 687 C1

C

C Av
10 LKOW 97034 656 F5
NE C Av
- ClkC 98684 538 E6
W C Av
1200 LCTR 98629 386 G7
C Ln
- PTLD 97218 567 D7
C St
- ORCY 97045 717 D1
- PTLD 97219 655 J3
- VCVR 98661 536 H4
- WasC 97224 685 A1
10 CMAS 98607 569 G5
10 WHGL 98671 569 H5
400 CBAC 97018 385 C3
500 ORCY 97045 687 F6
600 VCVR 98660 536 G5
900 WHGL 98671 570 A5
1300 VCVR 98663 536 G4
1700 FTGV 97116 591 H5
NW C St
- WasC 97006 594 C5
SE C St
10000 MWKE 97222 657 A2
C & D Row
- FTGV 97116 592 C4
SW Caballero Ct
12500 BRTN 97008 655 B1
Cabana Ln
700 LKOW 97034 656 F6
Cabana Pointe
100 LKOW 97034 656 F6
Cabernet Ct
- MCMV 97128 770 F3
SW Cabernet Ct
14600 WasC 97224 654 J6
S Cabernet Ln
14600 CmsC 97042 777 G6
SW Cabernet St
15000 WasC 97224 654 H6
SE Cabin Ln
58700 CmsC 97055 693 C5
SW Cable Av
1800 PTLD 97201 596 D6
SW Cabot St
11000 BRTN 97005 625 D2
11100 WasC 97005 625 D2
SW Cactus Dr
2300 PTLD 97205 596 B6
S Cadanau Rd
22200 CmsC 97023 750 C5
NW Cadbury Av
1900 HBRO 97006 594 C3
NE Caddis Dr
5500 HBRO 97124 593 J4
Caddis Pl
19200 ORCY 97045 717 C5
Caddy Ct
300 NWBG 97132 713 H7
SW Caddy Pl
13000 TGRD 97223 655 A4
Cade Dr
59300 STHN 97051 414 J1
NE Caden Av
400 HBRO 97124 593 J4
NE Caden St
20600 FRVW 97024 599 A4
NE Cadet Av
3200 PTLD 97220 597 G2
Cadillac Ln
- CmsC 97042 777 E7
S Cadle Rd
18300 CmsC 97045 718 D3
S Cadle Creek Ln
18300 CmsC 97045 718 D3
NW Cady Ct
4700 VCVR 98663 536 E1
SW Cady Ln
12300 BRTN 97005 625 B4

STREET
Block City ZIP Map# Grid

SW Caesar Ter
17400 KNGC 97224 685 A2
NE Cafe Wy
2400 HBRO 97124 593 A2
SW Cafield Ct
12600 TGRD 97223 655 B5
SW Cahalin Rd
- WasC 97140 715 C2
- WNVL 97140 715 C2
NW Caitlin Ter
1400 WasC 97229 595 B4
SW Calais Ct
- WNVL 97070 745 E2
Calaroga Cir
3800 WLIN 97068 686 J2
Calaroga Ct
4000 WLIN 97068 686 J2
Calaroga Dr
3800 WLIN 97068 686 J2
SW Calaveras Ct
7800 BRTN 97007 624 J1
SE Caldera Ct
13200 HPYV 97236 658 B2
SW Caldera Ct
15800 BRTN 97007 654 H1
SW Caldew Dr
700 PTLD 97219 626 D5
SW Caldew St
3500 PTLD 97219 626 B5
Caldwell Rd
6100 GLDS 97027 687 D3
SE Caleb Ln
18100 DAMA 97009 658 G1
Calgary Wy
13000 ORCY 97045 717 D5
N Calhoun Av
9200 PTLD 97203 565 J3
SW Calico Ct
12100 BRTN 97008 655 B1
Calico Ln
33600 ClbC 97056 444 E5
SE Calico Rd
34600 CmsC 97009 660 F3
Caliente Ct
2000 WLIN 97068 686 H4
California Ct
500 VCVR 98661 537 C6
California St
4500 VCVR 98661 537 B6
SW California St
3500 PTLD 97219 626 B5
5500 PTLD 97219 625 J5
NE Calkins Ln
16000 YmhC 97132 712 E2
Callahan Rd
- ClbC 97056 474 A4
SE Callahan Rd
12500 CmsC 97236 658 A1
12500 HPYV 97236 658 A1
SW Callahan Rd
31700 ClbC 97056 474 A4
33200 SPSE 97056 474 D3
NE Callan Ct
7500 HBRO 97124 594 B5
Calle Cte
- VCVR 98683 568 F4
SE Callister Rd
26300 MthC 97080 629 F6
NW Calumet Ter
2700 PTLD 97210 596 C5
SW Calusa Lp
5700 TLTN 97062 685 H4
N Calvert Av
8600 PTLD 97217 566 D3
Calvin St
600 CBAC 97018 385 B2
NW Calypso Ter
6000 WasC 97229 564 J6
SW Camas St
17900 WasC 97006 624 F1
NW Camas Meadows Dr
- ClkC 98607 538 J5
4100 CMAS 98607 539 A5
4800 CMAS 98607 538 J5
NW Cambray Pl
500 BRTN 97006 594 E5
500 WasC 97006 594 E5
NW Cambray St
17800 BRTN 97006 594 F5
17800 WasC 97006 594 F5
SE Cambray Wy
9200 CmsC 97236 657 H1
NE Cambrey Ct
700 HBRO 97124 593 D2
SW Cambria Ln
13000 TGRD 97223 655 D1
Cambria Ter
14400 ORCY 97045 717 G6
N Cambridge Av
7000 PTLD 97203 566 B5
Cambridge Ct
4700 LKOW 97035 656 A4
SW Cambridge Ct
16700 WasC 97007 624 G3
Cambridge Dr
300 NWBG 97132 713 C4
SW Cambridge Dr
16600 DRHM 97224 685 F1
16700 WasC 97007 624 G3
SE Cambridge Ln
9700 CmsC 97222 656 H1
9700 MWKE 97222 656 H1
Cambridge St
2500 WLIN 97068 687 A7
2700 CmsC 97068 687 A7
Camden Ln
600 NWBG 97132 713 C5
14200 LKOW 97035 655 J5
SW Camden Ln
6900 BRTN 97008 625 C5
Camden St
59500 STHN 97051 384 J7
Camdon St
13300 MOLA 97038 837 C1
13400 CmsC 97038 837 D1
NW Camelback Ln
17300 WasC 97006 594 F1
Camelia Av
- PTLD 97217 536 E7
Camellia Av NE
22000 MrnC 97002 775 D2
Camellia Ct NE
21900 MrnC 97002 775 D3
SE Camellia Ct
700 HBRO 97123 593 C6

Camellia Ln
4200 VCVR 98661 537 B4
SW Camellia St
12600 WasC 97005 595 B6
Camelot Ct
10 LKOW 97034 686 B2
SW Camelot Ct
- WasC 97225 595 H7
1900 BRTN 97225 595 H7
1900 BRTN 97225 625 H1
1900 WasC 97225 625 H1
SW Camelot Ln
6300 PTLD 97219 625 H7
SW Camelot St
29300 CmsC 97070 715 C7
29300 WNVL 97070 715 C7
Cameo Ct
13700 CmsC 97034 656 D5
13700 LKOW 97034 656 D5
NE Cameron Blvd
15800 PTLD 97230 598 E1
SW Cameron Ct
16100 WasC 97223 654 G5
SW Cameron Rd
4500 PTLD 97221 626 A4
5100 PTLD 97221 625 J4
Cameron Wy
6200 GLDS 97027 687 D3
NW Cami Pl
- NPNS 97133 563 B1
- WasC 97133 563 B1
SW Camille Ter
8900 WasC 97223 625 E6
E Camillia Dr
700 YmhC 97132 713 C3
Camino Dr
1600 FTGV 97116 591 H3
SW Camino Ln
16800 KNGC 97224 685 A1
Camino del Rio
- VCVR 98683 568 F4
Camino Rio Rd
- CmsC 97067 723 H1
23600 CmsC 97011 723 H1
SE Camp Rd
37600 CmsC 97023 750 H1
NE Campaign St
- PTLD 97230 598 D1
4200 PTLD 97211 597 B1
4200 PTLD 97218 597 C1
9400 MWDP 97220 597 H1
10900 PTLD 97220 597 J1
SE Campanario Rd
5400 CmsC 97222 657 C5
N Campbell Av
4600 PTLD 97217 596 E1
6500 PTLD 97217 566 E5
SW Campbell Ct
4700 PTLD 97239 626 C3
SW Campbell Ln
26000 CmsC 97068 716 D5
NW Campbell Rd
15000 YmhC 97128 770 A2
SW Campbell Rd
11500 WasC 97123 653 B3
NE Campbell St
5100 HBRO 97124 593 H2
SE Campbell St
3000 MWKE 97222 657 A2
SE Campfire Wy
13700 CmsC 97015 658 C6
SW Campion Ct
8100 BRTN 97008 625 D4
NW Camp Ireland St
100 HBRO 97124 593 B1
31400 WasC 97124 593 A1
SE Camplan Ct
14500 CmsC 97267 657 A6
NE Campus Ct
6100 HBRO 97124 593 J3
6300 HBRO 97124 594 A4
NE Campus Dr
6200 VCVR 98661 537 C3
NW Campus Dr
- CmsC 97023 750 A1
- ECDA 97022 750 A1
- ECDA 97023 750 A1
SW Campus Dr
500 PTLD 97239 626 E2
Campus Wy
1600 LKOW 97034 686 D1
NE Campus Wy
6700 HBRO 97124 594 A3
SE Camwal Dr
3000 HBRO 97123 593 F6
Canal Cir
16900 LKOW 97035 686 A1
Canal Rd
3900 LKOW 97034 686 A2
17800 LKOW 97035 686 A3
17900 RVGR 97034 686 A3
17900 RVGR 97035 686 A3
Canal Woods Ct
4000 LKOW 97034 686 A2
NE Canard Ct
5700 HBRO 97124 593 J4
NE Canard Dr
5500 HBRO 97124 593 J4
Canary Ln
50200 ClbC 97056 474 D5
S Canary Rd
22300 CmsC 97023 750 B4
SW Canby Ct
2200 PTLD 97219 626 C6
16700 BRTN 97007 624 G5
16900 WasC 97007 624 G5
Canby Fy
- CmsC 97013 746 C1
- CmsC 97068 746 C1
SW Canby Ln
7000 BRTN 97223 625 H6
7000 PTLD 97223 625 H6
SW Canby St
3400 PTLD 97219 626 B6
5900 PTLD 97219 625 H6
6400 BRTN 97223 625 H6
6400 PTLD 97223 625 H6
6800 WasC 97223 625 H6
Canby-Marquam Hwy
- CmsC 97013 776 D7
NE Candi Ct
200 PTLD 97220 597 G5
Candiana Rd
1500 MrnC 97137 772 F4

Candice Ln
20100 CmsC 97045 717 F6
20100 ORCY 97045 717 F6
Candlewood Ct
15200 CmsC 97035 655 J6
15200 LKOW 97035 655 J6
NE Candlewood Pl
4900 HBRO 97124 593 H5
SE Candy Ln
17800 CmsC 97267 687 C2
Canemah Ct
100 ORCY 97045 717 B2
Canemah Rd
100 ORCY 97045 717 C3
Canemah St
2000 WLIN 97068 687 A7
Canemah Wy
100 ORCY 97045 717 B3
NW Cannes Dr
21000 WasC 97229 564 C6
SW Canning St
800 PTLD 97201 626 D1
E Cannon Rd
20500 CmsC 97011 693 F6
SE Cannon St
- PTLD 97236 628 C4
NW Cannon Wy
2500 WasC 97229 595 D3
SW Canseco Ct
16600 WasC 97007 624 G6
Cantata Dr
19200 CmsC 97045 716 J5
19200 ORCY 97045 716 J5
SW Canter Ct
- BRTN 97008 655 A1
Canter Ln
6100 WLIN 97068 686 H5
NE Canter Ln
30400 YmhC 97140 713 J2
S Canter Ln
17600 CmsC 97045 718 D2
SW Canter Ln
- CmsC 97140 715 A3
Canterbury Dr
6600 GLDS 97027 687 D1
SE Canterbury Ln
24200 DAMA 97009 659 D3
SW Canterbury Ln
- PTLD 97219 626 A6
2900 PTLD 97205 596 B6
10300 TGRD 97224 655 D6
Canterbury Pl
- TGRD 97224 655 C6
Canterwood Ct
20100 ORCY 97045 717 H7
NW Canterwood Wy
16100 WasC 97229 594 H1
SE Canvasback Wy
12300 BRTN 97007 654 G4
Canyon Ct
13700 ORCY 97045 717 E1
17300 LKOW 97034 686 C1
SW Canyon Ct
4500 PTLD 97221 596 A7
4600 MthC 97221 596 A7
5800 PTLD 97221 595 H7
6100 WasC 97225 595 H7
Canyon Dr
16800 LKOW 97034 686 C1
NW Canyon Dr
100 DNDE 97115 742 H2
SW Canyon Dr
6600 MthC 97221 625 H1
6600 WasC 97225 595 H7
6600 WasC 97225 625 H1
8400 BRTN 97225 625 F2
Canyon Ln
400 YmhC 97132 713 B7
SW Canyon Ln
6600 WasC 97225 625 H1
6800 BRTN 97225 625 G1
Canyon Rd
- MthC 97231 535 B6
NE Canyon Rd
22400 ClkC 98604 449 C5
SW Canyon Rd
2200 PTLD 97201 596 C6
2200 PTLD 97205 596 C6
4000 PTLD 97221 596 B7
6800 BRTN 97225 625 G2
6800 WasC 97225 625 G2
9700 WasC 97005 625 C3
10700 BRTN 97005 625 D2
SW Canyon Rd SR-8
6800 BRTN 97225 625 G2
6800 WasC 97225 625 G2
9700 WasC 97005 625 C3
10700 BRTN 97005 625 D2
SW Canyon Ter
6700 WasC 97225 625 J1
Canyon Tr
- BRTN 97005 625 C2
Canyon Creek Rd S
28000 WNVL 97070 715 F6
SW Canyon Creek Rd
28000 WNVL 97070 715 F6
SW Canyon Creek Rd N
25500 WasC 97062 715 F3
26100 WNVL 97070 715 F4
SW Canyon Crest Dr
6600 WasC 97225 625 H1
7000 WasC 97225 625 H1
NW Canyon Crest Lp
6900 ClkC 98665 506 F6
NE Canyon Loop Rd
23300 ClkC 98604 449 B4
Canyon Ridge Cir
14000 CmsC 97045 717 F7
14000 ORCY 97045 717 F7
Canyon Ridge Dr
14100 CmsC 97045 717 F7
20100 ORCY 97045 717 F6
SE Canyon Valley Rd
19700 CmsC 97055 691 D5
Canyon View Dr
200 LFYT 97127 741 G7
Canyon View Ln
200 LFYT 97127 741 G7
SE Capella Ct
12500 HPYV 97236 658 D4
SW Cape Meares Ct
6300 BRTN 97007 624 J5
Capilano Ct
900 LKOW 97034 656 E4

SE Capistrano Ct
13000 CmsC 97222 657 C5
NW Capital St
- PTLD 97210 596 A2
SW Capitol Hwy
6000 PTLD 97239 626 D4
6600 PTLD 97219 626 A7
9700 PTLD 97219 656 A1
11200 PTLD 97219 655 J2
SW Capitol Hwy SR-10
6000 PTLD 97239 626 D4
Capitol St
7900 VCVR 98664 537 F6
Capitola Coms
- PTLD 97219 656 A2
SW Capitol Hill Rd
6700 PTLD 97219 626 C6
Caples Av
2500 VCVR 98661 537 B3
E Caples Ct
1100 LCTR 98629 386 H7
Caples Rd
800 CtzC 98674 385 E1
800 WDLD 98674 385 G2
NE Caples Rd
14800 ClkC 98606 478 A5
16700 ClkC 98604 478 A3
NE Caples Rd SR-503 BUS
14800 ClkC 98606 478 A5
16700 ClkC 98604 478 A3
SW Cappoen Rd
19100 WasC 97140 684 B4
SE Capps Rd
11300 CmsC 97015 687 J2
11300 CmsC 97015 688 A2
SW Capri Ct
800 WasC 97005 595 A6
SW Capriole Pl
8900 BRTN 97008 625 D4
SW Capstone Ct
15000 BRTN 97007 624 J7
Captains Ct
19100 ORCY 97045 717 C4
Caravatta Ct
19000 ORCY 97045 717 D4
SW Caraway Ct
3000 PTLD 97219 656 B2
5800 PTLD 97219 655 J1
NW Cardai Hill Rd
39800 ClkC 98674 386 B1
Cardinal Ct
17600 LKOW 97034 686 A2
SE Cardinal Ct
1200 VCVR 98683 538 F7
1200 VCVR 98683 568 F1
Cardinal Dr
17300 LKOW 97034 686 B2
SW Cardinal Ln
6600 TGRD 97224 655 G6
SW Cardinal Lp
15800 BRTN 97007 654 G3
Cardinal Pl
17800 LKOW 97034 686 A2
SE Cardinal St
4100 CmsC 97222 657 B5
4100 CmsC 97267 657 B5
SW Cardinal Ter
11300 BRTN 97008 625 C6
SW Cardinell Dr
1200 PTLD 97201 596 D7
N Carey Blvd
- PTLD 97203 566 A3
7000 PTLD 97203 565 J4
SW Carey Ln
200 MthC 97219 656 G2
SE Carey Pl
- PTLD 97233 598 D7
NW Caribou Ct
17700 WasC 97229 564 F7
NE Carillon Dr
1700 HBRO 97124 594 A3
Carissa Av NE
22000 MrnC 97002 775 D2
NW Carl Ct
17400 WasC 97229 594 F3
SW Carl Pl
- PTLD 97239 626 D3
Carl St
- PTLD 97218 567 E5
NE Carl St
- PTLD 97218 567 E5
SE Carl St
28100 MthC 97080 629 H6
SE Carla Ct
7400 CmsC 97267 657 E5
NE Carlaby Dr
1300 HBRO 97124 593 E2
SE Carleton St
13800 PTLD 97236 628 C5
SW Carlin Blvd
19800 WasC 97007 624 C5
SW Carlsbad Dr
14500 BRTN 97007 624 J6
Carlson Av
- SNDY 97055 690 J3
Carlson Ct
17100 LKOW 97034 686 D1
Carlson Rd
1800 VCVR 98661 537 C4
S Carlson Rd
17200 CmsC 97045 688 C3
SW Carlson St
7000 BRTN 97223 625 H1
NW Carlton Ct
- WasC 97229 594 E1
NW Carlton St
700 ECDA 97023 750 B3
SE Carlton St
1300 PTLD 97202 626 G6
2800 PTLD 97202 627 A5
4100 PTLD 97206 627 B5
8000 PTLD 97266 627 F5
12000 PTLD 97266 628 A5
14200 PTLD 97236 628 C5
Carlton Wy
200 NWBG 97132 713 D7
Carly Ct
- MCMV 97128 770 J2
SW Carlyle Av
- PTLD 97201 596 C6
- PTLD 97205 596 C6
SE Carlyle St
- HBRO 97123 624 A1
Carman Dr
- TGRD 97224 655 H7

Carman Dr
3500 LKOW 97035 656 A6
4600 CmsC 97035 656 A6
4700 CmsC 97035 655 H7
4700 LKOW 97035 655 H7
NW Carmel Cir
100 DNDE 97115 742 H2
SW Carmel Cir
8600 WNVL 97070 745 E3
Carmel Ct
10300 MWKE 97222 657 C2
SE Carmel Ct
16800 CmsC 97267 687 A1
SW Carmel Ct
8000 WasC 97223 625 F7
SE Carmel Dr
18800 DAMA 97009 658 H5
SW Carmel St
12900 KNGC 97224 685 A1
Carmelita Dr
19100 ORCY 97045 717 C4
Carmelita Pl
12900 ORCY 97045 717 C5
SW Carmen St
11600 TGRD 97223 655 B4
Carmen Heights Dr
700 DNDE 97115 742 H3
SE Carmichael Ct
14300 HPYV 97236 658 C1
SE Carnaby Wy
9400 CmsC 97236 657 H1
Carnation Rd
- WasC 97116 591 H7
SE Carnation St
8300 CmsC 97267 657 F6
Carnegie Av
16400 CmsC 97035 655 H7
Carol Av
1800 NWBG 97132 713 D6
SE Carol Av
14300 CmsC 97267 657 E6
Carol Ct
300 MOLA 97038 837 D1
SW Caroland Rd
7000 WasC 97223 625 H5
SW Carol Ann Ct
7900 TGRD 97224 655 F7
Carol Ann Dr
1700 NWBG 97132 713 D6
NE Carole Ct
1700 HBRO 97124 593 B2
SW Carole Ct
8100 TGRD 97224 655 F6
NE Carole St
400 ECDA 97023 750 C3
SW Carol Glen Pl
7800 BRTN 97007 624 J2
SW Carolina Ct
13800 WasC 97224 654 J6
13800 WasC 97224 655 A6
Carolina Ln
7300 VCVR 98664 537 E6
SW Carolina St
1800 PTLD 97239 626 D4
3300 PTLD 97221 626 B4
SW Caroline Dr
8800 WasC 97225 625 F4
E Caroline Ln
67700 CmsC 97067 724 B4
SW Carolwood Dr
14500 BRTN 97007 624 J6
14500 BRTN 97008 624 J6
SW Carousel Ct
14100 BRTN 97005 624 J2
14100 BRTN 97005 625 A2
SE Carpenter Dr
12300 CmsC 97015 688 A1
SE Carpenter Ln
32700 MthC 97080 630 F7
SW Carpenter Creek Rd
45800 WasC 97116 591 A6
S Carr St
100 CLTN 97111 711 C7
200 CLTN 97111 741 A1
SW Carr St
12700 BRTN 97008 625 A7
Carrera Ln
600 LKOW 97034 656 E4
S Carriage Ln
9900 CmsC 97013 746 F5
Carriage Wy
1600 CmsC 97068 686 G4
1600 WLIN 97068 686 H4
SW Carriage Wy
9200 BRTN 97008 655 A1
SW Carriage Oaks Ln
7600 WNVL 97070 715 F4
Carrie Ct
- CmsC 97045 717 H3
SE Carrie Lyn Ln
4000 MWKE 97222 657 C5
12900 CmsC 97222 657 C4
SE Carrington Ln
9800 HPYV 97236 658 B2
SW Carrollon Dr
7600 WasC 97007 624 E6
Carson Dr
2200 WLIN 97068 716 G1
SW Carson St
600 PTLD 97219 626 D6
SE Carson Corner Ct
16400 CmsC 97267 687 A1
SW Carter Av
- PTLD 97201 596 C6
- PTLD 97205 596 C6
Carter Ln
500 CmsC 97038 807 C6
500 MOLA 97038 807 C6
SW Carter Ln
1900 PTLD 97201 596 D7
Carter Pl
17000 LKOW 97034 686 D1
Carter Rd
30800 ClbC 97053 414 B2
Carter Park Vil
- VCVR 98660 536 F2
NE Carty Rd
- ClkC 98642 446 H3
NW Carty Rd
1300 ClkC 98642 446 D3
S Carus Rd
11600 CmsC 97013 746 J6
11600 CmsC 97045 746 J6
13100 CmsC 97045 747 F5
16200 CmsC 97004 748 D6

S Carus Rd
16200 CmsC 97045 748 A5
SE Caruthers Ct
13700 PTLD 97233 628 C1
SE Caruthers St
- PTLD 97215 627 D1
- PTLD 97216 627 G1
100 PTLD 97214 626 H1
2800 PTLD 97214 627 A1
16000 PTLD 97233 628 E1
17800 GSHM 97233 628 G1
SW Caruthers St
300 PTLD 97201 626 F1
SW Caruthers St US-26
300 PTLD 97201 626 E1
Carver Hwy
- CmsC 97009 658 D7
- CmsC 97015 658 B7
- DAMA 97009 658 D7
- DAMA 97015 658 D7
- HPYV 97015 658 D7
Carver Hwy SR-212
- CmsC 97009 658 D7
- CmsC 97015 658 B7
- DAMA 97009 658 D7
- DAMA 97015 658 D7
- HPYV 97015 658 D7
Carver Hwy SR-224
- CmsC 97009 658 D7
- CmsC 97015 658 B7
- DAMA 97009 658 D7
- DAMA 97015 658 D7
- HPYV 97015 658 D7
NW Cary St
200 ECDA 97023 750 B3
SE Casablanca Ct
8700 CmsC 97015 687 F2
SE Casa del Rey Dr
4800 CmsC 97222 657 C5
Casa Grande
- VCVR 98683 568 F3
SE Casa Verde Ct
4900 CmsC 97267 657 B7
S Casca Berry Ct
21000 CmsC 97045 747 H1
Cascade Av
500 ORCY 97045 717 D2
SE Cascade Av
1400 VCVR 98683 568 A1
SW Cascade Av
9700 BRTN 97008 655 E2
9700 TGRD 97223 655 E2
SW Cascade Blvd
8500 BRTN 97008 625 D7
8500 BRTN 97008 655 D1
8500 TGRD 97223 655 D1
NW Cascade Ct
600 GSHM 97030 628 J2
5400 CMAS 98607 539 B7
SE Cascade Ct
5000 HBRO 97123 593 H7
Cascade Dr
- CmsC 97011 723 H1
- CNBY 97013 776 D1
300 VCVR 98664 537 F7
SW Cascade Dr
3000 PTLD 97205 596 B6
18500 WasC 97006 624 E1
Cascade Hwy S
- CmsC 97004 747 G3
- CmsC 97013 777 E1
- CmsC 97038 807 E1
- CmsC 97038 837 B3
- CmsC 97042 747 F7
- CmsC 97042 777 E7
- CmsC 97042 807 E1
- CmsC 97045 687 E6
- CmsC 97045 717 F1
- CmsC 97045 747 G3
- CmsC 97045 777 E1
- MOLA 97038 807 C6
- MOLA 97038 837 B3
- ORCY 97045 687 E6
19600 ORCY 97045 717 F1
Cascade Hwy S SR-213
- CmsC 97004 747 G3
- CmsC 97013 777 E1
- CmsC 97038 807 E1
- CmsC 97038 837 B3
- CmsC 97042 747 F7
- CmsC 97042 777 E7
- CmsC 97042 807 E1
- CmsC 97045 687 E6
- CmsC 97045 717 F1
- CmsC 97045 747 G3
- CmsC 97045 777 E1
- MOLA 97038 807 C6
- MOLA 97038 837 B3
- ORCY 97045 687 E6
19600 ORCY 97045 717 F1
SE Cascade Hwy
8500 CmsC 97206 627 F7
8500 CmsC 97236 627 F7
8500 PTLD 97266 627 F7
9000 CmsC 97206 657 F1
9000 CmsC 97236 657 F3
9200 CmsC 97222 657 F3
12500 CmsC 97015 657 F4
SE Cascade Hwy SR-213
8500 CmsC 97206 627 F7
8500 CmsC 97236 627 F7
8500 PTLD 97266 627 F7
9000 CmsC 97206 657 F1
9000 CmsC 97236 657 F3
9200 CmsC 97222 657 F3
12500 CmsC 97015 657 F4
SE Cascade Hwy N
- CmsC 657 F6
- CmsC 97015 657 F5
SE Cascade Hwy N SR-213
- CmsC 657 F6
- CmsC 97015 657 F5
Cascade Ln
900 MOLA 97038 807 C7
SW Cascade Lp
28500 WNVL 97070 715 G6
SW Cascade Pl
23100 SRWD 97140 714 H1
Cascade St
- ORCY 97045 717 D2
5600 WLIN 97068 687 B6
34600 STHN 97051 414 H1
E Cascade St
21700 CmsC 97049 724 F1

NW Cascade St
1900 CMAS 98607 569 B3
Cascade Ter
3400 WLIN 97068 686 H7
SW Cascade Ter
3100 PTLD 97205 596 B6
NW Cascade Wy
900 MCMV 97128 770 E4
SE Cascade Park Dr
13600 VCVR 98683 568 D3
Cascade Park Ests
- ClkC 98684 538 E6
- VCVR 98684 538 E6
SE Cascades Av
- VCVR 98664 537 H7
NE Cascades Pkwy
- PTLD 97220 567 G5
SE Cascade View Ct
11300 CmsC 97236 657 J3
Cascade View Dr
56300 ClbC 97053 414 F7
Cascade View Ln
56300 ClbC 97053 414 G7
Cascade Vista Av
- CmsC 97045 688 B5
Cascade Vista Ln
- CmsC 97070 715 J2
S Cascadia Ct
13300 CmsC 97038 807 D4
SW Cascadia Ct
19300 WasC 97007 624 D2
NW Cascadia Pl
- PTLD 97210 596 A3
SW Cascadia St
19800 WasC 97007 624 C2
Cascadia Village Dr
38700 CmsC 97055 690 J4
38700 SNDY 97055 690 J4
39000 SNDY 97055 691 A4
39400 CmsC 97055 691 A4
SE Cascadia Village Dr
38400 CmsC 97055 690 J4
38400 SNDY 97055 690 J4
SW Cascara Ct
3100 CmsC 97070 716 B6
Cascara Ln
4900 LKOW 97035 655 J4
4900 LKOW 97035 656 A4
NE Cascara Ln
30800 ClkC 98675 419 D3
SW Cascara Ln
9200 TLTN 97062 685 E3
SW Cascara Ter
23700 SRWD 97140 714 G1
24000 CmsC 97140 714 G1
SW Case Ct
8700 WasC 97223 655 F1
Case Rd NE
18700 MrnC 97002 774 C4
19300 MrnC 97137 774 C3
Casey Ct
- CmsC 97034 686 A3
NW Casey Dr
15100 WasC 97229 594 J1
SW Cashew Wy
16900 BRTN 97006 594 G6
SW Cashmur Ln
8200 WasC 97225 625 F2
8600 BRTN 97225 625 F2
SW Casilda Ct
17500 WasC 97007 624 F7
Cason Cir
7400 GLDS 97027 687 F2
Cason Ct
8400 CmsC 97027 687 F2
Cason Ln
7500 CmsC 97027 687 F2
7500 GLDS 97027 687 F2
Cason Rd
8300 CmsC 97027 687 E3
8300 GLDS 97027 687 E3
17400 CmsC 97267 687 F2
NW Casper Pl
5800 HBRO 97124 563 J6
5800 WasC 97124 563 J6
SW Caspian Ct
- BRTN 97008 655 B1
S Cass St
24400 CmsC 97013 776 A1
NE Cassady Ct
12200 ClkC 98685 476 H7
12200 ClkC 98685 506 J1
Cassidy Ct
39700 SNDY 97055 691 A4
SE Cassie Ct
15700 CmsC 97267 657 A7
SW Casteel Ct
10200 TLTN 97062 685 C3
SW Casteel St
10100 TLTN 97062 685 C3
SW Casting St
29000 WNVL 97070 715 D7
N Castle Av
3900 PTLD 97227 596 E1
4000 PTLD 97217 596 E1
SE Castle Ct
9600 CmsC 97009 659 F2
SW Castle Ct
18300 WasC 97007 624 E5
SW Castle Dr
20500 WasC 97007 624 C5
NW Castle Ter
- PTLD 97210 595 J2
Castleberry Lp
19700 ORCY 97045 717 E5
SW Castleridge Ln
700 PTLD 97219 656 F4
NE Castlewood Ct
800 HBRO 97124 593 D2
SW Castlewood St
13000 BRTN 97008 625 B1
13000 WasC 97005 625 B1
S Casto Rd
11900 CmsC 97013 747 B6
11900 CmsC 97045 747 B6
SW Catalina Dr
14500 TGRD 97223 654 J5
14500 WasC 97223 654 J5
SE Catalina Ln
6700 CmsC 97222 657 E3
Catarin St
59500 STHN 97051 384 J7
SW Catbird Ln
15900 BRTN 97007 654 G4

STREET
Block City ZIP Map# Grid

Catching Ct
3300 FTGV 97116 591 E2
S Cate Ln
18800 CmsC 97004 748 F7
Cater Rd
32300 ClbC 97051 414 D1
32300 ClbC 97053 414 D1
SW Cathedral Dr
16100 BRTN 97007 624 G7
16100 WasC 97007 624 G7
NE Catherine Ct
7500 HBRO 97124 594 B5
Catherine Dr
100 CtzC 98674 386 B6
Cathy Adams Dr
18700 ORCY 97045 717 A4
SE Catina Pl
11700 HPYV 97236 658 C4
N Catlin Av
7400 PTLD 97203 565 G2
SW Catlin Crest Dr
1100 WasC 97225 595 G7
SE Catlyn Woods Dr
16500 CmsC 97267 687 D1
16500 GLDS 97027 687 D1
16500 GLDS 97267 687 D1
SW Cattail Ct
16000 WasC 97223 654 G5
Cattle Dr
16300 CmsC 97045 687 G6
16300 ORCY 97045 687 G6
SE Cat Track Rd
22700 CmsC 97022 720 E1
Caufield Rd
13800 CmsC 97045 717 E6
13800 ORCY 97045 717 E6
Caufield St
200 ORCY 97045 717 D2
6000 WLIN 97068 687 A6
SE Caufield St
- ORCY 97045 717 D2
SE Causey Av
- CmsC 97236 657 H3
- HPYV 97236 657 H3
7800 CmsC 97222 657 F3
SE Causey Lp
8800 CmsC 97236 657 F3
Causey Wy
4300 WLIN 97068 686 J5
SW Cavalier Ct
13100 BRTN 97008 655 A1
SE Cavalier St
6800 CmsC 97267 657 E6
SE Cavalier Wy
6300 CmsC 97267 657 D6
NW Cavens Ln
1200 WasC 97124 592 J3
NE Cavitt Rd
3200 ClkC 98607 539 H3
NW Caxton Ln
9400 PTLD 97229 595 E4
S Cayuse Ct
13400 CmsC 97038 807 D6
SW Cayuse Ct
21400 TLTN 97062 685 E6
NW Cazadero Ct
200 ECDA 97023 750 B2
CC St
100 WDLD 98674 386 A1
300 WDLD 98674 385 J1
NE C C Landon Rd
- ClkC 98675 419 E2
NE CC Landon Rd
24300 ClkC 98675 419 E2
NW CD Hale Rd
- ClkC 98642 386 C7
N Cecelia St
4900 PTLD 97203 566 B3
SW Cecelia Ter
8400 WasC 97223 625 F6
Cedar
- CmsC 97015 657 H7
- WasC 97006 594 D5
Cedar Av
600 LCTR 98629 386 H7
E Cedar Av
500 LCTR 98629 386 H7
N Cedar Av
300 YCLT 98675 419 F1
S Cedar Av
100 YCLT 98675 419 F1
SE Cedar Av
14000 CmsC 97267 656 H6
Cedar Ct
- ClkC 98671 570 C3
- WHGL 98671 570 C3
1800 LKOW 97034 686 C1
3300 WLIN 97068 686 J2
Cedar Ct NE
13700 MrnC 97002 775 C3
N Cedar Ct
800 CNBY 97013 746 B5
SE Cedar Ct
12200 HPYV 97236 658 A3
Cedar Dr
- MthC 97231 535 A6
10 VCVR 98661 537 B3
NE Cedar Dr
18200 ClkC 98604 478 C2
S Cedar Dr
1300 CNBY 97013 776 C1
Cedar Ln
100 WDVL 97060 599 D4
700 ORCY 97045 717 D2
3200 VCVR 98661 537 A3
NW Cedar Ln
8200 PTLD 97229 595 F4
SW Cedar Ln
7200 WasC 97225 625 G2
S Cedar Lp
1200 CNBY 97013 776 C1
Cedar Rd
17100 LKOW 97034 686 B1
SW Cedar Rd
500 ECDA 97023 750 B4
Cedar Sq
- BRTN 97225 625 D1
- WasC 97225 595 D7
- WasC 97225 625 D1
Cedar St
- PTLD 97218 567 D7
100 FRVW 97024 599 B4
300 VCVR 98661 537 A6
800 LKOW 97034 656 F7
1000 FTGV 97116 591 J4

STREET
Block City ZIP Map# Grid

Cedar St
1600 NWBG 97132 713 E6
3900 WHGL 98671 570 D3
N Cedar St
100 YMHL 97148 711 A1
200 CNBY 97013 746 B6
NE Cedar St
200 CMAS 98607 569 E4
NW Cedar St
2000 MCMV 97128 770 G3
14500 PTLD 97231 565 A1
14600 PTLD 97231 564 J1
S Cedar St
100 YMHL 97148 711 A1
300 YmhC 97148 711 A1
SE Cedar St
100 CMAS 98607 569 F5
400 HBRO 97123 593 C5
700 DNDE 97115 742 H4
1100 YmhC 97115 742 H4
5800 CmsC 97222 657 D1
SW Cedar St
- PTLD 97205 596 D5
200 ECDA 97023 750 B3
400 HBRO 97123 593 B5
7500 WasC 97225 625 G3
7800 BRTN 97225 625 G3
SE Cedar Wy
10900 HPYV 97236 658 A3
NW Cedar Acre Dr
19900 ClkC 98642 446 D7
NE Cedar Brook Rd
12500 CmsC 97002 745 B4
SW Cedar Brook Wy
- SRWD 97140 684 E6
Cedar Canyon Rd
- WasC 97106 531 D6
- WasC 97116 531 D6
NW Cedar Canyon Rd
- WasC 97116 531 B5
42500 BNKS 97106 531 J4
46100 WasC 97106 531 C5
SE Cedar Creek Ln
- ECDA 97023 750 C4
SE Cedar Creek Pl
1500 GSHM 97080 629 D4
SE Cedar Creek Rd
40200 CmsC 97055 691 B2
Cedar Creek Vil
- SRWD 97140 684 G6
SE Cedarcrest Dr
6300 MWKE 97222 657 D4
6400 CmsC 97222 657 D4
SW Cedarcrest St
7400 TGRD 97223 655 G1
9000 WasC 97223 655 E1
Cedar Edge Ct
3300 FTGV 97116 591 E2
E Cedar Glen Lp
25300 CmsC 97067 724 C4
NE Cedar Green Ln
30800 YmhC 97132 713 H4
SW Cedar Grove Ln
19900 WasC 97006 594 D6
Cedar Hill Lp
- CmsC 97067 724 C4
E Cedar Hill Lp
68900 CmsC 97067 724 C4
Cedar Hill Pl
- CmsC 97067 724 C3
E Cedar Hill Ter
24700 CmsC 97067 724 C4
E Cedar Hill Wy
24600 CmsC 97067 724 C3
NW Cedar Hills Blvd
- BRTN 97225 595 C5
- BRTN 97229 595 C5
- WasC 97225 595 C5
- WasC 97229 595 C5
SW Cedar Hills Blvd
100 BRTN 97225 595 C7
100 WasC 97225 595 D6
2000 BRTN 97005 625 B1
2000 BRTN 97225 625 C1
2000 WasC 97005 625 C1
2000 WasC 97225 625 C1
Cedar Mill Cross
- BRTN 97225 595 B5
- BRTN 97229 595 C5
- WasC 97225 595 B5
- WasC 97229 595 B5
Cedar Mill Vil
- WasC 97229 595 B4
S Cedaroak Dr
4300 WLIN 97068 686 J3
4300 WLIN 97068 687 A3
Cedaroak St
300 STHN 97051 415 A2
SE Cedar Park Ct
2100 HBRO 97123 593 E6
SE Cedar Park Dr
13200 CmsC 97015 657 J5
E Cedar Point Ct
23700 CmsC 97049 724 E3
SW Cedar Pointe Dr
6800 WNVL 97070 715 G7
SW Cedar Pointe Ln
6900 WNVL 97070 715 G7
SE Cedar Ridge Ct
10900 CmsC 97222 657 F3
NW Cedar Ridge Dr
1800 PTLD 97229 595 F4
NE Cedar Ridge Lp
1200 VCVR 98664 537 F5
Cedar Springs Ter
32600 ClbC 97053 444 D2
NE Cedars View Dr
14900 ClkC 98606 478 D3
NW Cedar View Ln
2100 PTLD 97229 595 E3
SW Cedarview Wy
17500 SRWD 97140 684 E5
SW Cedarwood Av
300 MCMV 97128 770 G6
SW Cedarwood Ln
8900 WasC 97225 625 E2
Cedarwood Rd NE
13300 MrnC 97002 775 C2
SE Celebration Ct
2100 HBRO 97123 624 A1
SW Celebrity Ct
20300 WasC 97007 624 C3
SW Celebrity Ln
20500 WasC 97007 624 C3

STREET
Block City ZIP Map# Grid

SW Celebrity St
19200 WasC 97007 624 D3
SE Celeste Ct
14000 CmsC 97267 657 A5
SW Celeste Ln
10600 BRTN 97225 595 D6
10600 WasC 97225 595 D6
SE Celestia Cir
3600 TDLE 97060 599 G7
Cellars Av
1500 VCVR 98661 537 A4
Cellini Ct
10 LKOW 97035 656 A4
SE Celsiana Ct
15900 DAMA 97009 688 D1
NW Celtis Ln
400 HBRO 97124 593 B3
Cemetery
- YmhC 97128 741 E6
Cemetery Rd
- CmsC 97023 750 C3
- ECDA 97023 750 C3
- PTLD 97219 626 E7
900 RDGF 98642 416 A7
2200 MCMV 97128 770 D4
2300 YmhC 97128 770 D4
NE Cemetery Rd
- ClkC 98685 506 H1
600 CmsC 97023 750 C3
600 ECDA 97023 750 C2
S Cemetery Rd
- CmsC 97045 716 J2
- CmsC 97045 717 A2
- ORCY 97045 716 J2
- ORCY 97045 717 A2
SE Cemetery Rd
- CmsC 97236 627 J7
- CmsC 97236 657 J1
- MthC 97266 627 J7
30000 CmsC 97023 750 C1
30000 ECDA 97023 750 C1
Centennial Cir
1500 FTGV 97116 592 D6
Centennial Ln
- CmsC 97013 776 D5
Center Av
200 MOLA 97038 837 E1
N Center Av
11900 PTLD 97217 536 F7
SE Center Av
- PTLD 97206 627 F3
- PTLD 97266 627 F3
NW Center Ct
4500 CMAS 98607 569 C1
SE Center Ct
9600 PTLD 97266 627 G3
Center Dr
- PTLD 97266 628 A7
Center Ln
- MrnC 97002 775 D4
Center St
- NWBG 97132 713 C5
- TLTN 97062 685 A3
- WasC 97224 655 D2
- WasC 97224 685 A1
100 ORCY 97045 717 C1
200 MOLA 97038 837 E1
600 ORCY 97045 687 C7
4100 WHGL 98671 570 D5
5700 GLDS 97027 687 D4
N Center St
3400 NWBG 97132 713 C4
NE Center St
300 MthC 97019 600 D7
S Center St
100 NWBG 97132 713 C7
100 ORCY 97045 717 B1
300 NWBG 97132 743 C1
SE Center St
100 MthC 97019 600 D7
800 PTLD 97202 626 H2
3600 PTLD 97202 627 B3
4200 PTLD 97206 627 B2
8000 PTLD 97266 627 F3
14900 PTLD 97236 628 D3
17400 CmsC 97267 687 A2
SW Center St
8800 TGRD 97223 655 E4
11000 BRTN 97005 625 D2
11600 WasC 97005 625 B2
NE Center Commons Wy
5800 PTLD 97213 597 C4
N Center Ct St
10 PTLD 97227 596 G4
Centerpointe Dr
10 LKOW 97035 655 H5
NE Centerpointe Dr
8700 ClkC 98662 507 E4
8700 ClkC 98665 507 E4
Centerwood St
4800 LKOW 97035 686 A3
4900 LKOW 97035 685 J2
5000 CmsC 97035 685 J2
NW Centine Ln
- WasC 97229 594 H1
Central Av
17800 CmsC 97035 685 J2
17800 LKOW 97035 685 J2
NW Central Dr
15000 WasC 97229 594 J1
15400 WasC 97229 564 H7
E Central Ln
28100 CmsC 97067 724 C7
N Central St
- PTLD 97203 566 A3
9700 PTLD 97203 565 G2
SE Central Park Ct
12400 HPYV 97236 658 A2
Central Park at Bethany
- WasC 97229 594 J1
Central Point Rd
18700 ORCY 97045 717 A5
19400 CmsC 97045 717 A5
S Central Point Rd
19900 CmsC 97045 717 A7
20200 CmsC 97045 747 A1
21000 CmsC 97013 746 J2
21000 CmsC 97045 746 J2
24000 CmsC 97013 747 A7
24000 CmsC 97013 777 A1
24800 CmsC 97013 776 J2
NE Centurian Ct
500 GSHM 97030 629 F2
SE Centurion Av
300 GSHM 97080 629 F3

STREET
Block City ZIP Map# Grid

NE Centurion Dr
1000 GSHM 97030 629 F1
SE Centurion Ln
- GSHM 97080 629 F4
NE Centurion Pl
1500 GSHM 97030 629 F1
SE Centurion Wy
- GSHM 97080 629 F5
NW Century Blvd
6700 HBRO 97124 564 A5
7100 WasC 97124 564 B5
SE Century Blvd
- HBRO 97007 623 J1
300 HBRO 97123 594 A6
1700 HBRO 97123 593 J7
2200 HBRO 97123 623 J1
SE Century Ct
6100 HBRO 97123 593 J7
W Century Ct
1300 MCMV 97128 770 F5
Century Dr
13100 ORCY 97045 717 D5
SW Century Dr
16100 SRWD 97140 684 G6
Century Ln
2300 WLIN 97068 687 A5
SW Century Oak Cir
15900 TGRD 97224 655 D7
SW Century Oak Dr
9900 TGRD 97224 655 D7
SW Cereghino Ln
17800 SRWD 97140 684 E6
18000 WasC 97140 684 E6
SE Cereghino Pl
1600 TDLE 97060 599 G5
SW Cerise Wy
1900 TDLE 97060 599 E5
Cervantes Cir
300 LKOW 97035 656 A3
NE Cerveny Rd
31400 ClkC 98629 417 F2
Cessna St NE
14000 MrnC 97002 775 D1
Chablis Ct
- DNDE 97115 742 G3
Chad Dr
4100 CmsC 97034 686 A3
Chalet Ct NE
21900 MrnC 97002 775 D3
S Chalet Dr
18100 CmsC 97045 718 H3
SE Chalet Pl
58900 CmsC 97055 693 B5
E Chalet Rd
- CmsC 97055 693 C5
NW Chalmers Ln
29500 WasC 97113 562 B3
29500 WasC 97116 562 B3
NE Chalmers Wy
2400 MCMV 97128 771 B6
NW Chamberlain Pl
10100 NPNS 97133 563 B2
NE Chamberlain Rd
32700 MthC 97019 600 D5
32700 MthC 97060 600 D5
SE Chambers Rd
19000 CmsC 97055 691 J5
E Chambreau Rd
23600 CmsC 97067 724 B3
SE Champagne Ln
10000 HPYV 97236 657 H2
SW Champion Ct
7800 WNVL 97070 715 F7
Champion Wy
- CmsC 97055 690 F2
- SNDY 97055 690 F2
SE Champion Wy
- CmsC 97055 690 F2
- SNDY 97055 690 F2
SW Champlain Dr
2800 PTLD 97205 596 B6
SW Champlin Ln
11400 WasC 97007 654 F3
SW Champoeg Ct E
11200 WNVL 97070 745 C2
SW Champoeg Dr E
11200 WNVL 97070 745 B1
Champoeg Rd NE
4800 MrnC 97137 743 G6
7600 MrnC 97137 744 A7
8000 MrnC 97137 774 E1
8800 MrnC 97002 774 E1
9100 MrnC 97002 744 F7
Champoeg Cemetery Rd
- MrnC 97002 774 C2
- MrnC 97137 774 C2
NE Chancellor Ct
100 HBRO 97124 593 B2
SW Chandelle Ct
20400 WasC 97007 624 C4
SE Chandler Av
300 MCMV 97128 770 H6
2700 TDLE 97060 599 H6
SW Chandler Dr
12100 TGRD 97224 655 B6
Chandler Pl
200 LKOW 97034 656 E6
Chandler Rd
1200 LKOW 97034 656 E6
NW Channa Dr
14900 WasC 97229 594 J1
N Channel Av
4600 PTLD 97217 566 C7
4600 PTLD 97217 596 C1
Chantal Ct NE
11000 DNLD 97020 774 G4
Chantal St NE
11100 DNLD 97020 774 H4
SW Chanterelle Dr
47100 WasC 97116 591 C6
NW Chanticleer Dr
4200 WasC 97229 594 H1
Chanticleer Pl
20100 ORCY 97045 717 F6
SW Chantilly
11200 WNVL 97070 745 C1
NE Chantler Ln
100 HBRO 97124 593 C4
NW Chaparral Ter
4100 WasC 97006 594 F1
Chaparrel Dr
- WLIN 97068 686 H7
Chaparrel Lp
3400 WLIN 97068 686 H7

STREET
Block City ZIP Map# Grid

SW Chapel Ct
7400 WasC 97223 625 G5
SW Chapel Ln
6900 WasC 97223 625 G5
NW Chapel Hill Dr
1300 ClkC 98674 386 F1
Chapin Ct
12000 ORCY 97045 717 B4
NW Chapin Dr
3000 MthC 97229 595 F2
3000 PTLD 97229 595 F2
Chapin Wy
16300 LKOW 97034 686 G1
SE Chapman Av
1100 TDLE 97060 599 G5
SW Chapman Av
200 TDLE 97060 599 G5
SW Chapman Ct
1500 TDLE 97060 599 H5
SW Chapman Rd
19400 WasC 97140 714 C2
21900 WasC 97140 713 J1
22600 WasC 97140 683 J7
Chapman Wy
4100 LKOW 97035 686 A1
SW Chaps Ct
12300 BRTN 97008 655 B1
SW Char Ct
8200 TGRD 97223 655 F5
8200 TGRD 97224 655 F5
SW Charbonneau Dr
31800 WNVL 97070 745 F2
Char Diaz Dr
13600 ORCY 97045 717 E5
SW Chardonnay Av
14500 WasC 97224 654 J6
SE Chardonnay Ct
15900 CmsC 97267 657 A7
Chardonnay Dr
- MCMV 97128 770 F3
NW Chardonnay St
100 DNDE 97115 742 H2
100 YmhC 97115 742 H2
SW Chariot Ct
13500 BRTN 97008 655 A1
SW Charity Ct
2800 TDLE 97060 599 E6
NE Charity Rd
29900 ClkC 98604 417 C4
29900 ClkC 98629 417 C4
SE Charjan St
14200 CmsC 97015 658 C6
NW Charlais St
16200 WasC 97006 594 G1
16200 WasC 97229 594 H1
SW Charlene Ct
19800 WasC 97006 594 D7
SW Charlene St
20800 WasC 97006 594 C7
Charles Av
- CmsC 97022 690 C5
Charles Cir
5600 LKOW 97035 655 J5
Charles Ct
200 NWBG 97132 743 B1
NE Charles Ct
1300 FRVW 97024 599 B5
SE Charles Ct
17500 CmsC 97015 687 F2
Charles St
900 NWBG 97132 743 C1
SE Charles St
6500 CmsC 97222 657 D3
SW Charles St
1200 DNDE 97115 742 H4
1300 YmhC 97115 742 H4
SW Charles Ter
- WasC 97007 624 C6
N Charleston Av
7300 PTLD 97203 565 H3
SW Charleston Ln
13500 WasC 97224 655 A7
13600 WasC 97224 654 J7
Charleston Wy
300 VCVR 98664 537 E6
Charleton Ct
5200 CmsC 97035 685 J2
S Charlie Ct
18100 CmsC 97045 718 C3
NE Charlois Ct
2800 HBRO 97124 593 D1
NE Charlois Dr
2500 HBRO 97124 593 D1
SE Charlotte Dr
10100 CmsC 97236 657 H3
SW Charlotte Dr
8000 WasC 97007 624 F6
SW Charlotte Ln
29100 WNVL 97070 715 C7
Charlotte Wy
300 VCVR 98664 537 F6
NE Charlson Dr
- ClkC 98604 448 E5
NW Charlton Rd
13700 MthC 97231 535 A1
Charman St
400 ORCY 97045 717 B2
2100 WLIN 97068 687 A7
SW Charming Wy
4000 WasC 97225 625 G3
Charolais Ct
7500 GLDS 97027 687 E2
Charolais Dr
7500 GLDS 97027 687 E3
Charolais Wy
17200 GLDS 97027 687 E2
S Charriere Rd
20800 CmsC 97045 719 A2
NE Charter Oak Rd
11300 ClkC 98604 417 J6
11300 ClkC 98604 418 A6
SE Charview Ct
11300 HPYV 97236 657 J3
N Chase Av
9100 PTLD 97217 566 C3
SE Chase Ct
17700 SNDY 97055 690 J3
SW Chase Ln
7600 WasC 97223 625 G7
SE Chase Lp
5600 GSHM 97080 629 H5
SE Chase Rd
4400 GSHM 97080 629 G5
5800 MthC 97080 629 J5
27900 MthC 97080 630 A5

STREET
Block City ZIP Map# Grid

SW Chastain Av
1400 GSHM 97080 629 A4
NW Chastain Ct
100 GSHM 97030 629 A2
SW Chastain Ct
1300 GSHM 97080 629 A4
SW Chastain Dr
1000 GSHM 97080 629 A4
NW Chastain Pl
10 GSHM 97030 629 A2
SW Chastain Pl
1200 GSHM 97080 629 A4
NE Chateau Dr
5200 ClkC 98661 537 C1
SW Chateau Ln
10800 TGRD 97224 685 C1
SW Chatelain Dr
17000 WasC 97006 624 F1
SE Chatfield Ct
9300 CmsC 97236 657 H1
N Chatham Av
7500 PTLD 97217 566 E5
Chatham Ct
- CmsC 97035 685 H3
- RVGR 97035 685 H3
14000 LKOW 97035 655 J5
SW Chaucer Ct
7600 DRHM 97224 685 F1
N Chautauqua Blvd
7100 PTLD 97203 566 C5
7100 PTLD 97217 566 C5
N Chautauqua Pl
9000 PTLD 97203 566 C3
9000 PTLD 97217 566 C3
E Cheeney Ln
25200 CmsC 97067 724 A4
NW Cheerio Dr
13100 MthC 97229 565 B6
SW Chehalem Av
3700 PTLD 97239 626 C2
SW Chehalem Ct
13900 TGRD 97223 654 J3
Chehalem Dr
500 YmhC 97132 713 B7
N Chehalem Dr
1000 YmhC 97132 713 B6
NE Chehalem Dr
1800 NWBG 97132 713 B4
15900 YmhC 97132 713 B3
17900 YmhC 97132 712 J1
18500 YmhC 97132 683 A7
S Chehalem St
300 NWBG 97132 713 D7
300 NWBG 97132 743 D1
SW Chehalem Station Rd
26000 WasC 97140 714 B3
SW Chehalis Ct
21700 TLTN 97062 685 B6
SW Chehalis St
21600 TLTN 97062 685 D6
SW Chelan Ct
8400 TLTN 97062 685 F5
Chelan Dr
3400 WLIN 97068 686 H7
3500 CmsC 97068 686 H6
Chelan Lp
3500 WLIN 97068 686 H7
21900 CmsC 97068 686 H7
SW Chelan Pl
9100 BRTN 97008 625 B7
9100 BRTN 97008 655 B1
SW Chelan St
8200 TLTN 97062 685 F5
SE Cheldelin Rd
17800 CmsC 97009 628 H7
17800 DAMA 97009 628 H7
17800 MthC 97236 628 H7
SW Chelmsford Av
2200 PTLD 97201 626 D1
SE Chelsea Av
1100 VCVR 98661 537 D7
1100 VCVR 98664 537 D7
W Chelsea Ct
900 MCMV 97128 770 G5
Chelsea Dr
13900 LKOW 97035 656 A5
Chelsea Ln
4600 LKOW 97035 656 A5
SE Chelsea Ln
4300 HBRO 97123 593 H5
SW Chelsea Lp
13100 TGRD 97223 655 E5
SW Chelsea Pl
6400 WasC 97223 625 G5
SE Chelsea St
4300 CmsC 97222 657 B5
4300 MWKE 97222 657 B5
SE Chelsea Morning Dr
15700 HPYV 97236 658 D4
SW Cheltenham Ct
1000 PTLD 97239 626 D4
SW Cheltenham Dr
5600 PTLD 97239 626 D4
SW Cheltenham St
500 PTLD 97239 626 D4
NW Chemeketa Ct
17700 WasC 97229 564 F6
NW Chemeketa Ln
18000 WasC 97229 564 F6
18300 WasC 97231 564 E7
NW Chemult Pl
3800 WasC 97229 594 D1
Chenowith Rd
- CmsC 97045 689 C5
Cherabon Ct
15700 ORCY 97045 687 G5
SW Cheraw Ct
9400 TLTN 97062 685 B6
SW Cherbourg Ct
- WNVL 97070 745 H2
Cherokee Ct
3400 WLIN 97068 686 J2
SW Cherokee Ln
8500 WNVL 97070 715 E6
SW Cherokee St
8500 TLTN 97062 685 E3
Cherry Av
100 ORCY 97045 717 B2
NW Cherry Av
2800 VCVR 98660 536 E3
SW Cherry Av
5100 BRTN 97005 625 E4
Cherry Cir
600 LKOW 97034 686 F1

STREET
Block City ZIP Map# Grid

S Cherry Cir
600 CNLS 97113 592 D5
Cherry Ct
17500 LKOW 97034 686 F1
NW Cherry Ct
- PTLD 97231 565 E4
SE Cherry Ct
16200 CmsC 97267 687 C1
NE Cherry Dr
6700 HBRO 97124 594 B4
7200 WasC 97124 594 B4
S Cherry Dr
400 CNLS 97113 592 D5
SW Cherry Dr
7400 TGRD 97223 655 G5
Cherry Ln
1100 LKOW 97034 686 G1
NE Cherry Ln
3100 VCVR 98663 537 A2
NW Cherry Ln
21000 HBRO 97124 594 B4
21600 WasC 97124 594 B4
S Cherry Ln
- LKOW 97034 686 G1
SW Cherry Ln
9400 TLTN 97062 685 E5
NE Cherry Rd
2800 VCVR 98663 537 A2
3000 ClkC 98661 537 A2
Cherry St
- NWBG 97132 713 F5
- WasC 97006 594 D5
NW Cherry St
- PTLD 97231 565 E4
100 DNDE 97115 742 J2
3900 VCVR 98660 536 E1
4700 VCVR 98663 536 E1
5000 VCVR 98663 506 E6
S Cherry St
800 CNLS 97113 592 D5
Cherry Wy
33400 ClbC 97056 474 E4
SW Cherry Blossom Ct
12900 BRTN 97008 625 B5
SE Cherry Blossom Dr
10200 PTLD 97216 597 J7
Cherry Blossom Mnr
- GSHM 97024 598 J4
- GSHM 97230 598 J3
Cherry Crest Av
1300 LKOW 97034 686 D1
Cherry Crest Dr
1400 LKOW 97034 686 E1
SW Cherryhill Ct
13800 BRTN 97008 625 A5
SW Cherryhill Dr
6000 BRTN 97005 625 A4
6000 BRTN 97008 625 A5
6700 BRTN 97008 624 J5
SE Cherry Hill Ln
14500 CmsC 97267 657 E6
SW Cherryhill Ln
6400 BRTN 97008 624 J5
SW Cherry Orchard Pl
20800 SRWD 97140 684 F5
SE Cherry Park Rd
300 GSHM 97030 599 D6
SW Cherry Park Rd
1900 TDLE 97060 599 E5
2400 GSHM 97030 599 D5
2400 WDVL 97060 599 D5
SE Cherryville Dr
49400 CmsC 97055 692 D6
Cherrywood Dr
59200 STHN 97051 415 A1
SW Cherrywood Ln
15700 WasC 97224 655 D2
Cheryl Ct
1900 LKOW 97034 686 C2
SE Cheryl Ct
9900 CmsC 97236 627 H7
Cheryl Dr
25500 WLIN 97068 716 F2
SW Cheryl Ln
7300 BRTN 97008 625 C6
SW Chesapeak Av
- PTLD 97239 626 C3
SW Chesapeake Av
3900 PTLD 97239 626 C2
SW Chesapeake Ct
19100 TLTN 97062 685 J4
Chesapeake Dr
8300 VCVR 98664 537 F6
SW Chesapeake Dr
19000 TLTN 97062 685 J4
SW Chesapeake Pl
22000 SRWD 97140 684 J7
NE Chesapeake St
7500 HBRO 97124 594 B5
SW Cheshire Ct
11700 BRTN 97008 625 C5
20500 WasC 97007 624 C4
Cheshire Ln
- MWKE 97222 657 B4
SW Cheshire Rd
11600 BRTN 97008 625 B5
SE Chesney St
6100 HBRO 97123 593 J6
Chessington Ct
16400 GLDS 97027 687 C1
Chessington Ln
6400 GLDS 97027 687 D2
SW Chesterfield Ln
14300 WasC 97224 654 J7
Chestnut Av
50500 ClbC 97056 474 E4
SW Chestnut Av
5100 BRTN 97005 625 E4
W Chestnut Ct
600 WHGL 98671 569 H3
SW Chestnut Dr
1100 PTLD 97219 626 D5
NW Chestnut Ln
17900 MthC 97231 504 F7
SW Chestnut Ln
6200 BRTN 97005 625 E5
SW Chestnut Pl
4700 BRTN 97005 625 E3
Chestnut St
- WLIN 97068 687 B7
700 VCVR 98660 536 F2
NE Chestnut St
6000 HBRO 97124 593 J4
6200 HBRO 97124 594 B3

STREET
Block City ZIP Map# Grid

NW Chestnut St
22800 HBRO 97124 594 A4
22800 WasC 97124 594 A4
SE Chestnut St
2300 CmsC 97267 656 J6
2900 CmsC 97267 657 A6
SW Chestnut St
500 PTLD 97219 626 E5
900 PTLD 97239 626 D5
7500 WasC 97223 655 G1
W Chestnut St
- WHGL 98671 569 H3
SE Chevy Ln
- ORCY 97045 687 F6
SW Chevy Pl
8300 BRTN 97008 625 A7
Cheyenne Ter
6100 WLIN 97068 686 H5
SW Cheyenne Wy
17300 TLTN 97062 685 E2
SW Chia Lp
31100 WNVL 97070 745 E2
SW Chianti Pl
4800 WasC 97007 624 G2
SE Chianti Ter
9400 HPYV 97236 658 C1
Chiara Dr
12000 ORCY 97045 717 A4
SW Chiara Pl
1100 WasC 97006 594 D6
Chicago Av
200 GLDS 97027 687 D4
N Chicago Av
9200 PTLD 97203 565 H2
Chickadee Ct
2300 WLIN 97068 686 H5
SW Chickadee Ter
11000 BRTN 97007 654 H2
Chickaree Dr
18000 ORCY 97045 717 E2
SW Chickasaw Ct
10000 TLTN 97062 685 D5
SW Chickasaw Dr
10300 TLTN 97062 685 D5
SW Chicory Ct
12800 TGRD 97223 655 C1
NW Chikeric St
1300 ClkC 98665 506 F5
Childs Ct
19200 CmsC 97035 685 J3
19200 RVGR 97035 685 J3
Childs Rd
58400 ClbC 97051 414 H2
SW Childs Rd
1500 CmsC 97034 686 C3
3200 LKOW 97034 686 A3
4300 LKOW 97035 686 A3
4500 CmsC 97035 686 A3
4700 CmsC 97035 685 J3
4700 LKOW 97035 685 J3
4700 RVGR 97035 685 J3
6200 TLTN 97035 685 H3
7300 DRHM 97224 685 G2
7300 TLTN 97224 685 G3
SW Chilkat Ter
22200 TLTN 97062 685 D7
NE Chilles Cir
24000 WDVL 97060 599 D5
NW Chiloquin Ct
20700 WasC 97229 594 C1
Chilwood Ct
- CmsC 97002 775 G6
SW Chimney Ridge Ct
13200 TGRD 97223 655 A3
SW Chimney Ridge St
13000 TGRD 97223 655 A3
SE Chin St
31500 CmsC 97009 660 C3
S China Rd
24500 CmsC 97013 776 A1
SW Chinn Ln
13800 WasC 97224 654 H7
Chinook Ct
5200 CmsC 97035 685 J2
E Chinook Ln
- CmsC 97049 724 G6
SW Chinook Plz
33400 SPSE 97056 474 E1
Chinook St
300 MOLA 97038 837 G1
NE Chinook St
- WDVL 97060 599 C4
SW Chinook St
8600 TLTN 97062 685 F3
NE Chinook Wy
21900 FRVW 97024 599 B5
SW Chinook Wy
52000 SPSE 97056 474 E1
E Chinquepin Dr
23600 CmsC 97049 724 C3
NW Chipmunk Ln
11700 WasC 97229 595 C2
E Chippawa Ln
65700 CmsC 97049 723 J1
Chippendale Ln
13200 ORCY 97045 717 D5
Chippewa Ct
- WasC 97005 624 J1
3400 WLIN 97068 686 J3
SW Chippewa Tr
17500 TLTN 97062 685 D2
SW Chirp St
12800 TGRD 97224 655 B6
SE Chitwood Rd
19400 DAMA 97009 658 H7
NE Chkalov Dr
10 VCVR 98683 537 J6
10 VCVR 98684 537 J6
SE Chkalov Dr
100 VCVR 98683 537 J7
100 VCVR 98684 537 J6
SE Chloe Ln
- CmsC 97236 657 G1
SW Choban Ln
11400 BRTN 97225 595 C6
SW Choctaw St
9800 TLTN 97062 685 D7
Chow Mein Ln
3500 WLIN 97068 686 J4
Chris Ct
18300 GLDS 97027 687 D3
SW Chris St
17300 WasC 97007 624 F3
SW Chrisben Ct
15100 WasC 97007 624 H4
SE Chrisman Rd
8500 YmhC 97114 772 C7
SE Christen Ct
- CmsC 97027 687 F2
- GLDS 97027 687 F2
SE Christensen Av
15700 CmsC 97015 657 H7
SW Christensen Ct
21400 TLTN 97062 685 G6
SE Christensen Rd
1100 MthC 97019 600 D7
1100 MthC 97019 630 D1
SE Christenson Ct
14200 CmsC 97015 658 C6
Christie Dr
- LKOW 97034 686 H1
Christie St
20100 MrnC 97137 773 B6
20100 STPL 97137 773 B6
SE Christina Ct
14400 CmsC 97015 658 B6
SE Christina Ln
13500 CmsC 97015 658 B6
SE Christina Wy
13500 CmsC 97015 658 B6
NW Christine Ct
1700 PTLD 97229 595 F4
1700 WasC 97229 595 F4
S Christine Ct
18100 CmsC 97045 718 H3
SE Christopher Ct
14300 CmsC 97267 657 A6
SW Christopher Dr
18700 WasC 97006 624 E1
Christopher St
300 MOLA 97038 837 E1
SW Christy Av
2900 WasC 97005 625 C1
Christy Ct
1700 WLIN 97068 716 G2
SE Chrysler Ln
34100 CmsC 97023 750 D5
NW Chrystal Dr
2100 MCMV 97128 770 G3
SW Chukar Ter
11900 BRTN 97007 654 H3
SE Chula Vista Ct
9500 CmsC 97236 657 H1
9500 HPYV 97236 657 H1
SE Chula Vista St
10500 HPYV 97236 657 H1
SW Chunut Ct
4500 TLTN 97062 685 J5
4500 TLTN 97062 686 A4
Church Av NE
4100 STPL 97137 773 C6
4300 MrnC 97137 773 C6
Church Av NE SR-219
4100 STPL 97137 773 C6
4300 MrnC 97137 773 C6
Church Rd
33100 ClbC 97053 414 F6
SE Church Rd
28800 CmsC 97009 659 J6
29000 CmsC 97009 660 A6
Church St
- CmsC 97038 807 E7
- MOLA 97038 807 E7
10 DAYT 97114 772 A4
10 LKOW 97034 656 G6
100 STHN 97051 415 B1
900 DAYT 97114 771 J4
N Church St
1500 PTLD 97217 566 E7
NE Church St
900 PTLD 97211 566 H7
5300 PTLD 97218 567 D7
S Church St
1500 NWBG 97132 713 D7
SE Church St
9200 CmsC 97015 657 G7
SW Churchill
11200 WNVL 97070 745 B1
Churchill Ct
1900 WLIN 97068 686 H5
SW Churchill Ct
7900 TGRD 97224 655 F7
Churchill Dr
6600 CmsC 97267 687 D1
6600 GLDS 97027 687 D2
Churchill Ter
1800 WLIN 97068 686 H5
SW Churchill Wy
7900 TGRD 97224 655 F7
Churchill Downs Dr
6100 WLIN 97068 686 H5
Churchill Downs St
10 LKOW 97035 656 B3
Chynoweth Rd
- CmsC 97023 719 F3
- CmsC 97045 719 F2
SW Cicero Ct
17800 WasC 97007 624 F7
NW Cider Ln
16200 WasC 97229 564 G6
SE Cielo Ct
15600 DAMA 97009 689 B1
SE Cinderella Ct
3100 CmsC 97222 657 A5
Cindy Ln
18200 GLDS 97027 687 D2
SE Cindy Ln
100 DAYT 97114 771 J5
10000 CmsC 97009 660 A2
SW Cindy St
11100 BRTN 97008 625 C6
SW Cinnabar Ct
16300 BRTN 97007 654 G1
Cinnabar St
- WNVL 97070 715 F6
Cinnamon Sq
- ORCY 97045 717 E4
S Cinnamon Hill Ln
14500 CmsC 97042 777 G6
SW Cinnamon Hills Pl
23100 SRWD 97140 684 G7
23300 SRWD 97140 714 G1
SW Cipole Rd
18800 WasC 97062 685 A3
19000 SRWD 97140 685 A4
19900 TLTN 97062 685 A5
19900 WasC 97062 684 J5
19900 WasC 97140 684 J5
19900 WasC 97140 685 A5
20000 TLTN 97140 685 A5
SW Cipole Rd
20200 SRWD 97062 685 A5
SE Circle Av
5100 MthC 97236 628 F4
5100 PTLD 97236 628 F4
Circle Dr
- SNDY 97055 690 J3
NW Circle A Dr
2900 WasC 97229 595 A3
Circle Crest Dr
3200 FTGV 97116 591 E2
S Circle Diamond Ln
21900 CmsC 97023 719 B7
21900 CmsC 97045 719 B7
Cirque Dr
- LKOW 97035 656 B4
SE Cirrus Av
3900 MCMV 97128 771 D7
SW Cirrus Dr
7600 BRTN 97008 625 C7
SE Citadel St
9800 CmsC 97015 657 G7
SW Citation Dr
10000 BRTN 97008 655 A2
SW Citation Pl
9900 BRTN 97008 655 A1
SW Citizens Dr
8600 WNVL 97070 715 E7
SW Citrine Lp
14800 BRTN 97008 624 J7
SW Citrine Wy
14700 BRTN 97008 624 J7
N City Dump Rd
- PTLD 97203 535 G7
SE City View Dr
9500 CmsC 97236 657 H1
9500 HPYV 97236 657 H1
NW Civic Dr
1000 GSHM 97030 629 B1
E Clackamas Blvd
200 GLDS 97027 687 E4
W Clackamas Blvd
100 GLDS 97027 687 D5
NE Clackamas Ct
19600 GSHM 97230 598 J4
Clackamas Hwy
- CmsC 97009 658 B7
- CmsC 97009 688 H3
- CmsC 97009 689 D3
- CmsC 97015 658 D7
- CmsC 97015 687 H1
- CmsC 97015 688 A1
- CmsC 97022 689 H6
- CmsC 97022 719 J1
- CmsC 97022 720 A7
- CmsC 97023 720 A7
- CmsC 97023 750 E7
- DAMA 97009 658 B7
- DAMA 97009 688 F2
- DAMA 97009 689 D3
- DAMA 97015 658 D7
- ECDA 97022 720 A7
- ECDA 97022 750 A1
- ECDA 97023 720 A7
- ECDA 97023 750 A2
- HPYV 97015 658 D7
Clackamas Hwy SR-211
- CmsC 97022 719 J1
- CmsC 97022 720 A7
- CmsC 97023 720 A7
- CmsC 97023 750 A1
- ECDA 97022 720 A7
- ECDA 97022 750 A1
- ECDA 97023 720 A7
- ECDA 97023 750 A3
Clackamas Hwy SR-212
- CmsC 97009 658 D7
- CmsC 97015 658 A7
- CmsC 97015 687 H1
- CmsC 97015 688 A1
- DAMA 97009 658 D7
- DAMA 97015 658 D7
- HPYV 97015 658 D7
Clackamas Hwy SR-224
- CmsC 97009 658 B7
- CmsC 97009 688 H3
- CmsC 97009 689 D3
- CmsC 97015 658 D7
- CmsC 97015 687 H1
- CmsC 97015 688 A1
- CmsC 97022 689 H6
- CmsC 97022 719 J1
- CmsC 97022 720 A7
- CmsC 97023 720 A7
- CmsC 97023 750 E7
- DAMA 97009 658 B7
- DAMA 97009 688 F2
- DAMA 97009 689 D3
- DAMA 97015 658 D7
- ECDA 97022 720 A7
- ECDA 97022 750 A1
- ECDA 97023 720 A7
- ECDA 97023 750 A2
- HPYV 97015 658 D7
SE Clackamas Rd
6400 CmsC 97267 657 E7
8300 CmsC 97015 657 F7
NE Clackamas St
200 PTLD 97232 596 G4
2600 PTLD 97232 597 A4
4900 PTLD 97213 597 C4
8500 PTLD 97220 597 G4
11600 PTLD 97220 598 A4
13400 PTLD 97230 598 B4
16800 GSHM 97230 598 F4
NW Clackamas St
300 ECDA 97023 750 B3
SE Clackamas St
7500 CmsC 97222 657 E1
8000 CmsC 97236 657 F1
NE Clackamas Ter
- GSHM 97230 598 G4
Clackamas Vil
- CmsC 97236 657 F3
Clackamas-Boring Rd
- CmsC 97009 658 D7
- CmsC 97009 659 F6
- CmsC 97009 688 D1
- CmsC 97015 658 F7
- CmsC 97015 688 D1
- DAMA 97009 658 G7
- DAMA 97009 659 A6
- DAMA 97009 688 D1
- DAMA 97015 658 F7
- HPYV 97009 658 E7
Clackamas-Boring Rd
- HPYV 97015 658 F7
Clackamas-Boring Rd SR-212
- CmsC 97009 658 D7
- CmsC 97009 659 F6
- CmsC 97009 688 D1
- CmsC 97015 658 F7
- CmsC 97015 688 D1
- DAMA 97009 658 G7
- DAMA 97009 659 A6
- DAMA 97009 688 D1
- DAMA 97009 658 F7
- HPYV 97009 658 E7
- HPYV 97015 658 F7
SE Clackamas-Boring Rd
28300 CmsC 97009 659 J5
29300 CmsC 97009 660 A5
SE Clackamas-Boring Rd SR-212
28300 CmsC 97009 659 J5
29300 CmsC 97009 660 A5
Clackamas-Boring Rdg
- CmsC 97009 659 H5
Clackamas-Boring Rdg SR-212
- CmsC 97009 659 H5
SE Clackamas-Boring Rdg
12500 CmsC 97009 659 H5
SE Clackamas-Boring Rdg SR-212
12500 CmsC 97009 659 H5
Clackamas River Dr
13000 ORCY 97045 687 E5
S Clackamas River Dr
13200 CmsC 97045 687 H2
13200 ORCY 97045 687 H2
16000 CmsC 97045 688 C2
Clackamette Dr
1700 ORCY 97045 687 C6
S Claim Rd
14400 CmsC 97038 837 F4
SE Clair Ln
10800 YmhC 97114 771 F5
Clair St
5800 VCVR 98661 537 C7
NW Claire Ct
10900 WasC 97229 595 D3
Clairmont Ct
5900 LKOW 97035 655 H5
S Clairmont Ct
21000 CmsC 97004 748 A1
21000 CmsC 97045 748 A1
Clairmont Dr
- CmsC 97045 717 F5
- ORCY 97045 717 F5
SW Clairmont St
600 MCMV 97128 770 G6
W Clairmont St
600 MCMV 97128 770 G6
Clairmont Wy
13100 ORCY 97045 717 D4
NW Clapshaw Hill Rd
45800 WasC 97116 561 A1
Clara Ct
600 LKOW 97034 686 D1
SW Clara Ct
2700 TDLE 97060 599 F6
NW Clara Ln
23500 HBRO 97124 563 J6
SW Clara Ln
12300 MthC 97034 656 C3
12300 MthC 97219 656 C3
12300 PTLD 97034 656 C3
12300 PTLD 97035 656 C3
12300 PTLD 97219 656 C3
SE Clara St
7700 CmsC 97267 687 E1
SW Clara St
1500 TDLE 97060 599 F5
SW Clara Mae Wy
200 PTLD 97219 626 F7
NE Clara Smith Rd
36900 MthC 97019 600 H4
SE Clare Ct
16100 CmsC 97267 687 E1
SE Clare Rd
6600 MthC 97080 630 C6
NE Claremont Av
6800 PTLD 97211 566 H5
NW Claremont Dr
15500 WasC 97229 594 H1
16200 WasC 97006 594 H1
SE Claremont St
13700 HPYV 97236 658 B3
SW Claremont Ter
1300 WasC 97225 595 D7
Clarendon Av
58400 ClbC 97051 414 G2
58400 ClbC 97053 414 G2
N Clarendon Av
9500 PTLD 97203 566 A3
E Clarendon St
500 GLDS 97027 687 E4
NE Clarendon St
2100 HBRO 97124 593 E3
W Clarendon St
100 GLDS 97027 687 D5
SW Claridge Dr
9200 WasC 97223 655 F1
SW Clarion Ct
19300 WasC 97006 624 D1
SW Clarion St
21400 WasC 97006 624 B1
Clark Av
3200 VCVR 98661 537 A6
N Clark Av
- PTLD 97227 596 F3
NE Clark Av
10 BGND 98604 448 C5
SE Clark Av
10 BGND 98604 448 C5
SE Clark Cir
10700 HPYV 97236 658 A2
NE Clark Ct
400 MCMV 97128 771 B6
SE Clark Ct
2500 TDLE 97060 599 H6
N Clark Ln
600 CNLS 97113 592 D4
S Clark Ln
17600 CmsC 97045 719 F3
NW Clark Rd
20100 MthC 97231 504 E6
SE Clark Rd
7900 CmsC 97080 660 B1
7900 MthC 97080 630 A7
Clark St
100 STHN 97051 415 B1
22400 WLIN 97068 687 A7
N Clark St
1000 CNLS 97113 592 E4
NE Clark St
- PTLD 97220 567 J7
SE Clark St
9000 CmsC 97015 657 G7
SW Clark Hill Rd
9400 WasC 97007 624 A7
9400 WasC 97007 654 A5
10000 WasC 97123 654 A3
NW Clarno Ct
18100 WasC 97229 594 F1
SE Clatsop Ct
8200 PTLD 97266 627 H7
SE Clatsop St
500 PTLD 97202 626 H7
2300 MWKE 97202 626 J7
2300 MWKE 97222 626 J7
7200 MthC 97206 627 E7
7200 PTLD 97206 627 E7
8200 CmsC 97236 627 F7
8200 PTLD 97266 627 F7
9200 PTLD 97236 627 G7
13300 HPYV 97236 628 E7
13300 PTLD 97266 628 B7
14200 PTLD 97236 628 C7
14900 CmsC 97236 628 E7
SW Claudia Ct
20600 SRWD 97140 684 F5
S Claus Ct
22100 CmsC 97045 689 D5
SW Clawson Cir
1000 TDLE 97060 599 F4
NW Claxter St
30800 NPNS 97133 563 B1
NW Claxton Ct
1600 PTLD 97229 595 E3
SE Clay Ct
15200 PTLD 97233 598 D7
20900 GSHM 97030 599 A7
20900 GSHM 97030 629 A1
SE Clay St
10 PTLD 97214 596 H7
200 MCMV 97128 770 J5
3700 PTLD 97214 597 B7
4100 PTLD 97215 597 B7
9200 PTLD 97216 597 G7
13300 PTLD 97233 598 B7
17700 GSHM 97233 598 G7
SW Clay St
1300 PTLD 97201 596 D6
5800 MthC 97221 595 J7
5800 PTLD 97221 595 J7
10600 WasC 97140 715 C2
10600 WNVL 97140 715 C2
SW Clay St US-26
700 PTLD 97201 596 E6
SE Claybourne St
1600 PTLD 97202 626 H5
3600 PTLD 97202 627 B5
7200 PTLD 97206 627 E5
8100 PTLD 97266 627 F5
12300 PTLD 97236 628 A5
12300 PTLD 97266 628 A5
NW Clay Horse Dr
- WasC 97106 531 E3
SE Clayson Av
5400 CmsC 97267 687 C2
Clayton Ct
39000 SNDY 97055 691 A4
Clayton Wy
1000 GLDS 97027 687 E2
Clear St
14000 ORCY 97045 687 F6
SW Clear St
10600 TLTN 97062 685 C7
S Clear Acres Dr
18000 CmsC 97045 688 E6
Clearbrook Ct
3100 NWBG 97132 713 C4
Clearbrook Dr
900 ORCY 97045 717 B3
SE Clearbrook St
5400 HBRO 97123 593 H6
5400 WasC 97123 593 H6
E Clear Creek Rd
71100 CmsC 97049 724 E1
S Clear Creek Rd
21300 CmsC 97023 749 D3
NE Clear Creek Wy
800 FRVW 97024 599 B5
SW Clear Hills Dr
7400 WasC 97225 625 G4
SW Clear Hills Ter
7500 WasC 97225 625 G4
Clear View Ct
21400 CmsC 97045 747 F2
SW Clearview Pl
13500 TGRD 97223 655 A5
SW Clearview Wy
13100 TGRD 97223 655 A5
SE Clearwater Ct
8600 HPYV 97236 628 D7
SW Clearwater Ct
17300 BRTN 97006 594 G7
NE Clearwater Dr
3500 MCMV 97128 771 B3
3500 YmhC 97128 771 B3
NW Cleary Ct
15800 WasC 97006 594 J4
NW Cleek Pl
4100 WasC 97229 594 H1
NW Cleetwood Av
19200 MthC 97231 504 E6
SE Clematis Ct
14600 HBRO 97123 623 E1
S Clematis Rd
700 CmsC 97068 686 F5
SW Clemell Av
3200 PTLD 97201 626 D2
3200 PTLD 97239 626 C2
SE Cleone Ct
10000 CmsC 97236 657 H2
NE Cleveland Av
10 GSHM 97030 629 D1
10 GSHM 97080 629 C2
1800 GSHM 97030 599 C7
3500 PTLD 97212 596 G2
4000 PTLD 97211 596 G1
NE Cleveland Av
5000 PTLD 97211 566 G6
SE Cleveland Av
10 GSHM 97030 629 C2
10 GSHM 97080 629 C3
400 MCMV 97128 770 H6
Cleveland St
- CLTN 97111 741 A1
14000 ORCY 97045 687 F6
W Cleveland St
100 CLTN 97111 741 A1
SW Cleveland Bay Ln
12600 BRTN 97008 655 B2
NW Cliff Dr
52900 SPSE 97056 444 D7
NW Cliff Ln
300 ECDA 97023 750 B3
NE Cliff St
9000 PTLD 97220 597 G2
SW Clifford Ct
15300 SRWD 97140 684 H7
SW Clifford St
11100 BRTN 97008 625 C6
S Cliffside Dr
13000 CmsC 97042 777 D3
SE Cliffside Dr
1300 ClkC 98671 570 B1
S Cliffview Rd
16300 CmsC 97045 688 B3
SW Clifton Ct
1200 MCMV 97128 770 F6
SW Clifton St
1400 PTLD 97201 596 D7
SW Cline St
8200 PTLD 97219 625 J6
SE Clinton Ct
8500 PTLD 97266 627 G1
13700 PTLD 97236 628 C1
Clinton St
100 ORCY 97045 717 B1
59500 STHN 97051 384 J7
SE Clinton St
- PTLD 97202 626 G1
2800 PTLD 97202 627 A1
6700 PTLD 97206 627 E1
9200 PTLD 97266 627 G1
11900 PTLD 97266 628 A2
16500 PTLD 97236 628 E2
17400 GSHM 97236 628 G2
18200 GSHM 97030 628 G2
SW Clinton St
6600 TGRD 97223 655 G3
Closher Dr
- CmsC 97049 724 H6
SW Cloud Ct
11500 TGRD 97224 655 C6
Cloud View Dr
21400 CmsC 97045 747 F2
SE Clover Ct
2400 HBRO 97123 623 E1
SE Clover Ln
11400 HPYV 97236 657 J2
11700 HPYV 97236 658 A1
SW Cloverdale Wy
1500 WasC 97006 594 C7
Cloverleaf Rd
1400 LKOW 97034 686 C1
Club House Cir
6200 WLIN 97068 686 H5
Club House Ct
3000 WLIN 97068 686 H5
SE Clubhouse Ct
19300 CmsC 97055 693 B5
Clubhouse Dr
200 ECDA 97023 750 B4
2100 WLIN 97068 686 H5
NW Clubhouse Dr
15600 WasC 97229 594 H2
SE Clubhouse Rd
19100 CmsC 97055 693 B5
SW Clubhouse Rd
500 ECDA 97023 750 D5
SW Club Meadow Ln
8900 WasC 97225 625 E3
9100 BRTN 97225 625 E3
SW Clutter Rd
10500 WasC 97140 715 C3
10500 WNVL 97070 715 C3
SW Clydesdale Ct
12200 TGRD 97223 655 D4
SW Clydesdale Pl
10400 TGRD 97223 655 D4
SW Clydesdale Ter
10100 BRTN 97008 655 B2
CM Dr
- CmsC 97049 724 D3
CO-74 Dayton Av
- YmhC 97115 742 J2
CO-74 NE Fox Farm Rd
9600 YmhC 97115 742 J2
10400 YmhC 97132 742 J1
11100 YmhC 97115 712 J7
11100 YmhC 97132 712 J7
SW Coach Ct
13500 BRTN 97008 655 A1
NW Coach House Ct
2000 ClkC 98685 476 E7
SE Coachman Ln
26800 CmsC 97009 659 G2
Coalca Ln
- CmsC 97045 716 G7
Coal Creek Rd
32200 ClbC 97056 474 C1
32200 SPSE 97056 474 C1
SE Coalman Rd
40800 CmsC 97055 691 E3
47000 CmsC 97055 692 A6
NE Coast Pine Av
100 VCVR 98684 538 C6
SE Coast Pine Av
14600 VCVR 98684 538 C6
SW Cobalt Ln
15400 BRTN 97007 654 E2
SW Cobb Ln
17500 WasC 97007 624 F7
Cobb Wy
4100 LKOW 97035 686 A1
SW Cobble Ct
17000 SRWD 97140 714 F1
Cobblecreek Dr
- NWBG 97132 743 F1
- YmhC 97132 743 F1
SW Cobblestone Dr
16800 SRWD 97140 684 F7
NW Coburg Ct
16900 WasC 97006 594 G2
NW Coburg Ln
16700 WasC 97006 594 G2
NE Coburn Dr
1600 MCMV 97128 770 J2
1600 MCMV 97128 771 A2
S Cochell Ln
14300 CmsC 97042 777 F3
NE Cochran Av
1000 GSHM 97030 629 E1
SE Cochran Dr
800 GSHM 97080 629 E4
SW Cochran Dr
22600 SRWD 97140 684 H7
SW Cochran St
14800 SRWD 97140 684 H7
SE Cochrane Rd
26400 GSHM 97030 629 F1
26400 MthC 97030 629 G1
26400 MthC 97060 629 G1
26400 TDLE 97060 629 F1
NW Cody Ct
100 HBRO 97124 593 B3
100 WasC 97124 593 B3
Cody Ln NE
21000 AURA 97002 775 F4
21000 MrnC 97002 775 F4
SW Cody Ln
17700 WasC 97007 624 F5
SW Cody St
17300 WasC 97007 624 F5
SW Coe Wy
16400 WasC 97007 624 G6
Coeur d'Alene Dr
3300 WLIN 97068 686 H7
3300 WLIN 97068 716 H1
Coffey Ln
1400 NWBG 97132 713 F6
NW Coffey Ln
21100 WasC 97124 564 C2
SE Coffey Rd
900 ClkC 98671 540 B7
1000 ClkC 98671 570 B1
SE Cohiba Ct
16300 DAMA 97009 688 E1
NE Coho Ct
- WDVL 97060 599 C5
SW Coho Ct
7300 TLTN 97062 685 G4
Coho Ln
4000 LKOW 97034 686 A3
4700 WLIN 97068 686 J7
Coho St
900 MOLA 97038 837 G1
Cokeron Dr
19200 ORCY 97045 717 E4
Colby Ct
5800 CmsC 97035 685 H3
N Cole Av
100 MOLA 97038 837 F2
S Cole Av
100 MOLA 97038 837 F2
Cole Ct
300 MOLA 97038 837 F2
SW Cole Ct
22000 TLTN 97062 685 D6
SE Cole Dr
15100 CmsC 97015 658 D7
Cole Ln NE
21800 MrnC 97002 775 E3
SW Cole Ln
11500 TGRD 97224 655 C5
N Cole St
100 MOLA 97038 837 F1
700 CmsC 97038 807 F7
700 MOLA 97038 807 F7
NW Coleman Dr
11900 WasC 97229 595 C4
SW Coleman Lp N
10400 WNVL 97070 715 C7
SW Coleman Lp S
10500 WNVL 97070 715 C7
Cole Valley Av
59400 ClbC 97051 384 H7
59400 ClbC 97051 414 H1
NE Cole Witter Rd
17400 ClkC 98604 418 G5
N Colfax St
1500 PTLD 97217 566 E6
NE Colfax St
9300 PTLD 97220 567 H6
SW Colfelt Ln
18300 SRWD 97140 714 D1
SW Colin Ct
8000 WasC 97223 625 F7
SE Colina Vista Av
17300 CmsC 97267 687 C2
SW Collard St
800 MCMV 97128 770 G5
SW Colleen Ct
16000 BRTN 97007 624 G5
SE College Av
300 MCMV 97128 770 H6
NW College Dr
- PTLD 97231 565 D4
11200 PTLD 97229 565 D4
N College St
100 NWBG 97132 713 C5
3100 YmhC 97132 713 C4
N College St SR-219
100 NWBG 97132 713 C5
3100 YmhC 97132 713 C4
S College St
100 NWBG 97132 713 C7
400 NWBG 97132 743 C1
1200 YmhC 97132 743 C1
SW College St
1200 PTLD 97201 596 D7
College Wy
2000 FTGV 97116 591 J4
College Hill Pl
2000 WLIN 97068 686 G2
College View Dr
2300 LKOW 97034 686 G2
2300 WLIN 97068 686 G2
SW Collina Av
10500 MthC 97219 656 G2
SW Collins Ct
1700 PTLD 97219 656 D1
NW Collins Rd
17800 WasC 97133 533 B1
SW Collins St
4200 PTLD 97219 656 D3

Portland Street Index

STREET
Block City ZIP Map# Grid

Collins Wy
4000 LKOW 97035 656 A6
Collins Crest Ct
400 GLDS 97027 687 D3
Collins Crest St
600 GLDS 97027 687 D3
N Colonial Av
3700 PTLD 97227 596 E1
4600 PTLD 97217 596 E1
NW Colonnade Dr
20200 HBRO 97124 594 C2
SE Colony Cir
5400 CmsC 97267 687 C2
SW Colony Ct
5200 BRTN 97005 624 J4
15900 WasC 97224 654 G6
SW Colony Dr
500 PTLD 97219 656 E2
15800 WasC 97223 654 G6
15800 WasC 97224 654 G6
SW Colony Ln
12500 BRTN 97005 625 B2
SW Colony Pl
15900 WasC 97224 654 G5
Colony Rd
- HBRO 97006 594 D5
SW Colony Creek Ct
8200 TGRD 97224 655 F6
NW Colorado Av
- PTLD 97231 565 F5
NW Colorado Ct
- PTLD 97231 565 F5
SE Colorado Rd
32300 CmsC 97009 690 C1
33500 CmsC 97055 690 F3
Color Connection
- WNVL 97070 715 F5
SW Colt Ct
12500 BRTN 97008 655 B1
SE Colt Dr
2800 PTLD 97202 626 J4
2800 PTLD 97202 627 A3
SW Colton Ln
8300 TGRD 97224 655 F7
Coltrane St
14600 ORCY 97045 717 F4
Colts Foot Ln
4000 LKOW 97035 656 A5
Columbia
- STHN 97051 385 C7
Columbia Av
1400 GLDS 97027 687 D3
E Columbia Av
- ClbC 97056 475 A1
33500 SPSE 97056 444 E7
33800 ClbC 97056 474 J1
33800 SPSE 97056 474 F1
NW Columbia Av
3600 WasC 97229 594 E1
4600 WasC 97229 564 E7
W Columbia Av
33400 SPSE 97056 444 E7
Columbia Blvd
10 STHN 97051 385 D7
2200 STHN 97051 415 A1
2700 STHN 97051 414 J2
2800 ClbC 97051 414 J2
N Columbia Blvd
10 PTLD 97211 566 G4
10 PTLD 97217 566 F4
3000 PTLD 97203 566 B2
6800 PTLD 97203 565 H1
9000 PTLD 97203 535 G7
NE Columbia Blvd
10 PTLD 97211 566 H4
10 PTLD 97217 566 G4
2300 PTLD 97211 567 B6
3600 PTLD 97218 567 B6
8200 PTLD 97220 567 G7
NE Columbia Blvd US-30 BYP
9200 PTLD 97220 567 G7
SW Columbia Cir
21700 TLTN 97062 685 B6
N Columbia Ct
5100 PTLD 97203 566 B2
NE Columbia Ct
2900 PTLD 97211 567 A5
Columbia Dr
- PTLD 97217 536 E6
600 MOLA 97038 807 D7
E Columbia Dr
100 NWBG 97132 713 C5
100 YmhC 97132 713 C5
SW Columbia Dr
21600 TLTN 97062 685 D6
21900 WasC 97062 685 D6
W Columbia Dr
100 NWBG 97132 713 B5
100 YmhC 97132 713 B5
SE Columbia Pkwy
4800 VCVR 98661 537 B7
NW Columbia Pl
- PTLD 97231 565 C1
Columbia Shrs
- VCVR 98661 536 H7
Columbia St
10 WDLD 98674 385 J1
100 VCVR 98660 536 F6
100 VCVR 98661 536 F6
NW Columbia St
3900 VCVR 98660 536 G2
4400 VCVR 98663 536 G1
4900 ClkC 98663 506 G7
4900 ClkC 98663 536 G1
4900 VCVR 98663 506 G7
18500 MthC 97231 534 E4
S Columbia St
500 NWBG 97132 743 D1
SW Columbia St
- PTLD 97221 595 J7
- SRWD 97140 684 G7
800 PTLD 97201 596 E7
Columbia Sta
- PTLD 97230 598 C1
N Columbia Wy
6200 PTLD 97203 566 A2
6800 PTLD 97203 565 J3
SE Columbia Wy
100 VCVR 98660 536 F6
100 VCVR 98661 536 G6
2700 VCVR 98661 537 A6
Columbia House Blvd
2200 VCVR 98661 536 J6
2600 VCVR 98661 537 A6
SE Columbia Ridge Dr
700 VCVR 98664 537 F7
SE Columbia River Dr
500 VCVR 98661 536 H7
Columbia River Hwy
- MthC - 599 H3
- MthC - 600 E4
- PTLD - 596 D4
- PTLD 97210 596 D3
- TDLE - 599 E3
- WDVL - 599 E3
50000 ClbC 97056 474 E5
50600 SPSE 97056 474 E4
52400 SPSE 97056 444 E6
52700 ClbC 97056 444 G2
55600 ClbC 97053 444 G2
56000 ClbC 97053 414 G7
57800 ClbC 97051 414 J4
58100 ClbC 97051 415 A3
58300 STHN 97051 415 A3
60700 ClbC 97051 385 C5
61100 CBAC 97018 385 C5
61100 ClbC 97018 385 C5
62900 ClbC 97054 385 B1
Columbia River Hwy I-5
- PTLD - 596 F3
Columbia River Hwy I-84
- MthC - 599 H3
- MthC - 600 E4
- TDLE - 599 E3
- WDVL - 599 E3
Columbia River Hwy US-30
- MthC - 599 H3
- MthC - 600 E4
- PTLD - 596 D3
- PTLD 97210 596 D3
- TDLE - 599 E3
- WDVL - 599 E3
50000 ClbC 97056 474 E5
50600 SPSE 97056 474 E4
52400 SPSE 97056 444 E6
52700 ClbC 97056 444 G2
55600 ClbC 97053 444 G2
56000 ClbC 97053 414 G7
57800 ClbC 97051 414 J4
58100 ClbC 97051 415 A3
58300 STHN 97051 415 A3
60700 ClbC 97051 385 C5
61100 CBAC 97018 385 C5
61100 ClbC 97018 385 C5
62900 ClbC 97054 385 B1
E Columbia River Hwy
- MthC 97060 599 G4
100 TDLE 97060 599 G4
N Columbia River Hwy
200 STHN 97051 385 B7
700 ClbC 97051 385 C6
N Columbia River Hwy US-30
200 STHN 97051 385 B7
700 ClbC 97051 385 C6
NE Columbia River Hwy
24400 TDLE 97060 599 E3
24400 WDVL 97060 599 E3
S Columbia River Hwy
100 STHN 97051 415 A2
S Columbia River Hwy US-30
100 STHN 97051 415 A2
SE Columbia Shores Blvd
500 VCVR 98661 536 H7
NW Columbia Summit Dr
1800 CMAS 98607 569 A3
Columbia View Dr
- VCVR 98661 537 B6
Columbine Ct
19300 CmsC 97045 717 A5
19300 ORCY 97045 717 A5
SE Columbine Ct
2300 HBRO 97123 593 G7
NE Columbine Dr
14800 VCVR 98682 538 C2
NW Columbine Ln
1700 PTLD 97229 595 G3
SW Colville Ct
20500 TLTN 97062 685 F5
NE Colvin Ct
1500 MCMV 97128 771 B4
SW Colvin Ln
26600 WNVL 97070 715 F4
NE Colwood Wy
6400 PTLD 97218 567 E6
SW Colyer Pl
15500 WasC 97224 654 J7
SW Colyer Wy
15500 WasC 97224 654 J7
NW Comadrona Ln
16400 WasC 97229 564 G7
SE Comanche Ct
13200 CmsC 97015 658 B7
SW Comanche Ter
20200 TLTN 97062 685 E5
SW Comanche Wy
8600 TLTN 97062 685 E5
SW Combine Ct
13100 BRTN 97008 655 C1
SW Combine St
13000 BRTN 97008 655 A2
NW Comet Ct
44500 WasC 97106 531 G3
Cominger Ct
12500 ORCY 97045 717 B5
Cominger Dr
12400 ORCY 97045 717 C4
S Cominger Dr
- ORCY 97045 717 C4
N Commando Av
7500 PTLD 97203 565 G1
SE Commerce Av
500 BGND 98604 448 C6
1600 ClkC 98604 448 D7
SW Commerce Cir
9300 WNVL 97070 715 D3
NW Commerce Ct
- ECDA 97022 750 A1
1700 TDLE 97060 599 D2
Commerce Pkwy
- NWBG 97132 743 E2
- YmhC 97132 743 E2
Commerce St
300 DAYT 97114 772 B4
N Commerce St
4300 PTLD 97217 566 B7
NE Commerce St
100 BNKS 97106 531 J5
Commercial Av
33500 ClbC 97056 444 E5
N Commercial Av
3500 PTLD 97227 596 F2
4000 PTLD 97217 596 F1
6500 PTLD 97217 566 G5
Commercial Dr
- MCMV 97128 770 G7
NW Commercial St
30600 NPNS 97133 563 B1
SW Commercial St
9300 TGRD 97223 655 E4
SW Commons Ct
9500 WasC 97005 625 E3
9500 WasC 97225 625 E3
Commons Wy
- STHN 97051 385 B7
SW Commonwealth Av
2400 PTLD 97201 626 D3
SW Commonwealth Ln
13200 WasC 97005 595 A7
NW Como Pl
- PTLD 97210 596 B5
NW Compton Dr
1000 HBRO 97006 594 D4
1500 HBRO 97124 594 D3
NW Compton Lp
- HBRO 97006 594 D4
SE Compton Rd
31300 CmsC 97009 660 D5
SW Comus Ct
- PTLD 97219 656 D2
SW Comus Pl
4500 PTLD 97219 656 A2
SW Comus St
- PTLD 97219 655 J2
1700 MthC 97219 656 G2
4700 PTLD 97219 656 A2
SE Con Battin Rd
8500 CmsC 97236 657 F1
SW Concho Ct
10000 TLTN 97062 685 D5
N Concord Av
3900 PTLD 97227 596 E1
4000 PTLD 97217 596 E1
6500 PTLD 97217 566 E5
SE Concord Ct
15000 CmsC 97267 657 B6
SE Concord Rd
2300 CmsC 97267 686 J1
2800 CmsC 97267 656 J7
3000 CmsC 97267 657 A7
Concord Wy
2900 FTGV 97116 591 H3
SW Concord Wy
600 WasC 97006 594 F6
SE Concorde Pl
5800 HBRO 97123 593 J6
NW Concordia Ct
17600 WasC 97229 564 F6
Condolea Ct
10 LKOW 97035 656 C4
10 PTLD 97035 656 C3
Condolea Dr
10 LKOW 97035 656 C4
10 PTLD 97035 656 C3
Condolea Ter
10 LKOW 97035 656 B4
10 PTLD 97035 656 B4
Condolea Wy
10 LKOW 97035 656 B4
SE Condor Av
2600 GSHM 97080 629 G5
SW Condor Av
3600 PTLD 97239 626 E2
NE Condor Dr
10 GSHM 97080 629 G3
SE Condor Dr
10 GSHM 97080 629 G3
SW Condor Ln
3700 PTLD 97239 626 E2
NW Condor Pl
5400 WasC 97229 564 C7
SE Condor Pl
1300 GSHM 97080 629 G4
SW Condor Wy
10 PTLD 97239 626 E3
SW Cone Pl
200 WasC 97006 594 D6
Cone St NE
10600 DNLD 97020 774 F4
SW Conestoga Dr
9900 BRTN 97008 655 B1
9900 BRTN 97223 655 C2
9900 TGRD 97223 655 C2
Conestoga Ln
2000 WLIN 97068 686 H5
Conestoga Pk
- BRTN 97008 655 C1
N Congress Av
4500 PTLD 97217 596 F1
8200 PTLD 97217 566 F4
Conifer Ct
18700 ORCY 97045 716 J3
S Conifer Ct
21900 CmsC 97045 747 F3
Conifer Dr
1700 LKOW 97034 656 E7
NE Conifer Dr
11100 ClkC 98662 507 J4
SW Conifer Dr
22600 WasC 97140 713 J1
Conifer Pl
700 DAYT 97114 772 B5
Conjuwac Rd
- CmsC 97067 724 A3
Conn St
11900 ORCY 97045 717 B4
NW Connell Av
100 HBRO 97123 593 B4
1200 HBRO 97124 593 B3
SW Connell Av
400 HBRO 97123 593 B5
NW Connell Rd
2200 HBRO 97124 593 B2
2300 WasC 97124 593 B2
SW Connemara Pl
8300 BRTN 97008 625 B7
SW Connemara Ter
7900 BRTN 97008 625 B7
NW Connery Ter
6400 WasC 97229 564 J6
NW Connett Meadow Ct
17700 WasC 97229 564 F7
Connie Ct
19800 ORCY 97045 717 G6
SW Connor Pl
14300 WasC 97224 654 J6
E Connors Ct
67300 CmsC 97067 724 B4
SW Conor Cir
14800 WasC 97006 594 J6
NW Conrad Ct
600 MCMV 97128 770 G5
2900 CMAS 98607 569 B2
SE Conrad Ct
3600 HBRO 97123 623 E2
NW Conrad St
3400 CMAS 98607 569 B2
SE Constance Dr
- PTLD 97236 627 G7
8500 CmsC 97236 627 G7
SW Constance St
17300 WasC 97007 624 F7
NW Continental Pl
4500 WasC 97006 594 F3
Convent Av
4000 STPL 97137 773 B5
SE Conway Ct
4500 MWKE 97222 657 B3
Conway Dr
13800 ORCY 97045 717 E6
SW Conzelmann Rd
19000 WasC 97140 684 C4
SE Cook Ct
10400 CmsC 97222 657 E2
SW Cook Ct
9700 TGRD 97224 685 E1
SW Cook Ln
10500 TGRD 97223 655 D5
SW Cook Rd
33000 WasC 97123 592 H7
Cook St
10 RDGF 98642 415 J6
18600 ORCY 97045 717 A3
N Cook St
10 PTLD 97212 596 G2
700 PTLD 97227 596 F2
NE Cook St
10 PTLD 97212 596 G2
10 PTLD 97227 596 G2
SE Cook St
17500 CmsC 97267 687 C2
SE Cooke Rd
2700 CmsC 97267 686 J2
2800 CmsC 97267 687 A2
NE Cooley Rd
25400 ClkC 98604 448 B1
SE Coop Rd
21300 CmsC 97022 690 A7
Cooper Dr
- YmhC 97128 770 E6
NE Cooper Ln
7700 YmhC 97148 711 C3
SW Cooper Ln
16100 WasC 97224 654 G6
NE Cooper Rd
2800 ClkC 98607 539 F3
SE Cooper St
3600 PTLD 97202 627 B5
5000 PTLD 97206 627 B5
8900 PTLD 97266 627 G5
12700 PTLD 97236 628 B6
SW Cooperhawk Ct
19600 WasC 97007 624 D6
SW Cooperidge Ct
20600 WasC 97007 624 C7
SW Cooper Mountain Rd
11400 TGRD 97223 655 C3
17500 WasC 97007 654 F3
Cooperspur Ct
59000 STHN 97051 414 H1
SE Coot Wy
5100 HBRO 97123 593 H6
SW Copel St
- WasC 97225 625 G1
7500 BRTN 97225 625 G1
NW Copeland St
10700 WasC 97229 595 D5
Copeland Wy
- LKOW 97035 656 B4
S Copley Ct
16500 CmsC 97045 718 B4
SW Copper Ct
15100 BRTN 97007 654 J1
SW Copper Ter
- SRWD 97140 684 E6
- WasC 97140 684 E6
NE Copper Beech Dr
6100 HBRO 97124 593 G3
6200 HBRO 97124 594 A3
SW Copper Creek Dr
16100 TGRD 97224 685 E1
SW Copper Hill Ln
14800 WasC 97224 654 J6
Coquille Ct
14900 ORCY 97045 717 G6
SW Coquille Ct
9700 TLTN 97062 685 B6
Coquille Dr
20000 ORCY 97045 717 G6
SW Coquille Dr
9900 TLTN 97062 685 D6
S Coquina Ct
19000 CmsC 97045 688 G3
SE Cora Dr
3400 PTLD 97202 627 A3
SE Cora St
800 PTLD 97202 626 H3
2800 PTLD 97202 627 A3
4200 PTLD 97206 627 C3
11700 PTLD 97266 628 A3
13000 PTLD 97236 628 B3
SW Coral St
8700 WasC 97223 655 F1
9000 TGRD 97223 655 F1
SW Coral Bell Ct
8100 BRTN 97008 625 D4
Coralburst St
37200 SNDY 97055 690 H1
NW Corazon Ter
4500 WasC 97229 595 C1
Corazon del Rio
- VCVR 98683 568 F4
SW Corbeth Ln
10 TDLE 97060 599 F6
3000 GSHM 97030 599 F7
3000 GSHM 97060 599 F7
Corbett Av
- VCVR 98660 536 E3
SW Corbett Av
2600 PTLD 97201 626 F1
3200 PTLD 97239 626 F4
6600 PTLD 97219 626 F5
9400 PTLD 97219 656 F1
SW Corbett Av US-26
2900 PTLD 97201 626 F1
SW Corbett Hill Cir
1300 MthC 97219 656 G3
NE Corbett Hill Rd
1500 MthC 97019 600 G4
2700 MthC 97060 600 G4
NE Corbin Rd
3200 ClkC 98686 477 A7
SW Corby Dr
11700 BRTN 97225 595 C6
SE Cordova Ct
15600 CmsC 97267 657 C7
NW Corey Rd
14600 WasC 97133 532 J4
14600 WasC 97133 533 A4
Corinne Dr
200 NWBG 97132 713 E7
200 YmhC 97132 713 E7
NW Corinthian St
18000 WasC 97229 594 F1
SE Cormack Ln
8600 CmsC 97015 657 F7
SW Cormorant Ct
16200 BRTN 97007 654 G2
SW Cormorant Dr
10200 BRTN 97007 654 G2
SW Cornelian Wy
16200 BRTN 97007 624 G7
NW Cornelius Pass Rd
- HBRO 97229 564 B7
10 HBRO 97124 594 B2
10 WasC 97006 594 B5
10 WasC 97124 594 B5
300 HBRO 97006 594 B5
5000 HBRO 97124 564 B7
5300 WasC 97229 564 B7
6100 WasC 97231 564 C5
8300 WasC 97124 564 F2
10900 MthC 97231 534 F5
SW Cornelius Pass Rd
10 WasC 97006 594 B7
400 HBRO 97006 594 B6
400 HBRO 97123 594 B7
400 WasC 97124 594 B6
800 HBRO 97123 594 B7
800 WasC 97123 594 B7
2200 HBRO 97123 624 B1
2200 WasC 97006 624 B1
2200 WasC 97123 624 B1
2700 HBRO 97006 624 B1
NW Cornelius Schefflin Rd
1000 CNLS 97113 592 E4
1000 WasC 97113 592 E3
4500 WasC 97113 562 D7
Cornell Av
1300 GLDS 97027 687 D3
Cornell Ct
100 LKOW 97034 686 E1
NW Cornell Dr
22000 ClkC 98642 446 A4
22000 RDGF 98642 446 A4
Cornell Pl
17800 GLDS 97027 687 D2
SW Cornell Pl
11400 TGRD 97223 655 C3
NE Cornell Rd
900 HBRO 97124 593 D4
6200 HBRO 97124 594 B3
NW Cornell Rd
- MthC 97210 595 H4
- MthC 97229 595 H4
2600 PTLD 97210 596 A5
3400 MthC 97210 595 A5
3400 PTLD 97210 595 J5
6500 PTLD 97229 595 H4
11000 BRTN 97229 595 A4
14400 BRTN 97229 594 J4
14400 WasC 97229 594 J4
14800 WasC 97006 594 J4
15600 BRTN 97006 594 G3
18400 HBRO 97006 594 C2
18400 HBRO 97124 594 B2
SW Cornell Rd
17300 CmsC 97034 686 F2
17300 LKOW 97034 686 F2
Cornell St
800 LKOW 97034 656 F7
2000 LKOW 97034 686 F1
16800 CmsC 97034 686 F1
SE Corner Rd
38100 CmsC 97023 750 J3
SW Cornerstone Ln
14500 SRWD 97140 714 J1
S Cornett Dr
1700 RDGF 98642 446 C2
NE Cornfoot Dr
6900 PTLD 97218 567 F6
NE Cornfoot Rd
4600 PTLD 97218 567 C5
SW Cornhusker Av
10300 BRTN 97008 655 A2
SE Cornish Ct
5400 CmsC 97267 657 C6
SE Cornog Rd
40800 CmsC 97055 691 C7
SW Cornus Ct
16400 SRWD 97140 714 G1
SE Cornutt St
2800 HBRO 97123 593 F6
NW Cornwall Ln
19900 HBRO 97124 594 D3
Cornwall St
4000 WLIN 97068 686 J7
4300 WLIN 97068 687 A7
SE Cornwell Av
8200 CmsC 97206 627 F7
8200 CmsC 97236 627 F7
SE Cornwell St
8000 CmsC 97206 627 F7
8000 CmsC 97236 627 F7
SW Corona Av
2600 PTLD 97201 626 C1
NE Corona Ct
3300 HBRO 97124 593 C1
SW Corona Ln
17500 WasC 97006 594 F6
SW Coronado Ct
- PTLD 97219 656 D2
SW Coronado St
- MthC 97219 656 F3
4100 PTLD 97219 656 A2
6400 PTLD 97219 655 H2
6400 TGRD 97223 655 H2
Corporate Dr
- ClkC 98682 508 A4
NW Corporate Dr
700 TDLE 97060 599 E3
Corral Ct
600 MOLA 97038 807 D7
NE Corral Ct
5200 HBRO 97124 593 H3
NE Corral Creek Rd
30700 YmhC 97132 713 H6
31700 YmhC 97132 743 H1
32000 YmhC 97132 744 C3
SW Corral Creek Rd
17800 CmsC 97140 744 D2
17800 YmhC 97132 744 D3
Corregidor Rd
6800 VCVR 98661 537 D7
6800 VCVR 98664 537 D7
NW Corridor Ct
17000 BRTN 97006 594 G3
17000 WasC 97006 594 G3
SW Corrine St
19600 WasC 97007 654 D1
SE Corsage Av
16800 CmsC 97027 687 F1
16800 CmsC 97267 687 F1
NW Corso Ln
13000 WasC 97229 595 B2
Cortez Ct
16800 LKOW 97035 685 J1
SW Cortez Ct
8600 BRTN 97008 625 A7
SW Cortland Ln
8800 TGRD 97224 655 E7
Corton Av
- MthC 97231 535 A5
SE Cortona Wy
11700 HPYV 97236 658 C4
NE Cory St
100 HBRO 97124 593 B2
NW Cory St
100 HBRO 97124 593 A3
SW Corylus Ct
12300 TGRD 97224 655 B6
Cosmo St
100 LFYT 97127 741 G7
SW Costa Cir
20700 WNVL 97070 715 B7
SW Costa Cir E
28600 CmsC 97070 715 B7
28600 WNVL 97070 715 B7
NW Cottage St
30800 NPNS 97133 563 B1
SE Cottingham St
17700 CmsC 97009 658 F5
17700 DAMA 97009 658 F5
17700 HPYV 97009 658 F5
SE Cottontail Dr
21000 CmsC 97055 690 H7
SW Cottontail Ln
13000 BRTN 97008 655 A2
SW Cottontail Pl
10500 BRTN 97008 655 C1
SE Cottonwood Av
- HBRO 97123 623 H1
Cottonwood Ct
3100 WLIN 97068 686 J4
17900 GLDS 97027 687 E3
SE Cottonwood Ct
4300 CmsC 97267 657 B6
Cottonwood Ln
- WasC 97006 594 D5
100 CtzC 98674 385 F1
SW Cottonwood Ln
11000 TGRD 97223 655 C2
E Cottonwood Rd
61300 CmsC 97011 693 E7
SE Cottonwood St
19500 CmsC 97267 687 B4
SW Cottonwood St
10500 TLTN 97062 685 C7
SE Cottrell Rd
6600 MthC 97080 630 F7
7800 CmsC 97009 660 F1
7800 MthC 97080 660 F1
NE Couch Ct
- GSHM 97030 599 B6
11100 PTLD 97220 597 J6
15300 PTLD 97230 598 D6
16500 GSHM 97230 598 F6
NE Couch Ln
18800 GSHM 97230 598 H6
NE Couch St
300 PTLD 97232 596 J5
2800 PTLD 97232 597 B5
4700 PTLD 97213 597 C5
8000 PTLD 97220 597 F5
11800 PTLD 97220 598 A6
13000 PTLD 97230 598 B6
19000 GSHM 97230 598 H6
20100 GSHM 97030 598 J6
21900 GSHM 97030 599 B6
NW Couch St
1200 PTLD 97209 596 E5
1800 CMAS 98607 569 D3
SE Cougar Ct
11000 HPYV 97236 658 A3
SW Cougar Ct
13400 BRTN 97008 655 A2
SW Cougar Ln
10400 BRTN 97008 654 J2
SE Cougar Pl
12300 HPYV 97236 658 A3
Cougar Mtn Rd
- YmhC 97128 770 A4
SW Cougar Mountain Rd
5900 YmhC 97128 770 A3
SW Cougar Ridge Dr
14100 BRTN 97008 654 J2
14400 BRTN 97007 654 J2
NW Council Dr
700 GSHM 97030 629 B1
1000 GSHM 97030 599 A7
Council St
1900 FTGV 97116 591 J5
Council Bluffs Wy
200 VCVR 98661 537 D6
SW Council Crest Dr
3400 PTLD 97239 626 C2
Country Ct
200 MCMV 97128 770 E5
NE Country Dr
3300 ClkC 98607 539 C3
NW Country Dr
17400 WasC 97006 594 F1
17400 WasC 97229 594 F1
SW Country Ln
13100 CmsC 97140 714 J7
13100 CmsC 97140 715 A6
Country Mdws
- ClkC 98662 507 J6
Country Mnr
- ClkC 98606 478 B4
S Country Air Ct
15800 CmsC 97045 717 J2
15800 CmsC 97045 718 A2
NE Country Club Av
1000 GSHM 97030 629 E1
3700 GSHM 97030 599 C6
3700 TDLE 97060 599 C6
SW Country Club Av
2700 GSHM 97030 599 E6
2700 TDLE 97060 599 E6
Country Club Ct
400 LKOW 97034 656 E5
NE Country Club Ct
2100 GSHM 97030 599 E7
E Country Club Dr
20800 CmsC 97011 693 F7
N Country Club Dr
1800 CmsC 97013 746 D4
1800 CNBY 97013 746 D4
NW Country Club Dr
- WasC 97006 594 H1
15800 WasC 97229 594 H2
Country Club Ests
- GSHM 97030 629 D1
E Country Club Ln
- CmsC 97011 723 F1
E Country Club Lp
20800 CmsC 97011 693 F7
Country Club Rd
500 CmsC 97034 656 E5
500 LKOW 97034 656 C5
2700 LKOW 97035 656 B5
E Country Club Rd
20500 CmsC 97011 693 F6
61800 CmsC 97011 723 F2
Country Commons Ln
900 LKOW 97034 656 D4
1000 CmsC 97034 656 D4
Country Edge Ln
- DNLD 97020 774 F5
Country Meadow Ests
- CNLS 97113 592 D4
Country Rambler
- GSHM 97233 598 H7
NW Countryridge Dr
16600 WasC 97229 594 G1
16800 WasC 97229 564 G7
NW Countryside Ct
1200 MCMV 97128 770 E4
1200 YmhC 97128 770 E4
15000 WasC 97229 564 H6
NE Countryside Dr
500 VCVR 98684 538 D5
Countryside Rd
14500 CmsC 97002 745 F6
NE Country View Cir
22900 ClkC 98604 539 B3
SW Country View Ct E
6900 WNVL 97070 745 H1
SW Country View Ct N
6800 WNVL 97070 745 G2
SW Country View Ct S
6800 WNVL 97070 745 G3
SW Country View Ct W
7000 WNVL 97070 745 G2
SW Country View Ln
31000 WNVL 97070 745 G2
SW Country View Lp
31000 WNVL 97070 745 G1
NW Countryview Wy
13400 WasC 97229 595 A3
Country Villa Ln
56500 ClbC 97053 414 G6
Country Village Dr
18000 CmsC 97045 717 G2
Country Woods Ct
4200 LKOW 97035 656 A6
NW Country Woods Ln
13900 PTLD 97231 565 A2
SE Coupland Rd
32500 ECDA 97023 750 C3
34700 CmsC 97023 750 J5
NE Courier Ct
5200 PTLD 97218 567 D4
SE Courser Ln
38200 CmsC 97023 750 H3
N Court Av
4000 PTLD 97217 596 E1
4000 PTLD 97227 596 E1
N Courtenay Av
8700 PTLD 97203 566 B4
NW Courting Hill Dr
14900 WasC 97106 532 A4
SE Courtney Av
1000 CmsC 97222 656 G5
1100 CmsC 97267 656 H5
2800 CmsC 97222 657 A5
2800 CmsC 97267 657 A5
NE Courtney Rd
16700 YmhC 97132 713 F2
17000 WasC 97140 713 G1
SW Courtney Rd
18100 WasC 97140 713 G1
18100 YmhC 97132 713 G1
NE Courtside Ct
41800 BNKS 97106 531 J6
SW Courtside Dr
28900 WNVL 97070 715 F7
SW Courtside Wy
7900 WNVL 97070 715 F7
NW Cove Ct
16800 WasC 97229 564 G7
Cove Ln
900 WLIN 97068 716 F2
Cove St
- CmsC 97045 719 B4
SE Covell Av
4200 MWKE 97222 657 B1

STREET
Block City ZIP Map# Grid

Coventry Ct
5100 LKOW 97035 655 J5
SW Coventry Pl
5700 WasC 97007 624 G4
NW Coventry St
14800 WasC 97229 594 J1
NW Coventry Wy
400 MCMV 97128 770 G5
NW Covey Ln
41500 WasC 97106 531 J3
41500 WasC 97106 532 A3
Covey Run Dr
1700 FTGV 97116 591 H4
SE Covina Ct
13400 CmsC 97015 657 J5
NE Covington Rd
9400 ClkC 98662 507 H6
SE Covington Rd
14800 CmsC 97015 658 C7
SE Covington St
6100 HBRO 97123 593 J6
Cowanlock Av
- MthC 97231 535 A5
Cowens Rd
50300 ClbC 97056 474 F4
SW Cowles Ct
13700 TGRD 97223 655 D5
SW Cowlitz Dr
22600 TLTN 97062 685 C7
NW Cowlitz Pl
- PTLD 97205 596 A4
- PTLD 97210 596 A4
Cowlitz St
10 STHN 97051 385 D7
1000 STHN 97051 415 C1
NE Cowls Ct
2300 MCMV 97128 770 H3
NE Cowls St
100 MCMV 97128 770 H4
SE Cowls St
300 MCMV 97128 770 H5
SE Cox Ln
8100 CmsC 97027 687 F2
8100 GLDS 97027 687 F2
NE Coxley Dr
10600 ClkC 98662 507 J7
NE Coyote Cir
18500 ClkC 98675 418 G4
SW Coyote Ct
15200 SRWD 97140 714 H1
NE Coyote Dr
30100 ClkC 98675 418 H4
NW Coyote Hill Rd
15500 WasC 97106 531 G3
NW Coyote Ridge Rd
2200 ClkC 98629 386 E5
SW Cozine Ln
800 MCMV 97128 770 G6
SW Cozine St
1500 MCMV 97128 770 F6
SE Cozy Dr
10900 CmsC 97222 657 E2
CR-16
29900 ClkC 98675 419 G5
CR-78
- YmhC 97115 742 E4
NW Crady Ln
5000 WasC 97229 565 A7
5400 WasC 97229 564 J7
Craig Ct
17200 GLDS 97027 687 E2
NW Craig Dr
3800 WasC 97006 594 G2
SE Cramer Ln
100 CMAS 98607 569 F4
Cramer Rd
- CmsC 97038 807 A7
- CmsC 97038 837 A1
NE Cramer Rd
17900 ClkC 98604 477 H2
S Cramer Rd
28000 CmsC 97013 807 A2
29600 CmsC 97038 807 A4
N Cramer St
1800 PTLD 97217 566 E6
NE Cramer St
1900 PTLD 97211 566 J6
Crammer St
1100 LFYT 97127 741 G7
Cranberry Ct
- CmsC 97002 775 G6
SW Cranberry Ct
5700 BRTN 97007 624 H4
SE Cranberry Dr
11300 CmsC 97015 657 J6
SE Cranberry Lp
10800 CmsC 97015 657 J6
NE Cranbrook Dr
2000 VCVR 98664 537 H4
2400 VCVR 98662 537 G3
SE Cranbrooke Ln
35300 CmsC 97023 750 F1
NW Crandall St
- PTLD 97231 565 D1
SW Crane Ct
14000 TGRD 97223 654 J3
SE Crane Rd
24000 CmsC 97022 720 F3
NE Crane St
1900 PTLD 97211 596 J1
Crater Ln
2000 NWBG 97132 713 B5
2000 YmhC 97132 713 B5
SW Crater Lp
11700 BRTN 97008 625 C6
Crater Lake Ct NE
13400 MrnC 97002 775 C7
NE Crawford Ln
4000 YmhC 97115 742 G7
4000 YmhC 97115 772 G1
NE Crawford Rd
24200 ClkC 98604 448 G3
N Crawford St
7600 PTLD 97203 565 H4
Creamery Creek Ln
600 MOLA 97038 807 D6
600 MOLA 97038 837 E1
SW Cree Cir
9200 TLTN 97062 685 E5
Creed St
- ORCY 97045 717 C1
SE Creek Ct
2900 HBRO 97123 623 F2
SW Creek Ct
21600 TLTN 97062 685 G6

SW Creek Dr
21700 TLTN 97062 685 E6
S Creek Rd
19100 CmsC 97045 718 C5
S Creek Haven Ln
16100 CmsC 97004 748 A4
NE Creeksedge Dr
800 HBRO 97124 593 D1
SW Creekshire Dr
12600 WasC 97223 654 J4
13000 TGRD 97223 654 J4
SW Creekshire Pl
12400 TGRD 97223 654 J4
12400 WasC 97223 654 J4
Creekside Ct
1400 NWBG 97132 713 B6
S Creekside Ct
16700 CmsC 97045 688 B5
NW Creekside Dr
3600 ClkC 98685 476 C6
12500 WasC 97229 595 B2
SE Creekside Dr
14400 CmsC 97267 657 D6
Creekside Ests
- VCVR 98682 538 A1
Creekside Ln
100 NWBG 97132 713 B6
1200 YmhC 97132 713 B6
SE Creekside Ln
30700 CmsC 97022 720 A3
SW Creekside Pl
8200 BRTN 97008 625 C7
Creekside Ter
10 LKOW 97035 655 J3
100 FRVW 97024 599 C4
NE Creekview Ct
- WasC 97124 594 A5
NW Creekview Dr
12600 WasC 97229 595 B2
SW Creekview Pl
51800 SPSE 97056 474 E2
NW Creekwood Pl
2100 FTGV 97116 591 D2
2100 WasC 97116 591 D2
SE Creighton Av
1800 CmsC 97267 656 J7
SW Creightonwood Pl
10800 PTLD 97219 656 C2
NW Creps Rd
15400 WasC 97106 531 H3
NE Cresap Rd
24800 ClkC 98604 449 B2
Crescent Dr
10 STHN 97051 385 B7
1200 FTGV 97116 592 A5
3300 WLIN 97068 686 J7
SE Crescent Rd
35200 CmsC 97009 660 F7
35200 CmsC 97009 690 F1
35200 CmsC 97055 690 F1
Crescent St
- PTLD 97231 565 B2
SW Crescent Wy
12600 BRTN 97005 625 B2
SE Crescent Ridge Dr
10200 CmsC 97236 657 H1
SE Crescent Ridge Lp
10200 CmsC 97236 657 H1
SW Cresmer Dr
13400 TGRD 97223 655 D5
SW Cresmoor Dr
7200 BRTN 97008 625 B6
NE Crest Av
10600 ClkC 98685 506 H2
Crest Ct
18000 ORCY 97045 717 E2
SE Crest Ct
16400 PTLD 97236 628 E4
Crest Dr
1800 LKOW 97034 656 C6
56300 ClbC 97053 414 G7
SE Crest Dr
12400 HPYV 97236 658 A2
28300 CmsC 97022 719 H7
SE Crest Wy
12200 HPYV 97236 658 A1
NW Crestbrook Ct
1000 MCMV 97128 770 F3
SW Crestdale Ct
7000 WasC 97225 625 H1
SW Crestdale Dr
2300 BRTN 97225 625 H1
2300 WasC 97225 625 H1
Crestfield Ct
10 LKOW 97035 655 J4
SE Crest Hill Rd
10000 HPYV 97236 658 A2
SE Cresthill Rd
10300 HPYV 97236 658 A2
Crestline Ct
1100 LKOW 97034 686 F2
SW Crestline Ct
13500 WasC 97224 655 A7
Crestline Dr
17600 LKOW 97034 686 F2
SW Crestline Dr
7900 PTLD 97219 626 E6
SW Crestmont Pl
20400 SRWD 97140 684 F5
NE Creston Av
4500 ClkC 98663 536 G1
NW Creston Av
4300 VCVR 98663 536 G1
NW Creston Rd
- MthC 97231 535 C6
12300 PTLD 97231 535 C6
SW Crestridge Ct
14500 WasC 97224 654 J6
SE Crestview Av
13900 CmsC 97222 657 B6
13900 CmsC 97267 657 B6
Crestview Cir
1600 NWBG 97132 713 D5
Crest View Dr
21400 CmsC 97045 747 F2
Crestview Dr
200 YmhC 97132 713 C5
2100 WLIN 97068 686 G7
3300 NWBG 97132 713 F5
16900 LKOW 97034 686 D1
17000 LKOW 97034 656 D7
NE Crestview Dr
- FRVW 97024 599 A3
4100 NWBG 97132 713 G5
4100 YmhC 97132 713 G5

SE Crestview Dr
100 HBRO 97123 593 C6
14200 CmsC 97015 657 J6
NE Crestview Ln
1300 MthC 97019 600 J5
SW Crestview Pl
7000 BRTN 97008 625 B5
SW Crestview St
7500 TGRD 97223 655 G5
NW Crestview Wy
2200 PTLD 97229 595 F3
SW Crestview Wy
600 TDLE 97060 599 F4
Crestwood Ct
2900 WLIN 97068 686 H4
NE Crestwood Ct
200 VCVR 98684 537 J6
NW Crestwood Ct
700 MCMV 97128 770 F3
SW Crestwood Ct
10100 BRTN 97008 625 D7
SE Crestwood Dr
15500 CmsC 97267 657 E7
SW Crestwood Dr
4100 WasC 97225 625 F3
4300 BRTN 97225 625 F3
10100 BRTN 97008 625 D7
28600 WNVL 97070 715 G6
SW Crestwood Ln
8300 WasC 97225 625 F3
Crestwood St
100 FRVW 97024 599 C4
NE Crestwood St
11700 VCVR 98684 537 J6
SW Crestwood St
8900 WasC 97223 625 E7
Crestwood Ter
- WHGL 98671 570 A4
SE Creswain Av
15500 CmsC 97267 656 J7
SW Crickhollow Ct
7900 DRHM 97224 685 F2
NW Crimson Ct
2300 MCMV 97128 770 G3
NE Crimson Pl
3100 HBRO 97124 593 B1
Crisell St NE
20900 DNLD 97020 774 F4
Crisp Dr
12400 ORCY 97045 717 B4
SW Crisp Dr
7100 WasC 97007 624 D5
SW Crist Ct
13800 TGRD 97223 655 B2
S Criswell Rd
20000 CmsC 97045 718 J1
20200 CmsC 97045 719 A1
SW Criterion Ter
15200 TGRD 97224 655 G6
S Criteser Rd
11900 CmsC 97045 747 B1
NE Crocus Ct
2500 HBRO 97124 593 E5
NW Croeni Rd
5000 HBRO 97124 564 B7
Cromptons Ln
12700 CmsC 97038 837 B1
SW Cromwell Ct
16300 WasC 97223 654 G4
NE CSB Rd
- ClkC 98665 506 J7
- VCVR 98663 506 J7
- VCVR 98665 506 J7
NW Crop Ct
22400 WasC 97106 531 J2
Crosby Rd
60100 ClbC 97051 384 B5
SW Cross Av
2600 PTLD 97201 626 E1
SW Crossbill Ter
11600 BRTN 97007 654 E3
SW Cross Creek Av
5800 WasC 97007 624 C4
SE Crosscreek Ct
14600 DAMA 97009 659 B7
SW Cross Creek Dr
6000 WasC 97007 624 C4
NE Cross Creek Rd
6900 YmhC 97115 742 G4
NW Crosshaven St
17100 WasC 97229 564 G7
NW Crossman Pl
16700 WasC 97106 531 G2
Cross Over Rd
16200 CmsC 97038 807 J7
SW Crossview Ct
17700 WasC 97006 624 F2
Crosswater
- ClkC 98686 477 A7
NW Crosswater Ter
2400 BRTN 97006 594 G3
2400 WasC 97006 594 G3
SE Crosswhite Wy
6400 CmsC 97206 657 D1
Crouse Wy
100 STHN 97051 415 B1
SW Crow Wy
10300 TLTN 97062 685 D7
NE Crown Cir
- MCMV 97128 771 E6
- YmhC 97114 771 E6
- YmhC 97128 771 E6
Crown Ct
22600 WLIN 97068 687 A7
NE Crown Ct
52700 ClbC 97056 444 F7
52700 SPSE 97056 444 F7
SE Crown Ct
6000 CmsC 97267 687 D1
SW Crown Dr
11400 KNGC 97224 655 C7
NE Crown Ln
1600 CMAS 98607 569 G4
NW Crown Pl
- PTLD 97210 595 J2
SE Crown Rd
2500 ClkC 98607 569 G3
3000 WHGL 98671 569 G3
3700 ClkC 98671 569 G4
3700 CMAS 98607 569 G3
3700 WHGL 98607 569 G4
Crown St
5100 WLIN 97068 687 A7
Crown Oak
- TGRD 97223 655 E1
Crown Point Hwy
- MthC 97060 599 H4

Crown Point Hwy
- TDLE 97060 599 G3
Crown View Ct
7100 GLDS 97027 687 E2
Crown View Dr
17300 GLDS 97027 687 E2
Crown Zellerbach Rd
31100 ClbC 97056 444 A2
NE Crown Zellerbach Rd
33600 ClbC 97056 444 E7
33600 SPSE 97056 444 E7
NE Crown Zellerbach Logging Rd
- ClbC 97056 444 F7
- SPSE 97056 444 F7
SE Cruickshank Rd
11300 YmhC 97114 771 F7
NE Crusher Rd
- ClkC 98685 506 G1
Crystal Ct
15000 CmsC 97045 717 G7
15000 ORCY 97045 717 G7
NE Crystal Ct
11300 ClkC 98686 506 J1
NW Crystal Ct
4300 CMAS 98607 569 C1
SE Crystal Ct
14200 PTLD 97236 628 C7
Crystal Ln
1100 LFYT 97127 741 G7
NE Crystal Ln
4400 PTLD 97218 567 C5
SE Crystal Ln
5700 CmsC 97267 687 C2
SE Crystal St
14400 PTLD 97236 628 C7
SW Crystal St
8500 WasC 97223 625 F6
10000 BRTN 97008 625 D7
10000 WasC 97008 625 D7
E Crystal Creek Dr
- CmsC 97067 724 A4
NW Crystal Creek Ln
10900 WasC 97229 595 D2
E Crystal Creek Rd
66100 CmsC 97067 723 J3
66100 CmsC 97067 724 A4
SE Crystal Lake Ln
10500 MWKE 97222 657 A2
Crystal Ridge Dr
50500 ClbC 97056 474 B4
SE Crystal Springs Blvd
2700 PTLD 97202 627 A6
7200 PTLD 97206 627 F7
8900 PTLD 97266 627 G7
16600 MthC 97236 628 F7
Crystal Springs Ct
32800 SPSE 97056 474 D1
SE Crystal Springs Ct
- PTLD 97206 627 D7
SE Crystal Springs St
14100 PTLD 97236 628 C7
Crystal Terrace Dr
23700 WLIN 97068 716 H1
NE Crystal View Ct
17000 YmhC 97140 713 H2
SE Crystal View Dr
9500 PTLD 97266 627 G7
NW Culebra Av
5700 PTLD 97210 565 H6
NW Culebra St
6000 PTLD 97210 565 H6
SW Cullen Blvd
3600 PTLD 97221 626 B4
NE Cullen Rd
14100 NWBG 97132 713 B5
14100 YmhC 97132 713 B5
NE Cully Blvd
3800 PTLD 97213 597 D2
4000 PTLD 97218 597 D1
5500 PTLD 97218 567 E7
NW Culpepper Dr
- TDLE 97060 599 F3
NW Culpepper Ter
600 PTLD 97210 596 C5
Cumberland Pl
- LKOW 97034 656 F4
Cumberland Rd
900 LKOW 97034 656 E4
NW Cumberland Rd
2800 PTLD 97210 596 B4
SW Cumberland Wy
17700 WasC 97006 594 G7
Cumberland II
- PTLD 97236 628 B5
Cummings Ct
6100 GLDS 97027 687 D3
S Cunningham St
700 CLTN 97111 741 A2
SW Curlew Wy
12300 BRTN 97007 654 G4
SW Curran Daniel Ln
6700 WasC 97225 595 H6
NW Currawong Ct
3900 CMAS 98607 569 C1
Current Dr
20100 ORCY 97045 717 F6
SE Currin Dr
1800 HBRO 97123 593 E7
SE Currin Ln
2000 HBRO 97123 593 E7
2000 WasC 97123 593 E7
SE Currin Rd
26500 CmsC 97022 720 B5
26500 CmsC 97023 720 B5
29300 CmsC 97023 750 E3
NE Currin St
100 ECDA 97023 750 B3
SE Currin St
100 ECDA 97023 750 B4
SW Curry Ct
8700 BRTN 97008 625 B7
SW Curry Dr
- WNVL 97070 745 E2
SW Curry St
900 PTLD 97239 626 D2
N Curtis Av
6500 PTLD 97217 566 D5
NE Curtis Ct
7500 HBRO 97124 594 B6

S Curtis Ct
15000 CmsC 97045 688 C4
NE Curtis Dr
10 MthC 97019 600 F6
SE Curtis Dr
10 MthC 97019 600 F7
SE Curtis Rd
20400 CmsC 97009 688 J1
20400 CmsC 97009 689 A1
Cushman Av
100 YCLT 98675 419 F1
SE Cushman Ct
2700 CmsC 97267 656 J7
SW Cushman Ct
7200 WasC 97223 655 G1
Cushman Dr
1300 WLIN 97068 687 B6
W Cushman St
100 YCLT 98675 419 E1
600 ClkC 98675 419 E1
SW Custer Dr
1200 PTLD 97219 626 D6
SW Custer St
1600 PTLD 97219 626 D6
5000 PTLD 97219 625 J6
SW Custer Wy
- PTLD 97219 626 F6
SW Cuthill Pl
23000 SRWD 97140 684 H7
N Cutter Cir
5900 PTLD 97217 566 C6
SE Cutter Ln
1500 VCVR 98661 536 H6
SW Cutter Pl
9200 BRTN 97008 655 B1
SW Cyber Ct
15000 WasC 97006 594 J6
S Cymry Ln
16000 CmsC 97004 747 J3
16000 CmsC 97004 748 A3
SW Cynthia Ct
11200 BRTN 97008 625 C6
15500 BRTN 97007 624 H6
SW Cynthia Ln
15400 BRTN 97007 624 H6
SW Cynthia St
9600 WasC 97008 625 E6
10300 BRTN 97008 625 D6
16400 BRTN 97007 624 G5
17000 WasC 97007 624 F5
Cypress Av
- PTLD 97217 536 E6
- WasC 97006 594 D5
SE Cypress Av
2000 PTLD 97214 596 H7
2000 PTLD 97214 626 J1
7000 CmsC 97267 657 E7
SE Cypress Ct
- CmsC 97267 657 F7
52200 SPSE 97056 474 F1
Cypress Dr
200 MCMV 97128 770 F5
Cypress Gdns
- TLTN 97062 685 E4
SW Cypress Ln
1100 MCMV 97128 770 F6
1400 YmhC 97128 770 F6
7700 TGRD 97224 655 F5
12800 BRTN 97005 625 B4
SW Cypress Pt
32000 WNVL 97070 745 E3
NW Cypress St
200 MCMV 97128 770 F4
SE Cypress St
2100 HBRO 97123 593 E7
SW Cypress St
100 MCMV 97128 770 F5
9500 BRTN 97005 625 E4
NW Cyrus Ln
11500 WasC 97229 595 C2

D

D Av
10 LKOW 97034 656 F5
W D Av
100 LCTR 98629 416 G1
500 LCTR 98629 386 G7
900 ClkC 98629 386 G7
D Ln
- PTLD 97218 567 D7
SE D Pl
2900 MWKE 97222 657 A2
D St
- ORCY 97045 717 D2
- PTLD 97219 655 J3
400 CBAC 97018 385 C3
500 ORCY 97045 687 E6
600 WHGL 98671 569 J5
1000 WHGL 98671 570 A5
1200 VCVR 98660 536 G5
1300 VCVR 98663 536 G4
2100 FTGV 97116 591 H4
NW D St
- WasC 97006 594 C5
SE D St
10200 MWKE 97222 657 A2
D & P Ln
57200 ClbC 97053 414 E5
SE Daffodil Pl
15300 CmsC 97015 658 D5
15300 HPYV 97015 658 D5
SW Daffodil St
16500 SRWD 97140 684 G5
SE Dagmar Ct
6500 CmsC 97027 687 D1
6500 CmsC 97267 687 D1
6500 GLDS 97027 687 D1
SE Dagmar Rd
16200 CmsC 97027 687 D1
16200 CmsC 97267 687 D1
16200 GLDS 97027 687 D1
16500 GLDS 97267 687 D1
SE Dagwood Ln
14100 HPYV 97236 658 C1
Dahlager St
18100 SNDY 97055 691 A4
Dahlgren Rd
54000 ClbC 97056 444 D4
NW Dahlia Ct
2800 CMAS 98607 569 B2
SW Dahlia Ct
16200 WasC 97223 654 G5
NW Dahlia Dr
2900 CMAS 98607 569 B2

NW Dahlia Dr
4700 CMAS 98607 539 B7
NW Dahlia Lp
3800 CMAS 98607 569 B1
N Dahlia Pl
600 CNBY 97013 746 B6
Dahlia Ter
11500 ORCY 97045 717 A5
SW Dahlke Ln
21400 SRWD 97140 685 A6
21400 WasC 97140 685 A6
Dahl Park Rd
- GLDS 97027 687 C5
SE Dahlquist Rd
16900 MthC 97236 628 F6
Daiquiri Lake Dr NE
13200 MrnC 97002 775 B7
Dairy Ln
34900 ClbC 97056 444 H4
NW Dairy Creek Rd
14600 WasC 97106 532 G4
14600 WasC 97133 532 F1
SW Daisy Dr
7300 WasC 97007 624 E6
Daisy Ln
32500 ClbC 97053 414 D6
SW Dakota Cir
21500 TLTN 97062 685 E6
SW Dakota Ct
8500 TLTN 97062 685 G6
SW Dakota Dr
8300 TLTN 97062 685 E7
SW Dakota St
2400 PTLD 97239 626 C4
3500 PTLD 97221 626 B4
NW Dale Av
500 WasC 97229 595 B5
SW Dale Av
6000 BRTN 97005 625 B4
6000 BRTN 97008 625 B5
SW Dale Cir
12800 BRTN 97008 625 B5
Dale Ct
- MOLA 97038 807 D7
SE Dale Ln
28100 CmsC 97022 689 H6
NW Dale Rd
6900 ClkC 98665 506 F6
Dale St
700 WDLD 98674 385 J2
700 WDLD 98674 386 A1
NW Dale St
200 HBRO 97124 593 B3
S Dales Av
15000 CmsC 97004 747 H3
Dallas Av
100 VCVR 98661 537 C6
NW Dallas Pl
3700 WasC 97229 595 D2
Dallas St
18800 ORCY 97045 717 C4
NE Dallas St
100 CMAS 98607 569 F4
NE Dallas St SR-500
200 CMAS 98607 569 F4
SE Dallas St
100 CMAS 98607 569 F5
Dallas Wy
- CmsC 97045 749 A2
S Dalmation Rd
28000 CmsC 97042 807 G2
SW Dalton Pl
- WasC 97007 624 C2
NW Dalton Ranch Ln
13100 WasC 97229 595 D1
Daly Ln NE
10900 MrnC 97002 744 G5
SW Daly Ln
12500 BRTN 97005 625 B4
NW Damascus Ct
10500 WasC 97229 595 D4
SE Damascus Ln
19700 DAMA 97009 658 H6
NW Damascus St
11500 WasC 97229 595 C4
NE Damsel Dr
5500 HBRO 97124 593 J5
N Dana Av
- PTLD 97217 566 C4
7900 PTLD 97203 566 C4
SE Dana Av
15400 CmsC 97267 656 H7
SW Dana Ct
21100 WasC 97006 594 C6
NE Danbury Av
100 HBRO 97124 594 A5
200 WasC 97124 594 B5
SW Danbush Ct
12600 TGRD 97223 655 D1
SE Dance Dr
400 ECDA 97023 750 C4
Dan Cupp Rd
32700 ClbC 97051 384 E2
S Dandelion Rd
22200 CmsC 97023 750 B4
NW Dane Ln
15100 WasC 97229 564 J7
Danee Pl
11700 CmsC 97045 717 A4
11700 ORCY 97045 717 A4
SW Daniel Rd
24100 WasC 97007 623 H7
Daniel Wy
3800 LKOW 97035 656 A5
SW Danielle Av
7200 BRTN 97008 625 A6
SW Daniels Ct
800 MCMV 97128 770 G6
Daniels St
2300 VCVR 98660 536 F3
NW Daniels St
3900 VCVR 98660 536 F5
4900 VCVR 98663 506 G7
4900 VCVR 98663 536 F1
SW Daniels St
100 MCMV 97128 770 G5
SE Danna Ct
2700 CmsC 97267 686 J1
Danny Ct
20200 CmsC 97045 717 J7
Danny Ln
15900 CmsC 97045 717 J7
Danny St
32800 ClbC 97056 444 D5

S Dans Av
22000 CmsC 97004 747 G3
NE Dans Ct
6400 ClkC 98607 509 G7
S Dans Ct
22200 CmsC 97004 747 G4
Daphne Av
- PTLD 97217 536 E7
SW Daphne Av
- MthC 97219 656 G2
SE Daphne Ct
6900 MWKE 97222 657 E4
31700 CmsC 97009 660 C6
SW Daphne Ct
12600 WasC 97005 595 B6
15000 BRTN 97007 624 J5
Daphne Ln
4200 VCVR 98661 537 B4
SW Daphne Pl
10200 MthC 97219 656 G1
SW Daphne St
14000 BRTN 97008 624 J5
Dapplegrey Ln
1200 LKOW 97034 656 E4
SW Dapplegrey Lp
9800 BRTN 97008 654 J1
NE Darby St
1700 HBRO 97124 593 E3
Darci Dr
- YmhC 97128 770 E6
Darcy St
59500 ClbC 97051 384 J7
59500 STHN 97051 384 J7
SE Daren Dr
3500 HBRO 97123 623 E2
3700 WasC 97123 623 E2
SW Darla Kay Ct
15400 SRWD 97140 684 H7
SW Darlene Ct
19100 WasC 97007 624 D4
SE Darling Av
2100 GSHM 97080 629 C5
SW Darmel Ct
9600 TGRD 97224 655 E7
S Darnell Rd
13400 CmsC 97042 777 E6
NE Darnielle Dr
500 HBRO 97124 593 C3
NW Darnielle St
400 HBRO 97124 593 B3
1000 WasC 97124 593 A3
SE Darrow Rd
800 CmsC 97023 750 C4
800 ECDA 97023 750 C4
S Dart Rd
11900 CmsC 97038 837 A4
Dart Creek Rd
61200 ClbC 97051 384 G2
SW Dartmoor Ct
13100 BRTN 97008 655 A1
Dartmouth St
500 NWBG 97132 713 C5
E Dartmouth St
100 GLDS 97027 687 D4
SW Dartmouth St
6800 TGRD 97223 655 G3
W Dartmouth St
100 GLDS 97027 687 D4
Date St
1500 VCVR 98661 537 A4
Dateline Av
19600 ORCY 97045 717 D5
SW Dauer Ct
14500 TGRD 97223 654 J4
14500 WasC 97223 654 J4
S Dave Rd
27100 CmsC 97013 776 B6
SW Davenport Ct
2600 PTLD 97201 626 D1
SW Davenport Ln
2600 PTLD 97201 626 D1
Davenport St
6100 WLIN 97068 687 A5
SW Davenport St
800 PTLD 97201 626 D1
NE Daventry St
5600 HBRO 97124 593 J4
NE David Cir
12900 PTLD 97230 598 B1
NE David Ct
14700 YmhC 97132 713 G4
NW David Ct
800 BRTN 97006 594 H5
SE David Ct
10900 HPYV 97236 658 A3
NE David Ln
29000 YmhC 97132 713 G4
NW David Hill Rd
44300 FTGV 97116 591 F2
44300 WasC 97116 591 F2
45100 WasC 97116 561 D7
SE Davidoff Ct
15500 DAMA 97009 658 E7
SE Davidoff Wy
16700 DAMA 97009 658 E7
Davidson Av
100 WDLD 98674 385 J2
700 CtzC 98674 385 J2
Davidson Dr
34100 ClbC 97056 444 G2
Davidson Rd NE
3900 MrnC 97137 773 B7
NW Davidson Rd
15600 WasC 97106 532 C2
E Davidson St
20200 CmsC 97011 693 E6
SE Davies Ct
2600 CmsC 97267 656 J7
SW Davies Ct
8300 WasC 97223 625 F7
SW Davies Rd
8900 BRTN 97008 624 H1
9200 BRTN 97008 654 F1
10900 BRTN 97007 654 J2
12700 BRTN 97008 625 A7
Da Vinci St
10 LKOW 97035 656 A4
Davis Av
1600 VCVR 98661 536 H5
Davis Ct NE
20100 STPL 97137 773 B5
N Davis Ct
2700 CNLS 97113 592 G4
NE Davis Ct
1200 HBRO 97124 593 E3

STREET / Block City ZIP Map# Grid

NE Davis Ct
2700 MCMV 97128 770 H2
13600 PTLD 97230 598 C6
SW Davis Ct
24200 WasC 97123 623 H2
Davis Dr
17700 SNDY 97055 691 A3
N Davis Dr
2900 CNLS 97113 592 G4
Davis Ln
14700 LKOW 97035 656 B6
NW Davis Ln
- WasC 97113 562 H5
- WasC 97124 562 H5
Davis Rd
1800 CmsC 97045 687 E7
1800 ORCY 97045 687 E7
NE Davis Rd
18400 ClkC 98606 508 G3
SE Davis Rd
4500 HBRO 97123 623 H2
4800 WasC 97123 623 H2
28500 CmsC 97023 720 F7
29200 CmsC 97023 750 F1
SW Davis Rd
14500 BRTN 97007 624 H5
14500 BRTN 97008 624 J5
15300 WasC 97007 624 H5
23700 WasC 97007 623 J2
23700 WasC 97123 623 H2
24500 HBRO 97123 623 H2
Davis St
17900 SNDY 97055 691 A3
N Davis St
1200 CNLS 97113 592 E4
NE Davis St
100 MCMV 97128 770 H4
1600 PTLD 97232 596 J5
2800 PTLD 97232 597 A5
4100 PTLD 97213 597 B5
9600 PTLD 97220 597 H5
11900 PTLD 97220 598 A6
12600 PTLD 97230 598 B6
18800 GSHM 97230 598 H6
NW Davis St
1600 PTLD 97209 596 D5
2100 PTLD 97210 596 D5
SE Davis St
100 MCMV 97128 770 H5
SE Davona Dr
- ClbC 97056 474 F2
33600 SPSE 97056 474 F2
SW Dawn Ct
15000 TGRD 97224 655 E7
NE Dawn Ln
- MCMV 97128 771 E6
4700 YmhC 97114 741 J7
Dawn St
4700 CmsC 97035 686 A3
5000 RVGR 97035 685 J3
6100 CmsC 97035 685 H3
6400 LKOW 97035 685 H3
SW Dawns Ct
11400 TGRD 97223 655 C3
NW Dawnwood Dr
14500 WasC 97229 564 J6
Dawson Ct
3200 WLIN 97068 686 H7
SW Dawson Ln
5600 YmhC 97128 770 D4
SE Dawson St
9600 CmsC 97015 687 H1
SW Dawson Wy
13000 BRTN 97005 625 A2
NE Dawson Creek Dr
4700 HBRO 97124 593 H1
4700 WasC 97124 593 H1
SW Day Ct
400 GSHM 97080 629 A3
NW Day Dr
800 GSHM 97030 629 B2
S Day Ln
23600 CmsC 97023 750 C7
Day Rd
- WasC 97140 715 C2
- WNVL 97140 715 C2
22400 WLIN 97068 686 H7
SW Day St
9400 WasC 97062 715 D2
9400 WasC 97140 715 D2
9400 WNVL 97070 715 D2
9400 WNVL 97140 715 D2
33200 SPSE 97056 474 E1
Daybreak Ct
19400 ORCY 97045 717 B6
Daybreak Dr
- NWBG 97132 743 F1
- YmhC 97132 743 F2
NE Daybreak Rd
26400 ClkC 98604 417 F7
26400 ClkC 98604 447 F1
Daybreak St
1700 TDLE 97060 599 E5
7800 WNVL 97070 715 F6
SW Daybreak Wy
1900 TDLE 97060 599 E5
S Day Hill Rd
22500 CmsC 97023 750 B7
SW Daylily St
16500 SRWD 97140 684 F5
SE Dayspring Ln
15100 CmsC 97015 658 C7
Dayton Av
- YmhC 97115 742 J3
300 NWBG 97132 713 D7
400 NWBG 97132 743 B1
800 YmhC 97132 743 B1
Dayton Av CO-74
- YmhC 97115 742 J3
NE Dayton Av
22700 YmhC 97115 742 J2
22700 YmhC 97132 742 J2
23200 YmhC 97132 743 A2
SE Dayton Av
200 MCMV 97128 770 J6
Dayton Byp
- DAYT 97114 771 J4
- DAYT 97114 772 A4
- YmhC 97114 771 J4
- YmhC 97114 772 B3
Dayton Byp SR-18
- DAYT 97114 771 J4
- DAYT 97114 772 A4
- YmhC 97114 771 J4
- YmhC 97114 772 B3
Dayton Byp SR-233
- DAYT 97114 771 J4
- DAYT 97114 772 A4
- YmhC 97114 771 J4
- YmhC 97114 772 B3
SE Dayton Byp
3000 YmhC 97114 772 C2
12200 YmhC 97114 771 G5
13400 DAYT 97114 771 J4
SE Dayton Byp SR-18
3000 YmhC 97114 772 C2
12200 YmhC 97114 771 G5
13400 DAYT 97114 771 J4
SE Dayton Byp SR-233
3000 YmhC 97114 772 C2
12700 YmhC 97114 771 J4
13400 DAYT 97114 771 J4
Dayton Wy
700 VCVR 98664 537 E5
SE Dean Dr
8900 CmsC 97015 687 F2
NE Dean St
1000 PTLD 97211 566 H6
SE Deana Ct
14700 CmsC 97015 658 B7
Deana Dr
1800 CmsC 97068 686 G4
1800 WLIN 97068 686 G4
SE Deana Wy
13500 CmsC 97015 658 B7
Deane Dr
31400 ClbC 97056 444 B2
SE Deardorff Rd
6900 PTLD 97236 628 B7
7900 PTLD 97266 628 B7
8000 HPYV 97236 628 B7
Debbie Ct
7000 GLDS 97027 687 E3
SE Debbie Ct
400 MCMV 97128 770 J6
SE Debbie St
800 MCMV 97128 770 H7
Debok Rd
1800 WLIN 97068 716 G1
2300 WLIN 97068 686 G7
SE Debora Dr
19000 DAMA 97009 658 H3
Deborah Ct
- NWBG 97132 713 E6
Deborah Rd
800 NWBG 97132 713 E6
Debra Ct
- CmsC 97022 690 B5
NE Debra Ct
100 HBRO 97124 593 C3
Debra Ln
- CmsC 97022 690 B5
Debring Rd
- ClbC 97056 444 D5
SE Decade Ct
2200 HBRO 97123 624 A1
E Decatur Rd
23900 CmsC 97067 724 B3
N Decatur St
9900 PTLD 97203 565 F2
NW Decatur Wy
15000 WasC 97229 564 H7
SE Decker Rd
17200 CmsC 97009 690 A3
SW Declaration Wy
17600 WasC 97006 594 F5
NW Decora Ln
19500 HBRO 97124 594 D2
SE Dee St
27600 CmsC 97009 659 G5
SW Deeann Ct
8300 TGRD 97223 655 F5
NW Deejay Ln
14800 WasC 97229 564 J7
Deemar Wy
17500 CmsC 97035 685 J2
17500 LKOW 97035 685 J2
SE Deep Creek Ct
13200 HPYV 97236 658 A1
Deep Creek Rd
14500 CmsC 97009 659 C7
14500 DAMA 97009 659 C7
SW Deepwell Ct
19600 WasC 97007 624 D4
NE Deer Dr
29600 ClkC 98675 419 J7
Deer Ln
18800 CmsC 97045 716 J4
SW Deer Ln
14000 BRTN 97008 654 J2
NW Deerbrook Ct
17500 WasC 97229 564 G6
Deerbrook Dr
100 ORCY 97045 717 A3
Deerbrush Av
17800 LKOW 97035 686 A2
NW Deercreek Ct
17000 WasC 97229 594 F1
SE Deer Creek Ln
8000 CmsC 97222 657 F5
SE Deer Creek Pl
4600 GSHM 97080 629 B7
SE Deer Creek Wy
- GSHM 97080 629 B6
SW Deercrest Ln
15700 BRTN 97007 654 G3
SE Deerfern Av
4500 ClkC 98607 568 J4
4500 CMAS 98607 568 J4
SE Deerfern Lp
20400 ClkC 98607 568 J4
NW Deerfern St
1200 ClkC 98607 568 J4
1200 CMAS 98607 568 J4
Deerfield Ct
13200 LKOW 97035 655 H4
NW Deerfield Dr
17800 WasC 97229 564 F7
SE Deerfield Dr
12000 HPYV 97236 658 B4
SE Deerfield Pl
12300 HPYV 97236 658 B4
NW Deerfield Wy
5300 WasC 97229 564 F7
NW Deerfoot Ln
14800 WasC 97229 564 J6
SW Deergrove Ln
13100 WasC 97224 685 A1
NE Deer Haven Dr
18600 YmhC 97132 712 E5
SE Deerhaven Dr
- PTLD 97266 628 A6
SE Deering Ct
6200 MWKE 97222 657 D3
NE Deering Dr
- PTLD 97220 567 J7
- PTLD 97220 568 A7
Deer Island Rd
300 STHN 97051 385 C6
1200 ClbC 97051 385 C6
Deer Lodge Ln
24000 CmsC 97049 724 D3
SE Deer Meadow Lp
16300 DAMA 97009 688 E1
Deer Meadows Rd
13200 ORCY 97045 717 D5
Deer Oak Av
18400 LKOW 97035 686 A2
Deer Oak Cir
18400 LKOW 97035 686 A2
Deer Park Rd
- CmsC 97067 724 C6
E Deer Park Rd
68300 CmsC 97067 724 C6
SW Deer Park Rd
35200 CmsC 97070 744 E6
NE Deer Ridge Dr
25700 ClkC 98675 419 F5
NE Deer Run St
6500 HBRO 97124 594 A5
6500 WasC 97124 594 A5
NW Deette Dr
- WasC 97229 595 F4
S Deininger Rd
17600 CmsC 97045 718 G2
SW DeKalb St
15700 WasC 97224 654 G6
SW Dekorte Ter
14500 TGRD 97224 655 F6
N Dekum St
10 PTLD 97211 566 G6
2500 PTLD 97217 566 D6
NE Dekum St
10 PTLD 97211 566 J6
10 PTLD 97217 566 G6
2600 PTLD 97211 567 A6
SE Del Dr
8100 JNCY 97267 687 F1
NW DeLamere Ter
- HBRO 97006 594 C5
NE Delancey Ct
2800 VCVR 98682 538 D3
2800 VCVR 98684 538 D3
SW Delaney Pl
3300 WasC 97225 625 F2
SW Delanois Pl
23600 WasC 97140 714 C1
N Delaware Av
- PTLD 97217 566 D3
SW Delaware Cir
7200 TLTN 97062 685 G5
Delaware Ln
7300 VCVR 98664 537 E6
SW Delaware St
7100 TLTN 97062 685 G5
Delenka Ln
18100 LKOW 97034 686 C2
NE Delfel Ct
17400 ClkC 98642 476 H2
NE Delfel Rd
18000 ClkC 98642 476 H1
19000 ClkC 98642 446 G7
SE Delia St
20100 DAMA 97009 658 J3
SW Deline Ct
16000 WasC 97007 624 G4
SW Deline St
19800 WasC 97007 624 C4
SW Delker Rd
5500 CmsC 97062 685 H7
Dell Av
100 ORCY 97045 717 C2
SW Dellwood Av
1300 WasC 97225 595 B7
SW Dellwood Ct
1500 WasC 97225 595 B7
Dellwood Dr
2300 LKOW 97034 686 B2
SW Dellwood Pl
1400 WasC 97225 595 B7
SW Del Mar Ct
13100 BRTN 97008 625 A7
SW Delmont Av
900 WasC 97225 595 C7
NW Del Monte Dr
900 MCMV 97128 770 F4
SW Del Monte Dr
10300 TGRD 97224 655 D6
32300 WNVL 97070 745 E3
SW Deloris Ln
18200 WasC 97007 624 E5
Delorme Av
4100 STPL 97137 773 B6
Delors Av
- SNDY 97055 690 J4
NE Delp Rd
300 ClkC 98607 539 E5
Delphi Ridge Rd
38100 CmsC 97023 750 H3
Del Prado St
10 LKOW 97035 656 A4
SE Del Rey Av
14900 CmsC 97267 657 E7
SE Del Rio Ct
5300 HBRO 97123 593 H7
7300 HBRO 97123 594 A7
SE Del Rio St
5500 HBRO 97123 593 J7
NE Delsey Rd
600 HBRO 97124 593 D4
SW Delta Ct
16500 BRTN 97006 594 G5
SW Delta Dr
100 BRTN 97006 594 G6
Del Verde
17400 GLDS 97027 687 E2
NW Demaris Rd
2200 ClkC 98665 506 D4
Demming Rd
36200 CmsC 97055 690 G4
SE Denali Dr
9100 HPYV 97236 658 D1
SW Denali Ln
23500 SRWD 97140 714 J1
Denbrook Rd
12900 CmsC 97002 745 C4
NE Denbrook Rd
- CmsC 97002 745 B4
SW Denfield St
11500 WasC 97005 625 C2
11700 BRTN 97005 625 C2
SE Denise Ct
17300 DAMA 97009 688 F1
SW Denney Rd
9500 BRTN 97008 625 D5
9500 WasC 97008 625 E5
NW Dennis Av
100 HBRO 97123 593 B4
100 HBRO 97124 593 B4
SW Dennis Av
100 HBRO 97123 593 B5
100 HBRO 97124 593 B4
Denny Ct
16800 CmsC 97035 685 H1
SE Denny St
1300 CmsC 97222 656 H5
Denton Dr
5000 LKOW 97035 655 J5
N Denver Av
4600 PTLD 97217 596 E1
7500 PTLD 97217 566 E6
N DePauw St
5000 PTLD 97203 566 A4
Depot Av
- ORCY 97045 687 E5
Depot Rd
- MthC 97231 534 F4
Depot St
10 FRVW 97024 599 B4
10 RDGF 98642 415 J6
100 BNKS 97106 531 J5
16800 LKOW 97035 686 A1
Derby Ct
19600 WLIN 97068 686 H4
Derby St
800 MCMV 97128 770 G6
19700 WLIN 97068 686 H4
SW Derby St
600 MCMV 97128 770 G6
13900 WasC 97005 594 J7
13900 WasC 97005 595 A7
SE Derdan Ct
5900 MWKE 97222 657 D3
NE Dereck Ln
6200 HBRO 97124 593 J5
SE Derek Ct
9800 CmsC 97236 657 H2
SE Derek Lp
10000 HPYV 97236 657 H2
SW Derrill Pl
1600 WasC 97006 594 E7
Derringer Dr
19600 ORCY 97045 717 A5
NW Derrington Ct
1300 BRTN 97006 594 F4
SE Derry Ln
4300 CmsC 97267 687 B1
SW Derry Dell Ct
10600 TGRD 97223 655 C4
NW Dersham Rd
10100 WasC 97113 532 G7
10100 WasC 97113 562 G1
11900 WasC 97133 532 G7
NW Deschutes Dr
5300 WasC 97229 564 C6
Deschutes Ln
3000 WLIN 97068 716 H1
NW Desert Canyon Dr
16500 WasC 97006 594 G1
Deskins St
700 NWBG 97132 713 C6
SE Deswell St
3100 CmsC 97267 687 A1
SE Determan Ct
14700 CmsC 97267 657 B6
N Detroit Av
5500 PTLD 97217 566 E6
Detroit Wy
600 VCVR 98664 537 E5
N Devine Rd
100 VCVR 98661 537 C5
S Devine Rd
100 VCVR 98661 537 C6
Devon Ln
800 LKOW 97034 686 F1
SW Devon Ln
300 WasC 97006 595 A6
8000 PTLD 97219 626 B6
NW Devonmoor Av
12300 BNKS 97106 531 J6
Devonshire Ct
35300 ClbC 97051 414 J2
SW Devonshire Ct
6800 WNVL 97070 745 G2
Devonshire Dr
3400 LKOW 97035 656 B6
6600 GLDS 97027 687 D1
6700 CmsC 97027 687 D1
6700 CmsC 97267 687 D1
SW Devonshire Dr
13100 WasC 97005 595 A7
13100 WasC 97225 595 B7
Devonshire Mnr
- WasC 97007 624 E4
SW Devonwood Av
10 WasC 97006 595 A6
200 WasC 97006 594 J6
NW Devoto Ln
3700 PTLD 97229 595 E1
4000 MthC 97229 595 E2
SW Dewberry Ln
16000 WasC 97223 654 G4
SW Dewberry Pl
23800 SRWD 97140 714 H1
E Dewey Av
23700 CmsC 97067 724 B3
SE Dewey Ct
5900 MWKE 97222 657 D3
SW Dewey Dr
22100 SRWD 97140 684 E7
Dewey St
400 ORCY 97045 717 D2
SW Dewitt St
- PTLD 97239 626 C4
NE Dexter Av
2700 GSHM 97030 599 E7
NE Dexter Ct
400 GSHM 97030 629 E2
SE Dexter Ct
9400 CmsC 97236 657 H1
SE Dexter Ln
1500 GSHM 97080 629 E4
SE Diamond Ct
15000 CmsC 97015 658 A7
NW Diamond Dr
12600 WasC 97229 595 B2
SE Diamond Dr
15000 CmsC 97015 657 J7
15000 CmsC 97015 658 A7
SE Diamond Ln
15100 CmsC 97267 657 A6
SW Diamond St
- BRTN 97007 654 E2
NW Diamondback Dr
4100 WasC 97006 594 G1
SE Diamond Creek Ct
8600 HPYV 97236 628 D7
SW Diamond Dr Vw
- BRTN 97007 654 E1
Diamond Head Rd
15300 LKOW 97034 656 D6
Diamond Lake Ct NE
13400 MrnC 97002 775 C7
SW Diamond View Dr
- BRTN 97007 654 G1
SE Diana Av
11100 DAMA 97009 658 H3
Diane Ct
- YmhC 97128 770 E6
Diane Dr
2900 LKOW 97035 656 B5
SW Diane Pl
11500 WasC 97005 625 C2
S Dick Dr
17500 CmsC 97045 688 D5
NW Dick Rd
7700 HBRO 97124 564 B4
7700 WasC 97124 564 B4
11500 WasC 97124 534 C7
SE Dick St
- MWKE 97222 657 C3
N Dickens St
8300 PTLD 97203 565 H3
Dickerson Ln
18300 GLDS 97027 687 D3
S Dickey Prairie Rd
32000 CmsC 97017 837 J3
32000 CmsC 97038 837 J5
SW Dickinson Ct
11800 PTLD 97219 656 C3
SW Dickinson Ln
1200 PTLD 97219 656 D3
SW Dickinson St
3900 PTLD 97219 656 A2
5700 PTLD 97219 655 H2
6400 TGRD 97223 655 H2
SW Dickson St
12500 WasC 97224 685 A1
NW Dierdorff Rd
23800 WasC 97124 563 J2
Dierick Rd
42800 WasC 97116 531 H7
Dierickx Ct
18500 GLDS 97027 687 D3
Dike Rd
- CtzC 98674 386 B5
1800 CtzC 98674 385 D2
3000 CtzC 98674 415 G1
50700 ClbC 97056 474 J2
SW Dillan Dr
600 BRTN 97006 594 J6
600 WasC 97006 594 J6
700 WasC 97005 594 J6
SW Dilley Rd
- WasC 97116 591 G7
S Dillman Rd
18000 CmsC 97045 718 E5
Dillon Ln
3000 WLIN 97068 686 H6
NE Dillon Rd
23200 YmhC 97132 712 J7
23200 YmhC 97132 713 A7
Dillow Dr
2000 WLIN 97068 687 A5
Dimick St
400 ORCY 97045 717 D2
SW Dipper Ln
12800 BRTN 97007 654 F4
SW Discovery St
3600 BRTN 97006 624 H2
NW District Ct
11000 WasC 97229 595 D2
NE Ditmer Av
- VCVR 98663 506 H7
SE Divers Rd
32100 CmsC 97023 750 H7
Division Av
3000 VCVR 98663 536 G3
3300 VCVR 98660 536 G2
NW Division Av
3900 VCVR 98663 536 G2
4500 ClkC 98663 536 G1
4500 VCVR 98660 536 G1
Division Ct
3700 LKOW 97035 656 A7
NE Division Dr
4000 GSHM 97030 629 G2
4600 MthC 97030 629 G2
SE Division Dr
27300 GSHM 97030 629 G2
27300 MthC 97030 629 G2
27600 MthC 97060 629 H3
28700 MthC 97060 630 A3
SE Division Pl
300 PTLD 97202 626 G1
300 PTLD 97214 626 G1
E Division Rd
35300 ClbC 97051 414 J3
S Division Rd
58200 ClbC 97051 414 J3
Division St
10 RDGF 98642 415 J6
200 ORCY 97045 717 D1
500 RDGF 98642 416 A6
600 CMAS 98607 569 E4
600 CmsC 97045 717 D1
1500 ORCY 97045 687 E7
1700 CmsC 97045 687 E7
19300 GLDS 97027 687 D3
NE Division St
10 GSHM 97030 629 C1
NW Division St
10 GSHM 97030 629 A1
1900 GSHM 97030 628 J1
SE Division St
300 PTLD 97214 596 G7
500 PTLD 97214 626 G1
900 PTLD 97202 626 H1
2800 PTLD 97202 627 A1
2800 PTLD 97214 627 A1
4100 PTLD 97206 627 D1
4100 PTLD 97215 627 D1
8100 PTLD 97216 627 J1
8100 PTLD 97266 627 J1
11500 PTLD 97216 628 A1
11500 PTLD 97266 628 A1
12100 PTLD 97233 628 B1
12100 PTLD 97236 628 B1
17400 GSHM 97233 628 H1
17400 GSHM 97236 628 F1
18000 GSHM 97030 628 H1
SW Division St
14800 SRWD 97140 684 H7
14900 BRTN 97007 624 J4
16700 WasC 97007 624 G4
W Division St
100 RDGF 98642 415 J6
SE Dix Ct
900 TDLE 97060 599 G4
NW Dixie Mountain Rd
15600 WasC 97133 533 D3
Dixon Av
100 MOLA 97038 837 D1
NE Dixon Ln
5500 YmhC 97114 742 E6
5500 YmhC 97115 742 E6
N Dixon St
300 PTLD 97227 596 F4
NW Doane Av
5500 PTLD 97210 565 J7
SE Doane Creek Rd
- CmsC 97009 660 B3
Dodge Wy
1600 WLIN 97068 716 G1
SE Dodge Park Blvd
28900 MthC 97080 629 J6
29500 MthC 97080 630 A6
34700 CmsC 97009 660 H1
34700 MthC 97009 630 G7
SW Dodson Dr
17500 SRWD 97140 714 E1
SW Doe Ln
13300 TGRD 97223 655 A4
NE Doe Ridge Rd
13800 YmhC 97111 711 F4
13800 YmhC 97148 711 F4
NE Dog Ridge Rd
7400 YmhC 97132 743 E3
7900 NWBG 97132 743 E2
Dogwood
- ClbC 97056 474 A4
- CmsC 97015 657 J7
- VCVR 98682 538 B2
Dogwood Av
- PTLD 97217 536 E6
3000 NWBG 97132 713 E5
E Dogwood Av
500 LCTR 98629 386 H7
Dogwood Blvd
1900 VCVR 98661 537 B4
S Dogwood Cir
200 CNLS 97113 592 C5
Dogwood Ct
17900 GLDS 97027 687 E2
NW Dogwood Ct
17600 BRTN 97006 594 F4
S Dogwood Ct
200 CNLS 97113 592 D5
SW Dogwood Ct
600 MCMV 97128 770 E6
W Dogwood Ct
- WHGL 98671 569 H3
Dogwood Dr
5500 RVGR 97035 685 H3
NW Dogwood Dr
100 DNDE 97115 742 H2
100 YmhC 97115 742 H2
6200 VCVR 98663 506 E6
S Dogwood Dr
200 CNLS 97113 592 D5
SW Dogwood Dr
4500 LKOW 97035 686 A4
4500 RVGR 97035 686 A4
4600 LKOW 97035 685 J3
4600 RVGR 97035 685 J3
Dogwood Ln
- HBRO 97006 594 D5
- WasC 97006 594 D5
58600 ClbC 97051 414 J2
58600 STHN 97051 414 J3
NE Dogwood Ln
- ClkC 98607 539 F6
SE Dogwood Ln
900 CmsC 97267 656 H6
900 GSHM 97080 629 G4
20500 DAMA 97009 658 J6
SW Dogwood Ln
3900 WasC 97225 625 H3
S Dogwood Pl
200 CNLS 97113 592 D5
SW Dogwood Pl
7000 WasC 97225 625 G4
SW Dogwood Rd
500 ECDA 97023 750 D5
NE Dogwood St
6000 HBRO 97124 593 J4
6300 HBRO 97124 594 B3
NW Dogwood St
6500 HBRO 97124 594 A4
6500 WasC 97124 594 A4
12700 WasC 97229 595 B4
S Dogwood St
400 CNLS 97113 592 E5
2800 WasC 97123 592 F5
SW Dogwood St
100 DNDE 97115 742 H2
10400 TLTN 97062 685 C7
W Dogwood St
100 WHGL 98671 569 H3
S Dogwood Ter
2300 CNLS 97113 592 F5
SE Dogwood Wy
1600 GSHM 97080 629 G4
SE Dohn Ct
1100 CmsC 97267 656 H6
S Dolan Rd
25400 ClkC 98642 446 F1
25400 RDGF 98642 446 F1
25700 RDGF 98642 416 F7
Dolash Ct
600 NWBG 97132 713 E7
SE Dolinda St
7600 CmsC 97267 687 E1
Dollar St
10 WLIN 97068 716 F1
Dolores Wy NE
21000 MrnC 97002 775 A3
Dolph Ct
14200 LKOW 97034 656 D5
SW Dolph Ct
2800 PTLD 97219 626 B7
5000 PTLD 97219 625 J7
SW Dolph Dr
6100 PTLD 97219 625 H7
SW Dolph St
1200 PTLD 97219 626 D7
5600 PTLD 97219 625 J7
8700 WasC 97223 625 F6
8800 BRTN 97008 625 F6
8800 WasC 97008 625 F6
SE Dolphin Rd
16300 CmsC 97009 688 J1
16300 DAMA 97009 688 J1
N Dolphin St
5500 PTLD 97217 566 B7
SW Doma Ln
19900 WasC 97006 594 D6
NW Domaine Pl
2900 HBRO 97124 594 C2
SW Dominie Ct
5200 WasC 97007 624 D3
NW Dominion Dr
14800 WasC 97229 594 J2
SW Domino St
13900 WasC 97005 594 J7
13900 WasC 97005 595 A7
NW Donahoo St
300 MCMV 97128 770 F5
E Donald Ln
300 NWBG 97132 713 C5
Donald Lp NE
12500 MrnC 97002 775 A5
Donald Rd NE
10000 DNLD 97020 774 H5
10000 MrnC 97002 774 E4
10000 MrnC 97020 774 E4
10900 MrnC 97032 774 G4
11200 MrnC 97002 775 A5
Donald St
100 ORCY 97045 717 C3
SE Donatello Lp
14300 HPYV 97236 628 C7
14300 PTLD 97236 628 C7
Doncaster Dr
6600 GLDS 97027 687 D1
NW Doncaster Ter
2300 HBRO 97124 594 D3
Donegal Ct
2400 WLIN 97068 686 G7
NW Donegal Ct
15500 WasC 97229 594 H1
SW Donelle Ln
19200 WasC 97140 714 D3
NE Donelson Rd
600 HBRO 97124 593 D4
NE Donelson St
200 HBRO 97124 593 C4
NW Donelson St
700 HBRO 97124 593 A4
NE Doneta Dr
15100 ClkC 98606 478 G5
NW Donin Ct
16100 BRTN 97006 594 H5
Donlee Wy
18400 CmsC 97035 685 H2
18400 LKOW 97035 685 H2
SE Don Lino Ct
16300 DAMA 97009 688 E2
SE Donna Cir
22200 DAMA 97009 659 B6
SE Donna Ct
21800 DAMA 97009 659 B6
SW Donna Ct
15400 WasC 97007 624 H3
Donna Lynn Wy
900 GLDS 97027 687 E3
Donnelly Ln
14600 AURA 97002 775 E3
14600 MrnC 97002 775 E3
SW Donner Wy
4300 PTLD 97239 626 D3
SW Donner Wy Ct
3200 PTLD 97239 626 C3
E Donneydell Ln
20300 CmsC 97049 693 G6
Donovan Rd
- CmsC 97045 687 F7
14100 CmsC 97045 717 F1
SE Don Tomas Ct
16200 DAMA 97009 688 F1
SE Don Vizo Ct
16400 DAMA 97009 688 F1
SW Doolittle Ct
1100 TDLE 97060 599 F5
NE Dopp Rd
14000 YmhC 97132 712 D4
Dora Av
100 TDLE 97060 599 G4
SE Dora Ct
2000 TDLE 97060 599 G6
NW Dorado Ln
20600 WasC 97006 594 C5
Doral Ct
2000 WLIN 97068 716 F2
NW Doral St
1600 MCMV 97128 770 F3
NW Dorchester Wy
19800 HBRO 97124 594 D3
NW Dorena St
19000 WasC 97229 594 E1
SW Dori Ct
6500 BRTN 97008 625 D5
Doris Av
14400 LKOW 97035 656 B6
Doris Ct
3000 LKOW 97035 656 B5
Doris Dr
200 NWBG 97132 713 E7
200 YmhC 97132 713 E7
NW Dorland Rd
26500 WasC 97133 533 E3

STREET / Block City ZIP Map# Grid

SW Dorothy Dr
20500 WasC 97006 594 C7
W Dorothy St
1300 MCMV 97128 770 F6
SE Dorset Ln
11700 HPYV 97236 657 J2
11800 HPYV 97236 658 A2
SE Dorsey Rd
- YmhC 97114 772 E7
SW Dosch Ct
3400 PTLD 97221 626 B2
3400 PTLD 97239 626 B2
SW Dosch Ln
- PTLD 97221 626 B2
- PTLD 97239 626 B2
SW Dosch Rd
2800 PTLD 97221 626 B1
2800 PTLD 97239 626 B2
SW Doschdale Ct
5400 PTLD 97239 626 B4
SW Doschdale Dr
3100 PTLD 97239 626 B4
SW Dosch Park Ln
4600 PTLD 97239 626 C3
SW Doschview Ct
3300 PTLD 97239 626 B2
3400 PTLD 97221 626 B2
Doty Ln
- YmhC 97128 770 B2
NW Doty Ln
1700 YmhC 97128 770 B2
Doublecreek Dr
36700 SNDY 97055 690 G2
Doubletree St
- FTGV 97116 591 G2
SE Dougie Rd
15200 CmsC 97015 658 D5
15200 HPYV 97015 658 D5
Douglas Av
2700 NWBG 97132 713 E6
SW Douglas Av
11800 BRTN 97225 595 C7
11800 WasC 97225 595 C7
12000 WasC 97225 625 B1
Douglas Cir
3100 LKOW 97035 656 B6
NW Douglas Ct
5500 CMAS 98607 539 B7
SE Douglas Ct
3700 TDLE 97060 599 G7
Douglas Dr
- STHN 97051 414 J1
1100 WLIN 97068 716 F1
35400 STHN 97051 415 A1
SW Douglas Dr
6200 CmsC 97219 655 H4
N Douglas Ln
500 CNBY 97013 746 B6
Douglas Lp N
- ORCY 97045 717 F5
NW Douglas Lp
1900 CMAS 98607 569 B3
NW Douglas Pl
800 WasC 97229 595 D5
SE Douglas Pl
1900 GSHM 97080 629 G5
SW Douglas Pl
1000 PTLD 97205 596 B6
Douglas St
2500 FTGV 97116 591 J4
2500 WasC 97116 591 J4
N Douglas St
900 CNBY 97013 746 B5
NW Douglas St
2000 CMAS 98607 569 B3
S Douglas St
500 CNBY 97013 746 C7
SW Douglas St
- CmsC 97219 655 H4
- LKOW 97035 655 H4
- PTLD 97219 655 H4
- TGRD 97223 655 H4
12400 BRTN 97005 625 B1
12400 WasC 97005 625 B1
12400 WasC 97225 625 B1
Douglas Wy
3900 LKOW 97035 656 A6
NE Douglas Wy
4300 VCVR 98662 537 F2
NE Douglas Fir Ct
14400 VCVR 98684 538 C6
SE Douglas Fir Ct
13900 CmsC 97267 657 B5
S Douglas Loop Rd
- ORCY 97045 717 F5
SE Douglass Rd
35700 CmsC 97022 720 F3
Dove Ct
- TGRD 97223 655 E3
5800 CmsC 97035 655 H6
SW Dove Ct
900 MCMV 97128 770 E6
E Dove Ln
27000 CmsC 97067 724 C6
SE Dove St
2300 CmsC 97222 656 J4
2300 HBRO 97123 623 E1
2400 MWKE 97222 656 J4
SW Dover Ct
5200 BRTN 97225 625 H4
10800 TGRD 97224 685 C1
SW Dover Ln
5000 BRTN 97225 625 H4
SW Dover Lp
5400 BRTN 97225 625 H4
NW Dover St
- MthC 97210 595 H5
- PTLD 97210 595 H5
SW Dover St
6300 BRTN 97225 625 H4
6300 PTLD 97221 625 H4
6700 WasC 97225 625 H4
Dover Wy
10 LKOW 97034 686 B3
SW Dow Dr
22400 SRWD 97140 684 F7
Dowd Rd
31000 ClbC 97051 384 A7
31400 ClbC 97051 414 B1
31400 ClbC 97053 414 B1
SE Dowery Ln
1600 HBRO 97123 593 D7
SE Down Wy
8400 CmsC 97267 687 F2

SE Downey Ln
23700 CmsC 97022 720 A2
SW Downing Ct
14700 WasC 97006 594 J6
SW Downing Dr
10 MCMV 97128 770 G5
9100 BRTN 97008 625 D6
9100 BRTN 97008 655 B1
SW Downing St
14000 WasC 97006 595 A6
14200 WasC 97006 594 J6
Down River Dr
1300 WDLD 98674 385 J1
SW Downs Post Rd
7500 WNVL 97070 745 F3
SW Downs View Ct
4500 MthC 97221 626 A2
5400 MthC 97221 625 J2
SW Downsview Ct
4000 PTLD 97221 626 B2
SW Downs View Ter
3400 PTLD 97221 626 B2
SE Dowsett Ln
600 GSHM 97080 629 C4
SE Dowty Rd
22400 CmsC 97022 689 H7
22500 CmsC 97022 719 G3
SW Doyle Pl
3000 WasC 97006 624 E1
SW Dozier Wy
15800 WasC 97224 654 G6
SE Drake Ct
7300 HBRO 97123 594 B7
SE Drake Rd
5000 HBRO 97123 593 H7
21600 DAMA 97009 689 A2
NW Drake St
1400 CMAS 98607 569 D4
SE Drake St
3700 MWKE 97222 657 B2
5800 HBRO 97123 593 J7
6000 WasC 97123 593 J7
6100 HBRO 97123 623 J1
6100 WasC 97123 623 J1
6300 HBRO 97123 624 A1
NW Drake Wy
1200 CMAS 98607 569 E4
NW Drakeway St
- CMAS 98607 569 E4
SW Draxton Ter
- WasC 97007 624 B5
SE Dream Ln
- CmsC 97009 659 F5
- DAMA 97009 659 F5
Dreamcatcher Av
15600 SNDY 97055 690 H1
SE Dreamweaver Ct
15700 HPYV 97236 658 E5
SE Dreamweaver Dr
15600 HPYV 97236 658 D4
SE Drefshill St
5500 MWKE 97222 657 C1
Dr Eldridge Dr
4600 WHGL 98671 570 E4
NW Dresden Pl
4600 WasC 97229 595 B1
NE Dresser Rd
24200 ClkC 98607 539 D3
NE Dresser Rd SR-500
24200 ClkC 98607 539 D3
S Dressler Ln
14000 CmsC 97038 837 D3
SE Drew Av
6800 CmsC 97222 657 E1
N Drew St
4700 PTLD 97203 566 B4
NE Drexel Av
5400 VCVR 98663 506 J7
N Drexler Dr
100 PTLD 97227 596 F4
Driftwood Dr
19000 CmsC 97045 718 C7
20300 CmsC 97045 748 D1
S Driftwood Dr
19000 ORCY 97045 717 B4
SW Driftwood Ln
10200 TGRD 97224 655 D6
14100 TGRD 97223 655 D5
NW Driftwood Pl
1200 MCMV 97128 770 F4
SW Driftwood Pl
13400 WasC 97005 625 E4
NW Driver Pl
4600 WasC 97229 594 H1
N Druid Av
8100 PTLD 97203 566 B4
Drummond Av
2900 VCVR 98661 537 A3
N Drummond Av
8400 PTLD 97217 566 D4
SW Drumwood Av
400 MCMV 97128 770 G6
NW Drury Ln
12600 MthC 97231 535 B6
12600 PTLD 97231 535 B6
Dry Gulch
- BRTN 97005 625 C2
S Dryland Rd
27200 CmsC 97013 776 F7
Duane St
13500 ORCY 97045 717 E2
Dubarko Rd
36200 CmsC 97055 690 J4
36200 SNDY 97055 690 J4
38900 SNDY 97055 691 A4
39000 CmsC 97055 691 A4
NW Dublin Ct
16600 WasC 97229 564 G7
NE Dublin Rd
24900 ClkC 98604 448 B2
Dubois Ct
100 VCVR 98661 537 C6
Dubois Dr
4500 VCVR 98661 537 B6
Du Bois Ln
10 STHN 97051 415 B1
S Dubois Creek Ln
25100 CmsC 97023 750 A6
SE Dubs Wy
- CmsC 97267 687 B2
SW Duchess Wy
11400 BRTN 97008 625 C5
SW Duchilly Ct
12200 TGRD 97224 655 B6

Duck Ct
12200 ORCY 97045 717 B4
SE Duckey Ln
15100 CmsC 97267 657 E7
SW Duckridge Pl
20500 SRWD 97140 684 F5
NE Duddleson St
8500 PTLD 97220 597 G2
NE Dudley Rd
11400 YmhC 97115 712 D7
11400 YmhC 97132 712 D7
SE Duke Dr
1200 HBRO 97123 593 D7
Duke Ln NE
7200 MrnC 97137 773 H4
7200 MrnC 97137 774 A4
SE Duke St
1400 PTLD 97202 626 H5
4900 PTLD 97206 627 C5
11000 PTLD 97266 627 J5
13100 PTLD 97236 628 B5
N Dumar Ln
10500 WasC 97229 595 D3
NW Dumar St
13000 WasC 97229 595 B3
SW Dumas Rd
6500 WasC 97123 623 G5
NW Dunbar Av
700 TDLE 97060 599 E3
NE Dunbar Ct
3400 HBRO 97124 593 D1
3400 WasC 97124 593 D1
SE Dunbar Dr
6300 PTLD 97236 628 F5
NW Dunbar Ln
14100 PTLD 97231 565 A2
SW Dunbar Pl
2200 TDLE 97060 599 E6
NE Dunberg Lp
23000 YmhC 97132 743 A1
Duncan Dr
2900 LKOW 97035 656 B5
SW Duncan Ln
9500 BRTN 97005 625 E3
NE Dunckley St
2400 PTLD 97212 596 J1
2600 PTLD 97212 597 A2
SE Dundee Ct
9300 CmsC 97236 657 G1
SE Dundee Dr
9300 CmsC 97236 657 H1
9800 HPYV 97236 657 H2
SW Dune Grass Ln
7800 TGRD 97224 655 F5
Dunes Dr
- ORCY 97045 687 C6
Dunham Av
200 WDLD 98674 385 J2
SE Dunhill Lp
16800 DAMA 97009 688 F1
Duniway Av
6000 GLDS 97027 687 C3
SW Duniway Av
- GSHM 97080 628 G3
300 GSHM 97030 628 H3
NE Duniway Rd
4300 LFYT 97127 741 H7
4300 YmhC 97114 741 H7
6800 YmhC 97114 742 A5
SE Dunlin Dr
14000 HPYV 97236 658 C2
SW Dunlin Pl
10300 BRTN 97007 654 H2
S Dunn Pl
100 MCMV 97128 771 B6
SE Dunn Rd
35200 CmsC 97009 660 G5
35200 CmsC 97055 660 G5
SW Dunsmuir Ln
7500 BRTN 97007 624 J6
NE Duran Dr
- MCMV 97128 771 B2
SE Durango Ct
11700 CmsC 97015 657 H5
SE Durango Pl
- GSHM 97080 629 C6
SW Durant Pl
8400 BRTN 97008 625 D3
SW Durdel Dr
24000 WasC 97140 714 A2
Durecka Rd
57000 ClbC 97053 414 C5
SW Durell Ct
19100 WasC 97006 624 D1
NW Durgan Ct
1100 CMAS 98607 569 B4
NE Durham Av
6300 PTLD 97211 566 H6
SW Durham Ln
8300 TGRD 97224 655 F7
Durham Pk
- TGRD 97224 655 D7
- TGRD 97224 685 C1
SW Durham Rd
7200 DRHM 97224 685 G1
7200 TGRD 97224 685 G1
7900 TGRD 97224 655 E7
11500 WasC 97224 655 C7
Durham St
10 LKOW 97034 656 G7
Durham Wy
200 VCVR 98664 537 E6
Durie Ct
17700 GLDS 97027 687 D3
NW Durrett St
9600 PTLD 97229 595 E2
Dusky Dr
1500 RDGF 98642 446 A1
SE Dustin Dr
1300 CmsC 97267 656 H6
NW Dustin Ln
17800 BRTN 97006 594 F5
18000 WasC 97006 594 F5
Dusty Ln
16100 CmsC 97055 691 C1
NW Dutch Ln
1300 HBRO 97006 594 C4
Dutch Canyon Rd
30700 ClbC 97056 474 A2
SW Dutch Canyon Rd
32700 ClbC 97056 474 D3
32700 SPSE 97056 474 D3
NE Dutch Vista Ct
2400 CmsC 97013 746 F4

SW Dutson Dr
23700 WasC 97140 713 H1
SW Dutton Ct
20800 WasC 97007 624 B4
SE Duus Rd
29600 CmsC 97023 720 D7
N Dwight Av
7000 PTLD 97203 566 B4
Dwight Dr
52400 ClbC 97056 444 B7
52400 ClbC 97056 474 B1
SE Dwyer Dr
3200 MWKE 97222 657 A1
Dyer St
1000 LKOW 97034 656 F7
NE Dyer St
8600 PTLD 97220 597 G2
SE Dykeman Ct
14300 CmsC 97267 657 A6
NW Dyreka Ct
400 MCMV 97128 770 G5

E

E Av
10 LKOW 97034 656 F5
W E Av
200 LCTR 98629 416 G1
500 LCTR 98629 386 G7
900 ClkC 98629 386 G7
E Ln
- PTLD 97218 567 E7
E St
- PTLD 97219 655 J3
10 CBAC 97018 385 C3
300 CMAS 98607 569 J5
300 WHGL 98671 569 J5
600 ClbC 97051 385 C3
900 WHGL 98671 570 B5
1300 VCVR 98660 536 G4
1500 VCVR 98663 536 G4
2000 FTGV 97116 591 H4
E St SR-8
2000 FTGV 97116 591 H4
NW E St
- WasC 97006 594 C5
S Eaden Rd
15600 CmsC 97045 689 D6
17000 CmsC 97045 719 F1
18100 CmsC 97023 719 C3
SE Eagle Av
- GSHM 97080 629 G5
SW Eagle Ct
9600 WasC 97008 625 E6
Eagle Dr
31900 ClbC 97056 444 B5
SE Eagle Dr
11900 CmsC 97015 658 A7
SE Eagle Ln
1000 GSHM 97080 629 G4
SW Eagle Ln
9600 WasC 97008 625 E6
9800 BRTN 97008 625 E6
NW Eagle St
1200 CMAS 98607 569 B4
SE Eagle St
1900 MWKE 97222 656 J3
SE Eagle Cliff Ln
31100 CmsC 97022 720 B3
SE Eagle Creek Rd
22600 CmsC 97022 719 J1
22600 CmsC 97022 720 A4
26200 CmsC 97023 720 A7
29200 CmsC 97023 750 B1
30500 ECDA 97023 750 B1
Eagle Creek-Sandy Hwy
- CmsC 97009 690 G5
- CmsC 97022 690 D6
- CmsC 97022 719 J1
- CmsC 97022 720 A1
- CmsC 97055 690 E6
- SNDY 97055 690 J4
- SNDY 97055 691 A3
Eagle Creek-Sandy Hwy SR-211
- CmsC 97009 690 G5
- CmsC 97022 690 D6
- CmsC 97022 719 J1
- CmsC 97022 720 A1
- CmsC 97055 690 E6
- SNDY 97055 690 J4
- SNDY 97055 691 A3
Eagle Crest
1900 WLIN 97068 686 H5
SW Eagle Crest
8500 WasC 97007 624 D7
Eagle Crest Dr
10 LKOW 97035 656 B3
10 PTLD 97219 656 B3
NW Eagle Crest Dr
31900 ClkC 98642 416 F1
Eaglecrest Ln
10600 YmhC 97115 742 D1
SE Eagle Fern Rd
25000 CmsC 97022 720 E4
27300 CmsC 97023 720 G7
SE Eagle Glen Dr
12200 CmsC 97236 658 A4
12200 HPYV 97236 658 A4
NE Eaglenest Ct
800 HBRO 97124 593 D2
NW Eagleridge Ln
14000 WasC 97229 595 A1
SW Eagles Nest Ln
2500 PTLD 97239 626 C4
SW Eagles View Ln
14000 WasC 97224 654 J7
SE Eagle View Dr
29800 CmsC 97022 689 J6
29800 CmsC 97022 690 A6
SE Eagle Woods Dr
32800 ClkC 98671 570 C3
SW Eaker Pl
7700 WasC 97007 624 F6
NW Earl Av
800 GSHM 97030 629 B2
Earl Ct
600 NWBG 97132 713 C4
600 YmhC 97132 713 C4
NW Earl Ct
2000 GSHM 97030 629 B1
NE Earlwood Rd
6500 CmsC 97132 744 D6
East Av
- BRTN 97005 625 A2

SE East Av
14800 CmsC 97267 657 A7
SW East Av
- DRHM 97224 685 G1
- TGRD 97224 685 G1
4200 BRTN 97005 625 B3
East Ln
- CNLS 97113 592 G4
- CNLS 97123 592 H5
- WasC 97124 592 G4
NW East Rd
11200 MthC 97229 595 C1
East St
- STHN 97051 415 C2
- TLTN 97062 685 A3
- WasC 97224 655 D2
- WasC 97224 685 A1
100 ORCY 97045 717 C2
NE East St
- PTLD 97217 566 G3
S East St
1700 MCMV 97128 770 F7
Eastborne Dr
13200 ORCY 97045 717 D5
SE Eastbourne Ln
11800 CmsC 97236 658 C4
11800 HPYV 97236 658 C4
NW Eastbrook Ct
1500 WasC 97006 594 F4
SE Eastbrook Dr
5800 CmsC 97222 657 D5
SW Easterday Rd
46100 WasC 97116 591 B5
Eastfield Dr
400 ORCY 97045 717 C2
Eastgate Dr
- CmsC 97062 715 H3
5000 CmsC 97070 715 H3
5000 CmsC 97070 716 A3
SE East Hampton St
12200 CmsC 97015 658 A6
SW East Lake Ct
7100 WNVL 97070 745 G2
SW East Lake Pt
32100 WNVL 97070 745 G3
SW Eastman Av
700 GSHM 97080 629 B3
SW Eastman Ct
400 GSHM 97080 629 B3
NW Eastman Pkwy
100 GSHM 97030 629 B2
100 GSHM 97080 629 B2
SW Eastman Pkwy
- GSHM 97030 629 B3
100 GSHM 97080 629 A3
SE Eastmont Dr
9800 CmsC 97009 659 F3
SW Eastmoor Ter
7300 WasC 97225 625 G5
NW Eastmoreland Ct
16800 BRTN 97006 594 G4
East Portland Frwy
- CmsC - 627 G7
- CmsC - 657 F7
- CmsC - 685 H5
- CmsC - 686 A5
- CmsC - 687 G1
- GLDS - 687 F3
- MWDP - 597 H1
- ORCY - 687 F4
- PTLD - 567 H7
- PTLD - 597 H1
- PTLD - 627 G7
- TLTN - 685 J5
- WLIN - 686 F7
- WLIN - 687 B7
- WLIN - 716 G1
- WLIN - 717 A1
East Portland Frwy I-205
- CmsC - 627 G7
- CmsC - 657 F6
- CmsC - 685 H5
- CmsC - 686 B5
- CmsC - 687 G1
- GLDS - 687 F3
- MWDP - 597 H1
- ORCY - 687 F4
- PTLD - 567 H7
- PTLD - 597 H1
- PTLD - 627 G7
- TLTN - 685 H5
- WLIN - 686 F7
- WLIN - 687 B7
- WLIN - 716 G1
- WLIN - 717 A1
East Portland Frwy SR-213
- CmsC - 657 F7
- CmsC - 687 G1
- GLDS - 687 F3
- ORCY - 687 F4
Eastridge Blvd
- ClkC 98682 508 A4
SE Eastridge Ct
14100 PTLD 97236 628 C7
Eastridge Ln
18000 LKOW 97034 686 G2
SE Eastridge St
13600 PTLD 97236 628 C7
SW Eastridge St
10100 WasC 97225 595 D7
East Ring Rd
- HBRO 97124 594 A1
Eastside Rd
18800 CmsC 97034 686 C3
Eastview Ct
1500 LKOW 97034 686 G2
SE East View Ct
16500 PTLD 97236 628 F3
NW Eastview Dr
52500 SPSE 97056 444 D7
SE East View Dr
9600 CmsC 97236 657 J2
9600 HPYV 97236 657 J2
Eastview Ln
51500 ClbC 97056 474 D2
SW Eastview Rd
21200 WasC 97140 684 C6
NW Eastway Ct
2600 WasC 97006 594 J2
NW Eastway Pl
2900 WasC 97006 594 J2
NW Eastwind Dr
800 TDLE 97060 599 D3

NE Eastwood Av
1000 GSHM 97030 628 H1
SW Eastwood Av
1800 GSHM 97080 628 H5
SE Eastwood Ct
1300 CmsC 97267 656 H7
SW Eastwood Ct
1500 GSHM 97080 628 H4
SW Eastwood Pl
3500 GSHM 97080 628 H6
Eastwood Vil
- PTLD 97236 628 D3
Easy St
1700 WLIN 97068 687 B6
59000 ClbC 97051 414 H1
E Easy St
23500 CmsC 97011 724 A2
23500 CmsC 97067 724 A2
N Easy St
5900 PTLD 97203 566 A3
SW Easystreet Ln
29800 WasC 97113 653 B1
29800 WasC 97123 653 B1
SW Eaton Ct
600 WasC 97006 594 B6
Eaton Ln NE
- MrnC 97002 744 G6
NE Eaton Lp
4300 ClkC 98686 477 B7
NW Ebberts Av
100 HBRO 97123 593 B4
100 HBRO 97124 593 B4
SW Ebberts Ct
11700 BRTN 97008 655 C1
NW Eberly Rd
13500 WasC 97106 531 F4
SE Eblen Ln
- CmsC 97009 660 E3
S Eby Rd
11700 CmsC 97013 807 C3
12500 CmsC 97038 807 B3
Echerd Av
200 MOLA 97038 837 E2
SW Echo Ct
3900 WasC 97229 594 E1
Echo Ln
35200 ClbC 97051 414 J3
Echo Wy
18500 GLDS 97027 687 D3
SE Echo Wy
16200 CmsC 97267 687 E1
NE Echo Ridge Rd
13900 ClkC 98606 479 B6
SE Echo Valley Ct
14100 CmsC 97015 658 A6
SE Echo Valley St
12000 CmsC 97015 658 A6
SE Eckert Ct
- DAMA 97009 688 E1
SE Eckert Ln
15800 CmsC 97009 688 D1
16100 DAMA 97009 688 E1
SE Eckler Av
9600 CmsC 97222 657 E1
NW Ecklund Rd
23300 ClkC 98642 446 F3
SW Eckman St
100 MCMV 97128 770 G5
S Eckmann Ct
800 MCMV 97128 770 F6
SW Ecola Pl
6500 BRTN 97007 624 G5
SW Ecole Av
2000 WasC 97005 595 A7
2000 WasC 97005 625 A1
SW Ecotopia Ln
19400 CmsC 97068 686 C4
Ed St
19300 CmsC 97045 717 D5
19300 ORCY 97045 717 D5
SE Ed Anna Ct
18100 CmsC 97267 687 C3
SE Eddies Wy
11900 CmsC 97015 658 A6
NW Eddy Rock Rd
2800 ClkC 98629 386 D6
NE Edelweiss Av
3100 VCVR 98682 538 C3
SE Edelweiss Dr
14500 CmsC 97009 660 F7
Edelweiss Ln
5300 YmhC 97114 771 J4
SW Eden Ct
11100 TGRD 97223 655 C5
Edenberry Ct
14000 LKOW 97035 655 J5
Edenberry Dr
14000 LKOW 97035 655 J5
S Edenwild Ln
- CmsC 97045 687 H6
NW Edgebrook Pl
5300 WasC 97229 564 D7
SW Edgecliff Rd
300 MthC 97219 656 G4
Edgecliff Ter
1500 LKOW 97034 656 D7
SW Edgefield Av
1100 TDLE 97060 599 F5
SW Edgefield Ct
1100 TDLE 97060 599 F4
SW Edgefield Pl
300 TDLE 97060 599 F4
NE Edgefield St
1200 HBRO 97124 593 E1
SW Edgefield Ter
13800 TGRD 97223 655 A5
13800 WasC 97223 655 A5
SW Edgefield Meadows Av
- TDLE 97060 599 E4
SW Edgefield Meadows Ct
1300 TDLE 97060 599 F3
SW Edgefield Meadows Ter
- TDLE 97060 599 E4
NE Edgehill Dr
700 ECDA 97023 750 C3
NW Edgehill Dr
1800 CMAS 98607 569 D3
NE Edgehill Pl
2800 PTLD 97212 597 A2
SW Edgemont Pl
5500 PTLD 97239 626 E4
Edgemont Rd
3000 LKOW 97035 656 B6
SW Edgemoor Av
2400 WasC 97005 625 B1

NE Edge Park Dr
1500 VCVR 98663 536 H1
NE Edge Park Lp
1800 VCVR 98663 536 J1
Edgeview Ln
3200 FTGV 97116 591 E2
SW Edgewater E
7900 WNVL 97070 745 F2
SW Edgewater W
8000 WNVL 97070 745 F2
Edge Water Ct
1500 WLIN 97068 687 B5
SW Edgewater Ct
12400 TGRD 97223 655 B2
NE Edgewater Dr
1900 PTLD 97211 566 J3
SW Edgewater Dr
8000 WNVL 97070 745 F2
Edgewater Rd
200 GLDS 97027 687 F4
N Edgewater St
6900 PTLD 97203 565 J4
SW Edgeway Dr
100 HBRO 97006 594 E5
300 BRTN 97006 594 E6
Edgewood Ct
3100 NWBG 97132 713 C4
3900 WLIN 97068 716 J1
18500 CmsC 97035 685 H2
S Edgewood Ct
18000 CmsC 97045 688 E5
SW Edgewood Ct
1800 WasC 97005 595 A7
10600 WNVL 97070 745 C1
Edgewood Dr
100 NWBG 97132 713 C4
3200 VCVR 98661 537 A5
NW Edgewood Dr
10200 PTLD 97229 595 D3
SE Edgewood Dr
- GSHM 97080 629 C6
W Edgewood Dr
100 NWBG 97132 713 B4
300 YmhC 97132 713 B4
S Edgewood Ln
17800 CmsC 97045 688 D4
NW Edgewood Pl
2200 PTLD 97229 595 D1
SE Edgewood Pl
- GSHM 97080 629 C6
SW Edgewood Rd
1800 PTLD 97201 626 C1
Edgewood St
6200 CmsC 97035 685 H2
6400 LKOW 97035 685 H2
S Edgewood St
17800 CmsC 97045 688 E4
SW Edgewood St
8800 TGRD 97223 655 E5
11800 BRTN 97225 595 C7
12000 WasC 97225 625 B1
12800 WasC 97225 595 A7
13100 WasC 97005 595 A7
Edie's Wy
35500 STHN 97051 415 A1
NW Edinburg Dr
2300 HBRO 97124 594 C2
Edison Av
- ORCY 97045 687 D6
N Edison St
8600 PTLD 97203 565 F2
NE Edison St
100 HBRO 97124 593 C4
SE Edison St
3500 MWKE 97222 657 A3
NW Edith Ln
12700 WasC 97229 595 B3
SW Edminston Rd
15700 CmsC 97070 744 G3
15700 CmsC 97140 744 G3
NE Edmunds Rd
17200 ClkC 98682 538 F3
SW Edmunston St
300 MCMV 97128 770 G6
W Edmunston St
500 MCMV 97128 770 G6
Edna Ln
34100 ClbC 97053 414 G3
Edna Barr Ln
34800 STHN 97051 384 J7
34800 STHN 97051 414 H1
NW Edward Ct
16000 WasC 97006 594 H2
SE Edward Dr
21600 DAMA 97009 659 A7
NE Edwards Dr
- DNDE 97115 742 J3
- YmhC 97115 742 J3
SE Edwards Dr
200 DNDE 97115 742 J3
200 YmhC 97115 742 J3
Edwards Ln
200 VCVR 98661 537 A6
Edwards Pl NE
- MrnC 97002 744 G6
N Edwards St
100 NWBG 97132 713 C7
S Edwards St
100 NWBG 97132 713 C7
400 NWBG 97132 743 C1
SW Edy Rd
16700 SRWD 97140 684 F5
17200 WasC 97140 684 F5
Eena Rd
3600 LKOW 97034 686 B1
Egan Wy
1700 LKOW 97034 656 C5
SW Egger Rd
29000 WasC 97123 653 C7
NW Eggers Ct
11000 BRTN 97225 595 D5
11000 BRTN 97229 595 D5
11000 WasC 97225 595 D5
11000 WasC 97229 595 D5
SW Eggert Wy
20700 WasC 97007 624 C3
SW Eggleston Ln
52000 SPSE 97056 474 D1
NE Egret Ct
3000 FRVW 97024 599 B3
Egret Ln NE
11500 MrnC 97002 744 H5
NE Egret Ln
34300 SPSE 97056 474 G1

Portland Street Index

STREET
Block City ZIP Map# Grid

SW Egret Pl
10100 BRTN 97007 654 G1
Ehlen Rd NE
10100 MrnC 97002 774 J3
12300 MrnC 97002 775 D3
14500 AURA 97002 775 E3
Ehlen St NE
21000 DNLD 97020 774 G4
SW Eider Av
11600 BRTN 97007 654 G3
NW Eider Ct
18500 BRTN 97006 594 E4
18500 HBRO 97006 594 E4
18500 WasC 97006 594 E4
SE Eider Ct
16000 DAMA 97009 688 E1
Eight Towncenter
- VCVR 98683 568 E2
SE Eikrem Ln
6000 CmsC 97267 687 D1
SE Eileen Ln
6800 HBRO 97123 594 A6
SE Eilers Cir
16800 DAMA 97009 688 F2
NE Eilers Rd
15500 CmsC 97002 745 H1
Eilertson St
100 STHN 97051 415 B2
SW Eirwen St
17400 WasC 97006 624 F1
Eisenschmidt Pl
1000 STHN 97051 385 C7
SE Eisert Cir
12000 HPYV 97236 658 A4
SE Eisert Ct
12100 HPYV 97236 658 A4
NW Ej Smith Rd
32000 ClbC 97056 444 B5
32400 SPSE 97056 444 D7
SW Ek Rd
1500 CmsC 97068 686 C6
2300 CmsC 97062 686 C6
SE Eklund Av
13900 CmsC 97009 660 F6
SE Eklund Ct
13900 CmsC 97009 660 E6
NW Elaina Ct
15000 WasC 97229 564 J7
NW Elaina Ln
14800 WasC 97229 564 J7
NW Elaine Ct
17300 BRTN 97006 594 H6
NE Elaine Dr
2700 MCMV 97128 771 A2
NE Elam Young Pkwy
5000 HBRO 97124 593 H4
NE El Camino Dr
4100 GSHM 97030 629 F2
SE El Camino Dr
3400 GSHM 97080 629 F3
3600 GSHM 97030 629 F3
SE El Camino Ter
18700 DAMA 97009 658 H5
SE El Camino Wy
14900 CmsC 97267 657 B7
SE El Centro Ct
5000 CmsC 97267 657 C6
SE El Centro Wy
4900 CmsC 97267 657 C7
Elder Av
50500 ClbC 97056 474 E4
S Elder Ct
1400 CNLS 97113 592 E5
S Elder Pl
2000 CNLS 97113 592 F5
Elder St
- ClbC 97056 474 B4
S Elder St
1000 CNLS 97113 592 E5
Elderberry Cir
- FRVW 97024 599 C3
- WDVL 97060 599 C3
Elderberry Ct
1700 NWBG 97132 713 D6
SE Elderberry Ln
14100 CmsC 97267 657 B6
SW Elderberry Ln
23300 CmsC 97068 716 E1
Elderberry St
- WDVL 97060 599 C3
Elder Tree Ct
19100 ORCY 97045 717 A4
SW Elder View Dr
17600 SRWD 97140 714 E1
SE Eldorado Ct
7100 CmsC 97267 657 E7
SW Eldorado Dr
- KNGC 97224 685 B1
17100 WasC 97224 685 B2
S Eldorado Rd
24100 CmsC 97042 747 F7
24100 CmsC 97045 747 F7
24300 CmsC 97042 777 E3
SE Eldorado St
7400 CmsC 97267 657 E7
SW Eldred Ln
17800 SRWD 97140 684 E6
Eldridge Dr
36700 SNDY 97055 690 G2
Eldridge Ln
59500 ClbC 97051 384 F7
Eleanor Ct
3700 LKOW 97035 656 A7
SW Eleanor Ln
4400 PTLD 97221 625 J3
NW Electric Av
- MthC 97210 595 H4
- MthC 97229 595 H4
- PTLD 97210 595 H4
- PTLD 97229 595 H4
Electric St
- ORCY 97045 717 C2
SW Electric St
9200 TGRD 97223 655 E4
13400 BRTN 97005 625 A2
SW Elemar Ct
11800 TGRD 97224 655 B6
Elevator Wy
1800 VCVR 98660 536 E4
NW Eleven Mile Av
100 GSHM 97030 628 J2
1900 GSHM 97030 598 J7
1900 GSHM 97233 598 J7
NW Eleven-Mile Ct
500 GSHM 97030 628 J2
SW Eleven Mile Rd
2200 GSHM 97080 628 J5
NW Elgin St
2300 CMAS 98607 569 D3
El Greco St
10 LKOW 97035 656 A5
S Elida Rd
18000 CmsC 97045 718 D3
SE Elina Av
900 HBRO 97123 593 D6
SE Elinor St
15300 CmsC 97015 658 D6
SW Elise Pl
1800 TDLE 97060 599 G6
S Elisha Rd
26500 CmsC 97013 776 H7
Elizabeth Ct
- DAYT 97114 772 A4
- YmhC 97114 772 A4
19200 CmsC 97045 716 J5
NW Elizabeth Ct
16000 BRTN 97006 594 H5
SW Elizabeth Ct
1500 PTLD 97201 596 D7
Elizabeth Ln
59000 STHN 97051 414 J1
SE Elizabeth Pl
3400 TDLE 97060 599 G7
SW Elizabeth St
1500 PTLD 97201 596 D7
SE Elk Ln
- CmsC 97023 750 J7
SW Elk Ln
2100 GSHM 97080 628 G5
SE Elk St
5100 MWKE 97222 657 C2
NW Elkcrest Ct
17700 WasC 97229 564 F7
SW Elk Horn Ct
20500 TLTN 97062 685 D5
NE Elkhorn Dr
23400 ClkC 98606 479 D6
Elk Lake Wy NE
19500 MrnC 97002 775 B7
Elk Meadow Dr
- STHN 97051 385 A6
NW Elk Meadow Ln
17700 WasC 97229 564 F7
NW Elk Mountain Rd
44200 WasC 97106 531 G3
E Elk Park Rd
26800 CmsC 97067 724 B6
27600 CmsC 97055 724 B6
Elk Rock Rd
12500 CmsC 97034 656 G4
12500 CmsC 97219 656 G4
NW Elk Run Dr
17000 WasC 97006 594 G1
17300 WasC 97229 594 F1
17700 WasC 97229 564 G6
NW Elkshire Ct
12500 BNKS 97106 531 J6
NW Elkton Ct
16900 WasC 97006 594 F3
SE Ella Av
2400 CmsC 97267 656 J7
Ella Ct
700 NWBG 97132 713 C6
SW Ella Pl
- WasC 97006 594 C6
Ella St
100 ORCY 97045 717 C3
SE Ellen Dr
13500 CmsC 97015 658 B5
NE Ellenease Av
13500 YmhC 97132 713 J6
SW Ellerson St
18900 WasC 97007 624 D4
SW Ellerson Ter
5800 WasC 97007 624 H1
SW Elligsen Rd
6900 WasC 97062 715 F3
7400 WNVL 97070 715 F3
8300 WasC 97070 715 F3
SW Elligsen Wy
11200 WasC 97140 715 C3
NE Ellington Ct
- SPSE 97056 444 G7
NE Elliot Av
1800 GSHM 97030 629 C2
2600 GSHM 97030 599 C7
NE Elliot Pl
1700 GSHM 97030 629 C1
NW Elliot St
900 CMAS 98607 569 B4
NE Elliott Av
10 GSHM 97030 629 C2
10 GSHM 97080 629 C2
SE Elliott Av
10 GSHM 97080 629 C3
1500 PTLD 97214 596 H7
2000 PTLD 97214 626 H1
2200 PTLD 97202 626 H1
SE Elliott Dr
2200 GSHM 97080 629 C5
NE Elliott Pl
2500 GSHM 97030 599 C7
SE Elliott Pl
1900 GSHM 97080 629 C5
N Elliott Rd
100 NWBG 97132 713 E6
NW Elliott Rd
16000 MthC 97231 534 C2
S Elliott Rd
100 NWBG 97132 713 E7
Elliott St
6100 WLIN 97068 687 A5
Ellis Av
600 LKOW 97034 656 F6
SW Ellis Av
- TDLE 97060 599 E4
NE Ellis Ln
24000 YmhC 97132 683 B6
S Ellis Rd
34000 CmsC 97038 837 H7
SE Ellis Rd
35100 MthC 97019 630 F1
SE Ellis St
1500 PTLD 97202 626 H4
3600 PTLD 97202 627 B4
7300 PTLD 97206 627 E4
8400 PTLD 97266 627 G4
12200 PTLD 97266 628 A4
13600 PTLD 97236 628 C4
Ellis Farm Rd
36600 ClbC 97056 445 B3
SW Ellman Ln
7600 DRHM 97224 685 F2
SW Ellson Ln
11100 TGRD 97223 655 C2
SE Ellsworth Av
100 VCVR 98664 537 H6
2000 VCVR 98664 567 H2
SE Ellsworth Rd
500 VCVR 98664 537 H7
1300 VCVR 98664 567 H1
Elm
- CmsC 97015 657 J7
- WasC 97006 594 D5
Elm Av
- PTLD 97217 536 E6
100 WDVL 97060 599 D4
E Elm Av
500 LCTR 98629 386 H7
23900 CmsC 97011 724 A3
23900 CmsC 97067 724 A3
SW Elm Av
5000 BRTN 97005 625 E4
S Elm Ct
700 CNBY 97013 746 C7
1100 CNBY 97013 776 C1
Elm Ln
1200 NWBG 97132 713 E6
SW Elm Ln
4700 PTLD 97221 596 A7
SW Elm Rd
400 ECDA 97023 750 B4
Elm St
- WasC 97116 591 J4
10 RDGF 98642 415 J6
10 STHN 97051 415 A1
500 ORCY 97045 687 C7
600 FTGV 97116 591 J5
1100 DNDE 97115 742 H4
1200 YmhC 97115 742 H4
2300 FTGV 97116 592 A4
N Elm St
100 YMHL 97148 711 A1
800 CNBY 97013 746 C5
NW Elm St
1000 CMAS 98607 569 D4
1000 MCMV 97128 770 G4
2400 YmhC 97128 770 G2
22500 HBRO 97124 594 A4
22500 WasC 97124 594 A4
S Elm St
100 CNBY 97013 746 C7
100 YMHL 97148 711 A1
300 YmhC 97148 711 A1
1100 CNBY 97013 776 C1
1600 CmsC 97013 776 C1
SE Elm St
600 DNDE 97115 742 H4
600 YmhC 97115 742 J3
1100 HBRO 97123 593 D6
33500 SPSE 97056 474 F1
34000 ClbC 97056 474 F1
SW Elm St
1600 PTLD 97201 596 D7
NW Elm Wy
400 CMAS 98607 569 D5
Elmar Dr
100 ORCY 97045 717 B3
SW Elmer Ct
11400 TLTN 97062 685 C2
SW Elmhurst Av
2300 WasC 97005 625 A1
NW Elmhurst Ct
42000 BNKS 97106 531 J6
SW Elmhurst St
7000 TGRD 97223 655 G4
SW Elmonica Pl
900 WasC 97006 594 G7
N Elmore Av
7500 PTLD 97217 566 E5
SE Elm Park Dr
14900 CmsC 97015 658 C5
Elmran Dr
3800 WLIN 97068 686 J3
4400 WLIN 97068 687 A3
SW Elmwood Av
100 MCMV 97128 770 G5
Elmwood Cir
- CNBY 97013 776 C1
Elmwood Ct
300 ORCY 97045 717 B2
Elmwood Dr
- CNBY 97013 776 C1
Elmwood Ln
- CNBY 97013 776 C1
SW Elmwood St
7400 TGRD 97223 655 G1
7400 WasC 97223 655 G1
NW Eloise Ln
1000 MthC 97229 595 H4
1000 PTLD 97229 595 G4
SE Elon St
9800 CmsC 97015 687 H1
SW El Rancho Ct
16000 BRTN 97007 624 H6
S El Rancho Rd
29100 CmsC 97038 807 E3
NW El Rey Dr
5700 CMAS 98607 539 B6
NE Elrod Dr
- PTLD 97211 567 B4
1300 PTLD 97218 567 B4
1400 PTLD 97211 566 J4
NE Elrod Rd
4200 PTLD 97211 567 C4
4200 PTLD 97218 567 C4
SW Elrose Ct
9100 TGRD 97224 655 E6
SW Elrose St
9500 TGRD 97224 655 E6
SE Elsa St
7200 MthC 97080 629 H6
SE Elsasser Ln
10800 PTLD 97266 627 J7
SE Elsewhere Ln
4300 MWKE 97222 657 B4
SW Elsner Rd
16800 WasC 97140 684 G2
16800 SRWD 97140 684 G2
SE Elston Ct
4600 CmsC 97267 687 B3
SW Elton Ct
11500 TGRD 97223 655 C4
Eluria St
100 ORCY 97045 717 D2
NW Elva Av
9400 PTLD 97231 565 E3
Elva Dr
200 NWBG 97132 713 D7
SW Elwert Rd
18800 WasC 97140 684 E4
21200 SRWD 97140 684 E4
NW Elwood Ct
4000 CMAS 98607 569 B1
NW Elwood Ln
- WasC 97229 564 G6
SE Ely Rd
30600 CmsC 97022 720 A6
30600 CmsC 97023 720 A6
SW Elysium St
11300 MthC 97219 656 F2
11300 PTLD 97219 656 F2
N Emerald Av
7500 PTLD 97217 566 D5
SW Emerald Av
2900 GSHM 97080 628 H6
SW Emerald Ct
15000 BRTN 97007 624 J7
SE Emerald Dr
17600 CmsC 97267 687 C2
SW Emerald Ln
2900 TDLE 97060 599 E6
S Emerald Lp
400 CNLS 97113 592 E5
SE Emerald Lp
9300 HPYV 97236 658 C1
SW Emerald St
15100 BRTN 97007 624 H7
NW Emerald Canyon Dr
17000 WasC 97006 594 H5
Emerald Cascade St
37200 SNDY 97055 690 H1
SW Emerald Creek Ln
- BRTN 97006 594 H6
SW Emeraldview St
- BRTN 97007 654 E1
- WasC 97007 654 E1
N Emerson Ct
2800 PTLD 97217 566 D7
NE Emerson Ct
5000 PTLD 97218 567 C6
N Emerson Dr
5000 PTLD 97217 566 D7
S Emerson Rd
11500 CmsC 97013 776 J7
11600 CmsC 97013 777 A7
N Emerson St
10 PTLD 97211 566 G7
10 PTLD 97217 566 F7
NE Emerson St
10 PTLD 97217 566 G7
400 PTLD 97211 566 H7
3300 PTLD 97211 567 A7
4200 PTLD 97218 567 C7
8700 PTLD 97220 567 G7
SW Emery Cir
7600 WNVL 97070 715 G4
SE Emery Ln
14700 CmsC 97015 658 D7
Emery St
1800 NWBG 97132 713 E6
SE Emi St
17800 DAMA 97009 658 G7
E Emigrant Tr
67500 CmsC 97067 724 B2
SE Emiko Ct
12600 HPYV 97236 658 A4
Emily Ct
- MCMV 97128 770 F7
Emily Dr
- MCMV 97128 770 E7
NW Emily Ln
1400 MCMV 97128 770 F6
Emily Pk
- GSHM 97230 598 G5
Emily Pl
14300 ORCY 97045 717 F6
Emily St
1200 FTGV 97116 592 A6
NW Emily Wy
4400 CMAS 98607 569 B1
SE Emily Park Wy
8800 CmsC 97236 657 H1
Emma Dr
- YmhC 97128 770 E6
NW Emma Wy
19300 HBRO 97124 594 D3
NW Emmaus Ln
17600 WasC 97231 564 F4
Emmerson Ct
14900 ORCY 97045 717 G6
SE Emmert Ct
17400 PTLD 97233 628 F1
Emmert Ter
- PTLD 97206 627 C7
SE Emmert View Ct
9200 CmsC 97236 657 G1
SE Empire Ct
9800 CmsC 97015 657 G6
SW Empire Ter
15300 TGRD 97224 655 F7
NW Empress Pl
11100 NPNS 97133 563 B1
11100 WasC 97133 563 B1
W Empress St
- WHGL 98671 569 H3
SW Em Watts Rd
33000 ClbC 97056 474 D1
33000 SPSE 97056 474 D2
N End Rd
17100 CmsC 97045 718 C4
N Endicott Av
8400 PTLD 97217 566 D4
SE Endicott Ln
52200 SPSE 97056 474 F1
NW Endicott St
3400 CMAS 98607 569 B2
S Endive Rd
22200 CmsC 97023 750 B4
SW Enduro Pl
4300 WasC 97007 624 D3
NW Energia St
15300 WasC 97229 564 H7
SE Engert Ridge Dr
16000 DAMA 97009 688 E1
Engle Av
100 MOLA 97038 837 E2
SW Engle St
28000 WNVL 97070 715 G6
NW Engleman St
9500 PTLD 97229 595 E3
SW Englewood Ct
1600 MthC 97034 656 C4
1600 PTLD 97034 656 C4
SE Englewood Dr
700 HBRO 97123 593 C6
SW Englewood Dr
600 LKOW 97034 656 E4
600 MthC 97034 656 D4
1600 MthC 97219 656 D4
1600 PTLD 97219 656 D4
SW English Ct
2700 PTLD 97201 626 B1
SW English Ln
2700 PTLD 97201 626 B1
Enid Av
100 VCVR 98661 537 D6
SW Enna Ct
15800 WasC 97224 654 G6
E Ennis Ct
1100 LCTR 98629 386 H7
SW Eno Pl
22600 TLTN 97062 685 D7
SW Enschede Dr
28600 WasC 97123 623 C5
N Ensign St
6200 PTLD 97217 566 B6
6400 PTLD 97203 566 B6
SE Enterprise Cir
1300 HBRO 97123 593 D7
Entrance Rd
- CmsC 97023 749 G2
S Entrance Rd
900 TDLE 97060 599 F3
24100 CmsC 97023 749 J3
N Entrance Wy
- TDLE 97060 599 F2
NE Enyeart Pl
300 HBRO 97124 593 G4
NE Equestrian Dr
- YmhC 97128 741 E7
SE Equestrian Dr
5900 GSHM 97080 628 F5
5900 GSHM 97236 628 F5
5900 MthC 97236 628 F6
5900 PTLD 97236 628 F6
SW Equestrian Dr
4400 GSHM 97080 628 G5
SE Equestrian Wy
16700 PTLD 97236 628 F3
Erasmus St
10 LKOW 97035 656 A3
SE Eric St
3000 HBRO 97123 623 E1
5900 CmsC 97222 657 D5
Erica Dr NE
21900 MrnC 97002 775 C2
SW Erica Pl
7500 BRTN 97008 625 B6
SW Erickson Av
4500 BRTN 97005 625 B4
5800 BRTN 97008 625 A4
NE Erickson Rd
18300 ClkC 98606 479 C2
SE Erickson Rd
42000 CmsC 97055 691 D6
Erickson St
800 LKOW 97034 656 F7
SW Ericwood Ln
3600 PTLD 97221 626 B2
SW Erie Ct
10000 TLTN 97062 685 D5
Erin Ct
17500 LKOW 97035 685 J1
SE Erin Ct
13400 CmsC 97015 658 B5
SW Erin Ct
21500 WasC 97006 594 B7
NE Erin Dr
- SPSE 97056 444 F7
SW Erin Pl
20300 WasC 97006 594 C7
SW Erin Ter
20900 WasC 97006 594 C7
NE Erin Wy
5900 ClkC 98686 507 D3
12000 PTLD 97220 598 A1
12000 PTLD 97230 598 A1
SW Erio Pl
22800 TLTN 97062 685 D7
NE Erion Rd
19200 ClkC 98604 479 D1
19800 ClkC 98604 449 D7
Ernest St NE
20800 DNLD 97020 774 F4
20800 MrnC 97002 774 F4
SW Ernst Rd
8100 BRTN 97225 625 F1
E Ernst St
20100 CmsC 97011 693 F6
SW Errol St
10500 TGRD 97223 655 C4
SW Erste Ct
11300 TGRD 97223 655 C4
NW Erwin O Rieger Memorial Hwy
- ClkC 98660 505 J5
- ClkC 98660 506 A3
- VCVR 98660 505 J5
SW Esau Pl
11400 TGRD 97223 655 E3
SW Escalon Pl
7500 BRTN 97008 625 B6
SW Eschman Wy
11000 TGRD 97223 655 A2
Escort St
200 MOLA 97038 807 E7
Esperanto Dr NE
14900 AURA 97002 775 F4
N Esperanza St
4900 PTLD 97203 566 B3
SE Espinosa Rd
400 ECDA 97023 750 C4
SW Esquiline Circus
10900 PTLD 97219 656 F2
11100 MthC 97219 656 F2
SW Essen Ct
20500 WasC 97007 624 B5
N Essex Av
2400 PTLD 97227 596 E3
Essex Cir
- ClkC 98686 507 D2
Essex Ct
10 LKOW 97034 686 B2
SW Essex Ct
6500 WNVL 97070 715 G6
SW Essex Dr
13000 TGRD 97223 655 A4
13300 TGRD 97223 654 J5
NW Essex St
- PTLD 97210 596 B3
SE Essex St
1500 MCMV 97128 770 H7
S Essig Ln
- CmsC 97004 748 B3
NW Esson Ct
9100 PTLD 97229 595 F3
S Estacada Rd
22200 CmsC 97023 750 A5
22600 CmsC 97023 749 J6
NE Estate Dr
500 HBRO 97124 593 C2
SW Estates Ct N
32200 WNVL 97070 745 G3
SW Estates Ct S
32300 WNVL 97070 745 G3
SW Estates Post Rd
32100 WNVL 97070 745 G3
SE Estella Av
13900 CmsC 97267 657 E5
NE Estelle Ct
1200 HBRO 97124 593 D1
S Ester Ct
25100 CmsC 97023 750 A7
SE Esther Ct
11900 HPYV 97236 658 A3
SW Esther Ct
7500 WasC 97223 625 G6
E Esther Ln
66200 CmsC 97011 724 A1
Esther St
2600 VCVR 98660 536 F3
NW Esther St
4900 VCVR 98663 536 F1
5200 VCVR 98663 506 F7
SW Estuary Dr
900 BRTN 97006 594 G6
NW Ethan Dr
12700 WasC 97229 565 B7
Ethan Ln
59800 ClbC 97051 385 A7
59800 STHN 97051 385 A7
Ethel St
100 ORCY 97045 717 C3
SW Eton Ct
7300 WasC 97225 595 G6
SE Eton Ln
1500 MWKE 97222 656 H2
SW Eucalyptus Pl
11300 TGRD 97223 655 C3
SW Eucalyptus Ter
23500 SRWD 97140 714 G1
NE Euclid Av
1300 PTLD 97213 597 C4
SW Euclid Ln
19300 WasC 97006 594 D7
NE Eugene Ct
14000 PTLD 97230 598 C4
16700 GSHM 97230 598 F4
NW Eugene Ln
15000 WasC 97229 594 H1
NE Eugene St
8200 PTLD 97213 597 F4
10600 PTLD 97220 597 J4
11700 PTLD 97220 598 A4
13700 PTLD 97230 598 C4
SE Eunice St
6400 CmsC 97222 657 D3
6400 MWKE 97222 657 D3
Eureka Wy
5000 VCVR 98661 537 C5
Evah Ln
1300 WLIN 97068 716 G2
SW Evan Ct
- BRTN 97223 625 H5
SE Evans Av
1300 TDLE 97060 599 H7
SE Evans Cir
1200 TDLE 97060 599 H5
S Evans Ct
15700 CmsC 97045 777 J2
SW Evans Ct
10900 TLTN 97062 685 C6
SE Evans Lp
1200 TDLE 97060 599 H5
NE Evans Rd
10 MthC 97019 600 G6
SE Evans Rd
10 MthC 97019 600 G7
300 MthC 97019 630 G1
Evans St
39200 SNDY 97055 691 A4
NE Evans St
2900 MCMV 97128 770 H2
SE Evans St
100 MCMV 97128 770 H5
SW Evans St
1700 PTLD 97219 626 D6
NE Evelyn Av
2700 GSHM 97030 599 D7
SE Evelyn Av
100 GSHM 97080 629 D3
SE Evelyn Ct
1400 GSHM 97080 629 D4
SE Evelyn Pl
2800 GSHM 97080 629 C5
SE Evelyn St
15800 CmsC 97015 687 G1
SW Evelyn St
3000 PTLD 97219 656 B1
6000 PTLD 97219 655 H1
6200 TGRD 97223 655 H1
SE Evening Star Ct
13400 HPYV 97236 658 B3
NE Evening Star Dr
1400 HBRO 97124 593 E2
SE Evening Star Dr
12800 HPYV 97236 658 B3
NW Evensong Pl
200 WasC 97229 595 B5
SW Everest Ct
23700 SRWD 97140 714 J1
N Everest Rd
100 NWBG 97132 713 D7
S Everest Rd
100 NWBG 97132 713 D7
300 NWBG 97132 743 D1
400 YmhC 97132 743 D1
NE Everett Ct
4100 CMAS 98607 569 E1
10600 PTLD 97220 597 J5
16000 PTLD 97230 598 E6
16800 GSHM 97230 598 F5
SW Everett Ct
7800 BRTN 97007 624 J1
NE Everett Dr
4300 CMAS 98607 569 E1
4600 CMAS 98607 539 F7
NE Everett Ln
19700 GSHM 97230 598 J6
SW Everett Pl
7600 BRTN 97007 624 J6
SE Everett Rd
- ClkC 98607 539 E7
800 CMAS 98607 539 E7
1000 CMAS 98607 569 E1
SE Everett Rd SR-500
100 ClkC 98607 539 F6
800 CMAS 98607 539 E7
1900 CMAS 98607 569 E1
NE Everett St
500 PTLD 97232 596 H5
1300 CMAS 98607 569 E4
2700 PTLD 97232 597 A5
4700 PTLD 97213 597 C5
10600 PTLD 97220 597 J5
11600 PTLD 97220 598 A5
14600 PTLD 97230 598 D5
19600 GSHM 97230 598 H6
NE Everett St SR-500
1400 CMAS 98607 569 E3
NW Everett St
10 PTLD 97209 596 F5
2000 PTLD 97210 596 D5
SE Everett St
200 CMAS 98607 569 F5
SE Everett Wy
33800 ClbC 97056 474 F1
33800 SPSE 97056 474 F1
SW Evergreen Av
10300 CmsC 97070 715 C7
10300 WNVL 97070 715 C7
E Evergreen Blvd
100 VCVR 98660 536 G5
500 VCVR 98663 536 G5
900 VCVR 98661 536 G5
2800 VCVR 98661 537 C6
5600 VCVR 98664 537 D7
SE Evergreen Blvd
34700 ClkC 98671 570 F6
34700 WHGL 98671 570 F6
W Evergreen Blvd
100 VCVR 98660 536 F5
Evergreen Ct
- PTLD 97216 628 A1
- PTLD 97266 628 A1
SE Evergreen Ct
14400 PTLD 97236 628 C6
SW Evergreen Ct
10100 CmsC 97070 715 D7
10100 WNVL 97070 715 D7
Evergreen Dr
- WLIN 97068 687 A6
100 VCVR 98661 537 B6
1100 NWBG 97132 713 C6
S Evergreen Dr
22000 CmsC 97004 748 D4
SE Evergreen Dr
15500 PTLD 97236 628 D6
SE Evergreen Hwy
6300 VCVR 98661 537 D7
6500 VCVR 98664 537 D7
8000 VCVR 98664 567 H2
11400 VCVR 98683 567 J2
12000 VCVR 98683 568 B3
16700 ClkC 98683 568 F4
17700 ClkC 98607 568 H4
SW Evergreen Hwy
20900 ClkC 98607 568 J5
20900 CMAS 98607 568 J5
Evergreen Ln
200 GLDS 97027 687 F4
56500 ClbC 97053 414 G6
NE Evergreen Ln
- ClkC 98607 539 F6
SE Evergreen Ln
16600 CmsC 97267 687 A2
SW Evergreen Ln
3100 PTLD 97205 596 B6
Evergreen Lp
58700 STHN 97051 414 J2
Evergreen Pkwy E
- MCMV 97128 771 A7
NW Evergreen Pkwy
7100 HBRO 97124 594 D2
17800 BRTN 97006 594 F3
17800 HBRO 97006 594 F3
17800 WasC 97006 594 F3
24000 HBRO 97124 593 J1
Evergreen Rd
200 LKOW 97034 656 E6
NW Evergreen Rd
21200 HBRO 97124 594 B1
24200 HBRO 97124 593 F1
26800 HBRO 97124 563 E7
26800 WasC 97124 563 E7
27600 WasC 97124 593 C1
Evergreen Rdg
- ClkC 98665 506 H7
NW Evergreen St
13500 WasC 97229 595 A2
14400 WasC 97229 594 J2
SE Evergreen St
1900 CmsC 97222 656 J4
2800 CmsC 97222 657 A4
3900 PTLD 97202 627 B5
7300 PTLD 97206 627 E5
SW Evergreen St
12600 WasC 97005 595 B6
SW Evergreen Ter
- PTLD 97205 596 B6
Evergreen Wy
2900 WHGL 98671 570 D6
4200 ClkC 98671 570 E6
SW Evergreen Wy
33200 SPSE 97056 474 E1
Evergreen Main
- HBRO 97124 594 A1

STREET
Block City ZIP Map# Grid

E Evergreen Park St
24000 CmsC 97067 724 B3
Evergreen Reservoir Rd
- HBRO 97124 593 J1
NW Evers Rd
6300 WasC 97116 562 B5
E Evert Ct
67600 CmsC 97067 724 B3
S Eves Rd
14100 CmsC 97038 837 E4
SW Ewen Dr
18000 WasC 97006 624 F1
18100 WasC 97006 594 E7
SW Excalibur Pl
8900 PTLD 97219 625 H7
Excalibur Mobile Home Ct
- CmsC 97045 747 F6
N Exeter Av
8900 PTLD 97203 566 B3
SE Exeter Dr
1800 CmsC 97202 656 H1
1800 CmsC 97222 626 G7
1800 CmsC 97222 656 H1
1800 PTLD 97202 626 G7
1800 PTLD 97202 656 H1
Exeter St
4200 WLIN 97068 687 A7
E Exeter St
500 GLDS 97027 687 E4
W Exeter St
100 GLDS 97027 687 D4
SW Exmoor Pl
10100 BRTN 97008 655 B1
Explorer Av
800 MOLA 97038 807 E7
N Expo Rd
- PTLD 97217 566 E1
NW Express Av
4000 PTLD 97210 596 A1
E EZ Ln
21800 CmsC 97049 724 F1

F

F Av
700 LKOW 97034 656 F5
W F Av
200 LCTR 98629 416 G1
F Cir
3900 WHGL 98671 570 D5
F Ln
- PTLD 97218 567 E7
F Pl
3200 WHGL 98671 570 C5
F St
- PTLD 97219 655 J3
10 CBAC 97018 385 C3
1200 WHGL 98671 570 A5
3900 VCVR 98663 536 G2
NW F St
- WasC 97006 594 C5
Faber Av NE
4100 MrnC 97137 773 C5
4100 STPL 97137 773 C5
SW Fagan Ct
18600 WasC 97006 624 G1
Fager Pl
- VCVR 98661 537 D7
E Fahie Ln
- CmsC 97067 724 C3
NE Failing Ct
13100 PTLD 97230 598 B2
Failing St
6500 WLIN 97068 687 B5
N Failing St
10 PTLD 97212 596 G2
10 PTLD 97227 596 F1
NE Failing St
10 PTLD 97212 596 H2
10 PTLD 97227 596 G2
4200 PTLD 97212 597 C2
4200 PTLD 97213 597 C2
8100 PTLD 97220 597 F2
9800 MWDP 97220 597 H2
13500 PTLD 97230 598 C2
22000 FRVW 97024 599 B2
NW Fair Acres Dr
15500 ClkC 98685 476 D4
NW Fairchild Dr
35600 ClkC 98674 386 C5
SW Faircrest Av
11800 WasC 97225 595 B7
Faircrest Dr
19300 ORCY 97045 717 B4
NE Faircrest Dr
12700 YmhC 97132 712 D6
SW Fairfax Pl
1100 WasC 97225 595 H7
NW Fairfax Ter
2800 PTLD 97210 596 B4
SW Fairfax Ter
- PTLD 97205 596 C6
SW Fairfield Ct
12500 WasC 97005 625 B2
SW Fairfield Pl
12400 WasC 97005 625 B2
E Fairfield St
300 GLDS 97027 687 E4
SW Fairfield St
11100 WasC 97005 625 C2
12600 BRTN 97005 625 B2
W Fairfield St
100 GLDS 97027 687 C4
NE Fairgrounds Av
10 BGND 98604 448 C5
SE Fairgrounds Av
10 BGND 98604 448 C5
NE Fairgrounds Dr
2100 MCMV 97128 771 A3
N Fairhaven Av
9200 PTLD 97203 565 J3
Fairhaven Ct
2100 WLIN 97068 686 J7
2100 WLIN 97068 716 J1
SW Fairhaven Ct
- TGRD 97223 655 D5
Fairhaven Dr
3600 WLIN 97068 686 J7
3700 WLIN 97068 716 J1
3800 WLIN 97068 717 A1
SW Fairhaven Dr
4400 PTLD 97221 596 A6
SW Fairhaven Ln
4900 PTLD 97221 596 A6

SW Fairhaven St
10500 TGRD 97223 655 C5
SW Fairhaven Wy
10600 TGRD 97223 655 C5
SW Fairlawn Ct
200 MCMV 97128 770 F5
SE Fairmont Dr
26900 CmsC 97009 659 G4
Fairmont Rd
400 LKOW 97034 656 F7
SW Fairmoor St
7500 WasC 97225 625 G2
Fairmount Av
1900 VCVR 98661 537 A4
NW Fairmount Av
- PTLD 97231 565 F4
SW Fairmount Blvd
- PTLD 97201 626 B1
3100 PTLD 97239 626 D3
SE Fairmount Dr
- CmsC 97009 659 F4
SW Fairmount Dr
4600 BRTN 97005 625 A3
SW Fairmount Ln
3300 PTLD 97239 626 B2
SE Fairoaks Av
13900 CmsC 97222 656 H5
13900 CmsC 97267 656 H7
SW Fairoaks Ct
22500 SRWD 97140 684 J7
NE Fair Oaks Dr
- ClkC 98682 538 A1
- VCVR 98682 507 J7
- VCVR 98682 538 A1
SE Fair Oaks Dr
13600 CmsC 97222 656 H5
SW Fairoaks Dr
14300 SRWD 97140 684 J7
SE Fairoaks Ln
14200 CmsC 97267 656 H6
Fair Oaks Vil
- WasC 97006 624 E1
SE Fairoaks Wy
13900 CmsC 97222 656 H5
13900 CmsC 97267 656 H5
N Fairport Pl
7000 PTLD 97217 566 F5
SW Fairridge Wy
8600 WasC 97223 625 F5
SW Fairvale Ct
- PTLD 97221 625 J4
4400 PTLD 97221 626 A4
SW Fairvale Dr
4000 PTLD 97221 626 B4
Fairview Av
1700 FRVW 97024 599 B4
SW Fairview Blvd
- PTLD 97221 596 B6
2700 PTLD 97205 596 B6
4100 MthC 97221 596 B6
SW Fairview Ct
13700 TGRD 97223 655 C5
Fairview Dr
100 STHN 97051 385 A7
NE Fairview Dr
16500 YmhC 97115 742 E2
NW Fairview Dr
1700 GSHM 97030 629 B1
Fairview Ln
53800 ClbC 97056 444 D5
SW Fairview Ln
11500 TGRD 97223 655 C5
Fairview Pl
- FRVW 97024 598 J4
SW Fairview Pl
8900 BRTN 97008 625 D7
8900 TGRD 97008 625 D7
8900 TGRD 97223 625 D7
8900 WasC 97008 625 D7
Fairview Wy
3100 WLIN 97068 686 H2
SW Fairview Circus
4300 PTLD 97221 596 A6
NE Fairview Lake Ct
3500 FRVW 97024 599 B2
NE Fairview Lake Wy
3700 FRVW 97024 598 J2
3700 FRVW 97230 598 J2
3900 GSHM 97230 598 J2
20300 FRVW 97024 599 B3
E Fairway Av
38200 CmsC 97067 724 C4
NE Fairway Av
6900 ClkC 98662 507 E6
Fairway Dr
1000 WHGL 98671 570 E5
NE Fairway Dr
2100 PTLD 97211 566 J3
SE Fairway Dr
10500 CmsC 97236 657 H3
19700 DAMA 97009 658 J5
SW Fairway Dr
7300 WNVL 97070 745 F3
7800 WasC 97225 625 F2
8600 BRTN 97225 625 F2
N Fairway Ln
700 CNBY 97013 746 D4
SW Fairway Lp
7300 WNVL 97070 745 G3
Fairway Rd
800 LKOW 97034 656 D6
Fairway St
100 NWBG 97132 713 H7
5000 NWBG 97132 743 G1
E Fairway Estates Rd
- CmsC 97067 724 C5
SW Fairway Village Lp
31600 WNVL 97070 745 H3
SE Fairwinds Lp
700 VCVR 98661 536 H6
SW Faith Ct
2800 TDLE 97060 599 F6
SE Falbrook Dr
11300 CmsC 97015 657 J5
Falcon
- FRVW 97024 599 A3
Falcon Ct NE
11600 MrnC 97002 744 J5
SW Falcon Ct
- BRTN 97007 654 H2
Falcon Dr
1500 RDGF 98642 416 A6
2300 WLIN 97068 686 G6
2300 WLIN 97068 716 H1
19400 CmsC 97045 717 E5

Falcon Dr
19400 ORCY 97045 717 E5
SW Falcon Dr
15700 BRTN 97007 654 G2
SW Falcon St
- PTLD 97219 626 C6
Falcon Crest Dr
- DNDE 97115 742 G3
NW Falconridge Ln
13800 WasC 97229 595 A1
14200 WasC 97229 594 J1
SW Falcon Rise Dr
12500 TGRD 97223 655 B3
NW Fales Rd
- ClkC 98642 445 J6
Falk Rd
2300 VCVR 98661 537 B3
3400 ClkC 98661 537 B3
SW Falkland Ct
14900 TGRD 97223 654 H5
14900 WasC 97223 654 H5
NW Fall Av
1100 BRTN 97006 594 F4
NW Fall Ct
17600 BRTN 97006 594 F4
NW Fall Pl
1400 BRTN 97006 594 F4
SW Fallatin Ct
18400 WasC 97007 624 E7
SW Fallatin Lp
18100 WasC 97007 624 E6
SW Fallbrook Pl
6400 BRTN 97005 625 E5
6400 BRTN 97008 625 E5
NW Fallcreek Pl
3900 WasC 97229 594 J1
SW Fallen Leaf St
7000 WNVL 97070 715 G6
SW Falling Creek Ct
4300 PTLD 97219 656 A2
SW Falling Leaf Dr
17600 WasC 97006 594 F7
NW Falling Waters Ln
- BRTN 97229 595 C5
Fall Oaks Ct
1100 WLIN 97068 716 G1
SW Fallow Ter
21400 SRWD 97140 684 H6
NE Falls Rd
27100 ClkC 98675 419 J1
Falls View Dr
4300 WLIN 97068 687 B7
Falls View St
- WLIN 97068 687 A7
NE Faloma Rd
500 PTLD 97211 566 H2
Falstaff St
10 LKOW 97035 656 B5
Fandango Dr
11200 CmsC 97045 716 J4
11200 ORCY 97045 716 J4
NW Fanning Wy
- GSHM 97030 629 A1
SW Fanno St
- BRTN 97008 625 D6
SW Fanno Creek Ct
14100 TGRD 97224 655 F6
SW Fanno Creek Dr
7800 TGRD 97224 655 F6
13800 TGRD 97223 655 F5
SW Fanno Creek Lp
14200 TGRD 97224 655 F6
SW Fanno Creek Pl
7300 TGRD 97224 685 G1
14000 TGRD 97224 655 F5
SW Fannowood Ln
8500 BRTN 97008 625 C7
Faraday Rd
33800 CmsC 97023 750 D6
NE Fargo Cir
16400 PTLD 97230 598 F3
NE Fargo Ct
11700 PTLD 97220 598 A3
15600 PTLD 97230 598 E3
NW Fargo Ct
2000 CMAS 98607 569 D3
NW Fargo Lp
2000 CMAS 98607 569 D3
NE Fargo Pl
15400 PTLD 97230 598 E3
Fargo Rd NE
11100 MrnC 97002 774 H1
12000 MrnC 97002 775 A1
N Fargo St
10 PTLD 97212 596 G2
600 PTLD 97227 596 F2
NE Fargo St
10 PTLD 97212 596 G2
10 PTLD 97227 596 G2
10200 PTLD 97220 597 J3
11200 PTLD 97220 598 A3
16200 PTLD 97230 598 F3
NW Fargo St
800 CMAS 98607 569 D4
NW Fariss Rd
500 GSHM 97030 629 B1
Farm Wy
300 FTGV 97116 591 F3
NE Farmcrest St
4900 HBRO 97124 593 H3
SW Farmer Wy
15500 SRWD 97140 684 G6
SW Farmington Rd
12000 BRTN 97005 625 A3
14100 BRTN 97005 624 J3
14300 BRTN 97007 624 J3
18500 WasC 97007 624 B7
22500 WasC 97007 654 A1
22900 WasC 97007 653 J1
24600 WasC 97123 653 F1
26700 WasC 97123 623 D7
SW Farmington Rd SR-10
12000 BRTN 97005 625 A3
14100 BRTN 97005 624 J3
14300 BRTN 97007 624 J3
18500 WasC 97007 624 B7
22500 WasC 97007 654 A1
22900 WasC 97007 653 J1
26700 WasC 97123 623 D7
28500 WasC 97123 653 C1
S Farm Pond Ct
21800 CmsC 97045 747 F3
NW Farmside Ln
37000 WasC 97113 592 D2

NW Farmstead Ct
14900 WasC 97006 594 J5
SE Farmstead Rd
29600 CmsC 97022 719 H7
29600 CmsC 97023 719 H7
29600 CmsC 97023 749 J1
NE Farnham St
5700 HBRO 97124 593 J4
SE Farr Dr
16000 CmsC 97267 657 F7
16000 CmsC 97267 687 F1
16000 JNCY 97267 687 F1
E Farragut St
23800 CmsC 97067 724 B3
N Farragut St
10 PTLD 97211 566 G5
500 PTLD 97217 566 F5
NE Farragut St
10 PTLD 97211 566 G5
10 PTLD 97217 566 G5
SW Farrin Ct
20400 WasC 97006 624 C1
Farrview Ct
1200 WLIN 97068 716 F1
Farrvista Dr
1300 WLIN 97068 686 F7
Farview Dr
100 VCVR 98661 537 B6
SW Farview Pl
- BRTN 97008 625 E7
- TGRD 97008 625 E7
- TGRD 97223 625 E7
SW Far Vista St
13400 WasC 97005 595 A7
SW Farwest Ln
17800 SRWD 97140 684 E5
SW Fast Pl
9200 WasC 97223 655 F1
N Fathom St
6800 PTLD 97217 566 B5
Faubian Lp
70800 CmsC 97049 724 E4
E Faubian Lp
70800 CmsC 97049 724 E4
Faurie Av
700 MOLA 97038 807 E7
700 MOLA 97038 837 E1
Fawn Ct
20900 WLIN 97068 686 F7
S Fawn Ct
1400 CNLS 97113 592 E5
S Fawn Dr
16700 CmsC 97045 688 B4
SE Fawn Dr
13000 HPYV 97236 658 B3
S Fawn Ln
16000 CmsC 97038 837 J2
S Fawn St
400 CNLS 97113 592 D5
NW Fawnlily Dr
14700 WasC 97229 564 J6
Fawver Rd
- CmsC 97013 745 J5
S Fawver Rd
7100 CmsC 97013 745 J5
7100 CmsC 97013 746 A5
NW Faxon Ter
3900 WasC 97229 595 A1
SE Fay Wy
33800 ClbC 97056 474 F1
33800 SPSE 97056 474 F1
NW Faye St
17900 WasC 97006 594 F5
NE Fazio Wy
- PTLD 97211 566 H3
NE Feather Ct
10 HBRO 97124 593 H6
SW Feiring Ln
13500 TGRD 97223 655 A3
S Feldheimer Rd
23100 CmsC 97023 719 F6
SW Feldspar Wy
15500 BRTN 97007 654 E1
Felisha Wy
33000 SPSE 97056 444 D7
Feller St NE
20900 DNLD 97020 774 G4
Fellers Rd NE
10000 MrnC 97002 774 F6
10000 MrnC 97032 774 J7
11500 MrnC 97002 775 A7
11500 MrnC 97032 775 A7
SW Fellows Ct
800 MCMV 97128 770 F6
S Fellows Rd
21100 CmsC 97023 749 D3
23300 CmsC 97004 749 D3
SW Fellows St
400 MCMV 97128 770 G6
2100 YmhC 97128 770 E6
E Feltz St
20200 CmsC 97011 693 E6
Fendle Wy
- MCMV 97128 770 E3
Fenton St
100 MOLA 97038 837 F1
NW Fenton St
600 MCMV 97128 770 F5
N Fenwick Av
6500 PTLD 97217 566 E6
S Ferguson Rd
17500 CmsC 97045 718 A5
20500 CmsC 97004 748 A4
20500 CmsC 97045 748 A2
S Ferguson Ter
19300 CmsC 97045 718 B5
SW Ferguson Ter
21400 SRWD 97140 684 H6
SE Fern Av
16700 CmsC 97206 627 E7
SE Fern Dr
27300 CmsC 97009 689 G1
Fern Pl
1700 LKOW 97034 656 E7
SW Fern Rd
19500 CmsC 97068 686 C4
SE Fern Sh
- GSHM 97080 629 H6
- MthC 97080 629 H6
SW Fern St
2700 PTLD 97201 626 C1
13500 TGRD 97223 655 A4
13800 TGRD 97223 654 J4
13800 WasC 97223 654 J4
13800 WasC 97223 655 A4

S Fern Bluff Dr
14800 CmsC 97045 747 G1
Fernbrook Cir
5800 CmsC 97035 685 H2
Fernbrook Ct
18300 CmsC 97035 685 J2
SW Fernbrook Ct
6700 WNVL 97070 715 G6
Fernbrook St
6000 CmsC 97035 685 H2
Fernbrook Wy
5500 CmsC 97035 685 H2
Ferndale Av
- ClbC 97056 474 A4
NE Ferngrove St
9200 VCVR 98664 537 G4
SW Fern Hill Rd
1200 FTGV 97116 592 A7
2700 WasC 97116 592 B7
3100 WasC 97113 592 B7
SW Fernhollow Ln
28700 WasC 97123 683 C2
SE Fernridge Av
13500 CmsC 97222 657 B5
SE Fernridge Ct
4600 ClkC 98607 568 J4
SE Fernridge Dr
20200 ClkC 98607 568 J4
NW Fern Ridge Ln
2300 PTLD 97229 595 E3
SW Fernridge Ter
13700 TGRD 97223 655 D2
13800 WasC 97223 655 A5
SW Fernshire Ln
19000 WasC 97006 624 D1
Fernview Rd
20000 CmsC 97068 686 F4
Fernwood Cir
2100 LKOW 97034 686 C1
E Fernwood Cir
56500 CmsC 97055 692 J6
Fernwood Dr
1500 LKOW 97034 686 C1
SE Fernwood Dr
15300 VCVR 98683 568 D2
21300 CmsC 97022 690 A7
E Fernwood Rd
3300 NWBG 97132 713 F7
3300 YmhC 97132 713 F7
3800 NWBG 97132 743 G1
3800 YmhC 97132 743 G1
NE Fernwood Rd
30100 NWBG 97132 743 H1
30100 YmhC 97132 743 H1
SW Ferrelo Pl
16900 BRTN 97007 624 G5
Ferry St
10 DAYT 97114 772 B4
SE Ferry St
400 DAYT 97114 772 A4
700 YmhC 97114 772 A4
NW Fescue Ct
16100 WasC 97229 564 H6
N Fessenden St
4500 PTLD 97203 566 A3
6800 PTLD 97203 565 J2
Fettig Ln
- NWBG 97132 743 G1
- YmhC 97132 743 G1
NE Fettig Ln
11200 NWBG 97132 743 G1
11200 YmhC 97132 743 G1
Feyrer Park Rd
- CmsC 97017 837 J3
- CmsC 97038 837 J3
S Feyrer Park Rd
- CmsC 97017 837 G2
14600 CmsC 97038 837 G2
14600 MOLA 97038 837 F2
SE Fieldcrest Av
4200 MWKE 97222 657 B1
SE Fieldcrest Dr
4300 MWKE 97222 657 B1
NW Fieldcrest Wy
800 HBRO 97006 594 C5
SW Fielding Ct
12300 BRTN 97008 625 B7
Fielding Rd
12700 CmsC 97034 656 G5
12800 LKOW 97034 656 G5
Fields Dr
2000 WLIN 97068 716 F1
SE Fieldstone Av
- HBRO 97123 623 G2
Fieldstone Dr
- LKOW 97035 655 J6
5600 CmsC 97035 655 J6
NW Fieldstone Dr
17300 BRTN 97006 594 F4
S Fieldstone Ln
17500 CmsC 97045 718 D2
SW Filbert Av
4900 BRTN 97005 625 C3
Filbert Ct
900 NWBG 97132 713 E6
Filbert Dr
11500 CmsC 97045 717 A4
11500 ORCY 97045 717 A4
Filbert Ln
33000 ClbC 97053 444 E1
SE Filbert Rd
22500 CmsC 97022 690 A7
22500 CmsC 97022 720 B3
Filbert St
1200 FTGV 97116 592 A5
Filbert St NE
20700 AURA 97002 775 F5
20700 MrnC 97002 775 F5
NW Filbert St
- WasC 97229 595 B4
SE Filbert St
3200 MWKE 97222 657 A1
SW Filbert St
- WNVL 97070 745 C1
100 MCMV 97128 770 E6
SE Filbert Creek Dr
14000 CmsC 97015 658 C6
SE Filly Ln
32800 CmsC 97023 750 C4
SW Filmont Av
1600 WasC 97225 595 B7
2100 WasC 97225 625 E4
2100 WasC 97225 625 D4
SW Finch Av
11800 BRTN 97007 654 H3

SE Findhorn Ln
26000 CmsC 97022 720 H4
SW Findlay Dr
7600 DRHM 97224 685 F1
SW Findlay Rd
7400 DRHM 97224 685 G1
7400 TGRD 97224 685 G1
SW Finis Ln
- WasC 97224 654 G7
Finnegans Wy
11300 CmsC 97045 716 J5
11600 ORCY 97045 716 J5
NE Finn Hill Lp
10800 YmhC 97111 711 G6
NE Finn Hill Rd
19400 ClkC 98604 449 C7
19400 ClkC 98606 449 C7
19400 ClkC 98606 479 B1
SW Finnigan Hill Rd
16400 WasC 97123 653 A7
16400 WasC 97123 683 A2
NW Finzer Ct
9200 PTLD 97229 595 F2
SW Fiord Ln
- WasC 97223 625 E7
Fir
- CmsC 97015 657 J7
Fir Av
- PTLD 97217 536 E6
E Fir Av
700 LCTR 98629 386 H7
NE Fir Av
- PTLD 97213 597 B5
SE Fir Av
6500 CmsC 97206 627 D7
Fir Ct
1600 FTGV 97116 592 B5
S Fir Ct
900 CNBY 97013 746 C7
SW Fir Ct
1200 DNDE 97115 742 G4
1200 YmhC 97115 742 G4
6900 BRTN 97008 625 B5
Fir Dr
16800 CmsC 97055 691 A2
16800 SNDY 97055 691 A2
Fir Ln
16600 LKOW 97034 656 C7
16600 LKOW 97034 686 C1
SW Fir Ln
33300 SPSE 97056 474 E1
SW Fir Lp
7000 TGRD 97223 655 G5
Fir Rd
1700 FTGV 97116 592 B5
17400 LKOW 97034 686 A1
Fir St
- ClbC 97056 474 A4
- CmsC 97022 719 G7
- DNDE 97115 742 G4
- PTLD 97218 567 E7
- YmhC 97115 742 G4
- YmhC 97148 711 A1
- YMHL 97148 711 A1
400 DAYT 97114 772 A4
13800 ORCY 97045 717 E4
35100 ClbC 97051 414 J2
N Fir St
100 CNBY 97013 746 C6
NW Fir St
1900 MCMV 97128 770 G3
4100 VCVR 98660 536 F2
22700 WasC 97124 594 A4
S Fir St
300 CNBY 97013 746 C7
300 YMHL 97148 711 A1
1100 CNBY 97013 776 C1
1200 CmsC 97013 776 C1
SW Fir St
7400 TGRD 97223 655 G5
30700 WNVL 97070 745 E1
Fir Ter
- TGRD 97223 655 D3
S Fir Cone Ct
17900 CmsC 97045 718 G2
Fircrest Av
58700 ClbC 97051 414 J2
58700 STHN 97051 414 J2
Fircrest Ct
1600 LKOW 97034 686 E1
SE Fircrest Ct
14100 PTLD 97236 628 C7
16700 CmsC 97267 687 C1
SW Fircrest Ct
13500 BRTN 97008 625 A6
Fircrest Dr
900 NWBG 97132 713 C5
1600 LKOW 97034 686 E1
2100 CmsC 97068 686 G7
2100 WLIN 97068 686 G7
Fircrest Mnr
- BRTN 97005 625 A4
- BRTN 97008 625 A4
SE Fircrest St
14000 PTLD 97236 628 C7
SW Firdale Rd
30300 WasC 97113 653 B2
30300 WasC 97123 653 B1
SE Fireman Wy
27200 CmsC 97009 659 G5
SE Firenze Ln
7500 PTLD 97206 627 H2
NW Firestone Ct
1400 MCMV 97128 770 F3
16700 BRTN 97006 594 G5
W Firestone Ln
2500 VCVR 98660 536 D2
S Firethorne Ct
14200 CmsC 97045 747 F3
NW Fireweed Ter
5800 WasC 97229 564 H5
Fir Grove Ct
15800 LKOW 97035 656 B7
SW Fir Grove Ln
9100 WasC 97225 625 E3
SE Fir Grove Lp
900 HBRO 97123 593 D7
SW Fir Grove Rd
3600 CmsC 97070 716 A2
SW Fir Ln Ter
8500 WasC 97223 625 H7
SW Firlock Wy
6600 WasC 97223 625 G5
Firlock Park Blvd
35100 ClbC 97051 414 J2

Firlock Park Blvd
35100 STHN 97051 414 J2
35200 ClbC 97051 415 A2
35200 STHN 97051 415 A2
Firlok Park St
58700 ClbC 97051 414 J2
Firridge Av
50500 ClbC 97056 474 E4
Fir Ridge Rd
3000 LKOW 97034 656 B6
3000 LKOW 97035 656 B6
SW Firtree Dr
15200 WasC 97223 654 H4
E Fir Tree Wy
21800 CmsC 97049 723 J1
NW Fir View Cir
3500 CMAS 98607 569 C2
SW Firview Pl
8700 WasC 97007 624 F7
Firway Ln
35400 ClbC 97051 415 A2
35500 STHN 97051 415 A2
Firwood Ct
5100 WLIN 97068 687 A6
SW Firwood Ct
12100 BRTN 97008 625 D6
Firwood Dr
5100 WLIN 97068 687 A6
NE Firwood Dr
16500 ClkC 98606 479 D4
NW Firwood Dr
300 ClkC 98665 506 G6
Firwood Ln
2600 FTGV 97116 592 A3
2600 WasC 97116 592 A3
Firwood Rd
4500 CmsC 97035 656 A7
4500 LKOW 97035 656 A7
4600 CmsC 97035 655 J7
4600 LKOW 97035 655 J7
SE Firwood Rd
20200 CmsC 97055 691 D7
SW Firwood Rd
4900 CmsC 97035 655 J7
4900 LKOW 97035 655 J7
SE Firwood St
5400 MWKE 97222 657 C1
5800 CmsC 97222 657 C1
SE Firwood Crest Ln
4900 HBRO 97123 593 H5
SE Firwood School Rd
42700 CmsC 97055 691 D6
SW Fischer Ln
- PTLD 97205 596 B6
- PTLD 97210 596 B6
- PTLD 97221 596 B6
SW Fischer Rd
11800 KNGC 97224 685 A1
11800 WasC 97224 685 A1
S Fischers Mill Rd
18100 CmsC 97045 718 G2
20000 CmsC 97045 719 A4
21000 CmsC 97023 719 B3
S Fish Rd
26500 CmsC 97013 777 C5
26500 CmsC 97042 777 C5
Fisher Av
- CmsC 97045 717 E1
- ORCY 97045 717 E1
SW Fisher Av
6000 BRTN 97005 624 J5
6000 BRTN 97008 624 J5
SE Fisher Dr
16400 VCVR 98683 568 E3
Fisher Ln
57400 ClbC 97051 414 J4
57400 ClbC 97053 414 J4
Fishermans Wy
12200 ORCY 97045 717 B5
12300 CmsC 97045 717 B5
SE Fish Hatchery Rd
- CmsC 97015 687 G2
39800 CmsC 97055 691 B2
SW Fisk Ter
22000 SRWD 97140 684 E7
N Fiske Av
8900 PTLD 97203 566 B3
SW Fitch Dr
17400 SRWD 97140 714 E1
17900 SRWD 97140 684 E7
NW Five Oaks Dr
5500 HBRO 97124 564 A7
SE Five Oaks Rd
27500 CmsC 97023 720 C6
NW Five Peak Ter
52700 ClbC 97056 444 D7
52700 SPSE 97056 444 D7
SW Flagstone Dr
15500 BRTN 97007 624 G7
16000 WasC 97007 624 G7
Flamm Pl
2500 WLIN 97068 716 H1
SW Flanders Ct
- WNVL 97070 745 H3
SE Flanders Ln
1700 HBRO 97123 593 D7
NE Flanders St
600 PTLD 97232 596 H5
2800 PTLD 97232 597 B5
4700 PTLD 97213 597 C5
10600 PTLD 97220 597 J5
11600 PTLD 97220 598 A5
12400 PTLD 97230 598 A5
16800 GSHM 97230 598 F5
NW Flanders St
1600 PTLD 97209 596 D5
2000 PTLD 97210 596 D5
NE Flanders Wy
17100 GSHM 97230 598 F5
SE Flavel Ct
10200 PTLD 97266 627 H6
SE Flavel Dr
4500 PTLD 97206 627 D7
6000 CmsC 97206 627 D7
8800 MWKE 97206 627 D7
8900 CmsC 97206 657 D1
8900 CmsC 97222 657 D1
8900 MWKE 97206 657 D1
8900 MWKE 97222 657 D1
15700 PTLD 97236 628 E6
SE Flavel St
1300 PTLD 97202 626 H6
3600 PTLD 97202 627 A6
7100 PTLD 97206 627 G6
10500 PTLD 97266 627 H6

STREET
Block City ZIP Map# Grid

SE Flavel St
11700 PTLD 97266 628 B6
12100 PTLD 97236 628 A6
S Flax Plant Rd
1000 CNLS 97113 592 E6
NW Fleetwood Dr
10000 WasC 97229 595 E4
NW Fleischner St
9400 PTLD 97229 595 E4
SW Fleishauer Ct
1300 MCMV 97128 770 F7
SW Fleishauer Ln
100 MCMV 97128 770 F6
NE Fleming Av
500 GSHM 97030 629 E2
SE Fleming Av
1400 GSHM 97080 629 E4
Fleming Pl
3100 FTGV 97116 591 F3
NE Fleming Ter
2300 GSHM 97030 599 E7
SE Fletcher Rd
13000 YmhC 97114 771 H4
14000 DAYT 97114 771 J4
SW Fletcher Ter
22000 SRWD 97140 684 E6
SW Flicka Pl
10000 BRTN 97008 655 A1
SW Flicker Ct
16000 BRTN 97007 654 G2
N Flint Av
1700 PTLD 97227 596 G3
Flint Dr
53100 ClbC 97056 444 C6
Flint Wy
300 VCVR 98664 537 E6
SE Flora Dr
5700 CmsC 97222 657 C1
Floral Av NE
22000 MrnC 97002 775 D2
Floral Ct NE
21900 MrnC 97002 775 D3
SE Floral Ct
8300 CmsC 97267 687 F1
NE Floral Pl
10 PTLD 97214 597 A5
100 PTLD 97232 597 A5
SE Floral Pl
10 PTLD 97214 597 A6
10 PTLD 97232 597 A6
NW Florence Av
10 GSHM 97080 629 A2
1900 GSHM 97030 629 A1
SW Florence Av
100 GSHM 97030 629 A3
100 GSHM 97080 629 A3
NW Florence Ct
400 GSHM 97030 629 A2
SW Florence Ct
900 GSHM 97080 629 A3
8500 WasC 97223 625 G7
SW Florence Dr
1000 GSHM 97080 629 A4
SW Florence Ln
- PTLD 97219 625 H7
6500 PTLD 97223 625 H7
6500 WasC 97223 625 G7
SW Florence St
20300 WasC 97007 624 C3
Florence Ter
- GSHM 97080 629 A3
SW Florendo Ln
18200 WasC 97007 624 E7
SW Florentine Av
13700 WasC 97223 654 G5
SW Flores St
10900 WNVL 97070 745 C1
SW Florida Ct
3000 PTLD 97219 626 B5
Florida Dr
600 VCVR 98664 537 F7
SW Florida St
1100 PTLD 97219 626 D5
5500 PTLD 97219 625 J5
SE Floss St
3200 MWKE 97222 627 A7
NW Flotoma Dr
10200 WasC 97225 595 D5
10200 WasC 97229 595 D5
SE Flower Av
16900 CmsC 97267 687 F2
SW Flower Ct
4700 PTLD 97221 626 A4
Flower Dr
- PTLD 97217 536 E7
Flower Ln
100 DAYT 97114 771 J5
100 YmhC 97114 771 J5
SW Flower Pl
4600 PTLD 97221 626 A4
SW Flower St
- PTLD 97221 626 B4
1500 PTLD 97239 626 D4
6200 PTLD 97221 625 H4
SW Flower Ter
3000 PTLD 97239 626 B4
NE Flying Feather Ln
15100 YmhC 97132 712 H3
SW Flynn St
28000 WNVL 97070 715 G5
Fobert Rd NE
19400 MrnC 97032 775 D7
NW Foley Ct
1600 PTLD 97229 595 F3
NW Folkenburg St
15000 MthC 97231 534 F4
SE Folsom Rd
27300 CmsC 97022 719 H5
29700 CmsC 97022 720 A4
30700 CmsC 97023 720 A5
SW Fonner St
10600 TGRD 97223 655 C4
SW Fonner Pond Pl
12800 TGRD 97223 655 C4
NE Foothill Dr
700 ECDA 97023 750 C2
SW Foothill Dr
11100 WasC 97225 595 B7
13100 WasC 97005 595 B7
S Foothills Av
21700 CmsC 97045 747 E3
Foothills Dr
5000 LKOW 97034 656 G6
E Foothills Dr
1000 NWBG 97132 713 D4
W Foothills Dr
100 NWBG 97132 713 B4
200 YmhC 97132 713 B4
Foothills Rd
10 LKOW 97034 656 G6
Foot of N Edgewater St
- PTLD 97203 565 J5
E Forbes Ct
- ClkC 98629 386 H6
N Force Av
9900 PTLD 97217 566 D1
11500 PTLD 97217 536 E7
S Ford Ct
20100 CmsC 97045 688 J5
Ford Pl
16500 CmsC 97035 655 H7
NE Ford St
2600 MCMV 97128 770 H3
S Ford St
2800 WHGL 98671 570 C6
SE Ford St
100 MCMV 97128 770 H6
12200 CmsC 97015 688 A1
SW Fordham Pl
1300 WasC 97006 594 E5
SW Ford St Dr
1500 PTLD 97201 596 D6
NW Forest Av
2800 WasC 97006 594 J3
SW Forest Av
14900 SRWD 97140 684 H7
Forest Ct
3200 WLIN 97068 686 H3
N Forest Ct
2000 CNBY 97013 746 E4
SW Forest Dr
14500 BRTN 97007 624 J6
NE Forest Ln
6500 HBRO 97124 594 A5
6500 WasC 97124 594 A5
NW Forest Ln
3100 MthC 97210 595 H1
3100 MthC 97229 595 H1
3100 PTLD 97210 595 H1
3500 PTLD 97210 565 H7
SE Forest Ln
31700 CmsC 97009 660 C6
SW Forest Ln
11100 TGRD 97223 655 C3
Forest Pl
200 FTGV 97116 591 F3
SW Forest Pl
14600 BRTN 97007 624 J6
S Forest Rd
24600 CmsC 97013 776 F1
30000 CmsC 97038 807 A5
SW Forest Rd
400 ECDA 97023 750 B4
Forest Rdg
- VCVR 98664 537 F6
NW Forest St
200 HBRO 97124 593 B4
SE Forest St
12600 VCVR 98683 568 A1
SW Foresta Ter
- WasC 97225 595 E6
NE Forest Canyon Rd
- ClkC 98686 506 H2
SW Forest Cove Rd
200 CmsC 97068 716 F7
200 CmsC 97068 746 E1
NW Forest Creek Dr
700 HBRO 97124 593 A2
SW Forest Creek Dr
- SRWD 97140 684 E7
NW Forest Creek Rd
- PTLD 97229 595 E3
NW Forestel Lp
14600 WasC 97006 594 J3
E Forest Fern Dr
20300 CmsC 97055 692 G6
Forest Gale Dr
2900 FTGV 97116 591 E3
SW Forest Glen Ct
13000 BRTN 97008 625 A5
SW Forest Glen Ln
14500 CmsC 97140 714 H5
S Forest Glen Rd
18800 CmsC 97023 719 B4
18800 CmsC 97045 719 B4
SE Forest Glen Rd
700 ECDA 97023 750 C4
S Forest Grove Lp
18700 CmsC 97045 717 H4
Forest Hideaway
- TGRD 97223 655 A3
S Forest Hill Dr
19800 CmsC 97045 718 F7
SE Forest Hill Dr
16900 DAMA 97009 689 A2
NW Forest Home Ln
1800 CMAS 98607 569 C3
NW Forest Home Rd
1100 CMAS 98607 569 C3
Forest Meadows Wy
1000 CmsC 97034 656 D4
1000 LKOW 97034 656 D4
Forest Park Dr
100 STHN 97051 385 D6
S Forest Park Rd
22000 CmsC 97004 749 D7
SW Forest Park Rd
18100 WasC 97123 683 C2
Forest Ridge Ln
10800 CmsC 97045 716 J4
11200 ORCY 97045 716 J4
SW Forest Ridge Pl
10300 WasC 97007 654 G2
NW Forest Spring Ln
12500 WasC 97229 595 B1
Forest View Dr
3700 WHGL 98671 570 D3
SE Forest View Ln
10700 CmsC 97236 657 H3
NW Forestview Wy
10200 WasC 97229 595 D4
Forge Dr
2400 FTGV 97116 591 G4
NE Fork Av
34700 ClkC 98629 386 J4
SE For Mor Ct
15400 CmsC 97015 658 A7
SE Forrester Rd
26900 CmsC 97009 689 F3
Forsythe Rd
13700 ORCY 97045 687 E5
14100 CmsC 97045 687 H4
S Forsythe Rd
15500 CmsC 97045 687 J4
15500 CmsC 97045 688 A4
SW Forsythia Pl
7700 BRTN 97008 625 A6
Fortuna Ct
13200 ORCY 97045 717 D4
N Fortune Av
8900 PTLD 97203 566 A3
N Fortune Ct
9200 PTLD 97203 566 A3
Fort Vancouver Wy
1000 VCVR 98661 536 G5
1000 VCVR 98663 536 G5
Fosberg Rd
- CmsC 97009 690 B2
12700 LKOW 97035 655 J4
12700 PTLD 97219 655 J4
13800 LKOW 97035 656 A5
SE Fosberg Rd
17000 CmsC 97009 690 B3
N Foss Av
7200 PTLD 97217 566 C5
7900 PTLD 97203 566 C4
N Foss Ct
4100 PTLD 97203 566 C4
SE Foss St
16200 DAMA 97009 688 E2
SW Fossil Ln
15300 BRTN 97007 654 E2
SW Foster Ln
15400 WasC 97007 624 H3
SE Foster Pl
11800 PTLD 97266 628 A5
13800 PTLD 97236 628 C5
SE Foster Rd
5000 PTLD 97206 627 C2
8100 PTLD 97266 627 H5
11100 PTLD 97266 628 A5
12000 PTLD 97236 628 A5
13800 YmhC 97114 771 J3
14100 YmhC 97114 772 A3
16400 MthC 97236 628 F7
17700 CmsC 97009 628 G7
17700 CmsC 97009 658 G1
17700 DAMA 97009 658 J6
S Foster Creek Ln
15600 CmsC 97045 689 A4
SW Foundry Av
22300 SRWD 97140 684 H7
SW Fountain Grove Ter
6000 WasC 97007 624 C5
SW Fountainlake Dr
7200 WNVL 97070 745 G4
SW Fountainwood Pl
15400 TGRD 97224 655 C7
Four Oaks St
12000 ORCY 97045 717 B4
NE Four Seasons Ln
2600 VCVR 98682 537 J3
2600 VCVR 98684 537 J3
Fourth St
- WasC 97140 715 C1
E Fourth Plain Blvd
100 VCVR 98660 536 G3
100 VCVR 98663 536 G3
1000 VCVR 98661 536 H3
2800 VCVR 98661 537 B3
NE Fourth Plain Blvd
5300 VCVR 98661 537 D3
7000 VCVR 98662 537 D3
9500 ClkC 98662 537 G1
10100 ClkC 98662 507 H7
W Fourth Plain Blvd
100 VCVR 98660 536 F3
100 VCVR 98663 536 G3
NE Fourth Plain Rd
11200 ClkC 98682 507 J7
11700 ClkC 98682 507 J7
11700 VCVR 98682 507 J7
11700 VCVR 98682 508 A7
16200 ClkC 98682 508 G7
NE Fourth Plain Rd SR-500
16200 ClkC 98682 508 G7
SE Foushee Wy
5700 CmsC 97267 687 C2
N Fowler Av
7900 PTLD 97217 566 C4
N Fowler Ct
8400 PTLD 97217 566 C4
SW Fox Ct
1100 TDLE 97060 599 F5
Fox Ln
1300 ORCY 97045 717 E3
NE Fox Ln
9600 YmhC 97115 742 F2
SW Fox Ln
2300 TDLE 97060 599 F6
14200 BRTN 97008 654 J2
SW Fox Pl
800 TDLE 97060 599 F4
Fox Run
- PTLD 97211 566 G3
13200 LKOW 97034 656 E4
N Fox St
- PTLD 97203 565 H2
NW Foxborough Cir
15900 BRTN 97006 594 H5
NE Fox Farm Rd
9600 YmhC 97115 742 J1
10400 YmhC 97132 742 J1
10900 YmhC 97115 712 J7
10900 YmhC 97132 712 J7
NE Fox Farm Rd CO-74
9600 YmhC 97115 742 J1
10400 YmhC 97132 742 J1
10900 YmhC 97115 712 J7
10900 YmhC 97132 712 J7
SW Foxfield Ct
6900 WasC 97225 595 H7
SE Foxfire St
5500 MWKE 97222 657 C4
SE Foxglove Ct
2200 HBRO 97123 623 E1
SE Foxglove Dr
1000 GSHM 97080 629 G4
SW Foxglove Pl
8000 BRTN 97008 625 D4
SE Foxglove Wy
1600 GSHM 97080 629 G4
NW Fox Hollow Ct
9300 WasC 97229 595 E5
NE Fox Hollow Ln
13300 YmhC 97132 712 F5
Fox Pointe
- VCVR 98661 537 C3
S Fox Pointe Dr
14900 CmsC 97045 717 G2
NW Fox Ridge Rd
5600 YmhC 97128 770 D4
11200 MCMV 97128 770 D4
SW Fox Run Pl
23800 SRWD 97140 714 F1
SW Foxtail Pl
16400 WasC 97123 653 A7
SW Foxwood Ct
15800 WasC 97224 655 A7
SW Fradeen Ln
8900 WasC 97225 625 F4
SE Fragrance Av
16800 CmsC 97027 687 F2
16800 CmsC 97267 687 F2
SW Frammy Wy
21500 HBRO 97006 594 B6
21500 WasC 97006 594 B6
SE Frances Av
8400 VCVR 98664 537 F7
SE Frances Ct
5200 HBRO 97123 593 H7
Frances St
100 MOLA 97038 837 E1
SE Frances St
5800 HBRO 97123 593 J7
5800 WasC 97123 593 J7
6400 HBRO 97123 594 A7
6400 WasC 97123 594 A7
7500 WasC 97006 594 B7
SW Frances St
20400 WasC 97006 594 C7
NW Francesca Dr
15000 WasC 97229 594 J1
SE Francesca Ln
14800 HPYV 97236 658 D4
NE Francis Av
900 GSHM 97030 629 D2
3300 GSHM 97030 599 D6
SE Francis Av
600 GSHM 97080 629 D3
15300 CmsC 97267 657 B7
NE Francis Ct
2300 GSHM 97030 599 D7
NE Francis Pl
3800 GSHM 97030 599 D6
SE Francis St
2600 PTLD 97202 626 J2
2800 PTLD 97202 627 A2
5400 PTLD 97206 627 D2
8000 PTLD 97266 627 F3
16800 PTLD 97236 628 F3
33300 MthC 97080 630 D3
SW Francis St
19700 WasC 97006 594 D7
Frank Av
16400 CmsC 97045 687 G6
SE Frank Av
13600 CmsC 97009 659 J6
SW Frank Av
- MthC 97219 656 F2
- PTLD 97219 656 F2
SW Frank Ct
18600 WasC 97007 624 E6
SW Franklin Av
4700 BRTN 97005 625 B4
NW Franklin Ct
3200 PTLD 97210 596 B4
SE Franklin Ct
17400 PTLD 97236 628 F2
SW Franklin Ln
10300 WNVL 97070 715 D7
Franklin St
600 CBAC 97018 385 B2
3600 VCVR 98660 536 F2
E Franklin St
300 NWBG 97132 713 C7
NE Franklin St
3700 CMAS 98607 569 E1
NW Franklin St
4400 VCVR 98663 536 E2
4500 VCVR 98660 536 F1
5900 VCVR 98663 506 F7
SE Franklin St
300 CMAS 98607 569 F3
500 PTLD 97202 626 H2
2800 PTLD 97202 627 A2
4100 MWKE 97222 657 B3
7000 PTLD 97206 627 E2
8200 PTLD 97266 627 F2
15100 PTLD 97236 628 D2
SW Franklin St
6600 TGRD 97223 655 H4
W Franklin St
100 NWBG 97132 713 B7
Franklin Wy
18300 GLDS 97027 687 D3
Frantz St
100 STHN 97051 415 A1
SW Fraser Av
4300 WasC 97225 625 H3
NW Frazier Ct
1100 PTLD 97229 595 F4
Frazier Ln
900 WDLD 98674 385 J1
SW Frederick Ln
17600 SRWD 97140 684 E7
Frederick St
16300 ORCY 97045 687 F6
S Frederick St
- ORCY 97045 687 F6
SE Frederick St
33800 SPSE 97056 474 E2
N Fredericksburg Wy
100 VCVR 98664 537 E6
S Fredericksburg Wy
100 VCVR 98664 537 E6
S Fredrick St
16200 ORCY 97045 687 F6
NE Freedom Rd
20400 ClkC 98604 448 G6
NW Freeman Av
100 HBRO 97123 593 B4
600 HBRO 97124 593 B4
SW Freeman Av
100 HBRO 97123 593 B5
100 HBRO 97124 593 B5
NW Freeman Ct
700 HBRO 97124 593 B3
SW Freeman Ct
- WNVL 97070 715 D4
5000 PTLD 97219 625 J6
Freeman Rd
54000 ClbC 97056 444 H4
S Freeman Rd
12600 CmsC 97013 777 B4
12600 CmsC 97042 777 B4
SE Freeman Rd
12700 MWKE 97222 657 B4
13000 CmsC 97222 657 B4
SW Freeman St
4200 PTLD 97219 626 A6
SE Freeman Wy
12400 MWKE 97222 657 B4
N Freemont Ln
900 CNLS 97113 592 D4
NE Fremont Ct
11200 PTLD 97220 597 J2
11300 PTLD 97220 598 A2
14800 PTLD 97230 598 D2
NE Fremont Dr
2600 PTLD 97220 597 G3
N Fremont St
10 PTLD 97212 596 G2
10 PTLD 97227 596 F2
1300 CNLS 97113 592 E4
NE Fremont St
10 PTLD 97212 596 J2
10 PTLD 97227 596 G2
2700 PTLD 97212 597 A2
4100 PTLD 97213 597 D2
8100 PTLD 97220 597 G2
10200 MWDP 97220 597 J2
11200 PTLD 97220 598 A2
14800 PTLD 97230 598 D2
NW Fremont St
1100 CMAS 98607 569 B4
SE French Rd
9200 VCVR 98664 567 G1
SE French Acres Dr
9700 HPYV 97236 657 J2
SW French Glen Ct
11400 WNVL 97070 745 B2
SW French Prairie Dr
9900 WNVL 97070 745 E2
32500 CmsC 97070 745 E3
32500 WNVL 97002 745 E3
French Prairie Rd NE
19100 MrnC 97137 773 H3
21700 MrnC 97002 774 A2
French Prairie Rd NE SR-219
19100 MrnC 97137 773 F7
SW French Prairie Rd
- CmsC 97002 745 G3
- WNVL 97002 745 G3
31100 WNVL 97070 745 G3
SW Frenwood Wy
10 WasC 97005 595 B6
S Fresh Air Ct
15800 CmsC 97045 717 J2
15800 CmsC 97045 718 A2
SW Frewing Ct
9500 TGRD 97223 655 E4
SE Frewing Rd
4400 HBRO 97123 593 G7
SW Frewing St
9500 TGRD 97223 655 D5
SW Friar Ln
22100 SRWD 97140 684 F6
Friars Ln
- CmsC 97045 717 B5
- ORCY 97045 717 B5
NW Friberg St
6800 ClkC 98607 538 J5
6800 CMAS 98607 538 J5
Friedel Av
500 VCVR 98664 537 E7
SW Friendly Ct
1500 MCMV 97128 770 F7
SE Friendly Ln
34100 CmsC 97023 750 E6
SW Friendly Ln
16500 WasC 97007 654 F4
SW Fritz Pl
1400 WasC 97006 594 D7
SW Frobase Rd
6500 CmsC 97062 715 F1
SE Frog Pond Ln
25300 CmsC 97022 719 J4
SW Frog Pond Ln
6700 CmsC 97070 715 G5
NW Front Av
1900 PTLD 97209 596 E3
2200 PTLD 97210 596 E3
3400 PTLD 97210 566 A7
4900 PTLD 97210 565 J7
10800 PTLD 97231 565 D1
SW Front Av
- PTLD 97219 626 E6
Front Pl
1800 CBAC 97018 385 C3
Front St
1500 WHGL 98671 570 A6
16000 ORCY 97045 687 F6
S Front St
- CMAS 98607 569 G5
- WHGL 98671 569 H5
Frontage Av
9100 MWKE 97222 626 J7
9100 MWKE 97222 656 J1
Frontage Rd
- ClbC 97051 385 C5
- ClbC 97053 414 H7
N Frontage Rd
- PTLD 97203 566 C3
- PTLD 97217 566 C3
NW Frontage Rd
300 TDLE 97060 599 F3
SE Frontage Rd
- CmsC 97222 657 E5
SW Frontage Rd
100 ECDA 97023 750 A3
SE Frontier Av
14100 CmsC 97015 658 C6
Frontier Cir
1500 FTGV 97116 592 C6
SE Frontier Ct
8500 CmsC 97015 687 H2
Frontier Dr
- MrnC 97002 775 D4
Frontier Ln
1100 NWBG 97132 743 B2
1100 YmhC 97132 743 B2
Frontier Pkwy
12800 CmsC 97045 717 C5
12800 ORCY 97045 717 C5
Frontier Wy
1300 FTGV 97116 592 C6
Frost Ln
5900 CmsC 97035 685 H1
5900 LKOW 97035 685 H1
Frost St
6300 CmsC 97035 685 H1
6300 LKOW 97035 685 H1
NW Frost St
- PTLD 97231 565 C1
Fruit Valley Rd
2600 VCVR 98660 536 E3
NW Fruit Valley Rd
3900 VCVR 98660 506 E7
3900 VCVR 98660 536 E2
3900 VCVR 98663 506 E7
3900 VCVR 98665 506 E7
7700 ClkC 98665 506 E4
Fruitwood Ct
4100 LKOW 97035 656 A5
Fry Rd NE
12100 MrnC 97002 774 J6
12100 MrnC 97002 775 A6
SE Frye St
14700 HPYV 97236 658 D4
NE Fryer Rd
6800 YmhC 97111 711 B4
6800 YmhC 97148 711 B4
Fryer Hill Rd
- YmhC 97115 742 H2
NE Fryer Hill Rd
22100 YmhC 97115 742 H2
S Fuchsia Rd
22200 CmsC 97023 750 B4
SW Fuji Ct
12200 WasC 97224 685 B1
NE Fuller Ct
600 MCMV 97128 770 H3
SW Fuller Dr
21600 TLTN 97062 685 C6
NE Fuller Rd
32600 ClkC 98629 417 D1
SE Fuller Rd
8500 CmsC 97236 627 F7
8500 PTLD 97266 627 G7
8900 CmsC 97236 657 F1
10500 CmsC 97222 657 F3
Fullerton Rd
54800 ClbC 97053 444 E2
55100 ClbC 97056 444 E2
NW Fullner Ct
9100 WasC 97229 595 F4
NW Fullner Pl
1300 WasC 97229 595 F4
SW Fulmar Ter
11900 BRTN 97007 654 G3
SE Fulquartz Landing Rd
22200 DNDE 97115 742 J5
23300 YmhC 97115 742 J4
SW Fulton Dr
10100 TLTN 97062 685 D2
10100 WasC 97062 685 D2
Fulton St
1800 NWBG 97132 713 D6
SW Fulton Park Blvd
7200 PTLD 97219 626 F5
SW Fulton Park Pl
7500 PTLD 97219 626 F6
SE Funny Farm Rd
33000 CmsC 97023 750 E4
Fur
- WasC 97006 594 D5
SE Furat Ct
- PTLD 97222 627 A7
SW Furlong Ct
14000 WasC 97005 595 A7
Furlong Pl
1900 WLIN 97068 686 H5
SW Furlong Wy
14000 WasC 97005 595 A7
14400 WasC 97005 594 J7
Furman Dr
- LKOW 97034 686 H2
Furnace St
10 LKOW 97034 656 G7
SE Furnberg St
6200 MWKE 97222 657 D3
6300 CmsC 97222 657 D3

G

G Av
800 LKOW 97034 656 F5
W G Av
200 LCTR 98629 416 G1
G Dr
2800 WHGL 98671 570 B5
G Ln
- PTLD 97218 567 D7
G St
- PTLD 97219 655 J3
- PTLD 97219 656 A3
300 CBAC 97018 385 C3
500 CBAC 97051 385 C3
500 ClbC 97051 385 C3
600 WHGL 98671 569 J5
900 WHGL 98671 570 A5
3900 VCVR 98663 536 G2
NW G St
- WasC 97006 594 B5
SW Gaarde St
10800 TGRD 97223 655 B5
10800 TGRD 97224 655 C5
SE Gabbert Rd
- GSHM 97080 629 C6
SW Gabbert Rd
10 GSHM 97080 629 B6
NE Gable Av
33400 ClkC 98629 417 H1
SW Gable Pkwy
6400 MthC 97221 625 H2
6400 WasC 97225 625 H2
Gable Rd
2100 ClbC 97051 415 B2
2100 STHN 97051 415 A2
2500 STHN 97051 414 J2
2700 ClbC 97051 414 J2
SW Gable Park Rd
7000 WasC 97225 625 G2
NW Gables Creek Ln
- BRTN 97006 594 G5
Gabreski St
- PTLD 97218 567 E5
NE Gabreski St
- PTLD 97218 567 D5
Gabrielle Ct
14100 LKOW 97035 656 A5
SE Gadroon St
6100 HBRO 97123 593 J7
SW Gadwall Ln
12800 BRTN 97007 654 F4
Gaffney Ln
13300 ORCY 97045 717 D5
13400 CmsC 97045 717 D5
SW Gage Ln
16000 BRTN 97006 594 G7
SW Gage Rd
23400 CmsC 97062 715 H2
23400 CmsC 97062 716 A1
23400 CmsC 97070 715 H2
23400 CmsC 97070 716 A1
SE Gaibler Ln
16000 MthC 97236 628 E7
16000 PTLD 97236 628 E7
SE Gail Ct
1700 HBRO 97123 623 E1
Gain St
14000 ORCY 97045 687 F6
SW Gaines Ct
5700 MthC 97221 625 J2
SW Gaines St
600 PTLD 97239 626 D2
SE Gaitgill Ct
5600 CmsC 97267 687 C1
E Gaither Av
- ClkC 98629 386 H6
SW Gala Ct
12200 KNGC 97224 685 B2
12200 WasC 97224 685 B2
SE Galaxy Av
- HBRO 97123 623 D2
- WasC 97123 623 D2
NW Galaxy St
2300 CMAS 98607 569 D3
SW Galbreath Dr
13700 SRWD 97140 684 J5
13700 WasC 97140 684 J5
SW Gale Av
3100 PTLD 97201 626 C1
3100 PTLD 97239 626 C2
SW Galeburn St
4000 PTLD 97219 656 A1
Galen Rd
10 LKOW 97035 655 J4
Galen St
4800 LKOW 97035 655 J4
4800 LKOW 97035 656 A4
SW Galena Wy
9200 BRTN 97007 654 H1
Gales Ct
1600 FTGV 97116 591 H4
Gales Wy
2300 FTGV 97116 591 H4
Gales Creek Rd
300 FTGV 97116 591 G3
1600 WasC 97116 591 E3
Gales Creek Rd SR-8
300 FTGV 97116 591 G3
1600 WasC 97116 591 E3
NW Gales Creek Rd
1600 FTGV 97116 591 D2
1600 WasC 97116 591 D2
4000 WasC 97116 561 B7
NW Gales Creek Rd SR-8
1600 FTGV 97116 591 D2
1600 WasC 97116 591 D2
4000 WasC 97116 561 B7
NW Gales Ridge Ln
7800 PTLD 97229 595 G3
SW Galewood Dr
17200 SRWD 97140 714 E1
Galewood St
4200 LKOW 97035 656 A6
NW Galice Ln
21000 HBRO 97124 564 C6
21000 HBRO 97229 564 C6
21000 WasC 97229 564 C6
NW Gallaher Rd
21300 MthC 97231 504 E5
NW Gallatin St
- HBRO 97006 594 D3
NW Gallatin Kinder Rd
34400 ClkC 98629 386 D6
Gallery Wy
1700 CmsC 97068 686 G4
1700 WLIN 97068 686 G4
NW Galliard Lp
20200 HBRO 97124 594 C2
SW Gallin Ct
12900 TGRD 97223 655 A5
SW Gallo Av
11400 TGRD 97223 655 C3
SW Gallop Ct
13300 BRTN 97008 625 A7
NE Galloway Ct
2600 MCMV 97128 770 H2
SW Galloway Ct
12600 BRTN 97008 655 B2
NE Galloway St
1700 MCMV 97128 770 H3
SE Galloway St
100 MCMV 97128 770 H5
SE Galway St
38400 CmsC 97055 690 J4
38400 SNDY 97055 690 J4
NE Gamma Dr
3200 GSHM 97030 599 E7
N Gammans Pl
2600 PTLD 97217 566 D5
Ganna
- WasC 97116 561 E5
NW Ganna Wy
46400 WasC 97116 561 E5
NW Gannet Ter
4600 WasC 97229 594 J1
SE Gannon Dr
13600 CmsC 97015 658 B6
Ganong St
300 ORCY 97045 717 B2
Gans St
1000 LKOW 97034 656 G7
N Gantenbein Av
3400 PTLD 97227 596 G2
4000 PTLD 97217 596 G1

STREET Block	City	ZIP	Map#	Grid
N Gantenbein Av				
4800	PTLD	97217	566	G7
N Gantenbein St				
-	PTLD	97217	566	G1
Garden Av				
-	PTLD	97217	536	E6
N Garden Dr				
3900	YmhC	97132	713	C3
NE Garden Dr				
18200	ClkC	98682	538	G3
S Garden Ln				
17300	CmsC	97045	717	H1
SE Garden Ln				
8300	CmsC	97236	627	F7
SW Garden Ln				
8500	WasC	97223	625	F6
Garden Mdws				
-	PTLD	97230	598	D2
Garden Mnr				
-	CNLS	97113	592	D4
SW Garden Pl				
11900	TGRD	97223	655	F4
Garden St				
1500	WLIN	97068	687	B6
SW Garden Acres Rd				
24900	WasC	97140	715	C3
24900	WNVL	97070	715	C3
SW Garden Home Rd				
3800	PTLD	97219	626	A6
5000	PTLD	97219	625	H6
6400	PTLD	97223	625	H6
6400	WasC	97223	625	F6
9400	BRTN	97008	625	E6
9400	WasC	97008	625	E6
Gardenia St				
2300	FTGV	97116	591	H4
Garden Meadow Dr				
13600	ORCY	97045	717	E5
Garden Park Ests				
-	PTLD	97236	628	C2
SW Garden Park Pl				
10500	TGRD	97223	655	C5
NE Gardenridge Ter				
100	HBRO	97124	593	F2
SW Garden View Av				
2200	WasC	97225	625	E2
Garden View Ct				
-	ClbC	97053	444	E1
Gardenview Ct				
55800	ClbC	97053	414	E7
55800	ClbC	97053	444	E1
Gardenview Dr				
33400	ClbC	97053	414	F7
SW Garden View Pl				
2800	WasC	97225	625	F1
SW Gardner Ct				
10300	TLTN	97062	685	D6
15500	WasC	97224	654	H6
NE Gardner Rd				
-	CMAS	98607	539	F7
SE Gardner Rd				
900	CMAS	98607	539	F7
Garen St				
53400	ClbC	97056	444	D5
NE Garfield Av				
3500	PTLD	97212	596	G2
4000	PTLD	97211	596	G1
5000	PTLD	97211	566	G7
NW Garfield Av				
5800	VCVR	98663	506	F7
NE Garfield Ct				
3500	CMAS	98607	569	F1
N Garfield St				
500	NWBG	97132	713	C7
NE Garfield St				
-	ClkC	98607	539	F7
-	CMAS	98607	539	F7
4300	CMAS	98607	569	F1
NE Garfield St SR-500				
300	CMAS	98607	569	F4
S Garfield St				
700	NWBG	97132	743	B1
SE Garfield St				
100	CMAS	98607	569	F4
SW Garibaldi Ct				
15400	BRTN	97007	624	H6
Garibaldi St				
10	LKOW	97035	656	A3
NW Garibaldi St				
100	HBRO	97124	593	B4
SE Garland Ct				
14400	CmsC	97267	657	B6
SE Garland Ln				
14500	CmsC	97267	657	B6
SW Garland Rd				
27500	WasC	97140	714	B5
27500	YmhC	97132	714	B5
SW Garnet Ct				
15100	BRTN	97007	624	H7
SE Garnet Wy				
5600	CmsC	97267	687	C2
SE Garrett Ct				
4500	MWKE	97222	657	B2
SW Garrett Ct				
13600	TGRD	97223	655	D5
SE Garrett Dr				
10800	MWKE	97222	657	B2
SW Garrett St				
9900	TGRD	97223	655	D5
11100	TLTN	97062	685	C2
Garrison Ct				
600	VCVR	98664	537	E5
Garrison Rd				
200	VCVR	98664	537	E6
N Garrison Rd				
100	VCVR	98664	537	E6
NE Garrison Rd				
500	VCVR	98664	537	E5
S Garrison Rd				
100	VCVR	98664	537	D6
NW Garswood Ter				
-	HBRO	97006	594	D5
Gary Ln				
16700	LKOW	97034	686	C1
SE Gary Ln				
19000	CmsC	97267	687	B4
SW Gary Ln				
21500	WasC	97006	594	B6
Gary St				
39300	SNDY	97055	691	A3
Gassner Ln				
16800	CmsC	97035	685	H1
SW Gassner Rd				
18500	WasC	97007	624	D7

STREET Block	City	ZIP	Map#	Grid
SW Gaston Av				
3000	PTLD	97239	626	B1
Gatepost Ct				
6700	WNVL	97070	745	G2
Gates Ln				
-	CmsC	97035	685	J3
-	RVGR	97035	685	J3
NW Gateway Av				
3100	VCVR	98660	536	B2
NW Gateway Ct				
15500	BRTN	97006	594	H4
Gateway Rd				
-	CmsC	97013	776	H2
SE Gateway Rd				
-	CmsC	97009	660	B6
NW Gatto Ct				
11200	WasC	97229	595	C3
SW Gault Ct				
12000	BRTN	97008	655	B1
SW Gavin Ct				
14900	BRTN	97006	594	J6
14900	WasC	97006	594	J6
N Gay Av				
5500	PTLD	97217	566	E6
SE Gayle Ct				
14700	CmsC	97267	657	B6
SW Gayle Ln				
8500	BRTN	97225	625	F1
SW Gaylord Wy				
-	WNVL	97070	715	D7
Geantry Villa Ln				
-	ClbC	97053	414	G6
SW Gearhart Ct				
15200	BRTN	97007	624	H6
SW Gearhart Dr				
7600	BRTN	97007	624	H6
SW Gearin Ct				
16300	WasC	97223	654	G5
Gearin Rd NE				
5900	MrnC	97137	773	F1
E Gedemke St				
68400	CmsC	97067	724	C6
S Gee Creek Lp				
-	RDGF	98642	416	B7
NE Geelan Rd				
17300	YmhC	97148	711	D1
SW Geer Rd				
35300	CmsC	97070	744	E6
35300	CmsC	97132	744	E6
Geer St				
6000	WLIN	97068	687	B5
S Geiger Rd				
20300	CmsC	97045	717	A7
SW Geiger Rd				
38700	FTGV	97116	592	B7
38700	WasC	97113	592	C7
38700	WasC	97116	592	B7
S Gelbrich Rd				
26000	CmsC	97013	776	D4
SW Gem Ln				
12500	BRTN	97005	625	B1
SW Gemini Dr				
8900	BRTN	97008	625	C7
8900	BRTN	97008	655	C1
Gemini Ln				
1400	NWBG	97132	713	F6
Gemini St				
1500	NWBG	97132	713	F6
SW Gemstone Ct				
-	BRTN	97007	654	G1
General Anderson Rd				
1800	VCVR	98661	537	C3
SW Genesis Lp				
13200	TGRD	97223	655	C5
N Geneva Av				
8900	PTLD	97203	566	A3
SW Geneva St				
10900	TGRD	97223	655	C2
SE Geneva Wy				
12700	HPYV	97236	658	B2
SW Genoa Ct				
20500	WasC	97007	624	C5
Gensman Rd				
60700	ClbC	97051	384	D5
Gentile St				
-	PTLD	97218	567	E5
NW Gentleman Ln				
7900	WasC	97116	561	C4
SW Gentle Woods Ct				
15200	TGRD	97224	655	G7
SW Gentle Woods Dr				
7600	TGRD	97224	655	G7
SW Gentry Ln				
12800	WasC	97005	595	B6
S Gentry Wy				
11800	ORCY	97045	717	A4
Gentry Highlands Ln				
19100	ORCY	97045	717	C4
Geo Ann Rd				
10600	CmsC	97045	746	H1
SW George Ct				
17800	WasC	97007	624	F3
George Rd				
-	CmsC	97023	750	H1
NE George Rd				
31100	ClkC	98607	540	B3
SE George Rd				
37700	CmsC	97022	720	H7
37700	CmsC	97023	720	H7
37700	CmsC	97023	750	J1
SW Georgene Ct				
20000	WasC	97007	624	C5
SW Georgetown Wy				
400	WasC	97006	594	E6
SW Georgian Pl				
2600	PTLD	97201	596	C7
2600	PTLD	97201	626	B1
SW Gerald Av				
2600	PTLD	97201	596	C7
2600	PTLD	97201	626	B1
NE Geraldine Dr				
500	HBRO	97124	593	C3
Geranium Pl				
11500	CmsC	97045	717	A5
11500	ORCY	97045	717	A5
SE Gerber Ct				
27900	CmsC	97022	689	H4
S Gerber Rd				
15700	CmsC	97045	689	A7
16900	CmsC	97045	719	A1
NW Gerber Ter				
6300	WasC	97229	564	H6
Gerber Woods Dr				
13400	ORCY	97045	717	D5

STREET Block	City	ZIP	Map#	Grid
SW Gerda Ln				
20500	SRWD	97140	684	J5
20500	WasC	97140	684	J5
SE Gerhard Dr				
1400	HBRO	97123	623	E2
Gerilyn Ct				
17700	SNDY	97055	690	J3
Gerkman Rd				
14700	CmsC	97045	687	G4
NW Germantown Ct				
-	PTLD	97231	565	E3
NW Germantown Rd				
9200	PTLD	97231	565	C4
9800	PTLD	97229	565	C3
12200	MthC	97231	565	C4
12200	MthC	97231	565	B3
16000	WasC	97229	564	G4
16000	WasC	97231	564	G4
18700	WasC	97124	564	G4
NW Gerrish Rd				
15000	WasC	97133	532	J4
NW Gerritz Ter				
3500	WasC	97229	595	D2
Gershwin Ct				
10	LKOW	97035	656	B4
NE Gertz Cir				
-	PTLD	97217	566	G3
9500	PTLD	97211	566	G3
NE Gertz Ct				
9400	PTLD	97211	566	G3
N Gertz Rd				
1000	PTLD	97211	566	G3
1000	PTLD	97217	566	G3
NE Gertz Rd				
-	PTLD	97217	566	H3
10	PTLD	97211	566	H3
NE Gher Rd				
-	ClkC	98682	507	J7
5100	ClkC	98662	507	J7
Ghiglieri Ct				
3500	WLIN	97068	716	J1
SE Gia Ct				
9900	CmsC	97236	657	H3
NW Gianola Ct				
16200	BRTN	97006	594	H5
Gibbons St				
4000	VCVR	98661	537	B3
Gibbs Cir				
-	MCMV	97128	771	A3
NW Gibbs Dr				
19500	HBRO	97006	594	D4
SW Gibbs St				
800	PTLD	97239	626	D2
SW Gibraltar Ct				
15400	BRTN	97007	624	H6
NE Gibson Rd				
6600	YmhC	97111	711	B4
6600	YmhC	97148	711	B3
SE Gibson Rd				
37000	ClkC	98671	570	H6
S Gideon St				
1200	PTLD	97202	626	H1
NW Giese Av				
100	GSHM	97030	628	G2
SW Giese Lp				
2300	GSHM	97080	628	G5
SW Giese Pl				
1900	GSHM	97080	628	G5
SE Giese Rd				
18200	GSHM	97080	628	G6
18200	MthC	97080	628	G6
18200	MthC	97236	628	G6
Gifford Pl				
3900	WHGL	98671	570	D5
Gift Pl				
32100	ClbC	97056	444	C3
N Gilbert Av				
7500	PTLD	97203	565	J3
9400	PTLD	97203	566	A2
Gilbert Ln				
50100	ClbC	97056	474	C5
NW Gilbert Ln				
17400	WasC	97229	594	F2
N Gilbert Pl				
8800	PTLD	97203	565	J3
SE Gilbertson Rd				
14000	CmsC	97055	660	J7
Gilbreath Dr				
-	ClkC	98671	570	C2
S Gilchrist Rd				
15600	CmsC	97042	807	J1
NE Gile Ter				
2200	PTLD	97212	596	J1
SE Gilesford St				
14700	CmsC	97015	658	C6
NE Gilham Av				
10	PTLD	97213	597	E5
10	PTLD	97215	597	E5
SE Gilham Av				
10	PTLD	97213	597	E6
10	PTLD	97215	597	E6
NW Gilkison Rd				
20700	ClbC	97056	474	B7
SE Gill St				
5300	CmsC	97267	687	C3
SW Gillcrest Ct				
5700	PTLD	97221	625	J4
SW Gillenwater Pl				
6500	WasC	97007	623	J5
SE Gillespie Ct				
12000	CmsC	97009	659	F4
SW Gillette Ln				
17800	SRWD	97140	684	E6
NW Gilliam Ln				
8500	PTLD	97229	595	F4
NW Gillihan Rd				
14000	MthC	97231	535	C4
14100	MthC	97231	505	E7
Gillis St				
700	VCVR	98661	537	A5
Gilman Dr				
2200	ORCY	97045	717	E1
Gilmore Rd				
32400	ClbC	97056	444	D6
SW Gilorr St				
1200	MCMV	97128	770	G7
W Gilson Ct				
1500	MCMV	97128	770	F6
W Gilson St				
700	MCMV	97128	770	G6
N Gilwood St				
500	CLTN	97111	711	A7
Gimley Ct				
18000	LKOW	97034	686	B2

STREET Block	City	ZIP	Map#	Grid
SW Gimm Ln				
25300	WasC	97140	714	C3
NW Gina Wy				
-	WasC	97006	594	C5
300	HBRO	97006	594	C5
S Ginger Ct				
1200	CNLS	97113	592	E5
S Ginger St				
1800	CNLS	97113	592	F5
2500	WasC	97113	592	F5
Ginger Wy				
11900	ORCY	97045	717	A4
SW Gingham Ln				
12100	BRTN	97008	655	B1
SW Gingko Ct				
15000	SRWD	97140	714	H1
SE Ginny Ln				
4100	CmsC	97267	657	B7
SE Gino Ln				
2600	MWKE	97222	656	J3
NE Ginseng Dr				
100	ECDA	97023	750	C3
SE Ginseng Dr				
100	ECDA	97023	750	C4
Girard St				
-	ORCY	97045	717	D4
N Girard St				
4700	PTLD	97203	566	B4
Glacier Av				
34500	STHN	97051	414	H1
SE Glacier Av				
1700	GSHM	97080	629	G5
SE Glacier Ct				
2500	GSHM	97080	629	G5
NW Glacier Ln				
14700	WasC	97006	594	J5
SE Glacier Ln				
1200	GSHM	97080	629	G4
Glacier St				
100	ORCY	97045	717	A3
SW Glacier Wy				
29300	WNVL	97070	715	C7
Glacier Lilly St				
4100	LKOW	97035	656	A5
Glacier Lily				
-	TGRD	97223	655	D3
SW Glacier Lily Cir				
12500	TGRD	97223	655	B3
SW Glade Ln				
14800	CmsC	97140	714	H5
SE Gladjen Av				
16800	CmsC	97027	687	E1
16800	CmsC	97267	687	E1
16800	GLDS	97027	687	E1
SE Gladstone Ct				
9900	PTLD	97266	627	H3
13000	PTLD	97236	628	B3
SE Gladstone Dr				
15000	PTLD	97236	628	D3
SE Gladstone St				
2200	PTLD	97202	626	J3
2800	PTLD	97202	627	A3
5200	PTLD	97206	627	C3
8000	PTLD	97266	627	F3
11800	PTLD	97266	628	A3
14800	PTLD	97236	628	D3
NE Glad Tidings Wy				
-	ClkC	98607	538	H6
-	ClkC	98684	538	H6
S Gladys Av				
16200	ORCY	97045	687	F5
SE Gladys St				
6600	HBRO	97123	594	A6
SE Gladys Rose Wy				
15500	DAMA	97009	658	E7
15500	DAMA	97009	688	E1
NE Glass Rd				
24300	CmsC	97002	745	H2
Glass Plant Rd				
-	PTLD	97220	567	H7
NE Glass Plant Rd				
9700	PTLD	97220	567	J6
SW Glastonbury Ln				
13900	WasC	97224	654	H7
SW Glaze Ct				
15700	WasC	97223	654	H4
Gleason Dr				
-	LKOW	97034	686	H1
Gleason St				
900	ORCY	97045	717	D3
NE Glen Ct				
900	ECDA	97023	750	C2
SW Glen Rd				
500	CmsC	97219	656	G4
Glen Ter				
3900	WLIN	97068	686	J3
SW Glenbrook Ct				
10800	WNVL	97070	745	B1
SW Glenbrook Rd				
14500	BRTN	97007	624	J4
SW Glenco Ct				
21500	SRWD	97140	684	F6
NW Glencoe Rd				
1900	HBRO	97124	593	B2
1900	WasC	97124	593	B3
4100	WasC	97124	563	B3
9400	WasC	97133	563	B2
9600	NPNS	97133	563	B2
SE Glencoe Rd				
7800	CmsC	97222	657	F2
8000	CmsC	97236	657	F2
NE Glencoe Oaks Pl				
3100	HBRO	97124	593	B1
NW Glencory St				
100	HBRO	97124	593	B2
SW Glencreek Ct				
14000	WasC	97223	625	G7
NW Glendale Av				
-	PTLD	97231	565	D3
SE Glendale Ct				
2100	HBRO	97123	594	A7
SE Glendon Dr				
13500	CmsC	97015	658	B5
SW Glendora Ln				
26700	WasC	97132	683	E7
NE Glendoveer Ct				
13600	PTLD	97230	598	C5
NW Glendoveer Dr				
8900	PTLD	97231	565	A2
S Glendover Ct				
15000	ORCY	97045	717	H6
Glendover Vil				
-	PTLD	97233	598	D6
SW Gleneagle Dr				
16400	SRWD	97140	684	F6

STREET Block	City	ZIP	Map#	Grid
Glen Eagles Ct				
15100	LKOW	97034	656	B6
Glen Eagles Pl				
2500	LKOW	97034	656	C6
NW Gleneagles Pl				
4000	WasC	97229	594	H1
Glen Eagles Rd				
2400	LKOW	97034	656	B6
2900	LKOW	97035	656	B6
Glen Echo Av				
5400	CmsC	97027	687	C4
5400	CmsC	97267	687	C3
5400	GLDS	97267	687	C4
6100	GLDS	97027	687	D3
SE Glen Echo Av				
4100	CmsC	97267	687	C4
5000	CmsC	97027	687	C4
5200	GLDS	97027	687	C3
5200	GLDS	97267	687	C4
Glen Echo Ct				
6100	GLDS	97027	687	C3
SW Gleneden Ct				
7900	BRTN	97007	624	H6
SW Gleneden Dr				
15300	BRTN	97007	624	H6
NE Glen Ellen Dr				
1300	HBRO	97124	593	C3
Glen Haven Rd				
2100	LKOW	97034	686	C1
SW Glenhaven St				
13100	WasC	97005	595	A7
13100	WasC	97225	595	A7
Glen Hollow Dr				
9400	YmhC	97132	743	A2
NW Glenlakes Pl				
4400	WasC	97006	594	F3
Glenmorrie Dr				
2500	LKOW	97034	686	G1
3100	LKOW	97034	656	G7
Glenmorrie Ln				
1900	LKOW	97034	686	G1
S Glenmorrie Ln				
1900	LKOW	97034	686	G1
Glenmorrie Ter				
1700	LKOW	97034	656	G7
1700	LKOW	97034	686	G1
SW Glenn Ct				
13000	BRTN	97008	625	A5
S Glenn Dr				
13000	CmsC	97042	777	D3
SW Glenn Dr				
12800	BRTN	97008	625	B5
Glenn Jackson Br				
-	MthC	-	567	J3
-	MthC	-	568	A4
-	PTLD	-	568	A6
-	VCVR	-	567	J3
Glenn Jackson Br I-205				
-	MthC	-	567	J3
-	MthC	-	568	A4
-	PTLD	-	568	A6
-	VCVR	-	567	J3
NE Glenn Widing Dr				
11300	PTLD	97220	568	A6
SW Glen Oak Pl				
18600	WasC	97007	654	D4
Glen Oak Rd				
14200	ORCY	97045	717	F6
15800	CmsC	97045	717	H6
SW Glen Park Ct				
17000	WasC	97006	594	G7
NW Glenridge Dr				
13000	WasC	97229	595	A5
SW Glenview Av				
1600	WasC	97225	595	B7
Glenview Ct				
19500	CmsC	97045	717	D5
19500	ORCY	97045	717	D5
Glenview Ln				
32500	ClbC	97056	474	C2
NW Glenway Dr				
-	PTLD	97210	595	J2
-	PTLD	97210	596	A2
Glenwood				
1100	WDLD	98674	385	J1
SW Glenwood Cir				
28600	WNVL	97070	715	G6
Glenwood Ct				
100	ORCY	97045	717	C2
1300	LFYT	97127	741	G7
16400	LKOW	97034	686	G1
SW Glenwood Ct				
6800	WNVL	97070	715	G6
11500	TGRD	97223	655	C2
NE Glenwood Dr				
7400	ClkC	98662	507	F5
SW Glenwood Dr				
7300	WNVL	97070	715	F6
Glenwood St				
100	WDLD	98674	385	J1
SE Glenwood St				
1400	PTLD	97202	626	H5
3400	PTLD	97202	627	B5
7400	PTLD	97206	627	E5
8200	PTLD	97266	627	F5
13000	PTLD	97236	628	B5
S Glisan Rd				
17700	CmsC	97045	718	D3
NE Glisan St				
-	PTLD	97232	596	J5
3900	PTLD	97232	597	A5
4100	PTLD	97213	597	D5
8200	PTLD	97220	597	F5
11400	PTLD	97220	598	C5
11900	PTLD	97230	598	A5
16000	GSHM	97230	598	F5
20000	GSHM	97024	598	J5
20000	GSHM	97030	598	J5
20200	FRVW	97024	598	J5
20400	FRVW	97024	599	A5
20400	GSHM	97024	599	A5
20400	GSHM	97030	599	A5
21400	FRVW	97030	599	B5
21900	WDVL	97060	599	B5
24100	TDLE	97060	599	D5
NW Glisan St				
100	PTLD	97209	596	E5
2000	PTLD	97210	596	D5
SE Gloria Ct				
-	CmsC	97222	657	A4
Gloria Dr				
2600	WLIN	97068	687	A6
NE Glory Ct				
13400	ClkC	98606	479	F7

STREET Block	City	ZIP	Map#	Grid
Glory Ln				
-	MOLA	97038	807	E7
NE Glory Rd				
13000	ClkC	98606	479	F7
N Gloucester Av				
7500	PTLD	97203	566	A4
E Gloucester St				
600	GLDS	97027	687	E4
W Gloucester St				
100	GLDS	97027	687	C4
NW Gloucester Wy				
19900	HBRO	97124	594	C2
Glover Ct				
39300	SNDY	97055	691	A4
SE Glover Rd				
28300	CmsC	97022	689	H7
SE Goboes Ct				
6200	HBRO	97123	593	J7
SE Goddard Av				
16100	CmsC	97015	687	G1
Godon Wy				
14600	ORCY	97045	687	G5
SW Godwin Ct				
8300	WasC	97223	625	F7
Goerig Rd				
800	CtzC	98674	385	G2
Goerig St				
500	WDLD	98674	385	J2
600	WDLD	98674	386	A2
N Goerig St				
1000	WDLD	98674	386	A1
Goetz Rd				
18500	GLDS	97027	687	D3
Goff Pl				
2200	FTGV	97116	591	G4
Goff Rd				
800	FTGV	97116	591	G3
N Going Ct				
1600	PTLD	97217	596	E1
NE Going Pl				
8200	PTLD	97218	597	F1
8200	PTLD	97220	597	G1
N Going St				
10	PTLD	97211	596	G1
10	PTLD	97217	596	G1
NE Going St				
10	PTLD	97211	596	J1
10	PTLD	97217	596	G1
2500	PTLD	97211	597	A1
5500	PTLD	97218	597	D1
8200	PTLD	97220	597	G1
SE Gold Rd				
23400	CmsC	97022	720	F2
NW Gold Canyon Ln				
17100	WasC	97006	594	G1
NW Golden Av				
9500	ClkC	98665	506	F3
Golden Ln				
4400	LKOW	97035	656	A4
SW Golden Ln				
1900	GSHM	97080	628	G4
SE Golden Rd				
5000	HBRO	97123	593	H7
SE Golden St				
5800	HBRO	97123	593	J7
NE Golden Ash Ln				
6400	HBRO	97124	594	B4
SE Goldenback Cir				
20400	ClkC	98607	568	J4
NW Goldendale St				
1000	CMAS	98607	569	B4
SW Goldeneye Ct				
16000	BRTN	97007	654	G4
SW Golden Gate Wy				
5300	WasC	97007	624	F3
Golden Leaf Ln				
-	MCMV	97128	770	H2
SW Golden Pond Ter				
23800	SRWD	97140	714	F1
Goldenrain St				
37200	SNDY	97055	690	H1
SE Golden Rod Ct				
2600	HBRO	97123	623	F1
NW Goldenweed Dr				
6300	WasC	97229	564	H4
SW Goldfinch Ter				
11000	BRTN	97007	654	G2
SE Goldfinch Wy				
9500	HPYV	97236	658	C1
NE Goldie Dr				
400	HBRO	97124	593	C2
Gold Leaf Ln				
57700	ClbC	97053	414	H4
NE Gold Nugget Dr				
22900	ClkC	98604	449	A4
SW Goldstone Pl				
8600	BRTN	97007	624	H7
SW Goldview Wy				
-	BRTN	97007	654	G1
NE Golf Ct				
1300	PTLD	97211	566	J3
SW Golf Course Rd				
2000	WasC	97113	592	D7
SW Golf Creek Dr				
-	BRTN	97225	595	G7
1700	WasC	97225	595	G7
SW Gonzaga St				
7000	TGRD	97223	655	G4
S Good Ln				
8800	CmsC	97013	776	D3
Goodall Ct				
2100	CmsC	97034	656	C4
2100	LKOW	97034	656	C4
Goodall Rd				
12800	CmsC	97034	656	C4
12800	LKOW	97034	656	C4
12800	PTLD	97034	656	C4
Goodfellow Lakes Rd				
-	CmsC	97011	693	F3
-	CmsC	97055	693	B2
Goodman Ln				
100	STHN	97051	415	A1
Goodrich Ln				
-	YmhC	97114	772	C5
S Goodtime Rd				
31600	CmsC	97038	837	A2
NE Goodwin Rd				
-	ClkC	98682	538	J5
2000	ClkC	98607	538	J5
2000	CMAS	98607	538	J5
2300	ClkC	98607	539	A3
2300	ClkC	98682	539	A4
Gooseberry Rd				
-	CmsC	97023	750	A3

STREET Block	City	ZIP	Map#	Grid
NW Goose Hill Rd				
-	ClkC	98674	386	D2
SE Goosehollow Dr				
15700	CmsC	97009	688	D1
15800	DAMA	97009	688	E1
16200	DAMA	97009	658	D7
Goose Lake Dr				
19500	MrnC	97002	775	C7
SW Gordana Ct				
7400	WasC	97223	655	G2
SE Gordon Ct				
16500	CmsC	97267	687	B1
NW Gordon Rd				
7400	WasC	97113	562	J3
7400	WasC	97124	562	J3
9600	WasC	97133	562	J1
10600	NPNS	97133	562	J2
11000	NPNS	97133	533	A7
11000	NPNS	97133	563	A1
11000	WasC	97133	533	A7
11000	WasC	97133	563	A1
Gordon St				
1000	WDLD	98674	385	J1
NW Gordon St				
3600	PTLD	97210	596	A3
SE Gordon St				
16400	CmsC	97267	687	B1
SE Gordon Creek Rd				
36100	MthC	97019	630	H6
SW Gordons Run				
7000	CmsC	97070	745	G1
7000	WNVL	97070	745	G1
SW Gordy Pl				
9500	WasC	97223	655	F1
SW Goshawk St				
16000	BRTN	97007	654	G3
NE Gospel Ln				
12900	YmhC	97132	711	J3
Goss Wy				
33400	ClbC	97056	474	E5
SW Goucher St				
100	MCMV	97128	770	F6
S Gould Ct				
20900	CmsC	97045	746	H1
Goya St				
10	LKOW	97035	656	A4
SW Grabel Rd				
30000	WasC	97113	623	B3
30000	WasC	97123	623	B3
SW Grabhorn Rd				
7300	WasC	97007	624	C6
9400	WasC	97007	654	C3
NE Grace Av				
10	BGND	98604	448	C4
900	ClkC	98604	448	C4
SE Grace Av				
10	BGND	98604	448	C7
1000	ClkC	98604	448	C7
Grace Ln				
-	CmsC	97013	776	J2
-	CmsC	97013	777	C3
-	CmsC	97042	777	C4
-	CmsC	97045	777	H2
SW Grace Ln				
3000	WasC	97225	625	G2
SE Grace Rd				
31700	MthC	97080	630	C6
Grace St				
900	VCVR	98661	536	J5
SE Grace St				
6600	HBRO	97123	594	A7
Graceland Pl				
700	WLIN	97068	716	E1
SW Gracie St				
20500	WasC	97006	594	C5
Graef Cir				
16600	LKOW	97035	656	A7
16600	LKOW	97035	686	A1
NW Graf St				
15400	WasC	97229	564	H6
NW Graham Cir				
2500	TDLE	97060	599	E2
NE Graham Pl				
6900	PTLD	97213	597	E3
NE Graham Rd				
1100	TDLE	97060	599	G2
24600	CmsC	97002	745	A4
NW Graham Rd				
1500	TDLE	97060	599	F2
46700	WasC	97106	531	D5
SE Graham Rd				
14700	CmsC	97045	568	C1
N Graham St				
10	PTLD	97212	596	G3
10	PTLD	97227	596	F3
NE Graham St				
10	PTLD	97212	596	G3
10	PTLD	97227	596	G3
14800	PTLD	97230	598	D3
SW Grahams Ferry Rd				
22000	TLTN	97062	685	D7
22000	WasC	97062	685	D7
23200	TLTN	97062	715	D1
23200	WasC	97062	715	D1
23200	WasC	97140	715	D1
23700	WNVL	97140	715	C2
27500	CmsC	97070	715	B7
28200	WNVL	97070	715	B7
29600	CmsC	97070	745	A1
29600	CmsC	97140	745	A1
30600	CmsC	97070	744	J2
SW Grainery Pl				
21500	SRWD	97140	684	G6
SW Gram St				
10900	TLTN	97062	685	C7
SW Granada Dr				
17300	WasC	97007	624	F5
NE Grand Av				
10	PTLD	97214	596	G5
10	PTLD	97232	596	G4
3500	PTLD	97212	596	G2
4000	PTLD	97211	596	G1
8000	PTLD	97211	566	H4
NE Grand Av SR-99E				
10	PTLD	97214	596	G5
10	PTLD	97232	596	G4
1600	PTLD	97212	596	G4
SE Grand Av				
-	CmsC	97009	659	G6
-	CmsC	97202	626	G7
-	CmsC	97222	626	G7
-	PTLD	97202	626	G7
10	PTLD	97214	596	G7
10	PTLD	97232	596	G5
2000	PTLD	97214	626	G1
7900	PTLD	97202	626	G6

STREET
Block City ZIP Map# Grid

SE Grand Av SR-99E
10 PTLD 97214 596 G7
10 PTLD 97232 596 G5
2000 PTLD 97214 626 G1
2800 PTLD 97202 626 G1
Grand Blvd
500 VCVR 98661 536 J5
500 VCVR 98661 537 A4
N Grand Blvd
100 VCVR 98661 536 J6
S Grand Blvd
100 VCVR 98661 536 J6
Grand Pl
1300 VCVR 98661 537 A5
SE Grand St
16100 DAMA 97009 688 E2
NE Grandhaven Dr
500 MCMV 97128 770 J2
3400 YmhC 97128 770 J2
3800 YmhC 97128 771 A1
Grandhaven St
- MCMV 97128 771 A2
NE Grandhaven St
900 MCMV 97128 770 J2
900 MCMV 97128 771 A2
NW Grandhaven St
800 MCMV 97128 770 J2
Grand Oak Dr
3500 NWBG 97132 713 F7
Grand Oaks Dr
5600 LKOW 97035 655 J4
SW Grandpa's Ln
- WasC 97225 595 E6
SE Grand Ridge Dr
4600 ClkC 98607 568 H4
NW Grandview Av
- PTLD 97231 565 F5
Grand View Ct
17200 LKOW 97034 686 G1
SE Grandview Ct
1900 CmsC 97267 656 J7
SW Grandview Ln
14500 WasC 97224 654 J6
NW Grandview Pl
13900 WasC 97106 531 F4
SE Grandview Ter
9200 CmsC 97236 627 G7
9200 PTLD 97236 627 G7
SE Grand Vista Dr
11800 CmsC 97015 657 J7
11900 CmsC 97015 658 A7
SW Grandvista Dr
24500 WasC 97140 683 H7
Grange St
100 MOLA 97038 837 E1
SE Grange St
27700 CmsC 97009 659 G5
NE Grange Hall Rd
- MthC 97019 600 H5
SW Granite Ct
16000 BRTN 97007 654 G1
SW Grant Av
12100 TGRD 97223 655 E4
S Grant Ct
1000 CNBY 97013 746 D7
SE Grant Ct
3800 PTLD 97214 627 B1
9700 PTLD 97216 627 H1
13100 PTLD 97233 628 B1
SW Grant Ct
- TGRD 97223 655 D4
Grant Dr
17900 CmsC 97045 717 G2
SE Grant Ln
17400 PTLD 97233 628 F1
NW Grant Pl
4600 VCVR 98663 536 F1
Grant St
1100 ORCY 97045 717 E1
2600 VCVR 98660 536 F2
4300 WLIN 97068 687 A7
N Grant St
- LFYT 97127 741 H6
- YmhC 97114 741 H6
100 CNBY 97013 746 C6
500 NWBG 97132 713 B7
NE Grant St
1800 HBRO 97124 593 F4
NW Grant St
4500 VCVR 98660 536 F1
4500 VCVR 98663 536 F1
S Grant St
100 CNBY 97013 746 C6
100 NWBG 97132 713 B7
400 NWBG 97132 743 B1
1100 CNBY 97013 776 C1
3700 WHGL 98671 570 C7
3700 WHGL 98671 600 D1
SE Grant St
600 PTLD 97214 626 H1
3900 PTLD 97214 627 B1
4100 PTLD 97215 627 B1
9300 PTLD 97216 627 G1
11400 PTLD 97216 628 A1
15700 PTLD 97233 628 E1
18700 GSHM 97233 628 H1
SW Grant St
- MthC 97221 595 J7
- PTLD 97221 595 J7
10 PTLD 97201 626 F1
400 PTLD 97201 596 B7
W Grant St
100 CLTN 97111 741 A1
600 CLTN 97111 711 A7
SW Grant Wy
- TDLE 97060 599 F5
SW Granville Ct
- WNVL 97070 745 H3
Grape St
- ClbC 97056 474 A4
S Grapevine Rd
21000 CmsC 97068 686 F6
21700 WLIN 97068 686 F7
SW Graphite Ter
9000 BRTN 97007 624 H7
9000 BRTN 97007 654 E1
S Grasle Rd
17800 CmsC 97045 718 D3
SW Grass Ct
7700 WNVL 97070 715 F7
Grassy Ln
35500 STHN 97051 415 A1
SE Gravel Ln
23900 CmsC 97022 720 C2

Gravel Pl
- ClkC 98604 417 D7
SW Graven St
11500 WasC 97224 685 C1
N Gravenstein Av
7500 PTLD 97217 566 D5
SW Gravenstein Ln
8800 TGRD 97224 655 E7
NW Gravenstein St
2900 CMAS 98607 569 B2
S Graves Rd
13900 CmsC 97042 777 E5
N Gray St
1300 CNLS 97113 592 E4
SE Gray St
8200 CmsC 97206 627 F7
8200 CmsC 97236 627 F7
SW Grayling Ln
14500 BRTN 97005 624 J4
14500 BRTN 97007 624 J4
SW Graystone Dr
- DNDE 97115 742 H3
Great Blue Rd
- RDGF 98642 446 A1
Great Oak Dr
- HPYV 97236 657 H3
SW Grebe Ln
14600 BRTN 97007 654 J1
N Greeley Av
3000 PTLD 97217 596 D1
3000 PTLD 97227 596 E2
4600 PTLD 97217 566 D7
NW Greeley St
700 CMAS 98607 569 D4
SW Green Av
700 PTLD 97205 596 D5
SE Green Ct
3100 CmsC 97267 687 A1
6000 HBRO 97123 593 J6
NW Green Ln
18600 WasC 97229 564 E5
18600 WasC 97231 564 E5
SW Green Ln
7800 BRTN 97008 625 B6
Green St
- LKOW 97034 656 G7
SE Green St
6200 HBRO 97123 593 J6
S Greenacres Dr
58900 STHN 97051 415 A2
Green Acres Ln
200 LKOW 97034 686 G1
Greenann Ct
8300 CmsC 97027 687 F2
Green Bluff Dr
17400 LKOW 97034 686 F2
Greenbrae Ct
2900 LKOW 97034 686 H1
Greenbrae Dr
2900 LKOW 97034 686 H1
NW Greenbriar Dr
8000 ClkC 98665 506 G4
Greenbriar Ln NE
11200 MrnC 97032 774 G7
NW Greenbriar Pl
1200 MCMV 97128 770 F3
NW Greenbriar Ter
3000 PTLD 97210 596 B4
NW Greenbrier Pkwy
14400 BRTN 97006 594 J5
Greenbrier Rd
16700 LKOW 97034 686 B1
Greenbrier Vil
- PTLD 97239 626 E4
SW Greenburg Rd
9200 BRTN 97008 655 E1
9200 WasC 97008 655 E1
9200 WasC 97223 655 E1
11500 TGRD 97223 655 E3
Greene St
2100 WLIN 97068 716 H1
S Greenfield Dr
17600 CmsC 97045 717 G2
SW Greenfield Dr
- KNGC 97224 655 B7
- TGRD 97224 655 A5
- WasC 97224 655 B7
13200 TGRD 97223 655 A5
Greenfield Vil
- TGRD 97223 655 A3
SE Green Fir Dr
11700 CmsC 97015 657 H5
SW Greengate Dr
16900 SRWD 97140 714 F1
SW Greengate Pl
23000 SRWD 97140 684 F7
23000 SRWD 97140 714 F1
NW Greenhaven Ter
4200 WasC 97229 595 A1
SW Green Heron Dr
17000 SRWD 97140 684 F4
SW Greenhill Ln
9000 WasC 97062 715 E1
SE Green Hills Ct
15400 CmsC 97236 658 D3
15400 HPYV 97236 658 D4
SW Greenhills Wy
4000 PTLD 97221 626 A1
SW Greenhouse Ln
7900 BRTN 97225 625 F1
SW Greening Ln
8800 TGRD 97224 655 E7
SW Greenland Dr
16300 TGRD 97224 685 D1
SW Greenleaf Ct
4100 PTLD 97221 626 B1
15600 TGRD 97223 655 D7
Greenleaf Dr
20600 CmsC 97055 691 E6
SW Greenleaf Dr
4000 PTLD 97221 626 B1
SW Greenleaf Pl
13400 WasC 97005 625 E4
NW Greenleaf Rd
300 MthC 97229 595 H5
600 PTLD 97229 595 G4
SW Greenleaf Ter
10200 TGRD 97224 655 D7
Greenlink Wy
200 NWBG 97132 713 G7
NE Green Meadows Wy
34300 SPSE 97056 474 G1
NW Green Mountain Rd
18100 WasC 97106 531 G1

Green Mountain St
37200 SNDY 97055 690 H1
SE Greenpark Cir
14900 VCVR 98683 568 C1
SE Greenpark St
15000 VCVR 98683 568 D1
Green Peace Ln
17400 CmsC 97045 718 B1
Greenridge Ct
10 LKOW 97035 656 C4
Greenridge Dr
200 LKOW 97035 656 B4
NE Greenridge Pl
200 HBRO 97124 594 B4
NE Greenridge Ter
100 HBRO 97124 594 A5
SW Greens Wy
15600 TGRD 97224 655 D7
SW Greensboro Wy
4500 WasC 97007 624 H3
Greensborough Ct
5000 LKOW 97035 655 J5
SE Green Slope Rd
21300 WasC 97007 654 B1
SW Greenspark Ter
8800 TGRD 97224 655 E6
E Greensprings St
65400 CmsC 97011 723 J1
SW Greens View Ct
7400 WNVL 97070 745 F3
SW Greensward Ln
8500 TGRD 97224 655 E6
NE Greensword Dr
1200 HBRO 97124 593 J3
NE Green Tee Ct
13400 PTLD 97230 598 B6
Greentree Av
16900 LKOW 97034 686 D1
Greentree Cir
1400 LKOW 97034 686 D1
S Green Tree Dr
14800 CmsC 97045 747 G1
Greentree Rd
1100 LKOW 97034 686 D1
1300 LKOW 97034 656 E7
Green Valley Dr
700 NWBG 97132 713 C5
SW Green Valley Ter
7600 WasC 97225 625 G4
SW Greenvalley Ter
- WasC 97225 625 G3
SE Greenview Av
14800 CmsC 97267 657 F7
NW Green View Ct
1200 MCMV 97128 770 F4
S Green View Dr
18300 CmsC 97045 718 E7
NW Green View Ln
10400 WasC 97229 595 D4
N Greenview Wy
700 CNBY 97013 746 D4
NW Greenville Rd
39500 WasC 97113 562 C2
39500 WasC 97116 562 A1
40700 WasC 97116 561 G1
SE Green Vista Dr
10800 CmsC 97222 657 F2
SW Greenway Av
2700 PTLD 97201 626 C1
2800 PTLD 97239 626 C1
SW Greenway Blvd
7000 BRTN 97008 625 B7
SW Greenway Cir
1700 CmsC 97068 686 C4
Greenway Dr
- NWBG 97132 713 G7
NE Greenway Dr
10 GSHM 97080 629 G3
1100 GSHM 97030 629 F1
23200 WDVL 97060 599 C4
SE Greenway Dr
200 GSHM 97080 629 F3
SE Greenway Ln
100 GSHM 97080 629 F3
NE Greenway Pl
1000 GSHM 97030 629 H2
Greenway Rdg
- BRTN 97008 655 B1
N Greenwich Av
6500 PTLD 97217 566 E5
SW Greenwich Dr
6800 WasC 97225 595 H7
E Greenwood Av
23800 CmsC 97011 724 B3
23800 CmsC 97067 724 B3
SW Greenwood Cir
5000 TLTN 97062 685 J4
NE Greenwood Dr
7700 VCVR 98662 537 E2
NW Greenwood Dr
13400 WasC 97229 565 A7
SW Greenwood Dr
7400 WasC 97223 625 G7
SW Greenwood Pl
5200 TLTN 97062 685 J4
Greenwood Rd
100 LKOW 97034 656 F6
SW Greenwood Rd
1600 MthC 97219 656 G3
SW Greenwood St
11900 WasC 97005 625 B1
Greenwood Acres
- ClkC 98665 506 H4
SE Greetings Dr
- CmsC 97236 658 E4
- HPYV 97236 658 E4
Gregory Ct
5000 CmsC 97068 686 J6
5000 WLIN 97068 686 J6
NW Gregory Dr
1400 ClkC 98665 506 E5
SW Gregory Dr
2300 CmsC 97068 716 C2
21400 WasC 97006 594 B5
SE Greiner Ln
12100 HPYV 97236 658 A2
Grenfell Lp
- MCMV 97128 770 E3
NE Gren Fels Dr
11000 ClkC 98604 447 J2
11000 ClkC 98604 448 A2
NW Grenoble Ln
- MthC 97229 595 B1
SW Grenoble St
11600 WNVL 97070 715 B7

SW Grenwolde Pl
2600 PTLD 97201 596 C7
2600 PTLD 97201 626 B1
Gresham-fairview Tr
- GSHM 97030 628 H3
Grey Av
18000 SNDY 97055 690 H4
Greycliffs Ct
400 STHN 97051 385 D6
Greycliffs Dr
- STHN 97051 385 D6
Grey Cliffs Rd
400 STHN 97051 385 D5
NW Greyhawk Dr
16700 WasC 97006 594 G1
Greystoke Dr
5300 CmsC 97035 655 J6
5300 LKOW 97035 655 J6
SW Greystone Ct
15600 BRTN 97006 594 H5
S Gribble Rd
8100 CmsC 97013 776 B6
SW Griffin Dr
6500 BRTN 97223 625 H5
SW Griffin Pl
6100 BRTN 97008 625 C4
NE Griffin Oaks St
1800 HBRO 97124 593 E2
SW Griffith Dr
4600 BRTN 97005 625 C3
S Griffith Ln
14000 CmsC 97042 747 F7
14000 CmsC 97042 777 F1
14000 CmsC 97045 747 F7
14000 CmsC 97045 777 F1
NW Griffith Rd
4100 ClkC 98674 386 C5
SE Griffy Ln
- CmsC 97015 687 H1
Grim Rd NE
19400 MrnC 97002 775 B6
19400 MrnC 97032 775 C7
SW Grimson Ct
16100 TGRD 97224 685 D1
NW Grist Mill Dr
26100 WasC 97124 533 G4
26100 WasC 97133 533 G4
NW Groce St
3600 PTLD 97210 596 B3
SE Grogran St
3600 MWKE 97222 657 A3
SW Groner Rd
- WasC 97123 683 E3
- WasC 97132 683 E3
S Gronlund Rd
17000 CmsC 97045 688 D4
SW Grosbeak Ter
11600 BRTN 97007 654 E3
NW Grossen Dr
23500 WasC 97124 563 J1
23500 WasC 97124 564 A1
NE Grouse Dr
35700 ClkC 98671 540 F4
Grouse Ln NE
11500 MrnC 97002 744 H6
Grouse Ter
10 LKOW 97035 656 A3
E Grove Av
28000 CmsC 97067 724 C7
Grove Cir S
- ORCY 97045 717 F5
SE Grove Ct
12300 MWKE 97222 657 D4
SW Grove Ln
19800 WasC 97007 654 C5
SE Grove Lp
12100 MWKE 97222 657 C4
NE Grove Rd
500 ClkC 98665 506 G4
SW Grove Rd
400 ECDA 97023 750 B4
Grove St
700 VCVR 98661 537 A5
5300 WLIN 97068 687 C6
NE Grove St
- ClkC 98665 506 G4
SE Grove Wy
- VCVR 98607 538 H7
NW Groveland Dr
24200 HBRO 97124 563 J6
24200 WasC 97124 563 H5
NW Groveland Rd
6900 WasC 97124 563 G5
SW Grover Ct
5700 MthC 97221 625 J1
SW Grover St
- PTLD 97201 626 D1
- PTLD 97239 626 D2
3500 PTLD 97221 626 B1
NW Groveshire Av
12300 BNKS 97106 531 J6
NW Guam St
3100 PTLD 97210 596 B2
SE Guido Bocci Dr
5000 MWKE 97222 657 C3
SW Guild Ln
- WasC 97123 653 F7
SE Guilford Ct
3400 MWKE 97222 657 A4
SE Guilford Dr
12200 MWKE 97222 657 A4
SW Guiss Wy
32000 WNVL 97070 745 C1
Gulf Dr
6800 VCVR 98661 537 D6
6800 VCVR 98664 537 D6
SW Gull Ct
15400 BRTN 97007 654 H2
SW Gull Dr
14700 BRTN 97007 654 H2
SW Gull Pl
10100 BRTN 97007 654 H1
Gum
- CmsC 97015 657 J7
E Gumjuwac Ln
23500 CmsC 97011 724 A2
23500 CmsC 97067 724 A2
Gun Club Rd
- YmhC 97111 741 A5
- YmhC 97128 741 A5
NE Gun Club Rd
10000 YmhC 97111 741 E6
10000 YmhC 97128 741 E6
SE Gunderson Rd
33100 CmsC 97009 690 D5

SE Gunderson Rd
33700 CmsC 97055 690 F4
SW Gunther Ln
5700 PTLD 97219 655 H3
S Gunzer Dr
16100 CmsC 97045 688 F6
SE Gurnee Av
16800 CmsC 97027 687 E2
16800 CmsC 97267 687 E1
17000 GLDS 97027 687 E2
NW Gurney St
- PTLD 97231 565 F4
NE Guston Ct
100 HBRO 97124 594 B5
100 WasC 97124 594 B5
NE Gwen Ct
300 HBRO 97124 593 C2
SW Gwen Dr
25500 WNVL 97070 715 F3

H

W H Av
400 LCTR 98629 416 G1
H Cir
3400 WHGL 98671 570 C5
H St
- PTLD 97219 655 J3
10 CBAC 97018 385 C3
600 CMAS 98607 569 J5
700 CBAC 97051 385 C3
700 ClbC 97051 385 C3
900 WHGL 98671 569 J5
1000 WHGL 98671 570 A5
3900 VCVR 98663 536 G2
NW H St
- WasC 97006 594 C5
Ha Ln
35100 ClbC 97051 414 J1
35100 STHN 97051 414 J1
59500 ClbC 97051 384 J7
59500 STHN 97051 384 J7
Haberman Rd
200 CtzC 98674 385 E1
NE Hacienda Av
1500 GSHM 97030 629 F1
SE Hacienda Av
1000 GSHM 97080 629 F4
SE Hacienda Cir
700 GSHM 97080 629 F3
NE Hacienda Ct
1400 GSHM 97030 629 H2
SE Hacienda Ct
100 GSHM 97080 629 F3
7200 HBRO 97123 594 A7
21900 DAMA 97009 659 B5
SE Hacienda Dr
12500 DAMA 97009 659 B5
NE Hacienda Ln
1100 GSHM 97030 629 H2
SE Hacienda Lp
2600 GSHM 97080 629 F5
NE Hacienda Pl
400 GSHM 97030 629 F2
SE Hacienda St
6000 HBRO 97123 593 J7
7400 HBRO 97123 594 B7
SW Hackamore Ct
12800 BRTN 97008 625 A7
SW Hackett Ln
23100 WasC 97007 623 J6
E Hackett Creek Ct
21500 CmsC 97049 693 J7
NW Hackney Dr
15600 WasC 97229 564 H7
Hadley Rd
1100 NWBG 97132 713 F6
SE Hagen Rd
16200 CmsC 97236 658 E3
16200 HPYV 97236 658 E3
16200 HPYV 97236 658 E3
SE Hager Ln
3500 CmsC 97267 657 B6
Hagey Rd
23000 YmhC 97115 742 J2
23000 YmhC 97115 743 A2
SW Hagg Ln
20700 WasC 97007 624 B3
NW Hahn Rd
35700 WasC 97133 532 G4
36800 WasC 97106 532 D4
Haida Ct
14900 ORCY 97045 717 G6
SW Haide Rd
18800 SRWD 97140 684 D6
18800 WasC 97140 684 D6
SE Haig Dr
17400 PTLD 97236 628 F2
17600 GSHM 97236 628 G2
18000 GSHM 97030 628 G2
SE Haig St
600 PTLD 97202 626 G2
3600 PTLD 97202 627 B2
4500 PTLD 97206 627 C2
15200 PTLD 97236 628 E2
N Haight Av
3500 PTLD 97227 596 F2
4000 PTLD 97217 596 F1
10900 PTLD 97217 566 G1
SW Hail Pl
22000 SRWD 97140 684 E6
S Haines Rd
22000 CmsC 97013 746 G5
23200 CNBY 97013 746 G5
SW Haines St
5500 PTLD 97219 655 H3
6400 TGRD 97223 655 H3
SW Halcyon Rd
3500 CmsC 97062 686 A4
4200 TLTN 97062 686 A4
NE Hale Av
2300 GSHM 97030 599 E7
3000 TDLE 97060 599 E7
SE Hale Av
700 GSHM 97080 629 E4
SE Hale Ct
1500 GSHM 97080 629 E4
NE Hale Dr
10 GSHM 97030 629 E2
10 GSHM 97080 629 E3
SE Hale Dr
200 GSHM 97080 629 E3
NE Hale Pl
1500 GSHM 97030 629 E1

SE Hale Pl
600 GSHM 97080 629 E3
SE Hale St
6600 CmsC 97222 657 D1
SE Hale Wy
2600 GSHM 97080 629 E5
Haley Ct
900 ORCY 97045 717 C3
SE Haley Rd
27100 CmsC 97009 659 H3
29700 CmsC 97009 660 A3
NW Half Mile Ln
3400 WasC 97116 591 A1
3800 WasC 97116 561 B7
SW Halite Ct
9800 BRTN 97007 654 H1
SW Hall Blvd
- WasC 97005 625 A2
3500 BRTN 97005 625 C7
5900 BRTN 97008 625 B4
8600 BRTN 97223 625 D7
8700 TGRD 97008 625 D7
8700 TGRD 97223 625 D7
8900 BRTN 97223 655 E1
9100 BRTN 97008 655 E1
9100 TGRD 97223 655 F7
9100 WasC 97008 655 E1
9100 WasC 97223 655 E1
13800 TGRD 97224 655 F5
Hall Cir
200 RDGF 98642 415 J6
Hall Ct
1800 WLIN 97068 716 H1
39900 SNDY 97055 691 B3
SE Hall Ct
3200 TDLE 97060 599 J7
SW Hall Ct
5200 BRTN 97005 625 B4
SE Hall Ln
3100 TDLE 97060 599 J7
Hall St
10 RDGF 98642 415 J6
1900 WLIN 97068 716 H1
SE Hall St
- CmsC 97009 659 G6
SW Hall St
400 PTLD 97201 596 E7
22100 SRWD 97140 684 H7
33400 SPSE 97056 444 E7
Hallberg Ct
18500 CmsC 97035 685 J2
N Halleck St
500 PTLD 97217 566 F4
NE Halleck St
100 PTLD 97211 566 G4
Hallinan Cir
1100 LKOW 97034 656 F7
1100 LKOW 97034 686 F1
Hallinan Ct
1100 LKOW 97034 656 F7
Hallinan St
1000 LKOW 97034 656 F7
1000 LKOW 97034 686 F1
Hallmark Dr
15400 LKOW 97035 656 A6
Hall PLace Rd
- ClkC 98642 415 H7
- ClkC 98642 445 G2
SW Halsey Lp
- TDLE 97060 599 F4
Halsey St
100 STHN 97051 385 A7
NE Halsey St
200 PTLD 97232 596 H4
2600 PTLD 97232 597 A4
3900 PTLD 97213 597 D4
8400 PTLD 97220 597 J4
11300 PTLD 97220 598 A4
11900 PTLD 97230 598 D4
16000 GSHM 97230 598 E4
20000 FRVW 97024 598 J4
20500 FRVW 97024 599 A5
22600 WDVL 97060 599 A5
24300 TDLE 97060 599 D4
SE Halsey St
500 TDLE 97060 599 E4
1900 WDVL 97060 599 D4
NE Halsey St Frontage Rd
- PTLD 97220 597 G4
SW Halter Ter
8400 BRTN 97008 625 A7
SE Halyard Ln
1500 VCVR 98661 536 H6
NE Hamblet St
2400 PTLD 97212 596 H2
2600 PTLD 97212 597 A2
NW Hamel Dr
12600 WasC 97229 565 B7
SW Hamilton Ct
2500 PTLD 97239 626 C3
4800 PTLD 97221 626 A3
6700 WasC 97225 625 H3
SW Hamilton St
2400 PTLD 97239 626 A3
3400 PTLD 97221 626 B3
5200 PTLD 97221 625 J3
6300 PTLD 97225 625 H3
6300 WasC 97225 625 H3
SW Hamilton Ter
4100 PTLD 97239 626 E3
SW Hamilton Wy
6000 PTLD 97221 625 H3
6000 WasC 97225 625 H3
Hamilton Ridge Dr
- SNDY 97055 690 H3
SW Hamlet Ct
8600 TGRD 97224 655 F7
SE Hamlet Dr
31200 CmsC 97009 660 B6
SW Hamlet St
8500 TGRD 97224 655 F7
N Hamlin Av
8900 PTLD 97217 566 C3
SW Hamlin Ct
16400 WasC 97007 624 G3
Hammerle St
2000 WLIN 97068 687 A6
NE Hammond Ct
29000 ClkC 98604 418 D5
NW Hammond Ct
12700 BNKS 97106 531 H5
12700 BNKS 97106 532 B6
NE Hammond Rd
14300 ClkC 98604 418 D4

SW Hammond Ter
- BRTN 97007 624 H5
SE Hampshire Ct
13700 CmsC 97236 658 B5
SE Hampshire Dr
13700 CmsC 97236 658 B5
SE Hampshire Ln
16300 CmsC 97267 687 C1
SW Hampshire St
3000 PTLD 97205 596 B5
SW Hampshire Ter
15800 WasC 97224 654 H7
SE Hampshire Wy
13700 CmsC 97236 658 B5
NW Hampson Av
- MthC 97229 565 C4
- PTLD 97229 565 C4
SE Hampton Av
2900 TDLE 97060 599 G7
Hampton Ct
1100 FTGV 97116 592 A6
4800 LKOW 97035 655 J4
4800 LKOW 97035 656 A4
E Hampton Ct
3900 WLIN 97068 686 J7
NE Hampton Ct
2500 HBRO 97124 593 F4
S Hampton Ct
3800 WLIN 97068 686 H7
3800 WLIN 97068 716 J1
SW Hampton Ct
13000 TGRD 97223 655 A4
Hampton Dr
12300 CmsC 97045 717 B4
12300 ORCY 97045 717 B4
Hampton Ln
600 NWBG 97132 713 C5
NW Hampton Ln
2300 PTLD 97229 595 D1
SE Hampton Lp
3100 TDLE 97060 599 G7
SW Hampton Pl
- WasC 97225 625 F4
NW Hampton Rd
- MthC 97231 535 C7
- PTLD 97231 535 C6
SW Hampton St
6600 TGRD 97223 655 G4
Hampton Hights
- TDLE 97060 599 F4
NE Hancock Ct
6600 PTLD 97213 597 E4
11200 PTLD 97220 597 J4
15200 PTLD 97230 598 D4
16700 GSHM 97230 598 F4
SW Hancock Ct
12200 TGRD 97223 655 B5
NE Hancock Dr
9200 PTLD 97220 597 G4
NE Hancock Rd
27600 ClkC 98607 509 H7
E Hancock St
2200 NWBG 97132 713 E7
3200 YmhC 97132 713 E7
E Hancock St SR-99W
100 NWBG 97132 713 C7
E Hancock St SR-219
700 NWBG 97132 713 C7
N Hancock St
10 PTLD 97212 596 G3
100 PTLD 97227 596 F4
NE Hancock St
10 PTLD 97227 596 G3
400 PTLD 97212 596 J4
2600 PTLD 97212 597 A4
4100 PTLD 97213 597 B4
8200 PTLD 97220 597 F4
11900 PTLD 97220 598 A4
14400 PTLD 97230 598 D4
22600 FRVW 97024 599 C4
W Hancock St
100 NWBG 97132 713 B7
W Hancock St SR-99W
100 NWBG 97132 713 B7
SW Hancock Wy
17500 WasC 97006 594 F6
SE Handel Av
1100 HBRO 97123 593 C7
SE Handel Pl
900 HBRO 97123 593 C7
SE Handley St
100 MCMV 97128 770 H6
SW Handley St
18000 SRWD 97140 684 E6
18200 WasC 97140 684 E6
N Haney Dr
- PTLD 97211 566 G2
- PTLD 97217 566 G2
NE Hanis St
- PTLD 97218 567 E5
Hankey Rd
- STHN 97051 384 G6
34000 ClbC 97051 384 G6
35400 ClbC 97051 385 A6
35400 STHN 97051 385 A6
Hankins Dr
100 STHN 97051 385 A7
300 ClbC 97051 385 A7
SE Hanna Ct
8400 CmsC 97015 687 H1
NE Hannah Ct
4300 HBRO 97124 593 G4
SE Hanna Harvester Dr
2000 MWKE 97222 656 J1
Hanneman Ct
17100 CmsC 97027 687 F2
17100 CmsC 97267 687 F2
SE Hanover Ct
2000 HBRO 97123 623 E2
SE Hanover St
1700 HBRO 97123 623 E2
Hansen Ln
100 WDLD 98674 386 A1
SE Hans Nagel Rd
3500 ClkC 98671 570 H6
SE Hanson Ct
17600 GLDS 97015 687 F3
SW Hanson Rd
12800 BRTN 97008 625 B6
NE Hantwick Rd
2300 ClkC 98604 419 D6
23100 ClkC 98675 419 C4
SE Hanwood Ln
15500 CmsC 97267 656 H7

Portland Street Index

STREET
Block City ZIP Map# Grid

SE Happiness Hill Ln
21400 CmsC 97022 690 A7
NE Happy Hill Ln
23500 YmhC 97132 713 B1
SE Happy Valley Ct
13800 HPYV 97236 658 C2
SE Happy Valley Dr
10600 HPYV 97236 658 C3
NE Haps Ln
13500 YmhC 97132 711 J4
13500 YmhC 97132 712 A4
NW Harbor Blvd
9400 PTLD 97231 565 E3
NW Harbor Ct
- PTLD 97231 565 E3
SW Harbor Dr
- PTLD 97201 596 F7
- PTLD 97201 626 F1
1400 MCMV 97128 770 F5
NW Harbor Ln
14000 WasC 97229 595 A1
SW Harbor Pl
1800 PTLD 97201 596 F7
SW Harbor Wy
1500 PTLD 97201 596 F7
N Harborgate St
8700 PTLD 97203 535 F6
NW Harborside Dr
1700 VCVR 98660 536 C3
NW Harborton Dr
12200 MthC 97231 535 C6
12200 PTLD 97231 535 C6
N Harbour Dr
900 PTLD 97217 566 F1
SW Harcourt Ter
15400 TGRD 97224 655 G7
N Harding Av
2100 PTLD 97227 596 E3
Harding Blvd
100 ORCY 97045 717 C2
NW Harding Ct
10500 WasC 97229 595 D3
S Harding Rd
- CmsC 97023 719 C2
15800 CmsC 97045 689 C7
17100 CmsC 97045 719 C2
Hardway Ct
18100 CmsC 97027 687 D2
18100 CmsC 97267 687 D2
18100 GLDS 97027 687 D2
NW Hardy Av
9300 PTLD 97231 565 E3
NE Harewood Pl
1900 HBRO 97124 593 D2
NE Harewood St
100 HBRO 97124 593 B3
100 WasC 97124 593 B3
SW Hargis Rd
13600 BRTN 97008 625 A6
13900 BRTN 97008 624 J6
16500 WasC 97007 624 G6
16800 BRTN 97007 624 G6
NW Harlan St
- HBRO 97124 593 J2
- HBRO 97124 594 A2
SE Harlene St
5400 MWKE 97222 657 C3
SW Harlequin Dr
12300 BRTN 97007 654 H4
Harley Av
15600 ORCY 97045 687 F5
SE Harlow Av
400 TDLE 97060 599 G4
SE Harlow Ct
900 TDLE 97060 599 G4
NE Harlow Pl
700 TDLE 97060 599 G3
SE Harlow Pl
1100 TDLE 97060 599 G4
SE Harlow St
5500 MWKE 97222 657 C3
SE Harmon Ct
14800 CmsC 97267 657 C6
SE Harmony Dr
7200 CmsC 97222 657 E3
N Harmony Ln
1100 YmhC 97132 713 G6
SE Harmony Pl
3900 ClkC 98607 568 H3
SW Harmony Pl
5800 WasC 97007 624 C4
SE Harmony Rd
5700 CmsC 97222 657 D4
5700 MWKE 97222 657 D4
8000 CmsC 97015 657 F4
8000 CmsC 97236 657 F4
S Harms Rd
26200 CmsC 97013 776 F5
SW Harness Ln
13500 BRTN 97008 655 A1
13700 BRTN 97008 654 F2
SE Harney Ct
3300 PTLD 97222 627 A7
9200 PTLD 97266 627 G7
SE Harney Dr
4500 PTLD 97206 627 C7
5800 CmsC 97206 627 D7
Harney St
2600 VCVR 98660 536 F3
NW Harney St
4600 VCVR 98663 536 F1
5800 VCVR 98663 506 F7
SE Harney St
- PTLD 97222 627 B7
10 PTLD 97202 626 G7
2700 PTLD 97202 627 A7
4200 PTLD 97206 627 B7
7400 MthC 97206 627 E7
8200 PTLD 97266 627 F7
14100 PTLD 97236 628 C7
Harney Wy
300 VCVR 98661 537 B6
Harney Heights Ln
1300 VCVR 98661 537 A4
SE Harnish St
7200 HBRO 97123 594 A6
SE Harold Av
15500 CmsC 97267 657 B7
16100 CmsC 97267 687 B1
Harold Ct
- MCMV 97128 770 G3
SE Harold Ct
3300 PTLD 97202 627 A4
4000 CmsC 97267 657 A7

SE Harold St
1500 PTLD 97202 626 H4
3800 PTLD 97202 627 B4
7000 PTLD 97206 627 E4
9200 PTLD 97266 627 H4
11500 PTLD 97266 628 A4
13900 PTLD 97236 628 C4
Harper Ln
700 STHN 97051 415 A2
Harriet Av
17400 CmsC 97045 717 E1
17400 ORCY 97045 717 E1
NW Harriet Ct
16000 WasC 97006 594 H2
Harrington Av
5900 CmsC 97035 655 H7
NW Harrington Rd
35500 WasC 97113 562 E2
37000 WasC 97106 562 D2
Harris Av
100 STHN 97051 415 A1
NW Harris Av
- PTLD 97231 565 E4
Harris Ln
400 ORCY 97045 717 D3
S Harris Rd
20900 CmsC 97045 689 B7
SE Harrison Ct
7100 PTLD 97215 627 E1
13500 PTLD 97233 628 B1
NE Harrison Rd
30000 ClkC 98604 418 A4
30400 ClkC 98604 417 J3
NW Harrison Rd
37500 WasC 97106 532 C5
37500 WasC 97133 532 E6
Harrison St
- CLTN 97111 741 A1
100 FRVW 97024 599 B4
500 ORCY 97045 717 D1
1500 ORCY 97045 687 D7
E Harrison St
400 CLTN 97111 741 B1
N Harrison St
100 NWBG 97132 713 B7
S Harrison St
100 NWBG 97132 713 B7
400 NWBG 97132 743 B1
SE Harrison St
500 PTLD 97214 596 G7
1900 MWKE 97222 656 J2
2800 MWKE 97222 657 A2
3200 PTLD 97214 597 B7
4100 PTLD 97215 597 B7
7400 PTLD 97215 627 E1
7700 CmsC 97222 657 E2
8200 PTLD 97216 627 F1
11400 PTLD 97216 628 A1
16900 PTLD 97233 628 F1
17700 GSHM 97233 628 G1
SW Harrison St
1400 PTLD 97201 596 D7
18000 SRWD 97140 714 E1
18000 WasC 97140 714 E1
W Harrison St
10 CLTN 97111 741 A2
NE Harrow St
5200 HBRO 97124 593 G3
NW Harrys Pl
15600 WasC 97106 532 C3
NE Hart Ct
- SPSE 97056 444 F7
SW Hart Dr
17800 WasC 97007 624 E6
SW Hart Pl
7400 BRTN 97008 625 D3
SW Hart Rd
12900 BRTN 97008 625 A6
13900 BRTN 97008 624 H6
14400 BRTN 97007 624 G6
18500 WasC 97007 624 E6
Hart St
100 MOLA 97038 837 E2
SW Hart Wy
17000 WasC 97007 624 F6
SE Hartcliffe Ct
8100 CmsC 97267 657 E6
Hartford Dr
1100 FTGV 97116 591 G2
Hartford Pl
4900 LKOW 97035 655 J6
NW Hartford St
12300 WasC 97229 595 B2
Hartke Lp
500 ORCY 97045 717 B3
NW Hartley Av
10 GSHM 97030 628 H2
SW Hartley Av
10 GSHM 97030 628 H3
1600 GSHM 97080 628 H5
SW Hartley Dr
2700 GSHM 97080 628 H5
N Hartman St
8100 PTLD 97203 565 H2
NW Hartmann Dr
12000 WasC 97106 531 F6
12000 WasC 97116 531 F6
SE Hartnell Av
15100 CmsC 97267 657 E7
NW Hartung Ct
13800 WasC 97229 595 A3
NW Hartwell Pl
1700 WasC 97229 595 D4
NW Hartwick Rd
44400 WasC 97106 531 F4
NW Hartwick Ter
44700 WasC 97106 531 F4
Harvard Av
900 GLDS 97027 687 D3
Harvard Ct
4900 LKOW 97035 655 J4
4900 LKOW 97035 656 A4
Harvard St
600 NWBG 97132 713 C4
N Harvard St
4700 PTLD 97203 566 A5
SE Harvard St
16100 CmsC 97015 687 H1
Harvest Ct
2700 FTGV 97116 591 F3
SW Harvest Ct
9600 BRTN 97005 625 E4
Harvest Dr
- MCMV 97128 770 J1

Harvest Ln
- MOLA 97038 807 C7
NW Harvest Ln
13900 WasC 97229 595 A2
SW Harvest Pl
1100 TDLE 97060 599 G5
NE Harvest St
5700 HBRO 97124 593 J3
NW Harvest St
13100 WasC 97229 595 A3
SW Harvester Ln
15600 SRWD 97140 684 H6
NW Harvest Moon Ct
900 HBRO 97124 593 A3
NW Harvest Moon Dr
600 HBRO 97124 593 A3
SE Harvey Ct
4200 MWKE 97222 657 B1
Harvey Ln
900 MOLA 97038 807 D7
SE Harvey St
3200 MWKE 97222 657 B1
Harvey Wy
4100 LKOW 97035 656 A6
SW Harvey Wy
1700 WasC 97006 594 C7
SE Harwell Wy
1700 HBRO 97123 623 D1
NE Hash Rd
8000 YmhC 97132 743 F4
NW Haskell Ct
12400 WasC 97229 595 B3
S Haskett Pl
18600 ORCY 97045 717 C3
SW Haskins Ct
1800 TDLE 97060 599 F5
Haskins Ln
2900 CmsC 97068 716 H1
2900 WLIN 97068 716 H1
Haskins Rd
2300 WLIN 97068 716 H1
2500 CmsC 97068 716 H1
Haskins St
38800 SNDY 97055 690 J5
38900 SNDY 97055 691 A5
NE Hassalo Ct
19700 GSHM 97230 598 J5
NE Hassalo St
200 PTLD 97232 596 G4
3400 PTLD 97232 597 B4
5700 PTLD 97213 597 D4
8200 PTLD 97220 597 G4
12300 PTLD 97230 598 B5
16600 GSHM 97230 598 F5
Hastings Ct
5000 LKOW 97035 655 J5
Hastings Dr
4800 LKOW 97035 655 J5
Hastings Pl
4500 LKOW 97035 656 A5
NW Hataya Ct
14700 WasC 97229 594 J2
NE Hathaway Rd
26700 ClkC 98607 539 G6
NW Hathaway Rd
1900 ClkC 98685 476 E6
SW Hathaway Ter
13500 TGRD 97223 655 B1
Hatheway Rd
400 VCVR 98661 536 G5
Hattan Ct
- GLDS 97027 687 F3
S Hattan Rd
15000 CmsC 97045 688 E7
16200 CmsC 97045 718 E1
NE Haugen Rd
32500 WasC 97132 714 A5
32600 WasC 97140 714 C6
SE Hauglum Rd
35200 CmsC 97009 660 G4
35800 CmsC 97055 660 J4
SE Haukebo Dr
12100 DAMA 97009 659 B4
Haun Dr
- MCMV 97128 770 E3
Hauser Ct
200 MOLA 97038 807 E7
N Haven Av
9100 PTLD 97203 566 B3
SE Haven Ln
- PTLD 97266 628 A6
SW Haven Ln
51200 ClbC 97056 474 D3
51200 SPSE 97056 474 D3
Haven Rd
19300 ORCY 97045 717 C4
Haven St
4100 LKOW 97035 686 A1
SW Havencrest St
13200 WasC 97005 595 A7
13200 WasC 97225 595 A7
Haverhill Ct
6200 WLIN 97068 686 H6
Haverhill Wy
1900 WLIN 97068 686 H5
SW Havlik Rd
33400 SPSE 97056 474 E3
Hawk
- FRVW 97024 599 A3
SE Hawk Ct
15700 PTLD 97236 628 E6
SW Hawk Ct
15600 SRWD 97140 714 G1
NW Hawk Pl
5300 WasC 97229 564 D7
NW Hawkins Blvd
7900 PTLD 97229 595 G4
SE Hawkins Ln
28600 CmsC 97022 719 H5
SW Hawk Ridge Rd
14500 WasC 97224 654 J7
SW Hawks Beard St
12800 TGRD 97223 655 A2
SE Hawks Crest Pl
12800 HPYV 97236 658 B4
NE Hawn Creek Rd
3400 YmhC 97128 771 D1
4000 YmhC 97128 741 D7
5100 YmhC 97111 741 D6
Haworth Av
2000 NWBG 97132 713 D6
NE Hawthorne Av
100 WDVL 97060 599 D4
900 HBRO 97124 593 D3

SE Hawthorne Blvd
500 PTLD 97214 596 G7
2800 PTLD 97214 597 B7
4100 PTLD 97215 597 C7
8200 PTLD 97216 597 F7
11500 PTLD 97216 598 A7
Hawthorne Br
- PTLD 97204 596 F7
- PTLD 97214 596 F7
N Hawthorne Ct
800 CNBY 97013 746 C5
S Hawthorne Ct
14300 CmsC 97045 747 F3
SE Hawthorne Ct
14600 PTLD 97233 598 D7
20700 GSHM 97030 599 A7
SW Hawthorne Ct
100 DNDE 97115 742 H3
Hawthorne Dr
2300 NWBG 97132 713 E6
16800 LKOW 97034 686 G1
SW Hawthorne Ln
9700 WasC 97225 625 E1
Hawthorne Lp
1200 NWBG 97132 713 D6
SW Hawthorne Rd
400 ECDA 97023 750 D5
Hawthorne St
- MCMV 97128 770 E6
- YmhC 97128 770 E6
1100 FTGV 97116 592 A5
2400 WasC 97116 592 A4
N Hawthorne St
1300 CNBY 97013 746 C5
1500 CmsC 97013 746 C5
SE Hawthorne St
15900 PTLD 97233 598 E7
SW Hawthorne St
800 MCMV 97128 770 E6
Hawthorne Ter
- NWBG 97132 713 E6
SW Hawthorne Ter
1600 PTLD 97201 596 D7
NW Hayden Ct
200 HBRO 97124 593 B3
SW Hayden Dr
8200 WasC 97007 624 E7
S Hayden Rd
- CmsC 97023 750 A5
24100 CmsC 97023 749 H4
N Hayden Bay Dr
10 PTLD 97217 536 F7
N Hayden Island Dr
10 PTLD 97217 536 F7
2500 MthC 97217 536 D6
N Hayden Meadows Dr
700 PTLD 97217 566 F3
NW Hayes Rd
5700 ClkC 98674 386 B1
Hayes St
2800 NWBG 97132 713 E7
NE Hayes St
100 HBRO 97124 593 B3
3800 CMAS 98607 569 F1
4200 ClkC 98607 569 F1
SW Haystack Dr
13000 BRTN 97008 655 A2
SW Haystack Pl
10100 BRTN 97008 655 A2
NE Haystack St
5700 HBRO 97124 593 J3
SE Hayward Wy
2400 CmsC 97267 656 J5
SE Haze Ct
14200 CmsC 97267 657 B6
SE Hazel Av
3800 MWKE 97222 657 B1
6200 CmsC 97206 627 E7
SE Hazel Pl
5700 CmsC 97222 657 D1
Hazel Rd
2100 CmsC 97034 656 C5
2100 LKOW 97034 656 C5
35100 ClbC 97051 414 J2
Hazel St
- ClbC 97056 474 B4
1300 ORCY 97045 717 C2
E Hazel St
23000 CmsC 97011 724 A1
SE Hazel St
1700 PTLD 97214 596 H7
SW Hazel St
13700 BRTN 97005 625 A4
SW Hazelbrook Ln
10000 TLTN 97062 685 D2
10000 WasC 97062 685 D2
SW Hazelbrook Rd
10300 TLTN 97062 685 C2
10400 WasC 97062 685 D2
10900 WasC 97224 685 C2
11100 TLTN 97224 685 C2
SW Hazelbrush Ct
3300 CmsC 97070 716 B7
Hazel Creek Dr
19400 ORCY 97045 717 B5
19500 CmsC 97045 717 B5
SW Hazelcrest Ter
14900 TGRD 97224 655 A6
SW Hazelcrest Wy
12900 TGRD 97224 655 A6
13000 WasC 97224 655 A6
Hazeldell Av
11900 ORCY 97045 717 A5
NE Hazel Dell Av
4700 ClkC 98663 536 G1
4700 VCVR 98663 536 G1
5100 ClkC 98663 506 G5
5400 ClkC 98665 506 G7
9600 ClkC 98685 506 G5
Hazel Dell Ests
- ClkC 98665 506 J5
NE Hazel Dell Plz
- ClkC 98665 506 H4
Hazel Dell Wy
- CmsC 97013 746 E5
- CNBY 97013 746 E5
NE Hazel Dell Wy
100 ClkC 98665 506 G6
NW Hazel Dell Wy
100 ClkC 98665 506 G6
SE Hazeldell Wy
- CNBY 97013 746 E6
NE Hazelfern Pl
400 PTLD 97232 597 B5
3900 PTLD 97213 597 B4

SW Hazelfern Rd
7100 TLTN 97224 685 G2
NW Hazelgrove Ct
16900 BRTN 97006 594 G5
Hazelgrove Dr
19300 ORCY 97045 717 A5
SW Hazel Hill Dr
14300 TGRD 97224 655 B6
SE Hazel Hill Rd
13300 CmsC 97236 657 J4
S Hazelhurst Ln
19600 CmsC 97068 686 G4
Hazelnut Ct
11600 CmsC 97045 717 A5
11600 ORCY 97045 717 A5
N Hazelnut Ct
1300 CNBY 97013 746 C5
Hazelnut Dr
- FRVW 97024 599 C3
- WDVL 97060 599 C3
100 NWBG 97132 713 B4
400 YmhC 97132 713 B4
SW Hazelnut Ln
8000 BRTN 97225 625 F3
8000 WasC 97225 625 F3
Hazel Park Dr
11900 CmsC 97045 717 B5
11900 ORCY 97045 717 B5
SE Hazeltine Av
- HBRO 97123 623 G2
SW Hazeltine Ln
16100 WasC 97224 654 G6
NW Hazeltine St
8000 MthC 97229 595 G3
8000 PTLD 97229 595 F3
SW Hazeltree Ter
14400 TGRD 97224 655 B6
14400 WasC 97224 655 B6
SW Hazelvern Wy
8800 WasC 97223 625 F5
Hazelwood Dr
10 VCVR 98661 537 A4
800 ORCY 97045 717 B3
SW Hazelwood Lp
11400 TGRD 97223 655 C2
Hazen Rd
55700 ClbC 97053 414 E7
55700 ClbC 97053 444 E1
Headlee Ln
1700 LKOW 97034 656 G7
SE Heart Pl
16300 CmsC 97267 687 C1
SW Hearth Ct
15500 BRTN 97007 624 H6
SW Hearthside Ct
8000 WasC 97223 625 G7
NE Hearthwood Blvd
100 VCVR 98684 538 C6
SE Hearthwood Blvd
100 VCVR 98683 538 C7
100 VCVR 98684 538 C7
SE Hearthwood Dr
16200 CmsC 97015 687 F1
NE Heartwood Cir
21800 FRVW 97024 599 B3
Heater Ct
1300 WLIN 97068 687 B6
SW Heater Rd
27000 CmsC 97140 714 E4
28200 CmsC 97132 714 E7
28200 CmsC 97132 744 E1
28200 CmsC 97140 744 E1
Heater St
3600 NWBG 97132 713 F5
SW Heath Pl
6900 BRTN 97008 625 A5
SE Heathcliff Ln
400 HBRO 97123 593 C6
SE Heather Ct
2400 HBRO 97123 623 E1
7700 CmsC 97222 657 E3
SW Heather Ct
7500 WasC 97223 625 G6
13000 BRTN 97008 625 A6
NE Heather Dr
- MCMV 97128 771 E6
SW Heather Dr
1400 MCMV 97128 770 F7
Heather Ln NE
13700 MrnC 97002 775 D2
SW Heather Ln
3300 PTLD 97201 626 B1
9800 BRTN 97008 625 D6
9800 WasC 97008 625 D6
SW Heather Pl
25900 WNVL 97070 715 E3
Heather St
4100 CNLS 97113 592 C5
4100 FTGV 97116 592 C5
S Heather St
10 CNLS 97113 592 D5
10 FTGV 97116 592 D5
Heather Wy
700 GLDS 97027 687 E3
2600 FTGV 97116 591 G3
E Heather Wy
- YCLT 98675 419 G1
Heather Ann Ct
18300 LKOW 97034 686 A2
Heather Glen Dr
14800 CmsC 97045 717 G3
Heatherwood
- VCVR 98661 537 E1
- VCVR 98662 537 D1
Heatherwood N
- ClkC 98661 537 E1
- ClkC 98662 537 E1
- VCVR 98661 537 D1
- VCVR 98662 537 D1
SW Heatherwood Ln
17500 SRWD 97140 714 E1
NW Heathman Ln
14600 WasC 97229 564 J7
Heathrow Ln
14100 LKOW 97034 656 D5
SW Heaton Creek Dr
25500 WasC 97132 683 F7
SW Hebb Park Rd
400 CmsC 97068 746 D1
SW Heceta Ct
16600 BRTN 97007 624 G5
SE Hector St
5800 CmsC 97222 657 C2
5800 MWKE 97222 657 C2

Hedge Nettle Ct
4100 LKOW 97035 656 A5
SW Hedges Ct
10000 TLTN 97062 685 D6
SW Hedges Dr
21600 TLTN 97062 685 D6
Hedges St
- ORCY 97045 717 B2
SW Hedlund Av
10500 MthC 97219 656 G2
SW Hedlund Ln
14800 BRTN 97007 654 H2
NW Heermann Dr
200 ClkC 98685 476 F7
NW Heesacker Rd
4000 WasC 97116 562 B7
Heia Ct
38100 SNDY 97055 690 J3
Heider Dr
20000 ORCY 97045 717 G6
SW Heidi Ct
14800 TGRD 97224 655 E6
SE Heidi Ln
15500 DAMA 97009 659 A7
15500 DAMA 97009 689 B1
S Heidi St
16500 CmsC 97045 718 B6
SE Heights Ct
15700 CmsC 97267 657 C7
SW Heights Ln
5900 BRTN 97007 624 H4
SW Heightsview Ct
18900 WasC 97007 624 E7
SW Heightsview Dr
19000 WasC 97007 624 D7
SE Heike Ct
6300 HBRO 97123 594 A6
SE Heike St
6000 HBRO 97123 593 J6
SW Heikes Dr
9300 WasC 97123 623 E7
9300 WasC 97123 653 E1
Hein St
18800 ORCY 97045 717 B4
Heindl Wy
51600 ClbC 97056 474 C2
SW Heiney Rd
1400 GSHM 97080 628 J4
E Heintz St
200 MOLA 97038 837 F1
W Heintz St
100 MOLA 97038 837 E1
SE Heiple Rd
27200 CmsC 97022 719 H6
29700 CmsC 97022 720 A6
30500 CmsC 97023 720 A6
SW Heiser St
21100 WasC 97006 594 B6
Heisinger Ln
- CmsC 97042 807 G3
S Heisinger Ln
28500 CmsC 97042 807 G2
NE Heisson Rd
- ClkC 98675 418 F6
22900 BGND 98604 448 E3
25900 ClkC 98604 448 G1
27900 ClkC 98604 418 F6
E Heitman Av
1400 ClkC 98629 386 J7
1400 LCTR 98629 386 J7
E Heitman Cir
- ClkC 98629 386 J6
SE Helen Ct
3600 TDLE 97060 599 H7
NW Helen Ln
13100 WasC 97229 595 B3
Helena Av
900 VCVR 98661 537 D5
Helena St
100 STHN 97051 415 B1
SE Helena St
9900 CmsC 97222 657 D2
SE Helene Ct
1000 HBRO 97123 593 J6
SE Helene St
5500 HBRO 97123 593 H6
SW Helenius Rd
10400 TLTN 97062 685 C7
10400 WasC 97062 685 C7
10900 WasC 97140 685 C7
SW Helenius St
- TLTN 97062 685 C7
- TLTN 97140 685 C7
- WasC 97062 685 C7
- WasC 97140 685 C7
Helens Wy
35100 ClbC 97051 384 J7
35300 STHN 97051 384 J7
35400 STHN 97051 385 A6
Hellens Wy
- ClbC 97051 384 J7
SW Hell's Canyon Rd
21200 WasC 97140 714 A4
22400 WasC 97140 713 J4
Helms Ct
18100 SNDY 97055 691 A4
NW Helvetia Rd
6600 HBRO 97124 563 J6
6600 WasC 97124 563 J4
8000 WasC 97124 564 A3
10500 WasC 97124 534 A7
10900 WasC 97124 533 H7
SE Helzer Wy
20300 DAMA 97009 658 J4
N Hembree St
800 MCMV 97128 770 J4
NE Hembree St
2400 MCMV 97128 770 J1
3200 YmhC 97128 770 J2
3800 YmhC 97128 771 A1
SE Hembree St
600 MCMV 97128 770 H6
Hemlock
- CmsC 97015 657 J7
Hemlock Av
- ClbC 97056 474 B5
- WasC 97006 594 D5
Hemlock Av NE
- AURA 97002 775 F5
SE Hemlock Av
1900 PTLD 97214 596 J7
SE Hemlock Ct
1900 HBRO 97123 593 E6
E Hemlock Dr
24500 CmsC 97049 724 E3

Hemlock Ln
800 NWBG 97132 713 C6
4100 VCVR 98661 537 B4
NE Hemlock Pl
10800 YmhC 97115 742 H1
Hemlock St
500 LKOW 97034 686 F1
1800 WLIN 97068 687 A6
N Hemlock St
100 YMHL 97148 711 A1
S Hemlock St
100 YMHL 97148 711 A1
300 YmhC 97148 711 A1
SE Hemlock St
4000 HBRO 97123 593 G7
6500 MWKE 97222 657 D4
SW Hemlock St
100 DNDE 97115 742 H3
8200 WasC 97223 655 F1
SE Hemmen Av
14400 CmsC 97015 658 C7
SE Hemrick Rd
17200 CmsC 97009 658 F2
17200 CmsC 97236 658 F2
17200 DAMA 97009 658 F2
17200 HPYV 97009 658 F2
17200 HPYV 97236 658 F2
SE Henderson Ct
7800 PTLD 97206 627 F6
SW Henderson Ct
16500 WasC 97007 624 G6
SE Henderson Dr
7100 PTLD 97266 627 J6
11900 PTLD 97266 628 A6
12200 PTLD 97236 628 A6
SE Henderson St
- PTLD 97236 628 A6
3900 PTLD 97202 627 B6
5200 PTLD 97206 627 D6
10400 PTLD 97266 627 H6
SE Henderson Wy
- MthC 97236 628 D6
15200 PTLD 97236 628 D6
NE Hendricks Rd
7300 CLTN 97111 711 B7
7300 YmhC 97111 741 C1
7500 YmhC 97111 711 D7
N Hendricks St
8300 PTLD 97203 565 H1
NW Hendrickx Rd
36700 WasC 97113 562 E6
SE Henkle Rd
1400 MthC 97019 630 D2
SW Hennig Ct
18600 HBRO 97006 594 E6
18600 WasC 97006 594 E6
SW Hennig St
19100 WasC 97006 594 D6
NW Henninger Ln
13500 WasC 97229 595 A1
SE Henningsen Rd
25000 CmsC 97009 659 E2
25000 DAMA 97009 659 E2
Henrici Rd
14700 CmsC 97045 717 G7
S Henrici Rd
15800 CmsC 97045 717 J7
15900 CmsC 97045 718 D6
NW Henry Ct
9600 PTLD 97229 595 E2
NW Henry Dr
10 WasC 97005 595 A5
SW Henry Dr
10 WasC 97005 595 A6
SE Henry Pl
7400 PTLD 97206 627 E5
E Henry Rd
700 NWBG 97132 713 C4
SE Henry St
1400 PTLD 97202 626 H5
3400 PTLD 97202 627 A5
7200 PTLD 97206 627 F5
10000 PTLD 97266 627 H5
13800 PTLD 97236 628 C5
SW Henry St
12700 BRTN 97005 625 B2
E Henry Creek Av
- CmsC 97049 724 H5
NE Henry Creek Rd
3900 YmhC 97114 771 J1
4800 YmhC 97114 741 J7
4800 YmhC 97114 742 A7
SW Hensley Rd
600 TDLE 97060 599 F6
N Heppner Av
7500 PTLD 97203 565 J3
SW Herb Wy
8900 WasC 97223 625 G7
8900 WasC 97223 655 G1
SW Herber Hoover Hwy W
4200 NWBG 97132 713 G6
30200 YmhC 97132 713 H6
SW Herber Hoover Hwy W SR-99W
4200 NWBG 97132 713 G6
30200 YmhC 97132 713 H6
SE Herbert Ct
8800 CmsC 97015 657 F6
Herbert Hoover Hwy W
1400 NWBG 97132 713 D7
Herbert Hoover Hwy W SR-99W
1400 NWBG 97132 713 D7
Herbert Hoover Hwy W SR-219
1400 NWBG 97132 713 D7
SW Herbert Hoover Hwy W
3200 NWBG 97132 713 F6
4300 YmhC 97132 713 G6
SW Herbert Hoover Hwy W SR-99W
3200 NWBG 97132 713 F6
4300 YmhC 97132 713 G6
SW Herd Ln
28100 WasC 97123 683 D3
NE Herd Rd
16200 YmhC 97132 713 D2
N Hereford Av
7500 PTLD 97203 566 B4
SE Hereford Ln
26500 CmsC 97022 719 J5
E Hereford St
100 GLDS 97027 687 E4
W Hereford St
100 GLDS 97027 687 D4

STREET Block	City	ZIP	Map#	Grid
Heritage Ct				
15400	LKOW	97035	656	A6
SE Heritage Ct				
8400	CmsC	97015	687	H1
SW Heritage Ct				
17000	BRTN	97006	624	G1
17000	WasC	97006	624	F1
Heritage Grn				
-	VCVR	98683	568	E2
Heritage Ln				
4500	LKOW	97035	656	A6
59000	ClbC	97051	414	G1
E Heritage Lp				
100	LCTR	98629	386	H7
1300	ClkC	98629	386	H7
NW Heritage Lp				
-	BRTN	97006	594	E5
-	WasC	97006	594	F5
Heritage Pk				
-	GSHM	97030	599	B7
NW Heritage Pkwy				
18200	BRTN	97006	594	E5
18200	WasC	97006	594	E5
18300	HBRO	97006	594	E5
SW Heritage Pkwy				
100	WasC	97006	594	F6
NW Heritage Ter				
18300	WasC	97006	594	E5
Heritage Wy				
2100	NWBG	97132	713	B5
2100	YmhC	97132	713	B5
S Herman Rd				
12900	CmsC	97038	837	D6
SW Herman Rd				
9500	TLTN	97062	685	A4
10800	WasC	97062	685	A4
13000	WasC	97140	685	A4
Herman St				
2300	NWBG	97132	713	E5
NW Hermosa Blvd				
10	PTLD	97205	596	B5
10	PTLD	97210	596	B5
SW Hermoso Wy				
7200	TGRD	97223	655	G4
NE Heron Cir				
9900	VCVR	98664	537	H4
SW Heron Cir				
10700	BRTN	97007	654	H2
SW Heron Ct				
15200	BRTN	97007	654	H2
Heron Dr				
1400	RDGF	98642	416	B6
2300	ClkC	98642	416	B6
N Heron Dr				
200	RDGF	98642	415	J6
200	RDGF	98642	416	A6
Heron Ln				
-	FTGV	97116	591	H2
SW Heron Pl				
10700	BRTN	97007	654	H2
SW Heron Lakes Dr				
23600	SRWD	97140	714	E1
NE Heron Meadows Dr				
34200	SPSE	97056	474	G1
SE Herrick Rd				
43100	CmsC	97055	691	G1
NW Herrin Ct				
8800	PTLD	97229	595	F2
NE Herring Ln				
19100	YmhC	97132	712	G6
NE Herrold Ct				
1400	HBRO	97124	593	E3
NW Hertel St				
500	HBRO	97124	593	B3
Hertrich Ct				
35700	CmsC	97055	690	F4
Hess Creek Ct				
1500	NWBG	97132	713	D6
SW Hessler Dr				
1200	PTLD	97239	626	D3
Heterodox View Av				
-	PTLD	97266	627	F3
SE Heuke Rd				
18800	DAMA	97009	658	H4
SW Hewett Blvd				
3800	PTLD	97221	626	A1
5000	PTLD	97221	625	J1
5400	MthC	97221	625	J1
5500	MthC	97221	595	J7
5500	PTLD	97221	595	J7
SW Hewitt Av				
100	TDLE	97060	599	F4
SW Hewitt Pl				
-	TDLE	97060	599	E5
7800	BRTN	97008	625	B6
N Hezzie Ln				
500	CmsC	97038	807	D7
500	CmsC	97038	837	D1
500	MOLA	97038	807	D7
500	MOLA	97038	837	D1
S Hezzie Ln				
31600	CmsC	97038	837	D1
31600	MOLA	97038	837	D1
SW Hialeah Dr				
9500	BRTN	97008	655	A1
SW Hialeah Pl				
9800	BRTN	97008	655	A1
SW Hiatt Rd				
43300	WasC	97116	591	G7
Hiawatha Ct				
6300	CmsC	97035	685	H3
E Hiawatha Rd				
22200	CmsC	97049	723	J1
NW Hibbard Dr				
12200	WasC	97229	595	B2
SE Hicklin Ct				
2600	TDLE	97060	599	H6
SW Hickman Ln				
6500	BRTN	97223	625	H5
SE Hickory Ct				
14900	CmsC	97267	657	C7
SW Hickory Ln				
14900	BRTN	97007	624	J5
SE Hickory Pl				
1400	GSHM	97080	629	G4
NE Hickory St				
15500	VCVR	98682	538	D2
NW Hickory St				
200	MCMV	97128	770	F5
SE Hickory St				
1400	PTLD	97214	626	H1
SE Hickory Wy				
1600	GSHM	97080	629	H4
SW Hicrest Av				
1600	WasC	97225	595	B7
SE Hidalgo Ct				
11400	CmsC	97015	657	J5
Hidalgo St				
10	LKOW	97035	656	A3
200	PTLD	97219	656	A3
SW Hidden Ct				
20500	WasC	97006	594	C7
S Hidden Rd				
15200	CmsC	97004	777	J4
15200	CmsC	97042	777	J4
Hidden Vil				
-	ClkC	98686	506	J2
SE Hidden Wy				
2300	VCVR	98661	536	J7
2600	VCVR	98661	537	A7
Hidden Bay Ct				
13200	LKOW	97035	655	J4
SE Hiddenbrook Dr				
3400	VCVR	98683	568	G3
NE Hidden Creek Dr				
5500	HBRO	97124	593	J4
SW Hidden Creek Pl				
13100	TGRD	97223	654	J5
NE Hidden Dell Dr				
17500	ClkC	98606	478	H3
SE Hidden Falls Rd				
37300	ClkC	98671	570	H4
SW Hidden Hills Ct				
15000	YmhC	97128	770	A3
NW Hidden Hills Ln				
14100	YmhC	97128	770	A3
SW Hidden Hills Ln				
14900	YmhC	97128	770	A3
S Hidden Lake Dr				
17200	CmsC	97045	717	H1
NE Hidden Meadows Rd				
24000	YmhC	97132	743	B2
Hidden Springs Ct				
2100	WLIN	97068	686	H5
Hidden Springs Rd				
-	CmsC	97068	686	G5
19400	WLIN	97068	686	G5
NE Hidden Springs Rd				
21400	YmhC	97115	742	H1
22100	YmhC	97115	712	H7
22100	YmhC	97132	712	H7
Hide-A-Way				
8900	CmsC	97009	659	E1
8900	DAMA	97009	659	E1
Hide-A-Way Ct				
1200	LKOW	97034	656	E4
Hide-A-Way Ln				
1200	LKOW	97034	656	E4
E Hideaway Ln				
21400	CmsC	97049	693	J7
SW Hideaway Ln				
28500	WasC	97123	683	C2
Hiefield Ct				
12700	ORCY	97045	717	C4
SE Higgins Dr				
2000	VCVR	98683	568	B2
High Ct				
300	GLDS	97027	687	D3
High Rd				
-	MthC	97231	534	F4
High St				
-	MthC	97231	534	F4
100	ORCY	97045	717	B1
500	ORCY	97045	687	C7
1000	GLDS	97027	687	E3
S High St				
100	ORCY	97045	717	B1
SE High St				
700	HBRO	97123	593	C6
SW High St				
1700	PTLD	97201	596	C7
1700	PTLD	97201	626	B1
High Creek Rd				
-	HPYV	97236	657	H4
SE Highfield Av				
1100	HBRO	97123	593	D7
SE Highgate Dr				
8800	CmsC	97236	657	H1
SW High Hill Ln				
16500	BRTN	97007	654	G3
16500	WasC	97007	654	G3
NE Highland Av				
400	LCTR	98629	386	J7
SW Highland Cir				
28400	WNVL	97070	715	G6
NW High Land Ct				
30700	NPNS	97133	563	B2
NW Highland Ct				
20500	WasC	97229	594	C1
SW Highland Ct				
6900	WNVL	97070	715	H6
15700	TGRD	97224	655	C7
Highland Dr				
5600	VCVR	98661	537	D6
6200	VCVR	98664	537	D7
18800	ORCY	97045	717	B4
SW Highland Dr				
800	GSHM	97030	628	G3
800	GSHM	97080	628	G4
10200	TGRD	97224	655	D7
22600	SRWD	97140	684	G7
SE Highland Lp				
11000	CmsC	97015	657	J6
SW Highland Pkwy				
1400	PTLD	97221	596	A7
SW Highland Rd				
1200	MthC	97221	596	A7
1200	PTLD	97221	596	A7
N Highland St				
10	PTLD	97211	566	G6
900	RDGF	98642	416	A7
1500	PTLD	97217	566	E6
NE Highland St				
10	PTLD	97217	566	G6
1300	PTLD	97211	566	J6
3900	PTLD	97211	567	B6
S Highland St				
15000	CmsC	97045	687	G4
S Highland Crest Dr				
23800	CmsC	97004	749	B7
NE Highland Meadows Dr				
26200	ClkC	98682	509	G6
Highlands Dr				
1500	LKOW	97034	656	D7
1500	LKOW	97034	686	D1
SE High Meadow Lp				
16400	PTLD	97236	628	E3
SW Highpoint Dr				
14900	SRWD	97140	714	G1
SE Highpointe Dr				
20700	ClkC	98607	568	J4
SE High Ridge Ct				
19400	DAMA	97009	658	J6
SE High School Wy				
33500	SPSE	97056	474	E2
High Tee Ct				
-	NWBG	97132	713	H7
100	NWBG	97132	743	H1
100	YmhC	97132	743	H1
SW High Tor Dr				
13800	TGRD	97224	654	J5
13800	WasC	97224	654	J5
High Touch St				
1300	WLIN	97068	716	F2
E Highview Ct				
25700	CmsC	97067	724	D4
E Highview Dr				
25700	CmsC	97067	724	D5
Highway 47				
-	CLTN	97111	711	A6
-	CLTN	97111	741	A2
-	YmhC	97111	711	A3
-	YmhC	97111	741	A2
-	YmhC	97128	741	B5
-	YmhC	97128	771	B1
-	YmhC	97148	711	A2
-	YMHL	97148	711	A2
Highway 47 SR-47				
-	CLTN	97111	711	A6
-	CLTN	97111	741	A2
-	YmhC	97111	711	A3
-	YmhC	97111	741	A2
-	YmhC	97128	741	B5
-	YmhC	97128	771	B1
-	YmhC	97148	711	A2
-	YMHL	97148	711	A2
SW Highway 47				
-	FTGV	97116	591	J6
-	FTGV	97116	592	B5
-	WasC	97116	591	H7
SW Highway 47 SR-47				
-	FTGV	97116	591	J6
-	FTGV	97116	592	B5
-	WasC	97116	591	H7
NE Highway 99				
-	VCVR	98663	536	G1
5400	ClkC	98665	506	G7
5400	VCVR	98663	506	G7
9800	ClkC	98686	506	G7
12200	ClkC	98686	476	J7
W Hilary Ct				
1200	MCMV	97128	770	F6
SW Hilary St				
700	MCMV	97128	770	G6
W Hilary St				
800	MCMV	97128	770	G6
Hilda St				
400	ORCY	97045	717	D2
Hildago Ln NW				
-	WasC	97229	564	H7
NW Hildago Ln				
-	WasC	97229	564	H7
SW Hilen Ct				
2100	PTLD	97219	656	C3
Hill Ct				
34300	ClbC	97053	414	G7
SW Hill Ct				
13200	TGRD	97223	655	E5
SW Hill Dr				
100	GSHM	97080	629	B4
SW Hill Pl				
6700	BRTN	97008	625	B5
NW Hill Rd				
400	MCMV	97128	770	E3
1200	YmhC	97128	770	E3
SE Hill Rd				
3300	CmsC	97267	657	A6
SW Hill Rd				
100	MCMV	97128	770	D7
100	YmhC	97128	770	D7
Hill St				
800	VCVR	98660	536	E5
56300	ClbC	97053	414	G7
NE Hill St				
4000	ClkC	98661	537	A2
NW Hill St				
700	CMAS	98607	569	D4
SE Hill St				
5800	MWKE	97222	657	D1
5900	CmsC	97222	657	D1
SW Hill St				
9000	TGRD	97223	655	E5
SW Hill Ter				
52000	SPSE	97056	474	D1
Hill Wy				
17400	LKOW	97035	685	J1
NE Hill Wy				
700	ECDA	97023	750	C2
8800	PTLD	97220	597	G2
NE Hillaire Ct				
1700	HBRO	97124	593	E4
NE Hillaire Dr				
1900	HBRO	97124	593	E4
SW Hillary Pl				
16000	WasC	97007	624	G4
NW Hillcourt Ln				
1200	PTLD	97229	595	G4
Hillcrest Av				
-	CmsC	97009	659	F4
Hillcrest Ct				
2400	WLIN	97068	686	H3
3300	FTGV	97116	591	E2
SW Hillcrest Ct				
11700	BRTN	97008	625	C6
Hillcrest Dr				
1700	WLIN	97068	686	G3
33200	ClbC	97056	474	D4
SE Hillcrest Dr				
8800	VCVR	98664	567	F1
10200	CmsC	97236	657	H2
SW Hillcrest Dr				
2500	PTLD	97201	596	C7
Hillcrest Ln				
400	ORCY	97045	717	D3
SW Hillcrest Pl				
2100	PTLD	97201	596	C7
7300	BRTN	97008	625	C6
Hillcrest Rd				
500	ClbC	97051	384	J7
SE Hillcrest Rd				
9200	CmsC	97236	657	G3
SW Hillcrest Rd				
22800	CmsC	97068	686	D7
22800	CmsC	97068	716	D1
NW Hillcrest St				
30600	NPNS	97133	563	B1
Hillcrest Wy				
3300	FTGV	97116	591	E2
SW Hillcroft Av				
900	WasC	97225	595	C7
SW Hilldale Av				
1200	WasC	97225	595	B7
SW Hillecke Rd				
28200	WasC	97123	623	C3
NW Hiller Ln				
12000	MthC	97229	595	C1
SE Hillgrove Ct				
14400	CmsC	97267	657	A6
Hill-House Dr				
1900	WLIN	97068	716	G2
NW Hillhurst Rd				
23000	ClkC	98642	446	D3
23600	RDGF	98642	446	C3
S Hillhurst Rd				
500	RDGF	98642	416	A7
800	RDGF	98642	446	A1
3100	ClkC	98642	446	C3
Hillis Rd				
37200	ClkC	98674	386	B4
SW Hillman Ct				
9000	WNVL	97070	715	D5
NW Hills Dr				
200	MCMV	97128	770	D5
NE Hillsboro Hwy				
17600	WasC	97132	713	C1
NE Hillsboro Hwy SR-219				
17600	WasC	97132	713	C1
SW Hillsboro Hwy				
2400	HBRO	97123	593	B7
2400	HBRO	97123	623	B6
2400	WasC	97123	593	B7
2400	WasC	97123	623	B6
2500	WasC	97113	623	B1
9600	WasC	97113	653	B1
9600	WasC	97123	653	C2
16300	WasC	97123	683	G1
16300	WasC	97140	683	G1
17400	WasC	97132	683	E4
23600	WasC	97132	713	D1
SW Hillsboro Hwy SR-219				
2400	HBRO	97123	593	B7
2400	HBRO	97123	623	B6
2400	WasC	97123	593	B7
2400	WasC	97123	623	B6
2500	WasC	97113	623	B1
9600	WasC	97113	653	B1
9600	WasC	97123	653	C2
16300	WasC	97123	683	G1
16300	WasC	97140	683	G1
20100	WasC	97132	683	D6
23600	WasC	97132	713	D1
SW Hillsboro St				
2700	PTLD	97239	626	C2
SW Hillsdale Av				
3800	PTLD	97239	626	C2
SW Hillsdale Ct				
-	PTLD	97221	626	A3
Hillsdale Dr				
1000	NWBG	97132	713	D4
Hillsdale Ter				
-	PTLD	97239	626	B4
Hillsdale Vil				
-	PTLD	97239	626	C4
Hillshire Dr				
10	LKOW	97034	686	B3
SW Hillshire Dr				
13200	TGRD	97223	655	A5
13500	TGRD	97223	654	J5
NW Hillside Blvd				
-	PTLD	97231	565	D4
Hillside Ct				
2100	LKOW	97034	686	C1
18000	WLIN	97068	686	G2
SE Hillside Ct				
2800	MWKE	97222	657	A2
10200	HPYV	97236	657	J2
Hillside Dr				
2100	LKOW	97034	686	C2
17700	LKOW	97068	686	G2
17700	WLIN	97068	686	G2
NE Hillside Dr				
15600	YmhC	97132	712	H1
22200	ClkC	98682	509	B3
SE Hillside Dr				
3500	CmsC	97267	687	A2
10500	HPYV	97236	657	J2
SW Hillside Dr				
4100	PTLD	97221	626	A1
4400	MthC	97221	626	A1
Hillside Ln				
-	CmsC	97055	692	H5
2300	LKOW	97034	686	C2
SE Hillside Ln				
16200	CmsC	97267	687	B1
Hillside Rd				
-	WasC	97116	531	A7
-	WasC	97116	561	A1
NW Hillside Rd				
46000	WasC	97116	561	B3
Hillside Wy				
3200	FTGV	97116	591	E2
17800	LKOW	97034	686	C2
Hillside Park Wy				
-	MCMV	97128	770	E5
S Hillsview Ln				
23000	CmsC	97004	749	E7
23000	CmsC	97023	749	E7
SE Hill Terrace Ct				
14200	CmsC	97267	657	B6
Hilltop Av				
400	ORCY	97045	717	D3
NW Hill Top Ct				
4400	MthC	97210	596	A5
4400	PTLD	97210	596	A5
SE Hilltop Ct				
11200	HPYV	97236	657	J2
Hilltop Dr				
700	NWBG	97132	713	C4
700	YmhC	97132	713	C4
59900	ClbC	97051	384	J7
59900	ClbC	97051	385	A7
NW Hilltop Dr				
200	MthC	97210	596	A5
200	PTLD	97210	596	A5
NE Hilltop Ln				
-	YmhC	97114	742	C4
SW Hilltop Ln				
5000	MthC	97221	625	J1
5000	MthC	97221	626	A1
SW Hilltop Ln				
5000	PTLD	97221	626	A1
Hill Top Rd				
18800	CmsC	97034	686	B3
S Hilltop Rd				
15900	CmsC	97045	687	J6
S Hill Valley Ln				
15400	CmsC	97045	717	H3
Hillview Ct				
9700	YmhC	97132	743	A2
SW Hillview Ct				
9600	TGRD	97223	655	E5
E Hillview Dr				
24600	CmsC	97049	724	E4
SW Hill View St				
10100	TGRD	97223	655	D5
SW Hillview St				
-	TGRD	97223	655	E5
SW Hill View Ter				
8700	WasC	97225	625	F4
SE Hillwood Av				
5100	CmsC	97267	687	C1
5200	CmsC	97267	657	C7
SE Hillwood Cir				
5400	CmsC	97267	657	C7
NE Hillwood Dr				
100	HBRO	97124	593	D4
SE Hillyard Dr				
29200	CmsC	97009	689	J2
SE Hillyard Rd				
2900	GSHM	97080	629	F5
Hilton Head Ct				
15000	ORCY	97045	717	H6
NW Hilton Head Ter				
3700	WasC	97229	595	D1
SW Himes St				
2700	PTLD	97239	626	C2
SE Hinckley Av				
8200	CmsC	97206	657	F1
8200	CmsC	97236	657	F1
SW Hindon Ct				
13800	TGRD	97223	655	B2
SE Hines Dr				
14000	CmsC	97015	658	D6
SW Hines Pl				
22000	SRWD	97140	684	E6
S Hinkle Rd				
18900	CmsC	97045	718	H5
SE Hinman Av				
31600	CmsC	97023	750	B1
NE Hinness Rd				
24500	ClkC	98606	479	E6
Hiram Av				
16200	ORCY	97045	687	F6
SE Hirters Ln				
2700	YmhC	97115	772	G2
Historic Columbia River Hwy				
800	MthC	97060	599	H6
800	TDLE	97060	599	H6
28200	MthC	97060	629	J1
28900	MthC	97060	600	A7
33900	MthC	97019	600	F6
W Historic Columbia River Hwy				
100	TDLE	97060	599	F4
SE Hite Ct				
8500	CmsC	97009	659	J1
SW Hiteon Ct				
13500	BRTN	97008	655	A2
SW Hiteon Dr				
13700	BRTN	97008	655	A2
13800	BRTN	97008	654	F2
SW Hiteon Ln				
13500	BRTN	97008	655	A2
SW Hiteon Pl				
10200	BRTN	97008	655	A2
SE Hittay Tr				
19200	DAMA	97009	658	H2
E Hiyu St				
25400	CmsC	97067	724	A4
E Hoag St				
100	ClkC	98675	419	G1
100	YCLT	98675	419	G1
W Hoag St				
100	YCLT	98675	419	F1
Hoag Ter				
52100	SPSE	97056	444	D7
SE Hobart Ct				
11700	CmsC	97236	657	J4
Hobbit Ct				
18000	LKOW	97034	686	B2
NW Hobbs Rd				
600	CNLS	97113	592	F3
800	WasC	97113	592	G3
SW Hocken Av				
2800	WasC	97005	625	A2
3200	BRTN	97005	625	A3
SE Hocker Rd				
-	MthC	97060	630	A1
NW Hocking Rd				
-	MthC	97231	535	C6
-	PTLD	97231	535	C6
NW Hodes Dr				
20600	HBRO	97006	594	C4
N Hodge Av				
8900	PTLD	97203	566	B3
Hods Ln				
35400	ClbC	97051	385	A5
E Hofeldt Dr				
24600	CmsC	97049	724	E4
Hofer Ct				
17100	LKOW	97034	686	D1
NW Hofer Rd				
15800	WasC	97106	531	D2
SW Hoffert Pl				
6400	WasC	97007	624	D5
Hoffman Av				
16800	SNDY	97055	691	A2
SW Hoffman Av				
2200	PTLD	97201	626	D3
NE Hoffman Dr				
1400	MCMV	97128	770	J2
1600	MCMV	97128	771	A2
S Hoffman Rd				
17300	CmsC	97045	688	C3
SW Hoffman Rd				
400	CmsC	97068	716	D7
Hoffman St				
600	WDLD	98674	385	J2
900	WDLD	98674	386	A1
SE Hoffmeister Ct				
13100	DAMA	97009	659	C5
SE Hoffmeister Rd				
-	CmsC	97009	659	E6
SE Hoffmeister Rd				
22200	DAMA	97009	659	B5
NE Hogan Av				
10	GSHM	97030	629	D2
10	GSHM	97080	629	D2
S Hogan Av				
10	GSHM	97030	629	D2
10	GSHM	97080	629	D4
2900	MthC	97080	629	D4
Hogan Mdws				
-	GSHM	97080	629	D3
NE Hogan Pl				
1200	GSHM	97030	629	D1
Hogan Rd				
9300	DAMA	97009	659	D5
NE Hogan Rd				
1000	GSHM	97030	629	D2
1600	GSHM	97030	599	D7
SE Hogan Rd				
6600	GSHM	97080	629	D5
6600	MthC	97080	629	D7
8400	DAMA	97009	629	D7
NW Hogan St				
13300	WasC	97229	595	A1
Hogan Ranch Rd				
34800	ClbC	97056	415	A7
34800	ClbC	97056	444	H3
34800	ClbC	97056	445	A2
NW Hoge Av				
9800	PTLD	97231	565	E2
Holaday Rd				
29900	ClbC	97056	444	A6
NW Holbrook Av				
-	MthC	97210	595	H4
NW Holbrook Ct				
3300	PTLD	97229	595	E2
Holcomb Blvd				
13600	CmsC	97045	687	E7
13600	ORCY	97045	687	E7
S Holcomb Blvd				
15500	CmsC	97045	687	J6
17000	CmsC	97045	688	C6
NW Holcomb Dr				
17000	WasC	97229	564	G7
17300	WasC	97006	564	F7
S Holcomb Rd				
-	CmsC	97045	688	D6
E Holden Rd				
27200	CmsC	97049	724	H6
SE Holgate Blvd				
1100	PTLD	97202	626	J3
2800	PTLD	97202	627	A3
7000	PTLD	97206	627	F3
8100	PTLD	97266	627	F3
11500	PTLD	97266	628	A3
12000	PTLD	97236	628	C3
Holgate Est				
-	PTLD	97236	628	A3
Holiday Ln				
2700	NWBG	97132	713	B5
N Holiday Ln				
1400	CNLS	97113	592	E4
NE Holladay Ct				
13000	PTLD	97230	598	B5
23500	WDVL	97060	599	C5
N Holladay Dr				
2500	CNLS	97113	592	G4
NE Holladay Pl				
12200	PTLD	97220	598	A5
12200	PTLD	97230	598	A5
19100	GSHM	97230	598	H5
23500	WDVL	97060	599	C5
N Holladay St				
400	CNLS	97113	592	D4
NE Holladay St				
10	PTLD	97227	596	G4
10	PTLD	97232	596	H4
3300	PTLD	97232	597	A4
6000	PTLD	97213	597	D5
8100	PTLD	97220	597	F5
11400	PTLD	97220	598	A5
12700	PTLD	97230	598	B5
19600	GSHM	97230	598	J5
19900	FRVW	97024	598	J5
23600	WDVL	97060	599	D5
23900	TDLE	97060	599	D5
NE Holland Ct				
3100	PTLD	97211	567	A5
SW Holland Ln				
11500	BRTN	97008	625	C5
SE Holland Lp				
14800	HPYV	97236	658	D4
15200	CmsC	97236	658	C4
N Holland St				
10	PTLD	97211	566	G5
3000	PTLD	97217	566	D5
NE Holland St				
10	PTLD	97217	566	G5
800	PTLD	97211	566	H5
SE Hollingshead Ct				
200	TDLE	97060	599	H4
SW Hollis Ct				
20000	WasC	97007	624	C3
SW Hollow Ln				
12100	TGRD	97223	655	B5
SE Hollow St				
700	HBRO	97123	593	C6
NW Holloway Dr				
2500	PTLD	97229	595	F2
Hollowell St				
1500	WLIN	97068	687	C6
SE Holly Av				
3000	CmsC	97222	657	A5
NE Holly Ct				
2100	VCVR	98664	537	G4
S Holly Ct				
1000	CNBY	97013	746	D7
SE Holly Ct				
-	PTLD	97215	597	C6
15600	CmsC	97267	657	C7
Holly Dr				
600	NWBG	97132	713	D7
Holly Ln				
17000	CmsC	97045	687	F7
17000	CmsC	97045	717	F2
SW Holly Ln				
8400	WasC	97223	625	F6
8800	WNVL	97070	745	E1
Holly St				
1400	WLIN	97068	687	C6
N Holly St				
600	CNBY	97013	746	C6
1400	CmsC	97013	746	C2
NE Holly St				
9800	VCVR	98664	537	G4
NW Holly St				
-	BRTN	97006	594	E5
18500	HBRO	97006	594	E5
S Holly St				
300	CNBY	97013	746	C7
1200	CNBY	97013	776	C1
SE Holly St				
1500	PTLD	97214	596	H7
SW Holly St				
8600	WNVL	97070	745	E1
SE Holly Wy				
400	MCMV	97128	770	H5
SW Hollybrook Ct				
6800	WNVL	97070	715	G6
Holly Brook Ln				
-	CmsC	97013	777	D1
S Hollybrook Ln				
24500	CmsC	97013	777	D1
SW Hollybrook Ter				
1500	GSHM	97080	629	A3
Holly Crest Ln				
14300	CmsC	97045	717	F1
SW Holly Hill Rd				
14600	WasC	97123	653	A6
SE Hollyhock Ct				
2700	HBRO	97123	623	D1
Holly Oak Ct NE				
-	DNLD	97020	774	H4
NE Hollyrood Ct				
3500	PTLD	97212	597	B3
NW Holly Springs Ln				
-	BRTN	97229	595	C5
Holly Springs Rd				
14300	LKOW	97035	656	B5
SE Hollyview Ct				
14300	DAMA	97009	659	D6
SE Hollyview Ln				
14000	DAMA	97009	659	E6
SE Hollyview Ter				
14000	CmsC	97009	659	E6
14000	DAMA	97009	659	E6
SE Hollywood Av				
9400	CmsC	97222	657	D1
9700	MWKE	97222	657	D2
SW Holly Woods Ct				
19800	WasC	97007	624	D3
NE Holman Pl				
4500	PTLD	97218	567	C6
N Holman St				
10	PTLD	97211	566	G6
800	PTLD	97217	566	F6
NE Holman St				
10	PTLD	97217	566	G6
800	PTLD	97211	566	J6
4200	PTLD	97211	567	C6
4500	PTLD	97218	567	C6
8800	PTLD	97220	567	G6
11200	PTLD	97220	568	A6
N Holmes Av				
7800	PTLD	97217	566	D4
Holmes Ln				
100	ORCY	97045	717	C3
S Holmes Rd				
15800	CmsC	97038	807	H6
Holmes St				
100	ORCY	97045	717	D1
5900	WLIN	97068	687	B5
SE Holst Rd				
29000	CmsC	97009	689	J3
29000	CmsC	97009	690	A3
NE Holt Ct				
1300	WDVL	97060	599	D5
Holveck Ct				
500	NWBG	97132	713	C4
Holy Names Ct				
2700	LKOW	97034	686	H1
Holy Names Dr				
17300	LKOW	97034	686	H1
Holy Names Pl				
2700	LKOW	97034	686	H1
SW Holznagel Rd				
-	WasC	97140	683	J2
18500	WasC	97140	684	A3
SE Homan Rd				
34200	MthC	97080	630	F5
SW Homar Av				
2700	PTLD	97201	626	C1
SE Home Av				
10300	MWKE	97222	657	C2
SE Home St				
11300	MWKE	97222	657	C3
SW Home St				
9300	TGRD	97224	655	E7
NE Home Wy				
1600	MCMV	97128	770	J4
NE Home Acres Rd				
23800	YmhC	97132	743	A1
E Homer St				
23100	CmsC	97011	724	A2
SE Homestead Ct				
7000	HBRO	97123	624	A1
Homestead Dr				
15000	ORCY	97045	717	H7
20300	CmsC	97045	717	H7
NE Homestead Dr				
17700	ClkC	98606	478	D2
SW Homestead Dr				
4200	PTLD	97239	626	E3
SW Homestead Ln				
10100	BRTN	97008	625	D7
Homestead Pl				
900	MOLA	97038	807	C7
Homestead Rd				
-	CmsC	97055	692	J4
-	CmsC	97055	693	A4
SW Homesteader Rd				
2800	CmsC	97068	716	B4
3500	CmsC	97070	716	A4
4500	CmsC	97070	715	H4
4500	WasC	97062	715	H4
Homewood Ct				
3100	NWBG	97132	713	C4
SW Homewood Ct				
8800	WasC	97225	625	F4
SW Homewood St				
8200	BRTN	97225	625	F4
8200	WasC	97225	625	F4
NE Honey Ln				
12100	YmhC	97132	713	B6
E Honeyman Rd				
52100	ClbC	97056	445	B6
52100	ClbC	97056	475	A1
N Honeyman Rd				
33900	ClbC	97056	444	F5
33900	SPSE	97056	444	F5

STREET
Block City ZIP Map# Grid
Honeyman Rd
35100 ClbC 97056 445 A2
W Honeysuckle Ct
500 MCMV 97128 770 E6
E Honeysuckle Wy
15300 CmsC 97015 658 D5
15300 HPYV 97015 658 D5
W Honeywood Ct
18800 WasC 97006 594 E7
W Honeywood Dr
18500 WasC 97006 594 E7
W Honors Dr
4600 GSHM 97080 629 C7
W Honors Pl
4600 GSHM 97080 629 C7
E Hood Av
10 GSHM 97080 629 C2
2000 GSHM 97030 629 C1
2700 GSHM 97030 599 C7
W Hood Av
7200 MthC 97229 595 G4
E Hood Av
10 GSHM 97030 629 C2
10 GSHM 97080 629 C3
W Hood Av
- PTLD 97201 626 F1
3100 PTLD 97239 626 F2
7400 PTLD 97219 626 F6
10400 PTLD 97219 656 F2
W Hood Av SR-43
3300 PTLD 97239 626 F2
Hood Ct
300 MOLA 97038 837 E2
17000 SNDY 97055 691 A2
NE Hood Ct
1900 GSHM 97030 629 C1
E Hood Ct
7800 CmsC 97267 657 F7
NW Hood Dr
1900 CMAS 98607 569 B3
NE Hood Pl
1700 GSHM 97030 629 C1
Hood St
100 ORCY 97045 717 C3
5500 WLIN 97068 687 B6
38200 SNDY 97055 690 J2
39200 SNDY 97055 691 A3
NE Hood St
800 HBRO 97124 593 D3
NW Hood St
1600 CMAS 98607 569 B3
E Hood St
8000 CmsC 97267 657 F7
8400 CmsC 97015 657 F7
38900 SNDY 97055 690 J2
38900 SNDY 97055 691 A2
E Hood Wy
1600 GSHM 97080 629 C4
SW Hoodoo Ct
17400 WasC 97007 624 F7
Hoodview
- CmsC 97045 749 A1
Hoodview Av
20000 CmsC 97068 686 H6
20000 WLIN 97068 686 H6
Hoodview Ct
20000 WLIN 97068 686 H6
SE Hoodview Dr
51300 SPSE 97056 474 F3
SW Hoodview Dr
10100 TGRD 97224 655 D7
Hood View Ln
800 CmsC 97034 656 D4
800 LKOW 97034 656 D4
SW Hood View Pl
7000 BRTN 97008 625 B6
Hood View St
1100 ORCY 97045 717 E1
SW Hoodvista Ln
13100 TGRD 97224 655 A6
13100 WasC 97224 655 A6
Hook Dr
- NWBG 97132 713 H7
- YmhC 97132 713 H7
SW Hooker St
- PTLD 97201 626 D1
SW Hoops Ct
16300 WasC 97223 654 G5
SW Hope Cir
2600 TDLE 97060 599 F6
SW Hope Ct
2800 TDLE 97060 599 E6
NW Hopedale Ct
9200 PTLD 97229 595 E3
SW Hopi Ct
19400 TLTN 97062 685 G4
SW Hopi Pl
28600 WNVL 97070 715 E6
Hopkins Ln
- LKOW 97035 656 A4
NW Hoquiam Ct
900 CMAS 98607 569 B4
SE Horace Rd
25800 CmsC 97022 720 J4
SW Horizon Blvd
14400 TGRD 97223 654 J4
14400 WasC 97223 654 J4
14500 BRTN 97007 654 J4
Horizon Dr
22100 WLIN 97068 686 H6
NW Horizon Dr
2200 MCMV 97128 770 D4
NE Horizon Lp
- HBRO 97124 594 A3
NE Horne Rd
17100 ClkC 98606 479 C3
Hornecker Av
- SNDY 97055 691 B3
NW Hornecker Rd
31000 HBRO 97124 593 A2
31000 WasC 97124 593 A2
31900 WasC 97124 592 G1
32400 WasC 97113 592 G1
Horseshoe Curv
1300 LKOW 97034 656 E7
SE Horseshoe Dr
34700 CmsC 97022 720 E3
S Horseshoe Ln
21500 CmsC 97023 719 C4
SW Horseshoe Wy
16200 BRTN 97007 624 G7
Horseshoe Lake Rd NE
1700 MrnC 97137 772 G5
SE Horsetail Ct
8700 HPYV 97236 628 B7

STREET
Block City ZIP Map# Grid
SE Horsetail Falls Ct
8600 HPYV 97236 628 D7
SW Horse Tale Dr
17200 WasC 97007 654 E3
Hort St
1800 MCMV 97128 770 F7
Horton Ct
21300 WLIN 97068 686 J5
NE Horton Ln
2500 MCMV 97128 771 A2
Horton Rd
4300 WLIN 97068 687 A5
6400 WLIN 97068 686 H5
SW Horton Wy
10 WasC 97006 594 F5
Hoskins St
1200 NWBG 97132 713 D6
SW Hosler Wy
22800 SRWD 97140 684 E7
SE Hosner Rd
5800 MthC 97080 630 E5
SE Hosner Ter
3300 MthC 97080 630 E3
Hotspur St
10 LKOW 97035 656 B5
N Houghton St
2700 PTLD 97217 566 D3
4200 PTLD 97203 566 C3
SW Houston Ct
17100 SRWD 97140 684 F5
SW Houston Dr
20600 SRWD 97140 684 F5
NE Houston Rd
37400 MthC 97019 600 H6
Hovland Wy
58700 ClbC 97051 414 G2
S Howard Ct
20500 CmsC 97023 719 E7
20500 CmsC 97023 749 F1
Howard Dr
- MCMV 97128 770 D5
SW Howard Dr
13000 TGRD 97223 655 C5
SE Howard Rd
1100 MthC 97019 600 J7
1100 MthC 97019 630 H1
Howard St
200 STHN 97051 385 B7
2300 VCVR 98661 537 A4
N Howard St
100 NWBG 97132 713 C7
S Howard St
100 NWBG 97132 713 C7
300 NWBG 97132 743 C1
SE Howard St
17500 CmsC 97267 687 D2
Howard James Lp
800 DAYT 97114 771 J4
800 YmhC 97114 771 J4
SW Howards Wy
2000 PTLD 97201 596 C6
S Howards Mill Rd
14700 CmsC 97042 777 G5
SW Howatt St
9000 WasC 97225 625 E2
SE Howe Ln
4400 MWKE 97222 657 B1
N Howe St
700 CLTN 97111 711 A7
S Howe St
200 CLTN 97111 741 A1
SE Howe St
4000 MWKE 97222 657 B1
SW Howell Av
2400 TDLE 97060 599 F6
S Howell Rd
22400 CmsC 97023 749 J5
Howell St
19900 GLDS 97027 687 C3
NW Howell Park Rd
12800 MthC 97231 535 B3
SE Howlett Rd
22000 CmsC 97022 690 C7
22100 CmsC 97022 720 E2
NE Hoyt Ct
18800 GSHM 97230 598 H5
Hoyt St
500 MOLA 97038 837 D1
NE Hoyt St
2400 PTLD 97232 596 J5
3900 PTLD 97232 597 B5
4300 PTLD 97213 597 C5
10700 PTLD 97220 597 J5
12200 PTLD 97220 598 A5
15100 PTLD 97230 598 D5
16700 GSHM 97230 598 F5
20000 GSHM 97024 598 J5
NW Hoyt St
1600 PTLD 97209 596 D5
2000 PTLD 97210 596 D5
NE Hoyt Ter
16500 GSHM 97230 598 F5
N Hubbard Av
100 YCLT 98675 419 F1
S Hubbard Av
100 YCLT 98675 419 F1
SE Hubbard Rd
12200 CmsC 97015 658 A7
SE Hubbard Ter
13400 CmsC 97015 658 B7
Hubbard Cut Off Rd NE
- MrnC 97032 775 D7
SW Huber Ct
2200 PTLD 97219 656 C1
SW Huber St
2500 PTLD 97219 656 B1
6100 PTLD 97219 655 H1
SW Huckleberry Ct
300 MCMV 97128 770 D6
12800 WasC 97140 714 E4
E Huckleberry Dr
68200 CmsC 97067 724 C4
SW Huckleberry Dr
100 MCMV 97128 770 D6
Huckleberry Ln NE
- DNLD 97020 774 G5
- MrnC 97032 774 G5
SW Huddleson Ln
600 PTLD 97219 656 F2
SW Huddleson St
5700 PTLD 97219 655 J1
SW Hudgik Ct
21700 WasC 97006 594 B6
SE Hudson Ct
2200 TDLE 97060 599 H6

STREET
Block City ZIP Map# Grid
Hudson Ln
9000 ClkC 98686 507 E2
SE Hudson Rd
37600 CmsC 97009 660 J3
38600 CmsC 97055 660 J4
N Hudson St
4900 PTLD 97203 566 B3
10100 PTLD 97203 565 G1
NW Huffman St
23500 HBRO 97124 563 J7
SE Hugh Av
15500 CmsC 97267 656 J7
16000 CmsC 97267 686 J1
Hughes Dr
2400 WLIN 97068 687 A5
NE Hughes Ln
19000 YmhC 97115 712 F7
19000 YmhC 97132 712 F7
S Hughes Ln
25000 CmsC 97013 777 D2
NE Hughes Rd
400 ClkC 98671 540 J5
Hughes St
1100 ORCY 97045 717 D3
SW Hugo Ct
- WNVL 97070 745 H3
Hulet Av
800 NWBG 97132 713 E6
Hulet Ln
400 NWBG 97132 713 E7
SE Hull Av
4200 CmsC 97267 687 D2
6000 CmsC 97027 687 C3
6000 GLDS 97027 687 C3
SE Hull Ct
18300 CmsC 97267 687 C3
S Hull Rd
- CmsC 97045 688 G7
- CmsC 97045 718 G1
SE Hult St
9800 PTLD 97266 627 H2
N Humboldt St
1500 PTLD 97217 566 E7
NE Humboldt St
1100 PTLD 97211 596 H1
8200 PTLD 97218 597 G1
8700 PTLD 97220 597 G1
SW Hume Ct
2500 PTLD 97219 626 C6
9400 TLTN 97062 685 B6
SW Hume St
500 PTLD 97219 626 D6
SE Humidor St
16700 DAMA 97009 688 E1
Hummingbird Ln
56700 ClbC 97053 414 E6
S Hummingbird Ln
20600 CmsC 97023 749 D1
SE Hummingbird Ln
20300 CmsC 97055 692 J6
SW Humphrey Blvd
3500 MthC 97221 626 A1
3500 PTLD 97201 626 B1
3500 PTLD 97221 626 A1
3500 PTLD 97239 626 B1
5100 MthC 97221 625 J1
5100 PTLD 97221 595 J7
5100 PTLD 97221 625 J1
5200 MthC 97221 595 J7
SW Humphrey Ct
4500 MthC 97221 626 A1
4500 PTLD 97221 626 A1
E Humphrey St
100 YCLT 98675 419 F1
W Humphrey St
100 YCLT 98675 419 F1
600 ClkC 98675 419 E1
SW Humphrey Park Rd
2200 MthC 97221 596 A7
2200 PTLD 97221 626 A1
5000 MthC 97221 626 A1
SW Humphrey Park Crest
4800 MthC 97221 596 A7
E Hunchback Ct
68200 CmsC 97067 724 C3
E Hunchback Dr
68800 CmsC 97067 724 C4
NW Hunsaker Ct
3300 CMAS 98607 569 B2
SW Hunt Ct
10800 WNVL 97070 745 C1
N Hunt St
700 PTLD 97217 566 F4
4100 PTLD 97203 566 B4
SW Hunt Club Dr
7000 WasC 97223 625 G5
SW Hunt Club Ln
7000 WasC 97223 625 G6
SW Hunt Club Pl
7700 PTLD 97219 625 H6
SW Hunt Club Rd
- BRTN 97223 625 G5
7000 WasC 97223 625 G5
Hunter Av
15900 CmsC 97045 687 F6
15900 ORCY 97045 687 F6
Hunter Ct
3000 WLIN 97068 686 H4
17300 LKOW 97035 685 J1
SE Hunter Dr
11700 HPYV 97236 658 B4
NW Hunter Ln
1900 ClkC 98629 386 E6
SW Hunter Ln
19500 WasC 97007 624 D6
SE Hunter St
5000 MWKE 97222 657 C3
Hunter Wy
2900 WLIN 97068 686 H4
SW Hunters Cir
4400 GSHM 97080 628 G4
NW Hunters Dr
14300 WasC 97006 594 J3
14300 WasC 97229 594 J3
Hunters Run
- BRTN 97006 594 G5
SE Hunters Bluff Av
9200 CmsC 97236 657 H1
SW Huntington Av
900 WasC 97005 595 B6
900 WasC 97225 595 B7
2100 WasC 97225 625 B1
2200 BRTN 97005 625 B1
2200 BRTN 97225 625 B1
2200 WasC 97225 625 B1

STREET
Block City ZIP Map# Grid
S Huntington Dr
10900 CmsC 97045 716 H6
SW Huntwood Ct
15700 WasC 97224 654 H7
SW Huntwood Wy
14700 WasC 97224 654 H7
SW Hunziker Rd
7200 TGRD 97223 655 F4
SE Hurlburt Rd
32500 MthC 97019 600 D7
32900 MthC 97019 630 D1
NE Hurleys Ln
11000 YmhC 97132 743 A1
N Huron Av
7400 PTLD 97203 566 B5
SW Huron Ct
8400 TLTN 97062 685 F6
SE Huron St
12200 CmsC 97015 658 A5
SW Hurrell Ln
17300 BRTN 97006 594 F6
17300 WasC 97006 594 F6
SE Hurse Ln
12200 HPYV 97236 658 A3
N Hurst Av
7200 PTLD 97217 566 C5
9700 PTLD 97203 566 C3
NE Hurt Rd
30200 MthC 97060 600 B5
NW Huserik Dr
4500 WasC 97229 594 J1
4900 WasC 97229 564 J7
NW HWY 47
- BNKS 97106 531 J6
- FTGV 97116 592 A3
- WasC 97116 592 A3
2400 FTGV 97116 591 J1
2400 WasC 97116 591 J1
4500 WasC 97116 561 J6
10000 WasC 97116 531 J7
16500 WasC 97106 531 H3
NW HWY 47 SR-47
- BNKS 97106 531 J4
- FTGV 97116 592 A3
- WasC 97116 592 A3
2400 FTGV 97116 591 J1
2400 WasC 97116 591 J1
4500 WasC 97116 561 J7
10000 WasC 97116 531 J7
11800 WasC 97106 531 J7
NE Hyde Cir
200 HBRO 97124 593 E4
NE Hyde St
1800 HBRO 97124 593 E4
NW Hyde Park Ln
20700 HBRO 97006 594 C4
SW Hyland Ct
7300 BRTN 97008 625 A6
NE Hyland Dr
- YmhC 97115 742 J1
22800 YmhC 97132 742 J1
22800 YmhC 97132 743 A1
NE Hyland Ln
10700 YmhC 97132 742 J1
SW Hyland Ter
13300 BRTN 97008 625 A6
SW Hyland Wy
6300 BRTN 97008 625 A5
SW Hyland Park Ct
7100 BRTN 97008 625 A6
SW Hyland Wy Ct
7100 BRTN 97008 625 A6
SE Hymie Wy
17900 CmsC 97267 687 C2
Hy Oaks Ln
33100 CmsC 97038 837 F5

I

I St
- PTLD 97219 655 J3
10 CBAC 97018 385 C3
400 WHGL 98671 569 J4
900 WHGL 98671 570 A5
3900 VCVR 98663 536 H2
5600 ClkC 98671 570 F5
I-5
- ClkC - 386 D6
- ClkC - 416 E4
- ClkC - 446 G2
- ClkC - 476 H1
- ClkC - 506 G6
- CmsC - 715 H7
- CmsC - 745 C7
- DRHM - 685 G3
- LKOW - 655 H5
- MrnC - 774 H6
- MrnC - 775 B1
- PTLD - 536 F7
- PTLD - 566 F6
- PTLD - 596 G5
- PTLD - 626 C7
- PTLD - 655 J2
- PTLD - 656 B1
- RDGF - 416 F6
- RDGF - 446 F1
- RVGR - 685 G3
- TGRD - 655 J1
- TGRD - 685 H1
- TLTN - 685 G3
- VCVR - 506 G6
- VCVR - 536 G1
- WasC - 685 G2
- WasC - 715 E2
- WDLD - 386 A2
- WNVL - 715 E7
- WNVL - 745 E1
I-5 TRK
- PTLD - 655 J2
I-5 Columbia River Hwy
- PTLD - 596 G3
I-5 Interstate Br
- PTLD - 536 F6
- VCVR - 536 F6
I-5 Marquam Br
- PTLD - 596 F7
- PTLD - 626 F1
I-84 Banfield Expwy
- FRVW - 598 J4
- FRVW - 599 A4
- GSHM - 598 J4
- MWDP - 597 H2
- PTLD - 596 H5
- PTLD - 597 C4
- PTLD - 598 B3

STREET
Block City ZIP Map# Grid
I-84 Banfield Expwy
- TDLE - 599 E3
- WDVL - 599 E3
I-84 Columbia River Hwy
- MthC - 599 J3
- MthC - 600 J4
- TDLE - 599 G3
- WDVL - 599 E3
I-205
- ClkC - 476 J7
- ClkC - 477 A7
- ClkC - 507 D3
- ClkC - 537 G1
- VCVR - 507 G7
- VCVR - 537 J7
- VCVR - 567 J2
I-205 East Portland Frwy
- CmsC - 627 G1
- CmsC - 657 G1
- CmsC - 685 J5
- CmsC - 686 B5
- CmsC - 687 F3
- GLDS - 687 F4
- MWDP - 597 G6
- ORCY - 687 F4
- PTLD - 567 J6
- PTLD - 568 A5
- PTLD - 597 G6
- PTLD - 627 G1
- TLTN - 685 J5
- WLIN - 686 F7
- WLIN - 687 C6
- WLIN - 716 J1
- WLIN - 717 A1
I-205 Glenn Jackson Br
- MthC - 567 J2
- MthC - 568 A4
- PTLD - 568 A5
- VCVR - 567 J2
I-405 Stadium Frwy
- PTLD - 596 E5
- PTLD - 626 E1
SW Ian Ct
- WasC 97006 624 D1
SW Ibach Ct
9100 TLTN 97062 685 E7
SW Ibach St
9500 TLTN 97062 685 D7
9500 WasC 97062 685 D7
SW Ibis Ter
11900 BRTN 97007 654 G3
Icarus Lp
10 LKOW 97035 656 B3
Icenogle Lp
- ClbC 97056 474 F1
SE Icenogle Lp
- ClbC 97056 474 F2
N Ida Av
9200 PTLD 97203 565 J3
Ida St
- MCMV 97128 770 D5
Idaho Ct
5300 VCVR 98661 537 C5
SW Idaho Dr
4300 PTLD 97219 626 A5
4300 PTLD 97221 626 A5
Idaho St
4100 VCVR 98661 537 C5
6700 VCVR 98664 537 D5
SW Idaho St
3000 PTLD 97239 626 B5
5000 PTLD 97221 625 J5
SW Idaho Ter
3700 PTLD 97219 626 B5
3700 PTLD 97221 626 A5
NW Idanha St
18800 WasC 97229 594 E1
SE Ide St
3600 HBRO 97123 593 G5
SE Idleman Rd
9200 CmsC 97236 657 G2
9800 HPYV 97236 657 G2
11700 HPYV 97236 658 A2
Idleman St
39300 SNDY 97055 691 A2
SE Idlewine Rd
21100 CmsC 97022 690 B6
SE Idyllwild Ct
11400 CmsC 97015 657 J5
SW Ihrig Rd
47300 WasC 97116 591 C4
NE Ilafern Ln
21900 YmhC 97115 742 J1
21900 YmhC 97132 742 J1
NW Illahe St
18800 WasC 97229 564 E7
SW Illahee Ct
8700 WNVL 97070 745 E2
SW Illahee Dr
8700 WNVL 97070 745 E2
SW Illinois Ln
20500 WasC 97007 624 C5
E Illinois St
100 NWBG 97132 713 C7
SW Illinois St
2700 PTLD 97239 626 B4
4500 PTLD 97221 626 A4
5000 PTLD 97221 625 J4
W Illinois St
- NWBG 97132 713 B6
SE Ilona Ct
17200 CmsC 97267 656 H6
NW Ilwaco Ct
1400 CMAS 98607 569 B4
NW Ilwaco St
300 CMAS 98607 569 B5
SE Image Ln
9000 VCVR 98664 567 G1
SE Image Rd
1900 VCVR 98664 567 F1
N Image Canoe Av
12800 PTLD 97217 536 E6
SW Imagination Wy
- TDLE 97060 599 E5
NW Imbrie Dr
21700 HBRO 97124 594 B1
SE Imlay Av
1100 HBRO 97123 593 J7
1100 WasC 97123 593 J7
2400 HBRO 97123 623 J1
NW Imnaha Ct
4500 WasC 97229 564 C7
4500 WasC 97229 594 C1
Impala Ln
19700 CmsC 97045 716 H6

STREET
Block City ZIP Map# Grid
NE Imperial Av
700 PTLD 97232 597 B4
SW Imperial Av
11600 KNGC 97224 655 B7
SE Imperial Ct
7300 CmsC 97222 657 E2
SW Imperial Ct
2300 WasC 97225 625 E1
21500 WasC 97006 624 B1
Imperial Dr
4000 WLIN 97068 716 J1
4000 WLIN 97068 717 A1
4100 WLIN 97068 687 A6
SW Imperial Dr
6500 BRTN 97008 625 C5
9400 WasC 97225 625 E1
SW Imperial Ln
20400 WasC 97006 624 C1
20600 WasC 97006 594 C7
SW Imperial Pl
20700 WasC 97006 624 B2
SW Imperial St
21200 WasC 97006 624 B1
NW Imperial Ter
2700 PTLD 97210 596 C5
SE Imperial Crest St
12200 CmsC 97236 658 A4
12200 HPYV 97236 658 A4
SE Ina Av
4500 CmsC 97267 687 B2
SE Ina Pl
17200 CmsC 97267 687 C2
Independence Av
10 LKOW 97035 656 B4
SE Independence Av
31400 CmsC 97023 750 D3
SW Independence Wy
17700 WasC 97006 594 F5
S Index St
2300 WHGL 98671 570 C7
3400 ClkC 98671 570 C7
SW Indian Ln
8800 WNVL 97070 715 E6
Indian Tr
1900 LKOW 97034 656 C6
Indiana Dr
6900 VCVR 98664 537 E5
Indian Creek Av
18800 CmsC 97035 685 J3
18800 LKOW 97035 685 J3
SW Indian Creek Av
19000 CmsC 97035 685 J3
19000 RVGR 97035 685 J3
Indian Creek Ct
4800 CmsC 97035 685 G3
Indian Creek Dr
18200 LKOW 97035 685 J2
18200 LKOW 97035 686 A2
Indian Creek Wy
18700 LKOW 97035 685 J2
SW Indian Hill Ln
8300 BRTN 97008 625 B7
SW Indian John Pl
2500 TDLE 97060 599 F6
SW Indian John St
2200 TDLE 97060 599 F6
SW Indian Mary Ct
2500 TDLE 97060 599 E6
Indian Oak Ct
100 MOLA 97038 837 F1
NW Indian Spring Dr
13400 ClkC 98685 476 F6
Indian Springs Cir
18800 CmsC 97035 686 A3
Indian Springs Rd
18800 CmsC 97035 686 A3
19100 LKOW 97035 686 A3
Indian Summer St
37200 CmsC 97055 690 H1
37200 SNDY 97055 690 H1
S Indigo Av
20400 CmsC 97045 718 G7
20400 CmsC 97045 748 G1
Indigo Wy
2700 FTGV 97116 591 G3
Industrial Pkwy
900 NWBG 97132 743 E1
NW Industrial St
2600 PTLD 97210 596 B3
Industrial Wy
- CmsC 97009 690 F1
400 MOLA 97038 807 C7
400 MOLA 97038 837 C1
35000 STHN 97051 415 A3
35000 STHN 97053 415 B3
35800 ClbC 97051 415 A3
36000 SNDY 97055 690 F1
NW Industrial Wy
500 ECDA 97023 750 A2
SE Industrial Wy
14300 CmsC 97015 657 G6
SW Industrial Wy
3400 WasC 97007 624 C2
10500 TLTN 97062 685 C6
11000 WasC 97062 685 C6
30000 WNVL 97070 715 D7
30000 WNVL 97070 745 D1
SW Inez St
9700 TGRD 97224 655 D6
Ingalls St
1200 VCVR 98660 536 F4
NW Ingle Av
- PTLD 97210 565 G5
- PTLD 97231 565 G5
NE Ingles Rd
2700 ClkC 98607 538 J2
2700 ClkC 98607 539 A3
2700 ClkC 98682 538 J2
2700 ClkC 98682 539 A3
NW Inglewood Ct
5800 CMAS 98607 539 B6
SW Inglewood Ct
9700 WasC 97225 625 F1
SW Inglewood Pl
9700 WasC 97225 625 F1
Inglewood St
1600 FTGV 97116 592 A5
SW Inglewood St
9400 WasC 97225 625 E1
10000 BRTN 97225 625 E1
SW Inglis Dr
19500 WasC 97007 624 D7
SW Ingrid Ter
18000 WasC 97007 624 E7

STREET
Block City ZIP Map# Grid
Inishbride Ct
19300 ORCY 97045 717 B5
SW Inkster Dr
17300 SRWD 97140 714 E1
NW Innisbrook Pl
5300 WasC 97229 564 D7
SW Innovation Ct
- BRTN 97006 624 H2
SE Innovation Wy
1100 VCVR 98683 538 E7
Inskeep Dr
- CmsC 97045 717 F5
- ORCY 97045 717 F5
SE Insley Ct
3600 PTLD 97202 627 A4
SE Insley St
2500 PTLD 97202 626 J4
3300 PTLD 97202 627 A4
5000 PTLD 97206 627 C4
8200 PTLD 97266 627 F4
11700 PTLD 97266 628 A4
NE Interlachen Ln
- FRVW 97230 598 J1
20100 FRVW 97024 598 J1
20100 FRVW 97024 599 A2
20100 GSHM 97230 598 J1
SW Intermark St
- BRTN 97225 595 G7
7900 WasC 97225 595 G7
NE International Pkwy
- PTLD 97220 567 G5
SE International Wy
3700 MWKE 97222 657 B3
5500 CmsC 97222 657 C4
N Interstate Av
- PTLD 97232 596 G5
1900 PTLD 97227 596 F3
4000 PTLD 97217 596 E1
4800 PTLD 97217 566 E7
Interstate Br
- PTLD - 536 F7
- VCVR - 536 F7
Interstate Br I-5
- PTLD - 536 F7
- VCVR - 536 F7
N Interstate Pl
8300 PTLD 97217 566 E4
NE Intervale Rd
10200 YmhC 97111 711 E7
11500 YmhC 97111 741 H1
SE Inverness Av
2100 GSHM 97080 629 H5
3100 MthC 97080 629 G6
SW Inverness Ct
10600 PTLD 97219 656 C2
NE Inverness Dr
11300 PTLD 97220 568 A7
11300 PTLD 97230 568 A7
NW Inverness Dr
2300 HBRO 97124 594 D3
SW Inverness Wy
9400 WasC 97007 654 C1
SW Inverurie Rd
15700 CmsC 97035 655 J7
15700 LKOW 97035 655 J7
16700 CmsC 97035 685 J1
16700 LKOW 97035 685 J1
NW Iona Ct
33900 WasC 97124 592 H4
NE Ione Lp
1600 CMAS 98607 569 F4
NE Ione St
3500 CMAS 98607 569 F1
NW Ione St
100 DNDE 97115 742 J2
100 YmhC 97115 742 J2
SW Iowa Dr
8800 TLTN 97062 685 D7
9800 WasC 97062 685 D7
Iowa Ln
900 VCVR 98664 537 E5
SW Iowa St
1800 PTLD 97239 626 D4
4700 PTLD 97221 626 A4
5000 PTLD 97221 625 J4
Ipswich St
100 GLDS 97027 687 D4
Ira Ln
18800 CmsC 97045 717 G4
Ireland Ln
4700 CmsC 97068 686 J6
4700 WLIN 97068 686 J6
NE Ireland Rd
29200 ClkC 98607 539 J1
29900 ClkC 98607 540 A1
NE Irene Ct
1100 HBRO 97124 593 D1
1100 WasC 97124 593 D1
SE Irina Ct
8100 PTLD 97206 627 C7
Iriquois Rd
- WasC 97005 594 J7
NW Iris Ct
2200 CMAS 98607 569 B3
SE Iris Ct
5900 CmsC 97267 657 C6
SW Iris Ct
13100 BRTN 97008 625 A5
SE Iris St
8100 JNCY 97267 687 F1
N Iris Wy
9500 PTLD 97203 565 H2
SE Iron Rd
35900 CmsC 97022 720 F2
NE Ironcreek Ter
100 HBRO 97124 593 J5
200 WasC 97124 593 J5
NW Iron Horse Ct
3200 CMAS 98607 569 B2
SW Iron Horse Ln
11600 BRTN 97008 625 C5
SW Iron Horse St
7000 WNVL 97070 715 G6
Iron Mountain Blvd
600 LKOW 97034 656 E5
2100 LKOW 97034 656 C6
SE Iron Mountain Blvd
12400 MthC 97219 656 G4
NW Ironside Ter
- PTLD 97209 596 F4
SW Ironstone Pl
8700 BRTN 97007 624 H7
Ironwood
- CmsC 97015 657 H7

STREET
Block City ZIP Map# Grid

SE Ironwood Av
3300 HBRO 97123 623 H1
3300 WasC 97123 623 H1
SE Ironwood Ct
52200 SPSE 97056 474 F1
SW Ironwood Ct
7000 WNVL 97070 745 F2
Ironwood Dr
300 NWBG 97132 713 G7
NW Ironwood Ln
10800 WasC 97229 595 D3
SE Ironwood Ln
1200 GSHM 97080 629 H4
SW Ironwood Ln
- SRWD 97140 714 J1
SW Ironwood Lp
11300 TGRD 97223 655 C2
SE Ironwood Pl
800 GSHM 97080 629 H4
800 MthC 97080 629 H4
S Ironwood Rd
14300 CmsC 97045 747 F3
SE Ironwood Wy
1800 GSHM 97080 629 H5
SW Iroquois Dr
8300 TLTN 97062 685 E5
N Irvine Ct
2700 CNLS 97113 592 G4
NE Irvine Ct
1800 MCMV 97128 770 J4
N Irvine St
2100 CNLS 97113 592 F4
NE Irvine St
100 MCMV 97128 770 J5
SE Irvine St
100 MCMV 97128 770 J5
NE Irving Ct
19400 GSHM 97230 598 H5
Irving St
400 ORCY 97045 717 D2
6100 WLIN 97068 687 B5
NE Irving St
400 PTLD 97232 596 G5
3000 PTLD 97232 597 A5
5200 PTLD 97213 597 D5
9000 PTLD 97220 597 G5
12700 PTLD 97230 598 B5
17200 GSHM 97230 598 F5
NW Irving St
- PTLD 97209 596 F5
2000 PTLD 97210 596 D5
8600 PTLD 97229 595 F4
8600 WasC 97229 595 F4
NW Irvington Ct
41800 BNKS 97106 531 H5
SE Irwin Ct
2700 HBRO 97123 624 A1
SE Isaac Dr
10300 HPYV 97236 658 A2
SE Isabella Ct
8500 PTLD 97266 627 F3
Isabella Ln
59900 ClbC 97051 385 A7
59900 STHN 97051 385 A7
SW Isabella St
2500 PTLD 97201 596 C7
Isberg RV Pk
- MrnC 97002 775 A3
NW Island Cir
200 BRTN 97006 594 H5
E Island Rd
69300 CmsC 97067 724 C7
SE Island Rd
28600 CmsC 97022 719 G7
NW Island Ter
800 BRTN 97006 594 H4
Island Aire Dr
200 ClkC 98674 386 A2
200 WDLD 98674 386 A2
300 WDLD 98674 385 J2
N Island Cove Ln
11600 PTLD 97217 566 F1
SW Isle Wy Ln
31100 CmsC 97068 746 F2
NE Issler St
5100 ClkC 98661 507 C5
SW Itel St
11700 TLTN 97062 685 B5
11800 WasC 97062 685 B5
NW Ithaca Ct
3000 WasC 97229 594 F2
SW Ivana Ct
9400 TGRD 97223 655 E1
N Ivanhoe St
7900 PTLD 97203 565 G3
N Ivanhoe St US-30 BYP
8200 PTLD 97203 565 H3
S Ivel Rd
16000 CmsC 97004 748 A2
SE Ivon Ct
12300 PTLD 97236 628 A1
18400 GSHM 97030 628 G2
SE Ivon St
1200 PTLD 97202 626 H1
3800 PTLD 97202 627 B1
6000 PTLD 97206 627 D1
16800 PTLD 97236 628 F1
SW Ivory Lp
1000 GSHM 97080 628 G4
1000 MthC 97236 628 G3
SW Ivory St
8900 BRTN 97007 624 H7
9100 BRTN 97007 654 E1
S Ivy
400 CNBY 97013 776 D1
NE Ivy Av
300 ClkC 98629 416 H1
300 LCTR 98629 416 H1
NW Ivy Cir
2600 CMAS 98607 569 D2
S Ivy Cir
500 CNLS 97113 592 D6
Ivy Ct
1500 LKOW 97034 686 E1
NW Ivy Ct
2600 CMAS 98607 569 D3
S Ivy Ct
900 CNBY 97013 746 D7
1100 CNBY 97013 776 D1
Ivy Dr
3500 NWBG 97132 713 D4
NW Ivy Dr
1000 CMAS 98607 569 D4
SW Ivy Dr
33000 SPSE 97056 474 D1

Ivy Ln
100 STHN 97051 385 A7
16300 LKOW 97034 656 G7
16300 LKOW 97034 686 G1
NE Ivy Ln
- MCMV 97128 771 E6
NW Ivy Ln
2800 CMAS 98607 569 D2
SW Ivy Ln
6900 BRTN 97225 625 H4
6900 PTLD 97225 625 H4
SW Ivy Rd
400 ECDA 97023 750 B4
N Ivy St
100 CNBY 97013 746 C6
100 PTLD 97227 596 G2
1400 CmsC 97013 746 C4
NE Ivy St
10 PTLD 97227 596 G2
400 PTLD 97212 596 G2
NW Ivy St
2300 CMAS 98607 569 D3
S Ivy St
100 CNBY 97013 746 D7
1000 CNLS 97113 592 E6
1100 CNBY 97013 776 D1
1300 CmsC 97013 776 D1
SW Ivy St
15400 BRTN 97007 624 H5
15400 WasC 97007 624 H5
NW Ivybridge St
17200 WasC 97229 564 G7
SE Ivy Creek St
15300 HPYV 97236 658 D5
SW Ivy Glen Ct
15000 BRTN 97007 624 H5
SW Ivy Glenn Dr
17300 WasC 97007 624 F5
SW Ivy Glenn St
16300 BRTN 97007 624 G5
16900 WasC 97007 624 G5

J

J St
- PTLD 97219 655 J3
10 CBAC 97018 385 D3
400 WHGL 98671 569 J4
3900 WHGL 98671 570 D5
5600 ClkC 98671 570 F5
NW J St
- WasC 97006 594 B5
NW Jack Ln
10000 PTLD 97229 595 E2
SE Jack Ln
- CmsC 97222 657 E2
NW Jack Rd
14000 WasC 97106 531 B4
SE Jack Rd
6200 CmsC 97222 657 D2
6200 MWKE 97222 657 D2
SE Jack St
7300 CmsC 97222 657 E2
SW Jack Burns Blvd
8300 WNVL 97070 715 E3
SW Jackie Ct
11400 TGRD 97224 655 C6
SE Jackknife Rd
30400 CmsC 97022 690 A7
Jackson Ct
800 LFYT 97127 741 H6
NW Jackson Ln
3300 PTLD 97229 595 E2
NW Jackson Lp
5300 CMAS 98607 539 B7
NW Jackson Pl
6000 CMAS 98607 539 A6
SE Jackson Rd
30200 MthC 97080 630 B6
Jackson St
300 LFYT 97127 771 G1
500 ORCY 97045 717 C1
700 LFYT 97127 741 H7
1000 ORCY 97045 687 D7
NE Jackson St
100 HBRO 97124 593 D4
NW Jackson St
100 HBRO 97124 593 A4
5700 CMAS 98607 539 B6
SE Jackson St
1900 MWKE 97222 656 J2
3700 MWKE 97222 657 B2
SW Jackson St
1800 PTLD 97201 596 D7
Jackson Wy
34900 ClbC 97056 444 H4
SW Jackson Wy
29500 WNVL 97070 715 C7
SE Jackson Hills Dr
14600 HPYV 97236 658 D1
SE Jackson Park Rd
700 TDLE 97060 599 H5
NW Jackson Quarry Rd
10400 WasC 97124 563 G1
10900 WasC 97124 533 G7
13000 WasC 97133 533 F5
NE Jackson Rd Lp
3100 HBRO 97124 593 D1
3300 WasC 97124 593 D1
NE Jackson School Rd
2300 HBRO 97124 593 D2
3700 WasC 97124 593 C1
NW Jackson School Rd
4000 HBRO 97124 593 D1
4000 WasC 97124 593 D1
7800 WasC 97124 563 D4
7800 WasC 97133 563 D7
12000 WasC 97124 533 E6
12000 WasC 97133 533 E6
NE Jackson Village Lp
500 HBRO 97124 593 C3
SW Jacktown Rd
7000 WasC 97007 623 J5
9100 WasC 97007 653 J1
SW Jacob Ct
13000 KNGC 97224 685 A2
13000 WasC 97224 685 A2
Jacob Ln
20700 FRVW 97024 599 A3
NW Jacob Rd
30400 WasC 97133 533 C4
Jacobs Wy
14000 ORCY 97045 687 F6
NW Jacobson Rd
21200 HBRO 97124 564 A6

NW Jacobson Rd
21200 HBRO 97229 564 C6
21200 WasC 97229 564 C6
22600 WasC 97124 564 A6
23300 HBRO 97124 563 J6
23300 WasC 97124 563 J6
SE Jacoby Rd
18500 SNDY 97055 691 A5
18700 CmsC 97055 691 A4
SE Jacquelin Dr
1200 HBRO 97123 623 D1
Jacqui Ct
800 NWBG 97132 713 C6
SW Jade Av
2700 BRTN 97225 625 G1
2700 WasC 97225 625 G1
SE Jade Ct
17000 CmsC 97267 687 D2
Jade Glen Av
15600 SNDY 97055 690 H1
Jaden Dr
59800 ClbC 97051 385 A7
59800 STHN 97051 385 A7
SW Jaden Dr
- WasC 97006 624 D1
SW Jadeview Wy
- BRTN 97007 654 G1
SW Jaeger Ter
11900 BRTN 97007 654 G3
Jaime Dr
59100 ClbC 97051 414 D1
59100 ClbC 97053 414 D1
NW Jakes Ct
600 MCMV 97128 770 G3
Jakobi St
35500 STHN 97051 385 A7
SW Jamaica
11500 CmsC 97070 745 B1
11500 WNVL 97070 745 B1
SW Jameco Ct
21000 TLTN 97062 685 E6
James Ct
13200 ORCY 97045 717 D6
SW James Ct
1100 DNDE 97115 742 H4
James St
700 CBAC 97018 385 B2
1000 NWBG 97132 743 C1
32900 ClbC 97056 444 D5
N James St
9700 PTLD 97203 565 G1
NE James St
100 CMAS 98607 569 H4
SE James St
100 CMAS 98607 569 H5
SW James St
1500 MCMV 97128 770 F6
12100 TGRD 97223 655 B4
NW James Arthur Ct
13100 WasC 97229 595 B3
James View Dr
50900 ClbC 97056 474 D3
Jamie Cir
1600 WLIN 97068 716 G2
SE Jamie Ct
13600 CmsC 97015 658 B6
NE Jamie Dr
600 HBRO 97124 593 C2
SW Jamieson Ct
9200 BRTN 97005 625 E3
SW Jamieson Rd
4600 BRTN 97005 625 F4
8400 WasC 97225 625 F4
9200 WasC 97005 625 F4
NE JA Moore Rd
3400 ClkC 98604 417 C5
3400 ClkC 98629 417 C5
SE Jane Ct
19000 DAMA 97009 658 H3
SW Janell Ct
17600 WasC 97006 594 F7
SW Janet Pl
5000 WasC 97007 624 F3
SW Jann Ct
19500 WasC 97006 624 D1
SW Jann Dr
18200 WasC 97006 624 E1
SW Jann Pl
20000 WasC 97006 624 D1
SE Jannsen Dr
37700 CmsC 97023 750 H1
SE Jannsen Rd
8400 CmsC 97267 657 F7
8800 CmsC 97015 657 G7
SW Jan Tree Ct
6000 PTLD 97219 625 J5
N Jantzen Av
1600 PTLD 97217 536 E7
N Jantzen Dr
11800 PTLD 97217 536 F7
N Jantzen St
- PTLD 97217 536 E7
N Jantzen Beach Av
11900 PTLD 97217 536 F7
N Jantzen Beach Ctr
1700 PTLD 97217 536 E7
SW Janzen Ct
9700 TGRD 97224 655 D6
NE Jaquith Rd
18500 WasC 97132 683 C7
18500 WasC 97132 713 D1
SW Jaquith Rd
20000 WasC 97132 683 C6
21300 WasC 97123 683 E3
SE Jarl Rd
- CmsC 97055 690 F1
33400 CmsC 97009 690 F1
NW Jarrel Rd
25100 MthC 97124 533 H2
25200 WasC 97133 533 H2
N Jarrett St
10 PTLD 97211 566 G7
1700 PTLD 97217 566 E7
NE Jarrett St
10 PTLD 97211 566 G7
10 PTLD 97217 566 G7
2500 PTLD 97211 567 A7
4200 PTLD 97218 567 B7
13200 PTLD 97230 568 C7
NW Jarvis Pl
12800 BNKS 97106 531 J6
SW Jasmine Ct
300 MCMV 97128 770 E5
Jasmine Ln
2600 FTGV 97116 591 G3

NW Jasmine Ln
1900 PTLD 97229 595 G3
SW Jasmine Pl
2700 WasC 97006 624 E1
NW Jasmine St
3500 CMAS 98607 569 D2
SE Jasmine Wy
1500 GSHM 97080 629 H4
NW Jason Ct
300 HBRO 97124 593 A4
SE Jason Ct
10800 HPYV 97236 658 A3
W Jason Ct
600 MCMV 97128 770 G3
S Jason Dr
20100 CmsC 97045 718 B7
SE Jason Ln
10600 HPYV 97236 658 A2
Jason Lee Dr
13400 ORCY 97045 717 E2
Jason Lee Wy
18000 ORCY 97045 717 E2
S Jasper Cir
400 CNLS 97113 592 D6
SW Jasper Dr
9300 BRTN 97007 654 H1
SW Jasper Ln
15100 BRTN 97007 654 H1
S Jasper St
1000 CNLS 97113 592 E6
NE Java Wy
2400 HBRO 97124 593 D2
Jay Ct
1300 WLIN 97068 716 G2
SW Jay Ct
1100 WasC 97006 594 F6
SW Jay St
15300 BRTN 97006 594 H7
15300 WasC 97005 594 H7
17600 WasC 97006 594 E7
21800 HBRO 97123 594 B7
S Jaybird Wy
15200 CmsC 97045 688 B4
SW Jaylee St
18900 WasC 97007 624 D3
S Jean Dr
17500 CmsC 97045 718 D2
NW Jean Ln
2400 PTLD 97229 595 E2
SE Jean Ln
1700 HBRO 97123 593 E7
Jean Rd
17700 LKOW 97035 685 H1
SW Jean Rd
4500 LKOW 97035 686 A2
4700 LKOW 97035 685 J2
5000 CmsC 97035 685 J2
S Jean Wy
24000 CmsC 97004 748 E7
NE Jeanette Ct
- PTLD 97230 598 E5
SE Jeanette St
26800 MthC 97080 629 G7
NW Jeanne Ct
15800 WasC 97006 594 H3
Jeep Tr
- CmsC 97055 691 C3
SE Jefferson Ct
7800 CmsC 97267 657 F7
7800 CmsC 97267 687 H1
Jefferson Pkwy
- LKOW 97035 655 J4
- PTLD 97219 655 J4
10 LKOW 97035 656 A4
SW Jefferson Rd
- PTLD 97201 596 C6
Jefferson St
- CLTN 97111 711 A7
100 ORCY 97045 717 C1
700 VCVR 98660 536 F5
800 LFYT 97127 741 H7
800 ORCY 97045 687 D7
E Jefferson St
300 CLTN 97111 711 B7
N Jefferson St
- LFYT 97127 741 G7
- YmhC 97114 741 G7
- YmhC 97128 741 G7
NE Jefferson St
1900 HBRO 97124 593 E4
SE Jefferson St
100 LFYT 97127 771 G1
300 LFYT 97127 741 G7
1800 MWKE 97222 656 J2
3700 MWKE 97222 657 B2
7800 CmsC 97267 687 E1
8600 CmsC 97015 687 H2
SW Jefferson St
10 PTLD 97204 596 F7
800 PTLD 97201 596 D6
800 PTLD 97205 596 D6
5500 PTLD 97221 595 J7
10100 TGRD 97223 655 F2
10100 WasC 97223 655 F2
W Jefferson St
200 CLTN 97111 711 A7
NW Jefferson Wy
2300 MCMV 97128 770 D4
2300 YmhC 97128 770 D4
Jeffery Ct
700 NWBG 97132 713 C5
Jeffrey Ln
- PTLD 97217 566 F3
NW Jeffrey Pl
1000 BRTN 97006 594 G4
Jeffries Rd
33600 ClbC 97056 444 E5
Jemtegaard Rd
32000 ClkC 98671 570 C2
Jenifers Wy
- CmsC 97035 685 J2
- LKOW 97035 685 J2
SW Jenine Ln
12300 BRTN 97008 625 C5
SW Jenkins Rd
12700 BRTN 97005 625 A1
12900 WasC 97005 625 A1
14200 WasC 97005 624 J1
14300 BRTN 97005 624 J1
14500 BRTN 97005 594 J7
14500 BRTN 97006 594 G6
14500 BRTN 97006 624 J1
14500 WasC 97005 594 J7
14900 WasC 97006 594 H7

SW Jenna Ct
13600 TGRD 97223 654 J5
13600 TGRD 97223 655 A5
NW Jenne Av
1200 WasC 97229 595 A4
SE Jenne Ln
5500 MthC 97236 628 F5
SE Jenne Rd
5100 GSHM 97080 628 F4
5100 GSHM 97236 628 F4
5100 MthC 97236 628 F5
5500 PTLD 97236 628 F5
NW Jenne Lake Ct
16100 BRTN 97006 594 H5
SW Jennett Ct
12700 BRTN 97008 625 B7
E Jennie Ln
70900 CmsC 97049 724 E4
E Jennie Welch Ct
67400 CmsC 97067 724 B4
SE Jennifer Ct
4100 MthC 97060 629 G1
4100 TDLE 97060 629 G1
NW Jennifer Pl
1500 WasC 97229 595 D4
Jennifer St
- CmsC 97015 687 G1
SE Jennifer St
10100 CmsC 97015 687 H1
11500 CmsC 97015 688 A1
Jennifer Lynn Ct
19500 ORCY 97045 716 J5
SE Jennings Av
6400 GLDS 97267 687 D2
6500 GLDS 97027 687 D1
8300 CmsC 97267 687 F1
SE Jennings Rd
34700 ClkC 98671 570 E2
Jennings Wy
- TDLE 97060 599 F4
SE Jennings Crest Ln
17100 CmsC 97267 687 D2
Jenny Ln
2100 WLIN 97068 716 F2
SW Jenny Ln
33200 SPSE 97056 474 E2
NE Jenny Creek Rd
35900 ClkC 98629 386 G5
38800 ClkC 98674 386 J2
Jenny Marie Ln
- AURA 97002 775 F4
- MrnC 97002 775 F4
SE Jensen Ln
12600 CmsC 97009 659 J5
SW Jenshire Ln
14600 WasC 97223 654 J4
SW Jerald Ct
3500 PTLD 97221 626 B2
SW Jerald Wy
3700 PTLD 97221 626 B2
3800 PTLD 97239 626 B2
SW Jeremy St
17900 WasC 97007 624 F7
Jerger St
38800 SNDY 97055 690 J5
38800 SNDY 97055 691 A5
NW Jericho Ct
10600 WasC 97229 595 D4
NW Jericho Ln
600 CMAS 98607 569 A5
NW Jericho Rd
11400 WasC 97229 595 C4
NE Jernstedt Rd
7300 YmhC 97111 741 D3
Jerome St
100 ORCY 97045 717 A2
E Jerrys Ln
66900 CmsC 97011 724 A2
Jersey St
100 ORCY 97045 717 C2
E Jersey St
100 GLDS 97027 687 D4
N Jersey St
9700 PTLD 97203 565 G2
SW Jersey St
17700 WasC 97007 624 F3
W Jersey St
100 GLDS 97027 687 D4
SE Jess Ct
6200 HBRO 97123 593 J7
NW Jessamine Wy
2100 WasC 97229 595 B3
SW Jesse Ct
16500 WasC 97007 624 G7
SE Jesse Ln
10100 PTLD 97266 627 H2
NE Jesse St
20600 FRVW 97024 599 A4
SW Jessica Ct
19500 WasC 97006 594 D6
Jessica Dr
100 FTGV 97116 591 F3
S Jessica Ln
- CmsC 97023 749 J5
NE Jessica Lp
1400 HBRO 97124 593 E3
SW Jessica St
8300 WNVL 97070 745 E1
SW Jessica Wy
18900 WasC 97006 594 E6
SE Jessica Erin Ln
16500 CmsC 97267 687 C1
S Jessie Av
19700 CmsC 97045 717 C5
19700 ORCY 97045 717 C6
Jessie Ct
19700 CmsC 97045 717 C5
NE Jessup Ct
7100 PTLD 97218 567 E7
N Jessup St
10 PTLD 97211 566 G7
1900 PTLD 97217 566 D7
NE Jessup St
10 PTLD 97217 566 G7
400 PTLD 97211 566 H7
3300 PTLD 97211 567 B7
5200 PTLD 97218 567 D7
Jette Ct
7800 MrnC 97137 744 A7
SW Jette Ln
20100 WasC 97006 594 D6
E Jett View Ln
61800 CmsC 97011 693 E6
Jewel Ln
5100 CmsC 97035 685 J2

Jewel Ln
5100 LKOW 97035 685 J2
Jewelberry Av
- CmsC 97055 690 H1
- SNDY 97055 690 H1
NW Jewell Ln
14600 WasC 97229 564 J7
NE Jewell St
14800 PTLD 97230 598 D4
SE Jewett Dr
18500 CmsC 97267 687 B3
SW Jex Ln
200 WasC 97116 591 C4
NW Jillanne Ct
1800 MCMV 97128 770 E4
SE Jo Ct
1800 CmsC 97267 656 H7
SW Joann Ct
19800 WasC 97006 594 D7
NE Joanne Cir
500 HBRO 97124 593 C2
NE Joanne Ct
600 HBRO 97124 593 C2
S Joanne Ln
17700 CmsC 97045 718 D2
SE Jobes Ct
4300 MWKE 97222 657 B4
SW Jobin Ln
52300 SPSE 97056 474 D1
Jodi Ct
2200 NWBG 97132 713 E6
SW Jody St
11300 WasC 97005 625 C1
SW Joe Ct
8900 WasC 97223 625 F7
SW Joelle Ct
8500 TGRD 97223 655 F2
Joel Palmer Wy
- DAYT 97114 772 A5
- YmhC 97114 772 A5
Joel's Pl
1100 LFYT 97127 741 G7
SW Joe's Dr
51400 SPSE 97056 474 E3
SE Joette Dr
30300 CmsC 97009 660 A3
W Johanna Ct
100 NWBG 97132 743 B1
SW Johanna Dr
52000 SPSE 97056 474 D2
N John Av
8500 PTLD 97203 565 H2
SW John Ct
8500 TGRD 97223 655 F5
John Adams St
100 ORCY 97045 717 C1
700 ORCY 97045 687 D7
S John Adams St
100 ORCY 97045 717 B1
SE John Ashley Dr
15000 CmsC 97015 658 D5
E John Lake Rd
27600 CmsC 97049 724 H6
NW John Olsen Av
2700 HBRO 97006 594 C3
2700 HBRO 97124 594 D2
NW John Olsen Pl
3200 HBRO 97124 594 D2
John Paul Jones Av
23800 CmsC 97067 724 B3
E John Paul Jones Av
23600 CmsC 97067 724 B2
John Q Adams St
500 ORCY 97045 717 D1
1000 ORCY 97045 687 D7
SE Johns Ct
9200 CmsC 97236 657 G1
N Johnson Av
100 YCLT 98675 419 E1
S Johnson Av
100 YCLT 98675 419 E1
Johnson Ct
1200 NWBG 97132 713 D5
NE Johnson Ct
1800 MCMV 97128 770 J3
SW Johnson Ct
10300 TGRD 97223 655 C4
Johnson Dr
1600 NWBG 97132 713 D6
Johnson Rd
23000 CmsC 97068 686 F7
23000 WLIN 97068 686 F7
23300 WLIN 97068 716 F1
NE Johnson Rd
3700 ClkC 98629 417 C1
11600 YmhC 97111 711 D7
NW Johnson Rd
15000 MthC 97124 533 J2
16500 MthC 97124 534 A1
16500 MthC 97231 534 A1
18000 MthC 97231 504 B7
SE Johnson Rd
13500 CmsC 97222 657 E5
13700 CmsC 97267 657 E6
15100 CmsC 97015 657 F7
15900 CmsC 97015 687 F1
SW Johnson Rd
22700 CmsC 97068 686 F7
23000 WLIN 97068 686 F7
Johnson St
- PTLD 97218 567 D5
- WLIN 97068 687 B5
900 ORCY 97045 717 C3
NE Johnson St
2500 MCMV 97128 770 J3
NW Johnson St
1200 PTLD 97229 595 F4
2000 PTLD 97210 596 C5
2600 PTLD 97210 596 D5
8500 WasC 97229 595 F4
SE Johnson St
6200 HBRO 97123 623 J1
6200 HBRO 97123 624 A1
6200 WasC 97123 624 A1
7500 WasC 97006 624 B1
SW Johnson St
9900 TGRD 97223 655 E4
17000 BRTN 97006 624 G1
18500 WasC 97006 624 E1
21600 HBRO 97006 624 B1
21600 WasC 97123 624 B1
W Johnson St
200 CLTN 97111 711 A7
Johnson Ter
13600 CmsC 97034 656 C5

Johnson Ter
13600 LKOW 97034 656 C5
SE Johnson Creek Blvd
4500 MWKE 97222 627 C7
4500 PTLD 97222 627 B7
5100 CmsC 97206 627 C7
5100 CmsC 97222 627 C7
5100 PTLD 97206 627 C7
5500 MWKE 97206 627 C7
5700 MWKE 97206 657 D1
6000 MWKE 97222 657 D1
6100 CmsC 97206 657 E1
6100 CmsC 97222 657 E1
8000 CmsC 97236 657 G1
SW Johnson School Rd
31900 WasC 97113 623 A5
Johnsons Landing Rd
33600 ClbC 97056 474 F4
SE Johnston Dr
16700 PTLD 97236 628 F5
NE Johnstone Ct
1400 MCMV 97128 770 J2
NE John Storm Av
300 ClkC 98629 416 J1
300 LCTR 98629 416 J1
N Johnswood Dr
8200 PTLD 97203 565 H1
SE John Thomas Ct
11500 HPYV 97236 658 A2
Johnye Ct
2100 WLIN 97068 716 F1
NW Jolie Pl
1500 WasC 97229 595 D4
Jolie Point Rd
2300 WLIN 97068 687 A4
2800 WLIN 97068 686 J4
NE Jolma Rd
24900 ClkC 98604 448 E2
SW Jonagold Ter
- TGRD 97224 655 F6
NW Jonathon Pl
2400 WasC 97229 595 A3
Jones St
3400 NWBG 97132 713 C4
E Jones St
100 YCLT 98675 419 G1
400 ClkC 98675 419 G1
W Jones St
100 YCLT 98675 419 F1
600 ClkC 98675 419 F1
NE Jones Farm Pkwy
- HBRO 97124 593 E2
NE Jonesmore St
7200 PTLD 97213 597 E4
8200 PTLD 97220 597 F4
SW Jonquil Terr
20500 SRWD 97140 684 F5
Jonsrud Rd
37900 SNDY 97055 690 J1
N Jordan Av
7100 PTLD 97203 566 B4
SE Jordan Av
6300 CmsC 97222 657 D1
SE Jordan Ct
13200 CmsC 97236 658 B4
S Jordan Rd
14500 CmsC 97042 807 F2
NW Jordan Wy
6400 ClkC 98665 506 G6
SW Jordan Wy
16600 KNGC 97224 685 A1
16600 WasC 97224 685 A1
SW Jordy Ct
14600 WasC 97224 654 H7
NW Joscelyn St
16000 WasC 97006 594 G2
N Joseph Ct
2200 CNLS 97113 592 F4
NW Joseph Ct
14500 WasC 97229 594 J1
Joseph Dr
- CmsC 97045 717 G2
N Joseph St
2500 CNLS 97113 592 G4
NE Josephine Ct
700 HBRO 97124 593 C2
NE Josephine Dr
2000 HBRO 97124 593 C2
Josephine St
- PTLD 97231 565 B3
900 ORCY 97045 717 A3
NE Josephine St
800 HBRO 97124 593 D2
SW Joshua Ct
4800 TLTN 97062 685 J5
SW Joshua St
1700 PTLD 97219 656 D3
1800 PTLD 97035 656 C3
4400 CmsC 97062 686 A4
4400 TLTN 97062 686 A4
4600 TLTN 97062 685 J5
Josi Ct
14900 ORCY 97045 687 H6
SW Jourdan Ct
20600 WasC 97006 594 C7
Journeay Ct
3200 WLIN 97068 686 H6
Journey Dr
14900 CmsC 97045 687 G6
14900 ORCY 97045 687 G6
NW Joy Av
600 WasC 97229 595 B5
NE Joy St
100 CMAS 98607 569 F4
Joyce Ct
18600 ORCY 97045 717 B3
NE Joyce Ct
500 HBRO 97124 593 C2
Joys Dr
12800 CmsC 97045 717 C5
12800 ORCY 97045 717 C5
JP West Rd
31400 ClbC 97056 444 B7
32400 ClbC 97056 474 C1
32400 SPSE 97056 474 C1
SW JP West Rd
32600 ClbC 97056 474 D1
32700 ClbC 97056 444 D7
32700 SPSE 97056 444 D7
33000 SPSE 97056 474 E1
SW JP West St
33400 SPSE 97056 474 E1
NE JR Anderson Rd
6100 ClkC 98629 417 E4
7200 ClkC 98604 417 F3

STREET Block City ZIP Map# Grid

SW Juanita Pl
13100 BRTN 97008 625 A7
Juarez St
10 LKOW 97035 656 A3
S Jubb Rd
20900 CmsC 97023 749 F2
SW Jubilee Pl
9500 TGRD 97224 655 E6
SE Jubilee St
12700 HPYV 97236 658 D5
SE Judd Rd
26300 CmsC 97009 689 G4
27000 CmsC 97022 689 J4
28300 CmsC 97022 690 A6
E Jude Ln
20000 CmsC 97011 693 G6
SW Julia Ct
5000 PTLD 97221 626 A3
SW Julia Pl
9300 TGRD 97224 685 E1
NW Julia St
2500 CMAS 98607 569 A2
SW Julia St
200 PTLD 97239 626 F3
4500 PTLD 97221 626 A3
SW Juliann Ln
16700 WasC 97007 624 G6
SE Juliano Ct
17000 PTLD 97236 628 F2
SW Julie Ct
33200 SPSE 97056 474 E1
Julie Ln
900 MOLA 97038 807 D7
SE Julie Ln
13800 CmsC 97222 657 E5
13800 CmsC 97267 657 E5
SE Julie Pl
17200 PTLD 97236 628 F2
Julie Ann Dr
300 ORCY 97045 717 A3
SW Juliet Ter
14500 WasC 97224 654 H6
SW Juliette Dr
32400 WNVL 97070 745 E3
SW Junction Pl
800 GSHM 97030 628 F4
800 GSHM 97080 628 F4
800 GSHM 97236 628 F4
900 MthC 97236 628 F3
N Junction St
6200 PTLD 97203 566 A2
SW June Ct
14600 SRWD 97140 684 H7
June Dr
700 MOLA 97038 807 D7
800 CmsC 97038 807 D7
1500 VCVR 98661 537 A4
June Ln
- SPSE 97056 474 E1
NW Juneau Ct
1600 CMAS 98607 569 B4
N Juneau St
3800 PTLD 97203 566 C3
3800 PTLD 97217 566 C3
NE Junior St
1300 PTLD 97211 566 J6
2700 PTLD 97211 567 A6
Juniper
- CmsC 97015 657 H7
NE Juniper Av
10 GSHM 97080 629 C2
100 VCVR 98684 538 C6
1600 GSHM 97030 629 C1
2800 GSHM 97030 599 C7
SE Juniper Av
10 GSHM 97030 629 C3
10 GSHM 97080 629 C3
14400 VCVR 98684 538 C6
N Juniper Ct
500 CNBY 97013 746 C6
NE Juniper Ct
1900 GSHM 97030 629 C1
2700 GSHM 97030 599 C6
SE Juniper Ct E
500 GSHM 97080 629 C3
SE Juniper Ct W
500 GSHM 97080 629 C3
Juniper Dr
3200 NWBG 97132 713 D4
35200 STHN 97051 414 J1
SE Juniper Dr
2200 CmsC 97267 686 J1
NE Juniper Pl
1400 CNBY 97013 746 C5
SW Juniper Rd
400 ECDA 97023 750 A4
Juniper St
- YMHL 97148 711 A1
2600 FTGV 97116 592 A3
2600 WasC 97116 592 A3
N Juniper St
500 CNBY 97013 746 C5
1600 CmsC 97013 746 C5
S Juniper St
100 CNBY 97013 746 C6
100 YMHL 97148 711 A1
SE Juniper St
11900 MWKE 97222 657 D4
SW Juniper Ter
6600 BRTN 97008 625 B5
Juniper Wy
33400 ClbC 97056 474 E5
Junker St
38900 SNDY 97055 690 J2
38900 SNDY 97055 691 A2
SE Junker St
38700 SNDY 97055 690 J3
SE Jupiter Ct
14300 CmsC 97267 657 B6
NW Jupiter Hills Ct
16600 BRTN 97006 594 H5
SW Jurgens Av
17200 TLTN 97062 685 D2
17200 WasC 97062 685 D2
SW Jurgens Ln
9900 WasC 97062 685 D1
10200 TLTN 97062 685 D1
SE Justin Ln
13100 CmsC 97015 658 B6
NW Justus Dr
9800 PTLD 97229 595 E3

K

K Ct
4000 WHGL 98671 570 D5
K St
- PTLD 97219 655 J3
100 CBAC 97018 385 C4
400 WHGL 98671 569 J4
500 ClbC 97018 385 C4
2600 VCVR 98663 536 H3
4900 ClkC 98671 570 E5
4900 WHGL 98671 570 E5
5700 WLIN 97068 687 B6
NW K St
- WasC 97006 594 B5
SW Kable Ln
7200 TGRD 97224 655 G7
SW Kable St
9800 TGRD 97224 655 D7
SE Ka-De Ct
19800 DAMA 97009 658 J5
NE Kadow Dr
13300 ClkC 98686 477 B6
Kae Ct
500 MOLA 97038 837 D1
Kaen Rd
1800 ORCY 97045 717 D4
Kafton Ter
12600 ORCY 97045 717 C5
Kahle Ln NE
21300 MrnC 97002 775 E3
SW Kahle Rd
5800 CmsC 97070 715 H4
NW Kahneeta Ct
4800 WasC 97229 564 F7
NW Kahneeta Dr
4400 WasC 97229 594 F1
4700 WasC 97229 564 E7
Kaicya St NE
- DNLD 97020 774 G4
- MrnC 97002 774 G4
SE Kaiser Av
600 VCVR 98661 536 J7
NW Kaiser Rd
3200 WasC 97229 594 J2
4800 WasC 97229 564 J7
9000 WasC 97231 564 H3
N Kaiser Center Dr
- PTLD 97227 596 E2
SE Kaitlin Wy
13200 CmsC 97015 658 B7
Kalal Ct
19500 CmsC 97045 717 C5
19500 ORCY 97045 717 C5
NW Kalama St
20900 WasC 97229 564 C6
Kalberer Rd
54000 ClbC 97056 444 D3
Kale Vala Vil
- WasC 97007 624 F4
Kalex Ln
700 FTGV 97116 591 F4
SW Kalispell St
11200 TLTN 97062 685 C2
Kallapuya St
- DAYT 97114 772 A4
N Kalmar St
9500 PTLD 97203 565 H1
Kalugin Ct
600 CmsC 97038 807 D7
600 MOLA 97038 807 D7
SW Kalyca St
8800 WNVL 97070 745 E2
SW Kalyca Wy
1100 WasC 97006 594 E6
Kama Dr
- YmhC 97128 770 E7
SW Kamalyn Pl
900 WasC 97005 595 A7
SW Kame Ter
26000 CmsC 97140 715 B4
SW Kamen Pl
6200 WasC 97007 624 B4
SW Kameron Wy
12800 WasC 97223 654 H4
SW Kame Ter Ct
12300 CmsC 97140 715 B4
N Kamiakan Dr
2100 CNLS 97113 592 F4
N Kamiakan St
- CNLS 97113 592 G4
Kamm St
1100 ORCY 97045 717 D3
Kammeyer Rd
33100 ClbC 97056 474 D5
S Kamrath Rd
22000 CmsC 97004 748 A6
22300 CmsC 97045 748 A6
SW Kanan Dr
3500 PTLD 97221 626 A4
SW Kanan St
1800 PTLD 97239 626 C4
5500 PTLD 97221 625 J4
SW Kandrea Ct
17300 WasC 97007 624 F3
SW Kandrea St
17200 WasC 97007 624 F3
SE Kane Av
2000 GSHM 97080 629 F5
NE Kane Dr
1600 GSHM 97030 629 F1
NE Kane Rd
600 GSHM 97030 629 E1
1800 GSHM 97030 599 F7
2900 TDLE 97060 599 F7
SE Kanne Rd
13200 HPYV 97236 658 B1
Kansas St
5600 VCVR 98661 537 D5
6300 VCVR 98664 537 D5
NW Kansas City Rd
6000 WasC 97116 561 E2
Kantara Ct
19000 WLIN 97068 686 H3
Kantara Wy
19000 WLIN 97068 686 H3
Kappel Ln
2100 FTGV 97116 592 A4
Kappler Rd W
59200 ClbC 97051 414 E1
59400 ClbC 97051 384 E7
E Kappler Rd
33800 ClbC 97051 384 G7
33800 ClbC 97051 414 F1

Kapteyns St
19100 WLIN 97068 686 G3
19300 CmsC 97068 686 G4
Kara Ln
16900 LKOW 97035 685 H1
Karen Ct
- MCMV 97128 771 A2
NE Karen Ct
1500 HBRO 97124 593 E2
SE Karen Ct
14500 DAMA 97009 659 B7
NE Karen Pl
33600 SPSE 97056 444 F7
SW Karen St
12500 TGRD 97223 655 B4
Karen Scott Dr
11200 ORCY 97045 716 J5
NW Karey Ct
11000 WasC 97229 595 D3
SW Kari Ln
1200 PTLD 97219 656 D2
Kari Ann Ct
19500 ORCY 97045 716 J5
SW Karla Ct
5900 PTLD 97239 626 B4
SW Karl Braun Dr
- WasC 97005 624 J1
14100 WasC 97005 625 A1
SW Karley Ct
14000 TGRD 97223 654 J4
NE Karlsen Dr
20200 ClkC 98606 478 J2
SW Karol Ct
12000 TGRD 97223 655 D3
SE Karry Av
14700 CmsC 97267 656 H6
NE Karvonen Rd
- ClkC 98604 448 J6
Kasel Ct NE
14600 AURA 97002 775 E3
Kaskela Mnr
- GSHM 97230 598 G4
NE Kaskillah Dr
- ClkC 98604 449 E3
SE Kaslin Ct
15500 CmsC 97267 657 E7
SE Kaslin Wy
15500 CmsC 97267 657 E7
NE Kaster Dr
2700 HBRO 97124 593 C1
Kaster Rd
600 STHN 97051 415 C2
SE Kate Schmitz Av
- CmsC 97055 690 H2
- SNDY 97055 690 H2
Kathaway Ct
11900 ORCY 97045 717 B5
Katherine Ct
25500 WLIN 97068 716 F3
SW Katherine Ln
8400 BRTN 97225 625 F1
SW Katherine St
11600 TGRD 97223 655 C3
NE Kathleen Ct
600 HBRO 97124 593 C2
NW Kathleen Dr
11900 WasC 97229 595 C3
SE Kathryn Ct
3400 MWKE 97222 627 A7
12900 CmsC 97236 658 A5
NE Kathryn St
1700 HBRO 97124 593 E2
SW Kathy Ct
14500 SRWD 97140 684 J7
18100 WasC 97007 624 E6
SE Kathy Ln
10700 CmsC 97009 659 H3
SW Kathy St
22600 SRWD 97140 684 J7
SE Katie Ct
16000 CmsC 97267 687 D1
NE Katie Dr
2500 HBRO 97124 593 B1
SE Katie Ln
31200 CmsC 97009 660 B6
Katie Rose Pl
100 DAYT 97114 772 A4
NW Katsules Pl
1000 BRTN 97006 594 H4
SW Kattegat Dr
16700 BRTN 97006 594 G5
Kauer Dr
- MCMV 97128 770 D5
Kauffman Av
1300 VCVR 98660 536 F3
NW Kauffman Av
4500 VCVR 98660 536 F1
4500 VCVR 98663 536 F1
5900 VCVR 98663 506 F7
SW Kaufman Dr
6900 WasC 97007 624 F5
Kavanaugh St
58500 ClbC 97051 415 A3
SW Kawanda Ct
20500 TLTN 97062 685 E5
SE Kay Ln
38000 CmsC 97009 660 J1
SE Kay Pl
500 GSHM 97080 629 C3
SE Kay St
19200 CmsC 97267 687 B4
19400 CmsC 97027 687 C4
19400 GLDS 97027 687 C4
NW Kaybern St
30500 WasC 97133 563 B1
31100 NPNS 97133 563 A1
Kayenta Pl
19200 ORCY 97045 717 C4
Kayla Ct
5600 CmsC 97222 657 C4
NW Kaylee St
9700 PTLD 97229 595 E3
SW Kaylynn Ln
15900 BRTN 97006 594 H7
NW Kearney St
900 PTLD 97209 596 E4
2000 PTLD 97210 596 D4
8700 WasC 97229 595 F4
S Kearney Estates Ln
25100 CmsC 97013 777 D2
SW Keas Ct
12000 BRTN 97008 655 B1
SW Keck St
400 MCMV 97128 770 G7

SW Keda Ct
16300 SRWD 97140 684 G6
SE Keegan Rd
24300 CmsC 97022 720 A3
SE Keeley Ct
13000 CmsC 97015 658 B7
SW Keena Ct
19500 WasC 97007 624 D5
NW Keenan Pl
4800 WasC 97229 595 A1
SW Keerins Ct
16100 WasC 97223 654 G5
NW Keeton Park Ln
13200 WasC 97229 595 D1
SE Kehrli Dr
11800 MWKE 97222 657 A3
Keil Rd NE
14000 MrnC 97002 775 D3
S Keirsey Ln
- CmsC 97045 777 J1
SE Kela Ct
9800 CmsC 97236 657 H2
SE Kela Pl
9900 CmsC 97236 657 H2
Keliher Dr
34500 ClbC 97053 414 H3
34500 ClbC 97053 414 H3
S Kelland Ct
10500 CmsC 97045 716 H5
SE Keller Av
- MthC 97080 629 G6
3100 GSHM 97080 629 G6
NW Keller Rd
18400 WasC 97133 532 G1
SE Keller Rd
15900 DAMA 97009 688 G1
16000 CmsC 97009 688 G1
Kelley Dr
36000 ClbC 97051 415 B2
36000 STHN 97051 415 B2
Kelley St
100 STHN 97051 385 B7
N Kelley Point Park Rd
- PTLD 97203 535 G2
SE Kellogg Av
14800 CmsC 97267 657 A6
SE Kellogg Ct
6100 CmsC 97267 657 D6
SW Kellogg Dr
10300 TLTN 97062 685 C3
SE Kellogg Rd
- CmsC 97222 657 B5
N Kellogg St
9000 PTLD 97203 565 G2
SE Kellogg St
- CmsC 97222 657 B5
SE Kellogg Creek Dr
5400 CmsC 97222 657 C5
5400 MWKE 97222 657 C5
NE Kelly Av
- GSHM 97030 599 C6
10 GSHM 97030 629 C1
10 GSHM 97080 629 C2
SE Kelly Av
100 GSHM 97080 629 C3
SW Kelly Av
2700 PTLD 97201 626 F1
3200 PTLD 97239 626 F3
7400 PTLD 97219 626 F6
9400 PTLD 97219 656 F1
SW Kelly Av SR-43
- PTLD 97239 626 F2
2900 PTLD 97201 626 F1
SW Kelly Av US-26
2700 PTLD 97201 626 F1
NW Kelly Cir
8500 MthC 97229 595 F2
8500 PTLD 97229 595 F2
NE Kelly Ct
600 HBRO 97124 593 C2
SE Kelly Ct
8300 CmsC 97015 657 F7
8300 CmsC 97015 687 F1
8300 CmsC 97267 687 F1
18000 GSHM 97236 628 G2
SW Kelly Ln
12200 TGRD 97223 655 B5
NE Kelly Pl
2700 GSHM 97030 599 C7
Kelly Rd
- CmsC 97023 750 E7
NE Kelly Rd
29100 ClkC 98675 418 F5
32500 ClkC 98604 418 G1
NW Kelly Rd
8100 ClkC 98665 506 E4
Kelly St
4300 WLIN 97068 687 A7
SE Kelly St
- PTLD 97202 626 G1
2800 PTLD 97202 627 A2
5900 PTLD 97206 627 D2
8200 PTLD 97266 627 F2
11900 PTLD 97236 628 A2
11900 PTLD 97266 628 A2
17700 GSHM 97236 628 G2
Kelly & Company Ests
- GSHM 97233 598 F6
SW Kelly View Lp
18300 WasC 97007 624 E6
Kelmsley Dr
14400 CmsC 97045 717 F7
14400 CmsC 97045 747 F1
Kelok Rd
17000 LKOW 97034 686 A1
17000 LKOW 97035 686 A2
Kelsey Ct
19100 GLDS 97027 687 E3
SW Kelsey Ct
22100 SRWD 97140 684 H7
Kelsey Ln
400 MOLA 97038 807 D7
Kelsey Lp
- MOLA 97038 807 D7
SW Kelsi Ct
7300 PTLD 97223 625 H6
SE Kelso Rd
26200 CmsC 97009 659 F7
34000 CmsC 97009 660 F7
36200 CmsC 97055 660 H7
36200 SNDY 97055 660 H7
N Kelsy Pl
- RDGF 98642 416 D7
SE Kelton St
2600 PTLD 97202 626 J2

SE Kelvin St
2700 MWKE 97222 657 A1
SW Kemmer Rd
- BRTN 97007 654 G1
16900 WasC 97007 654 F1
17600 WasC 97007 624 E7
SW Kemmer View Ct
17500 WasC 97007 624 F7
17500 WasC 97007 654 F1
SE Kemp Rd
36200 CmsC 97023 750 G5
NW Kemper Rd
41800 WasC 97116 561 G5
Kemper Crest Dr
300 NWBG 97132 713 B4
300 YmhC 97132 713 B4
SE Kempton Ct
15300 HPYV 97236 658 D5
NW Kenai Ct
21200 WasC 97229 564 B7
NE Kenasket Pl
23000 ClkC 98604 449 F4
SW Kendall Av
100 TDLE 97060 599 G4
SE Kendall Ct
17400 PTLD 97236 628 F3
SW Kendall Ct
2100 TDLE 97060 599 F6
SW Kendall Ln
19800 WasC 97006 624 D1
E Kenmore St
700 GLDS 97027 687 E3
W Kenmore St
200 GLDS 97027 687 D4
NW Kennedy Ct
2600 PTLD 97229 595 E2
SE Kennedy Ct
5300 CmsC 97267 687 C2
NE Kennedy Ln
1100 HBRO 97124 593 E3
SW Kennedy St
10000 BRTN 97005 625 D3
10000 WasC 97005 625 D3
Kennel St
100 MOLA 97038 837 E1
SW Kenneth Ct
21100 WasC 97006 594 B5
SW Kenneth Ter
- PTLD 97205 596 C6
Kenny St
5200 CmsC 97035 685 H2
5200 LKOW 97035 685 J2
NW Kenny Ter
3600 WasC 97229 595 B2
Kennycroft Wy
5800 CmsC 97035 685 H2
5800 LKOW 97035 685 H2
Kenola Ct
700 LKOW 97034 656 E7
SE Kens Ct
16500 CmsC 97267 687 A1
Kensington Ct
2500 CmsC 97068 716 H1
2500 WLIN 97068 716 H1
2600 CmsC 97068 686 H7
2600 WLIN 97068 686 H7
SE Kensington Dr
15300 CmsC 97015 658 D6
SW Kensington Dr
30500 WNVL 97070 745 C1
SW Kensington Pl
30500 WNVL 97070 745 C1
SW Kensington Rd
8000 WasC 97223 625 F7
SE Kensington St
6300 HBRO 97123 593 G7
6300 HBRO 97123 594 A7
6300 WasC 97123 594 A7
NW Kent Ct
- PTLD 97229 595 D1
SW Kent Ct
9800 TGRD 97224 685 D1
SW Kent Pl
10000 TGRD 97224 685 D1
Kent Rdg
- VCVR 98661 537 C2
NW Kent St
2600 CMAS 98607 569 D2
SE Kent St
1500 MCMV 97128 770 H7
5800 MWKE 97222 657 D3
SW Kent St
10300 TGRD 97224 685 D1
Kenthorpe Wy
3600 WLIN 97068 686 J3
3600 WLIN 97068 687 A3
SW Kenton Dr
14800 TGRD 97224 655 F7
Kentucky Dr
6900 VCVR 98664 537 D6
SW Kentucky Pl
14000 BRTN 97008 624 H1
SW Kenwood Ct
15000 WasC 97006 594 J5
Kenwood Rd
300 LKOW 97034 656 F6
NW Kenzie Ln
11300 WasC 97229 595 C4
S Kepler Dr
16100 CmsC 97045 688 C6
N Kerby Av
3500 PTLD 97227 596 F2
4500 PTLD 97217 596 F1
10000 PTLD 97217 566 F2
N Kerby Ct
- PTLD 97217 566 F2
NW Kerkman Rd
7000 WasC 97113 562 F4
Kern Ct NE
- SPSE 97056 444 F7
SE Kern Ct
6600 CmsC 97267 657 D7
Kerr Pkwy
- LKOW 97034 656 B5
10 LKOW 97035 656 A3
11800 PTLD 97219 656 A3
NE Kerr Rd
13100 ClkC 98682 508 B6
Kerry Ct
- MCMV 97128 770 J2
SE Kerslake Rd
29200 MthC 97060 629 J1
29200 MthC 97060 630 A1
SW Kessler Ln
16100 WasC 97224 654 G6

Kestrel Ct
13600 ORCY 97045 717 E2
SW Kestrel Ct
15800 BRTN 97007 654 H4
Ketreno Dr
55700 ClbC 97053 444 E1
NE Kettering St
5800 HBRO 97124 593 J4
NW Kevin Ct
16100 WasC 97006 594 G2
Kevin Ln
- CmsC 97045 719 F3
S Key Ct
11800 CmsC 97013 777 A6
SE Key Ct
16500 CmsC 97267 687 E1
NE Keyes Ct
14000 VCVR 98684 538 C5
NE Keyes Ln
9300 YmhC 97115 742 F2
NE Keyes Rd
1000 VCVR 98684 538 C5
SW Keylock Ln
20400 WasC 97006 594 C7
SW Keys Ct
- BRTN 97005 624 J3
- BRTN 97005 625 A3
SW Keys Rd
32000 SPSE 97056 474 D1
SW Keys Crest Dr
32800 SPSE 97056 474 D1
SW Keys Landing Wy
32800 SPSE 97056 474 D1
SW Keystone Ct
17500 WasC 97007 624 F6
SE Keystone Dr
16300 CmsC 97267 687 D1
NW Kian Ln
21500 HBRO 97124 594 B5
21500 WasC 97006 594 B5
SE Kibling Av
1200 TDLE 97060 599 G5
SE Kibling Ct
4000 TDLE 97060 599 G7
4000 TDLE 97060 629 G1
SE Kibling St
100 TDLE 97060 599 G4
SW Kickapoo Ct
10200 TLTN 97062 685 D6
Kiggins Av
2900 VCVR 98661 537 B3
SW Kilchis Ct
15000 BRTN 97007 624 H5
SW Kilchis St
14500 BRTN 97008 624 J5
15200 BRTN 97007 624 H5
Kilchurn Av
5500 LKOW 97035 655 J4
SW Kiley Wy
1100 BRTN 97006 594 G6
Kilkenney Rd
1700 LKOW 97034 656 D7
1700 LKOW 97034 686 E1
Kilkenny Ct
2500 WLIN 97068 686 G7
Kilkenny Dr
1700 LKOW 97034 686 E1
NW Killan Rd
13300 WasC 97106 531 D4
SW Killarney Ct
21100 TLTN 97062 685 D6
Killarney Dr
1400 WLIN 97068 686 F7
SW Killarney Ln
9300 TLTN 97062 685 D6
Killdeer Rd
- ORCY 97045 717 F5
S Killdeer Rd
17000 CmsC 97004 748 C2
NW Killin Rd
- WasC 97106 531 E3
N Killingsworth Ct
600 PTLD 97217 566 F7
NE Killingsworth Ct
600 PTLD 97211 566 H7
N Killingsworth St
10 PTLD 97211 566 G7
1700 PTLD 97217 566 D7
NE Killingsworth St
10 PTLD 97211 566 H7
10 PTLD 97217 566 G7
2500 PTLD 97211 567 A7
4100 PTLD 97218 567 C7
10000 PTLD 97220 567 H6
10800 PTLD 97220 597 J1
NE Killingsworth St US-30 BYP
7200 PTLD 97218 567 G7
7600 PTLD 97220 567 F7
Kilowatt Ln
30300 CmsC 97023 750 A2
N Kilpatrick St
2500 PTLD 97217 566 D4
3900 PTLD 97203 566 C4
NE Kilpatrick St
200 PTLD 97211 566 H4
Kim Ln
- FTGV 97116 591 G3
Kimball Av
15400 CmsC 97035 655 J6
N Kimball Av
8900 PTLD 97203 566 A3
Kimball Ct
5700 CmsC 97035 655 H6
S Kimball Rd
18600 CmsC 97045 718 J4
SW Kimball St
15800 CmsC 97035 655 J7
15800 LKOW 97035 655 J7
SW Kimber Pl
7800 WasC 97007 624 F7
Kimberly Cir
14100 LKOW 97035 655 H5
Kimberly Ct
600 MOLA 97038 837 F2
39400 SNDY 97055 691 A3
NE Kimberly Ct
2700 MCMV 97128 770 J2
S Kimberly Ct
15100 CmsC 97045 688 B4
SE Kimberly Ct
10500 HPYV 97236 658 A2
SW Kimberly Ct
7200 BRTN 97008 624 J6

Kimberly Dr
- LKOW 97035 655 H5
25500 WLIN 97068 716 G2
SW Kimberly Dr
9800 TGRD 97224 655 D7
14100 BRTN 97008 624 J6
Kimberly Rose Dr
20000 ORCY 97045 717 G7
NW Kimble Ct
11300 WasC 97229 595 D3
SE Kimbley Rd
34400 MthC 97019 630 E1
Kimmell Ln
59600 ClbC 97051 384 H7
SW Kimy Ter
4300 WasC 97007 624 H3
NE Kincaid Rd
15200 YmhC 97132 713 G3
NW King Av
100 PTLD 97205 596 D5
100 PTLD 97210 596 D5
SW King Av
700 PTLD 97205 596 D5
700 PTLD 97210 596 D5
SW King Blvd
- BRTN 97005 625 C4
6100 BRTN 97008 625 C5
King Rd
1000 ORCY 97045 717 A3
NW King Rd
18500 MthC 97231 504 E6
SE King Rd
3400 MWKE 97222 657 B2
5500 CmsC 97222 657 D2
8100 CmsC 97236 657 F2
12700 HPYV 97236 658 C2
King St
100 ORCY 97045 717 B3
1100 VCVR 98660 536 F5
S King St
7000 CmsC 97013 745 J7
7000 CmsC 97013 746 A7
SE King St
100 CMAS 98607 569 F4
King Vil
- KNGC 97224 685 B1
- WasC 97224 685 B2
SE King Wy
9600 CmsC 97236 657 H2
SW King Arthur St
- WasC 97224 655 B7
12000 KNGC 97224 655 D2
SW Kingbird Dr
15000 BRTN 97007 654 H3
SW King Charles Av
16000 KNGC 97224 685 B1
Kingfisher Ln NE
11600 MrnC 97002 744 H6
SW Kingfisher Ln
15700 BRTN 97007 654 F4
SW Kingfisher Wy
7700 DRHM 97224 685 F2
SE King George Ct
5200 CmsC 97267 687 C2
SW King George Dr
11600 KNGC 97224 655 B7
SW King Henry Pl
11900 KNGC 97224 655 D2
SW King James Pl
11800 KNGC 97224 685 B1
SW King John Pl
11800 KNGC 97224 655 D2
SW King Lear Wy
13300 KNGC 97224 685 A1
SW Kinglet Dr
17000 SRWD 97140 684 F7
SE King Me Two Ln
- CmsC 97022 689 J5
SW King Richard Dr
12000 KNGC 97224 685 B1
SW King Richards Ct
16600 SRWD 97140 684 F6
SW Kings Bywy
700 TDLE 97060 599 F5
SW Kings Ct
2100 PTLD 97205 596 D6
29400 WNVL 97070 715 C7
King's Mdw
- TDLE 97060 599 F6
King Salmon Ct
13000 CmsC 97045 717 D5
13000 ORCY 97045 717 D5
Kingsberry Hts
- ORCY 97045 717 F5
Kings Gate
- VCVR 98661 537 B4
Kingsgate Rd
10 LKOW 97035 655 J4
NE Kings Grade
16000 YmhC 97132 712 F2
SE Kingsley Rd
3400 CmsC 97267 687 A1
SE Kingsridge Ct
16600 CmsC 97267 687 E1
SE Kingston Av
14300 CmsC 97267 657 D6
SW Kingston Av
100 PTLD 97205 596 C6
SW Kingston Dr
- PTLD 97205 596 C6
- PTLD 97221 596 B7
SW Kingston Pl
13200 TGRD 97223 655 A5
SW Kingsview Ct
6600 TGRD 97223 655 H1
SE Kingswood Ct
22700 DAMA 97009 659 B1
SE Kingswood Wy
8400 DAMA 97009 659 C1
E Kingwood Ct
200 MCMV 97128 771 B6
NE Kingwood Dr
100 MCMV 97128 771 B6
100 YmhC 97128 771 B6
Kingwood St
2200 FTGV 97116 592 A4
2300 WasC 97116 592 A4
S Kingwood St
100 MCMV 97128 771 C6
Kinnaman Ct
- WasC 97007 624 F3
SW Kinnaman Rd
18500 WasC 97007 624 D3
NE Kinney Rd
13300 YmhC 97132 712 A5

STREET
Block City ZIP Map# Grid
Kinney St
- WLIN 97068 687 B5
NE Kinney St
1200 HBRO 97124 593 D1
E Kinnikinnick Av
23100 CmsC 97011 724 A1
NW Kino Springs Pl
4000 WasC 97006 594 G1
NE Kinsale Ct
200 HBRO 97124 593 B1
Kinsman Rd
- WNVL 97070 715 D4
SW Kinsman Rd
29100 WNVL 97070 715 D7
SW Kiowa Ct
10600 TLTN 97062 685 C2
SW Kiowa St
10300 TLTN 97062 685 D2
SW Kirby Ln
15400 WasC 97007 624 H4
NE Kirby St
1200 MCMV 97128 770 J4
SW Kirkwood Ct
19900 WasC 97006 594 D6
E Kirkwood Dr
54700 CmsC 97055 692 G6
SE Kirkwood Dr
- CmsC 97055 692 H6
SE Kirkwood Rd
17400 CmsC 97027 687 F2
17500 GLDS 97027 687 F2
SW Kirkwood St
20500 WasC 97006 594 C6
NE Kirra St
200 HBRO 97124 593 B1
SW Kirsten Ct
9900 WasC 97005 625 E3
N Kiska St
3800 PTLD 97203 566 C3
3800 PTLD 97217 566 C3
SE Kisor Ct
13200 HPYV 97236 658 B1
SW Kittiwake Ct
15800 BRTN 97007 654 E3
NW Kittridge Av
4400 PTLD 97210 566 A7
4400 PTLD 97210 595 J1
4400 PTLD 97210 596 A1
SE Kitty Kat Lp
34200 CmsC 97022 720 E1
SE Kitzmiller Rd
38400 CmsC 97022 720 H5
NW Kiwanda Dr
4500 WasC 97229 594 C1
4600 WasC 97229 564 C7
SW Kiwanda Ln
15300 BRTN 97007 624 H6
SW Klamath Cir
8500 WNVL 97070 715 E6
SW Klamath Ct
9200 TLTN 97062 685 E5
NE Klickitat Ct
13500 PTLD 97230 598 C2
SW Klickitat Ct
21600 TLTN 97062 685 D6
NW Klickitat Ln
1100 CMAS 98607 569 A4
NE Klickitat St
1300 PTLD 97212 596 J2
2700 PTLD 97212 597 C2
7000 PTLD 97213 597 F2
10400 PTLD 97220 597 J2
11200 PTLD 97220 598 A2
14800 PTLD 97230 598 D2
NW Klickitat St
900 CMAS 98607 569 A4
Klickitat Wy
23000 ClkC 98604 449 G4
Klickitat Mall
- PTLD 97212 596 H2
N Klimek Ln
1200 YmhC 97132 713 G6
NE Klineline Rd
11800 ClkC 98686 506 J1
S Klinger Rd
27100 CmsC 97013 777 A6
27700 CmsC 97013 807 A1
SW Klipsan Ct
14600 TGRD 97223 654 J5
14600 WasC 97223 654 J5
SW Klipsan Ln
14500 TGRD 97223 654 J5
Klupenger Rd NE
23600 CmsC 97002 745 A6
SE Knapp Cir
10700 PTLD 97266 627 J6
SE Knapp Ct
13300 PTLD 97236 628 B6
SE Knapp Dr
15200 PTLD 97236 628 D6
NW Knapp Ln
3500 CMAS 98607 569 A2
SE Knapp Ln
12100 PTLD 97236 628 A6
12100 PTLD 97266 628 A6
SE Knapp St
1600 PTLD 97202 626 J5
2700 PTLD 97202 627 B6
6200 PTLD 97206 627 D6
9700 PTLD 97266 627 H6
12200 PTLD 97266 628 A6
12600 PTLD 97236 628 B6
17700 MthC 97080 628 G6
17700 MthC 97236 628 G6
NW Knappton-General Rd
- PTLD 97231 565 F3
Knaps Al
1700 WLIN 97068 716 G2
SE Knarr Cir
4000 TDLE 97060 629 J1
SE Knarr Ct
1500 TDLE 97060 599 G5
SW Knaus Rd
2200 CmsC 97034 656 D4
2200 LKOW 97035 656 C4
13400 LKOW 97034 656 D5
SW Knee Ct
11800 CmsC 97236 657 J4
E Knieriem Rd
37400 MthC 97019 600 J7
NW Knight St
- CMAS 98607 568 H2
SE Knight St
11100 PTLD 97266 628 A5
1300 PTLD 97202 626 H4

STREET
Block City ZIP Map# Grid
SE Knight St
3600 PTLD 97202 627 B4
4600 PTLD 97206 627 C4
8000 PTLD 97266 627 F4
13400 PTLD 97236 628 C5
Knighton Wy
3200 FTGV 97116 591 E2
SW Knights Blvd
- PTLD 97205 596 B6
- PTLD 97221 596 B6
SW Knightsbridge Dr
5500 PTLD 97219 625 J7
N Knights Bridge Rd
200 CNBY 97013 746 B6
1000 CmsC 97013 746 B6
S Knights Bridge Rd
6500 CmsC 97013 745 H6
7100 CmsC 97013 746 A6
7100 CNBY 97013 746 A6
SE Knoll Ct
6700 CmsC 97267 687 C1
Knoll Dr
3200 NWBG 97132 713 D4
SW Knoll Dr
12300 TGRD 97223 655 F4
NE Knollcrest Av
1300 VCVR 98664 537 G5
SW Knollcrest Dr
1800 BRTN 97225 595 E7
1800 WasC 97225 595 E7
1900 WasC 97225 625 E1
SW Knollwood Ct
6500 CmsC 97062 715 G3
NE Knott Ct
14500 PTLD 97230 598 D3
NE Knott Pl
8400 PTLD 97220 597 G3
N Knott St
10 PTLD 97212 596 G3
400 CNBY 97013 746 C6
600 PTLD 97227 596 F3
NE Knott St
10 PTLD 97227 596 G3
400 PTLD 97212 596 J3
2700 PTLD 97212 597 A3
4100 PTLD 97213 597 B3
10200 PTLD 97220 597 J3
11200 PTLD 97220 598 A3
13800 PTLD 97230 598 C3
S Knott St
100 CNBY 97013 746 D6
N Knowles Av
6500 PTLD 97217 566 D5
NE Knowles Dr
1000 ClkC 98685 476 H6
SW Knowlton Rd
- WasC 97005 625 A2
SE Knox Rd
27200 CmsC 97009 689 J2
SW Knox Rd
400 ECDA 97023 750 A4
Knox St
2600 WLIN 97068 687 A6
Knox Ridge Ter
2700 FTGV 97116 591 G3
Knoxville Rd
100 VCVR 98664 537 E6
S Knoxville Wy
100 VCVR 98664 537 E6
NE Knudsen Ln
16500 YmhC 97115 742 C3
16900 YmhC 97114 742 C3
NW Koa Ct
14900 WasC 97229 594 J2
SE Koala Dr
11700 CmsC 97236 657 J3
11700 CmsC 97236 658 A3
Koawood Dr
1300 LKOW 97034 686 D1
SW Kobbe Dr
11700 WasC 97007 654 D3
Kobuk Ct
22700 WLIN 97068 687 A7
SE Kobus Wy
1400 HBRO 97123 623 D1
Koch Ct
17500 SNDY 97055 690 J3
NE Koch St
2000 MCMV 97128 771 A3
Koderra Av
- CmsC 97035 685 J2
- LKOW 97035 685 H2
Kodiak Ct
10000 CNLS 97113 592 E6
SW Koehler Rd
21300 WasC 97007 654 B1
NE Kogan Rd
8300 ClkC 98665 506 G4
Kokanee Ct
19400 LKOW 97034 686 A3
NE Kokanee Ln
- WDVL 97060 599 C5
SW Kokich Pl
- WasC 97007 624 G2
Koko St
53400 ClbC 97056 444 D6
Kolar Dr
19600 ORCY 97045 717 A5
SW Kolbe Ln
7500 WNVL 97070 715 F7
7500 WNVL 97070 745 F1
SW Kolding Ln
16800 BRTN 97007 624 F7
16900 WasC 97007 624 F7
SW Koll Pkwy
15000 BRTN 97006 594 H6
15000 WasC 97006 594 H6
Kollenborn Ln
13500 WasC 97229 595 A2
SW Koller St
10800 TLTN 97062 685 C7
SW Korbel Ter
6400 WasC 97007 624 B4
Korina
- CmsC 97015 657 H7
SW Koski Dr
11700 TGRD 97223 655 D3
SW Koso St
- TLTN 97062 685 D7
SW Kost Ln
20000 WasC 97007 624 C3
SW Kostel Ln
12900 TGRD 97224 655 A7
12900 WasC 97224 655 A7

STREET
Block City ZIP Map# Grid
Kotobuki Wy
1800 VCVR 98660 536 E4
NW Kotrik Pl
300 BRTN 97006 594 F5
SW Koven Ct
14200 WasC 97224 654 H6
S Kraeft Rd
16600 CmsC 97045 687 G7
SW Kraft Lp
14800 WasC 97223 654 H4
SW Kraft Pl
12700 WasC 97223 654 J4
Kramer Av
1400 FTGV 97116 591 G4
NW Kramer Dr
45000 WasC 97116 561 F7
S Kramer Rd
18800 CmsC 97023 719 B4
18800 CmsC 97045 719 B4
NE Kramien Rd
32800 YmhC 97132 744 C4
SW Kramien Rd
17600 CmsC 97070 744 E4
17600 CmsC 97132 744 E4
SE Krause Ln
14100 CmsC 97236 658 C3
14100 HPYV 97236 658 C3
S Kraxberger Rd
9100 CmsC 97013 776 F4
SE Kreder Rd
15000 YmhC 97114 772 A2
16200 DAYT 97114 772 C3
Kredor Dr
16000 DAYT 97114 772 B4
SW Kreick Pl
15800 TGRD 97224 655 G5
SE Krieger Ln
10900 PTLD 97266 627 J7
NW Krieger Rd
17900 ClkC 98642 475 J1
19200 ClkC 98642 445 J7
NW Krislynn Ter
6400 WasC 97229 564 H5
NE Kristen Cir
20700 ClkC 98606 479 A1
Kristi Wy
18500 CmsC 97035 685 H3
18500 LKOW 97035 685 H3
NE Kristie Ct
600 HBRO 97124 593 C2
NE Kristin Ct
1400 MCMV 97128 770 J2
SW Kristin Ct
21500 WasC 97006 594 B6
SW Kroese Lp
7900 TGRD 97224 655 F6
SE Krohn Rd
30700 ClkC 98671 540 A7
NW Kronan Ct
300 PTLD 97210 596 A5
SE Kronan Dr
12800 CmsC 97015 658 A7
SE Kronberg Av
14900 CmsC 97267 657 A6
SW Kruger Rd
- SRWD 97140 684 D7
18500 WasC 97140 684 A6
22400 WasC 97140 683 J7
S Krupicka Wy
32400 CmsC 97038 837 D3
SW Kruse Rd
5100 CmsC 97070 715 H6
Kruse Wy
- LKOW 97035 655 J6
- LKOW 97223 655 H5
- TGRD 97223 655 H5
4100 LKOW 97035 656 A6
Kruse Oaks Blvd
13600 LKOW 97035 655 H5
Kruse Oaks Dr
14800 LKOW 97035 655 H6
SW Kruse Ridge Dr
5600 PTLD 97219 655 H3
Kruse Villa
- CmsC 97035 655 H6
- LKOW 97035 655 H6
Kruse Woods Dr
10 LKOW 97035 655 J6
Kruse Wy Pl
4000 LKOW 97035 656 A6
SE Kubitz Rd
40200 CmsC 97055 691 B1
SE Kuehls Wy
14500 CmsC 97267 657 A6
SE Kuehn Ct
12400 CmsC 97222 657 B4
12400 MWKE 97222 657 B4
SE Kuehn Rd
12800 CmsC 97222 657 B5
12800 MWKE 97222 657 B4
NE Kuehne Rd
11700 YmhC 97111 711 H7
12100 YmhC 97111 712 A6
12100 YmhC 97132 712 A5
Kuhnis Rd
100 CtzC 98674 385 J6
SW Kummrow Av
18000 WasC 97062 684 H2
18000 WasC 97140 684 H2
NW Kurtz Pl
17300 WasC 97106 531 J1
17300 WasC 97106 532 A1
N Kutch St
100 CLTN 97111 711 A7
S Kutch St
200 CLTN 97111 741 A1
SE Kwanzan Ct
10500 CmsC 97236 657 H4
Kwong Toy Ct
- PTLD 97220 597 G5
Kwong Toy Ter
- PTLD 97233 628 D1
NW Kyla Ln
12700 WasC 97229 565 B7
NE Kyle Ct
20800 FRVW 97024 599 A4
N Kyle Pl
- RDGF 98642 416 D6
NW Kyle Pl
14700 WasC 97229 564 J7
S Kyllo Wy
31600 CmsC 97038 837 A2
NE Kyocera Rd
- VCVR 98661 537 C3

STREET
Block City ZIP Map# Grid
L
L Ct
5000 ClkC 98671 570 E5
N L Dr
2200 WHGL 98671 570 B5
L St
- PTLD 97219 655 J2
200 CBAC 97018 385 C4
2700 VCVR 98663 536 H3
4600 WHGL 98671 570 E5
5400 ClkC 98671 570 F5
N L St
2400 WHGL 98671 570 B5
L-1400
- ClkC 98604 479 J5
- ClkC 98606 479 J5
NE L-1400 Rd
- ClkC 98604 479 H6
- ClkC 98606 479 H6
L-1410
- ClkC 98604 449 H7
- ClkC 98604 479 J4
L-1500 G-I
- ClkC 98607 540 H1
L-1600H
- ClkC 98607 540 H1
Laas Dr
50900 ClbC 97056 474 E3
SW Labbe Av
2800 PTLD 97221 626 B1
SE Label Ln
7200 CmsC 97206 657 E1
SW Laber Ct
5800 MthC 97221 625 J2
SW Laber Rd
6400 MthC 97221 625 H2
6800 WasC 97225 625 H2
SE La Bonita Wy
15100 CmsC 97267 657 B7
SW Labrousse Rd
24600 WasC 97140 714 E4
Laburnum Wy
1400 LKOW 97034 686 D1
NW Lacamas Dr
1200 CMAS 98607 539 C7
1200 CMAS 98607 569 D1
NW Lacamas Ln
3400 CMAS 98607 569 D2
NE La Carter Ln
7700 HBRO 97124 594 D4
7700 WasC 97124 594 D4
NW La Cassel Crest Ln
10500 WasC 97229 595 D3
NW La Center Rd
10 ClkC 98642 416 G1
10 LCTR 98629 416 G1
32000 ClkC 98629 416 G1
NW Lacenter Rd
1800 ClkC 98642 416 E2
La Centre Dr
- MthC 97231 535 A6
Lacey Ln
- CmsC 97023 750 J7
NE Lachenview Ln
21700 FRVW 97024 599 B2
SE La Cour Ct
4600 CmsC 97267 687 B4
SE La Crescenta Wy
15100 CmsC 97267 657 B7
SE La Cresta Dr
12900 CmsC 97222 657 C4
SE Lacy Wy
19800 ClkC 98607 568 H3
19800 CMAS 98607 568 H3
SE Ladd Av
1500 PTLD 97214 596 H7
2000 PTLD 97214 626 J1
2200 PTLD 97202 626 J1
SE Ladd Ct
16500 CmsC 97267 687 A1
SW Ladd Ct
10200 TLTN 97062 685 C3
Ladd St
10 LKOW 97034 656 G7
SW Ladd Hill Rd
23600 SRWD 97140 714 G1
23700 CmsC 97140 714 G4
29900 CmsC 97140 744 E3
32100 CmsC 97070 744 E3
32100 CmsC 97132 744 E3
NE Laddington Ct
200 PTLD 97232 597 B5
4100 PTLD 97213 597 B5
SE Ladera Ct
9700 DAMA 97009 659 C2
SW Laducer Pl
4200 WasC 97007 624 G1
SW Lady Apple Ln
12700 TGRD 97224 655 H6
SW Ladyfern Dr
21100 SRWD 97140 684 E6
SW Lady Marion Dr
10000 TGRD 97224 655 D6
La Fave St
2500 WLIN 97068 687 A4
Lafayette Av
1100 ORCY 97045 717 A3
18700 ORCY 97045 716 J4
NE Lafayette Av
600 MCMV 97128 770 J4
1700 MCMV 97128 771 A3
SE Lafayette Ct
3600 PTLD 97202 627 B2
SE Lafayette Hwy
3100 LFYT 97127 771 G2
3100 YmhC 97114 771 H6
SE Lafayette Hwy SR-233
6500 YmhC 97114 771 H5
SW Lafayette Pl
2900 PTLD 97205 596 B5
SE Lafayette St
- PTLD 97202 627 B2
1900 PTLD 97202 626 J2
7000 PTLD 97206 627 E2
8000 PTLD 97266 627 F2
16800 PTLD 97236 628 F3
SW Lafayette Wy
8300 WNVL 97070 745 E3
SW Lafollett Rd
1900 WasC 97113 592 D6
La Frambois Rd
- ClkC 98660 506 B7
- ClkC 98660 536 C1

STREET
Block City ZIP Map# Grid
La Frambois Rd
2000 VCVR 98660 536 C1
SE Lagene St
21800 DAMA 97009 659 B4
N Lagoon Av
4600 PTLD 97217 566 B6
4600 PTLD 97217 596 C1
NE Lahdenpera Rd
17500 ClkC 98606 478 F3
NW Laidlaw Rd
10300 MthC 97229 595 C1
12500 WasC 97229 565 A7
14200 WasC 97229 564 J7
16900 WasC 97006 594 G1
16900 WasC 97229 594 G1
SW Laird Pl
7600 WasC 97007 624 F6
Laissez Faire Ests
- PTLD 97233 628 D1
SE La Jolla St
6200 CmsC 97222 657 D2
Lake Av
400 WDLD 98674 385 J2
NE Lake Ct
21900 FRVW 97024 599 B2
SW Lake Ct
7200 WNVL 97070 745 G3
SW Lake Dr
32100 WNVL 97070 745 G3
SW Lake Pl
1900 GSHM 97080 628 H4
NE Lake Rd
10 CMAS 98607 569 E2
NW Lake Rd
200 CMAS 98607 569 D1
400 CMAS 98607 539 A6
4200 CMAS 98607 538 J6
4200 VCVR 98607 538 J6
4800 ClkC 98607 538 J6
SE Lake Rd
2000 MWKE 97222 656 J3
2800 MWKE 97222 657 B4
6000 CmsC 97222 657 D5
7800 CmsC 97267 657 F6
NW Lake St
3500 PTLD 97210 596 B2
SW Lake St
9300 TGRD 97223 655 E5
Lake Bay Ct
300 LKOW 97034 656 F6
SW Lake Bluff Ct
7100 WNVL 97070 745 G2
NW Lakecrest Ct
8600 ClkC 98665 506 D4
NW Lakecrest Dr
8700 ClkC 98665 506 D4
SW Lake Forest Blvd
15800 CmsC 97035 655 H7
16600 LKOW 97035 655 H7
Lake Forest Dr
700 LKOW 97034 656 E6
Lake Front Rd
900 LKOW 97034 656 E7
Lake Garden Ct
1200 LKOW 97034 656 E5
Lake Grove Av
3200 LKOW 97035 656 A7
Lake Haven Dr
17800 LKOW 97035 686 A2
SW Lake Point Ct
32400 WNVL 97070 745 F3
NW Lakeridge Ct
16600 BRTN 97006 594 G5
Lakeridge Dr
16800 LKOW 97034 686 D1
NW Lakeridge Dr
3100 ClkC 98685 506 D2
Lake Ridge Wy
15100 CmsC 97045 717 H2
NW Lakeshore Av
7800 ClkC 98665 506 D4
7800 VCVR 98665 506 E5
9500 ClkC 98685 506 D2
NW Lakeshore Ct
14100 WasC 97229 595 A3
Lakeshore Dr
- ECDA 97023 750 A2
38300 ClkC 98674 386 A2
38300 WDLD 98674 386 A2
NE Lake Shore Dr
13600 YmhC 97132 713 G5
SW Lakeshore Dr
100 ECDA 97023 750 B4
Lake Shore Rd
700 LKOW 97034 656 F6
Lakeside
- VCVR 98665 506 D6
Lakeside Ct
- CmsC 97045 717 H1
NE Lakeside Dr
20300 FRVW 97024 599 A2
SW Lakeside Dr
7300 WNVL 97070 745 F2
9400 TGRD 97224 655 E7
SE Lakeside Ln
2700 MWKE 97222 656 J3
SW Lakeside Lp
7200 WNVL 97070 745 F2
Lakeview Blvd
2700 LKOW 97034 656 B7
2700 LKOW 97035 656 B7
4100 LKOW 97035 686 A1
5600 CmsC 97035 685 H2
5600 LKOW 97035 685 H2
Lake View Ct
5800 CmsC 97035 685 H2
5800 LKOW 97035 685 H2
NW Lakeview Dr
13500 WasC 97229 595 A1
NW Lakeview Rd
1200 ClkC 98665 506 E4
NW Lakeview St
- PTLD 97210 596 A2
SW Lakeview Ter
11400 TGRD 97223 655 B3
S Lake Vista Dr
17800 CmsC 97045 718 D7
NW Lakeway Ct
17700 WasC 97006 594 F4
NW Lakeway Ln
1500 WasC 97006 594 F4
Lakewood Ct NE
19500 MrnC 97002 775 C7
SW Lakewood Ct
11300 TGRD 97223 655 C2

STREET
Block City ZIP Map# Grid
Lakewood Dr NE
13100 MrnC 97002 775 B7
SE Lakewood Dr
2600 CmsC 97222 656 J4
2600 MWKE 97222 656 J4
Lakewood Rd
300 LKOW 97034 656 F7
NE Lakin Rd
19700 ClkC 98604 448 G7
Lakota Ln
600 MOLA 97038 807 E7
600 MOLA 97038 837 E1
SE Lala Dr
15100 CmsC 97015 658 D7
NE Lalonde Dr
- ClkC 98665 507 C3
- ClkC 98686 507 C3
SW La Mancha Ct
8300 TGRD 97224 655 F6
Lamareaux Dr
- CmsC 97049 724 H6
SE La Marquita Wy
15100 CmsC 97267 657 B7
SE Lambert Cir
700 GSHM 97080 629 E3
NW Lambert Rd
20900 ClkC 98642 446 F6
N Lambert St
2500 CNLS 97113 592 F4
NW Lambert St
- MthC 97229 565 C5
- PTLD 97229 565 C5
SE Lambert St
700 PTLD 97202 626 H6
2700 PTLD 97202 627 A6
7200 PTLD 97206 627 F6
8000 PTLD 97266 627 F6
NE La Mesa Av
1200 GSHM 97030 629 F1
SE La Mesa Av
1000 GSHM 97080 629 F4
La Mesa Ct
5600 LKOW 97035 655 J4
NE La Mesa Ct
500 GSHM 97030 629 F2
SE La Mesa Ct
200 GSHM 97080 629 F3
NE La Mesa Ln
1100 GSHM 97030 629 F1
SE La Mesa Ln
- GSHM 97080 629 F4
NE La Mesa Pl
1500 GSHM 97030 629 F1
SE La Mesa Pl
2500 GSHM 97080 629 F5
SE La Mesa Wy
4900 CmsC 97267 657 C6
S Lammer Rd
15400 CmsC 97045 747 J1
NW Lamonde Ter
400 WasC 97229 595 D5
Lamont Ct
4700 LKOW 97035 686 A1
Lamont Wy
4500 LKOW 97035 686 A1
4700 LKOW 97035 685 J1
SE Lamper Ct
18000 SNDY 97055 691 A3
SE Lampert Ct
10800 HPYV 97236 658 A3
NE Lampert Rd
29400 MthC 97060 599 J5
29400 MthC 97060 600 A5
SE Lamphier St
7000 CmsC 97222 657 E1
8100 CmsC 97236 657 F1
SE Lamplighter Av
11900 MWKE 97222 657 C3
Lamplighter Ct
2200 WLIN 97068 687 A5
NW Lancashire Ct
1300 BRTN 97006 594 F4
N Lancaster Av
7000 PTLD 97217 566 E5
Lancaster Dr
16600 GLDS 97027 687 D1
16600 GLDS 97267 687 D1
SW Lancaster Pl
9600 PTLD 97219 656 C1
NW Lancaster Rd
32400 ClkC 98642 385 H7
32400 ClkC 98642 415 J1
32400 ClkC 98642 416 A1
SW Lancaster Rd
9300 PTLD 97219 626 C7
9600 PTLD 97219 656 C1
Lancaster St
- SNDY 97055 690 J4
2400 WLIN 97068 687 A7
2700 WLIN 97068 686 J7
SW Lancaster Wy
15900 WasC 97007 624 H2
S Lance Ct
21500 CmsC 97004 747 J3
SE Lance Ct
12300 HPYV 97236 658 A3
SW Lancelot Ln
8900 PTLD 97219 625 J7
29600 WNVL 97070 715 C7
SW Lancewood St
13200 BRTN 97008 625 A6
NE Land Rd
- ClkC 98686 507 D2
SE Land Rd
33000 CmsC 97022 720 D1
SW Landau Pl
9700 TGRD 97223 655 G2
9700 WasC 97223 655 G2
SW Landau St
7200 TGRD 97223 655 F2
7200 WasC 97223 655 F2
NE Landerholm Rd
26000 ClkC 98629 417 B2
NW Landing Dr
5600 WasC 97229 564 C6
S Landing Wy
17200 CmsC 97042 777 D5
SW Landing Square Dr
4900 PTLD 97239 626 F3
SW Landis Ct
14700 CmsC 97015 657 J6
SE Landis Dr
11600 CmsC 97015 657 J6
Landis St
3600 CmsC 97068 686 J7

STREET
Block City ZIP Map# Grid
Landis St
3600 WLIN 97068 686 J7
SW Landmark Ln
7300 TGRD 97224 655 G6
Landmark St
18800 ORCY 97045 717 C4
SW Landon Ln
15000 WasC 97006 594 H6
Landon St
500 GLDS 97027 687 D3
NE Landover Dr
1900 VCVR 98684 538 B4
SW Landover Dr
6500 WNVL 97070 715 G6
Landreth Ln
61000 ClbC 97051 384 D4
SW Lane Ct
5800 MthC 97221 625 J2
SW Lane St
- PTLD 97239 626 D2
Lanewood St
3400 LKOW 97035 656 A6
SW Lanewood St
11400 WasC 97225 595 C6
S Langdon Ln
22700 CmsC 97023 749 E1
NE Lange Ct
2900 HBRO 97124 593 E2
SE Langensand Rd
17700 CmsC 97055 691 B5
17700 SNDY 97055 691 B5
SW Langer Dr
16000 SRWD 97140 684 G5
SW Langford Ln
5500 CmsC 97035 655 J6
NW Langley Ct
2000 PTLD 97229 595 E3
SW Langtree St
8200 TGRD 97224 655 F7
SE Langwood St
6800 HBRO 97123 594 A7
NW Langworthy Ter
10100 MthC 97229 595 E1
10100 PTLD 97229 595 D1
SE Lani Ln
12500 CmsC 97009 659 J5
SW Lanier Ln
- WasC 97224 654 G6
NW Lansbrook Ter
3500 WasC 97229 595 B2
SW Lansdowne Ln
12100 TGRD 97223 655 B4
SW Lansford Ct
16500 WasC 97007 624 G6
SE Lansing Ln
20700 DAMA 97009 659 A6
SW Lantana Ct
7600 BRTN 97008 625 A6
SW Lantana Pl
7900 BRTN 97008 625 D3
NW Lapaloma Ln
- WasC 97229 594 F1
17100 WasC 97006 594 F1
SE La Paz Av
7400 CmsC 97267 657 E6
SW Lapaz Ct
18400 WasC 97007 624 E5
NW Lapine St
18600 WasC 97229 564 E7
SW Lara St
7100 WasC 97223 625 G7
S La Rae St
13800 ORCY 97045 687 E5
SE Larch Av
1900 PTLD 97214 596 H7
NE Larch Ct
1400 MCMV 97128 770 F4
SW Larch Dr
4600 BRTN 97005 625 C3
SW Larch Ln
10900 BRTN 97005 625 D3
SW Larch Pl
13600 BRTN 97005 625 A3
SW Larch Rd
- ECDA 97023 750 B4
Larch St
1100 LKOW 97034 686 F1
1300 FTGV 97116 592 A6
S Larch St
600 CNBY 97013 746 D7
SW Larch St
8000 WasC 97223 655 F1
SE Larch Wy
1200 GSHM 97080 629 H4
NE Larena Pl
400 HBRO 97124 593 C3
NW Lariat Ct
13500 WasC 97229 595 A2
SE Lariat Ln
29400 CmsC 97009 659 J3
Lark
- FRVW 97024 599 A4
SE Lark Av
15500 CmsC 97267 657 F7
15900 CmsC 97267 687 H2
18700 JNCY 97267 687 F1
Lark Ct NE
11600 MrnC 97002 744 J6
Lark Dr
500 RDGF 98642 416 B6
SW Lark Ln
15200 BRTN 97007 654 H2
S Lark St
- CmsC 97013 776 C4
SE Lark St
- CmsC 97222 656 J4
- CmsC 97222 657 A4
2000 MWKE 97222 656 J4
Larkins Ln
2600 FTGV 97116 591 G3
NE Larkins Rd
23000 YmhC 97132 712 J6
23000 YmhC 97132 713 A6
NW Lark Meadow Ter
- WasC 97229 564 G6
S Larkspur Av
21700 CmsC 97045 747 F3
SE Larkspur Ct
2400 HBRO 97123 623 E1
Larkspur Ln
20000 WLIN 97068 686 J4
NE Larkspur Ln
21700 FRVW 97024 599 B3
SW Larkspur Pl
6700 BRTN 97008 625 B5

Portland Street Index

STREET
Block City ZIP Map# Grid

NW Larkspur St
5900 CMAS 98607 539 A6
N Larrabee Av
2500 PTLD 97227 596 F3
Larrabee St
3200 FTGV 97116 591 G2
Larrabee Oaks St
3300 FTGV 97116 591 G2
NW Larry Ct
12600 WasC 97229 565 B7
SW Lars Ter
2900 WasC 97006 624 G1
NW Larsen
- ClkC 98629 386 F7
NW Larsen Dr
33600 ClkC 98629 386 F7
SW Larsen St
13100 BRTN 97005 625 A4
Larson Av
6700 WLIN 97068 687 A5
SE Larson Ct
2000 HBRO 97123 623 E2
NW Larson Rd
14400 MthC 97231 535 A4
SW Larson Rd
25900 WasC 97123 623 F4
Larson Wy
1800 VCVR 98661 537 B4
SW Larsson Av
2100 TDLE 97060 599 D6
SE La Rue Ct
16900 CmsC 97267 687 A1
NE Las Brisas Ct
16400 PTLD 97230 598 F2
Lasic Ct
19700 ORCY 97045 717 D5
SW Lasich Ln
17500 WasC 97140 654 F7
17500 WasC 97224 654 F7
Lassen Ct
18600 ORCY 97045 717 B3
SE Last Rd
9400 CmsC 97015 687 G1
E Lataurelle Av
23000 CmsC 97011 724 A2
23300 CmsC 97067 724 A2
SW Latigo Cir
13700 BRTN 97008 655 A1
SW Latourell Pl
2300 TDLE 97060 599 E6
Latourell Wy
600 VCVR 98661 537 B5
S Latourette Rd
15200 CmsC 97045 689 C5
Latourette St
400 ORCY 97045 717 C2
NE Latte Wy
2300 HBRO 97124 593 A2
S Lau Ct
15100 CmsC 97045 688 B3
SW Laue Ln
- CmsC 97070 745 B2
SE Laugardia Wy
16900 CmsC 97267 687 B1
E Laugeson Av
22600 CmsC 97011 723 J1
NE Laughlin Rd
17200 YmhC 97148 711 D1
NE Laura Av
400 GSHM 97030 629 F2
SE Laura Av
2900 GSHM 97080 629 F6
6300 CmsC 97222 657 D1
SW Laura Av
2300 TDLE 97060 599 F6
NE Laura Ct
1900 HBRO 97124 593 E4
12300 VCVR 98684 538 A6
SW Laura Ct
2900 TDLE 97060 599 F6
SE Laura Dr
1100 GSHM 97080 629 F4
S Laura Ln
25300 CmsC 97023 750 A5
SE Laura Ln
1300 GSHM 97080 629 G4
SE Laura Pl
1000 GSHM 97080 629 F4
NE Laura St
2400 HBRO 97124 593 F4
Laurel Av NE
21900 MrnC 97002 775 C3
SE Laurel Ct
- HBRO 97123 623 E1
Laurel Dr
1800 NWBG 97132 713 D7
NE Laurel Dr
- MCMV 97128 771 E6
Laurel Ln
900 ORCY 97045 717 D3
Laurel Pl
2000 VCVR 98661 537 A4
S Laurel Rd
26100 CmsC 97013 776 C4
SW Laurel Rd
400 ECDA 97023 750 A3
10100 BRTN 97005 625 D3
10100 WasC 97005 625 D3
27500 WasC 97123 653 D5
Laurel St
10 LKOW 97034 656 F7
2000 FTGV 97116 592 A4
NE Laurel St
33600 SPSE 97056 444 E7
NW Laurel St
100 DNDE 97115 742 H2
100 YmhC 97115 742 H2
33000 SPSE 97056 444 E7
SE Laurel St
2400 CmsC 97267 656 J6
5700 CmsC 97222 657 D1
SW Laurel St
1600 PTLD 97201 596 D7
7500 WasC 97225 625 G3
7800 BRTN 97225 625 G3
NE Laurelee St
6000 HBRO 97124 593 J4
SW Laurel Glen Ct
11400 TGRD 97224 655 C6
SW Laurel Glen St
- CmsC 97070 715 G5
- WNVL 97070 715 G5
NE Laurelhurst Pl
10 PTLD 97214 597 B5
10 PTLD 97232 597 B5
NE Laurelhurst Pl
3900 PTLD 97213 597 B5
SE Laurelhurst Pl
10 PTLD 97214 597 B6
10 PTLD 97232 597 B6
SW Laurel Leaf Ln
8500 WasC 97225 625 F4
SW Laurel Leaf Ter
8800 WasC 97225 625 F4
SW Laurelview Rd
30500 WasC 97123 653 A7
SW Laurelwood Av
3800 BRTN 97225 625 F4
3800 WasC 97225 625 F4
NE Laurelwood Cir
1500 CNBY 97013 746 D4
Laurelwood Ct
400 ORCY 97045 717 B2
Laurelwood Dr
800 ORCY 97045 717 B2
SE Laurelwood Dr
2700 CmsC 97267 686 J2
2700 CmsC 97267 687 A2
NE Laurelwood Ln
- FRVW 97024 599 B3
N Laurelwood Lp
1700 CNBY 97013 746 C4
Lauren Ct
100 NWBG 97132 713 B6
NE Lauren Ct
300 HBRO 97124 593 C1
NE Lauren Ln
11500 YmhC 97132 713 J7
11500 YmhC 97132 714 A7
11500 YmhC 97132 744 A1
SW Lauren Ln
13500 TGRD 97223 655 A4
SE Laurie Av
13000 CmsC 97222 656 H5
13600 CmsC 97267 656 H5
SE Laurie Ct
14100 CmsC 97267 656 H6
SE Laurie Ln
100 DAYT 97114 771 J4
NE Laurin Rd
12500 ClkC 98662 477 H7
NW Laurinda Ct
10800 WasC 97229 595 D5
S Laurisa Ln
- CmsC 97045 719 F2
18200 CmsC 97045 717 J2
SW Laurmont Ct
13300 TGRD 97223 655 B2
SW Laurmont Dr
12900 TGRD 97223 655 A3
SW Lausanne St
11600 WNVL 97070 715 B7
SE Lauzon Ln
42000 CmsC 97055 691 D5
SW Lava Ct
8600 BRTN 97007 624 H7
SE Lava Dr
1300 CmsC 97222 656 H2
1300 MWKE 97222 656 H2
SW Lavender Av
20500 SRWD 97140 684 F5
SE Lavender Ln
- CmsC 97009 659 G3
SW Lavender Pl
20200 SRWD 97140 684 F5
SE Lavender St
1700 PTLD 97214 626 H1
SW Lavender Ter
20400 SRWD 97140 684 F5
SW Lavenir Ter
1700 WasC 97116 591 F6
SE Laver St
12800 VCVR 98683 538 A7
SW Laview Dr
7100 PTLD 97219 626 F5
NW Lavina Av
3200 VCVR 98660 536 F2
Lavina Dr
3000 FTGV 97116 591 E2
Lavina St
3600 VCVR 98660 536 F2
NW Lavina St
4300 VCVR 98660 536 F1
4300 VCVR 98663 536 F1
S Lavine Ln
17800 CmsC 97045 718 D2
SW Lavon Ln
- SRWD 97140 714 J1
SE Lavona Ct
11200 HPYV 97236 657 J3
SE Lawnfield Rd
9000 CmsC 97015 657 G6
NE Lawnview Cir
14700 CmsC 97002 745 F3
14700 CmsC 97070 745 F3
14700 WNVL 97070 745 F3
NE Lawrence Av
500 PTLD 97232 596 H4
SW Lawrence Ln
21100 WasC 97006 594 B6
SE Lawrence Rd
29900 CmsC 97023 750 D1
Lawson Ct
37700 SNDY 97055 690 H1
SE Lawson Ln
200 YmhC 97128 771 A7
300 YmhC 97128 770 J7
Lawton Rd
100 ORCY 97045 717 A3
SE Lawton Rd
34200 ClkC 98671 570 D3
34200 WHGL 98671 570 D3
SW Lawton St
17400 WasC 97006 594 F6
Lazy Acres Ln
57600 ClbC 97053 414 G4
SE Lazy B Ln
34400 CmsC 97022 720 E1
Lazy Creek Ln
13600 ORCY 97045 717 E5
19400 CmsC 97045 717 E5
SW Lazy River Pl
16800 WasC 97123 683 E1
Lazy River Wy
3000 WLIN 97068 686 H2
SE Leach Ln
11600 YmhC 97114 771 G3
NW Leadbetter Blvd
5500 CMAS 98607 539 C7
NE Leadbetter Dr
5900 CMAS 98607 539 A7
NW Leadbetter Pkwy
2700 CMAS 98607 539 B7
2700 CMAS 98607 569 B1
N Leadbetter Rd
7000 PTLD 97203 535 H4
NE Leadbetter Rd
100 ClkC 98607 539 C6
SE Leadbetter Rd
100 ClkC 98607 539 D7
100 ClkC 98607 569 E1
100 CMAS 98607 569 E1
Leafy Ln
17600 LKOW 97034 686 C1
31100 ClbC 97056 474 A1
SW Leah Ct
2700 PTLD 97219 656 C2
SW Leah Ter
13600 TGRD 97224 654 J6
13600 TGRD 97224 655 A6
13900 WasC 97224 654 J6
NW Leahy Rd
10900 WasC 97229 595 D5
11200 BRTN 97225 595 C5
11200 BRTN 97229 595 C5
11200 WasC 97225 595 C5
SW Leahy Rd
8100 WasC 97225 595 F6
NW Leahy Ter
8900 WasC 97229 595 F5
NE Leander Dr
16100 YmhC 97132 713 H3
16100 YmhC 97140 713 H3
SE Leander St
1000 HBRO 97123 593 D6
SE Le Ann Ct
13500 CmsC 97009 660 F6
SW Leann Ct
19000 WasC 97007 624 D6
Leann Marie Ln
11900 ORCY 97045 717 A4
NE Leaper Rd
15900 ClkC 98686 477 D4
NE Leathers Ln
2700 MCMV 97128 770 J2
SE Leavenworth Ct
30500 CmsC 97022 690 A6
NE Lea View Ct
2700 VCVR 98663 536 J1
2700 VCVR 98663 537 A1
N Leavitt Av
6700 PTLD 97203 565 G3
SW Lebeau Rd
18500 WasC 97140 684 A4
NE Lebeck Ln
2100 PTLD 97211 567 A3
Leberg Rd
54900 ClbC 97053 444 E3
54900 ClbC 97056 444 E3
SE Lechner St
100 CMAS 98607 569 J5
100 WHGL 98671 569 J5
200 CMAS 98671 569 J5
NW Ledum Ln
600 HBRO 97124 593 B3
SE Lee Av
13900 CmsC 97222 656 J5
13900 CmsC 97267 656 J6
SW Lee Av
- BRTN 97008 625 C4
5600 BRTN 97005 625 C4
S Lee Dr
21400 CmsC 97045 747 F2
SW Lee Dr
22300 SRWD 97140 684 G7
SE Lee Ln
2300 PTLD 97233 628 B1
Lee St
100 STHN 97051 415 A1
800 LKOW 97034 656 F7
1300 LKOW 97034 686 F1
NW Lee St
10100 WasC 97225 595 D5
10500 WasC 97229 595 D5
SW Lee St
4000 PTLD 97221 626 A3
5300 TLTN 97062 685 J5
SE Lee Anna Wy
4100 PTLD 97236 628 E3
SW Leeding Ln
16300 WasC 97223 654 G5
SW Leeds Ct
20500 WasC 97007 624 C3
SW Leewood Dr
1900 WasC 97006 594 C7
SE Leewood Ln
32100 CmsC 97009 690 D6
32700 CmsC 97022 690 C5
SW Leewood Ln
1900 WasC 97006 594 C7
SE Legacy Ct
15000 CmsC 97015 658 A7
Legacy Dr
2100 NWBG 97132 713 B5
2100 YmhC 97132 713 B5
Legacy Ln
- ClbC 97053 414 J5
Legato Dr
11300 CmsC 97045 716 J5
11300 ORCY 97045 716 J5
NW Legend Trail Pl
4400 WasC 97006 594 F3
SW Lehan Ct
29700 WNVL 97070 715 C7
NW Lehman Pl
3500 WasC 97006 594 H2
SW Lehman St
8600 WasC 97223 655 F1
9100 TGRD 97223 655 F1
SE Lehr Rd
3300 ClkC 98671 570 D3
3300 WHGL 98671 570 D3
NE Lehto Rd
19100 ClkC 98604 448 H7
SE Lei Ct
7900 CmsC 97267 687 F1
NE Leichner Rd
1800 ClkC 98686 476 J7
NW Leif Erickson Dr
- PTLD 97210 565 E4
- PTLD 97210 595 G1
NW Leif Erickson Dr
- PTLD 97210 596 A2
- PTLD 97231 565 E4
NW Leif Erikson Dr
- PTLD 97231 565 D3
Leigh Ct
1300 WLIN 97068 686 G2
NW Leighbrook Pl
3700 WasC 97229 595 A2
SE Leinan Rd
20500 CmsC 97022 690 A6
SW Leiser Ln
7900 TGRD 97224 655 F6
S Leisure Ln
23600 CmsC 97004 749 E7
NW Leisy Rd
3700 WasC 97124 562 J7
3700 WasC 97124 592 J1
SW Lela Ln
20200 WasC 97006 594 C6
SW Leland Dr
7600 WasC 97007 624 C6
Leland Rd
1300 ORCY 97045 717 C5
13500 CmsC 97045 747 F3
14500 CmsC 97004 747 G3
19400 CmsC 97045 717 C5
S Leland Rd
14700 CmsC 97004 747 H3
16000 CmsC 97004 748 A3
20000 CmsC 97045 717 C7
20600 CmsC 97045 747 C1
NW Le Mans Ct
10500 WasC 97229 595 D3
Lemont St
100 STHN 97051 385 D6
S Len Av
15400 CmsC 97045 688 C4
SE Lena Av
5100 CmsC 97222 657 C4
N Lena Ct
- YmhC 97128 741 G6
SE Lennon Ct
14000 PTLD 97236 628 C7
NW Lennox Ln
14400 PTLD 97231 565 A1
SE Lenore Cir
4000 TDLE 97060 599 G7
4000 TDLE 97060 629 G1
SW Lenore Ct
21100 WasC 97006 594 B7
SW Lenore Dr
2100 WasC 97006 594 C7
2300 WasC 97006 624 B1
NE Lenore St
1100 PTLD 97211 566 H6
SE Lenore St
10800 HPYV 97236 657 J3
NE Lenox St
100 HBRO 97124 593 C1
NW Lenox St
31000 HBRO 97124 593 B1
31100 WasC 97124 593 B1
31300 NPNS 97133 563 B1
SW Lenske Ln
27000 CmsC 97070 716 A5
Leo Ct
15900 ORCY 97045 687 F5
Leo Ln
1800 NWBG 97132 713 F6
Leo St
- MCMV 97128 770 D5
Leon Dr
1700 FTGV 97116 591 H3
SE Leona Ln
8100 JNCY 97267 687 F1
Leonard St
- WLIN 97068 687 A7
10 LKOW 97034 656 G6
900 ORCY 97045 717 C3
N Leonard St
9700 PTLD 97203 565 G2
SE Leonardo Ct
14400 HPYV 97236 628 C7
14400 PTLD 97236 628 C7
SW Leonardo Ln
20100 WasC 97007 654 C1
SE Leone Ln
4900 MWKE 97222 657 C1
SW Lepley Ln
27600 WasC 97123 653 D7
Leroy Av
200 CmsC 97038 837 D1
300 MOLA 97038 837 D1
500 CmsC 97038 807 D7
500 MOLA 97038 807 D7
Leroy Ln
16700 CmsC 97045 687 E6
16700 ORCY 97045 687 E6
NE Leroy Haagen Memorial Dr
- VCVR 98684 538 B5
NE Lesley Rd
32700 YmhC 97132 743 J4
32700 YmhC 97132 744 A4
S Leslie Av
22000 CmsC 97004 747 H3
Leslie Ct
13300 LKOW 97034 656 D4
SW Leslie Ct
14900 TGRD 97224 655 E6
SW Leslie St
8900 WasC 97223 625 F7
Leslies Wy
2000 WLIN 97068 716 H2
NE Lessard Rd
4900 ClkC 98607 539 J1
5100 ClkC 98607 540 A1
SW Lesser Rd
11500 PTLD 97219 655 H3
12700 LKOW 97035 655 J4
12700 PTLD 97035 655 J4
SW Lesser Wy
6100 PTLD 97219 655 H3
NE Levee Rd
8800 PTLD 97211 566 J3
SE Lever St
1200 MCMV 97128 770 H7
NE Leverich Ct
4600 VCVR 98663 536 H1
NE Leverich Pl
4700 VCVR 98663 536 H1
NE Leverich Park Wy
3900 VCVR 98663 536 H1
N Leverman St
3600 PTLD 97217 566 C6
SE Levern Ln
9300 CmsC 97236 657 G3
SW Leveton Dr
10800 TLTN 97062 685 B3
S Levi Ct
16100 CmsC 97004 748 A2
S Levi Rd
- CmsC 97045 748 A2
21300 CmsC 97004 748 A2
Levi Wy
200 NWBG 97132 713 B6
200 YmhC 97132 713 B6
SE Lewellyn Av
1600 TDLE 97060 599 H6
Lewis Av
3100 VCVR 98661 537 A5
N Lewis Av
2100 PTLD 97227 596 F3
SE Lewis Ct
2900 TDLE 97060 599 H6
NE Lewis Dr
8300 VCVR 98662 537 F2
NW Lewis Ln
3900 PTLD 97229 595 E1
SW Lewis Ln
9500 TGRD 97223 655 E3
Lewis St
- PTLD 97231 565 B3
1400 WLIN 97068 687 B6
SW Lewis & Clark Cir
- PTLD 97205 596 C5
Lewis & Clark Hwy
- ClkC 568 F4
- ClkC 98671 570 D6
- ClkC 98671 600 J1
- CMAS 98607 568 J5
- CMAS 98607 569 J5
- VCVR 536 G6
- VCVR 537 D7
- VCVR 567 J2
- VCVR 568 A2
- WHGL 98671 569 J5
- WHGL 98671 570 C6
Lewis & Clark Hwy SR-14
- ClkC 568 F4
- ClkC 98671 570 F7
- ClkC 98671 600 J1
- CMAS 98607 568 J5
- CMAS 98607 569 A5
- VCVR 536 G6
- VCVR 537 B6
- VCVR 567 F1
- VCVR 568 A2
- WHGL 98671 569 J5
- WHGL 98671 570 C6
Lewis River Rd
1000 WDLD 98674 386 A1
Lewis River Rd SR-503
1000 WDLD 98674 386 A1
NE Lewis Rogers Ln
16200 YmhC 97132 712 C2
NE Lewisville Hwy
24400 BGND 98604 448 A3
24400 ClkC 98604 448 A2
26200 ClkC 98604 418 C4
32900 ClkC 98675 418 D2
NE Lewisville Hwy SR-503
24400 BGND 98604 448 A3
24400 ClkC 98604 448 A2
26200 ClkC 98604 418 C4
32900 ClkC 98675 418 D2
Lewthwaite St
1800 WLIN 97068 687 B7
Lexington Ct
16400 LKOW 97034 656 G7
SE Lexington Ct
6800 PTLD 97206 627 E6
SE Lexington Dr
5600 HBRO 97123 593 J7
SW Lexington Dr
15300 BRTN 97007 654 E2
SE Lexington St
700 PTLD 97202 626 H6
3600 PTLD 97202 627 B6
5300 PTLD 97206 627 D6
10100 PTLD 97266 627 H6
11600 PTLD 97266 628 A7
Lexington Ter
2600 WLIN 97068 686 H4
Lexington Wy
400 VCVR 98664 537 E6
SW Lexington Wy
10 WasC 97006 594 F5
NW Lianna Wy
5300 WasC 97229 564 G6
SE Libby Ct
4400 HBRO 97123 593 H5
S Liberal Wy
12200 CmsC 97013 807 B1
12200 CmsC 97038 807 D3
NE Liberty Av
10 GSHM 97080 629 D2
1400 GSHM 97030 629 D1
2600 GSHM 97030 599 D7
SE Liberty Av
1400 GSHM 97080 629 D4
NE Liberty Ct
3200 PTLD 97211 567 A6
SE Liberty Ct
200 GSHM 97080 629 D3
NE Liberty Dr
24100 ClkC 98604 449 D3
SE Liberty Pl
2900 GSHM 97080 629 D6
Liberty St NE
21000 AURA 97002 775 F4
N Liberty St
3100 PTLD 97217 566 D6
NE Liberty St
600 PTLD 97211 566 H6
3300 PTLD 97211 567 B6
NE Liberty Ter
3700 PTLD 97211 567 B6
SW Liberty Bell Dr
2900 WasC 97006 594 E6
Liberty Hill Rd
26000 ClbC 97051 385 B5
Libra St
1400 NWBG 97132 713 F6
Library Ct
100 ORCY 97045 717 C4
SE Licyntra Ct
3700 MWKE 97222 657 A4
SE Licyntra Ln
3600 MWKE 97222 657 A4
SW Liden Dr
13500 TGRD 97223 655 A4
13800 TGRD 97223 654 J4
SW Lido St
20500 WasC 97007 624 C3
SE Liebe St
3700 PTLD 97202 627 B3
5500 PTLD 97206 627 C3
8200 PTLD 97266 627 F4
11800 PTLD 97236 628 A4
11800 PTLD 97266 628 A4
Liedtke Wy
3900 WHGL 98671 570 D5
Lieser Ct
8400 VCVR 98664 537 F6
N Lieser Rd
100 VCVR 98664 537 F6
SE Lieser Rd
100 VCVR 98664 537 F7
SE Lieser Point Dr
1500 VCVR 98664 567 F1
NW Lightning Ridge Dr
9400 PTLD 97229 595 E1
NE Lija Lp
900 PTLD 97211 566 H3
NW Lilac Av
- PTLD 97231 565 E3
NE Lilac Ct
900 HBRO 97124 593 D3
SE Lilac Dr
14800 CmsC 97267 657 F7
Lilac Ln
- MrnC 97002 775 C2
Lilac St
- FTGV 97116 591 G3
NE Lilac St
1700 HBRO 97124 593 E3
NW Lilium Dr
14300 WasC 97229 564 J7
14300 WasC 97229 565 A7
Lilli Ln
2000 LKOW 97034 686 G1
S Lilli Ln
25700 CmsC 97013 776 J4
SE Lillian Av
7500 CmsC 97267 687 E1
SE Lillian Ct
16100 CmsC 97267 687 E1
SW Lillian Ct
20700 WasC 97007 624 C6
Lillian Ln
34300 CmsC 97022 720 E1
SE Lillian Wy
16500 PTLD 97236 628 E3
Lilly Ct
1600 NWBG 97132 743 D1
Lilly Bay Ct
15100 LKOW 97034 656 D6
SW Lillyben Av
100 GSHM 97080 628 J3
SW Lillyben Ct
2200 GSHM 97080 628 H6
NW Lillyben Pl
10 GSHM 97030 628 J2
SW Lillyben Pl
2800 GSHM 97080 628 J5
SW Lily Pl
6700 BRTN 97008 625 A5
NW Lilywood Dr
12300 WasC 97229 595 B3
Limerick Ln
2500 WLIN 97068 686 G7
SE Limerick St
38400 SNDY 97055 690 J4
SW Limestone Ct
19500 WasC 97006 594 D7
Limpus Ln
3100 FTGV 97116 591 H3
Lincoln Av
3600 VCVR 98660 536 F2
4300 VCVR 98663 536 F1
NW Lincoln Av
4500 VCVR 98660 536 F1
4500 VCVR 98663 536 F1
5000 VCVR 98663 506 F7
SW Lincoln Av
11800 TGRD 97223 655 E3
NE Lincoln Ct
100 HBRO 97124 593 D5
SE Lincoln Ct
8900 PTLD 97216 627 G1
11400 PTLD 97216 628 A1
17200 PTLD 97233 628 F1
Lincoln St
200 FRVW 97024 599 B4
300 CBAC 97018 385 B2
1200 ORCY 97045 717 D1
N Lincoln St
- LFYT 97127 741 H7
- YmhC 97114 741 H7
300 NWBG 97132 713 B7
NE Lincoln St
1800 HBRO 97124 593 E5
4100 WasC 97124 593 G5
NW Lincoln St
100 HBRO 97124 593 B4
S Lincoln St
100 NWBG 97132 713 B7
400 NWBG 97132 743 B1
SE Lincoln St
- PTLD 97215 627 E1
200 MCMV 97128 770 H5
500 PTLD 97214 596 H7
2000 PTLD 97214 626 J1
2600 PTLD 97214 627 A1
3000 PTLD 97215 597 A7
8700 PTLD 97216 627 G1
11500 PTLD 97216 628 A1
12200 PTLD 97233 628 B1
18400 GSHM 97233 628 H1
SW Lincoln St
700 PTLD 97201 596 B7
12000 TGRD 97223 655 E2
12000 WasC 97223 655 E2
22200 SRWD 97140 684 H7
W Lincoln St
400 CLTN 97111 711 A7
SW Linda Ct
14800 WasC 97006 594 J5
Linda Dr
19300 CmsC 97045 716 J5
19300 ORCY 97045 716 J5
Linda Ln
2400 VCVR 98661 537 B3
SW Linda Ln
13600 WasC 97005 595 A6
13600 WasC 97006 595 A6
S Linda Rd
25800 CmsC 97013 776 E4
Linda Wy
600 NWBG 97132 713 D7
SE Linde Ln
31400 CmsC 97023 750 G3
Linden
- CmsC 97015 657 H7
NE Linden Av
10 GSHM 97080 629 C2
800 GSHM 97030 629 C1
1000 HBRO 97124 593 E3
3000 GSHM 97030 599 C7
SE Linden Av
100 GSHM 97080 629 C3
SE Linden Ct
800 GSHM 97080 629 C3
2600 CmsC 97267 656 J6
SE Linden Ln
- GSHM 97080 629 C6
- MthC 97080 629 C6
13100 CmsC 97222 656 J5
14600 CmsC 97267 656 J7
SW Linden Ln
700 DNDE 97115 742 H3
NE Linden Pl
2400 GSHM 97030 599 C7
SE Linden Pl
1900 GSHM 97080 629 C5
SW Linden Rd
7700 BRTN 97225 625 G2
7700 WasC 97225 625 G2
S Linden St
10 CNLS 97113 592 D6
10 FTGV 97116 592 D6
SW Linden St
33200 SPSE 97056 474 E2
SE Lindenbrook Ct
2200 CmsC 97222 656 J5
Lindgren Dr
300 NWBG 97132 743 B1
Lindquist Ct
3000 NWBG 97132 713 E6
Lindsay Ct
16000 LKOW 97035 685 J1
Lindsay Ln
58100 ClbC 97053 414 E3
SE Lindsay Ln
- HBRO 97123 624 A1
- WasC 97123 624 A1
NE Lindsey Ct
300 HBRO 97124 593 C2
NE Lindsey Dr
2100 HBRO 97124 593 C1
NW Lindy Ln
14500 MthC 97229 564 J6
SE Lindy St
8200 CmsC 97206 627 F7
8200 CmsC 97236 627 F7
SW Line Dr
9000 WasC 97113 623 A7
SW Linette Ct
7400 BRTN 97007 624 H6
SW Linette Wy
7100 BRTN 97007 624 H5
SE Linfield Av
100 MCMV 97128 770 H6
W Linfield Av
100 MCMV 97128 770 G6
Link Ct
100 NWBG 97132 713 G7
100 NWBG 97132 743 G1
SW Link Dr
9100 WasC 97113 623 A7
SW Link St
9000 WasC 97113 623 A7
S Linke Av
400 CLTN 97111 741 B1
W Linke St
400 MCMV 97128 770 G7
SE Links Av
9300 HPYV 97236 658 C1
NW Linmere Dr
2600 WasC 97229 595 A3
NW Linmere Ln
14100 WasC 97229 595 A2
Linn Av
100 ORCY 97045 717 C3
Linn Ct
- SNDY 97055 690 H3
Linn Ln
5000 WLIN 97068 686 J6
SE Linn St
600 PTLD 97202 626 H7
NW Linnea Dr
25500 WasC 97124 533 H6
NW Linneman Av
100 GSHM 97030 628 G2
SW Linneman Av
1100 GSHM 97080 628 G4
SW Linneman Ct
600 GSHM 97030 628 G3
SW Linneman Dr
2300 GSHM 97080 628 G5
3000 GSHM 97236 628 G5
3000 MthC 97080 628 G5
3000 MthC 97236 628 G5
NW Linnton Av
- PTLD 97231 535 D7
- PTLD 97231 565 D1
Linnton St
- MthC 97231 534 F5
Linnwood Dr
3700 WLIN 97068 686 J4
Linny Ln
- CmsC 97009 660 A3
SE Linwood Av
9300 CmsC 97206 657 D1
9300 CmsC 97222 657 D1
9300 MWKE 97206 657 D1
9300 MWKE 97222 657 D3
NW Lippert Ln
41600 WasC 97116 531 J7
41600 WasC 97116 532 A7
SW Lisa Ct
19500 WasC 97006 594 D6
SW Lisa Dr
19100 WasC 97006 594 E5
SE Lisa Ln
15900 CmsC 97267 656 J7

Portland Street Index

STREET Block City ZIP Map# Grid

SW Lisa Ln
13900 BRTN 97005 625 A4
14100 BRTN 97005 624 J4
SW Lisa St
16900 BRTN 97006 594 G6
17000 WasC 97006 594 G6
SW Lisbon Ct
6800 WasC 97007 624 B5
NW Lishan Rd
5200 ClkC 98674 386 B3
SW List Pl
22000 SRWD 97140 684 E6
SW List Ter
- SRWD 97140 684 E6
NW Listel Ln
14400 WasC 97229 594 J2
SW Little Ct
- WasC 97007 624 E3
SE Little Ln
21500 DAMA 97009 689 A1
S Little St
100 STHN 97051 415 B1
E Littlebrook Ln
- CmsC 97049 724 H6
SE Little Creek Ln
7400 CmsC 97267 687 E1
SE Littlegem St
1700 HBRO 97123 623 E1
Little John Ln
- CmsC 97045 716 G7
SW Little John Ter
22100 SRWD 97140 684 F6
Littlepage Av
17000 SNDY 97055 690 G2
NE Littlepage Rd
100 MthC 97019 600 J6
SE Littlepage Rd
100 MthC 97019 600 H7
1100 MthC 97019 630 H2
S Little Plain Pkwy
19100 CmsC 97045 717 B4
19100 ORCY 97045 717 B4
NE Littler Wy
3100 VCVR 98662 537 E3
E Little River Rd
21200 CmsC 97011 693 E7
Little Rock Wy
100 VCVR 98664 537 D6
Livesay Rd
13900 CmsC 97045 687 F7
13900 ORCY 97045 687 F7
Livingood Ln
400 LKOW 97034 686 E1
SW Livingston Pl
600 TDLE 97060 599 F4
NE Livingston Rd
5200 ClkC 98607 509 J7
5200 ClkC 98607 539 H1
NE Livingston Mountain Cir
29200 ClkC 98607 509 J4
NE Livingston Mountain Ct
9100 ClkC 98607 509 J4
NE Livingston Mountain Rd
8200 ClkC 98607 509 J4
SW Liz Pl
8100 WasC 97007 624 D6
SE Lizz Cir
10700 HPYV 97236 658 A2
SE Lizz Ct
10800 HPYV 97236 658 A3
SE Llewellyn St
2300 MWKE 97222 656 J2
3100 MWKE 97222 657 A2
SW Lloyd Av
4300 BRTN 97005 625 B3
NE Lloyd Blvd
- PTLD 97227 596 G5
200 PTLD 97232 596 G5
SE Lloyd St
5600 MWKE 97222 657 C3
NW Loan Pl
200 ClkC 98665 506 G4
SW Lobelia St
4100 PTLD 97219 626 A7
NW Lobo Ln
26300 WasC 97133 533 G5
SE Locks Rd
2600 YmhC 97114 771 H2
SE Locks Loop Rd
13000 LFYT 97127 771 H1
13000 YmhC 97114 771 H1
NE Lockwood Creek Rd
800 LCTR 98629 416 J1
1400 ClkC 98629 416 J1
1400 ClkC 98629 417 B2
SE Locust Av
1700 PTLD 97214 596 J7
Locust St
1100 DNDE 97115 742 H4
1100 YmhC 97115 742 H4
N Locust St
1200 CNBY 97013 746 C4
1400 CmsC 97013 746 C4
S Locust St
100 CNBY 97013 746 D6
SE Locust St
500 DNDE 97115 742 J3
SW Locust St
1600 MCMV 97128 770 F6
6500 PTLD 97219 655 H2
6500 PTLD 97223 655 H2
6900 TGRD 97223 655 E2
7100 WasC 97223 655 E2
Loder Rd
14800 CmsC 97045 717 H5
14800 ORCY 97045 717 G5
S Loder Rd
16000 CmsC 97045 717 J5
16000 CmsC 97045 718 A5
SW Lodestone Dr
9400 BRTN 97007 654 H1
E Lodge Ln
21400 CmsC 97049 693 J7
NW Lodge Rd
40600 WasC 97106 532 A2
41400 WasC 97106 531 J2
Lodge Pole
- MCMV 97128 771 A7
- YmhC 97128 771 A7
SW Lodgepole Av
- TLTN 97062 685 D7
- TLTN 97062 715 D1
SW Lodgepole Ter
23700 SRWD 97140 714 G1
SW Lodi Ln
4900 PTLD 97221 626 A2
8500 TGRD 97224 655 F7
SE Loeffelman St
3100 CmsC 97222 657 A5
NW Loftis Ln
31300 WasC 97133 533 A2
NW Loftus Ln
- WasC 97133 533 B3
NW Logan Cir
2800 CMAS 98607 569 C2
NW Logan Ct
3500 CMAS 98607 569 D2
9600 PTLD 97229 595 E2
SW Logan Ct
5700 PTLD 97219 625 J5
S Logan Dr
19200 CmsC 97004 748 G7
SE Logan Ln
600 DNDE 97115 742 J4
SW Logan Ln
- TLTN 97062 685 F4
NE Logan St
1200 MCMV 97128 770 J4
NW Logan St
2300 CMAS 98607 569 D3
SE Logan St
100 MCMV 97128 770 J5
SW Logan St
3500 PTLD 97219 626 B6
13400 WasC 97005 595 A6
E Loganberry Rd
20300 CmsC 97011 693 G6
NE Logger Ln
22000 YmhC 97115 742 J2
Logging Rd
- CmsC 97013 746 D2
- CNBY 97013 746 D2
NW Logie Trail Rd
13100 MthC 97124 533 J4
18200 MthC 97231 504 E7
19300 MthC 97231 534 D1
SE Logus Rd
4300 MWKE 97222 657 B1
5400 CmsC 97222 657 C2
Logus St
- CmsC 97045 717 D1
400 ORCY 97045 717 D1
Lois Ln
2200 WLIN 97068 716 H1
SW Lois Ln
- BRTN 97225 595 E7
- WasC 97225 595 E7
SE Lois St
- WasC 97006 594 B6
5900 HBRO 97123 593 J6
5900 WasC 97123 593 J6
6300 HBRO 97123 594 A6
SW Lois St
21400 WasC 97006 594 B6
21700 HBRO 97123 594 B6
NW Lois Elaine Ter
4000 WasC 97229 595 B1
Lola Av
100 MOLA 97038 837 E2
SE Lola Ln
15000 CmsC 97267 657 E7
SW Lola Ln
7000 TGRD 97223 655 G1
Lolo Pass Ct
59000 STHN 97051 414 H1
E Lolo Pass Rd
22200 CmsC 97049 724 D3
Loma Linda
- VCVR 98683 568 F3
SW Loma Vista St
17100 WasC 97007 624 F6
SW Lomax Ter
- TGRD 97223 655 A3
SW Lombard Av
4000 WasC 97005 625 B2
4400 BRTN 97005 625 C4
5900 BRTN 97008 625 C4
NE Lombard Ct
3400 PTLD 97211 567 B6
NE Lombard Pl
1000 PTLD 97211 566 H5
N Lombard St
10 PTLD 97211 566 G5
1700 PTLD 97217 566 D5
3900 PTLD 97203 566 A4
9600 PTLD 97203 565 G1
12300 PTLD 97203 535 F5
N Lombard St US-30 BYP
10 PTLD 97211 566 G5
1700 PTLD 97217 566 D5
3900 PTLD 97203 566 A4
6400 PTLD 97203 565 J3
NE Lombard St
10 PTLD 97211 566 J5
10 PTLD 97217 566 G5
2200 PTLD 97211 567 A6
4000 PTLD 97218 567 B6
NE Lombard St US-30 BYP
10 PTLD 97211 566 J5
10 PTLD 97217 566 G5
2200 PTLD 97211 567 A6
4000 PTLD 97218 567 B6
N Lombard Wy
8000 PTLD 97203 565 H3
SW Lomita Av
11300 TGRD 97223 655 F3
NW Lomita Ter
300 PTLD 97210 596 A4
SW London Ct
9700 TGRD 97223 655 E3
Londonderry Ln
6700 CmsC 97027 687 D1
6700 CmsC 97267 687 D1
6700 GLDS 97027 687 D1
Lone Pn
- ClkC 98665 507 B4
S Lone Elder Rd
5800 CmsC 97002 775 H4
6600 CmsC 97013 775 J4
7000 CmsC 97002 776 A4
7000 CmsC 97013 776 B4
SW Lone Fir Ln
25300 CmsC 97068 716 B3
SE Lone Oak Ln
14800 CmsC 97267 657 C6
Lone Oak Rd N
3000 YmhC 97128 771 C1
Lone Oak Rd N
3200 YmhC 97128 741 C7
SE Lone Oak Rd S
2800 YmhC 97128 771 C2
SW Lone Oak St
4500 HBRO 97123 623 H1
4600 WasC 97123 623 H1
SE Lone Pine Dr
14500 CmsC 97015 658 C6
Lone Pine Ln
- WasC 97007 654 B4
NW Lonerock Dr
17400 WasC 97006 594 F2
17400 WasC 97229 594 F1
NW Lone Rock Ln
17100 WasC 97006 594 G2
17300 WasC 97229 594 G2
Long Cir
38700 SNDY 97055 690 J3
NW Long Rd
35500 WasC 97113 592 F2
Long St
2000 WLIN 97068 687 A7
SE Long St
- PTLD 97236 628 B4
2500 PTLD 97202 626 J3
2800 PTLD 97202 627 A3
5200 PTLD 97206 627 D3
10400 PTLD 97266 627 J3
12200 PTLD 97266 628 A4
SW Longacre Ct
19500 WasC 97006 594 D6
SW Longacre St
18500 WasC 97006 594 E6
NW Longbow Ln
20700 WasC 97006 594 C5
SW Long Farm Rd
400 CmsC 97068 686 D4
Longfellow Av
18300 CmsC 97035 685 H2
SW Longfellow Av
18800 CmsC 97035 685 H3
18800 LKOW 97035 685 H3
19200 RVGR 97035 685 H3
S Longhorn Ln
18000 CmsC 97045 718 C3
SW Longhorn Ln
12100 BRTN 97008 655 B1
SW Longspur Ter
11600 BRTN 97007 654 E3
SW Longstaff St
9300 TGRD 97223 655 E2
Longstanding Ct
11700 CmsC 97045 717 A4
11700 ORCY 97045 717 A4
SE Longstreet Ln
19200 CmsC 97055 691 D5
N Longview Av
3700 PTLD 97227 596 E1
4000 PTLD 97217 596 E1
S Longview Wy
10 ORCY 97045 687 F5
SE Lonny Ct
2700 HBRO 97123 623 F1
Lookout Ct
2600 LKOW 97034 686 C1
E Lookout Dr
64300 CmsC 97049 693 H6
SW Lookout Dr
14800 TGRD 97224 655 B6
NE Lookout Rd
28500 ClkC 98607 509 H6
SW Lookout Ter
9700 BRTN 97008 655 B1
W Lookout Ridge Dr
- ClkC 98607 569 G3
700 WHGL 98671 569 G3
NW Lookover Dr
42100 WasC 97106 531 J1
SW Loon Dr
15900 BRTN 97007 654 G4
16400 WasC 97007 654 G4
SW Loop Dr
6400 PTLD 97221 626 A4
SE Loop Rd
10600 MCMV 97114 771 E6
10600 MCMV 97128 771 E6
10600 YmhC - 771 E6
10600 YmhC 97114 771 E6
10600 YmhC 97128 771 E6
NE Loowit Lp
7800 VCVR 98662 537 F1
SE Lopez Av
14700 HPYV 97236 658 C1
S Lora Ct
15800 CmsC 97045 687 J7
15800 CmsC 97045 688 A7
SE Lora St
16100 PTLD 97233 628 E1
SW Lorain Av
- PTLD 97239 626 C3
Lords Ln
4200 LKOW 97035 686 A1
SE Loren Ln
14500 CmsC 97267 657 C6
NW Lorenz St
- ClkC 98607 568 H2
- CMAS 98607 568 H3
SW Lorenzo Ln
16300 WasC 97223 654 G5
Lori Ln
54800 ClbC 97056 444 C3
SW Lori Wy
8100 BRTN 97007 624 G7
8100 WasC 97007 624 G7
NW Loriann Dr
3400 WasC 97229 595 C2
NE Lorie Dr
2500 HBRO 97124 593 C2
Lorinda Ln
2500 WLIN 97068 686 J7
2500 WLIN 97068 716 J1
N Loring St
800 PTLD 97227 596 F3
Lorna Ln
- RVGR 97035 685 J3
SW Lorna Ter
7000 WasC 97007 624 C5
Lorraine Av
- MthC 97231 535 A5
NW Lorraine Dr
12600 WasC 97229 595 B3
S Lorraine Dr
17800 CmsC 97045 719 F3
SE Lorry Av
8100 VCVR 98664 537 F7
Losalle Ln
23200 SRWD 97140 684 E7
23200 SRWD 97140 714 E1
S Lost Horse Ln
17200 CmsC 97045 717 J1
SE Lostine Ct
14800 CmsC 97015 658 A7
SE Lostine Dr
14800 CmsC 97015 658 A7
S Lost Mountain Rd
21800 CmsC 97023 719 C6
NW Lost Park Dr
10400 WasC 97229 595 D4
E Lost Shelter Rd
67200 CmsC 97049 724 B2
Los Verdes Dr
7100 GLDS 97027 687 E2
Lothlorien Wy
18200 LKOW 97034 686 B2
N Lotus Beach Dr
100 PTLD 97217 566 G1
SW Lotus Blossom Pl
7500 BRTN 97008 625 B6
N Lotus Isle Dr
300 PTLD 97217 566 G1
Lot Whitcomb Dr
19100 ORCY 97045 717 C4
SE Lou Ann Ct
15500 CmsC 97267 657 F7
SE Loudon Rd
37000 MthC 97019 630 J1
Louie Ct
58600 ClbC 97051 414 G2
58600 ClbC 97053 414 G2
SE Louise Av
800 VCVR 98664 537 F7
Louise Dr
- YmhC 97128 770 E6
SE Louise Ln
15200 CmsC 97015 658 D7
15200 HPYV 97015 658 D7
Louisiana Dr
6200 VCVR 98661 537 D6
6700 VCVR 98664 537 D6
Louisville Wy
400 VCVR 98664 537 E6
Loundree Dr
17700 SNDY 97055 691 A3
SE Lounsberry Ln
7500 PTLD 97206 627 H2
Lourie Ct
- ORCY 97045 717 D4
SW Louvonne Dr
32500 WNVL 97070 745 E3
Love Av
100 WDLD 98674 385 J2
SW Love Ct
7700 WNVL 97070 715 F7
NW Lovejoy Ct
12800 WasC 97229 595 B4
NW Lovejoy St
1200 PTLD 97209 596 C4
2000 PTLD 97210 596 A3
13100 WasC 97229 595 A4
NE Lovell St
900 HBRO 97124 593 D2
N Lovely St
5900 PTLD 97203 566 A4
SW Lovhar Dr
10 GSHM 97080 629 B4
SE Lovrien Av
500 GSHM 97080 629 F3
S Lowe Rd
13300 CmsC 97038 837 D1
13300 MOLA 97038 837 D1
Lowell Av
6800 WLIN 97068 686 J4
SW Lowell Ct
4700 PTLD 97221 626 A2
SW Lowell Ln
3900 PTLD 97239 626 E2
14800 SRWD 97140 714 H1
SW Lowell St
- PTLD 97221 626 A2
- PTLD 97239 626 D2
4900 PTLD 97221 625 J2
Lowenberg Ter
17100 LKOW 97034 686 D1
Lower Dr
4600 LKOW 97035 685 J1
4600 LKOW 97035 686 A1
SW Lower Dr
- PTLD 97201 596 C7
- PTLD 97221 596 C7
Lower Boones Ferry Rd
14000 LKOW 97034 656 B5
14000 LKOW 97035 656 A7
16200 CmsC 97035 656 A7
16500 CmsC 97035 655 J7
16500 LKOW 97035 655 J7
16800 LKOW 97035 685 J1
17500 TLTN 97035 685 H2
17700 TLTN 97224 685 H2
SW Lower Boones Ferry Rd
17800 TLTN 97224 685 G2
17900 DRHM 97224 685 G2
N Lower Columbia River Hwy
100 STHN 97051 385 B7
N Lwr Columbia River Hwy US-30
100 STHN 97051 385 B7
S Lower Columbia River Hwy
10 STHN 97051 415 B1
S Lwr Columbia River Hwy US-30
10 STHN 97051 415 B1
S Lower Highland Rd
18200 CmsC 97004 748 E7
20400 CmsC 97004 749 B7
Lower Meadows Dr
16900 LKOW 97035 685 J1
Lower Midhill Dr
18200 WLIN 97068 686 H2
Lower Perry Creek Rd
- STHN 97051 385 A6
NW Lower River Rd
2000 VCVR 98660 536 A1
5200 ClkC 98660 536 A1
6300 ClkC 98660 505 G2
6300 ClkC 98660 506 A7
6300 VCVR 98660 505 G2
NW Lower River Rd
6300 VCVR 98660 506 A7
10000 ClkC 98660 475 H2
NW Lower River Rd SR-501
2000 VCVR 98660 536 A1
5200 ClkC 98660 536 A1
6300 ClkC 98660 505 G2
6300 ClkC 98660 506 A7
6300 VCVR 98660 505 G2
6300 VCVR 98660 506 A7
10000 ClkC 98660 475 H2
SW Lower Roy St
22100 SRWD 97140 684 H6
SW Lowrie Ln
7500 WNVL 97070 715 F5
Lowry Dr
6400 WLIN 97068 687 A5
SW Loxley Dr
17700 WasC 97007 624 E6
NW Loy Ct
3800 WasC 97229 595 C2
SW Lucas Av
2800 TDLE 97060 599 E6
SW Lucas Ct
10500 TLTN 97062 685 C3
Lucas Dr
- MCMV 97128 770 J2
SW Lucas Dr
10600 TLTN 97062 685 C2
NE Lucas Rd
100 MthC 97019 600 C6
100 MthC 97060 600 C6
E Lucas St
- ClkC 98629 386 H6
SW Lucas Oaks Ln
20100 WasC 97007 624 C5
NW Lucerne Ct
10900 WasC 97225 595 D5
10900 WasC 97229 595 D5
Lucerne Pl
2200 WLIN 97068 686 G7
NE Lucia Falls Rd
15200 ClkC 98604 418 E5
16000 ClkC 98675 418 F5
22200 ClkC 98604 419 F5
22200 ClkC 98675 419 F5
SW Lucille Ct
- TGRD 97223 655 F2
8500 WasC 97223 655 F2
SE Lucille St
13200 PTLD 97236 658 B1
13900 HPYV 97236 658 C1
SW Lucille St
800 PTLD 97219 656 D1
S Lucky Ln
15800 CmsC 97045 688 D5
SE Lucky Ln
34600 CmsC 97023 750 E2
Lucy Ln
- CmsC 97045 718 C3
NW Lucy Reeder Rd
15700 MthC 97231 504 G3
NE Lucys Ln
- ClkC 98604 449 E3
SE Ludlow Ct
11200 HPYV 97236 657 J3
SW Ludwig St
16000 WasC 97007 624 G3
SE Luella Ln
14700 CmsC 97267 657 E6
SW Luelling Pl
9500 BRTN 97008 655 B1
SW Lukar Ct
14200 TGRD 97223 654 J4
SW Lukas Rd
30400 WasC 97113 653 A1
30400 WasC 97123 653 A1
SW Luke Ln
16300 WasC 97223 654 G4
SW Lumbee Ln
9800 TLTN 97062 685 D7
SW Lummi St
8100 TLTN 97062 685 F6
SE Luna Wy
6100 HBRO 97123 623 J1
Lund St
900 LKOW 97034 656 G7
SW Lundgren Ter
3200 BRTN 97005 625 C2
3200 WasC 97005 625 C2
SE Lundgren Wy
17200 GLDS 97027 687 E2
S Lundstrom Ln
16100 CmsC 97042 807 J4
NW Lupin St
6500 VCVR 98663 506 E6
NW Lupin Wy
6200 VCVR 98663 506 E6
Lupine Ct
21500 WLIN 97068 686 J6
N Lupine Ct
1200 CNBY 97013 746 C5
SE Lupine Ct
2600 HBRO 97123 623 F1
E Lupine Dr
64600 CmsC 97049 693 H7
S Lupine St
500 CNBY 97013 746 D7
1300 CmsC 97013 776 D1
1500 CNBY 97013 776 D1
SE Lupine St
7900 JNCY 97267 687 H2
SW Luradel Ct
5700 PTLD 97219 655 J1
SW Luradel Ln
2900 PTLD 97219 656 C1
SW Luradel St
3100 PTLD 97219 656 B1
5900 PTLD 97219 655 H1
NW Luray Ter
2800 PTLD 97210 596 B4
NW Luray Circus
3000 PTLD 97210 596 A3
SW Luree St
19800 WasC 97006 594 D7
NW Lusanne Ct
10900 WasC 97229 595 D5
SE Lusted Rd
6100 GSHM 97080 629 J4
6100 MthC 97080 629 J4
28200 MthC 97060 629 J4
28200 MthC 97060 630 A4
28200 MthC 97080 630 A4
35500 MthC 97009 660 J2
35500 MthC 97009 630 G7
SW Luster Ct
10100 TLTN 97062 685 D7
SE Luther Rd
7200 CmsC 97206 627 E7
7300 PTLD 97206 627 E7
8000 CmsC 97236 627 E7
Luttrell Ln
60800 ClbC 97051 384 D4
NW Luzon St
3100 PTLD 97210 596 B3
SE Lydia Ct
12600 PTLD 97236 628 B5
NW Lydia Pl
2300 WasC 97006 594 H3
SW Lyle Ct
3700 PTLD 97221 626 B3
SE Lynda Ln
12200 CmsC 97236 658 A4
NW Lyndel Ln
15800 WasC 97006 594 H3
SW Lynmar Pl
6000 WasC 97007 624 B4
NE Lynn Ct
2900 MCMV 97128 771 A2
SE Lynn Ct
12500 CmsC 97222 657 A4
Lynn Dr
100 NWBG 97132 713 B5
100 YmhC 97132 713 B5
Lynn Ln
800 MOLA 97038 837 D1
31000 ClbC 97056 444 A3
SE Lynn Ln
9000 CmsC 97236 657 G2
SW Lynn St
11600 TGRD 97223 655 C4
Lynne Ct
6100 GLDS 97027 687 D3
SW Lynnfield Ln
11700 BRTN 97005 625 C1
11700 BRTN 97225 625 C1
11700 WasC 97005 625 C1
11700 WasC 97225 625 C1
SW Lynnly Wy
17100 SRWD 97140 684 F5
SW Lynnridge Av
11100 BRTN 97225 625 C1
11100 WasC 97225 625 C1
11500 WasC 97225 595 C7
SW Lynnvale Dr
11300 WasC 97225 595 C7
SW Lynnwood Ct
7200 WNVL 97070 715 G6
Lynwood Dr
1600 FTGV 97116 592 A5
SW Lynwood Ter
9700 WasC 97225 625 E1
SW Lyon Ct
20500 WasC 97007 624 C3
S Lyons Rd
18500 CmsC 97045 748 G1
19600 CmsC 97045 718 H7
Lytle Dr
- ClbC 97051 384 A6

M

M Cir
4200 WHGL 98671 570 D5
M Ct
5100 ClkC 98671 570 E5
M Dr
4200 WHGL 98671 570 D4
M Lp
4200 WHGL 98671 570 D5
M St
100 CBAC 97018 385 D4
2900 VCVR 98663 536 H3
3900 WHGL 98671 570 D5
N M St
2200 WHGL 98671 570 B4
SE Mabel Av
6600 CmsC 97267 657 D7
6600 CmsC 97267 687 D1
SW Mabel St
20600 WasC 97006 594 C5
SW Macadam Av
3300 PTLD 97239 626 F7
6600 PTLD 97219 626 F5
8900 MthC 97219 656 G1
8900 PTLD 97219 656 G1
SW Macadam Av SR-43
3300 PTLD 97239 626 F7
8500 PTLD 97219 626 F7
8900 MthC 97219 656 G1
8900 PTLD 97219 656 G1
SE Macanudo St
16900 DAMA 97009 688 E1
MacArthur Blvd
5300 VCVR 98661 537 D6
6200 VCVR 98664 537 D6
MacArthur St
100 STHN 97051 385 A7
200 ClbC 97051 385 A7
SW MacBeth Dr
- KNGC 97224 685 A1
SW Maccorey Ct
12300 BRTN 97008 625 B6
SE Macduffee Ct
14300 PTLD 97233 628 C1
SE Macinnes Rd
35200 MthC 97019 630 F1
NW Mackay Av
- PTLD 97231 565 D2
SE Mackie Ln
7800 CmsC 97206 657 F1
7800 CmsC 97222 657 F1
S Macksburg Rd
9600 CmsC 97013 776 E6
11800 CmsC 97013 777 B6
13100 CmsC 97013 807 D1
13700 CmsC 97038 807 G4
NW Macleay Blvd
10 PTLD 97205 596 C5
10 PTLD 97210 596 C5
N Macrum Av
6800 PTLD 97203 565 J4
9500 PTLD 97203 566 A2
SE Macs Pl
13000 CmsC 97222 657 C4
NW Mactavish Ln
14400 PTLD 97231 565 A1
NE Macy St
1300 MCMV 97128 770 J4
SE Macy St
100 MCMV 97128 770 J5
NE Maddox Ct
16400 ClkC 98606 478 D3
Madeira Dr
12900 CmsC 97222 657 C5
12900 MWKE 97222 657 C5
SW Madeira Ter
21000 SRWD 97140 684 F5
Madeline Dr
14900 CmsC 97045 717 G2
SE Madeline Pl
15400 CmsC 97267 657 E7
SW Madeline Pl
20300 WasC 97007 624 C3
SW Madeline St
18500 WasC 97007 624 E4
SE Madera Ct
5600 HBRO 97123 623 J1
NW Madera Pl
- PTLD 97210 596 A3
SE Madera St
7300 HBRO 97123 624 A1
SW Mad Hatter Ln
6100 BRTN 97008 625 C5
SE Madison Ct
15500 PTLD 97233 598 D7
SW Madison Ct
6000 PTLD 97221 595 J6
13000 BRTN 97008 655 A1
Madison Dr
1000 NWBG 97132 713 C4
1000 YmhC 97132 713 D4
SE Madison Dr
10800 PTLD 97216 597 J7
SW Madison Dr
- PTLD 97201 596 C6
- PTLD 97205 596 C6
Madison St
100 ORCY 97045 717 C1
300 LFYT 97127 771 G1
400 LFYT 97127 741 G7
800 ORCY 97045 687 D7
E Madison St
300 CLTN 97111 711 B7
N Madison St
- LFYT 97127 741 H6
- YmhC 97114 741 H6
- YmhC 97128 741 H6
SE Madison St
100 LFYT 97127 771 G1
500 PTLD 97214 596 J7
2800 MWKE 97222 657 A3
3200 PTLD 97214 597 A7
5500 PTLD 97215 597 D7
6600 HBRO 97123 594 A6
8200 PTLD 97216 597 F7
11500 PTLD 97216 598 A7
14000 PTLD 97233 598 C7
SW Madison St
10 PTLD 97204 596 F7
2300 PTLD 97201 596 C6
2300 PTLD 97205 596 C6
W Madison St
200 CLTN 97111 711 A7
SE Madison Wy
18000 GSHM 97233 598 G7
NW Madras Ct
17200 WasC 97006 594 G2
SW Madrid Ct
20800 WasC 97007 624 C5
SW Madrid Dr
6700 WasC 97007 624 B5
Madrona Ct
100 ORCY 97045 717 A3
100 STHN 97051 385 D6
200 ClbC 97051 385 D5
1400 FTGV 97116 592 A6
17900 GLDS 97027 687 F2
NW Madrona Ct
1600 MCMV 97128 770 F5
Madrona Dr
1100 ORCY 97045 717 A3
3500 NWBG 97132 713 F6
18700 CmsC 97045 716 J3
18700 ORCY 97045 716 J3
SE Madrona Dr
6500 MWKE 97222 657 E4
E Madrona Ln
2300 CmsC 97013 746 F4
SE Madrona Ln
1500 CmsC 97267 656 H6
SW Madrona Ln
15700 SRWD 97140 684 G7
Madrona St
- ClbC 97056 474 A4
4700 CmsC 97035 655 J7
4700 LKOW 97035 655 J7
NE Madrona St
700 PTLD 97211 566 H6
NW Madrona St
2600 ClkC 98665 506 D3
SW Madrona St
4700 CmsC 97035 655 J7
4700 LKOW 97035 655 J7
SW Madrone Ct
11000 TLTN 97062 685 C7
SE Madsen Ct
3700 HBRO 97123 623 E2
SE Maduros Ct
16800 DAMA 97009 688 E1
SE Maduros Wy
16200 DAMA 97009 688 E1
SE Mae Hazel Ln
9200 CmsC 97206 657 F1
9200 CmsC 97222 657 F1
NE Magda Ln
1000 PTLD 97230 598 E5
Maggie Pl
13000 ORCY 97045 717 D2
SW Magnolia Av
30500 WNVL 97070 745 D1
Magnolia Cir
58600 STHN 97051 414 J2
SW Magnolia Ct
600 MCMV 97128 770 E6
Magnolia Ln
4100 VCVR 98661 537 B4
SW Magnolia Pl
7900 BRTN 97008 625 B6
Magnolia St
700 ORCY 97045 717 D2
NW Magnolia St
800 CMAS 98607 569 C4

Portland Street Index

STREET Block City ZIP Map# Grid

Magnolia St
10 CNLS 97113 592 D6
E Magnolia St
8300 CmsC 97267 657 F6
Magnolia Wy
900 FTGV 97116 591 G3
Magone Ln
2700 WLIN 97068 687 A5
W Magpie Ln
14500 BRTN 97007 654 J3
Mahala Wy
- MCMV 97128 770 F3
W Mahama Pl
19400 WasC 97229 594 D1
W Mahama Wy
19100 WasC 97229 594 D2
E Mahany Ct
15700 CmsC 97267 657 B7
E Mahnke Dr
14300 ClkC 98606 478 C6
Mahogany Ct
11700 ORCY 97045 717 A4
Mahogany Dr
19200 CmsC 97045 717 A4
19200 ORCY 97045 717 A5
Mahon Ct
- MCMV 97128 770 G3
Mahonia Ct
3100 FTGV 97116 591 F3
SW Maidenfern Ln
18100 SRWD 97140 714 E1
SW Maidenhair Pl
27200 WasC 97140 714 D4
NE Maidstone St
6000 HBRO 97124 593 G4
SE Mailwell Dr
2200 MWKE 97222 656 J1
N Main Av
10 GSHM 97030 629 C2
10 GSHM 97080 629 C2
100 RDGF 98642 415 J6
1000 ClkC 98642 415 J6
2000 GSHM 97030 599 C7
NW Main Av
28400 ClkC 98642 415 J5
28400 RDGF 98642 415 J5
S Main Av
10 GSHM 97030 629 B3
10 GSHM 97080 629 B3
100 RDGF 98642 415 J7
SW Main Av
5200 BRTN 97005 625 B4
5800 BRTN 97008 625 B4
SE Main Ct
22500 GSHM 97030 599 C7
SE Main Dr
20500 GSHM 97030 599 A7
Main St
- ClkC 98663 536 G1
10 FRVW 97024 599 B4
400 ORCY 97045 717 B1
500 ORCY 97045 687 C7
500 VCVR 98660 536 G5
700 DAYT 97114 772 A4
1300 VCVR 98663 536 G5
1500 FTGV 97116 591 H5
Main St SR-43
500 ORCY 97045 687 C7
Main St NE
20000 MmC 97137 773 B6
20000 STPL 97137 773 B5
21700 AURA 97002 775 F3
Main St NE SR-219
20200 STPL 97137 773 B5
20400 MmC 97137 773 C5
E Main St
10 BGND 98604 448 C5
100 CLTN 97111 711 B7
100 HBRO 97123 593 E5
100 MOLA 97038 837 F2
300 YMHL 97148 711 A1
800 YmhC 97111 711 B7
1000 YmhC 97148 711 A1
2000 ClkC 98604 448 E5
2000 HBRO 97124 593 G5
E Main St SR-211
100 MOLA 97038 837 F2
E Main St SR-240
300 YMHL 97148 711 A1
1000 YmhC 97148 711 A1
N Main St
100 BNKS 97106 531 J5
100 BRLO 97013 745 J7
100 BRLO 97013 775 J1
100 NWBG 97132 713 C6
100 WasC 97106 531 J5
1100 YmhC 97132 713 C6
N Main St SR-47
100 BNKS 97106 531 J5
100 WasC 97106 531 J5
N Main St SR-240
100 NWBG 97132 713 B7
NE Main St
100 ECDA 97023 750 B3
NW Main St
- MthC 97231 534 H2
10300 NPNS 97133 563 B1
11100 WasC 97133 563 B1
24100 WasC 97140 714 E1
S Main St
- BRLO 97013 775 J1
100 BNKS 97106 531 J6
100 NWBG 97132 713 C7
400 NWBG 97132 743 B1
500 WasC 97106 531 J6
600 WasC 97116 531 J6
S Main St SR-47
100 BNKS 97106 531 J6
500 WasC 97106 531 J6
600 WasC 97116 531 J6
SE Main St
10 PTLD 97214 596 H7
100 ECDA 97023 750 B4
2700 PTLD 97214 597 A7
6000 PTLD 97215 597 D7
8400 PTLD 97216 597 G7
8700 MWKE 97222 626 J7
9000 MWKE 97222 656 J2
11500 PTLD 97216 598 A7
12200 PTLD 97233 598 A7
17400 GSHM 97233 598 G7
21200 GSHM 97030 599 A7
SW Main St
10 PTLD 97204 596 F6
1800 PTLD 97205 596 D6
4500 BRTN 97005 625 B3
5700 PTLD 97221 595 J6
8300 WNVL 97070 745 E1
12000 TGRD 97223 655 E4
22300 SRWD 97140 684 G7
23200 SRWD 97140 714 G1
W Main St
10 BGND 98604 448 A5
100 CLTN 97111 711 A7
100 HBRO 97123 593 A4
100 HBRO 97124 593 A4
100 MOLA 97038 837 D1
800 CmsC 97038 837 D1
1500 BGND 98604 447 J5
2900 ClkC 98604 447 H5
W Main St SR-47
100 CLTN 97111 711 A7
W Main St SR-211
100 MOLA 97038 837 D1
800 CmsC 97038 837 D1
W Main St SR-502
1000 BGND 98604 448 A5
1500 BGND 98604 447 J5
2900 ClkC 98604 447 H5
Main Park Rd
- CmsC 97011 723 J2
24800 CmsC 97067 723 J2
SE Mair St
4500 HBRO 97123 593 H6
NE Maitland Rd
10300 ClkC 98686 507 D3
NE Majdali Dr
10 BGND 98604 447 H5
Majestic Ct
13800 LKOW 97035 656 B5
SE Majestic Ln
12600 CmsC 97236 658 A5
SW Majestic Ln
11500 KNGC 97224 655 D2
NW Majestic Sequoia Wy
12500 WasC 97229 595 B3
NE Major Ln
16100 YmhC 97148 711 D2
NE Major St
11700 VCVR 98684 537 J6
SW Major Oak Dr
14500 SRWD 97140 714 H1
SW Makah Ct
21200 TLTN 97062 685 F6
SW Makah St
21200 TLTN 97062 685 G6
NW Maki Rd
39300 ClkC 98674 386 C2
S Makin Ln
11600 CmsC 97013 746 J5
11600 CmsC 97013 747 A5
SW Malcolm Ct
3100 WasC 97225 625 E2
SE Malcolm St
2700 MWKE 97222 657 A1
SW Malcolm Glen St
9400 WasC 97225 625 E2
SE Malden Ct
7700 PTLD 97206 627 F6
8600 PTLD 97266 627 F6
11700 PTLD 97266 628 A6
SE Malden Dr
4500 PTLD 97206 627 C6
SE Malden St
1300 PTLD 97202 626 H6
3600 PTLD 97202 627 B6
5200 PTLD 97206 627 D6
8000 PTLD 97266 627 F6
NW Malhuer Av
4200 WasC 97229 594 D1
4300 WasC 97229 564 D7
NW Malia Ln
- HBRO 97124 593 B1
10900 WasC 97229 595 D2
Mall Dr N
- PTLD 97236 627 J7
- PTLD 97236 628 A7
- PTLD 97266 628 A7
Mall Dr S
- PTLD 97236 628 A7
- PTLD 97266 628 A7
SE Mall St
900 PTLD 97202 626 H3
3700 PTLD 97202 627 B3
6700 PTLD 97206 627 E3
11700 PTLD 97266 628 A3
12500 PTLD 97236 628 B3
SE Mallard Ct
15800 CmsC 97267 656 H7
SW Mallard Ct
7300 WasC 97223 625 G7
SW Mallard Dr
- BRTN 97007 654 H4
SE Mallard Ln
17000 YmhC 97114 772 D7
SE Mallard Wy
- MWKE 97222 657 B3
NW Maller Ln
39300 WasC 97106 532 C3
NW Maller Rd
14400 WasC 97106 532 B4
NE Mallory Av
3500 PTLD 97212 596 G2
4000 PTLD 97211 596 G1
5000 PTLD 97211 566 G7
SW Malloy Wy
11800 CmsC 97140 715 B5
Malo Av NE
4100 MmC 97137 773 B6
4100 STPL 97137 773 B6
Maloney Dr
- MCMV 97128 770 J2
NE Maloney Dr
3000 MCMV 97128 770 J2
SE Maloney Pl
9400 CmsC 97236 657 F1
Maloney St
1000 MCMV 97128 770 J2
SE Maloy Ln
13600 CmsC 97222 656 H5
13600 CmsC 97267 656 H5
SW Malsam Ct
5100 TLTN 97062 685 J4
NE Maltby St
2300 PTLD 97212 597 B2
E Manape Dr
68600 CmsC 97067 724 C7
Manchester Ct
1800 WLIN 97068 716 J1
1800 WLIN 97068 717 A1
Manchester Dr
15500 LKOW 97035 655 J6
SE Manchester Pl
500 PTLD 97202 656 H1
SW Manchester Pl
9300 BRTN 97007 654 E2
NW Manchester Wy
20000 HBRO 97124 594 D3
SW Mandan Ct
21800 TLTN 97062 685 E6
SW Mandan Dr
8500 TLTN 97062 685 F6
22300 WasC 97062 685 F7
SW Mandel Ln
17500 SRWD 97140 684 E7
Mandi Ln
17300 LKOW 97035 685 J1
NW Mandi St
100 HBRO 97124 593 A2
SW Mandy Ct
18500 WasC 97007 624 B6
SE Manewal St
- CmsC 97267 687 B4
SE Manfield Ct
8800 CmsC 97015 687 F2
SE Mangan Dr
9100 CmsC 97015 687 G2
SW Manhasset Dr
10300 TLTN 97062 685 D4
NW Manhattan Av
- MthC 97229 595 G4
- PTLD 97229 595 G4
Manitoba Av
10 YCLT 98675 419 F1
NE Manley Rd
24900 ClkC 98604 447 G1
SE Manley St
17100 PTLD 97236 628 F5
NW Mann Av
20300 MthC 97231 504 E5
SW Mannsland Pl
- WasC 97123 683 D1
SE Manor Av
1400 VCVR 98683 568 A1
Manor Dr
1300 GLDS 97027 687 C4
NE Manor Dr
10200 ClkC 98686 507 D3
NW Manor Dr
6300 PTLD 97210 595 H5
53000 ClbC 97056 444 E6
53000 SPSE 97056 444 E6
S Manor Dr
16700 CmsC 97045 688 B6
Manor Ln
1500 VCVR 98661 536 J4
SW Manor Wy
7100 WasC 97007 624 C5
NW Manresa Ct
15100 WasC 97229 564 J7
NW Mansfield St
- PTLD 97231 565 E4
SW Mansfield St
23000 SRWD 97140 684 H7
23100 SRWD 97140 714 H1
Manzanita Ct
4000 VCVR 98661 537 B5
S Manzanita Ct
300 CNBY 97013 746 D6
SW Manzanita Ct
11900 TGRD 97223 655 C3
Manzanita St
- ClbC 97056 474 A4
N Manzanita St
1000 CNBY 97013 746 D5
SW Manzanita St
100 MCMV 97128 770 E5
11500 TGRD 97223 655 C2
Manzanita Wy
700 VCVR 98661 537 B5
Maple
- CmsC 97015 657 H7
Maple Av
50500 ClbC 97056 474 E4
NE Maple Av
2000 GSHM 97030 629 D1
2500 GSHM 97030 599 D7
NW Maple Av
- MthC 97210 595 H4
- MthC 97229 595 H4
- PTLD 97229 595 H4
S Maple Av
- YCLT 98675 419 G1
SE Maple Av
1400 PTLD 97214 596 H7
7400 VCVR 98664 537 E7
SW Maple Av
4600 BRTN 97005 625 D3
Maple Blvd
100 WDVL 97060 599 D4
Maple Cir
16500 LKOW 97034 686 B1
SE Maple Cir
300 GSHM 97080 629 D3
Maple Ct
6700 WLIN 97068 687 A5
N Maple Ct
2500 CmsC 97013 746 D3
2500 CNBY 97013 746 D3
NE Maple Ct
2300 GSHM 97030 599 D7
SE Maple Ct
1600 HBRO 97123 593 E6
12300 MWKE 97222 657 D4
SW Maple Ct
8700 TGRD 97223 655 F2
Maple Dr
1900 NWBG 97132 713 D7
SW Maple Dr
7500 WasC 97225 625 G3
7800 BRTN 97225 625 F3
N Maple Ln
900 CNBY 97013 746 D5
NW Maple Ln
- CMAS 98607 569 C5
SE Maple Ln
13200 CmsC 97222 657 A5
13700 CmsC 97267 657 A5
SW Maple Ln
600 HBRO 97123 593 B6
2400 BRTN 97225 625 G1
2500 WasC 97225 625 H1
5000 MthC 97221 626 A1
SE Maple Lp
1400 GSHM 97080 629 D4
Maple Pl
1500 FTGV 97116 592 B5
SE Maple Pl
1100 GSHM 97080 629 D4
SW Maple Rd
400 ECDA 97023 750 A3
Maple Rdg
- VCVR 98664 537 H6
Maple St
- HBRO 97006 594 D5
- WasC 97006 594 D5
10 RDGF 98642 415 J6
700 DAYT 97114 772 B4
1100 LKOW 97034 656 E7
1500 WLIN 97068 687 B7
2200 FTGV 97116 592 B4
4100 VCVR 98660 536 F2
34900 ClbC 97051 414 J2
34900 STHN 97051 414 J2
E Maple St
68000 CmsC 97067 724 B6
N Maple St
100 BRLO 97013 745 J7
100 BRLO 97013 775 J1
100 CmsC 97013 745 J7
1000 CNBY 97013 746 D3
2300 CmsC 97013 746 D3
NW Maple St
3400 CMAS 98607 569 D2
S Maple St
500 CNBY 97013 746 D7
1300 CNBY 97013 776 D1
SE Maple St
400 DNDE 97115 742 H3
1200 YmhC 97115 742 H4
2800 CmsC 97267 656 G6
2800 CmsC 97267 657 A6
5700 CmsC 97222 657 C1
5700 MWKE 97222 657 C1
6000 HBRO 97123 593 J6
6400 HBRO 97123 594 A6
33500 SPSE 97056 474 F1
SW Maple St
400 HBRO 97123 593 B6
33300 SPSE 97056 474 E1
Maple Ter
2000 WLIN 97068 687 A5
SW Maplecrest Ct
500 PTLD 97219 656 D1
9900 BRTN 97008 625 E5
SW Maplecrest Dr
400 PTLD 97219 656 D1
NW Maplecrest Lp
12900 BNKS 97106 531 H5
NW Maplecrest Rd
22700 ClkC 98642 446 G3
NW Maplecrest Wy
12500 BNKS 97106 531 J5
SE Maple Finch Dr
14300 HPYV 97236 658 C2
NW Maple Hill Ln
11900 WasC 97229 595 C3
SE Maple Hill Ln
16200 CmsC 97236 658 F1
16200 HPYV 97236 658 F1
SE Maplehurst St
6700 CmsC 97222 657 E3
11100 MWKE 97222 657 D3
S Maplelane Rd
14200 CmsC 97045 717 H3
14200 ORCY 97045 717 F4
15800 CmsC 97045 718 A2
Mapleleaf Ct
1900 LKOW 97034 686 C1
Maple Leaf Ct NE
12800 MmC 97002 775 B7
SE Mapleleaf Ct
12200 CmsC 97015 658 A7
SW Mapleleaf Ct
7100 TGRD 97223 655 G2
Mapleleaf Rd
1600 LKOW 97034 686 C1
SW Mapleleaf St
- TGRD 97223 655 E2
7000 WasC 97223 655 F2
S Maple Ln Ct
14200 CmsC 97045 717 F4
14200 ORCY 97045 717 F4
Maple Ln Ests
- CmsC 97045 717 H3
Maple Ln Rd
- CmsC 97045 717 F4
- ORCY 97045 717 F4
SW Mapleoak Ln
3000 WasC 97006 624 E1
SW Mapleridge Dr
8200 WasC 97225 595 F6
NW Maple Ridge Rd
39300 ClkC 98674 386 F1
SW Maplethorpe Ln
17100 WasC 97140 714 F2
Mapleton Dr
3600 WLIN 97068 686 J4
3600 WLIN 97068 687 A4
SW Mapleview Ln
13500 WasC 97224 655 A7
Maplewood Ct
12500 MWKE 97222 657 B4
Maplewood Dr
600 STHN 97051 415 A1
NE Maplewood Dr
2700 ClkC 98665 507 A5
SW Maplewood Dr
9200 TGRD 97223 655 E4
SW Maplewood Rd
4500 PTLD 97219 626 A5
4900 PTLD 97219 625 J6
SW Mara Ct
7900 TGRD 97224 655 G6
S Maranna Ct
22500 CmsC 97023 750 B5
Marathon Av
- MthC 97231 535 A5
SE Marcella Ct
38000 SNDY 97055 690 J2
SE Marci Wy
14500 CmsC 97015 658 B7
NW Marcia Av
- PTLD 97231 565 F4
NW Marcia Ct
- PTLD 97231 565 F4
SE Marcia Ct
19400 CmsC 97267 687 B4
SW Marcia Dr
13500 TGRD 97223 655 A4
NW Marcia St
2500 PTLD 97210 596 C4
S Marci-June Wy
- ORCY 97045 717 A4
SW Marcile Ln
16100 WasC 97007 624 G7
16400 BRTN 97007 624 G7
NW Marcola Ct
16900 WasC 97006 594 G2
SW Marconi Av
100 PTLD 97205 596 C5
NW Marcotte Rd
3500 MthC 97229 595 C1
SE Marcus St
8700 CmsC 97236 657 F2
SE Marcy St
38000 CmsC 97055 690 J2
38000 SNDY 97055 690 J2
Mardee Av
17400 CmsC 97035 685 J2
17400 LKOW 97035 685 J2
SW Maree Ct
19200 CmsC 97035 685 J3
19200 RVGR 97035 685 J3
E Margaret Ln
- CmsC 97011 724 A2
SE Margaret Ln
1400 HBRO 97123 593 D7
NE Margaret Rd
14700 ClkC 98606 479 C5
SE Margaret St
31700 MthC 97080 630 C7
NE Margeaux Pl
1200 HBRO 97124 593 C3
Margery St
2300 WLIN 97068 686 F7
2300 WLIN 97068 716 G1
SE Margie Wy
8600 HPYV 97236 628 D7
8700 HPYV 97236 658 B1
NW Marguerite Ln
14700 WasC 97229 564 J6
Marguerite Wy
1100 NWBG 97132 713 C6
Maria Ct
2600 WLIN 97068 686 H2
SW Maria Ct
18500 WasC 97007 624 E5
Maria Ln
52500 SPSE 97056 444 D7
SW Mariah St
6700 WasC 97225 595 H6
SE Marian St
14800 CmsC 97267 656 J6
SW Marianne Ln
18400 WasC 97006 624 G1
SW Maricara St
3000 PTLD 97219 656 B1
SW Maricopa Dr
8500 TLTN 97062 685 E7
Marie Av
800 NWBG 97132 713 E6
Marie Ct
700 NWBG 97132 713 E7
SW Marie Ct
12700 TGRD 97223 655 B4
Marie Dr
- YmhC 97128 770 E6
SE Marie St
17600 PTLD 97236 628 G3
17700 GSHM 97030 628 G3
17700 GSHM 97236 628 G3
37400 CmsC 97055 660 H5
Marigold Ct
20000 WLIN 97068 686 J4
SE Marigold Ct
2500 HBRO 97123 623 E1
SE Marigold St
8200 CmsC 97267 657 F6
SW Marigold St
4100 PTLD 97219 626 A7
4900 PTLD 97219 625 J7
SE Marilyn Ct
10700 CmsC 97236 657 J3
SW Marilyn Ct
9600 TGRD 97224 655 E6
SW Marilyn St
10800 TLTN 97062 685 C7
S Marilyns Av
22100 CmsC 97004 747 H3
SW Marimar St
20400 WasC 97007 624 C4
NE Marina Ct
6300 HBRO 97124 593 J4
6300 HBRO 97124 594 A4
6400 WasC 97124 594 A4
NE Marina St
- HBRO 97124 594 A4
- WasC 97124 594 A4
NW Marina Wy
12200 MthC 97231 535 C6
12200 PTLD 97231 535 C6
S Marina Wy
10 WHGL 98671 569 H5
N Marine Dr
- PTLD 97203 536 B7
- PTLD 97203 566 C1
10 PTLD 97211 566 G2
10 PTLD 97217 566 E1
1600 PTLD 97217 536 D7
6000 PTLD 97203 535 H4
NE Marine Dr
10 PTLD 97211 566 G2
10 PTLD 97217 566 G2
2200 PTLD 97211 567 A2
3500 PTLD 97218 567 C2
5000 PTLD 97220 567 H4
10800 PTLD 97220 568 D7
11200 PTLD 97230 568 B7
15800 GSHM 97230 598 F1
15800 PTLD 97230 598 F1
18500 FRVW 97230 598 F1
18500 PTLD 97230 598 F1
20400 FRVW 97024 599 C1
22300 TDLE 97060 599 C2
NW Marine Dr
1900 TDLE 97060 599 D2
3500 FRVW 97024 599 C2
N Marine Wy
- PTLD 97217 566 F2
SE Marine Park Wy
- VCVR 98661 537 B6
SE Mariner Wy
6200 HBRO 97123 623 J1
SW Mariners Dr
8100 WNVL 97070 745 F2
NE Mariner's Lp
500 PTLD 97211 566 H2
SE Marinette Av
900 HBRO 97123 593 D6
NW Maring Dr
9600 WasC 97229 595 E4
SW Mario Ct
20100 WasC 97007 624 C3
Marion St NE
- MmC 97002 744 F6
SE Marion St
10 PTLD 97202 626 H7
SW Marion St
12100 TGRD 97223 655 B5
SE Mariposa Ct
2500 HBRO 97123 623 E1
SE Marisa Ct
12900 CmsC 97236 658 B5
SW Marissa Dr
8500 WasC 97223 625 F6
SE Maritime Av
500 VCVR 98661 536 J7
NW Marjo Ln
1400 YmhC 97128 770 A2
Marjorie Av
17200 LKOW 97034 686 D1
Marjorie Ln
14200 CmsC 97045 717 F4
14200 ORCY 97045 717 F4
SW Marjorie Ln
9900 BRTN 97008 625 D6
9900 WasC 97008 625 E6
Mark Ln
2400 WLIN 97068 686 J4
2400 WLIN 97068 687 A4
S Mark Rd
7000 CmsC 97002 775 J6
7000 CmsC 97013 775 J6
7000 CmsC 97013 776 A6
SE Mark Rd
21500 DAMA 97009 659 A7
SE Market Ct
14300 PTLD 97233 598 D7
Market Dr
- FRVW 97024 599 A4
NE Market Dr
700 FRVW 97024 599 B5
700 FRVW 97030 599 B5
700 GSHM 97030 599 B5
SE Market Dr
10200 PTLD 97216 597 H7
11600 CmsC 97015 657 J5
Market St
100 LFYT 97127 771 G1
300 LFYT 97127 741 G7
E Market St
200 CLTN 97111 711 A7
NE Market St
100 BNKS 97106 531 J5
SE Market St
2000 PTLD 97214 596 J7
3000 PTLD 97214 597 A7
4900 PTLD 97215 597 C7
8400 PTLD 97216 597 G7
11500 PTLD 97216 598 A7
14000 PTLD 97233 598 C7
17900 GSHM 97233 598 G7
SW Market St
1400 PTLD 97201 596 D6
SW Market St US-26
600 PTLD 97201 596 E6
SW Market St Dr
1900 PTLD 97201 596 D6
Markham Ct
17800 ORCY 97045 717 E2
SW Markhaven St
26400 WasC 97140 714 B4
SE Mark Kelly Ct
4300 CmsC 97267 657 B7
4300 CmsC 97267 687 B1
Markle Av
1500 VCVR 98660 536 F4
NW Markle St
- PTLD 97231 565 E4
S Marklund Dr
- CmsC 97045 718 D2
SW Marko Ln
18600 WasC 97007 624 E6
Markris Wy
100 NWBG 97132 713 B6
100 YmhC 97132 713 C6
SE Marla Pl
1200 HBRO 97123 593 H6
NW Marlborough Av
400 PTLD 97210 596 C5
Marlin Av
19300 CmsC 97035 685 J3
19300 RVGR 97035 685 J3
Marlin Ct
19200 CmsC 97035 685 J3
19200 RVGR 97035 685 J3
SW Marlin Ct
6900 WasC 97007 624 D5
SW Marlin Dr
19700 WasC 97007 624 D5
SW Marlow Av
1400 WasC 97225 595 D7
Marlynn Ter
- ORCY 97045 717 E4
Marlys Ct
1400 FTGV 97116 592 A6
E Marmot Rd
42200 CmsC 97055 691 D1
47300 CmsC 97055 692 B2
57400 CmsC 97055 693 A5
SE Marna Rd
16200 CmsC 97009 688 H2
SW Marne Ct
18700 WasC 97007 624 E6
NE Marok Rd
1700 MthC 97060 600 A4
Marquam Br
- PTLD 596 F7
- PTLD 626 F1
Marquam Br I-5
- PTLD 596 F7
- PTLD 626 F1
SW Marquam St
1200 PTLD 97201 626 D1
SW Marquam Hill Rd
3300 PTLD 97239 626 D2
Marquette Ct
6700 WLIN 97068 687 A5
Marquette Dr
6800 WLIN 97068 687 A5
Marquis Ct
3700 LKOW 97034 686 A3
Marracci Rd
55800 ClbC 97053 414 F7
55800 ClbC 97053 444 F1
55800 ClbC 97056 444 F1
NW Marsden Pl
2500 PTLD 97229 595 E2
SW Marseilles Dr
8600 WasC 97007 624 E7
NE Marsh Ln
800 MCMV 97128 771 A4
800 YmhC 97128 771 A4
NW Marsh Rd
4500 WasC 97116 562 C6
SE Marsha Ct
14000 CmsC 97009 660 F7
SE Marsha Ln
23700 DAMA 97009 659 D1
NW Marshall Ct
12800 WasC 97229 595 B4
NW Marshall Dr
100 HBRO 97124 593 A5
S Marshall Rd
28600 CmsC 97042 807 H4
Marshall St
100 STHN 97051 415 B1
600 ORCY 97045 717 C3
8600 YmhC 97128 771 D1
NW Marshall St
1200 PTLD 97209 596 D4
2000 PTLD 97210 596 D4
13200 WasC 97229 595 A4
SW Marshall St
22300 SRWD 97140 684 F7
SW Marsh Hawk Meadow Ln
31100 CmsC 97070 744 H2
Marson Ct
200 MOLA 97038 837 E1
SW Marsuda Wy
100 WasC 97006 594 C5
Marten St NE
- AURA 97002 775 F3
- MmC 97002 775 F3
SE Martenson Ct
15900 CmsC 97267 657 B7
SW Martha St
1500 PTLD 97239 626 D4
4500 PTLD 97221 626 A3
5000 PTLD 97221 625 J3
9200 TGRD 97224 685 E1
SW Martha Ter
5300 PTLD 97239 626 B4
Martin Ct
500 VCVR 98661 536 G5
20500 WLIN 97068 686 G5
SE Martin Ct
5300 PTLD 97206 627 C5
SW Martin Ct
22700 SRWD 97140 684 H7
Martin Ln NE
10900 MmC 97002 744 G6
SE Martin Ln
400 YmhC 97128 771 A7
NW Martin Rd
- WasC 97113 562 C7
- WasC 97116 562 C7
900 FTGV 97116 592 B4
2500 WasC 97113 592 C3
2500 WasC 97116 592 C3
SE Martin Rd
19300 CmsC 97055 690 H5
SW Martin St
19500 WasC 97007 624 D2
Martin Wy
600 VCVR 98661 537 A5
SW Martinazzi Av
18700 TLTN 97062 685 E6
SW Martinazzi Ct
8600 TLTN 97062 685 E6
SW Martine Ct
200 TDLE 97060 599 G4
SW Martingale Ct
13700 BRTN 97008 624 H1
13700 BRTN 97008 625 A7
N Martin Luther King Jr Blvd
9200 PTLD 97211 566 F2
9200 PTLD 97217 566 F2
N Martin L King Jr Blvd SR-99E
9200 PTLD 97211 566 F2
9200 PTLD 97217 566 F2
NE Martin Luther King Jr Blvd
10 PTLD 97214 596 G5
10 PTLD 97232 596 G5
1900 PTLD 97212 596 G3
4000 PTLD 97211 596 G1
4900 PTLD 97211 566 G7
9000 PTLD 97217 566 G3
NE ML King Jr Blvd SR-99E
10 PTLD 97214 596 G5
10 PTLD 97232 596 G5
1900 PTLD 97212 596 G3
4000 PTLD 97211 596 G1
4900 PTLD 97211 566 G7
9000 PTLD 97217 566 G3
SE Martin Luther King Jr Blvd
10 PTLD 97214 596 G6
10 PTLD 97232 596 G5
2100 PTLD 97214 626 G1
SE ML King Jr Blvd SR-99E
10 PTLD 97214 596 G6
10 PTLD 97232 596 G5
2100 PTLD 97214 626 G1
SE Martins Ct
12200 PTLD 97236 628 A5
12200 PTLD 97266 628 A5
SW Martins Ln
2900 PTLD 97221 626 B2
- PTLD 97239 626 B2
SE Martins St
- PTLD 97266 627 H5
1200 PTLD 97202 626 H5
3800 PTLD 97202 627 B5
6900 PTLD 97206 627 E5
12000 PTLD 97266 628 A5

STREET
Block City ZIP Map# Grid

SE Martins St
13800 PTLD 97236 628 C5
SW Marty Ln
17000 BRTN 97006 594 F7
17000 WasC 97006 594 F7
Marvin Ct
1200 FTGV 97116 592 A6
NW Marvin Ln
9400 PTLD 97229 595 E4
9400 WasC 97229 595 E4
NE Marx Dr
8200 PTLD 97220 567 G6
NE Marx Pl
11200 PTLD 97220 567 J7
11200 PTLD 97220 568 A7
NE Marx St
10100 PTLD 97220 567 J7
10900 PTLD 97220 597 J1
11200 PTLD 97220 598 B1
12100 PTLD 97230 598 A1
SE Mary Ct
3300 MWKE 97222 627 A7
Mary Dr
600 MOLA 97038 807 D7
SW Mary Pl
10700 TGRD 97223 655 C2
NE Maryann Ct
600 HBRO 97124 593 A1
SE Mary Ann Ln
15900 CmsC 97267 687 H2
15900 JNCY 97267 687 H2
SW Mary Failing Ct
1200 MthC 97219 656 F3
SW Mary Failing Dr
1400 MthC 97219 656 G3
SE Mary Jean Ct
9800 PTLD 97266 627 H6
N Maryland Av
4100 PTLD 97217 596 E1
8200 PTLD 97217 566 F4
NW Maryland Ln
- CMAS 98607 569 A3
NW Maryland St
2200 CMAS 98607 569 A3
Marylbrook Dr
17600 LKOW 97034 686 G2
Marylcreek Dr
17700 LKOW 97034 686 H2
NW Marylee Ct
11800 WasC 97229 595 C3
Marylhaven Pl
2400 LKOW 97034 686 G2
Marylhurst Cir
600 WLIN 97068 686 G3
Marylhurst Ct
18700 WLIN 97068 686 H3
NW Marylhurst Ct
17600 WasC 97229 564 F7
Marylhurst Dr
400 WLIN 97068 686 G3
NW Marylhurst Dr
17800 WasC 97229 564 G7
Marylshire Ln
2400 LKOW 97034 686 G2
Marylview Ct
2400 LKOW 97034 686 G2
Marylwood Ct
2000 WLIN 97068 686 G3
Marysville Ln
12800 ORCY 97045 717 C4
SE Masa Ln
11600 CmsC 97236 658 A4
11600 HPYV 97236 658 A4
Masaryk St
10 LKOW 97035 656 A3
S Maslow Rd
27200 CmsC 97013 776 J7
NE Mason Ct
4900 PTLD 97218 597 C1
16800 PTLD 97230 598 F1
SE Mason Ct
9300 MWKE 97222 657 C1
NE Mason Dr
8500 VCVR 98662 537 F2
SE Mason Ln
4200 MWKE 97222 657 C1
SW Mason Ln
16000 BRTN 97006 594 H6
N Mason St
10 PTLD 97211 596 G1
10 PTLD 97212 596 G1
1400 PTLD 97217 596 E1
1600 PTLD 97227 596 E1
NE Mason St
10 PTLD 97211 596 H1
10 PTLD 97217 596 G1
10 PTLD 97227 596 G1
1400 PTLD 97212 596 H1
2500 PTLD 97211 597 A1
2500 PTLD 97212 597 A1
4200 PTLD 97213 597 C1
4900 PTLD 97218 597 C1
9600 MWDP 97220 597 H2
11000 PTLD 97220 597 J2
14800 PTLD 97230 598 E2
21800 FRVW 97024 599 B2
NE Mason Creek Rd
8200 ClkC 98604 417 G3
8200 ClkC 98629 417 G3
Mason Heights Dr
- CmsC 97045 687 H4
SE Mason Hill Dr
4200 MWKE 97222 657 B1
NW Mason Hill Rd
12000 WasC 97124 533 E6
12000 WasC 97133 533 E6
Masonic Wy
2100 FTGV 97116 592 B4
N Massachusetts Av
3700 PTLD 97227 596 E2
4000 PTLD 97217 596 E2
SW Massey Ter
21400 SRWD 97140 684 G6
Masters Dr
4700 NWBG 97132 713 G7
SW Masters Lp
4500 WasC 97007 624 C3
SW Matador Ln
16800 KNGC 97224 685 A1
16800 WasC 97224 685 A1
Matheny Dr
2300 WLIN 97068 686 G7
SW Matheny Dr
7700 BRTN 97008 625 B6

N Mather Pl
2600 PTLD 97217 566 D5
SE Mather Rd
9200 CmsC 97015 657 G7
11800 CmsC 97015 658 A5
Mathias Ct
800 MOLA 97038 837 F3
Mathias Rd
100 CmsC 97038 837 F2
100 MOLA 97038 837 F2
S Mathias Rd
32300 CmsC 97038 837 F3
32300 MOLA 97038 837 F3
NE Mathison Pl
3500 PTLD 97212 597 B3
SE Matilda Dr
13800 CmsC 97222 657 E6
13800 CmsC 97267 657 E6
NE Matney Rd
3600 ClkC 98607 539 G3
Matney St
10 FRVW 97024 599 B4
NW Matomandy Ct
14800 WasC 97229 594 J2
Matterhorn Ct
2200 WLIN 97068 686 G7
NE Mattey Ln
10200 YmhC 97128 741 E7
10200 YmhC 97128 771 E1
Matthew Ct
16100 LKOW 97034 656 E7
S Matthew Ct
18100 CmsC 97045 718 C2
SW Matthew Ct
18500 WasC 97007 624 B6
SW Matthew Park St
8100 TGRD 97224 655 F6
Matthews Rd
23700 CmsC 97068 716 C2
Matthieu Ln NE
10000 MrnC 97002 774 F2
Matthieu St NE
20500 DNLD 97020 774 G5
20500 MrnC 97002 774 G5
20500 MrnC 97032 774 G5
S Mattoon Rd
18500 CmsC 97023 719 C5
18500 CmsC 97045 719 B4
20300 CmsC 97023 749 C1
SE Mattson Ln
26400 CmsC 97022 720 F4
NE Mattson Rd
19200 ClkC 98606 478 H1
SW Matzen Dr
10800 WNVL 97070 715 C7
10900 WNVL 97070 745 C1
Matzen St
500 STHN 97051 415 A1
NW Maudsley Ct
17900 BRTN 97006 594 F4
SW Maui Ct
8900 WasC 97223 655 E1
NE Maureen St
1200 HBRO 97124 593 D1
SW Maus St
- MthC 97219 656 G2
- PTLD 97219 656 F2
NW Mauzey Rd
21300 HBRO 97124 564 B6
21300 WasC 97124 564 B6
SW Maverick Ct
14000 BRTN 97008 624 J7
SW Maverick Pl
8400 BRTN 97008 624 J7
SW Maverick Ter
8200 BRTN 97008 624 J7
NW Mawcrest Dr
700 GSHM 97030 628 J2
SW Mawrcrest Av
10 GSHM 97030 628 J3
10 GSHM 97080 628 J3
SW Mawrcrest Ct
1900 GSHM 97080 628 J5
SW Mawrcrest Dr
300 GSHM 97080 628 J3
NW Mawrcrest Pl
500 GSHM 97030 628 J2
SW Mawrcrest Pl
700 GSHM 97080 628 J4
SW Maxine Ln
8100 WNVL 97070 715 F6
SE Maxon Rd
11200 VCVR 98664 567 J1
Maxwell Ct
11800 ORCY 97045 717 A4
SE Maxwell St
4700 HBRO 97123 593 H7
SW May Ct
14600 SRWD 97140 684 H7
S May Rd
20000 CmsC 97045 716 H7
20100 CmsC 97045 746 H1
May St
100 STHN 97051 415 A1
300 MOLA 97038 837 E2
300 ORCY 97045 717 D3
NE May St
3000 ClkC 98661 537 A2
3000 VCVR 98663 537 A2
SE May St
6400 CmsC 97222 657 D1
SE Maya Ct
4100 HBRO 97123 593 H6
SE Mayberry Ln
8500 CmsC 97009 660 H1
SW Mayberry Pl
8900 WasC 97007 624 E7
NW Maybrook Av
- PTLD 97231 565 E4
NW Maybrook Ct
- PTLD 97231 565 E4
NW Maybrook Pl
- PTLD 97231 565 E3
NW Mayer Ct
10400 PTLD 97229 595 D3
SW Mayfair Ct
5200 BRTN 97005 624 J2
Mayfair Dr
100 STHN 97051 385 A7
SW Mayfield Av
2000 BRTN 97225 595 C7
2000 WasC 97225 595 C7
2100 WasC 97225 625 C1
2500 WasC 97005 625 C1

SW Mayfield Pl
5600 WasC 97225 625 G4
NW Mayfield Rd
1200 PTLD 97229 595 E4
Mayfly Ct
19300 CmsC 97045 717 B5
19300 ORCY 97045 717 B5
SW Mayjohn Ct
18700 WasC 97007 624 E5
SW Maylinn Pl
11200 BRTN 97008 625 C6
SW Mayo St
6600 WasC 97223 625 H7
Mayors Ln
2300 LKOW 97034 686 C2
SW Maypark Ct
11200 WasC 97225 625 C1
SW Mayview Wy
12800 WasC 97223 654 H4
NE Mayward Ln
- MCMV 97128 771 D6
- YmhC 97128 771 D6
SW Mayway Dr
7700 WasC 97225 595 G6
SW Mayway St
- WasC 97225 595 H6
Maywood Ct
11200 ORCY 97045 716 J4
Maywood Dr
2700 FTGV 97116 592 A4
NW Maywood Dr
10 PTLD 97205 596 C5
10 PTLD 97210 596 C5
NE Maywood Pl
3500 MWDP 97220 597 H2
Maywood St
19000 ORCY 97045 716 J4
19200 CmsC 97045 716 J4
SW Mazama Pl
15300 TGRD 97224 655 D7
Mazour Dr
32900 ClbC 97053 444 E2
32900 ClbC 97056 444 E2
SE McAllister Ct
15500 CmsC 97267 656 J7
SW McAlpin Pl
12100 WasC 97007 654 C3
SW McBride Ct
11200 BRTN 97005 625 C2
NE McBride Ln
5800 HBRO 97124 593 J5
5800 WasC 97124 593 J5
NE McBride Rd
29900 ClkC 98604 418 C4
McBride St
10 STHN 97051 415 A1
SE McBride St
7600 CmsC 97222 657 E4
8100 CmsC 97236 657 E4
SE McBrod Av
8800 MWKE 97202 626 J7
8800 MWKE 97222 626 J7
8800 PTLD 97202 626 J7
8800 PTLD 97222 626 J7
9000 MWKE 97222 656 J1
S McBurney Rd
21600 CmsC 97004 747 J3
21600 CmsC 97045 747 J3
SE McCabe Ct
16400 CmsC 97267 687 C1
SE McCabe Rd
21000 CmsC 97055 691 H7
McCall Ct
18500 GLDS 97027 687 D3
McCallister Pl
4000 WHGL 98671 570 D5
SW Mccamant Dr
- TLTN 97062 685 B7
- TLTN 97140 685 B7
- WasC 97062 685 B7
- WasC 97140 685 B7
SW McCamant Dr
22200 WasC 97140 715 C1
SW McCamley Rd
1900 WasC 97005 595 A7
1900 WasC 97225 595 A7
NW McCann Rd
3600 ClkC 98685 476 B6
SE McCartney Ln
3400 CmsC 97267 657 A6
McCarver Av
100 ORCY 97045 717 C2
Mccarver Ct
- ORCY 97045 717 C3
NW McChesney Ct
2900 PTLD 97229 595 F2
SW McClarey Dr
18500 WasC 97007 624 E5
McClellan Rd
600 VCVR 98661 536 G5
N McClellan St
1700 PTLD 97217 566 E4
McClintock Rd
- ClbC 97051 385 A5
- STHN 97051 385 A5
McConnell Ct
18200 SRWD 97140 684 E7
NE McConnell Rd
3000 PTLD 97211 567 A3
SW McConnell Rd
25100 CmsC 97140 714 H3
McCord Rd
19400 CmsC 97045 717 B5
19400 ORCY 97045 717 B5
S McCord Rd
19500 CmsC 97045 717 B5
19500 ORCY 97045 717 B5
McCord Heights Ct
12000 ORCY 97045 717 B6
McCormick Ct
40200 SNDY 97055 691 B3
McCormick Dr
39400 SNDY 97055 691 A3
SW McCormick Hill Rd
14800 WasC 97123 653 D6
16500 WasC 97123 683 A4
21500 YmhC 97132 683 A4
N McCosh St
5400 PTLD 97203 566 A5
S McCown Rd
30400 CmsC 97038 807 F6
N McCoy Ct
4400 PTLD 97203 566 B3
McCoy Estates Dr
34000 ClbC 97053 414 G7

McCoy Estates Dr
34000 ClbC 97053 444 G1
SE McCreary Ln
10600 CmsC 97009 659 J3
11000 CmsC 97009 660 A3
Mccroskey St
- MthC 97231 534 F3
S McCubbin Rd
16600 CmsC 97045 688 H7
16600 CmsC 97045 718 G1
NE McDaniel Ln
1600 MCMV 97128 770 J3
NW McDaniel Rd
2900 MthC 97229 595 C3
2900 PTLD 97229 595 B3
McDonald Av
- STPL 97137 773 B5
SW McDonald Dr
7100 WNVL 97070 715 G7
NE McDonald Ln
1400 MCMV 97128 770 J3
3100 YmhC 97128 770 J2
NW Mcdonald St
- MthC 97231 534 F3
SW McDonald St
8900 TGRD 97223 655 D5
8900 TGRD 97224 655 D5
S McDonalds Pl
12900 CmsC 97045 747 D4
SW McDonnell Ter
4200 PTLD 97239 626 D3
NE McDougall Rd
14400 YmhC 97114 771 J1
14400 YmhC 97114 772 C1
McDowell Ln
19300 ORCY 97045 717 C5
McDuff Ct
6400 LKOW 97035 685 H3
6400 TLTN 97035 685 H3
SE Mceachron Av
- CmsC 97222 657 E3
- MWKE 97222 657 E3
McElroy St
39500 SNDY 97055 691 A2
NW McEnery Ln
11600 WasC 97229 595 C3
SW McEwan Av
17800 TLTN 97035 685 H2
17800 TLTN 97224 685 H2
McEwan Rd
5500 CmsC 97035 685 H3
5500 LKOW 97035 685 H3
SW McEwan Rd
- TLTN 97035 685 H2
6500 CmsC 97035 685 G2
6500 LKOW 97035 685 G2
6500 TLTN 97224 685 G2
SW McFarland Blvd
14200 TGRD 97224 655 C6
McFarland Rd
71200 CmsC 97049 724 E4
E McFarland Rd
70700 CmsC 97049 724 E4
Mcgarey Dr
- MCMV 97128 770 F3
McGary Ln
34400 ClbC 97053 414 G7
SE McGillivray Blvd
- VCVR 98664 537 J7
11600 VCVR 98683 537 J7
11900 VCVR 98683 538 A7
12500 VCVR 98683 568 D1
SW McGinnis Av
1200 TDLE 97060 599 E5
2800 GSHM 97030 599 E7
SW McGinnis Ct
1100 TDLE 97060 599 E4
NW McGrath Ct
4000 PTLD 97229 595 F2
NW McGregor Ter
6300 MthC 97229 564 J6
SE McGuffey Ln
24800 CmsC 97022 720 A3
SW McGwire Ct
16500 WasC 97007 624 G6
SW McInnis Ln
21100 WasC 97007 624 B3
NW McIntosh Rd
2800 CMAS 98607 569 A4
3400 CMAS 98607 568 J4
4600 ClkC 98607 568 J4
SW McIntosh Ter
15200 TGRD 97224 655 G6
E McIntyre Rd
64000 CmsC 97049 693 H6
SW McKay Ct
12100 BRTN 97008 625 B7
McKay Dr
53600 ClbC 97056 444 F5
McKay Rd NE
6100 MrnC 97137 773 G1
7300 MrnC 97002 774 A3
7300 MrnC 97137 774 A3
NW McKay Creek Ct
200 CNLS 97113 593 B2
N McKenna Av
6700 PTLD 97203 565 J5
6700 PTLD 97203 566 A4
SW McKenna Pl
10100 TGRD 97223 655 H2
NW McKenna St
9100 PTLD 97229 595 F1
McKenzie Ct
22400 WLIN 97068 686 J7
SW McKenzie Ct E
11200 WNVL 97070 745 B1
SW McKenzie Ct W
11200 WNVL 97070 745 B1
S McKenzie Ln
21300 CmsC 97023 719 B6
SW McKenzie Pl
9600 TGRD 97223 655 E4
NE McKenzie Rd
26600 ClkC 98604 417 E7
SW McKenzie St
9700 TGRD 97223 655 D4
E McKenzie Valley Ct
24600 CmsC 97067 724 B4
SE McKever Rd
3200 ClkC 98607 569 G3
3200 WHGL 98671 569 G3
NW McKibbin Rd
3200 WasC 97116 592 A2
McKillican Ln
5500 WLIN 97068 687 B6

McKillican St
1700 WLIN 97068 687 B6
McKilliken St
1900 WLIN 97068 687 B6
McKinley Av
700 ORCY 97045 717 C2
SE McKinley Av
15500 CmsC 97015 657 F7
16000 CmsC 97015 687 F1
NW McKinley Dr
6400 ClkC 98665 506 G6
SW McKinley Dr
14000 SRWD 97140 714 J1
14000 WasC 97140 714 J1
SE Mckinley Rd
- GSHM 97236 628 F5
SE McKinley Rd
16400 PTLD 97236 628 F5
16700 MthC 97236 628 F5
17300 GSHM 97080 628 G5
17300 MthC 97080 628 G5
W McKinley St
200 CLTN 97111 711 A7
SW McKinney St
10600 TLTN 97062 685 C7
SW McKnight Ln
17400 WasC 97006 594 F6
NW McLain Wy
13700 WasC 97229 595 A5
SW McLeod St
26700 WNVL 97070 715 F4
Mcloughlin Av
- ORCY 97045 687 D7
McLoughlin Blvd
10 ORCY 97045 717 B1
500 ORCY 97045 687 D7
19100 CmsC 97027 687 C4
19100 CmsC 97267 687 C4
19100 GLDS 97027 687 D7
19100 GLDS 97267 687 C4
McLoughlin Blvd SR-99E
10 ORCY 97045 717 B1
500 ORCY 97045 687 D7
19100 CmsC 97027 687 C4
19100 CmsC 97267 687 C4
19100 GLDS 97027 687 D7
19100 GLDS 97267 687 C4
E McLoughlin Blvd
100 VCVR 98660 536 G4
100 VCVR 98663 536 H4
1300 VCVR 98661 536 J4
2600 VCVR 98661 537 A4
S McLoughlin Blvd
100 ORCY 97045 717 B2
700 CmsC 97045 717 A2
S McLoughlin Blvd SR-99E
100 ORCY 97045 717 B2
700 CmsC 97045 717 A2
SE McLoughlin Blvd
2700 PTLD 97202 626 J6
8300 MWKE 97202 626 J7
8300 MWKE 97222 626 J7
10300 MWKE 97222 656 J2
12300 CmsC 97222 656 J4
13200 CmsC 97222 657 A5
13800 CmsC 97267 657 A5
15800 CmsC 97267 687 A1
18500 GLDS 97267 687 C3
18800 CmsC 97027 687 C4
18800 GLDS 97027 687 C4
SE McLoughlin Blvd SR-99E
2700 PTLD 97202 626 J6
8300 MWKE 97202 626 J7
8300 MWKE 97222 626 J7
10300 MWKE 97222 656 J2
12300 CmsC 97222 656 J4
13200 CmsC 97222 657 A5
13800 CmsC 97267 657 A5
15800 CmsC 97267 687 A1
18500 GLDS 97267 687 C3
18800 CmsC 97027 687 C4
18800 GLDS 97027 687 C4
W McLoughlin Blvd
100 VCVR 98660 536 G4
100 VCVR 98663 536 G4
SW McLoughlin Ct
23500 SRWD 97140 714 J1
SE McLoughlin Wy
14500 CmsC 97267 657 A6
McMichael Av
100 STHN 97051 415 A1
SW McMillan St
9600 WasC 97005 625 E2
9700 WasC 97225 625 E2
SE McMinn Rd
27500 CmsC 97022 719 G7
NW McNamee Rd
11700 MthC 97231 534 H6
11700 PTLD 97231 534 H6
McNary Pkwy
- LKOW 97035 656 B4
SE McNary Rd
5600 CmsC 97267 687 C1
SW McNay Rd
29000 WasC 97123 653 B6
NW McNew Rd
34100 WasC 97133 532 J1
McNulty Wy
58400 ClbC 97051 415 A2
58400 STHN 97051 415 A3
S McNulty Wy
- ClbC 97051 415 A3
- ClbC 97053 415 A3
SE McNutt Rd
24200 MthC 97080 629 D7
SE McQuaw Rd
18500 CmsC 97055 691 F4
McVey Av
600 LKOW 97034 656 F7
McVey Ln
19300 CmsC 97045 717 D5
19300 ORCY 97045 717 D5
SW Meacham Ln
52400 SPSE 97056 444 D7
NW Mead Ln
15300 WasC 97133 533 B3
NE Mead Rd
11000 ClkC 98682 509 B2
SW Meade Ct
6300 MthC 97225 625 H1
SW Meade St
- PTLD 97201 626 B3
9900 BRTN 97225 625 E1
9900 WasC 97225 625 E1

SE Meadehill Av
12600 HPYV 97236 658 D5
SW Meader Wy
12200 BRTN 97008 625 B6
Meadow
- VCVR 98664 537 F4
Meadow Av
- CmsC 97055 691 B4
- SNDY 97055 691 B4
20300 CmsC 97045 717 J7
Meadow Cr
- TGRD 97223 655 B2
NE Meadow Ct
2800 HBRO 97124 593 F5
SE Meadow Ct
1900 GSHM 97080 629 C5
Meadow Dr
800 MOLA 97038 807 C7
1400 CmsC 97038 807 C7
Meadow Dr NE
23500 MrnC 97002 744 H6
NE Meadow Dr
500 PTLD 97211 566 H3
NW Meadow Dr
10 BRTN 97006 594 J5
10 WasC 97006 594 J5
SW Meadow Dr
- BRTN 97006 594 J6
- WasC 97005 594 J6
10 WasC 97006 594 J6
33200 SPSE 97056 474 E2
Meadow Ln
1700 NWBG 97132 713 F6
32000 ClbC 97056 474 B2
NE Meadow Ln
1000 PTLD 97211 566 H3
3000 HBRO 97124 593 F5
SE Meadow Ln
8200 VCVR 98664 537 F7
SW Meadow Ln
9100 WasC 97225 625 E3
NE Meadow Lp
9300 YmhC 97132 743 B2
Meadow Pk
- WasC 97006 595 A6
SW Meadow St
10200 TGRD 97223 655 D3
SW Meadow Ter
21900 SRWD 97140 684 E6
SW Meadow Wy
21000 CmsC 97062 686 A6
NE Meadowbrook Cir
9100 VCVR 98664 537 G4
SW Meadowbrook Ct
19800 WasC 97007 624 B2
33200 SPSE 97056 474 D2
SW Meadowbrook Dr
11000 TGRD 97224 655 C7
33300 SPSE 97056 474 E2
S Meadowbrook Ln
30000 CmsC 97038 807 J5
SW Meadowbrook Ln
25300 CmsC 97140 715 A3
SW Meadowbrook Wy
20000 WasC 97007 624 B2
Meadowcreek Ct
5800 LKOW 97035 655 H4
Meadow Creek Ln
- CmsC 97009 660 A5
SE Meadow Creek Ln
13000 CmsC 97009 659 J5
SW Meadowcreek Wy
700 WasC 97006 594 C6
SE Meadowcrest Ct
4200 MWKE 97222 627 B7
E Meadow Crest Dr
21300 CmsC 97049 693 H7
Meadowcrest Farm Ests
- PTLD 97236 628 E3
SW Meadow Flower Ln
- WasC 97223 625 F7
NE Meadowgate Ct
6300 HBRO 97124 594 B4
NW Meadow Glade Rd
- CMAS 98607 569 C4
SE Meadowgold Pl
11500 CmsC 97015 657 H5
NW Meadow Grass Ct
16500 WasC 97006 594 G2
NW Meadow Grass Dr
16900 WasC 97006 594 G1
17200 WasC 97229 594 F1
Meadowgrass St
14200 LKOW 97035 656 A5
SE Meadowgreen Dr
14100 CmsC 97267 657 B5
SE Meadowland Ct
16400 PTLD 97236 628 E3
NW Meadowlands Ter
5400 WasC 97229 564 H7
Meadowlark Ct
15300 CmsC 97035 655 H6
NW Meadowlark Ct
400 MCMV 97128 770 D5
SE Meadowlark Dr
1700 WasC 97123 623 E1
2100 HBRO 97123 593 G7
2400 HBRO 97123 623 F1
Meadowlark Ln
- FTGV 97116 591 H2
17900 LKOW 97034 686 C2
SE Meadowlark Ln
15200 CmsC 97267 657 B7
SW Meadowlark Ln
11300 BRTN 97007 654 G3
Meadowlark Pl
800 MOLA 97038 807 C7
Meadowlark Wy
2200 MCMV 97128 770 D5
NW Meadowlark Wy
200 MCMV 97128 770 E5
S Meadow Lawn Dr
12000 CmsC 97045 717 C4
Meadowlawn Pl
800 MOLA 97038 807 C7
NW Meadowood Cir
700 MCMV 97128 770 E4
SW Meadowood Wy
16300 TGRD 97224 685 D1
SE Meadow Park Cir
15600 VCVR 98683 568 D1
SE Meadow Park Dr
14900 VCVR 98683 568 D1
SE Meadowpark Dr
13200 HPYV 97236 658 B2

Meadowridge Ct
- CmsC 97045 747 F
NW Meadowridge Dr
13800 WasC 97229 595 A
14200 WasC 97229 594 J
Meadow Ridge Ln
14700 CmsC 97045 687 G
NW Meadow Ridge Ln
700 CMAS 98607 569 D
NW Meadow Ridge St
700 CMAS 98607 569 D
NE Meadows Ct
8300 ClkC 98662 507 F
SW Meadows Ct
7200 WNVL 97070 715 F
Meadows Dr
- MCMV 97128 770 E
- YmhC 97128 770 E
1400 LKOW 97034 686 F1
NE Meadows Dr
6300 ClkC 98662 507 F
NW Meadows Dr
1300 MCMV 97128 770 E4
2200 YmhC 97128 770 E
SE Meadows Ln
14200 CmsC 97015 657 J6
SW Meadows Lp
28400 WNVL 97070 715 G
SW Meadows Pkwy
6800 WNVL 97070 715 G
NE Meadows Pl
1700 GSHM 97030 629 C1
SW Meadows Rd
4800 LKOW 97035 655 J6
4800 LKOW 97035 656 A
6200 CmsC 97035 655 H
SE Meadows Edge Ct
10600 HPYV 97236 657 H
NE Meadowside Wy
1000 HBRO 97124 593 A
Meadow Verde
- ClkC 98665 506 G
- ClkC 98685 506 G
Meadowview Ct
1100 WLIN 97068 716 F1
Meadowview Dr
59400 ClbC 97051 384 H7
59400 ClbC 97051 414 H1
59400 STHN 97051 384 H7
59400 STHN 97051 414 H1
S Meadow View Dr
17100 CmsC 97045 687 H7
17100 CmsC 97045 717 G1
Meadow View Rd
100 FTGV 97116 591 F3
S Meadow Wood Pl
20200 CmsC 97045 717 H6
NW Meares Dr
- PTLD 97229 595 E1
NW Mears Blvd
- PTLD 97231 565 D2
N Mears St
6200 PTLD 97203 566 A2
6800 PTLD 97203 565 J2
SE Medicine Song Rd
35700 CmsC 97023 750 F6
NW Medinah Dr
1100 MCMV 97128 770 F4
Medlik Dr
33400 ClbC 97056 474 E5
SW Medwyn Ter
- PTLD 97219 626 D7
SW Meek Lp
29000 WNVL 97070 715 G7
NW Meek Rd
24200 HBRO 97124 563 F5
24200 WasC 97124 563 F5
SE Meek St
2300 MWKE 97222 656 J2
3000 MWKE 97222 657 A2
Meeker St
37800 SNDY 97055 690 H2
NW Meersburg St
33000 SPSE 97056 444 E7
Meetin Hall Rd
- BRTN 97005 625 C2
Megan Ln
20300 FRVW 97024 599 A2
Megan Pl
19000 LKOW 97034 686 B3
NE Megan St
- HBRO 97124 593 H2
SW Megan Ter
- TGRD 97223 655 C3
SE Megan Wy
14500 CmsC 97015 658 B7
NW Mehama Ct
2600 WasC 97229 594 F3
SE Meier Ct
3600 HBRO 97123 623 E2
SW Meier Dr
10300 TLTN 97062 685 D7
SE Meier Ln
27000 CmsC 97009 659 F5
Meier Rd
54100 ClbC 97056 444 J4
54100 ClbC 97056 445 A5
NW Meier Rd
21900 WasC 97124 534 A7
NE Meikle Pl
10 PTLD 97213 597 B5
10 PTLD 97215 597 B5
10 PTLD 97232 597 B5
SW Meinecke Pkwy
- SRWD 97140 684 E6
SW Meinecke Rd
16300 SRWD 97140 684 F6
Meinig Av
17300 SNDY 97055 691 A3
Meinig Av SR-211
17400 SNDY 97055 691 A3
SE Meinig Av
17100 SNDY 97055 691 A2
Meinig Ct
39100 SNDY 97055 691 A2
Meinig Lp
18100 SNDY 97055 691 A4
NW Meisner Dr
4000 WasC 97229 595 A1
SW Meissinger Pl
200 SRWD 97140 684 H7
SE Mel Ct
2700 HBRO 97123 623 E1
SE Melbrook Wy
11900 CmsC 97015 658 A5

STREET
Block City ZIP Map# Grid

SE Meldrum Av
4300 CmsC 97267 687 B4
5100 GLDS 97267 687 C3
Meldrum Bar Park Rd
- GLDS 97027 687 B5
NW Melinda Av
600 PTLD 97210 596 C5
NE Melinda Ct
800 HBRO 97124 593 D2
SE Melinda Ct
15500 DAMA 97009 658 E7
SW Melinda Dr
15700 BRTN 97007 624 H6
Melinda Ln
- MrnC 97002 775 A3
Melinda St
13800 ORCY 97045 687 E5
SW Melinda St
16000 BRTN 97007 624 G6
Melissa Av
- CmsC 97055 690 H4
18100 SNDY 97055 690 H4
Melissa Dr
- CmsC 97034 686 A2
4000 LKOW 97034 686 A2
SW Melissa Pl
27200 WasC 97140 714 B5
SE Melita Dr
10500 HPYV 97236 658 B2
SE Mellmer Ln
4500 CmsC 97267 687 B3
Mellon Av
16600 CmsC 97035 655 H7
SW Melnore Ct
19300 WasC 97006 624 D1
SW Melnore St
9500 WasC 97225 625 E1
Melody Ct
100 NWBG 97132 713 B5
NW Melody Ct
15400 WasC 97006 594 H3
Melody Ln
100 NWBG 97132 713 C5
NW Melody Ln
14100 WasC 97229 595 A3
15500 WasC 97006 594 H3
SE Melody Ln
4300 MWKE 97222 657 B1
NE Melody Wy
2700 MCMV 97128 771 A3
SW Melrose Av
1200 MCMV 97128 770 G7
N Melrose Dr
3700 PTLD 97227 596 E2
NW Melrose Dr
19500 WasC 97229 594 D1
Melrose Pl
13600 LKOW 97035 656 A5
Melrose St
4500 LKOW 97035 656 A5
4800 LKOW 97035 655 J5
S Melva Ct
21900 CmsC 97004 747 G3
SW Melville Av
4200 PTLD 97239 626 C2
Melvin Av
10 STHN 97051 415 B1
Memorial Dr
- PTLD 97236 628 A7
- PTLD 97266 627 J7
- PTLD 97266 628 A7
SW Memorial Dr
8400 WNVL 97070 745 F1
SW Memory Ln
7600 BRTN 97225 625 G1
Memphis Wy
300 VCVR 98664 537 E7
NW Menco Av
- PTLD 97231 565 E5
NW Mendenhall St
8400 PTLD 97229 595 F3
SW Menefee Dr
700 PTLD 97239 626 E4
N Menlo Av
7000 PTLD 97203 566 B5
SE Menlo Dr
3000 VCVR 98683 568 C2
SW Menlo Dr
4600 BRTN 97005 625 A4
5800 BRTN 97008 625 A4
SW Menlor Ln
12700 BRTN 97007 654 H4
12700 BRTN 97223 654 H4
12700 WasC 97223 654 H4
13200 TGRD 97223 654 H4
SE Menser Ct
12000 DAMA 97009 659 D4
N Menzies Ct
2200 PTLD 97217 536 E6
N Menzies Dr
2200 PTLD 97217 536 E6
Mercantile Dr
3900 LKOW 97035 656 A6
SE Mercer Ct
22800 DAMA 97009 659 C7
SW Mercer Ter
3200 BRTN 97005 625 C2
SE Mercers Wy
16100 CmsC 97267 687 D1
Merchant Pl
- CmsC 97045 716 J4
- ORCY 97045 716 J4
NE Merchant Rd
12800 YmhC 97111 711 B4
Meredith Dr
200 NWBG 97132 713 D7
200 YmhC 97132 713 D7
SW Merestone Ct
12100 TGRD 97223 655 B3
SE Merganser Ct
16200 CmsC 97267 687 E1
SW Merganser Ln
12700 BRTN 97007 654 F4
12700 BRTN 97223 654 F4
12700 WasC 97223 654 F4
NE Merges Dr
3500 PTLD 97212 597 B2
NW Meridian Av
- MthC 97210 595 H4
Meridian Cir
6200 WLIN 97068 686 H5
Meridian Ct
5600 LKOW 97035 655 J5
S Meridian Rd
24000 CmsC 97002 775 G5
N Meridian St
3000 NWBG 97132 713 C4
S Meridian St
100 NWBG 97132 713 C7
300 NWBG 97132 743 C1
Meridian Vil
- TLTN 97062 685 H4
SW Meridian Wy
6200 CmsC 97062 685 H7
NW Meridian Ridge Ct
- PTLD 97210 595 H5
NW Meridian Ridge Dr
- PTLD 97210 595 H5
NW Meriwether Ct
1100 CMAS 98607 569 A4
Meriwether Dr
20100 ORCY 97045 717 H7
NE Merle Ct
300 HBRO 97124 593 C2
NW Merle Dr
100 HBRO 97124 593 B2
SW Merlin Ct
6300 PTLD 97219 625 H7
10800 CmsC 97070 715 C7
10800 WNVL 97070 715 C7
Merlin Ln
1600 NWBG 97132 743 D1
SW Merlin Pl
13000 TGRD 97223 655 A4
SW Merlo Ct
2000 BRTN 97006 594 G7
SW Merlo Dr
1700 BRTN 97006 594 G7
1700 WasC 97006 594 G7
SW Merlo Rd
15800 BRTN 97006 594 G7
16600 WasC 97006 594 G7
SW Merlyne Ct
8500 TGRD 97223 655 F5
SW Merridell Ct
5500 WasC 97225 625 G4
SW Merrill Ln
- BRTN 97005 625 C2
- WasC 97005 625 C2
NE Merritt Dr
18900 ClkC 98604 478 B1
SE Merriweather Dr
3000 HBRO 97123 593 F7
SW Merry Ln
6800 BRTN 97008 625 E5
6800 WasC 97008 625 E5
S Merry Lee Dr
15800 CmsC 97045 717 J6
SW Merryman St
15000 SRWD 97140 684 H7
S Merry Meadow Ct
17900 CmsC 97045 718 G2
NE Mershon Rd
30300 MthC 97060 600 D6
31400 MthC 97019 600 D6
NW Mery St
11000 WasC 97124 564 C1
SW Mesa Ct
12200 BRTN 97008 625 B6
NW Mesa View Ln
16900 WasC 97006 594 G1
SW Meteor Pl
1400 TDLE 97060 599 E5
Metlako Wy
300 CBAC 97018 385 C2
NW Metolius Ct
4400 WasC 97229 594 D1
SW Metolius Ct
31100 WNVL 97070 745 E2
NW Metolius Dr
19600 WasC 97229 564 D7
19800 WasC 97229 594 D1
SW Metolius Ln
8400 WNVL 97070 745 E2
E Metsger Island Rd
24400 CmsC 97067 723 J3
24400 CmsC 97067 724 A4
SW Metta Ter
12600 WasC 97223 654 J4
SW Metz St
12400 BRTN 97008 625 B5
Metzler Av
100 MOLA 97038 837 E2
NW Meuller Rd
23800 ClkC 98642 446 D3
Meury Ln
- WasC 97116 561 A2
SW Meyer Ln
16500 WasC 97224 684 H1
Meyer St
- PTLD 97218 567 E5
NE Meyers Ln
1300 MthC 97019 600 H5
Meyers Rd
- ORCY 97045 717 G6
19500 CmsC 97045 717 D5
S Meyers Rd
- CmsC 97045 717 E6
- ORCY 97045 717 D6
SE Meyers St
5500 CmsC 97267 687 C3
SE Mia Ct
15200 CmsC 97015 658 D7
SE Mia Garden Dr
14300 HPYV 97236 658 C4
SW Miami
800 WNVL 97070 745 E2
Miami Ct
600 VCVR 98664 537 F7
SW Miami Dr
22500 TLTN 97062 685 D7
SW Miami Pl
22900 TLTN 97062 685 D7
Miami Wy
300 VCVR 98664 537 F7
SE Miarly Ln
18200 DAMA 97009 688 G2
SW Mica Ln
15400 BRTN 97007 654 H1
SE Micah St
14200 HPYV 97236 658 C1
Michael Av
100 STHN 97051 415 A1
Michael Ct
2400 WLIN 97068 716 F1
NE Michael Ct
15600 PTLD 97230 598 E6
SW Michael Ct
14800 SRWD 97140 714 H1
Michael Dr
2200 WLIN 97068 716 F1
SE Michael Dr
7600 CmsC 97222 657 E3
NE Michael Rd
30900 YmhC 97132 713 H4
NW Michaelbrook Ln
2800 CMAS 98607 539 B6
NW Michelbook Ct
700 MCMV 97128 770 G4
NW Michelbook Ln
200 MCMV 97128 770 G4
SW Michelle Ct
13500 TGRD 97223 655 A4
SE Michelle Dr
15100 CmsC 97015 658 D7
Michelle St
500 NWBG 97132 743 C1
Michigan Av
- CmsC 97049 724 F1
E Michigan Av
71200 CmsC 97049 724 E1
N Michigan Av
3200 PTLD 97227 596 F2
4500 PTLD 97217 596 F1
4900 PTLD 97217 566 F6
Michigan Dr
7300 VCVR 98664 537 E5
Michlen Av
1600 WLIN 97068 686 G3
SE Middle Wy
6800 VCVR 98664 537 E7
E Middlebrook Dr
3000 NWBG 97132 713 E5
Middle Crest Rd
100 LKOW 97034 656 F6
NE Middlefield Rd
10 PTLD 97211 566 G2
10 PTLD 97217 566 G2
SW Middle Greens Rd
7500 WNVL 97070 745 F3
SW Middlesex Wy
17600 WasC 97006 594 G7
N Middle Shore St
2000 PTLD 97217 536 E7
SW Middleton Ct
15400 BRTN 97007 624 H6
SW Middleton Rd
23500 SRWD 97140 714 E1
24300 WasC 97140 714 E2
SW Midea Ct
9100 WasC 97225 625 E3
SW Midea Ln
8900 WasC 97225 625 F3
Midhill Cir
18600 WLIN 97068 686 H3
NW Midlake Ln
1500 WasC 97006 594 F3
Midland Mnr
- CNLS 97113 592 D4
SW Midline St
20100 WasC 97006 594 C6
SW Midmar Pl
6400 WasC 97223 625 H5
SE Midvale Rd
2000 TDLE 97060 599 H5
SW Midvale Rd
10 CmsC 97034 656 G4
10 CmsC 97219 656 G4
N Midway Av
9400 PTLD 97203 565 J2
NW Midway Av
8500 PTLD 97231 565 E4
E Midway Ln
28300 CmsC 97067 724 C7
SW Midway Rd
15500 WasC 97123 653 E7
16100 WasC 97123 683 E1
SE Midway St
17500 DAMA 97009 688 E3
NW Mignonette Av
800 GSHM 97030 629 B2
SE Mignonette Ct
2200 GSHM 97080 629 B5
S Mija Ln
21600 CmsC 97023 719 C6
NW Mikalo Ct
20800 WasC 97229 564 C7
SW Miken Ln
400 CmsC 97068 716 E1
SW Milan Ln
15900 WasC 97223 654 G5
SW Milan St
16300 WasC 97223 654 G5
SW Milano Ln
- WNVL 97070 715 B7
NW Milazzo Ln
12500 WasC 97229 595 B1
Milburn Ct
500 LKOW 97034 656 E5
NW Milburn St
13300 WasC 97005 595 A5
13300 WasC 97229 595 A5
SE Mildred Av
18800 CmsC 97267 687 C3
18800 GLDS 97027 687 C3
18800 GLDS 97267 687 C3
NW Mildred St
2500 PTLD 97210 596 C5
SW Miles Ct
2400 PTLD 97219 626 C5
6000 PTLD 97219 625 H5
6300 BRTN 97223 625 H5
6700 WasC 97223 625 H5
Miles Dr
21300 CmsC 97068 686 J6
21300 WLIN 97068 686 J6
SW Miles Pl
7300 PTLD 97219 626 F6
Miles St
19200 ORCY 97045 717 G4
SW Miles St
4900 PTLD 97219 625 J5
4900 PTLD 97219 626 A5
NE Miley Rd
8800 CmsC 97002 745 F3
8800 WNVL 97070 745 F3
14300 WNVL 97002 745 E3
14500 CmsC 97070 745 F3
SW Military Ct
- MthC 97219 656 H2
SW Military Ln
11500 MthC 97219 656 H3
19800 WasC 97007 654 C5
SW Military Rd
1300 MthC 97219 656 F3
1300 PTLD 97219 656 F3
S Milk Creek Wy
26100 CmsC 97042 777 E5
Milky Wy
56000 ClbC 97053 414 D6
Mill Ct
1500 NWBG 97132 743 D1
SE Mill Ct
10800 PTLD 97216 597 J7
11900 PTLD 97216 598 A7
11900 PTLD 97233 598 A7
17700 GSHM 97233 628 G1
Mill Pl
900 NWBG 97132 743 D1
1000 YmhC 97132 743 D1
NW Mill Rd
14900 MthC 97231 535 A4
Mill St
10 RDGF 98642 415 J7
100 STHN 97051 385 A7
100 STHN 97051 415 A1
200 DAYT 97114 772 B4
4800 WLIN 97068 687 B7
SE Mill St
300 PTLD 97214 596 G7
3700 PTLD 97214 597 B7
7200 PTLD 97215 597 E7
9600 PTLD 97216 597 H7
12200 PTLD 97216 598 A7
15600 PTLD 97233 598 E7
17400 PTLD 97233 628 G1
17500 GSHM 97233 628 G1
SW Mill St
900 PTLD 97201 596 E7
6000 MthC 97221 595 J7
6000 PTLD 97221 595 J7
W Mill St
100 RDGF 98642 415 J7
Millard Av
200 WDLD 98674 386 A1
Millard Rd
- ClbC 97056 415 A4
34300 ClbC 97051 414 G3
35400 ClbC 97053 414 J3
35400 ClbC 97053 415 A4
35500 ClbC 97051 415 A4
NW Millbrook St
17200 WasC 97229 564 G6
NW Mill Creek Dr
13100 WasC 97005 595 A5
13200 WasC 97229 595 A5
NW Millcrest Pl
1800 WasC 97229 595 E4
SW Millen Dr
9200 TGRD 97224 685 E1
Millenium Wy
13100 ORCY 97045 717 D5
SW Millennium Ter
7100 WasC 97007 624 C5
NW Miller Av
10 GSHM 97080 629 B2
2000 GSHM 97030 599 B7
2000 GSHM 97030 629 E1
SW Miller Ct
600 GSHM 97080 629 B3
8600 TGRD 97224 655 F7
10300 TLTN 97062 685 D7
SW Miller Dr
3300 GSHM 97080 629 B6
SE Miller Ln
52200 ClbC 97056 474 G1
52200 SPSE 97056 474 G1
SW Miller Pl
3300 GSHM 97080 629 B6
Miller Rd
- CmsC 97011 693 G7
- CmsC 97011 723 G1
- MrnC 97002 774 F6
- MrnC 97032 774 F6
38200 SNDY 97055 690 J3
E Miller Rd
21600 CmsC 97011 693 G7
NE Miller Rd
- ClbC 97056 444 G7
52200 ClbC 97056 474 G1
52200 SPSE 97056 474 G1
52400 SPSE 97056 444 G7
NW Miller Rd
- MthC 97231 535 B7
- PTLD 97231 535 B7
100 MthC 97229 595 G5
100 WasC 97225 595 G6
500 PTLD 97229 595 G5
SE Miller Rd
32200 MthC 97080 630 C7
SW Miller Rd
10 MthC 97229 595 G6
10 WasC 97225 595 G6
Miller St
100 MOLA 97038 807 E7
100 ORCY 97045 717 A2
NE Miller St
1300 MCMV 97128 771 B4
SE Miller St
700 PTLD 97202 626 H6
SW Millerglen Dr
7500 WasC 97007 624 D6
NW Miller Hill Ct
1700 PTLD 97229 595 E3
NW Miller Hill Dr
9500 PTLD 97229 595 H3
NW Miller Hill Pl
1700 PTLD 97229 595 E3
SW Miller Hill Rd
7000 WasC 97007 624 D6
NE Miller View Ln
29300 YmhC 97132 713 G3
NW Millford St
12500 WasC 97229 595 B1
NE Millican Ln
4500 YmhC 97128 741 E7
NW Millicomo Ct
20900 WasC 97229 564 C7
S Milligan Rd
21300 CmsC 97045 747 D2
SW Millikan Wy
12200 BRTN 97005 625 A2
13200 WasC 97005 625 A2
14100 BRTN 97005 624 J2
14100 WasC 97005 624 J2
14400 BRTN 97006 624 H2
SE Millmain Dr
15000 PTLD 97233 628 D1
SE Millmain Dr
15200 PTLD 97233 598 E7
SE Mill Plain Blv
- ClkC 98684 538 H7
- VCVR 98607 538 H7
E Mill Plain Blvd
100 VCVR 98660 536 G4
100 VCVR 98663 536 H5
1000 VCVR 98661 536 H5
2800 VCVR 98661 537 C5
6300 VCVR 98664 537 C5
E Mill Plain Blvd SR-501
100 VCVR 98660 536 G4
100 VCVR 98663 536 G4
SE Mill Plain Blvd
9900 VCVR 98664 537 H6
11100 VCVR 98683 537 J6
11100 VCVR 98684 537 J6
12000 VCVR 98683 538 D7
12000 VCVR 98684 538 D7
W Mill Plain Blvd
100 VCVR 98660 536 E4
100 VCVR 98663 536 G4
W Mill Plain Blvd SR-501
100 VCVR 98660 536 E4
100 VCVR 98663 536 G4
Mill Plain Ct
7800 VCVR 98664 537 E6
SE Mill Plane Blvd
- VCVR 98607 538 H7
17200 ClkC 98684 538 G7
17200 VCVR 98683 538 G7
17200 VCVR 98684 538 G7
NW Mill Pond Rd
1700 PTLD 97229 595 D3
2500 MthC 97229 595 D2
NW Mill Race Ct
700 MCMV 97128 770 G4
Mill Race Ln NE
- AURA 97002 775 E4
- MrnC 97002 775 E4
Mill Race Rd NE
- AURA 97002 775 F3
NW Mill Ridge Rd
1800 PTLD 97229 595 E3
NW Mills Av
8800 PTLD 97231 565 E4
Mills Ln
2300 FTGV 97116 591 G4
NW Mills St
- PTLD 97231 565 E4
SW Mill St Cir
- PTLD 97201 596 F7
SW Mill St Ter
1800 PTLD 97201 596 C7
NW Mills Terrace Rd
- PTLD 97231 565 E4
NW Millstone Wy
5000 WasC 97229 564 G6
SW Millview Ct
12100 TGRD 97223 655 B3
NE Milne Ct
300 HBRO 97124 593 C1
NE Milne Rd
100 HBRO 97124 593 B1
NW Milne Rd
7800 WasC 97113 562 H3
7800 WasC 97124 562 H3
9000 WasC 97133 562 H1
NW Milne St
100 HBRO 97124 593 B1
SW Milon Ln
8400 BRTN 97225 625 F2
8400 WasC 97225 625 F2
Miloris Wy
900 CBAC 97018 385 B4
900 ClbC 97018 385 B4
SE Milport Rd
1700 MWKE 97222 656 J1
NE Milton Ct
14100 PTLD 97230 598 C2
SW Milton Ct
14000 TGRD 97224 655 G6
NE Milton Pl
15600 PTLD 97230 598 E2
NE Milton St
3700 PTLD 97212 597 B2
5700 PTLD 97213 597 D2
8200 PTLD 97220 597 G2
15200 PTLD 97230 598 D2
Milton Wy
100 STHN 97051 415 B1
N Milton Wy
100 STHN 97051 415 B1
Milton Glen Rd
59500 ClbC 97051 384 F7
SE Milwaukie Av
2700 PTLD 97202 626 H6
SE Milwaukie Expwy
- CmsC 97015 657 F6
- CmsC 97222 657 A3
- CmsC 97267 657 F5
- MWKE 97222 656 J2
- MWKE 97222 657 A3
SE Milwaukie Expwy SR-224
- CmsC 97015 657 F6
- CmsC 97222 657 A3
- CmsC 97267 657 F5
- MWKE 97222 656 J2
- MWKE 97222 657 A3
Milwaukie-Foster Rd
9600 CmsC 97015 657 H4
9600 CmsC 97236 657 H4
11700 CmsC 97015 658 A4
11700 CmsC 97236 658 A4
SE Mimosa Dr
1200 GSHM 97080 629 H4
Mimosa St
3100 FTGV 97116 591 F2
SE Mindemere Pk
- CmsC 97267 657 F7
SW Mindi Ter
900 WasC 97006 594 C6
Mindy Ln
- YmhC 97132 712 H5
Mindy Wy
33000 SPSE 97056 444 D7
SW Miner Wy
7500 WasC 97225 625 G2
NE Mineral Springs Rd
4200 LFYT 97128 741 F7
4200 YmhC 97128 741 F7
6100 YmhC 97111 741 E4
9200 YmhC 97111 711 D7
N Minerva Av
7900 PTLD 97203 565 J4
9100 PTLD 97203 566 A3
SE Minerva Ln
15200 CmsC 97267 657 C7
E Minikanda Av
71500 CmsC 97049 724 F1
SE Miniview Ct
15700 CmsC 97267 656 J7
SW Minkler Ln
29700 WNVL 97070 715 D7
Minnehaha Ct
6100 CmsC 97035 685 H3
NE Minnehaha St
1100 ClkC 98665 506 H6
1200 VCVR 98665 506 H7
2600 ClkC 98665 507 B7
2600 VCVR 98663 507 A6
2600 VCVR 98665 507 B7
3200 ClkC 98661 507 A7
N Minnesota Av
4600 PTLD 97217 596 F1
7600 PTLD 97217 566 F5
SW Mint Pl
13500 TGRD 97223 654 J5
13500 TGRD 97223 655 A5
SE Minter Bridge Rd
1700 HBRO 97123 593 E7
2000 WasC 97123 593 E7
2300 HBRO 97123 623 E1
2300 WasC 97123 623 E1
SW Minter Bridge Rd
3700 HBRO 97123 623 D2
3700 WasC 97123 623 C5
SE Minthorn Lp
- MWKE 97222 657 B3
S Mint Lake Rd
22000 CmsC 97004 748 D4
SE Mintone Dr
4900 CmsC 97222 657 C4
Minuet Ct
19200 CmsC 97045 716 J5
19200 ORCY 97045 716 J5
SW Mira Ct
10900 TGRD 97223 655 C5
SW Miranda Pl
1600 TDLE 97060 599 F5
NE Mirimar Pl
400 PTLD 97232 597 A5
Mirkwood Dr
18700 LKOW 97034 686 B3
Mirkwood Ln
23700 CmsC 97067 724 C3
Mirror Rd
- CmsC 97023 750 B4
Mission Av NE
3900 STPL 97137 773 B5
Mission Dr
10 NWBG 97132 713 C6
Mission Rd NE
3600 MrnC 97137 772 J4
3600 MrnC 97137 773 A4
3600 STPL 97137 773 B5
NW Mission Oaks Dr
16100 BRTN 97006 594 G4
N Mississippi Av
2300 PTLD 97227 596 F3
4500 PTLD 97217 596 F1
7000 PTLD 97217 566 F5
Mississippi Dr
6800 VCVR 98664 537 D7
Missoula Av
10000 VCVR 98661 537 D5
N Missouri Av
3300 PTLD 97227 596 F2
4600 PTLD 97217 596 F1
7600 PTLD 97217 566 F5
Missouri Dr
6600 VCVR 98661 537 D6
6600 VCVR 98664 537 D6
Mistletoe Dr
- NWBG 97132 713 F7
SW Mistletoe Dr
13700 TGRD 97223 655 A5
13700 TGRD 97224 655 A5
13800 TGRD 97223 654 J5
13800 TGRD 97224 654 J5
SW Misty Ct
15700 BRTN 97007 624 H6
SE Misty Dr
- HPYV 97236 658 D5
Mitchell Av
600 WDLD 98674 385 J1
SW Mitchell Av
900 TDLE 97060 599 E4
Mitchell Ct
39900 SNDY 97055 691 A4
NW Mitchell Ct
500 CMAS 98607 569 C5
SE Mitchell Ct
6600 PTLD 97206 627 E4
SW Mitchell Ct
- TGRD 97223 654 J4
1100 TDLE 97060 599 E5
3100 PTLD 97239 626 B3
SW Mitchell Dr
1600 MCMV 97128 770 E7
1600 YmhC 97128 770 E7
S Mitchell Ln
15000 CmsC 97045 747 H2
SW Mitchell Ln
1400 PTLD 97239 626 D3
NW Mitchell St
500 CMAS 98607 569 C5
14700 WasC 97229 594 J1
SE Mitchell St
- PTLD 97202 627 A4
2300 PTLD 97202 626 H3
4100 PTLD 97206 627 B4
10200 PTLD 97266 627 H4
13900 PTLD 97236 628 C4
SW Mitchell St
2200 PTLD 97239 626 C3
5000 PTLD 97221 625 J3
5000 PTLD 97221 626 A3
SW Moapa Av
- MthC 97219 656 F2
N Mobile Av
7000 PTLD 97217 566 E5
Mobile Ln
33900 ClbC 97056 444 F7
33900 SPSE 97056 444 F7
SW Mobile Ln
18700 WasC 97006 594 E7
SW Mobile Pl
19000 TLTN 97062 685 H4
Moccasin Wy
13100 CmsC 97045 717 D5
13100 ORCY 97045 717 D5
NE Mocha Wy
2400 HBRO 97124 593 A3
Mock Ln
54700 ClbC 97056 444 B3
SW Mockingbird Ct
14800 BRTN 97007 654 J2
SW Mockingbird Wy
10200 BRTN 97007 654 J2
NW Moda Wy
2800 HBRO 97124 594 D2
NE Modaffari Rd
10800 CLTN 97111 711 B7
10800 YmhC 97111 711 B7
SW Modoc Ct
8500 TLTN 97062 685 F5
8800 WNVL 97070 715 E6
Moehnke St
- WLIN 97068 716 J2
SW Moet Ct
14500 WasC 97224 654 J6
SE Moffet Rd
38400 ClkC 98671 570 J3
Moffitt Dr
- CmsC 97070 715 B6
SW Moffitt Dr
12200 CmsC 97070 715 B6
NE Mohan Dr
3100 MCMV 97128 770 J2
SW Mohave Ct
19300 TLTN 97062 685 E4
SW Mohave Ter
28000 WNVL 97070 715 E6
N Mohawk Av
8500 PTLD 97203 565 H3
SW Mohawk Cir
8600 WNVL 97070 715 E6
SW Mohawk St
7500 TLTN 97062 685 F4
Mohawk Wy
3700 WLIN 97068 686 J4
SW Mohican St
19800 WasC 97006 594 D6
Molalla Av
100 ORCY 97045 717 D3
19400 CmsC 97045 717 E4
N Molalla Av
100 MOLA 97038 837 E1
600 MOLA 97038 807 E7
30100 CmsC 97038 807 E5
S Molalla Av
100 MOLA 97038 837 E3
700 CmsC 97038 837 E2
29900 CmsC 97038 807 E5
SW Molalla Ct
21500 TLTN 97062 685 E6
S Molalla Rd
29300 CmsC 97038 807 D3
SW Molalla Bend Rd
6700 WNVL 97070 745 G3
N Molalla Forest Rd
- CmsC 97013 746 E4
- CNBY 97013 746 E4
S Molalla Forest Rd
- CmsC 97038 837 C1
- MOLA 97038 807 C7
- MOLA 97038 837 C1
26000 CmsC 97013 776 J7
SW Moline Ct
20900 WasC 97006 594 C6
NW Molini Ter
2600 HBRO 97124 594 D3
SW Molly Ct
10000 TGRD 97223 655 D4
NE Molly St
5100 HBRO 97124 593 H2
SE Molly St
31700 MthC 97080 630 C6
Molony Dr
- ClbC 97056 444 F5
- SPSE 97056 444 F6
SE Molt St
6300 CmsC 97267 657 D7
SW Monaco Ln
16500 KNGC 97224 685 B1
16500 WasC 97224 685 B1
NW Monarch Ln
40500 WasC 97106 532 A2
SW Mondas Rd
600 MCMV 97128 770 G7
SE Monet Ct
13800 CmsC 97015 658 B6
SW Monica Ct
8300 WasC 97223 625 E7
SE Monner Rd
14700 CmsC 97236 658 D4
14700 HPYV 97236 658 D4
S Monpano Overlook Dr
20300 CmsC 97045 718 C7
20300 CmsC 97045 748 C1
Monroe Pkwy
- LKOW 97035 656 B4
SW Monroe Pkwy
10 LKOW 97034 656 C4
10 LKOW 97035 656 C4
Monroe St
200 ORCY 97045 717 C1
800 LFYT 97127 741 H7
900 ORCY 97045 687 D7
1400 YmhC 97114 741 H6
1400 YmhC 97128 741 H6
E Monroe St
100 CLTN 97111 711 A7
N Monroe St
10 PTLD 97212 596 G2
10 PTLD 97227 596 F2
NE Monroe St
10 PTLD 97212 596 G2
10 PTLD 97227 596 G2
SE Monroe St
300 LFYT 97127 771 G1
400 LFYT 97127 741 G7
1900 MWKE 97222 656 J2
3500 MWKE 97222 657 B2
6000 CmsC 97222 657 D2
W Monroe St
100 CLTN 97111 711 A7
SW Monson St
19800 WasC 97006 594 C6
NE Monstad Dr
13700 ClkC 98606 479 F7

STREET
Block City ZIP Map# Grid

SW Montague Wy
17100 KNGC 97224 685 A2
N Montana Av
3900 PTLD 97227 596 F1
4600 PTLD 97217 596 F1
7500 PTLD 97217 566 F5
Montana Ln
1100 VCVR 98661 537 C5
NW Montara Ct
2900 PTLD 97229 595 G2
NW Montara Dr
2900 PTLD 97229 595 E2
NW Montara Lp
3000 PTLD 97229 595 E2
SW Montauk Cir
6700 RVGR 97035 685 G3
6700 TLTN 97035 685 G3
SW Montclair Dr
7000 WasC 97225 625 G4
SW Montebello Dr
29400 CmsC 97070 715 D7
29400 WNVL 97070 715 D7
S Monte Carlo Wy
21900 CmsC 97004 747 G3
21900 CmsC 97045 747 G3
SE Montee Ct
3300 PTLD 97214 597 A6
SE Montego Dr
4700 HBRO 97123 593 H7
SE Montego St
5000 HBRO 97123 593 H7
SE Montego Bay St
6500 CmsC 97267 657 D6
N Monteith Av
6500 PTLD 97203 566 A5
SE Monterey Av
- HPYV 97236 657 H3
8200 CmsC 97222 657 F3
8200 CmsC 97236 657 F3
NW Monterey Dr
900 MCMV 97128 770 F4
SW Monterey Ln
16500 KNGC 97224 685 B1
16500 WasC 97224 685 B1
SW Monterey Pl
8900 WasC 97225 595 E7
Monterey Wy
300 VCVR 98661 537 C6
Monte Verde Dr
7100 GLDS 97027 687 E2
SW Monte Verdi Blvd
18000 WasC 97007 624 E5
NW Monteview Av
- MthC 97231 565 B3
- PTLD 97231 565 B3
SW Monte Vista Dr
19700 WasC 97007 624 D6
NW Monte Vista Ter
2900 PTLD 97210 596 B5
SW Montgomery Dr
1700 PTLD 97201 596 C7
2700 PTLD 97201 626 B1
SW Montgomery Pl
1800 PTLD 97201 596 D7
NE Montgomery St
2100 HBRO 97124 593 E3
SE Montgomery St
6200 MWKE 97222 657 D3
SW Montgomery St
100 PTLD 97201 596 F7
5700 PTLD 97221 595 J7
SW Montgomery Wy
6500 WNVL 97070 745 G1
Monticello Ct
6900 GLDS 97027 687 E2
SW Monticello Ct
8300 BRTN 97008 625 A7
Monticello Dr
10 LKOW 97035 656 B4
17400 GLDS 97027 687 D2
SW Monticello St
8500 BRTN 97008 625 A7
SW Montmore Wy
1700 TDLE 97060 599 E5
NW Montreux Ln
11000 WasC 97225 595 D5
11000 WasC 97229 595 D5
SW Moody Av
- PTLD 97201 596 F7
2500 PTLD 97201 626 F2
2500 PTLD 97239 626 F1
SE Moon Av
16400 CmsC 97267 687 B1
Moonbeam Dr
17800 CmsC 97055 690 D3
Moon Crater Rd
- CmsC 97049 724 G6
SE Moon Dust Ct
11400 HPYV 97236 658 B3
Mooney Av NE
22700 MrnC 97002 775 D1
SE Moonlight Av
- HBRO 97123 593 D7
SW Moonridge Pl
10 MthC 97229 595 F6
10 WasC 97225 595 F6
NE Moonridge Rd
1000 ClkC 98671 540 J5
NE Moon Rise Dr
1000 HBRO 97124 593 D2
SW Moonshadow Ct
6500 WasC 97223 625 H7
NW Moon Valley Ter
4300 WasC 97006 594 G1
N Moore Av
10900 PTLD 97217 566 G1
NE Moore Ct
5500 HBRO 97124 593 J4
SE Moore Ln
19000 CmsC 97022 689 F4
NE Moore Rd
34500 ClbC 97056 444 G4
34500 SPSE 97056 444 G4
S Moore Rd
16000 CmsC 97045 718 A6
SW Moore St
18100 WasC 97006 594 F7
SE Moores St
2100 MWKE 97202 626 J7
2300 MWKE 97222 626 J7
SW Moraine Ct
15200 BRTN 97007 654 H1
SW Moratoc Dr
10100 TLTN 97062 685 D6
10200 WasC 97062 685 D6

SW Morback Ct
14800 SRWD 97140 714 H1
NE Morcroft Rd
32900 ClkC 98629 417 E1
S Morel Dr
15300 CmsC 97045 687 H6
SW Morel Ln
48000 WasC 97116 591 C6
SE Moreland Ln
2900 PTLD 97202 627 A5
NW Moreland Rd
20000 MthC 97133 504 A5
20000 MthC 97231 504 A5
24500 WasC 97133 533 G1
NW Moresby Ct
15100 WasC 97229 564 H5
NW Moretti Ter
4500 WasC 97229 595 B1
SW Morey Ct
10800 WNVL 97070 745 C2
NE Morgan Cir
20700 ClkC 98606 478 J2
Morgan Ct
2700 WLIN 97068 686 H4
SW Morgan Ct
12900 BRTN 97008 625 B7
28200 WNVL 97070 715 G6
SW Morgan Dr
8200 BRTN 97008 625 B7
NW Morgan Ln
1400 PTLD 97229 595 D4
1400 WasC 97229 595 D4
SE Morgan Ln
400 MCMV 97128 770 H7
8700 YmhC 97128 770 J7
SW Morgan Ln
23900 CmsC 97140 715 A2
NW Morgan Rd
19100 MthC 97231 504 D6
SE Morgan Rd
1100 VCVR 98664 537 E7
1200 VCVR 98664 567 E1
1300 HBRO 97123 623 E2
1300 WasC 97123 623 E2
SW Morgan Rd
12500 CmsC 97140 715 A2
13500 CmsC 97140 714 J2
N Morgan St
10 PTLD 97211 566 G5
3000 PTLD 97217 566 D5
NE Morgan St
10 PTLD 97211 566 G5
10 PTLD 97217 566 G5
SW Morgan St
28000 WNVL 97070 715 G6
NW Morgan Wy
- CMAS 98607 539 A5
SE Morgan Wy
700 VCVR 98664 537 E7
SW Morgan Wy
- TDLE 97060 599 F5
SW Morganfield Ter
3800 WasC 97007 624 D2
SW Morgen Ct
11100 TGRD 97223 655 C4
Moria Ct
18200 LKOW 97034 686 B2
SW Morilon Ln
30000 WasC 97113 623 B1
30000 WasC 97123 623 B1
NE Morlan Av
2500 GSHM 97030 599 D7
SE Morlan Av
100 GSHM 97080 629 C3
SE Morlan Pl
2800 GSHM 97080 629 C5
SE Morlan Wy
2500 GSHM 97080 629 C5
SW Morlock Ct
12000 BRTN 97008 655 C1
Morning Vw
- WHGL 98671 570 C6
SE Morning Wy
14700 CmsC 97015 658 C7
14800 HPYV 97015 658 D7
SE Morning Glory Ct
15400 CmsC 97015 657 F7
15400 CmsC 97267 657 F7
SW Morning Hill Ct
12600 TGRD 97223 655 B4
SW Morning Hill Dr
11700 TGRD 97223 655 A3
SW Morningside Av
28300 WNVL 97070 715 F6
Morning Sky Ct
1300 LKOW 97034 686 G1
SW Morningstar Dr
12700 TGRD 97223 655 A5
SE Morning Sun Ct
14200 CmsC 97015 658 C6
SE Morning Sun Dr
14000 CmsC 97015 658 C6
NE Morning Sun Ln
1000 HBRO 97124 593 D2
Morningview Cir
10 LKOW 97035 656 A3
NW Morning View Ct
600 MCMV 97128 770 D4
Morningview Ln
10 LKOW 97035 656 A3
Morningview Pl
10 LKOW 97035 656 A3
NW Moro Pl
3300 WasC 97006 594 F2
SW Morocco St
12500 KNGC 97224 685 B1
NE Morrelli Dr
16900 YmhC 97148 711 E1
Morrie Dr
19400 CmsC 97045 717 C5
19400 ORCY 97045 717 C5
NE Morris Ct
10200 PTLD 97220 597 H3
14300 PTLD 97230 598 D3
NE Morris Pl
15400 PTLD 97230 598 E3
Morris St
3300 NWBG 97132 713 C4
3800 YmhC 97132 713 C3
N Morris St
10 PTLD 97212 596 G2
300 PTLD 97227 596 F2
NE Morris St
10 PTLD 97212 596 G2
10 PTLD 97227 596 G2

NE Morris St
3300 PTLD 97212 597 B3
6800 PTLD 97213 597 E3
10200 PTLD 97220 597 J3
11700 PTLD 97220 598 A3
12700 PTLD 97230 598 B3
SE Morris St
5700 CmsC 97222 657 D1
Morrison Av
600 VCVR 98664 537 E5
Morrison Br
- PTLD 97204 596 F6
- PTLD 97214 596 F6
SE Morrison Ct
- PTLD 97216 597 H6
6300 PTLD 97215 597 D6
14900 PTLD 97233 598 D7
17800 GSHM 97233 598 G7
20500 GSHM 97030 599 A7
N Morrison Rd
100 VCVR 98664 537 E6
S Morrison Rd
100 VCVR 98664 537 E6
SE Morrison Rd
400 VCVR 98664 537 E7
SE Morrison St
10 PTLD 97214 596 G6
4100 PTLD 97214 597 B6
4800 PTLD 97215 597 C6
8100 PTLD 97216 597 F6
11500 PTLD 97216 598 A7
14300 PTLD 97233 598 C7
22300 GSHM 97030 599 B7
SW Morrison St
10 PTLD 97204 596 F6
1100 PTLD 97205 596 E6
2000 PTLD 97209 596 D5
9500 WasC 97225 595 E6
12600 WasC 97005 595 B6
SE Morrison Ter
20200 GSHM 97030 598 J7
20200 GSHM 97233 598 J7
NE Morrow Rd
4100 VCVR 98682 537 J2
SE Morse Ct
18100 CmsC 97267 687 B3
SW Morse Ln
18200 WasC 97006 594 E7
N Morse Rd
57700 ClbC 97053 414 H4
57900 ClbC 97051 414 J3
S Morse Rd
56700 ClbC 97053 414 H5
Morten Ln
58700 ClbC 97051 414 H2
58700 ClbC 97053 414 H2
NW Mortensen Ter
3800 WasC 97229 595 A2
Morton Rd
100 CmsC 97045 717 E1
100 ORCY 97045 717 E1
N Morton St
100 NWBG 97132 713 B7
NE Morton St
1100 PTLD 97211 566 H6
SW Mortondale Ln
15900 BRTN 97006 594 H6
SE Moscato Ct
6700 HBRO 97123 594 A7
N Moses Ln
- PTLD 97203 565 H2
S Mosier Rd
19000 CmsC 97004 748 E4
19000 CmsC 97045 748 E4
S Mosier Creek Ln
23900 CmsC 97004 748 J7
Moss Av
- ClbC 97056 474 A4
SE Moss St
3000 MWKE 97222 657 A2
SW Moss St
4800 PTLD 97219 626 A6
5000 PTLD 97219 625 J6
9300 WasC 97223 625 E6
9400 BRTN 97008 625 E6
SE Moss Hill Rd
32500 CmsC 97023 750 D4
SW Mossy Brae Rd
1900 CmsC 97068 686 C4
Mossy Meadows Av
19900 ORCY 97045 717 G6
S Mossy Rock Ct
21000 CmsC 97045 747 G1
NE Mother Joseph Pl
200 VCVR 98664 537 F6
Mt Adams Av
8900 VCVR 98664 537 F7
NW Mt Adams Av
- PTLD 97231 565 D3
SW Mt Adams Dr
3500 PTLD 97239 626 C2
10300 BRTN 97007 654 G1
10300 WasC 97007 654 G1
Mount Adams Lp
- PTLD 97266 628 A7
Mountain Cir
10 LKOW 97035 656 B5
E Mountain Dr
70100 CmsC 97049 724 E3
SW Mountain Ln
2900 CmsC 97068 686 B7
2900 CmsC 97068 716 B1
Mountain Mdws
- TDLE 97060 599 F6
SW Mountain Rd
3500 CmsC 97062 686 A7
3500 CmsC 97068 686 B7
22800 CmsC 97068 716 C7
29400 CmsC 97068 746 C1
S Mountain Ter
23800 CmsC 97004 749 D7
SW Mountain Ter
- PTLD 97205 596 B6
Mountain Vw
- NWBG 97132 713 E7
- YmhC 97132 713 E7
SW Mountain Wy
33300 SPSE 97056 474 D2
E Mountain Air Dr
65500 CmsC 97067 723 J2
65500 CmsC 97011 723 J1
66100 CmsC 97011 724 A2
E Mountain Country Ln
20500 CmsC 97011 693 F6

E Mountain Creek Cir
21300 CmsC 97049 693 H7
SW Mountain Creek Rd
22400 WasC 97140 683 J3
NW Mountaindale Rd
32500 NPNS 97133 533 A7
32500 WasC 97133 532 E6
32500 WasC 97133 533 A7
33600 WasC 97106 532 E6
37500 WasC 97113 532 D7
SE Mountain Gate Rd
12900 HPYV 97236 658 B3
NE Mountain Home Rd
16000 WasC 97140 713 H2
16000 YmhC 97132 713 H2
SW Mountain Home Rd
17600 WasC 97123 683 G2
17600 WasC 97132 683 H6
17600 WasC 97140 683 H6
22500 WasC 97140 713 H1
E Mountain Meadow Ln
64800 CmsC 97049 693 H7
S Mountain Meadow Rd
21100 CmsC 97004 748 C2
E Mountain Quail Ct
65000 CmsC 97011 723 H1
SW Mountain Ridge Ct
13400 TGRD 97224 655 A5
Mountainside Ter
4000 LKOW 97035 656 A4
SE Mountain Sun Dr
11700 CmsC 97015 657 J7
11900 CmsC 97015 658 A6
SE Mountain Sun Ln
12400 CmsC 97015 658 A6
NE Mountain Top Rd
22300 YmhC 97132 683 B7
24300 WasC 97132 713 D1
29800 YmhC 97140 713 G3
Mountain View Ct
2100 WLIN 97068 686 G3
E Mountainview Ct
300 NWBG 97132 713 C5
NE Mountain View Ct
22700 ClkC 98642 446 H4
Mountain View Dr
1200 FTGV 97116 592 C6
1300 WasC 97113 592 C6
32700 ClbC 97056 474 D2
Mountainview Dr
- NWBG 97132 713 B5
E Mountain View Dr
28000 CmsC 97067 724 D7
E Mountainview Dr
1600 NWBG 97132 713 D5
1600 YmhC 97132 713 D5
SE Mountain View Dr
1800 PTLD 97215 597 E7
W Mountainview Dr
- NWBG 97132 713 B5
- YmhC 97132 713 B5
Mountain View Ln
10 LKOW 97035 655 J3
900 MOLA 97038 807 C7
1700 FTGV 97116 592 C5
59300 ClbC 97051 414 H1
59300 STHN 97051 414 H1
SE Mountain View Ln
400 CmsC 97023 750 C4
400 ECDA 97023 750 C4
13500 CmsC 97015 658 B5
13500 CmsC 97236 658 B5
SW Mountain View Ln
9000 TGRD 97224 655 E6
Mountain View Rd
51400 ClbC 97056 474 B2
52500 ClbC 97056 444 A7
NW Mountain View Rd
- MthC 97231 535 C6
- PTLD 97231 535 C6
- PTLD 97231 565 C4
NW Mountainview Rd
12500 MthC 97231 535 C6
12500 PTLD 97231 535 C6
Mountain View St
400 ORCY 97045 717 C2
SE Mountain View Ter
10 MCMV 97128 770 J6
10 YmhC 97128 770 J6
NW Mountain View Park Rd
- MthC 97210 595 J4
- MthC 97210 596 A4
- PTLD 97210 596 A4
E Mountain Vista Ct
65000 CmsC 97011 723 H1
Mt Baker Av
8800 VCVR 98664 537 F6
Mt Hood Av
400 ORCY 97045 717 D2
NE Mt Hood Av
- PTLD 97220 567 H5
Mt Hood Ct
200 CNBY 97013 776 D1
Mount Hood Dr
- PTLD 97266 628 A7
SE Mt Hood Dr
8900 VCVR 98664 567 F1
SW Mt Hood Dr
17000 WasC 97007 654 G2
Mt Hood Hwy
- CmsC 97009 659 H1
- CmsC 97009 660 A4
- CmsC 97009 690 E1
- CmsC 97011 693 F7
- CmsC 97011 723 J2
- CmsC 97011 724 A2
- CmsC 97049 724 F5
- CmsC 97055 690 H2
- CmsC 97055 693 B6
- CmsC 97067 723 H1
- CmsC 97067 724 A2
- DAMA 97009 659 G1
- GSHM 97080 629 E4
- MthC 97080 629 F6
- MthC 97080 659 G1
- SNDY 97055 690 G2
41600 CmsC 97055 691 B4
41600 SNDY 97055 691 B4
47300 CmsC 97055 692 D7
Mt Hood Hwy US-26
- CmsC 97009 659 H1
- CmsC 97009 660 A4
- CmsC 97009 690 E1
- CmsC 97011 693 F7
- CmsC 97011 723 J2

Mt Hood Hwy US-26
- CmsC 97011 724 A2
- CmsC 97049 724 F5
- CmsC 97055 690 H2
- CmsC 97055 693 B6
- CmsC 97067 723 H1
- CmsC 97067 724 A2
- DAMA 97009 659 G1
- GSHM 97080 629 E4
- MthC 97080 629 F6
- MthC 97080 659 G1
- SNDY 97055 690 G2
41600 SNDY 97055 691 B4
42800 CmsC 97055 691 E6
47300 CmsC 97055 692 D7
SW Mt Hood Ln
1800 PTLD 97239 626 D2
Mt Hood Ter
21600 WLIN 97068 687 B6
S Mt Hope Rd
11700 CmsC 97038 837 A4
Mt Jefferson Av
8800 VCVR 98664 537 G7
NW Mt Jefferson Av
- PTLD 97231 565 D3
Mt Jefferson Ter
10 LKOW 97035 656 B4
NW Mt Lake Wy
7100 ClkC 98665 506 F5
Mt Lassen Av
8900 VCVR 98664 537 F7
Mt McKinley Av
1100 VCVR 98664 537 F7
SE Mt Norway Dr
35700 ClkC 98671 540 F7
35700 ClkC 98671 570 G1
Mt Olympus Av
8400 VCVR 98664 537 F7
Mt Rainier Dr
8700 VCVR 98664 537 F7
SE Mt Rainier Dr
8600 VCVR 98664 537 F7
SE Mt Royale Ct
15000 CmsC 97267 657 C7
SE Mt Scott Blvd
9400 PTLD 97266 627 H7
10300 MthC 97266 627 H7
11600 CmsC 97236 627 J7
11600 PTLD 97236 627 J7
11800 CmsC 97236 658 A1
11800 HPYV 97236 658 A1
11800 PTLD 97236 658 A1
Mt Shasta Dr
300 VCVR 98664 537 G7
Mt Shuksan Av
8400 VCVR 98664 537 F6
NE Mt St Helens Av
- PTLD 97220 567 H6
Mt Stuart Av
8400 VCVR 98664 537 F7
Mt Thielsen Av
8400 VCVR 98664 537 F6
NW Mt View Av
- PTLD 97231 565 D1
NE Mountview St
8700 VCVR 98664 537 F5
SE Mt Whitney Dr
1100 VCVR 98664 537 F7
SW Mourning Dove Pl
10900 BRTN 97007 654 H2
E Mowich Ln
24000 CmsC 97067 724 B3
Mowitza Wy
- MthC 97231 535 A5
Moxie Ln
- CmsC 97055 720 J2
Mozarteum Ct
10 LKOW 97035 656 B4
NE Mueke Rd
14500 CmsC 97002 745 F5
Mueleck Dr
59600 ClbC 97051 384 H7
59600 STHN 97051 384 H7
SW Mueller Dr
4400 WasC 97007 624 H3
S Mueller Rd
13500 CmsC 97045 747 F4
NW Muirfield Ct
900 BRTN 97006 594 G4
SW Muirfield St
18500 WasC 97006 624 E1
SW Muirwood Dr
10700 WasC 97225 595 D7
SE Mulberry Av
1700 PTLD 97214 596 H7
Mulberry Ct
19200 ORCY 97045 717 A4
SE Mulberry Ct
1800 MCMV 97128 770 H7
SE Mulberry Dr
1900 CmsC 97267 686 J1
SW Muledeer Dr
8600 WasC 97007 624 G7
Mulholland Dr
4900 LKOW 97035 655 J4
4900 LKOW 97035 656 C5
S Mulino Rd
10000 CmsC 97013 776 F1
11500 CmsC 97013 777 A3
12200 CmsC 97042 777 B4
23200 CmsC 97013 746 F7
23200 CNBY 97013 746 F6
SE Mullan St
4900 MWKE 97222 657 C2
Mullen Ln NE
4100 MrnC 97137 773 B3
NW Mullerleile Rd
21000 WasC 97124 564 C1
NE Mulligan Ct
14500 CmsC 97002 745 E4
Mulligan Ln
- LKOW 97034 656 E6
Multnomah Av
3200 VCVR 98661 537 A6
E Multnomah Av
23600 CmsC 97011 724 A3
23600 CmsC 97067 724 A3
SW Multnomah Blvd
2100 PTLD 97219 626 B6
5000 PTLD 97219 625 H6
6400 PTLD 97223 625 H6
NE Multnomah Ct
19100 GSHM 97230 598 H5
SE Multnomah Ct
13200 HPYV 97236 658 B1

NE Multnomah Dr
1200 FRVW 97024 599 B5
17500 GSHM 97230 598 G5
N Multnomah St
- PTLD 97227 596 F5
- PTLD 97232 596 G5
NE Multnomah St
- PTLD 97227 596 G4
100 PTLD 97232 596 H4
3300 PTLD 97232 597 A4
6000 PTLD 97213 597 D4
9700 PTLD 97220 597 H4
11400 PTLD 97220 598 A4
12200 PTLD 97230 598 A5
19600 GSHM 97230 598 J5
NE Multnomah Ter
16600 GSHM 97230 598 F5
Munger Dr
2400 WLIN 97068 687 A4
SW Munger Ln
22200 WasC 97140 654 A7
NW Munson Rd
- MthC 97124 533 J2
SW Murdock Ct
10700 TGRD 97224 655 C6
SW Murdock Ln
10600 TGRD 97224 655 C6
SW Murdock Pl
10700 TGRD 97224 655 D6
SW Murdock Rd
22000 SRWD 97140 684 J7
23000 SRWD 97140 714 J1
23000 WasC 97140 714 H1
NW Murdock St
9000 PTLD 97229 595 E2
SW Murdock St
8300 TGRD 97224 655 F6
NW Murlea Dr
9700 WasC 97229 595 E5
NW Murlea Ln
9400 WasC 97229 595 E5
SE Murphy Ct
8300 CmsC 97015 657 F7
8300 CmsC 97267 657 F7
SW Murphy Ct
19100 WasC 97007 624 D4
SW Murphy Ln
11800 BRTN 97008 625 C7
20600 WasC 97007 624 B4
SW Murphy St
19600 WasC 97007 624 D4
SW Murray Blvd
10 WasC 97005 595 A6
10 WasC 97229 595 A5
900 WasC 97006 595 A6
1400 WasC 97005 594 J7
3000 BRTN 97005 624 J5
3000 WasC 97005 624 J1
3300 BRTN 97006 624 J5
3600 BRTN 97007 624 J5
5800 BRTN 97008 624 J4
9000 BRTN 97007 654 J3
9000 BRTN 97008 654 J3
Murray Ct
4800 VCVR 98661 537 C4
Murray Ln NE
13100 MrnC 97002 775 D3
SW Murray Ln
- PTLD 97201 596 C6
- PTLD 97205 596 C6
NW Murray Rd
100 WasC 97005 595 A5
100 WasC 97229 595 A5
600 BRTN 97229 595 A5
SW Murray St
- PTLD 97201 596 C6
- PTLD 97205 596 C6
7500 WNVL 97070 715 F5
Murray Crest
- BRTN 97005 624 J4
- BRTN 97007 624 J4
SW Murray Scholls Dr
- BRTN 97008 654 J2
14800 BRTN 97007 654 H3
SW Murray Scholls Pl
11100 BRTN 97007 654 J2
Murray Woods
- BRTN 97005 624 J4
- BRTN 97007 624 J4
SW Murre Ter
11700 BRTN 97007 654 E3
SW Murrelet Dr
15700 BRTN 97007 654 H4
Murton St
1600 VCVR 98661 537 A4
Murwood Ct
15700 LKOW 97035 656 B7
SE Music Camp Rd
42700 CmsC 97055 691 D7
Mustang Ct
2400 WLIN 97068 686 H5
SE Mustang Ln
21100 CmsC 97055 691 F7
NW Mustang Ter
5500 WasC 97229 564 H7
SE Mutch Rd
- MthC 97060 599 J7
SW Myers Dr
2500 GSHM 97080 628 J5
SW Myers Pl
1800 GSHM 97080 628 J4
Myra Ct
18200 SNDY 97055 690 H4
SE Myra Ln
15100 CmsC 97015 658 B7
SW Myrica Ct
16300 SRWD 97140 714 G1
SW Myrtle Av
900 GSHM 97030 628 H4
900 GSHM 97080 628 H4
16000 WasC 97224 684 J1
SE Myrtle Ct
18700 DAMA 97009 658 H6
SW Myrtle Ct
900 MCMV 97128 770 E6
1100 PTLD 97201 596 B7
SW Myrtle Dr
1000 PTLD 97201 596 D7
1000 PTLD 97201 626 D1
Myrtle St
200 ORCY 97045 717 D2
SE Myrtle St
- MWKE 97222 657 A2
33500 SPSE 97056 474 F1

SW Myrtle St
1100 DNDE 97115 742 H4
1300 YmhC 97115 742 H4
1500 PTLD 97201 596 D7
Myrtle Crest
- STHN 97051 385 C5
SE Myrtlewood Av
1100 GSHM 97080 629 D4
Myrtlewood Ct
200 NWBG 97132 713 C4
W Myrtlewood Dr
300 NWBG 97132 713 B4
300 YmhC 97132 713 B4
SE Myrtlewood Pl
600 GSHM 97080 629 D3
SE Myrtlewood Wy
2600 GSHM 97080 629 D5
SW Myslony St
11500 TLTN 97062 685 B4
SE Mystery Springs Ct
11000 CmsC 97015 657 J6
NE Mystic Ct
33800 ClkC 98675 419 E1
33800 YCLT 98675 419 E1
NE Mystic Dr
32800 ClkC 98675 419 D2
NW Mystic Dr
49900 WasC 97116 561 A4
SE Myway Ct
16200 CmsC 97267 687 B1

N

N Dr
- ClkC 98671 570 E4
N St
- ClkC 98671 570 E4
- WHGL 98671 570 E4
2900 VCVR 98663 536 H3
N N St
2600 WHGL 98671 570 B4
SW Nacira Ln
9600 TGRD 97223 655 E3
SW Nacira Pl
11600 TGRD 97223 655 E3
SW Nadina Ct
12000 BRTN 97005 625 C4
SE Naef Ct
15800 CmsC 97267 657 C7
SE Naef Rd
4800 CmsC 97267 657 C7
4800 CmsC 97267 687 B1
SE Naegeli Ct
4200 PTLD 97236 628 F3
SE Naegeli Dr
16600 PTLD 97236 628 F3
SW Naeve St
10400 TGRD 97224 655 C7
SW Nafus Ln
16600 WasC 97007 624 G7
SW Nahcotta Dr
13200 TGRD 97223 654 J5
NW Nahcotta St
2600 CMAS 98607 569 A2
NW Naito Pkwy
10 PTLD 97204 596 F5
10 PTLD 97209 596 F4
SW Naito Pkwy
- PTLD 97239 626 F2
10 PTLD 97204 596 F6
10 PTLD 97209 596 F5
1500 PTLD 97201 596 F7
1800 PTLD 97201 626 F1
SW Naito Pkwy SR-10
- PTLD 97239 626 F2
2600 PTLD 97201 626 F1
SW Naito Pkwy SR-99W
- PTLD 97239 626 F2
2400 PTLD 97201 626 F1
Namitz Ct
- DNDE 97115 742 H3
Nampa Ct
1200 VCVR 98661 537 C5
SW Nancy Av
200 GSHM 97030 628 G3
SW Nancy Cir
200 GSHM 97030 628 G3
SE Nancy Ct
9900 CmsC 97236 657 H2
SW Nancy Ct
600 GSHM 97030 628 G3
1300 GSHM 97080 628 G4
SW Nancy Dr
1500 GSHM 97080 628 G5
Nancy Ln
- CmsC 97055 691 B1
SW Nancy Ln
20000 WasC 97007 624 C7
NW Nancy Pl
100 GSHM 97030 628 G2
SW Nancy Pl
2200 GSHM 97080 628 G5
SE Nancy Rd
1000 VCVR 98664 537 J7
1000 VCVR 98664 567 J1
Nancy Marie Ln
18700 CmsC 97045 717 G3
Nansen Smt
10 LKOW 97035 656 A3
SW Nantucket Ln
20600 WasC 97006 594 C6
NE Naomi Ct
900 HBRO 97124 593 D2
SE Naomi Ct
22900 DAMA 97009 659 C7
SE Naomi Dr
22200 DAMA 97009 659 B7
NW Naomi Ln
12500 MthC 97229 565 B7
SE Naomi Wy
700 MCMV 97128 770 H6
SW Napa Ct
6800 TLTN 97062 685 G4
SW Napa Dr
6900 TLTN 97062 685 G4
E Naples Ct
1200 LCTR 98629 386 H7
SW Naples Ct
20700 WasC 97007 624 C3
Naples St
19400 CmsC 97045 717 E5
19400 ORCY 97045 717 E5
SW Naples St
20400 WasC 97007 624 C3

Each entry below lists: Block — City — ZIP — Map# — Grid

SW Napoleon Cir
1300 TDLE 97060 599 E5
SW Napoleon Pl
1200 TDLE 97060 599 E5
Napoleon Ct
- MrnC 97137 744 A7
Narain Ct
100 ORCY 97045 717 C2
Narrow Ln
32100 ClbC 97056 444 B4
NW Narup Rd
47500 WasC 97106 531 C4
SE Nase Ct
3500 MWKE 97222 657 A4
SE Nash Ct
2300 TDLE 97060 599 H6
N Nashton St
6800 PTLD 97203 566 A3
6800 PTLD 97203 566 A3
N Nashville Wy
100 VCVR 98664 537 E6
S Nashville Wy
100 VCVR 98664 537 E6
Natalie Ct
200 NWBG 97132 713 C4
NE Natalie St
200 HBRO 97124 594 B5
200 HBRO 97124 594 B5
SE Natalya St
14600 CmsC 97236 658 D5
14600 HPYV 97236 658 D5
SW Natchez Ct
4500 TLTN 97062 686 A4
SW Natchez St
5300 TLTN 97062 685 H4
NE Nates Rhodes
27400 ClkC 98675 419 H1
SE Nathan Ct
6300 HBRO 97123 594 A6
12700 CmsC 97015 658 A5
Nathan Dr
400 NWBG 97132 713 C6
Nathan Ln
20300 FRVW 97024 599 A2
SE Nature Wy
27400 687 C2
SE Nautilus Dr
16400 VCVR 98683 538 E7
Navaho Dr
- WasC 97005 590 J7
- WasC 97005 624 J2
SW Navajo Ct
4800 TLTN 97062 685 J5
SW Navajo Ter
28000 WNVL 97070 715 E5
Navajo Wy
10600 CmsC 97045 716 H5
SW Nazaneen Dr
17300 BRTN 97006 594 F5
17300 WasC 97006 594 F5
SE Nazomi Av
1000 HBRO 97123 593 D6
NW Neakahnie Av
4900 WasC 97229 564 D7
5400 WasC 97231 564 D7
Neals Ct
3000 VCVR 98661 537 A3
Neals Ln
2100 VCVR 98661 537 A3
SW Nebraska St
3000 PTLD 97239 626 B5
5000 PTLD 97221 626 A5
5000 PTLD 97221 626 A5
NW Necanicum Wy
5800 WasC 97229 564 C6
SE Neck Rd
700 DAYT 97114 772 B4
700 YmhC 97114 772 B4
S Nectarine St
100 CNLS 97113 592 D6
SE Needham Ct
6300 WasC 97222 657 D1
SE Needham St
6300 WasC 97222 657 D1
Neff Park Ln
5500 WasC 97035 685 J1
5500 WasC 97035 685 J1
SE Nehalem Ct
14200 CmsC 97236 628 C7
SW Nehalem Ct
4000 713 E6
31000 WNVL 97070 745 E1
SW Nehalem St
6300 BRTN 97007 624 J5
SE Nehalem St
- MthC 97236 628 E7
- PTLD 97202 626 H6
500 PTLD 97202 626 H6
3600 PTLD 97206 627 B6
3900 PTLD 97206 627 B6
SE Nehemiah Ln
- MCMV 97128 771 A6
1700 MCMV 97128 770 J6
1700 YmhC 97128 770 J6
S Neibur Rd
15300 CmsC 97045 688 A7
15300 CmsC 97045 717 H1
S Neil Rd
19200 CmsC 97023 719 B5
Neil St
20200 STPL 97137 773 B5
Neill Rd
- WasC 97132 683 G6
- WasC 97140 683 G6
SW Neill Rd
24500 WasC 97140 683 G6
25600 WasC 97132 683 G6
26700 WasC 97132 713 E1
NW Nela Rd
2700 PTLD 97210 596 C2
Nelco St
5100 WLIN 97068 687 A6
Nelco St
5100 WLIN 97068 687 A6
SE Nella Wy
12000 CmsC 97236 658 A4
12000 HPYV 97236 658 A4
NE Nelly St
7200 HBRO 97124 594 B5
7300 WasC 97124 594 B5
NW Nels Ct
17600 SRWD 97140 684 E5

NW Nelscott St
18500 WasC 97229 594 E2
Nelson Ct
1400 LKOW 97034 656 D7
Nelson Ln
- ClbC 97051 414 J4
- ClbC 97053 414 J4
100 GLDS 97027 687 D3
S Nelson St
19300 CmsC 97045 717 J5
NE Nelson Rd
15700 YmhC 97132 712 F2
SW Nelson St
10700 TLTN 97062 685 C7
SW Nemarnik Dr
14500 WasC 97224 654 H6
SW Neptune Ct
7400 BRTN 97007 624 H6
SW Neptune Pl
15500 BRTN 97007 624 J1
SW Neptune Ter
7400 BRTN 97007 624 J1
NW Neskowin Av
4500 WasC 97229 564 D7
4500 WasC 97229 594 C1
NW Neskowin Pl
4700 WasC 97229 564 D7
N Nesmith Av
2100 PTLD 97227 596 E3
S Nestle Ln
17800 CmsC 97045 718 D2
SW Nestucca Ct
8400 TLTN 97062 685 F5
NW Nestucca Dr
19800 WasC 97229 564 D7
19900 WasC 97229 594 D1
SW Netarts Ct
6900 BRTN 97007 624 G5
SW Netarts Pl
16800 BRTN 97007 624 G5
Nettie Connett Dr
37900 SNDY 97055 690 H3
Nettie Connett St
37900 SNDY 97055 690 H3
SW Nettle Pl
20700 SRWD 97140 684 F5
Netzel St
900 ORCY 97045 717 A3
NE Neumann Ln
9200 YmhC 97132 743 G2
SW Nevada Ct
4500 PTLD 97219 626 A5
6000 PTLD 97219 625 H5
SW Nevada St
300 CMAS 98607 569 F4
SW Nevada St
300 PTLD 97219 626 E5
SW Nevada Ter
7000 PTLD 97219 626 D5
Neville Av
2100 FTGV 97116 591 J2
Nevin Ct
19700 ORCY 97045 717 D6
New Cir
- SNDY 97055 690 G2
SE New Rd
32300 CmsC 97022 720 C1
Newall Rd
- NWBG 97132 713 F6
N Newark St
3600 PTLD 97217 566 C3
4500 PTLD 97203 566 B3
Newberg Hwy
2400 HBRO 97123 593 B7
2400 WasC 97123 623 B1
2400 WasC 97123 593 B7
2400 WasC 97123 623 B1
2500 WasC 97113 623 B3
Newberg Hwy SR-219
2400 HBRO 97123 593 B7
2400 WasC 97123 623 B1
2400 WasC 97123 593 B7
2400 WasC 97123 623 B1
2500 WasC 97113 623 B3
Newberg Ln
35900 SNDY 97055 690 G2
Newberg Vil
- NWBG 713 E6
NW Newberry Rd
12900 MthC 97231 535 A7
12900 MthC 97231 535 A7
15000 PTLD 97231 564 J1
15000 PTLD 97231 565 A1
Newberry Wy
19600 CmsC 97045 717 C5
SW Newbury Ct
8100 WasC 97007 624 C6
SW Newbury St
- PTLD 97239 626 E4
Newby St
- MCMV 97128 770 J2
- YmhC 97128 770 J1
NE Newby St
2700 MCMV 97128 770 J3
SW Newby Ter
3200 PTLD 97239 626 B2
N Newcastle Av
6500 PTLD 97217 566 E6
Newcastle Dr
5900 LKOW 97035 655 H5
SW Newcastle Dr
19900 WasC 97007 624 C4
SW Newcastle Pl
20300 WasC 97007 624 B4
N Newell Av
7100 PTLD 97203 565 J4
7500 PTLD 97203 566 A4
Newell Crest Dr
18000 ORCY 97045 717 E2
Newell Ridge Dr
18000 ORCY 97045 717 E2
S New Era Rd
10000 CmsC 97013 746 G3
10000 CmsC 97045 746 J2
11500 CmsC 97045 747 A2
SW New Forest Dr
9400 BRTN 97008 655 A1
NW New Hope Ct
1900 PTLD 97229 595 E3
NE Newhouse Rd
100 ClkC 98663 536 G1
100 VCVR 98663 536 G1

S Newkirchner Rd
24000 CmsC 97045 777 J1
24000 CmsC 97045 777 J1
25000 CmsC 97004 777 H3
25000 CmsC 97045 777 H3
New Kirk Rd
31100 ClbC 97056 444 A3
Newland Rd
- CmsC 97062 686 A7
SW Newland Rd
22400 CmsC 97062 686 A7
22400 CmsC 97070 716 A1
24700 CmsC 97070 716 A3
25600 CmsC 97068 716 A4
N Newman Av
8900 PTLD 97203 566 B3
New Mexico St
5200 CmsC 97045 537 C6
SW New Plymouth Ln
15100 BRTN 97007 624 H4
SW Newport Pl
16300 BRTN 97007 624 G5
NE Newport St
- PTLD 97230 598 D4
NW Newstead Ter
- HBRO 97006 594 D5
SW Newton Pl
7000 WasC 97225 625 G3
NW Newton Rd
- PTLD 97231 565 C3
Newton St
- CmsC 97045 691 A4
- SNDY 97055 690 J5
39200 CmsC 97055 691 A4
N New York Av
9000 PTLD 97203 565 H2
SW Nez Perce Ct
9300 TLTN 97062 685 E5
NF-9
- CmsC 97049 724 G5
NF-10
- CmsC 97049 724 G6
NF-12
- CmsC 97049 693 F2
NF-13
- CmsC 97049 724 G5
NF-14
16900 WasC 97123 683 C4
19300 WasC 97132 683 C4
NF-15
- CmsC 97049 724 G6
NF-20
- CmsC 97049 724 H6
NF-20C
- CmsC 97049 724 H6
NF-20D
- CmsC 97049 724 H7
NF-1200-500
- CmsC 97011 693 H4
NF-1401
- CmsC 97011 693 E2
- CmsC 97055 693 E2
NF-2503
- CmsC 97055 692 E1
- CmsC 97055 693 A2
NF-3626
- CmsC 97055 723 B7
SE Nia Dr
14900 HPYV 97236 658 D4
NW Niblick Pl
4100 WasC 97229 594 H1
Nicholas Ct
19900 WLIN 97068 686 G4
SW Nicholas St
21400 HBRO 97124 594 B4
SE Nicholas St
14000 CmsC 97009 660 E6
Nicholas Wy
100 WasC 97132 713 B6
100 YmhC 97132 713 B6
SW Nicholas View Dr
- WasC 97140 714 A5
Nichols Ln
1100 FTGV 97116 591 G3
1100 WasC 97116 591 G3
SE Nichols Hill Rd
38000 ClkC 98671 570 J7
NE Nicholson Lp
- VCVR 98661 537 B2
Nicholson Rd
3300 VCVR 98661 537 B3
NW Nichwana Ct
5200 WasC 97229 564 C7
NW Nick Wy
- HBRO 97006 594 C4
SE Nickel Rd
35600 CmsC 97022 720 F2
NE Nicki Ct
2400 HBRO 97124 593 C2
SE Nicklaus Ct
- WLIN 97068 686 J7
E Nicklaus Wy
67900 CmsC 97067 724 F5
S Nicks Pl
17700 CmsC 97045 748 C1
SW Nicol Rd
5500 BRTN 97225 625 E4
5500 WasC 97225 625 E4
5800 BRTN 97223 625 E4
5800 WasC 97223 625 E4
NW Nicolai St
2100 PTLD 97210 596 C3
Nicole Ct
800 WLIN 97068 716 F1
Nicole Dr
- YmhC 97128 770 E7
700 WLIN 97068 716 F1
SE Nicole Ln
10000 HPYV 97236 657 H2
NE Nicole Pl
- PTLD 97210 598 A1
SW Nicoli St
11600 KNGC 97224 655 C6
11600 TGRD 97224 655 C6
SW Nicota Ct
20500 WasC 97006 594 E5
NE Niederberger Rd
18700 YmhC 97115 742 F4
20700 DNDE 97115 742 G4

SW Niederberger Rd
200 DNDE 97115 742 G4
200 YmhC 97115 742 G4
SE Nielson Rd
30900 WasC 97060 600 B7
SW Nierman Ln
10800 TLTN 97062 685 C6
SW Nighthawk Dr
15600 BRTN 97007 654 G3
SW Night Heron Ln
12500 BRTN 97007 654 G4
SE Night Heron Pl
1900 GSHM 97080 629 H5
SE Night Heron Ln
1500 GSHM 97080 629 H4
SW Nightingale Ct
15300 BRTN 97007 654 H2
NW Nightshade Ct
14900 WasC 97229 564 J6
NW Nightshade St
5800 CMAS 98607 539 A6
Nike Dr
26900 WNVL 97070 715 D4
Nikki Crystal Dr
54000 ClbC 97056 444 D4
SW Niklas Ln
11900 WasC 97236 657 J4
SW Nik's Dr
- WasC 97006 624 E1
SW Nimbus Av
7600 BRTN 97008 625 D7
9000 BRTN 97008 655 C1
9900 TGRD 97223 655 C1
Nimbus Ct
- MCMV 97128 771 D7
SE Nimbus Lp
- MCMV 97128 771 E6
Nimitz Ct
100 STHN 97051 385 A7
SW Nipa Ct
7500 WasC 97223 655 G1
SW Nisqually Ct
8700 TLTN 97062 685 E5
NW Nitchman Rd
14600 WasC 97133 533 D4
Nixon Av
18300 WLIN 97068 686 J1
18300 WLIN 97068 687 A3
SE Nixon Ct
3400 MCMV 97128 771 E6
SW Noah Ln
- WasC 97007 624 A3
S Nobel Rd
13200 ORCY 97045 717 D6
13200 ORCY 97045 717 D6
Nob Hill Dr
- ClbC 97056 474 B5
- VCVR 98683 537 A5
Noble Ct
- STHN 97051 414 H2
N Noble Ct
200 YCLT 98675 419 F1
1000 CNBY 97013 746 D5
Noble Dr
16500 ORCY 97045 687 F6
Noble Ln
20300 CmsC 97068 686 H6
20300 WLIN 97068 686 H6
SE Noble Ln
14900 YmhC 97128 770 J7
Noble Rd
- ClbC 97051 414 H2
- ClbC 97053 414 H2
- STHN 97051 414 H2
N Noble St
1300 CNBY 97013 746 D5
NE Noble St
15500 VCVR 98682 538 E1
SW Noble St
22700 WasC 97007 624 A3
SW Noble Fir Ct
17200 SRWD 97140 684 F6
Noblewood Av
12900 CmsC 97045 717 C6
SW Nodaway Ln
24000 CmsC 97062 715 J2
24000 CmsC 97070 715 J2
NW Noelle Wy
12700 WasC 97229 595 B4
NW Noell Rd
- HBRO 97006 594 B5
Nokomis Ct
6200 CmsC 97035 685 H3
Nokora
- CmsC 97015 657 H7
Nola Ct
16100 LKOW 97035 656 A7
Nolan Ct
2000 WLIN 97068 716 H6
NW Nolana Ct
- HBRO 97006 594 C4
SE Noland St
3800 HBRO 97123 623 D2
4200 HBRO 97123 623 D2
Nomie Wy
3200 WLIN 97068 686 J7
Nonie Ct
20900 CmsC 97045 747 F1
SW Nootka St
11200 WasC 97140 715 C1
SW Nora Rd
15400 BRTN 97007 654 H1
15800 WasC 97007 654 H1
SE Norbert Dr
6900 CmsC 97222 657 E2
SW Nordic Dr
- WasC 97007 625 E7
SE Nordlund Ct
2100 HBRO 97123 594 A1
2100 HBRO 97123 624 A1
SW Norelius Wy
2600 VCVR 98683 568 C2
NW Norfolk Ct
1900 PTLD 97229 595 F3
SW Norfolk Ln
8400 TGRD 97224 655 H6
Norfolk St
3800 WLIN 97068 717 A1
13600 TGRD 97223 655 A4
SE Norma Cir
15300 CmsC 97267 657 D2
SE Norma Rd
15700 CmsC 97267 657 D2

NW Norman Av
2200 GSHM 97030 629 B2
2200 GSHM 97030 629 B3
SW Norman Ct
700 GSHM 97080 629 B3
S Norman Ct
18100 CmsC 97045 718 E3
SW Normandy Dr
- WNVL 97070 745 H3
SE Normandy Dr
12700 CmsC 97015 658 B6
SW Normandy Ln
- WNVL 97070 715 H7
SW Normandy Pl
4800 BRTN 97005 624 J3
Norris Ct
100 DAYT 97114 772 B5
SW Norris Ct
200 MCMV 97128 770 F5
Norris Rd
3000 VCVR 98661 537 A3
SW Norris St
200 MCMV 97128 770 G4
SW Norse Ln
4500 BRTN 97225 625 F3
4500 WasC 97225 625 F3
SE Norse Rd
20500 CmsC 97022 690 B6
SW Norse Hall Rd
7100 WasC 97062 685 F7
SW Norsehall Rd
6500 CmsC 97062 685 F7
NW Norstar Ranch Rd
33400 ClbC 98642 386 D7
NW North Av
30600 NPNS 97133 563 B1
30600 WasC 97133 563 B1
31600 NPNS 97133 533 A7
31600 WasC 97133 533 A7
SE North Ct
14800 DAMA 97009 658 H7
North Rd
- MthC 97231 534 F4
NE North Rd
- VCVR 98663 506 H7
52400 ClbC 97056 444 H7
52400 ClbC 97056 474 F1
52400 SPSE 97056 444 F7
52400 SPSE 97056 474 F1
NW North Dakota St
10500 TGRD 97223 655 B2
12600 BRTN 97008 655 B2
SW Northgate Av
8800 VCVR 98664 537 F6
SW Northgate Av
- PTLD 97219 656 F2
11300 MthC 97219 656 F2
SW Northgate Ct
- PTLD 97219 656 F3
SW Northgate Dr
12200 PTLD 97219 656 F3
12200 WasC 97219 656 F3
SW Northgate Rd
12200 PTLD 97219 656 F3
12200 WasC 97219 656 F3
NW North Grandview St
- PTLD 97231 565 F5
SE Northpoint Ct
9100 HPYV 97236 658 B1
SE Northridge Ct
4200 MWKE 97222 657 B4
NW Northridge Dr
100 NWBG 98642 416 A7
SE Northridge Dr
4100 MWKE 97222 657 B4
North Ring Rd
- HBRO 97123 593 J1
- HBRO 97124 594 A1
NW Northrup Rd
30000 WasC 97133 533 C2
NW Northrup St
800 PTLD 97209 596 E4
2000 PTLD 97210 596 C4
13100 WasC 97229 595 B4
SW Northshire Ln
7500 WasC 97225 625 G2
North Shore Blvd
10 LKOW 97034 656 E6
SE Northshore Cir
14800 VCVR 98683 568 C3
NW Northshore Dr
18900 WasC 97229 564 E7
SE Northshore Dr
15000 VCVR 98683 568 D3
North Shore Ests
- WHGL 98671 570 C6
Northshore Pl
1000 LKOW 97034 656 E6
SE North Star Dr
11300 HPYV 97236 658 B3
SW North Star Lp
1500 TDLE 97060 599 E5
SW North Star Wy
1900 TDLE 97060 599 E5
North Support Rd
- HBRO 97124 593 J1
NW Northumbria Ln
14800 WasC 97006 594 J3
SW Northvale Wy
- WasC 97007 625 G4
NE North Valley Rd
18500 YmhC 97132 712 H3
23700 YmhC 97132 713 H3
Northview Ct
10 LKOW 97035 656 B3
SW Northview Ct
12500 HPYV 97222 657 A4
SE Northview Dr
13600 TGRD 97223 655 A4
13600 TGRD 97223 655 A4
SE Northway Rd
6300 CmsC 97267 657 D2
Northwest View Wy
- WHGL 98671 570 A4

SW Northwood Av
4500 PTLD 97239 626 D3
SE Northwood Wy
3400 HBRO 97123 623 H1
NE Norton Wy
22600 SRWD 97140 684 H7
SW Norton Ct
2500 MCMV 97128 771 B6
S Norton Ln
200 MCMV 97128 771 B6
300 YmhC 97128 771 B7
S Norton Rd
- CmsC 97023 719 B4
- CmsC 97045 719 B4
NW Norwalk Dr
21000 MrnC 97002 775 D4
NW Norwalk Pl
2900 WasC 97006 594 G2
NW Norwich Cir
15400 WasC 97006 594 H3
NW Norwich Ct
16100 WasC 97006 594 H3
NW Norwich St
15300 WasC 97006 594 H3
NW Norwood Av
33400 ClbC 98642 386 D7
NW Norwood Cir
2800 CMAS 98607 569 C2
Norwood Rd
2500 NWBG 97132 713 E6
NW Norwood Ct
800 CMAS 98607 569 C4
SE Norwood Dr
1500 CMAS 98607 569 C5
SE Norwood Lp
11400 HPYV 97236 658 C3
NW Norwood Pl
2400 CMAS 98607 569 C3
SW Norwood Rd
6500 WasC 97062 685 E7
8900 TLTN 97062 685 E7
NW Norwood St
2600 CMAS 98607 569 D2
NE Notchlog Dr
10200 ClkC 98685 506 H3
SW Notdurft Rd
24700 WasC 97068 716 E2
NW Nottage Dr
9600 WasC 97229 595 E4
SW Nottingham Ct
22200 SRWD 97140 684 H7
Nottingham Dr
16500 GLDS 97027 687 D1
SW Nottingham Dr
3000 PTLD 97201 626 C2
3000 PTLD 97239 626 C2
Nottingham Pl
14100 LKOW 97035 655 J5
NW Notting Hill Ln
20600 HBRO 97006 594 C4
SE Nourse Rd
27600 ClkC 98607 569 G1
NE Nova Av
2500 HBRO 97124 593 B2
Nova Ct
10 LKOW 97035 655 J3
10 LKOW 97035 656 A3
1300 WLIN 97068 716 F1
SW Nova Ct
11300 TGRD 97223 655 C5
SW Novare Pl
11100 TGRD 97223 655 C5
SW Novato Ln
17300 WasC 97007 624 F4
Novella Av
59800 ClbC 97051 385 A7
SW November Ct
17400 WasC 97006 594 F6
Nugget Ln
20500 CmsC 97045 716 H7
20500 CmsC 97045 746 H1
SW Nutcracker Ct
10800 WasC 97007 654 H2
SW Nuthatch Ct
10800 WasC 97007 654 E3
SW Nutting Rd
31000 WNVL 97070 745 D1
NW Nut Tree Ln
1800 YmhC 97128 770 B2
SW Nyberg Ct
5400 TLTN 97062 685 J4
20400 CmsC 97062 685 J5
SW Nyberg Rd
6600 TLTN 97062 685 J5
SW Nymph Rd
400 ECDA 97023 750 A3
NW Nyssa Rd
3000 WasC 97006 594 G1
SW Nyssen St
3200 BRTN 97006 624 F2
3200 WasC 97006 624 F2

O

O St
2600 VCVR 98661 536 H3
2600 VCVR 98663 536 H3
N O St
1800 WHGL 98671 570 B4
Oak
- SNDY 97055 690 J5
Oak Av
- SNDY 97055 690 J5
NE Oak Av
19100 CmsC 97002 690 J4
NE Oak Cir
15700 CmsC 97013 746 D5
SE Oak Ct
3700 HBRO 97123 593 G5

SE Oak
4100 PTLD 97214 597 B6
4100 PTLD 97215 597 B6
13900 PTLD 97233 598 C6
14600 PTLD 97267 597 A6
SW Oak Ct
19800 WasC 97007 624 C4
Oak Dr
- ClbC 97056 474 B5
400 YmhC 97128 770 F2
1800 NWBG 97132 713 D7
NW Oak Dr
24300 WasC 97124 563 H6
SE Oak Dr
10600 MCMV 97128 771 F6
10600 YmhC 97114 771 F6
Oak Hvn
- ClkC 98661 507 A7
- VCVR 98663 507 A7
Oak Ln
- CmsC 97015 657 H7
Oak Ln NE
21000 MrnC 97002 775 D4
SW Oak Ln
8800 WasC 97223 625 F6
S Oak Pl
500 CNBY 97013 746 D7
S Oak Pl
900 RDGF 98642 446 A1
SW Oak Rd
400 ECDA 97023 750 A3
Oak St
200 DAYT 97114 772 A4
200 MOLA 97038 837 F1
1300 ORCY 97045 717 C1
1700 LKOW 97034 656 D7
1900 FTGV 97116 592 B4
1900 WLIN 97068 687 A2
2100 STHN 97051 415 B1
2300 WasC 97116 592 B4
Oak St NE
10600 MrnC 97002 774 F4
10600 MrnC 97020 774 F4
10800 DNLD 97020 774 G4
E Oak St
- YCLT 98675 419 G1
N Oak St
100 BRLO 97013 746 A4
100 BRLO 97013 776 A1
1000 CNBY 97013 746 D5
1800 CmsC 97013 746 D4
NE Oak St
300 CMAS 98607 569 F4
NW Oak St
8600 WasC 97229 595 F5
SE Oak St
900 DNDE 97115 742 J4
1800 PTLD 97214 596 H5
2800 HBRO 97123 593 F5
3300 PTLD 97214 597 B6
5500 PTLD 97215 597 D6
9400 PTLD 97216 598 A6
10800 MWKE 97216 657 A2
11700 PTLD 97216 598 A6
14200 PTLD 97233 598 C6
16600 GSHM 97030 599 B6
21400 GSHM 97030 599 B6
33500 SPSE 97056 474 F1
SE Oak St SR-8
100 HBRO 97123 593 C5
SW Oak St
10 HBRO 97123 593 B5
500 PTLD 97204 596 F5
500 PTLD 97205 596 F5
6500 PTLD 97223 655 H2
6500 PTLD 97223 655 H2
7100 WasC 97005 625 E4
9400 BRTN 97005 625 E4
19600 WasC 97007 624 G7
22400 SRWD 97140 684 G7
SW Oak St SR-8
100 HBRO 97123 593 A5
Oak Ter
900 LKOW 97034 656 D7
E Oak Wy
- BNKS 97106 531 J6
- WasC 97106 531 J6
NE Oak Wy
500 MCMV 97128 770 J5
NW Oak Wy
41600 BNKS 97106 531 J6
41600 BNKS 97106 532 A6
SW Oak Wy
8900 TGRD 97223 655 E2
SE Oak Acres Ct
8400 CmsC 97015 687 H2
8400 CmsC 97267 687 H2
Oak Bluff Blvd
- CmsC 97015 657 G5
NE Oakbrook Cir
10400 VCVR 98662 537 H3
NE Oakbrook Wy
- VCVR 98682 507 J1
NW Oak Creek Dr
- WasC 97229 594 G1
16500 WasC 97006 594 G1
SW Oak Creek Dr
11300 PTLD 97223 656 C2
Oak Crest
- STHN 97051 385 C5
Oakcrest Dr
3100 FTGV 97116 591 G2
3100 WasC 97116 591 G2
1800 HBRO 97123 593 E5
SW Oakenshield Ct
17200 DRHM 97224 685 E2
SE Oak Glen Ct
2800 CmsC 97267 656 J7
Oak Glen Dr
59100 STHN 97051 414 J1
SE Oak Glen Wy
- HBRO 97123 594 B6
SE Oak Grove Blvd
800 CmsC 97267 656 H6
2800 CmsC 97267 657 A6
SE Oak Grove Ct
51400 SPSE 97056 474 F2

Portland Street Index

STREET
Block City ZIP Map# Grid

S Oak Grove Rd
12200 CmsC 97013 777 B7
12200 CmsC 97013 807 A1
Oak Grove St
600 NWBG 97132 713 F7
SW Oak Hill Ln
21600 CmsC 97062 685 J7
SW Oakhill Ln
15600 TGRD 97224 655 E7
NW Oak Hills Dr
- WasC 97229 594 J3
14400 WasC 97006 594 H3
Oak Hollow Dr
600 NWBG 97132 713 F7
SE Oakhurst Ct
16300 CmsC 97267 687 C1
NE Oakhurst Dr
9800 VCVR 98662 537 H2
Oakhurst Ln
2300 LKOW 97034 686 G1
SE Oakhurst St
4200 HBRO 97123 623 G2
4200 WasC 97123 623 G2
NW Oak Island Rd
- MthC 97231 475 A7
23000 MthC 97231 504 J4
23000 MthC 97231 505 A5
Oak Knoll Ct
1200 NWBG 97132 713 D4
1800 LKOW 97034 656 C6
NW Oak Knoll Pl
2200 WasC 97006 594 G3
SE Oakland Av
4900 CmsC 97267 687 C1
5200 CmsC 97267 657 C7
SW Oakleaf Lp
- WNVL 97070 745 C1
Oak Leaf Mnr
- PTLD 97230 598 B4
Oak Leaf St
300 NWBG 97132 713 F7
NW Oakley Ct
17200 WasC 97229 564 G7
NE Oakmead Ln
31100 YmhC 97132 743 H4
Oak Meadow Ct
700 LKOW 97034 686 E1
SE Oak Meadow Ct
16500 DAMA 97009 688 E1
Oak Meadow Ln
17200 LKOW 97034 686 E1
Oak Meadow Ln NE
11000 MrnC 97002 744 G6
SW Oak Meadow Ln
15700 TGRD 97224 655 E7
Oak Meadows Lp
- NWBG 97132 713 F7
NW Oakmont Ct
900 MCMV 97128 770 F4
S Oakmont Ln
20200 CmsC 97045 688 J5
NW Oakmont Lp
15000 WasC 97006 594 J3
SW Oak Patch Ct
7800 WNVL 97070 715 F5
NW Oakpoint Wy
4400 WasC 97229 595 A1
5000 WasC 97229 565 A7
Oakridge Ct
16000 CmsC 97035 655 J7
16000 LKOW 97035 655 J7
Oakridge Dr
6500 GLDS 97027 687 D2
NW Oak Ridge Dr
2500 MCMV 97128 770 F3
NW Oakridge Dr
16600 WasC 97229 564 G7
SE Oakridge Dr
33900 ClbC 97056 474 F2
33900 SPSE 97056 474 F2
NW Oak Ridge Ln
- CMAS 98607 569 A4
Oakridge Rd
4200 LKOW 97035 656 A7
4400 CmsC 97035 656 A7
4900 CmsC 97035 655 J7
4900 LKOW 97035 655 J7
Oak Ridge St
59400 STHN 97051 414 J1
59500 STHN 97051 384 J7
59600 ClbC 97051 384 J7
NE Oaks Ln
3400 VCVR 98662 537 F2
SW Oaks Ln
9700 TGRD 97224 655 E7
NW Oak Shadow Ct
14500 WasC 97229 594 J1
SE Oak Shore Ct
1700 CmsC 97267 656 H7
SE Oak Shore Ln
1600 CmsC 97267 686 H1
1800 CmsC 97267 656 H7
SE Oaks Park Wy
- PTLD 97202 626 G6
NE Oak Springs Farm Rd
7000 YmhC 97111 741 G4
7000 YmhC 97114 741 G5
10200 YmhC 97111 711 H7
Oaktree Av
18700 ORCY 97045 717 A3
Oak Tree Ct
3100 WLIN 97068 686 H4
Oaktree Ct
18700 ORCY 97045 717 A3
SW Oaktree Ln
15300 TGRD 97224 655 E7
S Oaktree Ter
16100 ORCY 97045 687 G6
Oak Valley Dr
16100 ORCY 97045 687 G6
SW Oak Valley Ter
15100 TGRD 97224 655 A7
NE Oak View Dr
9300 VCVR 98662 537 G1
NE Oakview Dr
300 ECDA 97023 750 C3
SE Oakview Dr
33900 SPSE 97056 474 F2
Oak View Ln
- ECDA 97023 750 C4
SE Oakview Ln
22900 CmsC 97022 720 B1
SW Oakville Ct
18400 WasC 97007 624 B3

SE Oakwood Av
14200 CmsC 97267 657 D6
NW Oakwood Cir
900 MCMV 97128 770 F4
SW Oakwood Ct
2500 WasC 97006 624 F1
Oakwood Dr
100 STHN 97051 385 A7
35300 ClbC 97051 384 J7
35300 STHN 97051 384 J7
SW Oakwood Dr
6700 BRTN 97008 625 D5
SW Oakwood St
13100 WasC 97005 625 A1
NW Oatfield Ct
11900 WasC 97229 595 C3
SE Oatfield Ct
3800 CmsC 97267 657 A6
Oatfield Rd
17600 CmsC 97027 687 D2
17600 CmsC 97267 687 D2
17600 GLDS 97267 687 D2
18400 GLDS 97027 687 E3
SE Oatfield Rd
12100 MWKE 97222 657 A4
12300 CmsC 97222 657 A4
13700 CmsC 97267 657 B7
16100 CmsC 97267 687 C1
17400 GLDS 97027 687 D2
17500 CmsC 97027 687 D2
17500 GLDS 97267 687 D2
SE Oatfield Hill Rd
4300 CmsC 97267 657 B6
N Oatman Av
6700 PTLD 97217 566 D5
NW Oats Ter
6200 WasC 97229 564 H6
N Oberlin St
5000 PTLD 97203 566 A4
6500 PTLD 97203 565 J4
SW Oberst Ln
15700 CmsC 97140 714 G3
SW Oberst Rd
24500 WasC 97140 714 F2
O'Brien Rd
1000 LKOW 97034 656 G7
SW O'Brien St
7700 WasC 97223 625 G6
Observatory Wy
1200 MCMV 97128 770 G7
SW Obsidian St
9800 BRTN 97007 654 H1
SW Oceanspray Pl
27100 WasC 97140 714 D4
Ocho Casita
- VCVR 98683 568 E3
SW Ochoco Ct
9300 TLTN 97062 685 E5
SW Ochoco Dr
9300 TLTN 97062 685 D5
SE Ochoco St
900 CmsC 97202 626 G7
900 CmsC 97222 626 G7
900 PTLD 97202 626 G7
1700 MWKE 97202 626 J7
1700 MWKE 97222 626 J7
1700 PTLD 97222 626 J7
SW October Ct
17400 WasC 97006 594 F6
NW O'Day Pl
5500 WasC 97229 564 G7
NW O'Dell Ct
18200 WasC 97229 564 E7
18200 WasC 97229 594 E1
SE O'Dell Rd
26600 CmsC 97022 689 F5
NW Odeon Ln
11300 WasC 97229 595 C3
SW Odessa Av
20600 WasC 97140 714 B4
SW Odino Ct
14000 WasC 97224 654 J7
NE Oelrich Rd
5800 HBRO 97124 593 J5
5800 WasC 97124 593 J5
NW Oelrich Rd
6000 HBRO 97124 593 J5
6000 WasC 97124 593 J5
6300 HBRO 97124 594 A5
6400 WasC 97124 594 A5
Oester Rd
32600 ClbC 97053 444 D1
SE Oetkin Dr
5400 CmsC 97267 657 C7
SE Oetkin Rd
5300 CmsC 97267 657 D7
SE Oetkin Wy
5000 CmsC 97267 657 C7
Offenbach Pl
10 LKOW 97035 656 B4
Officers Row
600 VCVR 98661 536 H5
1200 VCVR 98663 536 H5
Ogan Ln
100 STHN 97051 415 A1
Ogden Av
1100 VCVR 98661 537 C5
Ogden Ct
5100 VCVR 98661 537 C5
NW Ogden Ct
2500 CMAS 98607 569 A2
SE Ogden Ct
12100 PTLD 97236 628 A6
12100 PTLD 97266 628 A6
Ogden Dr
100 ORCY 97045 717 B2
SE Ogden Dr
15200 PTLD 97236 628 D6
NE Ogden Rd
100 MthC 97060 600 A5
NW Ogden St
- PTLD 97231 565 E4
1400 CMAS 98607 569 A4
SE Ogden St
1400 PTLD 97202 626 H5
3600 PTLD 97202 627 B6
4100 PTLD 97206 627 C6
11200 PTLD 97266 627 J6
S Oglesby Rd
27600 CmsC 97013 776 B7
Ohio Dr
6900 VCVR 98664 537 E5
Ohlson Rd
1400 GLDS 97027 687 F3

SW Ohop Ct
9600 TLTN 97062 685 D6
NW Okanogan St
19000 HBRO 97006 594 E4
19100 WasC 97006 594 E4
SE Okja Ct
6300 HBRO 97123 593 G7
Oklahoma Dr
5800 VCVR 98661 537 C6
SW Olaf Ter
2900 WasC 97006 624 E1
S Old Acres Ln
15500 CmsC 97045 717 J7
SE Old Barn Ln
14500 DAMA 97009 658 J7
14500 DAMA 97009 659 A7
Old Bunker Hill Rd
32300 ClbC 97051 384 C7
Old Clapshaw Rd
10000 WasC 97116 531 B7
10000 WasC 97116 561 B1
NW Old Cornelius Pass Rd
8500 WasC 97124 564 E4
8500 WasC 97231 564 E4
10800 WasC 97231 534 E7
E Old County Rd
63200 CmsC 97011 693 G6
SE Oldenburg Ln
20200 CmsC 97055 690 G6
Old Farm Ct
- WNVL 97070 745 F2
SW Old Farm Rd
31400 WNVL 97070 745 F2
Old Forestry Coms
- PTLD 97210 596 C3
Old Gate Rd
4000 CmsC 97034 686 A3
4000 LKOW 97034 686 A3
NW Old Germantown Rd
12100 MthC 97229 564 J4
12100 MthC 97229 565 A4
12100 MthC 97231 564 J4
12100 MthC 97231 565 A4
12100 PTLD 97229 565 A4
SW Old Highway 47
1400 FTGV 97116 591 H6
1400 WasC 97116 591 H6
Old Highway 99 Rd
100 NWBG 97132 713 A7
SW Old Highway 99W
23100 SRWD 97140 714 D1
23700 WasC 97140 714 D1
SW Old Kruger Rd
20900 WasC 97140 684 B7
NW Old Laidlaw Rd
- MthC 97229 595 C1
NW Old Lower River Rd
- ClkC 98660 536 A1
2100 ClkC 98660 505 J7
2100 VCVR 98660 505 J7
2100 VCVR 98660 535 J1
2100 VCVR 98660 536 A1
NE Old McMinnville Hwy
5700 YmhC 97111 741 C5
SW Old Oak Dr
16000 BRTN 97007 624 G6
16000 WasC 97007 624 H6
SE Old Orchard Ct
4300 CmsC 97267 687 B4
NW Old Orchard Dr
200 ClkC 98665 506 G4
SW Old Orchard Ln
10100 WasC 97225 625 E2
SW Old Orchard Pl
15600 TGRD 97224 655 D7
SW Old Orchard Rd
2700 PTLD 97201 626 C1
SW Old Pacific Hwy W
20800 WasC 97140 714 B4
21400 WasC 97140 714 A5
NE Old Parrett Mountain Rd
32100 YmhC 97132 713 J6
33000 YmhC 97132 714 A7
NW Old Pass Rd
20500 WasC 97124 564 C5
20500 WasC 97231 564 C5
20800 HBRO 97124 564 C5
S Old Pioneer Wy
1000 RDGF 98642 416 A7
Old Portland Rd
400 STHN 97051 385 D7
800 STHN 97051 415 B2
2100 ClbC 97051 415 B2
56000 ClbC 97053 414 H6
57600 ClbC 97053 415 B3
57800 STHN 97053 415 A3
SW Old Portland Rd
50700 ClbC 97056 474 E4
50700 SPSE 97056 474 E3
NW Old Pumpkin Ridge Rd
12600 WasC 97133 532 J7
12600 WasC 97133 533 A6
NW Old Quarry Rd
11900 WasC 97229 595 C3
Old River Dr
18200 CmsC 97034 686 J2
18200 LKOW 97034 686 J2
18200 WLIN 97068 686 J2
Old River Lndg
18400 CmsC 97034 686 J2
18400 WLIN 97068 686 J2
Old River Rd
16500 LKOW 97034 656 G7
16500 LKOW 97034 686 G1
17100 CmsC 97034 686 H1
18100 WLIN 97068 686 J2
SE Olds Dr
15300 CmsC 97015 658 D6
NE Olds Ln
17300 YmhC 97132 712 D7
SW Old Scholls Ferry Rd
5700 WasC 97225 625 F4
5800 WasC 97223 625 E5
6400 BRTN 97005 625 E5
6400 WasC 97005 625 E5
NW Old Scotch Church Rd
29500 WasC 97124 563 C5
SW Old Sheridan Rd
1100 MCMV 97128 770 F7
1400 YmhC 97128 770 F7
NW Old Skyline Blvd
9200 PTLD 97231 565 B3
E Old Smokey Rd
24600 CmsC 97049 724 E4

NW Old Springville Rd
10800 PTLD 97229 565 D5
SW Old Well Rd
29500 CmsC 97068 716 D7
29500 CmsC 97068 746 D1
NW Old West Union Rd
30500 NPNS 97133 563 C1
30500 WasC 97133 563 C1
SW Old Wilsonville Rd
7000 WNVL 97070 715 G7
SE Old Woods Lp
5300 GSHM 97080 629 H4
NE Old Yamhill Rd
23000 YmhC 97132 712 J5
23000 YmhC 97132 713 A6
SW Oleander Ct
1900 MCMV 97128 770 E6
NE Oleander Ln
1200 HBRO 97124 593 D3
S Oleander Ln
1000 CNLS 97113 592 E6
S Oleander St
800 CNLS 97113 592 D6
SW Oleander St
1900 MCMV 97128 770 E5
NW Olepha Dr
53000 SPSE 97056 444 E6
SW Oleson Rd
4700 BRTN 97225 625 H4
4700 WasC 97225 625 H4
5700 PTLD 97225 625 H4
5800 BRTN 97223 625 G7
5800 PTLD 97223 625 H5
5800 WasC 97223 625 G7
8900 BRTN 97008 625 E7
8900 BRTN 97008 655 E1
8900 TGRD 97223 655 E1
8900 WasC 97008 625 E7
8900 WasC 97223 655 E1
N Olin Av
6700 PTLD 97203 566 B5
NW Olivares Ter
- WasC 97229 564 H7
- WasC 97229 594 H1
Olive
- CmsC 97015 657 H7
SE Olive Av
15300 CmsC 97267 657 A7
Olive Ln
57600 ClbC 97053 414 J4
Olive St
3600 VCVR 98660 536 E2
NW Olive St
3900 VCVR 98660 536 E1
4400 VCVR 98663 536 E1
SE Olive St
33600 SPSE 97056 474 G1
Oliver Ct
- DNDE 97115 742 H2
SW Oliver Ter
7100 WasC 97007 624 B5
Oliver Heights Ct
35000 ClbC 97051 384 J7
Oliver Heights Ln
59600 ClbC 97051 384 J7
59600 STHN 97051 384 J7
SE Olivewood St
4500 HBRO 97123 623 G1
SE Olivia Ct
16700 DAMA 97009 658 E7
SW Olivia Pl
5200 WasC 97007 624 G4
Olmstead Rd NE
19700 MrnC 97002 774 E7
SE Olsen Ct
3200 MWKE 97222 657 A1
Olson Av
18900 LKOW 97034 686 A3
Olson Ct
3600 LKOW 97034 686 A3
SW Olson Ct
16400 WasC 97007 624 G3
NE Olson Rd
24700 ClkC 98604 449 E7
SE Olson Rd
37200 CmsC 97055 690 H1
37200 SNDY 97055 690 H1
SE Olson St
37500 CmsC 97055 690 J1
37500 SNDY 97055 690 H1
SE Olvera Av
100 GSHM 97030 629 F3
100 GSHM 97080 629 F3
NE Olvera Ct
10 GSHM 97080 629 F2
1400 GSHM 97030 629 F1
SE Olvera Ct
1200 GSHM 97080 629 F4
SE Olympia Dr
400 VCVR 98683 538 C7
400 VCVR 98684 538 C7
1200 VCVR 98683 568 C1
N Olympia St
6200 PTLD 97203 566 A2
7900 PTLD 97203 565 H2
NE Olympic Ct
3800 HBRO 97124 593 G4
NW Olympic Dr
3500 WasC 97229 594 F2
SW Olympic Dr
31300 WNVL 97070 745 C1
NE Olympic St
3200 HBRO 97124 593 F4
S Olympus Rd
20100 CmsC 97045 718 B7
N Omaha Av
7500 PTLD 97217 566 E5
SW Omaha Ct
5500 TLTN 97062 685 J4
Omaha Wy
200 VCVR 98661 537 D6
SW O'Mara St
8600 TGRD 97223 655 E5
9700 TGRD 97224 655 D5
SE Omark Dr
9600 MWKE 97222 656 J1
SW Omega Dr
47500 WasC 97116 591 C7
S Ona Wy
31600 CmsC 97038 837 C2
31600 MOLA 97038 837 C2
SE Ondo Rivera Dr
14700 DAMA 97009 659 B7

O'Neal Ct
2500 WLIN 97068 686 F7
SW Oneida St
10900 TLTN 97062 685 C7
SW O'Neill Ct
16200 WasC 97223 654 G4
One Jefferson Pkwy
- LKOW 97035 656 A4
SE One Oak Ln
28300 CmsC 97022 719 H6
SE Oneonta Dr
10600 HPYV 97236 657 J2
NE Oneonta St
800 PTLD 97211 566 H6
SE One Rosa Dr
12200 CmsC 97236 658 A4
SW Onita Ct
19800 WasC 97006 594 D6
Onna Wy
33000 SPSE 97056 444 D7
SW Onnaf Ct
7500 TGRD 97224 655 G7
NW Onsdorff Blvd
10 BGND 98604 448 A4
10 ClkC 98604 448 A4
2000 BGND 98604 447 J4
2000 ClkC 98604 447 J4
SW Onyx Ct
14900 BRTN 97007 624 J7
SW Opal Dr
14900 BRTN 97007 654 H1
SW Opal Ln
2900 TDLE 97060 599 E6
SE Opal Wy
12500 CmsC 97015 658 A5
NW Oppenlander Ln
48400 WasC 97116 591 B2
SE Oral Hull Rd
42300 CmsC 97055 691 D2
SE Orange Av
2100 PTLD 97214 626 H1
2400 PTLD 97202 626 H1
SE Orangewood Ln
- HBRO 97123 623 H1
Orchard Av NE
14600 AURA 97002 775 E5
NE Orchard Av
1700 MCMV 97128 770 J3
2100 MCMV 97128 771 A3
NW Orchard Av
1600 GSHM 97030 629 A1
SW Orchard Av
1200 GSHM 97080 629 A4
NW Orchard Ct
3600 CMAS 98607 569 C1
SW Orchard Ct
2400 GSHM 97080 629 A5
Orchard Dr
1800 NWBG 97132 713 D6
4000 LKOW 97035 656 A5
NW Orchard Dr
10 WasC 97225 595 D5
10 WasC 97229 595 D5
SW Orchard Dr
30500 WNVL 97070 745 C1
SE Orchard Ln
8200 CmsC 97222 657 F2
8200 CmsC 97236 657 F2
SW Orchard Ln
4800 PTLD 97219 626 A6
NW Orchard Pl
10 GSHM 97080 629 A2
1500 GSHM 97030 629 A1
SW Orchard Pl
700 GSHM 97080 629 A3
Orchard St
1200 WLIN 97068 716 F1
Orchard Wy
4000 LKOW 97035 656 A5
NE Orchard Dell Ct
5000 VCVR 98663 537 A1
Orchard Grove Dr
19300 CmsC 97045 717 B5
19300 ORCY 97045 717 B5
SW Orchard Heights Pl
23200 SRWD 97140 714 G1
Orchard Hill Ln
2500 PTLD 97035 656 B3
SW Orchard Hill Ln
18200 SRWD 97140 684 D7
18400 WasC 97140 684 D7
Orchard Hill Pl
2500 PTLD 97035 656 C3
SW Orchard Hill Rd
12100 PTLD 97035 656 C3
12400 PTLD 97034 656 C3
Orchard Hill Wy
12000 PTLD 97035 656 C3
12000 PTLD 97219 656 C3
Orchard Spring Rd
14300 LKOW 97035 656 B5
SE Orchard View Ln
15900 DAMA 97009 688 D1
NW Orchard View Rd
13600 YmhC 97128 770 A1
SE Orchid Av
14400 CmsC 97267 657 F6
15000 CmsC 97015 657 F7
SW Orchid Ct
100 PTLD 97219 626 E7
5700 PTLD 97219 625 J7
SW Orchid Dr
5800 PTLD 97219 625 H7
SW Orchid St
1400 PTLD 97219 626 C7
4900 PTLD 97219 625 J7
6400 PTLD 97223 625 H7
6600 WasC 97223 625 H7
SW Orcutt Pl
22700 SRWD 97140 684 G7
SE Oregan Rd
1800 MthC 97019 630 J1
SE Oregold Ct
10700 HPYV 97236 658 B3
NW Oregon Ct
3500 CMAS 98607 569 C1
4600 CMAS 98607 539 C7
Oregon Dr
3800 VCVR 98661 537 B5
Oregon St
- MCMV 97128 770 J5
- MCMV 97128 771 A5
- YmhC 97128 770 J5
- YmhC 97128 771 A5
700 ClbC 97051 385 C6

Oregon St
700 STHN 97051 385 C6
E Oregon St
- CmsC 97067 724 B2
66700 CmsC 97011 724 A2
NE Oregon St
- PTLD 97220 598 A1
10 PTLD 97227 596 G5
10 PTLD 97232 596 G5
200 MCMV 97128 770 J5
2800 PTLD 97232 597 A5
7000 PTLD 97213 597 E5
10200 PTLD 97220 597 H5
12200 PTLD 97230 598 A5
16000 GSHM 97230 598 E5
20100 FRVW 97024 598 J5
23900 TDLE 97060 599 D5
23900 WDVL 97060 599 D5
NW Oregon St
4200 CMAS 98607 569 C1
SW Oregon St
14500 SRWD 97140 684 H6
21200 WasC 97140 684 J6
21500 SRWD 97140 685 A6
21500 WasC 97140 685 A6
Oregon City Blvd
2400 WLIN 97068 687 A7
Oregon City Lp
22500 WLIN 97068 687 A7
E Oregon Grape Ln
69000 CmsC 97067 724 C7
N Oregonian Av
9500 PTLD 97203 566 A2
SE Oregon Trail Dr
14700 CmsC 97015 658 D6
15300 HPYV 97015 658 D6
SW Oregon Trail Ln
14700 WasC 97006 594 J6
NE Orenco Gardens Dr
5600 HBRO 97124 593 J4
NE Orenco Ridge Ct
6400 HBRO 97124 594 B4
6400 WasC 97124 594 B4
NE Orenco Station Pkwy
- HBRO 97124 593 J3
1700 HBRO 97124 594 A3
SW Orepac Av
30100 WNVL 97070 745 D1
SE Orient Dr
1400 GSHM 97080 629 J6
3000 MthC 97080 629 J6
7900 MthC 97080 630 A7
8000 CmsC 97009 660 B3
8000 CmsC 97080 660 B1
14500 CmsC 97009 690 F1
15500 CmsC 97055 690 F1
Oriental Ct
600 MOLA 97038 807 C7
NW Origami Ct
2300 WasC 97229 595 B3
SW Orinda Wy
1200 WasC 97225 595 C7
SW Oriole Cir
10600 BRTN 97007 654 H2
SW Oriole Ct
15500 SRWD 97140 714 G1
Oriole Ln
10 LKOW 97035 656 B3
SW Oriole St
800 MCMV 97128 770 F6
NE Orion St
14700 VCVR 98682 538 C2
NW Orion Greens Ct
17000 WasC 97006 594 H4
SE Orland St
31400 MthC 97080 630 B7
SW Orland St
22100 SRWD 97140 684 H7
Orlando Wy
500 VCVR 98664 537 E7
SW Orlov Ct
- WasC 97007 624 E3
SE Ormae Rd
16300 CmsC 97027 687 D1
16300 CmsC 97267 687 D1
16300 GLDS 97027 687 D1
SW Ormandy Wy
4300 MthC 97221 626 A1
4300 PTLD 97221 626 A1
Orr Cir
36400 SNDY 97055 690 G3
SE Orville Av
15500 CmsC 97267 657 A7
SW Osage St
2300 PTLD 97205 596 D5
2300 PTLD 97210 596 D5
8800 TLTN 97062 685 E6
NE Osborne Ct
500 MCMV 97128 770 H2
NE Osburn Lp
21200 FRVW 97024 599 A3
NE Osman Rd
22200 ClkC 98604 449 C5
SE Osprey Av
3000 GSHM 97080 629 H6
Osprey Ct
- FTGV 97116 591 H2
SW Osprey Ct
14800 BRTN 97007 654 J2
S Osprey Dr
- RDGF 98642 446 B1
SW Osprey Dr
14300 BRTN 97007 654 J2
14300 BRTN 97008 654 J2
SE Osprey Lp
2800 GSHM 97080 629 H6
NW Osprey Pl
5400 WasC 97229 564 C7
NW Ostenson Canyon Rd
- CMAS 98607 569 D3
NW Ostenson-Canyon Rd
1100 CMAS 98607 569 D3
SW Oster Ct
20000 WasC 97007 624 C3
NW Osterman Rd
39400 WasC 97116 562 A6
41000 WasC 97116 561 J6
Ostman Rd
15100 WLIN 97068 716 F2
N Oswego Av
7500 PTLD 97203 565 H2
Oswego Dr
4200 VCVR 98661 537 B5
Oswego Smt
10 LKOW 97035 656 B3

Oswego Vil
- LKOW 97035 656 A5
Oswego Bay
- CmsC 97035 685 J1
- LKOW 97035 685 J2
Oswego Pointe Dr
300 LKOW 97034 656 G6
Oswego Shore Ct
15800 LKOW 97034 656 C7
Othello St
10 LKOW 97035 656 B5
NW Otis Ln
47000 WasC 97116 561 D5
SE Ott Ct
12500 CmsC 97015 658 A6
SE Ott St
12700 CmsC 97015 658 A6
NE Otter Dr
11100 YmhC 97132 713 A7
11100 YmhC 97132 743 A1
Otter Ln
1300 ORCY 97045 717 E3
SW Otter Ln
13600 BRTN 97008 655 A2
13800 BRTN 97008 654 J2
SW Otto Ln
30700 WNVL 97070 745 D1
Otto Rd
23000 CmsC 97013 746 F5
SW Ottowa St
6900 TLTN 97062 685 G5
Ottoway Rd NE
14500 AURA 97002 775 F4
15000 MrnC 97002 775 F4
SE Otty Pl
9200 CmsC 97236 657 G1
SE Otty Rd
7300 CmsC 97222 657 E1
8200 CmsC 97236 657 F1
SE Our Ct
6800 CmsC 97222 657 E2
Outer Dr
- PTLD 97236 627 J7
- PTLD 97236 628 A7
- PTLD 97236 658 A1
- PTLD 97266 627 J7
SW Outlook Ln
17500 WasC 97007 654 F2
S Outlook Rd
16500 CmsC 97045 688 B4
S Outlook Ter
15500 CmsC 97045 688 C5
SW Outrigger Ter
- BRTN 97006 594 H6
SW Overgaard St
12500 KNGC 97224 685 A1
12500 WasC 97224 685 A1
SE Overland St
6200 CmsC 97222 657 D1
8100 CmsC 97236 657 F1
Overlea Av
- MthC 97231 535 A5
NW Overlook Av
1000 GSHM 97030 629 A1
N Overlook Blvd
3700 PTLD 97227 596 E1
4000 PTLD 97217 596 E1
Overlook Cir
17700 LKOW 97034 686 B2
NW Overlook Ct
1000 GSHM 97030 629 A2
SW Overlook Ct
400 GSHM 97080 629 A3
Overlook Dr
1200 LKOW 97034 686 B2
1400 CmsC 97034 686 D2
NE Overlook Dr
20400 YmhC 97115 742 G1
NW Overlook Dr
200 ClkC 98665 506 F5
2500 HBRO 97006 594 D3
2500 HBRO 97124 594 D2
Overlook Ln
17700 LKOW 97034 686 B2
SE Overlook Ln
9700 HPYV 97236 657 H2
14000 CmsC 97267 656 H6
S Overlook Rd
17200 CmsC 97045 688 C3
25800 CmsC 97023 750 B5
NW Overlook St
32800 SPSE 97056 444 D7
N Overlook Ter
3900 PTLD 97227 596 E1
4100 PTLD 97217 596 E1
NW Overton Ct
2000 WasC 97006 594 H3
NW Overton Dr
15400 WasC 97006 594 H3
NW Overton St
- PTLD 97210 596 C4
1200 PTLD 97209 596 E4
12900 WasC 97229 595 A4
NE Overview Ct
- WasC 97124 594 A5
SW Oviatt Dr
7500 WasC 97007 624 F6
SW Oviatt St
17400 WasC 97007 624 F6
SE Owen Dr
8500 CmsC 97236 657 F2
SW Owens Pl
200 TDLE 97060 599 F3
Owl Ct
4300 WLIN 97068 686 J5
NW Owl Dr
3900 WasC 97116 561 C7
3900 WasC 97116 591 C1
NE Owls Ln
29300 YmhC 97132 713 G4
SE Owl's Rest Ct
19100 CmsC 97267 687 B4
NW Owyhee Ct
4500 WasC 97229 594 C1
SW Oxalis Ter
12900 TGRD 97223 654 J4
SE Oxbow Dr
30700 MthC 97060 630 D5
33100 MthC 97080 630 D5
SE Oxbow Pkwy
3200 MthC 97080 630 E3
SW Oxbow Ter
8700 BRTN 97008 625 B7
SE Oxbow Park Rd
- MthC 97080 630 F3

STREET Block City ZIP Map# Grid
NW Oxbow Ridge Crest Ct
10700 ClkC 98685 506 E2
NW Oxbridge Dr
4000 WasC 97229 595 B1
SW Oxford Av
5700 WasC 97225 625 G4
Oxford Dr
900 LKOW 97034 686 F1
SE Oxford Ln
1500 MWKE 97222 656 H1
SW Oxford Rd
- PTLD 97201 596 C6
- PTLD 97205 596 C6
Oxford St
100 NWBG 97132 713 C5
2300 WLIN 97068 687 A7
2700 CmsC 97068 687 A7
NW Oxford St
2200 CMAS 98607 569 A3
W Oxford St
100 NWBG 97132 713 B5
300 YmhC 97132 713 B5
Oyer Dr
15000 CmsC 97045 687 H5
15000 ORCY 97045 687 H5
SE Ozark Ct
4000 HBRO 97123 593 G6
SW Ozark Ln
24900 HBRO 97123 593 H6
SW Ozette Ct
8300 TLTN 97062 685 G6

P

P Cir
- WHGL 98671 570 C4
N P Cir
1100 WHGL 98671 570 A4
P Ct
- WHGL 98671 569 J4
P Lp
- WHGL 98671 570 C4
P St
2600 VCVR 98661 536 H3
2600 VCVR 98663 536 H3
4900 ClkC 98671 570 E4
4900 WHGL 98671 570 E4
N P St
- WHGL 98671 569 J4
800 WHGL 98671 570 A4
SW Pacer Ct
8600 BRTN 97008 625 B7
SW Pacer Dr
8600 BRTN 97008 625 B7
Pacific Av
1000 WDLD 98674 386 A1
1100 FTGV 97116 591 G4
1100 WasC 97116 591 G4
1900 WDLD 98674 385 J1
3100 FTGV 97116 592 B5
4300 CNLS 97113 592 C5
Pacific Av SR-8
1500 FTGV 97116 591 J5
3100 FTGV 97116 592 B5
4300 CNLS 97113 592 C5
NE Pacific Av
100 MCMV 97128 771 A6
200 MCMV 97128 770 J6
200 YmhC 97128 770 J6
200 YmhC 97128 771 A6
4500 VCVR 98663 536 G1
NW Pacific Av
40600 WasC 97106 532 A6
SW Pacific Av
4600 BRTN 97005 625 C3
Pacific Ct
600 MOLA 97038 807 C7
NE Pacific Ct
12900 PTLD 97230 598 B5
18100 GSHM 97230 598 G5
NE Pacific Dr
800 FRVW 97024 599 B5
16500 GSHM 97230 598 F5
SW Pacific Dr
17500 TLTN 97062 685 A3
18400 WasC 97062 685 A3
18600 TLTN 97062 684 J3
18600 WasC 97062 684 J3
18600 WasC 97140 684 J3
18600 WasC 97140 685 A3
Pacific Hwy
15000 LKOW 97034 656 G7
16400 LKOW 97034 686 G1
17700 WLIN 97068 686 H2
20600 WLIN 97068 687 B6
Pacific Hwy SR-43
15000 LKOW 97034 656 G7
16400 LKOW 97034 686 G1
17700 WLIN 97068 686 H2
20600 WLIN 97068 687 B6
Pacific Hwy E
- AURA 97002 775 E5
- BRLO 97013 746 A7
- BRLO 97013 775 J1
- BRLO 97013 776 A1
- CmsC 97002 775 J2
- CmsC 97013 746 G3
- CmsC 97013 775 J1
- CmsC 97013 776 A1
- CmsC 97045 716 H3
- CmsC 97045 717 A2
- CmsC 97045 746 F1
- CNBY 97013 746 A7
- MrnC 97032 775 D6
- ORCY 97045 716 H3
- ORCY 97045 717 A2
Pacific Hwy E SR-99E
- AURA 97002 775 E5
- BRLO 97013 746 A7
- BRLO 97013 775 J1
- BRLO 97013 776 A1
- CmsC 97002 775 J2
- CmsC 97013 746 A7
- CmsC 97013 775 J1
- CmsC 97013 776 A1
- CmsC 97045 716 H3
- CmsC 97045 717 A2
- CmsC 97045 746 F1
- CNBY 97013 746 A7
- MrnC 97032 775 D6
- ORCY 97045 716 H3
- ORCY 97045 717 A2
Pacific Hwy W
- LFYT 97114 771 H1
- LFYT 97127 771 H1
- MCMV 97128 770 H3
- MCMV 97128 771 B2
- NWBG 97132 713 B7
- NWBG 97132 743 B1
- YmhC 97114 771 H1
- YmhC 97115 742 J2
- YmhC 97115 743 A1
- YmhC 97127 771 H1
- YmhC 97128 741 F7
- YmhC 97132 713 B7
- YmhC 97132 743 A1
1300 DNDE 97115 742 H4
7800 YmhC 97128 771 E1
11300 LFYT 97127 741 F7
17500 KNGC 97224 685 B2
17500 TLTN 97062 685 A3
17500 TLTN 97224 685 B2
17500 WasC 97224 685 B2
17600 WasC 97062 685 B2
18600 YmhC 97114 772 C1
18600 YmhC 97115 772 E1
18700 WasC 97062 684 J3
18800 YmhC 97114 742 E7
20200 SRWD 97140 684 H4
22000 WasC 97140 684 D7
23000 SRWD 97140 714 D1
23000 WasC 97140 714 A5
27500 WasC 97132 714 A5
Pacific Hwy W SR-99W
- LFYT 97114 771 H1
- LFYT 97127 771 H1
- MCMV 97128 770 H3
- MCMV 97128 771 B2
- NWBG 97132 713 B7
- NWBG 97132 743 B1
- YmhC 97114 771 H1
- YmhC 97115 742 J2
- YmhC 97115 743 A1
- YmhC 97127 771 H1
- YmhC 97128 741 F7
- YmhC 97132 713 B7
- YmhC 97132 743 A1
- YmhC 97132 714 A5
1300 DNDE 97115 742 H4
7800 YmhC 97128 771 E1
11300 LFYT 97127 741 F7
17500 KNGC 97224 685 B2
17500 TLTN 97062 685 A3
17500 TLTN 97224 685 B2
17500 WasC 97224 685 B2
18200 WasC 97062 685 A3
18600 YmhC 97114 772 C1
18600 YmhC 97115 772 E1
18700 WasC 97062 684 J3
18800 YmhC 97114 742 E7
20200 SRWD 97140 684 H4
22000 WasC 97140 684 D7
23000 SRWD 97140 714 D1
23000 WasC 97140 714 A5
Pacific Hwy W SR-219
- NWBG 97132 713 C7
NW Pacific Hwy
- WDLD 98674 386 A1
300 LCTR 98629 416 G1
500 LCTR 98629 386 G7
900 ClkC 98629 386 G7
35200 ClkC 98674 386 B2
SW Pacific Hwy
11400 PTLD 97219 655 H2
11400 TGRD 97223 655 G3
14300 TGRD 97224 655 C7
15000 KNGC 97224 655 C7
15400 WasC 97224 655 C7
16000 TGRD 97224 685 C1
16100 KNGC 97224 685 B1
16100 WasC 97224 685 B2
SW Pacific Hwy SR-99W
11400 PTLD 97219 655 H2
12000 TGRD 97223 655 D5
13700 TGRD 97224 655 C7
15000 KNGC 97224 655 C7
15500 WasC 97224 655 C7
16000 TGRD 97224 685 C1
16100 KNGC 97224 685 B1
16100 WasC 97224 685 B2
Pacific St
100 CBAC 97018 385 B2
NE Pacific St
400 PTLD 97232 596 G4
2900 PTLD 97232 597 A5
4800 PTLD 97213 597 C5
8200 PTLD 97220 597 G5
11400 PTLD 97220 598 A5
12700 PTLD 97230 598 B5
19300 GSHM 97230 598 H5
NW Pacific St
30600 NPNS 97133 563 A1
S Pacific St
700 NWBG 97132 743 D1
NE Pacific Ter
16500 GSHM 97230 598 E5
NE Pacific Wy
3700 VCVR 98662 537 F2
SW Pacifica Ct
17300 BRTN 97006 594 F6
17300 WasC 97006 594 F6
N Pacific Gateway
- PTLD 97203 535 H3
N Pacific Gateway Blvd
- PTLD 97203 535 H3
NW Pacific Grove Dr
200 BRTN 97006 594 G5
SW Pacific Pointe Ct
11700 KNGC 97224 655 B7
NW Pacific Rim Blvd
4200 CMAS 98607 568 J3
4200 CMAS 98607 569 A2
4700 ClkC 98607 568 H3
SE Pacific Rim Blvd
6000 ClkC 98607 568 G3
6000 CMAS 98607 568 G3
6000 VCVR 98607 568 G3
NW Pacific Rim Dr
2900 CMAS 98607 569 A2
SW Packard Ln
13500 BRTN 97008 625 A7
NE Padden Pkwy
- ClkC 98661 507 D5
- ClkC 98662 507 J5
- ClkC 98665 507 D5
- ClkC 98682 507 J5
- ClkC 98682 508 B5
NE Padden Pkwy SR-500
- ClkC 98662 507 J5
- ClkC 98682 507 J5
- ClkC 98682 508 B5
NW Paddington Dr
16500 WasC 97006 594 G3
SE Paddington Rd
14800 CmsC 97015 658 C6
SW Paddock Ct
14000 BRTN 97008 654 J1
NW Padgett Rd
1100 HBRO 97124 593 A3
1100 WasC 97124 593 A3
32200 WasC 97124 592 J2
SE Padron Wy
16000 DAMA 97009 688 F1
SW Pag Pl
7400 PTLD 97223 625 H6
7400 WasC 97223 625 H6
SW Page Ct
19600 WasC 97007 624 D6
N Page St
10 PTLD 97212 596 G3
600 PTLD 97227 596 F3
SE Pagoda Ct
17000 CmsC 97267 687 D2
SE Paha Loop Dr
44900 CmsC 97055 691 G6
SE Painted Hills Ct
11500 HPYV 97236 658 C3
NW Painted Mountain Dr
20600 WasC 97006 594 D5
NW Paisley Ct
3500 WasC 97006 594 F3
NW Paisley Dr
16100 WasC 97006 594 G2
NE Palace Ct
- GSHM 97030 599 D5
- WDVL 97060 599 D5
NW Palace Dr
41900 WasC 97106 531 J2
SE Paladin Ln
4700 HBRO 97123 593 H5
SW Palater Rd
10 PTLD 97219 656 F1
SE Palatial Ct
10000 HPYV 97236 657 H2
SW Palatial Pl
10 WasC 97006 594 F5
SW Palatine Ct
11000 PTLD 97219 656 C2
SW Palatine St
1500 PTLD 97219 656 C2
5400 PTLD 97219 655 J2
SW Palatine Hill Rd
10 PTLD 97219 626 E7
300 PTLD 97219 656 F1
800 MthC 97219 656 F1
NW Palatka Pl
- PTLD 97205 596 B5
- PTLD 97210 596 B5
NW Palazza Wy
2600 HBRO 97124 594 D2
SW Palermo Ln
16100 WasC 97223 654 G5
Palermo St
- WNVL 97070 715 B6
SW Palermo St
11600 WNVL 97070 715 B7
NE Palisade Pl
21500 FRVW 97024 599 B3
Palisades Crest Dr
2300 LKOW 97034 686 B2
Palisades Lake Ct
1800 LKOW 97034 656 E7
Palisades Terrace Dr
800 LKOW 97034 656 E7
Pallari Dr
- ClkC 98686 476 J6
SW Pallay Ct
6300 PTLD 97219 655 H3
SW Palm Pl
11300 TGRD 97223 655 C3
SE Palm St
1300 PTLD 97214 596 H7
NE Palmblad Dr
10 GSHM 97080 629 E3
1000 GSHM 97030 629 E1
SE Palmblad Dr
100 GSHM 97030 629 E3
300 GSHM 97080 629 E3
SE Palmblad Pl
700 GSHM 97080 629 E3
SE Palmblad Rd
1500 GSHM 97080 629 E5
6600 MthC 97080 629 E5
NW Palmbrook Dr
- WasC 97229 594 G1
4300 WasC 97006 594 G1
Palmer Ct
59000 STHN 97051 414 H1
SE Palmer Ct
2700 HBRO 97123 624 A1
SE Palmer Ln
200 DAYT 97114 772 B4
NE Palmer Rd
17100 ClkC 98604 448 G2
S Palmer Rd
17400 CmsC 97045 719 F2
SW Palmer Wy
7000 BRTN 97007 624 J5
S Palmetto St
800 CNLS 97113 592 D6
SE Palmetto St
7100 CmsC 97267 657 E6
S Palmetto Wy
1000 CNLS 97113 592 E6
SE Palmire Ct
3700 HBRO 97123 623 E2
SE Palmquist Rd
1900 GSHM 97080 629 D4
Palmquist Ter
- GSHM 97080 629 E4
Palo Alto Dr
500 VCVR 98661 537 C5
NE Paloma Av
10 GSHM 97080 629 F3
1000 GSHM 97030 629 F1
1600 GSHM 97060 629 F1
1600 TDLE 97030 629 F1
1600 TDLE 97060 629 F1
SE Paloma Av
100 GSHM 97080 629 F3
3100 MthC 97080 629 F6
NE Paloma Ct
200 GSHM 97030 629 F2
SE Paloma Ct
1000 GSHM 97080 629 F4
SE Paloma Dr
1900 GSHM 97080 629 F5
SE Paloma Ter
2600 GSHM 97080 629 F5
NE Palomar Ct
200 HBRO 97124 593 F4
Palomino Cir
6500 WLIN 97068 686 J5
Palomino Ct
1300 NWBG 97132 713 C6
2500 WLIN 97068 686 J4
SW Palomino Pl
9200 BRTN 97008 654 J1
Palomino Wy
6300 WLIN 97068 686 H5
SW Palouse Ln
9200 TLTN 97062 685 A7
SW Palouse St
19800 WasC 97006 594 D6
NW Palo Verde Pl
4300 WasC 97006 594 G1
S Pam Dr
16400 CmsC 97045 687 J7
SW Pamela Ct
21100 WasC 97006 594 B7
SW Pamela St
6100 CmsC 97219 655 H4
6100 LKOW 97035 655 H4
6100 LKOW 97219 655 H4
SW Pamlico Ct
8700 TLTN 97062 685 E6
Pamrick Ln
7100 CmsC 97267 687 E1
NE Panache Pl
2900 FRVW 97024 599 B3
NW Panorama Av
- MthC 97210 595 H4
- MthC 97229 595 H4
SW Panorama Pl
9200 WasC 97225 625 E1
Pansy Ct
1400 FTGV 97116 591 G4
Paola Ct
6500 GLDS 97027 687 D1
Papago Rd
- WasC 97005 594 J7
SE Pappasloss Ct
1900 CmsC 97267 656 J6
Paquet St
- ORCY 97045 717 A3
NW Par Ct
15500 WasC 97229 594 H1
NE Par Ln
6700 ClkC 98662 507 F6
SE Paradise Ct
4200 CmsC 97267 687 B2
Paradise Dr
1500 NWBG 97132 743 D1
NW Paradise Dr
5700 WasC 97116 561 C6
SE Paradise Dr
17500 CmsC 97267 687 B2
Paradise Ln
54000 ClbC 97056 444 F4
S Paradise Ln
15000 CmsC 97042 807 H3
NE Paradise Rd
34500 ClkC 98671 540 E6
SE Paradise Rd
28200 CmsC 97022 719 F7
NW Paradise Park Rd
29900 ClkC 98642 416 E2
33000 ClkC 98642 386 D7
N Parcell Av
100 YCLT 98675 419 F1
NE Parcell Av
31100 ClkC 98675 419 F3
31200 YCLT 98675 419 F1
S Parcell Av
100 YCLT 98675 419 F1
500 ClkC 98675 419 F1
SE Pardee Dr
13300 PTLD 97236 628 B4
SE Pardee St
2300 PTLD 97202 626 J3
3300 PTLD 97202 627 A3
4100 PTLD 97206 627 B3
9600 PTLD 97266 627 H3
11800 PTLD 97236 628 A3
11800 PTLD 97266 628 A3
Parelius Cir
16000 LKOW 97034 656 E7
NE Paren Springs Rd
10800 YmhC 97115 742 H1
SW Par Four Dr
12000 KNGC 97224 655 B7
Paris Av
- MthC 97231 534 J6
- MthC 97231 535 A6
Park Av
500 LFYT 97127 771 G1
Park Av NE
4100 MrnC 97137 773 B6
4100 STPL 97137 773 B6
15000 AURA 97002 775 F4
15000 MrnC 97002 775 F4
E Park Av
300 MOLA 97038 837 F1
NW Park Av
- ECDA 97022 750 A1
- ECDA 97023 750 A1
- PTLD 97209 596 F5
10 PTLD 97205 596 F5
SE Park Av
1900 CmsC 97222 656 J4
2700 MWKE 97222 656 J4
2800 CmsC 97222 657 A4
SW Park Av
- PTLD 97209 596 F5
200 PTLD 97205 596 E6
1200 PTLD 97201 596 E7
Park Ct
200 NWBG 97132 713 C5
NW Park Ct
4700 CMAS 98607 539 C7
16900 BRTN 97006 594 G5
S Park Ct
8500 CmsC 97013 776 C4
Park Dr
100 ORCY 97045 717 B2
3100 CBAC 97018 385 C2
N Park Dr
33700 SPSE 97056 474 F2
NW Park Dr
100 MCMV 97128 770 G5
SE Park Dr
500 GSHM 97080 629 C3
SW Park Dr
33200 SPSE 97056 474 E2
Park Ln
1300 NWBG 97132 713 D6
NE Park Ln
- PTLD 97211 566 H6
1300 FRVW 97024 599 B3
22300 WDVL 97060 599 B5
Park Pl
- PTLD 97236 628 B2
- WasC 97223 655 F1
100 DAYT 97114 771 J5
100 YmhC 97114 771 J5
E Park Pl
300 MOLA 97038 837 F1
NE Park Pl
200 HBRO 97124 593 E4
NW Park Pl
13700 WasC 97229 595 A5
SW Park Pl
2600 PTLD 97205 596 C5
29400 WNVL 97070 715 E7
Park Rd
- WDLD 98674 386 A2
2200 LKOW 97034 686 C1
SE Park Rd
14200 CmsC 97267 656 J6
SW Park Row
22800 SRWD 97140 684 G7
Park St
100 STHN 97051 385 A7
200 WDLD 98674 385 J2
1000 WDLD 98674 386 A1
38400 SNDY 97055 690 J2
S Park St
100 CLTN 97111 711 C7
100 CLTN 97111 741 A1
1000 YmhC 97111 741 A1
SE Park St
300 BNKS 97106 531 J5
4800 MWKE 97222 657 C3
12600 VCVR 98683 568 A1
28700 CmsC 97022 719 F7
38900 SNDY 97055 690 J2
39000 SNDY 97055 691 A2
SW Park St
300 CMAS 98607 569 C5
10300 TGRD 97223 655 D5
22400 SRWD 97140 684 G7
Park Wy
300 STHN 97051 385 D7
300 STHN 97051 415 D1
6500 GLDS 97027 687 D2
SW Park Wy
9500 BRTN 97225 595 F7
10400 WasC 97225 595 D7
13000 WasC 97005 595 B7
SE Park Crest Av
2000 VCVR 98683 568 C2
SE Parkcrest Av
700 VCVR 98683 538 C7
700 VCVR 98684 538 C7
300 VCVR 98683 568 C1
Park Crest Coms
- VCVR 98683 538 C7
- VCVR 98684 538 C7
SE Park Entrance St
2200 CmsC 97267 656 J6
SW Parker Ct
20500 WasC 97007 624 C3
SE Parker Ln
28700 CmsC 97009 659 H5
Parker Rd
2600 CmsC 97068 686 G6
2600 WLIN 97068 686 J6
15800 CmsC 97035 655 H7
15800 LKOW 97035 655 H7
NW Parker St
3600 CMAS 98607 569 A2
3800 CMAS 98607 539 A7
SE Parkers Dr
17100 CmsC 97027 687 F2
17100 CmsC 97267 687 F2
Park Forest Av
1900 LKOW 97034 686 C1
Park Forest Ct
1900 LKOW 97034 686 C1
SW Parkhill Dr
6200 PTLD 97239 626 E5
Parkhill St
4900 LKOW 97035 655 J6
4900 LKOW 97035 656 A6
SW Parkhill Wy
6400 PTLD 97239 626 E5
SW Parkin Ln
21400 WasC 97006 594 B7
NE Parkinen Rd
14400 ClkC 98606 478 E5
S Parkland Ct
11100 CmsC 97045 716 J5
SW Parkland Ter
15200 TGRD 97224 655 G6
SE Park Mountain Ln
10200 CmsC 97015 657 H6
Park Place Ct
15800 ORCY 97045 687 E5
NE Park Plaza Dr
3000 VCVR 98684 538 A6
SE Park Plaza Dr
3000 VCVR 98684 538 A6
NW Park Ridge Ln
1100 PTLD 97229 595 G4
Parkrose Chateau
- PTLD 97230 598 D3
SE Parks Dr
200 DNDE 97115 742 H4
200 YmhC 97115 742 H4
Parks Rd
100 DNDE 97115 742 H4
100 YmhC 97115 742 H4
NE Parksedge Cir
1000 HBRO 97124 593 D2
Parkside Ct
1400 NWBG 97132 713 B6
2000 WLIN 97068 687 A5
E Parkside Ct
200 LCTR 98629 416 J1
NE Parkside Dr
8000 HBRO 97124 593 C3
SE Parkside Dr
13300 HPYV 97236 658 B2
SW Parkside Dr
200 PTLD 97205 596 B6
Parkside Ln
1300 NWBG 97132 713 B6
1300 YmhC 97132 713 B6
SW Parkside Ln
100 PTLD 97205 596 C5
SE Parktree Dr
15300 CmsC 97015 658 D6
15300 HPYV 97015 658 D6
SW Parkview Av
4000 WasC 97225 625 F3
NW Park View Blvd
17400 WasC 97006 594 F2
17400 WasC 97229 594 F2
SE Parkview Cir
1800 CmsC 97267 656 H7
Parkview Ct
2200 WLIN 97068 686 G4
SW Parkview Ct
1600 PTLD 97221 596 A7
Parkview Dr
100 NWBG 97132 713 D7
4500 LKOW 97035 656 A5
4800 LKOW 97035 655 J5
NE Parkview Dr
2000 ClkC 98686 506 J1
NW Parkview Dr
3000 WasC 97006 594 G2
3000 WasC 97229 594 F2
SW Parkview Dr
10700 WNVL 97070 745 C1
Parkview Ln
- CmsC 97023 749 H3
NW Park View Ln
2900 WasC 97229 594 F2
S Park View Ln
21600 CmsC 97023 749 G3
S Parkview Ln
21200 CmsC 97023 749 G3
SW Parkview Lp
8400 BRTN 97008 625 C7
Parkview Ter
21300 WLIN 97068 686 J6
SE Parkview Ter
6000 CmsC 97222 657 D5
SE Parkway E
- VCVR 98607 538 H7
SE Parkway W
- VCVR 98607 538 H6
N Parkway Av
10 BGND 98604 448 B4
1200 ClkC 98604 448 B4
S Parkway Av
10 BGND 98604 448 B6
1800 ClkC 98604 448 B7
SW Parkway Av
13200 WasC 97005 595 A7
13200 WasC 97225 595 A7
25000 WasC 97062 715 E3
25000 WNVL 97070 715 E3
30000 WNVL 97070 745 E2
SW Parkway Ct
29200 WNVL 97070 715 E7
NE Parkway Dr
7600 VCVR 98662 537 E1
SW Parkway Dr
10800 WNVL 97070 745 C1
SW Parkway Center Dr
25600 WasC 97062 715 F3
26200 WNVL 97070 715 E3
SW Parkwest Ln
6600 WasC 97225 625 H2
SW Parkwood Ct
10800 CmsC 97070 715 B7
10800 WNVL 97070 715 B7
Parkwood Dr
58600 ClbC 97051 414 J2
58600 STHN 97051 414 J2
SW Parkwood Dr
1300 WasC 97225 595 D7
1600 BRTN 97225 595 D7
SW Parkwood Ln
10500 WNVL 97070 715 C7
Parkwood Pl
18800 WLIN 97068 686 J2
NE Parkwood St
2500 HBRO 97124 593 F4
Parkwood Wy
3700 WLIN 97068 686 J2
SE Parkwood Wy
9500 HPYV 97236 658 B2
SE Parmenter Ct
6100 CmsC 97267 657 D5
SE Parmenter Dr
14000 CmsC 97267 657 D6
SE Parmley St
400 BNKS 97106 531 J5
Parnell Ln
61500 ClbC 97051 384 E3
NW Parnell Ter
2400 WasC 97229 595 C3
SE Paropa Av
700 GSHM 97080 629 E3
NE Paropa Ct
1400 GSHM 97030 629 E1
SE Paropa Ct
200 GSHM 97080 629 F3
SE Paropa Ln
2300 GSHM 97080 629 E5
NE Paropa Pl
3000 GSHM 97030 599 F7
3000 TDLE 97060 599 F7
SE Paropa Pl
500 GSHM 97080 629 F3
NE Paropa Wy
300 GSHM 97030 629 E2
NE Parrett Mountain Rd
- CmsC 97132 744 D4
9400 CmsC 97140 744 C1
9400 YmhC 97132 714 C7
13700 WasC 97140 714 D5
SW Parrett Mountain Rd
16000 WasC 97140 714 F4
18000 YmhC 97132 714 C7
Parrish Ln
17900 SRWD 97140 714 E1
Parrish Rd
11500 ORCY 97045 717 A5
19400 CmsC 97045 716 J5
19400 ORCY 97045 716 J5
NE Parrish Rd
8000 YmhC 97132 743 G4
Parrish St
1100 LKOW 97034 656 E7
1300 LKOW 97034 686 E1
S Parrot Creek Rd
22000 CmsC 97045 747 C3
S Parrott Creek Rd
- CmsC 97045 747 C3
SW Parrway Dr
7800 WasC 97225 625 F2
SW Pars Pl
17800 WasC 97007 624 F3
SW Parsons Ct
3200 PTLD 97219 656 B3
SE Partagas St
16700 DAMA 97009 688 E1
SW Par Three Dr
9000 WasC 97113 623 A7
Partlow Rd
11700 CmsC 97045 717 A4
11700 ORCY 97045 717 A4
Partridge Cir
6600 GLDS 97027 687 D2
Partridge Dr
15400 CmsC 97035 655 H6
Partridge Ln
- FTGV 97116 591 H3
10 LKOW 97035 656 B3
3200 NWBG 97132 713 C4
SW Partridge Lp
11100 BRTN 97007 654 H2
SW Parvenu Pl
10 WasC 97006 594 F5
SW Pasadena Dr
5500 PTLD 97219 655 H2
SW Pasadena St
4400 PTLD 97219 656 A2
5300 PTLD 97219 655 J2
Pasadena Wy
300 VCVR 98661 537 C6
SE Pascali Ct
11300 HPYV 97236 658 B3
SW Pascuzzi Ln
23100 WasC 97140 683 J1
23100 WasC 97140 684 A1
NW Paseo Dr
5200 WasC 97229 564 H7
SW Pasquinade Pl
10 WasC 97006 594 F5
S Passmore Rd
14000 CmsC 97042 777 E5
SW Pastern Pl
10100 BRTN 97008 655 B1
SW Pate Ct
20100 WasC 97006 624 C1
SW Pathfinder Ct
12500 TGRD 97223 655 D4
SW Pathfinder Wy
10500 TGRD 97223 655 C4
SW Patience Dr
21500 HBRO 97006 594 B6
21500 WasC 97006 594 B6
SW Patricia Av
13900 WasC 97123 653 G6
SE Patricia Ct
15500 CmsC 97267 656 J7
Patricia Dr
300 GLDS 97027 687 D3
Patricia Ln
21200 FRVW 97024 599 A2
SE Patricia Ln
6700 HBRO 97123 594 A5
SW Patricia St
1000 MCMV 97128 770 F6
SE Patricia Wy
33800 SPSE 97056 474 F1
NW Patricia Ann Pl
- HBRO 97006 594 D5
NW Patrick Ln
16800 WasC 97229 564 G7
SW Patrick Pl
4100 PTLD 97239 626 D2
S Patrick Wy
21900 CmsC 97023 719 C7
SW Patrick Wy
4100 PTLD 97239 626 D2
Patrol St
700 CmsC 97038 837 F1
700 MOLA 97038 837 F1
SE Patsy Av
15700 CmsC 97267 657 E7
15700 CmsC 97267 687 E1
Patsy Dr
20300 CmsC 97045 717 H7
SE Patteron St
5900 HBRO 97123 593 J6
5900 WasC 97123 593 J6
SW Patterson Ln
- CmsC 97035 685 J3
- RVGR 97035 685 J3
SE Patterson Pl
8500 VCVR 98664 537 F7
SE Patterson St
5200 HBRO 97123 593 H6
5300 WasC 97123 593 H6
SW Patti Ln
8200 TGRD 97224 655 F7
N Patton Av
- PTLD 97217 566 E3
SW Patton Ct
2500 PTLD 97201 626 B1
SW Patton Ln
2700 PTLD 97201 626 B1
Patton Rd
1100 LKOW 97034 656 E7
1300 LKOW 97034 686 E1
SW Patton Rd
2500 PTLD 97201 626 A2
3400 PTLD 97221 626 B1
3400 PTLD 97239 626 B1
4100 MthC 97221 626 A2
5200 MthC 97221 625 J2
5200 PTLD 97221 625 J2
SW Pattulo Wy
1800 CmsC 97068 686 C4
SW Patwin Ct
11000 TLTN 97062 685 C7
SW Paul Ct
18500 WasC 97006 624 G1
SE Paula Jean Ct
3500 HBRO 97123 623 E2
SE Paul Bunyan Ln
27400 CmsC 97022 689 G6
NW Pauley Rd
16500 MthC 97231 534 G6
SW Paulina Ct
31100 WNVL 97070 745 B2

STREET	Block	City	ZIP	Map#	Grid
NW Paulina Dr					
	19800	WasC	97229	594	D1
SW Paulina Dr					
	10000	TLTN	97062	685	D6
	10400	WasC	97062	685	D6
	11300	WNVL	97070	745	B2
Paulina Ln					
	23000	WLIN	97068	686	H7
SW Pauline Ln					
	16800	WasC	97007	624	G3
SE Paul Moore Rd					
	39200	CmsC	97055	691	A7
Paulsen Dr					
	18700	ORCY	97045	717	A4
SW Pawnee Lp					
	28600	WNVL	97070	715	E6
SW Pawnee Pth					
	9700	TLTN	97062	685	D2
NW Paxton Ct					
	9600	PTLD	97229	595	E2
NW Payne Ct					
	-	CMAS	98607	539	A4
NW Payne Dr					
	13300	WasC	97229	595	A1
SE Payne Rd					
	3400	ClkC	98607	568	H3
	3400	CMAS	98607	568	H3
NW Payne St					
	6000	CMAS	98607	539	A6
Payson Ln					
	11700	CmsC	97045	717	A6
	11700	ORCY	97045	717	A6
SE Peace Ct					
	15900	HPYV	97236	658	E5
NE Peaceful Dr					
	18500	ClkC	98606	478	G4
NW Peaceful Ln					
	32400	WasC	97133	532	J5
	32400	WasC	97133	533	A6
SE Peaceful Ln					
	33200	CmsC	97023	750	J5
SW Peaceful Ln					
	2800	PTLD	97239	626	C4
S Peach Av					
	21100	CmsC	97013	746	A7
SW Peach Ln					
	6500	BRTN	97008	625	A5
NW Peach St					
	100	DNDE	97115	742	H2
SW Peach Cove Ln					
	100	CmsC	97068	746	F2
SW Peach Cove Rd					
	30700	CmsC	97068	746	E2
SW Peachtree Dr					
	14400	TGRD	97224	655	A6
	14400	WasC	97224	655	A7
	14500	WasC	97224	654	J6
SW Peachvale St					
	12500	KNGC	97224	685	B1
	12500	WasC	97224	685	A1
	12900	WasC	97224	655	A7
Peacock Ct					
	300	NWBG	97132	713	C5
NW Peacock Ln					
	49200	WasC	97116	561	B7
SE Peacock Ln					
	500	PTLD	97214	597	B6
Peacock Pl					
	10	LKOW	97035	656	B3
Peak Ct					
	34400	STHN	97051	414	H2
SW Peak Ct					
	14600	WasC	97224	654	J5
NW Peak Rd					
	32700	SPSE	97056	444	D7
S Pear Rd					
	18500	CmsC	97045	718	F7
Pearcy St					
	900	LKOW	97034	656	F7
Pearl St					
	100	ORCY	97045	717	D2
SE Pearl St					
	-	CmsC	97045	717	D2
	-	ORCY	97045	717	D2
SW Pearl St					
	13100	BRTN	97005	625	A4
	18000	WasC	97140	714	E1
SW Pearson Ct					
	11800	BRTN	97008	625	C7
Pease Rd					
	18900	ORCY	97045	717	C4
	19200	CmsC	97045	717	B4
SW Peavine Rd					
	11900	YmhC	97128	770	A6
SW Pebble Ct					
	16100	BRTN	97007	654	G1
Pebble Dr					
	58500	ClbC	97053	414	B2
Pebble Ln					
	21100	FRVW	97024	599	A2
Pebble Beach Ct					
	700	LKOW	97034	656	E4
Pebble Beach Dr					
	15000	ORCY	97045	717	H6
SE Pebble Beach Dr					
	14500	HPYV	97236	658	D1
NW Pebble Beach Wy					
	800	BRTN	97006	594	G5
Pecan Ct					
	900	NWBG	97132	713	E6
SW Pecan Ct					
	19200	WasC	97006	624	D1
SW Pecan St					
	19900	WasC	97006	624	C1
NW Pederson Rd					
	23600	MthC	97124	533	H1
	23600	MthC	97124	534	A1
	23600	MthC	97231	534	A1
NE Peerless Pl					
	3200	PTLD	97232	597	A4
Pegasus Ct					
	500	MOLA	97038	837	E1
SE Pegasus St					
	6100	HBRO	97123	593	J7
SW Pegg Ct					
	12700	BRTN	97005	625	B4
SW Peggy Ct					
	21500	WasC	97006	594	B7
Peggy St					
	-	MCMV	97128	770	D5
SE Peggy Wy					
	11300	HPYV	97236	657	J3
	11400	CmsC	97236	657	J3
SE Peggy Ann Dr					
	22100	DAMA	97009	659	B7
N Pekin Rd					
	100	CtzC	98674	385	H2
	100	WDLD	98674	385	H1
S Pekin Rd					
	100	CtzC	98674	385	J3
	100	WDLD	98674	385	J3
	300	CtzC	98674	386	A4
NW Pekin Ferry Ct					
	33700	ClkC	98642	386	B7
NW Pekin Ferry Dr					
	33400	ClkC	98642	386	B7
NW Pekin Ferry Rd					
	32400	ClkC	98642	386	B7
	32400	ClkC	98642	416	B1
Pekkola Rd					
	-	YmhC	97111	741	A3
NE Pekkola Rd					
	4700	YmhC	97111	741	B3
NE Pelfrey Av					
	-	FRVW	97024	599	A3
SW Pelham Ct					
	8800	BRTN	97008	625	D4
S Pelican Ct					
	27100	CmsC	97013	776	A7
SW Pelican Wy					
	11900	BRTN	97007	654	H3
SE Pelton Av					
	3100	TDLE	97060	599	H7
SE Pelton Cir					
	3800	TDLE	97060	599	G7
SE Pelton Ct					
	1500	HBRO	97123	593	J7
	2500	TDLE	97060	599	H6
SE Pembroke Ct					
	11100	CmsC	97222	657	E3
SW Pembrook St					
	9700	TGRD	97224	655	D6
SW Pembrooke Ter					
	-	BRTN	97006	594	G5
SE Penance St					
	11000	MWKE	97222	657	A2
NW Pender Pl					
	5200	WasC	97229	564	H5
NE Pendle Hill Rd					
	29100	YmhC	97132	713	G3
SW Pendleton Ct					
	5900	PTLD	97221	625	H4
SW Pendleton St					
	1400	PTLD	97239	626	D4
	4700	PTLD	97221	626	A4
	5500	PTLD	97221	625	J4
SE Penguin Pl					
	400	TDLE	97060	599	G4
SW Peninsula Ct					
	16500	BRTN	97006	594	G6
N Peninsular Av					
	7500	PTLD	97217	566	D4
S Penman Rd					
	22000	CmsC	97045	747	B4
SW Penn Ct					
	11600	TGRD	97223	655	C2
Penn Ln					
	1700	CmsC	97045	687	E7
	1700	ORCY	97045	687	E7
Penn St					
	400	CBAC	97018	385	B2
SW Pennie Ln					
	14800	WasC	97224	654	J6
Pennington Ct					
	1000	NWBG	97132	713	C6
SE Pennington Ct					
	9200	CmsC	97236	657	H1
Pennington Dr N					
	1100	NWBG	97132	713	D6
Pennington Dr S					
	1100	NWBG	97132	713	D6
NW Pennington Pl					
	3200	WasC	97229	595	C2
SW Pennoyer St					
	10	PTLD	97239	626	F2
SE Penns Ln					
	11400	CmsC	97055	660	J4
Pennsylvania Ct					
	600	MOLA	97038	807	B7
Penny Av					
	15200	CmsC	97055	660	H7
	15200	SNDY	97055	660	H7
	15400	CmsC	97055	690	H1
	15400	SNDY	97055	690	H1
Penny Ct					
	18100	GLDS	97027	687	E2
Penny Ln					
	-	YmhC	97114	741	G5
	12000	YmhC	97111	741	G6
Penny St					
	15200	CmsC	97009	660	H7
	15200	SNDY	97009	660	H7
	15200	SNDY	97055	660	H7
	15200	SNDY	97055	690	H1
NE Penny Wy					
	4200	HBRO	97124	593	G2
SE Penny Lee Ct					
	15100	CmsC	97015	658	D7
Pennys Wy					
	11300	ORCY	97045	716	J5
SE Pennywood Ct					
	13000	MWKE	97222	657	B5
SE Pennywood Dr					
	4400	MWKE	97222	657	B4
	4500	CmsC	97222	657	B4
SW Pennywort Ter					
	14300	TGRD	97224	655	F6
NW Penridge Rd					
	7000	MthC	97229	595	G5
NW Pentland St					
	1700	PTLD	97229	595	G3
Pepper Ln					
	33100	ClbC	97053	444	E1
Pepperidge Ct					
	3000	FTGV	97116	591	H3
SW Peppermill Ct					
	15300	BRTN	97007	624	H4
S Peppermint Rd					
	18100	CmsC	97004	748	D3
SW Peppertree Ln					
	9800	TGRD	97224	655	D7
S Pepperwood St					
	1300	CNBY	97013	776	D1
SE Pepperwood Wy					
	3300	HBRO	97123	623	H1
	3300	WasC	97123	623	H1
Perch Ct					
	19500	LKOW	97034	686	A3
S Percheron Dr					
	17700	CmsC	97045	718	D2
SW Percheron Ln					
	12600	BRTN	97008	655	B2
Peregrine Ct					
	2100	WLIN	97068	686	J5
NW Peregrine Pl					
	5400	WasC	97229	564	D7
SW Perfecta Av					
	900	WasC	97005	595	A6
SW Periander St					
	2800	PTLD	97201	626	C1
Pericles					
	10	LKOW	97035	656	A3
SW Peridot Wy					
	15500	BRTN	97007	654	H1
NW Perimeter Dr					
	14400	WasC	97006	594	J2
NW Perimeter Pl					
	15500	WasC	97006	594	H3
Perimeter Wy					
	-	TDLE	97060	599	F2
NW Perimeter Wy					
	900	TDLE	97060	599	E2
Periwinkle St					
	3000	FTGV	97116	591	G3
NW Perl Wy					
	1000	HBRO	97006	594	D5
NW Permian Ct					
	11800	WasC	97229	595	C2
NW Permian Dr					
	11400	WasC	97229	595	C2
NE Perrault Dr					
	15400	VCVR	98684	538	D3
Perrin St					
	5700	WLIN	97068	687	B6
NE Perry Rd					
	600	ClkC	98671	539	H6
Perry Creek Rd					
	-	ClbC	97051	385	A5
	-	STHN	97051	385	A5
	60600	ClbC	97051	384	H4
N Perry Creek Rd					
	60700	ClbC	97051	384	J4
SE Pershing Ct					
	18000	GSHM	97236	628	G2
NE Pershing Ln					
	7700	HBRO	97124	594	B5
SE Pershing St					
	1100	PTLD	97202	626	H2
NW Persimmon Pl					
	600	BRTN	97006	594	H5
Persimmon Wy					
	15000	ORCY	97045	717	H7
SE Persons Ct					
	2900	CmsC	97267	657	A7
	2900	CmsC	97267	687	A1
NW Perthshire Av					
	5800	VCVR	98663	506	E7
NE Petal Av					
	3600	MCMV	97128	771	C4
	3600	YmhC	97128	771	C4
SW Pete Dr					
	15600	WasC	97007	624	H3
Peter Pl					
	-	CmsC	97055	693	D6
Peters Rd					
	13100	LKOW	97035	656	A4
SW Peters Rd					
	7700	DRHM	97224	685	F3
Peter Skene Wy					
	17600	ORCY	97045	717	E2
SE Peterson Rd					
	25800	CmsC	97009	659	F6
SW Petes Mountain Rd					
	1700	WLIN	97068	716	F3
	22000	CmsC	97068	716	E7
Petite Ct					
	18300	GLDS	97027	687	D3
SW Petrel Ct					
	15600	BRTN	97007	654	H1
SW Petrel Ln					
	15300	BRTN	97007	654	H2
NE Petticoat Ln					
	2700	VCVR	98663	537	A2
	2800	ClkC	98661	537	A2
	2800	VCVR	98661	537	A2
SE Petticoat Hill Av					
	8400	VCVR	98664	537	F7
NW Pettygrove St					
	1200	PTLD	97209	596	C4
	2000	PTLD	97210	596	D4
	13100	WasC	97229	595	A3
SW Peyton Ln					
	9200	WNVL	97070	715	E7
SW Peyton Rd					
	6300	BRTN	97223	625	H5
	6300	PTLD	97219	625	H5
	6800	WasC	97223	625	H5
SW Pfaffle St					
	7700	TGRD	97223	655	F3
Pfeifer Ct					
	4000	LKOW	97035	656	A5
Pfeifer Dr					
	14300	LKOW	97035	656	A5
Pfeifer Wy					
	14300	LKOW	97035	656	A5
PGE Rd					
	-	CmsC	97055	691	J1
	-	CmsC	97055	692	A1
Phantom Bluff Ct					
	16300	LKOW	97034	656	C7
SE Pheasant Av					
	3000	GSHM	97080	629	H6
SE Pheasant Ct					
	13200	CmsC	97222	657	E5
SW Pheasant Ct					
	18000	WasC	97006	594	F7
SW Pheasant Dr					
	1600	WasC	97006	594	F7
Pheasant Ln					
	-	FTGV	97116	591	H2
SW Pheasant Ln					
	17400	WasC	97006	594	F7
Pheasant Run					
	10	LKOW	97035	656	B3
SW Pheasant St					
	24700	WasC	97123	623	H2
SE Pheasant Wy					
	2600	GSHM	97080	629	H5
Pheasant Hill Ln					
	59500	ClbC	97051	384	H7
NW Pheasant Hill Rd					
	13500	YmhC	97128	770	A2
SE Pheasant Ridge Dr					
	11200	HPYV	97236	657	J2
N Philadelphia Av					
	7000	PTLD	97203	565	G3
N Philadelphia Av US-30 BYP					
	7200	PTLD	97203	565	G3
SW Philadelphia Wy					
	500	WasC	97006	594	F6
SE Philips Pl					
	9100	CmsC	97236	657	G1
SE Philips Creek Ln					
	7800	CmsC	97222	657	F3
NW Phillips Rd					
	19100	WasC	97124	564	D2
	19100	WasC	97231	564	E2
SE Phoebe Ct					
	800	GSHM	97080	629	C5
S Phoebe Dr					
	-	RDGF	98642	446	B1
NW Phoenix Dr					
	400	TDLE	97060	599	F3
NE Phoenix St					
	300	HBRO	97124	593	B1
Phoenix Wy					
	200	VCVR	98661	537	C6
SW Phyllis Av					
	1500	GSHM	97080	628	G4
Phyllis Ct					
	3200	LKOW	97035	656	B5
NW Phyllis Ct					
	10	GSHM	97030	628	G2
SW Phyllis Ct					
	200	GSHM	97030	628	G3
Phyllis Dr					
	-	YmhC	97128	770	D6
SW Phyllis Dr					
	2300	GSHM	97080	628	G5
SW Phyllis Pl					
	2200	GSHM	97080	628	G5
SE Piazza Av					
	15400	CmsC	97015	657	H7
SW Picadilly Ln					
	15400	BRTN	97007	654	E2
SW Picard Ct					
	6100	WasC	97223	625	F5
SW Picasso Pl					
	8900	TGRD	97223	655	G1
	8900	WasC	97223	625	E7
	8900	WasC	97223	655	G1
Piccadilly Ln					
	-	CmsC	97067	724	A4
Pickens St					
	-	WLIN	97068	687	B7
Pickle Pl					
	-	SPSE	97056	474	E1
SW Pickleweed Ln					
	7800	TGRD	97224	655	F5
SW Picks Ct					
	10000	TGRD	97224	685	D1
SW Picks Wy					
	10200	TGRD	97224	685	D1
N Pierce Av					
	6900	PTLD	97203	565	H4
NE Pierce Dr					
	8200	VCVR	98662	537	F2
Pierce Ln					
	9900	YmhC	97132	743	B2
Pierce St					
	700	ORCY	97045	717	D1
	1300	ORCY	97045	687	E7
NE Pierce St					
	100	ECDA	97023	750	B3
SE Pierce St					
	100	ECDA	97023	750	B4
	6800	CmsC	97222	657	E1
N Pier Park Pl					
	9100	PTLD	97203	565	H2
NE Pietila Rd					
	20800	ClkC	98604	449	A7
NE Pietz St					
	9100	VCVR	98664	537	G5
SW Pihas Ct					
	9800	TGRD	97223	655	D4
SW Pihas St					
	9500	TGRD	97223	655	E3
S Pike Av					
	25000	CmsC	97045	777	H2
SW Pike Ln					
	18800	WasC	97007	624	E2
NE Pike St					
	-	WDVL	97060	599	C5
SW Pike St					
	19600	WasC	97007	624	D2
SE Pilgrim Ct					
	17300	CmsC	97267	687	C2
SW Pilips Ln					
	9400	WasC	97008	625	E6
	9400	WasC	97223	625	E6
Pilkington Rd					
	17000	LKOW	97035	685	J1
	17700	CmsC	97035	685	J3
	18800	RVGR	97035	685	J3
SW Pima Av					
	22200	TLTN	97062	685	F7
Pimlico Dr					
	2200	WLIN	97068	686	J5
Pimlico Ter					
	10	LKOW	97035	656	B4
	2600	WLIN	97068	686	J5
SW Pimlico Ter					
	9700	BRTN	97008	655	A1
Pine					
	-	CmsC	97015	657	H6
SE Pine					
	-	CmsC	97055	690	J4
	-	SNDY	97055	690	J4
Pine Av					
	-	SNDY	97055	690	J5
N Pine Av					
	300	YCLT	98675	419	G1
SE Pine Ct					
	-	PTLD	97233	598	C6
	1100	HBRO	97123	593	J6
	6800	PTLD	97215	597	E6
	11200	PTLD	97216	597	J6
SE Pine Ln					
	2400	CmsC	97267	656	J6
Pine Pl					
	19100	CmsC	97045	717	A4
	19200	ORCY	97045	717	A4
Pine Rdg E					
	-	WasC	97007	624	D5
Pine Rdg N					
	-	WasC	97007	624	D5
Pine Rdg S					
	-	WasC	97007	624	D5
Pine Rdg W					
	-	WasC	97007	624	D5
Pine St					
	-	WasC	97006	594	D5
	100	STHN	97051	415	B1
	800	VCVR	98660	536	F2
	1200	LKOW	97034	686	E1
	4600	WLIN	97068	687	B7
N Pine St					
	400	CNBY	97013	746	D4
	1400	CmsC	97013	746	D5
S Pine St					
	-	CLTN	97111	711	A7
	-	CmsC	97013	776	D1
	100	CLTN	97111	741	A1
	100	CNBY	97013	746	D6
	1000	CNBY	97013	776	D1
S Pine St SR-47					
	100	CLTN	97111	741	A1
SE Pine St					
	300	PTLD	97214	596	J6
	1600	HBRO	97123	593	E6
	3900	PTLD	97214	597	B6
	5500	PTLD	97215	597	D6
	8100	PTLD	97216	597	F6
	11700	PTLD	97216	598	A6
	13300	PTLD	97233	598	B6
	17000	GSHM	97233	598	G6
SW Pine St					
	10	PTLD	97204	596	F6
	600	PTLD	97205	596	F5
	6600	TGRD	97223	655	G2
	7100	WasC	97223	655	G2
	9300	BRTN	97005	625	E4
	22800	SRWD	97140	684	G7
	23000	SRWD	97140	714	H1
W Pine St					
	1600	MCMV	97128	770	E5
SE Pine Wy					
	4300	HBRO	97123	593	G6
NE Pinebrook Av					
	600	VCVR	98684	538	A6
SW Pinebrook Ct					
	8900	TGRD	97224	655	E6
NE Pinebrook St					
	12600	VCVR	98684	538	A5
SW Pinebrook St					
	8500	TGRD	97224	655	E6
SW Pinecone Av					
	23700	SRWD	97140	714	F1
Pine Cone Ln					
	-	CmsC	97045	716	G7
SE Pine Cone Ln					
	17000	CmsC	97267	687	A2
Pinecreek Ln					
	13500	CmsC	97045	717	E5
	13500	ORCY	97045	717	E5
NE Pinecreek St					
	9200	VCVR	98664	537	G4
SE Pine Creek Wy					
	6300	CmsC	97267	657	D6
SW Pinecrest Ct					
	6600	BRTN	97008	625	D5
NW Pinefarm Pl					
	5800	HBRO	97124	563	J6
	5800	WasC	97124	563	J6
SE Pinegrove Ct					
	14900	CmsC	97015	658	C7
SE Pinegrove Lp					
	14900	CmsC	97015	658	C7
SE Pinehurst Av					
	3300	CmsC	97222	657	A6
	3300	CmsC	97267	657	A6
Pinehurst Ct					
	100	NWBG	97132	713	B6
Pinehurst Dr					
	100	NWBG	97132	713	C6
NW Pinehurst Dr					
	2000	MCMV	97128	770	G3
	2700	YmhC	97128	770	G2
SW Pinehurst Dr					
	9400	BRTN	97005	625	E4
	22500	SRWD	97140	684	E7
	23000	SRWD	97140	714	F1
Pinehurst St					
	700	NWBG	97132	713	C6
SE Pinelane St					
	2000	CmsC	97267	656	J6
SE Pineridge Ct					
	-	PTLD	97236	628	C7
SW Pineridge Ct					
	7300	WasC	97225	625	G2
E Pine Tree Wy					
	64700	CmsC	97049	693	H7
NW Pinetta Pl					
	-	PTLD	97210	596	B5
Pine Valley Rd					
	100	LKOW	97034	656	E6
SE Pineview Ct					
	-	ECDA	97023	750	C4
SW Pine View St					
	12800	TGRD	97224	655	A7
	12800	WasC	97224	655	A7
SE Pinewood Av					
	3400	HBRO	97123	623	G1
Pinewood Ct					
	100	ORCY	97045	717	A3
Pinewood Ln					
	22000	CmsC	97049	724	E1
E Pinewood Ln					
	22000	CmsC	97049	724	F1
SE Pinewood Wy					
	3500	HBRO	97123	623	G1
SW Pinewood Wy					
	3900	WasC	97007	624	F2
Pinkerton Dr					
	100	CtzC	98674	386	A2
Pinkney Rd					
	-	ClbC	97051	384	A1
NW Pinnacle Ct					
	8400	PTLD	97229	595	F2
NW Pinnacle Dr					
	-	PTLD	97229	595	F3
E Pinner Rd					
	25500	CmsC	97049	724	F4
Pin Oak Dr					
	300	ORCY	97045	717	B3
NW Pinon Ct					
	1300	CMAS	98607	569	A4
NW Pinon Hills Ter					
	3600	WasC	97229	595	B2
SW Pinot Ct					
	14500	WasC	97224	654	J6
SW Pinot Pl					
	-	WasC	97123	653	B7
	-	WasC	97123	683	B1
Pinot Noir Dr					
	-	MCMV	97128	770	F2
SW Pintail Ct					
	15200	BRTN	97007	654	H3
SW Pintail Lp					
	11200	BRTN	97007	654	H3
Pinto Ct					
	1900	WLIN	97068	686	H5
SW Pinto Ct					
	9000	BRTN	97008	625	D4
SW Pinto Dr					
	22100	TLTN	97062	685	E7
SW Pinto Ter					
	9200	BRTN	97008	655	A1
Pioneer Blvd					
	38200	SNDY	97055	690	J3
	38900	SNDY	97055	691	B3
	39700	CmsC	97055	691	B3
Pioneer Blvd US-26					
	38200	SNDY	97055	690	J3
	38900	SNDY	97055	691	B3
	39700	CmsC	97055	691	B3
Pioneer Cir					
	1500	FTGV	97116	592	C6
Pioneer Ct					
	18100	LKOW	97034	686	A2
	18100	LKOW	97035	686	A2
SW Pioneer Ct					
	9000	WNVL	97070	715	D3
Pioneer Dr					
	400	LFYT	97127	771	H1
SE Pioneer Dr					
	14700	CmsC	97015	658	D6
SW Pioneer Ln					
	12000	BRTN	97008	655	B2
Pioneer Lp					
	1100	LFYT	97127	771	H1
	1100	YmhC	97114	771	H1
E Pioneer Lp					
	600	LCTR	98629	386	H7
Pioneer Rd					
	55200	ClbC	97053	414	A4
	55200	ClbC	97053	444	B1
	55200	ClbC	97056	414	A4
	55200	ClbC	97056	444	A1
NW Pioneer Rd					
	13700	WasC	97229	595	A5
	13900	WasC	97006	595	A5
	17700	BRTN	97006	594	F5
	17700	WasC	97006	594	F5
Pioneer Rdg					
	-	ORCY	97045	717	E5
Pioneer St					
	-	DAYT	97114	772	A5
	100	RDGF	98642	415	J7
	900	NWBG	97132	713	C5
	5000	RDGF	98642	416	F7
Pioneer St SR-501					
	200	RDGF	98642	415	J7
	700	RDGF	98642	416	A7
Pioneer Wy					
	1300	FTGV	97116	592	C6
N Pioneer Canyon Dr					
	-	RDGF	98642	416	D6
S Pioneer Crossing Ln					
	18800	CmsC	97023	719	F5
NW Pioneer Park Wy					
	14400	BRTN	97006	594	J5
SE Pipeline Rd					
	30000	MthC	97060	630	C5
	30000	MthC	97080	630	C5
Piper Ct					
	3600	LKOW	97034	686	A2
SE Piper Dr					
	13200	CmsC	97236	658	C5
	13400	HPYV	97236	658	C5
NE Piper Rd					
	13900	VCVR	98684	538	B6
Piper St NE					
	14000	MrnC	97002	775	D1
SW Piper Ter					
	13600	TGRD	97223	655	B5
SE Pipers Dr					
	3700	HBRO	97123	623	F2
	3700	WasC	97123	623	F2
SW Pipit Ct					
	16100	BRTN	97007	654	G3
SW Pippen Ln					
	8800	TGRD	97224	655	E7
Pirelli Ln NE					
	19400	MrnC	97032	774	G7
Pisgah Home Rd					
	31000	ClbC	97056	444	A3
SW Pitic Ln					
	7700	WasC	97223	625	G6
NW Pittock Dr					
	200	PTLD	97210	596	A5
N Pittsburg Av					
	6500	PTLD	97203	565	G3
Pittsburg Rd					
	30700	ClbC	97051	384	B3
	34700	STHN	97051	384	J7
	35400	ClbC	97051	385	A7
	35400	STHN	97051	385	A7
SW Piute Ct					
	8100	TLTN	97062	685	F5
SE P Jay's Ct					
	15100	CmsC	97267	657	E7
NW Placido Ct					
	11300	WasC	97229	595	C3
NE Plains Wy					
	4400	VCVR	98662	537	F1
NW Plainview Rd					
	11000	MthC	97231	534	F7
	11000	MthC	97231	564	F1
NW Planet Ct					
	15200	WasC	97106	531	F3
Plantation Dr					
	56600	ClbC	97053	414	H6
NE Plantation Rd					
	12000	ClkC	98685	476	J7
	12000	ClkC	98685	506	H1
NW Plastics Dr					
	21500	WasC	97124	564	B4
SW Platanus Pl					
	23600	SRWD	97140	714	G1
SW Platinum Pl					
	9100	BRTN	97007	624	G2
	9100	BRTN	97007	654	E1
SE Platt Av					
	5900	MthC	97236	628	F5
	5900	PTLD	97236	628	F5
NE Platt St					
	1200	HBRO	97124	593	D1
SE Platz Ln					
	-	CmsC	97009	660	G4
SE Player Ct					
	2700	HBRO	97123	624	A1
Plaza Sq					
	10	STHN	97051	385	D7
NW Plaza St					
	-	PTLD	97210	596	A2
E Plaza Tr					
	26500	CmsC	97067	724	B6
Pleasant Av					
	300	ORCY	97045	717	D2
SW Pleasant Pl					
	10400	WNVL	97070	715	C7
Pleasant St					
	38500	SNDY	97055	690	J3
	38900	SNDY	97055	691	A3
NW Pleasant St					
	-	PTLD	97210	596	A2
SW Pleasant Hill Rd					
	15400	CmsC	97140	714	G4
SE Pleasant Home Rd					
	6000	MthC	97080	630	C6
	8200	CmsC	97009	660	C1
	8200	MthC	97080	660	C1
SW Pleasanton Ln					
	17000	WasC	97006	594	F7
SW Pleasant Valley Rd					
	13400	WasC	97007	654	C7
	16500	WasC	97007	684	B1
NW Pleasant View Av					
	10	GSHM	97030	628	H2
SW Pleasant View Av					
	10	GSHM	97030	628	H2
SW Pleasant View Ct					
	15600	WasC	97224	654	H6
NE Pleasant View Dr					
	100	ClkC	98629	386	G5
NW Pleasant View Dr					
	100	ClkC	98629	386	G5
SW Pleasant View Dr					
	1200	GSHM	97030	628	H4
	1200	GSHM	97080	628	H4
	2800	MthC	97080	628	H5
SE Pleides St					
	17000	DAMA	97009	688	F1
Plomondon Ln					
	3800	VCVR	98661	537	B3
Plomondon St					
	3900	VCVR	98661	537	B3
SW Plover Ct					
	17000	SRWD	97140	684	F4
SE Plover Dr					
	9500	HPYV	97236	658	C2
SW Plum Cir					
	2800	PTLD	97219	656	C1
N Plum Ct					
	1500	CmsC	97013	746	E5
	1500	CNBY	97013	746	E5
NW Plum Ct					
	-	PTLD	97231	565	E4
SW Plum Ct					
	2500	PTLD	97219	626	C7
	2700	PTLD	97219	656	C1
	11000	TLTN	97062	685	C6
NW Plum Dr					
	-	PTLD	97231	565	E4
S Plum Dr					
	14600	CmsC	97045	717	G3
SE Plum Dr					
	6300	MWKE	97222	657	D4
SW Plum Dr					
	800	PTLD	97219	656	D1
NW Plum St					
	100	DNDE	97115	742	H2
SW Plum St					
	200	PTLD	97219	656	E1
	4500	PTLD	97219	626	A7
SW Plum Ter					
	11300	TGRD	97223	655	C3
SW Plumeria Ln					
	4200	WasC	97007	624	D3
NW Plum Hill Ln					
	44600	WasC	97116	591	F1
SW Plumlee Rd					
	46400	WasC	97116	591	D7
NE Pluss Rd					
	22800	ClkC	98682	509	C4
NW Plymouth Ct					
	-	PTLD	97231	565	E3
SE Plymouth Ct					
	17300	CmsC	97267	687	C2
Plymouth St					
	300	STHN	97051	415	D1
SW Plymouth Wy					
	300	WasC	97006	594	F6
Pocatello Av					
	1100	VCVR	98661	537	D5
SE Poe Rd					
	-	CmsC	97055	690	H6
NW Poehler Ter					
	3500	WasC	97229	594	F2
N Point Rd					
	300	LKOW	97034	656	F6
S Point Rd					
	800	LKOW	97034	656	E6
W Point Rd					
	900	LKOW	97034	656	E7
SW Pointe Forest Ct					
	17600	WasC	97006	594	F7
SW Pointer Rd					
	7000	BRTN	97225	595	H7
	7000	BRTN	97225	625	G1
SW Pointer Wy					
	8200	WasC	97225	595	F7
NE Poison Oak Ln					
	32500	YmhC	97132	744	A2
Pokorny Rd NE					
	8000	MrnC	97137	774	A4
SE Polaris Wy					
	6200	HBRO	97123	623	J1
S Polehn Rd					
	19700	CmsC	97045	718	G7
	20300	CmsC	97045	748	G1
N Polk Av					
	8500	PTLD	97203	565	J2
SE Polk Cir					
	1100	CMAS	98607	569	G5
Polk St					
	-	CLTN	97111	741	A1
	900	ORCY	97045	717	D1
	1300	ORCY	97045	687	D7

Portland Street Index

STREET
Block City ZIP Map# Grid

Polk St
200 CLTN 97111 741 A1
E Polk St
600 CMAS 98607 569 G5
W Polk St
100 CLTN 97111 741 A1
Pollard Dr
34100 ClbC 97056 444 G1
W Pollard Ln
16100 WasC 97224 654 G6
W Pollock Rd
31700 ClkC 98642 416 G2
Polly Av
66700 CmsC 97049 724 A2
Polo Ct
2800 WLIN 97068 686 H4
W Polo Ct
13500 BRTN 97008 655 A1
Polo Ln
3500 FRVW 97024 599 A3
Polonius St
10 LKOW 97035 656 B5
W Polsky Rd
10800 WasC 97005 625 D2
E Pomfret Rd
14800 CmsC 97015 658 C6
W Pommel Ct
13500 BRTN 97008 625 A7
W Pomona Ct
3400 PTLD 97219 656 B2
W Pomona Dr
19000 WasC 97007 654 D1
19200 WasC 97007 624 D7
W Pomona St
1300 MthC 97219 656 F2
3500 PTLD 97219 656 A2
4900 PTLD 97219 655 J2
6400 PTLD 97223 655 H2
6400 TGRD 97223 655 H2
Pompei Dr
13800 CmsC 97045 717 E5
W Ponca Ct
8100 TLTN 97062 685 F6
Pond Dr
31000 ClbC 97056 444 A1
E Ponder Ln
37700 CmsC 97055 690 H4
37700 SNDY 97055 690 H4
Ponderay Dr
22300 WLIN 97068 686 H7
S Ponderosa Ct
600 CmsC 97013 746 E7
W Ponderosa Ct
500 MCMV 97128 770 E5
Ponderosa Dr
59300 STHN 97051 414 J1
W Ponderosa Ln
10600 TLTN 97062 685 D6
Ponderosa Lp
3400 WLIN 97068 686 H7
W Ponderosa Pl
10700 TGRD 97223 655 D2
N Ponderosa St
1500 CNBY 97013 746 E4
S Ponderosa St
- CNBY 97013 776 E1
500 CmsC 97013 746 D7
500 CNBY 97013 746 E7
NE Ponderosa Pine Av
14300 VCVR 98684 538 B7
NW Pondosa Ct
19400 WasC 97229 564 D7
NW Pondosa Dr
5200 WasC 97229 564 C7
Pony Ct
6300 WLIN 97068 686 H5
SW Pony Pl
9100 BRTN 97008 654 F1
Pope Ln
15800 ORCY 97045 687 E5
SE Popes Pl
5700 HBRO 97123 593 J7
SE Poplar Av
1500 PTLD 97214 596 H7
Poplar Blvd
- WasC 97006 594 D5
NE Poplar Ct
23900 WDVL 97060 599 D5
NW Poplar Ct
1800 CMAS 98607 569 A3
SW Poplar Ct
100 MCMV 97128 770 F5
Poplar Ln
56700 ClbC 97053 414 F6
SW Poplar Ln
4500 BRTN 97225 625 F3
4500 WasC 97225 625 F3
Poplar Pl
1600 FTGV 97116 592 B5
SE Poplar Pl
2500 CmsC 97267 656 J6
S Poplar Rd
22200 CmsC 97023 750 A4
Poplar St
1700 FTGV 97116 592 B5
NE Poplar St
15500 VCVR 98682 538 D1
16000 ClkC 98682 538 E2
Poplar Wy
2800 LKOW 97034 686 H1
SW Poplarwood Pl
19900 TLTN 97062 685 G4
SE Poppy St
8100 JNCY 97267 687 F1
NW Poppy Hills Dr
1700 MCMV 97128 770 F4
SE Poppy Hills Dr
14500 HPYV 97236 658 C2
Port Av
100 STHN 97051 415 B2
Port Wy
800 VCVR 98660 536 E5
NE Portal Wy
18400 GSHM 97230 598 H2
18400 PTLD 97230 598 H2
N Port Center Wy
4200 PTLD 97217 596 C1
SE Porter Cir
8600 VCVR 98664 567 F1
SE Porter Ct
1600 VCVR 98664 567 F1
Porter Ln NE
- SPSE 97056 444 F7
NW Porter Rd
1200 FTGV 97116 592 B1

NW Porter Rd
1200 WasC 97116 592 B1
SE Porter Rd
8900 VCVR 98664 567 F1
37900 CmsC 97023 750 J6
SW Porter St
- PTLD 97239 626 D1
10 PTLD 97201 626 F1
10300 WasC 97225 625 D1
Portland Av
- CmsC 97049 724 E1
100 GLDS 97027 687 D3
SE Portland Av
17600 CmsC 97267 687 C2
18100 GLDS 97027 687 C3
NE Portland Hwy
4200 PTLD 97211 567 C6
6500 PTLD 97218 567 E7
NE Portland Hwy US-30 BYP
4200 PTLD 97211 567 C6
4200 PTLD 97218 567 D6
Portland Rd
1400 NWBG 97132 713 D7
4300 YmhC 97132 713 G6
Portland Rd SR-99W
1400 NWBG 97132 713 D7
4300 YmhC 97132 713 G6
Portland Rd SR-219
1400 NWBG 97132 713 D7
N Portland Rd
10000 PTLD 97203 566 B1
11500 PTLD 97203 536 C7
11800 PTLD 97217 536 C7
NE Portland Blvd Ct
900 PTLD 97211 566 H6
Portland Fairview RV Pk
- FRVW 97024 599 B3
Portland Hubbard Hwy
- CmsC 97002 745 E6
SE Portlandia Av
900 HBRO 97123 593 D6
S Portland View Dr
15500 CmsC 97045 688 A4
SE Portland View Pl
13200 CmsC 97236 628 B7
13200 HPYV 97236 628 B7
SW Portola Av
1000 WasC 97225 595 D7
SW Port Orford St
5800 TLTN 97062 685 H5
N Portsmouth Av
6300 PTLD 97203 566 A5
SW Portsmouth Pl
500 WasC 97006 594 E4
Poseidon Ct
3800 WLIN 97068 686 J5
SE Posey St
7900 CmsC 97267 687 H1
7900 JNCY 97267 687 H1
SW Postrio Ct
8700 WasC 97007 624 E7
SW Potano St
9800 TLTN 97062 685 D4
Potomac Dr
8300 VCVR 98664 537 F6
SW Potomac St
6900 TLTN 97062 685 G5
NE Potter Rd
12400 ClkC 98604 418 B7
S Potter Rd
17000 CmsC 97045 688 C7
17200 CmsC 97045 718 C1
NW Potters Ct
1600 PTLD 97229 595 E3
Potters Rd
17600 LKOW 97034 686 B1
NE Pounder Rd
10 MthC 97019 600 G6
SE Pounder Rd
100 MthC 97019 600 H7
200 MthC 97019 630 H1
Poverty Ln
59400 ClbC 97051 384 H7
NE Poverty Bend Rd
5300 YmhC 97111 741 B6
5300 YmhC 97128 741 A6
S Powder Rd
23700 CmsC 97004 748 B7
23700 CmsC 97045 748 B7
E Powell Blvd
10 GSHM 97030 629 C2
10 GSHM 97080 629 C2
E Powell Blvd US-26
10 GSHM 97030 629 C2
10 GSHM 97080 629 C2
SE Powell Blvd
500 PTLD 97202 626 H2
2800 PTLD 97202 627 A2
6900 PTLD 97206 627 E2
8000 PTLD 97266 627 F2
11500 PTLD 97266 628 A2
12000 PTLD 97236 628 E3
17400 GSHM 97030 628 F3
17400 GSHM 97080 628 F3
17400 GSHM 97236 628 F3
SE Powell Blvd US-26
500 PTLD 97202 626 J2
2800 PTLD 97202 627 A2
6900 PTLD 97206 627 E2
8000 PTLD 97266 627 F2
11500 PTLD 97266 628 A2
12000 PTLD 97236 628 E2
17400 GSHM 97030 628 F3
17400 GSHM 97080 628 F3
17400 GSHM 97236 628 F3
W Powell Blvd
10 GSHM 97030 629 B2
10 GSHM 97080 629 B2
1800 GSHM 97030 628 H3
1800 GSHM 97080 628 H3
W Powell Blvd US-26
10 GSHM 97030 629 B2
10 GSHM 97080 629 B2
1800 GSHM 97030 628 H3
1800 GSHM 97080 628 H3
SE Powell Ct
11200 PTLD 97266 627 J2
11500 PTLD 97266 628 A2
12300 PTLD 97236 628 A2
W Powell Ct
- GSHM 97030 628 G4
- GSHM 97080 628 G4
W Powell Lp
3400 GSHM 97030 628 H4

W Powell Lp
3400 GSHM 97080 628 H4
NE Powell Rd
13200 ClkC 98606 479 B7
SE Powell Butte Pkwy
4400 PTLD 97236 628 F4
4600 MthC 97236 628 F4
NE Powell Hill Rd
8700 YmhC 97115 742 E3
Powellhurst Woods
- PTLD 97266 627 J4
SE Powell Valley Blvd
4200 GSHM 97030 628 G3
4200 GSHM 97080 628 G3
4900 GSHM 97236 628 G3
4900 PTLD 97236 628 G3
SE Powell Valley Blvd US-26
4200 GSHM 97030 628 G3
4200 GSHM 97080 628 G3
4900 GSHM 97236 628 G3
4900 PTLD 97236 628 G3
SE Powell Valley Rd
5000 GSHM 97080 629 G4
28100 MthC 97080 629 J6
SE Powell View Ct
16700 MthC 97236 628 F4
16700 PTLD 97236 628 F4
SW Power Ct
8200 WasC 97225 625 F2
NE Powers Ct
3400 VCVR 98682 538 C3
SW Powers Ct
800 PTLD 97219 656 F3
N Powers St
6600 PTLD 97203 566 A2
6800 PTLD 97203 565 J2
NE Powers St
14100 VCVR 98682 538 C3
SW Powhatan Av
5600 TLTN 97062 685 H4
NW Powhatan Ter
700 PTLD 97210 596 B4
NE Poyner Rd
21900 ClkC 98606 479 B4
NE Poynter St
1700 HBRO 97124 593 E4
NE Prahl Pkwy
- HBRO 97124 593 E1
NE Prahl Rd
- CmsC 97002 745 D3
NE Prairie Ln
33700 SPSE 97056 444 F7
NE Prairie Rd
13000 ClkC 98606 478 B3
NE Prairie St
33500 SPSE 97056 444 E7
NW Prairie St
33400 SPSE 97056 444 E7
SW Prairie Ter
9500 BRTN 97008 655 B1
NE Prairie View Ct
14600 CmsC 97002 745 F4
NE Prairie View Dr
24600 CmsC 97002 745 F4
25800 CmsC 97070 745 F3
25800 WNVL 97002 745 F3
25800 WNVL 97070 745 F3
S Prairieview Ter
19400 ORCY 97045 717 C5
SW Preakness
11500 CmsC 97070 745 B2
11500 WNVL 97070 745 B2
Preakness Ct
10 LKOW 97035 656 B4
Preakness Dr
6200 WLIN 97068 686 H5
NW Preakness Ter
5300 WasC 97229 564 H7
SE Premier Ct
6200 CmsC 97267 687 D1
SW Premier Ct
- WasC 97006 624 C1
NE Prescott Dr
12600 PTLD 97230 598 B1
NW Prescott Pl
200 WasC 97006 594 C5
Prescott St
1300 ORCY 97045 717 D1
1400 ORCY 97045 687 E7
N Prescott St
1600 PTLD 97217 596 E1
NE Prescott St
10 PTLD 97211 596 G1
10 PTLD 97217 596 G1
3700 PTLD 97211 597 B1
4100 PTLD 97218 597 B1
8100 PTLD 97220 597 J1
9100 MWDP 97220 597 G1
11300 PTLD 97220 598 A1
13500 PTLD 97230 598 C1
SW Preslynn Dr
6500 PTLD 97221 625 H2
6500 WasC 97225 625 H2
NW Preston Ct
2600 PTLD 97229 595 D1
SE Preston Ct
5700 HBRO 97123 593 J5
Preston's Cross
- BRTN 97007 654 J3
SW Prestwick Ct
10800 WNVL 97070 745 C1
Prestwick Rd
2100 LKOW 97034 656 C6
SW Price Ter
23100 SRWD 97140 684 E7
23200 SRWD 97140 714 E1
Prickett Rd
- WasC 97116 591 C3
SE Primo East Rd
20300 CmsC 97055 692 A6
SE Primrose Av
14400 CmsC 97267 657 F6
SE Primrose Ct
2800 HBRO 97123 623 E1
Primrose Ln
1100 FTGV 97116 591 G3
S Primrose Pth
27100 CmsC 97013 776 C7
SW Primrose St
1900 PTLD 97219 626 C7
Primrose Lane 2
- VCVR 98660 536 F2
SW Prince Av
900 PTLD 97201 626 D1

Prince Ct
600 MOLA 97038 837 D1
SW Prince Albert St
12400 KNGC 97224 655 B7
12700 WasC 97224 655 B7
SW Prince Edward Ct
12400 KNGC 97224 655 B7
SW Prince Phillip Ct
12500 KNGC 97224 655 B7
SW Princess Av
6600 BRTN 97008 625 C5
S Princess Ct
17900 CmsC 97045 718 G2
NW Princess Dr
- PTLD 97210 596 A1
Princeton Av
200 GLDS 97027 687 E4
Princeton Ct
3100 NWBG 97132 713 C4
13000 LKOW 97035 655 J4
13000 LKOW 97035 656 A4
SW Princeton Ln
12900 TGRD 97223 655 D1
Princeton St
2900 NWBG 97132 713 C4
N Princeton St
4700 PTLD 97203 566 A5
8000 PTLD 97203 565 H3
Princeton Vil
- CmsC 97015 658 C6
SE Princeton Village Wy
14200 CmsC 97015 658 C5
14400 HPYV 97015 658 C5
Printer Pkwy
- WNVL 97070 715 F4
NW Priscilla Ct
10000 WasC 97229 595 E4
S Priscilla Ln
15500 CmsC 97045 688 J5
Probe St
200 MOLA 97038 807 E7
Proctor Blvd
38200 SNDY 97055 690 J3
39000 SNDY 97055 691 A3
Proctor Blvd US-26
38200 SNDY 97055 690 J3
39000 SNDY 97055 691 A3
SE Proctor Rd
36200 CmsC 97009 660 G2
SE Proctor St
31700 MthC 97080 630 C6
NW Progress Ct
7100 HBRO 97124 564 A5
SE Progress Ct
17200 CmsC 97267 687 C2
NW Promenade Ter
4800 WasC 97229 564 J7
4800 WasC 97229 594 J4
NW Prominence Ct
7900 MthC 97229 595 G3
7900 PTLD 97229 595 G3
Promontory Av
100 ORCY 97045 717 C2
SW Prospect Ct
6300 WasC 97007 624 D5
Prospect Dr
2100 NWBG 97132 713 C5
SW Prospect Dr
1700 PTLD 97201 596 D6
SW Prospect Ln
19600 WasC 97007 624 D5
SW Prospect Pl
19200 WasC 97007 624 D5
Prospect St
900 ORCY 97045 717 D3
4900 WLIN 97068 687 A6
SW Prospect St
19600 WasC 97007 624 D4
Prospector Ter
19300 ORCY 97045 717 C5
SW Prosperity Park Rd
- TLTN 97062 685 H5
5100 CmsC 97062 685 H5
Providence Dr
2000 NWBG 97132 713 G6
SE Province Dr
400 ClkC 98607 569 G4
400 CMAS 98607 569 G4
Provincial Hill Dr
13700 LKOW 97035 655 J5
Provincial Hill Wy
13400 LKOW 97035 655 J4
Provisioner Ct
19400 ORCY 97045 717 C5
S Provisioner Dr
19300 ORCY 97045 717 C5
Prune St
- NWBG 97132 713 F5
- YmhC 97132 713 F5
Prune St NE
- MmC 97002 744 J7
- MmC 97002 774 J1
S Public Rd
- CmsC 97045 688 C3
NW Pubols Rd
- HBRO 97124 564 A5
23100 WasC 97124 563 J5
23100 WasC 97124 564 A5
SW Pueblo Ct
10600 TLTN 97062 685 D2
SE Pueblo St
5300 HBRO 97123 623 H1
SW Pueblo St
10300 TLTN 97062 685 D2
SW Pueblo Ter
28000 WNVL 97070 715 E6
SE Puente Vista Dr
18800 DAMA 97009 658 G5
SW Puma Dr
3700 WasC 97116 591 D7
SW Pumice Ln
15300 BRTN 97007 654 E2
NW Pumpkin Ridge Dr
30900 WasC 97133 533 B5
NW Pumpkin Ridge Rd
12900 WasC 97133 533 A2
16900 WasC 97133 532 J1
SE Punch Bowl Ct
13300 HPYV 97236 628 D7
NW Purdin Rd
41900 WasC 97116 561 G7
41900 WasC 97116 591 H1
SE Purple Finch Dr
14400 HPYV 97236 658 C2

SE Purplelily Av
- HBRO 97123 623 D1
NW Purvis Dr
14800 WasC 97229 594 J1
NE Putnam Rd
29200 NWBG 97132 713 G5
29200 YmhC 97132 713 G5

Q

Q Cir
4100 WHGL 98671 570 D4
N Q Cir
1200 WHGL 98671 570 A4
Q St
- WHGL 98671 569 J4
2600 VCVR 98661 536 H3
2600 VCVR 98663 536 H3
3200 WHGL 98671 570 C4
N Q St
1500 WHGL 98671 570 A4
Quail
- FRVW 97024 599 A3
SE Quail Cir
1800 HBRO 97123 593 E7
1800 HBRO 97123 623 D1
Quail Ct
- TGRD 97223 655 D3
16700 LKOW 97034 656 D7
16700 LKOW 97034 686 D1
NW Quail Ct
2300 MCMV 97128 770 D5
SE Quail Ct
17400 GLDS 97027 687 D2
Quail Dr
- FTGV 97116 591 H2
200 NWBG 97132 713 C4
400 YmhC 97132 713 C4
SE Quail Dr
2800 GSHM 97080 629 H5
Quail Ln
34100 ClbC 97056 444 F2
SE Quail Ln
3000 GSHM 97080 629 H6
SW Quail Ln
14500 BRTN 97007 654 J3
SW Quail Creek Ln
12100 TGRD 97223 655 B5
S Quail Crest Ln
14600 CmsC 97045 717 G7
14600 CmsC 97045 747 G1
Quail Grove Cir
14600 CmsC 97045 717 G3
NW Quail Hollow Dr
19600 WasC 97229 564 C6
SE Quail Pointe Ct
2000 HBRO 97123 594 B7
SW Quail Post Rd
9700 PTLD 97219 656 C1
Quail Ridge Ct
3300 WLIN 97068 686 J7
SE Quail Ridge Ct
9300 CmsC 97236 657 H1
SE Quail Ridge Dr
10300 CmsC 97236 657 H1
SE Quail Run Dr
11200 HPYV 97236 657 J2
SW Quailrun Ln
20000 WasC 97140 684 C6
SE Qualley Rd
19300 CmsC 97009 688 H2
Quandary Ln
- FTGV 97116 591 G4
Quarry Rd
15100 LKOW 97035 656 A6
NE Quarry Rd
13900 YmhC 97132 713 H3
13900 YmhC 97140 713 J5
NW Quarry Rd
- MthC 97231 535 A4
10700 MthC 97231 564 H1
SW Quarry Rd
7200 WasC 97007 624 C6
Quarry St
200 ORCY 97045 717 C1
SW Quarryview Dr
24500 CmsC 97070 715 J2
24500 CmsC 97070 716 A3
NW Quartz Ct
4700 CMAS 98607 539 C7
NW Quartz Pl
3100 CMAS 98607 569 C2
NW Quartz St
2400 CMAS 98607 569 C3
NW Quartz Ter
3500 WasC 97229 595 B2
NW Quatama Rd
20600 HBRO 97006 594 C5
20600 WasC 97006 594 C5
21200 HBRO 97124 594 B5
21200 WasC 97124 594 B5
SW Queen Ct
29400 WNVL 97070 715 C7
SW Queen Ln
6300 BRTN 97008 625 C5
SE Queen Rd
6200 CmsC 97222 657 D2
6200 MWKE 97222 657 D2
SW Queen Anne Av
16600 KNGC 97224 685 B1
16800 WasC 97224 685 B1
SE Queenborough Ct
1600 MCMV 97128 770 J6
SE Queenborough St
1600 MCMV 97128 770 J6
SW Queen Elizabeth Av
11600 KNGC 97224 655 C7
SW Queen Elizabeth St
11800 KNGC 97224 655 B7
SW Queen Mary Av
16500 KNGC 97224 685 B1
NW Queens Ct
500 HBRO 97124 593 B3
NE Queens Ln
800 HBRO 97124 593 D3
NW Queens Wy
6200 MthC 97210 595 J5
6200 PTLD 97210 595 H5
Queens Park Rd
6400 CmsC 97035 655 J7
6400 LKOW 97035 655 J7
SW Queen Victoria Pl
15600 KNGC 97224 655 B7
SW Quelle Pl
11200 TGRD 97223 655 C5

Querulous St
- PTLD 97218 567 E5
NE Quicksilver Dr
23100 ClkC 98604 449 A4
Quiet Glen Ct
15200 CmsC 97045 717 H7
SE Quiet Meadows Dr
5700 CmsC 97267 687 C1
Quiet Oak St
- ORCY 97045 717 F6
SE Quietwoods St
12200 CmsC 97236 658 A5
NW Quimby St
1100 PTLD 97209 596 E4
2100 PTLD 97210 596 C4
Quinalt Ct
14900 ORCY 97045 717 G7
Quinalt Dr
20000 ORCY 97045 717 G6
NW Quinault Ct
4400 WasC 97229 594 C1
SW Quinault Ct
2200 PTLD 97219 626 C7
SW Quinault Ln
9300 TLTN 97062 685 A7
NW Quinault St
- CMAS 98607 539 A5
3900 CMAS 98607 569 A4
Quince
- CmsC 97015 657 H7
Quince St
2100 FTGV 97116 592 B4
2300 WasC 97116 592 B4
Quince St SR-47
2100 FTGV 97116 592 B4
2300 WasC 97116 592 B4
SW Quinn Ct
- WasC 97006 624 E1
SW Quint Ter
9000 BRTN 97008 625 B7
9000 BRTN 97008 655 D1
SW Quintessa Ct
20800 WasC 97007 624 B4
SW Quiver Ct
22400 SRWD 97140 684 H7

R

R Cir
3700 WHGL 98671 570 D4
R Dr
4700 WHGL 98671 570 E4
R St
600 VCVR 98661 536 H5
2600 VCVR 98663 536 H3
3000 ClkC 98671 570 C4
3900 WHGL 98671 570 D4
N R St
1400 WHGL 98671 570 A4
SE R St
2600 ClkC 98671 570 C4
3000 WHGL 98671 570 B4
SW Raab Rd
6100 MthC 97221 595 J7
6100 PTLD 97221 595 J7
6400 WasC 97225 595 J7
Raasee Ln
56700 ClbC 97053 414 G6
NW Racely Ct
16400 WasC 97229 564 H7
SW Racely Pl
14300 TGRD 97224 654 J6
Rachael Dr
18000 SNDY 97055 690 H3
S Rachel Ct
16500 CmsC 97045 718 B6
Rachel Ln
- CmsC 97035 685 H2
- LKOW 97035 685 H2
SE Rachel Ln
3800 PTLD 97236 628 D3
NE Rachel St
- HBRO 97124 593 C4
NW Rachel St
1000 HBRO 97124 593 A4
SE Rachella Ct
12600 CmsC 97009 658 F5
12600 HPYV 97009 658 F5
S Rachel Larkin Rd
32300 CmsC 97038 837 D3
SW Rachelle Ct
20300 WasC 97007 624 C2
SW Racquet Ct
7800 WNVL 97070 715 F7
Radcliff Ct
1800 WLIN 97068 717 A1
SE Radcliff Ct
3400 HBRO 97123 623 F1
SW Radcliffe Ct
- MthC 97219 656 G1
- PTLD 97219 656 G1
SW Radcliffe Ln
1400 MthC 97219 656 G1
1400 PTLD 97219 656 G1
1500 PTLD 97219 655 J1
SW Radcliffe Rd
- PTLD 97219 656 G1
1300 MthC 97219 656 G1
SW Radcliffe St
6100 PTLD 97219 655 H1
SW Radford Ln
16400 WasC 97007 624 G3
NW Rae Ct
4500 CMAS 98607 569 C1
SE Raelyn Ter
14200 CmsC 97267 657 B6
NE Raenna Ln
34300 SPSE 97056 474 G1
NW Rafton Rd
- MthC 97231 534 J3
- MthC 97231 535 A3
Railroad Av
500 ORCY 97045 687 C7
500 ORCY 97045 717 C1
900 RDGF 98642 415 J6
1000 STHN 97051 415 B3
NE Railroad Av
100 YCLT 98675 419 F2
400 ClkC 98675 419 F1
29700 ClkC 98604 419 H5
SE Railroad Av
3100 MWKE 97222 657 A2
6000 CmsC 97222 657 D4
S Railroad Dr
7100 CmsC 97013 746 A7

S Railroad Dr
24100 BRLO 97013 746 A7
24400 BRLO 97013 776 A1
N Railroad St
- PTLD 97227 596 F3
SW Railroad St
- BRTN 97223 625 G6
- PTLD 97223 625 G6
16000 SRWD 97140 684 G7
SE Rainbow Ct
9100 MWKE 97222 657 C1
Rainbow Dr
3100 LKOW 97035 656 B6
NE Rainbow Dr
1900 ClkC 98642 446 J4
Rainbow Ln
- DNLD 97020 774 F4
NE Rainbow Ln
18200 YmhC 97132 712 E5
SE Rainbow Ln
4900 MWKE 97222 657 C1
5300 CmsC 97222 657 C1
SW Rainbow Ln
23500 WasC 97123 653 G5
S Rainbow Forest Ln
19900 CmsC 97045 718 H6
SE Rainbow Hill Dr
21200 CmsC 97055 691 J7
NW Raindance Ln
40400 WasC 97106 532 B3
NW Rainier Av
- PTLD 97231 565 C3
19500 MthC 97231 504 E6
SE Rainier Av
15500 CmsC 97015 657 F7
NW Rainier Ct
4800 CMAS 98607 539 C7
SE Rainier Ct
15400 CmsC 97015 657 F7
Rainier Pl
2600 WLIN 97068 686 J4
2600 WLIN 97068 687 A5
NW Rainier Ter
400 PTLD 97210 596 A4
4600 WasC 97229 594 J1
NW Rainmont Rd
10400 PTLD 97229 595 D3
10400 WasC 97229 595 D3
SE Raintree Ct
14600 CmsC 97267 657 A6
NE Raintree Dr
13600 ClkC 98604 418 C5
SW Raintree Dr
7600 BRTN 97008 625 B6
NE Raintree Ln
29600 YmhC 97132 743 G3
SE Rajessa Ct
17400 PTLD 97236 628 F2
Raleigh Dr
- PTLD 97231 565 B3
NW Raleigh St
1200 PTLD 97209 596 C4
3400 PTLD 97210 596 B4
SW Raleighview Ct
6600 WasC 97225 625 H2
SW Raleighview Dr
2800 WasC 97225 625 H2
SW Raleighwood Ct
6300 PTLD 97221 625 H2
SW Raleighwood Ln
6500 PTLD 97221 625 H2
6500 WasC 97225 625 H2
SW Raleighwood Wy
6600 WasC 97225 625 H3
Raley Av
- VCVR 98661 537 B7
SW Ralston Dr
- PTLD 97239 626 E4
SW Rambler Ln
8700 WasC 97223 625 F6
SW Ramblin Reck Rd
20600 WasC 97140 684 C5
SE Ramona Ct
11400 PTLD 97266 627 J5
14000 PTLD 97236 628 C5
NW Ramona Dr
15900 WasC 97006 594 G3
SE Ramona Dr
11100 CmsC 97009 659 H3
SE Ramona St
1300 PTLD 97202 626 H4
3800 PTLD 97202 627 B4
5200 PTLD 97206 627 D4
8200 PTLD 97266 627 F4
12200 PTLD 97266 628 A5
13600 PTLD 97236 628 C5
N Ramsey Blvd
9600 PTLD 97203 535 E5
NW Ramsey Dr
1700 MthC 97229 595 G3
1700 PTLD 97229 595 G3
NE Ramsey Rd
23200 YmhC 97132 742 J3
23200 YmhC 97132 743 A2
NW Ramsey Crest Dr
1700 MthC 97229 595 G3
1700 PTLD 97229 595 G3
Ranchet Mnr
- PTLD 97266 627 J2
S Ranch Hills Rd
26400 CmsC 97042 777 F6
SE Rancho Av
14800 CmsC 97267 657 D6
Rancho Dr
61500 ClbC 97051 384 B3
NE Rancho Dr
3900 VCVR 98682 538 C2
SE Rancho St
5300 HBRO 97123 593 H7
Rancho Lobo Ct
25100 WLIN 97068 716 F2
Rancho Lobo Ln
900 WLIN 97068 716 F2
N Ranck Av
100 YCLT 98675 419 F1
S Ranck Av
100 YCLT 98675 419 F1
NE Randall Av
600 PTLD 97232 597 A5
700 PTLD 97232 596 H4
Randall Ct
100 ORCY 97045 717 B2
NW Randall Ln
9500 PTLD 97229 595 E4
9500 WasC 97229 595 E4

STREET
Block City ZIP Map# Grid

Randall St
100 ORCY 97045 717 B3
2200 WLIN 97068 687 A5
N Randolph Av
2100 PTLD 97227 596 E3
NW Random Rd
- MthC 97229 595 G5
S Raney Ln
24200 CmsC 97023 749 J6
SE Ranger Dr
15300 CmsC 97015 658 D7
SW Rankin Ct
21500 WasC 97006 594 B6
NE Rankin Dr
6400 ClkC 98665 506 G6
SE Ranmar Dr
33300 CmsC 97009 660 D6
SE Ranstad Ct
13200 CmsC 97222 657 A5
NW Rapid St
17900 BRTN 97006 594 F5
NW Rapidan Ter
700 PTLD 97210 596 A3
SW Raptor Pl
13100 TGRD 97223 655 B4
SW Raritan Ct
9000 TLTN 97062 685 E5
SW Rask Ter
14600 WasC 97224 654 G6
SE Rasmussen Blvd
10 BGND 98604 448 C6
SW Rasmussen Blvd
- BGND 98604 448 B6
NE Rasmussen Rd
2400 MthC 97019 600 G4
SE Raspberry Ct
14000 CmsC 97267 657 F6
SW Raven Ct
15900 BRTN 97007 654 G3
Raven Dr
700 RDGF 98642 416 B6
SW Ravenna Lp
- WNVL 97070 715 B7
SW Ravensview Dr
2500 PTLD 97201 596 C7
2600 PTLD 97201 626 B1
SW Ravenswood St
20400 WasC 97007 624 C4
SW Ravhide Ter
- BRTN 97008 655 A1
SW Ravine Dr
8500 WasC 97007 624 F7
Rawhide Ct
2800 WLIN 97068 686 H4
SW Rawhide Ct
13600 BRTN 97008 655 A1
Rawhide St
2900 WLIN 97068 686 H4
NE Rawson Ml
14200 ClkC 98606 479 H6
NE Rawson Rd
25000 ClkC 98606 479 F5
NE Rawson Mill Rd
- ClkC 98606 479 G6
NE Ray Cir
5800 HBRO 97124 593 J3
NE Ray Ct
1300 HBRO 97124 593 J3
Ray Rd
- SPSE 97056 474 E1
Raybell Rd NE
3400 MrnC 97137 743 A6
SE Raymond Ct
6800 PTLD 97206 627 E4
8200 PTLD 97266 627 F4
Raymond St
3000 FTGV 97116 591 J3
3000 WasC 97116 591 J3
SE Raymond St
2300 PTLD 97202 626 J3
3200 PTLD 97202 627 A3
4100 PTLD 97206 627 C4
4200 CmsC 97267 657 B7
10200 PTLD 97266 627 H4
11800 PTLD 97266 628 A4
13600 PTLD 97236 628 C4
Raymond Creek Rd
31200 ClbC 97056 474 A3
SE Rayna Ct
16200 CmsC 97267 687 B1
SW Raynard Rd
27800 WasC 97123 653 D6
Ray Ridge Dr
18400 LKOW 97034 686 C3
Rays Wy
60100 ClbC 97051 384 H6
SW Raz Ct
7000 WasC 97223 625 H6
Reao Ct
18800 CmsC 97035 685 J3
18800 LKOW 97035 685 J3
Rebecca Ln
17100 LKOW 97035 685 J1
SW Rebecca Ln
8500 BRTN 97008 625 B7
SW Rebecca Ter
- TGRD 97223 655 A3
SW Rebekah St
30100 WNVL 97070 745 F1
SE Rebman Rd
25100 CmsC 97009 689 F1
SW Redbird St
15600 BRTN 97007 654 H3
SW Redbud Wy
14500 BRTN 97007 624 J4
14500 WasC 97007 624 J4
NW Red Cedar Ct
- MthC 97231 564 J2
- PTLD 97231 564 J2
12900 WasC 97229 565 B7
Red Cedar St
10 STHN 97051 385 B7
Red Cedar Wy
3500 LKOW 97034 656 B6
SW Red Cedar Wy
7300 TGRD 97223 655 G1
SW Redclover Ln
15800 SRWD 97140 684 G6
NW Redding Ln
16400 WasC 97229 564 G7
S Redding Ln
28000 CmsC 97042 807 H1
SE Red Dirt Rd
- DAMA 97009 658 H7

Redfern Av
17400 LKOW 97035 686 A1
SW Redfern Av
2100 GSHM 97080 628 H5
SW Redfern Dr
23500 SRWD 97140 714 F1
24000 WasC 97140 714 F1
SW Redfern Pl
2000 GSHM 97080 628 H5
23400 SRWD 97140 714 F1
NW Redfox Dr
5800 MthC 97229 565 B7
SW Red Haven Dr
13900 BRTN 97008 624 J5
13900 BRTN 97008 625 A5
SW Redhawk Ct
7700 DRHM 97224 685 F2
Red Hawk Dr
13300 CmsC 97045 717 D5
13300 ORCY 97045 717 D5
NW Redhawk Dr
30600 WasC 97133 533 B4
SE Redhawks Ln
11800 HPYV 97236 658 B4
SW Red Hills Dr
100 DNDE 97115 742 G3
700 YmhC 97115 742 G3
NE Red Hills Rd
9300 YmhC 97115 742 G1
11200 YmhC 97115 712 H7
11400 YmhC 97132 712 H6
Redland Rd
13500 CmsC 97045 687 F7
13500 ORCY 97045 687 E7
14600 CmsC 97045 717 G1
S Redland Rd
15000 CmsC 97045 717 J1
18000 CmsC 97045 718 G4
20400 CmsC 97045 748 J1
20700 CmsC 97045 749 A1
22400 CmsC 97023 749 F1
S Redland School Rd
- CmsC 97045 718 E2
SW Red Leaf Pl
16900 SRWD 97140 684 F5
Red Leaf St
5200 CmsC 97035 685 J3
SE Red Maple Ln
14100 CmsC 97015 658 C6
SW Red Maple Ln
14500 BRTN 97007 624 J4
Redmond Hill Rd
- MCMV 97128 770 D5
SW Redmond Hill Rd
2200 MCMV 97128 770 D6
2200 YmhC 97128 770 B5
Red Oak Ct NE
- DNLD 97020 774 G4
Red Oak Dr
3600 NWBG 97132 713 F7
SW Red Oak Ln
19500 WasC 97007 624 D5
Red Oak St
- NWBG 97132 713 F7
SW Redoaks Ln
8900 TGRD 97224 655 E6
SW Redondo Av
4200 PTLD 97239 626 B2
SW Red Rock Ct
16500 BRTN 97007 654 G1
16500 WasC 97007 654 G1
SW Red Rock Wy
9700 BRTN 97007 654 G1
16900 WasC 97007 654 G1
SE Red Rose Ln
13400 HPYV 97236 658 B3
Red Soils Ct
1600 ORCY 97045 717 D4
SW Redstone Dr
15500 BRTN 97007 624 H7
SE Red Sunset Av
13700 CmsC 97015 658 D6
NE Red Sunset Dr
2400 GSHM 97030 599 D7
SW Red Sunset Ln
7900 WasC 97007 624 E6
NW Redtail Dr
8400 WasC 97116 561 A3
SW Redtop Ter
21300 SRWD 97140 684 F6
SW Redtwig Dr
16300 SRWD 97140 714 F1
Red Wing Ct
19000 CmsC 97035 685 J3
SW Redwing Ter
10100 BRTN 97007 654 G1
Red Wing Wy
4700 CmsC 97035 685 J3
Redwood
- CmsC 97015 657 H7
SE Redwood Av
12000 MWKE 97222 657 E4
13900 CmsC 97222 657 A6
13900 CmsC 97267 657 A6
SE Redwood Cir
16700 VCVR 98683 538 E7
Redwood Ct
2500 NWBG 97132 713 E6
14100 LKOW 97034 656 D5
Redwood Ct N
1800 FTGV 97116 592 B5
Redwood Ct S
1700 FTGV 97116 592 B5
Redwood Dr
- WasC 97006 594 D5
NE Redwood Dr
2800 MCMV 97128 770 J2
S Redwood Ln
17000 CmsC 97004 748 B2
SW Redwood Ln
6600 TGRD 97224 655 G7
Redwood St
- CmsC 97055 690 J5
- SNDY 97055 690 J5
N Redwood St
900 CmsC 97013 746 E5
1900 CNBY 97013 746 E4
S Redwood St
300 CNBY 97013 746 E7
400 CmsC 97013 746 E7
1100 CNBY 97013 776 E1
1600 CmsC 97013 776 E1
SE Redwood St
1300 CmsC 97013 776 E1
1300 CNBY 97013 776 E1

SE Redwood St
4400 HBRO 97123 623 G2
Reed Cir
18000 SNDY 97055 691 A3
NW Reed Dr
8000 PTLD 97229 595 G3
NE Reed Rd
36700 MthC 97019 600 H4
Reed St
4100 CmsC 97068 686 J7
4100 WLIN 97068 686 J7
NW Reed St
2000 PTLD 97209 596 D3
2000 PTLD 97210 596 D3
SE Reed College Pl
6000 PTLD 97202 627 A5
NW Reeder Rd
18100 MthC 97231 534 J1
18100 MthC 97231 535 A1
18400 MthC 97231 505 A7
26200 ClbC 97231 475 F6
34900 ClbC 97231 445 D2
S Reeder Rd
20500 CmsC 97045 717 G7
SE Reedville Creek Dr
6600 HBRO 97123 594 A7
SE Reedway St
2600 PTLD 97202 626 J4
3700 PTLD 97202 627 B4
5200 PTLD 97206 627 D4
8800 PTLD 97266 627 G4
11500 PTLD 97266 628 A4
12200 PTLD 97236 628 B4
SW Reeher Pl
1000 WasC 97116 591 C5
Rees Ct NE
12000 DNLD 97020 774 H4
Rees St NE
10800 DNLD 97020 774 G4
Reese Rd
15900 LKOW 97035 656 A7
SE Reeves Ct
14500 CmsC 97015 658 B6
NW Reeves St
10700 WasC 97229 595 D4
SW Refectory Pl
16000 WasC 97224 655 A7
Reflection Ln
20000 CmsC 97045 716 H6
Reflections at Summer Cr
- BRTN 97007 654 J3
- BRTN 97008 654 J3
- TGRD 97223 654 J3
SE Regal Ct
11900 CmsC 97015 658 A6
SW Regal Ct
19300 WasC 97006 624 D1
SW Regal Dr
9600 WasC 97225 625 E1
SW Regal Ln
21200 WasC 97006 624 B1
NW Regal Ter
- PTLD 97210 595 J2
NE Regan Ct
600 HBRO 97124 593 C2
SE Regan Hill Lp
- CmsC 97023 750 C4
- ECDA 97023 750 C4
SW Regatta Ln
15900 BRTN 97006 594 G6
Regency Ct
- VCVR 98662 507 G7
- VCVR 98662 537 G1
13700 LKOW 97035 655 J4
SW Regency Pl
500 WasC 97225 595 G6
Regency St
1700 WLIN 97068 716 F2
SW Regency Ter
600 WasC 97225 595 H6
SE Regency View Dr
13200 CmsC 97236 658 B4
SE Regency View St
12600 CmsC 97236 658 B5
Regent Dr
- MCMV 97128 771 E6
NW Regent Dr
- PTLD 97210 596 A2
SW Regent Ter
15200 TGRD 97224 655 G6
SE Regents Ct
4900 MWKE 97222 657 C1
NE Regents Dr
2100 PTLD 97212 596 J2
2600 PTLD 97212 597 A2
3100 PTLD 97211 597 A1
13400 VCVR 98684 538 B4
SE Regents Dr
8800 MWKE 97222 627 C7
8800 MWKE 97222 657 C1
SW Reghetto St
16800 SRWD 97140 684 F5
NW Regina Ct
1800 MCMV 97128 770 E5
SE Regina Ct
10300 HPYV 97236 658 B2
SW Regina Ln
- TGRD 97223 655 F5
SE Reginald Ct
12000 HPYV 97236 658 A3
SE Regner Rd
1600 GSHM 97080 629 C5
4500 MthC 97080 629 B7
4800 DAMA 97009 629 B7
SE Regner Terrace Dr
14500 DAMA 97009 659 B7
Reich Ct
37500 SNDY 97055 690 H3
E Reid Ct
1200 LCTR 98629 386 H7
SW Reid Ct
11800 BRTN 97008 625 C7
SE Reid Ln
5000 YmhC 97114 771 E5
5000 YmhC 97128 771 E5
Reid Rd
54600 ClbC 97056 444 B3
S Reid Rd
22500 CmsC 97023 750 B6
NW Reiling Rd
39400 WasC 97113 562 C2
39400 WasC 97116 562 C2
40800 WasC 97116 561 J2
SW Reiling St
8600 TGRD 97224 655 F6

NE Reilly Rd
28200 ClkC 98607 539 H4
N Reiman Rd
10 RDGF 98642 416 B7
500 ClkC 98642 416 B7
SW Rein Rd
25300 WasC 97140 714 D3
NW Reindeer Dr
17300 WasC 97229 564 F7
SW Reiser Ln
18000 SRWD 97140 714 E1
Reisling Wy
- MCMV 97128 770 F3
SW Reisner Ln
17800 SRWD 97140 684 E6
E Relton Rd
64100 CmsC 97049 693 H6
Rembrandt Ln
4600 LKOW 97035 656 C5
NW Remembrance Ct
15200 WasC 97229 564 H7
Remington Dr
2400 WLIN 97068 716 G1
SW Remudo Ln
12700 BRTN 97008 625 B7
Ren Wy
61500 ClbC 97051 384 B3
SE Renada St
6700 CmsC 97267 657 D7
Renaissance Ct
2600 WLIN 97068 687 A6
NE Rene Av
2300 GSHM 97030 599 E7
3800 TDLE 97060 599 E6
SE Rene Av
500 GSHM 97080 629 D3
SW Renee Dr
7100 WasC 97225 625 H1
Renee Wy
19600 CmsC 97045 717 A5
19600 ORCY 97045 717 A6
NE Renne Rd
10000 YmhC 97132 743 J2
N Reno Av
9200 PTLD 97203 565 G1
SE Renoir Ct
13800 CmsC 97015 658 A6
NW Rentenaar Rd
- ClbC 97231 475 D1
Rentfro Wy
1000 NWBG 97132 713 C6
SE Renton Av
13700 CmsC 97222 656 H5
13700 CmsC 97267 656 H5
NE Repass Rd
600 ClkC 98665 506 H5
SE Reserve Lp
17400 CmsC 97267 687 B2
E Reserve St
- VCVR 98663 536 J4
500 VCVR 98661 536 H5
W Reserve St
800 VCVR 98660 536 G5
1800 VCVR 98663 536 G4
NE Retford Av
500 HBRO 97124 593 J4
SW Reusser Ct
17300 WasC 97007 654 F2
Reuter Ln
200 FTGV 97116 591 F3
Revenue Av
17000 SNDY 97055 691 A3
SE Revenue Rd
8500 CmsC 97009 660 C3
N Revere St
900 PTLD 97227 596 F2
E Reverie Ln
52800 CmsC 97055 692 G5
NW Rex Ct
10200 WasC 97229 595 D4
SE Rex Ct
- PTLD 97266 627 H6
SE Rex Dr
4500 PTLD 97206 627 C6
SE Rex St
1300 PTLD 97202 626 J6
2700 PTLD 97202 627 A6
3900 PTLD 97206 627 B6
10300 PTLD 97266 627 H6
NE Rex Hill Ct
14400 YmhC 97132 713 G4
Reymond
100 ClkC 98675 419 G1
100 YCLT 98675 419 G1
SE Reynolds St
900 PTLD 97202 626 H3
SW Rhett Ct
13500 WasC 97224 655 A6
SE Rhine Ct
14800 PTLD 97236 628 D2
SE Rhine St
1100 PTLD 97202 626 H2
3600 PTLD 97202 627 B2
7900 PTLD 97206 627 F2
8000 PTLD 97266 627 F2
15900 PTLD 97236 628 E2
SW Rhino Wy
3300 PTLD 97239 626 B4
NW Rhodes Ln
2500 PTLD 97229 595 E2
SE Rhodes Rd
37000 CmsC 97023 750 G2
SE Rhodesa St
4300 MWKE 97222 657 B2
Rhododendron Dr
500 VCVR 98661 537 B5
E Rhododendron Ln
69800 CmsC 97049 724 D3
Rhodora St
2100 FTGV 97116 592 B4
SE Rhone Ct
15400 PTLD 97236 628 D3
SE Rhone St
700 PTLD 97202 626 G2
4200 PTLD 97202 627 B2
4200 PTLD 97206 627 B2
8000 PTLD 97266 627 F2
12000 PTLD 97266 628 A3
16200 PTLD 97236 628 E2
S Rhoten Rd
25400 CmsC 97002 775 H3
SW Rhus Ct
16300 WasC 97223 654 G5
16300 WasC 97224 654 G5

NE Ribbon Ridge Rd
14700 YmhC 97132 712 B3
SW Ribera Ln
21500 CmsC 97068 686 D7
SW Rice Ct
7000 WasC 97223 625 H7
NW Rich Ct
14600 WasC 97229 564 J6
S Richard Ct
21000 CmsC 97023 749 A2
21000 CmsC 97045 749 A2
SW Richard Ct
1400 MCMV 97128 770 F6
17700 WasC 97007 624 F4
Richard Ln
- YmhC 97132 713 H4
NE Richard Ln
14500 YmhC 97132 713 H4
Richard St
32900 ClbC 97056 444 D5
NE Richards Rd
24300 ClkC 98606 479 D3
N Richards St
- PTLD 97203 566 A2
8100 PTLD 97203 565 J1
SW Richardson Ct
200 PTLD 97239 626 E3
SW Richardson Dr
4800 PTLD 97239 626 C3
SW Richardson St
2300 PTLD 97239 626 C3
SW Richenberg Ct
5100 PTLD 97239 626 C3
SW Richen Park Ter
- SRWD 97140 714 F1
SW Richen Park Wy
- SRWD 97140 714 F1
SW Richey Ln
6100 WasC 97223 625 F5
SE Richey Rd
12900 CmsC 97009 659 G6
17700 MthC 97080 628 G7
17700 MthC 97236 628 G7
Richland Ter
- BRTN 97006 594 H6
- WasC 97006 594 J6
Richlands Ln
- YmhC 97132 712 G6
NE Richlands Ln
12600 YmhC 97132 712 F6
N Richmond Av
7500 PTLD 97203 565 H3
N Richmond Av US-30 BYP
7300 PTLD 97203 565 H3
SE Richmond Ct
10800 HPYV 97236 657 J3
Richmond Pk
- BRTN 97006 594 E5
SW Richmond Pl
- PTLD 97205 596 C6
NE Richmond Rd
20700 ClkC 98606 508 J1
20700 ClkC 98606 509 A1
SW Richmond Wy
17500 WasC 97006 594 F6
Richter Ln NE
- MrnC 97002 775 E2
SW Rickard Pl
22500 SRWD 97140 684 F7
Rickenbacker St
- PTLD 97218 567 D5
NE Rickenbacker St
- PTLD 97218 567 D5
Rickert Rd
- MthC 97019 630 H2
SE Rickert Rd
36200 MthC 97019 630 G2
NW Rickey Ter
3500 HBRO 97124 594 C1
SE Rickshire Ln
15800 CmsC 97267 657 E7
15800 CmsC 97267 687 H1
Ridder Ln
1400 WLIN 97068 716 G1
SW Ridder Rd
9300 WNVL 97070 715 D3
10200 WasC 97140 715 D3
SW Riddle Ct
15300 BRTN 97007 624 H5
SW Rider Ln
17100 WasC 97007 654 F3
Ridge Ct
4000 WLIN 97068 686 J6
Ridge Dr
7400 GLDS 97027 687 F3
NE Ridge Dr
- WasC 97124 594 A5
NW Ridge Dr
32700 SPSE 97056 444 D6
SE Ridge Dr
13600 VCVR 98683 568 B1
SW Ridge Dr
2600 PTLD 97219 626 C7
2600 PTLD 97219 656 C1
Ridge Ln
3000 WLIN 97068 686 J6
4000 CmsC 97068 686 J6
NW Ridge Rd
- PTLD 97231 565 E5
10800 WasC 97229 595 D2
S Ridge Rd
18500 CmsC 97045 719 A4
20800 CmsC 97023 749 A2
20800 CmsC 97045 749 A3
21200 CmsC 97045 748 J4
21800 CmsC 97004 748 H7
Ridgebrook Dr
2000 WLIN 97068 686 G4
2200 CmsC 97068 686 G4
NW Ridgecrest Av
9900 ClkC 98685 506 E3
SE Ridgecrest Av
800 VCVR 98664 537 G7
SE Ridgecrest Ct
9400 HPYV 97236 658 A1
Ridgecrest Dr
400 ORCY 97045 717 B2
1300 LKOW 97034 656 C6
SE Ridgecrest Dr
20100 CmsC 97055 692 C6
SW Ridgecrest Dr
11200 BRTN 97008 625 C6
SE Ridgecrest Rd
12100 HPYV 97236 658 B1
12400 CmsC 97236 658 B1

Ridgecrest Timbers
- PTLD 97203 565 H1
SW Ridgefield Ln
12700 TGRD 97223 655 A5
12700 TGRD 97224 655 B5
12900 WasC 97223 655 B5
Ridgefield Wildlife Refuge Rd
- RDGF 98642 446 A1
Ridgegate Ct
18100 GLDS 97027 687 D2
Ridgegate Dr
7000 GLDS 97027 687 E2
Ridge Lake Dr
17900 LKOW 97034 686 C2
SW Ridgemont St
7000 WasC 97225 625 G4
NW Ridgemoor Ct
5400 WasC 97229 564 D7
Ridge Pointe Dr
2000 LKOW 97034 686 C2
3200 FTGV 97116 591 E2
S Ridge Runner Rd
- CmsC 97045 718 D7
S Ridgeside Ln
21900 CmsC 97045 748 J3
21900 CmsC 97045 749 A4
NE Ridgestone Ct
6100 HBRO 97124 593 F2
Ridgetop Ct
5600 LKOW 97035 655 H4
NW Ridgetop Ct
8200 MthC 97229 595 G2
8200 PTLD 97229 595 G2
14600 WasC 97006 594 J2
NW Ridgetop Ln
15600 WasC 97006 594 H2
NW Ridgetop St
13000 WasC 97229 595 B2
Ridgeview Dr
- STHN 97051 385 A6
SE Ridgeview Dr
22200 DAMA 97009 659 B5
SW Ridgeview Ln
10300 PTLD 97219 656 D1
NW Ridgeview Pl
11000 NPNS 97133 563 B1
11000 WasC 97133 563 B1
SW Ridgeview Ter
11600 BRTN 97008 625 C6
SE Ridgeway Dr
10600 CmsC 97236 657 J1
10600 HPYV 97236 657 J1
SW Ridgeway Dr
8000 WasC 97225 625 F2
S Ridgeway Ln
21000 CmsC 97045 719 B7
Ridgeway Lp
- ClbC 97051 385 A7
59900 STHN 97051 385 A7
Ridgeway Rd
100 LKOW 97034 656 F7
SW Ridgewood Av
2800 WasC 97225 625 G2
Ridgewood Dr
7400 GLDS 97027 687 E3
NE Ridgewood Dr
1900 PTLD 97212 596 J2
2700 PTLD 97212 597 A2
Ridgewood Ln
1900 LKOW 97034 656 C6
Ridgewood Rd
1500 LKOW 97034 656 C7
Ridgewood Wy
3600 WLIN 97068 686 J3
Ridings Av
100 MOLA 97038 837 D1
SW Riedwig Rd
31400 WasC 97113 623 A6
NW Riesling Ct
11300 WasC 97229 595 C4
SE Riesling Rd
3000 CmsC 97267 657 A7
SW Rigert Ct
8000 WasC 97007 624 G6
SW Rigert Rd
15500 BRTN 97007 624 H6
16000 WasC 97007 624 F6
SW Rigert Ter
16500 WasC 97007 624 G6
NW Riggs Dr
4000 PTLD 97229 595 E1
Riggs Rd
61500 ClbC 97051 384 C3
SW Riggs Rd
21700 WasC 97007 624 A6
SE Riggs Acres Ct
35200 CmsC 97009 660 F4
S Riggs Damm Rd
11200 CmsC 97013 776 H7
11600 CmsC 97013 807 A1
Rilance Ln
900 ORCY 97045 717 C3
NE Riley Ct
12500 ClkC 98686 477 B7
SW Riley Ct
10300 WasC 97005 625 D2
Rileys Ct
8600 CmsC 97027 687 F2
SE Rimrock Dr
10900 HPYV 97236 658 C3
Rimrock Ln
900 CmsC 97267 656 H5
SE Rinearson Av
4900 CmsC 97027 687 C4
4900 CmsC 97267 687 C4
4900 GLDS 97027 687 C4
SE Rinearson Ct
4900 CmsC 97027 687 C4
4900 CmsC 97267 687 C4
4900 GLDS 97027 687 C4
SE Rinearson Rd
- CmsC 97027 687 C4
- CmsC 97267 687 C4
- GLDS 97027 687 C4
NE Ring A Ring Rd
53600 ClbC 97056 444 G5
SW Ringer St
20600 WasC 97140 714 B2
S Ringo Rd
27500 CmsC 97042 777 H7
27700 CmsC 97042 807 G1
Rinkes Ct
3600 NWBG 97132 713 F5

Rio Villa
- WHGL 98671 570 A
SE Rio Vista St
4000 MWKE 97222 657 B
NW Rio Vista Ter
3000 PTLD 97210 596 B
SE Ripplewood Av
1500 HBRO 97123 593 F
SE Risberg Ln
30300 CmsC 97022 720 A
NE Rising Star Ln
8200 YmhC 97132 744 C
SE Risley Av
800 GLDS 97027 687 C
1700 CmsC 97267 686 J
2700 CmsC 97267 656 J
2800 CmsC 97267 657 B
SE Risley Ct
15300 CmsC 97267 657 A
NE Risto Rd
17600 ClkC 98604 448 J
17600 ClkC 98606 448 J
20100 ClkC 98604 449 A
Rita Dr
- ORCY 97045 717 D
SW Rita Dr
13000 WasC 97005 595 A
13500 WasC 97006 595 A
SW Ritchey Rd
43600 FTGV 97116 591 F
43600 WasC 97116 591 F
Riven Dell Ct
18800 CmsC 97034 686 B
18800 LKOW 97034 686 B
SW Rivendell Dr
17000 DRHM 97224 685 F
Riven Dell Rd
2600 LKOW 97034 686 B
NE Rivenwood Ln
10100 YmhC 97111 711 F
River Dr
- PTLD 97217 536 F
SE River Dr
4100 CmsC 97267 687 B
SW River Dr
1800 PTLD 97201 596 F
10500 TGRD 97224 685 D
River Ln
100 GLDS 97027 687 F
SW River Ln
- WasC 97123 623 H
14000 WasC 97224 684 J
SW River Pkwy
- PTLD 97201 596 F
300 PTLD 97201 626 F
3400 PTLD 97239 626 F
River Rd
19400 CmsC 97027 687 C
19400 CmsC 97267 687 C
19400 GLDS 97027 687 C
River Rd NE
18400 MrnC 97137 773 B
19200 STPL 97137 773 B
SE River Rd
1300 HBRO 97123 593 E
2400 HBRO 97123 623 F
3000 WasC 97123 623 F
11900 MWKE 97222 656 H
12300 CmsC 97222 656 H
13600 CmsC 97267 656 H
16100 CmsC 97267 686 J
16800 CmsC 97267 687 B
19100 CmsC 97027 687 B
SW River Rd
3200 HBRO 97123 623 G
5700 WasC 97123 623 G
6300 WasC 97007 623 G
9400 WasC 97007 653 F
9400 WasC 97123 653 F
SW River Sq
1900 PTLD 97201 596 F7
River St
- TLTN 97062 685 A2
200 STHN 97051 385 D
5300 WLIN 97068 687 C6
N River St
100 NWBG 97132 713 D
100 STHN 97051 385 D
800 PTLD 97227 596 F
S River St
100 NWBG 97132 713 C7
100 STHN 97051 385 D7
300 NWBG 97132 743 C1
1200 YmhC 97132 743 C2
E River Tr
28500 CmsC 97067 724 D7
SW River Wk
2000 PTLD 97201 596 F7
River Wy
10 STHN 97051 385 D6
River Bend Dr
400 CmsC 97068 746 D2
River Bend Ln
3200 CmsC 97034 686 B3
NE River Bend Rd
13800 ClkC 98604 418 C5
SE River Bluff Ct
3500 CmsC 97267 687 A2
River Cliff Dr
300 STHN 97051 385 D5
River Cliffs Dr
400 STHN 97051 385 D6
SE Rivercrest Av
3600 VCVR 98683 568 C3
SE Rivercrest Dr
13000 VCVR 98683 568 B2
SE River Crest Ln
19000 CmsC 97267 687 B3
Riverdale Dr
700 GLDS 97027 687 C5
SW Riverdale Rd
200 MthC 97219 656 G1
SE River Dr Ct
19200 CmsC 97267 687 B4
River Edge Ct
18200 WLIN 97068 686 J1
River Edge Ln
18300 WLIN 97068 686 J2
SE River Forest Ct
15300 CmsC 97267 656 G7
SE River Forest Dr
14700 CmsC 97267 656 G7
SE River Forest Ln
1200 CmsC 97267 656 H7

STREET
Block City ZIP Map# Grid
E River Forest Pl
15900 CmsC 97267 656 H7
E River Forest Rd
700 CmsC 97267 656 H7
W Riverfront Ter
2800 CmsC 97070 746 B1
Rivergate Blvd
9200 PTLD 97203 535 E6
E Rivergate St
2900 MCMV 97128 771 B4
E River Glen Ct
1700 CmsC 97267 656 H7
iverhead Pkwy
12400 CmsC 97045 717 B4
12400 ORCY 97045 717 B4
iver Heights Cir
2100 WLIN 97068 716 E1
E Riveridge Dr
11800 VCVR 98683 567 J1
12200 VCVR 98683 568 A1
W Riveridge Ln
5800 PTLD 97239 626 F4
verknoll Ct
2000 WLIN 97068 716 J1
verknoll Wy
3400 WLIN 97068 716 J1
River Lake Rd
25200 CmsC 97023 749 J2
25200 CmsC 97023 750 A4
W River Ln Rd
31200 CmsC 97068 746 D1
E River Mill Rd
29000 CmsC 97023 749 J2
30100 CmsC 97023 750 A1
30700 ECDA 97023 750 A1
E River Oaks
- PTLD 97202 626 H4
E River Oaks Dr
- PTLD 97202 626 H4
W River Park Pl
200 CmsC 97013 746 C1
W Riverpoint Ln
5600 PTLD 97239 626 F4
E River Pointe Cir
9400 PTLD 97211 566 H3
E River Ranch Rd
25100 CmsC 97022 720 C4
E River Ridge Dr
1500 CmsC 97222 656 H5
iver Royal Ter
- MWKE 97222 656 H2
iver Run Dr
19300 CmsC 97034 686 A3
19300 LKOW 97034 686 A3
ivers Ln
600 CmsC 97038 807 C7
600 MOLA 97038 807 C7
ivers Edge Dr
3600 LKOW 97034 686 A3
E Rivershore Dr
14400 VCVR 98683 568 D3
iverside Ct
- WLIN 97068 686 J2
iverside Dr
200 STHN 97051 385 D6
13000 CmsC 97034 656 G4
13000 CmsC 97219 656 G4
13100 LKOW 97034 656 G4
13100 LKOW 97219 656 G4
iverside Dr SR-43
13000 CmsC 97034 656 G4
13000 CmsC 97219 656 G4
13100 LKOW 97034 656 G4
13100 LKOW 97219 656 G4
iverside Dr NE
20300 MrnC 97137 772 J5
20800 MrnC 97137 743 C4
20800 MrnC 97137 773 A1
Riverside Dr
64700 CmsC 97011 693 H7
64700 CmsC 97011 723 H1
E Riverside Dr
1400 MCMV 97128 770 J4
1700 MCMV 97128 771 A4
3300 YmhC 97128 771 A4
E Riverside Dr
5600 VCVR 98661 537 C7
6600 VCVR 98664 537 D7
W Riverside Dr
9800 MthC 97219 656 G2
9800 PTLD 97219 656 G1
12400 CmsC 97034 656 H4
W Riverside Dr SR-43
9800 MthC 97219 656 G2
9800 PTLD 97219 656 G1
12400 MthC 97034 656 H4
iverside Ln
35300 ClbC 97056 474 J2
35300 ClbC 97056 475 A2
W Riverside Ln
5600 PTLD 97239 626 F4
iverside Lp
- YmhC 97128 771 D4
E Riverside Lp
3900 YmhC 97128 771 C5
E Riverside Lp
3900 YmhC 97128 771 C4
E Riverside Pkwy
17700 GSHM 97230 598 H1
17700 PTLD 97230 598 G1
W Riverside St
300 PTLD 97219 656 F1
E Riverside Wy
2000 PTLD 97211 566 J4
2000 PTLD 97211 567 A5
E Riverside Wy
30500 CmsC 97022 720 A3
iver View Av
4300 WLIN 97068 687 A7
W Riverview Av
- PTLD 97231 565 D4
1400 GSHM 97030 628 J1
W Riverview Av
200 GSHM 97080 628 J3
W Riverview Ct
10 GSHM 97080 628 H3
iver View Dr
4100 WLIN 97068 717 A1
iverview Dr
200 RDGF 98642 416 A7
W Riverview Dr
- PTLD 97229 565 D4
- PTLD 97231 565 D4
1000 GSHM 97030 628 J1
13500 MthC 97231 535 B5

STREET
Block City ZIP Map# Grid
NE Riverview Ln
15600 PTLD 97230 598 E2
SE Riverview Ln
8100 VCVR 98664 537 F7
SW Riverview Ln
11700 CmsC 97070 745 B2
NW Riverview Pl
500 GSHM 97030 628 H2
SW Riverview Pl
700 GSHM 97080 628 J4
NW Riverview Rd
- MthC 97231 535 B6
S Riverview Rd
16100 CmsC 97038 807 J6
16100 CmsC 97042 807 J6
NW Riverview Wy
400 GSHM 97030 628 H2
SW Riverview Wy
700 TDLE 97060 599 F5
NE River Vista Ln
14000 CmsC 97002 745 D2
SE Riverway Ln
10500 MWKE 97222 656 H2
SE Riverwood Ct
3300 VCVR 98683 568 A3
SW Riverwood Dr
29700 CmsC 97068 716 E7
29700 CmsC 97068 746 E2
Riverwood Hts
- KNGC 97224 685 B2
- WasC 97224 685 B1
E Riverwood Ln
27000 CmsC 97067 724 C6
SE Riverwood Ln
3300 VCVR 98683 568 B3
SW Riverwood Ln
9500 TGRD 97224 685 D1
SW Riverwood Pl
16600 TGRD 97224 685 D1
NE Riverwood Rd
19000 YmhC 97114 772 E1
19000 YmhC 97115 772 F1
SW Riverwood Rd
10800 MthC 97219 656 H3
River Woods Pl
3300 WLIN 97068 686 H2
Rivet Rd
- PTLD 97203 565 G1
Riviera Ct
6700 WLIN 97068 687 A5
SW Riviera Ln
16800 KNGC 97224 685 A1
32400 WNVL 97070 745 E3
SW Riviera Pl
4600 WasC 97007 624 F3
S Riviere Dr
3000 CmsC 97267 687 A1
SW Rivington Dr
1000 PTLD 97201 596 D7
1000 PTLD 97201 626 D2
NW Roads End
15600 WasC 97106 532 B3
SE Roads End
40200 CmsC 97055 691 B2
Roan Cir
19800 WLIN 97068 686 H4
SW Roan Ct
13500 BRTN 97008 655 A1
SE Roanoke Ct
3300 HBRO 97123 623 F1
SW Roanoke Dr N
7500 WNVL 97070 715 F4
SW Roanoke Dr S
7700 WNVL 97070 715 F4
NW Roanoke Ln
5300 WasC 97229 565 A7
NW Roanoke St
2600 PTLD 97210 596 C5
E Roaring River Rd
67400 CmsC 97049 724 B2
Robb Pl
17100 LKOW 97034 656 D7
17100 LKOW 97034 686 D1
SW Robbins Dr
9500 BRTN 97008 655 C1
SW Robbins Rd
6500 CmsC 97062 685 G5
Robbins St
- PTLD 97218 567 E5
100 MOLA 97038 837 E1
100 WDLD 98674 386 B2
SW Robby Ln
8300 WNVL 97070 745 E1
Roberson Rd
100 CtzC 98674 385 G5
SE Robert Av
16600 CmsC 97015 687 H1
SW Robert Ct
5000 PTLD 97219 625 J7
5000 PTLD 97219 626 A7
SW Robert Ln
17800 WasC 97007 624 F3
SE Roberta Ln
4800 MWKE 97222 657 C1
SW Robert Burns Dr
- WNVL 97070 715 E3
SW Robert Gray Ln
8900 WasC 97225 625 F3
Robert Moore St
5700 WLIN 97068 687 B6
N Roberts Av
- PTLD 97203 565 F1
NE Roberts Av
10 GSHM 97080 629 C2
1900 GSHM 97030 629 C1
2600 GSHM 97030 599 C7
SE Roberts Av
10 GSHM 97030 629 C2
10 GSHM 97080 629 C4
Roberts Ct
- MCMV 97128 770 H6
NE Roberts Ct
1900 GSHM 97030 629 E1
SW Roberts Ct
11400 TLTN 97062 685 C2
Roberts Ln
2500 YmhC 97132 713 E4
34900 STHN 97051 414 J1
NE Roberts Pl
2500 GSHM 97030 599 C6
E Roberts Rd
26600 CmsC 97067 724 C5
SW Roberts Rd
14800 CmsC 97140 744 F1

STREET
Block City ZIP Map# Grid
S Robertson Ln
17000 CmsC 97045 718 C2
Robin Cir
19300 WLIN 97068 686 J3
SE Robin Cir
2800 GSHM 97080 629 E6
3000 HBRO 97123 623 E1
NE Robin Ct
3100 GSHM 97030 629 E2
4300 YmhC 97132 713 G5
SE Robin Ct
1500 GSHM 97080 629 E4
4900 CmsC 97267 657 C6
SW Robin Ct
2500 TDLE 97060 599 G6
SE Robin Ln
2300 GSHM 97080 629 E5
Robin Pl
4000 WLIN 97068 686 J3
SE Robin Pl
2100 GSHM 97080 629 E6
SE Robin Rd
4300 CmsC 97267 657 B7
Robin St NE
11500 MrnC 97002 744 H6
NE Robin Wy
10 GSHM 97030 629 E3
10 GSHM 97080 629 E3
SE Robin Wy
200 GSHM 97080 629 E3
Robin Creek Ln
3600 WLIN 97068 686 J2
SE Robinette Ct
15000 CmsC 97267 657 D6
Robinette Rd
- ClbC 97051 385 A4
60000 ClbC 97051 384 G4
NW Robinia Ln
2500 WasC 97229 595 D3
SW Robins Crest Dr
2700 PTLD 97201 626 D3
NE Robinson Rd
26700 ClkC 98607 539 F6
SE Robinson Rd
27200 ClkC 98607 539 G7
SW Robinson Rd
9800 WasC 97123 653 D1
Robinview Ct
17800 WLIN 97068 686 J2
Robin View Dr
3600 WLIN 97068 686 J2
Robinwood Dr
2900 FTGV 97116 591 F3
SW Robinwood Pl
17100 SRWD 97140 684 F5
Robinwood Wy
2500 WLIN 97068 686 H2
SW Robson Ter
23500 SRWD 97140 714 J1
NE Rochelle Dr
- HBRO 97124 593 J5
SW Rochester Dr
13900 BRTN 97008 624 J5
13900 BRTN 97008 625 D6
N Rochester St
6800 PTLD 97203 565 J3
SW Rock Ct
1700 WasC 97006 594 B7
SW Rock Dr
19900 WasC 97006 594 D7
SW Rock Rd
19600 WasC 97006 594 D7
21800 WasC 97123 594 B7
Rock St
14000 ORCY 97045 687 E6
S Rock St
- ORCY 97045 687 F6
SW Rockbridge St
7800 WNVL 97070 715 F6
NW Rock Creek Blvd
18700 WasC 97229 594 D2
20800 WasC 97229 564 C7
21400 HBRO 97124 564 B7
21400 WasC 97124 564 B7
NW Rock Creek Cir
18800 HBRO 97229 594 E2
18800 WasC 97229 594 E2
NW Rock Creek Ct
4100 WasC 97229 594 D1
SE Rock Creek Ct
16500 CmsC 97015 658 E6
16500 DAMA 97009 658 E6
NW Rock Creek Dr
19600 WasC 97229 594 D1
Rock Creek Lndg
- HBRO 97124 594 D2
NE Rock Creek Ct
32000 ClkC 98604 418 D2
NW Rock Creek Rd
11300 WasC 97231 564 E1
11500 MthC 97231 534 C3
NW Rock Creek Wy
19600 WasC 97229 564 D7
NE Rock Creek Canyon Rd
- ClkC 98604 449 B3
SW Rockcress Ct
13400 BRTN 97008 625 D4
SW Rockingham Dr
13000 TGRD 97223 655 A5
Rockinghorse Ln
1200 LKOW 97034 656 E4
SW Rocklynn Pl
5000 BRTN 97005 624 J3
SW Rock of Ages Rd
14900 YmhC 97128 770 A7
SW Rockport Ln
20500 WasC 97006 594 C6
Rockridge Dr
1800 WLIN 97068 717 A1
SW Rockrose Ln
15700 WasC 97223 654 G5
NW Rock Spring Ln
20600 HBRO 97006 594 C3
NW Rockton Dr
11500 WasC 97124 534 D7
NE Rockwell Dr
12900 ClkC 98686 477 A7
NW Rockwell Ln
8900 PTLD 97229 595 F3
Rockwood Ct
5800 CmsC 97035 655 H7
SW Rockwood Ct
5600 BRTN 97007 624 H1
Rockwood Dr
700 STHN 97051 415 A2

STREET
Block City ZIP Map# Grid
SE Rockwood St
3200 MWKE 97222 657 A1
Rockwood Ter
- WHGL 98671 569 J5
E Rockwood Creek Ln
23700 CmsC 97049 724 D3
Rocky Ct
34600 STHN 97051 414 H1
SE Rocky Ln
1700 CmsC 97267 656 H6
Rocky Wy NE
11000 MrnC 97002 744 G6
S Rocky Bluff Ln
10000 CmsC 97045 716 G7
NE Rocky Brook St
7000 HBRO 97124 594 B4
NE Rocky Butte Ln
3000 PTLD 97220 597 H3
NE Rocky Butte Rd
3300 PTLD 97220 597 H2
NE Rocky Hill Rd
34600 YmhC 97132 744 C5
SW Rocky Mountain Ct
12700 TGRD 97224 655 B6
NW Rocky Point Rd
19000 MthC 97056 474 E7
19000 MthC 97056 504 B1
19000 MthC 97133 504 A2
19000 MthC 97231 474 E7
19000 MthC 97231 504 A2
NW Rocky Ridge Ln
- CMAS 98607 568 J4
- CMAS 98607 569 A4
NE Rodda Rd
20900 ClkC 98604 447 E5
Rodeo
- DAYT 97114 772 A4
SW Rodeo Pl
9700 BRTN 97008 654 J1
NW Roderick Rd
50100 WasC 97116 561 A7
Rodlun Ct
1500 FTGV 97116 591 H4
SE Rodlun Rd
- MthC 97080 628 J7
400 MthC 97080 628 J7
9300 DAMA 97009 659 A1
SW Rodlun Rd
3700 GSHM 97080 628 J7
3700 MthC 97080 628 J7
7800 DAMA 97009 629 A7
7800 MthC 97080 629 A7
8800 DAMA 97009 659 A1
NE Rodney Av
1900 PTLD 97212 596 G3
4000 PTLD 97211 596 G1
5000 PTLD 97211 566 G7
NE Rodney Ct
7000 PTLD 97211 566 G5
Rodney St
32900 ClbC 97053 414 D7
NE Roedel Rd
13300 YmhC 97132 713 A5
SW Roellich Av
21200 SRWD 97140 684 E6
SE Roethe Ln
15600 CmsC 97267 657 C7
SE Roethe Rd
3700 CmsC 97267 687 C1
5900 CmsC 97267 657 D7
SE Rofini Ct
8000 CmsC 97267 657 F7
SE Rofini St
7700 CmsC 97267 657 E7
NE Rogahn St
700 HBRO 97124 593 D2
SW Roger Blvd
28600 WNVL 97070 715 F6
SW Roger Ln
- WasC 97007 624 F2
SE Rogers Av
4000 CmsC 97267 687 B2
NW Rogers Cir
2700 MthC 97060 599 E2
2700 TDLE 97060 599 E2
SE Rogers Ln
13700 CmsC 97015 658 B6
Rogers Rd
12800 LKOW 97035 625 A3
SW Rogers Rd
33300 SPSE 97056 474 D2
SW Rogers Wy
33200 SPSE 97056 474 D1
Rogers Landing Rd
- YmhC 97132 743 D2
Roger Smith Dr
300 NWBG 97132 713 B5
SW Rogue Ct
30800 WNVL 97070 745 E1
SW Rogue Ln
8200 WNVL 97070 745 E1
Rogue Wy
2300 WLIN 97068 716 H1
SW Rogue River Ter
16500 BRTN 97006 594 G6
NW Rogue Valley Ter
2400 WasC 97006 594 G3
NE Rohrbach Rd
500 MthC 97019 600 H6
SW Roland Ct
10800 CmsC 97070 715 C7
10800 WNVL 97070 715 C7
Rolling St
- ClbC 97056 474 A4
E Rolling Green Ct
69300 CmsC 97067 724 C4
NW Rolling Hill Dr
1600 WasC 97006 594 F4
1800 BRTN 97006 594 F3
NW Rolling Hill Ln
17500 WasC 97006 594 F3
SE Rolling Hills Dr
33900 SPSE 97056 474 F2
SE Rolling Hills Ln
11000 HPYV 97236 658 C3
SE Rolling Hills St
- SPSE 97056 474 F2
SE Rolling Meadows Ct
14000 HPYV 97236 658 C3
Rolling Meadows Dr
4400 WHGL 98671 570 E4
4700 ClkC 98671 570 E4
SE Rolling Meadows Dr
13400 HPYV 97236 658 C3
Rolling Riggle Ln
- CmsC 97049 724 G6

STREET
Block City ZIP Map# Grid
SW Rollingwood Dr
6500 BRTN 97008 625 D5
6800 WasC 97008 625 D5
SE Rollins Ln
36000 CmsC 97023 750 F6
Rollins St
19300 CmsC 97045 717 G4
19300 ORCY 97045 717 G4
SW Romal Ct
8800 BRTN 97008 625 D4
Roman Ct
12500 ORCY 97045 717 C4
SW Ronald Ct
13800 WasC 97005 595 A6
13800 WasC 97006 595 A6
Ronald Ln
- CmsC 97045 747 J1
Rondevic Dr
23600 CmsC 97013 746 H7
NW Rondos Dr
15600 WasC 97229 564 H7
NE Ronler Wy
6900 HBRO 97124 594 A3
SE Rood Ct
3000 HBRO 97123 623 F1
SE Rood Bridge Dr
2400 HBRO 97123 623 E1
SE Rood Bridge Rd
2900 HBRO 97123 623 F2
3500 WasC 97123 623 F2
SW Rood Bridge Rd
4800 HBRO 97123 623 F3
4800 WasC 97123 623 F5
SW Roods Rd
29300 CmsC 97140 714 G7
29300 CmsC 97140 744 G1
SE Roork Rd
29400 MthC 97080 629 J6
29400 MthC 97080 630 A6
Roosevelt Av
2000 VCVR 98660 536 E3
16400 CmsC 97035 655 H7
Roosevelt St
- CmsC 97045 717 D2
400 ORCY 97045 717 D2
NW Roosevelt St
2100 PTLD 97209 596 D3
2100 PTLD 97210 596 D3
SW Roosevelt St
17100 SRWD 97140 684 F5
Rooster Rock Av NE
- AURA 97002 775 F5
SE Roots Rd
7300 CmsC 97267 687 F1
7700 JNCY 97267 687 F1
8300 CmsC 97015 687 F1
NE Roper Rd
12300 ClkC 98604 448 B1
S Rory Ct
17300 CmsC 97045 719 E2
SW Rosa Dr
20400 WasC 97007 624 C4
SW Rosa Pl
5600 WasC 97007 624 G4
SW Rosa Rd
19800 WasC 97007 624 C4
22900 WasC 97007 623 J4
24000 WasC 97123 623 H4
Rosalia Wy
5300 LKOW 97035 655 J4
SE Rosanne St
7600 CmsC 97267 657 E6
Rosa Parks Wy
600 PTLD 97211 566 H6
1800 PTLD 97217 566 E6
2900 PTLD 97211 567 A6
NW Rosaria Av
9500 PTLD 97231 565 E3
SW Rosario Ln
14700 WasC 97224 654 H7
Rose Ct
18400 WLIN 97068 686 J3
SW Rose Ct
2200 TDLE 97060 599 E6
SW Rose Dr
1300 MCMV 97128 770 G7
Rose Ln
- BRTN 97005 625 A3
21300 FRVW 97024 599 B3
SE Rose Ln
- PTLD 97206 627 F5
33700 SPSE 97056 474 F1
SW Rose Ln
2000 PTLD 97201 596 F7
4400 BRTN 97005 625 A3
29600 WNVL 97070 715 G7
30000 WNVL 97070 745 F1
NE Rose Pkwy
12200 PTLD 97230 598 C3
Rose Rd
18700 CmsC 97045 716 J4
18800 ORCY 97045 716 J4
18900 CmsC 97045 717 A4
18900 ORCY 97045 717 A4
Rose St
- ClbC 97056 474 A4
100 STHN 97051 415 B1
NE Rose St
16000 PTLD 97230 598 E3
NW Rose St
3900 VCVR 98660 536 E2
52900 SPSE 97056 444 D7
S Rose St
16400 ORCY 97045 687 F6
SE Rose St
17400 CmsC 97267 687 C2
Rose Wy
18600 WLIN 97068 686 J3
Rosearden Dr
1300 FTGV 97116 591 G3
NE Rosebay Dr
6100 HBRO 97124 593 J3
6200 HBRO 97124 594 A3
SW Roseberry Ln
- KNGC 97224 685 A1
- WasC 97224 685 A1
Rosebery Av
13200 ORCY 97045 717 D4
SW Rose Biggi Av
4200 BRTN 97005 625 A2
SE Rosebrier Ct
1800 CmsC 97267 656 H6
SW Rosebud Ct
18800 WasC 97007 624 E4

STREET
Block City ZIP Map# Grid
SE Rosebud Pl
3600 HBRO 97123 623 G2
SE Rosebud Wy
4500 HBRO 97123 623 G2
NW Roseburg Ter
2300 BRTN 97006 594 G3
2300 WasC 97006 594 G3
Rosecliffe Ct
2800 LKOW 97034 686 H1
Rosecliffe Dr
2800 LKOW 97034 686 H1
Rosecliffe Pl
2800 LKOW 97034 686 H1
Rosecrest Ln
35600 CmsC 97055 690 F4
SW Rosedale Ct
19200 WasC 97007 624 D5
SW Rosedale Rd
18900 WasC 97007 624 E5
23100 WasC 97007 623 H5
24000 WasC 97123 623 H5
SE Rosefinch Dr
2800 GSHM 97080 629 H6
NW Rosefinch Ln
1700 PTLD 97229 595 F3
SE Rosefinch Ln
3300 GSHM 97080 629 H6
SW Rose Garden Blvd
- PTLD 97205 596 C6
N Roselawn St
10 PTLD 97211 566 J7
10 PTLD 97217 566 J7
NE Roselawn St
900 PTLD 97211 566 H7
3700 PTLD 97211 567 B7
7200 PTLD 97218 567 F7
Rosemarie Dr
1400 WLIN 97068 686 G6
S Rosemary Ct
15600 CmsC 97045 689 B5
NE Rosemary Dr
37300 ClkC 98671 540 H6
Rosemary Ln
3000 LKOW 97034 686 B1
SE Rosemary Ln
- CmsC 97267 687 A1
Rose Meadow Dr
13200 CmsC 97015 658 B6
Rosemont Rd
10 CmsC 97034 686 D2
10 CmsC 97068 686 F4
1200 WLIN 97068 686 H6
1500 WLIN 97068 687 A6
SW Rosemount St
20400 WasC 97007 624 C5
S Rosenbaum Rd
15100 CmsC 97045 688 D4
S Rosencrantz Rd
13100 CmsC 97013 777 D7
Rosepark Ct
21400 WLIN 97068 686 J6
Rosepark Dr
3700 WLIN 97068 686 J6
SE Rosepetal Pl
4200 HBRO 97123 623 G2
SW Rose Quartz St
15500 BRTN 97007 624 H7
NW Roseshire Ct
41800 BNKS 97106 531 J6
SE Rosespring Dr
2700 HBRO 97123 593 F7
SE Rose Valley Pl
33700 SPSE 97056 474 F3
Rose Villa
- CmsC 97222 656 H5
SW Rose Vista Dr
11900 TGRD 97223 655 B5
11900 TGRD 97224 655 B5
NW Roseway Av
9200 PTLD 97231 565 E3
NE Rosewood Av
10500 ClkC 98662 507 J7
NE Rosewood Dr
- FRVW 97024 599 A3
Rosewood Ln
33300 ClbC 97056 444 E5
Rosewood St
4900 LKOW 97035 685 J1
6300 TLTN 97035 685 H1
6600 TLTN 97224 685 H1
SE Rosewood St
4300 HBRO 97123 623 G2
SW Rosewood Wy
8800 WasC 97225 625 F4
SW Roshak Dr
13600 WasC 97223 654 G5
SW Roshak Rd
- BRTN 97007 654 G4
15500 WasC 97224 654 H6
15700 WasC 97223 654 H5
SE Roslyn St
7900 CmsC 97222 657 F1
Ross Av
18300 SNDY 97055 691 A4
N Ross Av
2300 PTLD 97227 596 F3
Ross Rd
58200 ClbC 97051 414 H3
58200 ClbC 97053 414 H3
58700 STHN 97051 414 H2
SE Ross Rd
11500 HPYV 97236 658 B3
E Ross St
10 MOLA 97038 837 E1
NE Ross St
- VCVR 98663 506 H7
SW Ross St
8100 TGRD 97224 655 F6
W Ross St
100 MOLA 97038 837 E1
NE Ross Canyon Dr
- VCVR 98663 507 A7
Ross Island Br
- PTLD 97201 626 F1
- PTLD 97202 626 F1
- PTLD 97239 626 F1
Ross Island Br US-26
- PTLD 97201 626 F1
- PTLD 97202 626 F1
- PTLD 97239 626 F1
Rossiter Av
- CmsC 97067 724 C6
Rossiter Ln
2200 VCVR 98661 537 A3

STREET
Block City ZIP Map# Grid
Rossiter Pl
3700 VCVR 98661 537 A4
Rostrum Dr
- PTLD 97236 628 A7
- PTLD 97266 628 A7
SE Roswell Av
4200 MWKE 97222 627 B7
SW Roswell Av
2700 PTLD 97201 626 C1
SE Roswell St
2700 MWKE 97222 627 A7
3200 PTLD 97222 627 A7
SW Rosy Ct
13700 TGRD 97223 655 A4
SW Roth Ct
15900 WasC 97007 624 H3
SW Roth Dr
15900 WasC 97007 624 H3
NW Roth Rd
20900 ClkC 98642 445 J6
NE Roth St
300 PTLD 97211 566 G2
NE Rothbury Av
800 HBRO 97124 593 J4
SE Roundelay St
900 HBRO 97123 593 D7
SW Round Hill Wy
6200 MthC 97221 625 H1
NE Roundhouse Ln
52600 ClbC 97056 444 F7
52600 SPSE 97056 444 F7
SE Roundoak Ct
16600 CmsC 97267 687 B1
SW Roundtree Ct
6200 PTLD 97219 625 H7
Roundtree Dr
18800 ORCY 97045 717 B4
SW Roundtree Dr
15100 WasC 97223 654 H4
SW Rousseau Ct
- WNVL 97070 745 H3
E Routledge Ln
68200 CmsC 97067 724 C4
Rowell Rd
- WasC 97123 653 H7
- WasC 97123 683 H1
NE Rowland Rd
11500 YmhC 97111 711 C4
SW Roxanne Ct
8100 WasC 97223 625 F7
SW Roxbury Av
1900 WasC 97225 595 D7
2000 BRTN 97225 625 D1
2000 WasC 97225 625 D1
2600 BRTN 97005 625 C1
2600 WasC 97005 625 C1
Roxbury Ct
3000 WLIN 97068 686 J6
Roxbury Dr
3000 CmsC 97068 686 J6
3000 WLIN 97068 686 J6
Roxe Dr
600 FTGV 97116 591 F3
NW Roy Rd
6600 WasC 97113 562 C1
7900 WasC 97116 562 C1
10000 WasC 97106 562 C1
10400 WasC 97106 532 C7
Roy Wy
54000 ClbC 97056 444 H4
Royal Av
13200 ORCY 97045 717 D6
NW Royal Av
10 GSHM 97030 628 H2
SW Royal Av
1500 GSHM 97080 628 G4
NW Royal Blvd
200 PTLD 97210 595 H5
400 MthC 97210 595 H5
Royal Ct
1100 WLIN 97068 716 F1
17900 CmsC 97035 685 H2
NE Royal Ct
400 PTLD 97232 597 B5
4100 PTLD 97213 597 B5
SW Royal Ct
200 GSHM 97030 628 H3
1300 GSHM 97080 628 H4
7100 WasC 97223 625 G6
12000 KNGC 97224 655 B7
Royal Dr
1600 CmsC 97068 686 C4
NE Royal Dr
33200 SPSE 97056 444 F7
SE Royal Ln
16200 CmsC 97055 690 G2
16200 SNDY 97055 690 G2
SW Royal Pl
2100 GSHM 97080 628 H5
NW Royal Rd
- PTLD 97210 595 J2
- PTLD 97210 596 A2
NE Royal St
7700 VCVR 98662 537 E3
SW Royal Wy
2800 GSHM 97080 628 H5
Royalann Ln
- SRWD 97140 714 G1
SW Royal Anne Av
1200 TDLE 97060 599 E4
Royal Anne Ct
1200 TDLE 97060 599 E5
SW Royal Oak Ct
7000 WasC 97223 625 G6
Royal Oak St
100 NWBG 97132 713 F7
Royal Oaks Dr
5200 LKOW 97035 655 J6
5500 CmsC 97035 655 J6
NE Royal Oaks Dr
- VCVR 98662 537 F2
NW Royal Rose Ct
10200 WasC 97229 595 D4
SE Royalstar Av
3300 HBRO 97123 623 D2
3600 WasC 97123 623 D2
SW Royalty Ct
11900 KNGC 97224 655 B7
SW Royalty Pkwy
14900 TGRD 97224 655 C7
15300 KNGC 97224 655 C7
16200 KNGC 97224 685 B1
NE Royal View Av
3700 VCVR 98662 537 F2

STREET Block City ZIP Map# Grid

SE Royal View St
12500 CmsC 97236 658 A5
SW Royal Villa Dr
11400 WasC 97224 685 C1
SW Royal Woodlands Dr
9200 BRTN 97005 625 E4
SE Royce Ct
6500 HBRO 97123 594 A6
Royce Wy
3000 LKOW 97034 686 B2
Roydon Ter
- HBRO 97006 594 C5
SE Royer Rd
14400 DAMA 97009 658 J7
14400 DAMA 97009 659 A7
15400 DAMA 97009 689 B2
S Royle Rd
2600 ClkC 98642 446 D2
2600 RDGF 98642 446 D2
SW Roy Rogers Rd
12300 WasC 97007 654 F4
12300 WasC 97140 654 F7
12300 WasC 97223 654 F4
13400 WasC 97224 654 F7
16000 WasC 97140 684 F4
16000 WasC 97224 684 F1
19500 SRWD 97140 684 F4
Ruben Ln
17000 SNDY 97055 690 H2
NW Rubus Ln
600 HBRO 97124 593 A3
Ruby Ct
35000 STHN 97051 414 J1
SW Ruby Ct
500 MCMV 97128 770 F6
15100 BRTN 97007 624 H7
SE Ruby Dr
15500 CmsC 97267 656 J7
Ruby Ln
33500 ClbC 97051 414 F2
NW Ruby Ln
49100 WasC 97116 561 B3
SW Ruby Ln
2900 TDLE 97060 599 E6
SW Ruby St
14900 BRTN 97007 624 H7
SW Ruby Ter
7600 PTLD 97219 626 E6
SE Rudds Ct
34100 ClbC 97056 474 G1
34100 SPSE 97056 474 G1
SE Rude Rd
37700 CmsC 97055 720 J2
SE Rudiger Pl
19300 DAMA 97009 658 H3
SE Rudy Ct
13000 CmsC 97222 657 A5
E Rufus Ridge Ln
62700 CmsC 97011 693 F6
E Rufus Ridge Rd
62700 CmsC 97011 693 F6
SE Rugg Rd
24200 DAMA 97009 629 D7
24200 MthC 97080 629 D7
24500 MthC 97080 659 E1
25200 CmsC 97009 659 F1
25200 DAMA 97009 659 F1
Ruidoso Ct
3000 WLIN 97068 686 H5
SE Rummel St
600 MCMV 97128 770 H6
NW Runnymeade Ct
1900 PTLD 97229 595 F3
SE Rupert Dr
13900 CmsC 97222 656 J5
13900 CmsC 97267 656 J6
SE Rural Ct
16100 PTLD 97236 628 E6
SE Rural St
1300 PTLD 97202 626 H5
3600 PTLD 97202 627 B6
4100 PTLD 97206 627 C6
8700 PTLD 97266 627 G6
SE Ruscliff Rd
13300 CmsC 97222 657 D5
13300 CmsC 97267 657 D5
13300 MWKE 97222 657 D5
Rushing Ln
33800 ClbC 97056 444 F3
SE Rusk Rd
12600 CmsC 97222 657 C5
12600 MWKE 97222 657 C5
14000 CmsC 97267 657 C6
SW Russ Ct
300 MCMV 97128 770 F5
SW Russ Ln
500 MCMV 97128 770 F6
NE Russell Ct
10500 PTLD 97220 597 J3
14600 PTLD 97230 598 D3
SE Russell Ct
3500 HBRO 97123 593 G5
NE Russell Pl
8700 PTLD 97220 597 G3
15600 PTLD 97230 598 E3
N Russell St
10 PTLD 97212 596 G3
10 PTLD 97227 596 F3
NE Russell St
10 PTLD 97212 596 G3
10 PTLD 97227 596 G3
8200 PTLD 97213 597 F3
10700 PTLD 97220 597 J3
11700 PTLD 97220 598 A3
12200 PTLD 97230 598 A3
16000 GSHM 97230 598 F3
SE Russell St
600 CMAS 98607 569 G5
4000 HBRO 97123 593 G5
N Russet St
10 PTLD 97211 566 G5
4100 PTLD 97203 566 C5
4100 PTLD 97217 566 C5
NE Russet St
10 PTLD 97211 566 G5
10 PTLD 97217 566 G5
Russ Wilcox Wy
14200 ORCY 97045 717 F6
SE Rust Wy
13700 DAMA 97009 658 J6
13700 DAMA 97009 659 A6
SW Rustica Ter
- WasC 97225 595 D6
SW Rustling Leaves Pl
8600 WasC 97223 625 F7
SE Rustling Ridge Dr
11700 CmsC 97015 657 H5
Rusty Ter
19000 ORCY 97045 716 J4
SE Ruth Ct
2900 CmsC 97267 686 J1
SW Ruth Ct
19500 WasC 97007 624 D6
Ruth St NE
20800 DNLD 97020 774 G5
SW Ruth St
30400 WNVL 97070 745 E1
S Rutherford Ln
23200 CmsC 97004 748 J6
SW Rutland Ter
2700 PTLD 97205 596 C5
SE Ryan Av
13200 CmsC 97222 657 B5
13300 MWKE 97222 657 B5
Ryan Ct
1100 WLIN 97068 716 F1
SE Ryan Ct
4500 CmsC 97222 657 B5
4500 MWKE 97222 657 B5
NW Ryan St
8500 PTLD 97229 595 F4
8500 WasC 97229 595 F4
SW Rydell Pl
7100 WasC 97007 624 D5
SE Ryder Ln
- CmsC 97009 660 C5
Rydman Ct
19200 WLIN 97068 686 H3
Rye Rd
700 LKOW 97034 656 E5
NW Ryegrass St
15600 WasC 97229 564 H6
SW Rystadt Ln
9000 WasC 97225 625 E2
NW Rystadt Rd
- MthC 97229 565 B6

S

S Cir
3900 WHGL 98671 570 D4
W S Cir
900 WHGL 98671 569 G4
S St
500 VCVR 98661 536 J5
2400 VCVR 98663 536 J3
4900 WHGL 98671 570 E4
SE S St
3000 ClkC 98671 570 C4
3000 WHGL 98671 570 C4
W S St
600 WHGL 98671 569 H4
SW Sabin St
12400 BRTN 97008 625 B5
Sabina Ct
3300 LKOW 97035 656 B7
Sabo Ln
3000 CmsC 97068 686 J7
3000 WLIN 97068 686 J7
SW Sacajawea Blvd
- PTLD 97205 596 B6
NW Sacajawea Ct
1100 CMAS 98607 568 J5
SW Sacajawea Wy
8000 WNVL 97070 745 F3
SE Sacha Pl
900 HBRO 97123 593 C7
NE Sacramento Dr
13200 PTLD 97230 598 B3
NE Sacramento St
10 PTLD 97212 596 G3
10 PTLD 97227 596 G3
6400 PTLD 97213 597 E3
8200 PTLD 97220 597 G3
11200 PTLD 97220 598 A3
13200 PTLD 97230 598 C3
16900 GSHM 97230 598 F3
Saddle Ct
2400 WLIN 97068 686 J5
NE Saddle Ct
5000 HBRO 97124 593 H3
SW Saddle Dr
9400 BRTN 97008 654 J1
S Saddle Ln
15500 CmsC 97045 717 H7
NE Saddle St
5400 HBRO 97124 593 H3
SW Saddlebrook Ct
18200 WasC 97006 594 F7
Saddlehorn Ct
19500 ORCY 97045 717 D5
NW Sadie Ct
300 HBRO 97124 593 A2
SW Sage Pl
7500 BRTN 97008 625 B6
SE Sagebrush Dr
13200 CmsC 97236 658 B5
Sage Hen Cir
4800 LKOW 97035 686 A2
SW Sagehen St
11900 BRTN 97007 654 H3
Sage Hen Wy
4800 LKOW 97035 686 A2
SE Sager Rd
16200 CmsC 97236 658 F1
16200 PTLD 97236 658 F1
SW Sagert Ct
8900 TLTN 97062 685 E4
SW Sagert St
8700 TLTN 97062 685 E4
SW Sahnow Dr
1600 WasC 97006 594 E7
NE Saida Ln
5800 HBRO 97124 593 J4
SW Saige Ct
- WasC 97007 624 E2
St. Andrews Ct
20000 ORCY 97045 717 H7
St. Andrews Dr
15000 ORCY 97045 717 G6
NW St. Andrews Dr
15300 WasC 97229 594 H1
SE St. Andrews Dr
600 CmsC 97202 656 H1
600 CmsC 97222 656 H1
600 PTLD 97202 656 H1
1700 PTLD 97202 626 G7
W St. Andrews Dr
1800 MCMV 97128 770 G3
St. Andrews Ext
1200 MCMV 97128 770 F3
SE St. Andrews Pl
3800 GSHM 97080 629 B6
SW St. Barbara Wy
23000 SRWD 97140 684 G7
SW St. Charles Wy
23000 SRWD 97140 684 G7
23000 SRWD 97140 714 G1
SW St. Clair Av
700 PTLD 97205 596 D6
700 PTLD 97210 596 D5
St. Clair Dr
17900 LKOW 97034 686 D2
SE St. Clair Rd
3400 ClkC 98671 570 F3
St. Francis Ln
2100 VCVR 98660 536 D3
St. Helens Av
8400 VCVR 98664 537 F7
NW St. Helens Av
500 MthC 97229 595 H5
SE St. Helens Av
10900 VCVR 98664 537 J7
St. Helens Cir
10 LKOW 97035 656 B4
SW St. Helens Ct
2500 PTLD 97201 596 C7
SW St. Helens Dr
8500 WasC 97062 715 E2
8500 WNVL 97070 715 E2
NW St. Helens Rd
2200 PTLD 97210 596 A2
4300 PTLD 97210 595 J1
4600 PTLD 97210 565 J7
9600 PTLD 97231 565 D1
11600 PTLD 97231 535 D7
12300 MthC 97231 535 D7
15000 MthC 97231 534 G1
17700 MthC 97231 504 E2
25200 MthC 97056 474 E6
25200 MthC 97231 474 E6
NW St. Helens Rd US-30
2200 PTLD 97210 596 B3
4500 PTLD 97210 595 J1
4600 PTLD 97210 565 J7
9600 PTLD 97231 565 D1
11600 PTLD 97231 535 D7
12300 MthC 97231 535 D7
15000 MthC 97231 534 G1
17700 MthC 97231 504 E2
25200 MthC 97056 474 E6
25200 MthC 97231 474 E6
Saint Helens St
- ORCY 97045 717 D2
- STHN 97051 385 B7
St. Helens St
10 STHN 97051 385 D7
SE St. Helens St
9000 CmsC 97015 657 G7
SE St. James Ln
13000 TGRD 97224 655 A5
13000 WasC 97224 655 A5
St. James Pl
600 MOLA 97038 807 C7
SW St. James Pl
21400 CmsC 97068 686 D6
NE St. James Rd
3700 ClkC 98661 537 A2
3700 VCVR 98661 537 A2
3700 VCVR 98663 537 A1
5300 VCVR 98663 507 A7
6200 ClkC 98661 507 A6
NE St. Jean Pl
300 HBRO 97124 593 C3
SW St. John Pl
7400 WasC 97223 625 G5
N St. Johns Av
6900 PTLD 97203 565 G2
St. Johns Blvd
1600 VCVR 98661 536 J3
1600 VCVR 98663 536 J3
3500 VCVR 98661 537 A2
3500 VCVR 98663 537 A2
St. Johns Br
- PTLD 97203 565 G3
- PTLD 97210 565 F5
- PTLD 97231 565 F4
St. Johns Br US-30 BYP
- PTLD 97203 565 G3
- PTLD 97210 565 F5
- PTLD 97231 565 F4
N St. Johns Rd
5300 PTLD 97217 566 D7
NE St. Johns Rd
3600 ClkC 98661 537 A2
3600 VCVR 98661 537 A2
3600 VCVR 98663 537 A2
5200 ClkC 98661 507 A7
5200 VCVR 98663 507 A7
6700 ClkC 98665 507 B4
6700 VCVR 98665 507 A4
9800 ClkC 98686 507 D2
SW St. John Vianney Wy
4500 WasC 97007 624 H3
NE St. Joseph Rd
2700 YmhC 97128 771 D1
N St. Louis Av
6600 PTLD 97203 565 G2
St. Louis Wy
10 VCVR 98664 537 D6
SE St. Lucy Ln
10900 CmsC 97236 657 J3
SW St. Marys Dr
- BRTN 97007 624 J3
- WasC 97007 624 J3
St. Moritz Lp
2200 CmsC 97068 686 G7
2200 WLIN 97068 686 G7
NE St. Paul Av
- ClkC 98682 508 G7
- ClkC 98682 538 G1
St. Paul Hwy NE
900 NWBG 97132 743 F5
900 YmhC 97132 743 F5
4700 MmC 97137 773 G6
6500 MmC 97137 774 A7
8400 MmC 97002 774 A7
8400 MmC 97137 743 F7
20400 STPL 97137 773 C5
St. Paul Hwy NE SR-219
900 NWBG 97132 743 F5
900 YmhC 97132 743 F5
4500 MmC 97137 773 D6
4500 STPL 97137 773 C6
St. Paul Hwy NE SR-219
8400 MmC 97137 743 F7
St. Tropez Av
29200 WNVL 97070 715 B7
NE Sako Dr
32500 ClkC 98604 418 D1
NW Salada Pl
- PTLD 97210 596 B5
Salal Ct
- WasC 97007 624 D5
SW Salal Ct
13500 BRTN 97008 625 A6
Salal St
10 STHN 97051 385 B7
Salamo Rd
20000 CmsC 97068 686 H6
20000 WLIN 97068 686 H6
S Salamo Rd
23400 WLIN 97068 686 H7
23400 WLIN 97068 716 H1
23600 CmsC 97068 716 H1
N Salem Av
6600 PTLD 97203 565 G3
Salem-Dayton Hwy
- DAYT 97114 772 A3
- YmhC 97114 772 A3
Salem-Dayton Hwy SR-221
- DAYT 97114 772 A3
- YmhC 97114 772 A3
S Saling Rd
21900 CmsC 97023 749 J4
22000 CmsC 97023 750 A4
SW Salish Ln
8500 WasC 97062 715 E3
8500 WNVL 97070 715 E3
NW Salishan Dr
4500 WasC 97229 594 C1
4600 WasC 97229 564 C7
NW Salishan Pl
4900 WasC 97229 564 C7
SW Salix Ct
100 BRTN 97006 594 E5
SW Salix Pl
300 BRTN 97006 594 E6
300 WasC 97006 594 E6
SW Salix Ter
- HBRO 97006 594 E6
100 BRTN 97006 594 E6
SW Salix Ridge St
17900 BRTN 97006 594 E5
17900 WasC 97006 594 F5
Salmon Ct
12100 ORCY 97045 717 B4
SE Salmon Ct
4500 PTLD 97215 597 C7
9300 PTLD 97216 597 G7
12400 PTLD 97233 598 B7
22300 GSHM 97030 599 C6
NW Salmon Dr
2200 GSHM 97030 599 B7
SE Salmon Dr
22300 GSHM 97030 599 C6
SW Salmon Ln
30900 WNVL 97070 745 F2
Salmon St
10 STHN 97051 385 B7
E Salmon St
61700 CmsC 97011 693 E6
SE Salmon St
10 PTLD 97214 596 J7
2700 PTLD 97214 597 A7
7200 PTLD 97215 597 E7
8000 PTLD 97216 597 F7
11500 PTLD 97216 598 A7
12200 PTLD 97233 598 B7
20900 GSHM 97030 599 A7
SW Salmon St
10 PTLD 97204 596 F6
1000 PTLD 97205 596 D6
5700 MthC 97221 595 J6
5700 PTLD 97221 595 J6
9000 WasC 97225 595 E6
30800 WNVL 97070 745 F1
Salmonberry Dr
11500 CmsC 97045 716 J4
11500 CmsC 97045 717 A5
11500 ORCY 97045 716 J4
11500 ORCY 97045 717 A5
SW Salmonberry Dr
18000 WasC 97140 714 D4
Salmonberry Rd
- CmsC 97049 724 F3
E Salmonberry Rd
71000 CmsC 97049 724 E3
NE Salmon Creek Av
12000 ClkC 98686 477 A7
12000 ClkC 98686 507 A1
NE Salmon Creek St
4600 ClkC 98686 477 C5
Salmon River Hwy
- MCMV 97128 770 J7
- MCMV 97128 771 A6
- YmhC 97114 771 E6
- YmhC 97128 770 J7
- YmhC 97128 771 A6
Salmon River Hwy SR-18
- MCMV 97128 770 J7
- MCMV 97128 771 A6
- YmhC 97114 771 E6
- YmhC 97128 770 J7
- YmhC 97128 771 A6
NE Salmon River Hwy
2100 MCMV 97128 771 D6
2100 YmhC 97128 771 A6
4100 YmhC 97114 771 E6
NE Salmon River Hwy SR-18
2100 MCMV 97128 771 D6
2100 YmhC 97128 771 A6
4100 YmhC 97114 771 E6
SE Salmon River Hwy
- YmhC 97114 771 E6
SE Salmon River Hwy SR-18
- YmhC 97114 771 E6
Salmon River Rd
28300 CmsC 97067 724 D7
E Salmon River Rd
24900 CmsC 97049 724 D4
24900 CmsC 97067 724 C6
S Salo Rd
28100 CmsC 97042 807 J1
SE Salquist Rd
3900 GSHM 97080 629 G5
SW Saltus Ter
23000 SRWD 97140 684 F7
NW Saltzman Ct
12900 WasC 97229 595 B3
NW Saltzman Rd
- PTLD 97231 565 G6
1400 WasC 97229 595 B2
5800 PTLD 97210 565 H7
11100 PTLD 97229 565 D7
NW Salvia Ct
14500 WasC 97229 564 J7
NW Salzwedal Rd
36500 WasC 97113 562 F4
NE Samantha Ln
- HBRO 97124 594 B5
- WasC 97124 594 B5
SW Samantha Ln
21500 HBRO 97124 594 B5
21500 WasC 97006 594 B5
21500 WasC 97124 594 B5
SW Samaritan Ct
17800 WasC 97006 624 F1
Sam Blehm Rd
32200 ClbC 97056 444 C4
SW Samedy Ct
19100 WasC 97006 594 D7
SW Sam Jackson Park Rd
2700 PTLD 97201 626 D1
2900 PTLD 97239 626 D1
S Sam McGee Rd
18000 CmsC 97045 748 E1
SW Sammy Dr
18800 WasC 97006 624 E1
E Sampson Av
23800 CmsC 97067 724 B3
SW Sampson Ln
- TLTN 97062 685 C7
NW Samuel Dr
5800 WasC 97229 564 G7
SE Samuels Rd
26700 CmsC 97022 719 H5
Sand Rd
- CmsC 97023 750 B4
SW Sandalwood Av
2300 WasC 97005 625 E4
Sandalwood Ct
13100 LKOW 97035 655 J4
SW Sandalwood Ct
28500 WNVL 97070 715 G6
SW Sandalwood Dr
28500 WNVL 97070 715 G6
S Sandalwood Rd
15900 CmsC 97045 688 A7
SW Sandalwood St
1500 MCMV 97128 770 F5
NW Sandberg Rd
33000 SPSE 97056 444 D6
SW Sandburg St
6600 TGRD 97223 655 G5
NW Sandelie Ct
16700 BRTN 97006 594 G4
SE Sandercock Ln
44000 CmsC 97055 691 E6
SW Sanderling Ct
16300 BRTN 97007 654 G2
SW Sanders Ter
23500 SRWD 97140 714 E1
SW Sand Hill Ln
17000 SRWD 97140 684 F5
SW Sandhill Lp
14600 BRTN 97008 654 J3
SW Sandhill Ter
- BRTN 97007 654 H4
SW Sandlewood Av
1900 GSHM 97080 628 H4
SW Sandlewood Ln
3100 GSHM 97080 628 H6
SW Sandlewood Lp
100 GSHM 97030 628 H2
SW Sandlewood Pl
1900 GSHM 97080 628 H4
S Sandoz Rd
1300 NWBG 97132 743 E2
1700 YmhC 97132 743 E2
NW Sandpines Ln
- WasC 97229 594 G2
17200 WasC 97006 594 G2
Sandpiper Cir
18400 LKOW 97035 686 B3
NE Sandpiper Cir
9900 VCVR 98664 537 G3
SW Sandpiper Ln
15100 BRTN 97007 654 H1
Sandpiper St
18400 LKOW 97035 685 G3
Sandpiper Wy
18400 LKOW 97035 685 J2
18400 LKOW 97035 686 A2
SE Sandra Av
4900 CmsC 97267 687 C1
SW Sandra Ct
20000 WasC 97006 624 C1
SW Sandra Ln
18700 WasC 97006 624 E1
Sandra Lp
13600 CmsC 97045 717 E5
SW Sandridge Dr
13300 TGRD 97223 654 J5
SW Sands Ln
15500 WasC 97007 624 H2
SW Sandstone Ct
- BRTN 97007 654 G1
SW Sandstone Pl
9600 BRTN 97007 654 G1
SE Sandview Ln
10100 CmsC 97222 657 E2
SE Sandview St
6800 CmsC 97222 657 D2
Sandy Av
1500 TDLE 97060 599 G5
E Sandy Av
23200 CmsC 97049 724 B2
SE Sandy Av
300 TDLE 97060 599 G4
NE Sandy Blvd
1200 PTLD 97214 596 H5
1200 PTLD 97232 596 J5
2800 PTLD 97232 597 A4
3900 PTLD 97212 597 B4
4100 PTLD 97213 597 C3
8100 PTLD 97218 597 F2
8100 PTLD 97220 597 F2
9100 MWDP 97220 597 G1
9100 PTLD 97220 597 H1
11300 PTLD 97220 598 A1
11900 PTLD 97230 598 A1
16500 GSHM 97230 598 F2
19700 GSHM 97024 598 H3
20100 FRVW 97024 598 J3
20400 FRVW 97024 599 C3
23000 WDVL 97060 599 D3
NE Sandy Blvd US-30 BUS
1200 PTLD 97214 596 H5
1200 PTLD 97232 596 J5
2800 PTLD 97232 597 A4
3900 PTLD 97212 597 B4
4100 PTLD 97213 597 C3
8100 PTLD 97218 597 F2
8100 PTLD 97220 597 F2
9100 MWDP 97220 597 G1
NE Sandy Blvd US-30 BYP
9900 PTLD 97220 597 H1
11300 PTLD 97220 598 A1
15800 PTLD 97230 598 E1
16500 GSHM 97230 598 F2
19700 GSHM 97024 598 H3
20100 FRVW 97024 598 J3
20400 FRVW 97024 599 B3
SE Sandy Blvd
- PTLD 97232 596 H5
700 PTLD 97214 596 H6
SE Sandy Cir
3700 TDLE 97060 599 G7
SE Sandy Ct
1700 TDLE 97060 599 G5
SW Sandy Ct
30900 WNVL 97070 745 E1
NE Sandycrest Ter
5300 PTLD 97213 597 C3
NE Sandy Dell Rd
10 MthC 97060 599 H6
SE Sandy Dell Rd
10 MthC 97060 599 H7
1500 TDLE 97060 599 H7
Sandy Heights Rd
38200 SNDY 97055 690 J3
39000 SNDY 97055 691 A2
Sandy Heights St
37000 CmsC 97055 690 H3
37000 SNDY 97055 690 H3
SE Sandy River Dr
38200 CmsC 97055 690 J2
38200 SNDY 97055 690 J2
E Sandy River Ln
64600 CmsC 97049 693 H7
65200 CmsC 97049 723 J1
SE San Marcos Av
7100 CmsC 97267 657 D7
SE San Mareno Av
15200 CmsC 97267 657 D5
SE San Marino Av
3300 HBRO 97123 623 E1
SW San Mateo Ter
1600 WasC 97006 594 F7
NE San Rafael Dr
14800 PTLD 97230 598 D4
16200 GSHM 97230 598 F4
NE San Rafael St
10 PTLD 97212 596 G3
10 PTLD 97227 596 G3
11100 PTLD 97220 597 J4
11500 PTLD 97220 598 A4
12100 PTLD 97230 598 A4
19200 GSHM 97230 598 H4
20100 FRVW 97024 598 J4
21300 FRVW 97024 599 A4
SW Santa Anita Ct
13000 BRTN 97008 655 A1
Santa Anita Dr
- WLIN 97068 686 H5
1700 CmsC 97068 686 H6
S Santa Fe Ct
100 VCVR 98661 537 C6
N Santa Fe Dr
100 VCVR 98661 537 C5
SW Santa Fe Ter
20600 SRWD 97140 684 E5
SW Santa Maria Dr
19000 WasC 97132 683 F4
SW Santa Monica Ct
5000 PTLD 97221 625 J2
5000 PTLD 97221 626 A1
6300 PTLD 97225 625 H3
SW Santa Monica St
2900 PTLD 97239 626 B3
SW Santana Pl
200 WasC 97225 595 H6
NW Santanita Ter
2800 PTLD 97210 596 B5
SW Santa Rosa Ct
19000 WasC 97007 624 C4
SW Santee Ct
19700 TLTN 97062 685 G4
NW Santiam Ct
17600 WasC 97229 594 F2
NW Santiam Dr
17400 WasC 97006 594 F3
17400 WasC 97229 594 F3
SW Santiam Dr
8400 TLTN 97062 685 E5
SW Santolina Pl
7900 BRTN 97008 625 D3
SW Santoro Dr
18300 WasC 97007 624 E7
SE Santosh St
33500 SPSE 97056 474 E1
SW Sapphire Dr
15100 BRTN 97007 654 H1
SW Sapphire Ln
14500 BRTN 97007 654 J1
14500 BRTN 97008 654 J1
Sarah Dr
500 NWBG 97132 713 C6
SE Sarah Ln
15200 CmsC 97267 656 J7
Sarah Hill Ln
17800 LKOW 97035 686 A2
SW Sarala St
16700 WasC 97007 624 F6
SW Saratoga Ln
13200 BRTN 97008 655 A1
N Saratoga St
10 PTLD 97211 566 G6
2000 PTLD 97217 566 E5
NE Saratoga St
10 PTLD 97217 566 G6
1300 PTLD 97211 566 J6
2300 PTLD 97211 567 A6
NW Sargent Ln
- PTLD 97231 565 C3
Sargent St
200 RDGF 98642 415
NW Satellite Dr
14600 WasC 97106 531
Sattler Dr
50300 ClbC 97056 474
SW Sattler St
9100 TGRD 97224 655
Sauer Ct
- SPSE 97056 474
Saulser Rd
58600 ClbC 97051 414
58600 ClbC 97053 414
SW Saum Wy
4500 TLTN 97062 685
4500 TLTN 97062 686
SW Saunders Dr
22500 SRWD 97140 684
NW Sauvie Island Rd
15000 MthC 97231 535
18000 MthC 97231 534
18400 MthC 97231 504
24000 ClbC 97231 474
SE Savanna St
6800 CmsC 97267 657
SW Savannah Pl
4500 WasC 97007 624
SW Savaria Ct
10200 WasC 97005 625
NW Savier St
1300 PTLD 97209 596
3300 PTLD 97210 596
Savon Wy
16100 CmsC 97042 807
NW Savoy Ln
8700 WasC 97229 595
S Sawtell Rd
32700 CmsC 97038 837
SE Sawtooth St
17100 MthC 97236 628
17100 PTLD 97236 628
NW Sawyer Ct
9700 PTLD 97229 595
Sawyer St
38700 SNDY 97055 690
NE Sawyer St
52500 SPSE 97056 444
SW Saxon Pl
22300 SRWD 97140 684
Saxton Rd
58100 ClbC 97051 414
Sayre Dr NE
21100 AURA 97002 775
Scales Av
17100 SNDY 97055 690
Scappoose Vernonia Hwy
31100 ClbC 97056 444
33100 SPSE 97056 444
Scarborough Dr
10 LKOW 97034 686
Scarlet Ct NE
- DNLD 97020 774
SW Scarlett Dr
13600 WasC 97224 655
13700 WasC 97224 654
SW Scarlett Pl
14400 WasC 97224 654
14400 WasC 97224 655
Scenic Dr
1300 WLIN 97068 686
SW Scenic Dr
2200 WasC 97225 625
Scenic Ln
32800 ClbC 97056 444
SE Scenic Ln
5400 VCVR 98661 537
Scenic St
39100 CmsC 97055 691
39100 SNDY 97055 691
SW Scenic Dr Ct
2900 WasC 97225 625
SW Scenic Dr Ter
9300 WasC 97225 625
SE Scenic Ridge Rd
13000 CmsC 97015 658
NE Schaad Rd
31100 YmhC 97132 713
NE Schaad View Dr
31600 YmhC 97132 713
SW Schaber Ln
19100 CmsC 97062 686
SE Schacht Rd
9900 DAMA 97009 658
9900 DAMA 97009 659
Schaefer Dr
19600 ORCY 97045 717
NW Schaefer Rd
10200 WasC 97116 531
10200 WasC 97116 561
S Schaeffer Dr
19700 ORCY 97045 717
SW Schaeffer Rd
400 CmsC 97068 716
NW Schaff Rd
23300 WasC 97124 563
23300 WasC 97124 564
Schalit Wy
17300 LKOW 97035 685
SW Schaltenbrand Ln
22100 WasC 97140 684
SW Schamburg Dr
23000 SRWD 97140 684
SW Schatz Rd
4700 CmsC 97062 685
NE Schauer Dr
23000 ClkC 98604 449
SW Scheckla Dr
8800 TGRD 97224 655
NW Scheel Ter
5900 WasC 97229 564
NW Scheffin Lakes Ln
36700 WasC 97113 562
NW Schendel Av
15800 BRTN 97006 594
SW Schiffler Pl
- BRTN 97005 625
SE Schiller Ct
10300 PTLD 97266 627
SW Schiller Rd
- WasC 97225 625
7900 BRTN 97225 625
SE Schiller St
2400 PTLD 97202 626
2800 PTLD 97202 627
5200 PTLD 97206 627

Portland Street Index

STREET
Block City ZIP Map# Grid

SE Schiller St
9200 PTLD 97266 627 G3
11900 PTLD 97266 628 A4
13200 PTLD 97236 628 B4
SW Schiller Ter
2600 BRTN 97225 625 F1
NW Schlottman Pl
- BRTN 97006 594 H5
N Schmeer Rd
300 PTLD 97211 566 G4
300 PTLD 97217 566 F3
N Schmeer St
- PTLD 97217 566 E3
SW Schmeltzer Rd
21200 WasC 97132 683 H5
21200 WasC 97140 683 H7
23000 WasC 97140 713 G1
NW Schmidt Wy
2300 WasC 97006 594 G3
NE Schoeler Cir
5000 HBRO 97124 593 H5
S Schoenborn Rd
25000 CmsC 97042 777 F3
N Schofield St
1800 PTLD 97217 566 E4
SW Scholls Dr
15200 WasC 97140 653 J7
SW Scholls Ferry Ct
3200 MthC 97221 625 H1
SW Scholls Ferry Rd
- MthC 97221 625 J1
2000 MthC 97221 595 J7
2000 PTLD 97221 595 J7
3900 PTLD 97221 625 H2
4100 WasC 97225 625 F5
4200 PTLD 97225 625 H2
5400 BRTN 97225 625 F5
5800 WasC 97223 625 F4
6500 WasC 97005 625 E5
6700 BRTN 97005 625 E5
6700 BRTN 97008 625 E7
6700 WasC 97008 625 E7
8500 BRTN 97223 625 D7
8700 TGRD 97008 625 D7
8700 TGRD 97223 625 D7
9000 BRTN 97008 655 A2
9000 BRTN 97223 655 A2
9000 TGRD 97223 655 A2
11800 TGRD 97008 655 B2
13500 BRTN 97007 655 A2
13500 TGRD 97007 655 A2
14000 BRTN 97007 654 G4
14000 BRTN 97008 654 J2
16500 WasC 97007 654 F4
20300 WasC 97123 654 A5
22600 WasC 97123 653 H7
23600 WasC 97140 653 J6
24100 WasC 97123 683 H1
24100 WasC 97140 683 H1
SW Scholls Ferry Rd SR-210
4700 WasC 97225 625 F5
5400 BRTN 97225 625 F5
5800 WasC 97223 625 F4
6500 WasC 97005 625 E5
6700 BRTN 97005 625 E5
6700 BRTN 97008 625 E7
6700 WasC 97008 625 E7
8500 BRTN 97223 625 D7
8700 TGRD 97008 625 D7
8700 TGRD 97223 625 D7
9000 BRTN 97008 655 A2
9000 BRTN 97223 655 A2
9000 TGRD 97223 655 A2
11800 TGRD 97008 655 B2
13500 BRTN 97007 655 A2
13500 TGRD 97008 655 A2
14000 BRTN 97007 654 G4
14000 BRTN 97008 654 J2
17500 WasC 97007 654 E4
20300 WasC 97123 654 A5
22600 WasC 97123 653 H7
23600 WasC 97140 653 J6
24100 WasC 97123 683 H1
24100 WasC 97140 683 H1
Scholls Pointe
- BRTN 97007 654 J3
- BRTN 97007 655 A2
- BRTN 97008 655 A2
SW Scholls-Sherwood Rd
17900 WasC 97140 684 B2
22100 WasC 97140 654 A7
22500 WasC 97140 653 J6
23300 WasC 97123 653 H6
SW Schollwood Ct
11700 TGRD 97223 655 C2
SE School Av
12000 CmsC 97009 659 G5
N School St
100 NWBG 97132 713 C7
S School St
400 NWBG 97132 743 C1
SW School St
10200 TGRD 97223 655 D4
SW Schottky Rd
- BRTN 97005 624 J2
- WasC 97005 624 J2
SE Schroeder Av
13700 CmsC 97222 656 H5
13700 CmsC 97267 656 H5
SE Schroeder Ln
14200 CmsC 97267 656 H6
SW Schroeder Ln
18700 WasC 97140 684 D4
SW Schroeder Wy
7400 WNVL 97070 745 F1
S Schuebel School Rd
23800 CmsC 97004 748 D7
Schukart Ln
800 LKOW 97034 656 D7
Schuler Rd
- MrnC 97002 744 D7
- MrnC 97137 744 D7
Schuler Rd NE
10000 MrnC 97002 744 F7
Schultz Rd NE
22700 MrnC 97002 744 H5
22700 MrnC 97002 774 H1
NE Schuman Dr
6100 ClkC 98629 417 D5
NE Schuyler Ct
15200 PTLD 97230 598 D4
16600 GSHM 97230 598 F4
NE Schuyler St
100 PTLD 97212 596 H4
NE Schuyler St
3000 PTLD 97212 597 A4
7700 PTLD 97213 597 F4
9200 PTLD 97220 597 G4
11400 PTLD 97220 598 A4
14400 PTLD 97230 598 D4
22600 FRVW 97024 599 C4
SE Schwind Cir
8200 VCVR 98664 537 F7
NW Science Park Dr
13400 BRTN 97229 595 A4
13400 WasC 97229 595 A5
13800 BRTN 97229 594 J4
13800 WasC 97229 594 J4
SW Scoffins St
8600 TGRD 97223 655 F4
SE Scooter Ln
13800 DAMA 97009 658 H6
Scotsman Ct
- DNDE 97115 742 H3
Scott Av
3600 TDLE 97060 599 G7
NE Scott Av
400 GSHM 97030 629 F2
SE Scott Av
2000 GSHM 97080 629 F5
Scott Cir
3800 TDLE 97060 599 G7
Scott Ct
3600 TDLE 97060 599 G7
16800 LKOW 97034 656 D7
16800 LKOW 97034 686 D1
18300 GLDS 97027 687 D2
NE Scott Ct
1400 GSHM 97030 629 F1
SW Scott Ct
9800 TGRD 97223 655 D3
NE Scott Dr
10 GSHM 97030 629 F2
10 GSHM 97080 629 F3
SE Scott Dr
6200 PTLD 97215 597 D6
Scott Ln
- MthC 97060 629 G1
- TDLE 97060 629 G1
17700 GLDS 97027 687 D2
SW Scott Ln
- WNVL 97070 715 E3
N Scott St
800 CLTN 97111 711 A7
NW Scott St
100 HBRO 97124 593 B2
S Scott St
100 CLTN 97111 711 A7
200 CLTN 97111 741 A1
SE Scott St
1900 MWKE 97222 656 J2
SE Scott Creek Ln
13400 HPYV 97236 658 B3
SW Scottie Pl
4300 WasC 97007 624 D3
SE Scottish Ct
1400 CmsC 97267 656 H7
SE Scotton Wy
200 BGND 98604 448 C7
SW Scotton Wy
10 BGND 98604 448 A7
SE Scott Park Cir
9300 CmsC 97236 657 G1
SE Scott Park Ln
9400 CmsC 97236 657 G1
SW Scott Ridge Ter
23700 SRWD 97140 714 H1
SW Scotts Bridge Dr
13100 TGRD 97223 655 A4
NW Scottsdale Dr
4000 WasC 97006 594 G1
SE Scotts Ridge Ct
9400 CmsC 97236 657 H1
NW Scottston Ter
12800 BNKS 97106 531 J6
SE Scottstree Wy
8800 CmsC 97015 687 F2
N Scouler Av
12600 PTLD 97217 536 E6
E Scout Av
67400 CmsC 97049 724 B2
SW Scout Dr
12700 BRTN 97008 655 B1
Scout Camp Rd
- ClkC 98604 418 C7
Scouters Mountain Rd
- HPYV 97236 658 C3
SE Scrutton Ln
17500 CmsC 97267 687 D2
17700 CmsC 97027 687 D2
17700 GLDS 97027 687 D2
S Seal Ct
17100 CmsC 97045 718 B7
Seal Rd
500 STHN 97051 385 A7
500 STHN 97051 414 J1
500 STHN 97051 415 A1
Seal Rock Av NE
- AURA 97002 775 F5
Seaman Av
18000 SNDY 97055 690 J3
SW Sean Michael Pl
6700 WasC 97225 595 H6
NW Seavey Rd
10200 WasC 97116 531 B7
10200 WasC 97116 561 C1
SW Seaview Ln
14500 TGRD 97223 654 J5
Sebastian Wy
19500 CmsC 97045 717 E5
19500 ORCY 97045 717 E5
NW Seblar Ct
100 PTLD 97210 596 A5
NW Seblar Dr
200 PTLD 97210 596 A5
NW Seblar Ter
4500 PTLD 97210 596 A5
SW Seca Ct
13000 TGRD 97223 655 D1
SW Secretariat Ct
13900 BRTN 97008 625 D5
SW Secretariat Ln
13800 BRTN 97008 625 A7
SW Secretariat Ter
8200 BRTN 97008 625 A7
Section St
100 MOLA 97038 837 E2
E Section Line Rd
24000 CmsC 97049 724 F4
SW Sedge Ln
17600 SRWD 97140 684 E5
NW Sedgewick Ct
18100 BRTN 97006 594 E4
SW Sedlak Ct
10100 TLTN 97062 685 C3
SE Sedona Dr
14800 CmsC 97015 658 D7
NW Sedona Ln
20500 WasC 97006 594 C5
N Sedro St
6800 PTLD 97203 565 J3
SW See St
- WasC 97007 624 G3
SW Seely Av
9600 WNVL 97070 715 D7
SW Seely Ln
19800 SRWD 97140 684 F4
19800 WasC 97140 684 F4
Seiber Ln
20000 CmsC 97055 690 H5
NW Seibler Dr
35000 ClkC 98629 386 D5
35000 ClkC 98674 386 D5
NE Seidl Rd
300 MthC 97060 599 J5
SE Seifert Dr
11000 HPYV 97236 658 A3
SW Seiffert Rd
16700 WasC 97123 683 H1
16700 WasC 97140 683 H3
18600 WasC 97132 683 H3
NW Sell Rd
44300 WasC 97106 531 G1
NW Sellers Rd
14100 BNKS 97106 531 J1
14100 WasC 97106 531 J1
SW Selling Ct
4200 PTLD 97221 625 H3
SE Sellwood Blvd
700 PTLD 97202 626 G6
Sellwood Br
- PTLD 97202 626 G6
- PTLD 97219 626 G6
SW Sellwood Ln
- WasC 97007 624 F3
SE Sellwood St
3000 MWKE 97222 657 A3
Selma St
100 CmsC 97045 717 D1
100 ORCY 97045 717 D1
SW Seminole Ct
20300 WasC 97006 594 D6
SW Seminole Dr
100 WasC 97006 594 D5
SW Seminole Tr
8300 TLTN 97062 685 F5
SW Semler Wy
4400 PTLD 97221 625 H2
SE Semple Rd
18200 CmsC 97009 688 H4
NE Senate St
3500 PTLD 97232 597 B4
3900 PTLD 97213 597 B4
NW Seneca Ct
4300 CMAS 98607 569 C1
N Seneca St
6600 PTLD 97203 566 A3
9100 PTLD 97203 565 H2
SW Seneca St
7900 TLTN 97062 685 F3
NE Septan Dr
6700 ClkC 98604 447 E1
SW September Ln
17400 WasC 97006 594 F6
SE Sequoia Av
12000 MWKE 97222 657 D4
SE Sequoia Cir
- VCVR 98683 538 F7
SW Sequoia Cir
8500 WNVL 97070 715 E6
N Sequoia Ct
1800 FTGV 97116 592 C5
NE Sequoia Ct
300 HBRO 97124 593 F4
NW Sequoia Ct
1600 MCMV 97128 770 F4
S Sequoia Ct
1700 FTGV 97116 592 B5
SW Sequoia Ct
2200 PTLD 97035 656 C3
SW Sequoia Dr
5300 TLTN 97062 685 H4
SE Sequoia Pkwy
1400 CmsC 97013 746 E6
1400 CNBY 97013 746 E6
SW Sequoia Pkwy
14500 TGRD 97224 655 H7
SE Sequoia Pl
12100 MWKE 97222 657 D4
SE Sequoia St
16500 CmsC 97267 687 E1
SW Sequoia St
33200 SPSE 97056 474 E2
SW Sequoia Ter
22200 SRWD 97140 684 F6
SW Serah St
19700 WasC 97007 624 D6
Serango Ct
4000 WLIN 97068 686 J5
Serango Dr
21000 WLIN 97068 686 J5
SE Serban Rd
37700 CmsC 97055 660 J6
SW Serena Ct
15700 TGRD 97224 655 D7
SW Serena Wy
9600 TGRD 97224 685 D1
SW Serene Pl
10400 WNVL 97070 715 C7
SW Serenity Wy
29400 CmsC 97070 715 C7
29400 WNVL 97070 715 C7
Serne Rd
- CmsC 97023 750 A3
SW Sesame St
1600 MCMV 97128 770 E5
Setera Cir
13000 ORCY 97045 717 D5
NW Sethrich Ln
14600 WasC 97229 594 J1
NE Setting Sun Dr
1200 HBRO 97124 593 D2
SW Settlement Dr
20700 SRWD 97140 684 E5
SW Settlement Dr
20900 WasC 97140 684 E5
SW Settler Wy
11500 BRTN 97008 655 C1
Settlers Lp
1300 FTGV 97116 592 C6
SE Seven Oaks Dr
33800 SPSE 97056 474 F2
S Seven Oaks Ln
7000 CmsC 97002 775 J5
7000 CmsC 97002 776 A5
7000 CmsC 97013 775 J5
7000 CmsC 97013 776 A5
N Sever Rd
8900 PTLD 97203 535 F7
S Sevier Rd
1700 RDGF 98642 446 B2
SW Seville Av
5700 CmsC 97035 655 H7
N Seward Av
9100 PTLD 97217 566 C3
N Seward Ct
8700 PTLD 97217 566 C4
NW Seward Rd
3400 ClkC 98685 476 C4
NW Sewell Rd
4500 HBRO 97124 593 F1
4500 WasC 97124 563 F6
4500 WasC 97124 593 F1
SW Sexton Mountain Ct
8200 BRTN 97008 624 J7
SW Sexton Mountain Dr
14000 BRTN 97008 624 H7
14000 BRTN 97008 625 A7
15700 BRTN 97007 624 G7
16000 WasC 97007 624 G7
SW Seymour Ct
3200 PTLD 97239 626 B3
4700 PTLD 97221 626 A3
5400 PTLD 97221 625 J3
SW Seymour Dr
2400 PTLD 97239 626 C3
SW Seymour St
3100 PTLD 97239 626 D3
3500 PTLD 97221 626 B3
5400 PTLD 97221 625 J3
6100 WasC 97225 625 H3
Shadden Dr
- MCMV 97128 770 F3
SE Shade Tree Ln
21800 CmsC 97055 692 B7
35300 CmsC 97023 750 F3
Shadley Ln
58000 ClbC 97053 415 A4
SE Shadow Ct
17100 CmsC 97027 687 D1
17100 CmsC 97267 687 D1
17100 GLDS 97027 687 D1
17100 GLDS 97267 687 D1
E Shadow Ln
62200 CmsC 97011 693 F7
NW Shadow Ln
18600 WasC 97229 594 E2
SE Shadow Rd
21600 CmsC 97022 690 D7
SE Shadow Brook Ct
8800 CmsC 97015 687 H2
SE Shadowbrook Pl
5700 HBRO 97123 593 J6
NW Shadow Hills Ln
16700 WasC 97006 594 G3
Shadowood Dr
1500 CmsC 97068 686 C4
SW Shady Ct
7000 TGRD 97223 655 G1
E Shady Ln
54900 CmsC 97055 692 G6
SE Shady Ln
9700 CmsC 97009 659 F2
SW Shady Ln
7000 TGRD 97223 655 G1
SW Shady Pl
9400 TGRD 97223 655 G1
SE Shady St
800 MCMV 97128 770 H6
SE Shadybrook Dr
16800 CmsC 97267 687 A1
NW Shadybrook Rd
11100 NPNS 97133 563 C1
11100 WasC 97133 563 C1
11300 WasC 97133 533 D4
S Shady Dell Rd
31100 CmsC 97038 837 J2
NW Shadyfir Lp
17300 BRTN 97006 594 F5
17300 WasC 97006 594 F5
Shady Glen St
15000 CmsC 97045 717 G7
SW Shadygrove Dr
23700 SRWD 97140 714 F1
Shady Hollow Wy
18100 WLIN 97068 686 H2
Shadylane Ct
- VCVR 98661 537 A4
SE Shady Meadow Ct
12500 CmsC 97236 658 A4
SW Shady Meadow Ct
18100 WasC 97007 624 E6
SW Shadypeak Ln
17500 WasC 97007 624 F7
SE Shady View Ln
23300 CmsC 97022 720 D2
NW Shadywood Ln
9500 WasC 97229 595 E5
NW Shadywood St
1100 MCMV 97128 770 F4
SW Shaffer Ln
8000 TGRD 97224 685 F1
NE Shafford Av
100 ECDA 97023 750 C3
SE Shafford Av
100 ECDA 97023 750 C4
Shakespeare St
5900 CmsC 97035 655 H7
5900 LKOW 97035 655 H7
SW Shakespeare St
13100 KNGC 97224 685 A2
13100 WasC 97224 685 A2
NE Shaleen St
7200 HBRO 97124 594 B5
Shalimar Dr
14200 SNDY 97055 660 H7
SW Shallowbrook Ln
5900 BRTN 97007 624 H4
NE Shamrock Ct
23600 WDVL 97060 599 D5
NE Shamrock Dr
23600 WDVL 97060 599 D5
Shamrock Ln
11500 CmsC 97045 716 J5
33700 ClbC 97056 444 F1
SE Shamrock Ln
7400 HBRO 97123 594 B7
7400 WasC 97123 594 B7
Shamrock Wy
55500 ClbC 97056 444 F1
S Shandell Rd
30100 CmsC 97038 807 B5
SW Shane Ct
16500 SRWD 97140 684 F7
NE Shanghai St
12000 ClkC 98606 509 C1
12000 ClkC 98682 509 B1
NW Shaniko Ct
4700 WasC 97229 564 F7
NE Shannon Ct
1200 HBRO 97124 593 D2
23600 WDVL 97060 599 D5
SW Shannon Ct
6100 BRTN 97008 625 A4
NE Shannon Dr
1900 HBRO 97124 593 E3
Shannon Ln
21300 WLIN 97068 686 J6
Shannon Pl
2200 WLIN 97068 686 J5
SW Shannon Rd
- WasC 97005 625 A2
NE Shannon St
100 HBRO 97124 593 B2
23500 WDVL 97060 599 C5
SE Shannon Vw
13200 CmsC 97015 658 B5
SW Sharoaks Dr
19400 WasC 97006 624 D1
SE Sharon Dr
22000 DAMA 97009 659 B7
SW Sharon Ln
7100 WasC 97225 625 G2
Shartner Dr
16300 CmsC 97045 687 G6
16300 ORCY 97045 687 G6
SE Shasta Ln
14500 HPYV 97236 658 C1
SW Shasta Tr
17500 TLTN 97062 685 D2
17500 WasC 97062 685 D2
SW Shattuck Rd
3400 MthC 97221 626 A3
3400 PTLD 97221 626 A2
4500 PTLD 97221 625 J3
6500 PTLD 97219 625 H5
NW Shattuck Wy
1000 GSHM 97030 629 A1
NE Shaver Cir
4800 PTLD 97213 597 C2
NE Shaver Ct
22000 FRVW 97024 599 B2
Shaver St
100 MOLA 97038 837 D2
N Shaver St
10 PTLD 97212 596 G1
600 PTLD 97217 596 F1
800 PTLD 97227 596 E1
NE Shaver St
10 PTLD 97212 596 G1
10 PTLD 97227 596 G1
2900 PTLD 97212 597 A1
6200 PTLD 97213 597 D2
9700 MWDP 97220 597 H2
10200 PTLD 97220 597 J2
11300 PTLD 97220 598 A2
11600 PTLD 97230 598 B2
21500 FRVW 97024 599 B2
Shaw St
100 FRVW 97024 599 C4
SW Shaw St
16000 WasC 97007 624 F2
SW Shawmut Dr
8300 WasC 97007 624 C7
Shawn Ct
7100 GLDS 97027 687 E2
SW Shawn Pl
8500 WasC 97223 625 F7
Shawna Ln
18600 GLDS 97027 687 D3
SW Shawnee Tr
17600 TLTN 97062 685 E2
Shayer Av
- MOLA 97038 837 E1
NE Shea Ln
24000 WDVL 97060 599 D4
SW Shearwater Ct
15900 BRTN 97007 654 G2
SW Shearwater Lp
10000 BRTN 97007 654 G1
SW Shearwater Pl
10500 BRTN 97007 654 H2
NW Sheelar Rd
900 FTGV 97116 591 E3
900 WasC 97116 591 E3
NW Sheffield Av
2000 HBRO 97006 594 C3
2200 HBRO 97124 594 C3
SW Sheffield Av
2300 PTLD 97201 626 E1
SW Sheffield Cir
11500 TGRD 97223 655 A3
SE Shega Ct
- HBRO 97123 593 C5
Shelby Ct
12400 PTLD 97035 656 C3
SW Shelby Ct
16700 BRTN 97007 624 G6
16700 WasC 97007 624 G6
S Shelby Ln
16900 CmsC 97045 688 C7
Shelby Rose Dr
11300 ORCY 97045 716 J4
11400 ORCY 97045 717 A4
SW Sheldrake Wy
12100 BRTN 97007 654 H4
S Sheley Ln
16700 CmsC 97045 688 C7
SE Shell Ln
12300 MWKE 97222 657 A4
Shelley Av
17400 SNDY 97055 691 A2
SW Shelley Ct
20300 WasC 97007 624 C2
NE Shell Rock Ln
- VCVR 98663 536 H2
Shelly Ct
3800 NWBG 97132 713 C4
NE Shelly Ct
900 HBRO 97124 593 D2
SW Shelly St
18700 WasC 97007 624 E2
Shelly Scott Ln
- CmsC 97045 717 F7
NW Shelsam Ter
6400 WasC 97229 564 J6
NW Sheltered Nook Rd
15700 MthC 97231 534 F2
SW Shelton St
400 MCMV 97128 770 F5
16000 WasC 97007 624 G1
SW Shem Ter
- WasC 97007 624 H3
Shenandoah
- VCVR 98662 507 G7
Shenandoah Dr
600 MOLA 97038 807 D7
18600 ORCY 97045 717 B4
NW Shenandoah Ter
2800 PTLD 97210 596 B4
SW Shenandoah Wy
8100 TLTN 97062 685 F5
N Shepherd Rd
200 CMAS 98607 569 J4
200 WHGL 98671 569 J4
800 WHGL 98671 570 A4
NE Shepherd Rd
5300 YmhC 97115 742 F6
NW Shepherd St
- PTLD 97231 565 F4
Shepherds Ct
- LKOW 97035 686 A2
Shepherds Ln
- LKOW 97035 686 A1
SW Sheppard Ter
17800 WasC 97140 684 E2
Sher Ln
900 LKOW 97034 656 F4
NE Sherborne St
6000 HBRO 97124 593 G4
Sherbrook Pl
14200 LKOW 97035 656 B5
SW Sheridan Ct
5800 MthC 97221 625 J1
8900 BRTN 97008 625 C7
Sheridan Dr
2200 VCVR 98661 537 B4
E Sheridan St
100 NWBG 97132 713 C7
SW Sheridan St
- MthC 97225 625 H1
- PTLD 97221 625 H1
300 PTLD 97201 626 E1
6100 MthC 97221 625 J1
SW Sheridan St US-26
300 PTLD 97201 626 E1
W Sheridan St
300 NWBG 97132 713 B7
500 YmhC 97132 713 B7
SW Sherk Pl
23200 SRWD 97140 714 H1
SE Sherley Av
8100 VCVR 98664 537 F7
SE Sherley Ct
700 VCVR 98664 537 F7
NW Sherlock Av
- PTLD 97209 596 D3
2700 PTLD 97210 596 D2
SE Sherman Ct
11400 PTLD 97216 627 J1
11400 PTLD 97216 628 A1
17500 GSHM 97233 628 F1
SE Sherman Dr
13500 PTLD 97233 628 C1
Sherman Pl
100 STHN 97051 385 A7
E Sherman St
1300 NWBG 97132 713 D7
SE Sherman St
700 PTLD 97214 626 G1
4200 PTLD 97214 627 C1
5100 PTLD 97206 627 C1
9800 PTLD 97216 627 H1
12200 PTLD 97216 628 A1
15000 PTLD 97233 628 D1
SW Sherman St
600 PTLD 97201 626 F1
W Sherman St
200 NWBG 97132 713 B7
SE Sherman Cooper Dr
19800 CmsC 97022 689 F5
SE Sherrett St
- MWKE 97202 626 H7
2100 PTLD 97202 626 H7
2900 MWKE 97222 627 A7
2900 PTLD 97222 627 A7
7000 PTLD 97206 627 E7
7200 MthC 97206 627 E7
8200 PTLD 97266 627 F7
Sherri Ct
1300 WLIN 97068 716 F2
SE Sherrianne Ct
9300 CmsC 97222 657 F1
NW Sherry Ct
8900 WasC 97229 595 F5
SE Sherry Ln
3500 MWKE 97222 657 A1
NW Sherry St
- BRTN 97229 595 A5
13300 WasC 97229 595 A5
Sherwood Av
- CmsC 97023 719 B4
- CmsC 97045 719 B4
SW Sherwood Blvd
- PTLD 97201 596 C6
- PTLD 97205 596 C6
21100 SRWD 97140 684 G6
Sherwood Ct
10 LKOW 97034 686 B2
Sherwood Dr
100 STHN 97051 385 A7
NE Sherwood Dr
10500 ClkC 98686 507 A2
SW Sherwood Dr
2200 PTLD 97201 626 D1
Sherwood Ln
34000 ClbC 97053 414 G3
SW Sherwood Pl
2600 PTLD 97201 626 D1
2600 PTLD 97239 626 C1
5100 BRTN 97005 624 J2
N Sherwood Rd
- PTLD 97217 566 E3
SW Shetland Ct
8600 BRTN 97008 625 B7
Shetland Pl
6300 WLIN 97068 686 H5
Shilling St
- PTLD 97218 567 E5
SW Shilo Ln
11400 BRTN 97225 595 C6
S Shiloh Ln
17900 CmsC 97045 718 E2
Shine Dr
30500 WasC 97123 683 B4
30500 YmhC 97132 683 A5
SE Shingle Ln
58900 CmsC 97055 693 C5
NW Shipley Rd
31900 WasC 97133 532 J1
31900 WasC 97133 533 A1
SE Shipley Rd
42900 CmsC 97055 691 E1
SW Shire Ct
19600 WasC 97006 594 D7
Shireva Ct
13800 LKOW 97034 656 C5
Shireva Dr
13500 LKOW 97034 656 C5
SW Shirley Ln
7500 WasC 97223 625 G6
Shirley St
100 MOLA 97038 837 F1
900 CmsC 97038 837 G1
SW Shirley Ann Dr
1500 MCMV 97128 770 F7
Shobert Ln
600 RDGF 98642 416 A7
Shobert St
400 RDGF 98642 415 J7
500 RDGF 98642 416 A7
NW Shoe Factory Ln
52800 SPSE 97056 444 D7
NW Shoemaker Rd
52800 SPSE 97056 444 D7
N Shore Cir
100 LKOW 97034 656 F6
Shore Dr
10 STHN 97051 385 B7
NE Shore Dr
21000 FRVW 97024 599 A3
SW Shore Dr
13100 TGRD 97223 655 A3
NE Shore Crest Pl
20400 FRVW 97024 599 A3
NW Shoreline Wy
5200 WasC 97229 564 E7
5300 WasC 97231 564 E7
NE Shore View Dr
20400 FRVW 97024 599 A2
SW Shoreview Pl
11500 TGRD 97223 655 B3
S Shore Vista Dr
20100 CmsC 97045 718 D7
NW Shorewood Ct
1800 BRTN 97006 594 F4
1800 WasC 97006 594 F3
NW Shorewood Dr
17500 WasC 97006 594 F3
17600 BRTN 97006 594 F3
SE Shorewood Dr
5600 VCVR 98661 537 C6
SE Shorgorick Rd
29000 CmsC 97023 720 E7
29000 CmsC 97023 750 E1
Short Av
15900 ORCY 97045 687 E5
SW Short Av
4400 BRTN 97005 625 A2
SE Short Rd
7000 MthC 97080 629 J6
7200 MthC 97080 630 A7
Short St
400 ECDA 97023 750 B4
1300 WLIN 97068 716 F1
Short Oak Dr
3600 NWBG 97132 713 F7
SW Shoshone Ct
8800 WNVL 97070 715 E5
20700 TLTN 97062 685 E5
SW Shoshone Dr
20500 TLTN 97062 685 E5
SW Shoue Dr
14500 WasC 97224 654 J7
Shreveport Wy
200 VCVR 98664 537 D6
SW Shrope Ct
11400 TGRD 97223 655 C4
Shumard Ct NE
- DNLD 97020 774 G4
NE Shute Rd
2100 HBRO 97124 593 J2
NW Shute Rd
4600 HBRO 97124 563 J7
4600 HBRO 97124 593 J1
4800 WasC 97124 563 J6
Shute South
- HBRO 97124 593 J2
Shute Trailer Lp
- HBRO 97124 593 J2
Sibelius Ct
10 LKOW 97035 656 B4
NW Sichel Ct
10400 PTLD 97229 595 D3
NW Sickle Ter
5900 WasC 97229 564 H6
NW Sidewinder Pl
4600 WasC 97006 594 F3
SW Sidney Ln
16500 SRWD 97140 684 G5
SE Sieben Pkwy
13700 CmsC 97015 658 C6
SE Sieben Creek Dr
14200 CmsC 97015 658 C6
NE Siefken Ln
30400 YmhC 97132 743 H2
SW Sienna Ln
16300 BRTN 97007 624 G7
16300 WasC 97007 624 G7
Siercks Rd
31100 ClbC 97056 444 A3

STREET	Block	City	ZIP	Map#	Grid
Sierra Ct					
	12800	LKOW	97035	655	J4
NW Sierra Ct					
	4800	CMAS	98607	539	C7
SW Sierra Ct					
	15500	BRTN	97007	654	E2
NW Sierra Dr					
	2800	CMAS	98607	569	C1
SE Sierra Dr					
	13400	CmsC	97015	658	B5
NW Sierra Ln					
	1900	CMAS	98607	569	C5
SW Sierra Ln					
	15300	BRTN	97007	654	E2
NW Sierra Lp					
	1600	CMAS	98607	569	C2
NW Sierra Pl					
	2800	CMAS	98607	569	C2
NW Sierra St					
	600	CMAS	98607	569	C5
SE Sierra St					
	5500	HBRO	97123	593	J7
	6000	WasC	97123	593	J7
SW Sierra St					
	600	CMAS	98607	569	C5
SE Sierra Vista Ct					
	5100	CmsC	97267	657	C7
Sierra Vista Dr					
	12700	LKOW	97035	655	H4
	12700	PTLD	97219	655	H4
Sierra Vista St					
	600	NWBG	97132	713	C6
Sifton Gdns					
	-	ClkC	98682	508	B7
SE Sigrid St					
	6100	HBRO	97123	593	J6
	6300	HBRO	97123	594	A6
SE Sigs Wy					
	-	DAMA	97009	688	E1
NW Silent Ln					
	6100	MthC	97210	595	H4
	6100	MthC	97229	595	H4
SW Siler Ridge Ln					
	16700	WasC	97007	654	F2
Siletz Ct					
	5300	CmsC	97035	685	J2
SW Siletz Ct					
	15500	BRTN	97007	624	H6
	20600	TLTN	97062	685	E5
SW Siletz Dr					
	8900	TLTN	97062	685	D5
Sills Ct					
	1400	FTGV	97116	591	H3
NE Silo St					
	5600	HBRO	97124	593	J3
SW Silo Ter					
	21200	SRWD	97140	684	G5
NE Silvan Dr					
	17900	ClkC	98604	418	G3
	17900	ClkC	98675	418	H3
SE Silver Cir					
	13300	VCVR	98683	568	B2
Silver Ct					
	4300	LKOW	97035	656	A4
SW Silver Pl					
	9900	BRTN	97008	655	A1
NW Silverado Dr					
	200	BRTN	97006	594	G4
SE Silver Creek Ct					
	13200	HPYV	97236	628	D7
NW Silver Creek Pl					
	4600	WasC	97006	594	F1
Silverfox Pkwy					
	19300	ORCY	97045	717	C5
SE Silverleaf Ct					
	12800	CmsC	97222	657	C5
NW Silverleaf Dr					
	4200	WasC	97229	594	J1
	4500	WasC	97229	595	A1
SE Silverleaf Ln					
	3100	CmsC	97267	657	A7
NW Silver Ridge Lp					
	9600	PTLD	97229	595	E3
SE Silver Springs Dr					
	3000	VCVR	98683	568	B2
SE Silver Springs Rd					
	1700	CmsC	97222	656	J5
	3100	CmsC	97222	657	A5
Silver Star Av					
	8400	VCVR	98664	537	F6
S Silverwood Dr					
	18100	CmsC	97045	717	G2
NE Simmental St					
	900	HBRO	97124	593	D2
Simmons Ct					
	1100	GLDS	97027	687	D3
N Simmons Rd					
	15800	PTLD	97203	535	F3
NW Simnasho Dr					
	5800	WasC	97229	564	C6
Simons St					
	200	RDGF	98642	415	J7
	800	RDGF	98642	416	A7
Simpson Av					
	1600	VCVR	98660	536	E4
NE Simpson Ct					
	4200	PTLD	97211	567	C7
	4200	PTLD	97218	567	B7
SW Simpson Rd					
	30700	WasC	97113	623	A5
	30700	WasC	97123	623	B5
Simpson St					
	4400	WLIN	97068	687	A7
N Simpson St					
	1700	PTLD	97217	566	E6
NE Simpson St					
	100	PTLD	97220	568	A7
	400	PTLD	97211	566	H7
	3300	PTLD	97211	567	B7
	4200	PTLD	97218	567	C7
	10900	PTLD	97220	567	J7
SE Simtustus Ct					
	14500	CmsC	97009	660	B7
Sinclair St					
	5500	WLIN	97068	687	C6
Singer Hill Rd					
	-	ORCY	97045	687	C7
SE Singing Woods Dr					
	2100	HBRO	97123	623	E2
SE Singletary Ln					
	9400	YmhC	97128	770	H7
SE Single Tree Dr					
	1000	VCVR	98683	538	G7
	1200	VCVR	98683	568	G1

STREET	Block	City	ZIP	Map#	Grid
SW Singletree Dr					
	13500	BRTN	97008	655	A1
Single Tree St					
	-	FTGV	97116	591	G2
SW Sioux Ct					
	17800	TLTN	97062	685	D2
SW Sioux Ter					
	28000	WNVL	97070	715	E5
SW Sir Lancelot Ln					
	22100	SRWD	97140	684	F6
SW Siskin Ter					
	11600	BRTN	97007	654	G3
NE Siskiyou Ct					
	14900	PTLD	97230	598	D3
NE Siskiyou St					
	700	PTLD	97212	596	J2
	3300	PTLD	97212	597	A2
	6500	PTLD	97213	597	D2
	10400	PTLD	97220	597	J3
	11200	PTLD	97220	598	A3
	15800	PTLD	97230	598	E3
SW Sister Ln					
	16300	WasC	97006	594	E4
S Sisters Wy					
	15600	CmsC	97004	747	J2
	15600	CmsC	97045	747	J2
SW Sitka Ct					
	1000	MCMV	97128	770	E6
	10200	TLTN	97062	685	D7
	10700	TGRD	97223	655	F2
	10700	WasC	97223	655	F2
SW Sitka Dr					
	700	MCMV	97128	770	E6
Sitka St					
	400	NWBG	97132	713	E6
SW Sitkum Pl					
	300	WasC	97006	594	D6
SW Siuslaw Ln					
	9300	TLTN	97062	685	D6
Six Dees Ln					
	35000	ClbC	97051	414	J1
Skeet Av					
	61000	ClbC	97051	384	E4
Skellenger Wy					
	11700	ORCY	97045	717	A5
	11800	CmsC	97045	717	A5
N Skidmore Ct					
	1900	PTLD	97217	596	E1
N Skidmore St					
	10	PTLD	97211	596	G1
	10	PTLD	97217	596	F1
	1000	PTLD	97227	596	F1
NE Skidmore St					
	-	PTLD	97220	598	A1
	-	PTLD	97230	598	A1
	10	PTLD	97211	596	H1
	10	PTLD	97217	596	G1
	2500	PTLD	97211	597	A1
	3300	PTLD	97212	597	B1
	4900	PTLD	97218	597	C1
	8000	PTLD	97220	597	F1
	9000	MWDP	97220	597	G1
	21800	FRVW	97024	599	B2
N Skidmore Ter					
	2000	PTLD	97217	596	D1
SE Skill Center Dr					
	-	CmsC	97267	657	E6
NE Skipton St					
	5800	HBRO	97124	593	J4
Skirbin Ln					
	-	CmsC	97045	687	H3
SW Skiver Ct					
	6300	WasC	97007	624	C4
SW Skiver Dr					
	6300	WasC	97007	624	D5
SW Skiver St					
	20400	WasC	97007	624	C5
Skogan Rd					
	33900	CmsC	97055	690	F3
	33900	SNDY	97055	690	F3
SE Skoko St					
	-	CmsC	97015	657	J7
SW Skokomish Ln					
	9200	TLTN	97062	685	A7
E Skookum Ln					
	69800	CmsC	97049	724	D3
Sky Ln					
	400	FTGV	97116	591	F3
N Sky St					
	6800	PTLD	97203	565	J3
NW Skycrest Pkwy					
	4400	WasC	97229	595	A1
	4800	WasC	97229	594	J4
	4900	WasC	97229	564	J7
	5200	WasC	97229	565	A7
Skye Ct					
	1300	WLIN	97068	686	G2
Skye Ln					
	700	MOLA	97038	837	D1
Skye Pkwy					
	1300	WLIN	97068	686	G2
SW Skyhar Ct					
	7800	WasC	97223	625	G6
SW Skyhar Dr					
	7800	WasC	97223	625	G6
SE Sky High Ct					
	5800	CmsC	97267	687	C1
Skyland Cir					
	18800	LKOW	97034	686	F2
Skyland Dr					
	800	CmsC	97034	686	F2
	800	LKOW	97034	686	F2
S Skylane Dr					
	24000	CmsC	97013	746	G7
	24000	CmsC	97013	776	G1
NE Skylar St					
	100	HBRO	97124	593	B2
Skylark Ln					
	-	FTGV	97116	591	H2
NW Skyline Blvd					
	-	PTLD	97210	596	A2
	-	PTLD	97221	595	J6
	10	PTLD	97210	595	F1
	200	MthC	97229	595	H5
	700	PTLD	97229	595	G4
	4400	PTLD	97229	565	E7
	8300	PTLD	97231	565	D6
	9000	MthC	97231	565	B3
	10500	PTLD	97231	564	J1
	11200	PTLD	97231	534	H7
	11300	MthC	97231	564	G1
	11400	MthC	97231	534	F7
	17600	MthC	97231	504	A5
	19300	MthC	97133	504	A4
	23000	MthC	97056	504	A2

STREET	Block	City	ZIP	Map#	Grid
SW Skyline Blvd					
	300	PTLD	97210	595	J6
	300	PTLD	97221	595	J6
	700	MthC	97221	595	J6
	800	MthC	97221	596	A6
	800	PTLD	97221	596	A6
Skyline Cir					
	6000	WLIN	97068	687	A6
Skyline Dr					
	-	ClbC	97051	385	A6
	-	STHN	97051	385	A6
	1900	WLIN	97068	687	A6
NE Skyline Dr					
	25100	ClkC	98604	449	E5
NW Skyline Ln					
	-	MthC	97229	595	H5
	-	PTLD	97210	595	H5
NW Skyline Crest Rd					
	400	MthC	97229	595	G4
NW Skyline Heights Dr					
	9800	PTLD	97229	595	E1
SW Skyline Woods Ln					
	17500	WasC	97007	654	F2
NE Skyport Wy					
	5200	PTLD	97218	567	C5
S Sky Ranch Ln					
	15400	CmsC	97045	688	C4
Skyridge					
	-	ClkC	98682	508	B7
NW Skyview Ct					
	-	PTLD	97231	564	J2
SE Sky View Ct					
	1900	CmsC	97267	656	H7
Skyview Dr					
	-	WLIN	97068	686	H7
NE Skyview Dr					
	-	FRVW	97024	599	A3
NW Skyview Dr					
	9500	PTLD	97231	564	J2
	9500	PTLD	97231	565	A2
NE Skyway Dr					
	-	ClbC	97056	444	F5
	-	SPSE	97056	444	F5
NW Skyway Dr					
	29200	WasC	97133	533	D4
SE Sladen Av					
	5900	GLDS	97027	687	C3
E Sladky Ln					
	-	CmsC	97011	693	F6
Slavens Rd					
	33200	ClbC	97053	444	E1
	33600	ClbC	97056	444	F1
Slavens Wy					
	33400	ClbC	97053	444	E1
	33400	ClbC	97056	444	F1
SW Slavin Rd					
	4500	PTLD	97239	626	E3
E Sleepy Hollow Dr					
	58100	CmsC	97055	693	B5
NW Sleret Av					
	10	GSHM	97080	629	B2
	1000	GSHM	97030	629	B2
SE Sleret Av					
	800	VCVR	98664	537	D7
	900	VCVR	98661	537	D7
SW Sleret Av					
	600	GSHM	97080	629	B3
E Sleret Ln					
	27200	CmsC	97067	724	C6
NE Sliderberg Rd					
	-	ClkC	98606	478	J7
	11900	ClkC	98606	508	H1
NW Slocum Wy					
	12000	PTLD	97229	595	E4
NE Slope Ln					
	17000	YmhC	97132	713	E2
NW Sluman Rd					
	700	ClkC	98665	506	F5
	1500	VCVR	98665	506	E5
Small St					
	-	CmsC	97011	693	G6
Smith Av					
	17200	SNDY	97055	691	A3
SE Smith Av					
	17000	CmsC	97055	691	A2
	17000	SNDY	97055	691	A2
SW Smith Av					
	17100	SRWD	97140	684	F6
N Smith Ct					
	6600	PTLD	97203	566	A2
SE Smith Dr					
	2100	HBRO	97123	623	E2
	2100	WasC	97123	623	E2
Smith Ln NE					
	14700	AURA	97002	775	F2
	14700	MmC	97002	775	F2
Smith Rd					
	-	CBAC	97018	385	B3
	-	ClbC	97018	385	B3
	-	ClbC	97051	385	C3
	32700	ClbC	97051	384	J4
NE Smith Rd					
	18400	CmsC	97132	714	D7
	18400	CmsC	97132	744	D1
	18400	YmhC	97140	744	D1
SE Smith Rd					
	33900	MthC	97019	600	F7
N Smith St					
	9700	PTLD	97203	565	G1
Smithfield Dr					
	14800	ORCY	97045	687	G6
NW Smith Quarry Rd					
	5000	ClkC	98674	386	C4
Smith Rock Av NE					
	-	AURA	97002	775	F5
SE Smith Springs Ct					
	14600	DAMA	97009	658	G7
NE Smits Ln					
	30100	YmhC	97132	713	H5
SW Smock St					
	14600	SRWD	97140	714	H1
Smoke Tree Pl					
	13000	ORCY	97045	717	C5
SW Smokette Ln					
	18200	WasC	97006	594	E6
SE Smokey Ln					
	21600	CmsC	97022	690	D7
N Smythe Rd					
	2500	RDGF	98642	416	C7
Snapdragon Av					
	1200	FTGV	97116	591	G3
Snapdragon Ln					
	1400	FTGV	97116	591	G3
SW Snapdragon Ln					
	16000	WasC	97223	654	G5

STREET	Block	City	ZIP	Map#	Grid
NE Snell Ct					
	1300	HBRO	97124	593	E4
SE Snider Av					
	6800	CmsC	97222	657	E1
Snidow Dr					
	1000	WLIN	97068	716	F2
SE Snodgrass Ln					
	13800	CmsC	97236	658	C4
SW Snoopy Ct					
	8700	WasC	97223	625	G7
NW Snoqualmie St					
	-	WasC	97006	594	D3
	19000	HBRO	97006	594	D3
Snow St					
	34500	STHN	97051	414	H1
Snowberry Ct					
	13400	LKOW	97035	656	C5
SE Snowberry Ct					
	5800	HBRO	97123	593	J5
SW Snowberry Ct					
	17700	WasC	97140	714	E4
SE Snowberry Ln					
	27900	CmsC	97009	689	G2
NE Snowberry Lp					
	8200	VCVR	98664	537	F3
SE Snowberry St					
	3400	CmsC	97222	657	A5
Snowberry Ridge Ct					
	2100	WLIN	97068	716	G1
Snow Brush Ct					
	4300	LKOW	97035	656	A5
SW Snow Brush Ct					
	12600	TGRD	97223	655	C1
NW Snowden Ct					
	18300	WasC	97229	594	E2
Snowdrop Ct					
	20000	WLIN	97068	686	J4
SE Snowfire Dr					
	13000	HPYV	97236	658	B3
SW Snowgoose Ln					
	12300	BRTN	97007	654	F3
SW Snowgoose Pl					
	10100	BRTN	97007	654	G2
NW Snowlily Dr					
	5900	WasC	97229	564	J6
SW Snowshoe Ln					
	13100	BRTN	97008	655	A2
NE Snowy Owl Cir					
	52300	SPSE	97056	474	G1
SW Snowy Owl Ln					
	15500	BRTN	97007	654	G3
	16200	WasC	97007	654	G3
SE Snuffin Rd					
	35300	CmsC	97023	750	G1
	37300	CmsC	97022	720	G7
	37300	CmsC	97023	720	G7
SW Snyder Ct					
	51600	SPSE	97056	474	E2
SW Snyder Pl					
	4600	PTLD	97221	626	A3
S Soda Springs Rd					
	34700	CmsC	97038	837	C7
SE Sofich Ln					
	33100	CmsC	97022	690	D6
NE Sokol Blosser Ln					
	4100	YmhC	97114	742	D7
	4100	YmhC	97114	772	D1
NW Solano Ct					
	17200	WasC	97229	594	F1
NW Solano Ln					
	17400	WasC	97006	594	F1
	17400	WasC	97229	594	F1
NW Solberger Rd					
	-	WasC	97124	533	G1
	17400	WasC	97133	533	G1
SE Solomon Ct					
	11700	HPYV	97236	657	J2
	11700	HPYV	97236	658	A2
SE Solomon Lp					
	1500	VCVR	98683	568	D1
Solso Ct					
	37400	SNDY	97055	690	H4
Solso Dr					
	37100	CmsC	97055	690	H3
	37200	SNDY	97055	690	H3
SE Solstice Ct					
	12000	CmsC	97015	658	A6
Solstice Ln					
	3200	NWBG	97132	713	B4
Somera Dr					
	1500	FTGV	97116	591	H3
NW Somerset Dr					
	16000	WasC	97006	594	G2
	16000	WasC	97229	594	H2
S Somerset Dr					
	21700	CmsC	97045	747	F3
SW Somes Ln					
	16700	WasC	97007	624	G3
SE Somewhere Dr					
	4200	MWKE	97222	657	B4
Sommer St					
	100	ORCY	97045	717	D2
SW Songbird St					
	1700	MCMV	97128	770	E6
SW Sonne Ct					
	11300	TGRD	97223	655	C4
SW Sonnet Wy					
	17100	KNGC	97224	685	A2
NW Sonoma Ln					
	-	PTLD	97229	595	G3
SE Sonoma St					
	12600	CmsC	97015	658	A5
SE Sonora Wy					
	12700	HPYV	97236	658	D5
Sophia Ct					
	18800	ORCY	97045	717	G6
SW Sophia Ln					
	14800	WasC	97224	654	H6
NW Sophie Ct					
	14800	WasC	97229	564	J7
SW Sora Ct					
	15500	BRTN	97007	654	H4
SW Soren Ct					
	17100	WasC	97007	624	F7
NE Sorrel Dr					
	15000	VCVR	98682	538	C2
Sorrel Wy					
	6400	WLIN	97068	686	J5
SW Sorrel Dock Ct					
	12600	TGRD	97223	655	B2
SW Sorrento Rd					
	7400	BRTN	97008	625	B7
SW Sosa Pl					
	600	WasC	97006	594	C6

STREET	Block	City	ZIP	Map#	Grid
Sour Rd					
	49500	CmsC	97055	692	B7
NW South Av					
	30500	NPNS	97133	563	C2
	30500	WasC	97133	563	C2
NW South Dr					
	11800	WasC	97229	595	C2
South Ln					
	-	TLTN	97062	685	A3
South Pl					
	-	TLTN	97062	685	A3
South Rd					
	3500	WLIN	97068	716	H1
NW South Rd					
	3200	WasC	97229	595	C2
NE Southbrook Ct					
	6300	HBRO	97124	594	B4
S South End Ct					
	11400	CmsC	97045	716	J4
	11400	ORCY	97045	716	J4
S South End Rd					
	400	ORCY	97045	717	A4
	19000	CmsC	97045	717	A4
	19200	CmsC	97045	716	G7
	19200	ORCY	97045	716	G7
	20700	CmsC	97045	746	G1
SE Southern Lites Dr					
	11500	CmsC	97236	657	J3
	11700	CmsC	97236	658	A4
SE Southgate St					
	7600	CmsC	97222	657	E4
	8100	CmsC	97236	657	F4
NW South Parc St					
	-	WasC	97229	594	H1
South Point Vil					
	-	GSHM	97230	598	F4
SW South Ranch Rd					
	34200	CmsC	97070	744	E5
	34200	CmsC	97132	744	E5
SW Southridge Dr					
	10700	PTLD	97219	656	F2
South Ring Rd					
	-	HBRO	97124	593	J2
	-	HBRO	97124	594	A2
N South Shore Av					
	12200	PTLD	97217	536	E7
South Shore Blvd					
	600	LKOW	97034	656	D7
	1800	LKOW	97034	686	B1
	3600	LKOW	97035	686	A1
	4100	LKOW	97035	656	A7
NE South Shore Rd					
	200	PTLD	97211	566	H2
Southslope Wy					
	2300	WLIN	97068	687	A7
	2400	WLIN	97068	717	A1
SE Southview Av					
	15900	CmsC	97267	657	A7
	15900	CmsC	97267	687	A1
Southview Ct					
	-	ClkC	98675	418	H2
SW Southview Ct					
	19400	WasC	97007	624	D3
Southview Dr					
	34300	ClbC	97051	414	G1
NE Southview Dr					
	31100	ClkC	98675	418	H2
SW Southview Pl					
	5800	PTLD	97219	655	J3
	19500	WasC	97007	624	D3
SW Southview St					
	6200	PTLD	97219	655	H3
	19600	WasC	97007	624	C3
SW Southview Ter					
	4500	WasC	97007	624	B2
E Southview Heights Dr					
	900	LCTR	98629	386	H7
Southwood Ct					
	13500	LKOW	97035	655	J5
Southwood Dr					
	-	ORCY	97045	717	D4
	5300	LKOW	97035	655	J4
	5900	CmsC	97219	655	H4
SE Southwood Dr					
	100	ClkC	98671	540	C7
SW Southwood Dr					
	5900	CmsC	97219	655	H4
	5900	LKOW	97035	655	H4
SE Southwood Ln					
	-	HBRO	97123	623	H1
SE Sovereign Ct					
	11700	HPYV	97236	657	J3
	11700	HPYV	97236	658	A3
SE Sovereign Dr					
	11900	HPYV	97236	658	A3
S Spangler Rd					
	12600	CmsC	97045	747	C7
	13000	CmsC	97013	747	E7
	16000	CmsC	97045	748	A7
	16600	CmsC	97004	748	B6
SW Spaniel Ct					
	14200	BRTN	97008	654	J2
	14400	BRTN	97007	654	J2
SW Spaniel Pl					
	10300	BRTN	97008	654	J2
SW Spaniel St					
	14000	BRTN	97008	654	J2
NW Spanish Bay Dr					
	1800	MCMV	97128	770	E4
SE Spanish Bay Dr					
	14700	HPYV	97236	658	D1
S Sparrow Ct					
	24600	CmsC	97013	776	G1
SW Sparrow Lp					
	15000	BRTN	97007	654	H3
SE Sparrow St					
	2000	MWKE	97222	656	J4
NW Spartan Wy					
	16100	WasC	97229	564	H7
Spaulding Av					
	2600	VCVR	98661	537	C3
SE Spaulding Av					
	3700	CmsC	97267	657	A7
SW Spellman Dr					
	16800	WasC	97007	654	G1
SW Spence Av					
	1500	TDLE	97060	599	G5
SW Spence Ct					
	1400	TDLE	97060	599	H5
Spence Ln					
	-	TDLE	97060	599	F4
SW Spence Rd					
	1800	TDLE	97060	599	G4
Spence St					
	35400	ClbC	97051	385	A7

STREET	Block	City	ZIP	Map#	Grid
SW Spencer Av					
	4900	BRTN	97005	625	A3
E Spencer Ct					
	1200	LCTR	98629	386	H7
NW Spencer Ct					
	-	PTLD	97229	565	D4
SE Spencer Ct					
	10800	CmsC	97236	657	G3
	12300	HPYV	97236	658	A2
SE Spencer Dr					
	9000	CmsC	97236	657	G2
NW Spencer Rd					
	30700	ClkC	98642	416	G3
NW Spencer St					
	3000	PTLD	97229	595	E2
	3300	MthC	97229	595	E2
Sperling Dr					
	32000	ClbC	97051	384	C6
NW Spiesschaert Rd					
	36400	CNLS	97113	592	E4
	36400	WasC	97113	592	E4
SW Spinnaker Dr					
	14100	BRTN	97005	624	J2
Spinnaker Wy					
	200	CBAC	97018	385	C4
SE Spinnaker Wy					
	1600	VCVR	98661	536	H6
Spinosa					
	10	LKOW	97035	655	J3
SE Spirea Ct					
	-	CmsC	97009	660	C6
SW Spirea St					
	13900	BRTN	97008	625	A5
NE Spitz Rd					
	2100	CmsC	97013	746	F4
	2100	CNBY	97013	746	F4
SE Spitzenberg Ln					
	21000	CmsC	97022	690	B6
SW Spokane Ct					
	10200	TLTN	97062	685	D3
SE Spokane St					
	10	PTLD	97202	626	G6
NE Spokane Wy					
	-	VCVR	98662	537	F1
NW Spoon Pl					
	4100	WasC	97229	594	H1
SE Spoonbill Ct					
	800	HBRO	97123	593	H6
S Sprague Ln					
	19000	CmsC	97045	718	F5
S Sprague Rd					
	18700	CmsC	97045	718	G5
	20400	CmsC	97045	748	F1
	29000	CmsC	97038	807	E5
SW Spratlin Ln					
	17100	SRWD	97140	684	F5
SW Spratt Wy					
	4100	WasC	97007	624	H2
SE Spray Av					
	16800	CmsC	97267	687	F1
NW Spreadborough Rd					
	7700	WasC	97116	561	J4
NW Spring Av					
	600	MthC	97229	595	H4
SW Spring Ct					
	12100	WasC	97225	595	C6
SE Spring Dr					
	3200	HBRO	97123	593	F6
Spring Ln					
	3500	LKOW	97035	656	B6
SW Spring Ln					
	-	SRWD	97140	684	G7
	500	WasC	97225	595	C6
Spring St					
	700	ORCY	97045	717	C1
	71200	CmsC	97049	724	E4
SE Spring St					
	4000	HBRO	97123	593	G6
	4900	WasC	97123	593	G6
	27900	CmsC	97009	659	H5
SW Spring St					
	100	HBRO	97123	593	B6
	1500	PTLD	97201	596	D7
Springbrook Ct					
	15700	LKOW	97034	656	C7
Springbrook Gdns					
	-	WasC	97007	624	E5
SW Springbrook Ln					
	14000	BRTN	97007	654	J3
	14000	TGRD	97007	654	J3
	14000	TGRD	97223	654	J3
N Springbrook Rd					
	2600	NWBG	97132	713	F5
	2600	YmhC	97132	713	F5
NE Springbrook Rd					
	14500	YmhC	97132	713	F4
S Springbrook Rd					
	500	NWBG	97132	743	F1
	500	YmhC	97132	743	F1
E Springbrook St					
	65700	CmsC	97011	723	J2
	65700	CmsC	97011	724	A2
N Springbrook St					
	600	NWBG	97132	713	F6
	2100	YmhC	97132	713	F5
NE Springbrook St					
	15400	PTLD	97230	598	D2
S Springbrook St					
	100	NWBG	97132	713	F7
	200	YmhC	97132	713	F7
Spring Brook Vil					
	-	VCVR	98682	507	J7
	-	VCVR	98682	537	J1
Springbrook Wy					
	1600	NWBG	97132	713	F6
NE Spring Creek Ln					
	14300	YmhC	97132	713	H4
S Spring Creek Rd					
	22000	CmsC	97023	719	D5
SE Springcrest Dr					
	11500	CmsC	97015	657	H5
SW Spring Crest Dr					
	9500	WasC	97225	595	E6
SW Springdale Ct					
	15200	BRTN	97007	624	H4
NE Springer Ct					
	1900	MCMV	97128	771	A6
SW Springfield Ln					
	15600	BRTN	97007	624	H4
	16100	WasC	97007	624	H4
SW Springfield St					
	18200	WasC	97007	624	E4
SW Spring Garden Ct					
	3600	PTLD	97219	626	B7

STREET	Block	City	ZIP	Map#	Grid
SW Spring Garden St					
	3700	PTLD	97219	626	B6
Spring Garden Wy					
	1500	FTGV	97116	591	H3
SE Springhill Ct					
	7500	GLDS	97027	687	E2
SE Springhill Dr					
	7500	GLDS	97027	687	E2
SE Springhill Pl					
	17500	GLDS	97027	687	E2
NE Spring Hill Rd					
	30900	ClkC	98675	418	G3
SE Springhill Rd					
	200	MthC	97060	600	B6
SE Springlake Dr					
	33700	SPSE	97056	474	F3
SE Springlake Lp					
	51300	SPSE	97056	474	F3
NW Spring Meadows Wy					
	100	HBRO	97124	593	B1
SE Spring Mountain Ct					
	12700	HPYV	97236	658	A4
SE Spring Mountain Dr					
	12200	HPYV	97236	658	A4
Spring Ridge Dr					
	19700	WLIN	97068	686	G4
Springridge Dr					
	-	NWBG	97132	743	F2
Spring Rock Cir					
	4200	WLIN	97068	687	A6
	4200	WLIN	97068	717	A1
SW Springtooth Ln					
	15800	SRWD	97140	684	G6
Springtree Ln					
	100	WLIN	97068	716	G1
Spring Valley Dr					
	19300	ORCY	97045	717	A4
SW Springview Ct					
	20600	WasC	97006	594	E4
NW Springville Ct					
	8600	PTLD	97231	565	F4
NW Springville Ln					
	13200	MthC	97229	565	A6
NW Springville Rd					
	-	PTLD	97231	565	D5
	10800	MthC	97229	565	A6
	10800	PTLD	97229	565	A6
	13700	MthC	97229	564	J6
	18400	WasC	97231	564	E6
SW Springwater Ct					
	16600	BRTN	97006	594	H6
SE Springwater Dr					
	7700	MthC	97206	627	F7
	7700	PTLD	97206	627	F7
SW Springwater Ln					
	16700	BRTN	97006	594	G6
S Springwater Rd					
	-	CmsC	97009	688	E3
	-	DAMA	97009	688	E3
	-	DAMA	97045	688	E3
	14800	CmsC	97045	688	E3
	17100	CmsC	97045	719	A1
	18000	CmsC	97023	719	C3
	20300	CmsC	97023	749	J6
	23400	CmsC	97023	750	A7
NE Springwood Ct					
	3700	VCVR	98682	538	C2
SW Springwood Dr					
	10900	BRTN	97008	655	C2
	10900	TGRD	97223	655	C2
NW Springwood Ln					
	1000	MCMV	97128	770	G4
Spruce					
	-	CmsC	97015	657	H7
NE Spruce Av					
	2300	GSHM	97030	599	C7
S Spruce Av					
	-	YCLT	98675	419	G1
SE Spruce Av					
	200	GSHM	97080	629	C3
	2000	PTLD	97214	596	H7
	2200	PTLD	97214	626	H1
SW Spruce Av					
	5200	BRTN	97005	625	E4
NE Spruce Ct					
	1100	CNBY	97013	746	E5
SE Spruce Ct					
	900	GSHM	97080	629	C4
	14100	HPYV	97236	658	C1
Spruce St					
	-	WasC	97006	594	D5
	1000	LKOW	97034	656	E7
	2200	FTGV	97116	592	C4
NW Spruce St					
	4100	VCVR	98660	536	F1
SE Spruce St					
	2100	HBRO	97123	593	F6
SW Spruce St					
	100	DNDE	97115	742	H3
	7100	TGRD	97223	655	G2
	7100	WasC	97223	655	G2
Spruce Wy					
	33400	ClbC	97056	474	E4
NW Spruceridge Ln					
	14200	WasC	97229	595	A1
NE Spud Mountain Rd					
	29800	ClkC	98607	509	J4
SW Spur Ct					
	12000	BRTN	97008	655	B1
Spur St					
	3400	FTGV	97116	591	G2
Spyglass Ct					
	20100	ORCY	97045	717	H7
NW Spyglass Ct					
	1400	MCMV	97128	770	F3
NW Spyglass Dr					
	16100	WasC	97006	594	H2
SE Spy Glass Dr					
	9200	HPYV	97236	658	D2
SE Spyglass Dr					
	2300	VCVR	98683	568	D2
Spyglass Ln					
	15000	ORCY	97045	717	G6
SE Squaw Mountain Rd					
	35500	CmsC	97023	750	F5
Squire Dr					
	13200	ORCY	97045	717	D6
S Squire Dr					
	13400	ORCY	97045	717	E5
	13500	CmsC	97045	717	E5
NE Squire Rd					
	300	ClkC	98671	540	C6
SW Squirrel Ln					
	17000	WasC	97140	714	F3

STREET Block City ZIP Map# Grid

SR-6 NW Wilson River Hwy
- BNKS 97106 531 J6
- BNKS 97106 532 C6
- WasC 97106 532 C6
- WasC 97116 531 J6
50000 WasC 97106 531 B5
SR-8 SE 10th Av
300 HBRO 97123 593 D6
SR-8 19th Av
1800 FTGV 97116 591 H5
2500 FTGV 97116 592 A5
SR-8 19th Wy
- FTGV 97116 592 A5
SR-8 N Adair St
100 CNLS 97113 592 D4
100 FTGV 97116 592 D4
SR-8 B St
1900 FTGV 97116 591 J5
SR-8 E Baseline St
1200 CNLS 97113 592 H5
3100 CNLS 97123 592 G5
34300 WasC 97124 592 H5
SR-8 SE Baseline St
100 HBRO 97123 593 B5
SR-8 SW Baseline St
- CNLS 97113 592 H5
100 HBRO 97123 593 B5
32300 HBRO 97123 592 J5
32300 WasC 97123 592 J5
32300 WasC 97124 592 J5
33400 CNLS 97123 592 H5
33600 CNLS 97124 592 H5
SR-8 W Baseline St
100 CNLS 97113 592 D5
100 FTGV 97116 592 D5
SR-8 SW Canyon Rd
6800 BRTN 97225 625 H1
9500 WasC 97225 625 E2
9700 WasC 97005 625 E2
10700 BRTN 97005 625 D2
SR-8 E St
2000 FTGV 97116 591 H4
SR-8 Gales Creek Rd
1600 FTGV 97116 591 E3
1600 WasC 97116 591 E3
SR-8 NW Gales Creek Rd
1600 FTGV 97116 591 E3
1600 WasC 97116 591 C1
4000 WasC 97116 561 A5
SR-8 SE Oak St
100 HBRO 97123 593 B5
SR-8 SW Oak St
100 HBRO 97123 593 A5
SR-8 Pacific Av
1500 FTGV 97116 591 H5
4100 FTGV 97116 592 C5
4300 CNLS 97113 592 C5
SR-8 SE Tualatin Valley Hwy
900 HBRO 97123 593 D6
3600 HBRO 97123 623 H1
5800 HBRO 97007 623 J1
6300 HBRO 97007 624 A1
6300 HBRO 97123 624 A1
6700 WasC 97123 624 A1
7500 HBRO 97006 624 B1
SR-8 SW Tualatin Valley Hwy
13400 BRTN 97005 625 B3
14200 BRTN 97005 624 J3
14400 BRTN 97006 624 J3
14400 BRTN 97007 624 J3
14500 WasC 97007 624 J2
18500 WasC 97006 624 E2
21500 HBRO 97006 624 B1
21700 HBRO 97123 624 B1
32000 HBRO 97123 593 A5
32200 HBRO 97123 592 J5
SR-10 SW Barbur Blvd
3900 PTLD 97239 626 F2
SR-10 SW Beaverton Hwy
- PTLD 97221 625 H3
- PTLD 97221 626 B3
- PTLD 97225 625 H3
- PTLD 97239 626 C4
- WasC 97225 625 H3
SR-10 SW Beaverton-Hillsdl Hwy
6500 PTLD 97221 625 H3
6500 PTLD 97225 625 H3
6500 WasC 97225 625 H3
8100 BRTN 97225 625 F3
9500 BRTN 97005 625 E3
10300 WasC 97005 625 D3
SR-10 SW Capitol Hwy
6000 PTLD 97239 626 E4
SR-10 SW Farmington Rd
12000 BRTN 97005 625 A3
14100 BRTN 97005 624 J3
14300 BRTN 97007 624 J3
18500 WasC 97007 624 B6
22500 WasC 97007 654 A1
22900 WasC 97007 653 E1
26700 WasC 97123 623 E7
28500 WasC 97123 653 C1
SR-10 SW Naito Pkwy
- PTLD 97239 626 E4
2600 PTLD 97201 626 F1
SR-14 Lewis & Clark Hwy
- ClkC - 568 F4
- ClkC 98671 570 F7
- ClkC 98671 600 J1
- CMAS 98607 568 J5
- CMAS 98607 569 B5
- VCVR - 536 J6
- VCVR - 537 A6
- VCVR - 567 J2
- VCVR - 568 B2
- WHGL 98671 569 H5
- WHGL 98671 570 C6
SR-18 Dayton Byp
- DAYT 97114 771 J4
- DAYT 97114 772 A4
- YmhC 97114 771 J4
- YmhC 97114 772 C2
SR-18 SE Dayton Byp
3000 YmhC 97114 772 C2
12200 YmhC 97114 771 H5
13400 DAYT 97114 771 J4
SR-18 Salmon River Hwy
- MCMV 97128 770 H7
- MCMV 97128 771 B6
- YmhC 97114 771 E6
- YmhC 97128 770 H7
- YmhC 97128 771 B6
SR-18 NE Salmon River Hwy
2100 MCMV 97128 771 A6
4100 YmhC 97114 771 E6
4100 YmhC 97128 771 E6
SR-18 SE Salmon River Hwy
- YmhC 97114 771 F6
SR-18 Three Mile Ln
2100 MCMV 97128 771 A6
2100 YmhC 97128 771 A6
4100 YmhC 97114 771 E6
SR-18 E Three Mile Ln
4000 MCMV 97128 771 D6
SR-43 7th St
- ORCY 97045 687 C7
- WLIN 97068 687 C7
SR-43 SW Hood Av
3300 PTLD 97239 626 F2
SR-43 SW Kelly Av
- PTLD 97239 626 F2
2900 PTLD 97201 626 F1
SR-43 SW Macadam Av
3300 PTLD 97239 626 F2
6600 PTLD 97219 626 F4
8900 MthC 97219 656 G1
8900 PTLD 97219 656 G1
SR-43 Main St
500 ORCY 97045 687 C7
SR-43 Pacific Hwy
15000 LKOW 97034 656 G7
16400 LKOW 97034 686 H2
17700 WLIN 97068 686 H2
20600 WLIN 97068 687 B6
SR-43 Riverside Dr
13000 CmsC 97034 656 G4
13000 CmsC 97219 656 G4
13100 LKOW 97034 656 G4
13100 LKOW 97219 656 G4
SR-43 SW Riverside Dr
9800 MthC 97219 656 G6
9800 PTLD 97219 656 G6
12400 CmsC 97034 656 H4
SR-43 N State St
- LKOW 97219 656 G5
10 LKOW 97034 656 G6
800 CmsC 97034 656 G5
800 CmsC 97219 656 G5
SR-43 S State St
10 LKOW 97034 656 G6
SR-43 Willamette Dr
16800 LKOW 97034 686 G1
17700 WLIN 97068 686 H2
20600 WLIN 97068 687 A5
SR-47
- WasC 97106 531 G1
SR-47 Highway 47
- CLTN 97111 711 A6
- CLTN 97111 741 A1
- YmhC 97111 711 A4
- YmhC 97111 741 A1
- YmhC 97128 741 A2
- YmhC 97128 771 C2
- YmhC 97148 711 A2
- YMHL 97148 711 A2
SR-47 SW Highway 47
- FTGV 97116 591 J6
- FTGV 97116 592 A6
- WasC 97116 591 H7
SR-47 NW HWY 47
- BNKS 97106 531 J4
- FTGV 97116 592 B4
- WasC 97116 592 B4
2400 FTGV 97116 591 J2
2400 WasC 97116 591 J2
4500 WasC 97116 561 J6
10000 WasC 97116 531 J7
16500 WasC 97106 531 J6
SR-47 N Main St
100 BNKS 97106 531 J5
100 WasC 97106 531 J4
SR-47 S Main St
100 BNKS 97106 531 J5
500 WasC 97106 531 J6
600 WasC 97116 531 J6
SR-47 W Main St
100 CLTN 97111 711 A7
SR-47 S Pine St
200 CLTN 97111 741 A1
SR-47 Quince St
2100 FTGV 97116 592 B4
2300 WasC 97116 592 B4
SR-47 NW Sunset Hwy
45000 WasC 97106 531 F1
SR-47 N Yamhill St
100 CLTN 97111 711 A7
700 YmhC 97111 711 A6
SR-99E SE 1st Av
100 CNBY 97013 746 C6
1300 CmsC 97013 746 E5
SR-99E SW 1st Av
100 CNBY 97013 746 B7
1100 CmsC 97013 746 B7
SR-99E 5th St
- ORCY 97045 717 A2
100 ORCY 97045 687 C7
SR-99E NE Grand Av
10 PTLD 97214 596 G5
10 PTLD 97232 596 G5
1600 PTLD 97212 596 G4
SR-99E SE Grand Av
10 PTLD 97214 596 G6
10 PTLD 97232 596 G5
2000 PTLD 97214 626 G1
2800 PTLD 97202 626 G1
SR-99E N Martin L King Jr Blvd
9200 PTLD 97211 566 G3
9200 PTLD 97217 566 G3
SR-99E NE ML King Jr Blvd
10 PTLD 97214 596 G5
10 PTLD 97232 596 G5
1900 PTLD 97212 596 G1
4000 PTLD 97211 596 G1
4900 PTLD 97211 566 G5
9000 PTLD 97217 566 G3
SR-99E SE ML King Jr Blvd
10 PTLD 97214 596 G5
10 PTLD 97232 596 G5
2100 PTLD 97214 626 G1
SR-99E McLoughlin Blvd
10 ORCY 97045 717 B1
500 ORCY 97045 687 D6
19100 CmsC 97027 687 C4
19100 CmsC 97267 687 C4
19100 GLDS 97027 687 C4
19100 GLDS 97267 687 C4
SR-99E S McLoughlin Blvd
100 ORCY 97045 717 B1
700 CmsC 97045 717 A2
SR-99E SE McLoughlin Blvd
2700 PTLD 97202 626 G1
8300 MWKE 97202 626 J7
8300 MWKE 97222 626 J5
9100 MWKE 97222 656 J1
12300 CmsC 97222 656 J4
13200 CmsC 97222 657 A7
13800 CmsC 97267 657 A5
15800 CmsC 97267 687 B1
18500 GLDS 97267 687 C3
18800 CmsC 97027 687 C4
18800 GLDS 97027 687 C4
SR-99E Pacific Hwy E
- AURA 97002 775 F3
- BRLO 97013 746 A7
- BRLO 97013 775 J1
- BRLO 97013 776 A1
- CmsC 97002 775 J1
- CmsC 97013 746 G2
- CmsC 97013 775 J1
- CmsC 97013 776 A1
- CmsC 97045 716 H3
- CmsC 97045 717 A2
- CmsC 97045 746 F1
- CNBY 97013 746 E5
- MrnC 97032 775 D7
- ORCY 97045 716 J2
- ORCY 97045 717 A2
SR-99W E 1st St
100 NWBG 97132 713 C7
SR-99W W 1st St
100 NWBG 97132 713 B7
SR-99W SE 3rd St
100 LFYT 97127 741 G7
300 LFYT 97127 771 J1
1200 LFYT 97114 771 H1
1200 YmhC 97114 771 H1
1200 YmhC 97127 771 H1
SR-99W W 3rd St
100 LFYT 97127 741 G7
100 YmhC 97128 741 F7
SR-99W NE Adams St
100 MCMV 97128 770 H5
SR-99W SW Adams St
100 MCMV 97128 770 H5
SR-99W NE Baker St
100 MCMV 97128 770 H5
SR-99W SE Baker St
100 MCMV 97128 770 H5
SR-99W SW Baker St
700 MCMV 97128 770 H4
SR-99W SW Barbur Blvd
3900 PTLD 97239 626 E5
7200 PTLD 97219 626 B7
9400 PTLD 97219 656 B1
10400 PTLD 97219 655 G3
11400 TGRD 97223 655 H2
SR-99W E Hancock St
100 NWBG 97132 713 C7
SR-99W W Hancock St
100 NWBG 97132 713 B7
SR-99W SW Herber Hoover Hwy W
4200 NWBG 97132 713 G6
30200 YmhC 97132 713 H6
SR-99W Herbert Hoover Hwy W
1400 NWBG 97132 713 D7
SR-99W SW Herbert Hoover Hwy W
3200 NWBG 97132 713 F6
4300 YmhC 97132 713 G6
SR-99W SW Naito Pkwy
- PTLD 97239 626 E4
2400 PTLD 97201 626 E1
SR-99W Pacific Hwy W
- LFYT 97114 771 H1
- LFYT 97127 771 H1
- MCMV 97128 770 G7
- MCMV 97128 771 A3
- NWBG 97132 713 B7
- NWBG 97132 743 B1
- WasC 97132 714 A5
- WasC 97140 714 A5
- YmhC 97114 771 J1
- YmhC 97115 742 J2
- YmhC 97115 743 A1
- YmhC 97127 771 H1
- YmhC 97132 713 B7
- YmhC 97132 743 A1
1300 DNDE 97115 742 H4
7800 YmhC 97128 771 C2
10900 YmhC 97128 741 F7
11300 LFYT 97127 741 F7
17500 KNGC 97224 685 B2
17500 TLTN 97062 685 A3
17500 TLTN 97224 685 B2
17500 WasC 97224 685 B2
18200 WasC 97062 685 A3
18600 YmhC 97114 772 B2
18600 YmhC 97115 772 E1
18700 WasC 97062 684 J3
18800 YmhC 97114 742 E7
20200 SRWD 97140 684 E7
22000 WasC 97140 684 E7
23000 SRWD 97140 714 D1
SR-99W SW Pacific Hwy
11400 PTLD 97219 655 H2
12000 TGRD 97223 655 E4
14300 TGRD 97224 655 D5
15000 KNGC 97224 655 C7
15500 WasC 97224 655 D5
16000 TGRD 97224 685 C1
16000 WasC 97224 685 C1
16100 KNGC 97224 685 B1
SR-99W Portland Rd
1400 NWBG 97132 713 D7
4300 YmhC 97132 713 G6
SR-210 SW Scholls Ferry Rd
4700 WasC 97225 625 G3
5400 BRTN 97225 625 F4
5800 WasC 97223 625 F4
6500 WasC 97005 625 E5
6700 BRTN 97005 625 E5
6700 BRTN 97008 625 D7
6700 WasC 97008 625 E5
8500 BRTN 97223 625 D7
8700 TGRD 97008 625 D7
8700 TGRD 97223 625 D7
9400 BRTN 97008 655 A2
9400 BRTN 97223 655 D1
9400 TGRD 97223 655 D1
11800 TGRD 97008 655 B2
13500 BRTN 97007 655 A2
13500 TGRD 97007 655 A2
14000 BRTN 97007 654 J2
14000 BRTN 97008 654 J2
17500 WasC 97007 654 B5
20300 WasC 97123 654 B5
22600 WasC 97123 653 H7
23600 WasC 97140 653 H7
24100 WasC 97123 683 H1
24100 WasC 97140 683 H1
SR-211 Clackamas Hwy
- CmsC 97022 719 J2
- CmsC 97022 720 A5
- CmsC 97023 720 A6
- CmsC 97023 750 A1
- ECDA 97022 720 A7
- ECDA 97022 750 A1
- ECDA 97023 720 A7
- ECDA 97023 750 A2
SR-211 Eagle Creek-Sandy Hwy
- CmsC 97009 690 E6
- CmsC 97022 690 C7
- CmsC 97022 719 J1
- CmsC 97022 720 A1
- CmsC 97055 690 J4
- SNDY 97055 690 J4
- SNDY 97055 691 A3
SR-211 E Main St
100 MOLA 97038 837 E1
SR-211 W Main St
100 MOLA 97038 837 E1
800 CmsC 97038 837 D1
SR-211 Meinig Av
17400 SNDY 97055 691 A3
SR-211 Woodburn-Estacada Hwy
- CmsC 97023 750 A6
- CmsC 97038 807 H7
- CmsC 97038 837 C1
- ECDA 97023 750 B4
- MOLA 97038 837 C1
SR-212
- CmsC 97009 659 H5
SR-212 Carver Hwy
- CmsC 97009 658 D7
- CmsC 97015 658 B7
- DAMA 97009 658 D7
- DAMA 97015 658 D7
- HPYV 97015 658 D7
SR-212 Clackamas Hwy
- CmsC 97009 658 D7
- CmsC 97015 658 C7
- CmsC 97015 687 J1
- CmsC 97015 688 A1
- DAMA 97009 658 D7
- DAMA 97015 658 D7
- HPYV 97015 658 D7
SR-212 Clackamas-Boring Rd
- CmsC 97009 658 E7
- CmsC 97009 659 C6
- CmsC 97009 688 D1
- CmsC 97015 658 D7
- CmsC 97015 688 D1
- DAMA 97009 658 E7
- DAMA 97009 659 A6
- DAMA 97009 688 D1
- DAMA 97015 658 D7
- HPYV 97009 658 E7
- HPYV 97015 658 F7
SR-212 SE Clackamas-Boring Rd
28300 CmsC 97009 659 H5
29300 CmsC 97009 660 A5
SR-212 Clackamas-Boring Rdg
- CmsC 97009 659 H5
SR-212 SE Clackamas-Boring Rdg
12500 CmsC 97009 659 H5
SR-213 NE 82nd Av
10 PTLD 97213 597 F6
10 PTLD 97215 597 F6
10 PTLD 97216 597 F6
10 PTLD 97220 597 F1
3900 PTLD 97218 597 F1
5200 PTLD 97218 567 F7
5200 PTLD 97220 567 F7
SR-213 SE 82nd Av
- CmsC - 657 F5
- CmsC 97015 657 F5
10 PTLD 97213 597 F6
10 PTLD 97215 597 F6
10 PTLD 97216 597 F6
10 PTLD 97220 597 F6
2000 PTLD 97206 627 F7
2000 PTLD 97215 627 F1
2000 PTLD 97216 627 F1
2000 PTLD 97266 627 F7
8400 CmsC 97206 627 F7
8400 CmsC 97236 627 F7
SR-213 SE 82nd Av N
8500 CmsC 97206 627 F7
8500 CmsC 97236 627 F7
8500 PTLD 97266 627 F7
9000 CmsC 97206 657 F1
9000 CmsC 97236 657 F1
9200 CmsC 97222 657 F1
12500 CmsC 97015 657 F4
SR-213 Cascade Hwy S
- CmsC 97004 747 G3
- CmsC 97013 777 E1
- CmsC 97038 807 C6
- CmsC 97038 837 A3
- CmsC 97042 747 F7
- CmsC 97042 777 E1
- CmsC 97042 807 C6
- CmsC 97045 687 E6
- CmsC 97045 717 F7
- CmsC 97045 747 F6
- CmsC 97045 777 E1
- MOLA 97038 807 C6
- MOLA 97038 837 B1
- ORCY 97045 687 E5
19600 ORCY 97045 717 F3
SR-213 SE Cascade Hwy
8500 CmsC 97206 627 F7
8500 CmsC 97236 627 F7
8500 PTLD 97266 627 F7
9000 CmsC 97206 657 F1
9000 CmsC 97236 657 F5
9200 CmsC 97222 657 F5
12500 CmsC 97015 657 F4
SR-213 SE Cascade Hwy N
- CmsC - 657 F6
- CmsC 97222 657 F5
SR-213 East Portland Frwy
- CmsC - 657 F7
- CmsC - 687 F2
- GLDS - 687 F4
- ORCY - 687 F4
SR-217 Beaverton-Tigard Hwy
- BRTN - 595 E7
- BRTN - 625 D5
- BRTN - 655 D1
- LKOW - 655 H5
- TGRD - 655 E2
- WasC - 595 E7
- WasC - 625 D1
SR-219
- MrnC 97137 773 F6
SR-219 S 1st Av
300 HBRO 97123 593 B5
SR-219 E 1st St
700 NWBG 97132 713 C7
1700 YmhC 97132 713 E7
SR-219 Barr-Alex Rd
10900 WasC 97123 653 C2
16200 WasC 97123 683 G1
16300 WasC 97140 683 H1
SR-219 Church Av NE
4100 STPL 97137 773 B6
4300 MrnC 97137 773 C6
SR-219 N College St
100 NWBG 97132 713 C7
3100 YmhC 97132 713 C4
SR-219 French Prairie Rd NE
19100 MrnC 97137 773 F7
SR-219 E Hancock St
700 NWBG 97132 713 C7
SR-219 Herbert Hoover Hwy W
1400 NWBG 97132 713 D7
SR-219 NE Hillsboro Hwy
17600 WasC 97132 713 D1
SR-219 SW Hillsboro Hwy
2400 HBRO 97123 593 B6
2400 WasC 97123 593 B6
2500 HBRO 97123 623 B1
2500 WasC 97113 623 B1
2500 WasC 97123 623 B1
9600 WasC 97113 653 B1
9600 WasC 97123 653 B1
16200 WasC 97123 683 E4
16300 WasC 97140 683 H1
20100 WasC 97132 683 E4
23600 WasC 97132 713 D1
SR-219 Main St NE
20200 STPL 97137 773 B5
20400 MrnC 97137 773 C5
SR-219 Newberg Hwy
2400 HBRO 97123 593 B7
2400 WasC 97123 593 B7
2500 HBRO 97123 623 B1
2500 WasC 97113 623 B1
2500 WasC 97123 623 B1
SR-219 Pacific Hwy W
- NWBG 97132 713 C7
SR-219 Portland Rd
1400 NWBG 97132 713 D7
SR-219 St. Paul Hwy NE
900 NWBG 97132 743 F2
900 YmhC 97132 743 F2
8400 MrnC 97137 743 F5
20400 STPL 97137 773 C5
21800 MrnC 97137 773 E1
SR-219 Villa Rd
100 NWBG 97132 713 D7
SR-221
- YmhC 97114 772 A3
SR-221 3rd St
700 DAYT 97114 772 C4
700 YmhC 97114 772 C4
SR-221 SE 3rd St
100 DAYT 97114 772 A3
700 YmhC 97114 772 B4
SR-221 Salem-Dayton Hwy
- DAYT 97114 772 C6
- YmhC 97114 772 C6
SR-221 SE Wallace Rd
6000 DAYT 97114 772 C5
6000 YmhC 97114 772 C5
SR-224 SE 82nd Dr
14200 CmsC 97015 657 F6
SR-224 Carver Hwy
- CmsC 97009 658 D7
- CmsC 97015 658 B7
- DAMA 97009 658 D7
- DAMA 97015 658 D7
- HPYV 97015 658 D7
SR-224 Clackamas Hwy
- CmsC 97009 658 D7
- CmsC 97009 688 D1
- CmsC 97009 689 A3
- CmsC 97015 658 C7
- CmsC 97015 687 J1
- CmsC 97015 688 A1
- CmsC 97022 689 E4
- CmsC 97022 719 J2
- CmsC 97022 720 A5
- CmsC 97023 720 A6
- CmsC 97023 750 D6
- DAMA 97009 658 D7
- DAMA 97009 688 D1
- DAMA 97009 689 C3
- DAMA 97015 658 D7
- ECDA 97022 720 A7
- ECDA 97022 750 A1
- ECDA 97023 720 A7
- ECDA 97023 750 D6
- HPYV 97015 658 D7
SR-224 SE Milwaukie Expwy
- CmsC 97015 657 F6
- CmsC 97222 657 D5
- CmsC 97267 657 F5
- MWKE 97222 656 J2
- MWKE 97222 657 A2
SR-233 SE Amity-Dayton Hwy
10600 YmhC 97114 771 G7
SR-233 Dayton Byp
- DAYT 97114 771 J4
- DAYT 97114 772 A4
- YmhC 97114 771 J4
- YmhC 97114 772 C2
SR-233 SE Dayton Byp
3000 YmhC 97114 772 C2
12700 YmhC 97114 771 H5
13400 DAYT 97114 771 J4
SR-233 SE Lafayette Hwy
6500 YmhC 97114 771 G7
SR-240 E Main St
300 YMHL 97148 711 B1
1000 YmhC 97148 711 B1
SR-240 N Main St
100 NWBG 97132 713 B7
SR-240 Yamhill-Newberg Hwy
- NWBG 97132 713 B6
- YmhC 97132 711 G2
- YmhC 97132 712 A4
- YmhC 97148 711 E2
23000 YmhC 97132 713 B6
SR-500
- ClkC - 507 J7
- ClkC - 537 H1
- VCVR - 507 J7
- VCVR - 537 H1
- VCVR 98663 536 J2
- VCVR 98663 537 A2
SR-500 NE 3rd Av
500 CMAS 98607 569 F4
SR-500 NE 3rd St
26300 ClkC 98607 539 F6
SR-500 SE 6th Av
500 CMAS 98607 569 G5
SR-500 NE 14th Av
600 CMAS 98607 569 E4
SR-500 NE 25th St
24800 ClkC 98607 539 D4
SR-500 NE 44th St
23800 ClkC 98682 539 C2
SR-500 NE 54th St
23200 ClkC 98682 539 C1
SR-500 NE 58th St
19100 ClkC 98682 508 H7
20700 ClkC 98682 509 C7
SR-500 NE 117th Av
- VCVR 98682 507 J7
6300 ClkC 98662 507 J6
6300 ClkC 98682 507 J6
SR-500 NE 162nd Av
7000 ClkC 98682 508 E6
SR-500 NE 232nd Av
5300 ClkC 98682 509 C7
5300 ClkC 98682 539 C1
SR-500 NE 237th Av
4800 ClkC 98682 539 C1
SR-500 NE 238th Av
4400 ClkC 98682 539 C2
SR-500 NE 242nd Av
2800 ClkC 98607 539 D3
3400 ClkC 98682 539 D2
SR-500 NE 267th Av
300 ClkC 98607 539 F6
SR-500 NE Brunner Rd
25200 ClkC 98607 539 E4
SR-500 NE Dallas St
200 CMAS 98607 569 F4
SR-500 NE Dresser Rd
24200 ClkC 98607 539 D3
SR-500 SE Everett Rd
100 ClkC 98607 539 F6
800 CMAS 98607 539 E7
1000 CMAS 98607 569 E1
SR-500 NE Everett St
1400 CMAS 98607 569 E3
SR-500 NE Fourth Plain Rd
16200 ClkC 98682 508 G7
SR-500 NE Garfield St
300 CMAS 98607 569 F4
SR-500 NE Padden Pkwy
- ClkC 98662 507 J5
- ClkC 98682 507 J5
- ClkC 98682 508 B5
SR-500 SE Union St
600 CMAS 98607 569 G5
SR-500 NE Ward Rd
8300 ClkC 98682 508 E5
SR-501 E 15th St
100 VCVR 98660 536 G4
100 VCVR 98663 536 G4
SR-501 W 15th St
100 VCVR 98660 536 G4
100 VCVR 98663 536 G4
SR-501 NW Lower River Rd
2000 VCVR 98660 536 A1
5200 ClkC 98660 536 A1
6300 ClkC 98660 505 G1
6300 ClkC 98660 506 A7
6300 VCVR 98660 505 J7
6300 VCVR 98660 506 A7
10000 ClkC 98660 475 H4
SR-501 E Mill Plain Blvd
100 VCVR 98660 536 G4
100 VCVR 98663 536 G4
SR-501 W Mill Plain Blvd
100 VCVR 98663 536 G4
2300 VCVR 98660 536 D3
SR-501 Pioneer St
200 RDGF 98642 415 J7
700 RDGF 98642 416 B7
SR-502 NE 10th Av
17900 ClkC 98642 476 H1
19400 ClkC 98642 446 H7
SR-502 NE 219th St
1000 ClkC 98642 446 J5
2200 ClkC 98642 447 D5
4200 ClkC 98604 447 C5
9200 BGND 98604 447 H5
SR-502 W Main St
1000 BGND 98604 448 A5
1500 BGND 98604 447 J5
2900 ClkC 98604 447 H5
SR-503
- ClkC 98604 478 A3
- ClkC 98606 478 A3
SR-503 NW 10th Av
12200 BGND 98604 448 A4
12200 ClkC 98604 448 A4
SR-503 SW 10th Av
10 BGND 98604 448 A6
10 ClkC 98604 448 A7
SR-503 NE 117th Av
- VCVR 98682 507 J7
6300 ClkC 98662 507 J4
6300 ClkC 98682 507 J4
11700 ClkC 98606 507 J1
11900 ClkC 98606 477 J7
11900 ClkC 98662 477 J7
13100 ClkC 98606 478 A3
SR-503 NE 122nd Av
13300 BGND 98604 448 A3
17900 ClkC 98604 478 A2
17900 ClkC 98606 478 A2
19200 ClkC 98604 448 A7
SR-503 BUS NE Caples Rd
14800 ClkC 98606 478 A4
16700 ClkC 98604 478 A3
SR-503 Lewis River Rd
1000 WDLD 98674 386 A1
SR-503 NE Lewisville Hwy
24400 BGND 98604 448 A3
24400 ClkC 98604 448 A7
26200 ClkC 98604 418 B6
32900 ClkC 98675 418 D1
S Staben Ln
23000 CmsC 97004 748 B5
NE Stable Ct
5000 HBRO 97124 593 H3
NE Stable Dr
5100 HBRO 97124 593 H3
SW Stacey St
19200 WasC 97006 594 D7
SE Stacy Ct
10800 CmsC 97236 657 H2
Stadium Frwy
- PTLD - 596 E5
- PTLD - 626 E1
Stadium Frwy I-405
- PTLD - 596 E3
- PTLD - 626 E1
Stadium Frwy US-30
- PTLD - 596 E4
Stafford Rd
16500 LKOW 97034 686 D2
16700 CmsC 97034 686 E1
18400 CmsC 97068 686 D2
NW Stafford Rd
12400 WasC 97116 531 D6
SW Stafford Rd
19400 CmsC 97068 686 C4
19800 CmsC 97062 686 C5
22400 CmsC 97062 685 J7
22500 CmsC 97062 715 G4
23500 CmsC 97070 715 G4
27400 WNVL 97070 715 G5
N Stafford St
10 PTLD 97211 566 G5
10 PTLD 97217 566 F5
4600 PTLD 97203 566 B5
NE Stafford St
10 PTLD 97217 566 G5
1300 PTLD 97211 566 J5
SW Stafford Hill Ct
23400 CmsC 97068 716 C1
SW Stafford Hill Dr
23000 CmsC 97068 686 C7
23200 CmsC 97068 716 C1
SW Stafford Summit Ct
- CmsC 97068 716 E2
Stag Ct
35000 STHN 97051 414 J1
Stag St
34900 STHN 97051 414 J1
SW Stagecoach Ln
17500 SRWD 97140 684 F5
E Stage Stop Rd
67900 CmsC 97067 724 B3
NE Stag Hollow Rd
12000 YmhC 97111 711 F6
13500 YmhC 97148 711 F4
SW Stahl Dr
16200 WasC 97223 654 G5
SE Staley Av
12500 DAMA 97009 659 C5
SW Stallion Ct
9400 BRTN 97008 654 F1
9400 BRTN 97008 655 A1
SW Stallion Dr
14000 BRTN 97008 654 J1
SE Stamp Rd
31500 CmsC 97023 750 C3
31500 ECDA 97023 750 C3
Stampher Rd
- CmsC 97219 656 G5
200 LKOW 97034 656 G5
13800 CmsC 97034 656 G5
NE Stanchion Ct
5200 HBRO 97124 593 H3
NW Standish St
100 ECDA 97023 750 B3
N Stanford Av
6700 PTLD 97203 566 A4
SW Stanford Ct
6900 PTLD 97223 625 G6
6900 WasC 97223 625 G6
SE Stanhelma Dr
16900 CmsC 97027 687 E2
16900 CmsC 97267 687 F1
SW Stanhope Ct
2700 PTLD 97201 626 D3
SE Stanhope Rd
14800 CmsC 97015 658 C7
NW Stanley Av
2300 GSHM 97030 599 B7
SE Stanley Av
9000 CmsC 97222 657 C1
9000 MWKE 97206 657 C1
10400 MWKE 97222 657 C2
SE Stanley Ct
11400 MWKE 97222 657 D3
SW Stanley Ct
2500 PTLD 97219 626 C7
2700 PTLD 97219 656 B1
SE Stanley Pl
8900 MWKE 97206 627 D7
8900 MWKE 97206 657 D1
8900 MWKE 97222 657 D1

STREET
Block City ZIP Map# Grid

NE Stanley St
23500 WDVL 97060 599 D5
NE Stanton Ct
14500 PTLD 97230 598 D3
NE Stanton Pl
15500 PTLD 97230 598 E3
N Stanton St
10 PTLD 97212 596 G2
600 PTLD 97227 596 F3
NE Stanton St
10 PTLD 97212 596 G3
10 PTLD 97227 596 G2
2600 PTLD 97212 597 A3
4400 PTLD 97213 597 C3
11700 PTLD 97220 598 A3
15600 PTLD 97230 598 E3
SE Stanvick Ct
17100 CmsC 97267 687 A1
SE Stapleton Lp
1200 GSHM 97080 629 C4
NE Stapleton Rd
- ClkC 98661 537 C2
1800 VCVR 98661 537 C4
NW Star St
44700 WasC 97106 531 F3
SW Starbuck Ln
17200 WasC 97007 624 F3
SW Stardust Ln
14100 TGRD 97223 654 J4
NE Starflower Ct
8300 VCVR 98664 537 F4
NW Starflower Dr
6400 WasC 97229 564 J6
SE Starflower Dr
11700 CmsC 97009 659 E4
SE Stargazer Pl
4200 HBRO 97123 623 G2
SW Star Jasmine Pl
6700 BRTN 97008 625 B5
NW Stark Ct
9100 WasC 97225 595 F5
9100 WasC 97229 595 F5
SW Stark Rd
18000 WasC 97140 684 C3
SE Stark St
10 PTLD 97214 596 H6
2800 PTLD 97214 597 A6
7400 PTLD 97215 597 F6
8100 PTLD 97216 597 F6
11500 PTLD 97216 598 A6
11900 PTLD 97233 598 C6
16000 GSHM 97233 598 F6
20000 GSHM 97030 598 J6
20500 GSHM 97030 599 E7
24300 TDLE 97060 599 E7
25800 GSHM 97060 599 F7
28000 MthC 97060 629 J1
29200 MthC 97060 599 J7
SW Stark St
10 PTLD 97204 596 F6
500 PTLD 97205 596 F6
1200 PTLD 97209 596 E5
W Stark St
12000 BRTN 97225 595 B6
12000 BRTN 97229 595 B6
12000 WasC 97225 595 C6
12000 WasC 97229 595 B6
17300 BRTN 97006 594 F5
17300 WasC 97006 594 F5
NW Starkrest Av
9000 ClkC 98665 506 D3
SW Starlight Dr
23100 WasC 97140 683 G7
23100 WasC 97140 713 G1
SW Starling Ln
15700 BRTN 97007 654 H4
NW Star Mill Wy
200 MCMV 97128 770 G5
NE Star Mooring Ln
7000 YmhC 97132 743 J5
SW Starr Dr
10500 TLTN 97062 685 D2
SE Starr Rd
27500 CmsC 97022 719 G6
SW Starview Dr
12900 TGRD 97224 655 A6
NW Starview Pl
3900 WasC 97229 595 B2
State Hwy
19700 MmC 97002 775 D5
19700 MmC 97032 775 D5
23200 CmsC 97002 745 E7
N State St
- LKOW 97219 656 G5
10 LKOW 97034 656 G5
800 CmsC 97034 656 G5
800 CmsC 97219 656 G5
N State St SR-43
- LKOW 97219 656 G5
10 LKOW 97034 656 G5
800 CmsC 97034 656 G5
800 CmsC 97219 656 G5
S State St
10 LKOW 97034 656 G7
S State St SR-43
10 LKOW 97034 656 G7
SE State St
- VCVR 98661 537 D7
S Station Ln
1000 CmsC 97068 686 F4
NW Station Pl
1200 HBRO 97006 594 C4
NW Station Wy
900 PTLD 97209 596 F4
NE Stauffer Rd
29200 ClkC 98607 539 J3
30000 ClkC 98607 540 B3
SW Steamboat Dr
11800 BRTN 97008 625 B7
Steamboat Wy
18300 WLIN 97068 686 J2
S Steamer Ct
18100 CmsC 97045 718 H2
Steel Br
- PTLD 97209 596 F5
- PTLD 97227 596 F5
- PTLD 97232 596 F5
SE Steele St
2600 PTLD 97202 626 J4
2800 PTLD 97202 627 A4
4100 PTLD 97206 627 C4
10500 PTLD 97266 627 H4
12200 PTLD 97266 628 A4
13000 PTLD 97236 628 B4

SW Steele Wy
16900 BRTN 97006 594 G6
NE Steelhead Ln
22200 ClkC 98675 419 B4
Steelhead St
300 MOLA 97038 837 G1
Steelman Rd
- ClkC 97231 474 J3
- ClkC 97231 475 A2
SE Steen Ct
6200 CmsC 97222 657 D2
SW Steeplechase Cir
9900 BRTN 97008 654 J1
SW Steeplechase Ct
14000 BRTN 97008 654 J2
SW Steere Dr
11100 WasC 97007 654 G3
Stefanie Ct
39500 SNDY 97055 691 A3
NE Stegert Dr
23900 ClkC 98604 447 F3
SW Stein Ter
22000 SRWD 97140 684 E6
S Steiner Rd
17100 CmsC 97004 748 C3
E Steiner St
20100 CmsC 97011 693 G6
Steinke St
35700 STHN 97051 385 A7
SE Stella Ct
7000 HBRO 97123 594 A7
SW Stella Wy
1900 TDLE 97060 599 E5
SW Stellar Dr
16700 SRWD 97140 684 F7
Stenbock Wy
- MmC 97002 775 E1
Stenbock Wy NE
14300 MmC 97002 775 E1
NW Stent Ln
- MthC 97210 595 H4
- MthC 97229 595 H4
Steph Ct
16100 ORCY 97045 687 G6
Stephanie Ct
800 NWBG 97132 713 C4
15400 LKOW 97035 655 H6
NE Stephanie Ct
2300 HBRO 97124 593 C2
SE Stephanie Ct
7800 CmsC 97222 657 F3
SW Stephen Ln
7000 WasC 97225 625 G4
SE Stephens Cir
18400 GSHM 97233 628 G1
SE Stephens Ct
15200 PTLD 97233 628 D1
17500 GSHM 97233 628 F1
SE Stephens Pl
13500 PTLD 97233 628 B1
SE Stephens St
300 PTLD 97214 596 G7
3700 PTLD 97214 597 B7
6000 PTLD 97215 597 D7
8300 PTLD 97216 597 G7
11400 PTLD 97216 627 J1
11400 PTLD 97216 628 A1
12200 PTLD 97233 628 A1
18200 GSHM 97233 628 G1
SW Stephenson Ct
700 PTLD 97219 656 D3
SW Stephenson St
- LKOW 97219 656 B3
3400 PTLD 97035 656 B3
4100 LKOW 97035 656 A3
4100 PTLD 97219 656 A3
4900 PTLD 97219 655 J3
SE Sterling Cir
16200 CmsC 97267 686 J1
16200 CmsC 97267 687 A1
SE Sterling Ct
14600 CmsC 97015 658 A6
SE Sterling Ln
7100 HBRO 97123 624 A1
7100 WasC 97123 624 A1
Sterling Wy
5300 LKOW 97035 655 J4
Sterling Pointe
- BRTN 97008 654 J2
SW Sterns Dr
- PTLD 97205 596 C5
- PTLD 97210 596 C5
SW Stetson St
16100 SRWD 97140 684 G6
SW Steve St
8100 TGRD 97223 655 F3
SE Steven Ct
10000 CmsC 97236 657 H2
SW Steven Ct
13600 TGRD 97223 655 D5
SE Stevens Ct
12100 CmsC 97236 657 G4
12100 HPYV 97236 657 G4
S Stevens Rd
14900 CmsC 97045 688 G4
SE Stevens Rd
11000 CmsC 97236 657 G3
11200 HPYV 97236 657 G3
12000 CmsC 97015 657 H4
32500 MthC 97019 630 D2
SE Stevens Wy
10500 CmsC 97236 657 G2
SE Stevenson Dr
14900 VCVR 98683 568 C1
NE Stevenson Rd
10400 YmhC 97132 743 B1
SE Stewart Ct
4800 HBRO 97123 623 H1
SE Stewart Ln
26700 CmsC 97009 659 G5
SW Stewart St
7200 WasC 97223 625 G7
Stewart Glenn Ct
5800 LKOW 97035 655 H5
NE Stile Dr
1300 HBRO 97124 593 J3
1400 WasC 97124 593 J3
SE Stiles Rd
3400 ClkC 98671 570 C3
3400 WHGL 98671 570 C3
Still Creek Rd
- CmsC 97049 724 G5
E Still Creek Rd
- CmsC 97049 724 G6

NE Stillers Mill Rd
17400 YmhC 97148 711 B1
Stillmeadow Dr
19400 ORCY 97045 717 E5
SW Stillwell Ln
12500 BRTN 97008 625 B7
NW Stimpson Ln
2300 PTLD 97229 595 D1
SW Stirrup Ct
13500 BRTN 97008 625 A7
SW Stirrup Pl
14000 BRTN 97008 624 J7
SW Stirrup St
13800 BRTN 97008 625 A7
14000 BRTN 97008 624 J7
Stitt Ct
14600 ORCY 97045 717 G4
N St Johns Av
- PTLD 97203 565 F2
N St Louis Av
- PTLD 97203 565 G3
N Stockton Av
7400 PTLD 97203 566 B5
Stockton St
1400 FTGV 97116 592 A6
SW Stoddard Dr
4200 WasC 97007 624 C3
SE Stohler Rd
15300 CmsC 97267 657 D7
SW Stokesay Ln
19900 WasC 97007 624 D3
NW Stoller Dr
16600 WasC 97229 594 G1
17000 WasC 97229 564 G7
NE Stoller Pl
23400 CmsC 97002 745 D6
NE Stoller Rd
3000 YmhC 97114 772 A1
13100 LFYT 97127 741 H7
13100 YmhC 97114 741 J7
13700 YmhC 97114 771 J1
Stoltz Rd
16100 CmsC 97045 687 H6
Stone Rd
32900 ClbC 97053 414 E4
NE Stone Rd
13800 YmhC 97132 712 G3
SE Stone Rd
26800 DAMA 97009 659 G1
26800 MthC 97080 659 G1
27200 CmsC 97009 659 H1
28900 MthC 97080 629 J7
NE Stonebriar Ln
- WasC 97124 594 A5
NW Stonebridge Dr
13500 WasC 97229 595 A2
Stonebridge Wy
3000 LKOW 97034 686 H1
NW Stonebridge Wy
14100 WasC 97229 595 A1
SW Stonebrook Ct
4800 PTLD 97239 626 B3
Stonebrook Dr
- ClbC 97053 444 D2
- ClbC 97056 444 D2
SW Stonebrook Dr
3300 PTLD 97239 626 B3
Stone Brook Rd
32800 ClbC 97053 444 E2
Stonebrook Rd
32800 ClbC 97053 444 E2
32800 ClbC 97056 444 E2
S Stone Cliff Ln
- CmsC 97045 688 D3
E Stonecreek Dr
400 LCTR 98629 386 H7
400 LCTR 98629 416 H1
SW Stone Creek Dr
9400 WasC 97007 654 D1
SW Stonecrest Ln
1600 CmsC 97219 656 G5
Stonegate Dr
100 CMAS 98607 569 H4
100 WHGL 98671 569 H3
N Stonegate Dr
- WHGL 98671 569 J3
Stonegate Ln
- WLIN 97068 686 J7
Stonehaven Ct
1200 WLIN 97068 686 G2
Stonehaven Dr
1300 WLIN 97068 686 G3
SW Stonehaven St
23500 SRWD 97140 714 H1
23900 CmsC 97140 714 H1
NW Stonehedge Ct
18000 BRTN 97006 594 F4
NW Stonehedge Ln
15900 BRTN 97006 594 H4
Stonehill St
500 GLDS 97027 687 D3
Stonehurst Ct
2300 LKOW 97034 686 G2
S Stone Meadow Rd
- CmsC 97017 807 J7
- CmsC 97017 837 J1
- CmsC 97038 807 J7
SE Stonemill Dr
200 VCVR 98684 538 B6
200 VCVR 98683 538 B6
Stone Oaks Ct
8000 GLDS 97027 687 E3
Stoneridge
- VCVR 98663 537 A1
SW Stone Ridge Cir
- BRTN 97007 654 H1
NE Stonewater St
7000 HBRO 97124 594 B4
Stonewood Ct
1100 GLDS 97027 687 E3
Stonewood Dr
18000 GLDS 97027 687 E3
SE Stoneybrook Ct
16500 CmsC 97009 658 E5
16500 CmsC 97015 658 E5
16500 HPYV 97009 658 E5
16500 HPYV 97015 658 E5
NE Stoneybrook St
7200 HBRO 97124 594 B4
NE Stoney Meadows Dr
17000 ClkC 98682 538 F2
SW Stono Dr
8700 TLTN 97062 685 E7
9300 WasC 97062 685 E7

NE Storedahl Pit Rd
- ClkC 98604 417 D6
Storey Dr
600 MOLA 97038 807 C7
SE Storey St
700 MCMV 97128 770 H6
S Stormer Rd
- CmsC 97023 749 C1
22400 CmsC 97023 719 E7
SW Stott Av
4500 BRTN 97005 625 B3
SE Stott Cir
3100 TDLE 97060 599 G7
NE Stoughton Rd
2800 ClkC 98629 417 B4
Stowers Rd
100 MOLA 97038 837 F2
Straight St
- ORCY 97045 717 C2
Strand
100 STHN 97051 385 D7
NE Strand Rd
2000 ClkC 98686 476 J7
Strasburg Dr
2200 FTGV 97116 591 F4
SE Stratford Av
17000 CmsC 97027 687 F2
17000 CmsC 97267 687 F2
SW Stratford Ct
6500 WNVL 97070 715 G6
8500 TGRD 97224 655 G5
SW Stratford Lp
15700 TGRD 97224 655 E7
Stratford St
39200 SNDY 97055 691 A4
SW Strathfell Ln
4200 MthC 97221 596 A7
4200 PTLD 97221 596 A7
SW Strathmoor St
18100 WasC 97007 624 E5
SW Stratus St
11000 BRTN 97008 625 C7
SW Straughan Rd
6500 WasC 97123 623 F5
Straus Av
32400 CmsC 97038 837 A3
Strauss Av
17100 SNDY 97055 690 J3
SE Strawberry Dr
24200 DAMA 97009 659 D5
SE Strawberry Ln
7200 CmsC 97267 687 E1
7300 CmsC 97027 687 F2
8600 CmsC 97015 687 F2
SW Strawberry Hill Dr
27600 WasC 97123 683 D2
Strawbridge Pkwy
38200 SNDY 97055 690 J3
Streamside Ct
13300 LKOW 97035 655 J4
13300 LKOW 97035 656 A4
SW Streamside Ct
11400 PTLD 97219 656 C2
Streamside Dr
13400 LKOW 97035 655 J4
13400 LKOW 97035 656 C5
SW Streamside Dr
2700 PTLD 97219 656 C2
SE Strebin Rd
1000 TDLE 97060 629 G1
2500 MthC 97060 629 J2
Streeds Ln
- YmhC 97132 714 A7
- YmhC 97132 744 A1
SW Strickland St
18900 WasC 97007 624 E5
NW Stringtown Rd
10 WasC 97116 591 C2
SE Stringtown Rd
13400 YmhC 97114 771 J7
14100 YmhC 97114 772 B7
SW Stringtown Rd
100 WasC 97116 591 E5
SW Strobel Rd
12000 WasC 97007 654 E4
NW Strohmayer Rd
45000 WasC 97116 531 E7
45000 WasC 97116 561 E1
SE Strong Av
3700 ClkC 98607 569 G3
3700 WHGL 98671 569 G3
3900 CMAS 98607 569 G4
N Strong St
5400 PTLD 97203 566 A5
SW Strowbridge Ct
8000 BRTN 97008 625 B7
S Strowbridge Rd
17600 CmsC 97045 719 A3
SE Strubhar Ln
31100 CmsC 97023 750 B1
31100 ECDA 97023 750 B1
NW Strunk St
- ClkC 98607 538 J6
- CMAS 98607 538 J6
- VCVR 98607 538 J6
SW Stuart Ct
10200 TGRD 97224 685 D1
NE Stuart Dr
2600 PTLD 97212 596 J2
SE Stuart Ln
1300 CmsC 97267 656 H6
NE Stub Rd
- ClkC 98682 508 E6
SE Stubb St
2300 MWKE 97222 626 J7
SW Stubblefield Wy
18500 WasC 97006 624 E1
NW Stucki Av
2000 HBRO 97006 594 D3
2000 HBRO 97124 594 D3
NW Stucki Pl
3000 HBRO 97124 594 E2
NE Stugess Av
900 HBRO 97124 593 D4
SW Sturges Dr
1600 TDLE 97060 599 E5
SW Sturges Ln
1700 TDLE 97060 599 E5
NE Stutz Rd
11200 ClkC 98685 506 H1
NW Sue Ct
17600 BRTN 97006 594 F4
Sue Ln
17800 SNDY 97055 690 J3

NW Sue St
12900 WasC 97229 595 B5
SW Suffolk Ct
8600 BRTN 97008 625 D4
NW Suffolk St
2200 PTLD 97210 596 C3
NW Sugarberry Ter
6300 WasC 97229 564 H5
NW Sugarmaple Ct
1600 MCMV 97128 770 F4
SW Sugar Plum Ct
17000 WasC 97007 624 F5
SW Sugar Plum Ln
17000 BRTN 97007 624 F5
17000 WasC 97007 624 F5
NE Sullivan Ln
15700 YmhC 97132 712 E2
NE Sumac Ct
13000 ClkC 98606 478 B4
SW Sumac Ct
19600 WasC 97007 624 D5
Sumac Dr
- WasC 97007 624 D5
NE Sumac Dr
12800 ClkC 98606 478 B4
SW Sumac Ln
17500 WasC 97007 624 F5
SW Sumac St
16000 BRTN 97007 624 G5
NW Sumida Ln
14900 WasC 97229 594 J4
15000 WasC 97229 564 J7
NE Summer Dr
- ClkC 98606 509 C1
- ClkC 98682 509 C1
Summer Pl
16800 LKOW 97035 685 H1
SE Summer Pl
11700 CmsC 97015 657 J6
11700 CmsC 97015 658 A6
SE Summer Rd
33300 CmsC 97023 750 D3
SW Summer St
12100 TGRD 97223 655 B3
SW Summer Crest Dr
11600 TGRD 97223 655 B3
SW Summer Crest Pl
11700 TGRD 97223 655 C3
SW Summerfield Ct
9100 TGRD 97224 655 G4
SW Summerfield Dr
9400 TGRD 97224 655 D7
SW Summerfield Ln
15400 TGRD 97224 655 E7
SE Summerfield Lp
14000 CmsC 97236 658 C5
Summerfield St
- MCMV 97128 770 H2
SE Summerfield Wy
14200 CmsC 97236 658 C5
14300 HPYV 97236 658 C5
SW Summer Lake Dr
10600 BRTN 97008 655 B2
10600 TGRD 97223 655 B2
Summerlinn Dr
3100 WLIN 97068 716 G1
Summerlinn Wy
5100 WLIN 97068 716 G1
NE Summerplace Dr
15000 PTLD 97230 598 D4
Summer Run Dr
4700 WLIN 97068 686 J7
SE Summers Ct
14000 CmsC 97015 657 H5
SE Summers Ln
- CmsC 97015 657 J6
11800 CmsC 97015 658 A6
SE Summertime Dr
19300 CmsC 97045 692 G5
SW Summerton Av
7800 WNVL 97070 715 F6
SW Summerview Ct
12600 WasC 97224 655 C6
SW Summerview Dr
14900 WasC 97224 655 B6
15000 TGRD 97224 655 B6
SW Summerville Av
10600 MthC 97219 656 G2
NW Summerwood Dr
900 MCMV 97128 770 G4
SW Summerwood Dr
13200 TGRD 97223 655 A3
Summer Woods
6000 LKOW 97035 685 H1
NW Summit Av
- PTLD 97231 565 E5
800 PTLD 97210 596 C4
Summit Ct
2100 LKOW 97034 656 C7
NW Summit Ct
1200 PTLD 97210 596 A3
SE Summit Ct
14400 CmsC 97015 657 J6
Summit Dr
- MthC 97231 535 B5
1900 LKOW 97034 656 C7
2700 LKOW 97035 656 C7
NW Summit Dr
1200 ClkC 98665 506 E4
SE Summit Dr
14200 CmsC 97015 657 J6
SW Summit Dr
2700 PTLD 97201 626 C1
Summit Pl
2700 WLIN 97068 687 A6
Summit St
700 ORCY 97045 717 C2
4800 WLIN 97068 687 A5
5500 WLIN 97068 686 J5
SW Summit St
200 HBRO 97123 593 B6
Summit Ridge Ct
10 LKOW 97035 656 A3
NE Summit Ridge Dr
2300 ClkC 98686 506 J1
S Summit Ridge Ln
21100 CmsC 97045 719 B6
SW Summit Ridge St
- WasC 97224 655 A7
12700 TGRD 97224 655 A7
SE Summit Rock Wy
15700 DAMA 97009 688 E1
SW Summit View Ct
700 WasC 97225 595 G7

Summit View Dr
58800 ClbC 97051 414 H2
58800 STHN 97051 414 H2
NW Summitview Dr
- MthC 97229 595 H3
- PTLD 97229 595 H3
SW Summit View Dr
700 WasC 97225 595 G7
N Sumner St
10 PTLD 97211 566 F7
2000 PTLD 97217 566 D7
NE Sumner St
10 PTLD 97217 566 G7
200 CMAS 98607 569 G4
400 PTLD 97211 566 H7
3700 PTLD 97211 567 C7
5700 PTLD 97218 567 D7
8700 PTLD 97220 567 G7
11500 PTLD 97220 568 A7
SE Sumner St
600 CMAS 98607 569 G5
SE Sun Av
16200 CmsC 97267 687 B1
Sun Cir
19600 WLIN 97068 686 G4
SW Sun Pl
8600 WNVL 97070 715 E3
NW Sunbird Ter
- HBRO 97006 594 C5
- WasC 97006 594 C5
Sunbreak Ln
3000 CmsC 97068 686 H7
3000 WLIN 97068 686 H7
Sunbrook Dr
5800 LKOW 97035 655 H4
NE Sunburst Av
3000 HBRO 97124 593 C1
3300 WasC 97124 593 C1
SE Sunburst Ln
- HPYV 97236 658 A2
Sunburst Ter
1900 WLIN 97068 686 G4
SE Sunburst Wy
10300 HPYV 97236 658 A2
Suncreek Dr
5500 LKOW 97035 655 H5
Suncrest Av
19000 WLIN 97068 686 G3
19200 CmsC 97068 686 G3
NE Suncrest Ct
12000 VCVR 98684 538 A6
Suncrest Dr
19600 WLIN 97068 686 G4
20600 CmsC 97068 686 G4
SE Sun Crest Dr
9200 CmsC 97236 627 G7
9200 PTLD 97236 627 G7
9400 CmsC 97236 657 G1
SW Suncrest Ln
19100 WasC 97007 624 D7
Sundae Ln
- YmhC 97114 771 J4
NE Sundance Ct
600 HBRO 97124 593 C1
NW Sunday Dr
26300 WasC 97124 533 G7
SW Sunde Ct
20600 TLTN 97062 685 E5
Sundeleaf Dr
13900 LKOW 97034 656 C5
NE Sunderland Av
9100 PTLD 97211 567 A3
NW Sunderland Dr
19600 HBRO 97124 594 D3
Sundew Ct
4200 LKOW 97035 656 A5
SW Sundew Dr
15800 WasC 97223 654 H5
SW Sundial Av
3200 GSHM 97030 599 E6
3200 TDLE 97060 599 E6
SE Sundial Ct
5800 MWKE 97222 657 D3
SW Sundial Ct
2200 TDLE 97060 599 C6
NE Sundial Rd
5100 MthC 97060 599 E1
5100 TDLE 97060 599 E1
NW Sundial Rd
800 TDLE 97060 599 E2
1600 MthC 97060 599 E2
Sundown Ct
17800 LKOW 97034 686 C2
NE Sundown Ct
2000 HBRO 97124 593 B2
NW Sundown Ln
1800 PTLD 97229 595 F3
NW Sundown Wy
200 WasC 97229 595 F5
SW Sundrop Pl
20600 SRWD 97140 684 F5
SE Sunflower Ct
17200 HBRO 97123 623 D1
Sunflower St
- MCMV 97128 770 J2
300 YmhC 97128 770 J2
Sun Haven Ter
12300 ORCY 97045 717 B4
Sunlite Ct
18600 GLDS 97027 687 D3
SE Sun Meadow Ct
18100 CmsC 97267 687 C2
SE Sun Meadow Ter
5500 CmsC 97267 687 C2
Sunningdale Ct
1100 LKOW 97034 656 E5
NW Sunningdale Dr
11900 WasC 97229 595 B3
Sunningdale Rd
1000 LKOW 97034 656 E5
NW Sunningdale St
15600 WasC 97006 594 J4
Sunny Ln
11000 ORCY 97045 717 A3
SE Sunny Wy
11700 HPYV 97236 658 A4
SE Sunnybrook Blvd
- CmsC 97236 657 J4
8200 CmsC 97015 657 G5
8200 CmsC 97222 657 F4
SE Sunnybrook Dr
5700 HBRO 97123 593 J6
SE Sunnycreek Ln
11700 CmsC 97015 657 J5
11700 CmsC 97015 658 A5

NE Sunnycrest Rd
19400 YmhC 97132 712 J7
20000 YmhC 97115 712 G7
23100 YmhC 97115 713 A7
Sunnycrest Wy
- YmhC 97132 713 A7
Sunny Hill Dr
500 CmsC 97034 686 D1
500 LKOW 97034 686 D1
Sunny Hill Ln
33500 ClbC 97051 414 F2
SW Sunny Hill Ln
10600 WasC 97005 625 D2
10600 WasC 97225 625 D2
11000 BRTN 97005 625 D2
Sunnyridge Ct
19200 CmsC 97045 716 J4
19200 ORCY 97045 716 J4
NE Sunnyside Dr
8500 ClkC 98662 507 F5
SE Sunnyside Dr
7500 CmsC 97222 657 E4
8000 CmsC 97236 657 E4
SW Sunnyside Dr
10500 WNVL 97070 745 C1
Sunnyside Pl
- CmsC 97015 658 A5
SE Sunnyside Rd
8200 CmsC 97015 657 F4
8200 CmsC 97222 657 F4
8200 CmsC 97236 657 F4
11700 CmsC 97236 658 B5
13700 CmsC 97015 658 C5
14200 HPYV 97236 658 C5
16200 HPYV 97009 658 F5
16200 HPYV 97015 658 F5
17300 CmsC 97009 658 F5
17300 DAMA 97009 658 F5
SE Sunny Slope Rd
1900 CmsC 97267 656 J7
SE Sunnyview Ct
13600 CmsC 97015 658 A5
SE Sunnyview Dr
12700 CmsC 97015 658 B5
Sunny Vista Ct NE
20800 DNLD 97020 774 F5
NW Sunnywood Ct
800 MCMV 97128 770 G5
SE Sunpark Ct
14900 VCVR 98683 568 C1
SE Sunpark Dr
15000 VCVR 98683 568 C1
E Sunrae Dr
19900 CmsC 97055 693 E6
Sunray Cir
2000 WLIN 97068 686 G4
Sunray Ct
1900 WLIN 97068 686 G4
SE Sunray Dr
27600 CmsC 97009 659 H2
SW Sunridge Ct
6500 WasC 97062 715 G2
SE Sunridge Ln
16500 CmsC 97267 687 E1
SW Sunrise Cir
2000 TDLE 97060 599 G6
Sunrise Ct
16300 LKOW 97035 656 A7
NW Sunrise Ct
1100 MCMV 97128 770 E4
SE Sunrise Ct
15200 CmsC 97267 657 F7
Sunrise Dr
59900 STHN 97051 385 A7
SE Sunrise Dr
3500 ClkC 98607 568 H3
3500 VCVR 98607 568 H3
NE Sunrise Ln
2300 HBRO 97124 593 E3
NW Sunrise Ln
9700 PTLD 97229 595 E1
S Sunrise Ln
17300 CmsC 97004 748 C2
SW Sunrise Ln
- TGRD 97223 654 H5
- WasC 97223 654 H5
- WasC 97224 654 H5
14600 TGRD 97224 654 H5
SE Sunrise St
- PTLD 97236 628 D5
Sunrise Wy
19100 ORCY 97045 717 B4
Sunrise Acres
- ClkC 98682 508 A6
SE Sunrunner Ct
12700 HPYV 97236 658 D5
Sunset Av
1600 WLIN 97068 687 A7
2700 CmsC 97068 686 J7
2700 WLIN 97068 686 J7
SE Sunset Av
4600 CmsC 97267 687 B3
Sunset Blvd
100 STHN 97051 385 B7
100 STHN 97051 415 B1
SW Sunset Blvd
- SRWD 97140 684 E7
- WasC 97140 684 E7
1500 PTLD 97239 626 C3
14600 SRWD 97140 714 F1
NW Sunset Cir
3900 PTLD 97229 595 E1
Sunset Ct
500 NWBG 97132 713 C4
1800 WLIN 97068 687 A7
NW Sunset Ct
2600 CMAS 98607 569 C2
SE Sunset Ct
3800 CmsC 97267 657 A7
SW Sunset Ct
15800 SRWD 97140 714 G1
Sunset Dr
100 NWBG 97132 713 C4
2200 FTGV 97116 591 J3
2500 WasC 97116 591 J3
4000 LKOW 97035 656 A7
NW Sunset Dr
- FTGV 97116 591 J2
- WasC 97116 591 J2
- WasC 97116 592 A2
32800 SPSE 97056 444 D6
SW Sunset Dr
600 MCMV 97128 770 F6
2100 PTLD 97239 626 C4
5000 CmsC 97035 655 J7

Portland Street Index

STREET
Block City ZIP Map# Grid

SW Sunset Dr
5000 LKOW 97035 655 J7
Sunset Hwy
- BRTN - 594 G3
- BRTN - 595 A5
- BRTN - 625 F1
- HBRO - 563 J6
- HBRO - 564 A7
- HBRO - 594 F3
- MthC - 595 H7
- MthC - 596 A7
- NPNS - 562 J1
- NPNS - 563 D3
- PTLD - 595 H7
- PTLD - 596 B7
- PTLD - 626 B1
- WasC - 562 J1
- WasC - 563 D3
- WasC - 594 G3
- WasC - 595 A5
- WasC 97106 532 D5
- WasC 97113 532 E6
- WasC 97133 532 H7
Sunset Hwy US-26
- BRTN - 594 G3
- BRTN - 595 A5
- BRTN - 625 F1
- HBRO - 563 J6
- HBRO - 564 A7
- HBRO - 594 E2
- MthC - 595 H7
- MthC - 596 A7
- NPNS - 562 J1
- NPNS - 563 D3
- PTLD - 595 H7
- PTLD - 596 B7
- PTLD - 626 B1
- WasC - 562 J1
- WasC - 563 E4
- WasC - 594 E2
- WasC - 595 B6
- WasC 97106 532 D5
- WasC 97113 532 E6
- WasC 97133 532 H7
NW Sunset Hwy
39500 WasC 97106 532 A3
39700 WasC 97106 531 G1
NW Sunset Hwy SR-47
45000 WasC 97106 531 F1
NW Sunset Hwy US-26
39500 WasC 97106 532 A3
39700 WasC 97106 531 G1
NW Sunset Ln
4900 VCVR 98663 536 E1
S Sunset Ln
700 RDGF 98642 446 A1
NE Sunset Lp
34200 SPSE 97056 474 G1
Sunset Pl
10 STHN 97051 385 B7
Sunset St
500 ORCY 97045 717 B2
37600 SNDY 97055 690 H3
NE Sunset St
100 BNKS 97106 531 J5
300 WasC 97106 531 J5
Sunset Ter
- VCVR 98660 536 F3
NE Sunset Wy
8700 ClkC 98662 507 G3
SW Sunset Wy
600 TDLE 97060 599 F4
NE Sunset Falls Rd
28200 ClkC 98604 419 J6
28200 ClkC 98675 419 J6
Sunset Ridge Dr
- ClkC 98671 570 E5
400 WHGL 98671 570 E5
Sunset Springs Dr
19300 CmsC 97045 717 B4
19300 ORCY 97045 717 B5
SE Sunset View Ct
10600 HPYV 97236 657 H2
SE Sunset View Rd
34700 ClkC 98671 570 F5
34700 WHGL 98671 570 F5
NW Sunset View Ter
3500 WasC 97229 595 D2
SE Sunshadow St
13900 HPYV 97236 658 C1
SW Sunshine Ct
9600 BRTN 97005 625 E5
9600 BRTN 97008 625 E5
S Sunshine Ln
100 CmsC 97068 686 E4
SE Sunshine Valley Rd
24200 CmsC 97009 659 D3
24200 DAMA 97009 659 D2
SE Sunsprite Ct
13100 HPYV 97236 658 B3
SW Sunstead Ln
8900 WasC 97225 625 F3
SW Sunstone Lp
8300 BRTN 97007 624 H7
Suntree Ln
4900 LKOW 97035 655 J4
4900 LKOW 97035 656 C5
Sunview Ln
- ClkC 97056 444 E5
SE Sunview Ln
28900 CmsC 97023 720 C7
29400 CmsC 97023 750 C1
29400 ECDA 97023 750 C1
Sunwood Ct
3500 LKOW 97035 656 B7
N Superior St
5900 PTLD 97203 566 A4
NW Supreme Ct
10800 WasC 97229 595 D2
SE Surface Rd
34700 CmsC 97023 750 F6
SW Surrey Ct
14700 WasC 97006 594 J7
Surrey Ln
2600 WLIN 97068 686 H4
SW Surrey St
14800 WasC 97006 594 J6
SW Susan Ln
1400 MCMV 97128 770 F6
21400 WasC 97006 594 B7
Susan Marie
- WasC 97007 624 F4
NW Susbauer Rd
1200 CNLS 97113 592 G2
1200 WasC 97113 592 G2

NW Susbauer Rd
2600 WasC 97124 592 G2
3600 WasC 97113 562 G6
3600 WasC 97124 562 G6
SW Susquehanna Dr
10200 TLTN 97062 685 D5
NW Sussex Av
- PTLD 97210 596 A2
SE Sussex Ct
1600 HBRO 97123 593 E6
Sussex St
3900 WLIN 97068 686 J7
3900 WLIN 97068 687 A7
3900 WLIN 97068 716 J1
SW Sussex St
6500 BRTN 97008 625 B5
SE Suter Av
22800 CmsC 97022 720 A1
SW Sutherland Wy
200 WasC 97006 594 C5
N Suttle Rd
3600 PTLD 97203 536 C7
3600 PTLD 97217 536 C7
SE Suttle Rd
26400 CmsC 97022 689 F7
NE Suttle St
400 PTLD 97211 566 H2
SW Sutton Pl
9300 WasC 97223 655 F1
NW Suzanna Ct
1800 MCMV 97128 770 E5
SW Suzanne Ct
11300 TGRD 97223 655 C3
NW Svea Dr
25100 WasC 97124 533 H6
SE Swain Av
2200 CmsC 97267 656 J7
2800 CmsC 97267 657 A7
SE Swain Ct
15400 CmsC 97267 657 A7
Swan Av
15900 ORCY 97045 687 F6
SW Swan Ct
15200 BRTN 97007 654 H2
Swan St
16700 CmsC 97045 687 F7
S Swan St
15700 CmsC 97045 687 F5
15700 ORCY 97045 687 F5
SW Swank Rd
16200 WasC 97140 653 J7
16200 WasC 97140 683 J1
S Swansea Ln
16000 CmsC 97004 747 J3
16000 CmsC 97004 748 A3
SW Swanstrom Dr
17900 SRWD 97140 684 D6
18400 WasC 97140 684 E6
SW Sweek Dr
8900 TLTN 97062 685 E3
SW Sweeney Pl
12000 TGRD 97223 655 C4
SW Sweeney St
200 PTLD 97239 626 F4
4700 PTLD 97221 626 A4
5000 PTLD 97221 625 J4
SE Sweetbay St
1400 HBRO 97123 623 D1
S Sweetbriar Cir
21600 CmsC 97068 686 F6
SE Sweetbriar Ct
4200 TDLE 97060 629 G1
SW Sweetbriar Ct
6100 MthC 97221 625 H2
SW Sweetbriar Dr
3700 PTLD 97221 626 B2
SE Sweetbriar Ln
100 TDLE 97060 599 G7
900 TDLE 97060 629 G1
S Sweetbriar Rd
19600 CmsC 97068 686 F4
SE Sweetbriar Rd
900 TDLE 97060 629 H1
6900 MthC 97060 629 G1
SW Sweetbriar St
5500 MthC 97221 625 J2
SW Sweet Cider Ln
16700 YmhC 97114 772 B6
NW Sweetgale Ct
15400 WasC 97229 564 H5
NW Sweetgale Ln
15100 WasC 97229 564 J6
SW Sweet Gum Ct
19700 WasC 97007 624 D3
SE Sweetgum Wy
10300 CmsC 97236 657 H4
SE Sweet Meadow Ln
6700 HBRO 97123 624 A1
SE Sweet Valentine Dr
15600 HPYV 97236 658 D5
SE Sweetwater Ln
24600 CmsC 97022 720 A3
24800 CmsC 97022 719 J3
S Sweetwood Ln
20300 CmsC 97045 718 A7
SW Swendon Lp
11700 TGRD 97223 655 A3
N Swenson St
8100 PTLD 97203 565 H2
S Swiegle Av
100 MOLA 97038 837 E2
SW Swift Av
12100 BRTN 97007 654 H3
N Swift Ct
10400 PTLD 97203 565 H1
N Swift St
6600 PTLD 97203 566 A2
6800 PTLD 97203 565 J2
N Swift Wy
- PTLD 97203 565 H1
Swift Shore Cir
1100 WLIN 97068 716 F2
Swiftshore Dr
25100 WLIN 97068 716 F2
NW Swire Ln
20700 HBRO 97006 594 C4
Swordfern Ct
13700 ORCY 97045 717 E1
SW Swordfern Ln
- SRWD 97140 714 D1
- WasC 97140 714 E1
Syblon Ln
39800 SNDY 97055 691 A4
Sycamore
- WasC 97006 594 D5

SW Sycamore Av
19300 CmsC 97035 685 J4
19300 LKOW 97035 685 J4
19300 RVGR 97035 685 J4
Sycamore Ct
2700 FTGV 97116 591 G3
SW Sycamore Pl
11300 TGRD 97223 655 C3
S Sycamore St
900 CNBY 97013 746 E7
1100 CNBY 97013 776 E1
SE Sycamore St
- HBRO 97123 593 H5
SE Sydney Ln
12300 HPYV 97236 658 A3
NW Sydney St
21100 HBRO 97006 594 B4
Sykes Rd
2500 STHN 97051 415 A1
2700 STHN 97051 414 J1
32900 ClbC 97051 414 E1
NW Sylvan Av
- PTLD 97231 565 F5
S Sylvan Av
18700 CmsC 97023 719 B5
19300 CmsC 97045 719 B5
Sylvan Ct
16600 LKOW 97034 656 D7
16600 LKOW 97034 686 D1
SW Sylvan Ct
7100 BRTN 97225 625 G1
16300 TGRD 97224 685 D1
E Sylvan Dr
52200 CmsC 97055 692 E6
Sylvan Ln
1800 WLIN 97068 686 G3
NE Sylvan Ter
11000 ClkC 98686 506 J2
SE Sylvan Wy
27800 CmsC 97009 659 H6
NW Sylvania Ct
17700 WasC 97229 564 F7
SW Sylvania Ct
12000 PTLD 97219 656 C3
NW Sylvania Ln
17900 WasC 97229 564 F7
SW Sylvania Ter
2600 PTLD 97219 656 C3
NE Sylvan View Dr
10600 YmhC 97115 742 E1
NW Sylvia Ln
48100 WasC 97116 591 B3
48100 WasC 97117 591 A3
N Syracuse St
5200 PTLD 97203 566 A4
8600 PTLD 97203 565 G2
S Syth Rd
19500 CmsC 97023 719 B6
19500 CmsC 97045 719 B6

T

T Cir
3700 WHGL 98671 570 D4
T St
2400 VCVR 98661 536 J3
2400 VCVR 98663 536 J3
W T St
600 WHGL 98671 569 H4
N T-5 Access Rd
- PTLD 97203 535 F3
SW Tachi Ct
8600 TLTN 97062 685 E7
Tack Ct
6200 WLIN 97068 686 H5
SE Tacoma St
2600 PTLD 97202 626 J6
2600 PTLD 97202 627 A6
Tad Pl
20000 ORCY 97045 717 G6
NW Taennler Ct
15400 WasC 97229 564 H6
N Taft Av
9500 PTLD 97203 566 A3
SW Taft Ct
16400 BRTN 97007 624 G5
Taft St
- CLTN 97111 741 A1
SW Taft St
600 MCMV 97128 770 G7
W Taft St
10 CLTN 97111 741 A1
400 MCMV 97128 770 G7
SE Taggart Ct
5200 PTLD 97206 627 C1
15900 PTLD 97236 628 E2
SE Taggart St
400 PTLD 97202 626 G1
2800 PTLD 97202 627 A1
6700 PTLD 97206 627 E1
9100 PTLD 97266 627 G2
12500 PTLD 97236 628 B2
Tahoma Ct
300 CBAC 97018 385 C2
Tahoma St
3200 CBAC 97018 385 B1
S Tahyee Rd
21000 CmsC 97045 747 E2
SW Takena Ct
12800 TGRD 97224 655 A6
18500 WasC 97006 624 G1
NW Talamore Ter
3500 WasC 97229 595 B2
SW Talawa Ct
9100 TLTN 97062 685 G6
Talawa Dr
14300 ORCY 97045 717 F6
SW Talawa Dr
8600 TLTN 97062 685 E6
SE Talbert Dr
9700 CmsC 97015 657 H5
SW Talbot Pl
2400 PTLD 97201 626 C1
SW Talbot Rd
2600 PTLD 97201 626 C1
2700 PTLD 97239 626 C1
3400 PTLD 97221 626 B1
SW Talbot Ter
2800 PTLD 97239 626 B1
SW Talisha Ln
- CmsC 97062 685 H7
Talisman Ln
2800 FTGV 97116 591 G3
2800 WasC 97116 591 G3

NW Talkingstick Wy
16500 WasC 97006 594 G1
SW Tallac Wy
16800 WasC 97007 624 G6
SE Tallina Dr
15800 DAMA 97009 688 E2
W Tall Oaks Ct
1100 MCMV 97128 770 G6
SW Tall Oaks Dr
1000 MCMV 97128 770 G6
SW Tall Tree Pl
17200 WasC 97007 624 F7
SW Tallwood Ct
11500 TGRD 97223 655 C4
SW Tallwood Dr
11500 TGRD 97223 654 J3
11500 TGRD 97223 655 C4
SW Talon Ln
13500 TGRD 97223 655 A5
NW Talon Ter
3500 WasC 97229 595 C2
SE Talons Rd
25300 CmsC 97022 719 J3
25300 CmsC 97022 720 A3
SE Talton Av
1400 VCVR 98683 568 B1
SW Talus Ct
15700 BRTN 97007 654 H1
SW Talus Pl
15800 BRTN 97007 654 G1
SW Talus Wy
15500 BRTN 97007 654 H1
SE Talwood Ln
16200 CmsC 97267 687 C1
SE Tamango St
1000 HBRO 97123 593 D6
Tamara Av
17800 CmsC 97035 685 J2
17800 LKOW 97035 685 J2
NE Tamara Ln
1000 PTLD 97220 597 G5
SE Tamarack Av
2100 PTLD 97214 626 H1
2400 PTLD 97202 626 J1
Tamarack Ct
1800 FTGV 97116 592 C5
NE Tamarack Ct
14600 VCVR 98684 538 C5
SE Tamarack Ct
7200 CmsC 97267 657 E6
SW Tamarack Ct
600 MCMV 97128 770 D6
Tamarack Dr
59700 STHN 97051 385 A7
Tamarack Ln
3800 LKOW 97035 656 A5
SW Tamarack St
1600 MCMV 97128 770 E6
2100 YmhC 97128 770 E6
Tamarack Wy
1700 FTGV 97116 592 C5
NW Tamarack Wy
18300 WasC 97229 564 E7
SE Tamarack Wy
14300 CmsC 97267 657 E6
Tamarisk Dr
1300 WLIN 97068 686 F7
NW Tamarron Pl
5300 WasC 97229 564 D7
Tamaway Dr
18200 LKOW 97034 686 B3
SW Tamaway Ln
13600 TGRD 97223 655 A5
SE Tambara Ct
5500 MWKE 97222 657 C1
SW Tamera Ln
13000 TGRD 97223 655 A3
SW Tami Lp
- WNVL 97070 715 G7
SW Tammy Ct
20300 WasC 97007 624 C2
SE Tamora Av
- HBRO 97123 593 D6
NW Tam-O-Shanter Wy
4200 WasC 97229 594 H1
SE Tampa St
600 CMAS 98607 569 G5
Tampa Wy
400 VCVR 98664 537 F7
SE Tanager Cir
1700 HBRO 97123 623 E1
Tanager Dr
15400 CmsC 97035 655 H7
SW Tanager Ter
11000 BRTN 97007 654 G2
NW Tanasbourne Dr
18500 HBRO 97006 594 E3
20000 HBRO 97124 594 D2
Tanasbourne Ter
- HBRO 97124 594 E3
NW Tanasbrook Cir
- BRTN 97006 594 F3
- HBRO 97006 594 F3
NW Tanasbrook Ct
1500 WasC 97006 594 G4
NW Tanasbrook Dr
17800 WasC 97006 594 F4
18200 BRTN 97006 594 E4
18300 HBRO 97006 594 E4
NE Tandem Wy
10 HBRO 97124 593 H2
SW Tangela Ct
9300 TGRD 97223 655 E3
SW Tangela St
9300 TGRD 97223 655 F3
NE Tangen Rd
13500 YmhC 97132 712 J4
SW Tangent St
800 PTLD 97201 626 D3
NE Tanger Dr
2600 MCMV 97128 771 B6
NE Tangleberry Pl
3000 FRVW 97024 599 B3
SW Tanglewood Cir
600 MCMV 97128 770 G5
Tanglewood Dr
10 LKOW 97035 656 B4
NE Tanglewood Dr
9700 VCVR 98664 537 G6
SW Tanner Ln
15000 WasC 97006 594 J5
NW Tanner St
- CMAS 98607 569 C3
Tanner Creek Ln
2000 WLIN 97068 716 J1

Tannler Dr
2200 WLIN 97068 686 H7
2200 WLIN 97068 716 H1
SW Tanoak Ct
13700 TGRD 97223 655 A5
SW Tanoak Ln
9000 TLTN 97062 685 E3
SW Tapadera St
12800 BRTN 97008 625 A7
SW Taposa Ct
4800 TLTN 97062 685 J5
SW Taposa Pl
19700 TLTN 97062 685 J5
SE Tapp Rd
43200 CmsC 97055 691 E3
Tara Ct
1500 FTGV 97116 591 H4
SW Tara Ct
5600 PTLD 97221 625 J4
Tara Pl
15700 CmsC 97035 655 J6
15700 LKOW 97035 655 J6
NW Tara St
17900 BRTN 97006 594 F5
17900 WasC 97006 594 F5
SE Tara Lara Ln
20300 CmsC 97022 690 A5
SW Taralynn Av
5700 BRTN 97005 625 B4
5900 BRTN 97008 625 B4
SW Taralynn Pl
5800 BRTN 97005 625 B4
SW Tara Meadows Ct
18500 WasC 97007 624 E4
SE Tarbell Av
2400 CmsC 97267 686 J1
Tarbell Rd
33700 ClbC 97053 444 F1
33700 ClbC 97056 444 F2
NW Targhee Pl
1600 HBRO 97006 594 E4
SW Tarleton Ct
13500 WasC 97224 655 A6
SW Tarlow Ct
4500 PTLD 97221 626 A3
SE Tarnahan Ct
13900 HPYV 97236 658 C1
SE Tarnahan Dr
9100 HPYV 97236 658 C1
SW Tarpan Ct
10000 BRTN 97008 655 B1
SW Tarpan Dr
10100 BRTN 97008 655 B2
S Tarrybrooke Cir
200 CNLS 97113 592 D5
S Tarrybrooke Ct
300 CNLS 97113 592 D5
S Tarrybrooke Dr
200 CNLS 97113 592 D5
S Tarrybrooke Pl
500 CNLS 97113 592 C5
SE Taryn Ct
14700 HPYV 97236 658 C4
NW Tatum Ranch Pl
4500 WasC 97006 594 F3
SW Tauchmann St
9200 WNVL 97070 745 D2
SW Taurus Pl
6700 WasC 97007 624 D5
Taurus St
200 MOLA 97038 807 E7
Taverner Dr
1500 RDGF 98642 446 A1
SW Tawasa Ct
10300 TLTN 97062 685 C3
E Tawney Ln
68800 CmsC 97067 724 C7
SE Tawny Dr
12000 CmsC 97015 658 A5
Taylor Ct
1900 WLIN 97068 716 G1
SE Taylor Ct
8000 PTLD 97215 597 F7
8000 PTLD 97216 597 F7
14100 PTLD 97233 598 C7
21100 GSHM 97030 599 A7
SW Taylor Ct
5700 PTLD 97221 595 J6
12000 WasC 97225 595 C6
22700 SRWD 97140 684 H7
Taylor Dr
2300 CmsC 97068 686 G6
2300 WLIN 97068 686 G6
2300 WLIN 97068 716 G1
Taylor Ln
13900 ORCY 97045 687 E5
SW Taylor Ln
15700 WasC 97140 684 G1
15700 WasC 97224 654 G7
15700 WasC 97224 684 G1
Taylor St
600 ORCY 97045 717 D1
1400 ORCY 97045 687 D7
34500 ClbC 97051 414 H2
34500 ClbC 97053 414 H2
SE Taylor St
10 PTLD 97214 596 H7
2700 PTLD 97214 597 A7
4100 PTLD 97215 597 B7
9200 PTLD 97216 597 G7
11500 PTLD 97216 598 A7
15800 PTLD 97233 598 E7
SW Taylor St
10 PTLD 97204 596 F6
2100 PTLD 97205 596 D5
5700 MthC 97221 595 J6
5700 PTLD 97221 595 J6
9000 WasC 97225 595 E6
10400 BRTN 97225 595 D6
52200 ClbC 97056 474 D1
52200 SPSE 97056 474 D1
W Taylor St
100 CLTN 97111 741 A1
S Taylor Ter
16800 CmsC 97045 688 B4
Taylor Wy
2700 FTGV 97116 592 A6
SW Taylors Dr
22000 TLTN 97062 685 D7
SW Taylors Ln
9900 TLTN 97062 685 D6
9900 WasC 97062 685 D6
Taylors Crest Ct
14100 LKOW 97035 656 A5

Taylors Crest Ln
13800 LKOW 97035 656 A5
SW Taylors Ferry Ct
1300 PTLD 97219 626 D7
SW Taylors Ferry Rd
- PTLD 97219 656 D3
200 PTLD 97219 626 C7
5000 PTLD 97219 655 J1
6200 TGRD 97219 655 G1
6200 TGRD 97223 655 G1
6200 WasC 97223 655 G1
7800 WasC 97223 625 F7
SW T-Bird Dr
28300 WNVL 97070 715 E6
Teak
- CmsC 97015 657 J7
SE Teakwood Dr
52200 ClbC 97056 474 G1
52200 SPSE 97056 474 G1
NW Teakwood Pl
3900 WasC 97229 595 B2
N Teakwood St
1800 CNBY 97013 746 E4
2100 CmsC 97013 746 E4
S Teakwood St
- CmsC 97013 776 E1
- CNBY 97013 776 E1
900 CNBY 97013 746 E7
SE Teakwood St
4500 HBRO 97123 623 H1
SW Teal Blvd
14500 BRTN 97007 654 H2
14500 BRTN 97008 654 J2
SE Teal Ct
16400 DAMA 97009 688 D1
SE Teal Dr
- MthC 97080 629 H6
2900 GSHM 97080 629 H6
SW Teal Dr
14000 BRTN 97008 654 J2
14400 BRTN 97007 654 J2
Teal Ln NE
11600 MmC 97002 744 H5
S Team Ct
18200 CmsC 97045 718 C3
SW Tea Party Cir
6400 BRTN 97008 625 C5
SE Tear Ln
30800 CmsC 97022 690 B6
SW Tearose Wy
12900 WasC 97223 654 G4
S Teasel Creek Rd
14900 CmsC 97038 837 F7
SE Tech Center Dr
- VCVR 98683 568 E1
600 VCVR 98683 538 E7
600 VCVR 98684 538 F7
SW Tech Center Dr
7200 TGRD 97223 655 G5
SE Tech Center Pl
1400 VCVR 98683 568 E1
SW Teddi Rose Ct
19100 WasC 97006 624 D1
SE Teddy Ln
1300 CmsC 97267 656 H6
SE Teddy Bear Ln
37100 CmsC 97023 750 G4
NW Tee Ct
15400 WasC 97229 594 H2
SE Teeples Ln
31800 CmsC 97023 750 D3
SW Tegart Av
1400 GSHM 97080 628 H4
3300 MthC 97080 628 H6
Telford Rd
100 ORCY 97045 717 B2
SE Telford Rd
6700 MthC 97080 629 F7
8100 DAMA 97009 659 G1
8100 MthC 97080 659 G1
8900 CmsC 97009 659 G1
SW Telluride Ct
14900 BRTN 97007 624 H7
SW Telluride Ter
14900 BRTN 97007 624 J7
NW Telshire Dr
15800 WasC 97006 594 H2
NW Telshire Ln
15600 WasC 97006 594 H2
NW Telshire Ter
2900 WasC 97006 594 H2
Tempest Dr
3100 LKOW 97035 656 B5
SW Tempest Wy
16900 KNGC 97224 685 A1
SW Templar Pl
9200 BRTN 97008 655 C1
Temple Wy
- LKOW 97035 655 H5
S Tendril Ln
22700 CmsC 97068 686 F7
SE Ten Eyck Rd
- SNDY 97055 691 B3
15000 CmsC 97055 691 D1
SE Tenino Ct
4600 PTLD 97206 627 C7
9200 PTLD 97266 627 G7
9500 CmsC 97236 627 G7
9600 CmsC 97236 657 G1
SW Tenino Ct
20100 TLTN 97062 685 G5
SE Tenino Dr
4500 PTLD 97206 627 C7
SW Tenino Ln
7200 TLTN 97062 685 G5
SE Tenino St
500 PTLD 97202 626 J7
3600 PTLD 97202 627 B7
7200 PTLD 97206 627 E7
8900 PTLD 97266 627 G7
13700 PTLD 97236 628 B7
Tennessee Ln
6900 VCVR 98664 537 E6
SW Tennessee Ln
13800 BRTN 97008 625 D5
13900 BRTN 97008 624 J7
SW Tennessee Pl
14000 BRTN 97008 624 H1
NE Tenney Rd
800 ClkC 98685 476 H6
SW Tennis Ct
7800 WNVL 97070 715 F7
NE Tenny Creek Dr
9400 ClkC 98665 506 J3

NW Tennyson Ln
20700 HBRO 97006 594 C4
SW Tephra Ter
9400 BRTN 97007 654 H1
SW Tera Dr
800 MCMV 97128 770 G6
Teri Ln
- ORCY 97045 717 D4
SW Terlyn Ct
4200 PTLD 97221 626 A3
SW Terman Rd
- BRTN 97005 624 J1
13500 WasC 97005 625 A1
14000 WasC 97005 624 J1
Terminal
- PTLD 97209 596 F5
N Terminal Rd
8000 PTLD 97203 565 F1
NW Terminal St
2000 PTLD 97209 596 E3
SE Terra Cascade Dr
13200 CmsC 97236 658 B5
SE Terra Cascade Lp
13000 CmsC 97236 658 B5
Terrace Av
200 ORCY 97045 717 C1
Terrace Dr
10 VCVR 98661 537 B3
600 LKOW 97034 656 D7
5700 WLIN 97068 687 B6
E Terrace Dr
70300 CmsC 97049 724 E3
N Terrace Dr
3600 NWBG 97132 713 C4
3600 YmhC 97132 713 C3
SE Terrace Dr
14200 CmsC 97015 657 J6
SW Terrace Dr
1700 PTLD 97201 626 D1
1900 PTLD 97201 596 C7
N Terrace Ln
1100 CNBY 97013 746 D5
NW Terrace St
1700 ClkC 98685 506 E3
SE Terrace Trails Dr
7100 PTLD 97266 627 J6
SW Terrace Trails Dr
11500 TGRD 97223 655 C5
NW Terraceview Ct
8700 PTLD 97229 595 F3
E Terra Fern Dr
51400 CmsC 97055 692 D7
SE Terra Linda Ct
10000 HPYV 97236 657 J2
SW Terra Linda St
11300 WasC 97005 625 C1
SW Terrapin Dr
17200 SRWD 97140 684 F5
Terraplane Av
- ClkC 98686 507 E2
SW Terraview Dr
12600 WasC 97224 655 B6
12700 TGRD 97224 655 B6
Terra Vista Ct
4200 WLIN 97068 687 A3
Terrence Ln
1900 CmsC 97068 716 C2
SW Terreton Pl
8800 WasC 97223 625 F7
SW Terri Ct
6500 BRTN 97225 625 H4
6500 PTLD 97225 625 H4
SE Terri Wy
33800 ClbC 97056 474 F1
33800 SPSE 97056 474 F1
Terri Lee Mnr
- PTLD 97219 656 A1
Territorial Dr
5000 WLIN 97068 687 C7
NE Territorial Pl
2000 CmsC 97013 746 E4
2000 CNBY 97013 746 E4
E Territorial Rd
2300 CmsC 97013 746 F4
NE Territorial Rd
100 CNBY 97013 746 C4
1400 CmsC 97013 746 E4
NW Territorial Rd
400 CmsC 97013 746 B5
400 CNBY 97013 746 B5
S Territorial Rd
2500 CmsC 97013 746 F4
SE Territory Dr
14200 CmsC 97015 658 D6
Terry Av
18200 CmsC 97035 685 H2
SW Terry Av
18800 CmsC 97035 685 H3
18800 LKOW 97035 685 H3
19000 RVGR 97035 685 H3
NE Terry Cir
600 HBRO 97124 593 A1
Terry Ct
18200 CmsC 97035 685 H2
NE Terry Ct
600 HBRO 97124 593 C3
N Terry St
2300 PTLD 97217 566 D4
S Terry Michael Dr
18500 CmsC 97045 718 C4
S Terry Michael Ln
17200 CmsC 97045 718 C3
NE Terrys Ln
17500 YmhC 97132 712 D4
SW Terwilliger Blvd
- CmsC 97034 656 G5
2500 PTLD 97201 626 E1
4100 PTLD 97239 626 D3
6900 PTLD 97219 626 E7
9800 PTLD 97219 656 E1
11400 MthC 97219 656 F3
12700 LKOW 97034 656 F4
12700 LKOW 97219 656 F4
SW Terwilliger Pl
800 PTLD 97239 626 E5
10100 PTLD 97219 656 F1
SW Terwilliger Blvd Ext
11300 MthC 97219 656 F2
11300 PTLD 97219 656 F2
SW Tesoro Ct
20500 WasC 97006 594 E4
SE Tessa St
13000 PTLD 97233 628 B1
NW Testout Pl
- PTLD 97210 596 A4

STREET Block	City	ZIP	Map#	Grid
SW Teton Av				
18000	TLTN	97062	685	D5
SE Teton Dr				
7800	MthC	97080	630	A7
SW Teton Wy				
29300	WNVL	97070	715	C7
SW Teufel Hill Av				
13100	WasC	97007	654	C5
SW Tewkesbury Ct				
14200	WasC	97224	654	J7
SW Tewkesbury Dr				
14000	WasC	97224	654	J7
SW Texas Ct				
6000	PTLD	97219	625	H5
Texas Dr				
5700	VCVR	98661	537	C6
N Texas Dr				
100	VCVR	98661	537	C6
SW Texas St				
1200	PTLD	97219	626	D5
4900	PTLD	97219	625	J5
SW Thatcher Dr				
13100	BRTN	97008	655	A1
NW Thatcher Rd				
1300	FTGV	97116	591	G2
1300	WasC	97116	591	G2
3800	WasC	97116	561	F6
Thayer Ct				
14300	CmsC	97045	717	F4
Thayer Rd				
14300	CmsC	97045	717	G4
14300	ORCY	97045	717	G4
S Thayer Rd				
15800	CmsC	97045	717	J4
15800	CmsC	97045	718	A4
Thebes Av				
-	MthC	97231	535	A5
The Cove at Fisher's Lndg				
-	VCVR	98683	568	E2
The Greens Av				
-	NWBG	97132	743	G1
-	YmhC	97132	713	H7
-	YmhC	97132	743	G1
100	NWBG	97132	713	G7
The Grotto				
10	LKOW	97035	656	B5
SW Thelen Ln				
11800	PTLD	97219	656	B3
SE Thelma Cir				
14600	CmsC	97267	657	F6
The Montevideo				
-	GSHM	97230	598	G5
SW Theodore Wy				
16900	BRTN	97006	594	H6
SW Theresa Ct				
16000	BRTN	97007	624	G6
16000	WasC	97007	624	G6
Therese St				
-	SNDY	97055	691	B4
The Strand				
1900	CBAC	97018	385	C3
Thevor Ct				
18100	GLDS	97027	687	E2
SE Thiessen Ct				
15600	CmsC	97267	657	B7
SW Thiessen Pl				
3200	WasC	97006	624	E2
SE Thiessen Rd				
4500	CmsC	97267	657	D6
E Thimbleberry St				
71300	CmsC	97049	724	F4
Thimble Creek Dr				
19500	CmsC	97045	717	J5
SE Thistle Ct				
2400	HBRO	97123	623	E1
SW Thistlebrook Ct				
17300	DRHM	97224	685	E2
Thoma Rd				
13000	CmsC	97034	656	C4
13000	LKOW	97034	656	C4
NE Thomas Ct				
800	HBRO	97124	593	D2
NW Thomas Ct				
700	MCMV	97128	770	F5
SW Thomas Ct				
2200	GSHM	97080	628	G5
5800	MthC	97221	625	J2
SW Thomas Pl				
2300	GSHM	97080	628	G5
S Thomas Rd				
12000	CmsC	97038	837	C7
NE Thomas St				
1000	HBRO	97124	593	D3
SE Thomas St				
6400	CmsC	97222	657	D2
6400	MWKE	97222	657	D2
SW Thomas St				
-	PTLD	97239	626	D2
4900	MthC	97221	626	A2
4900	PTLD	97221	626	A2
5200	MthC	97221	625	J2
6000	PTLD	97221	625	H2
30200	WNVL	97070	745	E1
SW Thomas Wy				
2400	GSHM	97080	628	H5
Thomas Park Ct				
100	STHN	97051	415	A1
SE Thomas Smith Rd				
5000	CmsC	97267	687	C1
Thompson Av				
3500	VCVR	98660	536	E2
NE Thompson Ct				
14800	PTLD	97230	598	D3
SE Thompson Ct				
7500	CmsC	97222	657	E2
Thompson Ln				
-	DAYT	97114	772	B5
-	YmhC	97114	772	B5
SE Thompson Ln				
6100	YmhC	97114	772	C5
NE Thompson Rd				
13700	PTLD	97230	598	C3
20100	FRVW	97024	598	J4
20100	GSHM	97230	598	J4
20300	FRVW	97024	599	A4
34100	ClkC	98675	419	G1
NW Thompson Rd				
6100	MthC	97210	595	J3
6100	MthC	97229	595	G2
6100	PTLD	97210	595	J3
7000	PTLD	97229	595	G2
SE Thompson Rd				
1800	TDLE	97060	599	H5
7200	CmsC	97222	657	E3
Thompson St				
-	MthC	97231	534	F5
N Thompson St				
300	PTLD	97227	596	F3
NE Thompson St				
-	ClkC	98682	538	H1
10	PTLD	97227	596	G3
700	PTLD	97212	596	J3
2600	PTLD	97212	597	A3
5700	PTLD	97213	597	D3
8200	PTLD	97220	597	G3
11700	PTLD	97220	598	A4
14800	PTLD	97230	598	D4
16300	GSHM	97230	598	F3
S Thompson Gateway Rd				
22200	CmsC	97045	747	B4
NW Thomsen Ln				
1200	MCMV	97128	770	G4
Thomson Av				
-	ORCY	97045	687	D6
SE Thomson Ct				
12000	HPYV	97236	658	A4
SW Thomson Dr				
-	BRTN	97005	624	J2
-	WasC	97005	624	J2
-	WasC	97005	625	A1
SE Thorburn St				
6400	PTLD	97215	597	E6
SW Thorn St				
7900	TGRD	97223	655	F2
SE Thornapple Ln				
14500	CmsC	97267	657	D5
SE Thornbridge Dr				
15300	CmsC	97015	658	D6
NW Thorncroft Dr				
2000	HBRO	97006	594	E3
2000	HBRO	97124	594	E3
Thorne St				
2100	NWBG	97132	713	D5
2200	YmhC	97132	713	D5
Thornton Dr				
53000	SPSE	97056	444	E6
SE Thornton Dr				
14800	CmsC	97267	656	H7
SW Thornton Dr				
7500	WNVL	97070	715	F5
SW Thornwood Dr				
12200	TGRD	97224	655	B6
12200	WasC	97224	655	B6
NW Thornwood Ter				
-	WasC	97229	564	H4
SW Thoroughbred Pl				
8500	BRTN	97008	625	A7
SE Thorville Av				
15500	CmsC	97267	657	F7
SW Thrasher Wy				
15500	SRWD	97140	684	G6
SE Three Cedars St				
24200	DAMA	97009	659	D3
NE Three Creek Rd				
27600	ClkC	98675	419	H4
Three Mile Ln				
2100	MCMV	97128	771	B6
2100	YmhC	97128	771	A6
4100	YmhC	97114	771	G6
Three Mile Ln SR-18				
2100	MCMV	97128	771	B6
2100	YmhC	97128	771	A6
4100	YmhC	97114	771	G6
E Three Mile Ln				
4000	MCMV	97128	771	D6
E Three Mile Ln SR-18				
4000	MCMV	97128	771	D6
NE Three Mile Ln				
1800	MCMV	97128	770	J6
1800	YmhC	97128	770	J6
2000	MCMV	97128	771	A6
2000	YmhC	97128	771	A6
SE Three Mile Ln				
100	MCMV	97128	770	J5
200	YmhC	97128	770	J6
E Three Ring Rd				
23400	CmsC	97011	724	A2
23400	CmsC	97067	724	A2
SE Thrush Av				
2200	HBRO	97123	593	E7
Thrush Ct NE				
11600	MrnC	97002	744	J6
SW Thunder Ter				
11300	TGRD	97223	655	D3
NW Thunderbird Av				
5900	VCVR	98663	506	E7
SE Thunderbird Ct				
8500	CmsC	97015	687	F1
8500	CmsC	97267	687	F1
Thunderbird Dr NE				
-	MrnC	97002	774	J3
Thunderbird St				
100	MOLA	97038	807	E7
Thunderbird Vil				
-	VCVR	98661	537	B4
N Thunderbird Wy				
1100	PTLD	97227	596	F4
NW Thundercrest Dr				
4000	PTLD	97229	595	F1
SW Thunderegg Ct				
15300	BRTN	97007	654	H1
SW Thunderhead Wy				
12800	BRTN	97008	625	A6
Thunder Vista Ln				
4300	LKOW	97035	656	A4
SW Thurlow Dr				
9900	WasC	97225	625	E2
10000	WasC	97005	625	E2
Thurman St				
14100	ORCY	97045	687	F5
NW Thurman St				
1500	PTLD	97209	596	D4
2000	PTLD	97210	596	B3
SW Thurston Ln				
15200	TGRD	97224	655	F7
NE Thurston Wy				
4000	VCVR	98662	537	F1
5000	ClkC	98662	537	F1
SW Tia Ter				
17500	WasC	97007	624	F7
SE Tiara Dr				
13800	CmsC	97222	657	E6
13800	CmsC	97267	657	E6
SE Tibbetts Ct				
18200	GSHM	97030	628	G2
18200	GSHM	97236	628	G2
SE Tibbetts St				
1700	PTLD	97202	626	J1
2800	PTLD	97202	627	A2
4300	PTLD	97206	627	C2
10800	PTLD	97266	627	J2
11900	PTLD	97266	628	A2
15000	PTLD	97236	628	D2
17500	GSHM	97236	628	G2
18000	GSHM	97030	628	G2
S Tibbs Wy				
25500	CmsC	97023	750	B6
Tice Rd				
800	STHN	97051	414	J1
800	STHN	97051	415	A1
SW Tichner Dr				
2600	PTLD	97205	596	C5
2700	PTLD	97210	596	B5
SE Tickle Creek Ct				
18800	CmsC	97009	690	A5
SE Tickle Creek Rd				
-	CmsC	97055	690	B4
14700	CmsC	97009	659	J7
14700	CmsC	97009	689	J2
17200	CmsC	97009	690	B4
19500	CmsC	97022	690	B4
NW Tideland St				
1500	CMAS	98607	568	J3
SE Tidewater Pl				
1000	VCVR	98661	537	C7
SE Tidwells Wy				
15500	CmsC	97267	657	D7
SW Tiedeman Av				
11300	TGRD	97223	655	D3
SW Tierra del Mar Dr				
6800	BRTN	97007	624	J6
6800	BRTN	97008	624	J5
Tieton Ter				
2000	WLIN	97068	686	G4
SE Tiffany Ct				
8800	CmsC	97015	687	F2
NE Tiffany Dr				
12400	VCVR	98684	538	A5
NW Tiffany Ln				
100	HBRO	97124	593	B3
NE Tiffany St				
100	HBRO	97124	593	C3
SW Tigard Dr				
11500	TGRD	97223	655	C3
Tigard Plz				
200	TGRD	97223	655	F3
SW Tigard St				
9200	TGRD	97223	655	D3
Tigerlily Dr				
24800	CmsC	97049	724	E4
SW Tiger Lily Ln				
12400	BRTN	97008	625	B5
NW Tigon Ln				
-	WasC	97229	565	B7
SE Tikki Ct				
5800	CmsC	97267	657	C6
NE Tilbury St				
2000	MCMV	97128	771	A6
Tile Flat Rd				
-	WasC	97007	654	D4
SW Tile Flat Rd				
19000	WasC	97007	654	D4
21100	WasC	97123	654	D4
22400	WasC	97007	653	H2
22400	WasC	97123	653	H2
Tilia Ct NE				
13600	MrnC	97002	775	C2
NE Tillamook Ct				
13700	PTLD	97230	598	C4
16200	GSHM	97230	598	E4
SW Tillamook Ct				
20000	TLTN	97062	685	F5
NW Tillamook Dr				
17800	WasC	97229	594	F2
SW Tillamook Pl				
6200	BRTN	97007	624	G4
N Tillamook St				
10	PTLD	97212	596	G3
400	PTLD	97227	596	F3
NE Tillamook St				
10	PTLD	97212	596	G3
10	PTLD	97227	596	G3
2600	PTLD	97212	597	A4
4100	PTLD	97213	597	C3
10200	PTLD	97220	597	J4
12800	PTLD	97230	598	B4
16200	GSHM	97230	598	F4
E Tillicum Spur				
66300	CmsC	97067	724	A4
E Tillicum St				
24800	CmsC	97067	724	A4
SW Tillie Ln				
9400	TGRD	97224	655	G4
SE Tillstrom Rd				
11700	DAMA	97009	658	G1
20700	DAMA	97009	659	B3
SW Timara Ln				
12800	KNGC	97224	685	A2
12800	WasC	97224	685	A2
NW Timber Ct				
-	WasC	97229	595	A4
SE Timber Ln				
16900	CmsC	97015	658	F6
16900	HPYV	97009	658	F6
16900	HPYV	97015	658	F6
S Timber Wy				
-	YCLT	98675	419	G1
S Timber Creek Ln				
15700	CmsC	97045	689	B5
Timbercrest Ln				
58600	ClbC	97051	414	F2
S Timberdark Ln				
16200	CmsC	97045	688	C6
Timbergrove Ct				
18300	CmsC	97035	685	J2
18300	LKOW	97035	685	J2
Timbergrove St				
5100	CmsC	97035	685	J2
5100	LKOW	97035	685	J2
SE Timberlake Dr				
2900	HBRO	97123	623	F1
SW Timberland Dr				
16300	BRTN	97007	624	G5
16900	WasC	97007	624	G5
SW Timberland Pl				
6200	BRTN	97007	624	G4
Timberline Av				
58900	STHN	97051	414	H2
SW Timberline Ct				
11600	BRTN	97008	625	C6
Timberline Dr				
700	LKOW	97034	656	D4
1200	CmsC	97034	656	D4
E Timberline Dr E				
65200	CmsC	97049	693	J7
65300	CmsC	97049	723	J1
SW Timberline Dr				
2300	WasC	97225	625	E1
11100	BRTN	97008	625	C6
NW Timber Ridge Ct				
8300	PTLD	97229	595	F3
Timber Ridge Dr				
-	CmsC	97045	688	D6
Timbersky Wy				
20200	CmsC	97045	717	H7
SE Timber Valley Dr				
11700	CmsC	97236	658	A4
12000	HPYV	97236	658	A4
SW Timbrel Ln				
-	SRWD	97140	714	E1
N Time Oil Rd				
8900	PTLD	97203	535	F6
NW Timeric St				
11100	NPNS	97133	563	A1
SE Timm Ln				
22900	CmsC	97022	719	J1
S Timm Rd				
10	RDGF	98642	416	F7
10	RDGF	98642	446	F1
600	ClkC	98642	446	F2
E Timmen Ct				
1200	LCTR	98629	386	H7
NE Timmen Rd				
29200	ClkC	98642	416	H4
NW Timmen Rd				
31600	ClkC	98642	416	G2
NE Timmons Ln				
7200	YmhC	97114	742	D3
7200	YmhC	97115	742	C3
Timms Wy				
12900	ORCY	97045	717	C5
Timothy Ln				
1600	WLIN	97068	716	G2
NE Timothy Ln				
2500	HBRO	97124	593	F4
SW Timothy Pl				
11500	TGRD	97223	655	C3
NE Timothy Rd				
32000	ClkC	98607	540	B3
SE Timothy Wy				
17200	GLDS	97027	687	F2
Tims View Av				
17700	CmsC	97027	687	D2
17700	CmsC	97267	687	D2
17700	GLDS	97027	687	D2
NE Tina Ct				
400	HBRO	97124	593	C2
Tina St				
19300	ORCY	97045	717	D5
NE Tina St				
900	HBRO	97124	593	D2
SE Tindall Cir				
3100	PTLD	97202	627	A3
N Tioga Av				
8500	PTLD	97203	565	J2
Tioga Rd				
15200	CmsC	97045	747	H1
Tippecanoe Ct				
600	LKOW	97034	656	E5
Tipperary Ct				
2400	WLIN	97068	686	G7
SW Tippitt Pl				
12100	TGRD	97223	655	B4
NE Tipton Ct				
700	HBRO	97124	593	D2
S Titan Dr				
-	RDGF	98642	446	B1
SW Titan Ln				
10400	TGRD	97224	685	D1
S Titan Pl				
-	RDGF	98642	446	B2
NW Tivoli Ln				
1900	PTLD	97229	595	G3
SW Tobias Wy				
1000	WasC	97006	594	C6
Todd Ln				
17100	CmsC	97027	687	F2
17100	CmsC	97267	687	F2
Todd Rd				
1800	VCVR	98661	537	B4
N Todd St				
9500	PTLD	97203	565	H1
NW Todd St				
14700	WasC	97006	594	J5
SW Todd St				
10100	WasC	97225	595	D6
13500	WasC	97006	595	A5
14200	WasC	97006	594	J5
Todd Kelli Wy				
19200	CmsC	97045	716	J5
19200	ORCY	97045	716	J5
NW Toelle Ln				
-	MthC	97231	564	G3
NW Toenjes Rd				
34900	ClkC	98674	386	C5
NW Toketee Ct				
20900	WasC	97229	564	C6
NW Toketee Dr				
5400	WasC	97229	564	C7
SE Tolbert St				
8800	CmsC	97015	657	G7
Toliver Ct				
100	MOLA	97038	807	E7
Toliver Dr				
600	MOLA	97038	807	E7
600	MOLA	97038	837	E1
Toliver Rd				
100	MOLA	97038	837	E1
500	MOLA	97038	807	C7
600	CmsC	97038	807	C7
S Toliver Rd				
11500	CmsC	97038	807	A7
12200	MOLA	97038	807	B7
Tolkien Ln				
2600	LKOW	97034	686	B3
SE Tolman St				
1600	PTLD	97202	626	J5
2800	PTLD	97202	627	A5
5200	PTLD	97206	627	C5
8400	PTLD	97266	627	G5
NW Tolovana St				
18800	WasC	97229	594	E1
SW Toma Ct				
8700	WasC	97225	595	F6
Tomahawk Pl				
-	DNDE	97115	742	G3
N Tomahawk Island Dr				
10	PTLD	97217	566	G1
800	PTLD	97217	536	F7
NE Tomahawk Island Dr				
10	PTLD	97217	566	G1
Tompkins Ct				
6400	WLIN	97068	687	A5
Tompkins St				
1800	WLIN	97068	687	A5
SE Tom Thumb Ct				
12000	CmsC	97236	657	J4
SE Tong Rd				
15400	DAMA	97009	658	G7
15400	DAMA	97009	688	G2
16500	CmsC	97009	688	G2
SW Tongue Ln				
31000	WasC	97113	623	A3
31000	WasC	97123	623	B3
SW Tonka St				
8100	TLTN	97062	685	F4
SW Tonopah St				
9300	TLTN	97062	685	E5
SW Tonquin Lp				
10500	WasC	97062	715	C1
10500	WasC	97140	715	C1
SW Tonquin Pl				
11200	WasC	97140	715	C1
SW Tonquin Rd				
10600	WasC	97140	715	B1
12400	SRWD	97140	684	J6
12400	WasC	97140	684	J7
12400	WasC	97140	685	A7
S Tony Ct				
19500	ORCY	97045	717	D5
SW Tony Ct				
11100	TGRD	97223	655	B3
S Tonya Ct				
21800	CmsC	97004	747	G3
SW Tookbank Ct				
17000	DRHM	97224	685	E1
SW Tooze Rd				
11000	CmsC	97070	715	B5
11000	CmsC	97140	715	B5
13900	CmsC	97140	714	J4
SE Topaz Av				
14300	CmsC	97267	657	E6
SE Topaz Ct				
4100	TDLE	97060	599	H7
4100	TDLE	97060	629	J1
SW Topaz Ct				
14700	BRTN	97007	624	J2
SE Topaz Dr				
4200	TDLE	97060	629	H1
SW Topaz Ln				
14500	BRTN	97007	624	J6
Topeka Ln				
800	VCVR	98664	537	E5
SE Top O'Scott St				
9700	CmsC	97236	657	H3
9900	HPYV	97236	657	G3
SE Topper Dr				
6900	VCVR	98661	537	D7
6900	VCVR	98664	537	D7
6900	VCVR	98664	567	E1
Top View Ct				
3200	WLIN	97068	686	H4
SE Torbank Rd				
2500	CmsC	97222	656	J5
NW Tork Pl				
-	HBRO	97006	594	D5
SW Torland St				
11100	TGRD	97223	655	C3
SW Torr Ln				
4200	MthC	97221	596	A7
4200	PTLD	97221	596	A7
SE Torra Vista Ct				
11300	HPYV	97236	657	J2
NW Torres Pine Ct				
1200	MCMV	97128	770	F3
Torrey Pines Ct				
20000	ORCY	97045	717	G6
NW Torrey Pines Ct				
16600	BRTN	97006	594	G5
Torrey Pines Dr				
20000	ORCY	97045	717	G6
NW Torrey View Ct				
8900	WasC	97229	595	F5
NW Torrey View Dr				
200	WasC	97229	595	F5
NW Torrey View Ln				
400	WasC	97229	595	F5
SE Toscana Pl				
11700	HPYV	97236	658	C4
Touchstone Ct				
100	LKOW	97035	656	B5
Touchstone Dr				
100	LKOW	97035	656	B5
Touchstone St				
10	LKOW	97035	656	B5
Touchstone Ter				
100	LKOW	97035	656	B5
SW Touchstone Ter				
7100	WasC	97007	624	B6
SW Tournament Ct				
7600	WNVL	97070	715	F7
SE Tower Dr				
9400	CmsC	97009	659	F2
SW Tower Ln				
-	PTLD	97221	626	B4
2100	TDLE	97060	599	E6
SW Tower Wy				
3600	PTLD	97221	626	B4
Towercrest Dr				
19300	ORCY	97045	717	A4
Tower Hill Dr				
19300	ORCY	97045	717	B4
SW Towhee Ln				
15700	BRTN	97007	654	G4
NW Towle Av				
10	GSHM	97030	629	A2
10	GSHM	97080	629	A2
SW Towle Av				
10	GSHM	97030	629	A2
700	GSHM	97080	629	A6
NW Towle Ct				
1700	GSHM	97030	629	E1
Towle Dr				
17200	SNDY	97055	690	H3
NW Towle Ter				
1500	GSHM	97030	629	A1
NW Town Center Dr				
2000	HBRO	97006	594	E3
2000	WasC	97006	594	F3
SW Town Center Lp E				
29000	WNVL	97070	715	F7
SW Town Center Lp W				
29000	WNVL	97070	715	E7
30200	WNVL	97070	745	E1
Towne Ct				
500	FTGV	97116	591	F3
NW Townsend Ct				
5100	WasC	97229	564	H5
SW Townsend Ct				
2100	TDLE	97060	599	D6
NE Townsend Wy				
-	FRVW	97024	599	C3
S Township Rd				
1500	CNBY	97013	746	F7
1900	CmsC	97013	746	F7
11600	CmsC	97013	747	A7
11600	CmsC	97045	747	A7
SE Township Rd				
100	CNBY	97013	746	D7
1200	CmsC	97013	746	D7
NE Tracey Ln				
15500	PTLD	97230	598	E2
Traceylee Ct				
16200	ORCY	97045	687	G6
SW Trachsel Dr				
2100	WasC	97006	594	B7
SW Trachsel St				
-	PTLD	97219	656	C1
NE Traci Falls Rd				
22300	ClkC	98604	449	F5
Tracy Av				
16800	CmsC	97035	685	H1
SW Tracy Pl				
13600	TGRD	97223	654	J5
SE Tracy Rd				
35300	CmsC	97023	750	F2
SW Tracy Ann Ct				
14900	WasC	97007	624	J4
SE Tracy Suzanne Ct				
7300	CmsC	97267	657	E6
NW Tradewind St				
14000	WasC	97229	565	A7
NW Trafalgar Ln				
20700	HBRO	97006	594	C4
NW Trail Av				
1200	BRTN	97229	595	A4
1200	WasC	97229	595	A4
S Trail Av				
16000	CmsC	97045	687	H5
16000	ORCY	97045	687	H5
SW Trail Ct				
9100	PTLD	97219	626	D7
11900	BRTN	97008	625	D6
SE Trail Dr				
35700	CmsC	97023	750	F5
SW Trail Pl				
12100	BRTN	97008	625	B7
SW Trail Rd				
3400	CmsC	97062	686	A6
3400	CmsC	97068	686	B6
4500	CmsC	97062	685	J6
E Trailblazer Av				
23000	CmsC	97049	724	B2
SW Trailblazer Pl				
20700	SRWD	97140	684	F5
S Trail Ridge Rd				
17000	CmsC	97045	688	C5
SE Trails Ln				
11900	CmsC	97055	660	H4
SW Trails End Dr				
20500	SRWD	97140	684	E5
20800	WasC	97140	684	E5
NE Trails End Ln				
30300	YmhC	97132	713	H6
Trailview Dr				
16300	ORCY	97045	687	H6
NW Trail Walk Dr				
20600	HBRO	97006	594	C4
NW Trakehner Wy				
15400	WasC	97229	564	H7
NE Tralee Ct				
200	HBRO	97124	593	B1
SE Tranquil Ct				
5600	CmsC	97267	657	D7
5600	CmsC	97267	687	C1
Tranquil Ln				
-	YmhC	97132	713	A4
NE Tranquil Ln				
22900	YmhC	97132	712	J4
22900	YmhC	97132	713	A4
SW Tranquil Wy				
10400	WNVL	97070	715	C7
NW Tranquility Dr				
14600	WasC	97106	531	G4
Tranquility Ln				
20500	CmsC	97045	689	A4
SW Tranquility Ter				
-	WasC	97006	624	F1
NE Transport Wy				
5500	PTLD	97218	567	D4
SW Trapper Ter				
-	BRTN	97008	655	C2
SW Traveler's Ln				
-	TLTN	97224	685	G2
SW Travis Ct				
16500	SRWD	97140	684	F7
NW Treasure Ln				
37000	WasC	97113	562	E2
Treatment Plant Rd				
100	WDLD	98674	386	A1
Tree St				
5000	CmsC	97035	685	J2
5000	LKOW	97035	685	J2
NW Treehaven Dr				
500	HBRO	97124	593	B2
SW Treehill Ct				
11800	TGRD	97224	655	B6
NE Treehill Dr				
23800	WDVL	97060	599	D5
SE Treehill Ln				
25100	DAMA	97009	659	E2
SE Treehouse Ln				
-	CmsC	97267	687	C1
SW Treehouse Ln				
19400	WasC	97007	624	D2
SE Treeific Dr				
-	ClkC	98671	570	A3
-	WHGL	98671	570	A3
NE Treena St				
200	HBRO	97124	593	B2
E Tree Swallow Ln				
21700	CmsC	97049	693	J7
S Treetop Dr				
18100	CmsC	97045	717	G3
Tree Top Ln				
2800	WLIN	97068	686	J5
17400	LKOW	97034	686	C1
Tree Top Wy				
17400	LKOW	97034	686	C1
SW Treeview Ct				
11900	TGRD	97224	655	B6
NW Treglown Ct				
300	HBRO	97124	593	A4
SW Trelane St				
19500	WasC	97006	624	D1
SE Trellis Pl				
3600	HBRO	97123	623	G2
NW Trellis Wy				
42000	BNKS	97106	531	J6
NW Tremaine Ct				
1400	BRTN	97006	594	G4
SW Tremont St				
11800	BRTN	97225	595	C7
11800	WasC	97225	595	B7
SW Tremont Wy				
20100	WasC	97007	624	C6
SW Trenton Ct				
15000	WasC	97006	594	H6
N Trenton St				
3100	PTLD	97217	566	D3
4400	PTLD	97203	566	B3
Trestle View Ct				
1600	NWBG	97132	713	D6
E Trevino Ct				
25400	CmsC	97067	724	A4
E Trevino Pl				
25200	CmsC	97067	724	A4
NW Trevino St				
13400	WasC	97229	595	A1
SW Trevor Ln				
14500	WasC	97224	684	H1
Tribbett Ct				
-	DAYT	97114	772	B4
SW Trigger Ct				
9000	BRTN	97008	625	D4
SW Trigger Dr				
12600	BRTN	97008	655	B1
Trillium Av				
17200	ORCY	97045	687	E7
17200	ORCY	97045	717	E1
SW Trillium Av				
7100	BRTN	97008	625	B6
Trillium Ct				
14300	LKOW	97035	655	J5
15600	CmsC	97055	691	B1
SE Trillium Ct				
22700	DAMA	97009	659	C1
SW Trillium Ct				
7400	BRTN	97008	625	B6
Trillium Dr				
18300	WLIN	97068	686	J3
NE Trillium Ln				
9900	YmhC	97132	743	A2
NW Trillium Ln				
1700	VCVR	98663	506	E6
SW Trillium Ln				
15000	BRTN	97007	624	H4
Trillium St				
200	STHN	97051	385	B7
SW Trillium Creek Ter				
-	WasC	97225	595	D6
S Trillium Hollow Rd				
23000	CmsC	97045	719	F1
SE Trilva Jean Ct				
14200	CmsC	97267	657	B6
Trimble Ln				
38000	SNDY	97055	690	J3
Trinity Ln				
-	YmhC	97132	713	A4
NE Trinity Ln				
22900	YmhC	97132	712	J4
22900	YmhC	97132	713	A4
NW Trinity Pl				
10	PTLD	97205	596	D5
10	PTLD	97209	596	D5
SW Trinity Pl				
7200	WasC	97113	623	A5
NE Trisha Dr				
1700	HBRO	97124	593	C2
SE Tristin Av				
12600	CmsC	97009	658	F5
12600	CmsC	97236	658	F5
12600	HPYV	97009	658	F5
12600	HPYV	97236	658	F5
SE Troge Rd				
17300	CmsC	97009	658	G4
17300	DAMA	97009	658	G4
17300	HPYV	97009	658	G4
17300	HPYV	97236	658	G4
SE Troika Av				
11000	HPYV	97236	658	B3
SE Trolley Ln				
18300	CmsC	97267	687	C3
SE Trona Ln				
6100	CmsC	97222	657	D2
NW Troon Ct				
1700	MCMV	97128	770	F4
Troon Dr				
1300	WLIN	97068	686	G3
NW Troon Dr				
15000	WasC	97229	594	J1
Troon Rd				
1000	LKOW	97034	656	E6
NW Troon Wy				
15100	WasC	97229	594	J2
SW Tropicana Av				
900	WasC	97005	595	A6
SE Tropicana Ct				
13400	HPYV	97236	658	B2
SW Trotter Pl				
9900	BRTN	97008	655	A1
NW Trout Ct				
2100	CMAS	98607	539	C7
Trout Pl				
18800	CmsC	97045	719	A4
Trout St				
300	MOLA	97038	837	G1
NW Trout St				
4500	CMAS	98607	569	C1
SW Trout St				
600	CMAS	98607	569	C5
Trout Wy				
4000	LKOW	97034	686	A3
SW Trout Creek Ln				
14700	BRTN	97006	594	J6
14700	WasC	97006	594	J6
SE Trout Creek Rd				
37900	MthC	97019	630	J6
S Troutdale Rd				
1000	TDLE	97060	599	G7

STREET Block City ZIP Map# Grid

E Troutdale Rd
1100 MthC 97030 629 G1
1100 MthC 97060 629 G1
1100 TDLE 97060 629 G1
3600 MthC 97080 629 H3
W Troutman Ln
17600 WasC 97006 624 F1
roy Ct
2500 WLIN 97068 686 F7
W Troy St
1400 PTLD 97219 626 D6
E Trubel Rd
36800 CmsC 97055 690 H6
38800 CmsC 97055 691 D6
W Truitt Rd
27100 WasC 97133 533 E3
Truman Rd
3200 WHGL 98671 570 C7
Trumbull Av
4500 PTLD 97203 565 H2
W Trumpeter Dr
21500 SRWD 97140 684 G6
E Trunk Rd
18800 YmhC 97115 742 F5
ruth St
100 WDLD 98674 386 A2
W Tryon Av
11000 MthC 97219 656 G2
ryon Ct
18300 GLDS 97027 687 D3
W Tryon Hill Rd
12100 MthC 97219 656 G3
ualamere Av
19300 CmsC 97035 685 H3
19300 RVGR 97035 685 H3
W Tualasaum Dr
19000 CmsC 97062 686 A4
ualata Av
17800 CmsC 97035 685 J3
17800 LKOW 97035 685 J3
ualata Ct
5200 CmsC 97035 685 J2
ualata Ln
5000 LKOW 97035 685 J2
5200 CmsC 97035 685 J2
ualatin Av
1700 WLIN 97068 716 G3
W Tualatin Av
11800 PTLD 97229 565 C4
12100 MthC 97229 565 C4
W Tualatin Av
3900 PTLD 97239 626 C2
W Tualatin Dr
10400 TGRD 97224 685 C1
10600 WasC 97062 685 C1
ualatin Gdns
- TLTN 97062 685 E4
W Tualatin Lp
100 CmsC 97068 686 D7
W Tualatin Rd
8400 TLTN 97062 685 F3
ualatin St
10 STHN 97051 415 D1
16900 LKOW 97035 685 J1
W Tualatin St
15700 SRWD 97140 684 G7
W Tualatin-Sherwood Rd
8500 TLTN 97062 685 E4
11500 WasC 97062 685 B5
12400 SRWD 97140 685 A5
12400 WasC 97140 685 A5
13400 SRWD 97140 684 H5
E Tualatin Valley Hwy
900 HBRO 97123 593 D6
3600 HBRO 97123 623 H1
5800 HBRO 97007 623 J1
6300 HBRO 97007 624 A1
6300 HBRO 97123 624 A1
6700 WasC 97123 624 A1
7500 HBRO 97006 624 B1
E Tualatin Valley Hwy SR-8
1800 HBRO 97123 593 E7
3600 HBRO 97123 623 H1
5800 HBRO 97007 623 J1
6300 HBRO 97007 624 A1
6300 HBRO 97123 624 A1
6700 WasC 97123 624 A1
7500 HBRO 97006 624 B1
SW Tualatin Valley Hwy
13400 BRTN 97005 625 A3
14200 BRTN 97005 624 J3
14400 BRTN 97006 624 H2
14400 BRTN 97007 624 H2
14500 WasC 97007 624 H2
18500 WasC 97006 624 C1
21500 HBRO 97006 624 B1
21700 HBRO 97123 624 B1
32000 HBRO 97123 593 A5
32200 HBRO 97123 592 J5
SW Tualatin Valley Hwy SR-8
13400 BRTN 97005 625 A3
14200 BRTN 97005 624 J3
14400 BRTN 97006 624 H2
14400 BRTN 97007 624 H2
14500 WasC 97007 624 H2
18500 WasC 97006 624 C1
21500 HBRO 97006 624 B1
21700 HBRO 97123 624 B1
32000 HBRO 97123 593 A5
32200 HBRO 97123 592 J5
SW Tualaway Av
4000 BRTN 97005 625 A3
NW Tuality Wy
- MthC 97229 595 G5
100 WasC 97225 595 G6
SW Tucker Av
4700 BRTN 97005 625 B3
SW Tuckerwood Ct
11800 BRTN 97008 625 C7
NW Tucson St
16500 WasC 97006 594 G1
Tucson Wy
100 VCVR 98661 537 C6
Tudor Ct
6600 GLDS 97027 687 D2
Tudor Dr
16600 GLDS 97027 687 E2
NW Tudor Ln
10500 WasC 97229 595 D3
Tukta Wy
56800 ClbC 97053 414 F6
W Tukwila Dr
100 NWBG 97132 713 B4

Tulane St
2300 WLIN 97068 687 A5
SW Tulip Ct
13400 BRTN 97008 625 A5
Tulip Rd
700 ECDA 97023 750 A2
SE Tulip Tree Av
3300 HBRO 97123 623 D1
S Tull Av
7100 BRLO 97013 775 H1
7100 CmsC 97013 775 J1
7100 CmsC 97013 776 A1
NW Tullamorrie Wy
15900 WasC 97229 594 H1
Tulsa Av
100 VCVR 98661 537 D6
NW Tumalo Ct
4500 WasC 97229 564 C7
4500 WasC 97229 594 C1
SE Tumblestone Dr
2700 HBRO 97123 593 F7
SE Tumbleweed Ct
13200 CmsC 97236 658 B5
Tumwater Dr
100 ORCY 97045 717 B1
Tumwater St
2000 WLIN 97068 687 A7
NE Tunbridge St
5700 HBRO 97124 593 J4
Tundra Ct
58900 STHN 97051 414 H2
SW Tunica St
10900 TLTN 97062 685 C2
SW Tunnelwood St
3500 PTLD 97221 626 A2
SW Tupelo Ln
12500 BRTN 97008 625 B6
Tupper Rd
17700 SNDY 97055 690 J3
17700 SNDY 97055 691 A3
18400 CmsC 97055 690 J4
SE Tupper Rd
18400 CmsC 97055 690 J4
18400 SNDY 97055 690 J4
NW Turel Dr
30500 NPNS 97133 563 B1
30500 WasC 97133 563 B1
SW Turin Ct
20700 WasC 97007 624 C5
SE Turley Pl
12000 HPYV 97236 658 D4
Turley Rd
56100 ClbC 97053 414 C6
SW Turnagain Dr
- KNGC 97224 655 B7
- TGRD 97224 655 B7
15200 WasC 97224 655 B7
NW Turnberry Ter
800 BRTN 97006 594 H4
NE Turner Dr
1000 HBRO 97124 593 D4
SW Turner Rd
1300 CmsC 97068 686 C7
SE Turner Creek Dr
2900 HBRO 97123 593 F7
SW Turning Leaf Dr
17400 WasC 97006 594 F7
SW Turnstone Av
11800 BRTN 97007 654 H3
SW Turquoise Ct
15100 BRTN 97007 624 H7
SW Turquoise Lp
8500 BRTN 97007 624 H7
9200 BRTN 97007 654 E1
Turquoise Wy
19600 CmsC 97045 716 H5
Turtle Bay Dr
14900 ORCY 97045 717 G6
SW Turtledove Ln
16000 BRTN 97007 654 G1
SE Tuscany Ct
6600 CmsC 97267 657 D6
SW Tuscany St
15800 WasC 97223 654 G5
15800 WasC 97224 654 G5
SE Tuscany Wy
6800 CmsC 97267 657 E6
NW Tustin Ranch Dr
3600 WasC 97229 595 A2
SW Twelve Oaks Ct
13600 WasC 97224 655 A7
13800 WasC 97224 654 J7
SE Twelve Oaks St
3700 HBRO 97123 623 G2
Twenge Ct
24500 YmhC 97132 713 B6
Twilight Ln
18000 CmsC 97055 690 D3
NW Twilight Ter
4000 PTLD 97229 595 D1
Twilight Tr
200 CmsC 97068 686 E5
E Twinberry Lp
68100 CmsC 97067 724 B4
E Twin Bridges Ln
21300 CmsC 97011 693 F7
Twin Cedars Ln
- CmsC 97045 747 H2
Twin Creek Ct
13100 LKOW 97035 655 H4
Twin Creek Ln
13300 LKOW 97035 655 H4
Twin Fir Ct
14800 LKOW 97035 656 B6
Twin Fir Rd
14800 LKOW 97034 656 B6
14800 LKOW 97035 656 B6
NW Twinflower Dr
14600 WasC 97229 564 J6
Twinflower St
2900 FTGV 97116 591 G3
Twin Oaks Av NE
4100 MrnC 97137 773 C5
4100 STPL 97137 773 C5
NW Twin Oaks Dr
16500 BRTN 97006 594 G4
16500 WasC 97006 594 G4
SW Twin Park Pl
11400 TGRD 97223 655 C3
Twin Points Rd
1800 LKOW 97034 656 C7
SW Twombly Av
4200 PTLD 97239 626 C3
NW Twoponds Dr
15000 WasC 97229 564 J6

SW Tybalt Pl
17100 KNGC 97224 685 A2
SW Tygh Lp
8400 TLTN 97062 685 F6
N Tyler Av
9500 PTLD 97203 565 J2
N Tyler Ct
15600 LFYT 97127 741 G7
NW Tyler Ct
11800 WasC 97229 595 C2
SE Tyler Ct
10100 HPYV 97236 657 J2
Tyler Ln
20300 FRVW 97024 599 A2
SE Tyler Rd
10700 HPYV 97236 657 J2
SE Tyler St
52200 SPSE 97056 474 F1
N Tyndall Av
8700 PTLD 97217 566 D4
Tyndall Ct
1000 LKOW 97034 656 D7
SW Tyrol Cir
4900 PTLD 97239 626 D3
SW Tyrol St
2100 PTLD 97239 626 C3
SW Tyrone Ter
1400 WasC 97006 594 C7

U

U St
500 VCVR 98661 536 J5
2800 VCVR 98663 536 J3
3600 WHGL 98671 570 D4
N U St
- WHGL 98671 569 J3
W U St
600 WHGL 98671 569 H3
NW Uebel Rd
36300 WasC 97133 532 F1
NW Ukiah St
18600 WasC 97229 594 E1
SW Ulsky Rd
22600 CmsC 97068 686 E7
22600 CmsC 97068 716 E1
SE Umatilla Dr
- PTLD 97206 627 B7
Umatilla St
900 STHN 97051 415 C1
SE Umatilla St
400 PTLD 97202 626 H7
2700 PTLD 97202 627 A7
7200 PTLD 97206 627 E7
SW Umatilla St
8400 TLTN 97062 685 F5
Umatilla Wy
500 VCVR 98661 537 B5
Umbenhower Ln
16600 AURA 97002 775 E5
16600 MrnC 97002 775 E5
Umberview Ln
15900 CmsC 97045 687 H5
15900 ORCY 97045 687 H5
Umbrella
- CmsC 97015 657 J7
SW Umiat St
9300 TLTN 97062 685 E5
SW Umpqua Ct
21400 TLTN 97062 685 D6
Umpqua Ln
2600 WLIN 97068 686 H7
Unander Av
2600 VCVR 98660 536 E2
Underhill Ln
2700 WLIN 97068 686 J4
2700 WLIN 97068 687 A5
SW Underhill Rd
- CmsC 97034 656 G4
- LKOW 97034 656 G4
700 CmsC 97219 656 G4
SW Underwood Dr
2900 WasC 97225 625 D1
3300 WasC 97005 625 D1
SW Unger Rd
30500 WasC 97113 623 B7
30500 WasC 97123 623 B7
Union Av
300 GLDS 97027 687 E4
NW Union Av
- MthC 97210 595 H4
N Union Ct
10700 PTLD 97217 566 F2
NE Union Rd
15400 ClkC 98686 476 J4
15800 ClkC 98642 476 H2
Union St NE
- MrnC 97002 744 F6
SE Union St
600 CMAS 98607 569 G5
SE Union St SR-500
600 CMAS 98607 569 G5
S Union Hall Rd
11600 CmsC 97013 777 A2
13600 CmsC 97042 777 F2
14500 CmsC 97045 777 G2
NW Union Hills Ter
4600 WasC 97006 594 F1
S Union Mills Rd
13900 CmsC 97042 807 J2
S Unity Ln
17400 CmsC 97045 717 J1
University Av
2000 FTGV 97116 591 J4
17000 SNDY 97055 690 H3
N University Av
7000 PTLD 97203 566 B5
N Unnamed Rd
- PTLD 97203 535 G3
- PTLD 97217 566 D1
NE Unnamed Rd
- PTLD 97218 567 F5
NW Unnamed Rd
- PTLD 97210 565 F4
- PTLD 97231 535 C7
- PTLD 97231 565 E3
SW Uphill Pl
7100 WasC 97007 624 D6
Upland Dr
400 DNDE 97115 742 H3
N Upland Dr
7300 PTLD 97203 565 J1
SW Upland Dr
700 DNDE 97115 742 H3
1100 MthC 97221 596 A7

SW Upland Dr
1100 PTLD 97221 596 A7
Uplands Dr
14200 LKOW 97034 656 C6
SW Uplands Dr
13300 WasC 97223 654 G5
SE Upman Wy
15600 DAMA 97009 688 E1
Upper Dr
2800 LKOW 97035 656 B7
4300 CmsC 97035 656 B7
4700 CmsC 97035 655 J7
4700 CmsC 97035 685 J1
4700 LKOW 97035 685 J1
SW Upper Dr
2700 PTLD 97201 596 C7
2800 PTLD 97201 626 B1
S Upper Rd
19700 CmsC 97045 718 C6
SE Upper Aldercrest Dr
13900 CmsC 97222 657 C5
13900 CmsC 97267 657 C6
SW Upper Boones Ferry Rd
- CmsC 97035 655 H7
15600 TGRD 97224 655 H7
16000 TGRD 97224 685 G1
16100 DRHM 97224 685 G2
17900 TLTN 97224 685 G2
SW Upper Cascade Dr
3200 PTLD 97205 596 B6
Upper Cherry Ln
17400 LKOW 97034 686 F1
17800 CmsC 97034 686 F1
Upper Devon Ln
900 LKOW 97034 686 F1
SW Upper Dr Pl
2600 PTLD 97201 596 C7
2600 PTLD 97201 626 B1
SW Upper Hall St
1500 PTLD 97201 596 D7
Upper Midhill Dr
18000 WLIN 97068 686 G2
SW Upper Roy St
22600 SRWD 97140 684 H7
NW Upshur St
1700 PTLD 97209 596 D3
2100 PTLD 97210 596 D4
NW Upton Ct
9900 PTLD 97229 595 E1
NW Uptown Ter
200 PTLD 97205 596 C5
200 PTLD 97210 596 C5
US-26
- PTLD 97201 626 G1
- PTLD 97239 626 G1
US-26 E
- CmsC 97009 660 B5
US-26 SW 3rd Av
2400 PTLD 97201 626 E1
US-26 SW 5th Av
2300 PTLD 97201 626 E1
US-26 SW Arthur St
10 PTLD 97201 626 F1
US-26 SW Caruthers St
300 PTLD 97201 626 E1
US-26 SW Clay St
700 PTLD 97201 596 E7
US-26 SW Corbett Av
2900 PTLD 97201 626 F1
US-26 SW Kelly Av
2700 PTLD 97201 626 F1
US-26 SW Market St
700 PTLD 97201 596 E7
US-26 Mt Hood Hwy
- CmsC 97009 659 H1
- CmsC 97009 660 A4
- CmsC 97009 690 F1
- CmsC 97011 693 E6
- CmsC 97011 723 H1
- CmsC 97011 724 A3
- CmsC 97049 724 D4
- CmsC 97055 690 F1
- CmsC 97055 693 C6
- CmsC 97067 723 H1
- CmsC 97067 724 A3
- DAMA 97009 659 G1
- GSHM 97080 629 F6
- MthC 97080 629 F6
- MthC 97080 659 J3
- SNDY 97055 690 H2
41600 CmsC 97055 691 C4
41600 SNDY 97055 691 C4
47300 CmsC 97055 692 C7
US-26 Pioneer Blvd
38200 SNDY 97055 690 J3
38900 SNDY 97055 691 B3
39700 CmsC 97055 691 B3
US-26 E Powell Blvd
- GSHM 97080 629 E3
10 GSHM 97030 629 C2
US-26 SE Powell Blvd
500 PTLD 97202 626 J2
2800 PTLD 97202 627 A2
6900 PTLD 97206 627 J2
8000 PTLD 97266 627 J2
11500 PTLD 97266 628 C2
12000 PTLD 97236 628 A2
17400 GSHM 97030 628 F3
17400 GSHM 97080 628 F3
17400 GSHM 97236 628 F3
US-26 W Powell Blvd
10 GSHM 97030 629 A3
10 GSHM 97080 629 A3
1900 GSHM 97030 628 J2
1900 GSHM 97080 628 J2
US-26 SE Powell Valley Blvd
4200 GSHM 97030 628 G3
4200 GSHM 97080 628 G3
4900 GSHM 97236 628 F3
4900 PTLD 97236 628 F3
US-26 Proctor Blvd
38200 SNDY 97055 690 J3
39000 SNDY 97055 691 A3
US-26 Ross Island Br
- PTLD 97201 626 F1
- PTLD 97202 626 G1
- PTLD 97239 626 F1
US-26 SW Sheridan St
300 PTLD 97201 626 E1
US-26 Sunset Hwy
- BRTN - 594 F3
- BRTN - 595 H7
- BRTN - 625 G1
- HBRO - 563 J6

US-26 Sunset Hwy
- HBRO - 564 A7
- HBRO - 594 F3
- MthC - 595 H7
- MthC - 596 A7
- NPNS - 562 J1
- NPNS - 563 B2
- PTLD - 595 J7
- PTLD - 596 B7
- PTLD - 626 B1
- WasC - 562 J1
- WasC - 563 E4
- WasC - 594 E2
- WasC - 595 B6
- WasC 97106 532 E6
- WasC 97113 532 G7
- WasC 97133 532 E6
US-26 NW Sunset Hwy
39500 WasC 97106 532 B3
39700 WasC 97106 531 H2
US-30
- PTLD - 596 F3
US-30 BYP
- PTLD 97210 565 F4
- PTLD 97231 565 F4
US-30 Banfield Expwy
- FRVW - 598 J4
- FRVW - 599 C3
- GSHM - 598 J4
- MWDP - 597 H2
- PTLD - 596 J4
- PTLD - 597 C5
- PTLD - 598 B3
- TDLE - 599 E3
- WDVL - 599 E3
US-30 BYP NW Bridge Av
- PTLD 97210 565 F4
8700 PTLD 97231 565 F3
US-30 BUS E Burnside St
10 PTLD 97214 596 J5
10 PTLD 97232 596 J5
US-30 BYP NE Columbia Blvd
9200 PTLD 97220 567 H7
9600 PTLD 97220 597 J1
US-30 Columbia River Hwy
- MthC - 599 J3
- MthC - 600 A3
- PTLD - 596 D3
- PTLD 97210 596 D3
- TDLE - 599 G3
- WDVL - 599 E3
50000 ClbC 97056 474 E5
50600 SPSE 97056 474 E1
52400 SPSE 97056 444 E7
52700 ClbC 97056 444 E7
55600 ClbC 97053 444 G1
56000 ClbC 97053 414 H7
57800 ClbC 97051 414 J4
58100 ClbC 97051 415 A2
58300 STHN 97051 415 A2
60700 ClbC 97051 385 C6
61100 CBAC 97018 385 C6
61100 ClbC 97018 385 A4
62900 ClbC 97054 385 C6
US-30 N Columbia River Hwy
200 STHN 97051 385 B7
700 ClbC 97051 385 C6
US-30 S Columbia River Hwy
100 STHN 97051 415 B1
US-30 BYP N Ivanhoe St
8200 PTLD 97203 565 H3
US-30 BYP NE Killingsworth St
7200 PTLD 97218 567 E7
7600 PTLD 97220 567 F7
US-30 BYP N Lombard St
- PTLD 97211 566 G5
1700 PTLD 97217 566 E5
3900 PTLD 97203 566 A4
6500 PTLD 97203 565 J4
US-30 BYP NE Lombard St
10 PTLD 97211 566 J5
10 PTLD 97217 566 G5
2200 PTLD 97211 567 C6
4000 PTLD 97218 567 B6
US-30 N Lwr Columbia River Hwy
100 STHN 97051 385 B7
US-30 S Lwr Columbia River Hwy
10 STHN 97051 415 B1
US-30 BYP N Philadelphia Av
7200 PTLD 97203 565 J3
US-30 BYP NE Portland Hwy
4200 PTLD 97211 567 C6
4200 PTLD 97218 567 C6
US-30 BYP N Richmond Av
7300 PTLD 97203 565 H3
US-30 NW St. Helens Rd
2200 PTLD 97210 596 B3
4500 PTLD 97210 595 J1
4600 PTLD 97210 565 G5
7500 PTLD 97231 565 G5
11600 PTLD 97231 535 D7
12300 MthC 97231 535 A5
15000 MthC 97231 534 J3
17700 MthC 97231 504 F1
25200 MthC 97231 474 F7
27200 ClbC 97056 474 E5
US-30 BYP St. Johns Br
- PTLD 97203 565 G3
- PTLD 97210 565 F4
- PTLD 97231 565 F4
US-30 BUS NE Sandy Blvd
1200 PTLD 97214 596 H5
1200 PTLD 97232 596 H5
2700 PTLD 97232 597 C3
3900 PTLD 97212 597 B4
6800 PTLD 97213 597 G1
8100 PTLD 97218 597 G1
8100 PTLD 97220 597 G1
9100 MWDP 97220 597 H1
US-30 BYP NE Sandy Blvd
9900 PTLD 97220 597 H1
11300 PTLD 97220 598 C2
11900 PTLD 97230 598 A1
16500 GSHM 97230 598 F2
19700 GSHM 97024 598 J3
20100 FRVW 97024 598 J3
20400 FRVW 97024 599 A3

US-30 Stadium Frwy
- PTLD - 596 E3
US-30 NW Yeon Av
2500 PTLD 97210 596 C2
4400 PTLD 97210 595 J1
NE US Grant Pl
2800 PTLD 97212 597 A3
Usufruct Av
- PTLD 97236 628 A7
- PTLD 97266 628 A7
SW US Veterans Hospital Rd
3300 PTLD 97239 626 E2
NW Utah Ct
4500 CMAS 98607 569 C1
Utah St
5000 VCVR 98661 537 C5
NW Utah St
2800 CMAS 98607 569 C2
SW Utah St
600 CMAS 98607 569 B5
Ute Dr
- WasC 97005 594 J7
- WasC 97005 624 J1
SW Ute St
13300 TLTN 97062 685 A2
13500 WasC 97062 685 A2
13500 WasC 97140 685 A2

V

V St
500 VCVR 98661 536 J5
2800 VCVR 98663 536 J3
3900 WHGL 98671 570 D4
N V St
100 VCVR 98661 536 J6
300 WHGL 98671 569 J3
S V St
100 VCVR 98661 536 J6
W V St
- ClkC 98607 569 G3
- WHGL 98671 569 G3
SW Vacuna Ct
11500 PTLD 97219 656 C3
SW Vacuna St
- MthC 97219 656 F3
3500 PTLD 97219 656 A2
4900 PTLD 97219 655 J2
Vaden St
- CmsC 97009 659 H3
NW Vadis Rd
33500 WasC 97113 562 H1
33500 WasC 97124 562 J1
33500 WasC 97133 562 H1
33800 WasC 97113 532 H7
33800 WasC 97133 532 H7
Vail Ct
34400 STHN 97051 414 H2
NW Val Ct
800 HBRO 97124 593 B3
NW Val St
200 HBRO 97124 593 B3
NE Valarie Ct
600 HBRO 97124 593 C2
Vale Ct
2700 LKOW 97034 686 B2
SW Vale Ct
6700 BRTN 97008 625 B5
NW Vale St
18700 WasC 97229 594 E1
S Vale Garden Rd
7900 CmsC 97013 776 C2
SE Valemont Ln
13200 HPYV 97236 658 B1
SE Valencia Dr
14500 VCVR 98683 568 C2
NW Valencia Ter
4700 WasC 97229 595 B1
SW Valenta Ct
7000 WasC 97223 625 H7
SE Valentine Dr
8900 CmsC 97236 627 G7
SE Valentine Ln
32300 CmsC 97022 720 C3
Valeri Dr
1800 NWBG 97132 713 C5
SW Valeria View Dr
200 BRTN 97225 595 D6
200 WasC 97225 595 D6
NW Valle Vista Ter
2900 PTLD 97210 596 B5
NW Vallevue Ct
11500 WasC 97229 595 C4
NW Vallevue Pl
11900 WasC 97229 595 C4
SW Valley Av
6000 BRTN 97005 625 A4
6000 BRTN 97008 625 A5
SW Valley Cir
6100 BRTN 97008 625 A5
Valley Ct
2100 WLIN 97068 686 G3
NW Valley Ct
5100 CMAS 98607 539 C7
Valley Hwy
2300 WasC 97116 591 H7
Valley St
- MthC 97231 534 F4
E Valley St
300 YCLT 98675 419 F1
NW Valley St
- MthC 97231 534 F4
4500 CMAS 98607 539 C7
4500 CMAS 98607 569 C1
SW Valley St
600 CMAS 98607 569 B5
Valley Vw
- ClbC 97056 474 A4
SE Valley Wy
10800 HPYV 97236 658 B3
Valley Crest Wy
3200 FTGV 97116 591 E3
SW Valley Forge Wy
700 WasC 97006 594 F6
Valley Hideaway Ln
31900 ClbC 97056 444 B6
NW Valley View Ct
200 MCMV 97128 770 D5
SW Valley View Ct
7900 BRTN 97225 625 G1
Valley View Dr
- STHN 97051 385 A6
100 ORCY 97045 717 C2
1000 MCMV 97128 770 E4

Valley View Dr
1100 YmhC 97128 770 E4
1600 WLIN 97068 686 G3
7000 GLDS 97027 687 E2
SW Valley View Dr
8100 BRTN 97225 625 G1
NE Valley View Ln
4300 VCVR 98663 536 H1
NW Valley View Ln
13900 PTLD 97231 565 A2
Valley View Rd
16600 CmsC 97267 687 D2
16600 GLDS 97027 687 D2
S Valley View Rd
26100 CmsC 97023 750 C6
SE Valley View Rd
16600 CmsC 97267 687 D2
16600 GLDS 97027 687 D2
SW Valley View Rd
24300 CmsC 97068 716 D2
SE Valley View Ter
10900 HPYV 97236 657 J3
11300 CmsC 97236 657 J3
12100 CmsC 97015 657 J4
NW Valley Vista Rd
10000 WasC 97124 564 C1
11500 WasC 97124 534 C7
SW Valona Wy
4400 PTLD 97219 656 A1
NW Valros Ln
11300 WasC 97229 595 D4
NW Valsetz Ct
17100 WasC 97006 594 G2
Van Allman Av
2800 VCVR 98660 536 D3
N Van Buren Av
6700 PTLD 97203 565 H4
Van Buren St
500 ORCY 97045 717 D1
1700 ORCY 97045 687 D7
NW Vance Dr
14600 WasC 97229 564 J7
N Vancouver Av
1600 PTLD 97227 596 G4
4000 PTLD 97217 596 G1
4800 PTLD 97217 566 G7
8900 PTLD 97211 566 G3
Vancouver Ldg
- ClkC 98686 506 H2
NE Vancouver Pl
- ClkC 98662 507 J7
NE Vancouver Plz
- VCVR 98662 537 E2
Vancouver St
- MthC 97231 534 F5
N Vancouver Wy
9800 PTLD 97211 566 F2
9800 PTLD 97217 566 F2
NE Vancouver Wy
8900 PTLD 97211 566 G3
9600 PTLD 97217 566 G3
Vancouver Barracks
- VCVR 98661 536 G5
NE Vancouver Mall Dr
6900 ClkC 98661 537 D1
6900 VCVR 98661 537 E1
7300 VCVR 98662 537 F1
NE Vancouver Mall Lp
8600 VCVR 98662 537 F1
NE Vancouver Plaza Dr
7400 VCVR 98662 537 E2
SE Van Curen Rd
22000 CmsC 97022 690 C7
22200 CmsC 97022 720 C2
NW Vandehey Ln
42400 WasC 97116 561 H3
N Vanderbilt St
4700 PTLD 97203 566 B4
SW Vandermost Rd
13000 WasC 97007 654 E6
SW Vanderschuere Rd
25800 WasC 97123 683 E1
25800 WasC 97132 683 F2
25800 WasC 97140 683 F2
Vanderwood Ln
- DNLD 97020 774 G5
Van Dolah Ln
35600 ClbC 97051 385 A5
60500 STHN 97051 385 A6
SW Vandolah Ln
17700 SRWD 97140 684 E7
Van Fleet Av
17700 SNDY 97055 691 A3
NW Vanguard Pl
2900 CMAS 98607 569 C2
N Van Houten Av
8900 PTLD 97203 566 A3
N Van Houten Ct
- PTLD 97203 565 J5
N Van Houten Pl
5800 PTLD 97203 565 J5
5800 PTLD 97203 566 A5
NW Van Vleet Rd
- CMAS 98607 568 J2
SE Van Waters Ct
3600 PTLD 97222 627 A7
SE Van Waters St
2700 MWKE 97222 627 A7
3600 PTLD 97222 627 B7
SE Van Zyl Dr
15700 DAMA 97009 688 F1
NW Vardon Pl
3800 WasC 97229 594 H2
SW Varns St
7200 TGRD 97223 655 G5
NW Vaughan Ct
11800 WasC 97229 595 C4
S Vaughan Rd
14200 CmsC 97038 807 F7
14500 CmsC 97038 837 G1
NW Vaughn St
1800 PTLD 97209 596 D3
2000 PTLD 97210 596 D3
SE Velda St
25100 CmsC 97009 659 E3
25100 DAMA 97009 659 E3
SE Velma Ct
9100 PTLD 97236 627 G7
SW Vendla Park Ln
17000 BRTN 97006 624 G1
17000 WasC 97006 624 G1
SE Veneer Ln
18900 CmsC 97055 691 E5
NW Venetian Dr
2600 HBRO 97124 594 D3

STREET Block City ZIP Map# Grid

SW Venezia Ln
- WNVL 97070 715 B7
SW Venezia Ter
13800 WasC 97223 654 G5
Venice Ct
13900 CmsC 97045 717 E5
SW Venice Ct
20400 WasC 97007 624 C3
SE Venice Ridge Wy
15900 DAMA 97009 688 D1
Ventnor Ct
600 MOLA 97038 807 C7
SW Ventura Ct
9500 TGRD 97223 655 H1
SW Ventura Dr
6500 TGRD 97223 655 H2
SW Ventura Pl
6500 TGRD 97223 655 H1
SW Venus Ct
11400 TGRD 97223 655 C5
NE Vera St
6100 PTLD 97213 597 D5
Verandas at Hazel Grv
- HBRO 97124 594 C3
NW Verboort Rd
- WasC 97113 562 D7
39000 WasC 97116 562 C7
39600 WasC 97116 592 A1
40800 WasC 97116 591 J1
SW Verdant Ter
22500 SRWD 97140 684 F7
SW Verde Ter
11000 TGRD 97223 655 E3
NW Verde Vista Ter
3100 PTLD 97210 596 B5
Vergen Rd
- CmsC 97002 745 B4
NE Vergen Rd
12900 CmsC 97002 745 C4
NE Veritas Ln
31100 YmhC 97132 713 H6
Vermeer Dr
13100 LKOW 97035 656 A4
SW Vermillion Dr
22500 TLTN 97062 685 E7
22900 WasC 97062 685 E7
Vermillion St
600 NWBG 97132 713 C7
Vermilyea St
- ORCY 97045 717 D2
SW Vermont Ct
6900 BRTN 97223 625 G4
6900 BRTN 97225 625 G4
6900 WasC 97223 625 G4
SW Vermont St
10 PTLD 97219 626 F5
1000 PTLD 97239 626 D5
3400 PTLD 97221 626 A5
5000 PTLD 97221 625 J5
5500 PTLD 97219 625 J5
6500 BRTN 97223 625 J5
6500 PTLD 97223 625 H5
6500 PTLD 97225 625 H5
7500 BRTN 97225 625 G5
7500 WasC 97223 625 G5
7500 WasC 97225 625 G5
20900 WasC 97007 624 B4
SE Vernazza Ln
11100 CmsC 97236 657 J4
SE Vernelda St
6300 CmsC 97267 657 D6
SE Vernie Ct
4000 MWKE 97222 657 B4
SE Vernie Ln
12900 MWKE 97222 657 B4
SE Vernie Rd
12500 MWKE 97222 657 B4
NW Vernon Ct
- PTLD 97229 565 D7
NE Vernon Rd
37200 ClkC 98671 540 H6
SE Vernon Rd
35700 ClkC 98671 540 G7
SE Vernon St
12000 CmsC 97015 688 A2
N Vernonia Rd
100 STHN 97051 385 A7
200 STHN 97051 415 B1
500 ClbC 97051 384 J7
500 ClbC 97051 385 A7
500 STHN 97051 384 J7
S Vernonia Rd
100 STHN 97051 415 B1
SE Verns Wy
11500 HPYV 97236 658 A3
SW Verona Ct
20300 WasC 97006 594 E5
SW Veronica Pl
7700 BRTN 97008 625 D3
SW Versailles Ln
17000 KNGC 97224 685 B2
Verte Ct
13800 LKOW 97034 656 D5
NW Vesper Pl
300 WasC 97229 595 B5
SE Vest Ln
5800 MWKE 97222 657 D3
SW Vesta Ct
3300 PTLD 97219 656 B3
SW Vesta St
- MthC 97219 656 F3
4100 PTLD 97219 656 A3
4900 PTLD 97219 655 J2
SW Veta St
20100 WasC 97006 594 D7
Viamontemar Ct
7100 GLDS 97027 687 E3
S Vick Rd
13000 CmsC 97038 807 C6
13700 MOLA 97038 807 C6
SW Vicki Ln
20800 WasC 97007 624 C6
SE Victor Ln
9000 PTLD 97266 627 G2
NE Victoria Av
1600 PTLD 97212 596 G4
1600 PTLD 97232 596 G4
NW Victoria Av
1300 GSHM 97030 629 B1
Victoria Ct
- MCMV 97128 770 F3
5600 LKOW 97035 655 J5
SW Victoria Ct
400 GSHM 97080 629 B3

SW Victoria Ln
3600 GSHM 97080 629 B6
18800 WasC 97007 624 E5
Victoria Pl
600 CmsC 97068 686 D5
SW Victoria Pl
3500 GSHM 97080 629 B6
SE Victoria St
24700 CmsC 97009 659 D3
24700 DAMA 97009 659 D3
NE Victory Av
10 GSHM 97030 629 D2
10 GSHM 97080 629 D2
SE Victory Av
600 VCVR 98661 537 A7
N Victory Blvd
3500 PTLD 97217 566 D1
Victory Ln
2000 WLIN 97068 716 F2
NW Victory Ln
29800 WasC 97124 563 D3
SE Victory Ln
19800 CmsC 97055 692 G5
S Victory Rd
14900 CmsC 97045 688 B3
SE Victory Rd
31300 MthC 97060 630 C3
SW Vienna Ct
20300 WasC 97007 624 C5
SW Vienna Dr
20400 WasC 97007 624 C5
NE View Av
3300 GSHM 97030 599 D6
View Ct
10 LKOW 97034 656 G6
NE View Ct
1800 GSHM 97030 599 D7
SW View Ct
9800 TGRD 97224 655 E6
View Dr
19100 WLIN 97068 686 H3
NE View Pl
3700 GSHM 97030 599 D6
SW View Pl
3000 PTLD 97205 596 B6
NW View Rd
3000 ClkC 98685 506 C3
S View Rd
600 LKOW 97034 656 F7
NW View Ter
52800 SPSE 97056 444 D7
SE View Acres Rd
3900 CmsC 97267 657 B6
NE View Crest Ct
26000 YmhC 97132 713 D2
SW Viewcrest Ct
11800 TGRD 97224 655 B6
View Crest Dr
- DNDE 97115 742 G3
Viewcrest Dr
32100 ClbC 97053 444 C2
SE View Crest Dr
5500 CmsC 97267 657 C7
SW View Crest Dr
400 GSHM 97080 629 B4
600 DNDE 97115 742 G3
View Crest Ln
200 LKOW 97034 686 G1
Viewcrest Ln
32800 ClbC 97053 444 D1
SE Viewcrest Ln
- CmsC 97023 750 C4
- ECDA 97023 750 C4
Viewcrest Pl
55600 ClbC 97053 444 D1
View Glen St
15100 CmsC 97045 717 H7
View Lake Ct
1500 LKOW 97034 656 D6
SE View Meadows Ln
15200 CmsC 97267 657 B7
NW Viewmont Dr
100 DNDE 97115 742 H2
100 YmhC 97115 742 H2
SW Viewmont Dr
100 DNDE 97115 742 G3
100 YmhC 97115 742 G3
500 WasC 97225 595 H6
SW Viewmount Ct
11200 TGRD 97223 655 C5
SW Viewmount Ln
11400 TGRD 97223 655 C5
SW Viewpoint Ct
14000 WasC 97224 654 J7
SE Viewpoint Dr
4500 TDLE 97060 629 H1
4800 MthC 97060 629 H1
Viewpoint Ln
17300 LKOW 97034 686 F1
NW Viewpoint Pl
900 HBRO 97124 593 A4
S Viewpoint Rd
20700 CmsC 97068 686 H6
20700 WLIN 97068 686 H6
SW View Point Ter
3800 PTLD 97239 626 E2
7400 PTLD 97219 626 E6
9300 PTLD 97219 656 E1
NW View Ridge Ct
800 CMAS 98607 569 B4
NW View Ridge Ln
400 CMAS 98607 569 B5
NW View Ridge St
400 CMAS 98607 569 B5
NW View Ridge Wy
400 CMAS 98607 569 B5
NW View Terrace Pl
32800 SPSE 97056 444 D7
SW View Terrace St
9100 TGRD 97224 655 E6
SW Viking Ct
13100 BRTN 97005 625 A4
16400 BRTN 97007 624 G5
18500 WasC 97007 624 E5
SW Viking St
17300 WasC 97007 624 F5
Villa Rd
100 NWBG 97132 713 D7
Villa Rd SR-219
100 NWBG 97132 713 D7
NW Villa Rd
900 SRWD 97140 684 G7
SW Villa Rd
16200 SRWD 97140 684 G7

W Villa Rd
16900 SRWD 97140 684 F7
SE Villa St
5300 HBRO 97123 593 H7
7000 HBRO 97123 594 A7
NW Village Cir
2000 PTLD 97229 595 E3
SW Village Cir
15600 BRTN 97007 624 H4
Village Ct
- MCMV 97128 771 A6
14600 CmsC 97045 717 G3
NE Village Ct
2100 MCMV 97128 771 A6
23200 WDVL 97060 599 C4
SE Village Ct
2000 HBRO 97123 594 B7
SW Village Ct
15500 BRTN 97007 624 H4
Village Dr
600 MOLA 97038 807 D7
15300 LKOW 97034 656 D6
SW Village Ln
14500 BRTN 97005 624 J4
14600 BRTN 97007 624 H4
15800 WasC 97007 624 H4
SE Village Lp
2800 VCVR 98683 568 D1
SW Village Pl
5400 BRTN 97007 624 H4
5400 WasC 97007 624 H4
NE Village St
1300 FRVW 97024 599 B5
SE Village Wy
52200 ClbC 97056 474 G1
52200 SPSE 97056 474 G1
Village at the Pk
- VCVR 98662 507 G7
SW Village Crest Ct
31600 WNVL 97070 745 G2
SW Village Crest Ln
31700 WNVL 97070 745 G2
SW Village Glenn Cir
13200 TGRD 97223 655 F4
SW Village Glenn Ct
13300 TGRD 97223 655 E5
SW Village Glenn Dr
13200 TGRD 97223 655 E5
SW Village Green Ct
31300 WNVL 97070 745 G2
NE Village Green Dr
1800 VCVR 98684 538 B4
SW Village Greens Cir
7600 WNVL 97070 745 F2
NW Village Heights Dr
10200 PTLD 97229 595 E3
Village Park Ct
15500 LKOW 97034 656 C6
Village Park Ln
1600 LKOW 97034 656 D6
SW Village Park Ln
12800 TGRD 97223 655 B3
Village Park Pl
1400 WLIN 97068 716 G1
SE Village Slope Ct
14200 CmsC 97015 658 C6
NE Village Squire Av
10 GSHM 97080 629 E3
700 GSHM 97030 629 E2
NE Village Squire Ct
1000 GSHM 97030 629 E1
SE Villanova Pl
11700 HPYV 97236 658 C4
N Villard Av
5900 PTLD 97217 566 D6
SE Villard St
600 MCMV 97128 770 H6
Villa Ridge Rd
- TGRD 97223 655 G3
SW Villebois Dr S
- WNVL 97070 715 B6
NW Vinca Ln
800 CMAS 98607 568 J4
N Vincent Av
6900 PTLD 97217 566 D5
SW Vincent Ct
17000 WasC 97007 624 F3
Vincent Dr
19300 ORCY 97045 717 B4
S Vincent Dr
19400 ORCY 97045 717 A5
SW Vincent Pl
700 PTLD 97239 626 D4
SW Vincent St
18500 WasC 97007 624 E3
NW Vincola Ter
- WasC 97229 564 H7
- WasC 97229 594 H1
Vine
- CmsC 97015 657 J7
E Vine Av
67500 CmsC 97049 724 B2
Vine Ct
1800 FTGV 97116 592 C5
Vine St
- ClbC 97056 474 F2
- SPSE 97056 474 F2
100 ORCY 97045 717 B2
N Vine St
2000 CmsC 97013 746 F4
2000 CNBY 97013 746 F4
SE Vine St
700 MCMV 97128 770 H6
33800 SPSE 97056 474 F1
NW Vine Maple Ct
400 CMAS 98607 538 J5
Vine Maple Dr
- CmsC 97067 724 D3
E Vine Maple Dr
69000 CmsC 97067 724 C3
NE Vine Maple Dr
22200 YmhC 97115 742 H1
NW Vine Maple Dr
1800 ClkC 98674 386 F1
Vine Maple Rd
- CmsC 97049 724 G7
NE Vine Maple Rd
13000 ClkC 98606 479 F7
SE Vineyard Av
16600 CmsC 97267 687 A1
SW Vineyard Ct
7400 WasC 97223 625 G5
SE Vineyard Ln
16200 CmsC 97267 687 A1

SE Vineyard Rd
3500 CmsC 97267 687 A1
SE Vineyard Wy
2500 CmsC 97267 686 J1
NE Vinings Wy
6800 HBRO 97124 594 A3
SW Vintage Dr
21500 WasC 97123 654 A4
SE Vintage Pl
4800 CmsC 97267 687 C2
SW Vintner Ln
21700 SRWD 97140 684 F6
SW Vinwood Ter
6000 WasC 97007 624 B5
SW Viola St
8000 TGRD 97224 655 F6
SE Viola Vineyard
- CmsC 97236 658 C4
14200 HPYV 97236 658 C4
S Viola Welch Rd
22900 CmsC 97004 749 C6
Violet Av
- CmsC 97023 750 C1
SE Violet Av
9800 CmsC 97015 687 H1
SW Violet Ct
13200 BRTN 97008 625 A5
SE Violet St
- CmsC 97222 657 E2
SE Virginia Av
- MthC 97080 629 H6
3000 GSHM 97080 629 H6
SW Virginia Av
5900 PTLD 97239 626 F4
6600 PTLD 97219 626 F5
SE Virginia Ct
12000 CmsC 97055 660 J5
Virginia Ln
1900 WLIN 97068 716 G1
7500 VCVR 98664 537 E6
SW Virginia Pl
7100 PTLD 97219 626 F5
SE Virginia St
6200 HBRO 97123 593 G7
Virginia Wy
4000 LKOW 97035 686 A1
Visionary Ct
16400 ORCY 97045 687 F6
NW Visitation Rd
4100 WasC 97116 562 B6
NE Vista Av
1900 GSHM 97030 629 D1
2100 GSHM 97030 599 D7
NW Vista Av
- PTLD 97231 565 E5
7400 ClkC 98665 506 F5
21000 WasC 97124 564 C1
SE Vista Av
10 GSHM 97030 629 D2
10 GSHM 97080 629 D3
10000 CmsC 97015 687 H1
SW Vista Av
700 PTLD 97205 596 D5
700 PTLD 97210 596 D5
1400 PTLD 97201 596 C7
2600 PTLD 97201 626 D1
15400 SRWD 97140 684 H7
SE Vista Ct
- CmsC 97267 657 C6
Vista Dr
100 CtzC 98674 385 G1
2900 FTGV 97116 591 F3
3100 WasC 97116 591 F3
18300 WLIN 97068 686 H2
NW Vista Dr
5000 ClkC 98674 386 B3
SW Vista Dr
2600 WasC 97225 625 E2
3500 WasC 97005 625 E2
Vista Ln
33800 ClbC 97053 414 F3
NW Vista Ln
18700 MthC 97231 504 F7
SE Vista Ln
14200 CmsC 97267 657 C6
SW Vista Pl
9600 WasC 97225 625 E2
SW Vista St
18700 WasC 97006 594 E7
SE Vista Ter
500 GSHM 97080 629 D3
NE Vista Wy
1400 GSHM 97030 629 D1
SE Vista Wy
2600 GSHM 97080 629 D6
3000 GSHM 97080 629 D6
S Vista del Lago Ct
20800 CmsC 97045 748 D1
SE Vista Heights Dr
- HPYV 97236 658 C4
Vista Hill Ct
19300 ORCY 97045 717 A4
SE Vista Loop Dr
40900 CmsC 97055 691 C4
40900 SNDY 97055 691 C4
S Vista Montana Dr
20800 CmsC 97045 748 D1
NW Vista Ridge Ct
3200 CMAS 98607 569 B3
Vista Ridge Dr
3400 WLIN 97068 686 H7
3400 WLIN 97068 716 H1
SE Vista Sunrise Ct
15400 CmsC 97267 657 C7
Vista Verde
- VCVR 98683 568 F3
SE Vista View Ct
18200 CmsC 97055 691 C4
18200 SNDY 97055 691 C4
SW Vista View Ct
14200 TGRD 97224 655 B6
SE Vista View Ln
10800 CmsC 97236 657 J3
Vittoria Sq
- NWBG 97132 713 F6
Vittoria Wy
3200 NWBG 97132 713 F6
SE Vivaldi Ct
12000 MWKE 97222 657 C3
NW Vivian Ct
26600 WasC 97133 533 F5
Viviparous Wy
7500 PTLD 97219 626 A6
SW Vlahos Ct
7500 WNVL 97070 715 F6

SW Vlahos Dr
7500 WNVL 97070 715 F6
SE Vogel Ct
17600 CmsC 97009 658 G4
17600 DAMA 97009 658 F4
17600 HPYV 97009 658 F4
SE Vogel Rd
17200 CmsC 97009 658 F5
17200 CmsC 97236 658 F5
17200 HPYV 97009 658 F5
17200 HPYV 97236 658 F5
17700 DAMA 97009 658 G5
SE Vogel Wy
18400 DAMA 97009 658 G5
SW Volley St
29400 WNVL 97070 715 F7
SE Vollmer Ln
35200 CmsC 97055 690 F4
Volpp St
1800 CmsC 97068 716 G3
1800 WLIN 97068 716 H3
NW Von Neumann Dr
19500 HBRO 97006 594 D4
NW Von Neumann Rd
20600 HBRO 97006 594 C4
SW Voss Pl
23500 SRWD 97140 714 E1
SE Vrandenburg Rd
9200 CmsC 97236 658 D3
9200 HPYV 97236 658 D3
9200 PTLD 97236 658 E1
SW Vulcan Ct
14800 BRTN 97007 624 J6

W

W St
1500 VCVR 98661 536 J4
3000 VCVR 98663 536 J3
3200 ClkC 98671 570 C4
3200 WHGL 98671 570 C4
SE W St
34700 ClkC 98671 570 F4
34700 WHGL 98671 570 F4
N Wabash Av
7500 PTLD 97217 566 C5
SE Wabash Av
13200 CmsC 97222 656 J5
S Wachtman Rd
16500 CmsC 97045 688 B5
NW Waco Av
- PTLD 97210 565 G5
- PTLD 97231 565 G5
NE Waco Ct
200 HBRO 97124 593 F4
NW Waco Ct
- PTLD 97231 565 F5
S Waconda Wy
28200 CmsC 97013 807 D1
NW Wade St
100 ECDA 97023 750 B3
SW Wade St
200 ECDA 97023 750 B4
Wade Park Ests
- PTLD 97236 628 D2
NE Waggoner Dr
2700 MCMV 97128 771 A2
Wagner Av
10 STHN 97051 385 A7
SE Wagner Ln
14300 CmsC 97267 656 H6
SW Wagner Ln
19800 WasC 97007 624 C6
SE Wagner St
12100 HPYV 97236 658 A4
SW Wagner St
28000 CmsC 97070 715 G6
28000 WNVL 97070 715 G6
NW Wagon Wy
21700 HBRO 97124 564 B6
21700 HBRO 97229 564 B6
SE Wagoneer Lp
47400 CmsC 97055 691 J7
48300 CmsC 97055 692 A7
SW Wagoner Pl
14100 TGRD 97224 655 B7
SW Wagontrain Pl
20900 SRWD 97140 684 E5
Wagon Wheel Cir
4400 FTGV 97116 592 C6
SW Wagon Wheel Ct
11800 BRTN 97008 625 C7
Wahclellah Av
1900 VCVR 98661 537 C4
SE Wahkeena Ct
11400 HPYV 97236 657 J3
NW Wahkeena Ln
5200 WasC 97229 564 C7
SE Wake Ct
4100 MWKE 97222 657 B1
SE Wake St
3200 MWKE 97222 657 A1
SW Wakefield St
10600 WasC 97225 595 D7
SW Wakem Ln
17300 WasC 97006 624 F2
SW Wakem St
17500 WasC 97006 624 F2
NW Waker Dr
12300 WasC 97229 595 B3
Wakerobin Ct
2600 WLIN 97068 687 A6
Wake-Robin Dr
17300 ORCY 97045 717 E1
SW Wakheena Ct
12800 TGRD 97224 655 C6
SW Wakkila Ter
8500 WasC 97007 624 G7
8600 BRTN 97007 624 G7
NE Walbridge Dr
7000 HBRO 97124 594 A3
NW Walden Dr
2300 CMAS 98607 539 B7
SW Walden Ln
12000 BRTN 97008 625 B7
Walden St
2000 WLIN 97068 687 A7
NW Walden St
4500 CMAS 98607 569 C1
4600 CMAS 98607 539 B7
SE Walden Wy
15500 CmsC 97267 656 H7
NW Waldheim Wy
47700 WasC 97116 591 C4

SW Waldo Wy
11500 WasC 97140 715 B1
Waldow Rd
17800 CmsC 97045 717 H3
S Waldow Rd
18400 CmsC 97045 717 H3
SE Waldron Dr
13200 CmsC 97222 656 J5
SE Waldron Rd
1900 CmsC 97222 656 J5
SE Walgren Rd
20000 CmsC 97009 688 J1
20000 DAMA 97009 688 J1
21100 CmsC 97009 689 A1
21100 DAMA 97009 689 A1
NE Walker Ct
300 PTLD 97211 566 G3
NW Walker Rd
16600 BRTN 97006 594 F5
18500 HBRO 97006 594 E4
19000 WasC 97006 594 E4
19500 HBRO 97124 594 D3
S Walker Rd
18100 CmsC 97045 717 J3
18100 CmsC 97045 718 A3
SW Walker Rd
10000 WasC 97005 625 B1
10000 WasC 97225 625 D2
10800 BRTN 97005 625 D1
10800 BRTN 97225 625 D2
13400 WasC 97005 595 A7
14000 WasC 97006 595 A7
14200 WasC 97005 594 H6
14200 WasC 97006 594 J6
14500 BRTN 97006 594 H6
NE Walker St
10 PTLD 97211 566 G3
10 PTLD 97217 566 G3
Walking Woods Dr
10 LKOW 97035 656 B3
10 PTLD 97035 656 B3
10 PTLD 97219 656 B3
SW Walking Woods Dr
11800 LKOW 97035 656 B3
11800 PTLD 97035 656 B3
11800 PTLD 97219 656 B3
N Wall Av
6600 PTLD 97203 565 J5
6600 PTLD 97203 566 A3
Wall St
17100 LKOW 97034 656 D7
SW Wall St
- TGRD 97223 655 F5
E Wallace Av
23000 CmsC 97011 724 A2
SW Wallace Pl
21500 SRWD 97140 684 G6
Wallace Rd
10 CtzC 98674 385 H4
NW Wallace Rd
500 MCMV 97128 770 E4
1900 YmhC 97128 770 E4
SE Wallace Rd
6000 DAYT 97114 772 C6
6000 YmhC 97114 772 C6
15400 CmsC 97267 657 C7
27400 CmsC 97023 720 C6
SE Wallace Rd SR-221
6000 DAYT 97114 772 C6
6000 YmhC 97114 772 C6
NW Wallace Wy
200 MCMV 97128 770 G5
SE Wallace Wy
5100 CmsC 97267 657 C7
Walling Cir
18800 WLIN 97068 686 H3
Walling Wy
3300 WLIN 97068 686 H3
Wallingford Av
18900 SNDY 97055 691 A5
SW Wallingford Wy
10 PTLD 97229 594 G5
NW Wallowa Ct
4400 WasC 97229 594 C1
SW Wallowa Ct
31000 WNVL 97070 745 E2
NW Wallowa Pl
19900 WasC 97229 564 D7
19900 WasC 97229 594 C1
SE Wallowa Wy
14500 HPYV 97236 658 C1
NW Wallula Av
10 GSHM 97030 629 A2
10 GSHM 97080 629 A2
2000 GSHM 97030 599 A6
SW Wallula Av
10 GSHM 97030 629 A2
10 GSHM 97080 629 A3
NW Wallula Ct
20700 WasC 97229 564 C6
SW Wallula Ct
300 GSHM 97080 629 A3
SW Wallula Dr
1000 GSHM 97080 629 A4
SE Wally Rd
26200 CmsC 97009 659 F4
NW Walmar Dr
- MthC 97229 595 G3
- PTLD 97229 595 G3
NW Walmer Dr
1600 MthC 97229 595 G3
1600 PTLD 97229 595 G3
NE Walner
30000 ClkC 98642 416 H4
Walnut Av
2700 NWBG 97132 713 E6
NE Walnut Av
1300 YmhC 97128 771 C4
1600 WDVL 97060 599 D4
SE Walnut Av
31100 CmsC 97022 720 B2
SE Walnut Ct
4100 HBRO 97123 593 G6
SE Walnut Dr
10000 HPYV 97236 657 J2
Walnut Grv
- PTLD 97230 598 D2
Walnut Ln
- CmsC 97015 657 H7
SW Walnut Ln
7800 BRTN 97225 625 G1
13500 TGRD 97223 655 A4
14100 TGRD 97223 654 J4
Walnut Pl
- FRVW 97024 599 B4

SW Walnut Pl
9800 TGRD 97223 655 D4
Walnut St
- MCMV 97128 770 G6
2600 VCVR 98660 536 E3
4600 WLIN 97068 687 B7
Walnut St NE
- MrnC 97002 774 J1
20700 AURA 97002 775 F5
N Walnut St
2000 CmsC 97013 746 F4
NW Walnut St
100 DNDE 97115 742 G2
100 YmhC 97115 742 G2
5100 VCVR 98663 506 E7
S Walnut St
100 CmsC 97013 746 F6
100 CNBY 97013 746 F6
SE Walnut St
100 HBRO 97123 593 C5
2400 CmsC 97267 656 J6
SW Walnut St
100 DNDE 97115 742 G2
100 HBRO 97123 593 A5
500 MCMV 97128 770 G6
12900 TGRD 97223 655 A4
14000 BRTN 97007 654 J3
14000 TGRD 97223 654 J3
33500 SPSE 97056 474 D2
SW Walnut Ter
6500 PTLD 97219 655 H1
6500 TGRD 97223 655 H1
SW Walquin Ct
19600 WasC 97007 624 D4
SE Walta Vista Ct
2900 CmsC 97267 687 A2
SE Walta Vista Dr
17300 CmsC 97267 687 A2
SE Walter Cr
- TDLE 97060 629 H1
NW Walters Ln
10500 WasC 97229 595 D5
SW Walters Lp
1500 GSHM 97080 629 B4
SW Walters Rd
400 GSHM 97030 629 B3
400 GSHM 97080 629 B4
SW Walton Ct
14600 WasC 97006 594 J6
SW Walton St
14300 WasC 97006 594 J6
NW Waltuck Ct
17400 WasC 97229 594 F2
Waluga Dr
15300 CmsC 97035 655 J7
15300 LKOW 97035 655 J6
SW Wampanoag Dr
6700 TLTN 97062 685 G5
NE Wand Rd
31300 MthC 97060 600 C5
SE Wanda Ct
4800 CmsC 97267 657 B6
SE Wanda Dr
14600 CmsC 97267 657 C6
W Wanetah Wy
1100 MCMV 97128 770 F7
NW Wapato Av
16600 MthC 97231 534 H2
SW Wapato Av
3900 PTLD 97239 626 C2
NW Wapato Dr
16500 MthC 97231 534 H2
SW Wapato St
17500 SRWD 97140 684 F6
NW Wapinitia Ln
21100 WasC 97229 564 C6
NW Wapinitia Pl
20800 WasC 97229 564 C7
NW Wapitti Ln
49000 WasC 97106 531 A4
SW Warbler Ct
900 MCMV 97128 770 E6
Warbler Dr NE
- MrnC 97002 744 H6
Warbler Ln NE
11500 MrnC 97002 744 J6
SE Warbler Pl
14000 HPYV 97236 658 C2
SW Warbler Pl
23800 SRWD 97140 714 H1
SW Warbler Ter
- BRTN 97007 654 H4
SW Warbler Wy
15100 BRTN 97007 654 H4
S Ward Ct
23300 CmsC 97045 747 A6
Ward Dr
58700 ClbC 97051 414 G2
58700 ClbC 97053 414 G2
NE Ward Rd
8000 ClkC 98682 508 C6
8800 ClkC 98606 508 F3
NE Ward Rd SR-500
8300 ClkC 98682 508 E5
NE Ward St
8700 PTLD 97220 597 G1
NW Wardway St
2800 PTLD 97210 596 C3
SW Wareham Cir
8000 WasC 97223 625 F7
Wareham Ln
1800 NWBG 97132 713 E6
NE Warmington Rd
9300 YmhC 97128 771 D2
SW Warm Springs St
7500 TLTN 97062 685 F4
SW Warner Av
11700 TGRD 97223 655 F3
Warner St
100 ORCY 97045 717 D3
Warner Milne Ext
- ORCY 97045 717 D3
Warner Milne Rd
100 ORCY 97045 717 C3
Warner Parrott Rd
100 ORCY 97045 717 B3
SE Warnock Ln
16400 CmsC 97267 687 C1
S Warnock Rd
12900 CmsC 97045 717 D7
12900 CmsC 97045 747 C1
Warren Ct
600 ORCY 97045 717 D2
17100 LKOW 97035 685 J1

STREET
Block City ZIP Map# Grid

SE Warren Ct
13400 CmsC 97015 657 J5
NE Warren Rd
7600 YmhC 97115 742 F3
Warren St
100 ORCY 97045 717 D1
N Warren St
5300 PTLD 97203 566 A5
SW Warrens Wy
4200 PTLD 97221 626 A1
NW Warrenton Ter
700 PTLD 97210 596 A3
S Warrick Rd
13300 CmsC 97038 837 D3
SW Warwick Av
1700 WasC 97225 595 D7
2000 WasC 97225 625 C1
Warwick St
2400 WLIN 97068 687 A7
2700 WLIN 97068 686 J7
NE Wasco Ct
18700 GSHM 97230 598 H5
NE Wasco St
1700 PTLD 97232 596 J4
3500 PTLD 97232 597 B4
4900 PTLD 97213 597 C4
8100 PTLD 97220 597 F4
12200 PTLD 97220 598 A4
12600 PTLD 97230 598 B5
19600 GSHM 97230 598 J5
SW Wasco Wy
10000 TLTN 97062 685 D2
NW Wascoe St
- WasC 97133 563 A1
30900 NPNS 97133 563 B1
N Washburne Av
7500 PTLD 97217 566 C4
NW Washington Av
40700 WasC 97106 532 A6
SW Washington Av
4500 BRTN 97005 625 B3
Washington Ct
5200 LKOW 97035 685 H1
5400 CmsC 97035 685 H1
SE Washington Ct
2300 HBRO 97123 593 E5
17400 PTLD 97233 598 F7
19900 GSHM 97233 598 J7
SW Washington Ct
17400 WasC 97007 624 F3
SW Washington Dr
8600 WasC 97223 625 F7
9000 WasC 97223 655 F1
17500 WasC 97007 624 F3
SE Washington Pl
4700 MWKE 97222 657 C3
SW Washington Pl
9500 WasC 97225 595 E6
Washington St
- CLTN 97111 741 A2
100 LFYT 97127 771 G1
100 ORCY 97045 717 C1
200 WDLD 98674 386 B1
400 WDLD 98674 385 J1
700 ORCY 97045 687 C7
1100 LFYT 97127 741 G7
2600 VCVR 98660 536 G2
E Washington St
400 CLTN 97111 741 B1
N Washington St
- LFYT 97127 741 G6
- YmhC 97128 741 G6
100 NWBG 97132 713 C7
NW Washington St
3900 VCVR 98660 536 G1
4400 ClkC 98663 536 G1
4400 VCVR 98663 536 G1
S Washington St
100 NWBG 97132 713 C7
15700 ORCY 97045 687 E5
SE Washington St
- PTLD 97216 597 G7
100 HBRO 97123 593 B5
200 MCMV 97128 770 H5
1600 PTLD 97214 596 H6
1900 MWKE 97222 656 J2
3700 MWKE 97222 657 B2
4100 PTLD 97214 597 B6
5200 PTLD 97215 597 C6
11500 PTLD 97216 598 A6
13000 PTLD 97233 598 B6
17700 GSHM 97233 598 G7
SW Washington St
100 HBRO 97123 593 B5
200 PTLD 97204 596 F6
500 PTLD 97205 596 E6
10500 WasC 97225 595 D6
11000 BRTN 97225 595 D6
12700 WasC 97005 595 B6
22200 SRWD 97140 684 G7
W Washington St
10 CLTN 97111 741 A1
SW Washington Wy
- PTLD 97205 596 C5
SW Washington Park Dr
- PTLD 97205 596 C6
SW Washington Square Rd
- BRTN 97008 625 D7
- BRTN 97008 655 E1
- BRTN 97223 655 E1
- TGRD 97008 625 D7
- TGRD 97223 625 D7
9000 TGRD 97223 655 D1
NW Washington St Ext
4900 ClkC 98663 536 G1
5100 ClkC 98663 506 G7
SW Washo Ct
7300 TLTN 97062 685 G4
SW Washouga Av
4100 PTLD 97239 626 C2
N Washougal River Rd
1400 WHGL 98671 570 B4
2500 ClkC 98671 570 B4
NE Washougal River Rd
34700 ClkC 98671 540 F6
SE Washougal River Rd
10 ClkC 98671 540 C7
10 ClkC 98671 570 B1
2000 WHGL 98671 570 B4
Wassail Ln
13100 ORCY 97045 717 D4
SE Water Av
500 PTLD 97214 596 G7
1600 PTLD 97214 626 G1
17200 CmsC 97015 687 G2

SW Water Av
2200 PTLD 97201 626 F1
3200 PTLD 97239 626 F2
NW Water Rd
- MthC 97231 535 B7
- PTLD 97231 535 B7
Water St
- ORCY 97045 687 B7
500 DAYT 97114 772 C4
500 YmhC 97114 772 C4
E Water St
28000 CmsC 97067 724 C7
SE Water St
400 LFYT 97127 771 G1
500 DAYT 97114 772 B4
Waterboard Park Rd
- ORCY 97045 717 C1
SW Watercrest Ct
17100 BRTN 97006 594 G7
Watercrest Rd
500 FTGV 97116 591 F2
500 WasC 97116 591 F2
SE Water Edge Wy
4200 CmsC 97267 687 B3
SE Waterford Ct
10500 HPYV 97236 658 B2
Waterford Pl
21300 CmsC 97068 686 E5
NW Waterford Wy
16700 WasC 97229 564 G7
S Waterfront Dr
1600 YmhC 97132 743 C2
NW Waterhouse Av
600 BRTN 97006 594 H4
SW Waterleaf Ln
17300 BRTN 97006 594 F6
17300 WasC 97006 594 F6
SW Waterleaf St
16500 BRTN 97006 594 G6
SE Waterlily St
1700 HBRO 97123 623 E2
SW Watermark Ln
16900 BRTN 97006 594 G5
SW Water Parsley Ln
7800 TGRD 97224 655 F6
SW Waterthrush Ter
11600 BRTN 97007 654 E3
SW Watkins Av
12700 TGRD 97223 655 D5
NW Watkins Ct
2900 CMAS 98607 569 C2
SW Watkins Pl
10600 TGRD 97223 655 D4
Watson Av
2300 VCVR 98661 537 A3
SW Watson Av
4100 BRTN 97005 625 B3
SE Watson Pl
15800 CmsC 97267 657 A7
Watson Rd
- MthC 97231 474 E5
32400 ClbC 97056 474 C5
NW Watts Pl
3000 WasC 97116 561 D7
3000 WasC 97116 591 C1
N Watts St
2500 PTLD 97217 566 D4
NE Watts St
- SPSE 97056 444 E7
NW Watts St
33400 SPSE 97056 444 G7
SE Watts St
18900 GLDS 97027 687 D3
Wauna Vista Dr
3600 VCVR 98661 537 A6
S Wave Rd
15300 CmsC 97042 777 H6
SE Waverleigh Blvd
3300 PTLD 97202 627 A2
SE Waverly Ct
10000 MWKE 97222 656 H2
SE Waverly Dr
100 CmsC 97222 656 H1
1000 MWKE 97222 656 H1
SW Waverly Dr
8800 TGRD 97224 685 E1
SW Waverly Pl
11100 WasC 97225 625 C1
Wax Wing Cir
18400 LKOW 97035 685 J2
SW Waxwing Pl
16000 BRTN 97007 654 H2
Wax Wing Wy
18400 LKOW 97035 685 G3
SW Waxwing Wy
16000 BRTN 97007 654 G2
SE Waybill Rd
- CmsC 97009 690 B2
30100 CmsC 97009 660 B2
N Wayland Av
7200 PTLD 97217 566 C5
7900 PTLD 97203 566 C4
SE Waymire St
5600 MWKE 97222 657 C3
Wayne Dr
16300 ORCY 97045 687 F6
Wayne St
55500 ClbC 97053 444 E1
Wayside Dr
- ClbC 97056 474 B4
Wayside Ln
17600 LKOW 97034 686 G2
Way Wy Ln
56600 ClbC 97053 414 F6
Wayzata Wy
6200 CmsC 97035 685 H3
NE Weakley Rd
23200 ClkC 98607 539 C4
SW Weatherford Av
17700 SRWD 97140 684 E5
Weatherhill Rd
22800 CmsC 97068 686 G7
22800 WLIN 97068 686 G7
SE Weatherly Ln
22700 CmsC 97009 689 C1
22700 DAMA 97009 689 B1
Weaver Ct
18000 SNDY 97055 691 A3
SW Weaver Dr
30000 WasC 97132 683 B5
SW Weaver Wy
- TGRD 97224 655 G6
NE Weaver Creek Rd
27900 ClkC 98675 419 H2

S Webb Rd
700 CNLS 97113 592 G6
700 WasC 97113 592 G6
SW Webb Rd
- WasC 97113 592 F6
Webb St
1800 WLIN 97068 687 B6
SE Webber St
700 PTLD 97202 626 G7
SE Weber Rd
49500 CmsC 97055 692 B7
49900 CmsC 97055 723 A6
SE Webfoot Rd
6100 DAYT 97114 772 A5
6100 YmhC 97114 772 A6
7000 YmhC 97114 771 J7
Webster Av
19000 SNDY 97055 690 J5
NE Webster Ct
5300 PTLD 97218 567 C6
Webster Ln
3200 WHGL 98671 570 C5
SE Webster Ln
7200 CmsC 97267 657 E7
Webster Rd
16800 CmsC 97027 687 E1
16800 CmsC 97267 687 E1
16900 GLDS 97027 687 E3
NE Webster Rd
25900 ClkC 98604 448 F1
SE Webster Rd
13700 CmsC 97222 657 D6
13700 CmsC 97267 657 E7
15900 CmsC 97267 687 E1
16700 CmsC 97027 687 E1
N Webster St
10 PTLD 97211 566 J7
3100 PTLD 97217 566 C7
NE Webster St
400 PTLD 97211 566 H7
3300 PTLD 97211 567 A7
5400 PTLD 97218 567 C6
8200 PTLD 97218 597 G1
8200 PTLD 97220 597 G1
8700 PTLD 97220 567 G7
SW Wedgefield Ln
18800 WasC 97007 624 D2
SE Wedgewood Av
3300 HBRO 97123 623 H1
3300 WasC 97123 623 H1
NE Wedgewood Ct
300 CMAS 98607 569 H4
Wedgewood Dr
600 MOLA 97038 807 D7
Wedgewood Lp
5200 NWBG 97132 713 H7
SW Wedgewood St
10600 WasC 97225 595 D7
SE Weedman Ct
12600 MWKE 97222 657 B4
SE Weedman St
4200 MWKE 97222 657 B4
SE Weeks Ct
5000 CmsC 97267 657 C6
NW Weible Wy
14500 WasC 97006 594 J5
NE Weidler Cir
21300 FRVW 97024 599 A4
NE Weidler Pl
- FRVW 97024 599 A4
N Weidler St
10 PTLD 97227 596 F4
10 PTLD 97232 596 G4
NE Weidler St
- PTLD 97220 597 F4
10 PTLD 97227 596 G4
2400 PTLD 97232 596 J4
4200 PTLD 97213 597 B4
4200 PTLD 97232 597 B4
15700 PTLD 97230 598 E4
Weidman Ct
500 LKOW 97034 656 E7
Weigel Av
2600 VCVR 98660 536 D3
SE Weiko Wy
5800 CmsC 97222 657 D4
5800 MWKE 97222 657 D5
SW Weiland Pl
- WasC 97123 653 D7
- WasC 97123 683 D1
SW Weir Rd
- BRTN 97008 654 J1
13000 BRTN 97008 655 A1
14500 BRTN 97007 654 G1
16400 WasC 97007 654 G1
NE Weir St
100 CMAS 98607 569 J4
100 WHGL 98671 569 J5
SE Weir St
100 CMAS 98607 569 J5
SE Weitz Ln
29100 CmsC 97022 719 J2
30000 CmsC 97022 720 A2
SW Welch Ct
11500 BRTN 97008 655 C1
NE Welch Rd
16700 YmhC 97132 713 B2
SE Welch Rd
4200 GSHM 97080 629 G6
SW Welch Ter
11600 BRTN 97008 655 C1
Welches Ct
59000 STHN 97051 414 H2
E Welches Rd
24400 CmsC 97067 724 C3
Weleber St
400 ORCY 97045 717 C2
NE Weller Ct
5800 HBRO 97124 593 J5
5800 WasC 97124 593 J5
Wellesley Av
19000 SNDY 97055 691 A4
N Wellesley Av
7000 PTLD 97203 566 B5
SW Wellington Av
1600 WasC 97225 595 B7
Wellington Ct
3800 WLIN 97068 716 J1
SE Wellington Ct
12700 HPYV 97236 658 A1
Wellington Dr
2000 WLIN 97068 716 J1
2100 WLIN 97068 717 A1
SW Wellington Ln
10700 WNVL 97070 745 C1

Wellington Pl
3900 WLIN 97068 717 A1
SW Wellington Pl
13100 TGRD 97223 655 A5
NW Wellman Rd
2200 ClkC 98629 386 E6
NW Wells Ct
9400 PTLD 97229 595 E4
9400 WasC 97229 595 E4
Wells St
1200 LKOW 97034 656 G7
NW Welsh Dr
12000 WasC 97229 595 C2
Welter Cir
500 GLDS 97027 687 C4
Wembley Ct
2100 LKOW 97034 656 C5
Wembley Pl
1900 LKOW 97034 656 C5
Wembley Park Rd
1900 LKOW 97034 656 B6
2600 LKOW 97035 656 B6
SW Wembly Pl
4800 BRTN 97005 624 J3
E Wemme Tr
65200 CmsC 97011 723 J1
65200 CmsC 97067 723 J1
Wendlandt Wy
34800 ClbC 97056 444 H4
SW Wendover Ter
6200 WasC 97223 625 H5
SE Wendy Av
1000 GSHM 97080 629 F4
3100 MthC 97080 629 F6
Wendy Ct
800 WLIN 97068 716 F1
SE Wendy Ct
1700 GSHM 97080 629 F5
SE Wendy Dr
2100 GSHM 97080 629 F5
NE Wendy Ln
600 GSHM 97030 629 F2
NW Wendy Ln
14500 WasC 97229 564 J7
SE Wendy Ln
600 GSHM 97080 629 F3
1600 CmsC 97267 656 H7
SE Wenlock Av
1000 HBRO 97123 593 D6
NW Wenmarie Dr
6400 WasC 97229 564 J6
SW Wentworth Ter
4900 WasC 97007 624 G2
NW Werburgh Ln
11700 WasC 97229 595 C3
NW Werner Ln
14500 WasC 97229 564 J7
SW Wert Ct
15100 SRWD 97140 684 H7
S Wesley Ct
17800 CmsC 97045 718 D3
Wesley Ln
15400 CmsC 97035 655 J6
15400 LKOW 97035 655 J6
S Wesley Ln
18000 CmsC 97045 718 D2
Wesley Lynn St
- CmsC 97045 717 C5
- ORCY 97045 717 C5
NW Wessex Ter
2400 HBRO 97124 594 C2
SE Wessex Wy
9500 CmsC 97236 657 H1
West Av
- BRTN 97005 625 A2
SW West Av
4400 BRTN 97005 625 B3
West Ln
400 CmsC 97038 837 D1
400 MOLA 97038 837 D1
West Lp
- WasC 97124 592 G4
West Rd
- CmsC 97068 716 D3
500 STHN 97051 415 A1
4500 LKOW 97034 686 A3
4500 LKOW 97035 686 A3
4500 RVGR 97034 686 A3
4500 RVGR 97035 686 A3
NW West Rd
11400 WasC 97229 595 C2
West St
- TLTN 97062 685 A3
- WasC 97224 655 D2
- WasC 97224 685 A1
10 STHN 97051 385 C7
N Westanna Av
6800 PTLD 97203 565 J4
7300 PTLD 97203 566 A4
N Westanna Ct
9000 PTLD 97203 566 A3
Westberry Ct
1800 WLIN 97068 686 G4
West Bluff Ct
22700 WLIN 97068 686 H7
West Bluff Dr
22100 WLIN 97068 686 G7
23600 CmsC 97068 686 G7
Westboro Wy
34800 ClbC 97051 414 H1
34800 STHN 97051 414 H1
NW Westbrook Wy
15500 WasC 97229 564 H6
SW Westbury Ter
11900 TGRD 97223 655 B2
SE Westchester Av
11000 HPYV 97236 658 B3
SW Westchester Ct
6800 WNVL 97070 745 G2
Westcott Ct
13900 LKOW 97035 655 J5
SE Westcott Ln
7100 HBRO 97123 624 A1
7100 WasC 97123 624 A1
SW Westdale Dr
4000 PTLD 97221 626 A2
5300 MthC 97221 625 J2
SW Westdale St
12200 WasC 97225 595 B7
NE Westerholm Rd
23900 ClkC 98604 479 D1
23900 ClkC 98606 479 D1
SE Westerland St
900 HBRO 97123 593 D7

SW Western Av
4700 BRTN 97005 625 D3
5900 BRTN 97008 625 D4
NW Western Wy
- MCMV 97128 770 J6
100 HBRO 97123 593 A5
100 HBRO 97124 593 A5
SW Westfall Ct
10800 TLTN 97062 685 C7
SW Westfall Rd
12000 CmsC 97070 715 A5
12000 CmsC 97140 714 J5
12000 CmsC 97140 715 A5
SW Westfield Av
2100 WasC 97225 595 B7
2100 WasC 97225 625 B1
2300 WasC 97005 625 B1
Westfield Ct
5200 LKOW 97035 655 J5
SE Westfork St
5500 CmsC 97206 627 D7
NW Westgate Ct
9000 ClkC 98665 506 F4
NW Westgate Dr
1200 ClkC 98665 506 F4
SW Westgate Dr
- BRTN 97005 625 B2
5200 PTLD 97221 595 J7
SE Westgate Wy
11200 CmsC 97236 657 J4
11600 HPYV 97236 657 J4
SW Westgate Wy
7000 WasC 97225 625 G4
8000 BRTN 97225 625 F4
SW West Haven Dr
9000 WasC 97225 595 E6
Westhill Rd
59800 ClbC 97051 384 J7
West Hills Dr
- MCMV 97128 770 D6
- YmhC 97128 770 D6
Westlake Dr
14500 LKOW 97035 655 J5
SE Westlake Dr
51300 SPSE 97056 474 F2
Westlake Lp
1900 NWBG 97132 713 F5
SW Westland Ln
- WasC 97006 594 E7
NE Westlane Rd
52500 SPSE 97056 444 F7
52600 ClbC 97056 444 F6
NW Westlawn St
12200 WasC 97229 595 B4
NW Westlawn Ter
12700 WasC 97229 595 B4
Westling Dr
19400 ORCY 97045 717 A5
SW Westlund Ct
9000 TGRD 97224 655 E7
NW Westmark Dr
- WasC 97124 564 B5
22400 HBRO 97124 564 B5
Westminster Dr
10 LKOW 97034 686 B2
SW Westminster Dr
15800 WasC 97224 654 J7
SW Westmoor Wy
7500 WasC 97225 625 G3
SE Weston Landing Ln
18000 YmhC 97114 772 D7
NW Westover Cir
700 PTLD 97210 596 C5
NW Westover Rd
2300 PTLD 97210 596 C5
NW Westover Sq
700 PTLD 97210 596 C5
NW Westover Ter
600 PTLD 97210 596 C5
SE West Park Ct
14400 DAMA 97009 658 G7
NW Westphalian Ter
5300 WasC 97229 564 H7
SW West Point Av
2600 BRTN 97225 625 G1
SW West Point Ct
1700 PTLD 97201 596 D6
West Pond Dr
- FRVW 97024 599 A5
- GSHM 97024 599 A5
- GSHM 97030 599 A5
SE Westridge Blvd
- ClkC 98684 538 H7
100 ClkC 98607 538 H6
100 VCVR 98607 538 H7
Westridge Dr
10 LKOW 97034 686 B2
NW Westridge St
1100 ClkC 98665 506 F4
SW Westridge Ter
13500 TGRD 97223 655 A5
West Ring Rd
- HBRO 97124 593 J2
Westshire Ln
59100 STHN 97051 414 J1
N Westshore Dr
12200 PTLD 97217 536 E7
NE Westside Rd
2700 MCMV 97128 770 H2
2700 YmhC 97128 770 H1
SW Westside St
20300 WasC 97007 624 C4
SW West Slope Dr
7700 BRTN 97225 625 G1
NW West Union Rd
14300 WasC 97006 594 G1
14300 WasC 97229 594 G1
17000 WasC 97006 564 F7
18300 WasC 97231 564 E7
18600 WasC 97229 564 E7
20800 HBRO 97124 564 A5
20800 HBRO 97229 564 C6
20800 WasC 97124 564 A5
27700 WasC 97124 563 C1
28400 NPNS 97133 563 D1
28400 WasC 97133 563 D1
SW Westvale Ct
1900 MCMV 97128 770 E6
Westvale St
- MCMV 97128 770 E6
- YmhC 97128 770 E6
SW Westvale St
100 MCMV 97128 770 E5
Westview Cir
2900 LKOW 97034 686 B1

Westview Ct
3000 LKOW 97034 686 B2
SE Westview Ct
9600 HPYV 97236 657 H2
Westview Dr
16400 LKOW 97034 686 B2
18500 CmsC 97034 686 C3
SW Westview Dr
400 MCMV 97128 770 F6
NE Westview Ln
500 ECDA 97023 750 C3
SE Westview Rd
3100 CmsC 97267 687 A1
Westward Cir
4400 FTGV 97116 592 C6
Westward Wy
11700 MmC 97002 775 D4
Westward Ho Rd
1000 LKOW 97034 656 E6
NW Westway St
15300 WasC 97006 594 H3
SW Westwind Ct
4400 WasC 97007 624 H3
SW Westwind Dr
16000 WasC 97007 624 G3
SW Westwind Ln
16200 WasC 97007 624 G3
SW Westwood Ct
1000 PTLD 97239 626 D4
Westwood Dr
19600 ORCY 97045 717 A5
SW Westwood Dr
1000 PTLD 97239 626 D4
3000 BRTN 97225 625 D2
3000 WasC 97005 625 D2
3000 WasC 97225 625 D2
SE Westwood Ln
- HBRO 97123 623 H1
SW Westwood Ln
5100 PTLD 97239 626 D3
SW Westwood Vw
5100 PTLD 97239 626 D4
SW Westword St
18800 WasC 97007 624 D3
NE Wetherby St
5800 HBRO 97124 593 J4
Wewer Av
18000 SNDY 97055 690 H4
SE Wewer Ln
37500 SNDY 97055 690 H3
SW Wexford Pl
6400 WasC 97223 625 G5
NW Weybridge Wy
1100 BRTN 97006 594 G4
N Weyerhaeuser Av
7500 PTLD 97203 565 G1
WF Kirk Rd
- CmsC 97045 747 H5
Whalen Rd
- CtzC 98674 385 J3
- CtzC 98674 386 A4
Whalen Loop Rd
100 CtzC 98674 385 J4
SW Wheat Pl
21700 SRWD 97140 684 G6
NW Wheatfield Wy
2000 WasC 97229 595 A3
Wheatherstone Ct
10 LKOW 97035 656 D5
Wheatherstone Pl
10 LKOW 97035 656 D5
Wheatherstone St
10 LKOW 97035 656 B5
SW Wheatland Dr
11900 CmsC 97140 715 B3
SW Wheatland Run
6800 CmsC 97002 745 G2
6800 WNVL 97070 745 G2
SW Wheaton Ln
15000 BRTN 97007 624 J4
N Wheeler Av
1200 PTLD 97227 596 F4
1200 PTLD 97232 596 F4
SW Wheeler Ct
18200 WasC 97007 624 E3
Wheeler Ln
- WLIN 97068 686 J6
N Wheeler Pl
400 PTLD 97227 596 F4
SE Wheeler Rd
28700 CmsC 97009 659 J1
29500 CmsC 97009 660 A1
NW Wheeler St
33000 SPSE 97056 444 E6
SE Where Else Ln
12600 MWKE 97222 657 B5
SW Whetstone Wy
15500 SRWD 97140 684 G6
NE Wh Garner Rd
22300 ClkC 98675 419 C1
24300 YCLT 98675 419 E1
SE Whipperwill Ct
15900 DAMA 97009 688 D1
SE Whipple Av
16200 CmsC 97267 687 B1
Whipple Creek Vil
- ClkC 98642 476 J2
Whipple Creek 2
- ClkC 98642 476 J2
- ClkC 98642 477 A2
Whiskey Cr
- BRTN 97005 625 C2
E Whiskey Ln
20400 CmsC 97055 692 E6
SE Whisper Ct
12600 HPYV 97236 658 D4
SW Whisper Ct
6600 BRTN 97008 625 A5
SW Whispering Fir Dr
9100 WasC 97007 624 D7
9100 WasC 97007 654 D1
NW Whistler Ln
14200 WasC 97229 594 J2
14200 WasC 97229 595 A2
SW Whistler's Ln
12100 TGRD 97223 655 B5
SW Whistler's Lp
12000 TGRD 97223 655 B5
SW Whistling Ct
6600 BRTN 97008 625 A5
SW Whistling Wy
13100 BRTN 97008 625 A5
SW Whistling Swan Ln
16000 BRTN 97007 654 G4

N Whitaker Rd
9200 PTLD 97217 566 E3
SW Whitaker St
- PTLD 97239 626 D2
NE Whitaker Wy
12200 PTLD 97220 568 B7
12200 PTLD 97230 568 B7
14300 PTLD 97230 598 D1
SE Whitcomb Dr
12200 CmsC 97222 657 A4
12200 MWKE 97222 657 A4
SW White Ct
8600 WasC 97225 595 F6
White Ln
11700 CmsC 97045 717 A5
11700 ORCY 97045 717 A5
White Wy
100 STHN 97051 415 B1
SW Whitebark Ln
- TLTN 97062 715 D1
SW Whitebird Dr
15900 BRTN 97007 654 G3
SE White Cap Ln
55400 CmsC 97055 692 H6
SW White Cedar Pl
13600 TGRD 97223 655 A5
13600 TGRD 97224 655 A5
White Cloud Cir
19700 WLIN 97068 686 J4
SE White Crest Ct
19000 DAMA 97009 658 H3
NW White Fox Dr
15300 WasC 97006 594 H4
SE Whitehall Ct
9300 CmsC 97236 657 G1
SW Whitehall Ln
13500 TGRD 97223 655 D1
SE White Lake Rd
4400 MWKE 97222 657 B2
NW White Mountain Ter
4500 WasC 97006 594 F1
SW Whiteoak Ln
18500 WasC 97007 624 B6
White Oak St
100 NWBG 97132 713 F7
White Oaks Dr
15800 LKOW 97035 655 J6
SW Whiteoaks Ln
8900 TGRD 97224 655 G5
SW White Pine Ln
8400 WasC 97225 625 F3
8800 BRTN 97225 625 F3
White Salmon Ct
2800 WLIN 97068 686 J6
2800 WLIN 97068 687 A7
White Tail Av
- SNDY 97055 691 B4
Whitetail Av
34900 STHN 97051 414 J1
White Tail Dr
6300 WLIN 97068 687 A5
SW Whitetail Ln
16500 WasC 97007 624 G7
Whitetail St
59100 STHN 97051 414 J1
NE Whitewood Dr
6000 HBRO 97124 593 J5
6300 HBRO 97124 594 A5
SW Whitford Dr
7500 WasC 97223 625 E6
SW Whitford Ln
9200 WasC 97223 625 E6
9500 WasC 97008 625 E6
9800 BRTN 97008 625 E6
SW Whitfurrows Ct
7800 DRHM 97224 685 E1
SW Whitley Wy
16700 BRTN 97006 594 G6
17000 WasC 97006 594 F6
NE Whitlow Ln
13300 YmhC 97132 712 F5
NE Whitman Av
2500 VCVR 98662 537 E3
NW Whitman Ct
1200 CMAS 98607 568 J4
2800 WasC 97229 594 F3
NW Whitman St
1000 ClkC 98607 568 J4
1000 CMAS 98607 568 J4
Whitman Wy
13300 ORCY 97045 717 D2
Whitney Ln
19200 ORCY 97045 717 C4
S Whitney Ln
16800 CmsC 97004 748 B4
SW Whitney Ln
14100 SRWD 97140 714 J1
NW Whitney Rd
- VCVR 98660 506 E6
- VCVR 98665 506 E6
6300 VCVR 98663 506 E6
6600 ClkC 98665 506 E6
NE Whitney St
100 CMAS 98607 569 H4
NW Whitney St
- PTLD 97231 565 E4
SE Whitney St
100 CMAS 98607 569 H5
SW Whitney Wy
- BRTN 97005 625 A2
S Whitten Ln
18300 CmsC 97068 686 F3
SW Why Worry Ln
12000 BRTN 97008 625 B5
NE Wiberg Ln
2700 PTLD 97213 597 C3
SE Wichata Ct
11000 MWKE 97222 657 D3
SE Wichita Av
- MWKE 97206 657 D1
9300 CmsC 97222 657 D1
9300 MWKE 97222 657 D2
Wichita Dr
6600 VCVR 98661 537 D6
6700 VCVR 98664 537 D6
SW Wichita St
4600 TLTN 97062 685 J4
SE Wicker Ct
6200 HBRO 97123 593 J7
Wickiup Dr
13000 ORCY 97045 717 C5
NW Wickiup Wy
5200 WasC 97229 564 B7
Wickman Wy
33800 ClbC 97053 414 F3

STREET Block City ZIP Map# Grid

NE Wickson Rd
22600 ClkC 98604 449 C4
Wickstrom Dr
33300 SPSE 97056 444 E7
SE Widgeon Ct
16300 DAMA 97009 688 D1
SW Widgeon Ct
15200 BRTN 97007 654 H3
SE Widgeon Ln
16300 DAMA 97009 688 E1
NW Widgi Creek Ct
17200 WasC 97006 594 H4
Widman Ct
16100 ORCY 97045 687 H6
Wiedeman Rd
- WNVL 97070 715 E4
SE Wiese Ct
20500 DAMA 97009 658 J6
SE Wiese Rd
11600 DAMA 97009 658 J6
11700 DAMA 97009 659 A5
Wight Ln
16800 CmsC 97035 685 H1
16800 LKOW 97035 685 H1
Wikstrom Rd
32300 ClbC 97056 444 C4
NW Wilark Av
- PTLD 97231 565 E2
SW Wilbard St
3000 PTLD 97219 656 B1
6000 PTLD 97219 655 H1
6200 TGRD 97223 655 H1
N Wilbur Av
9000 PTLD 97217 566 D3
Wilbur St
10 LKOW 97034 656 G7
Wilcock Rd
- CmsC 97013 746 A4
S Wilcox Rd
22900 CmsC 97013 746 A5
NE Wilcox St
200 HBRO 97124 593 B1
S Wilda St
100 CmsC 97068 686 F3
NW Wildberry Ln
45200 WasC 97116 561 F6
Wild Bill Ct
19400 ORCY 97045 717 D5
SW Wildcat Ln
18900 WasC 97007 624 E5
E Wildcat Creek Rd
20100 CmsC 97055 693 C7
20100 CmsC 97055 723 D1
SE Wildcat Mountain Dr
30400 CmsC 97022 720 B3
NE Wilde Rd
10800 ClkC 98604 417 J4
SE Wilde Rd
17000 CmsC 97015 688 A2
SW Wilderland Ct
8100 DRHM 97224 685 F2
Wilderness Dr
19400 WLIN 97068 686 H3
E Wildfern Ln
21900 CmsC 97011 723 H1
SW Wildflower Dr
21300 WasC 97132 683 C6
E Wildflower Ln
63100 CmsC 97011 693 F6
S Wildflower Ln
15500 CmsC 97045 687 J6
SE Wildflower Pl
3600 HBRO 97123 623 G2
NW Wild Haven Ct
2000 YmhC 97128 770 A2
NW Wild Haven Ln
14100 YmhC 97128 770 A2
SW Wildhaven Ln
28500 WasC 97123 683 C1
SW Wildhorse Wy
14000 BRTN 97008 654 J1
NE Wild Horse Mountain Rd
35200 WasC 97140 714 D5
35200 YmhC 97132 714 D5
NE Wilding Rd
6000 ClkC 98686 507 D3
Wild Iris Av
- CmsC 97067 724 C7
SE Wildlife Estates Dr
6200 CmsC 97267 657 D7
SW Wildlife Haven Ct
16300 SRWD 97140 684 G7
SE Wild Rose Ct
4000 CmsC 97267 657 B6
Wild Rose Dr
3200 WLIN 97068 686 J6
NE Wildrose Dr
4400 VCVR 98682 538 C2
SE Wild Rose Ln
14500 CmsC 97267 657 B6
Wild Rose Lp
3200 CmsC 97068 686 H6
3200 WLIN 97068 686 H7
SW Wildrose Pl
20500 SRWD 97140 685 A5
20500 WasC 97140 685 A5
Wild Rose Wy
3600 WLIN 97068 686 H6
SE Wildwood Ct
15400 CmsC 97267 656 J7
SW Wildwood Ct
31500 WNVL 97070 745 B1
Wildwood Dr
19600 WLIN 97068 686 H4
31300 ClbC 97056 444 A2
NW Wildwood Dr
400 ClkC 98665 506 F3
SE Wildwood Dr
11600 DAMA 97009 659 D4
NW Wildwood Ln
52700 SPSE 97056 444 D7
Wildwood Pl
1800 WLIN 97068 686 H3
NE Wildwood Rd
24000 YmhC 97132 743 B2
Wildwood St
4500 LKOW 97035 686 A1
NW Wildwood St
- HBRO 97124 593 A1
SW Wildwood St
11700 TGRD 97224 655 B6
Wildwood Wy
58000 ClbC 97053 414 F3
Wild Woodland Dr
50200 ClbC 97056 474 A4
Wiles Ct
17100 CmsC 97027 687 F2
17100 CmsC 97267 687 F2
NW Wiley Ln
9100 PTLD 97229 595 F2
SE Wiley Wy
17000 CmsC 97267 686 J1
Wilhelm Rd
- CmsC 97062 685 H7
SW Wilhelm Rd
6100 CmsC 97062 685 H7
S Wilhoit Rd
32700 CmsC 97038 837 D7
SW Wilke Rd
5000 TLTN 97062 685 J4
5100 CmsC 97062 685 J4
SW Wilken Ln
26400 CmsC 97068 716 B4
26600 CmsC 97070 716 B5
SW Wilkens Ln
11600 BRTN 97008 655 C1
NE Wilkerson Wy
16100 YmhC 97132 713 E3
NE Wilkes Rd
17000 GSHM 97230 598 F3
SE Wilkes St
100 BNKS 97106 531 J5
NW Wilkesboro Rd
39300 WasC 97106 532 B7
39300 WasC 97106 562 B1
39300 WasC 97113 562 B1
40800 WasC 97116 532 A7
41300 WasC 97106 531 J7
41300 WasC 97116 531 J7
NW Wilkins St
21200 HBRO 97006 594 C4
SE Wilkinson Ct
14100 CmsC 97267 657 A6
NW Willalatin Rd
- PTLD 97229 565 D4
- PTLD 97231 565 D4
SE Willamette Av
3300 CmsC 97222 657 A5
N Willamette Blvd
1700 PTLD 97217 566 D6
3900 PTLD 97203 566 C5
5900 PTLD 97203 565 H4
Willamette Ct
4300 VCVR 98661 537 B5
NE Willamette Ct
52400 SPSE 97056 474 G1
NW Willamette Ct
500 MCMV 97128 770 E5
Willamette Dr
4500 VCVR 98661 537 B5
16900 LKOW 97034 686 G1
17700 WLIN 97068 686 H3
20600 WLIN 97068 687 A5
Willamette Dr SR-43
16900 LKOW 97034 686 G1
17700 WLIN 97068 686 H3
20600 WLIN 97068 687 A5
NW Willamette Dr
2000 MCMV 97128 770 E5
SE Willamette Dr
3700 CmsC 97267 687 A3
N Willamette Ln
5900 PTLD 97203 565 J4
Willamette St
- MthC 97231 534 F5
- STHN 97051 385 C7
200 ORCY 97045 717 D1
600 CmsC 97045 717 D1
S Willamette St
400 NWBG 97132 743 D1
SW Willamette St
14500 SRWD 97140 684 H7
Willamette Vw
- CmsC 97222 656 H4
Willamette Wy W
30900 CmsC 97070 745 B1
30900 WNVL 97070 745 B1
SW Willamette Wy E
- CmsC 97070 745 B1
- WNVL 97070 745 B1
Willamette Falls Dr
- CmsC 97068 716 E1
800 WLIN 97068 716 J2
2700 WLIN 97068 717 A1
4000 WLIN 97068 687 B7
SW Willamette Heights Ct
400 CmsC 97068 716 E2
Willamette Lock
10 WLIN 97068 687 B7
NW Willamette Stone Park Rd
- MthC 97229 595 H5
- PTLD 97210 595 H5
- WasC 97225 595 H6
Willamette Valley Dr
16300 ORCY 97045 687 G6
Willamette View Ct
2000 WLIN 97068 687 A5
Willamina Av
1400 FTGV 97116 591 G3
2100 WasC 97116 591 J3
NW Willamina Av
2300 FTGV 97116 591 J3
2300 FTGV 97116 592 A3
2300 WasC 97116 591 J3
2300 WasC 97116 592 A3
SW Willapa Ct
20900 TLTN 97062 685 E5
SW Willapa Wy
20800 TLTN 97062 685 E5
Willard Rd
- CmsC 97004 777 J3
SE Willard St
2200 MWKE 97222 656 J3
NW Willbridge Av
5500 PTLD 97210 565 H7
SE Willet Dr
14000 HPYV 97236 658 C1
SW Willet Ter
11600 BRTN 97007 654 E3
SW William Av
23000 SRWD 97140 684 J7
23100 SRWD 97140 714 H1
SE William Otty Rd
10700 CmsC 97236 657 H3
10700 HPYV 97236 657 J3
11900 HPYV 97236 658 A3
N Williams Av
1400 PTLD 97227 596 G3
1400 PTLD 97232 596 G4
1600 PTLD 97212 596 G3
4000 PTLD 97211 596 G1
4000 PTLD 97217 596 G1
6800 PTLD 97217 566 G5
10900 PTLD 97211 566 G1
NE Williams Av
10 GSHM 97030 629 G2
10 GSHM 97080 629 G2
SE Williams Av
10 GSHM 97030 629 G3
1200 GSHM 97080 629 G4
SE Williams Dr
1900 GSHM 97080 629 G5
SW Williams Dr
10 WasC 97005 595 A6
SE Williams Pl
24000 DAMA 97009 659 D3
S Williams Rd
16500 CmsC 97004 748 B4
Williams St
100 ORCY 97045 717 C3
900 NWBG 97132 713 D6
Williams St NE
20900 DNLD 97020 774 G4
NE Williams St
33500 SPSE 97056 444 E7
SW Williamsburg Wy
700 WasC 97006 594 F6
NE Williamson Rd
18600 YmhC 97132 712 E6
Willie Ln
34800 STHN 97051 384 H7
SE Willingham Ct
13500 CmsC 97015 657 J5
N Willis Blvd
3000 PTLD 97217 566 D4
3900 PTLD 97203 566 B4
Willis Dr
13000 ORCY 97045 717 C5
NW Willis Rd
12900 YmhC 97128 770 C2
SW Willis Rd
- WasC 97140 715 C1
Willow
- CmsC 97015 657 H6
- WasC 97006 594 D5
SE Willow Ct
2100 HBRO 97123 593 E6
SW Willow Ct
15600 SRWD 97140 714 G1
Willow Dr
2100 NWBG 97132 713 E6
NW Willow Dr
1900 CMAS 98607 569 C3
SE Willow Dr
3000 HBRO 97123 593 F6
SW Willow Dr
15800 SRWD 97140 714 G1
Willow Ln
5600 LKOW 97035 685 H1
NW Willow Ln
52700 SPSE 97056 444 D7
SE Willow Ln
5600 CmsC 97267 657 C6
SW Willow Ln
8800 BRTN 97225 625 F2
8800 WasC 97225 625 F2
SW Willow Pkwy
1600 GSHM 97080 629 A6
1700 GSHM 97080 628 J6
NE Willow St
6000 PTLD 97213 597 D5
SE Willow St
900 MCMV 97128 770 J6
3200 HBRO 97123 593 F6
5800 MWKE 97222 657 D1
5900 CmsC 97222 657 D1
SW Willow St
10700 TLTN 97062 685 C6
SW Willowbottom Wy
7600 DRHM 97224 685 F2
SW Willowbrook Av
1400 GSHM 97080 628 J4
NW Willow Brook Ct
1500 GSHM 97030 629 A1
NW Willowbrook Ct
10 GSHM 97030 628 J2
10 GSHM 97080 628 J2
SW Willowbrook Ct
1400 GSHM 97080 628 J4
SW Willowbrook Dr
200 GSHM 97080 629 A3
500 GSHM 97080 628 H3
15300 TGRD 97224 655 C7
SW Willowbrook Pl
10 GSHM 97080 629 A3
1700 GSHM 97080 628 J4
SW Willow Creek Ct
19200 WasC 97006 594 D6
SW Willow Creek Dr
500 WasC 97006 594 E6
600 HBRO 97006 594 E6
28000 CmsC 97070 715 G5
28000 WNVL 97070 715 G6
SW Willow Creek Ter
18800 HBRO 97006 594 E6
19100 WasC 97006 594 E6
NE Willow Glen Rd
21700 FRVW 97024 599 B3
NE Willowgrove St
6900 HBRO 97124 594 A5
6900 WasC 97124 594 A5
SW Willowmere Dr
7100 WasC 97225 625 G4
8000 BRTN 97225 625 G4
SW Willow Point Ln
12700 TGRD 97224 655 B7
SW Willow Top Ln
13500 WasC 97224 655 A7
SW Willowview Ter
- WasC 97006 594 E7
SW Willow Wood Ct
11200 TGRD 97223 655 C2
SW Wills Pl
12700 TGRD 97223 655 B3
Wills St
- SNDY 97055 690 H3
SE Wills Wy
15500 CmsC 97267 657 C7
S Willsada Park Wy
15400 CmsC 97045 688 E4
Willson St
1700 WLIN 97068 687 B6
E Willwood Rd
23200 CmsC 97011 724 A2
23400 CmsC 97067 724 A2
SE Wilma Ct
5000 MWKE 97222 657 C3
SW Wilmington Ln
12900 TGRD 97223 655 A5
12900 TGRD 97224 655 A6
13000 WasC 97224 655 A6
NW Wilmont Av
- MthC 97229 595 F5
SE Wilmot St
18400 CmsC 97267 687 B3
Wilmot Wy
- LKOW 97035 656 B6
Wilshire Cir
15800 CmsC 97045 717 J7
Wilshire Ct
700 NWBG 97132 713 C5
SE Wilshire Ct
7100 CmsC 97267 657 E6
NW Wilshire Ln
10000 PTLD 97229 595 D1
SE Wilshire St
6800 CmsC 97267 657 E6
SW Wilshire St
9200 WasC 97225 625 F1
9600 BRTN 97225 595 E7
9600 WasC 97225 595 D7
Wilson Av
1800 VCVR 98661 537 A4
Wilson Av NE
4100 MrnC 97137 773 C5
4100 STPL 97137 773 C5
E Wilson Av
23300 CmsC 97011 724 A2
NW Wilson Av
10 GSHM 97030 629 B2
10 GSHM 97080 629 B2
SW Wilson Av
6000 BRTN 97005 625 A5
6000 BRTN 97008 625 A5
S Wilson Ct
21000 CmsC 97004 748 A1
21000 CmsC 97045 748 A1
SE Wilson Ct
13700 HPYV 97236 658 B3
SW Wilson Ct
400 GSHM 97080 629 A3
14300 BRTN 97008 624 J6
SW Wilson Dr
13900 BRTN 97008 625 A6
14100 BRTN 97008 624 J6
Wilson Ln
35200 ClbC 97051 414 J4
35200 ClbC 97053 414 J4
SW Wilson Ln
8300 WNVL 97070 745 E1
33300 SPSE 97056 474 E1
S Wilson Rd
15900 CmsC 97004 748 A1
15900 CmsC 97045 747 J1
15900 CmsC 97045 748 A1
SE Wilson Rd
1800 MthC 97060 629 J1
Wilson St
400 LFYT 97127 771 H1
500 LFYT 97127 741 H7
E Wilson St
- YCLT 98675 419 F1
N Wilson St
- LFYT 97127 741 H7
- YmhC 97114 741 H7
NW Wilson St
2000 PTLD 97209 596 C3
2000 PTLD 97210 596 C3
SE Wilson St
300 MCMV 97128 770 H6
W Wilson St
100 CLTN 97111 741 A1
100 YCLT 98675 419 F1
NW Wilson River Hwy
- BNKS 97106 531 H6
- BNKS 97106 532 B6
- WasC 97106 531 H6
- WasC 97106 532 B6
- WasC 97116 531 H6
NW Wilson River Hwy SR-6
- BNKS 97106 531 H6
- BNKS 97106 532 B6
- WasC 97106 531 H6
- WasC 97106 532 B6
- WasC 97116 531 H6
NE Wilsonville Rd
28300 NWBG 97132 743 J3
28300 YmhC 97132 743 F2
33100 YmhC 97132 744 A5
36700 CmsC 97070 744 E6
SW Wilsonville Rd
- CmsC 97132 744 E6
8800 WNVL 97070 715 D7
10700 WNVL 97070 745 A2
11200 CmsC 97070 745 A2
12600 CmsC 97070 744 J3
28000 CmsC 97070 715 G6
Wilsonville Hubbard Hwy NE
19700 MrnC 97002 775 D6
19700 MrnC 97032 775 D7
23200 CmsC 97002 745 E7
SW Wilton Av
11600 TGRD 97223 655 A3
SW Wimbledon Cir N
7500 WNVL 97070 715 F7
SW Wimbledon Cir S
7500 WNVL 97070 715 F7
SW Wimbledon Ct
7500 WNVL 97070 715 F7
16000 WasC 97224 655 B7
Winchell Av
1600 VCVR 98661 536 J4
N Winchell St
3300 PTLD 97217 566 D4
3900 PTLD 97203 566 C4
NE Winchell St
10 PTLD 97211 566 G5
10 PTLD 97217 566 G4
SW Winchester Av
2100 WasC 97225 625 D1
2400 BRTN 97225 625 D1
Winchester Dr
2800 NWBG 97132 713 C4
3000 YmhC 97132 713 C4
SW Winchester Pl
2200 WasC 97225 625 D1
NW Winchester Ter
- PTLD 97210 596 A3
SW Winchester Wy
8000 WNVL 97070 745 F3
SW Windemere Lp
6700 WasC 97225 595 H6
SW Windfield Lp
5600 CmsC 97035 655 J6
SW Windfield Wy
- CmsC 97035 655 J6
SW Windflower Av
20600 SRWD 97140 684 G5
SW Windham Ter
15700 WasC 97224 654 J7
Windham Oaks Ct
2000 WLIN 97068 687 A4
NW Windhill Dr
15000 WasC 97106 531 E3
SW Windjammer Ct
14100 BRTN 97005 624 J2
SW Windjammer Wy
14100 BRTN 97005 624 J2
N Windle St
9100 PTLD 97203 565 H2
Windmill Dr
19300 CmsC 97045 717 B5
19300 ORCY 97045 717 B5
SW Windmill Dr
11700 BRTN 97008 625 C6
SE Windmill Ln
7300 CmsC 97267 657 E6
SW Windmill Pl
10100 BRTN 97008 655 A1
NW Wind Ridge Dr
9800 PTLD 97229 565 E7
SW Windrow Ln
15900 SRWD 97140 684 G5
NE Windrow St
5200 HBRO 97124 593 H3
SW Windsong Ct
14100 TGRD 97223 654 J4
NE Windsong Ln
29100 YmhC 97132 713 G3
Windsor Ct
10 LKOW 97034 686 B2
SE Windsor Ct
4300 PTLD 97206 627 B1
SW Windsor Ct
4800 MthC 97221 626 A2
5400 MthC 97221 625 J2
10500 TGRD 97223 655 D2
Windsor Dr
1200 GLDS 97027 687 C3
1600 CmsC 97267 687 C3
1600 GLDS 97267 687 C3
SW Windsor Pl
- PTLD 97201 596 C6
10500 TGRD 97223 655 D2
NW Windsor St
- PTLD 97210 596 A3
Windsor Ter
5200 WLIN 97068 687 B7
NW Windstone Ct
20900 HBRO 97006 594 C3
NW Windstone St
20600 HBRO 97006 594 C3
E Wind Tree Lp
23200 CmsC 97049 724 B2
SE Windward Pl
600 VCVR 98661 536 H6
SW Windwood Wy
- WasC 97225 595 D6
S Windy City Rd
15700 CmsC 97042 807 J1
Windy Ridge Rd
59900 ClbC 97051 385 A7
59900 STHN 97051 385 A7
NW Winema Ct
18400 WasC 97229 594 E1
SW Winema Ct
20800 TLTN 97062 685 D5
SW Winema Dr
20800 TLTN 97062 685 D5
SW Winery Ln
14600 WasC 97007 654 E6
Winfield Ct
6900 GLDS 97027 687 D2
NW Winged Foot Ter
800 BRTN 97006 594 G4
E Winnie Rd
22500 CmsC 97049 724 A2
N Winning Wy
10 PTLD 97227 596 F4
10 PTLD 97232 596 G4
NE Winona St
900 PTLD 97211 566 H6
NE Win Sivers Dr
5900 PTLD 97220 568 A7
SW Winslow Dr
19300 WasC 97007 624 D7
NE Winsor Ct
26300 ClkC 98606 479 F5
SE Winsor Ct
5200 MWKE 97222 657 C1
NE Winsor Dr
15000 ClkC 98606 479 F5
SE Winsor Dr
9300 MWKE 97222 657 C1
SW Winston Ct
16100 BRTN 97007 624 G7
16100 WasC 97007 624 G7
Winston Dr
16000 CmsC 97045 687 G6
16000 ORCY 97045 687 G6
NW Winston Dr
6400 PTLD 97210 595 H5
SE Winston Rd
12000 DAMA 97009 658 H4
SE Winter Ct
12400 CmsC 97015 657 H4
SW Winter Ct
6800 BRTN 97008 625 D5
NW Winter Ln
10100 PTLD 97210 596 B4
SW Winter Ln
10100 BRTN 97008 625 D5
SE Winterborne Ct
16000 DAMA 97009 688 D1
SE Winter Creek Ct
12400 CmsC 97236 658 A4
NE Winter Creek Rd
33700 ClkC 98675 418 E1
Wintercrest Dr
- MCMV 97128 770 H1
SW Winterfield Ln
21100 WasC 97006 594 B7
NW Wintergreen Ct
2300 MCMV 97128 770 D4
NW Wintergreen Dr
400 MCMV 97128 770 D5
800 YmhC 97128 770 D5
SW Wintergreen St
15300 WasC 97223 654 H4
SW Winterhawk Ln
12000 BRTN 97007 654 H3
SW Winter Lake Ct
13100 TGRD 97223 655 C3
SW Winter Lake Dr
11200 TGRD 97223 655 A3
NW Winter Park Ter
- BRTN 97229 595 C5
NE Winters Hill Rd
3900 YmhC 97114 742 A7
3900 YmhC 97114 772 A1
SW Winterview Dr
12300 TGRD 97224 655 B6
12300 WasC 97224 655 B6
S Winter View Ln
17000 CmsC 97045 718 C5
NW Winterwood Lp
1000 MCMV 97128 770 G4
SW Winthrop Av
1800 WasC 97225 595 D7
2000 BRTN 97225 595 D7
Winthrop Ct
4600 LKOW 97035 656 A5
Wintler Dr
2000 VCVR 98661 537 B4
SW Wintu Ct
11000 TLTN 97062 685 C3
SE Winworth Ct
4900 MWKE 97222 657 C1
SW Winya Ct
11000 TLTN 97062 685 C2
Wirta Wy
33500 ClbC 97056 474 F4
Wiseacre Ln NE
9900 MrnC 97002 774 E7
SW Wishram Ct
11000 TLTN 97062 685 C3
NW Wismer Dr
15400 WasC 97229 564 H7
NE Wispering Winds Cir
1000 ClkC 98642 446 H4
NE Wistaria Dr
3700 PTLD 97212 597 B2
3900 PTLD 97213 597 B3
SE Wister St
4000 MWKE 97222 657 B3
Wisteria Ct
2500 CmsC 97068 686 G7
2500 WLIN 97068 686 G7
Wisteria Ct NE
13500 MrnC 97002 775 D2
SW Wisteria Ct
6600 BRTN 97008 625 B5
Wisteria Dr NE
13600 MrnC 97002 775 D2
SW Wisteria Pl
17100 SRWD 97140 684 F6
Wisteria Rd
1400 WLIN 97068 686 G7
S Wisteria Rd
20600 CmsC 97068 686 F6
20600 WLIN 97068 686 G5
Wistful Vista Dr
700 FRVW 97024 599 B4
NE Wistful Vista Dr
20300 FRVW 97024 599 A4
SE Witch Hazel Rd
3400 WasC 97123 623 G1
4600 HBRO 97123 623 H1
NE Withycomb Rd
14800 YmhC 97111 711 B3
14800 YmhC 97148 711 B3
SW Withywindle Ct
17200 DRHM 97224 685 E2
Wittke Ct
16300 ORCY 97045 687 G6
SE WK Anderson Rd
28400 MthC 97080 629 H3
SW Wohler St
32600 WasC 97123 592 J7
SW Wolds Dr
8500 WasC 97007 624 C7
Wolf Dr
17500 SNDY 97055 691 A3
Wolf Berry Ct
4100 LKOW 97035 656 A5
SE Woll Pond Wy
5800 HBRO 97123 593 J5
SE Wolsborn Av
25300 WasC 97123 683 F1
S Wonderly Dr
100 STHN 97051 415 B1
NW Wonder View Av
- GSHM 97030 628 J2
NW Wonderview Av
1600 GSHM 97030 628 J1
1700 GSHM 97030 629 A1
SE Wonderview Av
3200 GSHM 97080 628 J6
NW Wonderview Ct
900 GSHM 97030 628 J1
SW Wonderview Ct
10 GSHM 97080 628 H3
SW Wonderview Dr
10 GSHM 97080 628 H3
SW Wonderview Pl
3100 GSHM 97080 628 J6
NW Wood Av
8600 PTLD 97231 565 E4
SE Wood Av
10800 MWKE 97222 657 C3
SW Wood Av
27100 WNVL 97070 715 F5
SE Wood Ct
5200 MWKE 97222 657 C3
SE Wood Dr
32700 ClkC 98671 540 D7
SW Wood Pkwy
4400 PTLD 97219 656 D3
9400 PTLD 97219 626 A7
SW Wood Pl
16400 WasC 97224 654 G6
SE Wood Rd
- CmsC 97055 691 A4
SE Wood Rd
- SNDY 97055 691 A4
NW Wood St
- PTLD 97231 565 F4
SW Wood St
200 HBRO 97123 593 B6
10400 WasC 97225 625 D1
SW Woodard Ct
14800 WasC 97007 624 J3
SW Woodard Ln
10000 TGRD 97223 655 D4
SE Woodard Rd
1700 MthC 97060 599 J6
1700 TDLE 97060 599 J6
29400 MthC 97060 600 A6
SW Woodberry Ct
17600 WasC 97007 624 F5
S Woodbine Rd
1100 CmsC 97068 686 F7
1100 WLIN 97068 686 F7
SW Woodbridge Ct
8100 WNVL 97070 745 F2
SE Woodburn Rd
3200 ClkC 98671 570 B3
3600 WHGL 98671 570 B4
Woodburn-Estacada Hwy
- CmsC 97023 750 A6
- CmsC 97038 807 H7
- CmsC 97038 837 G1
- ECDA 97023 750 A5
- MOLA 97038 837 G1
Woodburn-Estacada Hwy SR-211
- CmsC 97023 750 A6
- CmsC 97038 807 H7
- CmsC 97038 837 G1
- ECDA 97023 750 A5
- MOLA 97038 837 G1
Woodbury St
39200 SNDY 97055 691 A4
SE Woodcock Av
18400 CmsC 97267 687 C3
Woodcreek
- BRTN 97006 624 G2
- WasC 97006 624 G2
Woodcreek Dr
59400 ClbC 97051 384 H7
59400 ClbC 97051 414 H1
SW Woodcrest Av
16200 TGRD 97224 685 D1
Woodduck Ln NE
23900 MrnC 97002 744 H5
SW Wood Duck Pl
11100 BRTN 97007 654 H2
11500 TGRD 97223 655 C4
Wood Duck Wy
18600 LKOW 97035 685 J2
NW Wooded Wy
15300 WasC 97006 594 H2
SE Wooded Heights Rd
16800 CmsC 97236 658 F2
16800 HPYV 97009 658 F2
16800 HPYV 97236 658 F2
SE Wooded Hills Ct
8600 DAMA 97009 658 J1
SE Wooded Hills Dr
19200 DAMA 97009 658 H1
NW Woodfern Ter
- WasC 97229 564 H4
Woodfield Ct
100 ORCY 97045 717 A3
Woodglen Ct
15000 ORCY 97045 717 G7
Woodglen Dr
3200 FTGV 97116 591 E2
Woodglen Wy
15000 CmsC 97045 717 H7
20000 ORCY 97045 717 G7
Woodhaven Ct
2300 WLIN 97068 686 H3
SW Woodhaven Dr
17000 SRWD 97140 684 F7
SE Woodhaven St
5400 MWKE 97222 657 C3
Wood Hill Ct
4000 LKOW 97035 656 A5
Woodhill Ct
2400 WLIN 97068 686 H2
SW Woodhue St
14100 WasC 97224 654 J7
Woodhurst Pl
17600 LKOW 97034 686 G2
SE Wooding Rd
35700 ClkC 98671 570 G5
SE Woodland Cir
13200 CmsC 97236 658 B4
NW Woodland Ct
12300 WasC 97229 595 B2
SE Woodland Dr
4900 GSHM 97080 629 G4
SE Woodland Rd
31400 CmsC 97023 750 D2
Woodland Ter
1400 LKOW 97034 656 D7
1500 LKOW 97034 686 C1
59600 ClbC 97051 384 G7
S Woodland Wy
21800 CmsC 97023 749 H3
SE Woodland Wy
4800 GSHM 97080 629 G4
14100 CmsC 97267 656 J6
NE Woodland Loop Rd
17000 YmhC 97132 711 E1
17000 YmhC 97148 711 E1
E Woodlands Dr
- CmsC 97049 724 E4
Woodlands Ter
19400 ORCY 97045 717 D5
Woodlawn Av
900 ORCY 97045 717 B3
Woodlawn Ct
100 ORCY 97045 717 A3
SW Woodlawn Ct
11500 TGRD 97223 655 C2
SE Woodle Rd
34400 CmsC 97022 720 E3
SW Woodlee Heights Av
11700 PTLD 97219 656 C3
SW Woodlee Heights Ct
11400 PTLD 97219 656 C2
SE Woodleigh St
- HBRO 97123 623 G2
SE Woodman Av
200 BNKS 97106 531 J5

STREET Block City ZIP Map# Grid

NW Woodmere Ct
17200 BRTN 97006 594 F5
SE Woodmere Dr
51800 SPSE 97056 474 F2
E Woodmere St
65200 CmsC 97011 723 J1
SE Woodmill Ct
1900 MCMV 97128 770 H7
SW Woodridge Ln
- TGRD 97223 655 C1
NE Woodridge St
9100 VCVR 98664 537 G4
NW Woodrose Dr
2000 WasC 97229 595 B3
NW Wood Rose Lp
8900 PTLD 97229 595 F3
SW Woodruff Ct
14700 BRTN 97005 624 J3
14700 BRTN 97007 624 J3
14700 WasC 97007 624 J3
E Woodruff Wy
67800 CmsC 97067 724 B5
N Woodrush Wy
13100 PTLD 97203 535 F6
Woods Ct
100 NWBG 97132 743 H1
56300 ClbC 97053 414 D6
SW Woods Ct
6000 MthC 97221 625 J1
Woods Dr
32500 ClbC 97053 414 C7
SE Woods Rd
28500 CmsC 97022 719 G7
SW Woods St
10 PTLD 97201 626 E1
1000 PTLD 97239 626 D1
3500 PTLD 97221 626 B1
SW Woods Creek Ct
8200 PTLD 97219 625 J6
8200 PTLD 97219 626 A6
Woodsey Dr
- CmsC 97067 724 C3
E Woodsey Dr
24900 CmsC 97067 724 D4
SW Woodshire Ln
13000 TGRD 97223 655 A5
SE Woodside Av
14200 CmsC 97267 657 D6
Woodside Cir
4200 LKOW 97035 686 A2
SW Woodside Dr
8300 WasC 97225 625 F4
Woodside Ter
10 WDLD 98674 385 J1
NW Woodside Ter
4600 PTLD 97210 596 A6
Woodsman Ct
16500 LKOW 97034 656 D7
NE Woodsong St
100 HBRO 97124 594 A5
Woodsprite Ct
2600 WLIN 97068 687 A6
SE Woodstock Blvd
2800 PTLD 97202 627 A5
4100 PTLD 97206 627 D5
9100 PTLD 97266 627 G5
SE Woodstock Ct
9700 PTLD 97266 627 H5
Wood Thrush Cir
18200 LKOW 97035 685 J2
Woodthrush St
18200 LKOW 97035 685 G3
Wood Thrush Wy
18200 LKOW 97035 685 G3
NE Woodview Dr
6300 HBRO 97124 593 G2
6300 HBRO 97124 594 A5
S Woodview Ln
22700 CmsC 97004 749 D7
Woodview Vil
- NWBG 97132 743 C2
- YmhC 97132 743 C2
NE Wood Village Blvd
- FRVW 97024 599 C5
1000 GSHM 97030 599 C5
1000 WDVL 97060 599 C5
SE Wood Village Ct
8700 CmsC 97015 687 H2
8700 CmsC 97267 687 H2
Wood Village Grn
- WDVL 97060 599 C5
SE Wood Village Ln
- CmsC 97015 687 H2
Wood Village Pk
- WDVL 97060 599 C4
SE Woodward Ct
14700 PTLD 97236 628 C2
SE Woodward Pl
11900 PTLD 97266 628 A2
12100 PTLD 97236 628 A2
SE Woodward St
500 PTLD 97202 626 G1
2800 PTLD 97202 627 A1
4200 PTLD 97206 627 B1
11200 PTLD 97266 627 J2
14100 PTLD 97236 628 C2
SW Woodward Wy
1300 WasC 97225 595 D7
Woodway Ct
800 LKOW 97034 656 E4
SW Woodwind Ct
15400 BRTN 97007 624 J1
Woodwind Dr
11900 ORCY 97045 717 A5
SW Woodwind St
15200 BRTN 97007 624 H5
Woodwinds Ct
5000 WLIN 97068 687 A6
Woody Ln
- ClbC 97051 384 D6
SW Woody End St
8000 DRHM 97224 685 F2
NW Woollen Rd
41600 WasC 97106 532 A1
42100 WasC 97106 531 J1
N Woolsey Av
- PTLD 97203 566 B2
SW Worchester Pl
13100 TGRD 97223 655 D1
NE Worden Hill Rd
8100 DNDE 97115 742 F3
8100 YmhC 97115 742 F3
10800 YmhC 97115 712 C7
10800 YmhC 97132 712 C6
NE Work Av
4500 VCVR 98663 537 A1
SE Worthington Ln
15500 CmsC 97267 657 B7
Worthington St
1400 LKOW 97034 686 F1
Wren Ct
17300 LKOW 97034 686 B1
Wren Rd
- CmsC 97023 750 C1
NW Wren Rd
32300 WasC 97124 562 H6
32300 WasC 97124 563 A6
33600 WasC 97113 562 H6
SE Wren Rd
32000 CmsC 97023 750 B1
Wren St
3500 LKOW 97034 686 B1
SE Wren St
2300 MWKE 97222 656 J3
SE Wrenfield St
6500 HBRO 97123 594 A6
NE Wrenwood Ln
4700 HBRO 97124 593 H4
SW Wright Av
- PTLD 97210 596 C5
100 PTLD 97205 596 C5
100 TDLE 97060 599 F4
SW Wright Ct
2100 TDLE 97060 599 F6
18900 WasC 97007 624 D4
SW Wright Pl
1200 TDLE 97060 599 F5
S Wright Rd
30900 CmsC 97038 807 J7
31100 CmsC 97017 807 J7
31100 CmsC 97017 837 J1
31100 CmsC 97038 837 J1
SW Wright St
1300 MCMV 97128 770 F5
19200 WasC 97007 624 D4
SW Wrightwood Ct
13500 WasC 97224 655 A7
S Wrolstad Dr
15700 CmsC 97045 777 H2
WSU Entrance Rd
- ClkC 98686 477 A5
SW Wunderli Canyon Rd
23000 WasC 97140 683 H5
NE Wyatt Rd
- ClkC 98604 417 F7
SE Wy East Av
14400 DAMA 97009 658 G7
Wyeth St
10 STHN 97051 385 D7
N Wygant St
10 PTLD 97211 596 G1
1200 PTLD 97217 596 E1
3000 PTLD 97217 566 D7
NE Wygant St
10 PTLD 97217 596 G1
1400 PTLD 97211 596 J1
2500 PTLD 97211 597 A1
4200 PTLD 97218 597 C1
9500 PTLD 97220 597 J1
11200 PTLD 97220 598 A1
SE Wyler St
14200 HPYV 97236 658 C1
NE Wylie Rd
29200 ClkC 98607 539 J3
29200 ClkC 98607 540 A2
Wyman Rd
100 CtzC 98674 386 A5
SW Wyndham Ln
1300 MthC 97221 596 A7
1300 PTLD 97221 596 A7
SE Wyndham Wy
9000 CmsC 97236 657 G1
SW Wyndham Hill Ct
21000 CmsC 97062 686 B6
SW Wyngate St
20500 WasC 97007 624 C2
SE Wynnwood Dr
3900 HBRO 97123 623 G1
NE Wynooski Rd
2400 NWBG 97132 743 E2
2400 YmhC 97132 743 E2
Wynooski St
400 NWBG 97132 743 D1
800 YmhC 97132 743 D1
Wynton Dr
19100 CmsC 97045 717 G4
19100 ORCY 97045 717 G4
SW Wynwood Av
1400 WasC 97225 595 B7
2200 WasC 97005 625 E4
2200 WasC 97225 625 D4
Wyoming St
6300 VCVR 98661 537 D5

X

X St
1300 VCVR 98661 536 J4
2900 VCVR 98663 536 J3
3300 WHGL 98671 570 C3
N X St
100 WHGL 98671 569 H3
200 VCVR 98661 536 J6
W X St
800 WHGL 98671 569 H3
Xanthus Ct
- CmsC 97140 714 H5
SW Xanthus Ct
27000 CmsC 97140 714 G4
Xavier Av
3100 VCVR 98660 536 D2
SW Xavier St
600 CMAS 98607 569 B5
Xerox Dr
- WNVL 97070 715 E5
Xylopia
- CmsC 97015 657 H6

Y

Y St
2900 VCVR 98661 536 J3
3200 ClkC 98671 570 C3
3200 VCVR 98663 536 J3
3200 WHGL 98671 570 C3
N Y St
400 WHGL 98671 569 J3
W Y St
500 WHGL 98671 569 H3
SW Yachats Ct
21200 TLTN 97062 685 E6
N Yacht Harbor Dr
- PTLD 97217 566 H1
E Yacolt Rd
100 YCLT 98675 419 F1
500 ClkC 98675 419 G1
W Yacolt Rd
100 YCLT 98675 419 F1
600 ClkC 98675 419 E1
NE Yacolt Mountain Rd
18500 ClkC 98675 418 J1
18500 ClkC 98675 419 A1
NE Yacolt View Rd
28200 ClkC 98675 419 J1
SE Yahweh Ln
25500 CmsC 97009 659 E3
SW Yakima Ct
8600 TLTN 97062 685 E5
E Yakima Ln
22000 CmsC 97049 723 J1
Yakima St NE
- AURA 97002 775 F5
Yale Av
700 GLDS 97027 687 D4
SW Yale Pl
13200 TGRD 97223 655 D1
Yale St
300 NWBG 97132 713 C5
N Yale St
4700 PTLD 97203 566 A5
6600 PTLD 97203 565 J4
NE Yale St
100 CMAS 98607 569 H4
SE Yale St
100 CMAS 98607 569 H5
SE Yamaview Ln
35700 CmsC 97009 660 G6
35700 CmsC 97055 660 G6
SE Yamhill Cir
18400 GSHM 97233 598 G7
SE Yamhill Ct
6400 PTLD 97215 597 E6
SW Yamhill Ct
20100 WasC 97006 594 D5
SW Yamhill Dr
5900 MthC 97221 595 J6
5900 PTLD 97221 595 J6
NE Yamhill Rd
11900 YmhC 97111 711 C2
14200 YmhC 97148 711 C3
N Yamhill St
100 CLTN 97111 711 A7
700 YmhC 97111 711 A6
N Yamhill St SR-47
100 CLTN 97111 711 A7
700 YmhC 97111 711 A6
NW Yamhill St
1900 MCMV 97128 770 G3
S Yamhill St
100 CLTN 97111 711 C7
100 CLTN 97111 741 A1
SE Yamhill St
- PTLD 97216 597 H7
1200 PTLD 97214 596 H6
2700 PTLD 97214 597 B6
5500 PTLD 97215 597 D6
11500 PTLD 97216 598 A7
16200 PTLD 97233 598 E7
17500 GSHM 97233 598 G7
21000 GSHM 97030 599 A7
SW Yamhill St
10 PTLD 97204 596 F6
2100 PTLD 97205 596 D5
Yamhill-Newberg Hwy
- NWBG 97132 713 B6
- YmhC 97132 711 F2
- YmhC 97148 711 E2
23000 YmhC 97132 712 H5
23000 YmhC 97132 713 A6
Yamhill-Newberg Hwy SR-240
- NWBG 97132 713 B6
- YmhC 97132 711 F2
- YmhC 97148 711 E2
23000 YmhC 97132 712 H5
23000 YmhC 97132 713 A6
SW Yaquina Ct
17700 TLTN 97062 685 D2
Yarmer Ln
59400 ClbC 97051 384 H7
59400 ClbC 97051 414 H1
Yarmouth Cir
1700 LKOW 97034 656 G7
SW Yarrow Wy
13100 WasC 97223 654 H5
Yates St
900 LKOW 97034 656 F7
Yeagens Landing Rd NE
2900 MrnC 97137 743 A6
SW Yearling Ct
14100 BRTN 97008 624 J7
SE Yearling Ln
6900 CmsC 97267 657 E6
SW Yearling Pl
9000 BRTN 97008 624 J7
SW Yearling Wy
14200 BRTN 97008 624 J7
Yeary Ln NE
22700 MrnC 97002 774 J1
23000 MrnC 97002 744 J7
NW Yellowberry Wy
14700 WasC 97229 564 J6
SE Yellowbird Av
3300 HBRO 97123 623 D1
3400 WasC 97123 623 E1
E Yellow Brick Rd
61400 CmsC 97011 693 E7
SE Yellowhammer St
22700 DAMA 97009 659 B1
Yellow Oak Dr
- NWBG 97132 713 F7
NE Yellowstone Ct
14700 WasC 97006 594 J5
Yeoman Av
3100 VCVR 98660 536 D2
S Yeoman Rd
21000 CmsC 97004 748 B2
NW Yeon Av
3700 PTLD 97210 596 A1
4400 PTLD 97210 595 J1
NW Yeon Av US-30
2500 PTLD 97210 596 C2
4400 PTLD 97210 595 J1
Yergen Rd NE
9500 MrnC 97002 774 C3
Yew Ct
1800 FTGV 97116 592 C5
Yew St
- WasC 97113 592 C4
- WasC 97116 592 C4
2000 FTGV 97116 592 C4
SE Yew St
1200 CmsC 97267 656 H6
Yew Crest
- STHN 97051 385 C5
SE Yew Wood Dr
25100 CmsC 97009 689 E3
SW Yew Wood St
10 HBRO 97123 593 H5
SW Yocum Ln
19700 WasC 97007 624 D5
Yocum Lp
36200 SNDY 97055 690 G2
SE Yoder Dr
36600 CmsC 97023 750 G4
NW Yoncalla Ct
20800 WasC 97229 564 C7
NE Yonia Ct
400 HBRO 97124 593 A4
Yorick St
10 LKOW 97035 656 B5
SW York Pl
20400 WasC 97006 594 C7
York Rd
800 LKOW 97034 656 E4
York St
2500 WLIN 97068 687 A7
NW York St
2000 PTLD 97209 596 D3
2000 PTLD 97210 596 D3
SW York St
20300 WasC 97006 594 C7
21600 HBRO 97006 594 B7
21600 HBRO 97123 594 B7
Yorkshire Ct
5600 LKOW 97035 655 J5
NW Yorkshire Ln
1900 PTLD 97229 595 H3
Yorkshire Pl
5400 CmsC 97035 655 J7
5400 LKOW 97035 655 J7
NW Yorkshire St
30500 NPNS 97133 563 C1
30500 WasC 97133 563 C1
30600 NPNS 97133 533 B7
30600 WasC 97133 533 B7
NW Yorktown Dr
16600 WasC 97006 594 G2
Yosemite St NE
- AURA 97002 775 F5
SW Yosemite St
29300 CmsC 97070 715 C7
29300 WNVL 97070 715 C7
NW Yosemite Ter
200 WasC 97006 594 J5
SW Yosemite Wy
29500 WNVL 97070 715 C7
Young Rd
33900 ClbC 97051 384 G7
SW Young Wy
29600 WNVL 97070 715 C7
SW Youngberg Hill Rd
9300 YmhC 97128 770 A7
NE Youngman Ln
8000 YmhC 97128 771 D2
SE Youngs Ln
18100 DAMA 97009 658 G6
SW Yreka St
600 CMAS 98607 569 B5
Yucca
- CmsC 97015 657 H6
SE Yukon St
- PTLD 97236 628 B5
1300 PTLD 97202 626 H4
9600 PTLD 97266 627 H5
SE Yulan Wy
- HBRO 97123 623 D1
NW Yungen Rd
22400 WasC 97124 534 A6
NW Yvonne Ln
13300 WasC 97229 595 B2

Z

Z Cir
- WHGL 98671 570 D3
Z St
2800 VCVR 98661 536 J3
3400 WHGL 98671 570 D3
3500 VCVR 98663 536 J2
W Z St
800 WHGL 98671 569 H3
SW Zabaco Ter
6000 WasC 97007 624 C4
NE Zachary St
1200 HBRO 97124 593 D1
Zamia
- CmsC 97015 657 H7
NE Zander Ct
2500 HBRO 97124 593 B2
SW Zander Ct
8900 WasC 97223 655 F1
NE Zard Ln
24200 YmhC 97132 743 A1
SE Zee Ct
900 MCMV 97128 770 H7
NE Zeek Rd
28700 ClkC 98671 539 H6
S Zeller Rd
25000 CmsC 97013 777 C2
25400 CmsC 97042 777 C2
SW Zenith Pl
17700 WasC 97007 624 F6
NE Zenith St
100 CMAS 98607 569 H4
SE Zenith St
100 CMAS 98607 569 H5
Zentara Rd
- CmsC 97013 776 J6
Zephyr Wy
600 MOLA 97038 807 D7
NW Zermatt Ct
10900 WasC 97229 595 D5
Zeus Dr
21100 WLIN 97068 686 J5
N Ziegler Av
10200 PTLD 97203 565 H2
Ziegler St
- CmsC 97068 716 C1
E Zig Zag Dr
- CmsC 97067 724 C3
Zigzag Mountain Rd
- CmsC 97049 724 J6
Zigzag River Rd
- CmsC 97049 724 E3
E Zig Zag River Rd
70200 CmsC 97049 724 E3
Zigzag River Forest Camp Rd
- CmsC 97049 724 F4
SW Zillah St
600 CMAS 98607 569 B5
Zimmerman Ln
600 MOLA 97038 807 C7
NW Zimmerman Ln
30500 WasC 97124 563 B7
NE Zimri Dr
2700 NWBG 97132 713 F4
2700 YmhC 97132 713 F4
S Zina Ct
20100 CmsC 97045 718 C7
NE Zinser Rd
27900 ClkC 98604 418 E6
SW Zion Ct
16700 WasC 97007 624 G4
SW Zion St
- PTLD 97221 595 J6
NW Zion Church Rd
32300 WasC 97113 562 J4
32300 WasC 97124 562 J4
32300 WasC 97124 563 A4
SE Zion Hill Dr
11700 CmsC 97009 659 E4
SW Zivney Ln
1100 CmsC 97034 686 D3
1100 CmsC 97068 686 D3
NW Zobrist St
100 ECDA 97023 750 B3
SW Zobrist St
200 ECDA 97023 750 B4
Zoe Ct
800 NWBG 97132 713 C5
SW Zoe Ln
- WasC 97006 624 D1
SW Zoo Rd
- PTLD 97205 596 B7
- PTLD 97221 596 B7
SW Zoo Parking Rd
- PTLD 97221 596 B7
Zuni Dr
- WasC 97005 594 J7
- WasC 97005 624 J2
SW Zurich Ct
20700 WasC 97007 624 C5
SW Zworykin Av
- WasC 97005 625 A1
SW Zworykin Dr
- WasC 97005 625 A1

#

1st Av
- MthC 97231 534 F4
500 ORCY 97045 717 A2
E 1st Av
500 CMAS 98607 569 F4
N 1st Av
100 HBRO 97123 593 B4
100 HBRO 97124 593 B4
300 CNLS 97113 592 D4
900 RDGF 98642 415 J5
900 WasC 97124 593 B3
NE 1st Av
100 CNBY 97013 746 C6
100 ECDA 97023 750 B3
800 BGND 98604 448 B4
1600 PTLD 97212 596 G4
1600 PTLD 97232 596 G4
10800 PTLD 97211 566 G1
15000 ClkC 98685 476 G5
38900 ClkC 98674 386 H2
NW 1st Av
10 PTLD 97204 596 F5
10 PTLD 97209 596 F5
100 CNBY 97013 746 C6
1400 BGND 98604 448 B4
4900 ClkC 98663 536 G1
7800 ClkC 98665 506 G5
15000 ClkC 98685 476 G5
23500 ClkC 98642 446 G3
S 1st Av
100 CNLS 97113 592 D5
100 HBRO 97123 593 B5
100 HBRO 97124 593 B4
S 1st Av SR-219
300 HBRO 97123 593 B5
SE 1st Av
10 BGND 98604 448 B5
10 CNBY 97013 746 D6
1200 CMAS 98607 569 F4
1500 CmsC 97013 746 F5
SE 1st Av SR-99E
100 CNBY 97013 746 D6
1300 CmsC 97013 746 E5
SW 1st Av
- PTLD 97219 626 E5
- PTLD 97219 656 E2
10 ECDA 97023 750 B3
10 PTLD 97209 596 F5
100 CNBY 97013 746 B7
500 BGND 98604 448 B6
700 PTLD 97204 596 F6
1100 CmsC 97013 746 B7
1200 PTLD 97201 596 F7
2000 PTLD 97201 626 E1
4700 PTLD 97239 626 E3
SW 1st Av SR-99E
100 CNBY 97013 746 B7
1100 CmsC 97013 746 B7
W 1st Av
10 ECDA 97023 750 B3
NE 1st Cir
15800 VCVR 98684 538 E6
S 1st Cir
5500 RDGF 98642 416 E7
1st Ct
5500 WLIN 97068 687 B6
NE 1st Ct
700 BGND 98604 448 B4
2900 HBRO 97124 593 B1
6700 ClkC 98665 506 G6
11400 ClkC 98685 506 G1
13300 ClkC 98685 476 G7
NW 1st Ct
3600 GSHM 97030 628 H3
3700 HBRO 97124 593 B1
10400 ClkC 98685 506 G2
SW 1st Ct
600 BGND 98604 448 B6
1500 GSHM 97080 629 A3
W 1st Ct
1300 MCMV 97128 770 F5
1st Dr N
- PTLD 97236 627 J7
- PTLD 97266 627 J7
- PTLD 97266 628 A7
1st Dr S
- PTLD 97236 628 A7
- PTLD 97266 628 A7
NE 1st Dr
2500 HBRO 97124 593 B1
15300 VCVR 98684 538 D6
NW 1st Dr
2400 GSHM 97030 628 J2
NE 1st Pl
800 HBRO 97124 593 C3
10800 PTLD 97211 566 G1
13500 ClkC 98685 476 G6
NW 1st Pl
800 HBRO 97124 593 B3
SE 1st Pl
1900 BGND 98604 448 B7
1900 ClkC 98604 448 B7
3800 GSHM 97030 629 F3
3800 GSHM 97080 629 F3
1st St
- BRTN 97005 625 A2
- CLTN 97111 741 A1
- FTGV 97116 592 C4
- MthC 97231 534 J2
- PTLD 97233 598 B6
- TLTN 97062 685 A3
10 FRVW 97024 599 B4
200 DAYT 97114 772 B4
300 CMAS 98607 569 H5
300 GLDS 97027 687 E4
300 LKOW 97034 656 G5
300 WHGL 98671 569 H5
400 ORCY 97045 717 B1
1500 CBAC 97018 385 D3
1st St NE
14900 AURA 97002 775 F3
23600 MrnC 97002 744 G6
E 1st St
100 NWBG 97132 713 E7
300 YMHL 97148 711 A1
1000 YmhC 97132 713 E7
1300 ClkC 98629 416 J1
1300 LCTR 98629 416 J1
1700 YmhC 97132 713 E7
2700 VCVR 98661 536 J6
E 1st St SR-99W
100 NWBG 97132 713 E7
E 1st St SR-219
700 NWBG 97132 713 E7
1700 YmhC 97132 713 E7
N 1st St
100 BRLO 97002 775 J1
100 BRLO 97013 775 J1
100 CLTN 97111 711 A7
100 CmsC 97002 775 J1
100 STHN 97051 385 D6
NE 1st St
- ClkC 98671 540 E6
10 BGND 98604 448 C5
1400 MCMV 97128 770 J5
4200 GSHM 97030 629 G3
4200 GSHM 97080 629 G3
15800 VCVR 98684 538 D6
52500 SPSE 97056 444 E7
NW 1st St
- PTLD 97231 565 D1
600 GSHM 97030 629 A2
1200 BGND 98604 448 A5
2000 GSHM 97030 628 J2
4200 GSHM 97236 628 G2
52500 SPSE 97056 444 E7
S 1st St
10 WHGL 98671 569 H5
100 STHN 97051 385 D7
400 ORCY 97045 717 B1
900 CLTN 97111 741 A1
2000 STHN 97051 415 C3
SE 1st St
- VCVR 98684 537 J6
10 BGND 98604 448 C5
100 MCMV 97128 770 H5
1900 GSHM 97030 629 E3
2500 GSHM 97080 629 E3
14000 VCVR 98684 538 C6
16400 ClkC 98684 538 E6
18200 ClkC 98607 538 H6
18200 VCVR 98607 538 H6
19900 CMAS 98607 538 J6
34300 ClkC 98671 540 E7
52200 SPSE 97056 474 E1
SW 1st St
- WasC 97140 685 C7
10 BGND 98604 448 B5
1100 DNDE 97115 742 H2
1700 BGND 98604 447 J5
2200 GSHM 97080 628 J3
2300 GSHM 97080 628 J3
12000 BRTN 97005 625 C3
15700 SRWD 97140 684 G7
52200 SPSE 97056 474 E1
52400 SPSE 97056 444 G7
W 1st St
- WHGL 98671 569 H3
100 CLTN 97111 741 A1
100 LCTR 98629 416 G1
100 YmhC 97111 741 A1
400 NWBG 97132 713 B7
700 YmhC 97132 713 B7
W 1st St SR-99W
100 NWBG 97132 713 B7
SE 1st Ter
4200 GSHM 97080 629 G3
E 1st Wy
- ClkC 98629 416 J1
N 1st Wy
4500 RDGF 98642 416 D7
NW 1st Wy
1900 BGND 98604 447 J5
S 1st Wy
2100 RDGF 98642 416 B7
NE 2nd Av
- ClkC 98629 386 H2
- ClkC 98674 386 H2
100 CNBY 97013 746 C6
100 ECDA 97023 750 B3
100 HBRO 97123 593 C4
100 HBRO 97124 593 C4
200 CMAS 98607 569 F4
200 PTLD 97214 596 G5
800 BGND 98604 448 B4
1100 PTLD 97232 596 G4
1600 PTLD 97212 596 G4
3200 WHGL 98671 569 H4
5400 ClkC 98663 506 G7
6800 ClkC 98665 506 G6
10800 PTLD 97211 566 G2
11400 ClkC 98685 506 G1
14600 ClkC 98685 476 G5
17400 ClkC 98642 476 G2
27900 ClkC 98642 416 H6
NW 2nd Av
10 ECDA 97023 750 B3
10 PTLD 97204 596 F5
10 PTLD 97209 596 F5
100 CNBY 97013 746 C6
500 BGND 98604 448 B4
2900 CMAS 98607 569 B5
3200 HBRO 97124 593 B1
9400 ClkC 98665 506 G3
10300 ClkC 98685 506 G3
15400 ClkC 98685 476 G4
28200 ClkC 98642 416 G5
S 2nd Av
400 CNLS 97113 592 D5
SE 2nd Av
10 BGND 98604 448 B6
10 PTLD 97214 596 G6
10 PTLD 97232 596 G5
100 HBRO 97123 593 C5
100 HBRO 97124 593 C5
200 ECDA 97023 750 B4
700 CMAS 98607 569 F4
1000 CNBY 97013 746 D6
3400 WHGL 98671 569 J5
SW 2nd Av
- PTLD 97239 626 E5
10 PTLD 97204 596 F6
10 PTLD 97209 596 F5
100 CNBY 97013 746 C7
100 ECDA 97023 750 B4
400 BGND 98604 448 B6
1200 PTLD 97201 596 F7
2700 PTLD 97201 626 E1
8000 PTLD 97219 626 E6
9300 PTLD 97219 656 E1
NE 2nd Cir
1200 BGND 98604 448 C5
17200 ClkC 98684 538 F6
NW 2nd Cir
2800 BGND 98604 447 H5
3700 GSHM 97030 628 H2
SE 2nd Cir
12500 VCVR 98684 538 A6
NE 2nd Ct
700 BGND 98604 448 B4
1400 MCMV 97128 770 J5
3100 GSHM 97030 629 F2
3100 HBRO 97124 593 B1
11600 ClkC 98685 506 G1
13500 ClkC 98685 476 G6
18500 ClkC 98642 476 G1
NW 2nd Ct
1900 HBRO 97124 593 A2
10400 ClkC 98685 506 F3
11000 PTLD 97231 565 G1
14500 ClkC 98685 476 G5
S 2nd Ct
600 CNLS 97113 592 D5
SW 2nd Ct
200 BGND 98604 448 B5
1500 GSHM 97080 629 B4
2000 GSHM 97080 628 J3
4700 PTLD 97239 626 E3
2nd Dr N
- PTLD 97236 627 J7
- PTLD 97266 627 J7
NE 2nd Dr
2500 HBRO 97124 593 B1
SW 2nd Dr
1900 GSHM 97080 628 J3
1900 GSHM 97080 629 A3
NE 2nd Lp
17200 ClkC 98684 538 F6
2nd Pl
1600 CBAC 97018 385 C3
N 2nd Pl
300 CNLS 97113 592 D4
NE 2nd Pl
1700 HBRO 97124 593 B2
6700 ClkC 98665 506 G6
NW 2nd Pl
400 ECDA 97023 750 B3
S 2nd Pl
1200 CNLS 97113 592 D6
SE 2nd Pl
1600 BGND 98604 448 B7
1600 GSHM 97080 629 D3
1900 ClkC 98604 448 E7
SW 2nd Pl
1000 DNDE 97115 742 H3
2nd St
- BRTN 97005 625 A2
- CLTN 97111 741 A1
- FTGV 97116 592 C4
- PTLD 97233 598 B6
- TLTN 97062 685 A3
- WHGL 98671 569 H5
100 FRVW 97024 599 B4
100 LFYT 97127 771 G1
200 DAYT 97114 772 B4
300 LKOW 97034 656 F6
300 ORCY 97045 717 C1
400 WDLD 98674 385 J2
1200 CBAC 97018 385 D4
20500 STPL 97137 773 C5
2nd St NE
14900 AURA 97002 775 F3
23600 MrnC 97002 744 G6
E 2nd St
- ClkC 98629 416 J1
- LCTR 98629 416 J1
- YmhC 97132 713 E7
100 MOLA 97038 837 E2
400 YMHL 97148 711 A1
900 YmhC 97148 711 A1

STREET Block City ZIP Map# Grid

E 2nd St
1300 NWBG 97132 713 D7
2200 VCVR 98661 536 J6
N 2nd St
100 BRLO 97002 745 J7
100 BRLO 97013 745 J7
100 CLTN 97111 711 A7
100 CmsC 97013 745 J7
100 STHN 97051 385 D6
200 BRLO 97013 746 A7
NE 2nd St
100 MCMV 97128 770 H5
300 BGND 98604 448 C5
3700 GSHM 97030 629 F2
9700 VCVR 98664 537 G6
11400 VCVR 98684 537 J6
15300 VCVR 98684 538 D6
17000 ClkC 98684 538 E6
30600 ClkC 98671 540 A6
52500 SPSE 97056 444 E7
52700 ClbC 97056 444 E7
NW 2nd St
10 GSHM 97030 629 B2
100 MCMV 97128 770 G5
1700 BGND 98604 447 J5
1700 BGND 98604 448 A5
2500 YmhC 97128 770 C5
10400 PTLD 97231 565 C1
52600 SPSE 97056 444 E7
S 2nd St
10 WHGL 98671 569 H5
100 STHN 97051 385 D7
200 CLTN 97111 741 A1
200 ORCY 97045 717 B1
300 STHN 97051 415 D1
SE 2nd St
100 TDLE 97060 599 G4
500 BGND 98604 448 C5
3100 GSHM 97080 629 E3
10500 VCVR 98664 537 H6
15600 VCVR 98684 538 D6
52100 SPSE 97056 474 E1
52400 SPSE 97056 444 G7
SW 2nd St
- WNVL 97070 745 D1
100 TDLE 97060 599 G4
1000 DNDE 97115 742 H2
1100 BGND 98604 448 A5
1600 GSHM 97080 629 A3
1900 BGND 98604 447 J5
3300 GSHM 97030 628 H3
13000 BRTN 97005 625 A3
15800 SRWD 97140 684 G7
52300 SPSE 97056 474 E1
W 2nd St
- WHGL 98671 569 H3
100 LCTR 98629 416 G1
100 LFYT 97127 741 G7
100 NWBG 97132 713 B7
NW 2nd Ter
2500 GSHM 97030 628 J2
SE 2nd Ter
4100 GSHM 97080 629 G3
2nd Wy
- NWBG 97132 713 B7
N 2nd Wy
- RDGF 98642 416 D7
7800 ClkC 98642 416 H7
S 2nd Wy
3400 RDGF 98642 416 C7
SW 2nd Wy
1000 TDLE 97060 599 F4
W 2nd Place Cir
200 LFYT 97127 741 F7
200 LFYT 97127 771 F1
2nd St Al
- LKOW 97034 656 F6
3rd Av
- MthC 97231 534 F4
- ORCY 97045 717 A2
- WLIN 97068 716 H2
N 3rd Av
100 RDGF 98642 415 J7
NE 3rd Av
10 PTLD 97214 596 G5
100 CNBY 97013 746 C6
100 HBRO 97123 593 C4
200 CMAS 98607 569 F4
400 ECDA 97023 750 B3
900 BGND 98604 448 B4
1000 PTLD 97232 596 G4
1600 ClkC 98607 569 G4
1600 PTLD 97212 596 G4
3000 WHGL 98671 569 H4
3200 HBRO 97124 593 C1
3400 WasC 97124 593 C1
10800 PTLD 97211 566 G2
11400 ClkC 98685 506 G1
14400 ClkC 98685 476 G5
23100 ClkC 98642 446 H4
NE 3rd Av SR-500
500 CMAS 98607 569 F4
NW 3rd Av
- ClkC 98604 448 B3
- MthC 97231 534 F4
10 ECDA 97023 750 B3
10 PTLD 97204 596 F5
10 PTLD 97209 596 F5
100 CNBY 97013 746 C6
700 BGND 98604 448 B4
2300 HBRO 97124 593 B2
2600 WasC 97124 593 B1
3000 CMAS 98607 569 A5
6800 ClkC 98665 506 G5
11000 ClkC 98685 506 G1
14600 ClkC 98685 476 G5
38700 ClkC 98674 386 H2
S 3rd Av
100 RDGF 98642 415 J7
SE 3rd Av
- ECDA 97023 750 B4
10 BGND 98604 448 B5
10 PTLD 97214 596 G7
10 PTLD 97232 596 G5
100 HBRO 97123 593 C5
100 HBRO 97124 593 C5
200 CMAS 98607 569 F5
1100 CNBY 97013 746 D6
SW 3rd Av
- ECDA 97023 750 B4
10 BGND 98604 448 B5
10 PTLD 97204 596 F6
10 PTLD 97209 596 F5
100 CNBY 97013 746 C7
1200 PTLD 97201 596 F7

SW 3rd Av
2700 PTLD 97201 626 E1
3100 PTLD 97239 626 E2
6700 PTLD 97219 626 E5
9300 PTLD 97219 656 E1
SW 3rd Av US-26
2400 PTLD 97201 626 E1
E 3rd Cir
1400 ClkC 98629 416 J1
1400 LCTR 98629 416 J1
N 3rd Cir
- RDGF 98642 416 D7
NE 3rd Cir
14800 VCVR 98684 538 C6
NW 3rd Cir
1300 BGND 98604 448 A5
2900 BGND 98604 447 H5
SE 3rd Cir
20000 VCVR 98607 538 H7
35700 ClkC 98671 540 G7
NE 3rd Ct
2600 HBRO 97124 593 C1
6800 ClkC 98665 506 G6
13900 ClkC 98685 476 G6
NW 3rd Ct
1700 MCMV 97128 770 F5
1800 BGND 98604 448 B3
10100 PTLD 97231 565 C1
10900 ClkC 98685 506 G2
13200 ClkC 98685 476 G7
20900 ClkC 98642 446 G6
S 3rd Ct
900 CNLS 97113 592 D6
SW 3rd Ct
300 GSHM 97080 628 J3
W 3rd Ct
600 MCMV 97128 770 G5
3rd Dr N
- PTLD 97266 627 J7
NE 3rd Dr
9400 PTLD 97211 566 G3
SW 3rd Dr
1500 GSHM 97080 629 A3
E 3rd Lp
2300 VCVR 98661 536 J6
NE 3rd Lp
- ClkC 98607 569 G4
1800 CMAS 98607 569 G4
3rd Pl
1500 CBAC 97018 385 C4
N 3rd Pl
300 CNLS 97113 592 D4
NE 3rd Pl
300 CMAS 98607 569 F4
2600 HBRO 97124 593 C1
NW 3rd Pl
10400 ClkC 98685 506 F3
30000 ClkC 98642 416 G3
S 3rd Pl
1200 CNLS 97113 592 D6
SE 3rd Pl
52000 SPSE 97056 474 F1
3rd St
- BRTN 97005 625 A2
- FTGV 97116 592 C4
- NWBG 97132 713 C7
- PTLD 97233 598 B6
- SPSE 97056 474 E1
- STPL 97137 773 C5
- TLTN 97062 685 A3
10 FRVW 97024 599 B4
100 LKOW 97034 656 F6
300 CMAS 98607 569 H5
300 ORCY 97045 717 C1
300 WDLD 98674 385 J2
300 WHGL 98671 569 H5
700 DAYT 97114 772 B4
700 YmhC 97114 772 C4
1500 CBAC 97018 385 C3
3rd St SR-221
700 DAYT 97114 772 B4
700 YmhC 97114 772 B4
3rd St NE
14700 AURA 97002 775 F3
20400 STPL 97137 773 C5
23500 MrnC 97002 744 G6
E 3rd St
100 MOLA 97038 837 E2
300 YMHL 97148 711 A1
400 YmhC 97148 711 A1
800 CmsC 97038 837 F2
1500 NWBG 97132 713 D7
1700 YmhC 97132 713 D7
N 3rd St
100 CLTN 97111 711 B7
200 STHN 97051 385 D6
2400 WHGL 98671 569 J3
NE 3rd St
10 GSHM 97030 629 C2
100 MCMV 97128 770 H5
300 BGND 98604 448 B5
9700 VCVR 98664 537 G6
11500 VCVR 98684 537 J6
14700 VCVR 98684 538 C6
17400 ClkC 98684 538 F6
25200 ClkC 98607 539 E6
31200 ClkC 98671 540 B6
52500 SPSE 97056 444 E7
NE 3rd St SR-500
26300 ClkC 98607 539 F6
NW 3rd St
- PTLD 97231 565 D2
700 GSHM 97030 629 B2
1600 BGND 98604 447 J5
1600 BGND 98604 448 A5
2000 GSHM 97030 628 J2
4200 GSHM 97236 628 G2
S 3rd St
100 STHN 97051 385 D7
200 CLTN 97111 711 C7
200 CLTN 97111 741 A1
300 STHN 97051 415 D1
SE 3rd St
100 DAYT 97114 772 B4
100 DNDE 97115 742 J3
100 LFYT 97127 741 G7
100 TDLE 97060 599 G4
300 LFYT 97127 771 H1
700 YmhC 97114 772 B4
800 BGND 98604 448 C5
1200 LFYT 97114 771 H1
1200 YmhC 97114 771 H1
1200 YmhC 97127 771 H1
3600 GSHM 97080 629 F3
10500 VCVR 98664 537 H6

SE 3rd St
16100 VCVR 98684 538 E6
52200 SPSE 97056 474 F1
52400 SPSE 97056 444 G7
SE 3rd St SR-99W
100 LFYT 97127 741 G7
300 LFYT 97127 771 H1
1200 LFYT 97114 771 H1
1200 YmhC 97114 771 H1
1200 YmhC 97127 771 H1
SE 3rd St SR-221
100 DAYT 97114 772 B4
700 YmhC 97114 772 B4
SW 3rd St
10 BGND 98604 448 B5
100 DNDE 97115 742 H3
1700 BGND 98604 447 J5
2200 GSHM 97080 628 J3
3700 GSHM 97030 628 H3
4100 GSHM 97236 628 G3
12300 BRTN 97005 625 B3
15900 SRWD 97140 684 G7
52200 SPSE 97056 474 E1
W 3rd St
100 LCTR 98629 416 G1
100 LFYT 97127 741 F7
100 NWBG 97132 713 B7
100 YmhC 97128 741 F7
200 MOLA 97038 837 E2
200 VCVR 98660 536 F5
600 YmhC 97132 713 B7
1400 MCMV 97128 770 F5
W 3rd St SR-99W
100 LFYT 97127 741 F7
100 YmhC 97128 741 F7
NW 3rd Ter
2500 GSHM 97030 628 J2
E 3rd Wy
- ClkC 98629 416 J1
N 3rd Wy
1700 RDGF 98642 416 B6
NE 3rd Wy
600 BGND 98604 448 C5
NW 3rd Wy
10 BGND 98604 448 B5
2400 BGND 98604 447 J5
S 3rd Wy
3400 RDGF 98642 416 C7
SE 3rd Wy
13500 VCVR 98684 538 B6
4 Wheel Dr
- YmhC 97111 712 A7
- YmhC 97111 742 B1
- YmhC 97114 742 B1
- YmhC 97132 712 A6
4th Av
- MthC 97231 534 F4
200 ORCY 97045 717 A2
1700 WLIN 97068 716 G2
N 4th Av
10 CNLS 97113 592 D4
100 RDGF 98642 415 J7
800 WasC 97113 592 D3
NE 4th Av
100 CNBY 97013 746 D6
100 ECDA 97023 750 B3
100 HBRO 97123 593 C5
200 CMAS 98607 569 F4
3000 HBRO 97124 593 C1
3400 WHGL 98671 569 J4
6300 ClkC 98665 506 G6
10100 ClkC 98685 506 G3
10700 PTLD 97211 566 G2
14400 ClkC 98685 476 G5
21900 ClkC 98642 446 H5
39000 ClkC 98674 386 H2
NW 4th Av
- WasC 97124 593 A1
10 PTLD 97204 596 F5
10 PTLD 97209 596 F5
100 ECDA 97023 750 B3
300 CNBY 97013 746 B6
700 CMAS 98607 569 D5
2100 BGND 98604 448 B3
2100 ClkC 98604 448 B3
2400 HBRO 97124 593 B1
7900 ClkC 98665 506 G4
9800 ClkC 98685 506 G2
15100 ClkC 98685 476 G5
38900 ClkC 98674 386 G2
S 4th Av
10 CNLS 97113 592 D5
100 RDGF 98642 415 J7
SE 4th Av
- CMAS 98607 569 F5
- PTLD 97214 596 F7
10 BGND 98604 448 C5
100 ECDA 97023 750 D4
100 HBRO 97123 593 C5
100 HBRO 97124 593 C5
400 CNBY 97013 746 D6
1800 CmsC 97013 746 E6
2400 PTLD 97202 626 G1
2400 PTLD 97214 626 G1
32800 CmsC 97023 750 D4
SW 4th Av
10 PTLD 97204 596 F5
10 PTLD 97209 596 F6
100 ECDA 97023 750 B4
200 BGND 98604 448 B5
400 CNBY 97013 746 C7
1200 PTLD 97201 596 E7
2900 PTLD 97201 626 E1
3100 PTLD 97239 626 E3
6800 PTLD 97219 626 E5
9200 PTLD 97219 656 E1
E 4th Cir
1400 ClkC 98629 416 J1
1400 LCTR 98629 416 J1
NE 4th Cir
9700 VCVR 98664 537 G6
15000 VCVR 98684 538 D6
17500 ClkC 98684 538 F6
SW 4th Cir
2400 BGND 98604 447 J5
N 4th Cr
- RDGF 98642 416 D7
N 4th Ct
- WHGL 98671 569 J4
NE 4th Ct
1000 BGND 98604 448 C4
2800 HBRO 97124 593 C1
13600 ClkC 98685 476 G6
NW 4th Ct
1700 MCMV 97128 770 F5

NW 4th Ct
9600 ClkC 98665 506 G3
11200 ClkC 98685 506 G2
14700 ClkC 98685 476 G5
24500 ClkC 98642 446 G2
32000 ClkC 98642 416 G2
4th Pl
2300 CBAC 97018 385 C3
N 4th Pl
300 RDGF 98642 415 J6
NE 4th Pl
3000 HBRO 97124 593 C1
NW 4th Pl
- PTLD 97231 565 D2
500 BGND 98604 448 B5
15200 ClkC 98685 476 G5
S 4th Pl
100 CNLS 97113 592 D5
SW 4th Pl
100 BGND 98604 448 B5
4th St
- BRTN 97005 625 A2
- CMAS 98607 569 J4
- FRVW 97024 599 B4
- FTGV 97116 592 C4
- PTLD 97233 598 B6
- STPL 97137 773 C6
100 DAYT 97114 772 A4
100 LFYT 97127 741 G7
100 LKOW 97034 656 F6
300 ORCY 97045 717 C1
300 WDLD 98674 385 J2
500 LFYT 97127 771 G1
900 WHGL 98671 569 J4
1100 WLIN 97068 716 J2
1200 ClbC 97051 385 C4
2000 CBAC 97018 385 C3
4th St NE
14900 AURA 97002 775 F4
20000 MrnC 97137 773 B6
20000 STPL 97137 773 B6
E 4th St
100 LCTR 98629 416 H1
100 NWBG 97132 713 C7
500 NWBG 97132 743 C1
800 CmsC 97038 837 F2
800 MOLA 97038 837 F2
1600 VCVR 98661 536 H6
N 4th St
100 STHN 97051 385 D7
500 CLTN 97111 711 B7
2300 WHGL 98671 569 J3
NE 4th St
10 GSHM 97030 629 C2
100 MCMV 97128 770 H5
300 BGND 98604 448 C5
10000 VCVR 98664 537 H6
11700 VCVR 98684 537 J6
15300 VCVR 98684 538 D6
17200 ClkC 98684 538 F6
NW 4th St
- CNBY 97013 746 C6
- PTLD 97231 565 D2
600 GSHM 97030 629 B2
1100 BGND 98604 448 A5
1600 BGND 98604 447 J5
2500 GSHM 97030 628 J2
52800 SPSE 97056 444 E7
S 4th St
100 STHN 97051 385 D7
300 STHN 97051 415 D1
SE 4th St
10 BGND 98604 448 B6
100 TDLE 97060 599 G4
300 GSHM 97080 629 C3
400 DNDE 97115 742 J3
400 YmhC 97115 742 J3
10500 VCVR 98664 537 H6
16100 VCVR 98684 538 E6
52000 SPSE 97056 474 F1
52400 SPSE 97056 444 G7
SW 4th St
10 BGND 98604 448 B5
100 TDLE 97060 599 G4
200 GSHM 97080 629 A3
300 DNDE 97115 742 H3
2000 BGND 98604 447 J5
2200 GSHM 97080 628 J3
3700 GSHM 97030 628 H3
9100 WNVL 97070 745 E1
12500 BRTN 97005 625 B3
33000 SPSE 97056 444 E7
52100 SPSE 97056 474 E1
W 4th St
100 LCTR 98629 416 G1
100 LFYT 97127 741 G7
100 NWBG 97132 713 B7
200 MOLA 97038 837 E2
200 VCVR 98660 536 F5
1400 MCMV 97128 770 F5
E 4th Wy
- ClkC 98629 416 J1
NE 4th Wy
700 BGND 98604 448 C5
15700 VCVR 98684 538 D6
NW 4th Wy
- HBRO 97124 593 B1
S 4th Wy
2300 ClkC 98642 416 B7
3400 RDGF 98642 416 C7
SE 4th Wy
19700 VCVR 98607 538 H7
SW 4th Wy
10 BGND 98604 448 B6
2500 BGND 98604 447 J5
N 5th
300 CLTN 97111 711 B7
5th Av
- MthC 97231 534 F4
800 ORCY 97045 717 A2
2000 WLIN 97068 716 H2
N 5th Av
100 CNLS 97113 592 D4
100 RDGF 98642 415 J7
NE 5th Av
100 CNBY 97013 746 C6
100 HBRO 97123 593 C5
100 HBRO 97124 593 C4
200 CMAS 98607 569 F4
400 ECDA 97023 750 B3
8800 ClkC 98665 506 G4
10800 PTLD 97211 566 H1
10900 ClkC 98685 506 G2
14600 ClkC 98685 476 H5
40400 ClkC 98674 386 H1

NW 5th Av
10 PTLD 97204 596 F5
10 PTLD 97209 596 F5
100 CNBY 97013 746 C6
100 ECDA 97023 750 B3
700 CMAS 98607 569 D5
1600 BGND 98604 448 B4
7600 ClkC 98665 506 F5
11300 ClkC 98685 506 G1
14600 ClkC 98685 476 G5
21400 ClkC 98642 446 G5
27700 ClkC 98642 416 G6
S 5th Av
100 CNLS 97113 592 D5
100 RDGF 98642 415 J7
SE 5th Av
- ECDA 97023 750 B4
100 BGND 98604 448 C5
100 HBRO 97123 593 C5
100 HBRO 97124 593 C5
500 CNBY 97013 746 D6
SW 5th Av
- PTLD 97219 626 E5
10 BGND 98604 448 B5
10 PTLD 97204 596 E7
10 PTLD 97209 596 F5
400 CNBY 97013 746 C7
1700 CMAS 98607 569 C5
1900 PTLD 97201 596 E7
2300 PTLD 97201 626 E1
SW 5th Av US-26
2300 PTLD 97201 626 E1
N 5th Cir
- RDGF 98642 416 D6
NE 5th Cir
- ClkC 98684 538 E6
1700 BGND 98604 448 D5
9700 VCVR 98664 537 G6
14000 VCVR 98684 538 B6
S 5th Cir
1000 CNLS 97113 592 D6
1500 RDGF 98642 416 A7
SE 5th Cir
400 BGND 98604 448 C6
14700 VCVR 98684 538 C7
36500 ClkC 98671 540 G7
SW 5th Cir
2300 BGND 98604 447 J6
5th Ct
500 FRVW 97024 599 B4
NE 5th Ct
700 BGND 98604 448 C4
1600 CMAS 98607 569 F3
3400 GSHM 97030 629 F2
14800 ClkC 98685 476 H5
NW 5th Ct
- CMAS 98607 569 D5
1400 GSHM 97030 629 A2
1700 MCMV 97128 770 F5
1800 BGND 98604 448 B3
31100 ClkC 98642 416 G3
SW 5th Ct
300 CNBY 97013 746 C7
600 GSHM 97030 629 B3
3600 GSHM 97030 628 H3
NE 5th Dr
4000 GSHM 97030 629 F2
NW 5th Dr
700 CNBY 97013 746 B6
SW 5th Dr
- PTLD 97219 626 E7
- PTLD 97219 656 E1
3600 GSHM 97030 628 G3
5th Pl
700 ORCY 97045 717 A2
NW 5th Pl
1100 CNBY 97013 746 B6
14800 ClkC 98685 476 G5
S 5th Pl
300 CNLS 97113 592 D5
SW 5th Pl
1300 GSHM 97080 629 A3
5th St
- BRTN 97005 625 A2
- FTGV 97116 592 C4
- PTLD 97233 598 B6
- WasC 97140 715 C1
100 DAYT 97114 772 A4
100 LFYT 97127 741 G7
100 LKOW 97034 656 F5
100 ORCY 97045 687 B7
200 WDLD 98674 385 J2
300 FRVW 97024 599 B4
400 ORCY 97045 717 C1
700 LFYT 97127 771 H1
800 CMAS 98607 569 J4
800 WHGL 98671 569 J4
1400 ClbC 97018 385 C4
1400 ClbC 97051 385 C4
1500 WLIN 97068 716 H2
2300 CBAC 97018 385 C3
5th St SR-99E
- ORCY 97045 717 C1
100 ORCY 97045 687 B7
5th St NE
20000 MrnC 97137 773 B6
20000 STPL 97137 773 B6
E 5th St
100 LCTR 98629 386 H7
100 MOLA 97038 837 F2
100 NWBG 97132 743 D1
100 VCVR 98660 536 G5
400 VCVR 98661 536 J5
800 CmsC 97038 837 F2
2700 VCVR 98661 537 B6
N 5th St
100 CLTN 97111 711 B7
100 STHN 97051 385 D6
NE 5th St
10 BGND 98604 448 B5
100 MCMV 97128 770 J5
3000 GSHM 97030 629 E2
10200 VCVR 98664 537 H6
11700 VCVR 98684 537 J6
12200 VCVR 98684 538 A6
16700 ClkC 98684 538 E6
19300 ClkC 98684 538 G6
30400 ClkC 98671 540 A6
52400 SPSE 97056 444 F7
NW 5th St
- PTLD 97231 565 D2
100 MCMV 97128 770 G5
1500 GSHM 97030 629 A2
1900 GSHM 97030 628 J2
2300 BGND 98604 447 J5

NW 5th St
2900 ClkC 98604 447 H5
52800 SPSE 97056 444 E7
S 5th St
100 CLTN 97111 711 C7
100 CLTN 97111 741 B1
100 STHN 97051 385 D7
6500 RDGF 98642 416 G7
6700 ClkC 98642 416 G7
SE 5th St
- VCVR 98664 537 H7
100 DNDE 97115 742 J3
100 TDLE 97060 599 G4
400 YmhC 97115 742 J3
500 BGND 98604 448 C6
2900 GSHM 97080 629 E3
11700 VCVR 98683 537 J7
12500 VCVR 98683 538 A7
14800 VCVR 98684 538 C7
26400 ClkC 98607 539 F7
31300 ClkC 98671 540 B7
51800 SPSE 97056 474 F2
SW 5th St
10 GSHM 97080 629 B3
100 BGND 98604 448 B6
100 DNDE 97115 742 H3
2100 BGND 98604 447 J6
2300 GSHM 97080 628 J3
9100 WNVL 97070 745 D1
10000 BRTN 97005 625 B3
51500 SPSE 97056 474 E2
W 5th St
- WHGL 98671 569 H3
100 LCTR 98629 386 G7
100 LFYT 97127 741 G7
100 MOLA 97038 837 E2
100 NWBG 97132 743 B1
300 LCTR 98629 416 G1
400 VCVR 98660 536 F5
400 YmhC 97132 743 B1
1400 MCMV 97128 770 F5
N 5th Wy
1900 RDGF 98642 416 B6
NE 5th Wy
10100 VCVR 98664 537 H6
S 5th Wy
3400 RDGF 98642 416 C7
4500 ClkC 98642 416 D7
SE 5th Wy
1400 BGND 98604 448 D6
19700 VCVR 98607 538 H7
SW 5th Wy
- TDLE 97060 599 F4
2500 BGND 98604 447 J6
NE 5th Av Dr
800 HBRO 97124 593 C3
6th Av
- MthC 97231 534 F4
1500 WLIN 97068 716 G2
7400 CmsC 97027 687 E2
7400 CmsC 97267 687 E2
7400 GLDS 97027 687 E2
NE 6th Av
10 PTLD 97214 596 G5
100 CMAS 98607 569 E4
100 ECDA 97023 750 B3
100 HBRO 97123 593 C5
100 HBRO 97124 593 C4
700 PTLD 97232 596 G4
3500 PTLD 97212 596 G2
4800 PTLD 97211 596 H1
6000 PTLD 97211 566 H6
7800 ClkC 98665 506 G5
9900 ClkC 98685 506 G3
14300 ClkC 98685 476 H5
28800 ClkC 98642 416 H5
38900 ClkC 98674 386 H2
NW 6th Av
- CMAS 98607 569 A5
10 PTLD 97204 596 F5
10 PTLD 97205 596 F5
10 PTLD 97209 596 F5
100 CNBY 97013 746 C6
100 ECDA 97023 750 B3
900 BGND 98604 448 B4
1400 HBRO 97124 593 B3
2400 ClkC 98604 448 B3
8200 ClkC 98665 506 F4
10900 ClkC 98685 506 G2
15200 ClkC 98685 476 G5
16000 ClkC 98642 476 G4
18100 MthC 97231 534 F4
S 6th Av
100 CNLS 97113 592 D5
200 RDGF 98642 416 A7
SE 6th Av
10 PTLD 97214 596 G7
10 PTLD 97232 596 G5
100 HBRO 97123 593 C5
100 HBRO 97124 593 C5
500 CMAS 98607 569 F5
1100 BGND 98604 448 C6
2200 PTLD 97214 626 G1
2500 PTLD 97202 626 G1
6600 VCVR 98661 537 D7
7500 CmsC 97027 687 E2
SE 6th Av SR-500
500 CMAS 98607 569 F5
SW 6th Av
10 PTLD 97204 596 F6
10 PTLD 97205 596 F6
10 PTLD 97209 596 F5
100 CNBY 97013 746 C7
1200 BGND 98604 448 B6
1600 PTLD 97201 596 E7
2100 PTLD 97201 626 E1
4100 PTLD 97239 626 E2
4200 CMAS 98607 568 J5
4200 CMAS 98607 569 A5
7800 PTLD 97219 626 E6
9400 PTLD 97219 656 D1
NE 6th Cir
- ClkC 98671 540 C6
9800 VCVR 98664 537 G5
14400 VCVR 98684 538 C6
17500 ClkC 98684 538 F6
29800 ClkC 98671 539 J6
SE 6th Cir
200 BGND 98604 448 B6
26100 ClkC 98607 539 E7
32000 ClkC 98671 540 B7
SW 6th Cir
300 BGND 98604 448 B6
1100 TDLE 97060 599 F3

6th Ct
500 LFYT 97127 771 H1
1100 WHGL 98671 569 J4
NE 6th Ct
11100 ClkC 98685 506 H2
13400 ClkC 98685 476 H6
16100 ClkC 98642 476 H4
24600 ClkC 98642 446 H2
NW 6th Ct
600 MCMV 97128 770 F5
1500 GSHM 97030 629 A2
1700 CMAS 98607 569 C5
20900 ClkC 98642 446 G6
SE 6th Ct
600 BGND 98604 448 C6
SW 6th Ct
500 GSHM 97080 629 B3
600 PTLD 97219 656 E1
NE 6th Dr
2600 GSHM 97030 629 E2
9600 PTLD 97211 566 G2
NW 6th Dr
1700 GSHM 97030 628 J2
1700 GSHM 97030 629 A2
6th Pl
3000 CBAC 97018 385 B2
NE 6th Pl
2600 PTLD 97212 596 G3
NW 6th Pl
600 MCMV 97128 770 F5
900 CNBY 97013 746 B6
1500 CMAS 98607 569 C5
2100 GSHM 97030 628 H2
SE 6th Pl
500 CNBY 97013 746 D7
1900 BGND 98604 448 C7
1900 ClkC 98604 448 C7
SW 6th Pl
- PTLD 97219 656 E2
100 CNBY 97013 746 C7
1400 GSHM 97080 629 A3
6th St
- BRTN 97005 625 A2
- FTGV 97116 592 C4
- MCMV 97128 770 F5
10 FRVW 97024 599 B4
100 DAYT 97114 772 A4
100 LFYT 97127 741 G7
100 LKOW 97034 656 F5
100 ORCY 97045 687 C7
400 CMAS 98607 569 J5
400 CMAS 98671 569 J5
400 ORCY 97045 717 C1
400 WDLD 98674 385 J2
900 LFYT 97127 771 H1
900 WHGL 98671 569 J4
1500 CBAC 97018 385 C3
1500 ClbC 97018 385 C4
1500 WLIN 97068 716 H2
2000 CBAC 97051 385 C3
2000 ClbC 97051 385 C3
3400 ClbC 97054 385 B2
6th St NE
20100 MrnC 97137 773 C6
20100 STPL 97137 773 C6
E 6th St
100 LCTR 98629 386 H7
100 MOLA 97038 837 E2
100 VCVR 98660 536 G5
400 NWBG 97132 743 C1
800 CmsC 97038 837 F2
1600 VCVR 98661 536 J5
2700 VCVR 98661 537 A5
N 6th St
- WHGL 98671 569 J3
100 CLTN 97111 711 B7
100 STHN 97051 385 D7
NE 6th St
200 MCMV 97128 770 H5
1600 BGND 98604 448 D5
1700 ClkC 98604 448 D5
2600 GSHM 97030 629 E2
10700 VCVR 98664 537 H6
11800 VCVR 98684 537 J6
13800 VCVR 98684 538 B6
16700 ClkC 98684 538 E6
19200 ClkC 98607 538 H6
NW 6th St
100 MCMV 97128 770 H5
700 GSHM 97030 629 A2
2100 BGND 98604 447 J5
52800 SPSE 97056 444 E7
S 6th St
100 CLTN 97111 711 C7
100 CLTN 97111 741 B1
100 STHN 97051 385 D7
100 WHGL 98671 569 J5
300 STHN 97051 415 D1
SE 6th St
100 TDLE 97060 599 G4
600 DNDE 97115 742 J3
1400 BGND 98604 448 C6
1900 GSHM 97080 629 D3
9800 VCVR 98664 537 G7
13900 VCVR 98683 538 C7
16000 VCVR 98684 538 E7
28300 ClkC 98607 539 H7
32200 ClkC 98671 540 C7
51400 SPSE 97056 474 F2
51900 ClbC 97056 474 F2
SW 6th St
10 BGND 98604 448 B6
100 DNDE 97115 742 H3
200 GSHM 97080 629 B3
1700 BGND 98604 447 J6
3700 GSHM 97030 628 H3
13000 BRTN 97005 625 A3
14100 BRTN 97005 624 J4
14400 BRTN 97007 624 J4
14600 WasC 97007 624 J4
W 6th St
100 LCTR 98629 386 G7
100 LFYT 97127 741 G7
100 VCVR 98660 536 F5
1400 MCMV 97128 770 F5
2600 WHGL 98671 569 H3
NE 6th Ter
3500 GSHM 97030 629 F2
N 6th Wy
- RDGF 98642 416 D6
NE 6th Wy
28500 ClkC 98671 539 H6
S 6th Wy
900 RDGF 98642 416 A7
1500 RDGF 98642 446 F1

STREET
Block City ZIP Map# Grid

E 6th Wy
19700 VCVR 98607 538 H7
W 6th Wy
- TDLE 97060 599 F4
NE 6th Av Dr
1000 HBRO 97124 593 C3
W 6th Av Dr
4000 PTLD 97239 626 E2
7th Av
- MthC 97231 534 F4
N 7th Av
200 CNLS 97113 592 D4
NE 7th Av
10 PTLD 97214 596 G5
10 PTLD 97232 596 G5
100 HBRO 97123 593 C4
100 HBRO 97124 593 C5
200 CMAS 98607 569 E4
900 MCMV 97128 770 H5
1600 PTLD 97212 596 H1
4000 PTLD 97211 596 H1
5500 PTLD 97211 566 H7
9500 ClkC 98665 506 H3
9800 ClkC 98685 506 H3
12600 ClkC 98685 476 H7
NW 7th Av
200 CNBY 97013 746 C6
1200 CMAS 98607 569 D4
1600 HBRO 97124 593 B3
8200 ClkC 98665 506 F4
10500 ClkC 98685 506 F2
15000 ClkC 98685 476 F5
28500 ClkC 98642 416 G5
S 7th Av
100 RDGF 98642 416 A7
SE 7th Av
- PTLD 97214 626 G1
10 PTLD 97214 596 G7
10 PTLD 97232 596 G5
100 HBRO 97123 593 C6
100 HBRO 97124 593 C5
300 CNBY 97013 746 D7
1200 CmsC 97013 746 D7
1500 CMAS 98607 569 G5
2900 PTLD 97202 626 G2
SW 7th Av
10 BGND 98604 448 A5
400 CNBY 97013 746 C7
4200 PTLD 97239 626 E2
6800 PTLD 97219 626 E5
N 7th Cir
900 RDGF 98642 416 A6
NE 7th Cir
- ClkC 98607 569 G4
- ClkC 98671 569 G4
700 BGND 98604 448 C4
1800 CMAS 98607 569 G4
11600 VCVR 98684 537 J5
13900 VCVR 98684 538 B5
S 7th Cir
100 CNLS 97113 592 D5
1100 RDGF 98642 446 A1
SE 7th Cir
200 BGND 98604 448 B6
SW 7th Cir
1500 CMAS 98607 569 C5
7th Ct
200 WHGL 98671 569 J5
2000 CBAC 97018 385 C3
N 7th Ct
- CNLS 97113 592 D4
NE 7th Ct
2600 GSHM 97030 629 E2
11200 ClkC 98685 506 H2
13900 ClkC 98685 476 H6
NW 7th Ct
1500 GSHM 97030 629 A2
1800 BGND 98604 448 A3
11400 ClkC 98685 506 F1
15100 ClkC 98685 476 F5
S 7th Ct
300 CNLS 97113 592 D5
SE 7th Ct
800 BGND 98604 448 C6
SW 7th Ct
1300 BGND 98604 448 A6
2000 GSHM 97080 628 J3
3700 GSHM 97030 628 H3
W 7th Ct
1400 MCMV 97128 770 F4
N 7th Pl
800 RDGF 98642 416 A6
NE 7th Pl
- HBRO 97124 593 D4
7000 PTLD 97211 566 H5
12700 VCVR 98684 538 A5
13900 ClkC 98685 476 H6
NW 7th Pl
1700 GSHM 97030 628 J2
1700 GSHM 97030 629 A2
11100 ClkC 98685 506 F2
14500 ClkC 98685 476 F5
SE 7th Pl
500 CNBY 97013 746 D7
7th St
- FTGV 97116 592 C4
- WasC 97140 715 C1
- WLIN 97068 687 C7
10 FRVW 97024 599 B4
100 DAYT 97114 772 A4
100 LFYT 97127 741 H7
100 ORCY 97045 687 C7
300 WHGL 98671 569 J5
400 LKOW 97034 656 F5
600 ORCY 97045 717 C1
1100 YmhC 97114 741 H7
1300 WLIN 97068 716 H2
1600 ClbC 97018 385 C4
2300 ClbC 97051 385 C3
2800 CBAC 97018 385 B2
7th St SR-43
- ORCY 97045 687 C7
- WLIN 97068 687 C7
E 7th St
100 LCTR 98629 386 H7
100 VCVR 98660 536 G5
600 MOLA 97038 837 F3
700 NWBG 97132 743 D1
N 7th St
- WHGL 98671 569 J3
200 STHN 97051 385 C6
NE 7th St
10 BGND 98604 448 C4
100 MCMV 97128 770 H5
2800 GSHM 97030 629 E2
10000 VCVR 98664 537 H5
11200 VCVR 98684 537 J5
16100 ClkC 98684 538 E5
16100 VCVR 98684 538 E5
30300 ClkC 98671 539 J6
30300 ClkC 98671 540 A6
NW 7th St
10 BGND 98604 448 B4
100 MCMV 97128 770 H5
200 TDLE 97060 599 E3
2200 GSHM 97030 628 J2
2700 BGND 98604 447 H4
52800 SPSE 97056 444 E7
S 7th St
100 STHN 97051 385 D7
100 WHGL 98671 569 J6
300 STHN 97051 415 D1
SE 7th St
100 TDLE 97060 599 G4
400 BGND 98604 448 C6
400 DNDE 97115 742 J3
4000 GSHM 97080 629 F3
9600 VCVR 98664 537 G7
11600 VCVR 98683 537 J7
12100 VCVR 98683 538 A7
27600 ClkC 98607 539 G7
51700 SPSE 97056 474 F2
SW 7th St
100 DNDE 97115 742 H3
100 TDLE 97060 599 G4
300 GSHM 97080 629 B3
2100 BGND 98604 447 J6
3900 GSHM 97030 628 G3
12500 BRTN 97005 625 B4
W 7th St
- MOLA 97038 837 E2
100 LCTR 98629 386 G7
100 LFYT 97127 741 G7
900 VCVR 98660 536 E5
3000 WHGL 98671 569 H3
NE 7th Wy
13800 VCVR 98684 538 B5
NW 7th Wy
1100 CMAS 98607 569 D4
SE 7th Wy
200 CNBY 97013 746 D7
1400 BGND 98604 448 D6
14200 VCVR 98683 538 C7
19700 VCVR 98607 538 H7
8th Av
- ECDA 97023 750 B2
1500 WLIN 97068 716 G2
N 8th Av
100 RDGF 98642 416 A7
NE 8th Av
- ClkC 98604 448 C4
10 PTLD 97214 596 H5
100 HBRO 97123 593 D5
600 BGND 98604 448 C4
1500 PTLD 97232 596 H3
1600 PTLD 97212 596 H3
3400 HBRO 97124 593 D1
3400 WasC 97124 593 D1
4000 PTLD 97211 596 H1
7500 PTLD 97211 566 H5
8200 ClkC 98665 506 H4
10900 ClkC 98685 506 H2
13200 ClkC 98685 476 H7
37400 ClkC 98629 386 H4
NW 8th Av
- MthC 97231 534 F4
10 PTLD 97205 596 F5
10 PTLD 97209 596 F5
1200 CMAS 98607 569 D4
1500 BGND 98604 448 A3
1600 HBRO 97124 593 B3
5300 VCVR 98663 506 F7
9500 ClkC 98665 506 F5
9800 ClkC 98685 506 F3
14200 ClkC 98685 476 F6
S 8th Av
10 CNLS 97113 592 D5
100 RDGF 98642 416 A7
SE 8th Av
10 PTLD 97232 596 H5
100 HBRO 97123 593 D6
100 HBRO 97124 593 D6
200 BGND 98604 448 C5
500 PTLD 97214 596 H7
1300 CmsC 97013 746 E7
1300 CNBY 97013 746 D7
1400 CMAS 98607 569 G5
2200 PTLD 97214 626 H2
2200 WHGL 98671 569 G5
7900 PTLD 97202 626 G6
SW 8th Av
100 CNBY 97013 746 C7
200 PTLD 97205 596 F5
200 PTLD 97209 596 F5
1200 BGND 98604 448 A6
6800 PTLD 97219 626 E5
9600 PTLD 97219 656 E1
N 8th Cir
200 RDGF 98642 415 J6
NE 8th Cir
9800 VCVR 98664 537 G5
16000 VCVR 98684 538 D5
NW 8th Cir
3900 CMAS 98607 569 A4
SE 8th Cir
19700 VCVR 98607 538 H7
33500 ClkC 98671 540 D7
SW 8th Cir
400 TDLE 97060 599 F4
8th Ct
300 TDLE 97060 599 F4
1000 WHGL 98671 569 J4
2000 CBAC 97018 385 C3
2100 WLIN 97068 716 H2
N 8th Ct
1500 WHGL 98671 569 J4
NE 8th Ct
2200 HBRO 97124 593 D2
2600 GSHM 97030 629 E2
5800 ClkC 98665 506 H7
14300 ClkC 98685 476 H5
NW 8th Ct
700 HBRO 97124 593 B3
2200 GSHM 97030 628 J2
3600 CMAS 98607 569 A4
11300 ClkC 98685 506 F1
14300 ClkC 98685 476 F5
S 8th Ct
200 RDGF 98642 416 A7
SE 8th Ct
2400 GSHM 97080 629 E3
52000 ClbC 97056 474 F1
52000 SPSE 97056 474 F1
W 8th Ct
- WHGL 98671 569 H3
1300 MCMV 97128 770 F4
SW 8th Dr
1500 GSHM 97080 629 A3
1800 GSHM 97080 628 J3
9200 PTLD 97219 626 D7
9200 PTLD 97219 656 D1
N 8th Pl
900 RDGF 98642 416 A6
NE 8th Pl
900 CNBY 97013 746 D5
12700 VCVR 98684 538 A5
NW 8th Pl
500 CNBY 97013 746 B5
700 HBRO 97124 593 A3
11900 ClkC 98685 506 F1
SE 8th Pl
400 BGND 98604 448 C6
8th St
10 DAYT 97114 771 J4
10 DAYT 97114 772 A4
10 YmhC 97114 771 J4
10 YmhC 97114 772 A4
100 LFYT 97127 741 G7
100 ORCY 97045 687 C7
300 LKOW 97034 656 F5
300 WHGL 98671 569 J5
700 ORCY 97045 717 C1
1000 WLIN 97068 716 H2
1600 CBAC 97018 385 C4
1600 ClbC 97018 385 C4
E 8th St
300 VCVR 98660 536 G5
500 LCTR 98629 386 H7
700 NWBG 97132 743 C1
800 CmsC 97038 837 F3
800 MOLA 97038 837 F3
2300 VCVR 98661 536 J5
2800 VCVR 98661 537 A5
N 8th St
- WHGL 98671 569 J4
200 STHN 97051 385 C6
NE 8th St
- VCVR 98684 537 J5
100 MCMV 97128 770 H4
2200 GSHM 97030 629 E2
9200 VCVR 98664 537 G5
14800 VCVR 98684 538 D5
16200 ClkC 98684 538 E5
19200 ClkC 98607 538 H5
19700 CMAS 98607 538 H5
33000 ClkC 98671 540 C6
NW 8th St
10 GSHM 97030 629 B2
300 BGND 98604 448 B4
1400 MCMV 97128 770 F4
2400 BGND 98604 447 J4
S 8th St
100 STHN 97051 385 D7
300 STHN 97051 415 D1
SE 8th St
100 DNDE 97115 742 H3
100 TDLE 97060 599 G4
400 BGND 98604 448 C6
600 GSHM 97080 629 C3
15200 VCVR 98683 538 D7
19900 VCVR 98607 538 H7
26200 ClkC 98607 539 F7
51700 SPSE 97056 474 F2
SW 8th St
100 DNDE 97115 742 H3
700 GSHM 97080 629 B3
2100 BGND 98604 447 J6
3700 GSHM 97030 628 H3
12600 BRTN 97005 625 B4
W 8th St
100 LCTR 98629 386 G7
100 LFYT 97127 741 G7
100 NWBG 97132 743 B1
100 VCVR 98660 536 E5
500 ClkC 98629 386 G7
600 LCTR 98629 416 G1
800 ClkC 98629 416 G1
1900 WHGL 98671 569 H4
N 8th Wy
1800 RDGF 98642 416 B6
NE 8th Wy
- VCVR 98664 537 F5
NW 8th Wy
1000 CNBY 97013 746 B5
2800 CMAS 98607 569 B4
13100 ClkC 98685 476 F7
S 8th Wy
4500 ClkC 98642 446 D1
4500 RDGF 98642 446 D1
SE 8th Wy
31400 ClkC 98671 540 B7
NW 8th Av Dr
800 HBRO 97124 593 B3
900 WasC 97124 593 B3
9th Av
2300 FTGV 97116 591 J6
2300 WasC 97116 591 J6
N 9th Av
10 CNLS 97113 592 E5
100 RDGF 98642 416 A7
NE 9th Av
10 PTLD 97214 596 H5
100 CNBY 97013 746 C5
100 HBRO 97123 593 D5
800 PTLD 97232 596 H3
1100 MCMV 97128 770 J5
1600 HBRO 97124 593 D2
3500 PTLD 97212 596 H2
4000 PTLD 97211 596 H1
5300 PTLD 97211 566 H6
9900 ClkC 98665 506 H3
9900 ClkC 98685 506 H3
14300 ClkC 98685 476 H6
16300 ClkC 98642 476 H4
NW 9th Av
10 PTLD 97205 596 E5
10 PTLD 97209 596 E4
100 CNBY 97013 746 B5
1600 HBRO 97124 593 B2
2400 BGND 98604 448 A3
2400 ClkC 98604 448 A3
3100 CMAS 98607 569 B4
7400 ClkC 98665 506 F5
11900 ClkC 98685 506 F1
14900 ClkC 98685 476 F5
21400 ClkC 98642 446 F5
31600 ClkC 98642 416 G2
37900 ClkC 98629 386 G3
37900 ClkC 98674 386 G3
S 9th Av
100 CNLS 97113 592 D5
100 RDGF 98642 416 A7
SE 9th Av
10 PTLD 97214 596 H7
10 PTLD 97232 596 H5
100 HBRO 97123 593 D5
100 HBRO 97124 593 D5
200 CNBY 97013 746 D7
1100 BGND 98604 448 C6
1300 CmsC 97013 746 E7
1700 CMAS 98607 569 G5
2100 PTLD 97214 626 H1
7500 PTLD 97202 626 G7
8900 CmsC 97202 626 G7
8900 CmsC 97222 626 G7
SW 9th Av
- BGND 98604 448 A7
- ClkC 98604 448 A7
- PTLD 97239 626 D2
100 CNBY 97013 746 D7
200 PTLD 97205 596 E6
200 PTLD 97209 596 E6
8000 PTLD 97219 626 D6
N 9th Cir
10 RDGF 98642 415 J6
2400 RDGF 98642 416 B6
NE 9th Cir
15500 VCVR 98684 538 D5
NW 9th Cir
- ClkC 98629 386 G5
4400 CMAS 98607 568 J4
S 9th Cir
1100 RDGF 98642 446 A1
SE 9th Cir
10 BGND 98604 448 B6
19200 VCVR 98607 538 H7
SW 9th Cir
400 TDLE 97060 599 F4
2200 BGND 98604 447 J6
9th Ct
- LFYT 97127 741 H7
2000 CBAC 97018 385 C3
NE 9th Ct
11600 ClkC 98685 506 H1
14400 ClkC 98685 476 H5
NW 9th Ct
100 HBRO 97123 593 B4
100 HBRO 97124 593 B4
19400 ClkC 98642 446 F7
S 9th Ct
300 RDGF 98642 416 A7
SE 9th Ct
2200 GSHM 97080 629 D4
SW 9th Ct
- GSHM 97080 628 F3
- GSHM 97236 628 F3
3800 GSHM 97030 628 G3
W 9th Ct
1400 MCMV 97128 770 F4
NE 9th Dr
2500 HBRO 97124 593 D2
SW 9th Dr
8700 PTLD 97219 626 D7
NW 9th Lp
3700 CMAS 98607 569 A4
N 9th Pl
700 RDGF 98642 416 A6
NE 9th Pl
1100 CNBY 97013 746 D5
2300 HBRO 97124 593 D2
SW 9th Pl
2100 GSHM 97080 628 J3
9000 PTLD 97219 626 D7
9th St
100 DAYT 97114 771 J4
100 DAYT 97114 772 A4
300 LKOW 97034 656 F5
300 YmhC 97114 772 A5
500 ORCY 97045 687 C7
700 WHGL 98671 569 J5
900 ORCY 97045 717 D1
1000 WLIN 97068 716 H2
1600 CBAC 97018 385 C4
1900 CmsC 97045 717 D1
9th St SW
500 DNDE 97115 742 H3
900 YmhC 97115 742 G3
E 9th St
100 VCVR 98660 536 G5
1800 VCVR 98663 536 H5
2700 NWBG 97132 743 E1
2700 VCVR 98661 536 J5
2700 YmhC 97132 743 E1
2800 VCVR 98661 537 A5
N 9th St
200 STHN 97051 385 C6
1900 WHGL 98671 570 A3
NE 9th St
- ClkC 98607 538 F5
10 BGND 98604 448 B4
100 MCMV 97128 770 H4
800 GSHM 97030 629 C2
10800 VCVR 98664 537 J5
10800 VCVR 98684 537 J5
13800 VCVR 98684 538 D5
16300 ClkC 98684 538 E5
26700 ClkC 98607 539 G5
29500 ClkC 98671 539 J6
31200 ClkC 98671 540 B6
NW 9th St
10 BGND 98604 448 B4
100 MCMV 97128 770 G4
1300 GSHM 97030 629 A2
1600 BGND 98604 447 J4
S 9th St
100 STHN 97051 385 C7
300 STHN 97051 415 D1
SE 9th St
- ClbC 97056 474 F1
300 BGND 98604 448 C6
300 DNDE 97115 742 H4
700 GSHM 97080 629 C3
13200 VCVR 98683 538 B7
19700 VCVR 98607 538 H7
27300 ClkC 98607 539 G7
51600 SPSE 97056 474 F2
SW 9th St
100 DNDE 97115 742 H3
12000 BRTN 97005 625 B4
W 9th St
- ClkC 98607 569 G3
100 LCTR 98629 386 G7
100 LFYT 97127 741 G7
100 NWBG 97132 743 B1
100 VCVR 98660 536 F5
2300 WHGL 98671 569 G3
NW 9th Ter
- GSHM 97030 629 B2
N 9th Wy
1800 RDGF 98642 416 B6
NE 9th Wy
800 BGND 98604 448 C4
15400 VCVR 98684 538 D5
16400 ClkC 98684 538 E5
NW 9th Wy
- BGND 98604 447 J4
900 BGND 98604 448 A4
2700 CMAS 98607 569 B4
SW 9th Wy
2000 BGND 98604 447 J6
10th Av
2500 FTGV 97116 591 J6
N 10th Av
10 CNLS 97113 592 E4
700 WasC 97113 592 E4
NE 10th Av
10 PTLD 97214 596 H5
100 CNBY 97013 746 D5
100 HBRO 97123 593 D5
800 MCMV 97128 770 J5
1400 MCMV 97128 771 A5
1500 PTLD 97232 596 H3
1700 HBRO 97124 593 D2
3500 PTLD 97212 596 H2
4000 PTLD 97211 596 H1
5300 PTLD 97211 566 H6
6500 ClkC 98665 506 H6
10700 ClkC 98685 506 H2
13400 ClkC 98685 476 H5
17900 ClkC 98642 476 H1
19400 ClkC 98642 446 H7
25300 RDGF 98642 446 H1
25900 ClkC 98642 416 H6
25900 RDGF 98642 416 H6
NE 10th Av SR-502
17900 ClkC 98642 476 H1
19400 ClkC 98642 446 H7
NW 10th Av
10 PTLD 97205 596 E5
10 PTLD 97209 596 E5
500 CMAS 98607 569 D4
700 CNBY 97013 746 B5
800 WasC 97124 593 A3
1400 HBRO 97124 593 A3
7200 ClkC 98665 506 F5
12100 ClkC 98685 506 F1
12200 BGND 98604 448 A5
12200 ClkC 98604 448 A5
13300 ClkC 98685 476 F6
NW 10th Av SR-503
12200 BGND 98604 448 A5
12200 ClkC 98604 448 A5
S 10th Av
10 CNLS 97113 592 D6
1600 WasC 97113 592 D6
SE 10th Av
10 PTLD 97214 596 H7
10 PTLD 97232 596 H5
100 CNBY 97013 746 D7
100 HBRO 97123 593 D5
100 HBRO 97124 593 D5
1200 CmsC 97013 746 D7
2100 PTLD 97214 626 H1
2800 PTLD 97202 626 H2
8800 CmsC 97202 626 G7
8800 CmsC 97222 626 G7
SE 10th Av SR-8
300 HBRO 97123 593 D5
SW 10th Av
- PTLD 97209 596 E6
- PTLD 97239 626 D2
10 BGND 98604 448 A6
10 ClkC 98604 448 A6
100 CNBY 97013 746 C7
300 PTLD 97205 596 E6
2000 PTLD 97201 596 E7
8500 PTLD 97219 626 D6
SW 10th Av SR-503
10 BGND 98604 448 A6
10 ClkC 98604 448 A6
NE 10th Cir
16000 VCVR 98684 538 D5
NW 10th Cir
1500 BGND 98604 448 A4
SE 10th Cir
800 TDLE 97060 599 H4
19200 VCVR 98607 538 H7
SW 10th Cir
400 TDLE 97060 599 F5
10th Ct
700 LFYT 97127 741 H7
N 10th Ct
1800 WHGL 98671 570 A4
NE 10th Ct
10000 VCVR 98664 537 H5
NW 10th Ct
8600 ClkC 98665 506 F4
11900 ClkC 98685 506 F1
13800 ClkC 98685 476 F6
30700 ClkC 98642 416 G3
SW 10th Ct
1500 GSHM 97080 629 A4
N 10th Dr
1500 WHGL 98671 570 A4
NE 10th Dr
- GSHM 97030 629 C2
NW 10th Dr
- GSHM 97030 629 B2
SE 10th Dr
3900 GSHM 97080 629 F4
SW 10th Dr
1000 GSHM 97080 629 A4
N 10th Pl
900 RDGF 98642 416 A6
NE 10th Pl
300 HBRO 97124 593 D4
1500 CmsC 97013 746 E5
1500 CNBY 97013 746 E5
16500 ClkC 98684 538 E5
NW 10th Pl
14600 ClkC 98685 476 F5
SE 10th Pl
1500 CNBY 97013 746 E7
10th St
- ORCY 97045 717 D1
100 WHGL 98671 570 A5
200 LKOW 97034 656 F5
500 ORCY 97045 687 C7
1000 WLIN 97068 716 H2
E 10th St
- LFYT 97127 741 H7
1100 NWBG 97132 743 D1
N 10th St
200 STHN 97051 385 C7
4500 ClkC 98642 416 E6
4500 RDGF 98642 416 E6
NE 10th St
- ClkC 98604 448 C4
10 BGND 98604 448 B4
100 MCMV 97128 770 H4
700 GSHM 97030 629 C2
10200 VCVR 98664 537 H5
14000 VCVR 98684 538 C5
16700 ClkC 98684 538 E5
25400 ClkC 98607 539 E5
29500 ClkC 98671 539 J5
30200 ClkC 98671 540 A5
NW 10th St
100 ECDA 97023 750 B2
100 MCMV 97128 770 G4
200 BGND 98604 448 B4
2500 BGND 98604 447 H4
S 10th St
300 STHN 97051 415 D1
SE 10th St
100 DNDE 97115 742 H4
400 BGND 98604 448 C6
400 TDLE 97060 599 G4
3600 GSHM 97080 629 F4
9800 VCVR 98664 537 G7
11300 VCVR 98683 537 J7
12500 VCVR 98683 538 A7
15400 ClkC 98604 448 D6
19500 VCVR 98607 538 H7
37700 ClkC 98671 570 H1
SW 10th St
- DNDE 97115 742 H3
10 BGND 98604 448 B6
1200 TDLE 97060 599 F4
2200 BGND 98604 447 J6
12600 BRTN 97005 625 B4
16500 SRWD 97140 684 G6
W 10th St
100 LCTR 98629 386 G7
300 ClkC 98629 386 G7
2400 WHGL 98671 569 G3
NE 10th Ter
4000 GSHM 97030 629 F2
NW 10th Ter
- WasC 97229 595 D3
S 10th Ter
1400 CNLS 97113 592 E6
SE 10th Ter
4500 GSHM 97080 629 G4
N 10th Wy
800 RDGF 98642 416 A6
NE 10th Wy
1100 BGND 98604 448 C4
15800 VCVR 98684 538 D5
16700 ClkC 98684 538 E5
NW 10th Wy
1200 BGND 98604 447 J4
S 10th Wy
7700 ClkC 98642 446 H1
7700 RDGF 98642 446 H1
SE 10th Wy
1000 BGND 98604 448 C6
NW 10th Av Ct
800 HBRO 97124 593 A3
800 WasC 97124 593 A3
11th Av
2200 FTGV 97116 591 J6
N 11th Av
10 CNLS 97113 592 E4
NE 11th Av
10 PTLD 97214 596 H5
10 PTLD 97232 596 H5
100 CMAS 98607 569 E4
100 CNBY 97013 746 C5
1200 MCMV 97128 770 J4
1700 PTLD 97212 596 H3
2200 HBRO 97124 593 D2
4000 PTLD 97211 596 H1
5300 PTLD 97211 566 H7
6200 ClkC 98665 506 H6
10600 ClkC 98685 506 H2
12900 ClkC 98685 476 H7
23900 ClkC 98642 446 H3
NW 11th Av
10 PTLD 97205 596 E5
10 PTLD 97209 596 E4
100 CNBY 97013 746 C5
600 CMAS 98607 569 D4
700 BGND 98604 448 A4
9100 ClkC 98665 506 F4
9900 ClkC 98685 506 F2
13200 ClkC 98685 476 F5
15500 ClkC 98642 476 F3
21300 ClkC 98642 446 F4
27100 ClkC 98642 416 F5
27100 RDGF 98642 416 F5
34400 ClkC 98629 386 G6
S 11th Av
10 CNLS 97113 592 E5
SE 11th Av
10 PTLD 97214 596 H7
10 PTLD 97232 596 H5
400 HBRO 97123 593 D5
1500 CNBY 97013 746 E7
1700 CMAS 98607 569 G5
2200 PTLD 97214 626 H1
2300 WHGL 98671 569 G5
3000 PTLD 97202 626 H2
8900 CmsC 97202 626 H7
8900 CmsC 97222 626 H7
SW 11th Av
- PTLD 97239 626 D2
300 CNBY 97013 746 C7
300 PTLD 97205 596 E6
300 PTLD 97209 596 E6
1600 PTLD 97201 596 E7
7800 PTLD 97219 626 D7
NE 11th Cir
14300 VCVR 98684 538 C5
29000 ClkC 98671 539 H5
NW 11th Cir
4500 ClkC 98607 568 J4
4500 CMAS 98607 568 J4
S 11th Cir
6700 RDGF 98642 446 F1
SE 11th Cir
200 BGND 98604 448 B6
400 TDLE 97060 599 G5
10500 VCVR 98664 537 H7
15300 VCVR 98683 538 D7
SW 11th Cir
200 BGND 98604 448 B6
2300 BGND 98604 447 J6
11th Ct
800 LFYT 97127 741 H7
E 11th Ct
500 LCTR 98629 386 H7
1000 NWBG 97132 743 C1
NE 11th Ct
3100 HBRO 97124 593 A1
12700 ClkC 98685 476 H7
NW 11th Ct
9700 ClkC 98665 506 F3
11700 ClkC 98685 506 F1
12300 ClkC 98685 476 F7
20900 ClkC 98642 446 F6
33500 ClkC 98629 386 F7
S 11th Ct
10 RDGF 98642 416 A7
SE 11th Ct
500 TDLE 97060 599 G5
SW 11th Ct
16500 SRWD 97140 684 F6
N 11th Dr
1700 WHGL 98671 570 A4
SW 11th Dr
6700 PTLD 97219 626 D5
10400 PTLD 97219 656 D2
SE 11th Lp
1200 CNBY 97013 746 E7
N 11th Pl
- RDGF 98642 416 A6
NE 11th Pl
10 BGND 98604 448 C5
1100 CNBY 97013 746 D5
12700 ClkC 98685 476 H7
NW 11th Pl
800 BGND 98604 448 A4
13100 ClkC 98685 476 F7
SE 11th Pl
- HBRO 97124 593 D5
500 HBRO 97123 593 D5
1500 CNBY 97013 776 E1
11th St
100 DAYT 97114 771 J4
100 WHGL 98671 570 A5
100 YmhC 97114 771 J4
200 ORCY 97045 687 D7
1100 MCMV 97128 770 F4
1200 WLIN 97068 716 G2
1400 ORCY 97045 717 D1
E 11th St
100 VCVR 98660 536 G5
1100 NWBG 97132 743 D1
1500 YmhC 97132 743 D1
1900 VCVR 98661 536 J5
2000 VCVR 98663 536 J5
3300 VCVR 98661 537 A5
N 11th St
300 STHN 97051 385 C6
NE 11th St
100 MCMV 97128 770 H4
700 BGND 98604 448 C4
700 ClkC 98604 448 C4
10300 VCVR 98664 537 H5
15900 VCVR 98684 538 E5
16700 ClkC 98684 538 E5
19200 ClkC 98607 538 H5
19200 CMAS 98607 538 H5
26800 ClkC 98607 539 G5
NW 11th St
100 MCMV 97128 770 G4
400 BGND 98604 448 B4
600 GSHM 97030 629 B1
2500 BGND 98604 447 H4
53000 SPSE 97056 444 D6
S 11th St
- RDGF 98642 446 F1
100 STHN 97051 385 C7
100 STHN 97051 415 C1
SE 11th St
100 DNDE 97115 742 H4
500 BGND 98604 448 C6
1300 GSHM 97080 629 D4
10000 VCVR 98664 537 H7
11900 VCVR 98683 537 J7
12000 VCVR 98683 538 A7
SW 11th St
- MthC 97236 628 G4
10 BGND 98604 448 B6
200 DNDE 97115 742 G3
600 YmhC 97115 742 G4
1200 TDLE 97060 599 F4
2000 BGND 98604 447 J6
2700 ClkC 98604 447 H6
4400 GSHM 97080 628 G4
10900 BRTN 97005 625 D4
W 11th St
- WHGL 98671 569 G3
10 VCVR 98660 536 F5
11th Wy
- MCMV 97128 770 J4
NE 11th Wy
300 BGND 98604 448 C4
1100 MCMV 97128 770 J4
3100 HBRO 97124 593 D1
3100 WasC 97124 593 D1
4000 GSHM 97030 629 G1
9400 VCVR 98664 537 G5
S 11th Wy
4500 ClkC 98642 446 E1
4500 RDGF 98642 446 E1
SE 11th Wy
300 BGND 98604 448 C6
5000 GSHM 97080 629 G4
18800 VCVR 98683 538 G7
SW 11th Wy
2000 BGND 98604 447 J6
NE 11th St Dr
10 HBRO 97123 593 D5
100 HBRO 97124 593 D5
12th Av
2200 FTGV 97116 591 J6
2500 FTGV 97116 592 A6

STREET
Block City ZIP Map# Grid

N 12th Av
10 CNLS 97113 592 E4
NE 12th Av
10 PTLD 97214 596 H5
10 PTLD 97232 596 H5
100 CMAS 98607 569 E4
100 HBRO 97123 593 D5
300 CNBY 97013 746 D5
900 BGND 98604 448 C4
1000 ClkC 98604 448 C4
1100 MCMV 97128 770 J4
1700 PTLD 97212 596 H3
3100 HBRO 97124 593 D1
4000 PTLD 97211 596 H1
4300 VCVR 98663 536 H1
5300 PTLD 97211 566 H7
7000 ClkC 98665 506 H6
11200 ClkC 98685 506 H2
12800 ClkC 98685 476 H7
16500 ClkC 98642 476 H3
38200 ClkC 98629 386 J3
38900 ClkC 98674 386 J2
NW 12th Av
- ClkC 98607 568 J5
- CMAS 98607 568 J5
10 PTLD 97205 596 E5
10 PTLD 97209 596 E5
100 CMAS 98607 569 D4
600 CNBY 97013 746 B5
1200 BGND 98604 448 A4
1400 ClkC 98604 448 A4
8800 ClkC 98665 506 F4
9800 ClkC 98685 506 F3
S 12th Av
10 CNLS 97113 592 E6
SE 12th Av
10 PTLD 97214 596 H7
10 PTLD 97232 596 H5
100 HBRO 97123 593 D5
100 HBRO 97124 593 D5
1500 CNBY 97013 776 E1
1800 CMAS 98607 569 G5
2200 PTLD 97214 626 H1
3100 PTLD 97202 626 H2
SW 12th Av
10 BGND 98604 448 A5
100 CNBY 97013 776 C1
300 PTLD 97205 596 E5
300 PTLD 97209 596 E5
1100 PTLD 97201 596 E6
3700 PTLD 97239 626 D2
6700 PTLD 97219 626 D5
NW 12th Cir
2500 CMAS 98607 569 B4
SE 12th Cir
10400 VCVR 98664 537 H7
15900 VCVR 98683 538 D7
18300 VCVR 98683 568 G1
SW 12th Cir
100 BGND 98604 448 B6
400 TDLE 97060 599 F5
N 12th Ct
- RDGF 98642 416 A6
NE 12th Ct
12400 ClkC 98685 476 H7
16400 ClkC 98642 476 H3
30000 ClkC 98642 416 H4
NW 12th Ct
1500 GSHM 97030 629 A1
9500 ClkC 98665 506 F3
S 12th Ct
800 RDGF 98642 446 A1
SE 12th Ct
2700 HBRO 97123 623 D1
2700 WasC 97123 623 D1
4000 GSHM 97080 629 F4
SW 12th Ct
1100 TDLE 97060 599 F5
4100 GSHM 97080 628 G4
NE 12th Dr
- VCVR 98664 537 F5
SE 12th Dr
17500 VCVR 98683 568 F1
17700 VCVR 98683 538 F7
SW 12th Dr
6800 PTLD 97219 626 D5
9200 PTLD 97219 656 D1
NW 12th Lp
4200 CMAS 98607 569 A4
SE 12th Lp
1300 CNBY 97013 776 D1
NE 12th Pl
900 CNBY 97013 746 D5
9500 VCVR 98664 537 G5
SW 12th Pl
11800 PTLD 97219 656 D3
12th St
100 ORCY 97045 687 D7
500 WHGL 98671 570 A5
800 LFYT 97127 741 H7
1000 WLIN 97068 716 G2
1300 ORCY 97045 717 D1
E 12th St
- LFYT 97127 741 G7
100 VCVR 98660 536 G5
900 NWBG 97132 743 D2
1900 VCVR 98661 536 J5
1900 VCVR 98663 536 J5
3400 VCVR 98661 537 A5
N 12th St
300 STHN 97051 385 C6
1300 WHGL 98671 570 A4
NE 12th St
200 MCMV 97128 770 H4
1300 BGND 98604 448 D4
8700 VCVR 98664 537 F5
15800 VCVR 98684 538 D5
16200 ClkC 98684 538 E5
25800 ClkC 98607 539 E5
NW 12th St
10 BGND 98604 448 B4
100 MCMV 97128 770 G4
500 GSHM 97030 629 B1
2000 BGND 98604 447 J4
2000 GSHM 97030 628 J1
53100 SPSE 97056 444 D6
S 12th St
100 STHN 97051 385 C7
200 STHN 97051 415 C1
SE 12th St
300 TDLE 97060 599 G5
500 DNDE 97115 742 H4
500 YmhC 97115 742 H4
700 BGND 98604 448 C6
3300 GSHM 97080 629 F4

SE 12th St
6700 VCVR 98661 537 D7
9400 VCVR 98664 537 G7
15400 VCVR 98683 538 D7
15500 ClkC 98604 448 D6
SW 12th St
200 BGND 98604 448 B6
1200 TDLE 97060 599 E5
2100 BGND 98604 447 J6
12000 BRTN 97005 625 B4
16500 SRWD 97140 684 F6
W 12th St
700 VCVR 98660 536 F5
NE 12th Wy
1100 CNBY 97013 746 D5
2300 HBRO 97124 593 A2
9200 VCVR 98664 537 G5
15100 VCVR 98684 538 D5
NW 12th Wy
1100 BGND 98604 448 A4
2300 BGND 98604 447 J4
SE 12th Wy
10 BGND 98604 448 B6
5000 GSHM 97080 629 G4
19100 VCVR 98607 538 H7
19100 VCVR 98683 538 H7
13th Av
2200 FTGV 97116 591 J6
2500 FTGV 97116 592 A6
N 13th Av
10 CNLS 97113 592 E4
NE 13th Av
10 PTLD 97214 596 H5
10 PTLD 97232 596 H5
100 CMAS 98607 569 E4
500 CNBY 97013 746 D5
2500 PTLD 97212 596 H2
3400 HBRO 97124 593 D1
3400 WasC 97124 593 D1
4000 PTLD 97211 596 H1
7100 ClkC 98665 506 H5
9300 PTLD 97211 566 H2
9900 ClkC 98686 506 H3
14400 ClkC 98685 476 H5
16900 ClkC 98642 476 H3
NW 13th Av
10 PTLD 97205 596 E5
10 PTLD 97209 596 E5
100 CMAS 98607 569 E4
600 CNBY 97013 746 B5
900 BGND 98604 448 A4
8800 ClkC 98665 506 F4
11900 ClkC 98685 506 F1
13400 ClkC 98685 476 F6
31400 ClkC 98642 416 F2
S 13th Av
100 CNLS 97113 592 E5
SE 13th Av
- CmsC 97222 626 H7
10 PTLD 97214 596 H6
10 PTLD 97232 596 H5
300 CmsC 97013 776 D1
300 CNBY 97013 776 D1
500 HBRO 97123 593 D6
2500 PTLD 97202 626 H1
2500 PTLD 97214 626 H1
SW 13th Av
- PTLD 97201 626 D1
10 BGND 98604 448 A5
100 CNBY 97013 776 C1
200 CmsC 97013 776 C1
400 PTLD 97205 596 E5
400 PTLD 97209 596 E5
1100 PTLD 97201 596 E6
3300 PTLD 97239 626 D2
6700 PTLD 97219 626 D5
NE 13th Cir
15800 VCVR 98684 538 D5
16700 ClkC 98684 538 E5
NW 13th Cir
500 BGND 98604 448 A4
S 13th Cir
- RDGF 98642 446 B1
SE 13th Cir
10300 VCVR 98664 537 H7
15200 VCVR 98683 538 D7
18600 VCVR 98683 568 G1
31500 ClkC 98671 570 B1
SW 13th Cir
400 BGND 98604 448 B7
1500 TDLE 97060 599 E5
13th Ct
800 LFYT 97127 741 H7
NE 13th Ct
14600 ClkC 98685 476 H5
NW 13th Ct
8600 ClkC 98665 506 F4
11700 ClkC 98685 506 F1
S 13th Ct
10 RDGF 98642 416 A7
SE 13th Ct
400 GSHM 97080 629 C4
2700 HBRO 97123 623 D1
SW 13th Ct
1800 GSHM 97080 628 J4
1800 GSHM 97080 629 B5
12000 PTLD 97219 656 D3
NE 13th Dr
- VCVR 98664 537 G5
2900 HBRO 97124 593 A2
SW 13th Dr
7200 PTLD 97219 626 D5
13th Pl
2700 FTGV 97116 592 A6
E 13th Pl
- LFYT 97127 741 G7
3000 VCVR 98661 537 A5
N 13th Pl
- RDGF 98642 416 A6
NE 13th Pl
1100 CNBY 97013 746 D5
3100 HBRO 97124 593 E1
17100 ClkC 98642 476 H3
NW 13th Pl
200 CNBY 97013 746 C5
10700 ClkC 98685 506 F2
13100 ClkC 98685 476 F6
19700 ClkC 98642 446 F7
SE 13th Pl
300 CmsC 97013 776 D1
1100 CNBY 97013 776 D1
2900 PTLD 97202 626 H1
SW 13th Pl
1100 TDLE 97060 599 E5

13th St
100 LFYT 97127 741 G7
100 WHGL 98671 570 A5
500 ORCY 97045 687 C7
1800 ORCY 97045 717 D1
2100 WLIN 97068 716 G1
E 13th St
100 VCVR 98660 536 G4
400 LCTR 98629 386 H7
900 NWBG 97132 743 C2
900 YmhC 97132 743 C2
2000 VCVR 98661 536 J5
2000 VCVR 98663 536 J5
2800 VCVR 98661 537 A5
N 13th St
300 STHN 97051 385 C6
NE 13th St
300 MCMV 97128 770 H4
1300 BGND 98604 448 D4
2800 GSHM 97030 629 E1
8600 VCVR 98664 537 F5
16200 ClkC 98684 538 E5
16200 VCVR 98684 538 E5
19200 ClkC 98607 538 H5
19700 CMAS 98607 538 H5
25200 ClkC 98607 539 E5
33200 ClkC 98671 540 D5
NW 13th St
400 MCMV 97128 770 G4
700 GSHM 97030 629 A1
1200 BGND 98604 448 A4
2000 BGND 98604 447 J4
52700 SPSE 97056 444 D6
S 13th St
100 STHN 97051 385 C7
200 STHN 97051 415 C1
SE 13th St
10 BGND 98604 448 B6
200 TDLE 97060 599 G5
3900 GSHM 97080 629 F4
10500 VCVR 98664 537 H7
11900 VCVR 98683 537 J7
11900 VCVR 98683 538 A7
18800 VCVR 98683 568 G1
35700 ClkC 98671 570 G1
SW 13th St
200 BGND 98604 448 B6
200 DNDE 97115 742 H4
600 YmhC 97115 742 H4
1700 GSHM 97080 629 A4
12100 BRTN 97005 625 B4
W 13th St
- LCTR 98629 386 G7
10 VCVR 98660 536 F4
NE 13th Ter
4000 GSHM 97030 629 F1
SE 13th Ter
5400 GSHM 97080 629 H4
13th Wy
- MCMV 97128 770 J4
NE 13th Wy
1400 MCMV 97128 770 J4
2300 HBRO 97124 593 A2
15500 VCVR 98684 538 D5
SE 13th Wy
- VCVR 98607 568 H1
- VCVR 98683 568 H1
14th Av
2100 FTGV 97116 591 J6
2800 FTGV 97116 592 A6
N 14th Av
10 CNLS 97113 592 E4
NE 14th Av
10 PTLD 97214 596 H5
100 CMAS 98607 569 E4
100 HBRO 97123 593 E5
300 CNBY 97013 746 C5
1000 BGND 98604 448 D4
1500 PTLD 97232 596 H3
1600 PTLD 97212 596 H3
3200 HBRO 97124 593 E1
4000 PTLD 97211 596 H1
4300 VCVR 98663 536 H1
4900 PTLD 97211 566 H7
6500 ClkC 98665 506 H6
11600 ClkC 98685 506 H1
13000 ClkC 98685 476 H7
17600 ClkC 98642 476 H2
33900 LCTR 98629 386 J7
34100 ClkC 98629 386 J6
52300 ClbC 97056 474 G1
52300 SPSE 97056 474 G1
NE 14th Av SR-500
600 CMAS 98607 569 E4
NW 14th Av
- ClkC 98685 506 F1
10 PTLD 97205 596 E5
10 PTLD 97209 596 E4
100 CMAS 98607 569 E4
300 CNBY 97013 746 B5
1200 BGND 98604 448 A4
8600 ClkC 98665 506 E4
14800 ClkC 98685 476 F5
19600 ClkC 98642 446 F7
38400 ClkC 98629 386 F2
38400 ClkC 98674 386 F2
S 14th Av
10 CNLS 97113 592 E5
SE 14th Av
10 PTLD 97232 596 H5
200 PTLD 97214 596 H6
500 HBRO 97123 593 D5
1100 CNBY 97013 776 D1
2500 PTLD 97202 626 H1
2500 PTLD 97214 626 H1
SW 14th Av
- PTLD 97201 626 D1
400 PTLD 97205 596 E6
400 PTLD 97209 596 E5
1100 PTLD 97201 596 E6
5400 PTLD 97239 626 D4
6700 PTLD 97219 626 D5
E 14th Cir
1200 LCTR 98629 386 J7
NE 14th Cir
10100 VCVR 98664 537 H4
14000 VCVR 98684 538 C5
19200 ClkC 98607 538 H5
NW 14th Cir
1600 BGND 98604 448 A3
1700 BGND 98604 447 J4
3600 CMAS 98607 569 A4
5100 CMAS 98607 568 J4
SE 14th Cir
10300 VCVR 98664 537 H7

SE 14th Cir
17600 VCVR 98683 568 F1
SW 14th Cir
100 BGND 98604 448 B7
NE 14th Ct
10 BGND 98604 448 D5
6100 VCVR 98665 506 H7
7200 ClkC 98665 506 H5
27400 ClkC 98642 416 J6
NW 14th Ct
900 BGND 98604 448 A4
8300 ClkC 98665 506 E4
10500 ClkC 98685 506 F2
13400 ClkC 98685 476 F6
SE 14th Ct
400 GSHM 97080 629 C4
SW 14th Ct
400 CmsC 97013 776 C1
400 CNBY 97013 776 C1
1200 GSHM 97080 629 A4
NW 14th Dr
1500 GSHM 97030 629 A1
SW 14th Dr
2100 GSHM 97080 628 H4
10600 PTLD 97219 656 D2
NE 14th Ln
1200 GSHM 97030 629 D1
8400 VCVR 98664 537 F4
E 14th Pl
2900 VCVR 98661 537 A5
N 14th Pl
700 CNLS 97113 592 E4
NE 14th Pl
- VCVR 98664 537 F5
1100 CNBY 97013 746 D5
2200 HBRO 97124 593 E2
4500 PTLD 97211 596 H1
7600 PTLD 97211 566 H5
NW 14th Pl
10 GSHM 97030 629 B1
13600 ClkC 98685 476 F6
S 14th Pl
600 RDGF 98642 416 A7
600 RDGF 98642 446 A1
SE 14th Pl
300 CmsC 97013 776 D1
300 CNBY 97013 776 D1
500 BGND 98604 448 D6
14th St
- LFYT 97127 741 G6
100 ORCY 97045 687 D7
800 WHGL 98671 570 A5
1200 WLIN 97068 716 G2
1800 ORCY 97045 717 E1
E 14th St
100 LFYT 97127 741 H7
600 YmhC 97132 743 C2
2200 VCVR 98661 536 J4
3500 VCVR 98661 537 B5
N 14th St
500 STHN 97051 385 C6
NE 14th St
400 MCMV 97128 770 H4
7100 VCVR 98664 537 E4
11000 VCVR 98684 537 J5
12800 VCVR 98684 538 A5
20000 ClkC 98607 538 H5
27200 ClkC 98607 539 G5
NW 14th St
- ClkC 98604 447 H4
100 MCMV 97128 770 G4
400 BGND 98604 448 B4
1800 BGND 98604 447 J4
1900 GSHM 97030 628 J1
53000 SPSE 97056 444 D6
S 14th St
200 STHN 97051 415 C1
SE 14th St
200 TDLE 97060 599 G5
300 BGND 98604 448 C7
3400 GSHM 97080 629 F4
9500 VCVR 98664 537 G7
15400 VCVR 98683 538 C7
18100 VCVR 98683 568 F1
20000 ClkC 98607 568 H1
33900 ClkC 98671 570 D1
SW 14th St
200 BGND 98604 448 B7
600 TDLE 97060 599 F5
1400 GSHM 97080 629 A4
12100 BRTN 97005 625 B4
W 14th St
1000 VCVR 98660 536 F4
NE 14th Wy
2300 HBRO 97124 593 A2
9200 VCVR 98664 537 G5
15000 VCVR 98684 538 C5
SE 14th Wy
- VCVR 98607 568 H1
18800 VCVR 98683 568 G1
15th Av
2000 FTGV 97116 591 J5
2500 FTGV 97116 592 A5
N 15th Av
300 CNLS 97113 592 E4
NE 15th Av
- ClkC 98686 476 H4
- VCVR 98663 506 H7
10 BGND 98604 448 D5
10 PTLD 97214 596 H5
10 PTLD 97232 596 H5
100 CMAS 98607 569 E4
500 CNBY 97013 746 D5
1100 CmsC 97013 746 D5
1600 HBRO 97124 593 E1
1600 PTLD 97212 596 H3
3000 WasC 97124 593 E1
3900 VCVR 98663 536 H2
4000 PTLD 97211 596 H1
5500 PTLD 97211 566 H6
8800 ClkC 98665 506 H4
14900 ClkC 98642 476 H5
14900 ClkC 98685 476 H5
20900 ClkC 98642 446 J6
NW 15th Av
- PTLD 97205 596 E5
- PTLD 97209 596 E3
100 CMAS 98607 569 E4
700 BGND 98604 448 A4
8600 ClkC 98665 506 E3
9900 ClkC 98685 506 E2
15000 ClkC 98685 476 F5
S 15th Av
400 CNLS 97113 592 E5

SE 15th Av
10 PTLD 97214 596 H6
10 PTLD 97232 596 H5
400 HBRO 97123 593 E5
500 BGND 98604 448 D6
1100 CNBY 97013 776 D1
2500 PTLD 97202 626 H1
2500 PTLD 97214 626 H1
SW 15th Av
- PTLD 97201 596 D7
- PTLD 97201 626 D1
- PTLD 97209 596 E5
- PTLD 97239 626 D1
400 BGND 98604 448 A6
500 PTLD 97205 596 E6
6700 PTLD 97219 626 D5
15th Cir
500 ClkC 98629 386 H7
500 LCTR 98629 386 H7
NE 15th Cir
1800 BGND 98604 448 D4
14300 VCVR 98684 538 C5
19200 ClkC 98607 538 H5
30700 ClkC 98671 540 A5
NW 15th Cir
2400 CMAS 98607 569 B4
S 15th Cir
- RDGF 98642 446 B1
SE 15th Cir
14200 VCVR 98683 568 C1
38900 ClkC 98671 570 J1
W 15th Cir
- LCTR 98629 386 G7
N 15th Ct
900 RDGF 98642 416 A6
1800 WHGL 98671 570 A4
NE 15th Ct
200 HBRO 97124 593 E4
10200 VCVR 98664 537 H4
11200 ClkC 98685 506 H2
15600 ClkC 98686 476 H4
NW 15th Ct
- ClkC 98685 506 E1
1300 BGND 98604 448 A4
2000 GSHM 97030 628 J1
8400 ClkC 98665 506 E4
S 15th Ct
200 RDGF 98642 416 A7
700 RDGF 98642 446 A1
SE 15th Ct
4000 GSHM 97080 629 F4
SW 15th Ct
900 TDLE 97060 599 F5
1300 GSHM 97080 629 A4
3000 GSHM 97080 628 H4
SE 15th Dr
5400 GSHM 97080 629 H4
NE 15th Ln
1300 GSHM 97030 629 D1
SE 15th Ln
3900 GSHM 97080 629 F4
SE 15th Lp
5900 GSHM 97080 629 H4
15th Pl
2700 FTGV 97116 592 A5
E 15th Pl
- ClkC 98629 416 J1
N 15th Pl
700 CNLS 97113 592 E4
NE 15th Pl
15600 ClkC 98686 476 J4
NW 15th Pl
200 CNBY 97013 746 C5
SE 15th Pl
300 CmsC 97013 776 D1
300 CNBY 97013 776 D1
8800 PTLD 97202 626 H7
15th St
100 ORCY 97045 687 D7
200 LFYT 97127 741 G6
700 WHGL 98671 570 A5
1400 WLIN 97068 716 G2
E 15th St
- LFYT 97127 741 G6
100 VCVR 98660 536 G4
100 VCVR 98663 536 G4
3400 VCVR 98661 537 A4
E 15th St SR-501
100 VCVR 98660 536 G4
100 VCVR 98663 536 G4
N 15th St
100 STHN 97051 385 C7
1700 WHGL 98671 570 A4
NE 15th St
400 MCMV 97128 770 H4
2700 GSHM 97030 629 E1
10900 VCVR 98664 537 H4
11500 VCVR 98684 537 J4
15600 VCVR 98684 538 E5
16000 ClkC 98684 538 E5
29500 ClkC 98671 539 J5
30100 ClkC 98671 540 A5
NW 15th St
10 GSHM 97030 629 B1
100 MCMV 97128 770 H4
2000 BGND 98604 447 J4
S 15th St
100 STHN 97051 415 C1
SE 15th St
400 TDLE 97060 599 G5
4200 GSHM 97080 629 G4
10200 VCVR 98664 567 H1
11800 VCVR 98683 567 J1
16400 VCVR 98683 568 H1
18900 VCVR 98607 568 G1
26600 ClkC 98607 569 F1
26600 CMAS 98607 569 F1
33200 ClkC 98671 570 D1
SW 15th St
300 TDLE 97060 599 F5
1600 GSHM 97080 629 A4
2300 GSHM 97080 628 J4
W 15th St
100 LCTR 98629 386 G7
100 VCVR 98660 536 F4
100 VCVR 98663 536 G4
W 15th St SR-501
100 VCVR 98660 536 F4
100 VCVR 98663 536 G4
SE 15th Ter
- GSHM 97080 629 F4
15th Wy
1600 RDGF 98642 446 A2
SE 15th Wy
17300 VCVR 98683 568 F1

16th Av
1800 FTGV 97116 591 H5
2700 FTGV 97116 592 A5
N 16th Av
300 CNLS 97113 592 E4
NE 16th Av
10 PTLD 97214 596 H5
10 PTLD 97232 596 H5
200 BGND 98604 448 D5
300 HBRO 97124 593 E4
400 CNBY 97013 746 D4
700 CmsC 97013 746 D4
2100 PTLD 97212 596 H3
4000 PTLD 97211 596 H2
5000 PTLD 97211 566 J7
7200 ClkC 98665 506 H5
13400 ClkC 98685 476 H6
29000 ClkC 98642 416 J5
NW 16th Av
10 PTLD 97205 596 E5
10 PTLD 97209 596 E5
100 CMAS 98607 569 E4
700 BGND 98604 448 A4
1400 ClkC 98604 448 A4
4300 CMAS 98607 568 J4
7500 VCVR 98665 506 E5
8000 ClkC 98665 506 E4
10900 ClkC 98685 506 E1
15400 ClkC 98685 476 F4
35900 ClkC 98629 386 F5
S 16th Av
100 CNLS 97113 592 E5
SE 16th Av
10 PTLD 97214 596 H6
10 PTLD 97232 596 H5
400 HBRO 97123 593 E5
1100 CNBY 97013 776 D1
2200 PTLD 97214 626 H1
3300 PTLD 97202 626 H3
SW 16th Av
- PTLD 97201 626 D1
- PTLD 97239 626 D2
500 PTLD 97209 596 E5
1200 PTLD 97201 596 D6
1200 PTLD 97205 596 D6
E 16th Cir
1200 LCTR 98629 386 H7
NE 16th Cir
15900 VCVR 98684 538 D4
19200 ClkC 98607 538 H5
NW 16th Cir
400 BGND 98604 448 B4
5100 CMAS 98607 568 J4
SE 16th Cir
400 TDLE 97060 599 G5
11400 VCVR 98664 567 J1
12000 VCVR 98683 567 J1
17500 VCVR 98683 568 F2
SW 16th Cir
300 BGND 98604 448 B7
3000 GSHM 97080 628 H4
16th Ct
3300 FTGV 97116 592 B5
N 16th Ct
600 RDGF 98642 416 A6
NE 16th Ct
100 HBRO 97123 593 E5
100 HBRO 97124 593 E5
1600 BGND 98604 448 D4
4000 GSHM 97030 629 F1
9100 PTLD 97211 566 J3
NW 16th Ct
900 BGND 98604 448 A4
1700 GSHM 97030 629 A1
4800 CMAS 98607 568 J4
8400 ClkC 98665 506 E4
SE 16th Ct
10 GSHM 97080 629 C4
100 TDLE 97060 599 G5
SW 16th Ct
100 TDLE 97060 599 G5
2000 GSHM 97080 628 J4
SE 16th Dr
4800 GSHM 97080 629 G4
SW 16th Dr
11000 PTLD 97219 656 D2
NE 16th Ln
8500 VCVR 98664 537 F4
SE 16th Ln
18500 VCVR 98683 568 G1
NE 16th Lp E
1700 BGND 98604 448 D3
NE 16th Lp W
1700 BGND 98604 448 D3
SE 16th Lp
5800 GSHM 97080 629 H4
16th Pl
3500 FTGV 97116 592 B5
E 16th Pl
- ClkC 98629 416 J1
2900 VCVR 98661 537 A4
N 16th Pl
700 CNLS 97113 592 E4
SE 16th Pl
8800 PTLD 97202 626 H7
SW 16th Pl
2600 GSHM 97080 628 J4
16th St
10 WHGL 98671 570 A6
200 ORCY 97045 687 D6
1400 WLIN 97068 716 G2
E 16th St
100 VCVR 98660 536 G4
100 VCVR 98663 536 G4
100 YmhC 97114 741 G6
100 YmhC 97128 741 G6
700 LFYT 97127 741 H6
2100 VCVR 98661 536 J4
2700 VCVR 98661 537 A4
N 16th St
300 STHN 97051 385 C7
NE 16th St
1100 MCMV 97128 770 J4
1200 GSHM 97030 629 D1
1800 BGND 98604 448 D4
9500 VCVR 98664 537 G4
11200 VCVR 98684 537 J4
14000 VCVR 98684 538 B4
19900 ClkC 98607 538 H4
23900 ClkC 98607 539 C5
NW 16th St
100 BGND 98604 448 B4
100 MCMV 97128 770 H4
1600 GSHM 97030 629 A1
1800 GSHM 97030 628 J1

S 16th St
100 STHN 97051 415 C1
SE 16th St
300 BGND 98604 448 B7
2700 GSHM 97080 629 E4
10600 VCVR 98664 567 H1
17000 VCVR 98683 568 E1
32600 ClkC 98671 570 C1
SW 16th St
2300 GSHM 97080 628 J4
W 16th St
- ClkC 98629 386 G6
100 VCVR 98663 536 G4
1600 VCVR 98660 536 E4
16th Wy
- RDGF 98642 446 B2
NE 16th Wy
- BGND 98604 448 D3
1300 GSHM 97030 629 D1
8800 VCVR 98664 537 F4
S 16th Wy
- RDGF 98642 446 B1
SW 16th Wy
- TDLE 97060 599 F5
100 BGND 98604 448 B7
17th Av
1700 FTGV 97116 591 J5
2600 FTGV 97116 592 A5
N 17th Av
10 CNLS 97113 592 E5
NE 17th Av
- ClkC 98642 446 J3
10 PTLD 97214 596 H5
100 CMAS 98607 569 E4
700 CNBY 97013 746 D4
900 HBRO 97124 593 E3
1100 BGND 98604 448 D4
1100 ClkC 98604 448 D4
1200 PTLD 97232 596 J4
1600 PTLD 97212 596 J4
4000 PTLD 97211 596 J3
5800 VCVR 98663 506 H7
5800 VCVR 98665 506 H7
6900 ClkC 98665 506 H6
9000 PTLD 97211 566 J3
13900 ClkC 98686 476 J6
19000 ClkC 98642 476 J1
40100 ClkC 98674 386 J1
NW 17th Av
10 PTLD 97205 596 E5
10 PTLD 97209 596 E4
100 CMAS 98607 569 E3
700 BGND 98604 447 J4
8800 ClkC 98665 506 E4
11000 ClkC 98685 506 E2
12500 ClkC 98685 476 E7
SE 17th Av
10 PTLD 97232 596 H5
500 PTLD 97214 596 H6
1100 CmsC 97013 776 D1
1100 CNBY 97013 776 D1
2500 PTLD 97202 626 H1
2500 PTLD 97214 626 H1
9300 CmsC 97202 656 H1
9300 CmsC 97222 656 H1
9300 MWKE 97202 626 H7
9300 MWKE 97202 656 H1
9300 MWKE 97222 626 H7
9300 MWKE 97222 656 H1
9300 PTLD 97202 656 H1
SW 17th Av
- PTLD 97201 626 B1
- PTLD 97219 656 D3
100 BGND 98604 447 J6
300 HBRO 97123 593 A5
500 PTLD 97209 596 E5
1100 PTLD 97205 596 D6
2000 PTLD 97201 596 D7
7900 PTLD 97219 626 D6
17th Cir
1600 RDGF 98642 446 A2
E 17th Cir
- ClkC 98629 386 H6
NE 17th Cir
10100 VCVR 98664 537 H4
12300 VCVR 98684 538 A4
NW 17th Cir
800 BGND 98604 448 A3
5100 CMAS 98607 568 J3
SE 17th Cir
10800 VCVR 98664 567 H1
14100 VCVR 98683 568 C1
SW 17th Cir
200 BGND 98604 448 B7
17th Ct
3500 FTGV 97116 592 B5
N 17th Ct
500 RDGF 98642 416 B6
NE 17th Ct
15600 ClkC 98686 476 J4
19400 ClkC 98642 446 J7
NW 17th Ct
- ClkC 98642 416 F1
300 BGND 98604 447 J5
1700 GSHM 97030 629 A1
20900 ClkC 98642 446 F6
S 17th Ct
10 CNLS 97113 592 E5
SE 17th Ct
4500 GSHM 97080 629 G4
SW 17th Ct
1400 GSHM 97080 629 A4
3500 GSHM 97080 628 H4
NE 17th Dr
3200 GSHM 97030 629 F1
3900 GSHM 97060 629 F1
3900 MthC 97030 629 F1
3900 TDLE 97030 629 F1
3900 TDLE 97060 629 F1
SE 17th Dr
17700 VCVR 98683 568 F2
SW 17th Dr
7200 PTLD 97219 626 D6
SE 17th Ln
17800 VCVR 98683 568 F1
SE 17th Lp
5800 GSHM 97080 629 H4
17th Pl
2600 FTGV 97116 592 A5
E 17th Pl
- ClkC 98629 416 J1
NW 17th Pl
13600 ClkC 98685 476 E6
SW 17th Pl
2600 GSHM 97080 628 J4

STREET Block City ZIP Map# Grid

7th St
300 ORCY 97045 687 D6
400 WHGL 98671 570 A5
1600 CmsC 97045 687 E7
E 17th St
100 VCVR 98660 536 G4
100 VCVR 98663 536 G4
2100 VCVR 98661 536 J4
4200 VCVR 98661 537 B4
N 17th St
100 STHN 97051 415 B2
300 STHN 97051 385 C7
1700 WHGL 98671 570 A4
NE 17th St
200 MCMV 97128 770 H4
1500 BGND 98604 448 D4
2600 GSHM 97030 629 E1
8600 VCVR 98664 537 F4
13000 VCVR 98684 538 A4
29700 ClkC 98671 539 J5
34000 ClkC 98671 540 D5
NW 17th St
100 BGND 98604 448 B3
100 MCMV 97128 770 G4
1800 GSHM 97030 628 J1
1800 GSHM 97030 629 A1
S 17th St
100 STHN 97051 415 C1
SE 17th St
100 TDLE 97060 599 G5
200 BGND 98604 448 B7
2600 GSHM 97080 629 E4
10200 VCVR 98664 567 H1
15100 VCVR 98683 568 C1
31200 ClkC 98671 570 B1
SW 17th St
1600 GSHM 97080 629 A4
2000 GSHM 97080 628 J4
13400 BRTN 97008 625 A5
W 17th St
100 VCVR 98660 536 F4
100 VCVR 98663 536 G4
SE 17th Ter
5100 GSHM 97080 629 G4
S 17th Wy
- RDGF 98642 446 B2
SE 17th Wy
100 BGND 98604 448 B7
16200 VCVR 98683 568 E1
SW 17th Wy
600 TDLE 97060 599 F5
18th Av
1600 FTGV 97116 591 H5
2500 FTGV 97116 592 A5
NE 18th Av
- ClkC 98686 506 J1
10 PTLD 97214 596 J5
10 PTLD 97232 596 J5
100 CMAS 98607 569 E3
100 HBRO 97123 593 E5
100 HBRO 97124 593 E4
1200 BGND 98604 448 D4
2100 PTLD 97212 596 J3
4500 PTLD 97211 596 J1
4800 PTLD 97211 566 J7
4900 VCVR 98663 506 J7
4900 VCVR 98663 536 H1
8200 ClkC 98665 506 J4
12100 ClkC 98685 476 J7
12100 ClkC 98685 506 J1
15600 ClkC 98686 476 J3
NW 18th Av
10 BGND 98604 447 J5
10 PTLD 97205 596 E4
10 PTLD 97209 596 E4
600 CMAS 98607 569 D3
800 ClkC 98604 447 J4
4500 CMAS 98607 568 J3
9800 ClkC 98665 506 F3
9800 ClkC 98685 506 F3
15700 ClkC 98685 476 E4
20700 ClkC 98642 446 E6
31900 ClkC 98642 416 F2
38400 ClkC 98674 386 E2
S 18th Av
400 CNLS 97113 592 E5
SE 18th Av
- BGND 98604 448 D7
10 PTLD 97232 596 J5
100 HBRO 97124 593 E5
400 HBRO 97123 593 E6
1100 PTLD 97214 596 J6
2500 PTLD 97202 626 H1
2500 PTLD 97214 626 H1
12400 CmsC 97222 656 H4
12400 MWKE 97222 656 H4
SW 18th Av
- PTLD 97209 596 D5
600 PTLD 97205 596 D6
1900 PTLD 97201 596 D7
12100 PTLD 97219 656 C3
18th Cir
1700 RDGF 98642 446 B2
NW 18th Cir
- CMAS 98607 569 A3
800 BGND 98604 448 A3
SE 18th Cir
2800 GSHM 97080 629 E4
10800 VCVR 98664 567 H1
13900 VCVR 98683 568 A3
38700 ClkC 98671 570 J2
18th Ct
400 WHGL 98671 570 A5
3500 FTGV 97116 592 B5
NE 18th Ct
700 GSHM 97030 629 C1
1700 HBRO 97124 593 E3
4700 VCVR 98663 536 H1
15800 ClkC 98686 476 J4
25600 ClkC 98642 446 J1
NW 18th Ct
1000 BGND 98604 447 J4
1700 GSHM 97030 629 A1
S 18th Ct
10 CNLS 97113 592 F5
SE 18th Ct
4300 GSHM 97080 629 G5
SW 18th Ct
200 BGND 98604 447 J5
1600 GSHM 97080 629 A4
3200 GSHM 97080 628 H4
SW 18th Dr
- PTLD 97239 626 D3
SE 18th Ln
400 GSHM 97080 629 C4
NW 18th Lp
600 CMAS 98607 569 D4
18th Pl
3500 FTGV 97116 592 B5
E 18th Pl
- ClkC 98629 416 J1
N 18th Pl
300 CNLS 97113 592 F4
500 RDGF 98642 416 B6
NE 18th Pl
1300 CNBY 97013 746 E4
NW 18th Pl
29900 ClkC 98642 416 F4
S 18th Pl
100 CNLS 97113 592 F5
SE 18th Pl
1800 TDLE 97060 599 G5
SW 18th Pl
2600 GSHM 97080 628 J4
4600 PTLD 97239 626 D3
9200 PTLD 97219 626 D7
9200 PTLD 97219 656 D1
W 18th Pl
300 MCMV 97128 770 G3
18th St
300 ORCY 97045 687 D6
500 WHGL 98671 570 A5
1500 CmsC 97045 687 E7
2100 WLIN 97068 716 G1
E 18th St
300 ClkC 98629 386 H6
2200 VCVR 98661 536 J4
2200 VCVR 98663 536 J4
3100 VCVR 98661 537 A4
N 18th St
- STHN 97051 385 B7
100 STHN 97051 415 C1
1500 WHGL 98671 570 A4
NE 18th St
10 GSHM 97030 629 C1
600 MCMV 97128 770 J3
1700 MCMV 97128 771 A4
6500 VCVR 98661 537 D4
6500 VCVR 98664 537 D4
7000 VCVR 98662 537 E3
10700 VCVR 98684 537 J4
12100 VCVR 98684 538 C4
16400 ClkC 98684 538 H4
18700 ClkC 98607 538 H4
NW 18th St
600 BGND 98604 448 B3
1800 GSHM 97030 629 A1
S 18th St
100 STHN 97051 415 C1
SE 18th St
10 BGND 98604 448 B7
200 TDLE 97060 599 G5
5300 GSHM 97080 629 G4
10900 VCVR 98664 567 H1
13700 VCVR 98683 568 B1
32900 ClkC 98671 570 C1
SW 18th St
10 BGND 98604 448 B7
100 TDLE 97060 599 G5
2300 GSHM 97080 628 J4
12700 BRTN 97008 625 B5
W 18th St
600 MCMV 97128 770 G3
NE 18th Wy
16400 ClkC 98684 538 F5
SE 18th Wy
300 BGND 98604 448 C7
16100 VCVR 98683 568 E1
SW 18th Wy
900 TDLE 97060 599 F5
19th Av
1600 FTGV 97116 591 H5
2600 FTGV 97116 592 A5
19th Av SR-8
1800 FTGV 97116 591 J5
2600 FTGV 97116 592 A5
N 19th Av
10 CNLS 97113 592 F4
900 WasC 97113 592 F4
NE 19th Av
- ClkC 98686 506 J1
100 CMAS 98607 569 E3
400 HBRO 97124 593 E4
1200 PTLD 97232 596 J4
2000 CmsC 97013 746 F4
2000 CNBY 97013 746 E4
2100 PTLD 97212 596 J2
4500 PTLD 97211 596 J1
4800 PTLD 97211 566 J7
4800 VCVR 98663 536 J1
9600 ClkC 98665 506 J3
15600 ClkC 98686 476 J4
19400 ClkC 98642 446 J7
27900 ClkC 98642 416 J6
NW 19th Av
10 PTLD 97205 596 D5
10 PTLD 97209 596 D4
700 CMAS 98607 569 D3
900 BGND 98604 447 J4
3700 ClkC 98629 386 F5
7500 VCVR 98665 506 E5
8500 ClkC 98665 506 E4
11100 ClkC 98685 506 E2
14600 ClkC 98685 476 E5
18900 ClkC 98642 476 E1
S 19th Av
10 CNLS 97113 592 F5
SE 19th Av
- BGND 98604 448 D7
10 PTLD 97232 596 J5
1200 PTLD 97214 596 J6
2500 PTLD 97202 626 J1
2500 PTLD 97214 626 J1
11900 MWKE 97222 656 J3
SW 19th Av
- PTLD 97239 626 D3
100 BGND 98604 447 J5
600 PTLD 97209 596 D5
1100 PTLD 97205 596 D6
2000 PTLD 97201 596 D7
7200 PTLD 97219 626 D5
11500 PTLD 97219 656 C3
12400 MthC 97219 656 C3
12400 PTLD 97034 656 C3
12400 PTLD 97035 656 C3
12700 CmsC 97034 656 C3
12700 LKOW 97034 656 C3
NE 19th Cir
9000 VCVR 98664 537 G4
11300 VCVR 98684 537 J4
15000 VCVR 98684 538 D4
17700 ClkC 98684 538 F4
NW 19th Cir
800 BGND 98604 448 A3
2600 CMAS 98607 569 B3
SE 19th Cir
1300 TDLE 97060 599 H5
15500 VCVR 98683 568 D1
19800 ClkC 98607 568 H1
SW 19th Cir
600 TDLE 97060 599 F5
19th Ct
- FTGV 97116 592 B5
N 19th Ct
100 RDGF 98642 416 B7
NE 19th Ct
200 HBRO 97124 593 E4
1100 CmsC 97013 746 D4
1100 CNBY 97013 746 D4
8800 ClkC 98665 506 J4
15800 ClkC 98686 476 J4
NW 19th Ct
1200 BGND 98604 447 J4
9000 ClkC 98665 506 E4
11900 ClkC 98685 506 E1
S 19th Ct
500 CNLS 97113 592 F5
SW 19th Ct
1400 GSHM 97080 629 A4
2300 GSHM 97080 628 J5
SE 19th Dr
300 GSHM 97080 629 C5
SW 19th Dr
1200 GSHM 97080 629 A4
4800 PTLD 97239 626 D3
NE 19th Lp
1500 CmsC 97013 746 E4
1500 CNBY 97013 746 E4
NW 19th Lp
12600 ClkC 98685 476 E7
19th Pl
2700 FTGV 97116 592 A5
NE 19th Pl
9700 ClkC 98665 506 J3
S 19th Pl
200 CNLS 97113 592 F5
SE 19th Pl
1800 TDLE 97060 599 G5
SW 19th Pl
100 BGND 98604 447 J5
300 TDLE 97060 599 F5
19th St
500 WHGL 98671 570 A5
1400 WLIN 97068 716 F2
E 19th St
100 VCVR 98660 536 G4
100 VCVR 98663 536 G4
2500 VCVR 98661 536 J4
3500 VCVR 98661 537 A4
N 19th St
- STHN 97051 385 B7
100 STHN 97051 415 B1
NE 19th St
10 GSHM 97030 629 C1
100 MCMV 97128 770 H3
1700 MCMV 97128 771 A3
9200 VCVR 98664 537 G4
13400 VCVR 98684 538 B4
16400 ClkC 98684 538 F5
26700 ClkC 98607 539 F4
NW 19th St
10 BGND 98604 448 B3
10 ClkC 98604 448 B3
1300 GSHM 97030 629 A1
1800 GSHM 97030 599 A7
S 19th St
100 STHN 97051 415 C1
SE 19th St
100 TDLE 97060 599 G5
200 BGND 98604 448 B7
2700 GSHM 97080 629 E5
10800 VCVR 98664 567 H1
13100 VCVR 98683 568 B1
SW 19th St
200 BGND 98604 448 B7
1600 GSHM 97080 629 B5
2000 GSHM 97080 628 J4
12800 BRTN 97008 625 B5
W 19th St
100 MCMV 97128 770 G3
100 VCVR 98660 536 F4
100 VCVR 98663 536 F4
SW 19th Ter
1900 GSHM 97080 628 J4
19th Wy
- FTGV 97116 592 A5
19th Wy SR-8
- FTGV 97116 592 A5
NE 19th Wy
- VCVR 98664 537 E4
16400 ClkC 98684 538 F4
S 19th Wy
- RDGF 98642 446 B2
SE 19th Wy
12300 VCVR 98683 568 A1
SW 19th Wy
900 TDLE 97060 599 F5
N 20th Av
- CNLS 97113 592 F5
NE 20th Av
- ClkC 98642 476 J1
10 PTLD 97214 596 J5
10 PTLD 97232 596 J5
1100 BGND 98604 448 D4
1100 ClkC 98604 448 D4
1800 CNBY 97013 746 E4
2100 CmsC 97013 746 F4
4100 PTLD 97211 596 J1
4100 PTLD 97212 596 J1
4900 VCVR 98663 536 J1
6500 ClkC 98665 506 J6
9000 PTLD 97211 566 J3
10200 ClkC 98686 506 J2
15400 ClkC 98686 476 J4
25600 ClkC 98642 446 J1
27900 ClkC 98642 416 J6
NW 20th Av
10 BGND 98604 447 J5
10 PTLD 97205 596 D5
700 CMAS 98607 569 D3
1300 ClkC 98604 447 J4
1900 PTLD 97209 596 D3
9900 ClkC 98665 506 E3
9900 ClkC 98685 506 E3
14400 ClkC 98685 476 E5
30900 ClkC 98642 416 E2
S 20th Av
10 CNLS 97113 592 F5
700 WasC 97113 592 F6
SE 20th Av
10 PTLD 97214 596 J6
10 PTLD 97232 596 J5
400 HBRO 97123 593 E5
2100 PTLD 97214 626 J1
5300 PTLD 97202 626 J6
11900 MWKE 97222 656 J3
12300 CmsC 97222 656 J4
SW 20th Av
10 BGND 98604 447 J6
600 PTLD 97205 596 D6
600 PTLD 97209 596 D6
700 CmsC 97013 776 C2
1200 ClkC 98604 447 J6
1300 PTLD 97201 596 D6
8300 PTLD 97219 626 C6
NE 20th Cir
10200 VCVR 98664 537 H4
14700 VCVR 98684 538 C4
NW 20th Cir
800 BGND 98604 448 A3
3100 CMAS 98607 569 B3
SE 20th Cir
- CMAS 98607 569 E3
13400 VCVR 98683 568 B1
SW 20th Cir
600 TDLE 97060 599 F6
NE 20th Ct
6000 ClkC 98665 506 J7
10700 ClkC 98686 506 J2
NW 20th Ct
6300 VCVR 98660 506 D6
6300 VCVR 98663 506 D6
6300 VCVR 98665 506 D6
14800 ClkC 98685 476 E5
SE 20th Ct
600 HBRO 97123 593 E6
5900 GSHM 97080 629 H5
SW 20th Ct
1600 GSHM 97080 629 A5
1900 GSHM 97080 628 J5
12800 BRTN 97008 625 B5
NE 20th Dr
100 HBRO 97124 593 E5
300 GSHM 97030 629 C1
20th Pl
2700 FTGV 97116 592 A4
N 20th Pl
300 RDGF 98642 416 B6
500 CNLS 97113 592 F4
1500 WHGL 98671 570 B4
NE 20th Pl
700 HBRO 97124 593 E4
9400 ClkC 98665 506 J3
15700 ClkC 98686 476 J4
24900 ClkC 98607 539 D4
NW 20th Pl
10 PTLD 97205 596 D5
10 PTLD 97209 596 D5
SE 20th Pl
700 HBRO 97123 593 E6
SW 20th Pl
600 PTLD 97205 596 D5
600 PTLD 97209 596 D5
9300 PTLD 97219 626 C7
20th St
10 WHGL 98671 570 A5
E 20th St
100 VCVR 98660 536 G4
100 VCVR 98663 536 G4
2400 VCVR 98661 536 J4
2800 VCVR 98661 537 A4
N 20th St
- STHN 97051 385 B7
100 STHN 97051 415 B1
1400 WHGL 98671 570 B4
NE 20th St
1200 GSHM 97030 629 D1
2000 MCMV 97128 771 A3
9400 VCVR 98664 537 G4
15000 VCVR 98684 538 D4
17700 ClkC 98684 538 G4
NW 20th St
100 MCMV 97128 770 H3
500 GSHM 97030 629 B1
800 BGND 98604 448 A3
S 20th St
100 STHN 97051 415 B1
SE 20th St
4400 GSHM 97080 629 G5
14000 VCVR 98683 568 B1
18800 VCVR 98607 568 G1
19800 ClkC 98607 568 J1
20100 CMAS 98607 568 H1
32600 ClkC 98671 570 D2
SW 20th St
3000 GSHM 97080 628 H4
13800 BRTN 97008 625 A5
13900 BRTN 97008 624 J5
W 20th St
100 VCVR 98663 536 G4
900 MCMV 97128 770 G3
1600 VCVR 98660 536 E4
SE 20th Ter
4500 GSHM 97080 629 G5
N 20th Wy
800 CNLS 97113 592 F4
S 20th Wy
5500 ClkC 98642 446 F2
5500 RDGF 98642 446 F2
SE 20th Wy
1200 TDLE 97060 599 H6
14000 VCVR 98683 568 B1
SW 20th Wy
800 TDLE 97060 599 F6
21st Av
1600 FTGV 97116 591 H4
2500 FTGV 97116 592 A4
N 21st Av
600 CNLS 97113 592 F4
NE 21st Av
100 CMAS 98607 569 E3
500 CmsC 97013 746 D4
900 HBRO 97124 593 E3
1000 PTLD 97232 596 J4
1800 CNBY 97013 746 E4
2100 PTLD 97212 596 J2
4200 PTLD 97211 596 J1
4800 PTLD 97211 566 J7
4900 VCVR 98663 536 J1
8400 ClkC 98665 506 J4
38900 ClkC 98629 386 J2
38900 ClkC 98674 386 J2
NW 21st Av
- ClkC 98642 476 E1
10 PTLD 97205 596 D5
10 PTLD 97210 596 D4
700 BGND 98604 447 J4
700 CMAS 98607 569 D3
1900 PTLD 97209 596 D3
8500 ClkC 98665 506 E4
9900 ClkC 98685 506 E1
13800 ClkC 98685 476 E6
37200 ClkC 98629 386 F3
S 21st Av
200 CNLS 97113 592 F5
SE 21st Av
700 HBRO 97123 593 E6
1500 PTLD 97214 596 J6
2500 PTLD 97202 626 J1
2500 PTLD 97214 626 J1
10600 MWKE 97222 656 J2
12600 CmsC 97222 656 J4
SW 21st Av
400 BGND 98604 447 J5
700 PTLD 97205 596 D6
700 PTLD 97209 596 D5
700 PTLD 97210 596 D5
1200 ClkC 98604 447 J6
1300 PTLD 97201 596 D6
5900 PTLD 97239 626 C4
7200 PTLD 97219 626 C5
NE 21st Cir
900 PTLD 97232 596 J5
NW 21st Cir
500 BGND 98604 448 B3
SE 21st Cir
1100 TDLE 97060 599 H6
13500 VCVR 98683 568 B1
21st Ct
10 WHGL 98671 570 B6
NE 21st Ct
- ClkC 98686 506 J2
600 CNBY 97013 746 D4
9100 ClkC 98665 506 J4
21900 ClkC 98642 446 J5
S 21st Ct
500 CNLS 97113 592 F5
SE 21st Ct
700 HBRO 97123 593 E6
1000 GSHM 97080 629 D5
SW 21st Ct
- PTLD 97034 656 C4
800 BGND 98604 447 J6
2800 GSHM 97080 628 H5
SE 21st Dr
3500 GSHM 97080 629 F5
21st Pl
2300 FTGV 97116 591 J4
N 21st Pl
1500 WHGL 98671 570 B4
NE 21st Pl
9600 ClkC 98665 506 J3
9700 ClkC 98686 506 J3
NW 21st Pl
1200 BGND 98604 447 J4
2100 PTLD 97210 596 D3
21200 ClkC 98642 446 E5
S 21st Pl
400 RDGF 98642 416 B7
400 RDGF 98642 446 B1
SE 21st Pl
300 HBRO 97123 593 E5
900 GSHM 97080 629 C5
21st St
200 WHGL 98671 570 B5
E 21st St
2600 VCVR 98661 536 J4
3300 VCVR 98661 537 A4
N 21st St
100 STHN 97051 385 B7
100 STHN 97051 415 B1
NE 21st St
800 MCMV 97128 770 J3
1300 GSHM 97030 629 D1
9200 VCVR 98664 537 G4
16000 VCVR 98684 538 D4
16400 ClkC 98684 538 E4
NW 21st St
600 BGND 98604 448 B3
600 MCMV 97128 770 G3
S 21st St
10 STHN 97051 415 B1
SE 21st St
100 TDLE 97060 599 G5
2900 GSHM 97080 629 E5
9000 VCVR 98664 567 G1
13200 VCVR 98683 568 B1
SW 21st St
100 TDLE 97060 599 G6
13500 BRTN 97008 625 A5
W 21st St
100 VCVR 98660 536 F4
100 VCVR 98663 536 G4
1000 MCMV 97128 770 G3
SE 21st Ter
4500 GSHM 97080 629 G5
SW 21st Ter
1300 GSHM 97080 629 A5
NE 21st Wy
8000 VCVR 98664 537 E4
12400 VCVR 98684 538 A4
SE 21st Wy
17300 VCVR 98683 568 F1
22nd Av
2300 FTGV 97116 591 J4
2700 FTGV 97116 592 A4
NE 22nd Av
10 PTLD 97214 596 J5
100 CMAS 98607 569 E3
100 CmsC 97013 746 C4
500 CNBY 97013 746 C4
1100 HBRO 97124 593 E3
1200 PTLD 97232 596 J4
3900 PTLD 97212 596 J1
4000 PTLD 97211 596 J1
4500 VCVR 98663 536 J1
4800 PTLD 97211 566 J7
5200 VCVR 98663 506 J7
8200 ClkC 98665 506 J5
15000 ClkC 98686 476 J5
15600 ClkC 98642 476 J4
19700 ClkC 98642 446 J6
NW 22nd Av
10 PTLD 97205 596 D5
300 CmsC 97013 746 B4
600 BGND 98604 447 J4
700 CMAS 98607 569 D3
2000 PTLD 97210 596 D3
10400 ClkC 98685 506 E2
14600 ClkC 98685 476 E5
SE 22nd Av
10 PTLD 97232 596 J5
1000 PTLD 97214 596 J7
2000 PTLD 97214 626 J1
3100 PTLD 97202 626 J2
11900 MWKE 97222 656 J3
12600 CmsC 97222 656 J4
20200 ClkC 98604 448 D7
20600 BGND 98604 448 D6
SW 22nd Av
- PTLD 97239 626 C3
400 BGND 98604 447 J6
8300 PTLD 97219 626 C6
12700 CmsC 97034 656 C4
12700 PTLD 97034 656 C4
12700 PTLD 97035 656 C4
NE 22nd Cir
9700 VCVR 98664 537 G4
NW 22nd Cir
2200 CMAS 98607 569 C3
S 22nd Cir
2400 RDGF 98642 446 B2
SE 22nd Cir
1000 TDLE 97060 599 H6
14700 VCVR 98683 568 C1
N 22nd Ct
500 RDGF 98642 416 B6
NE 22nd Ct
800 GSHM 97030 599 C7
2600 GSHM 97030 629 E1
6100 ClkC 98665 506 J7
NW 22nd Ct
9400 ClkC 98665 506 E3
11100 ClkC 98685 506 E2
12700 ClkC 98685 476 E7
S 22nd Ct
500 CNLS 97113 592 F5
SE 22nd Ct
1000 GSHM 97080 629 D5
SW 22nd Ct
2100 TDLE 97060 599 E6
3600 GSHM 97080 628 H5
SE 22nd Dr
4100 GSHM 97080 629 G5
17500 VCVR 98683 568 G5
SW 22nd Dr
3700 GSHM 97080 628 G5
22nd Pl
1600 FTGV 97116 591 H4
3200 FTGV 97116 592 B4
NE 22nd Pl
- ClkC 98686 476 J6
8300 ClkC 98665 506 J4
10400 ClkC 98686 506 J2
NW 22nd Pl
10 PTLD 97205 596 D5
1200 BGND 98604 447 J4
2200 PTLD 97210 596 D3
12000 ClkC 98685 506 E1
S 22nd Pl
1900 RDGF 98642 446 B2
SW 22nd Pl
9300 PTLD 97219 626 C7
22nd St
400 WHGL 98671 570 B5
E 22nd St
100 VCVR 98660 536 G4
100 VCVR 98663 536 G4
2600 VCVR 98661 536 J4
N 22nd St
1500 WHGL 98671 570 B4
NE 22nd St
10 GSHM 97030 599 C7
10200 VCVR 98664 537 H4
10900 VCVR 98684 537 J4
15500 VCVR 98684 538 D4
16400 ClkC 98684 538 E4
22700 ClkC 98607 539 B4
38400 ClkC 98671 540 J4
NW 22nd St
10 GSHM 97030 599 B7
600 BGND 98604 448 B3
S 22nd St
10 STHN 97051 415 B1
SE 22nd St
4900 GSHM 97080 629 G5
15900 VCVR 98683 568 D1
31400 ClkC 98671 570 B2
SW 22nd St
2300 TDLE 97060 599 D6
3000 GSHM 97080 628 H5
13400 BRTN 97008 625 A5
14000 BRTN 97008 624 J5
14400 BRTN 97007 624 J5
W 22nd St
100 MCMV 97128 770 G3
1700 VCVR 98660 536 E4
SW 22nd Ter
1300 GSHM 97080 629 A5
NE 22nd Wy
17900 ClkC 98684 538 F4
SE 22nd Wy
18500 VCVR 98683 568 H2
34200 ClkC 98671 570 D2
23rd Av
1300 FTGV 97116 591 H4
2500 FTGV 97116 592 A4
NE 23rd Av
- ClkC 98629 417 A1
- ClkC 98686 476 J6
500 CMAS 98607 569 E3
600 PTLD 97232 596 J5
700 CNBY 97013 746 D4
2100 PTLD 97212 596 J3
4000 PTLD 97211 596 J1
4800 PTLD 97211 566 J7
5400 VCVR 98663 506 J7
9100 ClkC 98665 506 J4
9700 ClkC 98686 506 J3
15700 ClkC 98642 476 J4
21900 BGND 98604 448 D5
21900 ClkC 98604 448 D5
35200 ClkC 98629 386 J5
NW 23rd Av
10 PTLD 97205 596 D5
10 PTLD 97210 596 D4
500 GSHM 97030 599 B7
700 CMAS 98607 569 D3
1500 BGND 98604 447 J4
8800 ClkC 98665 506 E4
11900 ClkC 98685 506 E1
14600 ClkC 98685 476 E5
S 23rd Av
200 CNLS 97113 592 F5
SE 23rd Av
800 PTLD 97214 596 J7
1000 HBRO 97123 593 E6
2500 PTLD 97202 626 J1
2500 PTLD 97214 626 J1
10300 MWKE 97222 656 J2
12400 CmsC 97222 656 J4
20100 BGND 98604 448 E7
20100 ClkC 98604 448 E7
SW 23rd Av
1100 BGND 98604 447 J6
6000 PTLD 97239 626 C4
7200 PTLD 97219 626 C5
11800 PTLD 97219 656 C3
NE 23rd Cir
- VCVR 98684 537 J4
NW 23rd Cir
1900 CMAS 98607 569 C3
SE 23rd Cir
10700 VCVR 98664 567 H1
13800 VCVR 98683 568 B1
SW 23rd Cir
2400 TDLE 97060 599 C6
NE 23rd Ct
1800 HBRO 97124 593 E2
9300 ClkC 98665 506 J3
21900 ClkC 98642 447 A5
NW 23rd Ct
300 GSHM 97030 599 B7
8700 ClkC 98665 506 E4
11200 ClkC 98685 506 E2
15100 ClkC 98685 476 E4
S 23rd Ct
400 RDGF 98642 416 B7
400 RDGF 98642 446 B1
SE 23rd Ct
4500 GSHM 97080 629 G5
SW 23rd Ct
1400 GSHM 97080 629 A5
1900 GSHM 97080 628 J5
SE 23rd Dr
17100 VCVR 98683 568 F1
SW 23rd Dr
3700 GSHM 97080 628 G5
9100 PTLD 97219 626 C7
23rd Pl
2200 FTGV 97116 591 J4
N 23rd Pl
300 RDGF 98642 416 B6
NE 23rd Pl
- ClkC 98686 476 J6
500 GSHM 97030 599 C7
NW 23rd Pl
10 PTLD 97205 596 D5
2300 PTLD 97210 596 D3
23rd St
- MCMV 97128 770 E3
500 WHGL 98671 570 B5
NE 23rd St
- VCVR 98664 537 E4
1100 GSHM 97030 599 D7
11200 VCVR 98684 537 J4
15300 VCVR 98684 538 D4
18200 ClkC 98684 538 G4
30000 ClkC 98671 539 J4
30000 ClkC 98671 540 A4
NW 23rd St
10 GSHM 97030 599 C6
500 BGND 98604 448 B3
SE 23rd St
900 TDLE 97060 599 H6
2700 GSHM 97080 629 E5
10800 VCVR 98664 567 H1
13500 VCVR 98683 568 B1
28400 ClkC 98607 569 H2
28400 ClkC 98671 569 J2
SW 23rd St
100 TDLE 97060 599 G6
2100 GSHM 97080 628 J5
2600 GSHM 97030 599 E6
13500 BRTN 97008 625 A5
W 23rd St
100 VCVR 98663 536 G3
1200 VCVR 98660 536 E3
SE 23rd Ter
500 GSHM 97080 629 C5
SW 23rd Ter
1300 GSHM 97080 629 A5
NE 23rd Wy
18200 ClkC 98684 538 G4
S 23rd Wy
2100 RDGF 98642 446 C2
SE 23rd Wy
17300 VCVR 98683 568 F2
24th Av
2200 FTGV 97116 591 J4
3600 FTGV 97116 592 C4
3600 WasC 97116 592 C4
NE 24th Av
10 PTLD 97214 596 J5
100 HBRO 97123 593 E5
1200 PTLD 97232 596 J4
1700 HBRO 97124 593 F2
4000 PTLD 97211 596 J1
4000 PTLD 97212 596 J1
4800 PTLD 97211 566 J7
5100 VCVR 98663 536 J1
5200 VCVR 98663 506 J7
8800 ClkC 98665 506 J4
10900 ClkC 98686 506 J2
14400 ClkC 98686 476 J5
15700 ClkC 98642 476 J4
27900 ClkC 98642 417 A6
32900 ClkC 98629 417 A1
NW 24th Av
- ClkC 98642 446 E3
400 PTLD 97210 596 C4
700 CMAS 98607 569 D3
1000 BGND 98604 447 J4
8800 ClkC 98665 506 D4
9800 ClkC 98685 506 D3
14600 ClkC 98685 476 E5
32900 ClkC 98642 386 E7
32900 ClkC 98642 416 E1
35600 ClkC 98629 386 E4
S 24th Av
200 CNLS 97113 592 F5

Columns: **Block | City | ZIP | Map# | Grid**

SE 24th Av
Block	City	ZIP	Map#	Grid
10	PTLD	97214	596	J6
10	PTLD	97232	596	J5
100	HBRO	97123	593	E6
100	HBRO	97124	593	E5
2000	PTLD	97214	626	J1
3100	PTLD	97202	626	J2
10300	MWKE	97222	656	J3
12400	CmsC	97222	656	J4

SW 24th Av
–	PTLD	97219	626	C5
–	PTLD	97219	626	C5
400	BGND	98604	447	J6

E 24th Cir
–	ClkC	98629	386	H6

N 24th Cir
1300	WHGL	98671	570	B4

NE 24th Cir
9000	VCVR	98662	537	F3
10100	VCVR	98664	537	H3

NW 24th Cir
500	CMAS	98607	569	D3

SE 24th Cir
1200	TDLE	97060	599	H6
14500	VCVR	98683	568	C2

N 24th Ct
1300	WHGL	98671	570	B4

NE 24th Ct
2100	GSHM	97030	599	D7
9200	ClkC	98665	506	J3

SE 24th Ct
3600	GSHM	97080	629	F5

SW 24th Ct
–	GSHM	97080	628	J5

SW 24th Dr
1500	GSHM	97080	629	A5

NW 24th Pl
–	PTLD	97205	596	C5
2300	PTLD	97210	596	C3
8800	ClkC	98665	506	D4

S 24th Pl
–	RDGF	98642	446	B2

24th St
200	WHGL	98671	570	B5

E 24th St
200	VCVR	98663	536	G3
3200	VCVR	98661	537	A4

N 24th St
1200	WHGL	98671	570	B5

NE 24th St
200	MCMV	97128	770	H3
900	GSHM	97030	599	C7
10200	VCVR	98664	537	H4
10900	VCVR	98684	537	H4
12200	VCVR	98684	538	A4
16500	ClkC	98684	538	E4
37200	ClkC	98671	540	H4

NW 24th St
–	ClkC	98604	448	B3
100	MCMV	97128	770	H3
400	GSHM	97030	599	B7
600	BGND	98604	448	B3

SE 24th St
4300	GSHM	97080	629	G5
15000	VCVR	98683	568	D2

SW 24th St
2000	TDLE	97060	599	E6
2600	GSHM	97080	628	J5
13400	BRTN	97008	625	A5

W 24th St
100	VCVR	98663	536	G3
200	MCMV	97128	770	H3
1700	VCVR	98660	536	E3

SE 24th Ter
2900	GSHM	97080	629	E5

SW 24th Ter
3500	GSHM	97080	628	H5

NW 24th Ter
–	BGND	98604	448	B3

SE 24th Wy
18100	VCVR	98683	568	G2

25th Av
–	FTGV	97116	591	J4

E 25th Wy
–	FTGV	97116	592	A4

N 25th Av
600	CNLS	97113	592	F4

NE 25th Av
100	HBRO	97123	593	F4
800	HBRO	97124	593	F3
1500	PTLD	97232	596	J2
3800	WasC	97213	593	E1
4100	PTLD	97211	596	J1
4800	PTLD	97211	566	J7
5200	VCVR	98663	536	J1
7800	ClkC	98665	506	J6
9600	ClkC	98686	506	J3
13600	ClkC	98686	476	J6
15500	ClkC	98684	477	A4
17900	ClkC	98642	477	A2

NW 25th Av
–	CMAS	98607	568	H3
600	BGND	98604	447	J4
2300	PTLD	97210	596	C3
2400	CMAS	98607	569	B3
9400	ClkC	98665	506	D3
11700	ClkC	98685	506	D1
15100	ClkC	98685	476	E4

S 25th Av
100	CNLS	97113	592	F5

SE 25th Av
800	PTLD	97202	596	J7
2500	PTLD	97214	626	J1
8700	MWKE	97222	656	J1
9000	MWKE	97222	656	J1
12400	CmsC	97222	656	J4

SW 25th Av
–	PTLD	97219	626	C5
1100	BGND	98604	447	J7
1100	ClkC	98604	447	J6
6200	PTLD	97239	626	C1

N 25th Cir
1400	WHGL	98671	570	B4

NE 25th Cir
8600	VCVR	98662	537	F3
15200	VCVR	98684	538	D4
30500	ClkC	98607	540	A4
30500	ClkC	98671	540	A4

NW 25th Cir
2600	CMAS	98607	569	B3

SE 25th Cir
14000	VCVR	98683	568	B2

SW 25th Cir
10	TDLE	97060	599	G6

NE 25th Ct
500	HBRO	97124	593	F4
2800	GSHM	97030	599	E7
4800	VCVR	98663	506	J1
9400	ClkC	98665	506	J3
15000	ClkC	98686	477	A5

NW 25th Ct
12200	ClkC	98685	506	B1
12900	ClkC	98685	476	E7

S 25th Ct
600	CNLS	97113	592	F5

SE 25th Ct
800	HBRO	97123	593	F6

SW 25th Ct
1200	GSHM	97080	629	A5
1500	GSHM	97080	628	H5

SW 25th Dr
1500	GSHM	97080	629	A5

NE 25th Pl
8300	ClkC	98665	506	J4
10400	ClkC	98686	506	J2
10400	ClkC	98686	507	A2

NW 25th Pl
300	BGND	98604	447	J5
2500	PTLD	97210	596	C3

S 25th Pl
400	ClkC	98642	416	B7
400	ClkC	98642	416	B7
400	RDGF	98642	416	B7
400	RDGF	98642	416	B7
700	CNLS	97113	592	F6

SE 25th Pl
1300	HBRO	97123	593	F6

SW 25th Pl
9800	PTLD	97219	656	C1

25th St
500	WHGL	98671	570	B5

E 25th St
100	VCVR	98660	536	G3
100	VCVR	98660	536	G3
2100	VCVR	98661	536	J3
2100	VCVR	98661	537	A3

N 25th St
800	WHGL	98671	570	B4

NE 25th St
800	GSHM	97030	599	C7
800	MCMV	97128	770	J3
7300	VCVR	98662	537	E3
7300	VCVR	98664	537	E3
11200	VCVR	98684	537	J3
13200	VCVR	98684	538	B3
14900	VCVR	98684	538	D4
16300	ClkC	98684	538	D4
24800	ClkC	98607	539	D4
38600	ClkC	98671	540	J4

NE 25th St SR-500
24800	ClkC	98607	539	D4

NW 25th St
100	MCMV	97128	770	H3
300	GSHM	97030	599	B7

SE 25th St
3600	GSHM	97080	629	F5
14600	VCVR	98683	568	C2
19200	VCVR	98683	568	H2
36200	ClkC	98671	570	G2

SW 25th St
900	TDLE	97060	599	F6
3200	GSHM	97080	628	H5

W 25th St
200	MCMV	97128	770	H3
800	VCVR	98660	536	F3

N 25th Ter
–	CNLS	97113	592	F4

NE 25th Wy
–	VCVR	98682	538	A4
–	VCVR	98684	540	A4
29900	ClkC	98607	540	A4
29900	ClkC	98607	539	J4
29900	ClkC	98671	540	A4

SE 25th Wy
17200	VCVR	98683	568	F2

26th Av
2200	FTGV	97116	591	J3
2200	WasC	97116	591	J3
2400	FTGV	97116	592	A3
2400	WasC	97116	592	A3

N 26th Av
700	CNLS	97113	592	G4

NE 26th Av
10	PTLD	97214	596	J5
1200	PTLD	97232	596	J1
3800	PTLD	97212	596	J1
4100	PTLD	97211	597	A1
4100	PTLD	97212	597	A1
4400	VCVR	98663	537	A1
5500	PTLD	97211	567	A6
7100	ClkC	98665	506	J4
8300	ClkC	98665	506	J4
9800	ClkC	98665	506	J3
15300	ClkC	98686	477	A3
16400	ClkC	98642	477	A3
23900	ClkC	98642	447	A3
34700	ClkC	98629	386	E6

S 26th Av
10	CNLS	97113	592	F5
2000	RDGF	98642	446	B2
2000	WasC	97113	592	F5

SE 26th Av
6700	PTLD	97239	626	C5
6900	PTLD	97219	626	C5
10700	PTLD	97219	656	C2

W 26th Av
2200	VCVR	98660	536	D3

NW 26th Cir
1600	CMAS	98607	569	C3

S 26th Cir
2200	RDGF	98642	446	B2

NE 26th Ct
11500	VCVR	98664	567	J2
13400	VCVR	98683	568	B2

SW 26th Ct
200	TDLE	97060	599	G6

NE 26th Dr
500	HBRO	97124	593	F4
500	MCMV	97128	771	A3
4300	VCVR	98663	536	J2
9200	ClkC	98665	506	J3
9400	ClkC	98665	506	J3
15000	ClkC	98686	477	A5
15900	ClkC	98642	477	A4

NW 26th Ct
9400	ClkC	98665	506	D3

S 26th Ct
100	CNLS	97113	592	G5

SE 26th Ct
–	GSHM	97080	629	F5
100	TDLE	97060	599	H6

SW 26th Ct
1200	GSHM	97080	629	A5
2700	GSHM	97080	628	J5

SE 26th Dr
1100	GSHM	97080	629	D5

SW 26th Dr
4700	PTLD	97239	626	C3

NE 26th Pl
9600	ClkC	98665	506	J3
9700	ClkC	98665	507	A1
11800	ClkC	98686	507	A1

SE 26th Pl
3900	GSHM	97080	629	F5
8800	PTLD	97202	626	J7

26th St
1500	TDLE	97060	599	E6

E 26th St
700	VCVR	98663	536	G3
2100	VCVR	98663	536	J3
13900	VCVR	98684	537	A3

NE 26th St
–	VCVR	98682	538	A3
500	MCMV	97128	770	J3
1100	GSHM	97030	599	D7
9900	VCVR	98662	537	H3
10800	VCVR	98684	537	H3
16000	VCVR	98684	538	E3
16500	ClkC	98684	538	E3

S 26th St
1100	TDLE	97060	599	E6
2900	GSHM	97080	629	E5
14500	VCVR	98683	568	F2
35700	ClkC	98671	570	F2

SW 26th St
500	TDLE	97060	599	F6
3200	GSHM	97080	628	H5

N 26th Ter
–	CNLS	97113	592	G4

NE 26th Wy
16600	VCVR	98683	568	E2
19500	VCVR	98607	568	H2

SW 26th Wy
–	PTLD	97219	626	C7

N 27th Av
–	CNLS	97113	592	F4

NE 27th Av
200	PTLD	97232	596	J3
1500	PTLD	97232	597	A3
4000	PTLD	97211	597	A1
4000	PTLD	97212	597	A1
6800	ClkC	98665	506	J5
7100	ClkC	98665	567	A5
9000	ClkC	98665	507	A1
12300	ClkC	98686	507	A1
13000	ClkC	98686	477	A1
13000	ClkC	98642	477	A7

NW 27th Av
–	BGND	98604	447	H4
1400	PTLD	97210	596	C2
1500	CMAS	98607	569	C3
9500	ClkC	98665	506	D3
9800	ClkC	98685	506	D3
14000	ClkC	98685	476	D6

S 27th Av
100	CNLS	97113	592	G5

SE 27th Av
100	PTLD	97214	596	J6
2500	PTLD	97202	626	J1
2500	PTLD	97214	626	J1
7000	PTLD	97206	626	A5
12500	CmsC	97222	656	J4

SW 27th Av
–	BGND	98604	447	H6
4500	PTLD	97239	626	C3
7100	PTLD	97219	626	C1
11100	PTLD	97219	656	C1

NE 27th Cir
8600	VCVR	98662	537	F3
14500	VCVR	98683	568	C2

NW 27th Cir
2200	CMAS	98607	569	C2

SW 27th Cir
–	TDLE	97060	599	F6

NE 27th Ct
500	HBRO	97124	593	F5
2700	MCMV	97128	771	A3
4900	VCVR	98663	536	J1
10800	ClkC	98686	507	A1
14300	ClkC	98686	477	A1
16300	ClkC	98642	477	A4
20600	ClkC	98642	477	A4

NW 27th Ct
11500	ClkC	98685	476	D4
15500	ClkC	98685	476	D4

SE 27th Ct
–	HBRO	97123	623	F1
1500	TDLE	97060	599	H6

SE 27th Ct (col. 4)
2900	GSHM	97080	629	E5

SW 27th Ct
–	BRTN	97007	624	J6
–	PTLD	97239	626	C4

S 26th Cir ...

NE 27th Dr
2700	GSHM	97030	599	E7

SW 27th Dr
2100	GSHM	97080	628	J5

27th Pl
12400	PTLD	97035	656	C3

NW 27th Pl
20500	ClkC	98642	446	E6

SE 27th Pl
12800	CmsC	97222	656	J4

SW 27th Pl
11800	PTLD	97219	656	C3

27th St
500	WHGL	98671	570	B5

E 27th St
100	VCVR	98663	536	G3
100	VCVR	98663	536	G3
2100	VCVR	98661	536	J3
2200	VCVR	98661	537	A3

NE 27th St
10	GSHM	97030	599	C7
300	MCMV	97128	770	J2
1600	MCMV	97128	771	A3
3200	VCVR	98663	537	A3
7800	VCVR	98662	537	E3
11200	VCVR	98682	537	J3
14900	VCVR	98684	538	D3
16500	ClkC	98684	538	E3

S 27th St
400	WHGL	98671	570	B6

SE 27th St
700	GSHM	97080	629	C5
900	TDLE	97060	599	E6
12500	VCVR	98683	568	A2
13700	BRTN	97008	625	A6
13900	BRTN	97008	624	J6

W 27th St
100	VCVR	98663	536	G3
1900	VCVR	98660	536	E3

NE 27th Ter
1400	GSHM	97030	599	D7

NE 27th Wy
16500	VCVR	98684	538	A3
16500	VCVR	98682	538	E3
17200	ClkC	98682	538	F3

SW 27th Wy
300	TDLE	97060	599	F6

28th Av
1900	FTGV	97116	591	H3

N 28th Av
700	CNLS	97113	592	G4

NE 28th Av
10	PTLD	97214	597	A5
10	PTLD	97232	597	A5
100	HBRO	97123	593	F5
100	HBRO	97124	593	F4
3700	PTLD	97212	597	A1
4000	PTLD	97211	597	A1
4400	VCVR	98663	537	A1
5500	PTLD	97211	567	A7
10000	ClkC	98665	507	A3
15300	ClkC	98686	477	A3
17900	ClkC	98642	477	A4

NW 28th Av
100	BGND	98604	447	H5
1300	CMAS	98607	569	C3
2300	PTLD	97210	596	C3
9600	ClkC	98665	506	D3
11300	ClkC	98685	506	D2
17900	ClkC	98642	476	D2

SE 28th Av
100	HBRO	97123	593	F5
500	PTLD	97214	597	A7
1900	PTLD	97214	626	J7
2500	PTLD	97214	627	A1
2500	PTLD	97202	626	J1
5700	PTLD	97202	627	A1
8500	MWKE	97222	627	A7
10600	MWKE	97222	657	A2
11800	MWKE	97222	656	J3
12600	CmsC	97222	657	A4

SW 28th Av
–	PTLD	97219	656	C1

NE 28th Cir
10200	VCVR	98664	537	H3
28900	ClkC	98607	539	H4

NW 28th Cir
2500	CMAS	98607	569	B2

SE 28th Cir
13800	VCVR	98683	568	B2
15100	ClkC	98685	476	D5

28th Ct
900	WHGL	98671	570	C5

S 28th Ct
2100	RDGF	98642	446	C2

NE 28th Ct
10200	ClkC	98665	507	A3
10200	ClkC	98686	507	A3
15700	ClkC	98686	477	A4
16200	ClkC	98642	477	A4

NW 28th Ct
–	BGND	98604	447	H4
11000	ClkC	98685	506	D1
14000	ClkC	98685	476	D6

SE 28th Ct
1500	GSHM	97080	629	D5
1700	GSHM	97080	629	D5
20600	ClkC	98642	477	A4

SW 28th Ct
11500	ClkC	98685	476	B1
15500	ClkC	98685	476	D4

SE 28th Dr
2700	PTLD	97219	656	C2
4200	BRTN	97008	628	A5
7200	BRTN	97008	625	A6

SE 28th Dr (col. 5)
5100	GSHM	97080	629	G5

SW 28th Dr
2500	PTLD	97219	656	C2
9800	PTLD	97219	656	C1

NE 28th Dr
9600	ClkC	98665	507	A3

NW 28th Pl
1900	PTLD	97210	596	C3
14200	ClkC	98685	476	D6

SE 28th Pl
900	HBRO	97123	593	F6
900	TDLE	97060	599	G6
2000	PTLD	97214	597	A7
2100	PTLD	97214	627	A1
3300	PTLD	97202	627	A2
8600	MWKE	97222	627	A7
25900	ClkC	98607	539	E2

SW 28th Pl
11600	PTLD	97219	656	C3

E 28th St
100	VCVR	98663	536	G3
2200	VCVR	98661	536	J3
2800	VCVR	98661	537	A3

NE 28th St
–	ClkC	98684	538	E3
700	GSHM	97030	599	C7
800	MCMV	97128	770	J2
7800	VCVR	98662	537	E3
11200	VCVR	98682	537	J3
11900	VCVR	98682	538	A3
17700	VCVR	98682	538	F3
27600	ClkC	98607	539	G4
30200	ClkC	98607	540	A3

S 28th St
400	WHGL	98671	570	B6

SE 28th St
3100	GSHM	97080	629	F5
13900	VCVR	98683	568	B2
30000	ClkC	98671	569	J2

SW 28th St
1100	TDLE	97060	599	E6
1900	GSHM	97080	628	H5

W 28th St
1900	VCVR	98663	536	G3
1900	VCVR	98660	536	E3

SW 28th Ter
3500	GSHM	97080	628	H5

SE 28th Wy
15300	VCVR	98683	568	D2

N 29th Av
–	CNLS	97113	592	G5

NE 28th Av (col. 5)
10	PTLD	97214	597	A5
10	PTLD	97232	597	A5
100	HBRO	97123	593	F5
100	HBRO	97123	623	F1
700	CmsC	97013	746	D3
700	CNBY	97013	746 D3	

NE 29th Av
10	PTLD	97214	597	A5
10	PTLD	97232	597	A5
700	CmsC	97013	746	D3
700	CNBY	97013	746	D3
3900	GSHM	97080	628	A5
10800	ClkC	98685	507	A2
13500	BRTN	97008	625	A2

SW 29th Av
10	GSHM	97030	599	C7
1500	GSHM	97080	629	D5
1700	GSHM	97080	629	D5
20600	ClkC	98642	477	A4

NW 29th Pl
300	TDLE	97060	599	F6
2700	PTLD	97219	656	C2
4200	BRTN	97008	628	A5
7200	BRTN	97008	625	A6

SE 29th Pl
–	GSHM	97080	629	C5

SW 29th Pl
4600	PTLD	97239	626	C3
9800	PTLD	97219	656	C1

29th St
500	WHGL	98671	570	C5
1900	WHGL	98671	570	C4

NE 29th St
100	VCVR	98660	536	G3
100	VCVR	98660	536	G3
2200	VCVR	98661	536	J3

E 29th St
100	VCVR	98660	536	G3
100	VCVR	98663	536	G3
2200	VCVR	98661	536	J3

NE 29th St
1200	GSHM	97030	599	D7
7700	VCVR	98662	537	E3
11700	VCVR	98682	537	J3
16500	ClkC	98682	538	E3
25900	ClkC	98607	539	E2

NW 29th St
1100	VCVR	98660	536	F3
30300	ClkC	98671	570	A2

SE 29th St
2900	GSHM	97080	629	F5
3400	MthC	97080	628	H5

W 29th St
1800	GSHM	97030	599	E6
1800	TDLE	97060	599	E6

SW 29th St
100	VCVR	98660	536	F3
100	VCVR	98663	536	G3

NE 29th Wy
8600	VCVR	98662	537	F3
30600	ClkC	98607	540	A3

SE 29th Wy
6100	GSHM	97080	629	H6

SW 29th Wy
–	TDLE	97060	599	F6

30th Av
2000	FTGV	97116	591	H3

NE 30th Av
10	PTLD	97214	597	A5
10	PTLD	97232	597	A5
100	HBRO	97123	593	F4
200	HBRO	97124	593	F4
2200	PTLD	97212	597	A1
2200	PTLD	97211	597	A1
5000	PTLD	97211	567	A7
5400	VCVR	98663	507	A7
9500	ClkC	98665	507	A2
10600	ClkC	98686	507	A2
15700	ClkC	98686	477	A1
16100	ClkC	98642	477	A4
32800	ClkC	98629	417	B1

SW 30th Av
5800	PTLD	97239	626	C4
8200	PTLD	97219	627	A1
9800	PTLD	97219	656	B1

NE 30th Av
10	PTLD	97232	597	A6
200	HBRO	97123	593	F5
500	PTLD	97214	597	A7
2500	PTLD	97214	627	A1
2500	PTLD	97202	627	A1
6800	PTLD	97219	627	A1
11400	VCVR	98682	537	J3

NW 29th Av
2000	CMAS	98607	569	C2

SE 29th Av
14200	VCVR	98683	568	C2

SW 29th Av
–	TDLE	97060	599	F6
4000	GSHM	97080	629	F5
14600	VCVR	98683	568	G3
36200	ClkC	98671	570	G3

NE 30th Av (col. 6)
300	GSHM	97030	599	C7

SW 30th Dr
3600	GSHM	97080	626	H5
7600	PTLD	97219	626	C6

NE 30th Ln
1200	GSHM	97030	599	D7

NW 30th Pa
–	BGND	98604	447	H4

N 30th Pl
300	CNLS	97113	592	G4

NE 30th Pl
700	CmsC	97013	746	D3
5300	VCVR	98663	507	A7
10800	ClkC	98642	477	A3

S 30th Pl
60	GSHM	97030	599	C7

SE 30th Pl
10	PTLD	97214	597	A6
10	PTLD	97232	597	A6
1800	TDLE	97060	599	F6

SW 30th Pl
–	PTLD	97219	626	B6

30th St
600	WHGL	98671	570	C5

E 30th St
100	VCVR	98663	536	G3
2200	VCVR	98661	536	J3
2700	VCVR	98661	537	A3

NE 30th St
1100	MCMV	97128	770	J2
7800	VCVR	98662	537	E3
12500	VCVR	98682	538	A3
17300	VCVR	98682	538	F3
35500	ClkC	98671	540	F3

NW 30th St
1100	VCVR	98660	536	F3

SE 30th St
2900	GSHM	97080	629	E5
2900	MthC	97080	629	E6
15100	VCVR	98683	568	D2
19300	VCVR	98607	568	H2
29700	ClkC	98671	569	J2
30300	ClkC	98671	570	A2

SW 30th St
2900	GSHM	97080	628	H5
3400	MthC	97080	628	H5

W 30th St
100	VCVR	98660	536	F3
100	VCVR	98663	536	G3

SE 30th Wy
6000	GSHM	97080	629	H6
19600	VCVR	98607	568	H2

N 31st Av
–	CNLS	97113	592	G4

NE 31st Av
10	PTLD	97214	597	A3
10	PTLD	97232	597	A3
100	CmsC	97013	746	C3
700	CNBY	97013	746	D3
4000	PTLD	97211	597	A1
5000	PTLD	97211	567	A6
6800	PTLD	97211	507	A6
8700	ClkC	98665	507	A4
10600	ClkC	98686	507	A2
15700	ClkC	98686	477	A1
15900	ClkC	98642	477	A4

NW 31st Av
2200	PTLD	97210	596	B3
2600	CMAS	98607	569	B2
9600	ClkC	98665	506	D3
11300	ClkC	98685	506	D1
13100	ClkC	98685	476	D7
17400	ClkC	98642	476	D2
20900	ClkC	98642	446	D5
26800	RDGF	98642	416	D7
32300	ClkC	98642	416	D1
37400	ClkC	98629	386	D3
37400	ClkC	98674	386	D3

SE 31st Av
900	PTLD	97214	597	A7
2100	PTLD	97214	627	A1
3700	PTLD	97202	627	A2
8500	PTLD	97222	627	A7
8600	MWKE	97222	627	A7
10400	MWKE	97222	657	A2
12700	CmsC	97222	657	A4

SW 31st Av
6900	PTLD	97219	626	B5
10100	PTLD	97219	656	B1

NE 31st Cir
–	VCVR	98662	537	F3
18100	VCVR	98682	538	G3
28600	ClkC	98607	539	H3
36000	ClkC	98671	540	F3

NW 31st Cir
3300	CMAS	98607	569	B2

SE 31st Cir
15900	VCVR	98683	568	D2

NE 31st Ct
100	HBRO	97124	593	F5
5100	VCVR	98663	507	A7
8400	ClkC	98665	507	A4
14000	ClkC	98686	477	A6
26400	ClkC	98642	417	A7

NW 31st Ct
1600	CMAS	98607	569	C2
15700	ClkC	98685	476	D4

S 31st Ct
2100	RDGF	98642	446	C2

SE 31st Ct
600	HBRO	97123	593	F6
4400	GSHM	97080	629	G6

SW 31st Ct
11600	PTLD	97219	656	B2
13800	BRTN	97008	625	A6

SE 31st Dr
19300	VCVR	98683	568	H2

SE 31st Dr
4700	PTLD	97239	626	B3

SE 31st Pl
13100	MWKE	97222	657	A3

31st St
–	WHGL	98671	570	C5

E 31st St
100	VCVR	98660	536	G3
100	VCVR	98663	536	G3

NE 31st St
9700	VCVR	98662	537	J3
11600	VCVR	98682	537	J3
16200	VCVR	98682	538	D1
27300	ClkC	98607	538	D1

NW 31st St
1100	VCVR	98660	536	E3

SE 31st St
4000	GSHM	97080	629	F6
4000	MthC	97080	629	F6
17200	VCVR	98607	568	F2
19200	VCVR	98607	568	H2

SW 31st St
1300	GSHM	97080	629	A6
2700	GSHM	97080	628	H6
3400	MthC	97080	628	H6
13200	BRTN	97008	625	A6

W 31st St
100	VCVR	98663	536	G3
1600	VCVR	98660	536	E3

SE 31st Ter
6100	GSHM	97080	629	H6

NE 31st Wy
16800	VCVR	98682	538	E3

NW 31st Wy
2300	CMAS	98607	569	C2

S 31st Wy
3000	ClkC	98642	446	C2

SE 31st Wy
14500	VCVR	98683	568	C2
19600	VCVR	98607	568	H2

Portland Street Index

STREET
Block City ZIP Map# Grid

SE 31st Wy
34500 ClkC 98671 570 E3
E 32nd Av
1300 VCVR 98661 537 A5
NE 32nd Av
10 PTLD 97214 597 A5
100 HBRO 97123 593 F5
100 HBRO 97124 593 F5
1500 PTLD 97232 597 A4
1800 PTLD 97212 597 A3
4000 PTLD 97211 597 A1
6800 PTLD 97211 567 A6
8800 ClkC 98665 507 A4
11100 ClkC 98686 507 A2
17100 ClkC 98642 477 A3
NW 32nd Av
- NPNS 97133 563 A1
1200 CMAS 98607 569 D2
2100 PTLD 97210 596 B3
12100 ClkC 98685 506 D1
15100 ClkC 98685 476 D5
35100 ClkC 98629 386 D5
SE 32nd Av
10 PTLD 97232 597 A5
100 HBRO 97123 593 F6
100 HBRO 97124 593 F5
600 PTLD 97214 597 A6
2100 PTLD 97214 627 A1
2500 PTLD 97202 627 A1
8300 PTLD 97222 627 A7
8400 MWKE 97222 627 A7
9100 MWKE 97222 657 A1
12800 CmsC 97222 657 A4
SW 32nd Av
6100 PTLD 97239 626 B4
6700 PTLD 97219 626 B5
10200 PTLD 97219 656 B1
NE 32nd Cir
10300 VCVR 98662 537 H3
13700 VCVR 98682 538 B3
18500 ClkC 98682 538 G3
NW 32nd Cir
2300 CMAS 98607 569 C2
SE 32nd Cir
29700 ClkC 98671 569 J3
W 32nd Cir
1200 VCVR 98660 536 E3
N 32nd Ct
100 RDGF 98642 416 C7
NE 32nd Ct
2300 PTLD 97212 597 A3
4800 VCVR 98663 537 A1
11500 ClkC 98686 507 A1
12200 VCVR 98682 538 A3
NW 32nd Ct
12900 ClkC 98685 476 D7
S 32nd Ct
1600 ClkC 98642 446 C2
SE 32nd Ct
600 HBRO 97123 593 F6
4400 GSHM 97080 629 G6
SW 32nd Ct
2800 GSHM 97080 628 G6
SE 32nd Dr
19300 VCVR 98607 568 H2
32nd Pl
1100 FTGV 97116 591 G2
NE 32nd Pl
3600 PTLD 97212 597 A1
4000 PTLD 97211 597 A1
6600 PTLD 97211 567 A6
NW 32nd Pl
1100 VCVR 98660 536 F2
S 32nd Pl
- RDGF 98642 416 C7
SE 32nd Pl
1500 PTLD 97214 597 A7
2000 PTLD 97214 627 A1
SW 32nd Pl
10200 PTLD 97219 656 B1
32nd St
10 WHGL 98671 570 C5
1700 ClkC 98671 570 C4
E 32nd St
100 VCVR 98660 536 G3
100 VCVR 98663 536 G3
2400 VCVR 98661 536 J3
2700 VCVR 98661 537 A3
NE 32nd St
6200 VCVR 98661 537 D3
7800 VCVR 98662 537 E3
11500 VCVR 98682 537 J3
15500 VCVR 98682 538 D3
16200 ClkC 98682 538 E3
S 32nd St
400 WHGL 98671 570 C7
SE 32nd St
- VCVR 98607 568 H3
1400 TDLE 97060 599 H7
5400 MthC 97080 629 H6
6000 GSHM 97080 629 H6
15900 VCVR 98683 568 D3
SW 32nd St
1800 GSHM 97080 628 J6
13600 BRTN 97008 625 A6
W 32nd St
100 VCVR 98660 536 F3
100 VCVR 98663 536 G3
E 32nd Ter
6200 GSHM 97080 629 H6
SW 32nd Ter
2900 GSHM 97080 628 G6
NE 32nd Wy
11900 VCVR 98682 537 J3
33rd Av
1000 FTGV 97116 591 G2
NE 33rd Av
800 PTLD 97232 597 A5
1600 PTLD 97212 597 A3
4000 PTLD 97211 597 A1
4900 PTLD 97211 567 A7
5600 VCVR 98663 507 A7
11300 ClkC 98686 507 A2
15900 ClkC 98686 477 A4
17500 ClkC 98642 477 A2
NW 33rd Av
2000 PTLD 97210 596 B3
11600 ClkC 98685 506 D1
13000 ClkC 98685 476 D6
SE 33rd Av
100 HBRO 97123 593 F5
100 HBRO 97124 593 F5
100 PTLD 97214 597 A6
2500 PTLD 97202 627 A2
2500 PTLD 97214 627 A1

SE 33rd Av
8500 MWKE 97222 627 A7
8500 PTLD 97222 627 A7
9700 MWKE 97222 657 A1
SW 33rd Av
6700 PTLD 97219 626 B6
10600 PTLD 97219 656 B2
12200 LKOW 97035 656 B3
NE 33rd Cir
5900 VCVR 98661 537 D3
13100 VCVR 98682 538 B3
18200 ClkC 98682 538 G3
SE 33rd Cir
19200 VCVR 98607 568 G3
33rd Ct
2400 WHGL 98671 570 C3
NE 33rd Ct
300 HBRO 97124 593 F4
9400 ClkC 98665 507 A3
18800 ClkC 98642 477 A1
SE 33rd Ct
600 HBRO 97123 593 F6
4400 GSHM 97080 629 G6
NE 33rd Dr
7200 PTLD 97211 567 A4
SW 33rd Dr
5200 PTLD 97239 626 B4
33rd Pl
1000 FTGV 97116 591 G2
E 33rd Pl
1000 VCVR 98661 537 A5
NE 33rd Pl
3400 PTLD 97212 597 A2
SE 33rd Pl
700 PTLD 97214 597 A6
2500 PTLD 97202 627 A1
2500 PTLD 97214 627 A1
12000 MWKE 97222 657 A4
SW 33rd Pl
6700 PTLD 97219 626 B5
6700 PTLD 97239 626 B5
11600 PTLD 97219 656 B2
13800 BRTN 97008 625 A6
33rd St
600 WHGL 98671 570 C5
E 33rd St
100 VCVR 98660 536 G2
100 VCVR 98663 536 H3
2500 VCVR 98661 536 J3
2700 VCVR 98661 537 A3
NE 33rd St
- VCVR 98661 537 E3
- VCVR 98662 537 E3
2000 GSHM 97030 599 D6
2100 TDLE 97060 599 D6
11900 VCVR 98682 537 J3
11900 VCVR 98682 538 A3
16200 ClkC 98682 538 D1
28900 ClkC 98607 539 J3
SE 33rd St
- WHGL 98671 569 J3
600 TDLE 97060 599 H7
15200 VCVR 98683 568 D3
19300 VCVR 98607 568 H3
29300 ClkC 98671 569 J3
SW 33rd St
1200 GSHM 97080 629 A6
1800 GSHM 97080 628 J6
W 33rd St
100 VCVR 98660 536 F2
100 VCVR 98663 536 G2
NW 33rd Wy
1500 CMAS 98607 569 C2
SE 33rd Wy
6100 GSHM 97080 629 H6
14600 VCVR 98683 568 C3
W 33rd Wy
1100 VCVR 98660 536 E2
NE 34th Av
800 HBRO 97124 593 G4
900 CMAS 98607 569 F2
1400 PTLD 97232 597 A4
3700 PTLD 97212 597 A2
4200 PTLD 97211 597 A1
5900 PTLD 97211 567 A6
8800 ClkC 98665 507 A4
11500 ClkC 98686 507 A1
17600 ClkC 98642 477 B2
NW 34th Av
1400 CMAS 98607 569 C2
1800 PTLD 97210 596 B3
11600 ClkC 98685 506 D1
12100 ClkC 98685 476 D7
19900 ClkC 98642 446 D7
SE 34th Av
500 PTLD 97214 597 A6
1000 HBRO 97123 593 F6
2100 PTLD 97214 627 A1
3600 PTLD 97202 627 A2
8500 MWKE 97222 627 A7
8500 PTLD 97222 627 A7
10300 MWKE 97222 657 A1
SW 34th Av
4200 PTLD 97239 626 B3
6700 PTLD 97219 626 B5
12000 PTLD 97219 656 B3
NE 34th Cir
10000 VCVR 98662 537 H3
11000 VCVR 98682 537 H3
13300 VCVR 98682 538 B3
23000 ClkC 98607 539 C3
NW 34th Cir
2700 CMAS 98607 569 B2
SE 34th Cir
100 TDLE 97060 599 G7
14300 VCVR 98683 568 C3
NE 34th Ct
100 HBRO 97124 593 F5
11300 ClkC 98686 507 A2
NW 34th Ct
11400 ClkC 98685 506 D1
SE 34th Ct
300 HBRO 97123 593 F5
9600 MWKE 97222 657 A1
15700 VCVR 98683 568 D3
34th Pl
1100 FTGV 97116 591 G2
N 34th Pl
10 RDGF 98642 416 C7
NE 34th Pl
200 HBRO 97124 593 G4
700 CmsC 97013 746 D2
700 CNBY 97013 746 D2
S 34th Pl
- RDGF 98642 416 C7

SW 34th Pl
- PTLD 97219 626 B7
5300 PTLD 97221 626 B4
5300 PTLD 97239 626 B4
9700 PTLD 97219 656 B1
34th St
2400 WHGL 98671 570 C3
E 34th St
500 VCVR 98663 536 G2
2500 VCVR 98661 536 J2
2700 VCVR 98661 537 A2
NE 34th St
2100 GSHM 97030 599 C6
2100 GSHM 97060 599 C6
2100 TDLE 97060 599 C6
4700 VCVR 98661 537 C2
8200 VCVR 98662 537 F3
14800 VCVR 98682 538 D3
16000 ClkC 98682 538 D3
26100 ClkC 98607 539 F3
SE 34th St
- VCVR 98683 568 E3
19300 VCVR 98607 568 F3
19600 ClkC 98607 568 F3
19600 CMAS 98607 568 F3
32000 ClkC 98671 570 C3
32000 WHGL 98671 570 C3
SW 34th St
1800 GSHM 97080 628 J6
W 34th St
1900 VCVR 98660 536 E2
SW 34th Ter
2900 GSHM 97080 628 H6
NE 34th Wy
8600 VCVR 98662 537 F3
SE 34th Wy
6200 GSHM 97080 629 H6
16500 VCVR 98683 568 E3
W 34th Wy
1100 VCVR 98660 536 E2
NE 35th Av
1000 ClkC 98607 569 F2
1000 CMAS 98607 569 F2
1700 PTLD 97232 597 A4
3700 PTLD 97212 597 A2
4100 ClkC 98661 537 A2
4200 PTLD 97211 597 B1
6000 PTLD 97211 567 B6
6300 ClkC 98661 507 A6
8500 ClkC 98665 507 A4
11300 ClkC 98686 507 A1
14000 ClkC 98686 477 A6
16100 ClkC 98642 477 B4
NW 35th Av
800 CMAS 98607 569 D2
2700 PTLD 97210 596 B2
11600 ClkC 98685 506 C1
12700 ClkC 98685 476 D7
SE 35th Av
400 HBRO 97123 593 G6
800 PTLD 97214 597 A7
2500 PTLD 97202 627 A1
2500 PTLD 97214 627 A1
11300 MWKE 97222 657 A3
SW 35th Av
- CmsC 97062 686 B4
- PTLD 97221 626 B4
6400 PTLD 97219 626 B5
10000 PTLD 97219 656 B2
11700 LKOW 97035 656 B3
11700 PTLD 97035 656 B3
NE 35th Cir
3900 ClkC 98661 537 B2
5900 VCVR 98661 537 D2
11900 VCVR 98682 537 J3
14900 VCVR 98682 538 D3
16300 ClkC 98682 538 D1
NW 35th Cir
2500 CMAS 98607 569 B2
SE 35th Cir
1100 TDLE 97060 599 H7
16100 VCVR 98683 568 E3
35th Ct
19300 CmsC 97034 686 B3
19300 LKOW 97034 686 B3
NE 35th Ct
100 HBRO 97124 593 G5
9700 ClkC 98665 507 A3
12600 ClkC 98686 477 A7
18800 ClkC 98642 477 B1
19600 ClkC 98642 447 B7
NW 35th Ct
11400 ClkC 98685 506 B1
13100 ClkC 98685 476 D7
20900 ClkC 98642 446 D6
35600 ClkC 98629 386 D5
SE 35th Ct
300 HBRO 97123 593 G5
8700 MWKE 97222 627 A7
12200 MWKE 97222 657 A4
SW 35th Dr
9600 PTLD 97219 626 B7
9600 PTLD 97219 656 B1
28600 CmsC 97070 716 A7
29900 CmsC 97070 746 A1
SE 35th Lp
14000 VCVR 98683 568 B3
35th Pl
19000 LKOW 97034 686 B3
N 35th Pl
10 RDGF 98642 416 C7
700 ClkC 98642 416 C7
NE 35th Pl
3700 PTLD 97212 597 B2
4200 PTLD 97211 597 B1
6000 PTLD 97211 567 B6
S 35th Pl
- RDGF 98642 446 C4
2900 ClkC 98642 446 C3
2900 RDGF 98642 446 C3
SE 35th Pl
1500 PTLD 97214 597 A7
2000 PTLD 97214 627 A1
3600 PTLD 97202 627 A2
SW 35th Pl
4600 PTLD 97221 626 B3
35th St
10 WHGL 98671 570 C6
E 35th St
100 VCVR 98660 536 G2
100 VCVR 98663 536 G2
NE 35th St
2000 GSHM 97030 599 D6
4000 ClkC 98661 537 B2
9900 VCVR 98662 537 H3

NE 35th St
15500 VCVR 98682 538 D3
16400 ClkC 98682 538 E3
31000 ClkC 98607 540 A3
S 35th St
700 WHGL 98671 570 C7
SE 35th St
- VCVR 98607 568 H3
1300 MthC 97060 599 H7
1300 TDLE 97060 599 H7
14900 VCVR 98683 568 D3
37300 ClkC 98671 570 H3
SW 35th St
1800 GSHM 97080 628 J6
W 35th St
100 VCVR 98660 536 F2
100 VCVR 98663 536 G2
SE 35th Wy
16500 VCVR 98683 568 E3
19700 VCVR 98607 568 J3
W 35th Wy
1100 VCVR 98660 536 E2
NE 36th Av
- ClkC 98661 537 A1
100 HBRO 97124 593 G5
800 CMAS 98607 569 F2
1700 PTLD 97232 597 B4
3600 PTLD 97212 597 B2
4200 PTLD 97211 597 B1
5800 ClkC 98661 507 A7
6500 PTLD 97211 567 B6
8500 ClkC 98665 507 A4
11300 ClkC 98686 507 B2
15900 ClkC 98642 477 B4
15900 ClkC 98686 477 B4
NW 36th Av
2500 CMAS 98607 569 B2
11900 ClkC 98685 506 C1
12200 ClkC 98685 476 C7
22700 ClkC 98642 446 D4
SE 36th Av
300 HBRO 97123 593 G6
500 PTLD 97214 597 B6
2000 PTLD 97202 627 B2
2500 PTLD 97214 627 B1
8400 MWKE 97222 627 A7
8400 PTLD 97222 627 A7
9000 MWKE 97222 657 A1
SW 36th Av
6100 PTLD 97221 626 B4
7300 PTLD 97219 626 B5
NE 36th Cir
8400 VCVR 98662 537 F2
13100 VCVR 98682 538 B3
SE 36th Cir
3600 TDLE 97060 599 H7
14600 VCVR 98683 568 C3
NE 36th Ct
1900 GSHM 97030 599 D6
8100 ClkC 98665 507 A5
11600 ClkC 98686 507 A1
NW 36th Ct
20400 ClkC 98642 446 D6
SW 36th Ct
10000 PTLD 97219 656 B1
NE 36th Pl
4200 ClkC 98661 537 B2
9500 ClkC 98665 507 B3
13100 ClkC 98686 477 B7
SE 36th Pl
3600 PTLD 97202 627 B2
SW 36th Pl
3800 PTLD 97221 626 B2
10100 PTLD 97219 656 B1
36th St
2300 WHGL 98671 570 D4
E 36th St
100 VCVR 98660 536 G2
100 VCVR 98663 536 G2
NE 36th St
8600 VCVR 98662 537 F2
13400 VCVR 98682 538 B2
16300 ClkC 98682 538 E3
26800 ClkC 98607 539 F3
SE 36th St
1000 TDLE 97060 599 H7
13600 VCVR 98683 568 B3
19100 VCVR 98607 568 G3
19700 ClkC 98607 568 H3
SW 36th St
100 GSHM 97080 629 B6
W 36th St
100 VCVR 98663 536 G2
1900 VCVR 98660 536 E2
NE 36th Wy
17600 ClkC 98682 538 F2
SE 36th Wy
17700 VCVR 98683 568 F3
19900 VCVR 98607 568 H3
NE 37th Av
100 CmsC 97013 746 C2
100 HBRO 97123 593 G5
100 HBRO 97124 593 G5
1500 PTLD 97212 597 B4
1500 PTLD 97232 597 B4
4000 PTLD 97211 597 B1
4100 ClkC 98661 537 A2
5000 PTLD 97211 567 B7
9100 ClkC 98665 507 B4
10500 ClkC 98686 507 A2
16500 ClkC 98686 477 B3
24700 ClkC 98642 447 B1
26400 ClkC 98642 417 B7
NW 37th Av
2500 CMAS 98607 569 B1
10900 ClkC 98685 506 C2
15000 ClkC 98685 476 C5
SE 37th Av
100 HBRO 97124 593 G5
400 PTLD 97214 597 B7
2000 PTLD 97214 627 B1
3600 PTLD 97202 627 B1
8200 PTLD 97222 627 B7
9600 MWKE 97222 657 B1
SW 37th Av
3300 PTLD 97221 626 B2
7500 PTLD 97219 626 B6
9800 PTLD 97219 656 B1
11700 LKOW 97035 656 B3
NE 37th Cir
- VCVR 98682 538 B2
200 CMAS 98607 569 E1
8400 VCVR 98662 537 F2
11000 VCVR 98682 537 J2

NE 37th Cir
16300 ClkC 98682 538 E2
NW 37th Cir
1700 CMAS 98607 569 C2
SE 37th Cir
18100 VCVR 98683 568 G4
31600 ClkC 98671 570 B3
SW 37th Cir
300 GSHM 97080 629 B6
37th Ct
3000 WHGL 98671 570 D3
NE 37th Ct
10900 ClkC 98686 507 B2
12900 ClkC 98686 477 B7
NW 37th Ct
11600 ClkC 98685 506 C1
20400 ClkC 98642 446 D6
NE 37th Pl
17900 ClkC 98642 477 B2
37th St
2300 WHGL 98671 570 D4
E 37th St
100 VCVR 98660 536 G2
1800 VCVR 98663 536 J2
NE 37th St
5900 ClkC 98661 537 D2
9900 VCVR 98662 537 H2
11800 VCVR 98682 537 J2
14600 VCVR 98682 538 C2
17700 ClkC 98682 538 G3
30000 ClkC 98607 540 A3
S 37th St
500 WHGL 98671 570 D7
700 ClkC 98671 570 C7
SE 37th St
13500 VCVR 98683 568 B3
39100 ClkC 98671 570 J3
W 37th St
100 VCVR 98663 536 G2
1900 VCVR 98660 536 E2
SW 37th Ter
100 GSHM 97080 629 B6
SE 37th Wy
19600 VCVR 98607 568 H3
NE 38th Av
- ClkC 98665 507 B3
100 HBRO 97124 593 G5
300 CMAS 98607 569 F1
1000 ClkC 98607 569 F1
1600 PTLD 97212 597 B3
1600 PTLD 97232 597 B3
4000 PTLD 97211 597 B1
4900 ClkC 98661 537 B1
5300 ClkC 98661 507 B7
6300 PTLD 97211 567 B6
11000 ClkC 98686 507 B2
NW 38th Av
1600 CMAS 98607 569 C1
3500 ClkC 98607 568 J1
3500 CMAS 98607 568 J1
11000 ClkC 98685 506 C1
12500 ClkC 98685 476 C7
SE 38th Av
500 PTLD 97214 597 B6
1000 HBRO 97123 593 G7
2100 PTLD 97214 627 B1
2500 PTLD 97202 627 B1
9500 MWKE 97222 657 B1
SW 38th Av
3600 PTLD 97221 626 B2
9000 PTLD 97219 626 B7
NE 38th Cir
15700 VCVR 98682 538 D2
SE 38th Cir
15500 VCVR 98683 568 D3
19800 ClkC 98607 568 H3
38th Ct
3100 WHGL 98671 570 D3
NE 38th Ct
500 HBRO 97124 593 G4
8200 ClkC 98665 507 B5
10900 ClkC 98686 507 B2
18800 ClkC 98642 477 B1
NW 38th Ct
13400 ClkC 98685 476 C6
28600 ClkC 98642 416 D5
S 38th Ct
25400 ClkC 98642 446 D1
SE 38th Ct
2900 HBRO 97123 623 G1
NE 38th Dr
1900 GSHM 97030 599 E6
2200 TDLE 97060 599 E6
SE 38th Dr
600 GSHM 97080 629 C6
600 MthC 97080 629 C6
E 38th Lp
1800 VCVR 98663 536 J2
SW 38th Lp
200 GSHM 97080 629 B6
NE 38th Pl
1500 PTLD 97232 597 B4
10000 ClkC 98686 507 B3
SW 38th Pl
4600 PTLD 97221 626 B3
38th St
2800 WHGL 98671 570 D3
E 38th St
100 VCVR 98660 536 G2
100 VCVR 98663 536 G2
NE 38th St
6200 ClkC 98661 537 D2
14900 VCVR 98682 538 D2
16300 ClkC 98682 538 E2
25200 ClkC 98607 539 D3
25200 ClkC 98682 539 D3
SE 38th St
13900 VCVR 98683 568 B3
W 38th St
100 VCVR 98663 536 G2
600 VCVR 98660 536 F2
NE 38th Wy
17300 ClkC 98682 538 F2
SE 38th Wy
19700 VCVR 98607 568 H3
NE 39th Av
10 PTLD 97214 597 B5
10 PTLD 97232 597 B5
100 HBRO 97123 593 G5
200 HBRO 97124 593 G4
1300 PTLD 97213 597 B5
3500 PTLD 97212 597 B1
4000 PTLD 97211 597 B1
4900 ClkC 98661 537 B1
6300 PTLD 97211 567 B6

NE 39th Av
9400 ClkC 98665 507 B3
9900 ClkC 98686 507 B2
13300 ClkC 98686 477 B6
NW 39th Av
13400 ClkC 98685 476 C6
20900 ClkC 98642 446 C6
SE 39th Av
- HBRO 97123 623 G1
10 PTLD 97214 597 B7
10 PTLD 97232 597 B5
100 HBRO 97123 593 G5
100 HBRO 97124 593 G5
2100 PTLD 97214 627 B1
2400 PTLD 97202 627 B2
8900 MWKE 97222 627 B7
8900 MWKE 97222 657 B1
8900 PTLD 97222 627 B7
SW 39th Av
5700 PTLD 97221 626 B4
8100 PTLD 97219 626 B6
11500 PTLD 97219 656 A2
SE 39th Cir
15500 VCVR 98683 568 D3
39th Ct
3100 WHGL 98671 570 D3
NE 39th Ct
500 HBRO 97124 593 G4
3800 ClkC 98661 537 B2
6800 ClkC 98661 507 B6
SE 39th Ct
700 HBRO 97123 593 G6
12600 MWKE 97222 657 B4
SW 39th Dr
4500 PTLD 97221 626 B3
SE 39th Lp
2500 HBRO 97123 623 G1
39th St
100 WHGL 98671 570 D4
E 39th St
100 VCVR 98660 536 G2
100 VCVR 98663 536 H2
NE 39th St
3200 ClkC 98661 537 B2
3200 VCVR 98663 537 A2
9900 VCVR 98662 537 H2
10900 VCVR 98682 537 J2
12200 VCVR 98682 538 C2
16100 ClkC 98682 538 E2
23700 ClkC 98682 539 C2
24200 ClkC 98607 539 D2
SE 39th St
17900 VCVR 98683 568 F3
37300 ClkC 98671 570 H3
W 39th St
100 VCVR 98660 536 F2
100 VCVR 98663 536 G2
SE 39th Wy
19000 VCVR 98683 568 G3
E 40th Av
1100 VCVR 98661 537 B5
N 40th Av
- ClkC 98642 416 D6
- RDGF 98642 416 D6
NE 40th Av
100 HBRO 97123 593 G5
300 HBRO 97124 593 G4
1500 PTLD 97213 597 B4
1500 PTLD 97232 597 B4
3900 PTLD 97212 597 B1
4000 PTLD 97211 597 B1
4400 ClkC 98661 537 B1
5200 PTLD 97211 567 B7
6000 ClkC 98661 507 B7
7000 ClkC 98665 507 B6
11900 ClkC 98686 507 B1
16400 ClkC 98686 477 B3
19900 ClkC 98642 447 B7
31000 ClkC 98629 417 B2
NW 40th Av
1500 CMAS 98607 569 C1
11700 ClkC 98685 506 C1
13100 ClkC 98685 476 C6
SE 40th Av
200 HBRO 97123 593 G5
1100 PTLD 97214 597 B7
2200 PTLD 97214 627 B1
2400 PTLD 97202 627 B1
8600 MWKE 97222 627 B7
9400 MWKE 97222 657 B2
SW 40th Av
4100 PTLD 97221 626 B3
7700 PTLD 97219 626 B6
9600 PTLD 97219 656 D4
NE 40th Cir
700 CMAS 98607 569 F1
4800 ClkC 98661 537 C2
15500 VCVR 98682 538 D2
31500 ClkC 98607 540 B2
SE 40th Cir
15500 VCVR 98683 568 D3
36400 ClkC 98671 570 G4
40th Ct
2300 WHGL 98671 570 D3
SE 40th Ct
600 HBRO 97123 593 G6
SW 40th Ct
7500 PTLD 97219 626 B6
NE 40th Dr
8800 ClkC 98665 507 B4
N 40th Pl
10 RDGF 98642 416 D7
NE 40th Pl
- VCVR 98682 537 J2
8800 ClkC 98665 507 B4
11800 ClkC 98686 507 B1
15300 VCVR 98682 538 D2
SW 40th Pl
4000 PTLD 97221 626 B2
40th St
2800 WHGL 98671 570 D3
E 40th St
500 VCVR 98663 536 G2
NE 40th St
100 VCVR 98660 536 G2
100 VCVR 98663 536 G2
5400 ClkC 98661 537 C2
6500 VCVR 98661 537 D2
6900 VCVR 98662 537 E2
15800 VCVR 98682 538 D2
16400 ClkC 98682 538 E2
NW 40th St
100 VCVR 98663 536 G2
1100 VCVR 98660 536 E2

SE 40th St
100 TDLE 97060 599 G7
500 TDLE 97060 629 G1
18900 VCVR 98683 568 G3
19100 VCVR 98607 568 G3
20100 ClkC 98607 568 J3
20100 CMAS 98607 568 J3
29200 ClkC 98671 570 A4
29200 WHGL 98671 570 A4
E 41st Av
1400 VCVR 98661 537 B5
NE 41st Av
10 PTLD 97214 597 B5
10 PTLD 97215 597 B5
100 HBRO 97123 593 G5
300 HBRO 97124 593 G4
500 PTLD 97232 597 B5
900 CMAS 98607 569 F1
1500 PTLD 97213 597 B4
3900 PTLD 97212 597 B1
4000 PTLD 97211 597 B1
5800 ClkC 98661 507 B7
6000 PTLD 97211 567 B6
8800 ClkC 98665 507 B4
11500 ClkC 98686 507 B1
21900 ClkC 98642 447 B5
29700 ClkC 98629 417 C4
NW 41st Av
14800 ClkC 98685 476 C5
15300 ClkC 98642 476 C4
19100 ClkC 98642 446 C7
31300 ClkC 98642 416 C2
33200 ClkC 98642 386 D7
SE 41st Av
10 PTLD 97214 597 B6
10 PTLD 97215 597 B6
10 PTLD 97232 597 B5
100 HBRO 97123 593 G5
100 HBRO 97124 593 G5
2100 PTLD 97214 627 B1
2800 HBRO 97123 623 G1
3700 PTLD 97202 627 B2
8600 MWKE 97222 627 B7
8900 MWKE 97222 657 B1
SW 41st Av
4200 PTLD 97221 626 B3
8000 PTLD 97219 626 A6
9700 PTLD 97219 656 D3
11700 LKOW 97035 656 A3
NE 41st Cir
1500 VCVR 98663 536 J2
5800 ClkC 98661 537 C2
17000 ClkC 98682 538 F2
NW 41st Cir
1500 CMAS 98607 569 C1
SE 41st Cir
19500 ClkC 98607 568 H3
41st Ct
3100 WHGL 98671 570 D3
NE 41st Ct
3800 ClkC 98661 537 B2
6000 ClkC 98661 507 B7
9900 ClkC 98665 507 B3
10300 ClkC 98686 507 B2
13000 ClkC 98686 477 B7
NW 41st Ct
35900 ClkC 98674 386 C5
SE 41st Ct
200 GSHM 97080 629 B7
10200 MWKE 97222 657 B2
SE 41st Dr
- VCVR 98607 568 G3
18400 VCVR 98683 568 G3
SE 41st Lp
17900 VCVR 98683 568 F3
N 41st Pl
- RDGF 98642 416 D6
NE 41st Pl
- PTLD 97212 597 B3
- PTLD 97213 597 A3
- PTLD 97232 597 A3
SW 41st Pl
3800 PTLD 97221 626 A2
41st St
1700 WHGL 98671 570 D4
NE 41st St
- VCVR 98682 537 J2
100 VCVR 98660 536 G2
100 VCVR 98663 536 G2
3300 VCVR 98663 537 A2
6400 ClkC 98661 537 D2
7200 VCVR 98661 537 E2
7200 VCVR 98662 537 E2
11700 VCVR 98682 538 A2
17200 ClkC 98682 538 F2
NW 41st St
100 VCVR 98663 536 G2
1100 VCVR 98660 536 E2
SE 41st St
19600 ClkC 98607 568 H3
NE 41st Wy
5200 ClkC 98661 537 C2
SE 41st Wy
18000 VCVR 98683 568 F3
NE 42nd Av
800 PTLD 97232 597 B4
1400 PTLD 97213 597 B4
3500 PTLD 97212 597 B2
3900 ClkC 98661 537 B2
4000 PTLD 97211 597 B1
4100 PTLD 97218 597 B1
5000 PTLD 97211 567 B7
5000 PTLD 97218 567 B7
5600 ClkC 98661 507 B7
9000 ClkC 98665 507 B5
11900 ClkC 98686 507 B1
12600 ClkC 98686 477 B7
21900 ClkC 98642 447 B4
29600 ClkC 98629 417 C4
NW 42nd Av
2600 CMAS 98607 569 B1
13400 ClkC 98685 476 C6
SE 42nd Av
- PTLD 97215 597 B7
900 PTLD 97214 597 B6
2000 PTLD 97214 627 B1
2000 PTLD 97215 627 B1
2700 HBRO 97123 623 G1
3500 PTLD 97202 627 B2
5900 PTLD 97206 627 B6
8700 MWKE 97222 627 B7
9000 MWKE 97222 657 B1
SW 42nd Av
6700 PTLD 97219 626 A5
6700 PTLD 97221 626 A5

STREET Block	City	ZIP	Map#	Grid
SW 42nd Av				
10300	PTLD	97219	656	A1
NE 42nd Cir				
-	VCVR	98661	537	D2
600	CMAS	98607	569	F1
2700	VCVR	98663	536	J2
2700	VCVR	98663	537	A2
5200	ClkC	98661	537	C2
27200	ClkC	98607	539	G2
SE 42nd Cir				
400	TDLE	97060	629	G1
18400	VCVR	98683	568	G3
19400	ClkC	98607	568	H4
42nd Ct				
1800	WHGL	98671	570	D4
NE 42nd Ct				
500	HBRO	97124	593	G4
5100	ClkC	98661	537	B1
8700	ClkC	98665	507	B4
12000	ClkC	98686	507	B1
18900	ClkC	98642	477	B1
22000	ClkC	98642	447	B4
NW 42nd Ct				
12200	ClkC	98685	506	C1
13200	ClkC	98685	476	C6
38800	ClkC	98674	386	D2
SE 42nd Ct				
12200	MWKE	97222	657	B4
N 42nd Pl				
-	RDGF	98642	416	D6
SE 42nd Pl				
500	HBRO	97123	593	G6
SW 42nd Pl				
4500	PTLD	97221	626	A3
42nd St				
2000	WHGL	98671	570	D4
NE 42nd St				
2800	VCVR	98663	537	A2
6400	ClkC	98661	537	D2
10600	VCVR	98682	537	H2
14300	VCVR	98682	538	C2
16500	ClkC	98682	538	E2
26100	ClkC	98607	539	F2
NW 42nd St				
200	VCVR	98660	536	G2
SE 42nd St				
600	TDLE	97060	629	G1
18000	VCVR	98683	568	F3
19600	ClkC	98607	568	H4
NE 42nd Wy				
3600	ClkC	98661	537	A2
SE 42nd Wy				
200	HBRO	97123	593	G5
NE 43rd Av				
10	PTLD	97215	597	B5
100	HBRO	97123	593	G5
100	HBRO	97124	593	G5
100	WasC	97124	593	G5
300	CMAS	98607	569	F1
700	ClkC	98607	569	F1
1700	PTLD	97213	597	B3
5200	PTLD	97218	567	B7
6900	ClkC	98661	507	B6
6900	ClkC	98665	507	B6
9900	ClkC	98686	507	B3
12400	ClkC	98686	477	B7
NW 43rd Av				
1600	CMAS	98607	569	C1
11400	ClkC	98685	506	C1
14900	ClkC	98685	476	C5
21100	ClkC	98642	446	C5
27000	ClkC	98642	416	C4
SE 43rd Av				
100	HBRO	97123	593	G5
100	HBRO	97124	593	G5
1300	PTLD	97214	597	B7
1300	PTLD	97215	597	B7
2400	PTLD	97206	627	B1
2400	PTLD	97215	627	B1
8700	MWKE	97222	627	B7
9500	MWKE	97222	657	B1
SW 43rd Av				
3900	PTLD	97221	626	A2
8200	PTLD	97219	626	A6
11500	PTLD	97219	656	A2
NE 43rd Cir				
11000	VCVR	98682	537	J2
12300	VCVR	98682	538	A2
16500	ClkC	98682	538	E2
NW 43rd Cir				
1500	CMAS	98607	569	C1
SE 43rd Cir				
400	TDLE	97060	629	G1
43rd Ct				
1300	WHGL	98671	570	D5
N 43rd Ct				
-	RDGF	98642	416	D6
NE 43rd Ct				
5500	ClkC	98661	507	B7
13600	ClkC	98686	477	B6
NW 43rd Ct				
11500	ClkC	98685	506	C1
13200	ClkC	98685	476	C7
32800	ClkC	98642	416	C1
SE 43rd Ct				
2800	HBRO	97123	623	G1
SE 43rd Dr				
500	TDLE	97060	629	G1
SE 43rd Ln				
-	PTLD	97206	627	B4
18300	VCVR	98683	568	G4
N 43rd Pl				
-	RDGF	98642	416	D7
NE 43rd Pl				
10500	ClkC	98686	507	B2
NW 43rd Pl				
18700	ClkC	98642	476	C1
SE 43rd Pl				
-	HBRO	97123	593	G6
4300	TDLE	97060	629	G1
43rd St				
2000	WHGL	98671	570	D4
NE 43rd St				
100	VCVR	98660	536	G1
1200	VCVR	98663	536	H1
2900	VCVR	98663	537	A2
6400	VCVR	98661	537	D2
6900	VCVR	98661	537	E2
6900	VCVR	98662	537	E2
10400	VCVR	98682	537	H2
15300	VCVR	98682	538	D2
16200	ClkC	98682	538	E2
24400	ClkC	98682	539	D2
NW 43rd St				
100	VCVR	98660	536	G1
100	VCVR	98663	536	G1
NE 43rd Wy				
5500	ClkC	98661	537	C2
7200	VCVR	98662	537	E2
15800	VCVR	98682	538	D2
16300	ClkC	98682	538	E2
SE 43rd Wy				
18000	VCVR	98683	568	F4
NE 44th Av				
10	PTLD	97215	597	B5
1700	PTLD	97213	597	B3
4800	ClkC	98661	537	B1
9400	ClkC	98665	507	B3
12000	ClkC	98686	507	B1
12400	ClkC	98686	477	B7
NW 44th Av				
-	PTLD	97210	595	J1
-	PTLD	97210	596	A1
1400	CMAS	98607	569	C1
13700	ClkC	98685	476	C6
31400	ClkC	98642	416	C2
SE 44th Av				
10	PTLD	97213	597	B5
10	PTLD	97215	597	B6
300	PTLD	97214	597	B6
2000	HBRO	97123	593	G7
2000	HBRO	97123	623	G1
2000	PTLD	97215	627	B1
8200	PTLD	97206	627	B7
9600	MWKE	97222	657	B1
SW 44th Av				
3300	PTLD	97221	626	A2
9100	PTLD	97219	626	A7
NE 44th Cir				
-	VCVR	98662	537	E1
300	CMAS	98607	569	E1
6100	ClkC	98661	537	D1
6900	VCVR	98661	537	E1
14900	VCVR	98682	538	C2
NE 44th Ct				
9100	ClkC	98665	507	B4
9900	ClkC	98686	507	B3
12600	ClkC	98686	477	B7
NW 44th Ct				
14000	ClkC	98685	476	C5
33100	ClkC	98642	386	C7
33100	ClkC	98642	416	C1
SE 44th Ct				
2700	HBRO	97123	623	G1
9500	MWKE	97222	657	B1
SE 44th Ln				
18300	VCVR	98683	568	G4
N 44th Pl				
-	RDGF	98642	416	D6
NE 44th Pl				
-	ClkC	98607	539	E2
44th St				
2100	WHGL	98671	570	D4
NE 44th St				
100	VCVR	98660	536	G1
1200	VCVR	98663	536	H1
2900	VCVR	98663	537	A1
3300	ClkC	98661	537	B2
10400	VCVR	98682	537	H2
12200	VCVR	98682	538	B2
16300	ClkC	98682	538	E2
23200	ClkC	98682	539	C2
26100	ClkC	98607	539	F2
NE 44th St SR-500				
23800	ClkC	98682	539	C2
NW 44th St				
100	VCVR	98660	536	G1
100	VCVR	98663	536	G1
NE 44th Wy				
7200	VCVR	98662	537	E1
SE 44th Wy				
100	HBRO	97123	593	G5
18000	VCVR	98683	568	F4
N 45th Av				
10	RDGF	98642	416	D6
100	ClkC	98642	416	D6
NE 45th Av				
10	PTLD	97215	597	C5
1500	PTLD	97213	597	C3
4100	ClkC	98661	537	B2
5400	ClkC	98661	507	B7
6000	PTLD	97218	567	C6
8800	ClkC	98665	507	B4
10300	ClkC	98686	507	B2
13800	ClkC	98686	477	B6
19900	ClkC	98686	447	C7
25900	ClkC	98642	417	C7
25900	ClkC	98642	447	C1
NW 45th Av				
1600	CMAS	98607	569	C1
S 45th Av				
10	ClkC	98642	416	D7
10	RDGF	98642	416	D7
700	ClkC	98642	446	D1
700	RDGF	98642	446	D1
SE 45th Av				
10	PTLD	97213	597	C5
10	PTLD	97215	597	C6
1800	HBRO	97123	593	G7
2000	PTLD	97215	627	C1
2200	HBRO	97123	623	G1
2900	PTLD	97206	627	B2
9100	MWKE	97222	657	B1
13000	CmsC	97222	657	B5
SW 45th Av				
4500	PTLD	97221	626	A4
6400	PTLD	97219	626	A5
11000	PTLD	97219	656	A2
11700	LKOW	97035	656	A3
NE 45th Cir				
6300	ClkC	98661	537	D1
12600	VCVR	98682	538	A2
45th Ct				
400	WHGL	98671	570	D5
10200	MWKE	97222	657	B2
NE 45th Ct				
-	ClkC	98661	537	B1
14000	ClkC	98686	477	C6
NW 45th Ct				
13600	ClkC	98685	476	C6
SE 45th Ct				
2700	HBRO	97123	623	G1
SW 45th Dr				
8600	PTLD	97219	626	A7
26000	CmsC	97070	715	J6
26000	CmsC	97070	716	A4
NE 45th Pl				
4600	ClkC	98661	537	B1
5200	PTLD	97218	567	C7
9500	ClkC	98665	507	B3
9800	ClkC	98686	507	B3
13700	ClkC	98686	477	C6
SE 45th Pl				
600	VCVR	98661	537	B7
8400	MWKE	97222	627	B7
8400	PTLD	97206	627	B7
8400	PTLD	97222	627	B7
45th St				
-	ClkC	98671	570	D6
100	WHGL	98671	570	D6
NE 45th St				
-	VCVR	98662	537	E1
100	ClkC	98663	536	G1
100	VCVR	98660	536	G1
100	VCVR	98663	536	G1
2600	VCVR	98663	537	A1
3600	ClkC	98661	537	A1
7200	VCVR	98661	537	E1
10600	VCVR	98682	537	H1
15200	VCVR	98682	538	D2
28900	ClkC	98607	539	H2
NW 45th St				
100	ClkC	98663	536	G1
100	VCVR	98660	536	F1
100	VCVR	98663	536	F1
SE 45th Ter				
-	GSHM	97080	629	B7
NE 45th Wy				
6400	ClkC	98661	537	D1
6400	VCVR	98661	537	D1
NE 46th Av				
-	ClkC	98686	507	B3
1500	PTLD	97213	597	C4
5400	ClkC	98661	507	B7
6600	PTLD	97218	567	C6
13700	ClkC	98686	477	C6
25500	ClkC	98642	447	C1
NW 46th Av				
13000	ClkC	98685	476	C7
18800	ClkC	98642	476	C1
SE 46th Av				
500	PTLD	97215	597	C6
900	MthC	97060	629	G1
900	TDLE	97060	629	G1
2100	PTLD	97215	627	C1
2300	PTLD	97206	627	C1
4900	MWKE	97222	657	C1
SW 46th Av				
6700	PTLD	97219	626	A5
6900	PTLD	97221	626	A5
9600	PTLD	97219	656	A1
19100	TLTN	97062	685	J4
19100	TLTN	97062	686	A4
NE 46th Cir				
4400	ClkC	98661	537	B1
NW 46th Cir				
2300	CMAS	98607	569	C1
NE 46th Ct				
9600	ClkC	98665	507	B3
12300	ClkC	98686	507	C1
30500	ClkC	98629	417	C3
NW 46th Ct				
2500	CMAS	98607	569	B1
13600	ClkC	98685	476	B6
SE 46th Ct				
11500	MWKE	97222	657	B3
SE 46th Dr				
10	GSHM	97080	629	B7
NE 46th Pl				
5300	PTLD	97218	567	C7
SW 46th Pl				
6200	PTLD	97221	626	A4
NE 46th St				
2400	VCVR	98663	536	J1
2800	VCVR	98663	537	A1
5400	ClkC	98661	537	C1
10400	VCVR	98682	537	H1
12200	VCVR	98682	538	A1
27200	ClkC	98607	539	G2
NW 46th St				
200	ClkC	98663	536	G1
200	VCVR	98663	536	F1
SE 46th St				
20100	ClkC	98607	568	H4
38300	ClkC	98671	570	J4
NE 46th Wy				
29600	ClkC	98607	539	J2
SE 46th Wy				
20100	ClkC	98607	568	H4
NE 47th Av				
10	PTLD	97215	597	C5
2700	PTLD	97213	597	C2
4000	PTLD	97218	597	C2
4100	ClkC	98661	537	B1
6800	ClkC	98661	507	B6
8500	PTLD	97218	567	C4
9400	ClkC	98665	507	C3
11200	ClkC	98686	507	C2
17800	ClkC	98686	477	C2
22900	ClkC	98642	447	C4
NW 47th Av				
1900	CMAS	98607	539	C7
13400	ClkC	98685	476	B6
18500	ClkC	98642	476	B1
SE 47th Av				
10	PTLD	97213	597	C6
200	HBRO	97123	593	H5
500	PTLD	97215	597	C6
2300	PTLD	97206	627	C1
2400	PTLD	97215	627	C1
9200	MWKE	97222	657	B1
SW 47th Av				
4500	PTLD	97221	626	A3
7700	PTLD	97219	626	A6
9600	PTLD	97219	656	D3
11700	LKOW	97035	656	A3
NE 47th Cir				
-	ClkC	98665	507	C4
15400	VCVR	98682	538	D1
SE 47th Cir				
10	GSHM	97080	629	B7
NE 47th Ct				
9700	ClkC	98665	507	C3
12000	ClkC	98686	507	C1
NW 47th Ct				
-	ClkC	98642	386	C7
-	ClkC	98642	476	B2
SW 47th Dr				
4100	PTLD	97221	626	A2
N 47th Pl				
700	ClkC	98642	416	E6
700	RDGF	98642	416	E6
NE 47th Pl				
200	HBRO	97124	593	H5
6300	PTLD	97218	567	C6
SW 47th Pl				
2300	MthC	97221	626	A1
2300	PTLD	97221	626	A1
NE 47th Rd				
-	ClkC	98665	507	C4
47th St				
1200	WHGL	98671	570	E5
NE 47th St				
2500	VCVR	98663	536	J1
2900	VCVR	98663	537	A1
5300	ClkC	98661	537	D1
6400	VCVR	98661	537	D1
10500	VCVR	98682	537	J1
14900	VCVR	98682	538	D1
SE 47th St				
1200	HBRO	97123	593	H6
SW 47th Wy				
-	PTLD	97221	626	A2
NE 48th Av				
1200	HBRO	97124	593	H3
1500	PTLD	97213	597	C4
5200	ClkC	98661	537	B1
5500	PTLD	97218	567	C7
5600	ClkC	98661	507	B7
11200	ClkC	98686	507	C2
13700	ClkC	98686	477	C6
NW 48th Av				
100	PTLD	97210	596	A6
100	PTLD	97221	596	A6
13800	ClkC	98685	476	B6
SE 48th Av				
500	PTLD	97215	597	C6
1800	HBRO	97123	593	H7
2100	PTLD	97215	627	C1
2200	HBRO	97123	623	H1
7800	PTLD	97206	627	C6
9700	MWKE	97222	657	C1
SW 48th Av				
3100	MthC	97221	626	A2
3100	PTLD	97221	626	A2
7400	PTLD	97219	626	A5
9600	PTLD	97219	656	A1
19100	TLTN	97062	685	J4
NE 48th Cir				
6500	ClkC	98661	537	D1
6500	VCVR	98661	537	D1
11000	VCVR	98682	537	J1
15800	VCVR	98682	538	E1
19900	ClkC	98682	538	J1
NE 48th Ct				
30500	ClkC	98629	417	C3
NW 48th Ct				
12300	ClkC	98685	476	B7
SW 48th Dr				
300	PTLD	97210	596	A6
300	PTLD	97221	596	A6
10100	PTLD	97219	656	A1
10300	PTLD	97219	655	J1
NE 48th Pl				
4700	PTLD	97218	597	C1
SE 48th Pl				
1000	TDLE	97060	629	H1
SW 48th Pl				
3600	MthC	97221	626	A2
4000	PTLD	97221	626	A2
48th St				
-	WHGL	98671	570	E3
NE 48th St				
2600	VCVR	98663	536	J1
2900	VCVR	98663	537	A1
4000	ClkC	98661	537	B1
10800	VCVR	98682	537	H1
14800	VCVR	98682	538	D1
NW 48th St				
1100	VCVR	98663	536	F1
SE 48th Ter				
10	GSHM	97080	629	B7
10	MthC	97080	629	B7
NE 48th Wy				
-	ClkC	98661	537	C1
28300	ClkC	98607	539	H2
NE 49th Av				
100	HBRO	97123	593	H5
100	WasC	97124	593	H5
300	HBRO	97124	593	H4
2700	PTLD	97213	597	C2
4000	PTLD	97218	597	C1
4600	ClkC	98661	537	C1
5400	ClkC	98661	507	C7
6000	PTLD	97218	567	C7
NW 49th Av				
13500	ClkC	98685	476	B6
18400	ClkC	98642	476	B1
37900	ClkC	98674	386	C3
SE 49th Av				
500	PTLD	97215	597	C7
2200	HBRO	97123	593	H7
2200	HBRO	97123	623	H1
2400	PTLD	97206	627	C1
2400	PTLD	97215	627	C1
9600	MWKE	97222	657	C2
SW 49th Av				
4600	PTLD	97221	626	A3
7500	PTLD	97219	626	A6
9800	PTLD	97219	656	A1
11700	WasC	97035	656	A3
19700	TLTN	97062	685	J4
NE 49th Cir				
14500	VCVR	98682	538	C1
21200	ClkC	98682	539	A1
28300	ClkC	98607	539	H1
NW 49th Cir				
1100	ClkC	98663	536	G1
SE 49th Cir				
10	GSHM	97080	629	B7
NE 49th Ct				
6000	ClkC	98661	507	C7
11900	ClkC	98686	507	C1
13500	ClkC	98686	477	C6
NW 49th Ct				
900	VCVR	98663	536	F1
SE 49th Ct				
100	HBRO	97123	593	H5
100	HBRO	97124	593	H5
100	WasC	97123	593	H5
SW 49th Ct				
7400	PTLD	97219	626	A5
10000	PTLD	97219	656	A1
19100	TLTN	97062	685	J4
SW 49th Dr				
5100	PTLD	97221	626	A3
NE 49th Pl				
12200	ClkC	98686	507	C1
SE 49th Pl				
6800	PTLD	97206	627	C5
49th St				
1000	ClkC	98671	570	E4
1000	WHGL	98671	570	E4
NE 49th St				
1200	VCVR	98663	536	J1
2700	VCVR	98663	537	A1
5200	ClkC	98661	537	C1
11200	VCVR	98682	537	J1
11900	VCVR	98682	538	C1
19900	ClkC	98682	538	J1
31200	ClkC	98607	540	B1
NW 49th St				
200	ClkC	98663	536	F1
800	VCVR	98663	536	F1
NE 49th Wy				
14700	VCVR	98682	538	C1
NE 50th Av				
10	PTLD	97215	597	C6
1500	PTLD	97213	597	C3
3400	VCVR	98661	537	C2
5000	ClkC	98661	537	C2
5700	PTLD	97218	567	C7
6800	ClkC	98661	507	C6
9300	ClkC	98665	507	C4
9400	ClkC	98686	507	C3
14800	ClkC	98686	477	C1
19200	ClkC	98604	477	C1
19500	ClkC	98686	447	C7
19800	ClkC	98642	447	C3
19900	ClkC	98604	447	C5
NW 50th Av				
13900	ClkC	98685	476	B6
SE 50th Av				
10	PTLD	97213	597	C6
10	PTLD	97215	597	C6
100	HBRO	97123	593	H5
100	HBRO	97124	593	H5
2000	PTLD	97215	627	C1
3500	PTLD	97206	627	C2
9800	MWKE	97222	657	C1
SW 50th Av				
-	PTLD	97219	626	A4
3600	MthC	97221	626	A2
6100	PTLD	97221	626	A4
8800	PTLD	97219	625	J7
9900	PTLD	97219	655	J1
19000	TLTN	97062	685	J4
NE 50th Cir				
3100	VCVR	98663	537	A1
4800	ClkC	98661	537	C1
13100	VCVR	98682	538	B1
NE 50th Ct				
9200	ClkC	98665	507	C4
NW 50th Ct				
14100	ClkC	98685	476	B6
SW 50th Dr				
5600	PTLD	97221	625	J4
5600	PTLD	97221	626	A4
N 50th Pl				
10	RDGF	98642	416	E6
NE 50th Pl				
4700	PTLD	97218	597	C1
5600	ClkC	98661	507	C7
5900	PTLD	97218	567	C7
50th St				
1600	ClkC	98671	570	E4
1600	WHGL	98671	570	E4
NE 50th St				
4000	ClkC	98661	537	B1
14000	VCVR	98682	538	C1
24200	ClkC	98682	539	D1
28200	ClkC	98607	539	H1
NW 50th St				
100	ClkC	98663	536	G1
900	VCVR	98663	536	F1
NE 50th Wy				
2100	HBRO	97124	593	H2
NE 51st Av				
1100	HBRO	97124	593	H3
1500	PTLD	97213	597	C4
7300	ClkC	98661	507	C5
8600	ClkC	98665	507	C4
10100	ClkC	98686	507	C3
NW 51st Av				
14300	ClkC	98685	476	B5
17300	ClkC	98642	476	B4
22900	ClkC	98642	446	B4
26000	ClkC	98642	416	B2
26000	RDGF	98642	416	B6
SE 51st Av				
800	PTLD	97215	597	C6
1100	HBRO	97123	593	H6
1500	PTLD	97215	627	C1
2900	PTLD	97206	627	C2
9700	MWKE	97222	657	C1
12900	CmsC	97222	657	C4
SW 51st Av				
8800	PTLD	97219	625	J7
9600	PTLD	97219	655	J1
19000	TLTN	97062	685	J4
NE 51st Cir				
6600	ClkC	98661	537	D1
10400	VCVR	98682	537	H1
28200	ClkC	98607	539	H1
51st Ct				
-	WHGL	98671	570	E4
NE 51st Ct				
3200	VCVR	98661	537	C3
5600	ClkC	98661	507	C7
11000	ClkC	98686	507	C2
NW 51st Ct				
13900	ClkC	98685	476	B6
SW 51st Pl				
4200	PTLD	97221	626	A1
7600	PTLD	97219	625	J6
51st St				
400	WHGL	98671	570	E5
1200	ClkC	98671	570	E5
NE 51st St				
2200	VCVR	98663	536	J1
3400	VCVR	98663	537	A1
4000	ClkC	98661	537	B1
7200	ClkC	98662	537	E1
7200	VCVR	98661	537	E1
7200	VCVR	98662	537	E1
11000	VCVR	98682	537	J1
14600	VCVR	98682	538	C1
25000	ClkC	98682	539	D1
NW 51st St				
100	ClkC	98663	536	G1
900	VCVR	98663	506	F7
NE 51st Wy				
7500	VCVR	98662	537	E1
29700	ClkC	98607	539	J1
NE 52nd Av				
10	PTLD	97215	597	C6
1900	HBRO	97124	593	H2
2700	PTLD	97213	597	C3
4100	PTLD	97218	597	C1
4600	ClkC	98661	537	C1
5800	PTLD	97218	567	D6
9000	ClkC	98665	507	C4
23200	ClkC	98604	447	C4
NW 52nd Av				
14100	ClkC	98685	476	B5
SE 52nd Av				
10	PTLD	97213	597	C6
10	PTLD	97215	597	C6
1300	HBRO	97123	593	H7
2100	PTLD	97215	627	C1
2300	PTLD	97206	627	C5
10400	MWKE	97222	657	C2
SW 52nd Av				
4000	MthC	97221	625	J3
6700	PTLD	97219	625	J5
6700	PTLD	97221	625	J5
9800	PTLD	97219	655	J1
19100	TLTN	97062	685	J4
NE 52nd Cir				
4700	ClkC	98661	537	B1
14500	VCVR	98682	538	C1
52nd Ct				
2000	WHGL	98671	570	E4
NE 52nd Ct				
1500	HBRO	97124	593	H3
7800	ClkC	98661	507	C5
7800	ClkC	98665	507	C5
NW 52nd Ct				
14500	ClkC	98685	476	B5
SE 52nd Ct				
1100	HBRO	97123	593	H6
11100	MWKE	97222	657	C3
SW 52nd Ct				
19100	TLTN	97062	685	J4
NE 52nd Pl				
5700	ClkC	98661	537	D1
SE 52nd Pl				
900	PTLD	97215	597	C7
5000	HBRO	97123	593	H7
SW 52nd Pl				
3600	MthC	97221	625	J2
3600	MthC	97221	626	A2
NE 52nd St				
-	ClkC	98607	540	F1
2200	VCVR	98663	536	J1
3200	ClkC	98661	537	A1
3200	VCVR	98663	537	A1
7500	VCVR	98662	537	E1
7600	ClkC	98662	537	E1
13900	VCVR	98682	538	C1
NW 52nd St				
200	ClkC	98663	506	F7
200	VCVR	98663	506	F7
NE 52nd Wy				
12500	VCVR	98682	538	A1
25900	ClkC	98682	539	F1
NE 53rd Av				
10	PTLD	97215	597	C6
100	HBRO	97123	593	H5
100	HBRO	97124	593	H5
1500	PTLD	97213	597	C4
5600	PTLD	97218	567	D7
7400	ClkC	98661	507	C5
9900	ClkC	98665	507	C3
9900	ClkC	98686	507	C3
17300	ClkC	98686	477	C2
24200	ClkC	98604	447	C3
NW 53rd Av				
13900	ClkC	98685	476	B6
SE 53rd Av				
10	PTLD	97213	597	C6
10	PTLD	97215	597	C6
1400	HBRO	97123	593	H7
2100	PTLD	97215	627	C1
2200	HBRO	97123	623	H1
2300	PTLD	97206	627	C1
9900	MWKE	97222	657	C1
SW 53rd Av				
4100	PTLD	97221	625	J2
6800	PTLD	97219	625	J5
9800	PTLD	97219	655	J1
19500	TLTN	97062	685	J4
28100	CmsC	97070	715	J6
NE 53rd Cir				
2000	VCVR	98663	506	J7
3800	ClkC	98661	507	B7
5400	ClkC	98661	537	C1
NE 53rd Ct				
1700	HBRO	97124	593	H3
4300	PTLD	97218	597	C1
5100	ClkC	98661	537	C1
5300	ClkC	98661	507	C7
11100	ClkC	98686	507	C2
17900	ClkC	98686	477	C2
25600	ClkC	98642	447	D1
NW 53rd Ct				
20900	ClkC	98642	446	B6
SE 53rd Ct				
1100	HBRO	97123	593	H6
SW 53rd Ct				
5300	PTLD	97221	625	J3
19100	TLTN	97062	685	J4
NW 53rd Dr				
1000	PTLD	97210	595	J4
1100	MthC	97210	595	H2
1100	MthC	97210	596	A4
2900	MthC	97229	595	H2
SE 53rd Pl				
10400	MWKE	97222	657	C2
SW 53rd Pl				
-	PTLD	97219	625	J6
4000	MthC	97221	625	J2
4000	PTLD	97221	625	J2
53rd St				
400	WHGL	98671	570	E5
NE 53rd St				
2200	VCVR	98663	506	J7
2500	VCVR	98663	507	A7
2800	VCVR	98663	537	A1
5600	ClkC	98661	507	C7
5600	ClkC	98661	537	C1
7500	ClkC	98662	537	E1
9200	VCVR	98662	537	G1
13900	VCVR	98682	538	C1
23700	ClkC	98682	539	D1
30000	ClkC	98607	539	J1
30000	ClkC	98607	540	A1
NW 53rd St				
400	VCVR	98663	506	F7
NE 53rd Wy				
-	ClkC	98662	537	F1
-	VCVR	98662	537	F1
NE 54th Av				
1200	HBRO	97124	593	J3
3700	VCVR	98661	537	C2
4100	PTLD	97213	597	D1
4100	PTLD	97218	597	D1
4900	ClkC	98661	537	C1
5200	PTLD	97218	567	D7
6900	ClkC	98661	507	C6
11100	ClkC	98686	507	C2
SE 54th Av				
10	HBRO	97124	593	H5
500	PTLD	97215	597	C6
800	WasC	97123	593	H6
1600	HBRO	97123	593	H7
2100	PTLD	97215	627	C1
2900	PTLD	97206	627	C2
10200	MWKE	97222	657	C2
SW 54th Av				
-	MthC	97221	625	J1
6700	PTLD	97221	625	J5
7900	PTLD	97219	625	J6
9300	PTLD	97219	655	J1
NE 54th Ct				
1700	HBRO	97124	593	J3
5100	ClkC	98661	537	C1
7400	ClkC	98662	507	E7
9400	ClkC	98665	507	C4
11600	ClkC	98686	507	C1
SE 54th Ct				
2400	HBRO	97123	623	H1
10100	MWKE	97222	657	C2
NE 54th Pl				
7100	ClkC	98661	507	C6
SW 54th Pl				
3800	MthC	97221	625	J2
4200	PTLD	97221	625	J2
54th St				
1000	WHGL	98671	570	E5
1600	ClkC	98671	570	E4
NE 54th St				
2000	VCVR	98663	506	J7
2600	VCVR	98663	507	A7
5300	ClkC	98661	507	C7
6300	ClkC	98661	537	D1
6900	ClkC	98662	507	E7
8200	VCVR	98662	507	F7
9700	ClkC	98662	537	G1
12900	VCVR	98682	538	B1
23200	ClkC	98682	539	C1
32400	ClkC	98607	540	C1
NE 54th St SR-500				
23200	ClkC	98682	539	C1
NW 54th St				
400	VCVR	98663	506	F7
SW 54th Ter				
20000	TLTN	97062	685	J5
NE 54th Wy				
7900	ClkC	98662	507	E7
13700	VCVR	98682	538	B1
NW 54th Wy				
1100	VCVR	98663	506	E7
NE 55th Av				
10	PTLD	97213	597	C5
10	PTLD	97215	597	C6
100	HBRO	97123	593	J5
100	HBRO	97124	593	J5
100	WasC	97123	593	J5
100	WasC	97124	593	J5
3800	ClkC	98661	537	C2
4500	PTLD	97218	597	D1
6900	ClkC	98661	507	C6
7200	PTLD	97218	567	D6
8300	ClkC	98665	507	C4
10400	ClkC	98686	507	C2
23000	ClkC	98604	447	D3
28900	ClkC	98604	417	D5
NW 55th Av				
5400	PTLD	97210	565	H7
19300	ClkC	98642	446	B7
28000	ClkC	98642	416	B5
SE 55th Av				
10	PTLD	97213	597	C6
500	PTLD	97215	597	C7
1900	HBRO	97123	593	J7
2100	PTLD	97215	627	D1
2200	HBRO	97123	623	H1
2900	PTLD	97206	627	C2
8400	CmsC	97206	627	C7
8800	CmsC	97222	627	C7
8800	MWKE	97222	627	C7
8900	CmsC	97222	657	C1
8900	MWKE	97222	657	C1
SW 55th Av				
3200	MthC	97221	625	J1
6700	PTLD	97219	625	J5
6700	PTLD	97221	625	J5
9800	PTLD	97219	655	J1
22100	CmsC	97062	685	J7
NE 55th Cir				
4700	ClkC	98661	507	B7
8500	ClkC	98662	507	G7
8500	VCVR	98662	507	G
NE 55th Ct				
3700	ClkC	98661	537	C2
NW 55th Ct				
500	VCVR	98663	506	F7
SE 55th Ct				
2200	HBRO	97123	623	H1
SW 55th Ct				
19100	TLTN	97062	685	J4
SW 55th Dr				
-	PTLD	97219	625	J5
2800	MthC	97221	625	J1
3800	PTLD	97221	625	J1
NW 55th Lp				
1100	VCVR	98663	506	E7
NE 55th Pl				
4300	ClkC	98661	537	C2
SE 55th Pl				
700	HBRO	97123	593	H6
SW 55th Pl				
4300	PTLD	97221	625	J3
12300	LKOW	97035	655	J3
12300	PTLD	97219	655	J3
55th St				
1500	ClkC	98671	570	E4
1500	WHGL	98671	570	E4

Portland Street Index

STREET Block City ZIP Map# Grid

NE 55th St
4900 ClkC 98661 507 C7
7200 ClkC 98662 507 E7
8400 VCVR 98662 507 F7
12900 VCVR 98682 508 A7
27200 ClkC 98607 539 G1
NW 55th St
600 VCVR 98663 506 F7
SW 55th Ter
20000 TLTN 97062 685 J5
NE 56th Av
10 PTLD 97215 597 D6
1700 HBRO 97124 593 J3
4100 PTLD 97213 597 D1
4100 PTLD 97218 597 D1
4700 ClkC 98661 537 C1
5000 PTLD 97218 567 D7
7400 ClkC 98661 507 C5
9400 ClkC 98665 507 C4
11400 ClkC 98686 507 C1
NW 56th Av
5400 PTLD 97210 565 H7
17600 ClkC 98642 476 B2
32900 ClkC 98642 416 B1
33100 ClkC 98642 386 B7
SE 56th Av
10 PTLD 97213 597 D6
10 PTLD 97215 597 D6
600 HBRO 97123 593 J6
700 WasC 97123 593 J6
1500 PTLD 97215 627 D1
2900 PTLD 97206 627 D2
9500 MWKE 97222 657 C1
SW 56th Av
4800 PTLD 97221 625 J3
7900 PTLD 97219 625 J6
9800 PTLD 97219 655 J1
20000 TLTN 97062 685 J5
NE 56th Cir
6000 ClkC 98661 507 D7
8500 ClkC 98662 507 G7
8500 VCVR 98662 507 G7
11800 ClkC 98682 508 A7
11800 VCVR 98682 507 J7
11800 VCVR 98682 508 A7
NW 56th Cir
100 VCVR 98663 506 G7
500 VCVR 98663 506 F7
NE 56th Ct
1200 HBRO 97124 593 J3
7300 ClkC 98661 507 C6
9500 ClkC 98665 507 C3
SE 56th Ct
2800 HBRO 97123 623 J1
SW 56th Ct
12500 PTLD 97219 655 J3
19500 TLTN 97062 685 J4
NE 56th Pl
4300 ClkC 98661 537 C1
S 56th Pl
10 RDGF 98642 416 E7
100 RDGF 98642 446 E1
SE 56th Pl
2200 HBRO 97123 593 J7
2300 HBRO 97123 623 J1
SW 56th Pl
11400 PTLD 97219 655 J2
19100 TLTN 97062 685 J4
56th St
900 WHGL 98671 570 F5
1000 ClkC 98671 570 F5
NE 56th St
4000 ClkC 98661 507 B7
7100 ClkC 98662 507 E7
8400 VCVR 98662 507 F7
12100 ClkC 98682 508 A7
12100 VCVR 98682 508 A7
25400 ClkC 98682 539 E1
NW 56th St
1500 VCVR 98663 506 E7
NE 56th Wy
6500 ClkC 98661 507 D7
NW 56th Wy
1000 VCVR 98663 506 F7
NE 57th Av
10 PTLD 97215 597 D6
1500 HBRO 97124 593 J3
1500 PTLD 97213 597 D3
2900 VCVR 98661 537 C3
4100 PTLD 97218 597 D1
5100 ClkC 98661 537 C1
5700 PTLD 97218 567 D7
6600 ClkC 98661 507 C6
11100 ClkC 98686 507 D2
15600 ClkC 98686 477 D4
22900 ClkC 98604 447 D3
25900 ClkC 98642 447 D1
NW 57th Av
- ClkC 98642 416 B4
5700 PTLD 97210 565 H7
SE 57th Av
10 PTLD 97213 597 D6
10 PTLD 97215 597 D6
500 HBRO 97123 593 J6
2100 PTLD 97215 627 D1
2200 PTLD 97206 627 D1
8400 CmsC 97206 627 C7
SW 57th Av
800 MthC 97221 595 J6
800 PTLD 97221 595 J6
3500 MthC 97221 625 J2
4700 PTLD 97221 625 J3
8300 PTLD 97219 625 J6
9800 PTLD 97219 655 J1
19000 TLTN 97062 685 H4
NE 57th Cir
6200 ClkC 98661 507 D7
7600 ClkC 98662 507 E7
N 57th Ct
1000 ClkC 98642 416 E6
1000 RDGF 98642 416 E6
NE 57th Ct
7500 ClkC 98661 507 C5
12500 ClkC 98686 507 D1
14700 ClkC 98686 477 D5
NW 57th Ct
21000 ClkC 98642 446 B6
30100 ClkC 98642 416 B4
SE 57th Ct
2400 HBRO 97123 623 J1
NE 57th Pl
4300 ClkC 98661 537 C2
SW 57th Pl
- PTLD 97219 655 J2
800 PTLD 97221 595 J6

57th St
900 ClkC 98671 570 F4
1500 WHGL 98671 570 F4
NE 57th St
2300 VCVR 98663 506 J7
7200 ClkC 98661 507 E7
7200 ClkC 98662 507 E7
13400 ClkC 98682 508 B7
NW 57th St
800 VCVR 98663 506 F7
SW 57th St
19500 TLTN 97062 685 H4
SW 57th Ter
20000 TLTN 97062 685 J5
NE 58th Av
- ClkC 98661 537 C1
10 PTLD 97213 597 D5
10 PTLD 97215 597 D6
300 HBRO 97124 593 J4
400 WasC 97124 593 J4
5600 PTLD 97218 567 D7
6300 ClkC 98661 507 D5
7700 ClkC 98665 507 D5
10900 ClkC 98686 507 D2
17900 ClkC 98686 477 D2
18900 ClkC 98642 447 D7
18900 ClkC 98686 447 D7
29900 ClkC 98629 417 D4
NW 58th Av
17200 ClkC 98642 476 A3
SE 58th Av
100 PTLD 97215 597 D6
800 HBRO 97123 593 J6
1500 PTLD 97215 627 D1
8500 PTLD 97206 627 D7
8900 CmsC 97206 627 D7
8900 MWKE 97206 627 D7
8900 MWKE 97206 657 D1
8900 MWKE 97222 657 D1
SW 58th Av
- PTLD 97219 625 J6
- PTLD 97221 625 J3
1100 PTLD 97221 595 J6
10800 PTLD 97219 655 J2
NE 58th Cir
5800 ClkC 98661 507 C7
28800 ClkC 98607 509 H7
NE 58th Ct
1500 HBRO 97124 593 J3
5100 PTLD 97218 567 D7
5600 ClkC 98661 507 C7
SE 58th Ct
100 HBRO 97123 593 J5
100 HBRO 97124 593 J5
2700 HBRO 97123 623 J1
SW 58th Ct
11500 PTLD 97219 655 J2
SE 58th Dr
8800 CmsC 97206 627 D7
8800 MWKE 97206 627 D7
8900 CmsC 97206 657 D1
8900 MWKE 97206 657 D1
9200 MWKE 97222 657 D1
SW 58th Dr
3500 MthC 97221 625 J2
NE 58th Pl
300 HBRO 97124 593 J5
5400 ClkC 98661 507 D7
13900 ClkC 98686 477 D6
NE 58th St
2300 VCVR 98663 506 J7
3200 VCVR 98663 507 A7
3300 ClkC 98661 507 A7
7200 ClkC 98662 507 F7
19100 ClkC 98682 508 J7
20700 ClkC 98682 509 B7
28000 ClkC 98607 509 H7
NE 58th St SR-500
19100 ClkC 98682 508 H7
20700 ClkC 98682 509 B7
NW 58th St
700 VCVR 98663 506 F7
SW 58th Ter
19900 TLTN 97062 685 H5
NE 58th Wy
7500 ClkC 98662 507 E7
NE 59th Av
10 PTLD 97215 597 D5
3500 PTLD 97213 597 D2
4000 ClkC 98661 537 D1
5500 PTLD 97218 567 D7
5800 ClkC 98661 507 C7
9600 ClkC 98665 507 D3
9800 ClkC 98686 507 D3
24100 ClkC 98604 447 D3
29000 ClkC 98604 417 D5
32000 ClkC 98629 417 D2
NW 59th Av
38100 ClkC 98674 386 B2
SE 59th Av
700 HBRO 97123 593 J6
700 WasC 97123 593 J6
1500 PTLD 97215 597 D7
2100 PTLD 97206 627 D1
2100 PTLD 97215 627 D1
10600 MWKE 97222 657 D2
SW 59th Av
4900 PTLD 97221 625 J3
7400 PTLD 97219 625 J5
9600 PTLD 97219 655 J1
NE 59th Cir
5800 ClkC 98661 507 C7
7600 ClkC 98662 507 E7
SW 59th Cir
12600 PTLD 97219 655 H3
NE 59th Ct
3900 ClkC 98661 537 C2
6300 ClkC 98661 507 D6
25900 ClkC 98604 447 D1
25900 ClkC 98642 447 D1
NW 59th Ct
- ClkC 98642 446 A7
SE 59th Ct
500 HBRO 97123 593 J6
500 PTLD 97215 597 D6
2700 HBRO 97123 623 J1
SW 59th Ct
5800 PTLD 97221 625 J4
SW 59th Dr
10600 PTLD 97219 655 J1
SE 59th Ln
100 HBRO 97123 593 J5
NE 59th Pl
1400 HBRO 97124 593 J3
6200 PTLD 97218 567 D6

SW 59th Pl
10100 PTLD 97219 655 J1
NE 59th St
100 ClkC 98665 506 G7
2400 VCVR 98663 506 J7
2400 VCVR 98663 507 A7
7200 ClkC 98661 507 E7
7200 ClkC 98662 507 E7
13100 ClkC 98682 508 B7
27900 ClkC 98607 509 H7
NW 59th St
100 ClkC 98665 506 G7
1500 VCVR 98663 506 E7
SW 59th Ter
19900 TLTN 97062 685 H5
NE 60th Av
- ClkC 98661 537 D1
10 PTLD 97213 597 D5
10 PTLD 97215 597 D6
100 HBRO 97123 593 J5
100 WasC 97124 593 J5
1500 HBRO 97124 593 J3
4500 PTLD 97218 597 D1
5200 PTLD 97218 567 D7
7000 ClkC 98661 507 D6
9700 ClkC 98665 507 D3
11700 ClkC 98686 507 D1
33400 ClkC 98629 417 D1
NW 60th Av
3200 CMAS 98607 539 B6
6000 PTLD 97210 565 H6
SE 60th Av
- MWKE 97206 657 D1
10 PTLD 97213 597 D6
500 PTLD 97215 597 D7
600 HBRO 97123 593 J6
700 WasC 97123 593 J6
1900 PTLD 97215 627 D1
2400 PTLD 97206 627 D1
9300 CmsC 97222 657 D2
10800 MWKE 97222 657 D3
SW 60th Av
1500 MthC 97221 595 J7
1500 PTLD 97221 595 J7
6300 PTLD 97221 625 J4
6700 PTLD 97219 625 J5
9800 PTLD 97219 655 J1
19900 TLTN 97062 685 H5
28000 CmsC 97070 715 H6
NE 60th Cir
5900 ClkC 98661 507 D6
NE 60th Ct
1700 HBRO 97124 593 G3
3700 ClkC 98661 537 D2
5400 ClkC 98661 507 D7
10600 ClkC 98686 507 D2
22600 ClkC 98604 447 D4
SE 60th Ct
1500 HBRO 97123 593 J7
12300 MWKE 97222 657 D4
SW 60th Ct
12600 PTLD 97219 655 H3
NE 60th Pl
1600 HBRO 97124 593 J3
SE 60th Pl
6500 PTLD 97206 627 D5
SW 60th Pl
3500 MthC 97221 625 H2
4500 PTLD 97221 625 J3
NE 60th St
- ClkC 98661 507 D7
1900 ClkC 98665 506 J7
3200 VCVR 98663 507 A7
8400 ClkC 98662 507 F7
16200 ClkC 98682 508 E7
25800 ClkC 98682 509 E7
29200 ClkC 98607 509 J7
NW 60th St
1500 VCVR 98663 506 E6
NE 60th Wy
11700 VCVR 98682 507 J7
11700 VCVR 98682 508 A7
12100 ClkC 98682 508 A7
NE 61st Av
10 PTLD 97215 597 D6
1300 HBRO 97124 593 J3
3500 PTLD 97213 597 D2
3800 ClkC 98661 537 D2
7000 ClkC 98661 507 D6
7700 ClkC 98665 507 D5
10900 ClkC 98686 507 D2
15900 ClkC 98686 477 D4
26300 ClkC 98604 417 D7
26300 ClkC 98604 447 D1
26300 ClkC 98642 417 D7
26300 ClkC 98642 447 D1
29900 ClkC 98629 417 D4
NW 61st Av
5900 PTLD 97210 565 H6
19000 ClkC 98642 446 A7
19000 ClkC 98642 476 A1
28700 ClkC 98642 416 A5
SE 61st Av
10 PTLD 97213 597 D6
10 PTLD 97215 597 D6
700 HBRO 97123 593 J6
2400 PTLD 97206 627 D1
2400 PTLD 97215 627 D1
SW 61st Av
- PTLD 97219 655 H2
- PTLD 97221 625 J4
7900 PTLD 97219 625 H6
12800 CmsC 97219 655 H4
13300 LKOW 97035 655 H4
13300 PTLD 97219 655 H4
NE 61st Cir
1800 ClkC 98665 506 J7
5900 ClkC 98661 507 D7
9900 ClkC 98662 507 H7
NE 61st Ct
700 HBRO 97124 593 J4
3700 ClkC 98661 537 D2
5400 ClkC 98661 507 D7
9700 ClkC 98665 507 D3
9700 ClkC 98686 507 D3
SE 61st Ct
1700 HBRO 97123 593 J7
2700 HBRO 97123 623 J1
34800 ClkC 98671 570 E6
34800 WHGL 98671 570 E6
SW 61st Ct
1200 PTLD 97221 595 H6
SE 61st Dr
1700 HBRO 97123 593 J7

SW 61st Dr
800 MthC 97221 595 H7
800 PTLD 97221 595 H7
SE 61st Ln
2300 HBRO 97123 623 J1
NE 61st Pl
600 PTLD 97213 597 D5
1700 HBRO 97124 593 G3
12500 ClkC 98686 477 D7
12500 ClkC 98686 507 D1
SE 61st Pl
1300 HBRO 97123 593 J7
2100 WasC 97123 593 J7
SW 61st Pl
12500 PTLD 97219 655 H3
NE 61st St
- ClkC 98661 507 E7
200 ClkC 98665 506 G7
1000 VCVR 98665 506 H7
8100 ClkC 98662 507 F6
13700 ClkC 98682 508 B7
22800 ClkC 98682 509 B7
27200 ClkC 98607 509 G7
NW 61st St
- VCVR 98660 506 E7
1300 VCVR 98663 506 E7
NE 61st Ter
100 HBRO 97124 593 J5
NE 61st Wy
- ClkC 98662 507 E7
400 HBRO 97124 593 G4
SE 61st Wy
1000 HBRO 97123 593 J6
NE 62nd Av
10 PTLD 97215 597 D5
400 HBRO 97124 593 J4
2400 PTLD 97213 597 D3
3000 VCVR 98661 537 D3
3900 PTLD 97218 597 D1
4400 ClkC 98661 537 D1
5500 PTLD 97218 567 D7
7000 ClkC 98661 507 D6
8800 ClkC 98665 507 D4
NW 62nd Av
- PTLD 97210 565 H6
SE 62nd Av
10 PTLD 97213 597 D6
10 PTLD 97215 597 D6
700 HBRO 97123 593 J6
2400 PTLD 97215 627 D1
5000 PTLD 97206 627 D5
8700 CmsC 97206 627 D7
SW 62nd Av
- PTLD 97221 625 H3
8200 PTLD 97219 625 H6
9600 PTLD 97219 655 H1
12700 CmsC 97219 655 H4
13400 LKOW 97035 655 H4
13400 PTLD 97219 655 H4
NE 62nd Cir
10000 ClkC 98662 507 H7
13900 ClkC 98682 508 C7
NE 62nd Ct
6700 ClkC 98661 507 D6
SW 62nd Dr
9400 PTLD 97219 625 H7
9400 PTLD 97223 625 H7
10400 PTLD 97219 655 H1
SE 62nd Ln
2300 HBRO 97123 623 J1
NE 62nd Pl
200 HBRO 97124 593 J5
SE 62nd Pl
400 PTLD 97215 597 D6
SW 62nd Pl
6700 PTLD 97219 625 H5
6700 PTLD 97221 625 H5
10700 PTLD 97219 655 H2
NE 62nd St
- ClkC 98662 507 E7
200 ClkC 98665 506 G7
5900 ClkC 98661 507 D7
15200 ClkC 98682 508 D7
27900 ClkC 98607 509 H7
NW 62nd St
1100 VCVR 98663 506 E6
NE 62nd Wy
- ClkC 98662 507 F6
NE 63rd Av
10 PTLD 97213 597 D5
10 PTLD 97215 597 D6
100 HBRO 97123 593 J5
100 HBRO 97124 593 J5
1300 HBRO 97124 594 A3
4000 PTLD 97218 597 D2
5100 ClkC 98661 537 D1
6700 ClkC 98661 507 D6
6900 PTLD 97218 567 E6
29000 ClkC 98604 417 E5
NW 63rd Av
- PTLD 97210 565 H6
29500 ClkC 98642 416 A4
SE 63rd Av
10 PTLD 97213 597 D6
10 PTLD 97215 597 D6
600 HBRO 97123 593 J6
2600 PTLD 97206 627 D1
8500 CmsC 97206 627 D7
11600 MWKE 97222 657 D3
SW 63rd Av
4300 PTLD 97221 625 H3
6500 PTLD 97219 625 H5
10800 PTLD 97219 655 H2
12800 CmsC 97219 655 H4
17300 TLTN 97035 685 H1
NE 63rd Cir
16400 ClkC 98682 508 E7
29000 ClkC 98607 509 H7
NE 63rd Ct
- ClkC 98686 507 D2
300 HBRO 97124 593 J4
14400 ClkC 98686 477 D5
28300 ClkC 98604 417 D5
SE 63rd Ct
11000 MWKE 97222 657 D2
SE 63rd Dr
700 HBRO 97123 593 J6
SW 63rd Dr
10400 PTLD 97219 655 H1
SE 63rd Ln
1000 HBRO 97123 593 J6
NE 63rd Pl
200 HBRO 97124 593 F1
SW 63rd Pl
10700 PTLD 97219 655 H1

SW 63rd Pl
12800 CmsC 97219 655 H4
13700 CmsC 97035 655 H4
13700 LKOW 97035 655 H4
NE 63rd St
300 ClkC 98665 506 G6
5600 ClkC 98661 507 D6
7900 ClkC 98662 507 F7
16200 ClkC 98682 508 E7
21400 ClkC 98682 509 A7
27700 ClkC 98607 509 G7
NW 63rd St
1300 VCVR 98663 506 E6
NE 63rd Ter
100 HBRO 97124 593 J5
NE 63rd Wy
1000 HBRO 97124 594 A3
NE 64th Av
1500 HBRO 97124 594 A3
1700 VCVR 98661 537 D4
2500 PTLD 97213 597 D3
3900 PTLD 97218 597 E1
5200 ClkC 98661 537 D1
5300 ClkC 98661 507 D7
8400 ClkC 98665 507 D4
10900 ClkC 98686 507 D2
15100 ClkC 98686 477 D5
22800 ClkC 98604 447 D4
31900 ClkC 98629 417 E2
NW 64th Av
5900 PTLD 97210 565 H6
18400 ClkC 98642 476 A1
SE 64th Av
2100 PTLD 97215 627 D1
2400 PTLD 97206 627 D1
8400 CmsC 97206 627 D7
9100 CmsC 97206 657 D1
9100 CmsC 97222 657 D1
11600 MWKE 97222 657 D3
SW 64th Av
2300 MthC 97221 595 H7
2300 MthC 97221 625 H1
2300 PTLD 97221 595 H7
2300 PTLD 97221 625 H1
7900 PTLD 97219 625 H6
10800 PTLD 97219 655 H2
11500 TGRD 97219 655 H2
11500 TGRD 97223 655 H2
12800 CmsC 97219 655 H4
NE 64th Cir
8400 ClkC 98662 507 F6
13700 ClkC 98682 508 C7
NE 64th Ct
500 HBRO 97124 594 B3
7000 ClkC 98661 507 D6
10000 ClkC 98686 507 D3
NW 64th Ct
29100 ClkC 98642 416 A4
39600 ClkC 98674 386 B1
SE 64th Ct
1200 HBRO 97123 594 A7
10900 CmsC 97222 657 D2
10900 MWKE 97222 657 D2
SW 64th Ct
4200 PTLD 97221 625 H2
7300 PTLD 97219 625 H5
SW 64th Dr
10400 PTLD 97219 655 H1
NE 64th Ln
1100 HBRO 97124 594 A3
NE 64th Pl
700 HBRO 97124 594 A4
6700 ClkC 98661 507 D6
SW 64th Pl
2600 MthC 97225 625 H1
3300 MthC 97221 625 H1
NE 64th St
1000 ClkC 98665 506 H6
5300 ClkC 98661 507 C6
9600 ClkC 98662 507 G6
13500 ClkC 98682 508 B7
27200 ClkC 98607 509 G7
NE 64th Ter
100 HBRO 97124 594 A5
NE 64th Wy
400 HBRO 97124 594 A4
29400 ClkC 98607 509 J7
N 65th Av
10 ClkC 98642 416 F7
10 RDGF 98642 416 F7
NE 65th Av
10 PTLD 97215 597 D5
1300 VCVR 98661 537 D4
1500 HBRO 97124 594 A3
2500 PTLD 97213 597 E2
3900 PTLD 97218 597 E1
4000 ClkC 98661 537 D2
5500 PTLD 97218 567 E7
6700 ClkC 98661 507 D6
11400 ClkC 98686 507 D1
17100 ClkC 98686 477 D3
25400 ClkC 98604 447 E1
28100 ClkC 98604 417 E6
S 65th Av
10 RDGF 98642 416 F7
SE 65th Av
10 PTLD 97213 597 D6
10 PTLD 97215 597 D6
900 HBRO 97123 594 A6
2700 PTLD 97206 627 D2
8500 CmsC 97206 627 D6
9300 CmsC 97222 657 D1
SW 65th Av
- TGRD 97219 655 H2
5100 WasC 97225 625 H3
6700 BRTN 97223 625 H5
6700 PTLD 97221 625 H5
6700 PTLD 97223 625 H5
6700 PTLD 97225 625 H5
8300 WasC 97223 625 H6
9600 PTLD 97219 625 H7
9600 PTLD 97219 655 H1
9600 TGRD 97223 655 H1
9600 WasC 97223 655 H1
10800 PTLD 97223 655 H2
17500 TLTN 97224 685 H1
18500 CmsC 97035 685 H2
18500 LKOW 97035 685 H2
18700 TLTN 97035 685 H2
18900 RVGR 97035 685 H3
19200 TLTN 97062 685 H4
20100 CmsC 97062 685 H7
22900 CmsC 97062 715 H1
NE 65th Cir
8400 ClkC 98662 507 F6

NE 65th Cir
16400 ClkC 98682 508 E7
NE 65th Ct
- HBRO 97124 594 A4
- WasC 97124 594 A4
4300 ClkC 98661 537 D2
7600 ClkC 98661 507 D5
9900 ClkC 98686 507 D3
17500 ClkC 98686 477 D2
SE 65th Ct
12200 MWKE 97222 657 D4
SE 65th Ln
1500 HBRO 97123 594 A7
NE 65th Pl
7000 ClkC 98661 507 D6
SE 65th Pl
500 HBRO 97123 594 A6
NE 65th St
300 ClkC 98665 506 G6
2900 ClkC 98661 507 A6
3400 VCVR 98663 507 A6
7200 ClkC 98662 507 E6
11700 ClkC 98682 507 J6
18400 ClkC 98682 508 G7
27400 ClkC 98607 509 G7
NW 65th St
1500 VCVR 98663 506 E6
NE 66th Av
- HBRO 97124 594 A5
10 PTLD 97215 597 E5
100 WasC 97124 594 A5
2600 PTLD 97213 597 E2
3600 ClkC 98661 537 D2
3600 VCVR 98661 537 D2
3900 PTLD 97218 597 E2
6200 PTLD 97218 567 E6
7400 ClkC 98661 507 D5
7600 ClkC 98665 507 D5
12300 ClkC 98686 507 D1
12600 ClkC 98686 477 D7
28400 ClkC 98604 417 E5
32900 ClkC 98629 417 E1
NW 66th Av
28200 ClkC 98642 416 A5
SE 66th Av
10 PTLD 97213 597 E6
10 PTLD 97215 597 E6
900 HBRO 97123 594 A6
2200 PTLD 97215 627 E1
3500 PTLD 97206 627 E2
8500 CmsC 97206 627 D7
9600 CmsC 97222 657 D2
10900 MWKE 97222 657 D3
SW 66th Av
- PTLD 97221 595 H7
- PTLD 97225 595 H7
1000 WasC 97225 595 H7
2800 WasC 97225 625 H2
6800 BRTN 97223 625 H5
6800 PTLD 97223 625 H5
7500 WasC 97223 625 H6
9000 WasC 97223 655 H1
11100 PTLD 97223 655 H2
11500 TGRD 97223 655 H3
NE 66th Cir
200 ClkC 98665 506 F6
5600 ClkC 98661 507 C6
8400 ClkC 98662 507 F6
16300 ClkC 98682 508 E6
NW 66th Cir
1700 VCVR 98663 506 E6
SE 66th Ct
400 HBRO 97123 594 A6
SW 66th Ct
3000 WasC 97225 625 H2
6000 BRTN 97223 625 H5
6000 BRTN 97225 625 H5
6000 PTLD 97223 625 H5
6000 PTLD 97225 625 H5
NE 66th Pl
800 PTLD 97213 597 E5
SE 66th Pl
- PTLD 97215 597 E6
7600 PTLD 97206 627 E6
SW 66th Pl
8100 WasC 97223 625 H7
NE 66th St
300 ClkC 98665 506 G6
3100 ClkC 98661 507 A6
3100 VCVR 98663 507 A6
10400 ClkC 98662 507 H6
13500 ClkC 98682 508 B6
27900 ClkC 98607 509 H7
NE 66th Wy
7400 ClkC 98662 507 E6
16300 ClkC 98682 508 E6
SE 66th Wy
800 HBRO 97123 594 A6
NE 67th Av
10 PTLD 97215 597 E5
2600 PTLD 97213 597 E3
3900 PTLD 97218 597 E1
7400 ClkC 98661 507 D5
20900 ClkC 98604 447 E6
NW 67th Av
18100 ClkC 98642 476 A2
20900 ClkC 98642 446 A4
21900 RDGF 98642 446 A4
29900 ClkC 98642 416 A4
SE 67th Av
- VCVR 98661 537 D7
500 HBRO 97123 594 A6
900 PTLD 97215 597 E7
2200 HBRO 97123 624 A1
2400 PTLD 97206 627 E2
2400 PTLD 97215 627 E1
2400 WasC 97123 624 A1
2700 HBRO 97007 624 A1
8500 CmsC 97206 627 D7
9100 CmsC 97206 657 E1
11700 MWKE 97222 657 E3
12400 CmsC 97222 657 D4
SW 67th Av
6800 BRTN 97223 625 H5
7500 PTLD 97223 625 H6
7500 WasC 97223 625 H6
10400 TGRD 97223 655 H2
19400 TLTN 97062 685 G4
NE 67th Cir
1600 ClkC 98665 506 H6
6600 ClkC 98661 507 D6
NE 67th Ct
14000 ClkC 98686 477 E6
SW 67th Pl
- BRTN 97223 625 H5
- BRTN 97225 625 H4

SW 67th Pl
- PTLD 97223 625 H5
- PTLD 97225 625 H5
500 PTLD 97225 595 H6
500 WasC 97225 595 H6
8000 WasC 97223 625 H7
8800 TGRD 97223 655 H1
8800 WasC 97223 655 H1
NE 67th St
- ClkC 98662 507 E6
1900 ClkC 98665 506 J6
6100 ClkC 98661 507 D6
13500 ClkC 98682 508 B6
27900 ClkC 98607 509 H7
NE 67th Wy
6500 ClkC 98661 507 D6
NE 68th Av
- ClkC 98686 477 E6
10 PTLD 97215 597 E6
2600 PTLD 97213 597 E1
3900 PTLD 97218 597 E2
5000 PTLD 97218 567 E7
5100 ClkC 98661 537 D1
5600 ClkC 98661 507 D7
SE 68th Av
300 HBRO 97123 594 A6
400 PTLD 97215 597 E6
2200 PTLD 97206 627 E1
2200 PTLD 97215 627 E1
SW 68th Av
10 MthC 97229 595 H6
10 WasC 97225 595 H6
4300 WasC 97225 625 H2
6800 BRTN 97223 625 H6
7000 PTLD 97223 625 H6
11500 TGRD 97223 655 H4
19400 TLTN 97062 685 G4
NE 68th Cir
6600 ClkC 98661 507 D6
10700 ClkC 98662 507 H6
NE 68th Ct
- VCVR 98661 537 D2
25000 ClkC 98604 447 E2
SE 68th Ct
1500 HBRO 97123 594 A7
3000 PTLD 97206 627 E2
SW 68th Ct
6000 BRTN 97223 625 H5
6000 BRTN 97225 625 H5
6000 PTLD 97223 625 H5
6000 PTLD 97225 625 H5
SW 68th Pkwy
10900 TGRD 97223 655 H3
SE 68th Pl
800 HBRO 97123 594 A6
6300 PTLD 97206 627 E5
SW 68th Pl
8000 WasC 97223 625 H7
NE 68th St
100 ClkC 98665 506 G6
2700 ClkC 98665 507 A6
2700 VCVR 98665 507 A6
3400 VCVR 98663 507 A6
6100 ClkC 98661 507 D6
10500 ClkC 98662 507 H6
16300 ClkC 98682 508 E6
20700 ClkC 98682 509 C6
27500 ClkC 98607 509 G6
NW 68th St
100 ClkC 98665 506 G6
NE 68th Wy
15000 ClkC 98682 508 D6
NE 69th Av
- HBRO 97123 594 A5
- WasC 97124 594 A5
10 PTLD 97215 597 E5
3400 PTLD 97213 597 E2
3900 PTLD 97218 597 E2
7300 ClkC 98661 507 E5
26900 ClkC 98604 417 E7
31400 ClkC 98629 417 E2
NW 69th Av
17000 ClkC 98642 476 A3
17900 ClkC 98642 475 J2
SE 69th Av
10 PTLD 97213 597 D5
10 PTLD 97215 597 D5
300 HBRO 97123 594 A5
2300 PTLD 97215 627 E1
8200 PTLD 97206 627 E7
12200 MWKE 97222 657 E4
SW 69th Av
7200 BRTN 97223 625 H6
7500 PTLD 97223 625 H6
7500 WasC 97223 625 H6
9000 TGRD 97223 655 H1
9000 WasC 97223 655 H1
NE 69th Cir
6300 ClkC 98661 507 D6
10000 ClkC 98662 507 H6
NW 69th Cir
1900 VCVR 98663 506 E6
1900 VCVR 98665 506 E6
SE 69th Ct
500 HBRO 97123 594 A6
SW 69th Pl
8400 WasC 97223 625 H7
NE 69th St
- ClkC 98665 506 J6
5600 ClkC 98661 507 C6
10200 ClkC 98662 507 H6
15000 ClkC 98682 508 D6
NW 69th St
2000 ClkC 98665 506 E6
2000 VCVR 98665 506 E6
SW 69th St
20000 TLTN 97062 685 G5
NE 70th Av
10 PTLD 97215 597 E6
700 HBRO 97124 594 A4
1800 PTLD 97213 597 E4
3900 PTLD 97218 597 E1
5000 PTLD 97218 567 E7
7200 ClkC 98661 507 E6
11200 ClkC 98686 507 E1
14000 ClkC 98686 477 E6
SE 70th Av
10 PTLD 97213 597 E6
10 PTLD 97215 597 E6
900 HBRO 97123 594 A6
2200 PTLD 97206 627 E1
2200 PTLD 97215 627 E1
2600 HBRO 97123 624 A1
2700 HBRO 97007 624 A1
8500 CmsC 97206 627 E7

STREET Block City ZIP Map# Grid

SE 70th Av
9300 CmsC 97206 657 E1
9300 CmsC 97222 657 E1
11800 MWKE 97222 657 E3
SW 70th Av
- WasC 97223 625 H7
3000 WasC 97225 625 H2
7000 BRTN 97223 625 H6
7000 PTLD 97223 625 H6
9000 TGRD 97223 655 H1
9000 WasC 97223 655 H1
20000 TLTN 97062 685 G5
21500 WasC 97062 685 G6
NE 70th Cir
100 ClkC 98665 506 G6
5300 ClkC 98661 507 C6
10900 ClkC 98662 507 J6
16300 ClkC 98682 508 E6
29400 ClkC 98607 509 J6
NW 70th Cir
500 ClkC 98665 506 F6
NE 70th Ct
7400 ClkC 98661 507 E5
NW 70th Ct
- ClkC 98642 416 A5
SE 70th Ct
500 HBRO 97123 594 A6
SW 70th Pl
8400 WasC 97223 625 G7
10000 TGRD 97223 655 G2
NE 70th St
1600 ClkC 98665 506 J6
5800 ClkC 98661 507 D6
7200 ClkC 98662 507 E6
15600 ClkC 98682 508 D6
NW 70th St
300 ClkC 98665 506 G6
SE 70th St
38200 ClkC 98671 570 J7
SW 70th Ter
400 WasC 97225 595 H6
NE 71st Av
- HBRO 97123 594 A5
- WasC 97124 594 A5
10 PTLD 97215 597 E6
800 HBRO 97124 594 A4
1500 PTLD 97213 597 E3
3900 PTLD 97218 597 E2
5500 ClkC 98661 507 E7
12900 ClkC 98686 477 E7
33000 ClkC 98629 417 E1
NW 71st Av
29100 ClkC 98642 416 A4
SE 71st Av
10 PTLD 97213 597 E6
10 PTLD 97215 597 E6
500 HBRO 97123 594 A6
2400 PTLD 97206 627 E2
2400 PTLD 97215 627 E1
12000 MWKE 97222 657 E4
12500 CmsC 97222 657 E4
SW 71st Av
1900 BRTN 97225 625 H1
7500 PTLD 97223 625 G6
8100 WasC 97223 625 G6
10200 TGRD 97223 655 G2
20000 TLTN 97062 685 G5
NE 71st Cir
10800 ClkC 98662 507 H6
14400 ClkC 98682 508 C6
NE 71st Ct
- ClkC 98661 507 E7
15600 ClkC 98686 477 E4
SE 71st Ct
1300 HBRO 97123 594 A7
NE 71st Lp
8000 ClkC 98662 507 F6
SE 71st Pl
300 HBRO 97123 594 A6
SW 71st Pl
8400 WasC 97223 625 G7
10000 TGRD 97223 655 G2
NE 71st St
- ClkC 98682 507 J6
200 ClkC 98665 506 G6
3100 ClkC 98665 507 A6
7100 ClkC 98661 507 E6
7100 ClkC 98662 507 E6
14000 ClkC 98682 508 C6
SW 71st Ter
8500 WasC 97223 625 G7
NE 71st Wy
13700 ClkC 98682 508 B6
NE 72nd Av
10 PTLD 97215 597 E5
700 HBRO 97124 594 B4
3100 VCVR 98662 537 E2
3500 PTLD 97213 597 E2
3700 VCVR 98661 537 E2
4500 PTLD 97218 597 E1
5000 PTLD 97218 567 E7
5100 ClkC 98661 537 E1
5100 ClkC 98662 537 E1
5300 ClkC 98661 507 E7
9000 ClkC 98665 507 E2
11400 ClkC 98662 507 E1
11400 ClkC 98686 507 E1
12300 ClkC 98662 477 E6
12300 ClkC 98686 477 E6
16900 ClkC 98604 477 E3
19200 ClkC 98604 447 E2
19200 ClkC 98686 447 E7
28000 ClkC 98604 417 E6
30400 ClkC 98629 417 E3
SE 72nd Av
10 PTLD 97213 597 E6
400 HBRO 97123 594 B6
1100 PTLD 97215 597 E7
2000 PTLD 97215 627 E1
2200 HBRO 97123 624 A1
2400 WasC 97123 624 A1
5000 PTLD 97206 627 E4
8500 CmsC 97206 627 E7
9900 CmsC 97222 657 E2
SW 72nd Av
3000 WasC 97225 625 G2
7700 WasC 97223 625 G6
10000 TGRD 97223 655 G2
10000 WasC 97223 655 G2
13800 TGRD 97224 655 G5
16000 TGRD 97224 685 G1
16900 TLTN 97224 685 G1
19000 TLTN 97062 685 G4
NE 72nd Cir
100 ClkC 98665 506 G5
7000 ClkC 98661 507 D6
10000 ClkC 98662 507 H6
16300 ClkC 98682 508 E6
NW 72nd Cir
500 ClkC 98665 506 F6
SE 72nd Ct
1900 HBRO 97123 594 A7
NE 72nd Dr
2000 PTLD 97213 597 E3
2900 VCVR 98661 537 E3
2900 VCVR 98662 537 E3
NE 72nd Pl
4300 VCVR 98662 537 E2
7000 HBRO 97124 594 B5
7000 WasC 97124 594 B5
7200 ClkC 98661 507 E6
7200 ClkC 98662 507 E6
NE 72nd St
900 ClkC 98665 506 H6
2900 ClkC 98665 507 A6
8800 ClkC 98662 507 G6
15700 ClkC 98682 508 D6
NW 72nd St
700 ClkC 98665 506 F6
NE 72nd Wy
3100 ClkC 98665 507 A5
SE 72nd Wy
1500 HBRO 97123 594 A7
NE 73rd Av
10 PTLD 97215 597 E5
600 HBRO 97124 594 B4
3100 PTLD 97213 597 E2
4600 PTLD 97218 597 E1
5400 ClkC 98662 507 E7
5500 PTLD 97218 567 E7
27500 ClkC 98604 417 E6
SE 73rd Av
10 PTLD 97213 597 E6
400 HBRO 97123 594 B6
500 PTLD 97215 597 E7
800 VCVR 98664 537 E7
2300 WasC 97123 624 A1
2500 PTLD 97206 627 E1
2600 HBRO 97123 624 A1
2700 HBRO 97007 624 A1
8600 CmsC 97206 627 E7
9500 CmsC 97222 657 E1
SW 73rd Av
2400 BRTN 97225 625 G1
2400 WasC 97225 625 G1
8500 WasC 97223 625 G7
NE 73rd Cir
6000 ClkC 98661 507 D5
10000 ClkC 98662 507 J6
15000 ClkC 98682 508 D6
NW 73rd Cir
200 ClkC 98665 506 G5
NE 73rd Ct
6500 ClkC 98662 507 E6
SE 73rd Ct
1300 HBRO 97123 594 A7
10800 CmsC 97222 657 E2
SW 73rd Pl
8900 TGRD 97223 655 G1
8900 WasC 97223 625 G7
8900 WasC 97223 655 H1
NE 73rd St
- ClkC 98665 507 A6
100 ClkC 98665 506 G5
6500 ClkC 98661 507 D6
7200 ClkC 98662 507 E5
16300 ClkC 98682 508 E6
21800 ClkC 98682 509 A6
NW 73rd St
100 ClkC 98665 506 F6
NE 74th Av
- PTLD 97218 597 F1
10 PTLD 97215 597 E6
100 HBRO 97124 594 B5
100 WasC 97124 594 B5
2700 PTLD 97213 597 E3
5000 PTLD 97218 567 E7
7300 ClkC 98662 507 E5
32800 ClkC 98629 417 F1
NW 74th Av
- CMAS 98607 539 A5
SE 74th Av
10 PTLD 97213 597 E6
10 PTLD 97215 597 F6
700 HBRO 97123 594 B6
2200 HBRO 97123 624 A1
2400 PTLD 97206 627 E1
2400 PTLD 97215 627 E1
9000 CmsC 97206 657 E1
9500 CmsC 97222 657 E1
SW 74th Av
7500 PTLD 97223 625 G6
7500 WasC 97223 625 G6
9800 TGRD 97223 655 G2
10800 WasC 97223 655 G2
14600 TGRD 97224 655 G7
17800 TGRD 97224 685 G1
NE 74th Cir
5800 ClkC 98661 507 D5
16300 ClkC 98682 508 E6
NE 74th Ct
- ClkC 98604 477 E1
6500 ClkC 98662 507 E6
25500 ClkC 98604 447 F1
28500 ClkC 98604 417 E5
NW 74th Lp
- CMAS 98607 539 A5
NE 74th St
3600 ClkC 98665 507 A5
6100 ClkC 98661 507 D5
9900 ClkC 98662 507 H6
15900 ClkC 98682 508 E6
NW 74th St
300 ClkC 98665 506 F5
S 74th St
300 ClkC 98642 416 G7
300 RDGF 98642 416 G7
NE 74th Wy
9300 ClkC 98662 507 G5
SE 74th Wy
2700 HBRO 97123 624 A1
NE 75th Av
10 PTLD 97215 597 F6
100 HBRO 97124 594 B5
100 WasC 97124 594 B5
1500 PTLD 97213 597 F4
3900 PTLD 97218 597 F2
5100 VCVR 98662 537 E1
5500 PTLD 97218 567 F7
6700 ClkC 98662 507 E6
NW 75th Av
- CMAS 98607 539 A5
SE 75th Av
10 PTLD 97213 597 F6
10 PTLD 97215 597 F6
2200 PTLD 97215 627 E1
2600 HBRO 97123 624 B1
2600 WasC 97123 624 B1
4500 PTLD 97206 627 E3
8400 MthC 97206 627 E7
9500 CmsC 97222 657 E1
SW 75th Av
2000 BRTN 97225 625 G1
3800 WasC 97225 625 G3
8600 WasC 97223 625 G7
9000 WasC 97223 655 G1
10600 TGRD 97223 655 G2
18900 TLTN 97062 685 G3
21400 WasC 97062 685 G6
NE 75th Cir
5100 ClkC 98661 507 C5
16300 ClkC 98682 508 E5
20700 ClkC 98682 509 A6
NW 75th Cir
1100 ClkC 98665 506 F5
NE 75th Ct
- ClkC 98662 507 E7
15900 ClkC 98662 477 E4
19200 ClkC 98604 477 E1
SE 75th Ct
700 VCVR 98664 537 E7
1500 VCVR 98664 567 E1
1900 HBRO 97123 594 B7
11000 CmsC 97222 657 E3
NE 75th Pl
- ClkC 98629 417 F3
10300 ClkC 98662 507 H5
SE 75th Pl
7800 PTLD 97206 627 E6
8100 MthC 97206 627 E7
SW 75th Pl
13400 TGRD 97223 655 G5
NE 75th St
1100 ClkC 98665 506 H5
3600 ClkC 98665 507 B5
6900 ClkC 98661 507 E5
10900 ClkC 98662 507 H5
12400 ClkC 98682 508 A5
NW 75th St
700 ClkC 98665 506 F5
1500 VCVR 98665 506 E5
SW 75th Ter
2400 BRTN 97225 625 G1
NE 75th Wy
10100 ClkC 98662 507 H5
NE 76th Av
- WasC 97124 594 B5
10 PTLD 97215 597 F5
200 HBRO 97124 594 B5
3100 PTLD 97213 597 F2
3900 PTLD 97218 597 F1
5100 VCVR 98662 537 E1
5500 PTLD 97218 567 F7
8700 ClkC 98662 507 E4
13900 ClkC 98662 477 E6
NW 76th Av
- CMAS 98607 539 A4
SE 76th Av
- CmsC 97206 627 F7
- PTLD 97206 627 F1
10 PTLD 97213 597 F6
500 PTLD 97215 597 F7
1900 PTLD 97215 627 F1
8900 CmsC 97206 657 E1
9500 CmsC 97222 657 E1
SW 76th Av
2300 BRTN 97225 625 G1
4700 WasC 97225 625 G4
7000 WasC 97223 625 G6
7300 PTLD 97223 625 G6
13200 TGRD 97223 655 G5
14600 TGRD 97224 655 G6
22300 WasC 97062 685 G7
NE 76th Cir
6600 ClkC 98661 507 D5
10000 ClkC 98662 507 G5
15200 ClkC 98682 508 D5
NW 76th Cir
1100 ClkC 98665 506 F5
SE 76th Pl
8100 MthC 97206 627 F6
8100 PTLD 97206 627 E7
SW 76th Pl
8800 WasC 97223 625 G7
10800 TGRD 97223 655 G2
10800 WasC 97223 655 G2
NE 76th St
100 ClkC 98665 506 G5
6100 ClkC 98661 507 D5
8300 ClkC 98662 507 F5
11000 ClkC 98682 507 G5
15900 ClkC 98682 508 E5
NW 76th St
1000 ClkC 98665 506 F5
NE 76th Wy
15700 ClkC 98682 508 D5
SE 76th Cir Av
4600 PTLD 97206 627 H2
NE 77th Av
- HBRO 97124 594 D4
2100 VCVR 98664 537 E4
2600 PTLD 97213 597 F2
3900 PTLD 97218 597 F2
5100 ClkC 98662 537 E1
5100 VCVR 98662 537 E1
6600 ClkC 98662 507 E6
12900 ClkC 98662 477 E7
17300 ClkC 98604 477 F2
25100 ClkC 98604 447 F2
26600 ClkC 98604 417 F7
NW 77th Av
- CMAS 98607 539 A4
SE 77th Av
1500 PTLD 97215 597 F7
1900 PTLD 97215 627 F1
4500 PTLD 97206 627 F4
8400 MthC 97206 627 E7
9500 CmsC 97222 657 E1
SW 77th Av
4700 WasC 97225 625 G3
7000 PTLD 97223 625 G6
7000 WasC 97223 625 G6
9400 WasC 97223 655 G1
9700 TGRD 97223 655 G1
NE 77th Cir
10000 ClkC 98662 507 G5
16200 ClkC 98682 508 E5
NE 77th Ct
- VCVR 98664 537 E4
5400 ClkC 98662 507 E6
17900 ClkC 98604 477 F2
SE 77th Ct
900 VCVR 98664 537 E7
9200 CmsC 97206 657 E1
9300 CmsC 97222 657 E1
NE 77th Pl
- VCVR 98664 537 E4
2700 PTLD 97213 597 F3
6300 ClkC 98662 507 E6
S 77th Pl
- ClkC 98642 416 G7
- RDGF 98642 416 G7
- RDGF 98642 446 G1
SE 77th Pl
11400 CmsC 97222 657 E3
SW 77th Pl
2200 BRTN 97225 625 G1
12800 TGRD 97223 655 G4
NE 77th St
100 ClkC 98665 506 G5
6100 ClkC 98661 507 D5
10800 ClkC 98662 507 J5
15200 ClkC 98682 508 D5
26900 ClkC 98682 509 F6
NW 77th St
1000 ClkC 98665 506 F5
SW 77th Ter
15900 TGRD 97224 655 G7
NE 77th Wy
8600 ClkC 98662 507 F5
NE 78th Av
10 PTLD 97215 597 F6
2100 VCVR 98664 537 E4
3100 PTLD 97213 597 F2
3900 PTLD 97218 597 F2
5100 ClkC 98662 537 E1
5100 VCVR 98662 537 E1
6700 ClkC 98662 507 E6
NW 78th Av
- CMAS 98607 539 A4
SE 78th Av
10 PTLD 97213 597 F6
500 PTLD 97215 597 F7
800 VCVR 98664 537 E7
1200 VCVR 98664 567 E1
2400 PTLD 97206 627 F2
2400 PTLD 97215 627 F1
9500 CmsC 97222 657 F1
SW 78th Av
2000 BRTN 97225 625 G1
3200 WasC 97225 625 G2
6900 WasC 97223 625 G6
10800 TGRD 97223 655 G3
10800 WasC 97223 655 G2
21300 WasC 97062 685 F6
NE 78th Cir
10000 ClkC 98662 507 G5
13500 ClkC 98682 508 B5
NE 78th Ct
2400 VCVR 98664 537 E3
6000 PTLD 97218 567 F6
SE 78th Ct
10800 CmsC 97222 657 E3
N 78th Pl
10 ClkC 98642 416 H7
NE 78th Pl
4500 PTLD 97218 597 F1
S 78th Pl
10 ClkC 98642 416 H7
10 RDGF 98642 416 H7
SE 78th Pl
8400 PTLD 97206 627 E7
8900 CmsC 97206 627 F7
8900 CmsC 97206 657 F1
SW 78th Pl
8800 WasC 97223 625 G7
NW 78th Rd
1700 ClkC 98665 506 E5
1700 VCVR 98665 506 E5
NE 78th St
100 ClkC 98665 506 H5
2600 ClkC 98665 507 A5
4500 ClkC 98661 507 A5
10400 ClkC 98662 507 H5
15200 ClkC 98682 508 D5
21700 ClkC 98682 509 A5
NW 78th St
100 ClkC 98665 506 G5
1600 VCVR 98665 506 E5
NE 78th Wy
11700 ClkC 98662 507 J5
11700 ClkC 98682 507 J5
16300 ClkC 98682 508 E5
NE 79th Av
10 PTLD 97215 597 F5
800 PTLD 97213 597 F4
2100 VCVR 98664 537 E3
3300 VCVR 98662 537 F3
4700 PTLD 97218 597 F1
6500 ClkC 98662 507 E6
SE 79th Av
10 PTLD 97213 597 F6
10 PTLD 97215 597 F6
2400 PTLD 97206 627 F2
2400 PTLD 97215 627 F1
8600 CmsC 97206 627 F7
9500 CmsC 97222 657 F1
16100 CmsC 97267 687 E1
16100 JNCY 97267 687 E1
SW 79th Av
2000 BRTN 97225 625 G1
7500 WasC 97223 625 G6
10800 TGRD 97223 655 F3
14500 TGRD 97224 655 F7
NE 79th Cir
10800 ClkC 98662 507 J5
15000 ClkC 98682 508 D5
NW 79th Cir
1500 ClkC 98665 506 E5
NE 79th Ct
2400 VCVR 98664 537 E3
6600 PTLD 97218 567 F6
8800 ClkC 98662 507 E4
SE 79th Ct
1400 VCVR 98664 567 E1
11000 CmsC 97222 657 E3
SE 79th Pl
8900 CmsC 97206 627 F7
8900 CmsC 97206 657 F1
SW 79th Pl
17600 DRHM 97224 685 F2
NE 79th St
9400 ClkC 98662 507 G5
11700 ClkC 98682 507 J5
15200 ClkC 98682 508 D5
NW 79th St
800 ClkC 98665 506 F5
NE 79th Wy
15500 ClkC 98682 508 D7
NE 80th Av
10 PTLD 97215 597 F5
3100 PTLD 97213 597 F2
4800 PTLD 97218 597 F1
6000 PTLD 97218 567 F7
9300 ClkC 98662 507 F3
13100 ClkC 98662 477 F7
SE 80th Av
10 PTLD 97213 597 F6
10 PTLD 97215 597 F6
1100 VCVR 98664 537 E7
1900 PTLD 97215 627 F1
2500 PTLD 97206 627 F1
8600 CmsC 97206 627 F7
9000 CmsC 97206 657 F1
9000 CmsC 97222 657 F1
16100 JNCY 97267 687 F1
SW 80th Av
8100 WasC 97223 625 G7
9000 WasC 97223 655 F1
14600 TGRD 97224 655 F6
20500 TLTN 97062 685 F5
NE 80th Cir
- ClkC 98662 507 G5
14800 ClkC 98682 508 C5
NE 80th Ct
- ClkC 98604 477 F1
8800 ClkC 98662 507 F4
SE 80th Ct
5800 PTLD 97206 627 F4
SW 80th Ct
14100 TGRD 97224 655 F6
NE 80th Pl
2100 VCVR 98664 537 E4
SE 80th Pl
6400 PTLD 97206 627 F5
16600 JNCY 97267 687 F1
17000 CmsC 97267 687 F1
SW 80th Pl
7500 WasC 97223 625 G6
14200 TGRD 97224 655 F6
17600 DRHM 97224 685 F2
NE 80th St
2300 ClkC 98665 506 J5
3600 ClkC 98665 507 B5
10400 ClkC 98662 507 H5
11700 ClkC 98682 507 J5
15600 ClkC 98682 508 D7
NW 80th St
1100 ClkC 98665 506 E5
NE 80th Wy
20100 ClkC 98682 508 J5
NE 81st Av
2100 VCVR 98664 537 F4
3100 PTLD 97213 597 F2
3700 ClkC 98665 507 B5
4000 PTLD 97218 597 F2
5100 ClkC 98662 537 F1
5100 VCVR 98662 537 F1
10000 ClkC 98662 507 F3
15000 ClkC 98662 477 F4
18000 ClkC 98604 477 F2
SE 81st Av
10 PTLD 97213 597 F6
10 PTLD 97215 597 F6
2500 PTLD 97206 627 F1
2500 PTLD 97215 627 F1
9500 CmsC 97222 657 F1
16100 CmsC 97267 687 F1
16100 JNCY 97267 687 F1
SW 81st Av
2200 BRTN 97225 625 G1
6900 WasC 97223 625 F6
10900 TGRD 97223 655 F3
14500 TGRD 97224 655 F7
NE 81st Cir
17800 ClkC 98682 508 G5
NW 81st Cir
1000 ClkC 98665 506 F5
NE 81st Ct
9600 ClkC 98662 507 F3
SW 81st Ct
15800 TGRD 97224 655 F7
NE 81st Lp
- ClkC 98662 507 G5
NW 81st Pl
300 MthC 97229 595 G5
2500 PTLD 97229 595 G3
SE 81st Pl
6900 PTLD 97206 627 F6
SW 81st Pl
15900 TGRD 97224 655 F4
17700 DRHM 97224 685 F2
NE 81st St
300 ClkC 98665 506 G5
10400 ClkC 98662 507 H5
15900 ClkC 98682 508 E5
NE 81st Wy
9200 ClkC 98662 507 G5
15100 ClkC 98682 508 D5
NE 82nd Av
10 PTLD 97213 597 F5
10 PTLD 97215 597 F5
10 PTLD 97216 597 F6
10 PTLD 97220 597 F5
800 VCVR 98664 537 F5
3900 PTLD 97218 597 F1
5100 ClkC 98662 537 F1
5100 VCVR 98662 537 F1
5200 PTLD 97218 567 G5
5200 PTLD 97220 567 G5
5300 VCVR 98662 507 F7
8800 ClkC 98662 507 F3
15900 ClkC 98662 477 F4
19000 ClkC 98604 477 F1
23000 ClkC 98604 447 F4
26800 ClkC 98604 417 F7
31500 ClkC 98629 417 F2
NE 82nd Av SR-213
10 PTLD 97213 597 F5
10 PTLD 97215 597 F6
10 PTLD 97216 597 F6
10 PTLD 97220 597 F5
3900 PTLD 97218 597 F1
5200 PTLD 97218 567 F7
5200 PTLD 97220 567 F7
SE 82nd Av
- CmsC - 657 F6
- CmsC 97222 657 F5
10 PTLD 97213 597 F6
10 PTLD 97215 597 F6
10 PTLD 97216 597 F6
10 PTLD 97220 597 F6
2000 PTLD 97206 627 F6
2000 PTLD 97215 627 F1
2000 PTLD 97216 627 F1
2000 PTLD 97266 627 F6
8400 CmsC 97206 627 F7
8400 CmsC 97236 627 F7
SE 82nd Av SR-213
- CmsC - 657 F5
- CmsC 97015 657 F5
10 PTLD 97213 597 F6
10 PTLD 97215 597 F6
10 PTLD 97216 597 F6
10 PTLD 97220 597 F6
2000 PTLD 97206 627 F6
2000 PTLD 97215 627 F1
2000 PTLD 97216 627 F1
2000 PTLD 97266 627 F6
8400 CmsC 97206 627 F7
8400 CmsC 97236 627 F7
SE 82nd Av N
8500 CmsC 97206 627 F7
8500 CmsC 97236 627 F7
8500 PTLD 97266 627 F7
9000 CmsC 97206 657 F1
9000 CmsC 97236 657 F3
9200 CmsC 97222 657 F3
12500 CmsC 97015 657 F4
SE 82nd Av N SR-213
8500 CmsC 97206 627 F7
8500 CmsC 97236 627 F7
8500 PTLD 97266 627 F7
9000 CmsC 97206 657 F1
9000 CmsC 97236 657 F3
9200 CmsC 97222 657 F3
12500 CmsC 97015 657 F4
SW 82nd Av
3100 WasC 97225 625 G2
7000 WasC 97223 625 F6
9000 WasC 97223 655 F1
11000 TGRD 97223 655 F3
15600 TGRD 97224 655 F7
22100 WasC 97062 685 F7
23000 WasC 97062 715 F1
NE 82nd Cir
2600 ClkC 98665 507 A5
9100 ClkC 98662 507 G5
13500 ClkC 98682 508 B5
NW 82nd Cir
1700 ClkC 98665 506 F4
NE 82nd Ct
1500 VCVR 98664 537 F4
9300 ClkC 98662 507 F4
SE 82nd Ct
1000 VCVR 98664 537 F7
SW 82nd Ct
8800 WasC 97223 625 E7
82nd Dr
10 GLDS 97027 687 E4
700 GLDS 97015 687 F3
SE 82nd Dr
14200 CmsC 97015 657 G6
16000 CmsC 97015 687 G2
17500 GLDS 97015 687 F3
17700 GLDS 97027 687 F3
SE 82nd Dr SR-224
14200 CmsC 97015 657 F6
SW 82nd Pl
- WasC 97225 595 G7
8100 WasC 97223 625 F7
15300 TGRD 97224 655 F7
NE 82nd St
1800 ClkC 98665 506 J4
3000 ClkC 98665 507 A5
8800 ClkC 98662 507 G5
16300 ClkC 98682 508 E5
NW 82nd St
100 ClkC 98665 506 G5
NE 82nd Wy
2500 ClkC 98665 506 J4
2600 ClkC 98665 507 A4
E 83rd Av
5100 PTLD 97220 567 G7
NE 83rd Av
10 PTLD 97216 597 F6
2400 VCVR 98664 537 F3
3400 VCVR 98662 537 F2
4300 PTLD 97220 597 F1
9100 ClkC 98662 507 F4
SE 83rd Av
10 PTLD 97216 597 F6
10 PTLD 97220 597 F6
2400 PTLD 97216 627 F1
2400 PTLD 97266 627 F1
10100 CmsC 97236 657 F2
16100 CmsC 97267 687 F1
16100 JNCY 97267 687 F1
SW 83rd Av
600 WasC 97225 595 F6
2300 BRTN 97225 625 F1
4000 WasC 97225 625 F3
7000 WasC 97223 625 F6
10800 TGRD 97223 655 F3
15100 TGRD 97224 655 F6
NE 83rd Cir
9500 ClkC 98662 507 G5
14900 ClkC 98682 508 D5
NE 83rd Ct
1500 VCVR 98664 537 F4
9400 ClkC 98662 507 F3
27200 ClkC 98604 417 F7
SW 83rd Ct
14500 TGRD 97224 655 F6
NE 83rd Pl
- ClkC 98662 507 F7
- VCVR 98662 507 F7
- VCVR 98662 537 F1
NW 83rd Pl
300 MthC 97229 595 F5
2400 PTLD 97229 595 G3
SW 83rd Pl
9200 WasC 97223 655 F1
NE 83rd St
1900 ClkC 98665 506 J4
9800 ClkC 98662 507 H
15300 ClkC 98682 508 D
22700 ClkC 98682 509 C
NW 83rd St
100 ClkC 98665 506 G
NE 83rd Wy
2500 ClkC 98665 506 J4
3900 ClkC 98665 507 B4
14400 ClkC 98682 508 C
NE 84th Av
10 PTLD 97216 597 F6
1400 VCVR 98664 537 F4
2600 VCVR 98662 537 F3
4300 PTLD 97220 597 G
5400 VCVR 98662 507 F7
5800 ClkC 98662 507 F7
19100 ClkC 98604 477 F1
22200 ClkC 98604 447 F5
SE 84th Av
10 PTLD 97216 597 F6
10 PTLD 97220 597 F6
1900 PTLD 97216 627 F1
2500 PTLD 97266 627 F1
12900 CmsC 97015 657 F4
12900 CmsC 97236 657 F4
16100 CmsC 97267 687 F1
16100 JNCY 97267 687 F1
SW 84th Av
- TGRD 97224 655 F7
600 WasC 97225 595 F6
2000 BRTN 97225 625 F1
7000 WasC 97223 625 F6
11100 TGRD 97223 655 F3
18800 TLTN 97062 685 F3
21900 WasC 97062 685 F7
NE 84th Cir
11100 ClkC 98662 507 J5
17700 ClkC 98682 508 F5
NW 84th Cir
200 ClkC 98665 506 G4
NE 84th Ct
9100 ClkC 98662 507 F4
32900 ClkC 98629 417 G1
SE 84th Ct
1600 VCVR 98664 567 F1
SW 84th Ct
700 WasC 97225 595 F6
14600 TGRD 97224 655 F6
20500 TLTN 97062 685 F5
NE 84th Lp
5300 VCVR 98662 507 G7
5300 VCVR 98662 537 F1
NW 84th Lp
2100 ClkC 98665 506 E4
NE 84th Pl
6300 ClkC 98662 507 F6
NW 84th Pl
- MthC 97229 595 F5
SE 84th Pl
2500 PTLD 97216 627 F1
2500 PTLD 97266 627 F1
SW 84th Pl
2600 BRTN 97225 625 F1
3000 WasC 97225 625 F2
15600 TGRD 97224 655 F7
NE 84th St
1800 ClkC 98665 506 J4
6400 ClkC 98665 507 D4
10700 ClkC 98662 507 J5
13500 ClkC 98682 508 B5
NW 84th St
600 ClkC 98665 506 F4
NE 84th Wy
9600 ClkC 98662 507 H4
NE 85th Av
10 PTLD 97216 597 F6
1000 VCVR 98664 537 F5
4300 PTLD 97220 597 G1
5200 VCVR 98662 537 F1
5600 ClkC 98662 507 F7
5600 VCVR 98662 507 F7
18500 ClkC 98604 477 F1
SE 85th Av
10 PTLD 97216 597 G6
10 PTLD 97220 597 G6
2100 PTLD 97216 627 F1
2500 PTLD 97266 627 G2
10500 CmsC 97236 657 F2
SW 85th Av
10 MthC 97229 595 F6
10 WasC 97225 595 F6
2000 BRTN 97225 625 F1
5100 WasC 97225 625 F4
8300 WasC 97223 625 F7
10000 WasC 97223 655 F2
10600 TGRD 97223 655 F2
16000 TGRD 97224 685 F1
16200 WasC 97224 685 F1
NE 85th Cir
2100 ClkC 98665 506 J4
2700 ClkC 98665 507 A4
10200 ClkC 98662 507 H4
14500 ClkC 98682 508 C4
28900 ClkC 98607 509 J5
NE 85th Ct
27200 ClkC 98604 417 G7
SW 85th Ct
2400 BRTN 97225 625 F1
20100 TLTN 97062 685 F5
NE 85th Dr
8400 ClkC 98662 507 F4
NE 85th Pl
11200 ClkC 98662 507 J4
NE 85th St
200 ClkC 98665 506 G4
3400 ClkC 98665 507 B4
10900 ClkC 98662 507 J4
15300 ClkC 98682 508 D4
22200 ClkC 98682 509 B5
NW 85th St
300 ClkC 98665 506 F4
NE 85th Wy
17900 ClkC 98682 508 G5
NE 86th Av
10 PTLD 97216 597 G6
2000 VCVR 98662 537 F3
2000 VCVR 98664 537 F4
4800 PTLD 97220 597 G1
5100 PTLD 97220 567 G7
5400 VCVR 98662 507 F7
10200 ClkC 98662 507 F3
19100 ClkC 98604 447 G7
19100 ClkC 98604 477 F1

STREET Block City ZIP Map# Grid

NW 86th Av
10 WasC 97225 595 F6
900 WasC 97229 595 F5
SE 86th Av
10 PTLD 97216 597 G6
10 PTLD 97220 597 G6
3500 PTLD 97266 627 G2
10400 CmsC 97236 657 F2
SW 86th Av
3300 WasC 97225 625 F2
3900 BRTN 97225 625 F3
6300 WasC 97223 625 F5
14300 TGRD 97224 655 F6
20000 TLTN 97062 685 F5
NE 86th Cir
2000 ClkC 98665 506 J4
2700 ClkC 98665 507 A4
10700 ClkC 98662 507 H4
15800 ClkC 98682 508 E4
NW 86th Cir
1900 ClkC 98665 506 E4
NE 86th Ct
9900 ClkC 98662 507 F3
NW 86th Ct
500 WasC 97229 595 F5
SE 86th Ct
1500 VCVR 98664 567 F1
4500 PTLD 97266 627 G4
SW 86th Ct
21000 TLTN 97062 685 F6
NE 86th Pl
11200 ClkC 98662 507 J4
SE 86th Pl
5900 PTLD 97266 627 F5
NE 86th St
500 ClkC 98665 506 G4
2900 ClkC 98665 507 A4
8400 ClkC 98662 507 G4
12200 ClkC 98682 508 A4
NW 86th St
1300 ClkC 98665 506 E4
NE 86th Wy
9700 ClkC 98662 507 H4
NW 86th Wy
1500 ClkC 98665 506 E4
NE 87th Av
10 PTLD 97216 597 G6
2000 VCVR 98662 537 F4
2000 VCVR 98664 537 F4
4300 PTLD 97220 597 G1
5700 PTLD 97220 567 G7
10000 ClkC 98662 507 F3
11900 ClkC 98662 477 F7
20000 ClkC 98604 447 G6
27200 ClkC 98604 417 H7
30500 ClkC 98629 417 G3
NW 87th Av
10 WasC 97225 595 F5
1100 PTLD 97229 595 F4
1100 WasC 97229 595 F4
SE 87th Av
10 PTLD 97216 597 G6
10 PTLD 97220 597 G6
1900 PTLD 97216 627 G1
2500 PTLD 97266 627 G2
8400 CmsC 97236 627 G7
SW 87th Av
- WasC 97225 595 F7
- WasC 97225 625 F1
3000 BRTN 97225 625 F2
7200 WasC 97223 625 F6
10100 TGRD 97223 655 F2
10100 WasC 97223 655 F2
14500 TGRD 97224 655 F6
NE 87th Cir
- ClkC 98665 506 H4
2700 ClkC 98665 507 A4
7400 ClkC 98662 507 E4
15700 ClkC 98682 508 D4
NW 87th Cir
1600 ClkC 98665 506 E4
NE 87th Ct
9100 ClkC 98662 507 F4
SE 87th Ct
- PTLD 97266 627 G4
SW 87th Ct
13900 TGRD 97223 655 E5
13900 TGRD 97224 655 E5
20800 TLTN 97062 685 E5
NE 87th Pl
2800 VCVR 98662 537 F3
3100 PTLD 97220 597 G2
SW 87th Pl
22500 TLTN 97062 685 E7
NE 87th St
- ClkC 98665 506 H4
11000 ClkC 98662 507 J4
11200 ClkC 98682 507 J4
16100 ClkC 98682 508 E4
NW 87th St
300 ClkC 98665 506 F4
NW 87th Ter
400 WasC 97229 595 F5
NE 87th Wy
- ClkC 98665 506 H4
9000 ClkC 98662 507 G4
NE 88th Av
100 VCVR 98664 537 F6
3300 VCVR 98662 537 F3
4300 PTLD 97220 597 G1
9500 ClkC 98662 507 F3
15000 ClkC 98604 477 G4
15000 ClkC 98662 477 G5
29000 ClkC 98604 417 G5
NW 88th Av
10 WasC 97225 595 F5
1300 WasC 97229 595 F4
SE 88th Av
10 PTLD 97216 597 G6
10 PTLD 97220 597 G6
100 VCVR 98664 537 F6
1500 VCVR 98664 567 F1
1900 PTLD 97216 627 G1
3600 PTLD 97266 627 G2
8400 CmsC 97236 627 G7
SW 88th Av
10 WasC 97225 595 F6
10 WasC 97229 595 F6
5100 WasC 97223 625 F4
8200 WasC 97223 625 F7
9200 WasC 97223 655 F1
11500 TGRD 97223 655 F3
14900 TGRD 97224 655 F7
NE 88th Cir
800 ClkC 98665 506 H4
11100 ClkC 98662 507 J4
13500 ClkC 98682 508 B4
NE 88th Ct
3500 VCVR 98662 537 F2
8400 ClkC 98662 507 F4
NE 88th Pl
2900 PTLD 97220 597 G3
SW 88th Pl
6500 WasC 97223 625 F5
16600 TGRD 97224 685 E1
NE 88th St
1200 ClkC 98665 506 J4
2700 ClkC 98665 507 A4
10300 ClkC 98662 507 H4
13700 ClkC 98682 508 C4
22200 ClkC 98682 509 B4
NW 88th St
200 ClkC 98665 506 G4
NE 88th Wy
4000 ClkC 98665 507 B4
16300 ClkC 98682 508 E4
NE 89th Av
- ClkC 98604 477 G1
10 PTLD 97216 597 G6
1100 VCVR 98664 537 F5
4500 PTLD 97220 597 G1
5000 PTLD 97220 567 G7
5400 VCVR 98662 507 F7
10400 ClkC 98662 507 G3
14100 ClkC 98662 477 G6
19200 ClkC 98604 447 G7
NW 89th Av
10 WasC 97225 595 F5
10 WasC 97229 595 F5
SE 89th Av
10 PTLD 97220 597 G6
100 VCVR 98664 537 F6
1100 PTLD 97216 597 G7
1900 PTLD 97216 627 G1
2500 PTLD 97266 627 G2
8400 CmsC 97236 627 G7
SW 89th Av
- WasC 97062 685 E7
10 WasC 97225 595 F6
10 WasC 97229 595 F6
2500 WasC 97225 625 F1
7900 WasC 97223 625 F7
10800 TGRD 97223 655 F2
14000 TGRD 97224 655 E6
19300 TLTN 97062 685 E4
NE 89th Cir
2500 ClkC 98665 506 J4
2700 ClkC 98665 507 A4
10500 ClkC 98662 507 H4
13900 ClkC 98682 508 C4
NW 89th Cir
300 ClkC 98665 506 G4
NE 89th Ct
1500 VCVR 98664 537 F4
8100 ClkC 98662 507 G5
SW 89th Ct
14800 TGRD 97224 655 F6
20900 TLTN 97062 685 E5
SE 89th Dr
12700 CmsC 97015 657 G4
12700 CmsC 97236 657 G4
NE 89th Pl
- ClkC 98629 417 G2
1600 VCVR 98664 537 F4
22700 ClkC 98604 447 G4
SE 89th Pl
- PTLD 97266 627 G6
SW 89th Pl
6500 WasC 97223 625 F5
15000 TGRD 97224 655 E7
16600 TGRD 97224 685 E1
22700 TLTN 97062 685 E7
NE 89th St
2200 ClkC 98665 506 J4
4000 ClkC 98665 507 B4
10400 ClkC 98662 507 H4
13500 ClkC 98682 508 B4
NW 89th St
1200 ClkC 98665 506 E4
NE 89th Wy
3800 ClkC 98665 507 B4
NE 90th Av
10 PTLD 97216 597 G6
1900 VCVR 98664 537 F4
2200 VCVR 98662 537 F4
4300 MWDP 97220 597 G1
4500 PTLD 97220 597 G1
10100 ClkC 98662 507 G3
26800 ClkC 98604 417 G7
NW 90th Av
10 WasC 97225 595 F5
10 WasC 97229 595 F5
SE 90th Av
10 PTLD 97216 597 G6
10 PTLD 97220 597 G6
100 VCVR 98664 537 F6
2100 PTLD 97216 627 G1
2100 PTLD 97266 627 G1
11400 CmsC 97236 657 G3
15000 CmsC 97015 657 G7
SW 90th Av
10 WasC 97225 595 F6
10 WasC 97229 595 F6
5500 WasC 97225 625 F4
6300 WasC 97223 625 F5
9400 WasC 97223 655 F1
10100 TGRD 97223 655 E2
14300 TGRD 97224 655 E6
18300 TLTN 97062 685 E3
NE 90th Cir
1900 ClkC 98665 506 J4
3300 ClkC 98665 507 A4
NW 90th Cir
300 ClkC 98665 506 G4
NE 90th Ct
5000 ClkC 98665 507 C4
10500 ClkC 98662 507 G2
13100 ClkC 98662 477 G7
SW 90th Ct
19100 TLTN 97062 685 E4
NE 90th Pl
9100 ClkC 98662 507 G4
NW 90th Pl
600 WasC 97229 595 F5
SE 90th Pl
2000 PTLD 97216 627 G1
2800 PTLD 97266 627 G2
SW 90th Pl
7500 WasC 97223 625 F6
16600 TGRD 97224 685 E1
22700 TLTN 97062 685 E7
NE 90th St
2100 ClkC 98665 506 J4
5100 ClkC 98665 507 C4
10400 ClkC 98662 507 H4
14200 ClkC 98682 508 C4
NW 90th St
1700 ClkC 98665 506 E4
NE 91st Av
1300 VCVR 98664 537 G4
4600 PTLD 97220 597 G1
5100 PTLD 97220 567 G7
10200 ClkC 98662 507 G3
27900 ClkC 98604 417 G6
NW 91st Av
1000 WasC 97229 595 F4
SE 91st Av
10 PTLD 97216 597 G6
100 VCVR 98664 537 G6
1600 VCVR 98664 567 G1
3600 PTLD 97266 627 G2
8700 CmsC 97236 627 G7
8700 PTLD 97236 627 G7
9200 CmsC 97236 657 G1
14900 CmsC 97015 657 G7
SW 91st Av
3400 WasC 97225 625 E2
4500 BRTN 97225 625 E3
7500 WasC 97223 625 E6
9000 BRTN 97223 625 E7
9000 WasC 97223 655 E1
11400 TGRD 97223 655 E3
14500 TGRD 97224 655 E6
21400 TLTN 97062 685 E6
NE 91st Cir
1500 ClkC 98665 506 H4
4000 ClkC 98665 507 B4
11500 ClkC 98662 507 J4
13000 ClkC 98682 508 B4
21800 ClkC 98682 509 A4
NW 91st Cir
1500 ClkC 98665 506 E4
NE 91st Ct
5600 ClkC 98662 507 G7
SW 91st Ct
3900 WasC 97225 625 F3
11200 TGRD 97223 655 E3
21300 TLTN 97062 685 E6
NE 91st Pl
- VCVR 98664 537 G4
9000 ClkC 98662 507 G4
NW 91st Pl
1600 WasC 97229 595 F4
SE 91st Pl
3600 PTLD 97266 627 G3
SW 91st Pl
9800 WasC 97223 655 E1
NE 91st St
2000 ClkC 98665 506 J4
2600 ClkC 98665 507 A5
8100 ClkC 98662 507 F4
15800 ClkC 98682 508 D4
NW 91st St
900 ClkC 98665 506 F4
SW 91st Ter
18500 TLTN 97062 685 E3
NE 91st Wy
2700 ClkC 98665 507 A4
NE 92nd Av
1400 VCVR 98664 537 G4
2400 VCVR 98662 537 G3
4300 MWDP 97220 597 G1
4300 PTLD 97220 597 G1
9700 ClkC 98662 507 G3
13200 ClkC 98662 477 G7
15600 ClkC 98604 477 G4
21900 ClkC 98604 447 G5
30000 ClkC 98604 417 G4
NW 92nd Av
1200 WasC 97229 595 F4
SE 92nd Av
100 VCVR 98664 537 G6
500 PTLD 97216 597 G6
1900 PTLD 97216 627 G1
2400 PTLD 97266 627 G4
8400 PTLD 97236 627 G7
8700 CmsC 97236 627 G6
9000 CmsC 97236 657 G1
15100 CmsC 97015 657 G7
SW 92nd Av
6600 BRTN 97005 625 E5
6600 BRTN 97008 625 E5
6600 BRTN 97223 625 E5
6600 WasC 97005 625 E5
6600 WasC 97223 625 E5
6700 WasC 97008 625 E5
9500 WasC 97223 655 E1
11200 TGRD 97223 655 E3
15100 TGRD 97224 655 E6
16000 TGRD 97224 685 E1
21300 TLTN 97062 685 E6
NE 92nd Cir
2700 ClkC 98665 507 A4
10800 ClkC 98662 507 H4
29300 ClkC 98607 509 J4
NE 92nd Ct
5400 VCVR 98662 507 G7
6800 ClkC 98662 507 G6
SE 92nd Ct
1600 VCVR 98664 567 G1
11000 CmsC 97236 657 G3
SW 92nd Ct
21400 TLTN 97062 685 E6
NE 92nd Dr
5500 PTLD 97220 567 G7
NE 92nd Pl
10 PTLD 97216 597 G6
10 PTLD 97220 597 G5
NW 92nd Pl
500 WasC 97229 595 F5
SE 92nd Pl
10000 CmsC 97236 657 G2
SW 92nd Pl
7500 WasC 97223 625 E6
22700 TLTN 97062 685 E7
NE 92nd St
- ClkC 98682 508 E4
100 ClkC 98665 506 G4
4300 ClkC 98665 507 B4
11500 ClkC 98662 507 J4
NW 92nd St
1800 ClkC 98665 506 E3
SW 92nd Ter
- TGRD 97223 655 E6
- TGRD 97224 655 E5
18500 TLTN 97062 685 E3
NE 92nd Wy
14200 ClkC 98682 508 C4
NE 93rd Av
100 VCVR 98664 537 G6
2400 PTLD 97220 597 G3
2400 VCVR 98662 537 G3
10300 ClkC 98662 507 G3
12500 ClkC 98662 477 G7
NW 93rd Av
1200 WasC 97229 595 F4
SE 93rd Av
10 PTLD 97216 597 G6
100 VCVR 98664 537 G6
2400 PTLD 97216 627 G1
6100 PTLD 97266 627 G5
12400 CmsC 97236 657 G4
13000 CmsC 97015 657 G7
SW 93rd Av
10 WasC 97225 595 E6
10 WasC 97229 595 E6
3400 WasC 97225 625 E2
7400 WasC 97223 625 E6
11000 TGRD 97223 655 E3
14000 TGRD 97224 655 E6
16000 TGRD 97224 685 E1
19800 TLTN 97062 685 E5
NE 93rd Cir
9300 ClkC 98662 507 G4
13500 ClkC 98682 508 B4
NW 93rd Cir
1700 ClkC 98665 506 E3
NE 93rd Ct
2100 VCVR 98664 537 G4
6800 ClkC 98662 507 G6
SE 93rd Ct
8500 PTLD 97236 627 G7
8500 PTLD 97266 627 G7
10600 CmsC 97236 657 G2
NE 93rd Pl
9200 ClkC 98662 507 G4
NW 93rd Pl
1700 WasC 97229 595 E4
NE 93rd St
100 ClkC 98665 506 G4
5100 ClkC 98665 507 C4
8000 ClkC 98662 507 F4
16300 ClkC 98682 508 E4
NW 93rd St
100 ClkC 98665 506 G4
SW 93rd Ter
18500 TLTN 97062 685 E3
NE 94th Av
10 PTLD 97216 597 G6
100 VCVR 98664 537 G6
500 PTLD 97220 597 G5
4700 VCVR 98662 537 G1
5300 VCVR 98662 507 G7
7600 ClkC 98662 507 G4
17700 ClkC 98604 477 G2
NW 94th Av
1200 WasC 97229 595 E4
SE 94th Av
10 PTLD 97216 597 G6
10 PTLD 97220 597 G6
100 VCVR 98664 537 G6
2100 PTLD 97216 627 G1
3800 PTLD 97266 627 G3
10000 CmsC 97236 657 G2
15200 CmsC 97015 657 G7
SW 94th Av
3600 WasC 97225 625 E2
7400 WasC 97223 625 E6
11300 TGRD 97223 655 E3
15000 TGRD 97224 655 E7
20500 TLTN 97062 685 E5
NE 94th Cir
5500 ClkC 98665 507 C3
9300 ClkC 98662 507 G4
NE 94th Ct
1900 VCVR 98664 537 G4
7400 ClkC 98662 507 G5
13700 ClkC 98682 508 B4
SE 94th Ct
9400 VCVR 98664 567 G1
SW 94th Ct
14400 TGRD 97224 655 E6
NE 94th Pl
1200 VCVR 98664 537 G5
SE 94th Pl
10500 CmsC 97236 657 G2
NE 94th St
100 ClkC 98665 506 G3
2600 ClkC 98665 507 A3
8100 ClkC 98662 507 F3
13400 ClkC 98682 508 B4
NW 94th St
1800 ClkC 98665 506 E3
NW 94th Ter
500 WasC 97229 595 E5
SW 94th Ter
22700 TLTN 97062 685 E7
22700 WasC 97062 685 E7
NE 94th Wy
3000 ClkC 98665 507 A3
NE 95th Av
100 VCVR 98664 537 G6
2100 VCVR 98662 537 G4
4500 MWDP 97220 597 H1
4500 PTLD 97220 597 H1
10300 ClkC 98662 507 G3
17600 ClkC 98604 477 G3
31000 ClkC 98604 417 H3
31000 ClkC 98629 417 H3
NW 95th Av
10 WasC 97225 595 E6
10 WasC 97229 595 E6
SE 95th Av
10 VCVR 98664 537 G6
1500 VCVR 98664 567 G1
SW 95th Av
10 WasC 97225 595 E6
10 WasC 97229 595 E6
10500 TGRD 97223 655 E2
19700 TLTN 97062 685 E5
26000 WNVL 97070 715 D5
NE 95th Cir
- ClkC 98682 508 C4
4700 ClkC 98665 507 C3
NW 95th Cir
200 ClkC 98665 506 G3
NE 95th Ct
2400 VCVR 98662 537 G3
10000 ClkC 98662 507 G3
NW 95th Ct
1500 ClkC 98665 506 E3
SE 95th Ct
1800 VCVR 98664 567 G1
10700 CmsC 97236 657 G2
SW 95th Ct
21300 TLTN 97062 685 E6
NE 95th Pl
2000 PTLD 97220 597 H4
NW 95th Pl
3000 ClkC 98665 506 D3
NE 95th St
1000 ClkC 98665 506 H3
5200 ClkC 98665 507 C3
8200 ClkC 98662 507 F3
11700 ClkC 98682 507 J4
20900 ClkC 98682 508 J4
20900 ClkC 98682 509 A4
NW 95th St
900 ClkC 98665 506 F3
NE 95th Wy
4500 ClkC 98665 507 B3
NE 96th Av
2000 VCVR 98664 537 G4
2400 VCVR 98662 537 G3
4100 MWDP 97220 597 H1
4400 PTLD 97220 597 H1
11900 ClkC 98662 507 G1
17700 ClkC 98604 477 G2
19900 ClkC 98604 447 G7
27900 ClkC 98604 417 H6
NW 96th Av
1300 WasC 97229 595 E4
SE 96th Av
10 VCVR 98664 537 G6
500 PTLD 97216 597 H7
1400 VCVR 98664 567 G1
1800 PTLD 97216 627 H1
4300 PTLD 97266 627 G3
9400 CmsC 97236 657 G1
SW 96th Av
1800 BRTN 97225 595 F6
1800 WasC 97225 595 F6
3600 WasC 97005 625 E3
3600 WasC 97225 625 E2
4400 BRTN 97005 625 E3
14800 TGRD 97224 655 E7
NE 96th Cir
- ClkC 98665 507 B3
NE 96th Ct
2100 VCVR 98664 537 G4
26600 ClkC 98604 417 H7
SE 96th Ct
1900 VCVR 98664 567 G1
10700 CmsC 97236 657 G2
SE 96th Dr
2200 PTLD 97216 627 H1
2200 PTLD 97266 627 H1
SW 96th Dr
22500 TLTN 97062 685 D7
SW 96th Pl
12000 TGRD 97223 655 E4
NE 96th St
100 ClkC 98665 506 G3
4500 ClkC 98665 507 C3
7800 ClkC 98662 507 F3
11600 ClkC 98682 507 J3
13300 ClkC 98682 508 B3
21200 ClkC 98682 509 A4
NW 96th St
2100 ClkC 98665 506 E3
NE 96th Wy
2100 ClkC 98665 506 J3
2700 ClkC 98665 507 A3
13000 ClkC 98682 508 B3
NE 97th Av
10 PTLD 97216 597 H5
100 VCVR 98664 537 G5
3200 VCVR 98662 537 G2
4500 MWDP 97220 597 H1
4500 PTLD 97220 597 H1
7400 ClkC 98662 507 G5
13400 ClkC 98662 477 G6
17600 ClkC 98604 477 H2
27400 ClkC 98604 417 H6
NW 97th Av
300 WasC 97229 595 E5
SE 97th Av
10 PTLD 97216 597 H6
10 PTLD 97220 597 H6
700 VCVR 98664 537 G7
1300 VCVR 98664 567 G1
1900 PTLD 97216 627 H1
3900 PTLD 97266 627 H3
9900 CmsC 97236 657 G1
12400 CmsC 97015 657 H6
SW 97th Av
10 WasC 97225 595 E6
10 WasC 97229 595 E6
1800 BRTN 97225 595 E7
3700 WasC 97005 625 E2
3700 WasC 97225 625 E2
14000 TGRD 97223 655 E5
14000 TGRD 97224 655 E6
19300 TLTN 97062 685 D4
NE 97th Cir
2100 ClkC 98665 506 J3
3100 ClkC 98665 507 B5
10500 ClkC 98662 507 H3
14300 ClkC 98682 508 C3
NW 97th Cir
3000 ClkC 98665 506 D3
NE 97th Ct
10000 ClkC 98662 507 G3
24000 ClkC 98604 447 H3
SE 97th Ct
10300 CmsC 97236 657 H2
SW 97th Ct
11200 TGRD 97223 655 E3
SW 97th Pl
12000 TGRD 97223 655 E3
14100 TGRD 97224 655 E6
NE 97th St
2200 ClkC 98665 506 J3
5900 ClkC 98665 507 D3
10400 ClkC 98662 507 H3
13400 ClkC 98682 508 B3
NW 97th St
1700 ClkC 98665 506 E3
NE 97th Wy
2800 ClkC 98665 507 A3
NE 98th Av
1800 VCVR 98664 537 G4
3400 VCVR 98662 537 G2
4500 MWDP 97220 597 H1
4500 PTLD 97220 597 H1
10200 ClkC 98662 507 G3
31100 ClkC 98604 417 H3
31100 ClkC 98629 417 H3
SE 98th Av
100 VCVR 98664 537 G7
1900 VCVR 98664 567 G1
2100 PTLD 97216 627 H1
2500 PTLD 97266 627 H1
15600 CmsC 97015 657 G7
15800 CmsC 97015 657 H7
SW 98th Av
1900 WasC 97225 595 E7
3100 WasC 97225 625 E2
4700 BRTN 97005 625 E3
11400 TGRD 97223 655 E3
14000 TGRD 97224 655 E5
20500 TLTN 97062 685 D5
NE 98th Cir
700 ClkC 98665 506 H3
4400 ClkC 98665 507 B3
10900 ClkC 98662 507 H3
NW 98th Cir
1400 ClkC 98665 506 E3
NE 98th Ct
- VCVR 98664 537 G4
24600 ClkC 98604 447 H2
SE 98th Ct
10400 CmsC 97236 657 H2
13800 CmsC 97015 657 G6
SW 98th Ct
7800 WasC 97008 625 E6
14100 TGRD 97224 655 E6
20500 TLTN 97062 685 D5
NE 98th Lp
1900 VCVR 98664 537 G4
NE 98th Pl
11400 ClkC 98662 507 J3
24900 ClkC 98604 447 H2
NW 98th Pl
1400 PTLD 97229 595 E4
1400 WasC 97229 595 E4
NE 98th St
1900 ClkC 98665 506 J3
3400 ClkC 98665 507 B3
11000 ClkC 98662 507 J3
13200 ClkC 98682 508 B3
NW 98th St
1800 ClkC 98665 506 E3
NE 98th Wy
2800 ClkC 98665 507 B5
NE 99th Av
10 PTLD 97216 597 H5
500 PTLD 97220 597 H5
1400 VCVR 98664 537 G5
3600 VCVR 98662 537 G2
3900 MWDP 97220 597 H1
11900 ClkC 98662 507 G2
18700 ClkC 98604 477 H1
23400 ClkC 98604 447 H3
29100 ClkC 98604 417 H5
NW 99th Av
10 WasC 97225 595 E5
10 WasC 97229 595 E5
SE 99th Av
10 PTLD 97216 597 H6
500 VCVR 98664 537 G7
2000 VCVR 98664 567 G1
3600 PTLD 97266 627 H3
SW 99th Av
10 WasC 97225 595 E6
10 WasC 97229 595 E6
3800 WasC 97005 625 E2
3800 WasC 97225 625 E2
4300 BRTN 97005 625 E3
21400 TLTN 97062 685 B6
NE 99th Cir
4100 ClkC 98686 507 B3
8200 ClkC 98662 507 F3
SE 99th Ct
300 VCVR 98664 537 G6
2000 VCVR 98664 567 G1
9900 CmsC 97236 657 H2
SE 99th Dr
10000 CmsC 97236 657 H2
10000 HPYV 97236 657 H2
NE 99th Pl
24600 ClkC 98604 447 H2
SW 99th Pl
7000 WasC 97008 625 E6
NE 99th St
100 ClkC 98665 506 G3
100 ClkC 98685 506 G3
1100 ClkC 98686 506 G3
5000 ClkC 98665 507 C3
5500 ClkC 98686 507 D3
10400 ClkC 98662 507 J3
11500 ClkC 98682 507 J3
11700 ClkC 98682 508 A3
16800 ClkC 98606 508 F3
21100 ClkC 98682 509 A3
NW 99th St
1800 ClkC 98665 506 D3
1800 ClkC 98685 506 D3
NE 99th Wy
13100 ClkC 98682 508 B3
NE 100th Av
10 PTLD 97216 597 H5
1800 VCVR 98664 537 G4
4700 PTLD 97220 597 H1
10200 ClkC 98662 507 H3
17600 ClkC 98604 477 H2
SE 100th Av
- PTLD 97216 597 H6
100 VCVR 98664 537 G6
1900 PTLD 97216 627 H1
3600 PTLD 97266 627 H4
SW 100th Av
3000 WasC 97225 625 E2
13800 TGRD 97223 655 D5
13800 TGRD 97224 655 D7
NE 100th Cir
7100 ClkC 98665 507 E3
7100 ClkC 98686 507 E3
8000 ClkC 98662 507 F3
13900 ClkC 98682 508 C3
22200 ClkC 98682 509 B3
NE 100th Ct
500 VCVR 98664 537 G6
3800 VCVR 98662 537 G2
7000 ClkC 98662 507 H6
SE 100th Ct
2000 VCVR 98664 567 G1
SW 100th Ct
18100 TLTN 97062 685 D3
SE 100th Dr
10000 CmsC 97236 657 H2
SW 100th Dr
21600 TLTN 97062 685 D6
NE 100th St
- ClkC 98682 507 J3
2300 ClkC 98686 506 J3
2600 ClkC 98686 507 A3
2700 ClkC 98665 507 A3
10400 ClkC 98662 507 H3
14000 ClkC 98682 508 C3
14600 ClkC 98606 477 H5
NW 100th St
2400 ClkC 98685 506 D3
NW 100th Ter
- WasC 97229 595 E4
SW 100th Ter
7000 BRTN 97008 625 D6
7000 WasC 97008 625 D6
NE 100th Wy
9400 ClkC 98662 507 G3
NE 101st Av
1900 VCVR 98664 537 H4
2600 VCVR 98662 537 H3
4700 PTLD 97220 597 H1
5200 PTLD 97220 567 H7
8000 ClkC 98662 507 H5
19100 ClkC 98604 477 H1
20000 ClkC 98604 447 H7
NW 101st Av
10 WasC 97225 595 E5
3100 MthC 97229 595 E2
3100 PTLD 97229 595 E2
SE 101st Av
100 VCVR 98664 537 G6
1700 PTLD 97216 597 H7
1800 PTLD 97216 627 H1
1800 VCVR 98664 567 H1
5300 PTLD 97266 627 H4
SW 101st Av
10 WasC 97225 595 E6
10 WasC 97229 595 E6
4400 BRTN 97005 625 D3
7200 BRTN 97008 625 D6
NE 101st Cir
5300 ClkC 98686 507 C3
8000 ClkC 98662 507 F3
15200 ClkC 98682 508 D3
22800 ClkC 98682 509 C3
NW 101st Cir
300 ClkC 98685 506 G3
NE 101st Ct
1100 VCVR 98664 537 H5
3300 VCVR 98662 537 G3
6900 ClkC 98662 507 H6
23900 ClkC 98604 447 H3
31100 ClkC 98604 417 H3
31100 ClkC 98629 417 H3
NW 101st Ct
1200 ClkC 98685 506 F3
SW 101st Ct
3500 WasC 97005 625 E2
NE 101st Lp
20000 ClkC 98604 447 H7
NE 101st Pl
- ClkC 98662 477 G5
8600 ClkC 98662 507 H4
14800 ClkC 98606 477 H5
SE 101st Pl
7400 PTLD 97266 627 H6
NE 101st St
100 ClkC 98685 506 G3
7200 ClkC 98662 507 E3
7200 ClkC 98686 507 E3
12000 ClkC 98682 508 A3
21800 ClkC 98682 509 B3
NW 101st St
1500 ClkC 98685 506 E3
NE 101st Wy
14400 ClkC 98682 508 C3
NE 102nd Av
10 PTLD 97216 597 H6
2100 VCVR 98664 537 H4
3000 PTLD 97220 597 H5
3500 MWDP 97220 597 H5
3600 VCVR 98662 537 H2
4900 PTLD 97220 567 H7
5400 ClkC 98662 537 H1
11000 ClkC 98662 507 H1
15600 ClkC 98606 477 H4
18900 ClkC 98604 477 H4
21900 ClkC 98604 447 H5
23100 BGND 98604 447 H4
27200 ClkC 98604 417 H6
31400 ClkC 98629 417 H2
NW 102nd Av
1000 WasC 97229 595 D4
SE 102nd Av
10 PTLD 97216 597 H6
100 VCVR 98664 537 H7
1500 VCVR 98664 567 H1
1900 PTLD 97216 627 H1
5500 PTLD 97266 627 H5
10700 CmsC 97236 657 H3
15500 CmsC 97015 657 H7
SW 102nd Av
10 WasC 97225 595 D6
3700 BRTN 97005 625 E3
3700 WasC 97005 625 E3
7200 BRTN 97008 625 D6
13800 TGRD 97223 655 D5
13800 TGRD 97224 655 D5
NE 102nd Cir
11600 ClkC 98662 507 J3
NW 102nd Cir
1100 ClkC 98685 506 F3
NE 102nd Ct
2900 VCVR 98662 537 H3
8000 ClkC 98662 507 F3
NW 102nd Ct
1400 ClkC 98685 506 E3
SE 102nd Ct
2200 VCVR 98664 567 H1
SW 102nd Ct
10100 TLTN 97062 685 D6
SW 102nd Pl
22200 TLTN 97062 685 D7
NE 102nd St
100 ClkC 98685 506 G3
1300 ClkC 98686 506 H3
2700 ClkC 98665 507 A3

Portland Street Index

STREET Block	City	ZIP	Map#	Grid
NE 102nd St				
5000	ClkC	98686	507	C3
8600	ClkC	98662	507	G3
20700	ClkC	98682	508	J3
21100	ClkC	98682	509	A3
NW 102nd St				
1700	ClkC	98685	506	E3
NE 102nd Wy				
-	ClkC	98682	508	D3
NE 103rd Av				
2600	VCVR	98662	537	H3
2600	VCVR	98664	537	H3
4700	PTLD	97220	597	H1
11900	ClkC	98662	507	H1
19400	ClkC	98604	447	H7
29900	ClkC	98604	417	H4
SE 103rd Av				
100	PTLD	97216	597	H6
100	VCVR	98664	537	H7
1500	VCVR	98664	567	H1
2500	PTLD	97216	627	H1
2500	PTLD	97266	627	H2
10800	CmsC	97236	657	H2
SW 103rd Av				
3300	WasC	97005	625	D2
3300	WasC	97225	625	D2
4500	BRTN	97005	625	D3
7000	BRTN	97008	625	D6
14100	TGRD	97223	655	D5
14100	TGRD	97224	655	D6
16000	TGRD	97224	685	D1
20500	TLTN	97062	685	D5
NE 103rd Cir				
-	ClkC	98682	508	A3
6500	ClkC	98686	507	D3
9900	ClkC	98662	507	H3
NW 103rd Cir				
1000	ClkC	98685	506	F3
NE 103rd Ct				
1200	VCVR	98664	537	H5
7900	ClkC	98662	507	H5
NW 103rd Ct				
1400	ClkC	98685	506	E2
SW 103rd Ct				
10200	TLTN	97062	685	D6
NE 103rd Dr				
-	ClkC	98682	508	D3
SE 103rd Dr				
300	PTLD	97216	597	H6
2000	PTLD	97216	627	H1
2900	PTLD	97266	627	H2
SW 103rd Dr				
20800	TLTN	97062	685	D5
NE 103rd Lp				
2900	VCVR	98662	537	H3
NE 103rd Pl				
1500	PTLD	97220	597	H4
SE 103rd Pl				
6100	PTLD	97266	627	H5
NE 103rd St				
200	ClkC	98685	506	G2
5300	ClkC	98686	507	C3
9200	ClkC	98662	507	G3
NW 103rd St				
1600	ClkC	98685	506	E2
NE 104th Av				
2400	VCVR	98664	537	H4
4100	VCVR	98682	537	H2
4700	PTLD	97220	597	J1
11900	ClkC	98662	507	H1
19400	ClkC	98604	447	H7
31000	ClkC	98604	417	J3
31000	ClkC	98629	417	J3
SE 104th Av				
100	VCVR	98664	537	H7
1400	VCVR	98664	567	G2
1700	PTLD	97216	597	H7
1800	PTLD	97216	627	H1
3600	PTLD	97266	627	H3
7600	MthC	97266	627	H6
10800	CmsC	97236	657	H3
SW 104th Av				
10	WasC	97225	595	D6
10	WasC	97229	595	D6
3500	WasC	97005	625	D2
6800	BRTN	97008	625	D5
13800	TGRD	97223	655	D5
13800	TGRD	97224	655	D5
16100	TGRD	97224	685	D1
17400	TLTN	97062	685	D2
NE 104th Cir				
-	ClkC	98662	507	F3
3300	ClkC	98686	507	A3
19800	ClkC	98606	508	H3
NW 104th Cir				
400	ClkC	98685	506	F2
NW 104th Cr				
100	ClkC	98685	506	G2
NE 104th Ct				
9900	ClkC	98662	507	H3
SE 104th Ct				
1500	VCVR	98664	567	H1
1700	PTLD	97216	597	H7
12000	CmsC	97236	657	H4
12200	CmsC	97015	657	H4
SE 104th Dr				
2100	PTLD	97216	627	H1
2400	PTLD	97266	627	H1
NW 104th Lp				
700	ClkC	98685	506	F2
NE 104th Pl				
6400	ClkC	98662	507	H6
NE 104th St				
-	ClkC	98682	508	A3
1700	ClkC	98686	506	J2
6600	ClkC	98686	507	E3
9200	ClkC	98662	507	G3
21800	ClkC	98682	509	B3
NW 104th St				
1600	ClkC	98685	506	E2
SW 104th Ter				
-	TLTN	97062	685	D7
-	TLTN	97062	715	D1
NE 104th Wy				
4500	ClkC	98686	507	B2
NE 104th St Lp				
1800	ClkC	98686	506	J3
NE 105th Av				
2200	VCVR	98664	537	H4
3500	PTLD	97220	597	J1
4400	VCVR	98682	537	H1
5100	PTLD	97220	567	J7
11900	ClkC	98662	507	H1
19400	ClkC	98604	447	H7
26900	ClkC	98604	417	J7
NW 105th Av				
-	PTLD	97231	565	D2
SE 105th Av				
10	PTLD	97216	597	H6
10	PTLD	97220	597	H6
1100	VCVR	98664	537	H7
2100	PTLD	97216	627	J1
3800	PTLD	97266	627	H3
7800	MthC	97266	627	H7
10800	CmsC	97236	657	H3
12500	CmsC	97015	657	H4
SW 105th Av				
6700	BRTN	97008	625	D5
14000	TGRD	97223	655	D6
14000	TGRD	97224	655	D6
17300	WasC	97062	685	D2
20600	TLTN	97062	685	D5
NE 105th Cir				
4700	ClkC	98686	507	C2
12800	ClkC	98682	508	A3
NW 105th Cir				
2600	ClkC	98685	506	D2
NE 105th Ct				
2600	VCVR	98662	537	H3
8900	ClkC	98662	507	H4
12500	ClkC	98662	477	H7
18000	ClkC	98604	477	H2
SE 105th Ct				
1300	VCVR	98664	537	H7
1400	VCVR	98664	567	H1
SW 105th Ct				
17800	TLTN	97062	685	D2
SE 105th Dr				
12000	CmsC	97236	657	H4
12200	CmsC	97015	657	H4
SW 105th Pl				
11200	TGRD	97223	655	D3
NE 105th St				
200	ClkC	98685	506	G2
2200	ClkC	98686	506	J2
3900	ClkC	98686	507	B2
8600	ClkC	98662	507	G2
15700	ClkC	98682	508	E3
22800	ClkC	98682	509	C3
NW 105th St				
1400	ClkC	98685	506	E2
SW 105th Ter				
10	WasC	97225	595	D6
200	BRTN	97225	595	D6
NE 106th Av				
10	VCVR	98664	537	H6
4000	VCVR	98682	537	H1
4700	PTLD	97220	597	J1
9000	ClkC	98662	507	H4
SE 106th Av				
10	PTLD	97216	597	J6
1300	VCVR	98664	537	H7
1500	VCVR	98664	567	H1
1800	PTLD	97216	627	J1
7900	PTLD	97266	627	H7
12100	CmsC	97015	657	H4
12100	CmsC	97236	657	H4
15900	CmsC	97015	687	H1
SW 106th Av				
2400	WasC	97225	625	D1
3200	WasC	97005	625	D2
10700	TGRD	97223	655	D2
14600	TGRD	97224	655	D6
17300	TLTN	97062	685	D2
22900	WasC	97062	685	D7
NE 106th Cir				
6300	ClkC	98686	507	D2
8900	ClkC	98662	507	G2
NW 106th Cir				
3000	ClkC	98685	506	D2
NE 106th Ct				
9400	ClkC	98662	507	H3
SE 106th Ct				
1100	VCVR	98664	537	H7
SW 106th Dr				
12200	TGRD	97223	655	D4
NE 106th Pl				
500	PTLD	97220	597	J5
8100	ClkC	98662	507	H5
SW 106th Pl				
10	WasC	97225	595	D5
2000	BRTN	97225	625	D1
2000	WasC	97225	625	D1
22000	TLTN	97062	685	D6
NE 106th St				
-	ClkC	98682	508	A2
1000	ClkC	98685	506	H2
2200	ClkC	98686	506	J2
4300	ClkC	98686	507	B2
9100	ClkC	98662	507	G2
NW 106th St				
1600	ClkC	98685	506	E2
NE 106th Wy				
5900	ClkC	98686	507	D2
NE 107th Av				
1900	VCVR	98664	537	H4
4700	PTLD	97220	597	J1
5400	ClkC	98662	537	H1
11700	ClkC	98662	507	H1
16000	ClkC	98604	477	J3
19900	ClkC	98604	447	J7
NW 107th Av				
10	WasC	97225	595	D5
1900	WasC	97229	595	D4
9900	PTLD	97231	565	E2
SE 107th Av				
100	VCVR	98664	537	H7
1300	PTLD	97216	597	J7
2500	PTLD	97216	627	J1
2500	PTLD	97266	627	J1
SW 107th Av				
2600	BRTN	97225	625	D1
2600	WasC	97225	625	D1
3000	WasC	97005	625	D1
4400	BRTN	97005	625	D3
5600	BRTN	97008	625	D4
13200	TGRD	97223	655	D5
17300	TLTN	97062	685	D2
NW 107th Cir				
2700	ClkC	98685	506	D2
SW 107th Ct				
12700	TGRD	97223	655	D4
16300	TGRD	97224	685	D1
NE 107th Pl				
3700	PTLD	97220	597	J2
6400	ClkC	98662	507	H6
NW 107th Pl				
2100	WasC	97229	595	D3
SE 107th Pl				
10700	PTLD	97266	627	J3
SW 107th Pl				
11400	TGRD	97223	655	D3
NE 107th St				
300	ClkC	98685	506	G2
1800	ClkC	98686	506	J2
3100	ClkC	98686	507	A2
9400	ClkC	98662	507	H2
11400	ClkC	98682	507	J2
NW 107th St				
100	ClkC	98685	506	G2
SW 107th Ter				
15000	TGRD	97224	655	D7
NE 108th Av				
-	ClkC	98604	447	J3
10	PTLD	97216	597	J6
500	VCVR	98664	537	H5
4000	VCVR	98682	537	H2
4700	PTLD	97220	597	J1
11900	ClkC	98662	507	J1
13100	ClkC	98662	477	J7
29900	ClkC	98604	417	J4
NW 108th Av				
-	PTLD	97231	565	D2
1800	WasC	97229	595	D4
SE 108th Av				
10	PTLD	97216	597	J6
10	PTLD	97220	597	J6
4800	PTLD	97266	627	J4
8000	MthC	97266	627	J7
11500	CmsC	97236	657	H4
11500	HPYV	97236	657	J3
SW 108th Av				
3100	WasC	97005	625	D2
3100	WasC	97225	625	D2
10800	TGRD	97223	655	D2
16000	TGRD	97224	655	D6
16000	TGRD	97224	685	C1
18000	TLTN	97062	685	C3
18500	WasC	97062	685	C3
NE 108th Ct				
3100	ClkC	98686	507	A2
7500	ClkC	98662	507	H5
SE 108th Ct				
7600	PTLD	97266	627	J6
SW 108th Ct				
10800	TGRD	97223	655	D2
NE 108th Pl				
3900	PTLD	97220	597	J2
NW 108th Pl				
-	PTLD	97231	565	D2
SE 108th Pl				
4500	PTLD	97266	627	J3
SW 108th Pl				
17300	TLTN	97062	685	C2
NE 108th St				
1000	ClkC	98685	506	H2
2200	ClkC	98686	506	J2
3100	ClkC	98686	507	A2
23200	ClkC	98682	509	C2
NW 108th St				
100	ClkC	98685	506	G2
NE 109th Av				
10	PTLD	97216	597	J6
1400	VCVR	98664	537	H5
2800	VCVR	98682	537	H3
2800	VCVR	98684	537	H3
5000	PTLD	97220	567	J7
5000	PTLD	97220	597	J1
6600	ClkC	98662	507	H6
12500	ClkC	98662	477	J7
18900	ClkC	98604	477	J1
19600	ClkC	98604	447	J7
26900	ClkC	98604	417	J7
NW 109th Av				
-	PTLD	97231	565	D2
700	WasC	97229	595	D5
SE 109th Av				
10	PTLD	97216	597	J6
2500	PTLD	97216	627	J1
2500	PTLD	97266	627	J2
SW 109th Av				
4000	WasC	97005	625	D3
4500	BRTN	97005	625	D3
10800	TGRD	97223	655	D2
14600	TGRD	97224	655	C7
17800	TLTN	97062	685	C2
NE 109th Cir				
900	ClkC	98685	506	H2
NW 109th Cir				
400	ClkC	98685	506	F2
NE 109th Ct				
500	PTLD	97220	597	J5
2200	VCVR	98684	537	H4
8600	ClkC	98662	507	J4
19800	ClkC	98604	447	J7
SE 109th Pl				
1700	VCVR	98664	567	G2
SW 109th Pl				
16300	TGRD	97224	685	C1
NE 109th St				
-	ClkC	98606	508	F2
1100	ClkC	98685	506	H2
2100	ClkC	98686	506	J2
4700	ClkC	98686	507	C2
10900	ClkC	98662	507	J2
20700	ClkC	98682	508	J2
20800	ClkC	98606	509	A2
20800	ClkC	98682	509	A2
NW 109th St				
2600	ClkC	98685	506	D2
NW 109th Ter				
3400	WasC	97229	595	D2
SW 109th Ter				
21500	TLTN	97062	685	C6
22900	WasC	97062	685	C7
NE 109th Wy				
600	ClkC	98685	506	H2
NE 109th Av Lp				
3600	VCVR	98682	537	H2
NE 110th Av				
600	VCVR	98664	537	H5
2400	VCVR	98684	537	H3
4700	PTLD	97220	597	J1
4800	VCVR	98682	537	J1
9500	ClkC	98662	507	J4
12900	ClkC	98662	477	J7
17400	ClkC	98604	477	J2
NW 110th Av				
10	WasC	97225	595	D5
700	WasC	97229	595	D5
10200	PTLD	97231	565	D1
SE 110th Av				
500	VCVR	98664	537	H7
1400	PTLD	97216	597	J7
2000	PTLD	97216	627	J1
2000	PTLD	97266	627	J1
SW 110th Av				
-	BRTN	97225	595	D6
-	WasC	97225	595	D6
-	WasC	97229	595	D6
3100	WasC	97005	625	D2
3200	BRTN	97005	625	D2
6500	BRTN	97008	625	D5
10700	CmsC	97070	715	C6
10700	WNVL	97070	715	C6
13200	TGRD	97223	655	C5
13900	TGRD	97224	655	C5
17400	TLTN	97062	685	C2
28200	CmsC	97140	715	C5
NE 110th Cir				
10200	ClkC	98662	507	H2
NW 110th Cir				
3600	ClkC	98685	506	C2
NE 110th Ct				
2000	VCVR	98684	537	H4
19900	ClkC	98604	447	J7
NW 110th Ct				
1900	WasC	97229	595	D4
SE 110th Ct				
1700	VCVR	98664	567	H1
12400	CmsC	97015	657	J4
12400	CmsC	97236	657	J4
SE 110th Dr				
6400	PTLD	97266	627	J5
NE 110th Pl				
2300	ClkC	98686	506	J2
3200	PTLD	97220	597	J3
SW 110th Pl				
-	TGRD	97223	655	C3
21500	TLTN	97062	685	C6
NE 110th St				
1100	ClkC	98685	506	H2
1900	ClkC	98686	506	J2
7300	ClkC	98662	507	E2
7300	ClkC	98686	507	E2
12000	ClkC	98682	508	A2
NW 110th St				
300	ClkC	98685	506	G2
NW 110th Wy				
500	ClkC	98685	506	F2
NE 111th Av				
4700	PTLD	97220	597	J1
12000	ClkC	98662	507	J1
18200	ClkC	98604	477	J2
NW 111th Av				
-	PTLD	97231	565	D1
2000	WasC	97229	595	D3
SE 111th Av				
10	PTLD	97216	597	J6
1800	PTLD	97216	627	J1
2500	PTLD	97266	627	J2
SW 111th Av				
6500	BRTN	97008	625	C5
10700	TGRD	97223	655	C2
17400	TLTN	97062	685	C2
17400	WasC	97224	685	C2
NE 111th Cir				
5000	ClkC	98686	507	C2
12200	ClkC	98682	508	A2
NW 111th Cir				
3700	ClkC	98685	506	C2
NE 111th Ct				
-	ClkC	98662	507	J2
2000	VCVR	98684	537	J4
3000	ClkC	98686	507	A2
NW 111th Ct				
2800	WasC	97229	595	D3
SE 111th Ct				
1700	VCVR	98664	567	H1
NE 111th Dr				
2800	PTLD	97220	597	J3
NW 111th Lp				
100	ClkC	98685	506	G2
SW 111th Pl				
2100	WasC	97225	625	D1
11000	TGRD	97223	655	C2
NE 111th St				
100	ClkC	98685	506	G2
2600	ClkC	98686	506	H1
5900	ClkC	98686	507	D2
8700	ClkC	98662	507	G2
12400	ClkC	98682	508	A2
NW 111th St				
700	ClkC	98685	506	F2
NW 111th Ter				
3000	WasC	97229	595	D2
SW 111th Ter				
10	BRTN	97225	595	D6
10	WasC	97225	595	D6
112th Av				
-	WasC	97140	715	C2
-	WNVL	97140	715	C2
NE 112th Av				
-	VCVR	98662	537	J1
300	VCVR	98684	537	J5
2500	VCVR	98682	537	J1
3500	PTLD	97220	597	J1
6400	PTLD	97220	567	J6
6400	PTLD	97220	568	A6
9300	ClkC	98662	507	J4
15400	ClkC	98606	477	J5
18600	ClkC	98604	477	J1
22500	BGND	98604	447	J3
26500	ClkC	98604	447	J1
30800	ClkC	98604	417	J3
NW 112th Av				
-	PTLD	97231	565	D1
10	BRTN	97225	595	D5
10	BRTN	97229	595	D5
10	WasC	97225	595	D5
10	WasC	97229	595	D5
SE 112th Av				
-	MthC	97266	627	J7
500	PTLD	97216	597	J7
1700	PTLD	97216	627	J1
2200	PTLD	97266	627	J2
2500	VCVR	98664	567	J2
SW 112th Av				
6000	BRTN	97008	625	C5
11200	TGRD	97223	655	C3
14000	TGRD	97224	655	C6
17700	TLTN	97062	685	C2
22700	TLTN	97140	685	C7
22700	WasC	97140	685	C7
22800	WasC	97140	715	C1
NE 112th Cir				
300	ClkC	98685	506	G2
4600	ClkC	98686	507	B2
NW 112th Cir				
1900	ClkC	98685	506	E2
NE 112th Ct				
9900	ClkC	98662	507	J3
14800	ClkC	98606	477	J5
SE 112th Ct				
1700	VCVR	98664	567	J1
NE 112th Pl				
9900	ClkC	98662	507	J3
NW 112th Pl				
3000	WasC	97229	595	D2
SE 112th Pl				
1800	VCVR	98664	567	J1
SW 112th Pl				
2400	WasC	97225	625	C1
NE 112th St				
100	ClkC	98685	506	G2
1600	ClkC	98686	506	J2
6400	ClkC	98686	507	D2
12800	ClkC	98682	508	B2
19300	ClkC	98606	508	H2
NW 112th St				
1700	ClkC	98685	506	E2
NW 112th Wy				
3900	ClkC	98685	506	C2
NE 113th Av				
-	ClkC	98604	477	J1
10	PTLD	97216	597	J6
3500	PTLD	97220	597	J2
10500	ClkC	98662	507	J2
24200	ClkC	98604	447	J2
27000	ClkC	98604	418	A7
NW 113th Av				
900	BRTN	97229	595	C5
900	WasC	97229	595	D4
SE 113th Av				
10	PTLD	97216	597	J6
10	VCVR	98683	537	J6
10	VCVR	98684	537	J6
1700	VCVR	98664	567	J1
2100	PTLD	97216	627	J1
2100	PTLD	97266	627	J1
SW 113th Av				
2800	WasC	97005	625	C1
2800	WasC	97225	625	C1
3500	BRTN	97005	625	C2
16000	TGRD	97224	655	D6
16000	TGRD	97224	685	C1
16200	WasC	97224	685	C1
17700	TLTN	97062	685	C2
NE 113th Cir				
5500	ClkC	98686	507	C2
10200	ClkC	98662	507	H2
NW 113th Cir				
3200	ClkC	98685	506	D1
NE 113th Ct				
8900	ClkC	98662	507	J4
SE 113th Ct				
1500	VCVR	98664	567	J1
13900	CmsC	97015	657	J6
NE 113th Pl				
10	PTLD	97216	597	J6
10	PTLD	97220	597	J6
4500	PTLD	97220	598	A1
NW 113th Pl				
3200	WasC	97229	595	D2
SW 113th Pl				
11600	TGRD	97223	655	C3
NE 113th St				
-	ClkC	98685	506	G2
1600	ClkC	98686	506	J2
5500	ClkC	98686	507	D2
11700	ClkC	98662	507	J2
11700	ClkC	98682	507	J2
11700	ClkC	98682	508	A2
22800	ClkC	98682	509	C2
NW 113th St				
1200	ClkC	98685	506	E2
SW 113th Ter				
11000	TGRD	97223	655	C1
NE 114th Av				
2600	VCVR	98682	537	J3
2600	VCVR	98684	537	J3
3500	PTLD	97220	598	A2
9600	ClkC	98662	507	J3
31400	ClkC	98604	418	A2
NW 114th Av				
10	BRTN	97225	595	C5
10	WasC	97225	595	C5
10	WasC	97229	595	C5
SE 114th Av				
1300	PTLD	97216	597	J7
7600	PTLD	97266	627	J6
15300	CmsC	97015	657	J7
16500	CmsC	97015	687	J1
SW 114th Av				
3600	BRTN	97005	625	C2
13600	TGRD	97223	655	C5
14000	TGRD	97224	655	C6
17700	TLTN	97062	685	C2
NE 114th Cir				
6500	ClkC	98686	507	D2
9800	ClkC	98662	507	H2
NW 114th Cir				
3100	ClkC	98685	506	D1
NE 114th Ct				
10500	ClkC	98662	507	J2
14600	ClkC	98606	477	J5
SE 114th Ct				
1600	VCVR	98664	567	J1
7600	PTLD	97266	627	J6
12100	CmsC	97015	657	J4
12100	CmsC	97236	657	J4
SW 114th Ct				
15300	TGRD	97224	655	C7
NE 114th Pl				
1600	PTLD	97220	598	A4
1800	PTLD	97220	597	J4
SE 114th Pl				
500	PTLD	97216	597	J6
1800	PTLD	97216	627	J1
5400	PTLD	97266	627	J4
SW 114th Pl				
11000	TGRD	97223	655	C3
NE 114th St				
100	ClkC	98685	506	G1
2600	ClkC	98686	506	H1
4300	ClkC	98686	507	C1
8700	ClkC	98662	507	G2
12400	ClkC	98682	508	A2
NW 114th St				
1600	ClkC	98685	506	E1
NW 114th Ter				
3000	WasC	97229	595	C2
SW 114th Ter				
12200	TGRD	97223	655	C4
NE 115th Av				
1400	VCVR	98684	537	J4
2900	VCVR	98682	537	J3
5000	PTLD	97220	568	A7
5000	PTLD	97220	598	A1
9900	ClkC	98662	507	J3
NW 115th Av				
3600	WasC	97229	595	C2
SE 115th Av				
500	PTLD	97216	597	J6
2300	PTLD	97216	627	J1
2500	PTLD	97266	627	J2
11900	CmsC	97236	657	J4
13700	CmsC	97015	657	J6
16500	CmsC	97015	687	J1
SW 115th Av				
-	BRTN	97005	625	C3
10700	TGRD	97223	655	C3
13900	TGRD	97224	655	C5
17500	TLTN	97062	685	C2
17500	TLTN	97224	685	C2
17500	WasC	97224	685	C2
NE 115th Cir				
400	ClkC	98685	506	G1
3000	ClkC	98686	507	A1
NW 115th Cir				
900	ClkC	98685	506	F1
SE 115th Cir				
14000	CmsC	97015	657	J6
NE 115th Ct				
9700	ClkC	98662	507	J3
14600	ClkC	98606	477	J5
SE 115th Ct				
1700	VCVR	98664	567	J1
SE 115th Pl				
2000	PTLD	97216	628	A1
6600	PTLD	97266	627	J5
6600	PTLD	97266	628	A5
NE 115th St				
1300	ClkC	98685	506	H1
4100	ClkC	98686	507	B1
8700	ClkC	98662	507	G2
21200	ClkC	98606	509	A2
23000	ClkC	98682	509	C2
NW 115th St				
3200	ClkC	98685	506	D1
NE 116th Av				
-	VCVR	98683	537	J6
200	VCVR	98684	537	J6
2800	VCVR	98682	537	J3
4400	PTLD	97220	598	A1
10100	ClkC	98662	507	J3
18900	ClkC	98604	478	A1
NW 116th Av				
1400	WasC	97229	595	C4
SE 116th Av				
500	VCVR	98683	537	J7
2300	PTLD	97216	628	A1
2300	PTLD	97266	628	A1
6900	PTLD	97266	627	J6
14000	CmsC	97015	657	J6
SW 116th Av				
-	BRTN	97005	625	C2
2900	WasC	97005	625	C2
11700	TGRD	97223	655	C3
15000	KNGC	97224	655	C7
15000	TGRD	97224	655	C6
15800	WasC	97224	655	C7
NE 116th Cir				
1300	ClkC	98685	506	H1
9900	ClkC	98662	507	H1
22200	ClkC	98682	509	B2
NW 116th Cir				
700	ClkC	98685	506	F1
NE 116th Ct				
500	PTLD	97220	598	A5
10200	ClkC	98662	507	J3
15100	ClkC	98606	477	J5
SE 116th Ct				
1000	VCVR	98683	537	J7
12000	CmsC	97236	657	J4
13500	CmsC	97015	657	J5
NE 116th Pl				
1500	PTLD	97220	598	A4
10300	ClkC	98662	507	J3
NW 116th Pl				
3100	WasC	97229	595	C2
SW 116th Pl				
12900	TGRD	97223	655	C4
14900	KNGC	97224	655	C6
14900	TGRD	97224	655	C6
NE 116th St				
-	ClkC	98662	507	G1
1700	ClkC	98686	506	J1
2600	ClkC	98686	507	A1
19400	ClkC	98606	508	H2
21800	ClkC	98606	509	A2
NW 116th St				
3700	ClkC	98685	506	C1
SW 116th Ter				
-	BRTN	97008	625	C6
14000	TGRD	97224	655	C6
NE 116th Wy				
12700	ClkC	98682	508	A1
NW 116th Wy				
3200	ClkC	98685	506	D1
NE 117th Av				
-	VCVR	98682	507	J7
10	PTLD	97216	598	A6
100	VCVR	98684	537	J5
2000	PTLD	97220	598	A3
6300	ClkC	98662	507	J6
6300	ClkC	98682	507	J4
11700	ClkC	98606	507	J1
11900	ClkC	98662	477	J7
13100	ClkC	98606	478	A6
15400	ClkC	98606	477	J4
24300	ClkC	98604	448	A3
27400	ClkC	98604	418	A6
NE 117th Av SR-500				
-	VCVR	98682	507	J7
6300	ClkC	98662	507	J6
6300	ClkC	98682	507	J7
NE 117th Av SR-503				
-	VCVR	98682	507	J7
6300	ClkC	98662	507	J6
6300	ClkC	98682	507	J4
11700	ClkC	98606	507	J1
11900	ClkC	98606	477	J7
11900	ClkC	98662	477	J7
13100	ClkC	98606	478	A6
SE 117th Av				
10	PTLD	97216	598	A7
100	VCVR	98683	537	J6
100	VCVR	98684	537	J6
1700	PTLD	97216	628	A1
4200	PTLD	97266	628	A3
11500	CmsC	97236	657	J4
12000	HPYV	97236	657	J4
14700	CmsC	97015	657	J6
SW 117th Av				
400	BRTN	97225	595	C6
3600	BRTN	97005	625	C3
14000	TGRD	97223	655	C6
14000	TGRD	97224	655	C6
NE 117th Cir				
14600	ClkC	98606	508	D1
14600	ClkC	98682	508	D1
NW 117th Cir				
3000	ClkC	98685	506	D1
NE 117th Ct				
2900	VCVR	98682	537	J3
NW 117th Ct				
1500	WasC	97229	595	C4
SE 117th Ct				
13700	CmsC	97015	657	J5
NW 117th Dr				
3000	WasC	97229	595	C3
SE 117th Dr				
7500	PTLD	97266	627	J6
7500	PTLD	97266	628	A6
SE 117th Pl				
3800	PTLD	97266	628	A3
SW 117th Pl				
14700	TGRD	97224	655	C6
NE 117th St				
600	ClkC	98685	506	H1
1400	ClkC	98686	506	J1
4100	ClkC	98686	507	B1
NW 117th St				
1800	ClkC	98685	506	E1
SW 117th Ter				
11100	TGRD	97223	655	C3
NW 117th Wy				
2700	ClkC	98685	506	D1
NE 118th Av				
-	ClkC	98682	507	J3
10	PTLD	97216	598	A6
1600	VCVR	98684	537	J4
4500	PTLD	97220	598	A1
4600	VCVR	98682	537	J1
18900	ClkC	98604	478	A1
24300	ClkC	98604	448	A3
33300	ClkC	98629	418	A1
NW 118th Av				
-	BRTN	97229	595	C5
3500	MthC	97229	595	C1
SE 118th Av				
200	VCVR	98683	537	J7
200	VCVR	98684	537	J7
2100	PTLD	97216	628	A1
2500	PTLD	97266	628	A2
SW 118th Av				
-	TGRD	97223	655	C4
2700	WasC	97005	625	C1
19300	TLTN	97062	685	B4
NE 118th Cir				
21900	ClkC	98606	509	B1
NW 118th Cir				
1200	ClkC	98685	506	F1
NE 118th Ct				
-	ClkC	98604	478	A2
4900	VCVR	98682	537	J1
NW 118th Ct				
1500	WasC	97229	595	C4
SE 118th Ct				
900	VCVR	98683	537	J7
10900	HPYV	97236	657	J3
SW 118th Ct				
10700	TGRD	97223	655	C2
13600	TGRD	97224	655	B5
SE 118th Dr				
7000	PTLD	97266	628	A6
14000	CmsC	97015	657	J6
NW 118th Pl				
3700	WasC	97229	595	C2
SE 118th Pl				
4000	PTLD	97266	628	A3
NE 118th St				
-	VCVR	98682	537	J2
5600	ClkC	98686	507	D1
10600	ClkC	98662	507	H1
NW 118th St				
2600	ClkC	98685	506	D1
NW 118th Ter				
2500	WasC	97229	595	C3
NW 118th Wy				
3900	ClkC	98685	506	C1
NE 119th Av				
1800	VCVR	98684	537	J4
4500	PTLD	97220	598	A1
4700	VCVR	98682	537	J1
11900	ClkC	98606	508	A1
11900	ClkC	98682	508	A1
18600	ClkC	98604	478	A1
25600	ClkC	98604	448	A1
26900	ClkC	98604	418	A7
NW 119th Av				
1000	BRTN	97229	595	C4
1000	WasC	97229	595	C4
SE 119th Av				
10	PTLD	97216	598	A6
700	VCVR	98683	537	J7
1500	VCVR	98683	567	J1
2100	PTLD	97216	628	A1
2500	PTLD	97266	628	A2
11700	CmsC	97236	658	A3
11700	HPYV	97236	658	A4
14400	CmsC	97015	658	A7
SW 119th Av				
2700	BRTN	97005	625	C1
2700	WasC	97005	625	C1
11000	TGRD	97223	655	C2
15100	KNGC	97224	655	B6
15100	WasC	97224	655	B6
19000	TLTN	97062	685	B4
NE 119th Cir				
-	ClkC	98606	509	C1
-	ClkC	98682	509	C1
7600	ClkC	98682	507	J5
NE 119th Ct				
3500	VCVR	98682	537	J2
SE 119th Ct				
7600	PTLD	97266	628	A6
11000	HPYV	97236	658	A3
13300	CmsC	97015	658	A5

Portland Street Index

STREET
Block City ZIP Map# Grid

SE 119th Dr
7500 PTLD 97266 628 A6
11200 HPYV 97236 657 J3
11200 HPYV 97236 658 A2
12900 CmsC 97015 657 J5
12900 CmsC 97015 658 A5
13000 CmsC 97236 658 A5
NW 119th Pl
2400 WasC 97229 595 C3
SW 119th Pl
2300 BRTN 97005 625 C1
2300 BRTN 97225 625 C1
2300 WasC 97225 625 C1
14000 TGRD 97223 655 B5
14000 TGRD 97224 655 B5
NE 119th St
2100 ClkC 98686 506 J1
2100 ClkC 98686 507 D1
7200 ClkC 98662 507 G1
11100 ClkC 98606 507 J1
11100 ClkC 98682 507 J1
11700 ClkC 98682 508 A1
15200 ClkC 98606 508 G1
21200 ClkC 98606 509 A1
NW 119th St
400 ClkC 98685 506 G1
NW 119th Ter
3700 WasC 97229 595 C2
NE 120th Av
10 PTLD 97216 598 A6
400 VCVR 98684 537 J6
500 PTLD 97220 598 A5
4600 VCVR 98682 538 A2
11000 ClkC 98682 508 A2
17600 ClkC 98604 478 A2
17600 ClkC 98606 478 A2
26400 ClkC 98604 418 A7
NW 120th Av
3500 MthC 97229 595 C1
SE 120th Av
100 VCVR 98683 537 J6
100 VCVR 98684 537 J6
1000 PTLD 97216 598 A7
1500 VCVR 98683 567 J1
2100 PTLD 97216 628 A1
2700 PTLD 97266 628 A1
16400 CmsC 97015 688 A1
SW 120th Av
- TLTN 97062 685 B5
2700 WasC 97005 625 C1
20700 WasC 97062 685 B6
NW 120th Cir
1000 ClkC 98685 506 F1
NE 120th Ct
9900 ClkC 98682 508 A3
23500 ClkC 98604 448 A3
SE 120th Ct
13200 CmsC 97015 658 A5
NW 120th Pl
1100 WasC 97229 595 C4
SE 120th Pl
7500 PTLD 97266 628 A6
14000 CmsC 97015 658 A6
SW 120th Pl
14100 TGRD 97224 655 B6
14500 WasC 97224 655 B6
NE 120th St
2100 ClkC 98686 506 J1
4000 ClkC 98686 507 B1
NW 120th St
1300 ClkC 98685 506 E1
NW 120th Ter
3700 WasC 97229 595 C2
SE 120th Wy
13500 CmsC 97015 658 A5
NE 121st Av
1800 VCVR 98684 538 A4
5100 ClkC 98682 538 A1
5100 PTLD 97220 598 A1
5100 VCVR 98682 538 A1
5300 VCVR 98682 508 A7
7200 ClkC 98682 508 A6
15900 ClkC 98606 478 A4
26400 ClkC 98604 418 A7
SE 121st Av
100 VCVR 98683 538 A6
100 VCVR 98684 538 A6
500 VCVR 98683 537 J7
1300 VCVR 98683 568 A1
2200 PTLD 97216 628 A1
2200 PTLD 97266 628 A1
SW 121st Av
- BRTN 97005 625 C2
2700 WasC 97005 625 C1
10500 BRTN 97008 655 C2
10500 TGRD 97008 655 C2
10500 TGRD 97223 655 B5
13800 TGRD 97224 655 B6
NW 121st Cir
2400 ClkC 98685 506 D1
NE 121st Ct
9900 ClkC 98682 508 A3
19000 ClkC 98604 478 A1
SE 121st Ct
11000 HPYV 97236 658 A3
13200 CmsC 97015 658 A5
NE 121st Pl
4300 PTLD 97220 598 A1
4500 PTLD 97230 598 A1
NW 121st Pl
2300 WasC 97229 595 C3
SE 121st Pl
13400 CmsC 97015 658 A5
SW 121st Pl
300 WasC 97225 595 C6
2600 WasC 97005 625 C1
NE 121st St
2100 ClkC 98686 506 J1
11900 ClkC 98606 508 A1
22700 ClkC 98682 509 B1
NW 121st St
900 ClkC 98685 506 F1
NE 121st Wy
5000 ClkC 98686 507 C1
NE 122nd Av
10 PTLD 97216 598 A6
10 PTLD 97230 598 A5
10 PTLD 97233 598 A6
1000 VCVR 98684 538 A5
3000 PTLD 97220 598 A3
3800 VCVR 98682 538 A2
9900 ClkC 98682 508 A3
11900 ClkC 98606 508 A1
17900 ClkC 98604 478 A1
17900 ClkC 98606 478 A2
NE 122nd Av
19200 BGND 98604 448 A7
19200 ClkC 98604 448 A7
31500 ClkC 98604 417 J2
31500 ClkC 98604 418 A2
NE 122nd Av SR-503
17900 ClkC 98604 478 A1
17900 ClkC 98606 478 A2
19200 BGND 98604 448 A7
19200 ClkC 98604 448 A7
NW 122nd Av
1000 WasC 97229 595 C4
SE 122nd Av
10 PTLD 97216 598 A7
10 PTLD 97233 598 A7
800 VCVR 98683 538 A7
1800 PTLD 97216 628 A1
1800 PTLD 97233 628 A1
2300 PTLD 97236 628 A5
6800 PTLD 97266 628 A6
11800 HPYV 97236 658 A4
12100 CmsC 97236 658 A4
13000 CmsC 97015 658 A6
15900 CmsC 97015 688 A1
SW 122nd Av
2700 BRTN 97005 625 B1
3300 WasC 97005 625 C2
12400 TGRD 97223 655 B4
15000 WasC 97224 655 B7
15200 KNGC 97224 655 B7
NE 122nd Blvd
- PTLD 97220 568 B7
- PTLD 97220 598 A1
- PTLD 97230 568 B7
- PTLD 97230 598 A1
NE 122nd Cir
22800 ClkC 98682 509 C1
SE 122nd Ct
700 VCVR 98683 538 A7
SW 122nd Ct
11900 TGRD 97223 655 B3
SE 122nd Dr
6800 PTLD 97236 628 A6
NE 122nd St
1900 ClkC 98686 506 J1
4100 ClkC 98686 507 B1
20200 ClkC 98606 508 J1
21200 ClkC 98606 509 A1
NW 122nd St
3600 ClkC 98685 506 C1
4300 ClkC 98660 506 B1
NE 123rd Av
- ClkC 98604 418 A6
2400 VCVR 98684 538 A4
2700 PTLD 97230 598 A3
4200 VCVR 98682 538 A2
8300 ClkC 98682 508 A4
14900 ClkC 98606 478 A5
18800 ClkC 98604 478 A1
NW 123rd Av
1400 WasC 97229 595 B4
SE 123rd Av
300 VCVR 98683 538 A7
300 VCVR 98684 538 A6
1000 PTLD 97233 598 A7
1500 VCVR 98683 568 A1
3500 PTLD 97236 628 A2
12500 CmsC 97236 658 A4
13500 CmsC 97015 658 A5
SW 123rd Av
2700 WasC 97005 625 B1
3300 BRTN 97005 625 B2
6500 BRTN 97008 625 B5
12500 TGRD 97223 655 B4
15400 KNGC 97224 655 B7
16900 KNGC 97224 685 B1
16900 WasC 97224 685 B1
NE 123rd Cir
4400 ClkC 98686 507 B1
10500 ClkC 98662 507 H1
22700 ClkC 98606 509 B1
NW 123rd Cir
1000 ClkC 98685 476 F7
NE 123rd Ct
4600 VCVR 98682 538 A1
10000 ClkC 98682 508 A3
SE 123rd Ct
13700 CmsC 97015 658 A6
SW 123rd Ct
800 WasC 97225 595 B6
12100 TGRD 97223 655 B4
NE 123rd Pl
- ClkC 98682 508 A3
- PTLD 97230 598 A4
29900 ClkC 98604 418 A4
NW 123rd Pl
3600 WasC 97229 595 C2
SW 123rd Pl
11100 TGRD 97223 655 B2
NE 123rd St
6600 ClkC 98662 507 E1
6600 ClkC 98686 507 E1
13300 ClkC 98606 508 B1
24100 ClkC 98606 509 D1
NW 123rd St
2100 ClkC 98685 476 E7
SW 123rd Ter
- TGRD 97223 655 B5
- TGRD 97224 655 B5
NE 124th Av
2100 VCVR 98684 538 A4
3500 PTLD 97230 598 A2
4400 VCVR 98682 538 A2
9900 ClkC 98682 508 A3
17900 ClkC 98604 478 A2
29300 ClkC 98604 418 B4
NW 124th Av
5000 MthC 97229 565 B7
5000 MthC 97229 595 B1
SE 124th Av
- HPYV 97236 658 A4
10 PTLD 97233 598 B6
100 VCVR 98683 538 A6
100 VCVR 98684 538 A6
1500 VCVR 98683 568 A1
2200 PTLD 97233 628 A1
2400 PTLD 97236 628 A1
13100 CmsC 97015 658 A5
13100 CmsC 97236 658 A5
SW 124th Av
- WasC 97062 685 B5
3100 WasC 97005 625 B2
6000 BRTN 97005 625 B5
6000 BRTN 97008 625 B5
12100 TGRD 97223 655 B4
SW 124th Av
16600 KNGC 97224 685 B1
16800 WasC 97224 685 B1
19000 TLTN 97062 685 B3
NE 124th Cir
24100 ClkC 98606 509 D1
NE 124th Ct
4700 VCVR 98682 538 A1
6000 ClkC 98682 508 A7
15600 ClkC 98606 478 A4
SE 124th Ct
1900 VCVR 98683 568 A1
NE 124th Pl
2400 PTLD 97230 598 B3
NW 124th Pl
3600 WasC 97229 595 B2
SE 124th Pl
13600 CmsC 97015 658 A5
SW 124th Pl
11100 TGRD 97223 655 B3
NE 124th St
1300 ClkC 98685 476 H7
5500 ClkC 98686 507 D1
NW 124th St
3100 ClkC 98685 476 D7
NE 125th Av
- ClkC 98604 478 A3
2100 VCVR 98684 538 A4
3500 PTLD 97230 598 B2
5000 VCVR 98682 538 A1
8300 ClkC 98682 508 A4
29900 ClkC 98604 418 B4
NW 125th Av
4200 WasC 97229 595 B1
SE 125th Av
700 VCVR 98683 538 A7
1400 VCVR 98683 568 A1
2500 PTLD 97233 628 A1
2500 PTLD 97236 628 A1
12500 CmsC 97236 658 A4
12500 HPYV 97236 658 A4
13100 CmsC 97015 658 A5
SW 125th Av
- BRTN 97008 625 B7
3200 BRTN 97005 625 B2
9200 BRTN 97008 655 B1
12100 TGRD 97223 655 B4
14000 TGRD 97224 655 B6
NE 125th Cir
500 ClkC 98685 476 G7
4600 ClkC 98686 477 C7
NE 125th Ct
2500 VCVR 98684 538 A3
3700 VCVR 98682 538 A2
16200 ClkC 98606 478 A4
16900 ClkC 98606 478 A3
SE 125th Ct
1500 PTLD 97233 598 A7
1900 VCVR 98683 568 A1
15400 CmsC 97015 658 A7
15400 CmsC 97015 688 A1
SW 125th Ct
11600 TGRD 97223 655 B3
19000 TLTN 97062 685 B4
NE 125th Pl
4000 PTLD 97230 598 B1
18900 ClkC 98604 478 A1
NW 125th Pl
3100 WasC 97229 595 B2
SE 125th Pl
- PTLD 97236 628 A2
SW 125th Pl
7000 BRTN 97008 625 B5
11100 TGRD 97223 655 B2
16900 KNGC 97224 685 B2
16900 WasC 97224 685 B1
NE 125th St
1300 ClkC 98685 476 H7
2500 ClkC 98686 476 J7
5000 ClkC 98686 477 C7
14600 ClkC 98606 508 D1
NW 125th St
4600 ClkC 98685 476 B7
NE 125th Wy
2300 ClkC 98686 476 J7
18200 ClkC 98606 478 G7
18200 ClkC 98606 508 G1
NE 126th Av
10 PTLD 97233 598 B6
1800 VCVR 98684 538 A4
3500 PTLD 97230 598 B2
4400 VCVR 98682 538 A1
11600 ClkC 98606 508 A1
11600 ClkC 98682 508 A1
14900 ClkC 98606 478 A5
NW 126th Av
4100 WasC 97229 595 B1
SE 126th Av
- VCVR 98683 538 A6
- VCVR 98684 538 A6
10 PTLD 97230 598 B6
10 PTLD 97233 598 B6
1400 VCVR 98683 568 A1
4200 PTLD 97236 628 A3
12200 HPYV 97236 658 A4
12400 CmsC 97236 658 A5
13200 CmsC 97015 658 A6
SW 126th Av
500 WasC 97005 595 B6
3200 BRTN 97005 625 B2
12100 TGRD 97223 655 B4
14500 TGRD 97224 655 B6
16600 KNGC 97224 685 B1
16800 WasC 97224 685 B1
NE 126th Cir
- ClkC 98686 477 C7
10400 ClkC 98662 477 H7
10600 ClkC 98662 507 H1
NE 126th Ct
- VCVR 98682 538 A2
1500 VCVR 98684 538 A4
3100 PTLD 97230 598 B3
7200 ClkC 98682 508 A6
SE 126th Ct
1500 VCVR 98683 568 A1
SW 126th Ct
7100 BRTN 97008 625 B6
NE 126th Lp
1100 ClkC 98685 476 H7
NE 126th Pl
- VCVR 98684 538 A4
1800 PTLD 97230 598 B4
5000 VCVR 98682 538 A1
NW 126th Pl
4500 WasC 97229 595 B1
SE 126th Pl
2100 PTLD 97233 628 B1
SW 126th Pl
11700 TGRD 97223 655 B3
18400 TLTN 97062 685 B3
NE 126th St
700 ClkC 98685 476 H7
2300 ClkC 98686 476 J7
6600 ClkC 98662 477 E7
6600 ClkC 98686 477 E7
NW 126th St
3400 ClkC 98685 476 C7
NW 126th Ter
5400 WasC 97229 565 B7
SW 126th Ter
16100 WasC 97224 685 B1
NE 126th Wy
9200 ClkC 98662 477 G7
NE 127th Av
10 PTLD 97230 598 B5
10 PTLD 97233 598 B6
1100 VCVR 98684 538 A5
4600 VCVR 98682 538 A1
7600 ClkC 98682 508 A5
16900 ClkC 98604 478 B3
NW 127th Av
4100 WasC 97229 595 B1
SE 127th Av
10 PTLD 97230 598 B6
10 PTLD 97233 598 B6
1500 VCVR 98683 568 A1
2600 PTLD 97236 628 B2
12800 CmsC 97236 658 A5
13200 CmsC 97015 658 A5
SW 127th Av
12100 TGRD 97223 655 B4
NE 127th Cir
100 ClkC 98685 476 G7
3700 ClkC 98686 477 B7
18800 ClkC 98606 478 G7
18800 ClkC 98606 508 H1
NE 127th Ct
9900 ClkC 98682 508 A3
SE 127th Ct
700 VCVR 98683 538 A7
12500 CmsC 97236 658 A5
SW 127th Ct
6000 BRTN 97005 625 B5
6000 BRTN 97008 625 B5
10600 TGRD 97223 655 B2
NE 127th Pl
- VCVR 98682 538 A4
- VCVR 98684 538 A4
500 PTLD 97230 598 B5
NW 127th Pl
2000 WasC 97229 595 B3
SE 127th Pl
3200 PTLD 97236 628 B2
SW 127th Pl
- TLTN 97062 685 B3
11700 TGRD 97223 655 B3
16100 WasC 97224 685 D1
NE 127th St
- ClkC 98606 478 B7
500 ClkC 98685 476 G7
3400 ClkC 98686 477 A7
NW 127th St
3100 ClkC 98685 476 D7
NW 127th Ter
1500 WasC 97229 595 B4
5500 WasC 97229 565 B7
NE 127th Wy
4500 ClkC 98686 477 C7
NE 128th Av
10 PTLD 97233 598 B6
1900 VCVR 98684 538 A4
3300 PTLD 97230 598 B2
4400 VCVR 98682 538 A2
11500 ClkC 98606 508 B1
11500 ClkC 98682 508 B1
18100 ClkC 98604 478 B2
25400 ClkC 98604 448 B2
NW 128th Av
- MthC 97229 565 B6
4100 WasC 97229 595 B1
SE 128th Av
500 PTLD 97233 598 B6
1000 VCVR 98683 538 A7
3400 PTLD 97236 628 B2
12700 CmsC 97236 658 B5
13800 CmsC 97015 658 A6
SW 128th Av
11500 TGRD 97223 655 B4
16000 KNGC 97224 655 B7
16000 WasC 97224 655 B7
16400 KNGC 97224 685 B1
16400 WasC 97224 685 B1
NE 128th Cir
21900 ClkC 98606 479 B7
21900 ClkC 98606 509 B1
NW 128th Cir
3600 ClkC 98685 476 C7
NE 128th Ct
4600 VCVR 98682 538 A1
29100 ClkC 98604 418 B5
NW 128th Ct
2600 WasC 97229 595 B3
SE 128th Ct
1600 VCVR 98683 568 A1
12600 CmsC 97236 658 B5
NE 128th Pl
29900 ClkC 98604 418 B4
NW 128th Pl
3100 WasC 97229 595 B2
SW 128th Pl
13300 TGRD 97223 655 D1
14200 TGRD 97224 655 B6
16200 WasC 97224 685 D2
NE 128th St
700 ClkC 98685 476 H7
3400 ClkC 98686 477 A7
23800 ClkC 98606 479 D7
23900 ClkC 98606 509 D1
NW 128th St
3200 ClkC 98685 476 D7
NW 128th Ter
- WasC 97229 595 B4
5300 WasC 97229 565 B7
NE 129th Av
1800 VCVR 98684 538 A4
2300 PTLD 97230 598 B2
4900 VCVR 98682 538 A1
5500 VCVR 98682 508 A7
10000 ClkC 98682 508 B3
19300 BGND 98604 448 B7
NE 129th Av
19300 ClkC 98604 448 B7
30700 ClkC 98604 418 B3
NW 129th Av
400 WasC 97229 595 B5
SE 129th Av
10 PTLD 97233 598 B6
700 VCVR 98683 538 A7
2500 PTLD 97233 628 B2
2500 PTLD 97236 628 B2
9200 CmsC 97236 658 B1
10500 HPYV 97236 658 A3
13500 CmsC 97015 658 B5
SW 129th Av
12300 TGRD 97223 655 A4
16800 KNGC 97224 685 A1
16900 WasC 97224 685 A1
19400 TLTN 97062 685 A4
NE 129th Cir
5000 ClkC 98686 477 C7
NW 129th Cir
3600 ClkC 98685 476 C7
NE 129th Ct
1400 VCVR 98684 538 A4
4600 VCVR 98682 538 A1
SE 129th Ct
2600 VCVR 98683 568 A2
12900 CmsC 97236 658 B4
NE 129th Pl
4000 PTLD 97230 598 B2
NW 129th Pl
2000 WasC 97229 595 B3
SE 129th Pl
6400 PTLD 97236 628 B5
SW 129th Pl
11600 TGRD 97223 655 B3
NE 129th St
100 ClkC 98685 476 H7
1800 ClkC 98686 476 J7
6000 ClkC 98686 477 D7
7000 ClkC 98662 477 D7
14400 ClkC 98606 478 D7
NW 129th St
3300 ClkC 98685 476 D7
NW 129th Ter
- WasC 97229 565 B7
SW 129th Ter
8000 BRTN 97008 625 B7
15900 WasC 97224 655 A7
15900 WasC 97224 685 A1
NE 130th Av
1500 VCVR 98684 538 B4
3200 PTLD 97230 598 B2
4000 VCVR 98682 538 B1
11100 ClkC 98682 508 B2
16500 ClkC 98606 478 B3
17600 ClkC 98604 478 B2
25400 ClkC 98604 448 B1
NW 130th Av
- WasC 97229 565 B7
1300 WasC 97229 595 B5
SE 130th Av
500 PTLD 97233 598 B7
1000 VCVR 98683 538 A7
1800 PTLD 97233 628 B2
1900 VCVR 98683 568 A2
3400 PTLD 97236 628 B3
12500 CmsC 97236 658 B5
13100 CmsC 97015 658 B5
15700 CmsC 97015 688 B1
SW 130th Av
10 WasC 97005 595 B6
6000 BRTN 97005 625 B5
6000 BRTN 97008 625 B5
9000 BRTN 97008 655 B1
10500 TGRD 97223 655 A2
14300 TGRD 97224 655 A6
NE 130th Cir
1400 ClkC 98685 476 H7
4200 ClkC 98686 477 B7
11000 ClkC 98662 477 J7
18800 ClkC 98606 478 H7
NW 130th Cir
3300 ClkC 98685 476 D7
NE 130th Ct
800 VCVR 98684 538 A5
8800 ClkC 98682 508 B4
SE 130th Ct
600 VCVR 98683 538 A7
SE 130th Dr
14500 CmsC 97015 658 B7
NE 130th Pl
4000 PTLD 97230 598 B2
9600 ClkC 98682 508 B3
SE 130th Pl
5700 PTLD 97236 628 B5
SW 130th Pl
13600 TGRD 97223 655 A5
NE 130th St
700 ClkC 98685 476 H7
4000 ClkC 98686 477 B7
19300 ClkC 98606 478 H7
25500 ClkC 98606 479 F7
NW 130th St
3100 ClkC 98685 476 D7
SW 130th Ter
16000 WasC 97224 655 A7
16100 WasC 97224 685 A1
NE 131st Av
2000 VCVR 98684 538 B4
3200 PTLD 97230 598 B2
5100 VCVR 98682 538 B1
5500 VCVR 98682 508 B7
9900 ClkC 98682 508 B3
NW 131st Av
1300 WasC 97229 595 B4
SE 131st Av
200 VCVR 98683 538 B7
200 VCVR 98684 538 B7
1800 PTLD 97233 598 B7
1800 PTLD 97233 628 B1
1900 VCVR 98683 568 A1
2500 PTLD 97236 628 B2
10100 HPYV 97236 658 B2
13600 CmsC 97015 658 B5
SW 131st Av
10 WasC 97005 595 B6
7400 BRTN 97008 625 A6
12000 TGRD 97223 655 A4
14300 TGRD 97224 655 A6
14300 WasC 97224 655 A6
16100 WasC 97224 685 A1
16500 KNGC 97224 685 A1
NE 131st Cir
1100 ClkC 98685 476 H7
NE 131st Cir
24500 ClkC 98606 479 D7
NE 131st Ct
4900 VCVR 98682 538 B1
9700 ClkC 98682 508 B3
SE 131st Ct
600 VCVR 98683 538 A7
5300 PTLD 97236 628 B4
12500 CmsC 97236 658 B4
SE 131st Dr
14500 CmsC 97015 658 B7
NE 131st Pl
4000 PTLD 97230 598 B1
NW 131st Pl
3100 WasC 97229 595 B2
SE 131st Pl
- PTLD 97230 598 B5
10 PTLD 97233 598 B5
6600 PTLD 97236 628 B5
SW 131st Pl
11000 TGRD 97223 655 A2
14100 TGRD 97224 655 D2
NE 131st St
3900 ClkC 98686 477 B7
10600 ClkC 98662 477 J7
11000 ClkC 98606 477 J7
16300 ClkC 98606 478 E7
NW 131st St
2600 ClkC 98685 476 D7
SW 131st Ter
14000 TGRD 97224 655 A5
NE 131st Wy
7800 ClkC 98662 477 E7
NW 131st Wy
1100 ClkC 98685 476 F7
NE 132nd Av
500 VCVR 98684 538 B5
4000 PTLD 97230 598 B2
4500 VCVR 98682 538 B2
9400 ClkC 98682 508 B4
11300 ClkC 98606 508 B1
12300 ClkC 98606 478 B7
18700 ClkC 98604 478 B1
19200 BGND 98604 448 B7
23200 ClkC 98604 448 B3
29900 ClkC 98604 418 B4
NW 132nd Av
2700 WasC 97229 595 B3
SE 132nd Av
200 PTLD 97233 598 B6
500 VCVR 98683 538 B7
1300 VCVR 98683 568 A3
2100 PTLD 97233 628 B1
3500 PTLD 97236 628 B2
8500 CmsC 97236 628 B7
8500 HPYV 97236 628 B7
8500 PTLD 97266 628 B7
8900 HPYV 97236 658 B2
8900 PTLD 97236 658 B2
12300 CmsC 97236 658 B4
13200 CmsC 97015 658 B6
SW 132nd Av
100 WasC 97005 595 B6
1400 WasC 97225 595 B7
12700 TGRD 97223 655 A4
NE 132nd Cir
24100 ClkC 98606 479 D7
NW 132nd Cir
3500 ClkC 98685 476 C7
NE 132nd Ct
200 PTLD 97230 598 B5
3900 VCVR 98682 538 B2
6900 ClkC 98682 508 B6
SE 132nd Ct
1900 VCVR 98683 568 B1
SW 132nd Ct
12300 TGRD 97223 655 A4
NE 132nd Pl
4000 PTLD 97230 598 B2
4600 VCVR 98682 538 B1
NW 132nd Pl
3100 WasC 97229 595 B2
SW 132nd Pl
14200 TGRD 97224 655 D2
NE 132nd St
300 ClkC 98685 476 G7
7800 ClkC 98662 477 F7
19000 ClkC 98606 478 H7
NW 132nd St
800 ClkC 98685 476 F7
SW 132nd Ter
14100 WasC 97224 655 D2
15000 TGRD 97224 655 A6
16400 WasC 97224 685 A1
NE 132nd Wy
5000 ClkC 98686 477 C7
NE 133rd Av
10 PTLD 97233 598 B6
3900 VCVR 98682 538 B2
4000 PTLD 97230 598 B2
8800 ClkC 98682 508 B3
29900 ClkC 98604 418 C3
NW 133rd Av
1300 WasC 97229 595 B4
SE 133rd Av
10 PTLD 97230 598 B6
10 PTLD 97233 598 B6
2500 PTLD 97233 628 B1
2500 PTLD 97236 628 B2
2500 VCVR 98683 568 B2
SW 133rd Av
200 WasC 97005 595 A6
8000 BRTN 97008 625 D4
10200 BRTN 97008 655 A2
11400 TGRD 97223 655 B3
14100 TGRD 97224 655 A6
14600 WasC 97224 655 A7
NE 133rd Cir
300 ClkC 98685 476 G7
14500 ClkC 98606 478 C7
NW 133rd Cir
600 ClkC 98685 476 F6
NE 133rd Ct
4400 VCVR 98682 538 B2
12100 ClkC 98606 508 B1
16000 ClkC 98606 478 B4
24900 ClkC 98604 448 B2
SE 133rd Ct
2400 VCVR 98683 568 B2
SE 133rd Dr
4600 PTLD 97236 628 B4
NE 133rd Pl
2600 PTLD 97230 598 C3
NW 133rd Pl
2000 WasC 97229 595 A3
SE 133rd Pl
700 VCVR 98683 538 B7
7200 PTLD 97236 628 B6
8600 HPYV 97236 628 B7
SW 133rd Pl
10500 BRTN 97008 655 A2
11500 TGRD 97223 655 B3
NE 133rd St
800 ClkC 98685 476 H7
6800 ClkC 98662 477 E7
6800 ClkC 98686 477 E7
NW 133rd St
2800 ClkC 98685 476 D6
SW 133rd Ter
- KNGC 97224 685 A1
16400 WasC 97224 685 A1
18100 TLTN 97062 685 A3
NE 134th Av
2400 VCVR 98684 538 B3
3100 VCVR 98682 538 B3
4000 PTLD 97230 598 C2
9400 ClkC 98682 508 B3
24900 ClkC 98604 448 B2
NW 134th Av
1900 WasC 97229 595 A4
SE 134th Av
600 PTLD 97233 598 B7
700 VCVR 98683 538 B7
2600 VCVR 98683 568 B2
2900 PTLD 97236 628 B2
9600 HPYV 97236 658 B1
12900 CmsC 97236 658 B5
SW 134th Av
1400 WasC 97005 595 A7
12700 TGRD 97223 655 A4
NE 134th Cir
300 ClkC 98685 476 G7
4200 ClkC 98686 477 B6
22700 ClkC 98606 479 C7
NW 134th Cir
400 ClkC 98685 476 G6
NE 134th Ct
4000 VCVR 98682 538 B2
8900 ClkC 98682 508 B4
18200 ClkC 98604 478 B2
31400 ClkC 98604 418 C3
SE 134th Ct
2500 VCVR 98683 568 B2
SE 134th Dr
4500 PTLD 97236 628 B4
8400 HPYV 97236 628 B7
9800 HPYV 97236 658 B2
SW 134th Dr
14100 TGRD 97224 655 A6
14200 WasC 97224 655 A6
NE 134th Pl
100 PTLD 97230 598 C6
19500 BGND 98604 448 B7
19500 ClkC 98604 448 B7
19500 ClkC 98604 478 B1
NW 134th Pl
2600 WasC 97229 595 A3
SE 134th Pl
10 PTLD 97233 598 C6
2700 PTLD 97236 628 B2
SW 134th Pl
11500 TGRD 97223 655 A3
NE 134th St
1200 ClkC 98685 476 H7
2200 ClkC 98686 476 J6
3900 ClkC 98686 477 B6
8700 ClkC 98662 477 G7
14000 ClkC 98606 478 C7
NW 134th St
1100 ClkC 98685 476 F6
NW 134th Ter
4000 WasC 97229 595 A1
SW 134th Ter
- KNGC 97224 685 A1
- WasC 97224 685 A1
11600 TGRD 97223 655 A3
18100 TLTN 97062 685 A3
NE 134th Wy
2700 ClkC 98686 477 A7
NW 134th Wy
1200 ClkC 98685 476 F6
NE 135th Av
4400 PTLD 97230 598 C1
4500 VCVR 98682 538 B2
8900 ClkC 98682 508 B4
NW 135th Av
2000 WasC 97229 595 A3
SE 135th Av
500 PTLD 97233 598 B7
1800 PTLD 97233 628 B1
2000 VCVR 98683 568 B1
4400 PTLD 97236 628 B3
15300 CmsC 97015 658 B7
15500 CmsC 97015 688 B1
SW 135th Av
1300 WasC 97005 595 A7
7800 BRTN 97008 625 A7
9000 BRTN 97008 655 A1
10700 TGRD 97008 655 A2
10700 TGRD 97223 655 A2
NE 135th Cir
1100 ClkC 98685 476 H6
NW 135th Cir
4600 ClkC 98685 476 B6
NE 135th Ct
9400 ClkC 98682 508 B4
NW 135th Ct
- ClkC 98685 476 F6
SE 135th Ct
700 VCVR 98683 538 B7
SW 135th Pl
17400 KNGC 97224 685 A2
NE 135th St
100 ClkC 98685 476 G6
4500 ClkC 98686 477 C6
18500 ClkC 98606 478 G7
NW 135th St
4700 ClkC 98685 476 B6
NW 135th Ter
- WasC 97229 595 D1
SW 135th Ter
18000 TLTN 97062 685 A3
18000 WasC 97062 685 A3
NE 136th Av
10 PTLD 97233 598 C6
2000 VCVR 98684 538 B4
4400 PTLD 97230 598 C1
4500 VCVR 98682 538 B1
8800 ClkC 98682 508 B4
31900 ClkC 98604 418 C2

Portland Street Index

STREET Block City ZIP Map# Grid

NW 136th Av
1400 WasC 97229 595 A4
SE 136th Av
10 PTLD 97233 598 C6
100 VCVR 98684 538 B6
400 VCVR 98683 538 B7
1100 VCVR 98683 568 B1
2500 PTLD 97233 628 C1
2500 PTLD 97236 628 B4
SW 136th Av
600 WasC 97005 595 A6
7200 BRTN 97008 625 A6
16900 KNGC 97224 685 A1
NE 136th Cir
4200 ClkC 98686 477 B6
NW 136th Cir
3700 ClkC 98685 476 C6
NE 136th Ct
3900 VCVR 98682 538 B2
29800 ClkC 98604 418 C4
SE 136th Ct
3400 VCVR 98683 568 B3
6400 PTLD 97236 628 B5
SW 136th Ct
12600 TGRD 97223 655 A4
14600 WasC 97224 655 A6
SE 136th Dr
12700 CmsC 97236 658 B5
NE 136th Pl
3700 PTLD 97230 598 C2
SW 136th Pl
10400 BRTN 97008 655 A2
13200 TGRD 97223 655 A5
15100 WasC 97224 655 A7
NE 136th St
100 ClkC 98685 476 G6
3800 ClkC 98686 477 B6
18400 ClkC 98606 478 G7
24200 ClkC 98606 479 D7
NW 136th St
1100 ClkC 98685 476 F6
NE 136th Wy
300 ClkC 98685 476 G6
3300 ClkC 98686 477 A6
NE 137th Av
3900 VCVR 98682 538 B1
4000 PTLD 97230 598 C2
5500 ClkC 98682 508 B4
5500 VCVR 98682 508 B7
14400 ClkC 98606 478 B5
NW 137th Av
1300 WasC 97229 595 A4
5100 WasC 97229 565 A7
SE 137th Av
500 PTLD 97233 598 C6
2300 PTLD 97233 628 C1
2300 PTLD 97236 628 C1
8700 HPYV 97236 628 C7
8700 HPYV 97236 658 C1
SW 137th Av
10 WasC 97006 595 A6
16000 WasC 97224 654 H7
16000 WasC 97224 684 J1
NE 137th Cir
4100 ClkC 98686 477 B6
NE 137th Ct
2000 VCVR 98684 538 B4
19800 BGND 98604 448 C7
19800 ClkC 98604 448 C7
SE 137th Ct
2000 VCVR 98683 568 B1
SE 137th Dr
12600 CmsC 97236 658 B5
NE 137th Pl
3700 PTLD 97230 598 C2
8800 ClkC 98682 508 B4
SE 137th Pl
10 PTLD 97233 598 C6
SW 137th Pl
10400 BRTN 97008 655 A2
14900 WasC 97224 655 A6
NE 137th St
6100 ClkC 98662 477 D6
6100 ClkC 98686 477 D6
NW 137th St
1400 ClkC 98685 476 F6
NW 137th Ter
- WasC 97229 595 A1
NE 138th Av
400 VCVR 98684 538 B6
4500 PTLD 97230 598 C1
4600 PTLD 97230 568 C7
5000 VCVR 98682 538 B1
9100 ClkC 98682 508 B4
NW 138th Av
1400 WasC 97229 595 A4
SE 138th Av
800 PTLD 97233 598 C7
1000 VCVR 98683 538 B7
1200 VCVR 98683 568 A3
1800 PTLD 97233 628 C1
2500 PTLD 97236 628 C2
SW 138th Av
10 WasC 97006 595 A6
12600 TGRD 97223 655 A4
NE 138th Cir
4200 ClkC 98686 477 B6
NW 138th Cir
1400 ClkC 98685 476 F6
NE 138th Ct
4600 VCVR 98682 538 B1
9400 ClkC 98682 508 C3
SE 138th Ct
2000 VCVR 98683 568 B1
SW 138th Ct
4400 BRTN 97005 625 A3
SE 138th Dr
- HPYV 97236 628 B7
8000 PTLD 97236 628 B7
SE 138th Lp
2600 VCVR 98683 568 B2
NE 138th Pl
3300 PTLD 97230 598 C2
4500 VCVR 98682 538 B1
31000 ClkC 98604 418 C3
NW 138th Pl
4600 WasC 97229 595 A1
SE 138th Pl
4300 PTLD 97236 628 C3
NE 138th St
2000 ClkC 98686 476 J6
4700 ClkC 98686 477 C6
NW 138th St
2100 ClkC 98685 476 E6
NW 138th Ter
- WasC 97229 595 A1
NE 138th Wy
4500 ClkC 98686 477 C6
NW 138th Wy
1100 ClkC 98685 476 F6
NE 139th Av
10 PTLD 97233 598 C6
900 VCVR 98684 538 B5
3800 PTLD 97230 598 C2
4700 VCVR 98682 538 C1
11500 ClkC 98682 508 C1
11900 ClkC 98606 508 C1
25800 ClkC 98604 448 C1
25900 ClkC 98604 418 C7
NW 139th Av
10 WasC 97229 595 A5
SE 139th Av
10 PTLD 97233 598 C7
400 VCVR 98683 538 B7
400 VCVR 98684 538 B7
1800 PTLD 97233 628 C1
1900 VCVR 98683 568 B1
4800 PTLD 97236 628 C4
8500 HPYV 97236 628 C7
8700 HPYV 97236 658 C1
12800 CmsC 97236 658 B5
13400 CmsC 97015 658 B6
SW 139th Av
- TGRD 97223 655 A4
- WasC 97223 655 A4
10 WasC 97006 595 A6
1600 WasC 97005 595 A7
2000 WasC 97005 625 E4
4700 BRTN 97005 625 A3
7900 BRTN 97008 625 A6
14500 TGRD 97224 654 J6
14500 WasC 97224 654 J6
NE 139th Cir
2200 ClkC 98686 476 J6
NE 139th Ct
9000 ClkC 98682 508 C4
SE 139th Ct
1400 VCVR 98683 568 B1
8400 PTLD 97236 628 C7
NE 139th Lp
5100 VCVR 98682 538 B1
23400 ClkC 98606 479 C7
NW 139th Lp
4600 ClkC 98685 476 B6
NW 139th Pl
3000 WasC 97229 595 A2
SW 139th Pl
13900 BRTN 97005 625 A3
NE 139th St
500 ClkC 98685 476 H6
2000 ClkC 98686 476 J6
4200 ClkC 98686 477 D6
8700 ClkC 98662 477 G6
16700 ClkC 98606 478 F6
20200 ClkC 98606 479 A6
NW 139th St
100 ClkC 98685 476 G6
NW 139th Ter
- WasC 97229 595 A1
SW 139th Wy
4000 BRTN 97005 625 A3
NE 140th Av
10 PTLD 97233 598 C6
1300 VCVR 98684 538 B5
3500 PTLD 97230 598 C2
4000 VCVR 98682 538 C2
8500 ClkC 98682 508 C4
16900 ClkC 98606 478 C3
24900 ClkC 98604 448 C2
NW 140th Av
4800 WasC 97229 595 A1
5000 WasC 97229 565 A7
SE 140th Av
1100 PTLD 97233 598 C7
1100 VCVR 98683 538 B7
1200 VCVR 98683 568 B1
1900 PTLD 97233 628 C1
2900 PTLD 97236 628 C2
13000 CmsC 97236 658 C5
13200 CmsC 97015 658 C5
SW 140th Av
10 WasC 97006 595 A6
7200 BRTN 97008 624 J6
NE 140th Cir
4700 ClkC 98686 477 C6
NW 140th Cir
1800 ClkC 98685 476 E6
NE 140th Ct
8400 ClkC 98682 508 C4
31900 ClkC 98604 418 C2
SE 140th Ct
1000 VCVR 98683 538 B7
1400 VCVR 98683 568 B1
8300 PTLD 97236 628 C7
SW 140th Ct
14100 BRTN 97008 624 J6
SE 140th Dr
7600 PTLD 97236 628 C7
NW 140th Pl
200 WasC 97006 595 A5
200 WasC 97229 595 A5
SE 140th Pl
500 PTLD 97233 598 C6
3900 PTLD 97236 628 C3
8500 HPYV 97236 628 C7
SW 140th Pl
7100 BRTN 97008 625 A5
NE 140th St
2200 ClkC 98686 476 J6
NW 140th St
800 ClkC 98685 476 F6
SW 140th Ter
12300 TGRD 97223 655 B4
NW 140th Wy
4300 ClkC 98685 476 C6
NE 141st Av
10 PTLD 97233 598 C6
2800 VCVR 98684 538 C3
3000 PTLD 97230 598 C3
4700 VCVR 98682 538 C1
8300 ClkC 98682 508 C4
SE 141st Av
10 PTLD 97233 598 C6
600 VCVR 98683 538 B7
1400 VCVR 98683 568 B1
2000 PTLD 97233 628 C1
2000 PTLD 97236 628 C1
8400 HPYV 97236 628 C7
13700 CmsC 97015 658 C6
SW 141st Av
300 WasC 97006 595 A6
3700 WasC 97005 625 A2
4600 BRTN 97005 625 A4
5900 BRTN 97005 624 J4
7500 BRTN 97008 624 J6
9900 BRTN 97008 654 J1
14100 WasC 97224 654 J6
NE 141st Cir
4300 ClkC 98686 477 B6
NE 141st Ct
5100 VCVR 98682 538 C1
10000 ClkC 98682 508 C3
SE 141st Ct
1000 VCVR 98683 538 C7
8500 HPYV 97236 628 C7
8500 PTLD 97236 628 C7
NE 141st Dr
3800 PTLD 97230 598 C2
NW 141st Pl
2300 WasC 97229 595 A3
SE 141st Pl
2000 VCVR 98683 568 C1
5000 PTLD 97236 628 C4
SW 141st Pl
- BRTN 97005 625 A2
- WasC 97005 625 A2
7000 BRTN 97008 624 J5
12400 TGRD 97223 654 J4
12400 WasC 97223 654 J4
NE 141st St
- ClkC 98662 477 G6
700 ClkC 98685 476 H6
2900 ClkC 98686 477 A6
NW 141st St
2100 ClkC 98685 476 E6
NE 141st Wy
2200 ClkC 98686 476 J6
NW 141st Wy
900 ClkC 98685 476 F6
NE 142nd Av
1000 VCVR 98684 538 C5
3800 PTLD 97230 598 C2
4900 VCVR 98682 538 C1
7600 ClkC 98682 508 C5
15900 ClkC 98606 478 C2
17600 ClkC 98604 478 C2
19100 BGND 98604 448 C7
19100 BGND 98604 478 C1
22900 ClkC 98604 448 C3
30500 ClkC 98604 418 C3
SE 142nd Av
500 PTLD 97233 598 C7
1800 PTLD 97233 628 C1
6200 PTLD 97236 628 C5
13600 CmsC 97015 658 C5
13600 CmsC 97236 658 C6
SW 142nd Av
10 WasC 97006 595 A5
4300 BRTN 97005 624 J3
6800 BRTN 97008 624 J5
NW 142nd Cir
2700 ClkC 98685 476 D6
NE 142nd Ct
- ClkC 98606 508 C1
1500 VCVR 98684 538 C4
7000 ClkC 98682 508 C6
SE 142nd Ct
3800 VCVR 98683 568 C3
SW 142nd Ct
7500 BRTN 97008 624 J6
SE 142nd Pl
1700 PTLD 97233 598 C7
2900 PTLD 97236 628 C2
SW 142nd Pl
7000 BRTN 97008 624 J5
NE 142nd St
- ClkC 98685 476 H6
6700 ClkC 98662 477 E6
6700 ClkC 98686 477 E6
NW 142nd St
700 ClkC 98685 476 F6
NW 142nd Ter
3800 WasC 97229 595 A2
NW 142nd Wy
2800 ClkC 98685 476 D6
NE 143rd Av
10 PTLD 97233 598 C6
1000 VCVR 98684 538 C5
3700 PTLD 97230 598 C2
4900 VCVR 98682 538 C1
8300 ClkC 98682 508 C4
NW 143rd Av
1500 BRTN 97229 594 J4
1500 WasC 97229 594 J3
1900 WasC 97006 594 J3
SE 143rd Av
600 PTLD 97233 598 C7
700 VCVR 98683 538 C7
1800 PTLD 97233 628 C1
2900 PTLD 97236 628 C2
9300 HPYV 97236 658 C1
SW 143rd Av
10 WasC 97006 594 J5
NE 143rd Cir
4700 ClkC 98686 477 C6
9000 ClkC 98662 477 G6
NW 143rd Cir
2100 ClkC 98685 476 E6
NE 143rd Ct
5100 VCVR 98682 538 C1
10000 ClkC 98682 508 C3
SE 143rd Ct
6400 PTLD 97236 628 C5
SE 143rd Dr
10600 HPYV 97236 658 C2
NE 143rd Pl
2900 PTLD 97230 598 D3
6900 ClkC 98682 508 C6
SE 143rd Pl
1300 PTLD 97233 598 C7
12100 CmsC 97236 658 C4
12100 HPYV 97236 658 C4
NE 143rd St
600 ClkC 98685 476 G6
3100 ClkC 98686 477 A6
21100 ClkC 98606 479 A6
NW 143rd St
800 ClkC 98685 476 F5
NW 143rd Wy
2800 ClkC 98685 476 D5
NE 144th Av
300 VCVR 98684 538 C6
3900 PTLD 97230 598 C2
5000 VCVR 98682 538 C1
9900 ClkC 98682 508 C3
NW 144th Av
2300 WasC 97006 594 J3
SE 144th Av
- CmsC 97015 658 C6
- HPYV 97236 658 C1
1100 PTLD 97233 598 C7
2000 VCVR 98683 568 C1
2800 PTLD 97236 628 C2
SW 144th Av
10 WasC 97006 594 J6
1700 WasC 97005 594 J7
3600 BRTN 97005 624 J2
10200 BRTN 97008 654 J2
14000 WasC 97224 654 J6
NE 144th Cir
300 ClkC 98685 476 G5
7900 ClkC 98662 477 F5
NW 144th Cir
1000 ClkC 98685 476 F5
NE 144th Ct
4900 VCVR 98682 538 C1
9400 ClkC 98682 508 C3
SE 144th Ct
1000 VCVR 98683 538 C7
1700 VCVR 98683 568 C1
SE 144th Dr
8000 PTLD 97236 628 C7
SE 144th Ln
6400 PTLD 97236 628 C5
SE 144th Lp
10500 HPYV 97236 658 C3
NW 144th Pl
3700 WasC 97229 594 J2
SE 144th Pl
- PTLD 97236 628 C5
SW 144th Pl
6800 BRTN 97008 624 J5
15800 WasC 97224 654 J7
NE 144th St
1000 ClkC 98685 476 H5
2000 ClkC 98686 476 J5
6300 ClkC 98686 477 D6
6800 ClkC 98662 477 D6
16800 ClkC 98606 478 F6
26400 ClkC 98606 479 F6
NW 144th St
1900 ClkC 98685 476 E5
SW 144th Ter
15300 WasC 97224 654 J7
NE 145th Av
1100 VCVR 98684 538 C5
3100 PTLD 97230 598 D2
5000 VCVR 98682 538 C1
10000 ClkC 98682 508 C3
15700 ClkC 98606 478 C4
25600 ClkC 98604 448 D1
NW 145th Av
- MthC 97229 564 J6
- MthC 97229 565 A5
2300 WasC 97006 594 J3
SE 145th Av
1400 PTLD 97233 598 C7
2000 PTLD 97233 628 C1
2600 VCVR 98683 568 C2
8500 HPYV 97236 628 C7
8500 PTLD 97236 628 C7
8800 HPYV 97236 658 C2
8800 PTLD 97236 658 C1
13500 CmsC 97015 658 C5
13500 HPYV 97015 658 C5
SW 145th Av
27100 CmsC 97140 714 J5
NE 145th Cir
200 ClkC 98685 476 G5
2400 ClkC 98686 476 J5
2500 ClkC 98686 477 A5
NW 145th Cir
1900 ClkC 98685 476 E5
NE 145th Ct
7300 ClkC 98682 508 C6
SE 145th Ct
1000 VCVR 98683 538 C7
11600 VCVR 98683 568 C1
7900 PTLD 97236 628 C7
NE 145th Pl
7600 ClkC 98682 508 C5
NW 145th Pl
6100 WasC 97229 564 J6
SE 145th Pl
8400 PTLD 97236 628 C7
NE 145th St
- ClkC 98662 477 G6
- ClkC 98685 476 G5
400 ClkC 98685 476 G5
3000 ClkC 98686 477 A5
NW 145th St
5100 ClkC 98685 476 B5
SW 145th Ter
15300 WasC 97224 654 J7
NE 146th Av
10 PTLD 97230 598 D6
10 PTLD 97233 598 D6
1800 VCVR 98684 538 C4
5000 VCVR 98682 538 C1
10000 ClkC 98682 508 C3
25100 ClkC 98604 448 D2
30600 ClkC 98604 418 D3
NW 146th Av
5200 WasC 97229 564 J7
SE 146th Av
10 PTLD 97233 598 D7
700 VCVR 98683 538 C7
2000 PTLD 97233 628 D1
2000 VCVR 98683 568 C1
3900 PTLD 97236 628 D3
SW 146th Av
15700 WasC 97224 654 J7
16000 WasC 97224 684 J1
NW 146th Cir
3200 ClkC 98685 476 D5
NE 146th Ct
2700 VCVR 98684 538 C3
3500 VCVR 98682 538 C2
SE 146th Ct
1000 VCVR 98683 538 C7
1600 VCVR 98683 568 C1
14200 CmsC 97015 658 C6
NE 146th Dr
2400 PTLD 97230 598 D3
NE 146th Pl
3100 VCVR 98682 538 C3
NW 146th Pl
4800 WasC 97229 594 J1
4900 WasC 97229 564 J7
SE 146th Pl
1600 PTLD 97233 598 D7
3100 VCVR 98683 568 C2
8400 PTLD 97236 628 C7
NE 146th St
100 ClkC 98685 476 G5
5000 ClkC 98686 477 C5
NW 146th St
1300 ClkC 98685 476 F5
NW 146th Ter
5000 WasC 97229 564 J7
SW 146th Ter
8000 BRTN 97007 624 J6
9200 BRTN 97007 654 J1
NE 146th Wy
3000 VCVR 98682 538 C3
11500 ClkC 98606 477 J5
25700 ClkC 98606 479 E6
NW 146th Wy
500 ClkC 98685 476 G5
NE 147th Av
100 PTLD 97233 598 D6
1100 VCVR 98684 538 C5
4000 PTLD 97230 598 D2
4900 VCVR 98682 538 C1
9400 ClkC 98682 508 C3
25700 ClkC 98604 448 D1
26500 ClkC 98604 418 D7
NW 147th Av
4100 WasC 97229 594 J1
SE 147th Av
- CmsC 97015 658 C6
- HPYV 97015 658 C5
800 PTLD 97233 598 D7
800 VCVR 98683 538 C7
1400 VCVR 98683 568 C1
1800 PTLD 97233 628 D1
2800 PTLD 97236 628 D2
8300 HPYV 97236 628 D7
11200 CmsC 97236 658 C4
12100 HPYV 97236 658 C5
SW 147th Av
- BRTN 97007 654 J1
15700 WasC 97224 654 J7
16400 WasC 97224 684 J1
27100 CmsC 97140 714 H5
NE 147th Cir
600 ClkC 98685 476 H5
2400 ClkC 98686 477 A5
NW 147th Cir
300 ClkC 98685 476 G4
NE 147th Ct
2300 VCVR 98684 538 C4
17700 ClkC 98606 478 C2
30500 ClkC 98604 418 D4
SE 147th Ct
3000 VCVR 98683 568 C2
3500 PTLD 97236 628 D2
NW 147th Pl
2400 WasC 97006 594 J3
3200 WasC 97229 594 J2
5500 WasC 97229 564 J7
SE 147th Pl
3100 VCVR 98683 568 C2
SW 147th Pl
10 WasC 97006 594 J6
12800 WasC 97223 654 J4
NE 147th St
2600 ClkC 98686 477 A5
21200 ClkC 98606 479 A6
NW 147th St
1500 ClkC 98685 476 E5
NW 147th Ter
2000 WasC 97006 594 J4
SW 147th Ter
- BRTN 97008 624 J7
8100 BRTN 97007 624 J7
11600 BRTN 97007 654 J3
14000 TGRD 97224 654 J5
14000 WasC 97224 654 J5
NW 147th Wy
700 ClkC 98685 476 F5
NE 148th Av
10 PTLD 97230 598 D6
10 PTLD 97233 598 D6
1400 VCVR 98684 538 C4
4300 VCVR 98682 538 C2
5100 PTLD 97230 568 D7
9100 ClkC 98682 508 D4
NW 148th Av
5500 WasC 97229 564 J7
SE 148th Av
10 PTLD 97233 598 D7
100 VCVR 98684 538 C7
500 VCVR 98683 538 C7
1600 PTLD 97233 628 D2
2900 VCVR 98683 568 C2
3800 PTLD 97236 628 D3
SW 148th Av
10 WasC 97006 594 J5
4200 BRTN 97007 624 J3
4200 WasC 97007 624 J3
10000 BRTN 97007 654 J1
13300 TGRD 97223 654 H5
13300 WasC 97223 654 H5
NW 148th Cir
300 ClkC 98685 476 G4
NE 148th Ct
2300 VCVR 98684 538 C4
3600 VCVR 98682 538 C2
SW 148th Ct
6900 BRTN 97007 624 J1
NE 148th Pl
2800 PTLD 97230 598 D3
3100 VCVR 98682 538 C3
NW 148th Pl
3100 WasC 97006 594 J2
3900 WasC 97229 594 J2
SE 148th Pl
2100 PTLD 97233 628 D1
SW 148th Pl
14400 WasC 97224 654 H6
NE 148th St
- ClkC 98686 476 J5
500 ClkC 98685 476 H5
2400 ClkC 98686 477 A5
9800 ClkC 98686 477 H5
16200 ClkC 98606 478 E5
23200 ClkC 98606 479 C6
NW 148th St
100 ClkC 98685 476 G5
SW 148th Ter
400 WasC 97006 594 J6
8400 BRTN 97007 624 J2
8400 BRTN 97008 624 J2
15000 WasC 97224 654 J6
NE 149th Av
2400 VCVR 98684 538 C4
3300 PTLD 97230 598 D2
4600 VCVR 98682 538 C1
10000 ClkC 98682 508 D3
18100 ClkC 98606 478 D2
19300 ClkC 98604 478 D1
19400 BGND 98604 448 D7
19400 ClkC 98604 448 D7
27900 ClkC 98604 418 D6
SE 149th Av
1800 PTLD 97233 628 D1
2200 VCVR 98683 568 C1
3700 PTLD 97236 628 D3
SW 149th Av
100 WasC 97006 594 J6
4800 WasC 97007 624 J3
7500 BRTN 97007 624 H6
9100 BRTN 97007 654 J1
NE 149th Cir
1700 ClkC 98686 476 J5
NW 149th Cir
2500 ClkC 98685 476 D5
NE 149th Ct
2200 VCVR 98684 538 C4
6800 ClkC 98682 508 D6
NW 149th Ct
5500 WasC 97229 564 J7
SE 149th Ct
200 VCVR 98684 538 C6
2900 VCVR 98683 568 C2
SW 149th Ct
6900 BRTN 97007 624 J5
NE 149th Pl
100 PTLD 97230 598 D6
NW 149th Pl
3300 WasC 97006 594 J2
3300 WasC 97229 594 J2
SE 149th Pl
800 PTLD 97233 598 D7
SW 149th Pl
15000 WasC 97224 654 H6
NE 149th St
- ClkC 98686 476 J5
100 ClkC 98685 476 H5
9300 ClkC 98606 477 H5
18200 ClkC 98606 478 G5
24700 ClkC 98606 479 D5
NW 149th St
3100 ClkC 98685 476 D5
NW 149th Ter
5400 WasC 97229 564 H5
SE 149th Ter
13500 CmsC 97015 658 D5
SW 149th Ter
400 WasC 97006 594 J7
10100 BRTN 97007 654 J1
14700 WasC 97224 654 H6
NE 150th Av
- VCVR 98684 538 C3
3300 PTLD 97230 598 D2
4800 VCVR 98682 538 D1
9300 ClkC 98682 508 D3
25500 ClkC 98604 448 D1
NW 150th Av
10 WasC 97006 594 J5
5500 WasC 97229 564 J7
SE 150th Av
1300 PTLD 97233 598 D7
1800 PTLD 97233 628 D1
2300 VCVR 98683 568 C2
2900 PTLD 97236 628 D2
8500 CmsC 97236 628 D7
8500 HPYV 97236 628 D7
SW 150th Av
10 WasC 97006 594 J6
400 BRTN 97006 594 J6
5900 BRTN 97007 624 J4
14000 TGRD 97224 654 H6
14000 WasC 97224 654 H7
15900 WasC 97224 684 H1
NE 150th Cir
200 ClkC 98685 476 G4
12000 ClkC 98606 478 A5
NW 150th Cir
500 ClkC 98685 476 F5
NE 150th Ct
700 VCVR 98684 538 C6
4300 PTLD 97230 598 D1
8600 ClkC 98682 508 D4
22300 BGND 98604 448 D5
22300 ClkC 98604 448 D5
SE 150th Ct
200 VCVR 98684 538 C6
SW 150th Ct
5600 BRTN 97007 624 J4
5600 WasC 97007 624 J4
NE 150th Pl
500 PTLD 97230 598 D5
6800 ClkC 98682 508 D6
15900 ClkC 98606 478 D4
NW 150th Pl
4200 WasC 97229 594 J1
5300 WasC 97229 564 J7
SE 150th Pl
14700 CmsC 97015 658 D7
SW 150th Pl
4800 WasC 97007 624 J3
7600 BRTN 97007 624 H6
NE 150th St
- ClkC 98686 476 J5
100 ClkC 98685 476 G5
2500 ClkC 98686 477 A5
20900 ClkC 98606 479 A5
NW 150th St
100 ClkC 98685 476 G5
SE 150th Ter
13500 CmsC 97015 658 D6
NE 150th Wy
25700 ClkC 98606 479 F5
NW 150th Wy
200 ClkC 98685 476 G5
NE 151st Av
10 PTLD 97233 598 D6
2400 VCVR 98684 538 D4
3300 PTLD 97230 598 D2
3600 VCVR 98682 538 D2
8100 ClkC 98682 508 D5
25900 ClkC 98604 448 D1
27900 ClkC 98604 418 D6
NW 151st Av
5500 WasC 97229 564 J7
SE 151st Av
10 PTLD 97233 598 D7
100 VCVR 98684 538 D6
1800 PTLD 97233 628 D1
2400 VCVR 98683 568 C2
2500 PTLD 97236 628 D2
15300 CmsC 97015 658 C7
SW 151st Av
9200 BRTN 97007 654 H1
NE 151st Cir
2000 ClkC 98686 476 J5
6800 ClkC 98662 477 E5
6800 ClkC 98686 477 E5
8800 ClkC 98604 477 G5
NW 151st Cir
3900 ClkC 98685 476 C5
NE 151st Ct
2100 VCVR 98684 538 D4
3500 VCVR 98682 538 C3
9400 ClkC 98682 508 D4
SE 151st Ct
3600 VCVR 98683 568 D3
NW 151st Pl
2900 WasC 97006 594 J2
3300 WasC 97229 594 J2
SW 151st Pl
200 WasC 97006 594 J6
8100 BRTN 97007 624 H6
10000 BRTN 97007 654 H1
NE 151st St
200 ClkC 98685 476 G5
12100 ClkC 98606 478 B5
25200 ClkC 98606 479 E5
NW 151st St
1400 ClkC 98685 476 E4
NW 151st Ter
5000 WasC 97229 564 J7
SE 151st Ter
13500 CmsC 97015 658 D5
NE 152nd Av
- VCVR 98684 538 D4
3500 PTLD 97230 598 D2
4400 VCVR 98682 538 D1
7600 ClkC 98682 508 D7
11300 ClkC 98606 508 D3
12500 ClkC 98606 478 D3
23000 BGND 98604 448 D4
24400 ClkC 98604 448 D2
29500 ClkC 98604 418 D5
NW 152nd Av
100 WasC 97006 594 J5
SE 152nd Av
- CmsC 97015 658 D5
- HPYV 97015 658 D5
- HPYV 97236 658 D4
100 VCVR 98684 538 D6
800 VCVR 98683 538 D7
1500 PTLD 97233 598 D7
2000 PTLD 97233 628 D1
2400 VCVR 98683 568 D2
6600 PTLD 97236 628 D6
8500 CmsC 97236 628 D7
8500 CmsC 97236 658 D1
8500 HPYV 97236 628 D7
SW 152nd Av
10 WasC 97006 594 J5
4800 WasC 97007 624 H3
5400 BRTN 97007 624 H4
10200 BRTN 97007 654 H2
NE 152nd Cir
2200 ClkC 98686 476 J5
2500 ClkC 98686 477 A5
20200 ClkC 98606 478 J5
NE 152nd Ct
2000 PTLD 97230 598 D4
5000 VCVR 98682 538 D1
7500 ClkC 98682 508 D5
SE 152nd Ct
300 VCVR 98684 538 D7
1300 VCVR 98683 538 D7
1300 VCVR 98683 568 D1
SW 152nd Ct
5000 WasC 97007 624 H4
SE 152nd Dr
13500 CmsC 97015 658 D7
13500 HPYV 97015 658 D6
13500 HPYV 97236 658 D5
NE 152nd Pl
1900 VCVR 98684 538 D4
4300 VCVR 98682 538 D2
5200 PTLD 97230 598 E1
NW 152nd Pl
5200 WasC 97229 564 J7
SE 152nd Pl
1300 PTLD 97233 598 D7
NE 152nd St
100 ClkC 98685 476 G5
1700 ClkC 98686 476 J5
12200 ClkC 98606 478 A5
NW 152nd St
200 ClkC 98685 476 G5
NW 152nd Ter
4000 WasC 97229 594 J1
SW 152nd Ter
12800 BRTN 97007 654 H4
12800 BRTN 97223 654 H4
12800 WasC 97223 654 H4
NE 153rd Av
2000 VCVR 98684 538 D4
2100 PTLD 97230 598 D4
4100 VCVR 98682 538 D2
8400 ClkC 98682 508 D4
25700 ClkC 98604 448 D1
NW 153rd Av
1600 WasC 97006 594 H3
SE 153rd Av
10 PTLD 97230 598 D6
10 PTLD 97233 598 D6
800 VCVR 98683 538 D7
2100 PTLD 97233 628 D1
2500 PTLD 97236 628 D2
2800 VCVR 98683 568 D2
SW 153rd Av
- WasC 97224 654 H5
4900 WasC 97007 624 H3
6200 BRTN 97007 624 H5
9300 BRTN 97007 654 H1
NE 153rd Cir
2700 ClkC 98686 477 A5
19700 ClkC 98606 478 J5
NE 153rd Ct
4700 VCVR 98682 538 D1
8100 ClkC 98682 508 D5
SE 153rd Ct
300 VCVR 98684 538 D7

STREET Block	City	ZIP	Map#	Grid
SE 153rd Ct				
3800	VCVR	98683	568	D3
SE 153rd Dr				
13400	CmsC	97015	658	D6
13400	HPYV	97015	658	D5
SW 153rd Dr				
2200	BRTN	97006	594	H7
2200	BRTN	97006	624	H1
2200	WasC	97006	594	H7
NE 153rd Pl				
2300	PTLD	97230	598	D3
NW 153rd Pl				
2100	WasC	97006	594	J3
5200	WasC	97229	564	J7
SE 153rd Pl				
15100	VCVR	98683	568	D3
SW 153rd Pl				
10600	BRTN	97007	654	H2
NE 153rd St				
100	ClkC	98685	476	G5
600	VCVR	98684	538	D6
1800	ClkC	98686	476	J5
2600	ClkC	98686	477	A5
12200	ClkC	98606	478	A5
24800	ClkC	98606	479	E5
NW 153rd St				
100	ClkC	98685	476	G5
NW 153rd Ter				
4000	WasC	97229	594	J1
4800	WasC	97229	564	J7
SW 153rd Ter				
12900	WasC	97223	654	H4
NE 154th Av				
10	PTLD	97233	598	D6
2500	VCVR	98684	538	D4
3200	PTLD	97230	598	E2
3400	VCVR	98682	538	D3
8300	ClkC	98682	508	D5
25400	ClkC	98604	448	E2
NW 154th Av				
2800	WasC	97006	594	H2
SE 154th Av				
-	PTLD	97230	598	D6
10	PTLD	97233	598	D6
1700	VCVR	98683	568	D1
1800	PTLD	97233	628	D1
2500	PTLD	97236	628	D2
11600	CmsC	97236	658	D4
11600	HPYV	97236	658	D4
SW 154th Av				
2700	BRTN	97006	624	H1
4600	WasC	97007	624	H3
8000	BRTN	97007	624	H7
12900	BRTN	97007	654	H4
12900	WasC	97223	654	H5
NE 154th Cir				
2100	ClkC	98686	476	J5
8300	ClkC	98604	477	F5
8300	ClkC	98662	477	F5
NE 154th Ct				
2000	PTLD	97230	598	D4
2600	VCVR	98684	538	D3
4200	VCVR	98682	538	D2
7800	ClkC	98682	508	D7
SE 154th Ct				
200	VCVR	98684	538	D6
3800	VCVR	98683	568	D3
SE 154th Dr				
13500	CmsC	97015	658	D5
13600	HPYV	97015	658	D6
NE 154th Pl				
2300	PTLD	97230	598	E3
NW 154th Pl				
2300	WasC	97006	594	H3
SE 154th Pl				
3900	PTLD	97236	628	D3
15300	VCVR	98683	568	D3
SW 154th Pl				
5400	WasC	97007	624	H4
6200	BRTN	97007	624	H5
NE 154th St				
100	ClkC	98685	476	H4
1000	ClkC	98642	476	H4
1500	ClkC	98686	476	J5
2800	ClkC	98686	477	A5
7200	ClkC	98662	477	E5
11200	ClkC	98606	477	J5
11700	ClkC	98606	478	A5
21200	ClkC	98606	479	A5
NW 154th St				
100	ClkC	98685	476	G4
SW 154th Ter				
7100	BRTN	97007	624	H6
14800	WasC	97224	654	H6
NE 154th Wy				
21200	ClkC	98606	479	A5
NE 155th Av				
1900	VCVR	98684	538	D4
2700	PTLD	97230	598	E3
4200	VCVR	98682	538	D1
8500	ClkC	98682	508	D4
27400	ClkC	98604	418	E7
SE 155th Av				
100	VCVR	98684	538	D7
500	PTLD	97233	598	D7
500	VCVR	98683	538	D7
1400	VCVR	98683	568	D1
2100	PTLD	97233	628	D1
7400	PTLD	97236	628	D6
8500	CmsC	97236	628	D7
8500	HPYV	97236	628	D7
8500	HPYV	97236	658	D1
SW 155th Av				
6200	BRTN	97007	624	H7
6200	WasC	97007	624	H5
9200	BRTN	97007	654	H2
NE 155th Cir				
800	ClkC	98685	476	H4
1900	ClkC	98686	476	J3
NW 155th Cir				
1100	ClkC	98685	476	F4
NE 155th Ct				
2000	PTLD	97230	598	E4
3700	VCVR	98682	538	D2
8200	ClkC	98682	508	D7
SW 155th Ct				
15400	BRTN	97007	654	H1
SE 155th Dr				
13300	CmsC	97015	658	D5
13600	HPYV	97015	658	D5
NE 155th Pl				
2300	PTLD	97230	598	E3
SE 155th Pl				
10	PTLD	97230	598	D6
10	PTLD	97233	598	D6
1900	PTLD	97233	628	D1
15400	VCVR	98683	568	D3
NE 155th St				
2000	ClkC	98686	476	J4
NW 155th St				
2700	ClkC	98685	476	D4
SW 155th Ter				
5200	WasC	97007	624	H4
11500	BRTN	97007	654	H3
NE 155th Wy				
2200	ClkC	98686	476	J4
NE 156th Av				
1900	VCVR	98684	538	D4
3600	PTLD	97230	598	E2
4400	VCVR	98682	538	D2
9900	ClkC	98682	508	D3
NW 156th Av				
1900	WasC	97006	594	H3
SE 156th Av				
-	HPYV	97236	658	D1
100	VCVR	98684	538	D6
600	PTLD	97233	598	E6
1600	VCVR	98683	568	D1
1900	PTLD	97233	628	E1
6800	PTLD	97236	628	E6
8700	CmsC	97236	628	D7
8700	CmsC	97236	658	D1
14000	CmsC	97015	658	D6
SW 156th Av				
4500	WasC	97007	624	H3
6800	BRTN	97007	624	H5
NE 156th Ct				
2000	PTLD	97230	598	E4
7800	ClkC	98682	508	D5
15500	ClkC	98606	478	D4
28800	ClkC	98604	418	E5
SE 156th Ct				
1300	VCVR	98683	538	D7
1300	VCVR	98683	568	D1
NE 156th Pl				
2300	PTLD	97230	598	E3
7800	ClkC	98682	508	D5
NW 156th Pl				
2800	WasC	97006	594	H2
SE 156th Pl				
700	PTLD	97233	598	E7
SW 156th Pl				
7500	BRTN	97007	624	H6
9700	BRTN	97007	654	H1
NE 156th St				
1500	ClkC	98686	476	H4
2900	ClkC	98686	477	A4
9200	ClkC	98604	477	H4
9200	ClkC	98606	477	H4
11900	ClkC	98606	478	A4
NW 156th St				
-	ClkC	98685	476	G4
SW 156th Ter				
-	WasC	97223	654	H5
11600	BRTN	97007	654	H3
NE 156th Wy				
14700	ClkC	98606	478	C4
NE 157th Av				
-	BGND	98604	448	E7
10	PTLD	97233	598	E5
2500	VCVR	98684	538	D3
3000	VCVR	98682	538	D3
3600	PTLD	97230	598	E2
9900	ClkC	98682	508	E3
19300	ClkC	98604	448	E7
19300	ClkC	98604	478	E1
26900	ClkC	98604	418	E7
SE 157th Av				
-	CmsC	97236	628	D7
-	HPYV	97015	658	D5
-	VCVR	98683	538	D7
10	PTLD	97233	598	E6
300	VCVR	98684	538	D7
2000	PTLD	97233	628	E1
2100	PTLD	97236	628	E2
3000	VCVR	98683	568	D3
12500	HPYV	97236	658	E4
SW 157th Av				
7500	BRTN	97007	624	H6
12600	BRTN	97007	654	H4
12900	WasC	97223	654	H4
NE 157th Cir				
-	ClkC	98686	476	J4
2100	ClkC	98642	476	J3
NW 157th Cir				
3300	ClkC	98685	476	D4
NE 157th Ct				
600	VCVR	98684	538	D5
4700	VCVR	98682	538	D1
8500	ClkC	98682	508	D4
SE 157th Dr				
1800	PTLD	97233	598	E7
1800	PTLD	97233	628	E1
SE 157th Lp				
500	VCVR	98684	538	D7
NE 157th Pl				
100	VCVR	98684	538	D6
3300	PTLD	97230	598	E2
NW 157th Pl				
3100	WasC	97006	594	H2
SW 157th Pl				
5400	WasC	97007	624	H4
14000	WasC	97224	654	H5
NE 157th St				
100	ClkC	98685	476	G4
2000	ClkC	98686	476	J4
2200	ClkC	98642	476	J4
2500	ClkC	98642	477	A4
2500	ClkC	98686	477	A4
NW 157th St				
1600	ClkC	98685	476	E4
NE 158th Av				
2800	VCVR	98684	538	D3
3800	PTLD	97230	598	E2
4400	VCVR	98682	538	D1
9200	ClkC	98682	508	D4
NW 158th Av				
10	BRTN	97006	594	H4
1200	WasC	97006	594	H4
SE 158th Av				
100	VCVR	98684	538	D6
1300	PTLD	97233	598	E7
1600	VCVR	98683	568	D1
1800	PTLD	97233	628	E1
3000	PTLD	97236	628	E2
11900	CmsC	97236	658	D4
11900	HPYV	97236	658	D4
SW 158th Av				
10	BRTN	97006	594	H7
700	WasC	97006	594	H6
4900	WasC	97007	624	H3
6500	BRTN	97007	624	H5
9200	BRTN	97007	654	H1
NE 158th Cir				
2000	ClkC	98686	476	J4
2100	ClkC	98642	476	J4
NE 158th Ct				
1400	VCVR	98684	538	D5
1900	PTLD	97230	598	F4
3700	VCVR	98682	538	D2
SE 158th Ct				
2200	VCVR	98683	568	D1
SE 158th Lp				
2000	VCVR	98683	568	D1
NE 158th Pl				
2000	PTLD	97230	598	E4
3500	VCVR	98682	538	D3
7900	ClkC	98682	508	E5
SW 158th Pl				
7200	BRTN	97007	624	H6
NE 158th St				
1800	ClkC	98686	476	J3
2200	ClkC	98642	476	J4
2500	ClkC	98642	477	A4
3000	ClkC	98686	477	A4
17900	ClkC	98606	478	G4
SW 158th Ter				
9000	BRTN	97007	624	H7
11600	BRTN	97007	654	H3
13800	WasC	97223	654	H5
13800	WasC	97224	654	H5
NE 158th Wy				
18900	ClkC	98606	478	H4
NE 159th Av				
1800	VCVR	98684	538	D4
2500	PTLD	97230	598	E3
3400	VCVR	98682	538	D2
9100	ClkC	98682	508	E4
18000	ClkC	98606	478	E2
19900	ClkC	98604	448	E7
32900	ClkC	98604	418	E1
32900	ClkC	98675	418	E1
SE 159th Av				
200	VCVR	98684	538	D6
1200	VCVR	98683	538	D7
1300	PTLD	97233	598	E7
1300	VCVR	98683	568	D1
2000	PTLD	97233	628	E1
2700	PTLD	97236	628	E2
13100	HPYV	97015	658	D5
13100	HPYV	97236	658	D5
SW 159th Av				
4200	WasC	97007	624	H3
NE 159th Cir				
-	ClkC	98642	477	A4
NW 159th Cir				
2400	ClkC	98685	476	E4
NE 159th Ct				
700	VCVR	98684	538	D5
1500	PTLD	97230	598	E4
25500	ClkC	98604	448	E1
SE 159th Ct				
1800	VCVR	98683	568	D1
SW 159th Ct				
12600	BRTN	97007	654	G4
SE 159th Dr				
6200	PTLD	97236	628	E5
NW 159th Pl				
3100	WasC	97006	594	H2
6200	WasC	97229	564	H6
SE 159th Pl				
1800	VCVR	98683	568	D1
7300	PTLD	97236	628	E6
SW 159th Pl				
-	WasC	97007	624	H3
8000	BRTN	97007	624	H7
NE 159th St				
-	ClkC	98606	477	J4
2000	ClkC	98642	476	J4
2000	ClkC	98686	476	J4
2200	ClkC	98642	477	A4
5000	ClkC	98686	477	B4
7000	ClkC	98662	477	C4
8200	ClkC	98604	477	F4
12600	ClkC	98606	478	C4
20200	ClkC	98606	479	A4
NW 159th Ter				
2900	WasC	97006	594	H2
SW 159th Ter				
13700	WasC	97223	654	G5
NE 160th Av				
-	ClkC	98682	508	E4
-	VCVR	98684	538	E3
10	PTLD	97233	598	E6
2000	PTLD	97230	598	E4
4300	VCVR	98682	538	E2
14500	ClkC	98606	478	E5
NW 160th Av				
2000	WasC	97006	594	H3
SE 160th Av				
-	VCVR	98683	568	D1
10	PTLD	97233	598	E6
400	VCVR	98684	538	D7
800	VCVR	98683	538	D7
1800	PTLD	97233	628	E1
2500	PTLD	97236	628	E2
SW 160th Av				
-	BRTN	97006	624	H4
-	BRTN	97223	654	G4
-	WasC	97223	654	G4
1000	BRTN	97006	594	H7
4000	WasC	97007	624	H3
8000	BRTN	97007	624	H7
9400	BRTN	97007	654	G2
NE 160th Cir				
20500	ClkC	98606	478	J4
NE 160th Ct				
3400	VCVR	98682	538	E3
15700	ClkC	98606	478	E4
NW 160th Ct				
2900	WasC	97006	594	H2
NE 160th Dr				
2900	PTLD	97230	598	E3
NE 160th Lp				
2300	VCVR	98684	538	E4
NE 160th Pl				
1900	PTLD	97230	598	E4
7200	ClkC	98682	508	E6
SE 160th Pl				
1300	PTLD	97233	598	E7
1900	VCVR	98683	568	D1
NE 160th St				
2900	ClkC	98642	477	A4
11800	ClkC	98606	478	A4
SW 160th Ter				
12600	BRTN	97007	654	F4
NE 161st Av				
800	GSHM	97230	598	E5
800	PTLD	97230	598	E5
1100	VCVR	98684	538	E5
4300	VCVR	98682	538	E2
10300	ClkC	98682	508	E3
18300	ClkC	98606	478	E2
25600	ClkC	98604	448	E1
NW 161st Av				
2200	WasC	97006	594	H3
SE 161st Av				
200	VCVR	98684	538	E6
1800	PTLD	97233	628	E1
2900	VCVR	98683	568	D2
3000	PTLD	97236	628	E2
SW 161st Av				
-	BRTN	97007	654	E1
-	WasC	97007	654	E1
5700	WasC	97007	624	H4
14200	WasC	97224	654	G6
NW 161st Cir				
300	ClkC	98642	476	G4
NE 161st Ct				
1200	VCVR	98684	538	E5
3700	VCVR	98682	538	E2
10500	ClkC	98682	508	E2
SE 161st Ct				
2000	PTLD	97233	628	E1
2400	VCVR	98683	568	E2
SW 161st Ct				
10500	BRTN	97007	654	G2
SW 161st Dr				
7500	BRTN	97007	624	G6
7500	WasC	97007	624	G6
NE 161st Pl				
2100	VCVR	98684	538	E4
8900	ClkC	98682	508	E4
17000	ClkC	98606	478	E3
NW 161st Pl				
-	WasC	97006	594	H3
1000	BRTN	97006	594	H4
SE 161st Pl				
1600	VCVR	98683	568	D1
SW 161st Pl				
4600	WasC	97007	624	G2
6600	BRTN	97007	624	G5
13100	WasC	97223	654	G5
NE 161st St				
2500	ClkC	98642	477	A4
9200	ClkC	98604	477	G4
19700	ClkC	98606	478	J4
NW 161st Ter				
900	BRTN	97006	594	H4
SW 161st Ter				
-	BRTN	97006	594	H7
7100	BRTN	97007	624	G6
NE 161st Wy				
3500	ClkC	98642	477	B4
NW 161st Wy				
3600	ClkC	98642	476	C4
NE 162nd Av				
-	ClkC	98604	418	E7
10	GSHM	97230	598	E3
10	GSHM	97233	598	E6
10	VCVR	98684	538	E5
400	ClkC	98684	538	E5
500	PTLD	97230	598	E3
2300	ClkC	98682	538	E3
2300	VCVR	98682	538	E3
8600	ClkC	98682	508	E4
24400	ClkC	98604	448	E2
NE 162nd Av SR-500				
7000	ClkC	98682	508	E6
SE 162nd Av				
10	GSHM	97233	598	E6
1200	VCVR	98683	568	E1
1300	PTLD	97233	598	E7
1600	PTLD	97233	628	E2
6700	PTLD	97236	628	E6
8400	CmsC	97236	628	E7
8600	PTLD	97236	658	E1
11500	CmsC	97236	658	E4
11500	HPYV	97236	658	E4
14400	CmsC	97015	658	E7
14400	DAMA	97009	658	E7
14400	HPYV	97009	658	E7
14400	HPYV	97015	658	E7
SW 162nd Av				
1100	BRTN	97006	594	H7
5400	WasC	97007	624	G4
14100	WasC	97224	654	G5
NE 162nd Ct				
19700	ClkC	98604	448	E7
SE 162nd Ct				
4100	VCVR	98683	568	E3
SW 162nd Ct				
4800	WasC	97007	624	G3
SW 162nd Dr				
6600	BRTN	97007	624	G5
SE 162nd Pl				
1700	VCVR	98683	568	C3
SW 162nd Pl				
4200	WasC	97007	624	G2
6900	BRTN	97007	624	G5
NE 162nd St				
3300	ClkC	98642	477	A4
6700	ClkC	98662	477	E4
6700	ClkC	98686	477	E4
8700	ClkC	98604	477	G4
18700	ClkC	98606	478	H4
NW 162nd Ter				
-	WasC	97229	564	H7
-	WasC	97229	594	H1
900	BRTN	97006	594	H5
SW 162nd Ter				
13700	WasC	97223	654	G5
14800	WasC	97224	654	G6
NE 163rd Av				
2100	ClkC	98684	538	E4
2400	GSHM	97230	598	E3
4300	ClkC	98682	538	E2
8800	ClkC	98682	508	E4
19400	ClkC	98604	448	E7
19400	ClkC	98604	478	E1
SE 163rd Av				
1300	PTLD	97233	598	E7
1400	VCVR	98683	568	E1
SW 163rd Av				
900	BRTN	97006	594	G6
4400	WasC	97007	624	G1
9600	BRTN	97007	654	G1
14500	WasC	97224	654	G6
NE 163rd Cir				
10200	ClkC	98604	477	H4
10900	ClkC	98606	477	J4
20400	ClkC	98606	478	J4
NE 163rd Ct				
2500	ClkC	98684	538	E4
3800	ClkC	98682	538	D1
24200	ClkC	98604	448	E3
NW 163rd Ct				
3500	WasC	97006	594	G2
SW 163rd Dr				
6500	BRTN	97007	624	G5
NE 163rd Pl				
2100	ClkC	98684	538	E4
3400	PTLD	97230	598	E2
7100	ClkC	98682	508	E6
NW 163rd Pl				
300	BRTN	97006	594	G5
6000	WasC	97229	564	H6
SE 163rd Pl				
1100	VCVR	98683	538	E7
1200	PTLD	97233	598	E7
1600	VCVR	98683	568	E1
SW 163rd Pl				
6100	WasC	97007	624	G4
7000	BRTN	97007	624	G6
13600	WasC	97223	654	G5
NE 163rd St				
2500	ClkC	98642	477	A4
11900	ClkC	98606	478	A4
NW 163rd Ter				
3600	WasC	97006	594	G2
SW 163rd Ter				
13800	WasC	97223	654	G5
NE 164th Av				
100	ClkC	98684	538	E6
100	VCVR	98684	538	E6
2400	GSHM	97230	598	F3
3900	ClkC	98682	538	E2
8800	ClkC	98682	508	E4
17000	ClkC	98606	478	E3
23000	ClkC	98604	448	F4
29000	ClkC	98604	418	F5
29000	ClkC	98675	418	F5
NW 164th Av				
5200	WasC	97229	564	G7
SE 164th Av				
100	ClkC	98684	538	E6
100	VCVR	98684	538	E6
500	GSHM	97233	598	E6
500	PTLD	97233	598	E7
600	VCVR	98683	538	E7
1200	VCVR	98683	568	E3
1800	PTLD	97233	628	E1
2500	PTLD	97236	628	E2
SW 164th Av				
-	BRTN	97007	654	G1
4100	WasC	97007	624	G3
14000	WasC	97223	654	G5
14000	WasC	97224	654	G6
NE 164th Cir				
-	ClkC	98606	479	A4
8900	ClkC	98604	477	G4
17800	ClkC	98606	478	G4
NE 164th Ct				
1200	ClkC	98684	538	E5
3300	ClkC	98682	538	E3
7100	ClkC	98682	508	E6
SW 164th Ct				
5400	WasC	97007	624	G4
NE 164th Lp				
3200	PTLD	97230	598	F3
NE 164th Pl				
-	ClkC	98682	508	E5
2000	GSHM	97230	598	G4
2700	ClkC	98682	538	E3
2700	ClkC	98684	538	E3
SE 164th Pl				
1300	PTLD	97233	598	E7
SW 164th Pl				
4400	WasC	97007	624	G1
NE 164th St				
-	ClkC	98604	477	G4
100	ClkC	98642	476	G3
2400	ClkC	98642	477	A3
8200	ClkC	98662	477	F4
18200	ClkC	98606	478	J4
21700	ClkC	98606	479	A4
NW 164th St				
100	ClkC	98642	476	F3
NW 164th Ter				
3200	WasC	97006	594	G2
SW 164th Ter				
4600	WasC	97007	624	G3
7000	BRTN	97007	624	G5
NE 165th Av				
10	GSHM	97230	598	F5
10	GSHM	97233	598	F6
2400	ClkC	98684	538	E3
3400	PTLD	97230	598	F2
4300	ClkC	98682	538	E2
9900	ClkC	98682	508	E3
14500	ClkC	98606	478	E6
25400	ClkC	98604	448	F1
33400	ClkC	98604	418	F1
33400	ClkC	98675	418	F1
SE 165th Av				
10	GSHM	97230	598	F6
10	GSHM	97233	598	E6
800	PTLD	97233	598	F7
2300	VCVR	98683	568	E2
2500	PTLD	97233	628	E2
2500	PTLD	97236	628	E2
SW 165th Av				
-	BRTN	97007	654	G1
-	WasC	97007	654	G1
4000	WasC	97007	624	G3
6100	BRTN	97007	624	G4
NE 165th Cir				
6200	ClkC	98686	477	D3
NE 165th Ct				
1200	ClkC	98684	538	E5
3500	ClkC	98682	538	E2
SW 165th Ct				
5800	WasC	97007	624	G4
NE 165th Dr				
1900	GSHM	97230	598	F4
NE 165th Ln				
3200	PTLD	97230	598	F3
NE 165th Pl				
1900	GSHM	97230	598	F4
4000	ClkC	98682	538	E2
NW 165th Pl				
3100	WasC	97006	594	G2
5500	WasC	97229	564	G7
SE 165th Pl				
1800	PTLD	97233	628	E1
3000	PTLD	97236	628	F2
SW 165th Pl				
7300	BRTN	97007	624	G6
9300	BRTN	97007	654	G1
9300	WasC	97007	654	G1
NE 165th St				
1400	ClkC	98642	476	H3
2400	ClkC	98642	477	A3
NW 165th Ter				
6000	WasC	97229	564	G6
NE 165th Wy				
1100	ClkC	98642	476	H3
1100	ClkC	98686	476	H3
NW 165th Wy				
5800	ClkC	98642	476	A3
NE 166th Av				
-	PTLD	97230	598	F1
800	GSHM	97230	598	F5
1200	ClkC	98684	538	E5
3200	ClkC	98682	538	E3
8100	ClkC	98682	508	E5
NW 166th Av				
3100	WasC	97006	594	G2
4500	WasC	97229	594	G1
SE 166th Av				
100	GSHM	97233	598	F6
2400	VCVR	98683	568	E2
2600	PTLD	97236	628	F2
SW 166th Av				
500	BRTN	97006	594	G6
4700	WasC	97007	624	G3
6100	BRTN	97007	624	G4
9300	WasC	97007	654	G1
9600	BRTN	97007	654	G1
NE 166th Cir				
-	ClkC	98604	477	G3
NW 166th Cir				
6100	ClkC	98642	476	A3
NE 166th Ct				
2200	GSHM	97230	598	F3
2400	ClkC	98684	538	E4
SE 166th Ct				
3800	PTLD	97236	628	F3
SW 166th Ct				
5800	WasC	97007	624	G4
NE 166th Dr				
2000	GSHM	97230	598	F4
NW 166th Dr				
3600	WasC	97006	594	G2
NE 166th Pl				
2600	ClkC	98684	538	E3
2700	ClkC	98682	538	E3
SE 166th Pl				
-	PTLD	97233	628	F1
500	GSHM	97233	598	F6
500	PTLD	97233	598	F7
3400	PTLD	97236	628	F2
4400	VCVR	98683	568	E4
SW 166th Pl				
6300	BRTN	97007	624	G5
7700	WasC	97007	624	G6
NE 166th St				
1200	ClkC	98642	476	H3
2600	ClkC	98642	477	A3
NW 166th St				
3200	ClkC	98642	476	C3
NW 166th Ter				
2600	WasC	97006	594	G3
SW 166th Ter				
6900	BRTN	97007	624	G5
7300	WasC	97007	624	G5
NE 166th Wy				
2900	ClkC	98642	477	A3
NE 167th Av				
-	ClkC	98684	538	E4
16900	ClkC	98606	478	F2
18900	ClkC	98606	448	F7
23100	ClkC	98604	448	F3
NW 167th Av				
100	BRTN	97006	594	G5
2500	WasC	97006	594	G3
SE 167th Av				
10	GSHM	97233	598	F6
1000	PTLD	97233	598	F7
2500	PTLD	97233	628	F1
2500	PTLD	97236	628	F2
SW 167th Av				
10	BRTN	97006	594	G6
4100	WasC	97007	624	G3
SE 167th Ct				
3500	VCVR	98683	568	E3
NE 167th Pl				
2300	GSHM	97230	598	F4
NW 167th Pl				
1200	BRTN	97006	594	G4
3000	WasC	97006	594	G2
5000	WasC	97229	564	G7
SW 167th Pl				
800	BRTN	97006	594	G6
6700	BRTN	97007	624	G5
7200	WasC	97007	624	G6
9700	BRTN	97007	654	G1
NE 167th St				
1100	ClkC	98642	476	H3
1100	ClkC	98686	476	H3
13800	ClkC	98606	478	C3
NW 167th Ter				
3900	WasC	97006	594	G2
NE 168th Av				
100	GSHM	97230	598	F6
2300	ClkC	98684	538	E4
3100	ClkC	98682	538	E3
SE 168th Av				
500	GSHM	97233	598	F6
500	PTLD	97233	598	F7
500	VCVR	98684	538	E7
600	VCVR	98683	538	E7
2500	PTLD	97233	628	F2
2500	PTLD	97236	628	F2
3100	VCVR	98683	568	E3
SW 168th Av				
7800	BRTN	97007	624	G6
7800	WasC	97007	624	G6
NE 168th Cir				
2900	ClkC	98642	477	A3
NE 168th Ct				
9900	ClkC	98682	508	E3
SE 168th Ct				
3300	VCVR	98683	568	F5
NE 168th Pl				
800	GSHM	97230	598	F5
NW 168th Pl				
2200	WasC	97006	594	G3
5100	WasC	97229	564	G7
SE 168th Pl				
1300	PTLD	97233	598	F7
SW 168th Pl				
4800	WasC	97007	624	G3
6700	BRTN	97007	624	G5
9700	BRTN	97007	654	G1
NE 168th St				
1100	ClkC	98642	476	H3
13200	ClkC	98606	478	B3
SW 168th Ter				
6100	WasC	97007	624	G4
NE 169th Av				
1600	GSHM	97230	598	F4
1900	ClkC	98684	538	E4
3300	ClkC	98682	538	E3
8500	ClkC	98682	508	F4
29700	ClkC	98675	418	F4
NW 169th Av				
3800	WasC	97006	594	G1
SE 169th Av				
200	VCVR	98684	538	E6
300	GSHM	97233	598	F6
1000	PTLD	97233	598	F7
1700	PTLD	97233	628	F1
1700	VCVR	98683	568	E1
3000	PTLD	97236	628	F2
SW 169th Av				
7000	WasC	97007	624	G5
9100	BRTN	97007	624	G7
NE 169th Ct				
800	ClkC	98684	538	E5
SE 169th Ct				
3100	VCVR	98683	568	F5
SW 169th Ct				
300	BRTN	97006	594	G6
NE 169th Dr				
900	GSHM	97230	598	F5
SE 169th Dr				
700	PTLD	97233	598	F7
NE 169th Pl				
-	GSHM	97230	598	F5
NW 169th Pl				
1800	BRTN	97006	594	G3
1800	WasC	97006	594	G3
4700	WasC	97229	594	G1
5300	WasC	97229	564	G7
SE 169th Pl				
1300	PTLD	97233	598	F7
2600	VCVR	98683	568	F5
3600	PTLD	97236	628	F3
SW 169th Pl				
300	BRTN	97006	594	G6
5300	WasC	97007	624	G4
6500	BRTN	97007	624	G5
9700	BRTN	97007	654	G1
NE 169th St				
1200	ClkC	98642	476	H3
6900	ClkC	98662	477	E3
6900	ClkC	98686	477	E3
10200	ClkC	98604	477	H3
12300	ClkC	98604	478	A3
17500	ClkC	98606	478	G3
20600	ClkC	98606	479	B3
NW 169th St				
4300	ClkC	98642	476	B3
NE 170th Av				
-	ClkC	98682	538	F3
100	GSHM	97230	598	F6
1900	ClkC	98684	538	F4
15400	ClkC	98606	478	F4
SE 170th Av				
-	ClkC	98684	538	E6
-	VCVR	98684	538	E6
1600	VCVR	98683	568	E1
2000	PTLD	97233	628	F1
2600	PTLD	97236	628	F2
8400	CmsC	97236	628	F7
SW 170th Av				
800	BRTN	97006	594	G7
1100	WasC	97006	594	G7
2300	BRTN	97006	624	G1
2300	WasC	97006	624	G1
3800	WasC	97007	624	G6
6100	BRTN	97007	624	G4
9500	WasC	97007	654	F1
9600	BRTN	97007	654	F1
27000	WasC	97140	714	F5
NW 170th Cir				
6200	ClkC	98642	476	A3
NE 170th Ct				
1100	ClkC	98684	538	E5
SE 170th Ct				
3300	VCVR	98683	568	F5
NW 170th Dr				
300	BRTN	97006	594	G5
SE 170th Dr				
700	PTLD	97233	598	F7
NE 170th Pl				
3100	ClkC	98682	538	F3
3400	GSHM	97230	598	F3
NW 170th Pl				
900	BRTN	97006	594	G4
2300	WasC	97006	594	H4
NE 170th St				
2200	ClkC	98642	477	A3
9700	ClkC	98604	477	H3
14000	ClkC	98606	478	C3
NE 171st Av				
1600	GSHM	97230	598	F4
1900	ClkC	98684	538	F4
3900	ClkC	98682	538	F2
32900	ClkC	98604	418	F1
32900	ClkC	98675	418	F1
NW 171st Av				
4100	WasC	97006	594	G1
5000	WasC	97229	564	G7
SE 171st Av				
10	GSHM	97233	598	F6
200	VCVR	98684	538	F6
1900	PTLD	97233	628	F1
2700	VCVR	98683	568	F5
3900	PTLD	97236	628	F3
SW 171st Av				
10	BRTN	97006	594	G5
5900	WasC	97007	624	F4
9100	WasC	97007	654	F1
NE 171st Ct				
1100	ClkC	98684	538	F5
24000	ClkC	98604	448	F3

STREET Block City ZIP Map# Grid

SE 171st Ct
2600 VCVR 98683 568 F5
SE 171st Dr
3000 PTLD 97236 628 F2
SW 171st Dr
7100 WasC 97007 624 F5
NW 171st Pl
3800 WasC 97006 594 G1
SE 171st Pl
1500 VCVR 98683 568 F1
SW 171st Pl
200 BRTN 97006 594 G6
2300 WasC 97006 624 F1
4100 WasC 97007 624 G2
NE 171st St
1200 ClkC 98642 476 H3
6300 ClkC 98604 477 E3
6300 ClkC 98662 477 E3
6300 ClkC 98686 477 E3
17000 ClkC 98606 478 E3
22400 ClkC 98606 479 B3
NW 171st St
5800 ClkC 98642 476 A3
SE 171st St
3100 VCVR 98683 568 E2
SW 171st Ter
1600 WasC 97006 594 G7
NE 172nd Av
10 GSHM 97230 598 F5
10 GSHM 97233 598 F6
100 ClkC 98684 538 F5
100 VCVR 98684 538 F6
2700 ClkC 98682 538 F3
9400 ClkC 98606 508 F2
9400 ClkC 98682 508 F2
11900 ClkC 98606 478 F7
30100 ClkC 98675 418 G4
SE 172nd Av
- VCVR 98683 568 F2
10 GSHM 97233 598 F6
100 ClkC 98684 538 F7
100 VCVR 98684 538 F7
400 VCVR 98683 538 F7
1000 PTLD 97233 598 F7
8500 CmsC 97236 628 F7
8500 CmsC 97236 658 F2
9200 DAMA 97236 658 F1
9200 HPYV 97236 658 F1
9500 HPYV 97009 658 F7
9800 CmsC 97009 658 F7
13100 HPYV 97015 658 F7
13300 CmsC 97015 658 F7
13700 DAMA 97009 658 F7
13900 DAMA 97015 658 F6
SW 172nd Av
10 BRTN 97006 594 F6
10 WasC 97006 594 F6
3300 WasC 97006 624 F2
3800 WasC 97007 624 F2
NE 172nd Cir
2500 ClkC 98642 477 A3
14200 ClkC 98606 478 C3
SW 172nd Ct
2300 WasC 97006 624 F1
NE 172nd Pl
3400 GSHM 97230 598 F3
NW 172nd Pl
800 BRTN 97006 594 G5
3800 WasC 97006 594 G1
5000 WasC 97229 564 G7
SE 172nd Pl
1800 VCVR 98683 568 F1
SW 172nd Pl
7600 WasC 97007 624 F6
NE 172nd St
1300 ClkC 98642 476 J3
2700 ClkC 98642 477 A3
20500 ClkC 98606 478 J3
20700 ClkC 98606 479 A3
NW 172nd St
6200 ClkC 98642 476 A3
NW 172nd Ter
2800 WasC 97006 594 G3
5800 WasC 97229 564 G7
SW 172nd Ter
1600 WasC 97006 594 F7
NE 172nd Wy
16100 ClkC 98606 478 E3
NE 173rd Av
600 GSHM 97230 598 F5
2600 ClkC 98684 538 F3
2800 ClkC 98682 538 F3
21500 ClkC 98604 448 F5
NW 173rd Av
10 BRTN 97006 594 G4
10 WasC 97006 594 G4
5900 WasC 97229 564 G6
SE 173rd Av
200 VCVR 98684 538 F6
1500 VCVR 98683 568 F3
SW 173rd Av
10 BRTN 97006 594 F6
10 WasC 97006 594 F6
3100 WasC 97006 624 F2
3900 WasC 97007 624 F2
NE 173rd Cir
2500 ClkC 98642 477 A3
14400 ClkC 98606 478 C3
NE 173rd Ct
2800 ClkC 98682 538 F3
22500 ClkC 98604 448 F4
SE 173rd Ct
2200 VCVR 98683 568 F1
SW 173rd Ct
2300 WasC 97006 624 F1
NW 173rd Pl
4600 WasC 97006 594 F1
5000 WasC 97229 564 F7
SE 173rd Pl
2100 VCVR 98683 568 G5
SW 173rd Pl
6700 WasC 97007 624 F5
NE 173rd St
1200 ClkC 98642 476 H3
1200 ClkC 98686 476 H3
3000 ClkC 98642 477 A3
9900 ClkC 98604 477 H3
NW 173rd St
5500 ClkC 98642 476 A3
NW 173rd Ter
2800 WasC 97006 594 G2
SW 173rd Ter
1600 WasC 97006 594 F7
173rd Rd Ct
- ClkC 98604 448 F5

NE 174th Av
700 GSHM 97230 598 F5
2700 ClkC 98684 538 F3
3600 ClkC 98682 538 F3
27900 ClkC 98604 418 G6
NW 174th Av
2600 BRTN 97006 594 F3
2600 WasC 97006 594 F1
2600 WasC 97229 594 F1
5700 WasC 97229 564 F6
SE 174th Av
500 GSHM 97233 598 F6
500 PTLD 97233 598 F7
1600 PTLD 97233 628 F1
2100 PTLD 97236 628 F2
3000 VCVR 98683 568 F5
3300 GSHM 97030 628 F2
3300 PTLD 97030 628 F2
4500 MthC 97236 628 F3
SW 174th Av
1600 WasC 97006 594 F7
2900 WasC 97006 624 F2
3900 WasC 97007 624 F2
NE 174th Ct
3300 ClkC 98682 538 F2
23600 ClkC 98604 448 F3
SE 174th Ct
1800 VCVR 98683 568 F1
NW 174th Pl
1400 BRTN 97006 594 F4
SE 174th Pl
- VCVR 98683 568 F2
1300 PTLD 97233 598 F7
SW 174th Pl
600 WasC 97006 594 F6
5000 WasC 97007 624 F3
NE 174th St
- ClkC 98642 477 A3
3500 ClkC 98686 477 B3
7200 ClkC 98604 477 F3
12700 ClkC 98604 478 B3
18200 ClkC 98606 478 H3
21200 ClkC 98606 479 A3
NW 174th Ter
400 BRTN 97006 594 F5
SW 174th Ter
500 BRTN 97006 594 F6
500 WasC 97006 594 F6
5200 WasC 97007 624 F4
NE 175th Av
100 ClkC 98684 538 F6
100 VCVR 98684 538 F6
900 GSHM 97230 598 G5
3400 ClkC 98682 538 F3
SE 175th Av
100 ClkC 98684 538 F7
100 VCVR 98684 538 F7
1600 VCVR 98683 568 F1
SW 175th Av
300 BRTN 97006 594 F6
1200 WasC 97006 594 F7
2500 WasC 97006 624 F1
4200 WasC 97007 624 F3
9100 WasC 97007 654 F4
NE 175th Cir
5500 ClkC 98686 477 D2
SE 175th Ct
1900 VCVR 98683 568 F1
NW 175th Pl
1500 BRTN 97006 594 F4
4500 WasC 97229 594 F1
SE 175th Pl
- VCVR 98683 568 F1
500 GSHM 97233 598 F7
2500 GSHM 97233 628 F1
2500 GSHM 97236 628 F2
2500 PTLD 97233 628 F1
3100 PTLD 97236 628 F2
SW 175th Pl
600 WasC 97006 594 G7
6300 WasC 97007 624 F5
NE 175th St
2500 ClkC 98642 477 A2
SW 175th Ter
800 WasC 97006 594 G7
7300 WasC 97007 624 F6
NE 175th Wy
16200 ClkC 98606 478 E2
NW 175th Wy
4800 ClkC 98642 476 B2
NE 176th Av
10 GSHM 97233 598 G6
100 ClkC 98684 538 F6
900 GSHM 97230 598 G5
3600 ClkC 98682 538 F2
7100 ClkC 98682 508 F6
22600 ClkC 98604 448 G4
33100 ClkC 98604 418 G1
33100 ClkC 98675 418 G1
NW 176th Av
700 BRTN 97006 594 F5
4500 WasC 97229 594 F1
SE 176th Av
1500 GSHM 97233 598 G7
1500 GSHM 97233 628 G1
1500 PTLD 97233 628 G1
2000 VCVR 98683 568 F2
2200 GSHM 97236 628 G1
SW 176th Av
- WasC 97007 654 F1
2800 WasC 97006 624 F1
5600 WasC 97007 624 F4
NE 176th Cir
10200 ClkC 98604 477 H2
NE 176th Ct
700 ClkC 98684 538 F5
17900 ClkC 98606 478 F2
NW 176th Ct
600 BRTN 97006 594 F4
3300 WasC 97229 594 F2
5400 WasC 97229 564 F7
SE 176th Ct
1200 VCVR 98683 568 F1
NE 176th Pl
27900 ClkC 98604 418 G6
NW 176th Pl
1400 BRTN 97006 594 F4
SE 176th Pl
10 GSHM 97233 598 G6
1700 VCVR 98683 568 F2
2500 GSHM 97233 628 G1
2500 GSHM 97236 628 G2
NE 176th St
9700 ClkC 98604 477 H2
12200 ClkC 98604 478 B2

NE 176th St
21200 ClkC 98606 479 A3
SW 176th Ter
- WasC 97007 624 F6
900 WasC 97006 594 F7
NE 177th Av
- ClkC 98682 538 F2
800 GSHM 97230 598 G5
2200 ClkC 98684 538 F4
NW 177th Av
3300 WasC 97229 594 F2
5000 WasC 97229 564 F7
SE 177th Av
1200 VCVR 98683 568 F1
1500 GSHM 97233 598 G7
1600 GSHM 97233 628 G1
3100 GSHM 97236 628 G2
13500 CmsC 97009 658 F6
13500 DAMA 97009 658 F6
13500 HPYV 97009 658 F5
SW 177th Av
4000 WasC 97007 624 F3
NE 177th Cir
11400 ClkC 98604 477 J2
11400 ClkC 98604 478 A2
11400 ClkC 98606 478 A2
NW 177th Cir
4300 ClkC 98642 476 C2
NW 177th Ct
3300 WasC 97229 594 F2
SE 177th Ct
13800 CmsC 97009 658 F6
13800 DAMA 97009 658 F6
NE 177th Pl
800 GSHM 97230 598 G5
NW 177th Pl
1400 BRTN 97006 594 F4
SE 177th Pl
- VCVR 98683 568 F1
SW 177th Pl
3100 WasC 97006 624 F1
6300 WasC 97007 624 F5
NE 177th St
9200 ClkC 98604 477 G2
SW 177th Ter
900 WasC 97006 594 F6
NE 178th Av
2000 GSHM 97230 598 G4
2500 ClkC 98684 538 F3
2800 ClkC 98682 538 F3
NW 178th Av
700 BRTN 97006 594 F4
2900 WasC 97229 594 F2
5500 WasC 97229 564 F7
SE 178th Av
700 GSHM 97233 598 G7
1800 VCVR 98683 568 F1
2200 GSHM 97233 628 G1
3200 GSHM 97236 628 G2
13500 DAMA 97009 658 G6
SW 178th Av
1200 WasC 97006 594 F7
2200 WasC 97006 624 F1
3800 WasC 97007 624 F2
NE 178th Cir
11100 ClkC 98604 477 J2
NE 178th Ct
3700 ClkC 98682 538 F2
25900 ClkC 98604 448 G1
SE 178th Ct
1200 VCVR 98683 538 F7
1200 VCVR 98683 568 F1
SW 178th Ln
2100 WasC 97006 594 F7
2100 WasC 97006 624 F1
NW 178th Pl
1300 BRTN 97006 594 F4
4000 WasC 97229 594 F1
SE 178th Pl
1700 VCVR 98683 568 F1
2000 GSHM 97233 628 G1
SW 178th Pl
900 WasC 97006 594 F6
6500 WasC 97007 624 F5
NE 178th St
4500 ClkC 98686 477 C2
10000 ClkC 98604 477 H2
13700 ClkC 98604 478 C2
18800 ClkC 98606 478 H2
23200 ClkC 98606 479 C3
NE 179th Av
10 GSHM 97233 598 G6
900 GSHM 97230 598 G5
2600 ClkC 98684 538 F3
2700 ClkC 98682 538 F3
NW 179th Av
1900 BRTN 97006 594 F3
1900 HBRO 97006 594 F3
1900 WasC 97006 594 F3
3100 WasC 97229 594 F2
5500 WasC 97229 564 F7
SE 179th Av
500 GSHM 97233 598 G7
1200 VCVR 98683 538 F7
1200 VCVR 98683 568 F1
2000 GSHM 97233 628 G1
2500 GSHM 97236 628 G2
SW 179th Av
800 WasC 97006 594 F6
4300 WasC 97007 624 F3
NE 179th Cir
- ClkC 98604 477 J2
15200 ClkC 98606 478 D2
NE 179th Ct
18900 ClkC 98604 478 G1
18900 ClkC 98606 478 G1
22400 ClkC 98604 448 G5
SE 179th Ct
1100 VCVR 98683 538 F7
1900 VCVR 98683 568 F1
SW 179th Ct
1300 WasC 97006 594 F7
NE 179th Pl
1900 ClkC 98684 538 F4
8400 ClkC 98682 508 G4
NW 179th Pl
4000 WasC 97229 594 F1
SW 179th Pl
7500 WasC 97007 624 E6
NE 179th St
100 ClkC 98642 476 H2
2300 ClkC 98642 477 A2
3700 ClkC 98686 477 D2
6500 ClkC 98604 477 H2
12000 ClkC 98604 478 A2

NE 179th St
12000 ClkC 98606 478 A2
23000 ClkC 98606 479 C2
NW 179th St
100 ClkC 98642 476 F2
6900 ClkC 98642 475 J2
SW 179th Ter
3200 WasC 97006 624 F2
NE 180th Av
2800 ClkC 98684 538 F3
3500 ClkC 98682 538 G3
NW 180th Av
10 BRTN 97006 594 F5
300 WasC 97006 594 F5
SE 180th Av
500 GSHM 97233 598 G7
2000 GSHM 97233 628 G1
2000 VCVR 98683 568 F1
3100 GSHM 97236 628 G2
13500 DAMA 97009 658 G6
SW 180th Av
4300 WasC 97007 624 F3
NE 180th Cir
- ClkC 98604 478 A2
9700 ClkC 98604 477 H2
NE 180th Ct
3200 ClkC 98682 538 F3
25900 ClkC 98604 448 G1
NW 180th Ct
4000 WasC 97229 594 F1
SE 180th Ct
2400 VCVR 98683 568 F2
SW 180th Ct
1400 WasC 97006 594 F7
NE 180th Pl
2000 ClkC 98684 538 F4
NW 180th Pl
3500 WasC 97229 594 F2
5600 WasC 97229 564 F7
SE 180th Pl
3800 GSHM 97236 628 G3
4200 VCVR 98683 568 F4
SW 180th Pl
3000 WasC 97006 624 F2
7000 WasC 97007 624 F5
NE 180th St
12200 ClkC 98604 478 A2
15700 ClkC 98606 478 E2
23200 ClkC 98606 479 C2
NW 180th Ter
4900 WasC 97229 564 F7
SW 180th Ter
2500 WasC 97006 624 F1
4000 WasC 97007 624 F2
NE 180th Wy
- ClkC 98604 477 G2
- ClkC 98604 478 A2
SE 180th Wy
1300 GSHM 97233 598 G7
NE 181st Av
10 GSHM 97233 598 G6
2100 GSHM 97230 598 G3
2300 ClkC 98684 538 G4
3000 ClkC 98682 538 F3
30500 ClkC 98675 418 G4
NW 181st Av
10 BRTN 97006 594 E5
200 WasC 97006 594 F5
5600 WasC 97229 564 F6
SE 181st Av
10 GSHM 97233 598 G7
1100 VCVR 98683 538 F7
1100 VCVR 98683 568 F1
2000 GSHM 97233 628 G1
SW 181st Av
1000 WasC 97006 594 F7
7600 WasC 97007 624 E6
NE 181st Cir
- ClkC 98686 477 C2
11000 ClkC 98604 477 J2
13400 ClkC 98604 478 C2
21600 ClkC 98606 479 B2
NE 181st Ct
8100 ClkC 98682 508 G5
SE 181st Ct
4400 VCVR 98683 568 F4
NE 181st Lp
15200 ClkC 98606 478 D2
NE 181st Pl
300 GSHM 97230 598 G6
NW 181st Pl
3600 WasC 97229 594 F2
5400 WasC 97229 564 F7
SE 181st Pl
1800 VCVR 98683 568 F2
SW 181st Pl
6400 WasC 97007 624 F7
NE 181st St
10400 ClkC 98604 477 H2
13100 ClkC 98604 478 B2
18700 ClkC 98606 478 H2
NE 182nd Av
- ClkC 98604 418 G6
2800 ClkC 98684 538 G3
3300 ClkC 98682 538 G3
6700 ClkC 98682 508 G6
11900 ClkC 98606 508 G1
12500 ClkC 98606 478 G7
25000 ClkC 98604 448 G2
30300 ClkC 98675 418 G4
NW 182nd Av
200 WasC 97006 594 F5
SE 182nd Av
1000 GSHM 97233 598 G7
1100 VCVR 98683 538 G7
1200 VCVR 98683 568 G1
1600 GSHM 97233 628 G3
2000 GSHM 97030 628 G1
4200 GSHM 97080 628 G3
6500 GSHM 97236 628 G5
6500 MthC 97080 628 G6
6500 MthC 97236 628 G6
SW 182nd Av
1100 WasC 97006 594 E6
2400 WasC 97006 624 F1
4200 WasC 97007 624 E3
NE 182nd Cir
19800 ClkC 98606 478 J2
NE 182nd Ct
100 VCVR 98684 538 G6
2400 ClkC 98684 538 G4
29500 ClkC 98675 418 G5
SE 182nd Ct
3800 VCVR 98683 568 F3

NE 182nd Pl
100 GSHM 97230 598 G6
NW 182nd Pl
3500 WasC 97229 594 F2
SE 182nd Pl
1800 VCVR 98683 568 F2
SW 182nd Pl
3900 WasC 97007 624 E2
NE 182nd St
- ClkC 98604 477 J2
- ClkC 98604 478 A2
SW 182nd Ter
6100 WasC 97007 624 E4
NE 183rd Av
800 GSHM 97230 598 G5
2000 ClkC 98684 538 G4
20400 ClkC 98604 448 G7
NW 183rd Av
300 WasC 97006 594 E5
900 BRTN 97006 594 E4
3500 WasC 97229 594 E1
5500 WasC 97229 564 F7
SE 183rd Av
2100 VCVR 98683 568 G2
SW 183rd Av
5400 WasC 97007 624 E4
NE 183rd Ct
2800 ClkC 98682 538 G3
14700 ClkC 98606 478 G5
SE 183rd Ct
3700 VCVR 98683 568 G3
SW 183rd Ct
4600 WasC 97007 624 E3
SE 183rd Lp
2400 VCVR 98683 568 G2
NE 183rd Pl
100 GSHM 97230 598 G6
3000 ClkC 98682 538 G3
SE 183rd Pl
1800 VCVR 98683 568 F2
SW 183rd Pl
1100 WasC 97006 594 E6
2600 WasC 97006 624 E1
7300 WasC 97007 624 E6
NE 183rd St
10500 ClkC 98604 477 J2
15900 ClkC 98606 478 E2
20800 ClkC 98606 479 A2
SW 183rd Ter
6100 WasC 97007 624 E4
NE 184th Av
2800 ClkC 98682 538 G3
2800 ClkC 98684 538 G3
SE 184th Av
1000 GSHM 97233 598 G7
2000 GSHM 97233 628 G1
2200 VCVR 98683 568 G1
SW 184th Av
- WasC 97006 594 E6
6800 WasC 97007 624 E5
NE 184th Ct
24900 ClkC 98604 448 G2
SE 184th Ct
3700 VCVR 98683 568 G4
SW 184th Dr
- WasC 97007 624 E7
NE 184th Pl
300 GSHM 97230 598 G6
SE 184th Pl
- VCVR 98683 568 G3
2900 GSHM 97030 628 G2
SW 184th Pl
1100 WasC 97006 594 E7
7300 WasC 97007 624 E6
NE 184th St
900 ClkC 98642 476 H2
3500 ClkC 98642 477 B2
10000 ClkC 98604 477 H2
12200 ClkC 98604 478 A2
17600 ClkC 98606 478 G2
NW 184th St
6100 ClkC 98642 476 A1
SW 184th Ter
2100 WasC 97006 594 E7
SE 184th Wy
1900 GSHM 97233 628 G1
NE 185th Av
1800 ClkC 98684 538 G4
3200 GSHM 97230 598 H2
3200 PTLD 97230 598 H2
15800 ClkC 98606 478 G4
NW 185th Av
- HBRO 97229 594 E2
- WasC 97124 594 E2
10 BRTN 97006 594 E5
10 HBRO 97006 594 E3
10 WasC 97006 594 E5
1700 HBRO 97124 594 E3
3100 WasC 97229 594 E2
4800 WasC 97229 564 E5
5200 WasC 97231 564 E7
SE 185th Av
- GSHM 97230 598 G6
200 GSHM 97233 598 G6
1500 VCVR 98683 568 G1
1900 GSHM 97233 628 G1
2400 GSHM 97030 628 G1
SW 185th Av
10 BRTN 97006 594 E5
10 WasC 97006 594 E6
900 HBRO 97006 594 E6
2000 WasC 97006 624 E2
3600 WasC 97007 624 E6
NE 185th Cir
22800 ClkC 98606 479 C2
NE 185th Ct
3100 ClkC 98682 538 G3
12200 ClkC 98606 508 G1
NW 185th Ct
11000 MthC 97231 534 F7
11000 MthC 97231 564 F1
SE 185th Ct
2000 VCVR 98683 568 H1
NE 185th Pl
500 GSHM 97230 598 H5
3200 ClkC 98682 538 G3
SE 185th Pl
1700 VCVR 98683 568 G1
NE 185th St
8700 ClkC 98604 477 G1
11400 ClkC 98604 478 A2
20400 ClkC 98606 478 J2
20700 ClkC 98606 479 A2
NE 185th Wy
14400 ClkC 98606 478 G6

NE 186th Av
1300 GSHM 97230 598 H4
14400 ClkC 98606 478 G6
NW 186th Av
4500 WasC 97229 594 E1
4700 WasC 97229 564 E7
SE 186th Av
1700 GSHM 97233 628 H1
2100 VCVR 98683 568 H2
SW 186th Av
2400 WasC 97006 624 E1
4000 WasC 97007 624 E3
NE 186th Cir
11500 ClkC 98604 477 J1
NE 186th Ct
2800 ClkC 98682 538 G3
18400 ClkC 98606 478 G2
SE 186th Ct
1500 VCVR 98683 568 H1
2400 GSHM 97030 628 H1
2400 GSHM 97233 628 H1
NE 186th Dr
1100 GSHM 97230 598 H5
SE 186th Ln
1500 VCVR 98683 568 H1
NE 186th Pl
3000 ClkC 98682 538 G3
SE 186th Pl
1800 VCVR 98683 568 G1
2900 GSHM 97030 628 H2
SW 186th Pl
2600 WasC 97006 624 E1
5300 WasC 97007 624 E4
NE 186th St
12000 ClkC 98604 478 A2
SW 186th Ter
5800 WasC 97007 624 E4
NE 186th Wy
16400 ClkC 98606 478 E1
NE 187th Av
100 GSHM 97230 598 H6
1800 ClkC 98684 538 G4
2500 ClkC 98682 538 G3
7300 ClkC 98682 508 G6
16000 ClkC 98606 478 G4
NW 187th Av
4400 WasC 97229 594 E1
4800 WasC 97229 564 E7
SE 187th Av
500 GSHM 97233 598 H7
1000 VCVR 98683 538 G7
1000 VCVR 98683 568 G1
14200 DAMA 97009 658 G6
SW 187th Av
1500 WasC 97006 594 E7
2300 WasC 97006 624 E2
4000 WasC 97007 624 E2
NE 187th Ct
16400 ClkC 98606 478 G4
23900 ClkC 98604 448 H3
SW 187th Dr
5800 WasC 97007 624 E4
SE 187th Lp
3900 VCVR 98683 568 G3
SE 187th Pl
1800 VCVR 98683 568 G1
2500 GSHM 97030 628 H1
2500 GSHM 97233 628 H1
SW 187th Pl
5700 WasC 97007 624 E4
NE 187th St
10300 ClkC 98604 477 H1
NW 187th Wy
4200 ClkC 98642 476 C1
NE 188th Av
10 GSHM 97230 598 H5
10 GSHM 97233 598 H6
11600 ClkC 98606 508 G1
16400 ClkC 98606 478 H3
21900 ClkC 98604 448 H5
NW 188th Av
2300 HBRO 97006 594 E3
2300 HBRO 97124 594 E3
4700 WasC 97229 564 E7
4700 WasC 97229 594 E1
SE 188th Av
10 GSHM 97230 598 H6
10 GSHM 97233 598 H6
1100 VCVR 98683 538 G7
1300 VCVR 98683 568 G1
SW 188th Av
3600 WasC 97007 624 E2
NE 188th Ct
17500 ClkC 98606 478 H2
25500 ClkC 98604 448 H1
SW 188th Ct
2200 WasC 97006 624 E1
6200 WasC 97007 624 E5
NE 188th Pl
1100 GSHM 97230 598 H5
SW 188th Pl
4800 WasC 97007 624 E3
NE 188th St
2700 ClkC 98642 477 A1
9900 ClkC 98604 477 H1
NW 188th St
3800 ClkC 98642 476 C1
NE 189th Av
4100 GSHM 97230 598 H2
7300 ClkC 98682 508 G6
18100 ClkC 98606 478 H2
NW 189th Av
4700 WasC 97229 564 E7
SE 189th Av
- VCVR 98683 568 G1
2200 GSHM 97233 628 H1
SW 189th Av
2000 WasC 97006 594 E7
2100 WasC 97006 624 E1
5100 WasC 97007 624 E3
NE 189th Cir
16100 ClkC 98606 478 E1
NE 189th Ct
18400 ClkC 98606 478 H2
23100 ClkC 98604 448 H4
SE 189th Ct
1900 VCVR 98683 568 G1
SW 189th Ct
4300 WasC 97007 624 E3
NE 189th Pl
1100 GSHM 97230 598 H5
SE 189th Pl
1300 VCVR 98683 568 G1
SW 189th Pl
4100 WasC 97007 624 E2

NE 189th St
2000 ClkC 98642 476 J1
2300 ClkC 98642 477 A1
10200 ClkC 98604 477 J1
17200 ClkC 98604 478 G1
17200 ClkC 98606 478 G1
20700 ClkC 98606 479 A1
22800 ClkC 98604 479 C1
NW 189th St
1900 ClkC 98642 476 E1
NW 189th Wy
- HBRO 97006 594 E4
NE 190th Av
500 GSHM 97230 598 H5
12900 ClkC 98606 478 H7
19900 ClkC 98604 448 H7
NW 190th Av
- HBRO 97006 594 E4
4000 WasC 97229 594 E1
4800 WasC 97229 564 E7
SE 190th Av
500 GSHM 97233 598 H7
1000 GSHM 97233 628 H1
1800 VCVR 98683 568 G1
2300 GSHM 97030 628 H1
7000 GSHM 97080 628 H6
7000 MthC 97080 628 H6
7000 MthC 97236 628 H7
SW 190th Av
- WasC 97007 654 D1
5400 WasC 97007 624 E4
NE 190th Cir
- ClkC 98606 478 H1
2900 ClkC 98642 477 A1
NE 190th Ct
15300 ClkC 98606 478 H5
SE 190th Ct
11100 DAMA 97009 658 H3
SW 190th Ct
5100 WasC 97007 624 E3
SE 190th Dr
3000 GSHM 97080 628 H6
3000 MthC 97080 628 H6
7600 CmsC 97009 628 H7
7600 DAMA 97009 628 H7
7600 MthC 97236 628 H7
8500 CmsC 97009 658 H1
8500 DAMA 97009 658 H1
NE 190th Ln
4500 GSHM 97230 598 H1
NE 190th Pl
10 GSHM 97230 598 H6
10 GSHM 97233 598 H6
NW 190th St
- ClkC 98642 476 E1
NE 191st Av
600 GSHM 97230 598 H5
18900 ClkC 98606 478 H1
NW 191st Av
1600 HBRO 97006 594 E4
4600 WasC 97229 564 E7
4600 WasC 97229 594 E1
SE 191st Av
1000 GSHM 97233 598 H7
1100 VCVR 98683 538 G7
1200 VCVR 98683 568 G1
SW 191st Av
500 WasC 97006 594 E6
2900 WasC 97006 624 C2
4100 WasC 97007 624 D2
NE 191st Cir
- ClkC 98604 477 J1
1700 ClkC 98642 476 J1
17900 ClkC 98604 478 G1
17900 ClkC 98606 478 G1
NW 191st Cir
3300 ClkC 98642 446 D7
3300 ClkC 98642 476 C1
NE 191st Ct
23500 ClkC 98604 448 H4
SW 191st Ct
900 WasC 97006 594 E6
5300 WasC 97007 624 D4
NW 191st Pl
1500 HBRO 97006 594 E4
1500 WasC 97006 594 E4
SE 191st Pl
100 GSHM 97230 598 H6
100 GSHM 97233 598 H6
1800 VCVR 98683 568 G1
2500 GSHM 97030 628 H2
SW 191st Pl
8100 WasC 97007 624 D6
NE 191st St
9800 ClkC 98604 477 H1
12000 ClkC 98604 478 A1
SW 191st Ter
2400 WasC 97006 624 E1
NE 192nd Av
10 GSHM 97233 598 H6
100 ClkC 98607 538 H5
100 ClkC 98684 538 H5
100 VCVR 98607 538 H6
1500 GSHM 97230 598 H4
6500 ClkC 98682 508 H6
10200 ClkC 98606 508 H3
17400 ClkC 98606 478 H2
21200 ClkC 98604 448 H6
27700 ClkC 98604 418 H6
NW 192nd Av
- HBRO 97124 594 E3
1800 HBRO 97006 594 E3
3900 WasC 97229 594 E1
SE 192nd Av
- ClkC 98607 568 G2
- ClkC 98683 568 H4
- VCVR 98607 568 G3
10 GSHM 97230 598 H6
10 GSHM 97233 598 H6
100 ClkC 98607 538 H6
100 ClkC 98684 538 H7
100 VCVR 98607 538 H7
1000 VCVR 98683 538 H7
1200 VCVR 98683 568 G2
SW 192nd Av
1300 WasC 97006 594 D7
2100 WasC 97006 624 D2
3900 WasC 97007 624 D2
16300 WasC 97140 684 D1
NE 192nd Cir
4200 ClkC 98642 477 B1
4200 ClkC 98686 477 B1
22600 ClkC 98606 479 B1
NE 192nd Ct
16400 ClkC 98606 478 H4

STREET / Block	City	ZIP	Map#	Grid
SW 192nd Ct				
900	WasC	97006	594	E6
NW 192nd Pl				
4200	WasC	97229	594	E1
SW 192nd St				
	WasC	97007	594	E6
100	WasC	97007	594	E6
9300	WasC	97007	654	D1
NE 192nd St				
4400	ClkC	98686	477	C1
12000	ClkC	98604	478	A1
19200	ClkC	98606	478	A1
21200	ClkC	98606	479	A1
NW 192nd St				
6100	ClkC	98642	446	A7
6100	ClkC	98642	475	J1
6700	ClkC	98642	475	J1
NE 192nd Wy				
7200	ClkC	98604	477	E1
NE 193rd Av				
	ClkC	98682	508	H7
10	GSHM	97230	538	H6
500	GSHM	97230	538	H5
700	GSHM	97230	538	H5
13500	ClkC	98606	478	H7
NW 193rd Av				
	HBRO	97006	594	D4
	WasC	97006	594	D3
SE 193rd Av				
10	GSHM	97230	598	H6
10	GSHM	97233	598	H6
3100	VCVR	98607	568	H2
SW 193rd Av				
3800	WasC	97007	624	D2
NE 193rd Cir				
	ClkC	98604	477	A1
3600	ClkC	98642	477	A1
NW 193rd Cir				
3500	ClkC	98642	446	A7
3500	ClkC	98642	476	B1
NE 193rd Ct				
	ClkC	98606	478	H5
1800	ClkC	98607	538	H4
1800	ClkC	98684	538	H4
SW 193rd Ct				
900	WasC	97006	594	D6
NW 193rd Pl				
1600	HBRO	97006	594	D4
1600	WasC	97006	594	D4
SE 193rd Pl				
	VCVR	98607	568	H1
SW 193rd Pl				
5100	WasC	97007	624	D3
NE 193rd Pl				
	ClkC	98604	477	J1
NE 194th Av				
	ClkC	98675	418	H5
10	GSHM	97230	598	H6
10	GSHM	97233	598	H6
1300	ClkC	98607	538	H4
8000	ClkC	98682	508	H5
19000	ClkC	98606	448	H1
25900	ClkC	98604	448	H1
28000	ClkC	98604	418	J6
SE 194th Av				
10	GSHM	97230	598	H6
10	GSHM	97233	598	H6
SW 194th Av				
500	WasC	97006	594	D6
2100	WasC	97006	624	D1
5600	WasC	97007	624	D4
NE 194th Ct				
1100	GSHM	97230	538	H5
15600	ClkC	98606	478	H4
21000	ClkC	98604	448	H6
SE 194th Ct				
3200	VCVR	98607	568	H2
SW 194th Ct				
200	WasC	97006	594	D6
4400	WasC	97007	624	D3
NE 194th Pl				
600	ClkC	98607	538	H6
SE 194th Pl				
	VCVR	98607	568	H1
SW 194th Pl				
3700	WasC	97007	624	D2
NE 194th St				
100	ClkC	98642	446	G7
2000	ClkC	98642	477	A1
14900	ClkC	98604	478	D1
NW 194th St				
100	ClkC	98642	446	F7
NW 194th Ter				
2500	HBRO	97006	594	D3
2500	HBRO	97124	594	D3
SW 194th Ter				
6700	WasC	97007	624	D5
NE 195th Av				
10	GSHM	97233	598	J5
500	GSHM	97230	598	J5
13900	ClkC	98606	478	J5
25600	ClkC	98604	448	J1
NW 195th Av				
10000	WasC	97124	564	E2
SE 195th Av				
10	GSHM	97230	598	J6
10	GSHM	97233	598	J6
900	VCVR	98607	538	H7
1000	VCVR	98607	568	H1
SW 195th Av				
100	WasC	97006	624	D1
2300	WasC	97006	624	D1
4900	WasC	97007	624	D2
NW 195th Cir				
	ClkC	98642	446	A7
NE 195th Ct				
11700	ClkC	98606	478	H6
21600	ClkC	98604	448	H6
SW 195th Ct				
500	WasC	97006	594	D6
5800	WasC	97007	624	D3
SW 195th Pl				
5100	WasC	97007	624	D3
23700	WasC	97140	714	C1
SW 195th Ter				
3800	WasC	97007	624	D2
NE 196th Av				
10	GSHM	97233	598	J6
10	GSHM	97233	598	J6
800	GSHM	97230	598	J5

STREET / Block	City	ZIP	Map#	Grid
SE 196th Av				
1100	VCVR	98607	568	H1
SW 196th Av				
1400	WasC	97006	594	D7
2800	WasC	97006	624	D1
3700	WasC	97007	624	D2
SE 196th Av				
4000	ClkC	98607	568	H3
14900	DAMA	97009	658	H7
SW 196th Ct				
2600	WasC	97006	624	D1
NW 196th Pl				
5300	WasC	97229	564	D7
SW 196th Pl				
7300	WasC	97007	624	D6
NE 196th St				
7200	ClkC	98604	447	H7
16700	ClkC	98604	448	F7
16700	ClkC	98606	448	F7
19600	ClkC	98604	478	J1
NW 196th St				
5600	ClkC	98642	446	A7
NW 196th Ter				
3200	HBRO	97006	594	D2
SW 196th Ter				
7000	WasC	97007	624	D5
NE 197th Av				
10	GSHM	97230	598	J6
10	GSHM	97233	598	J6
500	GSHM	97230	598	J5
1300	ClkC	98607	538	J6
16400	ClkC	98606	478	H4
19700	ClkC	98604	478	H1
24100	ClkC	98604	448	J3
27400	ClkC	98604	418	J6
SE 197th Av				
10	GSHM	97230	598	J6
10	GSHM	97233	598	J6
700	VCVR	98607	538	H7
3500	VCVR	98607	568	J3
13000	DAMA	97009	658	H5
18500	CmsC	97009	688	H4
SW 197th Av				
700	WasC	97006	594	D7
NE 197th Cir				
10800	ClkC	98604	447	J7
21000	ClkC	98606	479	A1
SE 197th Ct				
1100	VCVR	98607	538	H7
3100	VCVR	98607	568	H3
NE 197th Pl				
2700	GSHM	97230	598	J3
SE 197th Pl				
	VCVR	98607	538	H7
SW 197th Pl				
7300	WasC	97007	624	D6
NE 197th St				
10300	ClkC	98604	447	H7
10300	ClkC	98606	508	H3
12700	ClkC	98604	448	B7
NE 198th Av				
10	GSHM	97233	598	J6
500	GSHM	97230	598	J5
17700	ClkC	98604	478	J2
25900	ClkC	98604	448	J1
SE 198th Av				
10	GSHM	97230	598	J6
10	GSHM	97233	598	J6
3500	VCVR	98607	568	H3
SW 198th Av				
500	WasC	97006	594	D7
2200	WasC	97006	624	D1
3500	WasC	97007	624	D5
NE 198th Ct				
4600	ClkC	98686	447	C7
SE 198th Ct				
13700	ClkC	98606	478	H6
SW 198th Ct				
200	VCVR	98607	538	H7
NE 198th St				
7200	ClkC	98604	447	H7
24400	ClkC	98604	479	D1
SW 198th Pl				
700	WasC	97006	594	D6
19100	WasC	97140	684	C3
NE 199th Av				
10	GSHM	97230	598	J6
10	GSHM	97233	598	J6
700	GSHM	97230	598	J7
SW 199th Av				
400	WasC	97006	594	D6
8100	WasC	97007	624	D6
NE 199th Ct				
13700	ClkC	98606	478	H6
21400	ClkC	98604	448	J5
SW 199th Ct				
1100	WasC	97006	594	D7
2200	WasC	97006	624	D1
7600	WasC	97007	624	D5
SE 199th Dr				
12500	DAMA	97009	658	J5
NE 199th Pl				
24000	ClkC	98607	448	J3
24000	ClkC	98604	449	A3
SW 199th Pl				
2700	WasC	97006	624	D1
6000	WasC	97007	624	D4
NE 199th St				
100	ClkC	98642	446	J7
2200	ClkC	98642	447	D7
4200	ClkC	98686	447	D7
5800	ClkC	98604	447	F7
11000	BGND	98604	447	J7
11200	BGND	98604	448	A7
15900	ClkC	98604	448	G7
16300	ClkC	98606	448	F7
23200	ClkC	98606	449	C7
NW 199th St				
100	ClkC	98642	446	F7
SW 199th St				
3100	WasC	97006	624	D1
NE 200th Av				
13900	ClkC	98606	478	J5
27400	ClkC	98604	418	J6
SE 200th Av				
300	WasC	97006	594	D6
4300	WasC	97007	624	D3

STREET / Block	City	ZIP	Map#	Grid
NE 200th Cir				
17400	ClkC	98604	448	F7
NE 200th Ct				
14800	ClkC	98606	478	J5
SW 200th Ct				
1500	WasC	97006	594	D7
2400	WasC	97006	624	D1
NE 200th Pl				
500	GSHM	97230	598	J5
SE 200th Pl				
700	VCVR	98607	538	H7
SW 200th Pl				
4000	WasC	97007	624	D2
NE 200th St				
22300	ClkC	98606	449	B7
NE 201st Av				
500	FRVW	97024	598	J5
500	GSHM	97230	598	J5
500	GSHM	97230	598	J5
8000	ClkC	98682	508	J3
27900	ClkC	98604	418	J6
SE 201st Av				
400	VCVR	98607	538	J7
1100	ClkC	98607	538	H7
1100	ClkC	98607	568	H1
4000	CMAS	98607	568	H4
SW 201st Av				
600	WasC	97006	594	D6
2500	WasC	97006	624	D1
4400	WasC	97007	624	C3
NE 201st Ct				
17800	ClkC	98606	478	J2
SE 201st Ct				
900	VCVR	98607	538	H7
NE 201st Pl				
300	ClkC	98604	538	H7
SW 201st Pl				
6400	WasC	97007	624	C4
NE 202nd Av				
10	GSHM	97030	598	J6
10	GSHM	97233	598	J6
1300	ClkC	98607	538	J6
1600	ClkC	98607	568	H1
11000	DAMA	97009	658	J3
SW 202nd Av				
3000	WasC	97006	624	C1
NW 202nd Cir				
5700	WasC	97006	594	C4
SE 202nd Ct				
	ClkC	98607	538	H7
	CMAS	98607	568	H3
300	WasC	97006	594	C6
6200	WasC	97007	624	C4
NE 202nd St				
17600	ClkC	98604	448	G7
SW 202nd Ter				
700	WasC	97006	594	C6
NE 203rd Av				
	FRVW	97024	598	J2
2200	WasC	97006	624	C1
3800	WasC	97007	624	C2
NE 203rd Ct				
4700	ClkC	98682	538	H1
6600	WasC	97007	624	C4
NW 203rd Pl				
5600	WasC	97229	564	D6
5700	WasC	97231	564	D6
SW 203rd Pl				
6200	WasC	97007	624	C4
NW 203rd St				
3200	ClkC	98642	446	D7
NE 204th Av				
3700	FRVW	97024	599	A2
7800	ClkC	98682	508	J3
18100	ClkC	98606	478	J2
25900	ClkC	98604	448	J1
SW 204th Av				
1400	WasC	97006	594	C7
5700	WasC	97006	624	C1
NW 204th Cir				
22000	ClkC	98604	448	J5
NE 204th Ct				
6500	ClkC	98682	508	J6
NW 204th Pl				
5600	WasC	97229	564	D6
SW 204th Pl				
4200	WasC	97007	624	C3
24200	ClkC	98604	449	D7
SW 204th Ter				
100	WasC	97006	594	C5
NE 205th Av				
3800	FRVW	97024	599	A2
7300	ClkC	98682	508	J6
15900	ClkC	98606	478	J3
SE 205th Av				
	HBRO	97006	594	D5
27400	ClkC	98604	418	J7
SW 205th Av				
100	WasC	97006	594	C5

STREET / Block	City	ZIP	Map#	Grid
SW 205th Av				
2700	WasC	97006	624	C1
3800	WasC	97007	624	C2
NE 205th Cir				
3300	WasC	97007	624	B5
NE 205th Ct				
17900	ClkC	98604	448	G7
NE 205th Ct				
19200	ClkC	98606	478	J1
SW 205th Ct				
5200	WasC	97007	624	C4
SE 205th Dr				
600	GSHM	97030	598	J7
NE 205th Pl				
600	GSHM	97030	599	A6
NE 205th Pl				
20400	ClkC	98604	448	J6
20400	ClkC	98604	449	A7
SE 205th Pl				
10	GSHM	97030	598	J6
10	GSHM	97030	599	A6
SW 205th Pl				
1400	WasC	97006	594	C7
2200	WasC	97006	624	B2
SW 205th Ter				
1200	WasC	97006	594	E5
7500	WasC	97007	624	B4
NE 206th Av				
21700	ClkC	98604	448	J5
25900	ClkC	98604	449	A1
NW 206th Av				
800	HBRO	97006	594	C4
2400	HBRO	97124	594	C3
SW 206th Av				
10	WasC	97006	594	C5
5500	WasC	97007	624	C4
NE 206th Cir				
6900	ClkC	98604	447	E6
SE 206th Ct				
6500	WasC	97007	624	B4
NE 206th Dr				
	FRVW	97024	599	A3
SW 206th Pl				
700	WasC	97006	594	C6
2300	WasC	97006	624	C1
6800	WasC	97007	624	B5
NE 206th St				
22400	ClkC	98606	449	B7
23300	ClkC	98604	449	B7
NW 206th St				
27500	ClkC	98604	418	J7
SW 206th Ter				
10	WasC	97006	594	E4
NE 207th Av				
10	GSHM	97030	599	A5
3700	FRVW	97024	599	A2
4900	ClkC	98682	538	J1
6800	ClkC	98604	508	J2
10900	ClkC	98606	508	J2
20600	ClkC	98604	449	A5
NW 207th Av				
600	GSHM	97030	599	A7
1000	HBRO	97006	594	C4
SE 207th Av				
600	GSHM	97030	599	A7
SW 207th Av				
300	WasC	97006	594	C6
2800	WasC	97006	624	C1
5700	WasC	97007	624	C4
27200	WasC	97140	714	B5
NE 207th Cir				
9100	ClkC	98604	447	G6
NW 207th Cir				
3400	ClkC	98642	446	D6
SW 207th Ct				
4600	WasC	97007	624	C3
NE 207th Dr				
	ClkC	98675	419	A1
1600	FRVW	97024	599	A1
SW 207th Pl				
1100	WasC	97006	594	C6
NE 207th St				
8000	ClkC	98604	447	F6
10400	ClkC	98606	508	J3
21200	ClkC	98604	449	A6
NE 207th Ter				
1400	WasC	97006	594	C7
NE 208th Av				
10100	ClkC	98682	508	J3
18300	ClkC	98606	479	A2
NW 208th Av				
3400	FRVW	97024	599	B2
5800	WasC	97229	564	C6
6100	WasC	97231	564	C6
SE 208th Av				
500	GSHM	97030	599	A7
SW 208th Av				
100	WasC	97006	594	C5
NE 208th Ct				
	ClkC	98682	508	J3
18500	ClkC	98606	479	A1
SW 208th Ct				
2600	WasC	97006	624	B1
NW 208th Ln				
1300	HBRO	97124	564	C5
NE 208th Pl				
1500	FRVW	97024	599	A4
12000	ClkC	98606	508	J1
NW 208th Pl				
1600	HBRO	97006	594	C4
SW 208th Pl				
1100	WasC	97006	594	C6
6000	WasC	97007	624	B4
NE 208th St				
10500	ClkC	98682	508	J2
10500	ClkC	98682	508	J2
NW 208th Ter				
3300	FRVW	97024	599	B2
NE 208th Ter				
4800	WasC	97007	624	C3
NE 209th Av				
7300	ClkC	98682	509	A3
15900	ClkC	98606	478	J3
SE 209th Av				
800	GSHM	97030	599	A7

STREET / Block	City	ZIP	Map#	Grid
SW 209th Av				
1100	WasC	97006	594	C7
2600	WasC	97006	624	C3
3300	WasC	97007	624	B5
SW 209th Ct				
2000	WasC	97006	594	C7
NW 209th Ln				
1300	HBRO	97006	594	C4
NE 209th Pl				
15000	ClkC	98606	479	A5
SW 209th Pl				
900	WasC	97006	594	C6
NE 209th St				
300	ClkC	98642	446	A6
2200	ClkC	98642	447	A6
6500	ClkC	98604	447	E6
17500	ClkC	98606	479	A3
22500	ClkC	98604	449	B5
NW 209th St				
1800	WasC	97006	624	B1
6700	WasC	97007	624	B5
NE 210th Av				
24500	ClkC	98604	449	A2
NW 210th Av				
	HBRO	97006	594	C5
NE 210th Cir				
1700	ClkC	98642	446	E6
SW 210th Ct				
2500	WasC	97006	624	C1
NW 210th Ln				
1300	HBRO	97006	594	C4
SW 210th Pl				
900	WasC	97006	594	C6
NW 210th Wy				
1400	WasC	97006	594	C4
NE 211th Av				
3600	FRVW	97024	599	A2
7500	ClkC	98682	509	A5
SW 211th Av				
1200	WasC	97006	594	C7
1400	WasC	97030	629	C1
SW 211th Av				
300	WasC	97006	594	C6
3000	WasC	97006	624	C1
6500	WasC	97007	624	B5
NW 211th Av				
3600	ClkC	98642	446	C6
NE 211th Ct				
6400	ClkC	98682	509	A7
SE 211th Ct				
1000	GSHM	97030	599	A7
SW 211th Ct				
2500	WasC	97006	624	C1
NE 211th Pl				
2100	WasC	97006	594	C6
NW 211th Ter				
3200	HBRO	97124	594	C2
NE 212th Av				
5000	ClkC	98682	539	A1
8300	ClkC	98682	509	A4
10100	ClkC	98604	509	A3
18900	ClkC	98606	479	A1
25300	ClkC	98604	449	A1
26700	ClkC	98604	419	A7
SE 212th Av				
500	GSHM	97030	599	A7
SW 212th Av				
300	WasC	97006	594	C6
2800	WasC	97006	624	C1
5700	WasC	97007	624	C4
SW 212th Ct				
1500	WasC	97006	594	B7
NE 212th Pl				
19100	ClkC	98606	479	A1
NW 212th Pl				
7300	WasC	97124	564	C3
NE 213th Av				
	FRVW	97024	599	A2
6500	ClkC	98682	509	A6
17900	ClkC	98606	479	A2
SE 213th Av				
1000	GSHM	97030	599	A7
SW 213th Av				
1000	WasC	97006	594	B6
5800	WasC	97007	624	B4
NE 213th Cir				
22000	ClkC	98604	449	B6
NE 213th Ct				
17700	ClkC	98606	479	A3
NE 213th Pl				
5800	WasC	97229	564	C6
SW 213th Pl				
2100	WasC	97006	594	B7
NW 214th Av				
3400	FRVW	97024	599	B2
5800	ClkC	98682	509	A4
6100	WasC	97231	564	C6
SE 214th Av				
500	GSHM	97030	599	A7
SE 214th Av				
100	GSHM	97030	599	A6
SW 214th Av				
2600	WasC	97006	594	B7
NW 214th Cir				
400	ClkC	98642	446	G6
NW 214th Pl				
7300	WasC	97124	564	C5
SW 214th Pl				
2300	WasC	97006	624	B1
NE 214th St				
	ClkC	98604	447	G6
	ClkC	98682	447	A6
20200	ClkC	98604	448	J6
21200	ClkC	98604	449	A6
SE 215th Av				
4000	FRVW	97024	599	B2
10900	ClkC	98682	509	A4
15400	ClkC	98604	479	A5
NW 215th Av				
3300	HBRO	97124	594	B2
SW 215th Av				
4800	WasC	97007	624	B3
SW 215th Av				
3000	WasC	97006	624	B1
NE 215th Cir				
19000	ClkC	98604	448	H6
NW 215th Ct				
5100	WasC	97229	564	C6
NE 215th Dr				
	GSHM	97030	599	A7

STREET / Block	City	ZIP	Map#	Grid
SE 215th Ct				
13500	ClkC	98009	659	A6
NE 215th Pl				
17800	ClkC	98606	479	A2
NE 215th St				
17900	ClkC	98604	448	G6
NE 215th Ter				
200	WasC	97006	594	B5
NE 215th Wy				
100	GSHM	97030	599	B6
NE 216th Av				
3900	FRVW	97024	599	B2
17500	ClkC	98606	479	A3
22500	ClkC	98604	449	B5
SW 216th Av				
100	GSHM	97030	599	B6
1700	WasC	97006	594	B7
2600	WasC	97006	624	B1
NE 216th Cir				
6700	ClkC	98604	447	B5
NW 216th Cir				
1000	ClkC	98642	446	F5
NE 216th Ct				
3500	FRVW	97024	599	B3
SW 216th Pl				
1300	WasC	97006	594	B7
20100	WasC	97140	684	A5
NE 217th Av				
	ClkC	98682	539	A1
3600	FRVW	97024	599	B2
6900	ClkC	98682	509	A6
16900	ClkC	98606	479	A3
22100	ClkC	98604	449	B5
NE 217th Av				
500	GSHM	97030	599	B7
SW 217th Av				
800	WasC	97006	594	B7
NE 217th Ct				
3500	FRVW	97024	599	B3
5900	ClkC	98682	509	A7
SW 217th Ct				
1600	WasC	97006	594	B7
NE 217th Pl				
14500	ClkC	98606	479	A3
SW 217th Pl				
2100	WasC	97006	594	B3
NW 217th Wy				
3100	ClkC	98642	446	D5
NE 218th Av				
4000	FRVW	97024	599	B2
22400	ClkC	98604	449	B5
NE 218th Cir				
100	GSHM	97030	599	B6
SE 218th Cir				
5100	ClkC	98642	446	B5
NE 218th Ct				
11500	ClkC	98606	509	A2
SW 218th Ct				
1600	WasC	97006	594	B7
SW 218th Dr				
2200	WasC	97006	624	B3
SW 218th Pl				
2200	WasC	97006	594	B7
NE 218th St				
24200	ClkC	98604	449	D6
SW 218th Ter				
1400	WasC	97006	594	B6
SE 219th Av				
500	HBRO	97123	594	B7
1500	HBRO	97123	594	B7
NE 219th Av				
200	FRVW	97024	599	B5
200	FRVW	97030	599	B5
9900	ClkC	98682	509	A3
11600	ClkC	98606	509	B1
15400	ClkC	98606	479	B5
26100	ClkC	98604	449	B1
NE 219th Ln				
	GSHM	97030	599	B6
NE 219th St				
2000	BGND	98642	446	E5
5800	WasC	97007	624	B4
6800	ClkC	98604	447	H5
9200	BGND	98604	447	H5
15300	ClkC	98604	448	J5
NE 219th St SR-502				
2100	ClkC	98642	447	D5
6800	ClkC	98604	447	H5
9200	BGND	98604	447	H5
NW 219th St				
14300	ClkC	98606	479	A6
27100	ClkC	98604	419	B7
NE 220th Av				
10	GSHM	97030	599	B6
4000	FRVW	97024	599	B2
25000	ClkC	98604	449	B2
26900	ClkC	98604	419	B7
NW 220th Av				
22000	MthC	97231	534	B5
22000	WasC	97124	534	B5
SE 220th Av				
10	GSHM	97030	599	B6
18700	ClkC	98604	448	H5
20900	ClkC	98604	449	A5
NE 220th Pl				
2300	WasC	97006	624	B1
NE 221st Av				
20200	ClkC	98604	449	B5
22500	ClkC	98604	449	B5
SE 221st Av				
700	GSHM	97030	599	B7
NE 221st Cir				
20300	ClkC	98604	448	J5
20800	ClkC	98604	449	A5
NE 221st St				
2300	ClkC	98642	446	H5
2900	ClkC	98642	447	A5
NW 221st St				
19000	ClkC	98604	448	H6
NW 222nd Av				
19100	ClkC	98607	539	B3
5500	ClkC	98682	509	B3
8300	ClkC	98682	509	B3
18900	ClkC	98606	479	B3
24400	ClkC	98604	449	B3

STREET / Block	City	ZIP	Map#	Grid
SE 222nd Dr				
8700	DAMA	97009	659	B5
NE 223rd Av				
500	FRVW	97024	599	B7
500	WDVL	97060	599	B6
900	WDVL	97024	599	B5
3300	TDLE	97060	599	B3
4000	FRVW	97024	599	B1
8100	ClkC	98682	509	B1
NE 223rd Cir				
8900	ClkC	98604	447	G5
15000	BGND	98604	448	D5
15000	ClkC	98604	448	D5
NE 223rd Ct				
13600	ClkC	98606	479	B7
24000	ClkC	98604	449	B3
NE 223rd St				
7200	ClkC	98604	447	E5
22300	ClkC	98604	449	B5
NE 224th Av				
5100	ClkC	98682	509	B1
11600	ClkC	98606	509	B1
19600	ClkC	98606	479	B1
SE 224th Av				
800	GSHM	97030	599	B7
NE 224th Av				
2500	ClkC	98642	447	A4
21100	ClkC	98604	449	A3
NE 224th Ct				
17400	ClkC	98606	479	B3
22500	ClkC	98604	449	B5
NE 224th St				
20200	ClkC	98604	448	J5
20600	ClkC	98604	449	A5
NE 225th Av				
20000	ClkC	98606	449	B7
NW 225th Av				
800	HBRO	97124	594	A4
900	WasC	97124	594	A4
SE 225th Av				
900	GSHM	97030	599	B7
NE 225th Cir				
2900	ClkC	98642	447	A4
NE 225th St				
17200	ClkC	98604	448	G5
NE 226th Av				
1800	FRVW	97024	599	C4
NW 226th Av				
900	HBRO	97124	594	A4
SE 226th Av				
800	GSHM	97030	599	C7
NE 226th Cir				
8900	ClkC	98604	447	G4
16200	ClkC	98604	448	E4
20600	ClkC	98604	449	A4
NE 226th Ct				
8800	ClkC	98682	509	B4
13900	ClkC	98682	479	B6
NE 226th St				
17200	ClkC	98604	448	H4
NE 227th Av				
1800	FRVW	97024	599	C4
10700	ClkC	98682	509	B2
12000	ClkC	98606	509	B1
18900	ClkC	98606	479	C1
21000	ClkC	98604	449	C5
NW 227th Av				
500	FRVW	97024	594	A4
1200	HBRO	97124	594	A4
NE 227th Ct				
1800	FRVW	97024	599	C4
19200	ClkC	98604	479	B1
NE 227th St				
24200	ClkC	98604	449	D5
NE 228th Av				
6100	ClkC	98682	509	B7
NW 228th Av				
600	HBRO	97124	594	A4
900	WasC	97124	594	A4
NE 228th Cir				
24700	ClkC	98604	449	D5
NE 228th Ct				
2000	FRVW	97024	599	C4
13400	ClkC	98606	479	C7
29600	ClkC	98604	419	C7
NE 228th St				
	ClkC	98682	509	B7
1900	ClkC	98607	539	B4
NW 229th Av				
800	WasC	97124	594	A4
2100	WasC	97124	594	A1
4400	HBRO	97124	564	A7
SW 229th Av				
2900	HBRO	97007	624	A2
2900	HBRO	97123	624	A2
2900	WasC	97007	624	A2
NE 229th Ct				
2000	FRVW	97024	599	C4
5300	ClkC	98682	539	B1
7800	ClkC	98682	509	B5
18700	ClkC	98606	479	C2
20900	ClkC	98604	449	C4
NE 229th St				
300	ClkC	98642	446	H4
4700	ClkC	98604	447	F4
7200	ClkC	98604	447	E4
20300	ClkC	98604	448	J4
20800	ClkC	98604	449	A4
NW 229th St				
2900	ClkC	98642	446	B4
229th Main				
	HBRO	97124	594	A1
NE 230th Av				
2900	ClkC	98682	539	C1
3100	ClkC	98682	509	C1
NW 230th Av				
900	HBRO	97124	594	A4
1100	HBRO	97124	594	A4
NE 230th Ct				
	ClkC	98682	539	B1
1600	WDVL	97060	599	C4
2000	FRVW	97024	599	C4

Portland Street Index

STREET
Block City ZIP Map# Grid

NE 230th Ct
5300 ClkC 98682 509 C7
17600 ClkC 98606 479 C3
NE 230th St
17600 ClkC 98604 448 G4
25200 ClkC 98604 449 F4
NE 231st Av
22400 ClkC 98604 449 C5
NW 231st Av
100 HBRO 97123 594 A5
100 HBRO 97124 594 A4
100 WasC 97124 594 A4
NE 231st Ct
1600 WDVL 97060 599 C4
SW 231st Pl
11700 WasC 97007 653 J3
11700 WasC 97123 653 J3
NE 231st St
7200 ClkC 98604 447 E4
16300 ClkC 98604 448 E4
24900 ClkC 98604 449 E4
NE 231st Wy
18200 ClkC 98604 448 G4
NE 232nd Av
600 ClkC 98607 539 C6
5300 ClkC 98682 539 C1
10200 ClkC 98682 509 C2
11500 ClkC 98606 509 C1
18900 ClkC 98604 479 C1
18900 ClkC 98606 449 C7
18900 ClkC 98606 479 C1
22900 ClkC 98604 449 C4
NE 232nd Av SR-500
5300 ClkC 98682 509 C7
5300 ClkC 98682 539 C1
SE 232nd Av
10600 DAMA 97009 659 C3
NE 232nd Cir
6000 ClkC 98604 447 E4
SE 232nd Dr
14500 CmsC 97009 659 C7
14500 DAMA 97009 659 C7
15400 CmsC 97009 689 C1
15400 DAMA 97009 689 C3
NE 232nd St
4100 ClkC 98642 447 C4
5600 ClkC 98604 447 D4
15200 BGND 98604 448 D4
15200 ClkC 98604 448 D4
NE 233rd Av
4000 ClkC 98682 539 C2
NE 233rd Ct
- ClkC 98604 449 C3
NE 233rd St
5000 ClkC 98604 447 C4
5000 ClkC 98642 447 C4
SW 234th Av
- HBRO 97123 623 J2
2900 HBRO 97007 623 J2
3000 WasC 97007 623 J1
NE 234th Ct
22400 ClkC 98604 449 C5
NE 234th St
1000 ClkC 98642 446 J3
9200 ClkC 98604 447 H4
16300 ClkC 98604 448 F4
19100 ClkC 98604 449 A4
NW 234th St
5100 ClkC 98642 446 B3
NE 235th Av
1600 WDVL 97060 599 D4
NW 235th Av
4300 HBRO 97124 563 J7
4300 HBRO 97124 593 J1
NE 235th Cir
11200 ClkC 98604 447 J3
23000 ClkC 98604 449 C4
NE 235th St
600 ClkC 98642 446 H3
NE 236th Av
- ClkC 98604 419 D6
1300 WDVL 97060 599 D4
23500 ClkC 98604 449 D3
NE 236th Cir
24300 ClkC 98604 449 D4
NE 236th Ct
8900 ClkC 98604 447 G3
16400 ClkC 98606 479 C4
SE 236th Ct
300 GSHM 97030 599 D6
NE 236th Pl
600 GSHM 97030 599 D5
600 WDVL 97060 599 D5
NE 236th St
1000 ClkC 98642 446 J3
2100 ClkC 98642 447 A3
6900 ClkC 98604 447 E3
16000 ClkC 98604 448 E4
NE 237th Av
700 ClkC 98607 539 C6
1300 WDVL 97060 599 D5
4800 ClkC 98682 539 C1
19700 ClkC 98604 479 D1
21900 ClkC 98604 449 D5
NE 237th Av SR-500
4800 ClkC 98682 539 C1
NE 237th Cir
22100 ClkC 98604 449 D5
NE 237th Ct
22900 ClkC 98604 449 D4
NE 237th St
23200 ClkC 98604 449 C4
NE 238th Av
1000 WDVL 97060 599 D5
4400 ClkC 98682 539 C2
6500 ClkC 98682 509 C6
12200 ClkC 98606 479 C7
12200 ClkC 98606 509 C1
NE 238th Av SR-500
4400 ClkC 98682 539 C2
SE 238th Av
300 GSHM 97030 599 D6
NE 238th Ct
12800 ClkC 98606 479 C7
NE 238th Dr
1000 TDLE 97060 599 D5
1000 WDVL 97060 599 D4
SE 238th Dr
- GSHM 97030 599 D5
- TDLE 97060 599 D5
- WDVL 97060 599 D5
NE 238th Pl
600 GSHM 97030 599 D5
600 WDVL 97060 599 D5
1300 ClkC 98607 539 C5

STREET
Block City ZIP Map# Grid

SW 238th Pl
20700 WasC 97140 683 H5
NE 238th St
13200 BGND 98604 448 B3
16200 ClkC 98604 448 F3
NE 238th Wy
13200 BGND 98604 448 B3
13200 ClkC 98604 448 B3
NE 239th Av
1600 ClkC 98607 539 C5
12300 ClkC 98606 509 D1
16300 ClkC 98606 479 D4
19600 ClkC 98604 449 D7
19600 ClkC 98604 479 D1
NE 239th Ct
25000 ClkC 98604 449 E3
NE 239th Pl
600 GSHM 97030 599 D5
600 WDVL 97060 599 D5
NE 239th St
1100 ClkC 98642 446 J3
2900 ClkC 98642 447 B3
4100 ClkC 98642 447 C3
13600 ClkC 98604 448 C3
NE 240th Av
2000 WDVL 97060 599 D4
13500 ClkC 98606 479 D7
23100 ClkC 98604 449 D4
NE 240th Cir
19800 ClkC 98604 448 J3
19900 ClkC 98604 449 A3
NE 240th Cr
- ClkC 98604 448 J3
SE 240th Ct
400 GSHM 97030 599 D6
NE 240th Pl
600 GSHM 97030 599 D5
600 WDVL 97060 599 D5
SE 240th Pl
10700 DAMA 97009 659 D3
SW 240th Pl
7000 WasC 97007 623 H6
NE 240th St
1000 ClkC 98642 446 H3
2500 ClkC 98642 447 A3
13600 ClkC 98604 448 C3
NE 240th Wy
11900 ClkC 98604 448 A3
NE 241st Av
- ClkC 98682 539 C1
NE 241st Cir
15900 ClkC 98604 448 E3
NE 241st Ct
6000 ClkC 98682 509 D7
12000 ClkC 98606 509 D1
SE 241st Ct
400 GSHM 97030 599 D6
NE 241st Pl
600 GSHM 97030 599 D5
600 WDVL 97060 599 D5
18000 ClkC 98604 479 D2
18000 ClkC 98606 479 D2
NE 242nd Av
2800 ClkC 98607 539 D3
4900 ClkC 98682 539 D1
22300 ClkC 98604 449 D5
NE 242nd Av SR-500
2800 ClkC 98607 539 D3
3400 ClkC 98682 539 D3
SE 242nd Av
- CmsC 97009 659 D7
8400 DAMA 97009 629 D7
8400 MthC 97080 629 D7
8600 DAMA 97009 659 D7
NE 242nd Ct
12800 ClkC 98606 479 D7
NE 242nd Dr
400 GSHM 97030 599 D6
400 TDLE 97060 599 D6
800 WDVL 97060 599 D6
SE 242nd Dr
2000 GSHM 97030 599 D6
NE 242nd St
13200 BGND 98604 448 B3
13500 ClkC 98604 448 C3
NE 243rd Av
6400 ClkC 98682 509 D7
NE 243rd Ct
23200 ClkC 98604 449 D4
NE 243rd St
- ClkC 98604 449 A3
NE 244th Av
1800 ClkC 98607 539 D4
2100 TDLE 97060 599 D4
2100 WDVL 97060 599 D4
15100 ClkC 98606 479 D5
21900 ClkC 98604 449 D5
SE 244th Av
1100 GSHM 97030 599 D7
NE 244th Cir
5000 ClkC 98642 447 D3
7200 ClkC 98604 447 E3
NE 244th St
2400 ClkC 98642 447 A2
6100 ClkC 98604 447 E3
12000 BGND 98604 448 A3
14200 ClkC 98604 448 D3
NE 245th Av
900 ClkC 98607 539 D5
12300 ClkC 98606 509 D1
13500 ClkC 98606 479 D6
20300 ClkC 98604 449 D6
30600 ClkC 98675 419 D4
SE 245th Av
8600 DAMA 97009 629 D7
8600 DAMA 97009 659 D1
8600 MthC 97080 629 D7
NE 245th Ct
- ClkC 98604 447 E2
11900 ClkC 98606 509 D1
NE 245th St
14200 ClkC 98604 448 C2
20800 ClkC 98604 449 A3
NE 246th Av
3800 ClkC 98607 539 D2
3800 ClkC 98682 539 D2
12800 ClkC 98606 479 D7
NE 246th Cir
300 ClkC 98642 446 H2
9900 ClkC 98604 447 H2
13200 ClkC 98604 448 B2
21900 ClkC 98604 449 B3
NE 246th Ct
12400 ClkC 98606 509 D1
23400 ClkC 98604 449 D4

STREET
Block City ZIP Map# Grid

NE 246th St
2900 ClkC 98642 447 B2
14200 ClkC 98604 448 C2
NE 247th Av
5000 ClkC 98682 539 D1
14900 ClkC 98606 479 D5
20100 ClkC 98604 449 E7
30600 ClkC 98675 419 E4
SE 247th Av
7400 MthC 97080 629 D6
SW 247th Pl
16900 WasC 97123 683 E1
NE 248th Av
1000 ClkC 98607 539 D5
5000 ClkC 98682 539 D1
NE 248th Cir
4600 ClkC 98642 447 C2
NE 249th Av
1300 ClkC 98607 539 D4
14900 ClkC 98606 479 E5
20900 ClkC 98604 449 E6
NE 249th St
1000 ClkC 98642 446 J2
5000 ClkC 98642 447 C2
6300 ClkC 98604 447 E2
18000 ClkC 98604 448 G2
NE 249th Wy
6300 ClkC 98604 447 E2
NE 250th Av
14500 ClkC 98606 479 E6
SE 250th Av
9600 DAMA 97009 659 E2
10000 CmsC 97009 659 E2
SE 250th Pl
10800 CmsC 97009 659 E3
10800 DAMA 97009 659 E3
NE 250th St
14200 ClkC 98604 448 C2
NE 251st Av
5000 ClkC 98682 539 E1
22500 ClkC 98604 449 E5
NE 251st St
7200 ClkC 98604 447 E2
NE 251st Wy
6500 ClkC 98604 447 E2
NE 252nd Av
2500 ClkC 98607 539 E3
5100 ClkC 98682 539 E1
5300 ClkC 98682 509 E7
23000 ClkC 98604 449 E4
SE 252nd Av
100 ClkC 98607 539 E7
1500 GSHM 97080 629 E5
7000 MthC 97080 629 E7
7800 DAMA 97009 659 E1
7800 MthC 97080 659 E1
8500 CmsC 97009 659 E1
NE 252nd Ct
6000 ClkC 98682 509 E7
SE 252nd Dr
10200 CmsC 97009 659 E2
NE 252nd St
7700 ClkC 98604 447 F2
NE 252nd Wy
6800 ClkC 98604 447 E2
NE 253rd Av
15100 ClkC 98606 479 E5
NW 253rd Av
- WasC 97124 563 G7
4800 HBRO 97124 563 H7
4800 HBRO 97124 593 H1
4800 WasC 97124 593 H1
NE 253rd Cir
19900 ClkC 98604 448 J2
NE 253rd Ct
5500 ClkC 98682 539 E1
NE 253rd St
10 ClkC 98642 446 H2
2100 ClkC 98642 447 A2
12800 ClkC 98604 448 B2
NW 253rd St
400 ClkC 98642 446 G2
400 RDGF 98642 446 G2
NE 254th Cir
13700 ClkC 98604 448 C2
NE 254th Ct
22600 ClkC 98604 449 E4
NE 254th St
- ClkC 98604 447 G2
2900 ClkC 98642 447 B2
12100 ClkC 98604 448 B2
NW 254th St
3100 ClkC 98642 446 C1
3100 RDGF 98642 446 D1
NE 255th Cir
9200 ClkC 98604 447 G1
18300 ClkC 98604 448 G2
NE 255th St
6100 ClkC 98604 447 E1
NE 256th Av
5300 ClkC 98682 539 E1
20600 ClkC 98604 449 E7
NE 256th Cir
19300 ClkC 98604 448 H1
NE 256th Ct
2000 ClkC 98642 446 J1
NE 256th St
12900 ClkC 98604 448 B1
NE 257th Av
15100 ClkC 98606 479 E5
22700 ClkC 98604 449 E4
SE 257th Av
7800 MthC 97080 629 F7
8500 CmsC 97009 659 F1
8500 MthC 97080 659 F1
14000 DAMA 97009 659 E6
SW 257th Av
1100 TDLE 97060 599 F5
2900 GSHM 97030 599 F7
NE 257th Cir
20000 ClkC 98604 449 F7
NE 257th Dr
- GSHM 97080 629 F3
100 GSHM 97030 629 F2
1800 GSHM 97030 599 F7
2900 TDLE 97060 599 F7
SE 257th Dr
- GSHM 97030 629 F3
- GSHM 97080 629 F3
9500 CmsC 97009 659 E3
SW 257th Dr
100 TDLE 97060 599 F4
NE 257th St
8000 ClkC 98604 447 F1
13700 ClkC 98604 448 C1

STREET
Block City ZIP Map# Grid

NW 257th Wy
100 TDLE 97060 599 G3
NE 258th Av
6000 ClkC 98682 509 E7
20500 ClkC 98604 449 F7
26300 ClkC 98675 419 F4
NE 258th Cir
16100 ClkC 98604 448 F1
SE 258th Pl
10500 CmsC 97009 659 F3
NE 258th St
13700 ClkC 98604 448 C1
NE 259th Av
2400 ClkC 98607 539 E4
5300 ClkC 98682 539 E1
NE 259th St
400 ClkC 98642 446 J1
400 RDGF 98642 446 H1
2000 ClkC 98642 447 A1
6600 ClkC 98604 447 F1
13800 ClkC 98604 448 C1
20400 ClkC 98604 449 A1
NW 259th St
4100 ClkC 98642 446 C1
26000 RDGF 98642 446 C1
NE 259th Wy
19500 ClkC 98604 448 J1
NE 260th Av
14600 ClkC 98606 479 F6
NE 260th Ct
- CMAS 98607 539 E7
NE 260th Pl
21900 ClkC 98604 449 F5
NE 261st Av
2900 ClkC 98607 539 F3
NE 261st Cir
12000 ClkC 98604 448 A1
NE 262nd Av
1000 ClkC 98607 539 F5
1100 TDLE 97060 599 F5
5500 ClkC 98682 509 F7
5500 ClkC 98682 539 F1
22700 ClkC 98604 449 F5
SE 262nd Av
6400 GSHM 97080 629 F6
6400 MthC 97080 629 F6
14500 CmsC 97009 659 F7
15500 CmsC 97009 689 F1
NE 262nd St
14300 ClkC 98604 448 D1
NE 263rd St
- ClkC 98642 447 B1
14300 ClkC 98604 448 D1
21200 ClkC 98604 449 A1
NW 264th Av
3300 HBRO 97124 593 F1
3300 WasC 97124 593 F1
NE 264th Pl
22900 ClkC 98604 449 F4
NE 264th St
- ClkC 98604 447 G1
- ClkC 98642 447 B1
200 ClkC 98642 416 H7
200 RDGF 98642 416 H7
14300 ClkC 98604 418 D7
NE 265th Av
14400 ClkC 98606 479 F6
NE 265th Ct
3400 ClkC 98607 539 F3
14100 ClkC 98606 479 F6
NW 265th Pl
14200 WasC 97124 533 G5
14200 WasC 97133 533 G4
NE 265th St
5300 ClkC 98642 417 D7
20300 ClkC 98604 448 J1
20800 ClkC 98604 449 A1
NE 266th Cir
18200 ClkC 98604 448 G1
NE 266th Pl
14100 ClkC 98606 479 F6
NE 266th St
11200 ClkC 98604 417 J7
11200 ClkC 98604 418 A7
21200 ClkC 98604 449 B1
NE 267th Av
4400 ClkC 98607 539 F2
NE 267th Av SR-500
300 ClkC 98607 539 F5
SE 267th Av
6800 GSHM 97080 629 G6
6800 MthC 97080 629 F7
7900 DAMA 97009 659 F1
7900 MthC 97080 659 F1
8600 CmsC 97009 659 G1
NE 267th Ct
21900 ClkC 98604 449 F5
NE 267th St
- ClkC 98642 417 A7
20200 ClkC 98604 418 J7
20200 ClkC 98604 419 A7
NE 268th Av
10 GSHM 97030 629 G2
10 GSHM 97080 629 G2
NW 268th Av
3400 HBRO 97124 593 F1
4000 WasC 97124 593 F1
SE 268th Ct
13900 CmsC 97009 659 G6
NW 268th Pl
6000 WasC 97124 563 F6
NE 268th St
- ClkC 98642 417 C7
NE 269th Av
4600 ClkC 98607 539 F2
7300 ClkC 98682 509 F6
22300 ClkC 98604 449 G5
NE 269th St
2900 ClkC 98642 417 B7
9200 ClkC 98604 417 J7
14700 ClkC 98604 418 D7
20800 ClkC 98604 419 A7
NE 270th Av
5600 ClkC 98682 539 G1
NE 270th Cir
15400 ClkC 98604 418 E7
SE 270th Pl
1500 ClkC 98607 569 F1
NE 270th St
15700 ClkC 98604 418 E7
NE 271st Av
14600 ClkC 98606 479 G5
33600 ClkC 98675 419 G1
NW 271st Av
6600 WasC 97124 563 F5

STREET
Block City ZIP Map# Grid

SE 271st Av
600 ClkC 98607 539 F7
800 ClkC 98607 569 F1
SE 271st Ct
300 ClkC 98607 539 F7
NE 271st St
20200 ClkC 98604 419 A7
NE 272nd Av
3400 ClkC 98607 539 G3
SE 272nd Av
11300 CmsC 97009 659 G4
NE 272nd St
10600 ClkC 98604 417 J7
12000 ClkC 98604 418 A7
NE 272nd Wy
14100 ClkC 98604 418 D7
NW 273rd Av
4500 HBRO 97124 563 F7
4500 WasC 97124 563 F7
SE 273rd Av
1800 ClkC 98607 569 G1
NE 273rd St
20200 ClkC 98604 418 J7
20200 ClkC 98604 419 A7
NE 274th Av
5500 ClkC 98607 509 G7
5500 ClkC 98607 539 G1
NE 274th Ct
4900 ClkC 98607 539 G1
SE 274th Ct
1000 ClkC 98607 569 G1
NE 274th St
14200 ClkC 98604 418 D7
NE 275th Av
5200 ClkC 98607 539 G1
NE 275th Cir
15200 ClkC 98604 418 D7
NE 275th St
7200 ClkC 98604 417 E6
NE 276th Av
5400 ClkC 98607 539 G1
NE 276th St
8200 ClkC 98604 417 F6
20100 ClkC 98604 418 J7
NE 276th Wy
20700 ClkC 98604 419 A7
NE 277th Av
- ClkC 98607 509 G7
1900 ClkC 98607 539 G4
SE 277th Av
- ClkC 98607 569 G1
NW 277th Cir
300 ClkC 98642 416 G6
NE 278th Av
2800 ClkC 98607 539 G3
5600 ClkC 98607 509 G7
NE 278th St
15100 ClkC 98604 418 D6
NE 279th Av
6200 ClkC 98607 509 G7
SE 279th Av
1700 ClkC 98607 569 G1
12600 CmsC 97009 659 H5
NE 279th St
- ClkC 98604 419 B6
100 ClkC 98642 416 J6
2000 ClkC 98642 417 A6
6700 ClkC 98604 417 J6
15500 ClkC 98604 418 H6
NW 279th St
200 ClkC 98642 416 G6
500 RDGF 98642 416 G6
NE 280th Av
5600 ClkC 98607 509 G7
NE 280th Cir
8300 ClkC 98604 417 F6
13000 ClkC 98604 418 B6
SE 280th Ct
1700 ClkC 98607 569 G1
NE 280th St
14300 ClkC 98604 418 D6
NW 280th St
5100 ClkC 98642 416 B6
5100 RDGF 98642 416 B6
NE 281st Av
4600 ClkC 98607 539 H1
NE 281st Cir
15300 ClkC 98604 418 E6
NE 282nd Av
5300 ClkC 98607 509 H7
5300 ClkC 98607 539 H1
SE 282nd Av
1000 GSHM 97080 629 H6
1000 MthC 97080 629 H6
2500 MthC 97060 629 H1
2500 TDLE 97060 629 H1
8600 CmsC 97009 659 H2
8600 MthC 97080 659 H1
SE 282nd Ct
2800 ClkC 98607 569 G2
SE 282nd Dr
- MthC 97060 629 H1
SE 282nd Ln
13400 CmsC 97009 659 H6
NE 282nd St
13200 ClkC 98604 418 C6
NE 283rd Av
100 ClkC 98607 539 H6
SE 283rd Av
100 ClkC 98607 539 H7
700 ClkC 98607 569 H1
1700 ClkC 98671 569 H1
NE 283rd Cir
13000 ClkC 98604 418 B6
NE 283rd St
19200 ClkC 98604 418 J6
NE 284th Av
1700 ClkC 98607 539 H4
NE 284th St
6000 ClkC 98604 417 E6
SE 285th Av
13200 CmsC 97009 659 H5
NE 285th St
10500 ClkC 98604 417 J5
NE 286th Av
4800 ClkC 98607 539 H1
SE 286th Ln
13200 CmsC 97009 659 H5
SE 287th Av
2500 MthC 97060 629 J2
8600 CmsC 97009 659 H1
8600 MthC 97080 659 H1
15100 CmsC 97009 689 H1
NE 287th Cir
13200 ClkC 98604 418 C5

STREET
Block City ZIP Map# Grid

NE 287th Pl
600 ClkC 98671 539 H6
NE 287th St
19400 ClkC 98604 418 J5
NW 287th St
6100 ClkC 98642 416 A5
NE 288th Av
3500 ClkC 98607 539 H3
NE 288th Cir
19400 ClkC 98604 418 J5
NE 289th Av
2900 ClkC 98607 539 H3
NE 289th Cir
7800 ClkC 98604 417 F5
16800 ClkC 98604 418 F5
NE 289th Ct
5000 ClkC 98607 539 H1
NW 289th Pl
10500 NPNS 97133 563 D1
10500 WasC 97133 563 D1
NE 289th St
1000 ClkC 98642 416 J5
8300 ClkC 98604 417 G5
NW 289th St
100 ClkC 98642 416 F5
NE 290th St
500 ClkC 98642 416 H5
4300 ClkC 98629 417 B5
17800 ClkC 98604 418 G5
NE 291st Av
12700 ClkC 98604 418 B5
NW 291st St
6100 ClkC 98642 416 A5
7100 ClkC 98642 415 J5
NE 291st Wy
6300 ClkC 98604 417 E5
NE 292nd Av
- ClkC 98675 419 J1
900 ClkC 98671 539 J5
2200 ClkC 98607 539 J2
5300 ClkC 98607 509 J7
NE 292nd Cir
1600 ClkC 98642 416 J5
NE 292nd Ct
5500 ClkC 98607 509 J7
5500 ClkC 98607 539 J1
SE 292nd Pl
- MthC 97080 629 J7
SE 293rd Av
- ClkC 98671 569 J2
NE 293rd St
- ClkC 98604 417 J5
- ClkC 98604 418 A5
1500 ClkC 98642 416 J5
NE 294th Cir
5300 ClkC 98629 417 D4
NW 294th Cir
- ClkC 98642 416 C4
NE 294th St
- ClkC 98604 418 D5
6500 ClkC 98604 417 E5
25500 ClkC 98604 419 F5
25500 ClkC 98675 419 F5
NW 294th St
- ClkC 98642 416 H4
NE 295th Av
800 ClkC 98671 539 J6
NE 295th St
5800 ClkC 98629 417 D4
15300 ClkC 98604 418 E5
NE 296th Av
- ClkC 98607 539 J2
- ClkC 98671 539 J5
NE 296th St
7300 ClkC 98604 417 F4
SE 297th Av
2900 ClkC 98671 569 J3
NW 297th Cir
700 ClkC 98642 416 G4
NE 297th Ct
8200 ClkC 98607 509 J5
NE 297th Pl
5000 ClkC 98607 539 J1
NE 297th St
4500 ClkC 98604 417 C4
4500 ClkC 98629 417 C4
16100 ClkC 98604 418 F4
16100 ClkC 98675 418 F4
NE 298th Ct
7800 ClkC 98607 509 J5
NE 298th St
15200 ClkC 98604 418 E4
NW 298th St
6200 ClkC 98642 416 A4
NE 299th Av
2900 ClkC 98607 539 J3
NE 299th Cir
6100 ClkC 98629 417 D4
NE 299th St
200 ClkC 98642 416 H4
5100 ClkC 98629 417 D4
7400 ClkC 98604 417 H4
11500 ClkC 98604 418 B4
16800 ClkC 98675 418 G4
26300 ClkC 98675 419 F4
NW 299th St
1500 ClkC 98642 416 F4
300 St
2700 CmsC 97015 657 H7
SE 300th Av
2800 ClkC 98671 569 J3
NE 300th Ct
5600 ClkC 98607 539 J1
NE 301st Cir
14100 ClkC 98604 418 C4
NE 301st St
12200 ClkC 98604 418 B4
NE 302nd Av
500 ClkC 98671 539 J6
3100 ClkC 98607 540 A3
SE 302nd Av
1000 MthC 97060 630 A3
3600 MthC 97080 630 A3
SE 302nd Ln
9500 CmsC 97009 660 A2
NE 302nd St
9500 ClkC 98604 417 H4
11400 ClkC 98604 418 A4
SE 303rd Av
1900 ClkC 98671 570 A2
NE 303rd Wy
- ClkC 98629 417 C4
NE 304th Av
1000 ClkC 98671 540 A5
3300 ClkC 98607 540 A3

STREET
Block City ZIP Map# Grid

NW 304th Cir
- ClkC 98642 416 F3
NE 304th Ct
3600 ClkC 98607 540 A3
NE 304th St
11500 ClkC 98604 418 A4
NW 304th St
5100 ClkC 98642 416 A3
NW 304th Wy
300 ClkC 98642 416 G3
NE 305th Av
500 ClkC 98671 540 A6
NE 306th Cir
4400 ClkC 98629 417 C3
NE 306th Ct
2900 ClkC 98607 540 A3
NE 306th St
10000 ClkC 98604 417 J3
14300 ClkC 98604 418 D3
NE 307th Av
1900 ClkC 98671 540 A4
2500 ClkC 98607 540 A3
NW 307th Av
9600 NPNS 97133 563 B2
SE 307th Av
- MthC 97080 630 B7
7300 CmsC 97009 660 A1
7300 CmsC 97080 660 A1
SE 308th Av
3700 ClkC 98671 570 A3
3700 WHGL 98671 570 A3
NE 308th St
12200 ClkC 98604 418 B3
18300 ClkC 98675 418 H3
NW 309th Av
10800 NPNS 97133 563 B1
10900 WasC 97133 563 B1
11200 NPNS 97133 533 B7
11200 WasC 97133 533 B7
NE 309th Cir
- ClkC 98642 416 G3
NE 309th St
24400 ClkC 98675 419 E3
NW 309th St
- ClkC 98642 415 J3
5200 ClkC 98642 416 B3
NE 310th Av
1000 ClkC 98671 540 A5
3100 ClkC 98607 540 A3
SW 310th Av
9100 WasC 97113 623 A7
NE 310th Cir
100 ClkC 98642 416 H3
NE 310th St
15200 ClkC 98604 418 E3
NW 310th St
1500 ClkC 98642 416 F3
NW 311th Av
10300 NPNS 97133 563 B1
NE 311th Cir
14300 ClkC 98604 418 D3
NE 311th St
10300 ClkC 98604 417 J3
15100 ClkC 98604 418 D3
25800 ClkC 98675 419 F3
312th Av
10000 NPNS 97133 563 B2
NE 312th Av
10 ClkC 98671 540 B6
4800 ClkC 98607 540 B1
NW 312th Av
1300 HBRO 97124 593 B3
1300 WasC 97124 593 B3
SE 312th Av
10 ClkC 98671 540 A7
11000 CmsC 97009 660 B4
14500 CmsC 97009 690 B1
NW 312th Cir
4800 ClkC 98642 416 C3
NE 312th St
15200 ClkC 98604 418 E3
24400 ClkC 98675 419 E3
NE 312th Wy
25200 ClkC 98675 419 E3
NW 313th Av
3400 HBRO 97124 593 B1
3400 WasC 97124 593 B1
10800 NPNS 97133 563 B1
11000 WasC 97133 563 B1
SW 313th Av
9000 WasC 97113 623 A7
NE 313th St
15200 ClkC 98604 418 E3
SE 313th St
3000 ClkC 98671 570 A3
NE 314th Av
900 ClkC 98671 540 B5
NW 314th Av
9500 WasC 97124 563 A2
10000 NPNS 97133 563 B2
SE 314th Av
3200 ClkC 98671 570 B3
5600 MthC 97080 630 B5
NW 314th Cir
5100 ClkC 98642 416 B2
NE 314th St
9700 ClkC 98604 417 J3
9700 ClkC 98629 417 H3
13400 ClkC 98604 418 C3
SE 315th Av
3900 ClkC 98671 570 B3
3900 WHGL 98671 570 B3
NW 315th Cir
- ClkC 98642 416 A2
NE 315th St
5900 ClkC 98629 417 D2
15200 ClkC 98604 418 E3
NW 316th Cir
600 ClkC 98642 416 G2
NE 316th Ct
4700 ClkC 98607 540 B1
NE 316th St
8200 ClkC 98629 417 G2
NW 317th Av
- NPNS 97133 563 A1
- WasC 97133 563 A1
300 HBRO 97124 593 A4
500 WasC 97124 593 A4
SE 317th Av
3500 MthC 97080 630 C3
NE 317th St
15400 ClkC 98604 418 E2
18100 ClkC 98675 418 H2
NW 318th Av
10900 NPNS 97133 563 A1

Portland Street Index

STREET Block	City	ZIP	Map#	Grid
NE 318th Pl				
600	ClkC	98671	540	B7
NW 318th St				
3100	ClkC	98642	416	C2
NE 319th Av				
200	ClkC	98671	540	B6
NW 319th Av				
10900	NPNS	97133	563	A1
NE 319th Cir				
26300	ClkC	98675	419	G3
SE 319th Pl				
7100	MthC	97080	630	C6
NE 319th St				
13200	ClkC	98604	418	C2
NW 319th St				
600	ClkC	98642	416	G2
NE 320th Av				
4900	ClkC	98607	540	B1
NW 321st Av				
10300	NPNS	97133	563	A1
NE 321st Ct				
5600	ClkC	98607	540	C1
NE 321st St				
14700	ClkC	98604	418	D2
NW 321st St				
4100	ClkC	98642	416	C2
NE 322nd Av				
1000	ClkC	98671	540	B5
SE 322nd Av				
3800	MthC	97060	630	C4
6700	MthC	97080	630	C6
13700	CmsC	97009	660	C6
15300	CmsC	97009	690	C1
SE 322nd Pl				
8100	MthC	97080	630	C7
8100	MthC	97080	660	C1
NE 322nd St				
9400	ClkC	98629	417	H2
26100	ClkC	98675	419	F2
NE 323rd Cir				
15500	ClkC	98604	418	E2
NE 324th Av				
4800	ClkC	98607	540	C1
NW 324th Av				
10600	NPNS	97133	563	A1
NE 324th Cir				
15600	ClkC	98604	418	E2
NE 324th St				
5000	ClkC	98629	417	D2
NW 324th St				
2600	ClkC	98642	416	E1
SW 325th Av				
1600	WasC	97123	592	J7
NE 325th St				
8200	ClkC	98629	417	G2
13700	ClkC	98604	418	C2
NE 326th Av				
5300	ClkC	98607	540	C1
SE 326th Av				
900	ClkC	98671	570	C1
NE 326th St				
13700	ClkC	98604	418	D1
SE 327th Av				
3200	ClkC	98671	570	C3
3200	WHGL	98671	570	C3
9000	CmsC	97080	660	C1
9500	CmsC	97009	660	C2
NW 327th Rd				
-	ClkC	98642	386	C7
-	ClkC	98642	416	C1
NE 327th St				
13900	ClkC	98604	418	C1
SE 328th Av				
1600	ClkC	98671	570	C1
3100	WHGL	98671	570	C3
NE 328th Cir				
14500	ClkC	98604	418	D1
NE 328th St				
8200	ClkC	98629	417	G1
NW 328th St				
4200	ClkC	98642	416	D1
SE 329th Av				
500	ClkC	98671	540	C7
1100	ClkC	98671	570	C1
14600	CmsC	97009	660	D7
14600	CmsC	97009	690	D1
14600	CmsC	97055	690	D1
SE 329th Pl				
16600	CmsC	97055	690	D2
NE 329th St				
9500	ClkC	98629	417	H1
13700	ClkC	98604	418	C1
NW 329th St				
2400	ClkC	98642	416	E1
NE 330th Av				
1500	ClkC	98671	540	C5
SE 330th Ct				
3200	ClkC	98671	570	C3
3200	WHGL	98671	570	C3
NE 330th St				
-	ClkC	98629	417	D1
SE 331st Av				
1100	ClkC	98671	570	C1
SW 331st Av				
10	WasC	97123	592	J7
10	WasC	97124	592	J5
NE 331st St				
10300	ClkC	98629	417	H1
NW 331st St				
5600	ClkC	98642	386	B7
NE 332nd Av				
900	ClkC	98671	540	C5
NE 332nd Ct				
2000	ClkC	98671	540	D4
NE 332nd St				
7800	ClkC	98629	417	F1
16100	ClkC	98604	418	F1
16100	ClkC	98675	418	F1
NW 332nd St				
-	ClkC	98642	416	C1
4100	ClkC	98642	386	C7
NW 332nd Wy				
3500	ClkC	98642	416	D1
NE 333rd St				
13800	ClkC	98604	418	C1
13800	ClkC	98675	418	C1
NW 334th Av				
100	WasC	97123	592	H5
100	WasC	97124	592	H5
NE 334th St				
2400	ClkC	98629	417	A1
NW 334th St				
5500	ClkC	98642	386	B7
NE 335th Av				
1600	ClkC	98671	540	D4
NE 335th Cir				
-	ClkC	98604	418	H1
-	ClkC	98675	418	H1
NE 335th St				
6800	ClkC	98629	417	E1
NW 336th Av				
10	CNLS	97123	592	H5
10	WasC	97124	592	H5
NE 336th St				
15600	ClkC	98675	418	E1
SE 337th Av				
600	ClkC	98671	540	D7
NE 338th Av				
1500	ClkC	98671	540	D4
NW 338th Av				
100	CNLS	97123	592	H5
100	CNLS	97124	592	H5
100	WasC	97124	592	H5
NE 339th Av				
2300	ClkC	98671	540	D4
SE 339th Av				
100	ClkC	98671	540	D7
NE 339th St				
1400	LCTR	98629	386	J7
1900	ClkC	98629	386	J7
SE 340th Av				
-	ClkC	98671	570	D1
SE 340th Ct				
14300	CmsC	97009	660	E7
NE 341st Av				
1500	ClkC	98671	540	D5
NW 341st Av				
10	CNLS	97123	592	H5
10	CNLS	97124	592	H5
10	WasC	97124	592	H5
NE 342nd Av				
1100	ClkC	98671	540	D5
SE 342nd Av				
2000	ClkC	98671	570	D2
2600	WHGL	98671	570	D2
SE 343rd Ct				
2200	ClkC	98671	570	E2
SE 344th Av				
1500	ClkC	98671	570	E2
SE 345th Av				
100	ClkC	98671	540	E7
SW 345th Av				
10	CNLS	97113	592	G6
10	CNLS	97123	592	G6
10	WasC	97123	592	G6
SE 347th Av				
2500	ClkC	98671	570	E3
8200	CmsC	97009	660	E1
NE 348th St				
100	ClkC	98629	386	G6
NE 349th Av				
5400	ClkC	98607	540	E1
NE 349th Ct				
100	ClkC	98671	540	E6
SE 349th Pl				
100	ClkC	98671	540	E7
NE 349th St				
100	ClkC	98629	386	H6
NE 352nd Av				
10	ClkC	98671	540	E7
SE 352nd Av				
10	ClkC	98671	540	E7
10	ClkC	98671	570	E1
9500	CmsC	97009	660	F2
NW 352nd Cir				
600	ClkC	98629	386	G6
NE 353rd Av				
10	ClkC	98671	540	F6
NW 353rd St				
600	ClkC	98629	386	G6
NE 354th Av				
5200	ClkC	98607	540	F1
SE 354th Av				
5800	ClkC	98671	570	F6
NE 354th St				
-	ClkC	98629	386	D6
NW 354th St				
1500	ClkC	98629	386	F5
SE 356th Av				
6200	ClkC	98671	570	F6
NW 356th St				
2000	ClkC	98629	386	F5
NE 357th Av				
2400	ClkC	98671	540	F4
SE 357th Av				
600	ClkC	98671	540	F7
900	ClkC	98671	570	F1
NE 357th Ct				
3100	ClkC	98671	540	F3
SE 358th Ct				
11700	CmsC	97009	660	G4
NE 359th Av				
1900	ClkC	98671	540	F4
SE 359th Pl				
19000	CmsC	97055	690	F4
359th St NW				
800	ClkC	98629	386	G5
NE 359th St				
500	ClkC	98629	386	H5
NW 359th St				
1100	ClkC	98629	386	F5
NE 360th Av				
2000	ClkC	98671	540	F3
NE 360th Ct				
3400	ClkC	98607	540	F3
3400	ClkC	98671	540	F3
SE 362nd Av				
2000	ClkC	98671	570	F3
9500	CmsC	97009	660	G2
13000	CmsC	97055	660	G7
14500	CmsC	97009	690	G1
16500	SNDY	97055	690	G2
16800	CmsC	97055	690	G4
NW 363rd Pl				
5600	WasC	97113	562	F6
NW 363rd St				
-	ClkC	98629	386	D5
NE 365th Av				
100	MthC	97019	600	G6
SE 365th Ct				
4700	ClkC	98671	570	G5
NE 366th Av				
1400	MthC	97019	600	H5
NW 366th Pl				
3000	WasC	97113	592	E2
NW 366th St				
2900	ClkC	98629	386	E4
NE 367th Av				
100	ClkC	98671	540	G6
SE 367th Av				
20100	CmsC	97055	690	G5
SE 367th Ct				
3700	ClkC	98671	570	G3
SE 369th Ct				
100	ClkC	98671	540	G7
NW 369th St				
2100	ClkC	98629	386	E4
SE 370th Av				
2300	ClkC	98671	570	G2
17700	CmsC	97055	690	G3
17700	SNDY	97055	690	G3
NW 372nd St				
2900	ClkC	98629	386	D4
2900	ClkC	98674	386	D4
NE 373rd St				
1300	ClkC	98629	386	J4
NE 375th Av				
2000	ClkC	98671	540	H4
SE 377th Av				
1600	ClkC	98671	570	H2
14900	CmsC	97055	660	H7
14900	SNDY	97055	660	H7
15100	CmsC	97055	690	H1
15100	SNDY	97055	690	H1
NE 378th St				
800	ClkC	98629	386	H3
SE 379th Av				
4500	ClkC	98671	570	H4
NW 379th St				
400	ClkC	98629	386	E3
4500	ClkC	98674	386	C3
NE 380th Av				
1700	ClkC	98671	540	H4
SE 380th Av				
1000	ClkC	98671	570	H1
SE 380th Ct				
500	ClkC	98671	540	H7
500	ClkC	98671	570	H1
NE 381st St				
100	ClkC	98629	386	H3
NW 381st St				
100	ClkC	98629	386	H3
100	ClkC	98674	386	G3
SE 382nd Av				
3500	ClkC	98671	570	H3
NE 382nd St				
600	ClkC	98629	386	H2
NW 382nd St				
-	ClkC	98674	386	C3
NW 384th Cir				
1000	ClkC	98629	386	F2
1000	ClkC	98674	386	F2
NE 384th Ct				
2000	ClkC	98671	540	J4
NE 384th St				
800	ClkC	98629	386	J2
SE 385th Av				
1200	ClkC	98671	570	J1
NE 386th St				
100	ClkC	98629	386	H2
100	ClkC	98674	386	H2
NE 387th Av				
2000	ClkC	98671	540	J4
NW 387th St				
4100	ClkC	98674	386	C2
SE 389th Av				
1400	ClkC	98671	570	J1
NE 389th St				
100	ClkC	98674	386	J2
1200	ClkC	98629	386	J2
NW 389th St				
700	ClkC	98629	386	G2
5700	ClkC	98674	386	B2
NE 390th Av				
10	ClkC	98671	540	J6
SE 390th Av				
1700	ClkC	98671	570	J2
SE 391st Av				
3700	ClkC	98671	570	J4
NE 391st Dr				
100	ClkC	98671	540	J7
NE 394th St				
100	ClkC	98674	386	H1
NW 394th St				
-	ClkC	98674	386	G2
NW 395th St				
5600	ClkC	98674	386	B1
400 St				
-	CmsC	97015	657	J7
NW 402nd St				
-	ClkC	98674	386	A1
NE 403rd St				
400	ClkC	98674	386	H1
NE 404th St				
-	ClkC	98674	386	J1
NW 404th St				
100	ClkC	98674	386	G1
SE 412th Av				
-	CmsC	97055	691	C4
-	SNDY	97055	691	C4
SE 422nd Av				
16900	CmsC	97055	691	D4
17600	SNDY	97055	691	D4
SE 427th Av				
21500	CmsC	97055	691	D7
SE 502nd Av				
18900	CmsC	97055	692	C5

Portland Points of Interest Index

FEATURE NAME Address City ZIP Code	MAP#	GRID

Airports

FEATURE NAME	MAP#	GRID
Aurora State, MrnC	775	E1
Big Sky Ranch, CmsC	688	H6
Cedars North, ClkC	447	F7
Country Squire Airpark, CmsC	720	H1
Evergreen Field, VCVR	538	B6
Fairways, CmsC	717	H6
Fly For Fun, ClkC	508	C4
Goheen, ClkC	417	G6
Grove Field, ClkC	539	F6
Hutchinson Airfield, CmsC	837	A2
McMinnville Municipal, MCMV	771	D7
Mulino Airfield, CmsC	777	D5
Olinger Airstrip, WasC	562	J7
Pearson Airfield, VCVR	536	H6
Portland-Hillsboro, HBRO	593	G3
Portland International, PTLD	567	F4
Portland-Troutdale, TDLE	599	F2
Sandy River, CmsC	691	D2
Scappoose Industrial Airpark, SPSE	444	G5
Skyport, WasC	562	F3
Sportsman Airpark, YmhC	743	E1
Sunset Airstrip, WasC	563	A2
Valley View, CmsC	750	C1
Woodland State, WDLD	386	A2

Beaches, Harbors & Water Rec

FEATURE NAME	MAP#	GRID
A-1 Boat Moorage, PTLD	535	C6
Big Eddy Marina, GSHM	598	J1
Cliff's Marina, PTLD	567	B2
Columbia Corinthian Marina, PTLD	567	A2
Columbia Harbor, PTLD	566	G1
Columbia Ridge Marina, GSHM	598	H1
Czapszys Marina, PTLD	566	G7
Dillards Moorage, STHN	385	D7
Donaldson Marina, PTLD	567	B2
Ducks Moorage, GSHM	598	H1
Fred's Marina, PTLD	535	C6
Happy Rock Moorage, MthC	504	F2
Hayden Island Marina, PTLD	566	G1
Kadows Caterpillar Island Marina, ClkC	505	G2
Kadows Marina, VCVR	537	H5
Larsons Moorage, MthC	535	B5
McCuddy's Marina, PTLD	567	A2
Oregon City Marina, CmsC	716	J2
Parker Marina, MthC	535	A2
Rocky Pointe Marina, MthC	504	F2
Rodgers Marina, PTLD	567	B2
Scappoose Boat Moorage, ClbC	474	G3
Sportcraft Marina, ORCY	687	C6
Sundance Marina, PTLD	566	H1
Tomahawk Bay Marina, PTLD	566	H1
Tomahawk Island Marina, PTLD	566	H1
Waverly Marina, PTLD	626	G7

Buildings

FEATURE NAME	MAP#	GRID
Clean Water Services SW Hillsboro Hwy, HBRO, 97123	623	B1
Fountain Plaza 1414 SW 3rd Av, PTLD, 97201	596	F7
Intel-Aloha Campus WasC, 97007	624	C2
Intel-Ronler Acres Campus HBRO, 97124	594	A1
Jackson Bottom Wetlands 2600 SW Hillsboro Hwy, HBRO, 97123	623	B1
KOIN Center 222 SW Columbia St, PTLD, 97201	596	F7
Mikado Building 117 SW Taylor St, PTLD, 97204	596	F6
Minnehaha Grange NE 51st St, ClkC, 98661	537	A1
Nike World Campus WasC, 97005	594	J7
Pacwest Bank Tower SW Madison St, PTLD, 97204	596	E6
Pittock Block 921 SW Washington St, PTLD, 97205	596	E5
Portland International Center PTLD, 97220	567	G6
Tektronix-Howard Vollum Park WasC, 97005	625	A1
Town Plaza 5411 E Mill Plain Blvd, VCVR, 98661	537	C5
US Bancorp Tower 111 W Burnside St, PTLD, 97204	596	F5
Wells Fargo Bank Tower 1300 SW 5th Av, PTLD, 97201	596	E7
World Trade Center 121 SW Salmon St, PTLD, 97204	596	F6

Buildings - Governmental

FEATURE NAME	MAP#	GRID
Aurora City Hall 21420 Main St NE, AURA, 97002	775	F4
Banks City Hall 100 NE Market St, BNKS, 97106	531	J5
Barlow City Hall 106 N Main St, BRLO, 97013	775	J1
Battle Ground City Hall 109 W Main St, BGND, 98604	448	B5
Beaverton City Hall 4755 SW Griffith Dr, BRTN, 97005	625	C3
Beaverton Municipal Court 4755 SW Griffith Dr, BRTN, 97005	625	C3
Camas City Hall 616 NE 4th Av, CMAS, 98607	569	F4
Camas Court 631 NE 4th Av, CMAS, 98607	569	F4
Canby City Hall 182 N Holly St, CNBY, 97013	746	C6
Canby Municipal Court 122 N Holly St, CNBY, 97013	746	C6
Carlton City Hall 191 E Main St, CLTN, 97111	711	A7
Clackamas County Courthouse 807 Main St, ORCY, 97045	687	C7
Clark County Courthouse 1200 Franklin St, VCVR, 98660	536	F4
Columbia City Hall 1840 2nd St, CBAC, 97018	385	C3
Columbia County Courthouse 230 Strand, STHN, 97051	385	D7
Cornelius City Hall 1355 N Barlow St, CNLS, 97113	592	E4
Cornelius Municipal Court 1311 N Barlow St, CNLS, 97113	592	E4
County Office N 1st Av, HBRO, 97124	593	B4
Dayton City Hall 416 SE Ferry St, DAYT, 97114	772	B4
Donald City Hall 10790 Donald Rd NE, DNLD, 97020	774	G4
Dundee City Hall 620 SW 5th St, DNDE, 97115	742	H3
Durham City Hall 17160 SW Upper Boones Ferry Rd, DRHM, 97224	685	G2
Estacada City Hall 475 SE Main St, ECDA, 97023	750	B4
FAA/AFS Office Building NE Unnamed Rd, PTLD, 97218	567	F5
Fairview City Hall 1300 NE Village St, FRVW, 97024	599	B5
Fairview Municipal Court 300 Harrison St, FRVW, 97024	599	B4
Federal Building 500 W 13th St, VCVR, 98660	536	F4
Federal Courthouse 620 SW Main St, PTLD, 97205	596	E6
Fire Department Training Center NE 66th St, ClkC, 98662	507	J6
Forest Grove City Hall 1924 Council St, FTGV, 97116	591	J5
Gladstone City Hall 525 Portland Av, GLDS, 97027	687	D4
Gladstone Municipal Court 525 Portland Av, GLDS, 97027	687	D4
Green Wyatt Federal Building 1220 SW Madison St, PTLD, 97204	596	F7
Gresham City Hall 1333 NW Eastman Pkwy, GSHM, 97030	629	B1
Gresham District Court 150 W Powell Blvd, GSHM, 97080	629	B3
Happy Valley City Hall 12915 SE King Rd, HPYV, 97236	658	B2
Hillsboro City Hall 123 W Main St, HBRO, 97123	593	B5
Hillsboro Municipal Court 205 SE 2nd Av, HBRO, 97123	593	C5
Johnson City City Hall 16120 SE 81st Av, JNCY, 97267	687	F1
King City City Hall 15300 SW 116th Av, KNGC, 97224	655	C7
King City Municipal Court 15300 SW 116th Av, KNGC, 97224	655	C7
Lafayette City Hall 486 SE 3rd St, LFYT, 97127	771	G1
Lake Oswego City Hall 380 A Av, LKOW, 97034	656	F6
Lake Oswego Municipal Court A Av, LKOW, 97034	656	F6
Mark O Hatfield US Courthouse 1000 SW 3rd Av, PTLD, 97204	596	F6
Maywood Park City Hall 10100 NE Prescott St, MWDP, 97220	597	H1
McMinnville City Hall 230 NE 2nd St, MCMV, 97128	770	H5
Milwaukie City Hall 10722 SE Main St, MWKE, 97222	656	J2
Milwaukie Municipal Court 10722 SE Main St, MWKE, 97222	656	J2
Molalla City Hall 117 N Molalla Av, MOLA, 97038	837	E1
Multnomah County District Court 1021 SW 4th Av, PTLD, 97204	596	F6
Multnomah County Inverness Jail 11540 NE Inverness Dr, PTLD, 97220	568	A7
Municipal Court 100 Davidson Av, WDLD, 98674	385	J2
Newberg City Hall 414 E 1st St, NWBG, 97132	713	C7
Newberg Municipal Court 115 S Howard St, NWBG, 97132	713	C7
North Plains City Hall 31360 NW Commercial St, NPNS, 97133	563	B1
North Plains Municipal Court 31360 NW Commercial St, NPNS, 97133	563	B1
Oregon City City Hall 320 Warner Milne Rd, ORCY, 97045	717	D3
Oregon City Municipal Court 320 Warner Milne Rd, ORCY, 97045	717	D3
Oregon Department of Transportation NW Glisan St, PTLD, 97209	596	F5
Pioneer Courthouse 555 SW Yamhill St, PTLD, 97204	596	F6
Police Headquarter 1120 SW 3rd Av, PTLD, 97204	596	F6
Portland City Hall 1221 SW 4th Av, PTLD, 97204	596	E6
Rivergrove City Hall 19598 Marlin Av, RVGR, 97035	685	J3
St. Helens City Hall 265 Strand, STHN, 97051	385	D7
St. Paul City Hall 20239 Main St NE, STPL, 97137	773	B6
Sandy City Hall 39250 Pioneer Blvd, SNDY, 97055	691	A3
Sandy Municipal Court 39250 Pioneer Blvd, SNDY, 97055	691	A3
Scappoose City Hall 33560 E Columbia Av, SPSE, 97056	444	E7
Scappoose Municipal Court E Columbia Av, SPSE, 97056	444	E7
Sherwood City Hall 20 SW Washington St, SRWD, 97140	684	G7
Sherwood Municipal Court 22566 SW Washington St, SRWD, 97140	684	G7
State Building 800 NE Lloyd Blvd, PTLD, 97232	596	H5
State Office Building Harney St, VCVR, 98660	536	F5
Tigard City Hall 13125 SW Hall Blvd, TGRD, 97223	655	F5
Tigard Courthouse 13125 SW Hall Blvd, TGRD, 97223	655	F5
Troutdale City Hall 104 SE Kibling St, TDLE, 97060	599	G4
Troutdale Municipal Court 104 SE Kibling St, TDLE, 97060	599	G4
Tualatin City Hall 18888 SW Martinazzi Av, TLTN, 97062	685	F3
Tualatin Municipal Court 18884 SW Martinazzi Av, TLTN, 97062	685	F3
US Federal Building 511 NW Broadway, PTLD, 97209	596	E5
Vancouver City Hall 210 E 13th St, VCVR, 98660	536	G4
Wapato Corrections Facility 14355 N Bybee Lake Ct, PTLD, 97203	535	G4
Washington County Circuit Court 150 N 1st Av, HBRO, 97124	593	B4
Washington County Courthouse 145 NE 2nd Av, HBRO, 97124	593	C4
Washington County Jail 215 SW Adams Av, HBRO, 97123	593	B5
Washington County Justice Court 3700 SW Murray Blvd, BRTN, 97005	624	J2
Washougal City Hall 1701 C St, WHGL, 98671	570	A5
West Linn City Hall 22500 Salamo Rd, WLIN, 97068	686	H7
West Linn Municipal Court 22825 Pacific Hwy, WLIN, 97068	687	C7
Wilsonville City Hall 30000 SW Town Center Lp E, WNVL, 97070	715	F7
Wilsonville Municipal Court 8445 SW Elligsen Rd, WNVL, 97070	715	F3
Woodland City Hall 230 Davidson Av, WDLD, 98674	385	J2
Wood Village City Hall 2055 NE 238th Dr, WDVL, 97060	599	D4
Yamhill County Circuit Court 535 NE 5th St, MCMV, 97128	770	H5

Cemeteries

FEATURE NAME	MAP#	GRID
Ahavai Shalom Memorial Cem, PTLD	626	E7
Aurora Cem, MrnC	775	D4
Bakers Prairie Cem, CNBY	746	B6
Bayview Cem, ClbC	414	J5
Bethany Lutheran Cem, ClbC	414	H5
Bethany Presbyterian Cem, WasC	564	J5
Bethel Cem, ClkC	478	B4
Beth Israel Cem, PTLD	626	E7
Brainard Cem, PTLD	597	G5
Brookside Cem, DAYT	772	B4
Brush Prairie Cem, ClkC	508	A2
Butteville Cem, MrnC	744	H5
Camas Cem, CMAS	569	F3
Canemah Cem, CmsC	716	J2
Champoeg Cem, MrnC	774	C2
Chimes Memorial Gardens Cem, CmsC	657	G3
Clackamas County Cem, CmsC	657	F5
Cliffside Cem, CmsC	691	C1
Columbia Masonic Cem, PTLD	597	H1
Columbia Memorial Cem, ClbC	444	F3
Columbian Cem, PTLD	566	F4
Cooper Mountain Cem, WasC	624	E7
Cornelius Lutheran Cem, CNLS	592	E4
Cornelius Methodist Cem, WasC	592	D3
County Farm Cem, ClkC	506	H6
Crescent Grove Cem, TGRD	655	E1
Damascus Pioneer Cem, DAMA	658	H7
Douglass Cem, TDLE	599	F5
Elim Cem, ClkC	478	F4
Evangle Cem, TGRD	655	C6
Evergreen Memorial Cem, VCVR	537	J5
Fairview Cem, ClbC	474	E4
Fernwood Pioneer Cem, YmhC	743	D1
Finn Hill Cem, ClkC	478	H2
Fir Hill Cem, SNDY	690	H2
Fir Lawn Cem, HBRO	593	A4
Fisher Cem, VCVR	568	E4
Forest Lawn Cem, GSHM	629	B3
Forest View Cem, FTGV	591	G4
Friends Cem, YmhC	743	D1
Gethsemane Cem, CmsC	657	H3
Gibbs Cem, YmhC	713	J2
Goodrich Family Cem, YmhC	772	B5
Grand Army of the Republic Cem, PTLD	626	E7
Gresham Poineer/Escobar Cem, GSHM	629	B3
Hillcrest Cem, YmhC	743	A1
Hillsboro Pioneer Cem, HBRO	593	A5
IOOF Cem, ECDA	750	C2
IOOF Cem, ORCY	717	E2
IOOF Cem, PTLD	626	F7
IOOF Cem, YmhC	741	H7
Jones Cem, MthC	595	J7
Kilpatrick Post Gar Cem, YmhC	743	D1
Lincoln Memorial Cem, MthC	627	J7
Lone Fir Cem, PTLD	596	J6
Maple Lane Cem, SRWD	684	F5
Masonic Cem, ClbC	384	E7
Masonic Cem, ORCY	717	D2
Masonic Cem, PTLD	626	E7
Memory Memorial Park Cem, ClkC	477	E5
Meridian Cem, WasC	715	G2
Middleton Cem, WasC	714	D1
Milwaukie Cem, MWKE	656	H1
Mountainside Cem, WasC	683	F2
Mountain View Cem, MthC	600	G6
Mountain View Cem, ORCY	717	E3
Mountain View Cem, TDLE	599	F7
Mountain View Memorial Gardens Cem, FTGV	591	F2
Mt Calvary Cem, PTLD	595	J5
Mt Zion Cem, LCTR	386	J7
Multnomah Cem, PTLD	627	F3
Northwood Park Cem, ClkC	476	J3
Odd Fellows Cem, YmhC	772	C5
Old Colony Cem, MrnC	775	E3
Oswego Pioneer Cem, LKOW	686	D1
Park Hill Cem, VCVR	537	C5
Patton Cem, WasC	625	F4
Pleasant Home Cem, MthC	630	B7
Post Military Cem, VCVR	536	H3
Powell Grove Cem, PTLD	598	A1
Redland Pioneer Cem, CmsC	718	H7
Ridgefield Cem, RDGF	416	A7
Riverview Cem, PTLD	626	F7
Robert Bird Cem, CmsC	716	A1
Rose City Cem, PTLD	597	C2
Sacred Heart Cem, LKOW	686	D1
St. Anthony Cem, TGRD	655	C5
St. Francis Cem, WasC	532	C7
St. James Acres Cem, VCVR	536	H3
St. Johns Cem, ClkC	506	H1
St. Johns Cem, ORCY	717	D3
St. Matthews Cem, HBRO	623	F2
St. Paul Cem, SRWD	684	F5
St. Wenceslaus Cem, SPSE	474	E2
Salmon Creek Cem, ClkC	506	H1
Scandinavian Cem, SNDY	690	H2
Shaarie Torah Cem, PTLD	627	D7
Shadybrook Cem, WasC	533	D3
Sifton Cem, ClkC	508	A6
Skyline Memorial Gardens, PTLD	595	D1
Sunset Hills Memorial Park, WasC	595	H7
Tualatin Plains Cem, WasC	563	B4
Union Cem, WasC	594	J3
Union Point Cem, WasC	532	A5
Valley Memorial Park Cem, HBRO	593	F7
Vancouver City Cem, VCVR	536	J5
Visitation Cem, WasC	562	B5
Washougal Memorial Cem, WHGL	570	C4
West Cem, WasC	564	B5
White Birch Cem, GSHM	629	B3
Willamette National Cem, PTLD	628	A7
Winona Cem, TLTN	685	D2
Yacolt Cem, ClkC	419	G2
Yankton Hillcrest Cem, ClbC	384	F6
Zion Cem, CmsC	746	F7
Zoar Cem, CNBY	746	F6

Colleges & Universities

FEATURE NAME	MAP#	GRID
Art Institute of Portland 1122 NW Davis St, PTLD, 97209	596	E5
Ashmead College-Vancouver 120 NE 136th Av, VCVR, 98684	538	B6

Portland Points of Interest Index

FEATURE NAME	Address City ZIP Code	MAP#	GRID
usiness Computer Training Institute	204 SE Stonemill Dr, VCVR, 98684	538	B6
ascade College	9101 E Burnside St, PTLD, 97220	597	G6
hemeketa Community College	NW Hill Rd, MCMV, 97128	770	D4
ity University	SE 126th Av, VCVR, 98684	538	A6
lackamas Community College	19600 Cascade Hwy S, ORCY, 97045	717	F5
lark College	1800 E McLoughlin Blvd, VCVR, 98663	536	H4
oncordia University	2811 NE Holman St, PTLD, 97211	567	A6
eorge Fox University	414 N Meridian St, NWBG, 97132	713	C7
olden Gate Baptist Theological Smnry-Northw	3200 NE 109th Av, VCVR, 98682	537	H3
eald College Sch of Bus & Tech-Portland	625 SW Broadway, PTLD, 97205	596	E6
nternational Air Academy Inc	Grand Blvd, VCVR, 98661	537	A5
T Technical Institute-Portland	6035 NE 78th Ct, PTLD, 97218	567	F6
ewis & Clark College	615 SW Palatine Hill Rd, PTLD, 97219	656	F1
ewis & Clark Law School	10015 SW Terwilliger Blvd, PTLD, 97219	656	E1
infield College-McMinnville	900 SE Baker St, MCMV, 97128	770	G6
infield College-Portland	2255 NW Northrup St, PTLD, 97210	596	D4
Marylhurst University	17600 Pacific Hwy, LKOW, 97034	686	H2
Mt Hood Community College	26000 SE Stark St, GSHM, 97030	599	F7
Multnomah Bible College	8435 NE Glisan St, PTLD, 97220	597	G5
National College of Naturopathic Medicine	049 SW Porter St, PTLD, 97201	626	F1
Oregon College of Art & Craft	8245 SW Barnes Rd, WasC, 97225	595	F7
Oregon College of Oriental Medicine	SE Cherry Blossom Dr, PTLD, 97216	597	H7
Oregon Graduate Institute of Science & Tech	20000 NW Walker Rd, HBRO, 97006	594	D4
Oregon Health & Science University	3181 SW Sam Jackson Park Rd, PTLD, 97239	626	D1
Oregon Institue of Technology-Portland West	NW Walker Rd, HBRO, 97006	594	E4
Pacific Northwest College of Art	1241 NW Kearney St, PTLD, 97209	596	E4
Pacific University	2043 College Wy, FTGV, 97116	591	J4
Pioneer Pacific College	SW Parkway Av, WNVL, 97070	715	E5
Portland Community College-Cascade	705 N Killingsworth St, PTLD, 97217	566	F7
Portland Community College-Rock Creek	17705 NW Springville Rd, WasC, 97229	564	F6
Portland Community College-SE Center	2305 SE 82nd Av, PTLD, 97215	627	F1
Portland Community College-Sylvania	K St, PTLD, 97219	655	J3
Portland State University	1633 SW Park Av, PTLD, 97201	596	E7
Reed College	SE Woodstock Blvd, PTLD, 97202	627	A4
University of Oregon-Portland Center	722 SW 2nd Av, PTLD, 97204	596	F6
University of Phoenix-Hillsboro	3600 NW John Olsen Pl, HBRO, 97124	594	D2
University of Phoenix-Oregon	13190 SW 68th Pkwy, TGRD, 97223	655	G5
University of Portland	5000 N Willamette Blvd, PTLD, 97203	566	A5
Warner Pacific College	2219 SE 68th Av, PTLD, 97215	627	D1
Washington State University-Vancouver	14204 NE Salmon Creek Av, ClkC, 98686	477	B5
Western Business College	425 SW Washington St, PTLD, 97204	596	F6
Western Business College	120 SE 136th Av, VCVR, 98684	538	B6
Western Seminary	SE Hawthorne Blvd, PTLD, 97215	597	C7
Western States Chiropractic College	2900 NE 132nd Av, PTLD, 97230	598	B3

Entertainment & Sports

FEATURE NAME	Address City ZIP Code	MAP#	GRID
Aladdin Theatre & Performance Center	3116 SE 11th Av, PTLD, 97202	626	H1
Ambridge Event Center	300 NE Multnomah St, PTLD, 97232	596	G4
Amphitheater at Clark County	17200 NE Delfel Rd, ClkC, 98642	476	H3
Arlene Schnitzer Concert Hall	1037 SW Broadway, PTLD, 97205	596	E6
Artists Repertory Theater	1111 SW 10th Av, PTLD, 97205	596	E6
Brody Theater	1904 NW 27th Av, PTLD, 97210	596	C3
Buckeroo Rodeo Grounds	MOLA, 97038	837	F1
Chips & Palace Casino	318 NW Pacific Hwy, LCTR, 98629	416	H1
Clackamas County Fairgrounds	694 NE 4th Av, CNBY, 97013	746	D6
Clark County Exhibition Center	17402 NE Delfel Rd, ClkC, 98642	476	G2
Clark County Fairgrounds	ClkC, 98642	476	G3
Classic Greek Theater	3131 NE Glisan St, PTLD, 97232	597	A5
Clinton Street Theatre	2522 SE Clinton St, PTLD, 97202	626	J1
Columbia Arts Center	400 W Evergreen Blvd, VCVR, 98660	536	F5
Columbia County Event Complex	58892 Saulser Rd, ClbC, 97051	414	F1
Echo Theatre	1515 SE 37th Av, PTLD, 97214	597	A7
Firehouse Theatre	1436 SW Montgomery St, PTLD, 97201	596	D7
Hazel Dell Golf O Rama	7120 NE Highway 99, ClkC, 98665	506	H5
Hillsboro Actors Repertory Theatre	230 E Main St, HBRO, 97123	593	C4
Hillsboro Stadium	4450 NW 229th Av, HBRO, 97124	594	A1
Hollywood Theatre	4122 NE Sandy Blvd, PTLD, 97212	597	B4
Imago Theater	17 SE 8th Av, PTLD, 97214	596	G5
Interstate Firehouse Cultural Center	5340 N Interstate Av, PTLD, 97217	566	E7
Keller Auditorium	222 SW Clay St, PTLD, 97201	596	E7
Ladybug Theatre	2315 SE Grant St, PTLD, 97214	626	J1
Lakewood Theatre	368 S State St, LKOW, 97034	656	F6
Main Street Playhouse	904 SW Main St, PTLD, 97205	596	E6
Memorial Coliseum	300 N Winning Wy, PTLD, 97227	596	F4
Miracle Theatre	525 SE Stark St, PTLD, 97214	596	G6
New Phoenix Casino	225 W 4th St, LCTR, 98629	416	H1
Old Slocum House Theatre Company	605 Esther St, VCVR, 98660	536	F5
Oregon Ballet Theatre	818 SE 6th Av, PTLD, 97214	596	G6
Oregon Convention Center	777 NE Martin Luther King Jr Bl, PTLD, 97232	596	G5
Oregon Theater	3530 SE Division St, PTLD, 97202	627	A1
Oregon Zoo	4001 SW Canyon Rd, PTLD, 97221	596	B7
Pats Acres Racing Complex	6255 S Arndt Rd, CmsC, 97013	745	H6
PGE Park	1844 SW Morrison St, PTLD, 97205	596	D5
Portland Center for Performing Arts	1111 SW Broadway, PTLD, 97205	596	E6
Portland International Raceway	PTLD, 97217	566	E3
Portland Meadows	1001 N Schmeer Rd, PTLD, 97217	566	F3
Portland Metropolitan Expo Center	PTLD, 97217	566	E1
Portland Opera Plaza	211 SE Caruthers St, PTLD, 97214	626	G1
Roehr Park Amphitheater	350 Oswego Pointe Dr, LKOW, 97034	656	G6
Rose Garden Arena	1 N Center Ct St, PTLD, 97227	596	G4
Roseland Theatre	8 NW 6th Av, PTLD, 97209	596	F5
Stark Raving Theatre	2257 NW Raleigh St, PTLD, 97210	596	D4
Sykart Indoor Racing	8205 SW Hunziker Rd, TGRD, 97223	655	F4
Tears of Joy Puppet Theatre	601 Main St, VCVR, 98660	536	G5
Theatre in the Grove	2028 Pacific Av, FTGV, 97116	591	H4
Washington County Fairgrounds	873 NE 34th Av, HBRO, 97124	593	F4
Yamhill County Fairgrounds	2070 NE Lafayette Av, MCMV, 97128	771	A3

Golf Courses

FEATURE NAME	City	MAP#	GRID
Arrowhead GC	CmsC	807	E2
Broadmoor GC	PTLD	567	B5
Camas Meadows GC	CMAS	539	A5
Cedars GC	ClkC	478	D2
Charbonneau GC	WNVL	745	F2
Chehalem Glenn GC	NWBG	713	G7
Children's GC	GLDS	687	C5
Claremont GC	WasC	594	H2
Club Green Meadows	ClkC	507	E5
Columbia Edgewater CC	PTLD	566	J2
Colwood National GC	PTLD	567	E7
Eagle Creek GC	CmsC	719	H4
Eagle Landing GC	HPYV	657	H3
Eastmoreland GC	PTLD	626	J5
Fairway Village GC	VCVR	568	D2
Glendoveer GC	PTLD	598	C5
Greenlea GC	CmsC	659	F7
Green Mountain GC	ClkC	538	J3
Gresham GC	GSHM	629	E1
Hartwood GC	ClkC	478	D7
Heron Lakes GC	PTLD	566	C1
Killarney West GC	WasC	592	H4
King City GC	KNGC	655	C7
Lake Oswego GC	LKOW	686	D1
Lakeview Par 3 GC	ClkC	506	D6
Langdon Farms GC	CmsC	745	E5
McKay Creek GC	HBRO	593	A4
McMenamins Pub Course	TDLE	599	E4
Meriwether National GC	WasC	623	F3
Michelbrook CC	MCMV	770	G4
Mountain View GC	CmsC	659	G6
Orchard Hills Golf & CC	WHGL	570	D5
Oregon City GC	CmsC	717	H6
Oregon GC	CmsC	716	F4
Oswego Lake CC	LKOW	656	E6
Persimmon CC	GSHM	629	C6
Pine Crest GC	ClkC	476	E6
Pleasant Valley GC	HPYV	658	E4
Portland GC	WasC	625	F4
Portland Meadows GC	PTLD	566	F3
Pumpkin Ridge GC	WasC	533	A6
Quail Valley GC	WasC	532	A6
Ranch Hills GC	CmsC	777	F5
Red Tail GC	BRTN	625	D7
Reserve Vineyards & GC	WasC	624	A3
Resort at the Mountain	CmsC	724	C5
Riverside Golf & CC	PTLD	567	A4
Rock Creek CC	WasC	564	D7
Rose City GC	PTLD	597	E3
Royal Oaks CC	VCVR	537	F2
Sah-Hah-Lee GC	CmsC	688	B2
St. Helens GC	ClbC	414	F5
Sandelie GC	CmsC	716	C7
Stone Creek GC	CmsC	747	G2
Summerfield Golf & CC	TGRD	655	D7
Sunset Grove GC	WasC	561	J6
Tri-Mountain GC	ClkC	416	F4
Tualatin CC	TLTN	685	E2
Waverley CC	CmsC	656	H2
Wildwood GC	MthC	504	E4
Willamette Valley CC	CNBY	746	D3

Historic Sites

FEATURE NAME	Address City ZIP Code	MAP#	GRID
Albert Tanner House	2248 NW Johnson St, PTLD, 97210	596	C5
Ayer-Shea House	1809 NW Johnson St, PTLD, 97209	596	D4
Bybee House	NW Howell Park Rd, MthC, 97231	535	A2
Captain Vancouver Monument	Esther St, VCVR, 98660	536	F5
Covington House	4201 Main St, VCVR, 98663	536	G1
Cox-Williams House	280 S 1st St, STHN, 97051	385	D7
Fort Vancouver National Historic Site	612 E Reserve St, VCVR, 98661	536	H5
George Huesner House	333 NW 20th Av, PTLD, 97209	596	D5
Henry J Kaiser Shipyard Memorial	SE Marine Park Wy, VCVR, 98661	537	B7
Howard House	750 Anderson St, VCVR, 98661	536	G5
Japanese-American Historical Plaza	2 NW Naito Pkwy, PTLD, 97209	596	F5
Joseph Bergman House	2134 NW Hoyt St, PTLD, 97210	596	D5
Mary Smith House	2256 NW Johnson St, PTLD, 97210	596	D4
McLoughlin House	713 Center St, ORCY, 97045	687	C7
Nathan Loeb House	726 NW 22nd Av, PTLD, 97210	596	D5
Officers Row-Marshall House	1301 Officers Row, VCVR, 98661	536	H5
Oregon Holocaust Memorial	SW Washington Wy, PTLD, 97205	596	C5
Oregon Korean War Memorial	29600 SW Park Pl, WNVL, 97070	715	E7
Overlook House	3839 N Melrose Dr, PTLD, 97227	596	E2
Parkersville Site	WHGL, 98671	569	H5
Pettygrove House	2287 NW Pettygrove St, PTLD, 97210	596	D4
Philip Foster Farm	29912 Eagle Creek-Sandy Hwy, CmsC, 97022	720	A1
Pittock House	114 NE Leadbetter Rd, ClkC, 98607	539	C6
Queen Anne Victorian Mansion	1441 N McClellan St, PTLD, 97217	566	E4
Sprague-Marshall-Bowie House	2234 NW Johnson St, PTLD, 97210	596	D5
Stevens-Crawford House	603 6th St, ORCY, 97045	717	C1
Trevett-Nunn House	2347 NW Flanders St, PTLD, 97210	596	D5
Vietnam Veterans of Oregon Memorial	4000 SW Canyon Rd, PTLD, 97221	596	B7

Hospitals

FEATURE NAME	Address City ZIP Code	MAP#	GRID
Adventist Med Ctr	10123 SE Market St, PTLD, 97216	597	H7
Columbia District Hosp	500 N Columbia River Hwy, STHN, 97051	385	B7
Doernbecher Childrens Hosp	3181 SW Sam Jackson Park Rd, PTLD, 97239	626	D2
Eastmoreland Hosp	2900 SE Steele St, PTLD, 97202	627	A4
Kaiser Permanente-Sunnyside	10180 SE Sunnyside Rd, CmsC, 97015	657	H4
Legacy Emanuel Hosp	2801 N Gantenbein Av, PTLD, 97227	596	F2
Legacy Good Samaritan Hosp	1015 NW 22nd Av, PTLD, 97210	596	D4
Legacy Meridian Park Hosp	19300 SW 65th Av, TLTN, 97062	685	H4
Legacy Mt Hood Med Ctr	24800 SE Stark St, GSHM, 97030	599	E7
Legacy Salmon Creek Hosp	2211 NE 139th St, ClkC, 98686	476	J6
Oregon Health & Science University Hosp	3181 SW Sam Jackson Park Rd, PTLD, 97239	626	D2
Physicians Hosp	10300 NE Hancock St, PTLD, 97220	597	J4
Providence Milwaukie Hosp	10150 SE 32nd Av, MWKE, 97222	657	A2
Providence Newberg Hosp	1001 Providence Dr, NWBG, 97132	713	G6
Providence Portland Med Ctr	4805 NE Glisan St, PTLD, 97213	597	C5
Providence St. Vincent Med Ctr	9205 SW Barnes Rd, WasC, 97225	595	E7
Shriners Hosp for Children	3101 SW Sam Jackson Park Rd, PTLD, 97239	626	E1
Southwest Washington Med Ctr	400 NE Mother Joseph Pl, VCVR, 98664	537	F5
Tuality Community Hosp	335 SE 8th Av, HBRO, 97123	593	C5
Tuality Forest Grove Hosp	1809 Maple St, FTGV, 97116	592	B5
Veterans Affairs Med Ctr	3710 SW US Veterans Hospital Rd, PTLD, 97239	626	E2
Willamette Falls Hosp	1500 Division St, ORCY, 97045	717	E1
Willamette Valley Med Ctr	2700 SE Stratus Av, MCMV, 97128	771	B7

Law Enforcement

FEATURE NAME	Address City ZIP Code	MAP#	GRID
Beaverton Police Dept	4755 SW Griffith Dr, BRTN, 97005	625	C3
Camas Police Dept	2100 NE 3rd Av, CMAS, 98607	569	G4
Canby Police Dept	122 N Holly St, CNBY, 97013	746	C6
Clackamas County Sheriff Dept-N Station	12800 SE Cascade Hwy, CmsC, 97015	657	F4
Clackamas County Sheriff's Dept	2223 Kaen Rd, ORCY, 97045	717	C4
Clackamas County Sheriff's Dept	8445 SW Elligsen Rd, WNVL, 97070	715	F3
Clark County Sheriff's Dept	707 W 13th St, VCVR, 98660	536	F4
Columbia City Police Station	Fulbright Pl, CBAC, 97018	385	C3
Cornelius Police Dept	1311 N Barlow St, CNLS, 97113	592	E4
Davidson Police Dept	230 Davidson Av, WDLD, 98674	385	J2
Fairview Police Dept	1300 NE Village St, FRVW, 97024	599	B5
Forest Grove Police Dept	2102 Pacific Av, FTGV, 97116	591	J5
Gladstone Police Dept	535 Portland Av, GLDS, 97027	687	D4
Gresham Police Dept	1333 NW Eastman Pkwy, GSHM, 97030	629	B1
Hillsboro Northeast Precinct	20795 NW Cornell Rd, HBRO, 97124	594	C3
Hillsboro Police Dept	205 SE 2nd Av, HBRO, 97123	593	B5
Kenton Community Police Office	8134 N Denver Av, PTLD, 97217	566	E4
King City Police Dept	15300 SW 116th Av, KNGC, 97224	655	C7
La Center Police Dept	105 W 5th St, LCTR, 98629	386	G7
Lake Oswego Police Dept	380 A Av, LKOW, 97034	656	F6
McMinnville Police Dept	130 NE Baker St, MCMV, 97128	770	H5
Milwaukie Police Dept	3200 SE Harrison St, MWKE, 97222	657	A2

Portland Points of Interest Index

Law Enforcement

FEATURE NAME	Address City ZIP Code	MAP#	GRID
Multnomah County Sheriff's Dept	12240 NE Glisan St, PTLD, 97230	598	A5
Newberg Police Dept	414 E 1st St, NWBG, 97132	713	C7
North Plains Police Dept	31360 NW Commercial St, NPNS, 97133	563	B1
Oregon City Police Dept	320 Warner Milne Rd, ORCY, 97045	717	D3
Oregon State Police Dept-McMinnville	1502 Pacific Hwy W, MCMV, 97128	770	J3
Oregon State Police Dept-Portland	10526 SE Washington St, PTLD, 97216	597	H6
Portland Police Dept-Central Precinct	1111 SW 2nd Av, PTLD, 97204	596	F6
Portland Police Dept-East Precinct	737 SE 106th Av, PTLD, 97216	597	J6
Portland Police Dept-North Precinct	7214 N Philadelphia Av, PTLD, 97203	565	G3
Portland Police Dept-SE Precinct	4735 E Burnside St, PTLD, 97213	597	C5
St. Helens Police Dept	150 S 13th St, STHN, 97051	385	C7
Sandy Police Dept	38970 Proctor Blvd, SNDY, 97055	691	A3
Scappoose Police Dept	33568 E Columbia Av, SPSE, 97056	444	E7
Sherwood Police Dept	20495 SW Borchers Dr, SRWD, 97140	684	F5
Tigard Police Dept	13125 SW Hall Blvd, TGRD, 97223	655	F4
Troutdale Police Dept	141 Dora Av, TDLE, 97060	599	G4
Tualatin Police Dept	8650 SW Tualatin Rd, TLTN, 97062	685	F3
Vancouver Police-Central Precinct	2800 NE Stapleton Rd, VCVR, 98661	537	C3
Vancouver Police Dept	300 E 13th St, VCVR, 98660	536	G4
Vancouver Police-East Precinct	1201 SE Tech Center Dr, VCVR, 98683	538	E7
Washington County Sheriff's Dept	215 SW Adams Av, HBRO, 97123	593	B5
Washington State Patrol	605 E Evergreen Blvd, VCVR, 98661	536	G5
Washington State Patrol	1121 NE 136th Av, VCVR, 98684	538	B5
Washougal Police Dept	1400 A St, WHGL, 98671	570	A6
West Linn Police Dept	22825 Pacific Hwy, WLIN, 97068	687	B7
Yamhill County Sheriff's Dept	535 NE 5th St, MCMV, 97128	770	H5

Libraries

FEATURE NAME	Address City ZIP Code	MAP#	GRID
Albina	3605 NE 15th Av, PTLD, 97212	596	H2
Banks Public	111 NE Market St, BNKS, 97106	531	J5
Battle Ground Community	12 W Main St, BGND, 98604	448	B5
Beaverton City	12375 SW 5th St, BRTN, 97005	625	B3
Belmont	1038 SE 39th Av, PTLD, 97214	597	B7
Canby Public	292 N Holly St, CNBY, 97013	746	C6
Capitol Hill	10723 SW Capitol Hwy, PTLD, 97219	656	A2
Cascade Park Community	301 SE Hearthwood Blvd, VCVR, 98684	538	C6
CDRC	707 SW Gaines St, PTLD, 97239	626	E2
Cedar Mill Community	12505 NW Cornell Rd, WasC, 97229	595	B5
Central	801 SW 10th Av, PTLD, 97205	596	E6
Clackamas Corner	11750 SE Cascade Hwy, CmsC, 97236	657	F3
Cornelius Public	1355 N Barlow St, CNLS, 97113	592	E4
Dayton (M Gilkey)	416 SE Ferry St, DAYT, 97114	772	B4
Estacada Public	475 SE Main St, ECDA, 97023	750	B4
Fairview-Columbia	1520 NE Village St, FRVW, 97024	599	B4
Forest Grove City	2114 Pacific Av, FTGV, 97116	591	J5
Garden Home Community	7475 SW Oleson Rd, PTLD, 97223	625	G6
Gladstone Public	135 E Dartmouth St, GLDS, 97027	687	D4
Gregory Heights	7921 NE Sandy Blvd, PTLD, 97213	597	F2
Gresham Regional	385 NW Miller Av, GSHM, 97030	629	B2
Hillsboro Main	2300 NE Brookwood Pkwy, HBRO, 97124	593	H2
Hillsboro Public-Shute Park	775 SE 10th Av, HBRO, 97123	593	D6
Hillsboro Public-Tanasbourn	2453 NW 185th Av, HBRO, 97124	594	E3
Hillsdale	1525 SW Sunset Blvd, PTLD, 97239	626	D4
Holgate	7905 SE Holgate Blvd, PTLD, 97206	627	F3
Hollywood	4040 NE Tillamook St, PTLD, 97212	597	B3
Hoodland	68256 Mt Hood Hwy, CmsC, 97067	724	B3
Lake Oswego Public	706 4th St, LKOW, 97034	656	F5
Ledding	10660 SE 21st Av, MWKE, 97222	656	J2
McMinnville Public	225 NE Adams St, MCMV, 97128	770	H5
Midland Regional	805 SE 122nd Av, PTLD, 97216	598	A7
Molalla Public	201 E 5th St, MOLA, 97038	837	E2
Newberg Public	503 E Hancock St, NWBG, 97132	713	C7
North Portland	512 N Killingsworth St, PTLD, 97217	566	F7
Northwest	2300 NW Thurman St, PTLD, 97210	596	D4
NWREL Information Center	101 SW Main St, PTLD, 97204	596	F6
Oak Lodge	16201 SE McLoughlin Blvd, CmsC, 97267	687	A1
Oregon City Public	362 Warner Milne Rd, ORCY, 97045	717	D3
Otto F Linn	2219 SE 68th Av, PTLD, 97215	627	E1
Port of Portland	121 NW Everett St, PTLD, 97209	596	F5
Reed College	3203 SE Woodstock Blvd, PTLD, 97202	627	A4
Ridgefield Community	210 N Main Av, RDGF, 98642	415	J7
Rockwood	17917 SE Stark St, GSHM, 97233	598	G6
St. Helen's Public	375 S 18th St, STHN, 97051	415	C1
Saint Johns	7510 N Charleston Av, PTLD, 97203	565	H3
Sandy Public	38980 Proctor Blvd, SNDY, 97055	691	A3
Scappoose Public	52469 SE 2nd St, SPSE, 97056	474	E1
Sellwood-Moreland	7860 SE 13th Av, PTLD, 97202	626	H6
Sherwood Public	955 SW Sherwood Blvd, SRWD, 97140	684	G6
Three Creeks Community	800 NE Tenney Rd, ClkC, 98685	476	H6
Tigard Public	13500 SW Hall Blvd, TGRD, 97223	655	F5
Tualatin Public	18880 SW Martinazzi Av, TLTN, 97062	685	F3
Vancouver Community	1007 E Mill Plain Blvd, VCVR, 98663	536	H5
Vancouver Mall Community	8700 NE Vancouver Mall Dr, VCVR, 98662	537	F1
WA Budden Memorial	2900 NE 132nd Av, PTLD, 97230	598	B3
Washougal Community	1661 C St, WHGL, 98671	570	A5
West Linn Public	1595 Burns St, WLIN, 97068	687	B6
West Slope Community	3678 SW 78th Av, WasC, 97225	625	G2
Wilsonville Public	8200 SW Wilsonville Rd, WNVL, 97070	745	F1
Woodland Community	770 Park St, WDLD, 98674	385	J2
Woodstock	6008 SE 49th Av, PTLD, 97206	627	C5

Military Installations

FEATURE NAME	Address City ZIP Code	MAP#	GRID
Camp Bonneville	ClkC, 98682	509	D5
Camp Withycombe	CmsC, 97015	657	J7
Portland Air National Guard Base	PTLD, 97218	567	D5
Vancouver Barracks	VCVR, 98661	536	H5

Museums

FEATURE NAME	Address City ZIP Code	MAP#	GRID
American Advertising Mus	211 NW 5th Av, PTLD, 97209	596	F5
Archer Gallery, The	1800 Fort Vancouver Wy, VCVR, 98663	536	J4
Brougher Mus	E Sherman St, NWBG, 97132	713	D7
Canby Depot Mus	888 NE 4th Av, CNBY, 97013	746	D6
Clark County Historical Mus	1511 Main St, VCVR, 98663	536	G4
Contemporary Crafts Musuem & Gallery	3934 SW Corbett Av, PTLD, 97239	626	F2
Evergreen Aviation Mus	3850 NE Salmon River Hwy, YmhC, 97128	771	C6
Gresham Pioneer Mus	410 N Main Av, GSHM, 97030	629	C2
Harlow House Mus	726 E Columbia River Hwy, TDLE, 97060	599	G4
Hoover-Minthorne House Musuem	115 S River St, NWBG, 97132	713	C7
Jeff Morris Memorial Fire Mus	55 SW Ash St, PTLD, 97204	596	F5
Kidd Toy Mus	1300 SE Grand Av, PTLD, 97214	596	G7
Lilah C Holden Elephant Mus	4001 SW Canyon Rd, PTLD, 97221	596	B7
Milwaukie Historical Society Mus	3737 SE Adams St, MWKE, 97222	657	A2
Museum of Oregon Territory	211 Tumwater Dr, ORCY, 97045	717	B1
Newell House Mus	8089 Champoeg Rd NE, MrnC, 97137	774	A1
Old Aurora Colony Mus	15018 2nd St NE, AURA, 97002	775	F3
Oregon City Carnegie Center	606 John Adams St, ORCY, 97045	717	C1
Oregon Historical Society	1200 SW Park Av, PTLD, 97205	596	E6
Oregon Maritime Center & Mus	113 SW Naito Pkwy, PTLD, 97204	596	F6
Oregon Military Mus	10101 SE Clackamas Rd, CmsC, 97015	657	H7
Oregon Mus of Science & Industry	1945 SE Water Av, PTLD, 97214	626	F1
Oregon Nikkei Legacy Center	121 NW 2nd Av, PTLD, 97209	596	F5
Oregon Sports Hall of Fame & Mus	321 SW Salmon St, PTLD, 97204	596	F6
Oregon Trail Interpretive Center	1726 Washington St, ORCY, 97045	687	D6
Pacific University Mus	2043 College Wy, FTGV, 97116	591	J4
Pearson Air Mus	1115 E 5th St, VCVR, 98661	536	H6
Pioneer Mothers Memorial Cabin Mus	8239 Champoeg Rd NE, MrnC, 97137	774	B1
Pittock Mansion	3229 NW Pittock Dr, PTLD, 97210	596	B5
Portland Art Mus	1219 SW Park Av, PTLD, 97205	596	E6
Portland Children's Mus	4015 SW Canyon Rd, PTLD, 97221	596	B7
Sandy Historical Mus	39260 Pioneer Blvd, SNDY, 97055	691	A3
Troutdale Depot Rail Mus	473 E Columbia River Hwy, TDLE, 97060	599	G3
Two Rivers Heritage Mus	1 16th St, WHGL, 98671	570	A6
Vancouver Fire Department Mus	900 W Evergreen Blvd, VCVR, 98660	536	F5
Washington County Mus	17677 NW Springville Rd, WasC, 97229	564	F6
Water Resources Education Center	4600 SE Columbia Wy, VCVR, 98661	537	B7
Watts Pioneer Mus	52432 SE 1st St, SPSE, 97056	474	E1
Wendel Mus of Animal Conservation	8303 SE Evergreen Hwy, VCVR, 98664	567	F1
Willamette Falls Locks & Mus	1 Willamette Lock, WLIN, 97068	687	B7
Wings of Freedom Showcase	13515 SE McLoughlin Blvd, CmsC, 97222	656	J5
Yamhill County Historical Mus	605 Market St, LFYT, 97127	741	G7

Open Space

FEATURE NAME	MAP#	GRID
Beaver Marsh Nature Preserve, VCVR	537	G2
Bull Run Reserve, CmsC	693	F2
Carlton Lake State Game Refuge, YmhC	711	A5
Fern Hill Wetlands, FTGV	592	C6
Henry J Biddle Nature Preserve, VCVR	567	J2
Jackson Bottom Wetlands, HBRO	593	C7
Loretta Norene Forest Preserve, ClkC	477	G6
Molalla Wetlands, CmsC	837	F3
Mt Hood Wilderness Area, CmsC	724	H2
Oaks Bottom Wildlife Refuge, PTLD	626	H5
Ridgefield National Wildlife Refuge, ClkC	445	H3
Rock Creek Open Space Park, WasC	564	E7
Salmon Huckleberry Wilderness, CmsC	723	F6
Sand Island Marine Pk, STHN	385	E6
Shillapoo Wildlife Refuge, ClkC	505	H3
Smith & Bybee Lakes Wildlife Area, PTLD	535	H5
South Shore Open Space, LKOW	656	C7
Steigerwald National Wildlife Refuge, ClkC	570	F7
Vancouver Lake Wildlife Area, ClkC	536	C1
Wilderness Pk, WLIN	687	A6

Other

FEATURE NAME	Address City ZIP Code	MAP#	GRID
Audubon Bird Sanctuary	5151 NW Cornell Rd, MthC, 97210	595	J4
Benson Hotel	309 SW Broadway, PTLD, 97205	596	F5
Berry Botanic Garden	11505 SW Summerville Av, MthC, 97219	656	G3
Blitz-Weinhard Brewery	1137 W Burnside St, PTLD, 97209	596	E5
Bridgeport Brewing	1313 NW Marshall St, PTLD, 97209	596	E4
Burnt Tree Farm	20707 SW Chapman Rd, WasC, 97140	714	B1
Camp Ireland Cub Scout Camp	31615 NW Camp Ireland St, WasC, 97124	593	A1
Chinatown	55 NW 4th Av, PTLD, 97209	596	F5
Clear Creek Distillery	2389 NW Wilson St, PTLD, 97210	596	C3
Clyde Hotel	1022 SW Stark St, PTLD, 97205	596	E5
Crystal Springs Rhododendron Garden	6001 SE 28th Av, PTLD, 97202	627	A4
Fantasy Trail Wenzel Farm	19754 S Ridge Rd, CmsC, 97045	719	A6
First Christian Church	1315 SW Broadway, PTLD, 97201	596	E6
Governor Hotel	614 SW 11th Av, PTLD, 97205	596	E5
Heathman Hotel	1001 SW Broadway, PTLD, 97205	596	E6
Hotel Lucia	400 SW Broadway, PTLD, 97205	596	F6
Hotel Vintage Plaza	422 SW Broadway, PTLD, 97205	596	F6
Hoyt Arboretum	4000 SW Fairview Blvd, PTLD, 97205	596	A6
Hulda Klager Lilac Gardens	115 S Pekin Rd, WDLD, 98674	385	J3
International Rose Test Garden	400 SW Kingston Av, PTLD, 97205	596	C6
Japanese Gardens	611 SW Kingston Av, PTLD, 97205	596	B6
Mallory Hotel	729 SW 15th Av, PTLD, 97205	596	E5
Medical Research Foundation of Oregon	Colony Rd, HBRO, 97006	594	D5
North Clackamas Aquatic Park	7300 SE Harmony Rd, CmsC, 97222	657	E4
Old Church	1422 SW 11th Av, PTLD, 97201	596	E6
Old Scotch Church	30685 NW Old Scotch Church Rd, WasC, 97124	563	B4
Oregon City Municipal Elevator	700 Railroad Av, ORCY, 97045	687	B7
Pioneer Courthouse Square	701 SW 6th Av, PTLD, 97205	596	E6
Portland Art Center	33 NW 4th Av, PTLD, 97209	596	F5
Portland Saturday Market	108 W Burnside St, PTLD, 97204	596	F5
Powell's City of Books	1005 W Burnside St, PTLD, 97209	596	E5
Rouge Blanc Gallery	720 E 1st St, NWBG, 97132	713	C7
Scouters' Mountain Boy Scout Camp	11300 SE 147th Av, HPYV, 97236	658	D3
Temple Beth Israel	1972 NW Flanders St, PTLD, 97209	596	D5
Vancouver Hatchery	12208 SE Evergreen Hwy, VCVR, 98683	568	A2
World Forestry Center	4033 SW Canyon Rd, PTLD, 97221	596	B7

Park & Ride

FEATURE NAME	MAP#	GRID
Park & Ride-7th-Day Adventist Church, BRTN	624	J5
Park & Ride-7th Street, VCVR	536	G5
Park & Ride-10th Church of Christ, PTLD	626	H4
Park & Ride-181st Av, GSHM	598	G6
Park & Ride-Barbur Boulevard, PTLD	656	B1
Park & Ride-Battleground, BGND	448	C5
Park & Ride-Beaverton Creek, BRTN	624	H1
Park & Ride-Bethel Congregational, BRTN	625	B4
Park & Ride-Boones Ferry Community, TLTN	685	E5
Park & Ride-BPA, VCVR	536	G1
Park & Ride-Canby Christian, CNBY	746	C6
Park & Ride-Carver, DAMA	688	E2
Park & Ride-Cedar Hills, WasC	595	C6
Park & Ride-Central Bible, PTLD	597	G5
Park & Ride-Christ Church Parish, LKOW	656	E6
Park & Ride-Christ the King Lutheran, TGRD	655	C6
Park & Ride-City of Estacada, ECDA	750	B4
Park & Ride-Clackamas Community College, - ORCY	717	F5
Park & Ride-Clackamas Town Center, CmsC	657	F3
Park & Ride-Clark County Fairgrounds, ClkC	476	H2
Park & Ride-Cleveland, GSHM	629	C2
Park & Ride-Community Church-Cedar Hills, - WasC	595	C7
Park & Ride-Cornell, WasC	594	H4
Park & Ride-Eleventh Church of Christ, PTLD	626	B5
Park & Ride-Elmonica-SW 170th Av, BRTN	594	G6
Park & Ride-Emmanuel United Presbyterian, - WLIN	686	J3
Park & Ride-Evergreen Transit Center, VCVR	538	B4
Park & Ride-Expo Center, PTLD	566	E1
Park & Ride-Fair Complex-Airport, HBRO	593	G4
Park & Ride-First Presbyterian, ORCY	717	C3
Park & Ride-Fisher's Landing, VCVR	568	E3

FEATURE NAME Address City ZIP Code	MAP#	GRID
Park & Ride-Forest Grove-7th Day Adventist, - FTGV	592	C5
Park & Ride-Gateway, PTLD	597	H5
Park & Ride-GI Joes, CmsC	657	A7
Park & Ride-Gresham City Hall, GSHM	629	B1
Park & Ride-Gresham Parking Garage, GSHM	629	C2
Park & Ride-Hillsboro Parking Garage, HBRO	593	B5
Park & Ride-Hope Church, LKOW	656	B6
Park & Ride-Kern Park Christian, PTLD	627	E3
Park & Ride-Lake Grove-United Presbyterian, - LKOW	656	A7
Park & Ride-Lake Oswego-United Methodist, - LKOW	656	E7
Park & Ride-Mall 205, PTLD	597	H6
Park & Ride-Menlo Park-122nd, PTLD	598	A6
Park & Ride-Millikan Way, WasC	625	A2
Park & Ride-Milwaukie Elks Lodge, CmsC	656	J4
Park & Ride-Milwaukie Presbyterian, MWKE	656	J3
Park & Ride-Mohawk, TLTN	685	F4
Park & Ride-New Life Foursquare, CmsC	746	F4
Park & Ride-Orenco, HBRO	593	J4
Park & Ride-Parkrose, PTLD	597	H1
Park & Ride-Pilgrim Lutheran, PTLD	627	G3
Park & Ride-Prince of Peace Lutheran, WasC	595	A4
Park & Ride-Progress, BRTN	625	D7
Park & Ride-Quatama-NW 205th Av, WasC	594	C5
Park & Ride-Reynolds School District, FRVW	598	J5
Park & Ride-Rose City Church, PTLD	597	E2
Park & Ride-St. Alexander Catholic, CNLS	592	E4
Park & Ride-St. Andrew's Presbyterian, PTLD	626	B3
Park & Ride-Salmon Creek, ClkC	476	J6
Park & Ride-Sandy 7th Day Adventist, SNDY	690	H2
Park & Ride-Sandy Sentry Market, SNDY	691	A3
Park & Ride-Sauvie Island, MthC	534	J1
Park & Ride-Sherwood, SRWD	684	G7
Park & Ride-Sherwood Regal Cinemas, SRWD	684	G5
Park & Ride-Somerset Christian Church, WasC	594	H3
Park & Ride-Southgate Theater, MWKE	656	J1
Park & Ride-Southminster Presbyterian Church, - BRTN	625	B5
Park & Ride-Sunset Transit Center, BRTN	595	D7
Park & Ride-Tigard, TGRD	655	G3
Park & Ride-Tualatin, TLTN	685	G2
Park & Ride-University Park Baptist, PTLD	566	C5
Park & Ride-Valley Comm United Presbyterian, - BRTN	625	G3
Park & Ride-Vancouver Mall Transit, VCVR	537	F1
Park & Ride-Vernon United Presbyterian, PTLD	567	A7
Park & Ride-Washougal, WHGL	569	H5
Park & Ride-West Beaverton, BRTN	624	H2
Park & Ride-Willow Creek, HBRO	594	E6
Parl & Ride-Delta Park/Vanport, PTLD	566	E2

Parks & Recreation

FEATURE NAME Address City ZIP Code	MAP#	GRID
11th Street Pk, DAYT	771	J5
Abernethy Green Pk, ORCY	687	D6
Abrams Pk, RDGF	416	A6
Adams Acres Pk, WasC	564	C7
Adams Pk, PTLD	596	A5
Airport Pk, MCMV	771	D7
Alberta Pk, PTLD	566	J7
Albert Kelly Pk, PTLD	626	B3
Alderman Pk, DAYT	772	B4
Alex Belisle Memorial Pk, ClkC	507	G1
Allenbach Acres Pk, WasC	564	F7
Alma Myra Pk, CmsC	657	E6
Aloha Pk, WasC	624	E2
Alohawood Pk, WasC	624	F1
Alpine Pk, CNLS	592	F5
Angella Pk, YmhC	770	J7
Ann-Toni Schreiber Pk, CmsC	657	D7
Apollo Ridge Pk, BRTN	594	F4
April Hill Pk, PTLD	625	J5
Arboretum Pk, CNLS	592	E5
Arbor Lodge Pk, PTLD	566	D5
Ardenwald Pk, MWKE	627	A7
Argay Pk, PTLD	598	C2
Arleda Pk, WasC	594	D6
Arnada Pk, VCVR	536	G3
Arnold Pk, VCVR	536	J2
Ash Creek Pk, CMAS	569	A3
Ashley Meadows Pk, HPYV	658	D6
Aspen Crest Pk, BRTN	624	H7
Aspen-Highland Pk, GSHM	599	C7
Atfalati Pk, TLTN	685	G5
Atkinson Pk, ORCY	687	D7
Austin Pk, CNLS	592	E5
Autumn Ridge Pk, BRTN	594	F4
Avalon Pk, WasC	685	B2
Bagley Pk, HBRO	593	C4
Bagley Pk, VCVR	537	B3
Bales Wetlands Pk, WasC	624	F4
Barclay Hills Pk, ORCY	717	E2
Barclay Pk, ORCY	687	D7
Bard Pk, FTGV	592	A4
Barsotti Pk, WasC	624	G2
Barton County Pk, CmsC	689	E5
Battle Ground Lake State Pk, ClkC	448	F1
Bauman Pk, BRTN	625	G4
Beacon Hill Pk, BRTN	624	H7
Beaver Pk, WHGL	570	A6
Beaverton Creek Wetlands, BRTN	624	H2
Beech Pk, PTLD	598	B2
Beggars Tick Pk, PTLD	627	J5
Bella Vista Pk, GSHM	628	J2
Bella Vista Pk, VCVR	568	C1
Bell Vue Point, MthC	535	F1
Benal Pk, HBRO	593	C6
Ben Franklin Pk, VCVR	506	E7
Benski Pk, WLIN	686	H4
Berkeley Pk, PTLD	627	A5
Berrydale Pk, PTLD	597	G7
Bethany Crest Pk, WasC	564	J7
Bethany Lake Pk, WasC	564	E7
Bethany Meadows Pk, WasC	564	H7
Bethany Wetlands Pk, WasC	594	H2
Beulan City Pk, YMHL	711	A1
Bicentennial Pk, HBRO	593	E4
Biddlewood Pk, VCVR	568	A1
Bill Hamlik Pk, WHGL	570	D6
Billick-Dundee School Pk, DNDE	742	H3
Bloomington Pk, PTLD	627	H4
Bluegrass Downs Pk, BRTN	594	F4
Blue Lake Regional Pk, FRVW	599	A1
Bluffs, The, WasC	595	B2
Bonita Pk, TGRD	655	G6
Bonnie Lure State Rec Area, CmsC	719	G2
Bonny Slope Pk, WasC	595	D2
Boones Ferry Pk, WNVL	745	D2
Brentwood Pk, PTLD	627	D5
Brockview Pk, BRTN	624	H4
Bronson Creek Pk, BRTN	594	F3
Brookhaven Pk, BRTN	624	J5
Brooklyn Pk, PTLD	626	H2
Brooklyn School Pk, PTLD	626	H2
Brown's Ferry Pk, TLTN	685	H3
Bryant Woods Nature Pk, LKOW	686	A3
Buckman Field, PTLD	596	H5
Buckskin Mini Pk, BRTN	655	A1
Bundy Pk, PTLD	628	C6
Bunnell Pk, CmsC	656	J6
Burlingame Pk, PTLD	626	D6
Burnside Pk, WLIN	687	B5
Burnsridge Pk, WasC	624	E5
Burnt Bridge Creek Pk, VCVR	537	A3
Burntwood Powerline Pk, BRTN	624	G5
Burntwood Upper West Pk, BRTN	624	G5
Burton Pk, WasC	595	A3
Butler Creek Pk, GSHM	628	J5
Butterfly Pk, PTLD	626	F6
Butternut Pk, WasC	624	D3
Camassia Natural Area, WLIN	687	B7
Camille Pk, BRTN	625	D6
Campbell Pk, STHN	415	A1
Camp Currie, ClkC	539	B4
Canal Acres Pk, LKOW	686	A3
Canby Community Pk, CNBY	746	B7
Canemah Pk, ORCY	717	A2
Carl Gustafson Pk, VCVR	537	E6
Carlson Pk, MCMV	770	G5
Carolwood Pk, BRTN	624	H6
Carter Pk, VCVR	536	G3
Cascade Pk, VCVR	538	A7
Cascadia Pk, SNDY	691	A5
Caterpillar Island Rec Area, ClkC	505	G2
Cathedral Pk, PTLD	565	F3
Cedar Hills Pk, BRTN	625	B1
Cedar Island Pk, WLIN	687	A3
Cedar Mill Pk, WasC	595	D4
Cedar Mill Woods Pk, WasC	595	E4
Cedar Oak Pk, WLIN	686	J3
CE Mason Wetlands Pk, BRTN	625	C2
Centerpointe Pk, VCVR	537	E2
Central Pk North, VCVR	536	H4
Central Street Pk, BRTN	625	C2
Century Pk, MWKE	657	A3
Champoeg State Heritage Area, MrnC	744	B7
Channing Heights Pk, BRTN	625	A5
Chantal Village Pk, WasC	594	D6
Chapin Pk, ORCY	717	B3
Chapman Square, PTLD	596	F6
Cherry Blossom Pk, PTLD	627	H1
Cherry Pk, PTLD	627	J1
Chimney Pk, PTLD	565	G1
Chinook Landing Marine Pk, FRVW	599	B1
City-College Pk, VCVR	536	H4
City Pk, AURA	775	F4
City Pk, BRTN	625	B3
City Pk, STPL	773	B6
Clackamette Pk, ORCY	687	C5
Clark Pk, MOLA	837	F1
Clark-Wilson Pk, PTLD	565	D3
Clatsop Pk, PTLD	627	E7
Clearmeadows Pk, VCVR	568	F2
Cleone Pk, FRVW	599	A4
Clinton Pk, PTLD	627	C1
Coe Circle Pk, PTLD	597	B5
Cold Creek Pk, ClkC	506	J6
College Pk, NWBG	713	D6
College Pk, WasC	564	F7
Colonel Summers Pk, PTLD	596	H6
Columbia Lancaster Pk, VCVR	537	D5
Columbia Pk, PTLD	566	C5
Columbia Pk, TDLE	599	E5
Columbia River Gorge National Scenic Area, - MthC	600	G5
Columbia View Pk, GSHM	598	F5
Commonwealth Pk, WasC	595	B6
Cook Pk, TGRD	685	E2
Cooks Butte Pk, LKOW	686	C2
Cooper Pk, WasC	624	F4
Coop Pk, VCVR	537	F5
Cottonwood Beach Pk, WHGL	570	C7
Couch Pk, PTLD	596	D5
Cougar Creek Greenway Pk, ClkC	506	G4
Council Crest Pk, PTLD	626	B1
Countryside Pk, VCVR	538	C5
Courthouse Square Pk, DAYT	772	A4
Courtside Pk, WNVL	715	F7
CP Pk, TDLE	599	F6
Crabtree Pk, YmhC	742	D3
Crater Pk, NWBG	713	B4
Creston Pk, PTLD	627	B2
Crestwood Pk, MCMV	770	G4
Cross Memorial Pk, GLDS	687	E5
Crowell Court Pk, WasC	594	F7
Crown Continental Pk, ClkC	506	H2
Crown Pk, CMAS	569	E4
Crown Point State Pk, MthC	600	C4
Crystal Creek Pk, WasC	594	G2
Custer Pk, PTLD	626	C5
Dabney State Pk, MthC	600	A7
Dahl Beach, GLDS	687	C5
Dairy Creek Pk, HBRO	593	A5
David Douglas Pk, VCVR	537	E5
Davids Windsor Pk, BRTN	654	H4
Davis Pk, GSHM	598	H5
Davis Pk, RDGF	415	J6
Dawson Pk, PTLD	596	G2
Daybreak Pk, ClkC	447	G1
DC Latourette Pk, ORCY	687	D7
Deerfield Pk, WasC	564	F7
Deline Pk, WasC	624	E4
Dement Pk, ORCY	717	C2
Depot Pk, TDLE	599	G4
DeWitt Pk, PTLD	626	D4
Diamond Pk, VCVR	538	C3
Dickinson Pk, PTLD	655	J1
Dogwood Pk, CNLS	592	F5
Dogwood Pk, MWKE	656	J3
Donald R Robertson Pk, WDVL	599	D4
Dorothy Fox Pk, CMAS	569	C3
Dubois Pk, VCVR	537	C6
Duniway Pk, PTLD	626	E1
Durham City Pk, DRHM	685	F2
Durkee Pk (Undeveloped), ClkC	448	F5
Dwight S Parr Junior Pk, BRTN	594	H6
Eagle Fern Pk, CmsC	720	G6
Earl Boyles Pk, PTLD	627	J3
Eastbank Riverfront Pk, PTLD	596	F6
East Delta Pk, PTLD	566	F2
East Gresham Pk, GSHM	629	G3
Eastridge Pk, PTLD	628	C7
Ed Benedict Community Pk, PTLD	627	H2
Edgewood Pk, VCVR	537	A5
Eichler Pk, BRTN	625	A3
Eisenhower Pk, ClkC	506	F4
Elizabeth Meadows Pk, WasC	624	D1
Elizabeth Pk, WHGL	570	A5
Elk Rock Island, MWKE	656	H3
Ellsworth Pk, VCVR	537	H7
Elsie Stuhr Center Pk, BRTN	625	B4
Emerald Estates Pk, WasC	564	G7
Errol Heights Pk, PTLD	627	C7
Essex Pk, PTLD	627	F3
Esther Short Pk, VCVR	536	F5
Evelyn Schiffler Memorial Pk, BRTN	625	A4
Evergreen Memorial Pk, YmhC	771	C1
Evergreen Park-East, HBRO	594	D3
Evergreen Park-North, HBRO	594	D2
Evergreen Park-West, HBRO	594	D2
Evergreen Pk, VCVR	537	A4
Ewing Young Historical Pk, NWBG	743	B2
Fairgrounds Pk, BGND	448	C5
Fairview Community Pk, FRVW	599	B5
Falcon Crest Pk, DNDE	742	G3
Fallen Leaf Pk, CMAS	569	E3
Fanno Pk, TGRD	655	E5
Farragut Pk, PTLD	566	F4
Father Blanchet Pk, VCVR	537	E6
Felida Pk, ClkC	476	C7
Fernhill Pk, PTLD	567	B6
Feyrer Memorial Pk, CmsC	837	J2
Fields Bridge Pk, WLIN	716	E1
Fifth Street Pk, BRTN	625	C3
Fir Crest Pk, VCVR	538	A5
Firgarden Pk, VCVR	538	D2
Fir Grove Pk, BRTN	625	A5
Firland Parkway, PTLD	627	E3
First Place Pk, VCVR	538	D4
Fisher Basin Community Pk, VCVR	538	H7
Flag Island County Pk, MthC	600	C3
Flavel Pk, PTLD	627	E6
Florence Pointe Pk, WasC	625	G7
Floyd Light Pk, PTLD	597	J6
Foothills Pk, WasC	595	B7
Forest Glen Pk, BRTN	655	A1
Forest Glen Pk, FTGV	591	E3
Forest Hills Pk, WasC	595	C6
Forest Home Pk, CMAS	569	D5
Forest Pk, PTLD	565	B1
Forest Ridge Pk, VCVR	537	G4
Fort Vancouver National Historic Site Pk, - VCVR	536	G5
Four Seasons Pk, VCVR	537	J3
Fox Pk, MOLA	837	E2
Frances Street Pk, HBRO	593	J7
Fraser Pk, PTLD	597	C4
Free Orhard Pk, CNLS	592	E5
Freepons Pk, LKOW	686	F1
Frenchman's Bar Regional Pk, ClkC	505	G4
Frimble Pk, MOLA	807	C7
Fruit Valley Pk, VCVR	536	D2
Fulton Pk & Community Center, PTLD	626	E6
Furnberg Pk, MWKE	657	D3
Gabriel Pk, PTLD	626	A5
Gaiser Pk, ClkC	507	A3
Gammans Pk, PTLD	566	D5
Garden Home Pk, WasC	625	F7
Garden Home Recreation Center, PTLD	625	G6
Gary Island Pk, MthC	600	B2
General Anderson Pk, VCVR	537	C6
George Foegue Pk, BRTN	595	D5
George Himes Pk, PTLD	626	E4
George Pk, PTLD	565	J2
George Rogers Pk, LKOW	656	G7
Gilbert Heights Pk, PTLD	628	B3
Gilbert Primary Pk, PTLD	628	B5
Glenfair Pk, PTLD	598	D6
Glenhaven Pk, PTLD	597	F3
Glenmorrie Pk, LKOW	686	G1
Glenn Otto Community Pk, TDLE	599	H4
Glenwood Pk, PTLD	627	F5
Goat Island Pk, WLIN	687	B5
Godfrey Pk, STHN	385	D7
Goot Pk, CMAS	569	H5
Governors Pk, PTLD	596	D7
Governor Tom McCall Waterfront Pk, PTLD	596	F7
Gradin Community Sports Pk, GSHM	629	E4
Graf Meadows Pk, WasC	564	H6
Granada Pk, WasC	624	E5
Grass Vally Pk, CMAS	569	B1
Greentree Pk, LKOW	686	D1
Greenville Pk, BNKS	531	J6
Greenway Pk, BRTN	655	C1
Griffin Oaks Pk, HBRO	593	E2
Griffith Pk, BRTN	625	C3
Grotto, The, PTLD	597	G2
Haagen Pk, VCVR	538	A5
Hall Pk, GSHM	599	E7
Hamilton Pk, PTLD	626	A3
Hammerle Pk, WLIN	687	B6
Hancock Pk, PTLD	597	G4
Handy Pk, FRVW	599	B4
Happy Valley Pk, HPYV	658	B1
Harleman Pk, CNLS	592	D6
Harrison Pk, PTLD	627	F1
Hartke Pk, ORCY	717	B3
Hartwood Highland Pk, BRTN	624	J5
Hathaway Pk, WHGL	570	B5
Hathaway Pk, WNVL	715	G7
Hazeldale Pk, WasC	624	D5
Hazel Dell Pk, ClkC	506	J6
Hazel Sills Pk, FTGV	591	H3
Hazelwood Pk, ORCY	717	B3
HB Fuller Pk, ClkC	476	G6
Healy Heights Parlk, PTLD	626	D2
Hearthwood Pk, VCVR	538	B6
Heather Glen Pk, YmhC	770	E7
Hebb Memorial Pk, CmsC	746	D1
Heddie Notz Pk, CmsC	687	E1
Heinie Heumann Pk, STHN	415	C1
Helen Althaus Pk, TDLE	599	G4
Hembree Pk, CNLS	592	F4
Herbert Hoover Pk, NWBG	713	D7
Heritage Pk, CMAS	569	E2
Heritage Pk, SPSE	474	E1
Heritage Pk, VCVR	568	E2
Hidden Pk, VCVR	536	F2
Hideaway Pk, BRTN	625	H5
Hillendale Pk, ORCY	717	D4
Hillsdale Pk, PTLD	626	C4
Hillside Community Center, PTLD	596	C5
Hi Rocks Pk, GLDS	687	E4
Hiteon Meadows Pk, BRTN	655	A2
Hiteon Pk, BRTN	625	A7
Hoffman Pk, WDLD	385	J2
Holladay East Pk, PTLD	598	B5
Holladay Pk, PTLD	596	H4
Hollybrook Pk, GSHM	628	J3
Holman Pk, PTLD	596	A3
Homestead Pk, VCVR	568	D1
Horseshoe Lake Pk, WDLD	386	A2
Howard M Terpenning Complex, BRTN	594	H5
Howell Territorial Pk, MthC	535	B2
Hubert Lee Cain Pk, WasC	624	F6
Hyland Forest Pk, BRTN	625	A6
Ibach Nature Pk, WLIN	686	J6
Ibach Pk, TLTN	685	D6
Indian John Island, MthC	630	G7
Intel Aloha Wetlands Pk, WasC	624	C1
Iron Mountain Pk, LKOW	656	C6
Irving Pk, PTLD	596	H2

Portland Points of Interest Index

FEATURE NAME Address City ZIP Code	MAP#	GRID
Jack Pk, TGRD	655	B4
Jacobs Memorial Pk, ORCY	717	C1
Jaggy Road Pk, VCVR	537	E1
James Abele Pk, CmsC	658	A5
James Pk, MCMV	770	F6
Jamison Square, PTLD	596	E4
Jandina Pk, MCMV	770	E6
Jaquith Pk, NWBG	713	C6
Jason Lee School Pk, ClkC	506	F4
Jenkins Estate, WasC	624	B6
Jenne Butte Pk, GSHM	628	G5
Jessie Mays Comm Center & Pk, NPNS	563	B1
JJ Collins Memorial Pk, ClbC	445	B6
Joe Dancer Pk, MCMV	771	A5
John Ball Pk, VCVR	536	F3
John Luby Pk, PTLD	598	B3
John Marty Pk, WasC	594	G2
Johnson Creek Pk, PTLD	626	J7
Jones Farm Pk, HBRO	593	E1
Jordan Pk, WasC	595	D4
Jorgenson Pk, ClkC	506	F6
Joseph Gale Pk, FTGV	592	A5
Joseph Wood Hill Pk, PTLD	597	G2
Jurgens Pk, TLTN	685	D2
Kaiser Ridge Pk, WasC	594	J1
Kane Road Pk, GSHM	629	F2
Keller Pk, MWKE	656	H4
Kelley Point Pk, PTLD	535	G2
Kelly Butte Pk, PTLD	627	H2
Kenilworth Pk, PTLD	627	A3
Kennedy Pk, BRTN	625	D3
Kenton Pk, PTLD	566	D4
Kern Pk, PTLD	627	E3
Kiku Pk, TDLE	599	H5
King School Pk, PTLD	596	H1
Kingsley Pk, PTLD	565	D1
Kirk Pk, GSHM	598	H5
Kiwanis Marine Pk, MCMV	770	J6
Kiwanis Pk, BGND	448	B6
Klickitat Pk, CMAS	569	A4
Knott Pk, PTLD	598	A3
Knox Ridge Pk, FTGV	591	F4
Koll Center Wetlands Pk, BRTN	625	C7
Lacamas Creek Pk, CMAS	569	F3
Lacamas Pk, ClkC	569	F2
La Center Bottoms, ClkC	416	G1
Ladds Circle & Squares Pk, PTLD	626	H1
Lafky Pk, TLTN	685	D5
Lair Hill Pk, PTLD	626	E1
Lake at the Commons, TLTN	685	F3
Lake Grove Swim Pk, LKOW	656	A7
Langer Pk, SRWD	684	G6
Laurelhurst Pk, PTLD	597	A6
Laurelhurst Pk Theatre Annex, PTLD	597	B6
Laurelwood Pk, PTLD	627	D3
Lawndale Pk, WasC	624	F4
Leach Botanical Garden, PTLD	628	A5
Leach Pk, VCVR	536	H3
Leavitt Pk, NWBG	743	D1
Legacy Pk, CNBY	746	D7
Leghtenberg Pk, ClkC	538	J4
Legion Field, DAYT	772	A4
Lents Pk, PTLD	627	G4
Leonard Long Pk, MOLA	837	E1
Lesser Pk, PTLD	655	J3
Leverich Pk, VCVR	536	H2
Lewellyn Pk, TDLE	599	H5
Lewis & Clark State Pk, MthC	599	H3
Lewisville Pk, ClkC	418	B7
Lexington Pk, WasC	594	B5
Liberty Ship Memorial Pk, PTLD	596	F4
Lieser Crest Pk, VCVR	537	E6
Lillis-Albina Pk, PTLD	596	F3
Lilly Johnson Pk, WasC	624	H3
Lincoln Pk, FTGV	591	J4
Lincoln Pk, PTLD	628	B1
Linnton Pk, PTLD	565	C2
Little Peoples Pk, BRTN	625	C3
Little Woodrose Nature Pk, TLTN	685	E5
Locks Pk, YmhC	771	H2
Locust Street Pk, CNBY	746	D6
Lost Pk, WasC	595	D3
Lotus Isle Pk, PTLD	566	F1
Louis Bloch Pk, CMAS	569	F4
Lovejoy Pk, PTLD	596	E7
Lowami Hart Woods Pk, BRTN	624	H5
Lownsdale Square, PTLD	596	F6
Lucia Falls South Pk, ClkC	419	B4
Luscher Farm Pk, CmsC	686	E2
Luscher Pk Farm, CmsC	686	D2
Lynchview Pk, PTLD	598	E7
Lynchwood Pk, PTLD	628	F2
Lyons View Pk, CmsC	748	E1
Madrona Heights Pk, WasC	624	F7
Madrona Pk, PTLD	596	D1
Magness Memorial Tree Farm, CmsC	744	E1
Main City Community Pk, GSHM	629	B3
Maplecrest Pk, ClkC	538	F4
Maple Street Pk, CNBY	746	D5
Maricara Pk, PTLD	656	C1
Marine Pk, VCVR	537	B7
Marks Memorial Pk, CmsC	776	A6
Marquam Nature Pk, PTLD	626	C1
Marshall Community Pk, VCVR	536	G4
Marshall Pk, PTLD	656	D1
Marylhurst Heights Pk, WLIN	686	G3
Mary S Young Pk, WLIN	687	A4
Mason Hill Pk, MthC	533	J2
Matrix Hill Pk, BRTN	624	J7
Max Patterson Memorial Pk, GLDS	687	D4
McCormick Pk, STHN	415	B2
McCoy Pk, PTLD	566	B3
McKenna Pk, PTLD	566	A4
McKinney Pk, HBRO	593	B4
McLean House Pk, WLIN	687	C6
McLoughlin Promenade, ORCY	717	B1
McMillan Pk, BRTN	625	E3
McMinnville City Pk, MCMV	770	G5
Meadowbrook Marsh Pk, VCVR	537	F4
Meadowbrook North Pk, VCVR	537	F3
Meadowbrook Pk, WasC	624	C3
Meadow Homes Pk, VCVR	537	B4
Meadow Pk, WasC	594	J6
Meinig Memorial Pk, SNDY	691	A3
Meldrum Bar State Pk, GLDS	687	B5
Melilah Pk, WasC	624	F1
Memorial Pk, BRTN	625	B4
Memorial Pk, NWBG	743	C1
Memory Mill Plain Pk, VCVR	536	H5
Merrifield Pk, PTLD	598	A4
Merritt Orchard Pk, WasC	595	D6
Metzger County Pk, WasC	655	F1
Midhill Pk, WLIN	686	H2
Midland Pk, PTLD	598	A7
Millenium Plaza Pk, LKOW	656	F6
Miller Pk, SPSE	474	G1
Mill Pk, CmsC	657	D1
Mill Pk, PTLD	628	A1

FEATURE NAME Address City ZIP Code	MAP#	GRID
Mill Plain One Pk, VCVR	538	A6
Milo McIver State Pk, CmsC	749	G1
Mitchell Pk, WasC	595	E6
Molalla River State Pk, CmsC	746	A2
Montavilla Pk, PTLD	597	F5
Moon Shadow Pk, WasC	625	H7
Morgans Run Pk, WasC	564	H7
Morrison Woods Pk, BRTN	624	G7
Moshofsky Woods Pk, BRTN	594	G4
Moulton Falls State Pk, ClkC	419	H6
Mt Hood National Forest, CmsC	724	G4
Mt Scott Pk, PTLD	627	E4
Mt Tabor Pk, PTLD	597	D7
Mt Talbert Pk, CmsC	657	J5
Mt Zion, ClkC	386	J6
Mud Lake Pk, ClkC	416	C2
Murray Hill Pk, BRTN	654	H2
Murrayhill Pk, BRTN	654	H2
Nehalem Pk, PTLD	627	C7
Neighborhood Pk, CmsC	657	E4
Nicholas Acres Pk, WasC	624	B3
Noble Woods Pk, HBRO	593	J5
Normandale Pk, PTLD	597	D4
North Clackamas City Pk, MWKE	657	C5
Northgate Pk, PTLD	566	A3
North Gresham Pk, GSHM	599	A7
North Lake Shore Pk, FRVW	599	B2
North Pk Blocks, PTLD	596	E5
North Powellhurst Pk, PTLD	598	C7
Northridge Pk, WasC	624	D6
Northshore Estates Pk, WasC	564	D7
Northview Pk, TGRD	654	J4
North Willamette Neighborhood Pk, WLIN	686	G7
Oakbrook Pk, VCVR	537	G3
Oak Hills Pk, WasC	594	J3
Oak Pk, CMAS	569	F5
Oaks Pioneer Pk, PTLD	626	G6
Odd Fellows Pk, MOLA	837	E1
Old Apple Tree Pk, VCVR	536	G6
Old Canemah Pk, ORCY	717	B2
Oppenlander Fields, WLIN	686	H6
Orchard Highlands Pk, ClkC	507	J3
Orchard Pk, HBRO	594	C3
Orchards Pk, ClkC	507	G7
Oregon Electric Right of Way Path, WasC	625	F5
Oregon Pk, PTLD	597	A5
Orenco Pk West, HBRO	594	A3
Ostenson Canyon, CMAS	569	D4
Overlook Pk, PTLD	596	E2
Oxbow Regional Pk, MthC	630	F3
Pacific Community Pk, ClkC	538	E5
Palomino Pk, WLIN	686	H5
Paradise Pk, CmsC	719	F7
Paradise Point State Pk, ClkC	386	D7
Park at Merryfield, WNVL	715	C7
Parker's Landing, WHGL	569	G5
Parklane Pk, PTLD	598	D7
Park Place Pk, ORCY	687	F5
Pat Pfeifer Barrier-Free Pk, GSHM	598	F5
Patton Square, PTLD	566	E7
Paula Jean Pk, WasC	594	B6
Pebble Creek Pk, ClkC	508	B5
Pelfrey Pk, FRVW	599	A3
Pendleton Pk, PTLD	625	J4
Peninsula Pk Rose Garden, PTLD	566	F6
Peppertree Pk, WasC	595	B6
Peter Kerr Pk, MthC	656	H3
Peter S Ogden Pk, VCVR	537	F3
Pettygrove Pk, PTLD	596	E7
Pheasant Pk, WasC	594	F7
Philip Foster Farm Historic Pk, CmsC	720	A1
Piccolo Pk, PTLD	626	J1
Pidgeon Pk, CmsC	688	G2
Pier Pk & Swim Pool, PTLD	565	G1
Pioneer Pk, BRTN	594	J5
Pioneer Pk, SNDY	690	G2
Pioneer Square, PTLD	596	E6
Pittock Acres Pk, PTLD	596	B5
Pixie Pk, CBAC	385	D3
Pleasant Valley Pk, ClkC	477	B5
Pool Pk, NWBG	713	D6
Portland Classical Chinese Garden, PTLD	596	F5
Portland Heights Pk, PTLD	626	B1
Portsmouth Pk, PTLD	566	A5
Powell Butte Nature Pk, PTLD	628	D4
Powell Pk, PTLD	626	J2
Powers Marine Pk, PTLD	626	F7
Prune Hill Sports Pk, CMAS	569	A4
Quarnberg Pk, VCVR	536	J5
Quarry Pk, MCMV	770	E5
Quimby Pk, BRTN	625	B6
Raleigh Pk, WasC	625	G2
Raleigh Scholls Pk, WasC	625	G4
Raleighwood Pk, WasC	625	G3
Raymond Pk, PTLD	628	A4
Red Sunset Pk, GSHM	599	D7
Reed Island State Pk, ClkC	600	F2
Reedville Creek Pk, WasC	594	B7
Reservior Pk, WasC	625	E1
Ridgewood Pk, BRTN	595	E7
Ridgewood View Pk, BRTN	625	D1
Risley Pk, CmsC	656	J7
Rivercrest Pk, ORCY	717	C2
River Fox Pk, WNVL	745	B1
Riverfront Pk, STHN	385	E7
River Run Pk, LKOW	686	A4
Riverside County Pk, CmsC	687	G2
Riverside Pk, PTLD	626	G2
River Villa Pk, CmsC	656	H5
Robinwood Pk, WLIN	686	H2
Rock Creek Landing Pk, WasC	564	B6
Rock Creek North Soccer Field Pk, WasC	564	C7
Rock Creek Pk, HBRO	593	H5
Rock Creek Pk, WasC	594	D1
Rockwood Central Pk, GSHM	598	G7
Rocky Butte State Pk, PTLD	597	H3
Rod Harman Swim Center & Pk, BRTN	625	E6
Roehr Pk, LKOW	656	G6
Rogers Pk, FTGV	591	J5
Rood Bridge Pk, WasC	623	F2
Rosa Pk, WasC	624	D4
Rose City Pk, PTLD	597	D3
Roselawn Pk, PTLD	566	H7
Rossman Pk, LKOW	656	F5
Roxbury Pk, BRTN	625	D1
Roy Dancer Pk, BRTN	624	J4
Ruth R Rose Pk, CBAC	385	C3
Saarinen Wayside Pk, TLTN	685	E5
Sacajawea Pk, PTLD	597	F1
Sahallie Illahee Pk, WLIN	686	J6
St. Francis Pk, PTLD	596	H6
St. Helens Pk, VCVR	537	B5
St. Johns Pk, PTLD	565	H2
Salish Ponds Wetlands Pk, FRVW	599	A5
Salix Pk, WasC	594	F5
Salmon Creek Greenway Pk, ClkC	476	E7
Sam Brown Pk, VCVR	537	C5
Sandee Palisades Pk, TDLE	599	H6

FEATURE NAME Address City ZIP Code	MAP#	GRID
San Salvador State Pk, MrnC	772	F4
Satterberg Heights Parks, WasC	624	G7
Scappoose Airport Pk, SPSE	444	F5
Scatterberg Heights Parks, BRTN	624	G7
Schrunk Plaza, PTLD	596	F6
Schuepbach Pk, BRTN	625	H4
Scott Pk, MWKE	656	J2
Scotts Place Pk, WasC	624	F1
Sellwood Pk, PTLD	626	G6
Sellwood Riverfront Pk, PTLD	626	G6
Seminole Pk, WasC	594	D6
Serah Lindsay Estates Pk, WasC	564	G7
Sewallcrest Pk, PTLD	597	A7
Sexton Mountain Pk, BRTN	624	J5
Shadow Creek Pk, BRTN	654	J1
Shadywood Pk, HBRO	593	E4
Sheets Field, MOLA	807	C7
Shenandoah Pk, ORCY	717	B4
Sherwood North Pk, ClkC	507	A1
Shute Pk, HBRO	593	D6
Sieben Pk, CmsC	658	C6
Singer Creek Pk, ORCY	717	C2
Skyline Pk, WLIN	686	F3
Skyview Pk, WasC	594	H4
Somerset Meadows Pk, WasC	594	G2
Somerset West Pk, WasC	594	E2
South Cliff Pk, VCVR	537	B5
Southeast Community Pk, GSHM	629	F5
Southeast Neighborhood Pk, GSHM	629	F6
Southern Lites Pk, CmsC	658	A4
South Pk Blocks, PTLD	596	E7
Southwest Community Pk, WasC	624	E5
Southwest Pk, GSHM	628	H3
Southwood Pk, LKOW	655	H5
Springbrook Pk, LKOW	656	B6
Spring Garden Pk, PTLD	626	B7
Spring Meadow Pk, NWBG	713	F6
Spring Pk, MWKE	656	H4
Springville Meadows Pk, WasC	564	H6
Springwater Trail Corridor, GSHM	629	C3
Spyglass Pk, WasC	594	G2
Stafford Pk, ORCY	717	C2
Stanley Pk, MWKE	657	D3
Status Pk, CNLS	592	F4
Steamboat Landing Pk, WHGL	570	A6
Steamboat Pk, CNLS	592	E6
Stella Olson Pk, SRWD	684	G7
Stevens Meadow, CmsC	686	C3
Stewart Glen Burnt Bridge Creek Greenway, - VCVR	506	E6
Stocker Pk, GLDS	687	E4
Stoller Farms Pk, WasC	594	G1
Stonegate at Willow Creek, BRTN	594	G4
Stonegate Pk, BRTN	594	G5
Stonemist Pk, WasC	624	F6
Stoneridge Pk, TLTN	685	G4
Summercrest East Pk, BRTN	624	G6
Summercrest West Pk, WasC	624	F7
Summerfield Pk, CmsC	658	B5
Summer Lake Pk, TGRD	655	A3
Summer's Walk Pk, VCVR	568	F1
Sunburst Pk, WLIN	686	G4
Sunrise Pk, TDLE	599	F6
Sunset Pk, BNKS	531	H6
Sunset Pk, BRTN	595	A4
Sunset Pk, WLIN	687	A7
Sutherland Meadows Pk, WasC	594	C6
Swan Ponds Pk, ClkC	506	J3
Sweetbriar Pk, TDLE	599	G7
Swift Shore Pk, WLIN	716	F2
Taleisen Pk, BRTN	625	A6
Talisman Pk, FTGV	591	G3
Tallac Terrace Pk, BRTN	624	G5
Tall Oaks Pk, MCMV	770	F7
Tanner Creek Pk, WLIN	686	H6
Tarrybrooke Pk, CNLS	592	D5
Terra Linda Pk, WasC	595	A3
Terry Pk, LFYT	771	G1
Terwilliger Pk, PTLD	626	D3
Thom Pk, GSHM	629	C3
Thompson Pk, PTLD	598	C3
Thornbrook Pk, BRTN	624	G5
Tice Pk, MCMV	770	H2
Tideman Johnson Pk, PTLD	627	B7
Tiger Tree Pk, ClkC	508	C4
Timber Pk, CmsC	750	A2
Tokola Wetlands Pk, WasC	594	H2
Tom Gail Pk, NWBG	713	D4
Tower Crest Pk, ClkC	537	D1
Town Center Pk, WNVL	715	F7
Trachsel Meadows Pk, WasC	624	B1
Tranquil Nature Pk, WNVL	715	C7
Trenton Pk, PTLD	566	C3
Tryon Creek State Pk, PTLD	656	E2
Tualatin Community Pk, TLTN	685	F3
Tualatin Hills Nature Pk, BRTN	624	H1
Tualatin River Pk, WLIN	716	F1
Tupper Pk, SNDY	690	J3
Turner Creek Pk, HBRO	593	F6
Twin Cedars Pk, WasC	624	G3
UJ Hamby Pk, HBRO	593	C3
US Grant Pk, PTLD	597	A3
University Pk, PTLD	566	C3
Unthank Pk, PTLD	596	F1
Upper Macleay Pk, PTLD	596	A4
Vale Pk, BRTN	624	H6
Valley Pk, BRTN	625	A5
Valley West Pk, BRTN	625	A4
Vance Pk, GSHM	598	G7
Vancouver Lake Lowlands, ClkC	506	D6
Vancouver Lake Pk, ClkC	505	J4
Van Fleet Pk, VCVR	537	E5
Vendla Pk, WasC	624	F1
Ventura Pk, PTLD	598	A6
Vietnam Veterans Memorial Pk, PTLD	596	A7
Village Green, CmsC	658	C6
Vista Brook Pk, WasC	625	F5
Wait Pk, CNBY	746	C6
Wake Robin Pk, BRTN	625	A6
Wallace Pk, PTLD	596	C4
Walnut Street Pk, HBRO	593	E5
Walt Morey Pk, WNVL	745	C1
Waluga Pk, LKOW	656	A6
Wanda Peck Memorial Pk, WasC	625	A6
Washington Pk, PTLD	596	B7
Washington School Pk, VCVR	536	H3
Washougal River Greenway, CMAS	569	G4
Waterboard Pk, ORCY	717	C1
Waterfront Pk, VCVR	536	G6
Waterhouse Pk, BRTN	594	G5
Waterhouse South Pk, BRTN	594	G6
Water Pk, CNLS	592	F4
Water Tower Pk, MWKE	657	B1
Waterworks Pk, VCVR	536	J4
Weber Pk, MWKE	657	E4
Weedin Pk, TDLE	599	G5
Wellington Pk, PTLD	597	D1
Wennerberg Pk, YmhC	741	A1

Portland Points of Interest Index

FEATURE NAME / Address City ZIP Code	MAP#	GRID
West Bridge Pk, WLIN	687	C7
Westlake Pk, LKOW	655	J5
Westmoreland Pk, PTLD	626	J6
West Powellhurst Pk, PTLD	628	A2
Westridge Pk, LKOW	686	B2
West Slope Pk, WasC	625	G1
West Sylvan Pk, BRTN	625	F1
West Union Estates Pk, WasC	564	G7
Westvale Pk, MCMV	770	E5
Whipple Creek Pk, ClkC	476	D3
Whispering Woods Pk, WasC	594	D7
White Fox Pk, WasC	594	H3
Wichita Pk, MWKE	657	D2
Wildhorse Mini Pk, BRTN	654	J1
Wildwood Mini Pk, BRTN	624	J7
Wilkes Pk, PTLD	598	D2
Willamette Greenway State Pk, YmhC	744	A6
Willamette Pk, PTLD	626	F5
Willamette Pk, WLIN	716	H3
Willamette Stone State Heritage Site, PTLD	595	J5
William Pk, WasC	684	H7
Willow Creek Landover Pk, WNVL	715	G6
Willow Creek Nature Pk, BRTN	594	G4
Willow Creek Pk, WasC	594	E6
Willow Pk, BRTN	624	J2
Willsada Pk, CmsC	688	E4
Wilshire Pk, PTLD	597	A1
Wilsonville Memorial Pk, WNVL	745	F1
Wintler Pk, VCVR	537	D7
Woldwood Pk, VCVR	568	B2
Wonderland Pk, BRTN	625	C5
Woodale Pk, TDLE	599	D6
Woodard Pk, TGRD	655	D4
Woodlawn Pk & Swim Pool, PTLD	566	H5
Woods Memorial Pk, PTLD	626	A7
Woodstock Pk, PTLD	627	C4
Wortman Pk, MCMV	771	A3
Wy'East Pk, VCVR	538	B7
Yakolt Burn State Forest, ClkC	419	D6
Yamhill Landing State Pk, YmhC	772	D4
Yamhill Neighborhood Pk, GSHM	598	H7
Zimmerman Historic Pk, GSHM	598	F2

Post Offices

FEATURE NAME / Address City ZIP Code	MAP#	GRID
Aurora 14682 Ottoway Rd NE, AURA, 97002	775	E5
Banks 135 NW Oak Wy, BNKS, 97106	531	J6
Battle Ground 418 W Main St, BGND, 98604	448	B5
Beaver Creek 16101 S Leland Rd, CmsC, 97004	747	J3
Beaverton 4550 SW Betts Av, BRTN, 97005	625	B3
Beaverton-Aloha 3800 SW 185th Av, WasC, 97007	624	E2
Beaverton-Evergreen 3685 NW Aloclek Pl, HBRO, 97124	594	C1
Boring 28515 SE Clackamas-Boring Rd, CmsC, 97009	659	H4
Brush Prairie 12012 NE 150th Cir, ClkC, 98606	478	A5
Camas 440 NE 5th Av, CMAS, 98607	569	E4
Canby 615 NW 2nd Av, CNBY, 97013	746	B6
Carlton 438 W Main St, CLTN, 97111	711	A7
Cascade Park 304 SE Hearthwood Blvd, VCVR, 98684	538	C6
Clackamas 9009 SE Adams St, CmsC, 97015	657	G7
Columbia City 1905 2nd St, CBAC, 97018	385	C3
Cornelius 1639 E Baseline St, CNLS, 97113	592	E5
Dayton 530 SE Ferry St, DAYT, 97114	772	A4
Donald 10751 Donald Rd NE, DNLD, 97020	774	G4
Dundee 279 SW 5th St, DNDE, 97115	742	H3
Eagle Creek 24200 SE Eagle Creek Rd, CmsC, 97022	720	A2
Estacada 205 SW 2nd Av, ECDA, 97023	750	B3
Fairview 1700 NE Market Dr, FRVW, 97024	599	B5
Forest Grove 1822 21st Av, FTGV, 97116	591	H4
Gladstone 605 Portland Av, GLDS, 97027	687	D4
Gresham 103 W Powell Blvd, GSHM, 97080	629	B2
Hillsboro 125 S 1st Av, HBRO, 97123	593	B6
Lafayette 491 SE 3rd St, LFYT, 97127	771	G1
Lake Oswego 501 4th St, LKOW, 97034	656	F5
Lake Oswego 15875 Lower Boones Ferry Rd, LKOW, 97035	656	A7
Lents 8100 SE Crystal Springs Blvd, PTLD, 97206	627	F7
Lents 3850 SE 82nd Av, PTLD, 97266	627	F3
Marylhurst 17600 Pacific Hwy, LKOW, 97034	686	H2
McMinnville 650 NE 2nd St, MCMV, 97128	770	H5
Milwaukie 11222 SE Main St, MWKE, 97222	656	J3
Molalla 215 Robbins St, MOLA, 97038	837	E1
Newberg 401 E 1st St, NWBG, 97132	713	C7
North Plains 31700 NW Commercial St, NPNS, 97133	563	A1
Oak Grove 3860 SE Naef Rd, CmsC, 97267	687	A1
Orchards 11909 NE 65th St, ClkC, 98682	507	J6
Oregon City 19300 Molalla Av, ORCY, 97045	717	E4
Parkrose Station 4048 NE 122nd Av, PTLD, 97230	598	A2
Portland 5010 SE Foster Rd, PTLD, 97206	627	C2
Portland-Brooklyn 1410 SE Powell Blvd, PTLD, 97202	626	H2
Portland-Central 204 SW 5th Av, PTLD, 97204	596	F6
Portland-Cherry Blossom 10445 SE Cherry Blossom Dr, PTLD, 97216	597	J7
Portland-East Portland 1020 SE 7th Av, PTLD, 97214	596	H6
Portland-Forest Park 1706 NW 24th Av, PTLD, 97210	596	C4
Portland-Holladay Park 815 NE Schuyler St, PTLD, 97212	596	H4
Portland-Kenton 2130 N Kilpatrick St, PTLD, 97217	566	E4
Portland-Midway 400 SE 103rd Dr, PTLD, 97216	597	H6
Portland-Multnomah 7805 SW 40th Av, PTLD, 97219	626	A6
Portland-Piedmont 630 NE Killingsworth St, PTLD, 97211	566	H7
Portland-Rose City Park 2425 NE 50th Av, PTLD, 97213	597	C3
Portland-Saint Johns 8420 N Ivanhoe St, PTLD, 97203	565	H3
Portland-Sellwood 6723 SE 16th Av, PTLD, 97202	626	H5
Portland-Tigard 12210 SW Main St, TGRD, 97223	655	E4
Portland-University 1505 SW 6th Av, PTLD, 97201	596	E7
Portland-West Slope 3225 SW 87th Av, BRTN, 97225	625	F2
Ridgefield 205 N Main Av, RDGF, 98642	415	J7
St. Helens 1571 Columbia Blvd, STHN, 97051	385	C7
Saint Paul 20180 Main St NE, STPL, 97137	773	B6
Sandy 17570 Wolf Dr, SNDY, 97055	691	A3
Scappoose 52643 Columbia River Hwy, SPSE, 97056	444	E7
Sherwood Main 16300 SW Langer Dr, SRWD, 97140	684	G5
Troutdale 647 SW Cherry Park Rd, TDLE, 97060	599	F5
Tualatin 19190 SW 90th Av, TLTN, 97062	685	E4
Vancouver 1211 Daniels St, VCVR, 98660	536	F4
Vancouver 2700 Caples Av, VCVR, 98661	537	B3
Washougal 129 17th St, WHGL, 98671	570	A6
West Linn 5665 Hood St, WLIN, 97068	687	B6
Wilsonville 29333 SW Town Center Lp E, WNVL, 97070	715	F7
Woodland 190 Bozarth Av, WDLD, 98674	385	J2

Schools

FEATURE NAME / Address City ZIP Code	MAP#	GRID
Abernethy Elementary School 2421 SE Orange Av, PTLD, 97214	626	H1
Ackerman Middle School 350 SE 13th Av, CNBY, 97013	776	D1
Ackerman Middle School (Lee Campus) 350 SE 13th Av, CNBY, 97013	746	D7
Agape Christian School 18380 SW Kinnaman Rd, WasC, 97007	624	E3
Ainsworth Elementary School 2425 SW Vista Av, PTLD, 97201	596	C7
Alameda Elementary School 2732 NE Fremont St, PTLD, 97212	597	A2
Alder Creek Middle School 13801 SE Webster Rd, CmsC, 97267	657	D5
Alder Elementary School 17200 SE Alder St, PTLD, 97233	598	F7
Alice Ott Middle School 12500 SE Ramona St, PTLD, 97236	628	A5
Alki Middle School 1800 NW Bliss Rd, ClkC, 98685	476	E6
All Saints School 601 NE 39th Av, PTLD, 97232	597	B5
Aloha High School 18550 SW Kinnaman Rd, WasC, 97007	624	E3
Aloha Park Elementary School 17770 SW Blanton St, WasC, 97007	624	F2
Anderson Elementary School 2215 NE 104th St, ClkC, 98686	506	J2
Arbor School of Arts & Science 4201 SW Borland Rd, CmsC, 97062	686	A5
Archbishop Howard School 5309 NE Alameda St, PTLD, 97213	597	C3
Archer Glen Elementary School 16155 SW Sunset Blvd, SRWD, 97140	714	G1
Ardenwald Elementary School 8950 SE 36th Av, MWKE, 97222	627	A7
Arleta Elementary School 5109 SE 66th Av, PTLD, 97206	627	D4
Arts-Communnication Magnet Academy 11375 SW Center St, BRTN, 97005	625	C2
Astor Elementary School 5601 N Yale St, PTLD, 97203	565	A5
Athey Creek Middle School 2900 Sw Borland Rd, CmsC, 97062	686	B5
Atkinson Elementary School 5800 SE Division St, PTLD, 97206	627	D1
Ball Elementary School 4221 N Willis Blvd, PTLD, 97203	566	C4
Banks Elementary School 42350 NW Trellis Way, BNKS, 97106	531	J6
Banks High School 450 S Main St, BNKS, 97106	531	J5
Banks Junior High School 450 S Main St, BNKS, 97106	531	J5
Barlow High School 5105 SE 302nd Av, MthC, 97080	630	A4
Barnes Elementary School 13730 SW Walker Rd, WasC, 97005	595	A7
Battle Ground High School 416 W Main St, BGND, 98604	448	A5
Beach Elementary School 1710 N Humboldt St, PTLD, 97217	566	E7
Beaumont Middle School 4043 NE Fremont St, PTLD, 97212	597	B2
Beaver Acres Elementary School 2125 SW 170th Av, WasC, 97006	594	G7
Beavercreek Elementary School 21944 S Yeoman Rd, CmsC, 97004	748	B3
Beaverton High School 13000 SW 2nd St, BRTN, 97005	625	A3
Belmont Academy 3841 SE Belmont St, PTLD, 97214	597	B6
Benson Polytechnic High School 546 NE 12th Av, PTLD, 97232	596	H5
Bethany Elementary School 3305 NW 174th Av, WasC, 97229	594	F2
Bethel Christian School 501 NW Baker Creek Rd, MCMV, 97128	770	G3
Bilquist Elementary School 15708 SW Webster Rd, CmsC, 97267	657	E7
Binnsmead Middle School 2225 SE 87th Av, PTLD, 97216	627	G1
Boeckman Creek Primary School 6700 SW Wilsonville Rd, WNVL, 97070	715	G7
Boise-Eliot Elementary School 620 N Fremont St, PTLD, 97227	596	F2
Bolton Primary School 5933 Holmes St, WLIN, 97068	687	B6
Boones Ferry Primary School 11495 SW Wilsonville Rd, CmsC, 97070	745	B1
Boring Middle School 27801 SE Dee St, CmsC, 97009	659	H5
Bridgeport Elementary School 5505 SW Borland Rd, TLTN, 97062	685	J4
Bridger Elementary School 7910 SE Market St, PTLD, 97215	597	F7
Bridlemile Elementary School 4300 SW 47th Dr, PTLD, 97221	626	A2
Brookwood Elementary School 3960 SE Cedar St, HBRO, 97123	593	G6
Brown Middle School 1505 SW Cornelius Pass Rd, HBRO, 97123	594	B7
Bryant Elementary School 4750 Jean Rd, LKOW, 97035	685	J2
Buckman Elementary School 320 SE 16th Av, PTLD, 97214	596	H6
Burnt Bridge Creek Elementary School 14619 NE 49th St # A, VCVR, 98682	538	C1
Burton Elementary School 14015 NE 28th St, VCVR, 98684	538	C3
Butler Creek Elementary School 2789 SW Butler Rd, GSHM, 97080	628	J6
Butternut Creek Elementary School 20395 SW Florence St, WasC, 97007	624	C3
Byrom Elementary School 21800 SW 91st Av, TLTN, 97062	685	E6
Camas High School 26900 SE 15th St, ClkC, 98607	569	F1
Campbell Elementary School 11326 SE 47th Av, MWKE, 97222	657	B3
Canby High School 721 SW 4th Av, CNBY, 97013	746	C7
Candy Lane Elementary School 5901 SE Hull Av, CmsC, 97267	687	C3
Capitol Hill Elementary School 8401 SW 17th Av, PTLD, 97219	626	D6
Captain Strong Elementary School 1002 NW 6th Av, BGND, 98604	448	B4
Carlton Elementary School 420 S 3rd St, CLTN, 97111	741	B1
Carus Elementary School 14412 S Carus Rd, CmsC, 97045	747	F5
Cascade Middle School 13900 NE 18th St, VCVR, 98684	538	B4
Cascadia Montessori School 10606 NE 14th St, VCVR, 98664	537	H5
Cathedral Elementary School 110 NW 17th Av, PTLD, 97209	596	E5
Catlin Gabel School 8825 SW Barnes Rd, WasC, 97225	595	F7
Cedar Mill Elementary School 10265 NW Cornell Rd, WasC, 97229	595	D5
Cedaroak Park Primary School 4515 Cedar Oak Dr, WLIN, 97068	686	J3
Cedar Park Middle School 11100 SW Park Way, BRTN, 97225	595	D7
Cedar Ridge Middle School 17225 Smith Av, SNDY, 97055	691	A3
Cedar Tree Christian School 5201 NE Minnehaha, ClkC, 98661	507	C7
Cedarwood Waldorf School 3030 SW 2nd Av, PTLD, 97201	626	E1
Centennial High School 3505 SE 182nd Av, GSHM, 97030	628	G2
Centennial Middle School 17650 SE Brooklyn St, GSHM, 97236	628	G2
Center Advanced Learning Charter School 1484 NW Civic Dr, GSHM, 97030	629	B1
Central Catholic High School 2401 SE Stark St, PTLD, 97214	596	J6
Century High School 2000 SE Century Blvd, HBRO, 97123	593	J7
Chapman Elementary School 1445 NW 26th Av, PTLD, 97210	596	C4
Chehalem Elementary School 15555 SW Davis Rd, BRTN, 97007	624	H4
Chehalem Valley Middle School 403 W Foothills Dr, NWBG, 97132	713	B4
Cherry Park Elementary School 1930 SE 104th Av, PTLD, 97216	627	H1
Chief Joseph Elementary School 2409 N Saratoga St, PTLD, 97217	566	D5
Chief Umtuch Primary School 700 NW 9th St, BGND, 98604	448	B4
Childpeace Montessori School 1516 NW Thurman St, PTLD, 97209	596	E4
Chinook Elementary School 1900 NW Bliss Rd, ClkC, 98685	476	E6
Christ the King School 7414 SE Michael Dr, CmsC, 97222	657	E3
City Christian School 9200 NE Fremont St, PTLD, 97220	597	G2
Clackamas Elementary School 15301 SE 92nd Av, CmsC, 97015	657	G7
Clackamas High School 14486 SE 122nd Av, CmsC, 97015	658	A6
Clackamas River Elementary School 301 NE 2nd Av, ECDA, 97023	750	B3
Clackamas Web Academy 4444 SE Lake Rd, MWKE, 97222	657	B4
Clarendon Elementary School 9325 N Van Houten Av, PTLD, 97203	566	A3
Clark Elementary School 1231 SE 92nd Av, PTLD, 97216	597	G7
Class Academy 2730 NW Vaughn St, PTLD, 97210	596	C3
Clear Creek Middle School 219 NE 219th Av, GSHM, 97030	599	B6
Cleveland High School 3400 SE 26th Av, PTLD, 97202	626	J2
Columbia Adventist Academy 11100 NE 189th St, ClkC, 98604	477	H1
Columbia Christian Schools 413 NE 91st Av, PTLD, 97220	597	G5
Columbia City School 2000 2nd St, CBAC, 97018	385	C3
Columbia River High School 800 NW 99th St, ClkC, 98685	506	F3
Columbia Valley Elementary School 17500 SE Sequoia Cir, VCVR, 98683	538	F7
Columbus Elementary School 1600 SW Fellows St, MCMV, 97128	770	F6
Community Christian School 7400 SW Sagert St, TLTN, 97062	685	F5
Concord Elementary School 3811 SE Concord Rd, CmsC, 97267	657	A7
Conestoga Middle School 12250 SW Conestoga Dr, BRTN, 97008	655	B1
Cook Elementary School 800 NE Lafayette Av, MCMV, 97128	770	J5

Portland Points of Interest Index

FEATURE NAME Address City ZIP Code	MAP#	GRID
Cooper Mt Elementary School 7670 SW 170th Av, BRTN, 97007	624	G6
Cornelius Elementary School 200 N 14th Av, CNLS, 97113	592	E4
Cornerstone Christian School 7708 NE 78th St, ClkC, 98662	507	E5
Cottrell Elementary School 36225 SE Proctor Rd, CmsC, 97009	660	G2
Covington Middle School 11200 NE Rosewood Av, ClkC, 98662	507	J7
Crater Elementary School 203 W Foothills Dr, NWBG, 97132	713	B4
Crestline Elementary School 13003 SE 7th St, VCVR, 98683	538	A7
Creston Elementary School 4701 SE Bush St, PTLD, 97206	627	C2
Crossroads Christian School 2505 NE 102nd Av, PTLD, 97220	597	H3
CS Lewis Academy 609 Wynooski St, NWBG, 97132	743	D1
Damascus Christian School 14251 SE Rust Way, DAMA, 97009	658	J6
Damascus Middle School 14151 SE 242nd Av, DAMA, 97009	659	D6
David Douglas High School 1001 SE 135th Av, PTLD, 97233	598	B7
David Hill Elementary School 440 SE Oak St, HBRO, 97123	593	C5
Davis Elementary School 19501 SE Davis St, GSHM, 97230	598	J6
Dayton Grade School 526 Ferry St, DAYT, 97114	772	A4
Dayton High School 801 Ferry St, DAYT, 97114	772	A5
Dayton Junior High School 801 Ferry St, DAYT, 97114	772	A4
Deep Creek Elementary School 15600 SE 232nd Dr, CmsC, 97009	689	C1
Deer Creek Elementary School 16155 SW 131st Av, WasC, 97224	685	A1
De La Salle High School 7654 N Delaware Av, PTLD, 97217	566	D4
Dexter McCarty Middle School 1400 SE 5th St, GSHM, 97080	629	D3
Discovery Middle School 800 E 40th St, VCVR, 98663	536	G2
Dorothy Fox Elementary School 2623 NW Sierra St, CMAS, 98607	569	C3
Dundee Elementary School 140 SW 5th St, DNDE, 97115	742	H3
Duniway Elementary School 7700 Ee Reed College Pl, PTLD, 97202	627	A6
Duniway Middle School 575 NW Michelbook Ln, MCMV, 97128	770	G5
Durham Elementary School 8048 SW Schaeffer Ln, TGRD, 97224	685	F1
Eagle Creek Elementary School 30391 SE Hwy 211, CmsC, 97022	690	A7
Earl Boyles Elementary School 10822 SE Bush St, PTLD, 97266	627	J3
East Gresham Elementary School 900 SE 5th St, GSHM, 97080	629	C3
East Orient Elementary School 7431 SE 302nd Av, MthC, 97080	630	A7
Eastside Christian School 5001 W Powell Blvd, GSHM, 97030	628	F3
East Sylvan Middle School 1849 SW 58th Av, PTLD, 97221	595	J7
Eastwood Elementary School 2100 NE Lincoln St, HBRO, 97124	593	E5
Eccles Elementary School 562 NW 5th Av, CNBY, 97013	746	B6
Echo Shaw Elementary School 914 S Linden St, CNLS, 97113	592	D6
Edwards Elementary School 715 E 8th St, NWBG, 97132	743	C1
Eisenhower Elementary School 9201 NW 9th Av, ClkC, 98665	506	F3
Ellsworth Elementary School 512 SE Ellsworth Rd, VCVR, 98664	537	H7
Elmonica Elementary School 16950 SW Lisa Ct, BRTN, 97006	594	G6
El Puente Magnet School 11250 SE 27th Av, MWKE, 97222	657	A3
Emmaus Christian School 460 S Heather St, CNLS, 97113	592	D5
Environmental Middle School 3421 SE Salmon St, PTLD, 97214	597	A7
Errol Hassell Elementary School 18100 SW Bany Rd, WasC, 97007	624	E6
Estacada High School 355 NE 6th Av, ECDA, 97023	750	B3
Estacada Junior High School 500 NE Main St, ECDA, 97023	750	B3
Evergreen High School 14300 NE 18th St, VCVR, 98684	538	C4
Evergreen Middle School 29850 NW Evergreen Rd, HBRO, 97124	593	C1
Ewing Young Elementary School 17600 NE North Valley Rd, YmhC, 97132	712	D3
Fairview Elementary School 225 Main St, FRVW, 97024	599	B4
Faith Bible Christian School 16860 SW Blanton St, WasC, 97007	624	G2
Faith Bible High School 4435 SE Tualatin Valley Hwy, HBRO, 97123	623	G1
Farmington View Elementary School 8300 SW Hillsboro Hwy, WasC, 97123	623	B6
Faubion Elementary School 3039 NE Portland Blvd, PTLD, 97211	567	A6
Felida Elementary School 2700 NW 119th St, ClkC, 98685	506	D1
Fern Hill Elementary School 4445 Heather St, FTGV, 97116	592	C5
Fernwood Middle School 1915 NE 33rd Av, PTLD, 97212	597	A4
Findley Elementary School 4155 NW Saltzman Rd, WasC, 97229	595	B1
Fircrest Elementary School 12001 NE 9th St, VCVR, 98684	537	J5
Fir Grove Elementary School 6300 SW Wilson Av, BRTN, 97008	625	A5
Firm Foundation Christian School 19919 NE 107th Av, ClkC, 98604	447	J7
First Baptist Church School 1905 N Maple St, CNBY, 97013	746	C4
Firwood Elementary School 42900 SE Trubel Rd, CmsC, 97055	691	D6
Fisher's Landing Elementary School 3800 SE Hiddenbrook Dr, VCVR, 98683	568	F3
Five Oaks Middle School 1600 NW 173rd Av, BRTN, 97006	594	G4
Floyd Light Middle School 10800 SE Washington St, PTLD, 97216	597	J6
Forest Grove High School 1401 Nichols Ln, FTGV, 97116	591	H2
Forest Hills Elementary School 1133 Andrews Rd, LKOW, 97034	656	E5
Forest Park Elementary School 9935 NW Durrett St, PTLD, 97229	595	E2
Fort Vancouver High School 5700 E 18th St, VCVR, 98661	537	C4
Fowler Middle School 10865 SW Walnut St, TGRD, 97223	655	D4
Franciscan Mont Earth School 14750 SE Clinton St, PTLD, 97236	628	D2
Franklin Elementary School 5206 NW Franklin St, VCVR, 98663	506	F7
Franklin High School 5405 SE Woodward St, PTLD, 97206	627	C1
French-American School 8500 NW Johnson St, PTLD, 97229	595	F4
Frontier Middle School 7600 NE 166th Av, ClkC, 98682	508	E5
Full Circle Countryside School 16077 SE Highway 224, DAMA, 97009	688	E2
Gaarde Christian School 11265 SW Gaarde St, TGRD, 97224	655	C5
Gaffney Lane Elementary School 13521 Gaffney Ln, ORCY, 97045	717	D5
Gaiser Middle School 3000 NE 99th St, ClkC, 98665	507	A3
Gardiner Middle School 180 Ethel St, ORCY, 97045	717	C3
Gardner School 16413 NE 50th Av, ClkC, 98686	477	C4
Gause Elementary School 1100 34th St, WHGL, 98671	570	C5
George Middle School 10000 N Burr Av, PTLD, 97203	565	J2
Gilbert Heights Elementary School 12839 SE Holgate Blvd, PTLD, 97236	628	B3
Gilbert Park Elementary School 13132 SE Ramona St, PTLD, 97236	628	B5
Gladstone High School 18800 Portland Av, GLDS, 97027	687	D3
Glencoe Elementary School 825 SE 51st Av, PTLD, 97215	597	C6
Glencoe High School 2700 NW Glencoe Rd, HBRO, 97124	593	B2
Glenfair Elementary School 15300 NE Glisan St, PTLD, 97230	598	D5
Glenwood Heights Primary School 9716 NE 134th St, ClkC, 98662	477	H7
Good Shepherd School 28986 SE Haley Rd, CmsC, 97009	659	J3
Gordon Russell Middle School 3625 SE Powell Valley Rd, GSHM, 97080	629	F3
Grace Christian School 6460 Glen Echo Av, GLDS, 97027	687	D3
Grandhaven Elementary School 3200 NE McDonald Ln, MCMV, 97128	770	J2
Grandview Christian Academy 14855 S Leland Rd, CmsC, 97004	747	G3
Grant High School 2245 NE 36th Av, PTLD, 97212	597	A3
Grant Watts Elementary School 52000 SE 3rd Pl, SPSE, 97056	474	F2
Gray Middle School 5505 SW 23rd Av, PTLD, 97239	626	C4
Greenway Elementary School 9150 SW Downing Dr, BRTN, 97008	655	B1
Gregory Heights Middle School 7334 NE Siskiyou St, PTLD, 97213	597	E3
Gresham High School 1200 N Main Av, GSHM, 97030	629	C1
Groner Elementary School 23405 SW Scholls Ferry Rd, WasC, 97123	653	J5
Grout Elementary School 3119 SE Holgate Blvd, PTLD, 97202	627	A3
Hall Elementary School 2505 NE 23rd St, GSHM, 97030	599	E7
Hallinan Elementary School 16800 Hawthorne Dr, LKOW, 97034	686	F1
Happy Valley Elementary School 13865 SE King Rd, HPYV, 97236	658	C2
Harmony Elementary School 17404a NE 18th St, ClkC, 98684	538	F4
Harney Elementary School 3212 E Evergreen Blvd, VCVR, 98661	537	A5
Harold Oliver Intr School 15840 SE Taylor St, PTLD, 97233	598	E7
Harold Oliver Primary School 15811 SE Main St, PTLD, 97233	598	E7
Hartley Elementary School 701 NE 185th Pl, GSHM, 97230	598	H5
Harvey Clarke Elementary School 2516 B St, FTGV, 97116	591	H4
Hathaway Elementary School 630 24th St, WHGL, 98671	570	B5
Hayhurst Elementary School 5037 SW Iowa St, PTLD, 97221	626	A4
Hazelbrook Middle School 11300 SE Hazelbrook Rd, TLTN, 97062	685	C2
Hazeldale Elementary School 20080 SW Farmington Rd, WasC, 97007	624	C5
Hazel Dell Elementary School 511 NE Anderson St, ClkC, 98665	506	G6
HB Lee Middle School 1121 NE 172nd Av, GSHM, 97230	598	F5
Hearthwood Elementary School 801 NE Hearthwood Blvd, VCVR, 98684	538	C5
Helen Baller Elementary School 1954 NE Garfield St, CMAS, 98607	569	F3
Heritage Christian School 1679 SE Enterprise Cir, HBRO, 97123	593	D7
Heritage High School 7825 NE 130th Av, ClkC, 98682	508	B5
Highland Elementary School 295 NE 24th St, GSHM, 97030	599	C7
Highland Park Middle School 7000 SW Wilson Av, BRTN, 97008	625	A5
Hillsboro High School (Hilhi) 3285 SE Rood Bridge Rd, HBRO, 97123	623	F1
Hilltop Christian School 5700 SW Dosch Rd, PTLD, 97239	626	C4
Hiteon Elementary School 13800 SW Brockman Rd, BRTN, 97008	625	A7
Hockinson Heights Int'l School 19912 NE 164th St, ClkC, 98606	478	J4
Hockinson Heights Primary School 20000 NE 164th St, ClkC, 98606	478	J4
Hockinson High School 16819 NE 159th St, ClkC, 98606	478	E4
Hockinson Middle School 15916 NE 182nd Av, ClkC, 98606	478	G4
Hogan Cedars Elementary School 1770 SE Fleming Av, GSHM, 97080	629	E4
Holcomb Elementary School 14625 Holcomb Blvd, ORCY, 97045	687	G5
Hollydale Elementary School 505 SW Birdsdale Dr, GSHM, 97080	628	J3
Hollyrood Elementary School 3560 NE Hollyrood Ct, PTLD, 97212	597	B3
Holy Cross Area School 5202 N Bowdoin St, PTLD, 97203	566	B4
Holy Family School 7425 SE 39th Av, PTLD, 97202	627	B6
Holy Redeemer School 127 N Portland Blvd, PTLD, 97217	566	G6
Holy Trinity School 13755 SW Walker Rd, WasC, 97005	595	A7
Hood View Junior Academy 26505 SE Kelso Rd, CmsC, 97009	659	F6
Hosanna Christian School 4120 NE St Johns Rd, VCVR, 98663	537	A2
Hosford Middle School 2303 SE 28th Pl, PTLD, 97214	626	J1
Hough Elementary School 1900 Daniels St, VCVR, 98660	536	F4
Hudson's Bay High School 1206 E Reserve St, VCVR, 98663	536	H5
Humboldt Elementary School 4915 N Gantenbein Av, PTLD, 97217	566	G7
Illahee Elementary School 19401 SE 1st St, VCVR, 98607	538	H6
Image Elementary School 4400 NE 122nd Av, VCVR, 98682	538	A2
Imlay Elementary School 5900 SE Lois St, HBRO, 97123	593	J6
Indian Hills Elementary School 21260 SW Rock Rd, WasC, 97006	594	B7
International School 25 SW Sherman St, PTLD, 97201	626	F1
Inza R Wood Middle School 11055 SW Wilsonville Rd, WNVL, 97070	745	C1
Irvington Elementary School 1320 NE Brazee St, PTLD, 97212	596	H3
Islamic School of MET 10330 SW Scholls Ferry Rd, TGRD, 97223	655	C2
Jackson Elementary School 675 NE Estate Dr, HBRO, 97124	593	C2
Jackson Middle School 10625 SW 35th Av, PTLD, 97219	656	B1
Jacob Wismer Elementary School 5477 NW Skycrest Pkwy, WasC, 97229	565	A7
James John Elementary School 7439 N Charleston Av, PTLD, 97203	565	H3
Jason Lee Middle School 8500 NW 9th Av, ClkC, 98665	506	F4
JC Hopkins Elementary School 21920 SW Sherwood Blvd, SRWD, 97140	684	G6
Jefferson High School 5210 N Kerby Av, PTLD, 97217	566	F7
Jemtegaard Middle School 35300 SE Evergreen Blvd, ClkC, 98671	570	E6
Jennings Lodge Elementary School 18521 SE River Rd, CmsC, 97267	687	B3
Jesuit High School 9000 SW Beaverton Hillsdale Hw, BRTN, 97225	625	F3
Joan Austin Elementary Mountainview Dr, NWBG, 97132	713	D5
John Wetten Elementary School 250 E Exeter St, GLDS, 97027	687	D4
Joseph Gale Elementary School 3130 18th Av, FTGV, 97116	592	A5
Joseph Meeks Technical High School 4039 NE Alberta Ct, PTLD, 97211	597	B1
Kellogg Middle School 3330 SE 69th Av, PTLD, 97206	627	E2
Kelly Creek Elementary School 2400 SE Baker Way, GSHM, 97080	629	G5
Kelly Elementary School 9030 SE Cooper St, PTLD, 97266	627	G5
Kelso Elementary School 34651 SE Kelso Rd, CmsC, 97009	660	E7
King Elementary School 995 S End Rd, ORCY, 97045	717	A3
King Elementary School 4906 NE 6th Av, PTLD, 97211	566	H7
King Elementary School 4801 Idaho St, VCVR, 98661	537	C5
Kings Way Christian School 3300 NE 78th St, ClkC, 98665	507	A5
Kinnaman Elementary School 4205 SW 193rd Av, WasC, 97007	624	D2
Knight Elementary School 501 N Grant St, CNBY, 97013	746	C6
Kraxberger Middle School 17777 Webster Rd, GLDS, 97027	687	E2
Lacamas Heights Elementary School 4600 NE Garfield St, CMAS, 98607	569	F1
La Center Elementary School 700 E 4th St, LCTR, 98629	416	H1
La Center Middle School 700 E 4th St, LCTR, 98629	416	H1
Ladd Acres Elementary School 2425 SW Cornelius Pass Rd, HBRO, 97123	624	B1
Lake Grove Elementary School 15777 Boones Ferry Rd, LKOW, 97035	656	A7
Lake Oswego High School 2501 Country Club Rd, LKOW, 97034	656	C5
Lake Oswego Junior High School 2500 Country Club Rd, LKOW, 97034	656	C5
Lakeridge High School 1235 Overlook Dr, LKOW, 97034	686	D2
Lake Shore Elementary School 9300 NW 21st Av, ClkC, 98665	506	E3
Lane Middle School 7200 SE 60th Av, PTLD, 97206	627	D6
La Salle High School 11999 SE Fuller Rd, CmsC, 97222	657	E3
Laurelhurst Elementary School 840 NE 41st Av, PTLD, 97232	597	B5
Laurin Middle School 13601 NE 97th Av, ClkC, 98662	477	H6
Lee Elementary School 2222 NE 92nd Av, PTLD, 97220	597	G4
Lenox Elementary School 21200 NW Rock Creek Blvd, WasC, 97229	564	C7
Lent Elementary School 5105 SE 97th Av, PTLD, 97266	627	H4
Lewelling Elementary School 5325 SE Logus Rd, MWKE, 97222	657	C1
Lewis & Clark Campus 111 S 9th St, STHN, 97051	385	C7
Lewis Elementary School 4401 SE Evergreen St, PTLD, 97206	627	B5
Lewisville Middle School 406 NW 5th Av, BGND, 98604	448	A5
Liberty High School 21945 NW Wagon Way, HBRO, 97124	564	B6
Life Christian School 5585 SW 209th Av, WasC, 97007	624	B4
Lincoln Elementary School 4200 NW Daniels St, VCVR, 98660	536	F2
Lincoln High School 1600 SW Salmon St, PTLD, 97205	596	D6
Lincoln Park Elementary School 13200 SE Lincoln St, PTLD, 97233	628	B1
Linwood Elementary School 11909 SE Linwood Av, MWKE, 97222	657	D3
Llewellyn Elementary School 6301 SE 14th Av, PTLD, 97202	626	H5

Portland Points of Interest Index

FEATURE NAME / Address City ZIP Code	MAP#	GRID
ynch Meadows Elementary School 18009 SE Brooklyn St, GSHM, 97236	628	G2
ynch View Elementary School 1546 SE 169th Pl, PTLD, 97233	598	F7
ynch Wood Elementary School 3615 Ee 174th Av, PTLD, 97236	628	F2
Mabel Rush Elementary School 1441 Deborah Rd, NWBG, 97132	713	E6
Madeleine School 3240 NE 23rd Av, PTLD, 97212	596	J2
Madison High School 2735 NE 82nd Av, PTLD, 97220	597	F3
Maple Grove Middle School 12500 NE 199th St, BGND, 98604	448	B7
Maple Grove Primary School 12500 NE 199th St, BGND, 98604	448	B7
Maplewood Elementary School 7452 SW 52nd Av, PTLD, 97219	625	J5
Markham Elementary School 10531 SW Capitol Hwy, PTLD, 97219	656	A1
Marrion Elementary School 10119 NE 14th St, VCVR, 98664	537	H5
Marshall Elementary School 6400 MacArthur Blvd, VCVR, 98661	537	D6
Marshall High School 3905 SE 91st Av, PTLD, 97266	627	G3
Marysville Elementary School 7733 SE Raymond St, PTLD, 97206	627	F4
Mary Woodward Elementary School 12325 SW Katherine St, TGRD, 97223	655	B3
McBride Elementary School 2774 Columbia Blvd, STHN, 97051	414	J1
McKay Elementary School 7485 SW Scholls Ferry Rd, BRTN, 97008	625	E6
McKinley Elementary School 1500 NW 185th Av, BRTN, 97006	594	E4
McLoughlin Elementary School 19230 S End Rd, ORCY, 97045	717	A4
McLoughlin Middle School 5802 MacArthur Blvd, VCVR, 98661	537	C6
McMinnville High School 615 NE 15th St, MCMV, 97128	770	H4
Meadow Glade School 18717 NE 109th Av, ClkC, 98604	477	J1
Meadow Park Middle School 14100 SW Downing St, WasC, 97006	595	A6
Memorial Elementary School 501 NW 14th St, MCMV, 97128	770	G4
Menlo Park Elementary School 12900 NE Glisan St, PTLD, 97230	598	B5
Metzger Elementary School 10255 SW Lincoln St, TGRD, 97223	655	E2
Middleton Elementary School 23505 SW Old Highway 99w, SRWD, 97140	714	D1
Miller Educ Center-West Campus 215 SE 6th Av, HBRO, 97123	593	C5
Mill Park Elementary School 1900 SW 117th Av, PTLD, 97216	628	A1
Mill Plain Elementary School 400 SE 164th Av, VCVR, 98684	538	E7
Milwaukie Elementary School 11250 SE 27th Av, MWKE, 97222	657	A3
Milwaukie High School 11300 SE 23rd Av, MWKE, 97222	656	J2
Minnehaha Elementary School 2800 NE 54th St, VCVR, 98663	507	A7
Minter Bridge Elementary School 1750 SE Jacquelin Dr, HBRO, 97123	623	E1
MITCH Charter School 19945 SW Boones Ferry Rd, TLTN, 97062	685	E4
MITCH-Sherwood Charter School 950 S Sherwood Blvd, SRWD, 97140	684	G7
Molalla Elementary School 910 Toliver Rd, MOLA, 97038	807	C7
Molalla High School 357 E Francis St, MOLA, 97038	837	F1
Molalla River Middle School 318 Leroy St, MOLA, 97038	837	D1
Montclair Elementary School 7250 SW Vermont St, WasC, 97223	625	G5
Mooberry Elementary School 1230 NE 10th Av, HBRO, 97124	593	D3
Mountain View Christian School 2810 NE 259th St, ClkC, 98642	447	A1
Mountain View High School 1500 SE Blairmont Dr, VCVR, 98683	568	C1
Mountain View Middle School 2015 N Emery Dr, NWBG, 97132	713	E5
Mountain View Middle School 17500 SW Farmington Rd, WasC, 97007	624	F4
Mt Pleasant Elementary School 1232 Linn Av, ORCY, 97045	717	C3
Mount Scott Elementary School 11201 SE Stevens Rd, CmsC, 97236	657	G3
Mount Tabor Middle School 5800 SE Ash St, PTLD, 97215	597	D6
Mulino School 26600 S Highway 213, CmsC, 97042	777	E5
Multisensory Learning Charter Academy 402 NE 172nd Av, GSHM, 97230	598	F5
Naas Elementary School 12240 SE School Av, CmsC, 97009	659	G4
Nancy Ryles Elementary School 10250 SW Cormorant Dr, BRTN, 97007	654	G2
N Clackamas Christian School 19575 Sebastian Way, CmsC, 97045	717	E5
Neil Armstrong Middle School 1777 Mountain View Ln, FTGV, 97116	592	C5
Newberg High School 2400 Douglas Av, NWBG, 97132	713	E6
Newby Elementary School 1125 NW 2nd St, MCMV, 97128	770	G5
New Generation Christian School 10702 NE 117th Av, ClkC, 98662	507	J2
New Urban Charter High School 14450 SE Johnson Rd, CmsC, 97267	657	E6
North Gresham Elementary School 1001 SE 217th Av, GSHM, 97030	599	B7
North Marion High School 20167 Grim Rd Ne, MrnC, 97002	775	A6
North Marion Intr School 20237 Grim Rd Ne, MrnC, 97002	775	B6
North Marion Middle School 20246 Grim Rd Ne, MrnC, 97002	775	B6
North Marion Primary School 20257 Grim Rd Ne, MrnC, 97002	775	B6
North Plains Elementary School 32030 NW North Av, NPNS, 97133	533	A7
Oak Creek Elementary School 55 Kingsgate Rd, LKOW, 97035	655	J4
Oak Grove Elementary School 2150 SE Torbank Rd, CmsC, 97222	656	J5
Oak Hills Elementary School 2625 NW 153rd Av, WasC, 97006	594	H3
Ockley Green Middle School 6031 N Montana Av, PTLD, 97217	566	F6
Ogden Elementary School 8100 NE 28th St, VCVR, 98662	537	E3
Ogden Middle School 14133 Donovan Rd, CmsC, 97045	717	F1
Open Bible Christian School 1605 N College St, NWBG, 97132	713	C6
Open Door Christian Academy 27710 SE Strebin Rd, MthC, 97060	629	H1
Open Meadow Alternative School 7602 N Emerald Av, PTLD, 97217	566	D5
Orchards Elementary School 7000 NE 117th Av, ClkC, 98662	507	J6
Oregon City High School 19761 Beavercreek Rd, ORCY, 97045	717	G5
Oregon Episcopal School 6300 SW Nicol Rd, WasC, 97223	625	G5
Oregon Trail Elementary School 13895 SE 152nd Av, CmsC, 97015	658	D6
Orenco Elementary School 22550 NW Birch St, HBRO, 97124	594	A4
Our Lady of Lourdes School 4701 NW Franklin St, VCVR, 98663	536	F1
Our Lady of the Lake School 716 A Av, LKOW, 97034	656	F6
Our Lady of Sorrows School 5239 SE Woodstock Blvd, PTLD, 97206	627	C5
Pacific Crest Academy 324 NE Oak St, CMAS, 98607	569	F4
Pacific Crest Community School 116 NE 29th Av, PTLD, 97232	597	A5
Pacific Middle School 2017 NE 172nd Av, ClkC, 98684	538	F4
Palisades Elementary School 1500 Greentree Av, LKOW, 97034	686	D1
Park Place Elementary School 16075 Front St, ORCY, 97045	687	F5
Parkrose High School 12003 NE Shaver St, PTLD, 97220	598	A2
Parkrose Middle School 11800 NE Shaver St, PTLD, 97220	598	A2
Patton Middle School 1175 NE 19th St, MCMV, 97128	770	J3
Paul L Patterson Elementary School 261 NE Lenox St, HBRO, 97124	593	B1
Peninsula Elementary School 8125 N Emerald Av, PTLD, 97217	566	D4
Peter Boscow Elementary School 452 NE 3rd Av, HBRO, 97124	593	C4
Petersen Elementary School 52181 SW Em Watts Rd, ClbC, 97056	474	D1
Phonics Phactory School 2229 NE Burnside Rd # 283, GSHM, 97030	629	E2
Pilgrim Lutheran School 5650 SW Hall Blvd, BRTN, 97005	625	B4
Pioneer Elementary School 7212 NE 166th Av, ClkC, 98682	508	E6
Pleasant Valley Elementary School 17625 SE Foster Rd, MthC, 97236	628	G7
Pleasant Valley Middle School 14320 NE 50th Av, ClkC, 98686	477	C5
Pleasant Valley Primary School 14320 NE 50th Av, ClkC, 98686	477	C5
Portland Adventist Academy 1500 SE 96th Av, PTLD, 97216	597	H7
Portland Adventist Elementary School 3990 NW 1st St, GSHM, 97030	628	G2
Portland Christian Elementary School 11845 SE Market St, PTLD, 97216	598	A7
Portland Christian High School 12425 NE San Rafael St, PTLD, 97230	598	A4
Portland Christian School-Vancouver 7915 NE Burton Rd, VCVR, 98664	537	E3
Portland Evening High School 546 NE 12th Av, PTLD, 97232	596	H5
Portland French School 6318 SW Corbett Av, PTLD, 97239	626	F4
Portland Jewish Academy 6651 SW Capitol Hwy, PTLD, 97239	626	C5
Portland Lutheran School 740 SE 182nd Av, GSHM, 97233	598	G6
Portland Night High School 2245 NE 36th Av, PTLD, 97212	597	B3
Portsmouth Middle School 5103 N Willis Blvd, PTLD, 97203	566	B4
Powell Valley Elementary School 4825 SE Powell Valley Rd, GSHM, 97080	629	G4
Poynter Middle School 1535 NE Grant St, HBRO, 97124	593	E4
Prescott Elementary School 10410 NE Prescott St, PTLD, 97220	597	J1
Prune Hill Elementary School 1601 NW Tidland St, CMAS, 98607	569	A3
Raleigh Hills Elementary School 5225 SW Scholls Ferry Rd, WasC, 97225	625	G4
Raleigh Park Elementary School 3670 SW 78th Av, WasC, 97225	625	G2
Redland School 18131 S Redland Rd, CmsC, 97045	718	E3
Reedville Elementary School 2695 SW 209th Av, WasC, 97006	624	C1
Rex Putnam High School 4950 SE Roethe Rd, CmsC, 97267	687	C1
Reynolds Arthur Charter Academy 123 SW 21st St, TDLE, 97060	599	G6
Reynolds High School 1698 SW Cherry Park Rd, TDLE, 97060	599	E5
Reynolds Middle School 1200 NE 201st Av, FRVW, 97024	598	J5
Richmond Elementary School 2276 SE 41st Av, PTLD, 97214	627	B1
Ridgefield High School 2630 S Hillhurst Rd, RDGF, 98642	446	B2
Ridgewood Elementary School 10100 SW Inglewood St, WasC, 97225	625	E1
Rieke Elementary School 1405 SW Vermont St, PTLD, 97219	626	D5
Rigler Elementary School 5401 NE Prescott St, PTLD, 97218	597	D1
Riverdale Grade School 11733 SW Breyman Av, MthC, 97219	656	G3
Riverdale High School 9727 SW Terwilliger Blvd, PTLD, 97219	656	E1
Rivergate SDA Elementary School 1505 Ohlson Rd, GLDS, 97027	687	F3
River Grove Elementary School 5850 McEwan Rd, LKOW, 97035	685	H3
River Mill Elementary School 850 N Broadway St, ECDA, 97023	750	B2
Riverside Elementary School 16303 SE River Rd, CmsC, 97267	686	J1
Riverview Elementary School 12601 SE Riverridge Dr, VCVR, 98683	568	A1
Rock Creek Elementary School 4125 NW 185th Av, WasC, 97229	594	E1
Ron Russell Middle School 3955 SE 112th Av, PTLD, 97266	627	J3
Roosevelt Elementary School 2921 Falk Rd, VCVR, 98661	537	B3
Roosevelt High School 6941 N Central St, PTLD, 97203	565	J3
Rose City Park Elementary School 2334 NE 57th Av, PTLD, 97213	597	D3
Rosemont Ridge Middle School 20001 S Salamo Rd, WLIN, 97068	686	H6
Rowe Middle School 3606 SE Lake Rd, MWKE, 97222	657	A4
Russell Academy 2700 NE 127th Av, PTLD, 97230	598	B3
Sabin Elementary School 4013 NE 18th Av, PTLD, 97212	596	J1
Sabin-Schellenberg Center 14211 Johnson Rd, CmsC, 97267	657	F6
Sacajawea Elementary School 700 NE 112th St, ClkC, 98685	506	H2
Sacramento Elementary School 11400 NE Sacramento St, PTLD, 97220	598	A3
St. Agatha School 7960 SE 15th Av, PTLD, 97202	626	H6
St. Andrew Nativity School 4925 NE 9th Av, PTLD, 97211	566	H7
St. Anthony School 12645 SW Pacific Hwy, TGRD, 97223	655	E4
St. Cecilia School 12250 SW 5th St, BRTN, 97005	625	B4
St. Clare School 1807 SW Freeman St, PTLD, 97219	626	D7
St. Francis of Assisi School 39085 NW Harrington Rd, WasC, 97106	562	C1
St. Francis School 410 NE Oregon St, SRWD, 97140	684	G7
St. Helens High School 2375 Gable Rd, STHN, 97051	415	A2
St. Helens Middle School 345 N 15th St, STHN, 97051	385	C7
St. Ignatius School 3330 SE 43rd Av, PTLD, 97206	627	B2
St. James School 206 NE Kirby St, MCMV, 97128	770	J5
St. John Fisher School 7101 SW 46th Av, PTLD, 97219	626	A5
St. John the Apostle School 516 5th St, ORCY, 97045	717	C1
St. John the Baptist School 10956 SE 25th Av, MWKE, 97222	656	J2
St. Joseph School-Vancouver 6500 Highland Dr, VCVR, 98661	537	D6
St. Mary of the Valley School 4440 SW 148th Av, BRTN, 97007	624	J3
St. Mary's Academy 1615 SW 5th Av, PTLD, 97201	596	E7
St. Matthew School 221 SE Walnut St, HBRO, 97123	593	C5
Saint Paul Elementary School 20449 Main St Ne, STPL, 97137	773	C5
Saint Paul High School 20449 Main St Ne, STPL, 97137	773	B5
St. Paul Lutheran School 17500 SW Cedarview Way, SRWD, 97140	684	F5
St. Paul Parochial School 20327 Christie St Ne, STPL, 97137	773	B5
St. Pius X School 1260 NW Saltzman Rd, WasC, 97229	595	B4
St. Therese School 1260 NE 132nd Av, PTLD, 97230	598	B4
St. Thomas More School 3521 SW Patton Rd, PTLD, 97221	626	B1
Salish Ponds Elementary School 1210 NE 201st Av, FRVW, 97024	598	J5
Salmon Creek Elementary School 1601 NE 129th St, ClkC, 98685	476	J7
Sandy Grade School 38955 Pleasant Av, SNDY, 97055	691	A3
Sandy High School 17100 SE Bluff Rd, SNDY, 97055	690	J3
Sauvie Island Elementary School 14445 NW Charlton Rd, MthC, 97231	535	A1
Scappoose High School 33700 High School Way, SPSE, 97056	474	E2
Scappoose Middle School 52265 Columbia River Hwy, SPSE, 97056	474	E1
Schellenburg Campus Learning Center 14450 SE Johnson Rd, CmsC, 97267	657	F6
Scholls Heights Elementary School 16400 SW Loon Dr, BRTN, 97007	654	G4
Scott Elementary School 6700 NE Prescott St, PTLD, 97218	597	E1
Scott Elementary School 14700 NE Sacramento St, PTLD, 97230	598	D3
Sellwood Middle School 8300 SE 15th Av, PTLD, 97202	626	H7
Sexton Mt Elementary School 15645 SW Sexton Mountain Rd, BRTN, 97007	624	H7
Shahala Middle School 601 SE 192nd Av, VCVR, 98607	538	H7
Shaver Elementary School 3701 NE 131st Pl, PTLD, 97230	598	B2
Sherwood High School 16956 SW Meinecke Rd, SRWD, 97140	684	F7
Sherwood Middle School 400 N Sherwood Blvd, SRWD, 97140	684	G6
Sifton Elementary School 7301 NE 137th Av, ClkC, 98682	508	B6
Silver Star Elementary School 10500 NE 86th St, ClkC, 98662	507	H4
Sitton Elementary School 9930 N Smith St, PTLD, 97203	565	G1
Skinner Elementary Montessori School 5001 NE 66th Av, VCVR, 98661	537	D1
Skyline Elementary School 11536 NW Skyline Blvd, MthC, 97231	534	G7
Skyridge Middle School 5220 NW Parker St, CMAS, 98607	539	A7
Skyview High School 1300 NW 139th St, ClkC, 98685	476	F6
Sojourner Elementary School 1901 SE Oak Grove Blvd, CmsC, 97267	656	J6
South Ridge Elementary School 502 NW 199th St, ClkC, 98642	446	G7
Southridge High School 9625 SW 125th Av, BRTN, 97008	655	B1
Southwest Christian School 14605 SW Weir Rd, BRTN, 97007	654	J1
Spring Mountain Elementary School 11645 SE Masa Ln, HPYV, 97236	658	A3
Springwater Trail High School 1440 SE Fleming Av, GSHM, 97080	629	D4
Stafford Primary School 19875 SW Stafford Rd, CmsC, 97068	686	C4
Stephenson Elementary School 2627 SW Stephenson St, PTLD, 97219	656	C3
Stoller Middle School 14141 NW Laidlaw Rd, WasC, 97229	565	A7
Sunnyside Elementary School 13401 SE 132nd Av, CmsC, 97015	658	B5
Sunnyside Elementary School 3421 SE Salmon St, PTLD, 97214	597	A7
Sunrise Middle School 14331 SE 132nd Av, CmsC, 97015	658	B6

Schools

Portland Points of Interest Index

FEATURE NAME Address City ZIP Code	MAP#	GRID
Sunset Elementary School 9001 NE 95th St, ClkC, 98662	507	G4
Sunset High School 13840 NW Cornell Rd, BRTN, 97229	595	A4
Sunset Primary School 2351 Oxford St, WLIN, 97068	687	A7
Sweetbriar Elementary School 501 SE Sweetbriar Ln, TDLE, 97060	599	G7
Templeton Elementary School 9500 SW Murdock St, TGRD, 97224	655	E6
Terra Linda Elementary School 1998 NW 143rd Av, WasC, 97229	595	A3
Thomas Jefferson Middle School 3000 NW 119th St, ClkC, 98685	506	D1
Thomas Middle School 645 NE Lincoln St, HBRO, 97124	593	C4
Three Rivers Charter School 4975 Willamette Falls Dr, WLIN, 97068	687	B7
Tigard Elementary School 12855 SW Grant Av, TGRD, 97223	655	D4
Tigard High School 9000 SW Durham Rd, TGRD, 97224	685	E1
Tobias Elementary School 1065 SW 206th Av, WasC, 97006	594	C6
Tom McCall Upper Elementary School 1341 Pacific Av, FTGV, 97116	591	G4
Touchstone School 2 Touchstone, LKOW, 97035	656	B4
Trillium Charter School 116 N Page St, PTLD, 97227	596	G3
Trinity Lutheran School 5520 NE Killingsworth St, PTLD, 97218	567	D7
Trost Elementary School 800 S Redwood St, CNBY, 97013	746	E7
Troutdale Elementary School 648 SE Harlow Av, TDLE, 97060	599	G4
Truman Elementary School 4505 NE 42nd Av, ClkC, 98661	537	B1
Tualatin Elementary School 20405 SW 95th Av, TLTN, 97062	685	E5
Tualatin High School 22300 SW Boones Ferry Rd, TLTN, 97062	685	E7
Tualatin Valley Junior Academy 21975 SW Baseline Rd, HBRO, 97124	594	B6
Tubman Middle School 2231 N Flint Av, PTLD, 97227	596	G3
Twality Middle School 14650 SW 97th Av, TGRD, 97224	655	E6
Union Ridge Elementary School 330 N 5th St, RDGF, 98642	416	A7
Uplands Elementary School 2055 Wembley Park Rd, LKOW, 97034	656	C5
Valley Catholic Middle High School 4275 SW 148th Av, BRTN, 97007	624	J3
Vancouver Christian High School 8100 E Mill Plain Blvd, VCVR, 98664	537	E5
Vancouver School Arts-Academics 3101 Main St, VCVR, 98663	536	G3
Ventura Park Elementary School 145 SE 117th Av, PTLD, 97216	598	A6
Veritas School 401 Mission Dr, NWBG, 97132	713	C6
Vernon Elementary School 2044 NE Killingsworth St, PTLD, 97211	566	J7
Vestal Elementary School 161 NE 82nd Av, PTLD, 97213	597	F5
View Acres Elementary School 4828 SE View Acres Rd, CmsC, 97267	657	B6
View Ridge Middle School 510 Pioneer St, RDGF, 98642	416	A7
Visitation School 4189 NW Visitation Rd, WasC, 97116	562	B7
Vose Elementary School 11350 SW Denney Rd, BRTN, 97008	625	C5
Walker Elementary School 11940 SW Lynnfield Ln, BRTN, 97005	625	C1
Walnut Grove Elementary School 6103 NE 72nd Av, ClkC, 98662	507	E7
Walt Morey Middle School 2801 SW Lucas Av, TDLE, 97060	599	E6
Waluga Junior High School 4700 Jean Rd, LKOW, 97035	686	A2
Warren Elementary School 34555 Berg Rd, ClbC, 97053	414	H7
Wascher Elementary School 986 7th Street Ext, LFYT, 97127	741	H7
Washington Elementary School 2908 S St, VCVR, 98663	536	J3
Washougal High School 1201 39th St, WHGL, 98671	570	C5
Welches Elementary School 24901 E Salmon River Rd, CmsC, 97067	724	D4
Welches Middle School 24903 E Salmon River Rd, CmsC, 97067	724	D4
Westgate Christian School 12930 SW Scholls Ferry Rd, TGRD, 97223	655	A2
West Gresham Elementary School 330 W Powell Blvd, GSHM, 97030	629	B3
West Hills Christian School 7945 SW Capitol Hill Rd, PTLD, 97219	626	C6
West Hills Montessori School 4920 SW Vermont St, PTLD, 97219	626	A5
West Linn High School 5464 W A St, WLIN, 97068	687	B7
West Orient Middle School 29805 SE Orient Dr, MthC, 97080	630	A7
West Powellhurst Elementary School 2921 SE 116th Av, PTLD, 97266	628	A2
Westridge Elementary School 3400 Royce Way, LKOW, 97034	686	B2
Westside Christian High School 4565 Carman Dr, LKOW, 97035	656	A5
West Sylvan Middle School 8111 SW West Slope Dr, BRTN, 97225	625	G1
West Tualatin View Elementary School 8800 SW Leahy Rd, WasC, 97225	595	F6
West Union Elementary School 23870 NW West Union Rd, WasC, 97124	563	J4
Westview High School 4200 NW 185th Av, WasC, 97229	594	E1
Whitcomb Elementary School 7400 SE Thompson Rd, CmsC, 97222	657	E3
Whitford Middle School 7935 SW Scholls Ferry Rd, BRTN, 97008	625	E6
Whitman Elementary School 7326 SE Flavel St, PTLD, 97206	627	E6
Wichita Elementary School 6031 SE King Rd, CmsC, 97222	657	D2
Wilkes Elementary School 17020 NE Wilkes Rd, GSHM, 97230	598	F3
Willamette Primary School 1403 12th St, WLIN, 97068	716	G2
Wilson High School 1151 SW Vermont St, PTLD, 97219	626	D5
Wilsonville High School 6800 SW Wilsonville Rd, WNVL, 97070	715	G7
Winterhaven School 3830 SE 14th Av, PTLD, 97202	626	H2
Witch Hazel Elementary School 4950 SE Davis St, HBRO, 97123	623	H2
WL Henry Elementary School 1060 SE 24th Av, HBRO, 97123	593	E6
Woodland Elementary School 21607 Ne Glisan St, FRVW, 97024	599	B5
Woodland High School 757 Park St, WDLD, 98674	385	J2
Woodland Middle School 755 Park St, WDLD, 98674	385	J2
Woodland Primary School 600 Bozarth Av, WDLD, 98674	385	J2
Woodlawn Elementary School 7200 NE 11th Av, PTLD, 97211	566	H5
Woodmere Elementary School 7900 SE Duke St, PTLD, 97206	627	F5
Woodstock Elementary School 5601 SE 50th Av, PTLD, 97206	627	C4
W Verne McKinney Elementary School 535 NW Darnielle St, HBRO, 97124	593	B3
Wy'east Middle School 1112 SE 136th Av, VCVR, 98683	538	B7
Yacolt Primary School 406 W Yacolt Rd, YCLT, 98675	419	F1
Yamhill Grade School 310 E Main St, YMHL, 97148	711	A1
York Elementary School 9301 NE 152nd Av, ClkC, 98682	508	D4
Zellerbach Elementary School 841 NE 22nd Av, CMAS, 98607	569	F3

Shopping Centers

FEATURE NAME Address City ZIP Code	MAP#	GRID
Cedar Hills Crossing BRTN, 97005	625	B1
Clackamas Promenade SE 89th Dr, CmsC, 97015	657	G4
Clackamas Town Center CmsC, 97236	657	F4
Jantzen Beach Supercenter PTLD, 97217	536	F7
Lloyd Center 2201 NE Halsey St, PTLD, 97232	596	H4
Mall 205 PTLD, 97216	597	H6
Pioneer Place 700 SW 5th Av, PTLD, 97204	596	F6
Tanasbourne Town Center 2000 NW Allie Av, HBRO, 97124	594	D3
Washington Square 9585 SW Washington Square Rd, TGRD, 97223	655	D1
Westfield Vancouver VCVR, 98662	537	F1

Subdivisions & Neighborhoods

FEATURE NAME	MAP#	GRID
Albina, PTLD	596	F3
Arleta, PTLD	627	E3
Bolton, WLIN	687	A6
Brooklyn, PTLD	627	A3
Bryant, LKOW	656	A7
Burlingame, PTLD	626	E6
Canemah, ORCY	717	A2
Capitol Hill, PTLD	626	D6
Carnation, FTGV	591	J6
Chutes, PTLD	626	G6
Clackamas Heights, ORCY	687	F5
Cook, LKOW	685	J1
Council Crest, PTLD	626	C3
East Moreland, PTLD	627	A5
East Parkrose, PTLD	598	A3
East Portland, PTLD	596	H6
East St. Johns, PTLD	566	B2
Errol Heights, PTLD	627	C6
Gasco, PTLD	565	G4
Gilbert, PTLD	628	A5
Glen Cullen, PTLD	626	A3
Green Hills, MthC	626	A1
Harbor Track, MthC	535	E5
Hillsdale, PTLD	626	D4
Hollywood, PTLD	597	A4
Irvington, PTLD	596	H3
Kenton, PTLD	566	F4
Kings Heights, PTLD	596	C4
Lake Grove, LKOW	686	A1
Lake Yard, PTLD	596	B1
Laurelhurst, PTLD	597	A5
Lents, PTLD	627	G5
Linnton, PTLD	565	E1
Maplewood, PTLD	626	A5
Marquam Hill, PTLD	626	D2
McLoughlin Heights, VCVR	537	D5
Midway, PTLD	598	B7
Montavilla, PTLD	597	F6
Mt Pleasant, ORCY	717	C3
Multnomah, PTLD	626	C6
Oak Park, CMAS	569	G5
Park Place, ORCY	687	E5
Parkrose, PTLD	597	H1
Piedmont, PTLD	566	G6
Portland Heights, PTLD	626	C1
Powellhurst, PTLD	627	H1
Riverdale, MthC	656	G1
Robinwood, WLIN	686	H2
Rosemont, WLIN	686	H6
Russellville, PTLD	597	J6
St. Johns, PTLD	565	H3
Sellwood, PTLD	626	H6
Six Corners, SRWD	684	G5
Sunset, WLIN	687	A7
Sylvan, PTLD	595	J7
Twelve Mile, GSHM	599	B6
Vermont Hills, PTLD	626	A4
West Moreland, PTLD	626	H5
West Portland, PTLD	655	J1
West Portland Park, PTLD	656	A1
West St. Helens, STHN	415	B1
Willamette, WLIN	716	G2
Willbridge, PTLD	565	J7
Willsburg Junction, MWKE	627	A7
Woodstock, PTLD	627	C5

Transportation

FEATURE NAME	MAP#	GRID
Albina-Mississippi Station, PTLD	596	F3
Amtrak-Union Station, PTLD	596	F5
Amtrak-Vancouver, VCVR	536	E5
Barbur Blvd Station, PTLD	656	A1
Beaverton Central Station, BRTN	625	B2
Beaverton Creek Station, BRTN	624	J1
Beaverton Transit Center Station, BRTN	625	C2
Clackamas Town Center Station, CmsC	657	F3
Cleveland Av Station, GSHM	629	D2
Convention Center Station, PTLD	596	G4
Delta Park-Vanport Transit Center Station, - PTLD	566	E2
E 102nd Av Station, PTLD	597	H6
E 181st Av Station, GSHM	598	G6
Elmonica Station, BRTN	594	F7
Expo Center Station, PTLD	566	E1
Fair Complex-Hillsboro Airport Station, HBRO	593	F4
Fisher's Landing Transit Center, VCVR	568	D
Galleria Station, PTLD	596	E6
Gateway Transit Center Station, PTLD	597	H
Goose Hollow Station, PTLD	596	D
Gresham City Hall Station, GSHM	629	B1
Gresham Transit Center Station, GSHM	629	C2
Greyhound-Portland, PTLD	596	F5
Greyhound-Tigard, TGRD	655	E4
Greyhound-Vancouver, VCVR	536	G5
Hatfield-Government Center Station, HBRO	593	B4
Hawthorn Farm Station, HBRO	593	H
Hillsboro Central Transit Center Station, - HBRO	593	C5
Hollywood Station, PTLD	597	B4
Interstate-Rose Garden Station, PTLD	596	G
Kenton-N Denver Av Station, PTLD	566	E4
Kings Hill Station, PTLD	596	D6
Library & 9th Av Station, PTLD	596	E6
Lloyd Center Station, PTLD	596	H4
Mall-SW 4th Av Station, PTLD	596	F6
Mall-SW 5th Av Station, PTLD	596	F6
Merlo Road Station, BRTN	594	H7
Millikan Way Station, WasC	625	A
Morrison Station, PTLD	596	F6
NE 7th Av Station, PTLD	596	H4
NE 60th Av Station, PTLD	597	D5
NE 82nd Av Station, PTLD	597	F4
NE 122nd Av Station, PTLD	598	A6
NE 148th Av Station, PTLD	598	D6
NE 162nd Av Station, GSHM	598	E6
NE 172nd Av Station, GSHM	598	F6
N Killingsworth Station, PTLD	566	E7
N Lombard Station, PTLD	566	E5
N Portland Blvd Station, PTLD	566	E6
N Prescott St Station, PTLD	596	E1
Oak St Station, PTLD	596	F6
Old Town-Chinatown Station, PTLD	596	F5
Oregon City Transit Center Station, ORCY	687	C7
Orenco Station, HBRO	594	A4
Overlook Park Station, PTLD	596	E2
Parkrose Sumer Station, PTLD	597	H1
PGE Park Station, PTLD	596	D5
Pioneer Square Station North, PTLD	596	F6
Pioneer Square Station South, PTLD	596	E6
Portland International Airport Station, PTLD	567	E4
Quatama Station, HBRO	594	C5
Rockwood Transit Center Station, GSHM	598	H6
Rose Quarter Center Station, PTLD	596	G4
Ruby Junction Station, GSHM	598	J7
Skidmore Fountain Station, PTLD	596	F5
Sunset Transit Center Station, BRTN	595	D7
Tigard Transit Center Station, TGRD	655	F4
Tuality Hospital Station, HBRO	593	D5
Washington Park Station, PTLD	596	B7
Washington Station, HBRO	593	D5
Willow Creek Station, WasC	594	E5
Yamhill District Station, PTLD	596	F6

Visitor Information

FEATURE NAME Address City ZIP Code	MAP#	GRID
I Visitor Center 621 High St, ORCY, 97045	687	C7
Mount Hood Information Center 65000 Mt Hood Hwy, CmsC, 97011	723	H1
Portland Oregon Visitors & Service Center 701 SW 6th Av, PTLD, 97205	596	E6
Portland-Oregon Visitors Assoc 1000 SW Broadway, PTLD, 97205	596	E6

The Thomas Guide®

Thank you for purchasing this Rand McNally Thomas Guide!
We value your comments and suggestions.

Please help us serve you better by completing this postage-paid reply card.
This information is for internal use ONLY and will not be distributed or sold to any external third party.

Missing pages? Maybe not... Please refer to the "Using Your Street Guide" page for further explanation.

Thomas Guide Title: Portland   ISBN-13# 978-0-5288-6665-4   **MKT: POR**

Today's Date: _____   Gender: ☐M ☐F   Age Group: ☐18-24 ☐25-31 ☐32-40 ☐41-50 ☐51-64 ☐65+

1. What type of industry do you work in?

   ☐Real Estate   ☐Trucking   ☐Delivery   ☐Construction   ☐Utilities   ☐Government
   ☐Retail   ☐Sales   ☐Transportation   ☐Landscape   ☐Service & Repair
   ☐Courier   ☐Automotive   ☐Insurance   ☐Medical   ☐Police/Fire/First Response
   ☐Other, please specify: _____

2. What type of job do you have in this industry?_____

3. Where did you purchase this Thomas Guide? (store name & city) _____

4. Why did you purchase this Thomas Guide? _____

5. How often do you purchase an updated Thomas Guide? ☐Annually ☐2 yrs. ☐3-5 yrs. ☐Other: _____

6. Where do you use it?   ☐Primarily in the car ☐Primarily in the office ☐Primarily at home ☐Other: _____

7. How do you use it?   ☐Exclusively for business   ☐Primarily for business but also for personal or leisure use
   ☐Both work and personal evenly   ☐Primarily for personal use   ☐Exclusively for personal use

8. What do you use your Thomas Guide for?
   ☐Find Addresses   ☐In-route navigation   ☐Planning routes   ☐Other: _____
   Find points of interest: ☐Schools ☐Parks ☐Buildings ☐Shopping Centers ☐Other:_____

9. How often do you use it? ☐Daily ☐Weekly ☐Monthly ☐Other:_____

10. Do you use the internet for maps and/or directions?   ☐Yes ☐No

11. How often do you use the internet for directions? ☐Daily ☐Weekly ☐Monthly ☐Other:_____

12. Do you use any of the following mapping products in addition to your Thomas Guide?
    ☐Folded paper maps ☐Folded laminated maps ☐Wall maps ☐GPS ☐PDA ☐In-car navigation ☐Phone maps

13. What features, if any, would you like to see added to your Thomas Guide? _____
    _____

14. What features or information do you find most useful in your Rand McNally Thomas Guide? (please specify)
    _____
    _____

15. Please provide any additional comments or suggestions you have. _____
    _____
    _____

We strive to provide you with the most current updated information available if you know of a map correction, please notify us here.

Where is the correction?   Map Page #:_____   Grid #:_____   Index Page #:_____

Nature of the correction: ☐Street name missing   ☐Street name misspelled   ☐Street information incorrect
    ☐Incorrect location for point of interest   ☐Index error   ☐Other:_____

Detail: _____

I would like to receive information about updated editions and special offers from Rand McNally
    ☐via e-mail   E-mail address: _____
    ☐via postal mail
    Your Name: _____   Company (if used for work):_____
    Address: _____   City/State/ZIP:_____

Thank you for your time and help. We are working to serve you better.
This information is for internal use ONLY and will not be distributed or sold to any external third party.

TG-noCD.06

2ND FOLD LINE

1ST FOLD LINE